FRONTIERS OF FINANCE
THE BATTERYMARCH FELLOWSHIP PAPERS

To future Fellows
and
the freedom to pursue inspiration

Frontiers of Finance
The Batterymarch Fellowship Papers

Edited by

DEBORAH H. MILLER

and

STEWART C. MYERS

Basil Blackwell

First published 1990

Basil Blackwell, Inc.
3 Cambridge Center
Cambridge, Massachusetts 02142, USA

Basil Blackwell Ltd
108 Cowley Road, Oxford, OX4 1JF, UK

Library of Congress Cataloging in Publication Data

Frontiers of finance : the Batterymarch Fellowship papers / edited by Deborah H. Miller and Stewart C. Myers.
p. cm.
Includes bibliographical references.
ISBN 1-55786-085-8
1. Finance. I. Miller, Deborah H. II. Myers, Stewart C.
HG173.F76 1990
332—dc20 89-18620
CIP

British Library Cataloguing in Publication Data

A CIP catalogue record for this book is available from the British Library

Typeset in 11 on 13pt Plantin by
Mathematical Composition Setters Ltd, Salisbury, UK
Printed in Great Britain by The Alden Press Ltd., Oxford

Contents

Acknowledgments

The successful completion of this volume represents the combined efforts of many people at Batterymarch Financial Management and Basil Blackwell, as well as the authors of the papers and the journal publishers who granted reprint permission. In particular, special thanks go to Susan A. Gula, consultant, who acted as project coordinator for this endeavor. Without her dedication, hard work, and gentle persuasion this book would still be merely an idea. Others who made significant contributions to this volume include Christine Sharrock, copy-editor, for her painstaking attention to the manuscript, and Diane Keitt for her counsel and support throughout the project.

Foreword

The decision was made in a matter of five minutes.

I do not know who started it, but in a conversation with Evan Schulman, one of us – we worked so closely those days it was hard to remember who – asked, "Shouldn't we do something to repay our debt to the academic community?" The discussion of creating a research fellowship for creative financial academics began to unfold. One of us asked, "What if these young creative financial academics were free of all those committee responsibilities we loathe as well as the teaching loads they find distracting?" The other no doubt said, "Let's call it the Batterymarch Fellowship and provide nontenured academics a generous stipend, coupled with support services by their institution. Let's make it a yearly competition."

"O.K." The Batterymarch Fellowship became a reality ten years ago in 1980, with the first award made in the following year.

It may be true that the best ideas are the simple ones. The Batterymarch Fellowship is now a quarter of a million dollar per year project to repay our steadily growing debt to the academic community for advice, critique, counsel, and friendship throughout the 20 year existence of Batterymarch Financial Management. Curiously enough it has a commercial benefit as well, but the Fellowship was created to operate for the public good in the investment area and not for Batterymarch's own personal success as an investment manager or for the interest of Batterymarch clients. And yet, while it was intended as a "good work," it has also become one that stimulates ideas that we can all use in this business. From time to time Batterymarch Fellows have visited with clients, but on no special topic. The early Batterymarch Fellows are now Senior Professors and have continued to increase their flow of research work. We have all been beneficiaries.

When Batterymarch first started, academics were held in some disdain by most investment people. Twenty years ago, when I suggested that a senior portfolio manager meet a finance professor he responded, "Tell me the value of his personal portfolio, and I'll tell you if his advice is worthwhile." Today, academics are involved in many investment organizations and Batterymarch has been one of the pioneers in making academic thinking practical in an investment sense. From its inception, Batterymarch has utilized research found in the leading academic journals – work that was going unheeded. Our early devotion to efficient market principles came from this research. Academics said that investment management was very inefficient because of high trading costs, and, in response, we emphasized trading cost efficiency to reduce the friction between the theoretical ideas and actual portfolio results. Indexing first led to tilt funds, to active management done under quantitative disciplines, and to derivative products, and is now going on to global management. In each case, academia pulled investment professionals along behind them in this quest.

Research is the principal function at Batterymarch. As many comment when they visit our offices, it seems more like a library or a laboratory than an investment office. Quiet thinking, as well as the noisy exchange by colleagues, replaces the normal clatter of telephones and operations that takes place in most day-to-day investment offices. Research is where the investment process starts at Batterymarch, with ideas generated that lead to specific strategies. Research challenges us to adhere to our disciplines far more severely than the vagaries of short-term performance figures. Finally, research gives us a sense of quality in our activities because our conclusions are ultimately subjected to the discipline of the marketplace and the critique of our peers in other firms.

In Japan, the major research activities are centered within the companies themselves; here in the United States they are treated in a more theoretical fashion and relegated to the universities. Batterymarch, however, thinks of itself as being in a fast-moving technological business and, as a technologically driven company, we know that we must remain competitive in the world of ideas. Most corporations dedicated to excellence strive for a high research input even when it may not be the cultural norm for that business. Fresh forward-thinking ideas from current research have given Batterymarch a leading edge over investment houses that ignore such input.

Our early commitment to research not only has enhanced our quest for novel ideas in finance, but also has resulted in our close association with academics. I have many friends who are teaching in the exceptional universities in Boston and elsewhere. I occasionally contemplated a teaching career, and I have filled in for teachers at a few business schools when they have been ill or just thought that an outside person would perk up their class. I have avoided, however, all those aspects of academia that we try to eliminate for the Batterymarch Fellow – notably committee meetings and internal politics. The network of close associations among peers who exchange insights and even confidences about their work is an important aspect of the academic–corporate relationship. Batterymarch people have often been part of this network of mutual respect and help in obtaining data and assistance on many projects.

The Fellowship Program begins with people. Through the Fellowship applications we become familiar with the careers of the best and brightest of young financial investment academics. We learn about their lives and aspirations; they share their plans with us. We learn what their teachers think of them, about their strengths, and even about their weaknesses. Then we compile the best single compendium of the forward-looking research plans of a quite outstanding group of researchers. Although I cannot point to a particular investment idea that came from this exposure, I know that Batterymarch people and our clients have benefited from the stimulation of being exposed to this group.

The selections are important to the Fellowship winners and indirectly important in their absence to the nonwinners. The award is considered within academia to be the most prestigious designation of its type for promising academics. We undertake this selection process with extraordinary care because we fully realize the impact that our decisions will have on researchers; we also know that the research selected provides a base from which we draw inspiration for our work. Each year winners are judged by the quality of their peers who have been winners previously. Fellowship candidates know that this is a group with which they wish to be associated. We have called for selection help from a diverse group of senior finance professors. Professor Stewart C. Myers from the Alfred P. Sloan School of Management at the Massachusetts Institute of Technology, a co-editor of this volume, was the first academic selector and was instrumental in shaping that role in later years. Stew and subsequent senior academics provide counsel on submitted projects. They often laboriously explain to people like me, who might be more concerned with a candidate's more general achievements as seen through the curriculum vitae and references, the underlying merit of a research idea.

Each year we ask a Batterymarch client to participate in this program. Not only does this give us an opportunity to work with truly outstanding individuals from a variety of our client organizations, but it has also tended to bring a note of pragmatism to what might otherwise be the seduction of a new theoretical breakthrough. Clients have a keen eye for quality as well as practicality and often insert the useful question: "What will the payoff be for the work of this candidate?" The client is often the deciding factor when we are fighting over the last spot, and the insertion of a constructive dimension often carries the argument. Instead of mentioning each person who assisted in the selection process by name, let me give a blanket thank-you to these people. The academic selectors have told us about the merits of the project and the Batterymarch client has told us about the merits of the individual along with the dozens of finance professors who face an annual Christmas chore of writing long letters of recommendation for their outstanding students. Together these judges have become a powerful combination and each of them, many of whom have contributed to this volume as well, should share the same pride that we feel in looking at the record that has been built by them. The Fellows owe a great deal of gratitude to this group, as do we, for their assistance in making the Batterymarch Fellowship a success.

This volume will reveal the diverse range of work that has been done by Fellows while they were sponsored by the Fellowship. Nearly all of them are tenured now; many are bringing along other Fellows. This volume will mark a standard which new Fellows should surpass because improvement over time is, after all, the function of research.

We hope to reach different readers with this volume. Fellowship winners, of course, will have the volume to commemorate their work as Fellows. The work itself will act as a stimulus for further research from which we shall all draw. Academics will be kept abreast of who is doing what, as we document the esteem with which the Fellowship Award is held. At a minimum, the book will reflect the pride that everyone should feel by participation in this effort.

And finally, to the general readers of whom I trust there will be many, we hope that it will be worthwhile to do more than, as an old professor said to me, "Feel the binding." This volume should convey the solid underpinning of the investment work that is going on today and leave a sense of the progress that is being made by extraordinarily talented and bright people represented by Batterymarch Fellows.

We owe them our admiration and thanks.

Dean LeBaron

Boston, Massachusetts

Introduction

The Batterymarch Fellowship Program is the inspiration for this volume. Top-notch research has resulted from the Fellowship awards, and recipients have become recognized experts in their fields. This book celebrates the quality of the work that has been accomplished by Fellows during the first seven years of the Fellowship Program from 1981 to 1987. Here we assemble a diverse collection of previously published papers with Batterymarch as the common link, and provide commentary by way of an introduction which lends a new perspective to this body of work.

As we began to think about the composition and organization of this collection, the idea of grouping papers by topics was proposed. Seminal works in many areas such as asset pricing, signaling theory, market microstructure, and capital structure were all represented by the work done, and such an organizational scheme lent itself to a graduate course syllabus. However, the Fellowship's spirit of freeing the researcher to be creative and productive prevailed, and we decided to ask each Fellow to make his or her own paper selection. As a result, papers were chosen for a variety of reasons: a favorite, a most important, most famous, or most overlooked paper, as well as one most representative of that person's research. Organized into 21 chapters in chronological order by Fellowship year, each highlights not only a unique project, but also the individual scholar.

The centerpiece of each chapter is a paper which resulted from the Fellowship. Many of these share joint authorship, and some are collaborations by Fellows representing different award years. Professor Stewart C. Myers, from the Alfred P. Sloan School of Management at the Massachusetts Institute of Technology, has written the opening remarks in "Background and Comments" for each paper, and each Fellow has contributed a new introduction for his or her paper specifically for this book.

Each chapter also has a bibliography of the other papers written by the Fellow which benefited from the Fellowship. Some 100 papers are listed in all.

The freedom and simplicity of the book's organizational approach is mirrored in the Fellowship Program itself and accounts in part for the Program's uniqueness and success. Simplicity is also translated into an efficient selection process, uncomplicated program administration, and a flexible relationship with each Fellow.

The five minute decision to create the Batterymarch Fellowship in 1980 was a very efficient use of executive time, and set the tone for the evolving process. We decided to allocate project resources by targeting youth – those untenured faculty fighting for peer recognition and tenure within their universities. Furthermore, we chose to award the grant directly to the three successful candidates, each a motivated individual struggling to find the time to think, research, write, and publish. A conscious decision to bypass the fund-raising arms of universities allowed the Fellowship to remain independent of other institutions.

We began our search for candidates by announcing the Batterymarch Fellowship Program Competition in the annual mailing of the American Finance Association. We expected to be inundated with applications but only 30 individuals had responded by year end. We indicated that this was a serious endeavor by asking candidates to submit a list of their published papers, a research proposal, letters of recommendation, a curriculum vitae, and a letter from their school freeing them from teaching and administrative responsibilities for a year, should they win, as well as granting full secretarial and computer support. We also enlisted a senior academic and client colleague to join the selection committee. As a result there was a certain amount of self-selection implied in requiring an individual to proclaim to departmental associates that he or she felt capable of winning a contest which was to be judged by outstanding members of both the academic and practitioner worlds.

The final step in the process of choosing Fellows was to design a procedure that maximized the efficient use of committee members' time. It was determined that one person at Batterymarch would act as Program Administrator, and together with Dean LeBaron, the senior academic, and the client colleague, the selection committee was completed. It was the administrator's responsibility to write an evaluation of each candidate dividing the group into "consider" candidates and all "others." This classification then went to the full committee by mid-January so that each committee member could study the administrator's classifications. A candidate could be moved from the "other" to the "consider" group, but only if the proposing member felt strongly that the candidate should be considered as one of the three winners. In that way, time-consuming discussions over ranking differences at the margin were avoided. In over nine years of the Program only one candidate was so moved, and indeed he did win a Fellowship that year.

This first full committee meeting lasted only about four hours. Most of the time was spent discussing the merits of all the suggested research proposals together with their possible data and methodological problems. For the remaining time, the committee focused on the "consider" group, and the important decision at hand. Winners were announced in early February. The only stipulation that the award carried was that all research undertaken during the Fellowship year be publicly available, simply acknowledging Batterymarch support when published.

The selection process as described above remains essentially the same today as in 1981 when the first Fellows were chosen. New Year's Day and the first weeks of each new year continue to be an intensely busy – and rewarding – time for all those involved. While simple in concept and execution, the selection process represents hard work and dedication by many people who devoted themselves to this endeavor. It is these individuals, together with the Fellows, who have made the Fellowship Program a success over the years. It is with pride that we list the selection committees (with their then affiliation) which served between 1981 and 1987 and share with you some of their present comments on the Fellowship written especially for this volume.

1981 Stewart C. Myers, Massachusetts Institute of Technology
Jon L. Hagler, Ford Foundation

1982 Stephen A. Ross, Yale University

This volume makes it timely to comment on the impact of the Batterymarch Fellowships on financial scholarship. Of course, there is no doubt that young scholars have been supported in their work with the freedom to focus on their research at a time when they are at the peak of their energy and in the midst of what for most will be amongst the most important work of their career. I now number nine students and co-authors among the recipients and, as a consequence, I have had a chance to observe close up the effect of the award on the participants. In every case, as the scholar was growing in importance and the academic version of the Peter Principle, i.e. rising committee assignments, was growing apace, the Fellowship freed the scholar of those necessary but unwelcome intrusions for a special year. The result was fine research, some of which has changed the way we now think of finance.

Beyond this direct benefit, though, the Fellowships have had at least two wonderful additional effects. The incentive effect of an award can be at least as important as the direct effect. Bright young scholars do not work solely for such awards, but perhaps the prestige that now attaches to the Batterymarch Fellowships makes their light glow just a touch brighter. Just as importantly, the prestige of the award is one of the signs of the new maturity of financial economics, and "the Batterymarch" surely has had a marginal impact on inducing young economists to turn their attention to our science.

S.A.R.

Charles D. Ellis, Greenwich Associates

The evolution of new knowledge and understanding is never a smooth process. It is lumpy, risky, disruptive, and unpopular.

Surprisingly large parts of intellectual progress are accomplished by solo practitioners – often by quite young people who are risking their dreams and careers when they are without institutional security or professional independence of financial resources. They are pioneers on what may be the world's harshest frontier – the boundary between what is known and what is not known, between what is understood and what is not, between great and valuable discovery and the waste of time.

Batterymarch, through its grants to the most promising – but not yet proven – researchers in finance gives international recognition to the most exciting members of the academy when they will benefit most and can contribute most, honoring them not for long past achievements but for the capacity to achieve in the future... .

C.D.E.

1983 **Merton H. Miller**, University of Chicago
John W. English, Ford Foundation

1984 **Robert C. Merton**, Massachusetts Institute of Technology
Peter L. Bernstein, Peter L. Bernstein Inc.

When I was invited to serve on the selection committee in 1984, I was deeply flattered. I must confess that my anticipation of the duties involved fell well short of the load of cerebral material that soon came my way. Reading and understanding the papers was hard enough; coming to some kind of a conclusion as to which most merited the Fellowship was a brain-cracking process.

We are all victims of parochial views and biases all too easily established. Naturally, I believe that the three people we picked are the superior trio. I am equally convinced that each year's committee feels the same way about their trio, and with equal justification.

Yet, I suspect that those who preceded and followed me on the selection committee share still one more emotion: how far more marvelous it would have been to have been a recipient instead of a selector!

P.L.B.

1985 **Barr Rosenberg**, BARRA Inc.
John C. Bogle, The Vanguard Group Inc.

As a result of my day-long foray at Batterymarch (not counting a ton of homework), I came to this conclusion: while there is a lot of witchcraft in the academic lore, a certain naivete among the practitioners about what is truly susceptible to proof, and far too much reliance on the misbegotten idea that the past is inevitably prologue to the future, the most solid academic thinking, however complex, abstruse, and precise, is worth even a busy financial executive's perusal. For sound theory, sooner or later, will find its way into actual practice in the financial markets, and into the investor marketplace as well.

J.C.B.

1986 **Jay O. Light**, Harvard University
Marvin L. Damsma, City of New York

1987 **Myron S. Scholes**, Stanford University
Greta E. Marshall, California Public Employees' Retirement System

The Batterymarch Fellowship Awards are well represented by the words of these committee members. The papers which follow are themselves the best testament to Batterymarch's continuing commitment to further the frontiers of finance.

Deborah H. Miller
Evan Schulman

Boston, Massachusetts

Chapter 1

Douglas T. Breeden

Background and Comments

It is a pleasure to begin with a comment on the work of Douglas Breeden, the first of the three Batterymarch Fellows that I helped to choose in 1981. Note how quickly they and the Fellows chosen later have advanced to senior positions in the profession of financial research.

Breeden is well known for his development of the consumption capital asset pricing model (CCAPM), in which the risk of individual assets is not measured by betas with respect to the market but by the covariance of the assets' returns with changes in investors' consumption. This steps over the chief theoretical problem of the standard CAPM, which defines "the market" to include all the economy's assets, including all debt securities, commodities, real estate, human capital, and so on – not just the Standard & Poor's 500. Obviously the return on the portfolio of all assets is unobservable. Consumption, however, can be directly estimated.

Tests of the simple CCAPM have not worked out very well, but new models extending the CCAPM's basic ideas show considerable promise (for a review and development of recent theory, see G. M. Constantinides, forthcoming).

The following paper applies the machinery of the CCAPM to address several important issues. For example, it clarifies how "complete" securities markets really are.

Ideally the menu of investment options should be diverse enough to allow investors to construct a portfolio to cover or hedge any possible future event. However, since the number of securities is far less than the number of possible events, it appears that the market is seriously incomplete.

Suppose that a restaurant's menu includes 100 dishes but does not allow customers to order *à la carte*. They can only buy ten set menus. None of the menus contains both lasagna and cheesecake, and if that is what you want, you are out of luck. The restaurant menu is *incomplete*.

If the set menus were securities, things would be a little easier. You could order from two or more menus, perhaps short others, and have some lasagna and some cheesecake along with other things. Still, there is no way of obtaining every possible combination of 100 dishes by mixing only ten set menus.

Securities markets seem to be incomplete in the same sense. There may be 10,000 securities on investors' menus, but there are millions of distinct future events that investors may wish to provide for.

Now here is the real insight: under certain conditions, *continuous trading* in a *limited* number of assets or securities is sufficient to generate *any* desired portfolio characteristic – to generate any pattern of payoffs over the millions of future events investors may contemplate. I will leave it to Breeden's article to describe how this is done.

Reference

Constantinides, G. M. (forthcoming) "Habit Formation: A Resolution of the Equity Premium Puzzle," *Journal of Political Economy*.

Author's Introduction

This paper makes contributions to research in the following areas: (a) general portfolio theory in an intertemporal economy, (b) definition and optimality of hedging and reverse hedging behavior, (c) discrete Pareto-optimal allocations in a continuous-time economy with multiple goods, (d) incomplete capital markets that give complete-market allocations by dynamic trading strategies, and (e) supply and demand for future contracts.

Merton (1969, 1971, 1973), Breeden (1979), and Cox, Ingersoll, and Ross (1985) preceded this paper with well-known continuous-time models of consumption and portfolio choice. Important discrete-time multiperiod models were presented by Fama (1970), Hakansson (1970), Long (1974), Kraus and Litzenberger (1975), Dieffenbach (1976), Rubinstein (1976, 1981), Breeden and Litzenberger (1978), and Grauer and Litzenberger (1979). This paper extended or generalized results in those papers.

In the area of general portfolio theory, the paper carefully examines the "hedging demands" for the investment opportunity set, which Merton (1973) shows were the principal differences between single-period and multiperiod optimal portfolios. A hedge portfolio is defined here as a portfolio that stabilizes an individual's expected utility of *lifetime* consumption. Individuals who are infinitely risk averse are shown to hold portfolios that do hedge fully and give a certain utility for the lifetime consumption path.

In a new result, the paper shows that Merton's "hedging terms" are really composed of two separate effects. The first is the vector of compensating variations in wealth for opportunity set changes. This is the vector that would give a perfect hedge of lifetime consumption. However, those demands are multiplied by $1 - T^\star$, where $T^\star$ is the individual's Arrow–Pratt measure of relative risk tolerance, which is positive, but may be greater or less than unity. Thus, if risk tolerance exceeds unity, individuals will "reverse hedge."

The reason that this portfolio behavior is optimal for some individuals is that reverse hedging provides a higher multiperiod mean return than does a hedging strategy. For individuals with $T^\star > 1$, this higher mean offsets their distaste for the higher multiperiod variance. An example of this possibility is when one faces an opportunity set next period that may have a 25 percent or a 5 percent expected return on investment for the following period. A hedger would consume more both now and later with the 25 percent reinvestment opportunity. A reverse hedger would reduce current consumption in that situation to take advantage of the excellent investment opportunity. This strategy would provide for an average lifetime consumption path that is higher but more volatile. Optimally, it is shown that different individuals may rationally choose different strategies, depending on risk tolerance.

Futures contracts provide payoffs that are linear in commodity prices. However, Pareto-optimal risk allocations lead to nonlinear sharing rules. It is demonstrated that dynamic trading in linear futures contracts creates the optimal nonlinear allocations. The intuition for this result is very similar to the option replication intuition of Black and Scholes (1973). However, this is extended by handling the optimal allocations that are general functions of many commodity prices $C(P_1, P_2, \ldots, P_N)$. This development also shows how Ross's (1976) options with multiple contingencies can be created by continuous trading of the underlying assets. Thus, the paper shows that markets which appear to be incomplete may be dynamically complete.

Finally, the supply and demand positions of individuals in both financial and commodity futures contracts are derived. Demands for opportunity set hedges depend on risk aversion, on the compensating variations in wealth for opportunity set changes, and on the aggregate of all investors' exposures and risk tolerances. Correspondingly, demands for various commodity futures depend on the individual's consumption bundle compared with the aggregate consumption bundle in the economy. The risks of price uncertainty for the aggregate consumption bundle are shared by investors in relation to their respective risk tolerances.

References

Black, F. and Scholes, M. S. (1973) "The Pricing of Options and Corporate Liabilities," *Journal of Political Economy*, 81: 3, May–June, 637–54.

Breeden, D. T. (1979) "An Intertemporal Asset Pricing Model with Stochastic Consumption and Investment Opportunities," *Journal of Financial Economics*, 7: 3, September, 265–96.

Breeden, D. T. and Litzenberger, R. H. (1978) "Prices of State-Contingent Claims Implicit in Option Prices," *Journal of Business*, 51: 4, October, 621–51.

Cox, J. C., Ingersoll, J. E. and Ross, S. A. (1985) "A Theory of the Term Structure of Interest Rates," *Econometrica*, 53: 2, March, 385–407.

Dieffenbach, B. C. (1976) "A Theory of Securities Markets under Uncertainty," *Review of Economic Studies*, 43: 2, June, 317–27.

Fama, E. F. (1970) "Efficient Capital Markets: A Review of Theory and Empirical Work," *Journal of Finance*, 25: 2, May, 383–417.

Grauer, F. L. A. and Litzenberger, R. H. (1979) "The Pricing of Commodity Futures Contracts, Nominal Bonds and other Risky Assets under Commodity Price Uncertainty," *Journal of Finance*, 34: 1, March, 69–83.

Hakansson, N. H. (1970) "Optimal Investment and Consumption Strategies under Risk for a Class of Utility Functions," *Econometrica*, 38: 5, September, 587–607.

Kraus, A. and Litzenberger, R. H. (1975) "Market Equilibrium in a Multiperiod State Preference Model with Logarithmic Utility," *Journal of Finance*, 30: 5, December, 1213–27.

Long, J. B. (1974) "Stock Prices, Inflation, and the Term Structure of Interest Rates," *Journal of Financial Economics*, 1: 2, 131–70.

Merton, R. C. (1969) "Lifetime Portfolio Selection Under Uncertainty: The Continuous-Time Case," *Review of Economics and Statistics*, 51: 3, August, 247–57.

Merton, R. C. (1971) "Optimum Consumption and Portfolio Rules in a Continuous-Time Model," *Journal of Economic Theory*, 3: 4, December, 373–413.

Merton, R. C. (1973) "An Intertemporal Capital Asset Pricing Model," *Econometrica*, 41: 5, September, 867–87.

Ross, S. A. (1976) "Options and Efficiency," *Quarterly Journal of Economics*, 90: 1, February, 75–89.

Rubinstein, M. (1976) "The Valuation of Uncertain Income Streams and the Pricing of Options," *Bell Journal of Economics*, 7: 2, Autumn, 407–25.

Rubinstein, M. (1981) *A Discrete-Time Synthesis of Financial Theory* (Greenwich, CT: JAI Press).

Bibliographical Listing

"Empirical Tests of the Consumption-Oriented CAPM" (with Michael R. Gibbons and Robert H. Litzenberger), *Journal of Finance*, 44: 2, June 1989, 231–62.

"Consumption, Production, Inflation and Interest Rates: A Synthesis," *Journal of Financial Economics*, 16: 1, May 1986, 3–39.

"Allocational Roles of Options on Bonds," *Stanford GSB Working Paper 720*, revised December 1983.

"Hedging and Valuation Uses of Commodity Options," *Working Paper*, Yale University School of Organization and Management, March 1982.

Futures Markets and Commodity Options: Hedging and Optimality in Incomplete Markets

DOUGLAS T. BREEDEN

1 Introduction

Recent works by Hakansson [21–23], Ross [32], and Breeden and Litzenberger [8] have considered alternative structures of capital markets that are considerably less extensive than a complete Arrow–Debreu securities market but permit all unconstrained Pareto-optimal allocations of time–state contingent consumption claims within the contexts of their models. A difficulty with their results is that they do not explicitly consider a multi-good economy, which has greater complexity of efficient allocations than does the single-good model.[1] This paper demonstrates that efficient allocations in a multi-good economy can be attained with a limited number of markets that include "unconditional" futures contracts or commodity options.[2]

The role of contingent commodity contracts in the allocation of goods under uncertainty has been amply demonstrated by Debreu [13]. However, contingent-claims markets are much less prevalent than would appear to be optimal. To quote a recent paper by Townsend [36, p. 54]:

> In particular, the existence of futures or forward markets in which unconditional rather than contingent claims are traded is regarded by some as a phenomenon in need of an explanation, and by others as prima facie evidence of some inefficiency.

Townsend then proves that if there are as many linearly independent spot commodity prices as there are states of the world, then unconditional forward contracts have the spanning property that Arrow–Debreu securities have, and they therefore constitute a Pareto-optimal capital market. Unfortunately, this is a very weak theorem in answer to the effi-

Reproduced from *Journal of Economic Theory*, 32: 2, April 1984, 275–300.

I am grateful for the helpful comments of Philip Dybvig, Stephen Ross, an anonymous referee, and especially Robert Litzenberger. Of course, I am solely responsible for any remaining errors.

ciency question raised in the quotation, since there are surely more economic states of the world than there are commodities. For example, with just two commodities that can each have prices \$1 or \$2, four states of the world are necessary to provide a complete description of these prices: {(\$1, \$1), (\$1, \$2), (\$2, \$1), (\$2, \$2)}. Two unconditional futures contracts cannot span these state payoffs. Thus the efficiency question remains unanswered for many interesting cases. In this paper (section 3) we show that, with continuous trading in unconditional futures contracts, contingent futures contracts are not necessary for optimality of capital markets. Without continuous trading, options on specified portfolios of commodity options and aggregate nominal consumption are shown (section 6) to comprise a Pareto-optimal capital market; again, contingent futures contracts are not necessary, as they are spanned by this capital market.

In sections 4 and 5, in a multi-good extension of Merton's [28] continuous-time economic model, we derive individuals' long or short positions in the various futures contracts in terms of their measures of relative risk aversion, their consumption preferences, and their reinvestment risks. These sections generalize and extend some of the hedging and "reverse hedging" results that were presented by Merton [28], Long [26], Fischer [18], Dieffenbach [16], and Grauer and Litzenberger [19]. An individual's futures portfolio is considered as part of his overall asset portfolio. Since an individual chooses a portfolio that is mean–variance efficient in his real wealth, the futures portfolio is related to the effects of those holdings on the mean and variance of real wealth. It is shown that the variance-reducing effects of hedging (on real wealth) can be offset (in lifetime utility terms) by the mean-expanding impact of reverse hedging. Consistent with prior works, logarithmic utility is the dividing line between portfolios dominated by mean effects and those dominated by variance effects of futures. Throughout the hedging analysis, the effects of futures holdings on the mean and variance of lifetime utility are distinguished from their effects upon the mean and variance of current consumption.

2 Optimal Allocations in a Multi-good Multiperiod Economy

In this section, characteristics of Pareto-optimal allocations of consumption goods in a multi-good multiperiod economy are derived. In particular, using a preference assumption and an assumption on probability beliefs, it is shown that any individual *k*'s optimal state-contingent consumption bundle of the *N* goods at time *t*, $\boldsymbol{c}_t^k = (c_{1t}^k, \dots, c_{Nt}^k)'$, can be written as a function of (only) the vector of aggregate consumption goods at that time,

$\boldsymbol{C}_t = \Sigma_k \boldsymbol{c}_t^k$. Furthermore, for any given date it is shown that all states of the world with the same level of aggregate nominal expenditure and consumption goods prices have the same optimal allocation of consumption goods to individuals. The results of these theorems are used in the next section to determine optimal capital market structures.

The restriction on individuals' preferences that is assumed is as follows.

Assumption 1 Each individual's von Neumann–Morgenstern utility function is time additive and state independent in terms of consumption bundles. Mathematically, individual k maximizes

$$U^k(\boldsymbol{c}_1^k, \boldsymbol{c}_2^k, \ldots, \boldsymbol{c}_{T_k}^k) = \sum_t \sum_{s \in S_t} \pi_{ts}^k u^k(\boldsymbol{c}_{ts}^k, t), \tag{1}$$

where T_k is k's time of death, S_t is the set of possible states at time t, and π_{ts}^k is k's subjective probability for state s at time t. The utility function u^k is monotonically increasing and strictly quasi-concave.

In each of the paper's theorems, either homogeneous beliefs or one of the following two assumptions of conditionally homogeneous beliefs is used.[3]

Assumption 2 Given the vector of aggregate consumption of all goods at date t, individuals agree upon the probabilities of states at date t.[4] That is, $\pi_{ts}^k = \pi_{tC}^k \pi_{ts|C}$, where π_{tC}^k is k's subjective probability for an aggregate consumption vector $\boldsymbol{C}$ at time t, and $\pi_{ts|C}$ is k's probability that state s occurs at time t, conditional upon an aggregate consumption vector $\boldsymbol{C}$ at time t.

Assumption 3 Given the $(N+1)$-vector $(E, \boldsymbol{P})$ of aggregate nominal consumption expenditure and goods prices at time t, individuals agree upon the probabilities of states at time t.

The following two theorems characterize all Pareto-optimal allocations in this class of economies, which includes many of the models in the literature of financial economics.

Theorem 1 If assumptions 1 and 2 hold, then any unconstrained Pareto-optimal allocation of time–state contingent consumption goods is such that, at each date, all states with the same vector of aggregate goods consumption have the same allocation of goods to individuals. Furthermore, given assumption 1, assumption 2 is both necessary and sufficient for the theorem.

Theorem 2 If assumptions 1 and 3 hold, then any unconstrained Pareto-optimal allocation of time–state contingent consumption goods is such that, at each date, all states with the same consumption goods' prices and aggregate nominal consumption expenditure have the same allocation of consumption goods and consumption expenditure to individuals. Furthermore, given assumption 1, assumption 3 is both necessary and sufficient for the theorem.

The proofs of theorems 1 and 2 are given in appendix A.

Theorem 1 implies that each individual's optimal vector of consumption goods at time t can be written as a function of (only) time and the aggregate vector of consumption goods at that time, that is, $\tilde{\boldsymbol{c}}_t^k = \boldsymbol{c}^k(\tilde{\boldsymbol{C}}_t, t)$. A special case of this theorem is Breeden and Litzenberger's [8] single-good version, $\tilde{c}_t^k = c^k(\tilde{C}_t, t)$, which was a part of the consumption-oriented CAPM theory. Their single-good result implied that (with homogeneous beliefs) each individual's optimal consumption rate was locally perfectly correlated with every other person's and with the aggregate consumption rate. In this multi-good economy with homogeneous beliefs, marginal utilities of consumption dollars will be perfectly correlated. However, in a multi-good economy, the consumption rates of all individuals for a single good (such as cheese) will not be locally perfectly correlated but will depend upon the aggregate supplies of *all* goods. The power of theorem 1 is its statement that other economic variables such as interest rates, prospective returns on risky assets, and aggregate output affect individuals' optimal consumption rates if and only if they affect optimal aggregate consumption rates.

Theorem 2 is just the dual problem version of theorem 1, stating the same basic result in terms of aggregate expenditure and the vector of goods' prices. The result is that individual k's optimal nominal expenditure rate $\tilde{e}_t^k$ at time t can be written in terms of the aggregate nominal expenditure rate, the vector of consumption goods' prices, and time, that is, $\tilde{e}_t^k = e^k(\tilde{E}_t, \tilde{\boldsymbol{P}}_t, t)$.

From the result of theorem 2 that the Pareto-optimal allocation of nominal consumption expenditure at date t depends only upon aggregate expenditure and consumption goods' prices at t, it is not surprising that futures contracts, forward contracts, and commodity options have significant roles in risk allocation. However, with the generality and diversity of preferences permitted by the analysis, futures, forwards, and options are *not* sufficient to span all possible Pareto-optimal allocations with simple buy and hold strategies. The risk-sharing limitations of buying and holding these contracts are well appreciated, and so they will only be outlined prior to the analysis of risk sharing with continuous trading given in the next section.

Forward contracts can be viewed as having payoffs at maturity that are linear in (equal to) the underlying commodity's price at maturity. Consequently, these contracts and futures contracts for aggregate nominal consumption span the space of efficient allocations if and only if all individuals have optimal nominal consumption levels that are linear in aggregate consumption and consumption goods' prices at each date, that is, only if

$$e_t^k(\tilde{E}, \tilde{\boldsymbol{P}}) = a_t^k + \sum_i b_{ti}^k \tilde{P}_{ti} + c_t^k \tilde{\boldsymbol{E}}, \qquad \forall\, k, t. \tag{2}$$

Schrems [34], Ross [32], Breeden and Litzenberger [8], and Banz and Miller [3] showed that portfolios of call or put options on an asset with price $\tilde{P}_t$ can achieve any desired contingent payoff function $f(\tilde{P}_t)$. Thus portfolios of commodity options and options on aggregate consumption span the set of allocations that are additive (but not necessarily linear) functions of $(E, \boldsymbol{P})$ such as

$$e_t^k(\tilde{E}_t, \tilde{\boldsymbol{P}}_t) = a_t^k + \sum_i f_{ti}^k(\tilde{P}_{ti}) + f_{te}^k(\tilde{E}_t). \tag{3}$$

Neither portfolios of futures contracts nor portfolios of commodity options can span the general space of efficient allocations as given by theorem 2, since these simple portfolios do not capture the interactions among consumption goods prices and aggregate expenditure that determine the optimal allocation $\{e_t^k(\tilde{E}, \tilde{\boldsymbol{P}})\}$. For example, the payoff function $e^k(\tilde{P}_1, \tilde{P}_2) = \tilde{P}_1 \cdot \tilde{P}_2$ cannot be achieved by simple buying and holding of futures, forwards, or commodity options on goods 1 and 2. More powerful sequential trading strategies are examined in the following sections.

3 Continuous Trading and the Optimality of Futures Markets

Now consider an economy with continuous trading and with all economic variables following diffusion processes, as in the models of Merton [28], Cox, Ingersoll, and Ross [11], and Breeden [6]. In these models (as well as in discrete-time multiperiod models), individual k uses dynamic programming to determine his indirect utility function for current wealth W^k and makes consumption–investment decisions for the current period based upon that function and the utility of current consumption. If the relevant characteristics of consumption, income, and investment opportunities are stochastic over time and are represented by the "state" vector s, then individual k's indirect utility function is written as $J^k(W^k, s, t)$.

Individual k's demands for risky assets in the continuous-time multicommodity model are[5]

$$\boldsymbol{w}^k W^k = T^k \mathbf{V}_{aa}^{-1}(\boldsymbol{\mu} - \boldsymbol{r}) + \mathbf{V}_{aa}^{-1}\mathbf{V}_{as}\boldsymbol{H}_s^k, \tag{4}$$

where $\boldsymbol{w}^k$ is the $A \times 1$ vector of the individual's wealth shares invested in various risky assets, and $1-\Sigma_i w_i^k = w_0^k$ is the fraction of wealth invested in the (nominally) riskless asset. The $A \times A$ incremental covariance matrix for instantaneous nominal rates of return on assets is $\mathbf{V}_{aa}$, and $\mathbf{V}_{as}$ is the $A \times S$ matrix of incremental covariances of assets' returns with the various state variables describing the investment, income, and consumption opportunity sets. Individual k's absolute risk tolerance in terms of the indirect utility function is $T^k = -\mathcal{J}_W^k / \mathcal{J}_{WW}^k$ and k's relative risk tolerance is $T^{\star k} = T^k / W^k$. The $S \times 1$ vector denoted by $\boldsymbol{H}_s^k = -\mathcal{J}_{sW}^k / \mathcal{J}_{WW}^k$ gives individual k's "hedging demands against adverse changes in the consumption–investment opportunity set," in Merton's [28] terminology. The instantaneous expected rates of return on risky assets are given by the $A \times 1$ vector $\boldsymbol{\mu}$ and $\boldsymbol{r} = r \cdot \boldsymbol{1}$ where $\boldsymbol{1}$ is an $A \times 1$ vector of ones and r is the instantaneous riskless interest rate (in nominal terms).

Aggregating the demand vectors in (4) gives the market portfolio $\boldsymbol{w}^M M = \Sigma_k \boldsymbol{w}^k W^k$. Individual k's risky asset holdings can be stated in terms of his amount in the market portfolio and his amounts in the S portfolios having the highest correlation with the S state variables respectively:

$$\boldsymbol{w}^k W^k = \frac{T^k M}{T^M}(\boldsymbol{w}^M) + \mathbf{V}_{aa}^{-1}\mathbf{V}_{as}\left(\boldsymbol{H}_s^k - \frac{T^k}{T^M}\boldsymbol{H}_s^M\right), \tag{5}$$

where $T^M = \Sigma_k T^k$ and $\boldsymbol{H}_s^M = \Sigma_k \boldsymbol{H}_s^k$.

Define a "futures contract of instantaneous maturity on state variable s_1" as an asset with a gross payoff in the next instant that is equal to the first state variable s_1. If s_1 is the price of corn, then this futures contract would have a gross payoff equal to the price of corn in the next instant, just as a standard futures contract *at maturity* can be regarded as having a gross payoff equal to the value of the underlying commodity. When an instantaneous maturity futures contract is assumed to exist at all times for a variable like s_1, the implication is that at every instant a futures contract on s_1 expires and another one is created that matures in the instant.[6] This is analogous to the assumption that there always exists an instantaneous riskless discount bond but that the interest rate on it changes stochastically over time.

Assume that there exist S such futures contracts of instantaneous maturity that have zero net supplies in aggregate, and whose returns (by definition) are perfectly correlated with changes in the various state variables.[7] The assumption that aggregate supplies of futures are zeros (as is true with futures contracts traded on organized exchanges) implies that their fractions of the market portfolio are also zeros. The fact that the payoffs of the futures contracts are the levels of the various state variables implies that $\mathbf{V}_{aa}^{-1}\mathbf{V}_{as} = (\mathbf{I0})'$, where $\mathbf{I}$ is the $S \times S$ identity matrix and $\mathbf{0}$ is the $S \times (A-S)$ matrix of zeros.[8] The subvector $\boldsymbol{w}_s^k W^k$ of individual k's demands for futures contracts is obtained by combining these two facts with (5):[9,10]

$$w_s^k W^k = \boldsymbol{H}_s^k - \frac{T^k}{T^M} \boldsymbol{H}_s^M. \tag{6}$$

From (5) and (6), it is seen that individual k's portfolio consists of $T^k M/T^M$ dollars in the market portfolio, S holdings of the form $H_{sj}^k - H_{sj}^M T^k/T^M$ in the futures contract for state variable j, and the remainder of wealth in the nominally riskless asset. Since the indirect utility function $\mathcal{J}^k(W^k, s, t)$ and its derivatives (which determine $\boldsymbol{H}_s^k$ and T^k) are all dependent upon the state of the world, each individual's portfolio weights will in general change over time in response to changing wealth, changing consumption and investment opportunities, and life cycle considerations.

The paper's principal theorem on allocational efficiency is theorem 3 below. This theorem states that if individuals hold the market portfolio, the riskless asset, and the S futures contracts in the proportions just derived, then the resulting intertemporal allocation of consumption goods to individuals is an unconstrained Pareto-optimal allocation. The proof of the theorem demonstrates that the marginal rate of substitution of dollars at any one time and state for dollars at any other time and state is the same for all individuals, which is the criterion for an unconstrained Pareto optimum. The theorem is a global theorem, in the sense that it is true for allocations that are discrete distances apart in time, as well as for allocations that are at adjacent points in time; of course, continuous trading is assumed throughout the theorem. Furthermore, it is also shown that if there do not exist futures contracts or portfolios whose returns are locally perfectly correlated with changes in state variables, then the allocation will not be an unconstrained Pareto optimum for all preferences within the time-additive class, given that there is at least one stochastic state variable for opportunities.

Theorem 3 In the multi-good continuous-time economic model with individuals who have time-additive preferences as in assumption 1 and who have fully homogeneous beliefs, the following $S+2$ funds (or any nonsingular transformation of them) are necessary and sufficient for the capital markets to permit all possible unconstrained Pareto-optimal allocations of time–state contingent consumption: an instantaneously riskless asset in nominal terms, the market portfolio, and S futures contracts (of instantaneous maturity) for the elements describing the consumption–income–investment opportunity set.

Since the proof is not an obvious extension of proofs in the literature, it is presented in the text. Readers may skip to the next section, where the actual supplies and demands for futures contracts are examined, without losing the main points of the paper.

PROOF The criterion for an unconstrained Pareto optimum is that the marginal rate of substitution (MRS) of a unit of the numeraire ("dollars") between any two time–states be the same for all individuals. An optimal policy has the marginal utility of expenditure $u_c^k(e^k, \boldsymbol{P}, t)$ for individual k equal to the marginal utility of wealth $\mathcal{J}_W^k(W^k, \boldsymbol{s}, t)$. Thus the sufficiency part of the theorem can be shown by proving that (where θ is the state of the world at time t)

$$\frac{\mathcal{J}_W^k[W^k(\theta), \boldsymbol{s}(\theta), t]}{\mathcal{J}_W^k(W_{t_0}^k, \boldsymbol{s}_{t_0}, t_0)} = \frac{\mathcal{J}_W^j[W^j(\theta), \boldsymbol{s}(\theta), t]}{\mathcal{J}_W^j(W_{t_0}^j, \boldsymbol{s}_{t_0}, t_0)}, \qquad \forall\, \theta, \{j, k\}, t > t_0. \tag{7}$$

The equivalence of MRSs in (7) is shown in logarithm form by showing that

$$\ln \mathcal{J}_W^k(\theta, t) - \ln \mathcal{J}_W^k(t_0) = f(\theta, t), \qquad \forall\, k, \tag{8}$$

where $f(\theta, t)$ is independent of k. As seen today (at time t_0), the difference between the logarithm of the marginal utility of wealth today and at a future time and state is given by Itô's stochastic integral as

$$\ln \mathcal{J}_W^k(t) - \ln \mathcal{J}_W^k(t_0) = \int_{t_0}^{t} \left[\frac{\mathrm{d} \ln \mathcal{J}_W^k(\tau)}{\mathrm{d}\tau}\right] \mathrm{d}\tau. \tag{9}$$

It will be shown that the Itô stochastic differential $\mathrm{d} \ln \mathcal{J}_W^k$ is the same for all k at all points in time. This implies that the integral in (9) is the same for all k, which gives an $f(\theta, t)$ for which (8) is true, thereby proving sufficiency.

The drift and diffusion parameters for $\mathrm{d} \ln \mathcal{J}_W^k$ are obtained from those for $\mathrm{d}\mathcal{J}_W^k$ by Itô's lemma as follows:

$$\mathrm{d}\mathcal{J}_W^k \equiv \mu_{J_W}^k \,\mathrm{d}t + \sigma_{J_W}^k \,\mathrm{d}Z^k$$

$$\Rightarrow \mathrm{d} \ln \mathcal{J}_W^k = \left[\frac{1}{\mathcal{J}_W^k} \mu_{J_W}^k - \frac{1}{2(\mathcal{J}_W^k)^2} (\sigma_{J_W}^k)^2\right] \mathrm{d}t + \frac{1}{\mathcal{J}_W^k} \sigma_{J_W}^k \,\mathrm{d}Z^k. \tag{10}$$

Cox, Ingersoll, and Ross [11] have shown that $\mu_{J_W}^k / \mathcal{J}_W^k = -r$, which is stochastic but the same for all k.[11] Thus it only remains to show that the remaining two terms of (10) are the same for all individuals.

The third term in (10) is the locally stochastic component of the change in marginal utility. Since $\mathcal{J}_W^k = \mathcal{J}_W^k(W^k, \boldsymbol{s}, t)$, the stochastic movement in k's marginal utility can be derived from the stochastic movements in k's wealth and in the state vector for opportunities. Itô's lemma gives

$$\sigma_{J_W}^k \,\mathrm{d}Z^k = \mathcal{J}_{WW}^k(\sigma_W^k \,\mathrm{d}Z_W^k) + \boldsymbol{\mathcal{J}}_{Ws}^k(\boldsymbol{\sigma}_s \,\mathrm{d}\boldsymbol{Z}_s). \tag{11}$$

The random wealth impact upon marginal utility derives from k's portfolio weights. Given the market portfolio holding of MT^k/T^M and the futures holdings as in (6), we have

$$\frac{1}{\mathcal{J}_W^k}\,\sigma_{J_W}^k\,\mathrm{d}Z^k = \frac{1}{\mathcal{J}_W^k}\left\{\mathcal{J}_{WW}^k\left[\frac{MT^k}{T^M}\,\sigma_M\,\mathrm{d}Z_M + \left(\boldsymbol{H}_s^k - \frac{T^k}{T^M}\,\boldsymbol{H}_s^M\right)\boldsymbol{\sigma}_s\,\mathrm{d}\boldsymbol{Z}_s\right]\right.$$
$$\left. + \boldsymbol{\mathcal{J}}_{Ws}^k\boldsymbol{\sigma}_s\,\mathrm{d}\boldsymbol{Z}_s\right\}$$
$$= -\frac{M}{T^M}\,\sigma_M\,\mathrm{d}Z_M + \frac{\boldsymbol{H}_s^M}{T^M}\,\boldsymbol{\sigma}_s\,\mathrm{d}\boldsymbol{Z}_s, \tag{12}$$

which is the same for all individuals k. This demonstrates that, with futures, all individuals' marginal utilities are locally perfectly correlated.

The remaining second term of (10) is proportional to $(\sigma_{J_W}^k)^2/(\mathcal{J}_W^k)^2$. Again, Itô's lemma can be used to find the variance of k's marginal utility as follows:

$$(\sigma_{J_W}^k)^2 = (\mathcal{J}_{WW}^k\boldsymbol{\mathcal{J}}_{Ws}^k)\begin{pmatrix} V_{WW}^k\boldsymbol{V}_{Ws}^k \\ \boldsymbol{V}_{sW}^k\mathbf{V}_{ss}\end{pmatrix}\begin{pmatrix}\mathcal{J}_{WW}^k \\ \boldsymbol{\mathcal{J}}_{sW}^k\end{pmatrix}. \tag{13}$$

This can be computed by using k's portfolio weights to compute k's wealth variance V_{WW}^k and k's covariances of wealth with the state vector $\boldsymbol{V}_{sW}^k$, and then substituting those into (13). The result is that the second term of (10) is proportional to

$$\frac{(\sigma_{J_W}^k)^2}{(\mathcal{J}_W^k)^2} = \left(\frac{M}{T^M}\right)^2\sigma_M^2 + \frac{2M}{(T^M)^2}\,\boldsymbol{V}_{Ms}\boldsymbol{H}_s^M + \frac{1}{(T^M)^2}\,\boldsymbol{H}_s^M\mathbf{V}_{ss}\boldsymbol{H}_s^M, \tag{14}$$

which is the same for all individuals. Equation (14) could also be obtained straight from (12) and the variance–covariance matrix for $(M, \boldsymbol{s})$.

Sufficiency has now been proved since all parts of the change in the logarithm of marginal utility in (10) are the same for all individuals.

Consider individuals' portfolio demands (5) when there are no portfolios that perfectly hedge against all state variables' changes: each individual's net hedging demands $\boldsymbol{H}_s^k - (T^k/T^M)\boldsymbol{H}_s^M$ go to the portfolios $\mathbf{V}_{aa}^{-1}\mathbf{V}_{as}$, which were shown by Breeden [6] to have maximum correlations with respect to state variables. Now reformulate the portfolio problem slightly, letting the first S assets be those portfolios $\mathbf{V}_{aa}^{-1}\mathbf{V}_{as}$, and letting the remaining assets be those $A - S$ assets that, when combined with the hedge portfolios, span the same space as the original A assets. Clearly, the same returns are possible and optimal as before. However, if we let $\boldsymbol{\sigma}_p\,\mathrm{d}\boldsymbol{Z}_p$ be the stochastic components of returns on the hedge portfolios, the stochastic component of k's marginal utility that corresponds to equation (11) is

$$\frac{1}{\mathcal{J}_W^k}\,\sigma_{J_W}^k\,\mathrm{d}Z^k = \frac{1}{\mathcal{J}_W^k}\left\{\mathcal{J}_{WW}^k\left[\frac{MT^k}{T^M}\,\sigma_M\,\mathrm{d}Z_M + \left(\boldsymbol{H}_s^k - \frac{T^k}{T^M}\,\boldsymbol{H}_s^M\right)\boldsymbol{\sigma}_p\,\mathrm{d}\boldsymbol{Z}_p\right]\right.$$

$$\left. + \boldsymbol{\mathcal{J}}_{Ws}^k\boldsymbol{\sigma}_s\,\mathrm{d}\boldsymbol{Z}_s\right\}$$

$$= -\frac{M}{T^M}\,\sigma_M\,\mathrm{d}Z_M + \frac{\boldsymbol{H}_s^M}{T^M}\,\boldsymbol{\sigma}_p\,\mathrm{d}\boldsymbol{Z}_p - \frac{\boldsymbol{H}_s^k}{T^k}\,(\boldsymbol{\sigma}_p\,\mathrm{d}\boldsymbol{Z}_p - \boldsymbol{\sigma}_s\,\mathrm{d}\boldsymbol{Z}_s). \tag{15}$$

If there are no perfect hedges available, $\boldsymbol{\sigma}_p\,\mathrm{d}\boldsymbol{Z}_p \neq \boldsymbol{\sigma}_s\,\mathrm{d}\boldsymbol{Z}_s$ for some states of the world. In those cases, preferences ($\boldsymbol{H}_s^k$) can be chosen so that individuals' marginal utilities are not perfectly correlated, which implies a nonoptimal allocation. ∎

4 Supply and Demand for Futures Contracts

In the previous section, theorem 3 demonstrated that continuous trading in "futures contracts" for elements of the consumption and investment opportunity set allow individuals to achieve an unconstrained Pareto-optimal allocation of risk. The characteristics of Pareto-optimal allocations, as given earlier by theorems 1 and 2, have not changed since a central planner is not concerned with whether trading is continuous, discrete, or once and for all; the planner simply maximizes expected utilities subject to resource constraints. Thus continuous trading in "unconditional" futures contracts achieves a sharing of commodity prices' risks and aggregate expenditure's risk that is not necessarily linear or additive in commodity prices and expenditure. For example, continuous trading in futures contracts can achieve the contingent payoff function at a future time t of $\tilde{e}_t = \tilde{p}_{1t}^{\alpha_1}\tilde{p}_{2t}^{\alpha_2}$, where buy and hold strategies of futures and commodity options could not. This construction utilizes the important insights of Black and Scholes [5] in their demonstration that the nonlinear payoffs of an option can be replicated by continuous trading in the underlying asset and a bond.

This section examines individuals' holdings of these futures contracts and relates them to individuals' preferences for the various consumption goods and to individuals' differential exposures to reinvestment risks. The analysis of this section generalizes and extends some of the results obtained by Merton [28], Long [26], Fischer [18], Dieffenbach [16], and Grauer and Litzenberger [19] in their examinations of the consumption and investment hedging aspects of individuals' portfolios. Since the continuous-time model is the same as that of Breeden [6], which is a multi-good version of Merton's [28] model, the consumption-oriented asset pricing theory applies. Given that, the focus of this section is entirely upon portfolio theory and hedging.

Individual k's portfolio of futures contracts was shown in section 3 to be (equation (6))

$$\boldsymbol{w}_s^k W^k = \boldsymbol{H}_s^k - \frac{T^k}{T^M} \boldsymbol{H}_s^M.$$

Thus it is clear that whether in equilibrium an individual demands (is net long) or supplies (is net short) a particular futures contract depends critically upon the magnitude of his element of $\boldsymbol{H}_s^k$ relative to his risk tolerance share of the aggregate vector $\boldsymbol{H}_s^M$. To understand these supplies and demands for futures, an analysis of the $\boldsymbol{H}_s^k$ vector follows.

Applying the implicit function theorem to the function for marginal utility of wealth $J_W^k(W^k, \boldsymbol{s}, t)$ gives that $H_{s_j}^k$ is the compensating variation in wealth for a change in state variable j that is required to maintain the current level of marginal utility of wealth, that is,

$$H_{s_j}^k = \frac{-J_{Ws_j}^k}{J_{WW}^k} = \frac{\partial W^k}{\partial s_j}\bigg|_{J_W}. \tag{16}$$

As noted, at the individual's optimum, his marginal utility of wealth must equal his marginal utility of nominal consumption expenditure:

$$J_W^k(W^k, \boldsymbol{s}, t) = u_e^k(e^k, \boldsymbol{P}, t). \tag{17}$$

An alternative calculation of $H_{s_j}^k$ is given by finding $J_{Ws_j}^k$ and J_{WW}^k by implicit differentiation of (17) and then using the implicit function theorem for the expenditure function:[12]

$$H_{s_j}^k = \frac{\partial W^k}{\partial s_j}\bigg|_{e^k} = \frac{\partial W^k}{\partial s_j}\bigg|_{u^k} \quad \text{for elements of the investment opportunity set,} \tag{18}$$

$$H_{s_j}^k = \left(\frac{\partial e^k}{\partial P_j}\bigg|_{u_e^k} - \frac{\partial e^k}{\partial P_j}\right)\bigg/\left(\frac{\partial e^k}{\partial W^k}\right) \quad \text{for consumption goods' prices } P_j. \tag{19}$$

It is shown in appendix B that the vector of *commodity* futures demand components, given by (19) and now denoted $\boldsymbol{H}_c^k$, can be rewritten in a more instructive form:

$$\begin{aligned}\boldsymbol{H}_c^k &= e^k\left(\boldsymbol{\alpha}_c^k - \frac{\partial \ln e^k}{\partial \ln \boldsymbol{P}}\right)\bigg/\left(\frac{\partial e^k}{\partial W^k}\right) - T^k \boldsymbol{m}^k \\ &= \frac{\partial W^k}{\partial \boldsymbol{P}}\bigg|_{u^k} - T^k \boldsymbol{m}^k,\end{aligned} \tag{20}$$

where $\boldsymbol{\alpha}_c^k$ is individual k's current vector of budget shares spent on the various consumption goods (his average propensities to consume) and the $\boldsymbol{m}^k$ are individual k's marginal propensities to consume, $\boldsymbol{P}(\partial c^k/\partial e^k)$. That is, $\boldsymbol{m}^k$ represents the fractions of an additional dollar's consumption expenditure that k would spend on the various commodities.

Two examples will be given to indicate the implications of this analysis for individuals' holdings of futures contracts. First, consider the effect on an individual of an increase in an interest rate, *ceteris paribus*. Assume that the interest rate increase has a real wealth effect that is positive, thereby tending to increase current consumption expenditure e. However, the change has a negative effect on current consumption in that the price of current consumption has increased relative to the price of future consumption. The net result on current consumption is ambiguous; thus individual k's demand component $H_{s_j}^k$ may be either positive or negative. In any case, those who consume more with an increase in interest rates would tend to be long in bonds, and those whose consume less would tend to be short in bonds. Since equilibrium prohibits all investors from being net short or net long, equilibrium expected excess returns must create asset demands such that markets are cleared; this effect explains the second component of futures demands in (6), $-(T^k/T^m)\boldsymbol{H}_s^M$.

The second example of an individual's futures market position is of an increase in a consumption goods' price P_j. From (20), an individual who increases current total consumption expenditure would tend to be short in this commodity's futures market, whereas an individual who decreases current expenditures would tend to be long in this futures market. Furthermore, an individual with a very low income elasticity of demand for the given commodity would tend to be long in this futures market, as the good would have a relatively small share of his marginal consumption bundle. This has an intuitive basis in that goods that are "necessities" (low income elasticities of demand) are "hedged" more than "luxuries" (goods with high income elasticities).

A more complete analysis of individuals' supplies and demands for commodity futures contracts is given in section 3 for the case where an invariant price index exists, that is, when individuals have unitary income elasticities of demand for all goods. First, however, consideration will be given to the more general concept of hedging against changes in consumption *and* investment opportunities in this multiperiod model, with particular emphasis upon the role of futures markets as hedging instruments.

Merton [28], in a single-good model with changing investment opportunities, has characterized the $\boldsymbol{H}_s^k$ demands as "hedging" demands. The sense in which this is an apt characterization should be examined. From (18), futures contracts for investment set state variables held due to

$\boldsymbol{H}_s^k$ will provide state-contingent wealth that combines in effect with investment opportunity changes to maintain the utility of current consumption precisely. This is a myopic view of hedging, as only the stability of an individual's utility of *current* consumption is considered. Since an individual chooses a consumption bundle and asset portfolio to maximize his expected utility of *lifetime* consumption, a more appropriate concept of hedging considers the use of futures contracts in stabilizing an individual's expected utility of lifetime consumption.

A perfect hedge, as defined here, is a portfolio of assets whose return in the various states of the world is such that the individual's utility of lifetime consumption $J^k(W^k, s, t)$ is the same in all states of the world. Consequently, an individual's hedging portfolio would have weights that are the compensating variations in wealth required to maintain expected lifetime utility, that is, the weights would be $(-\boldsymbol{J}_s^k/J_W^k)$.

To examine the relation of the portfolio demand component $\boldsymbol{H}_s^k$ (which is Merton's hedging portfolio) to the lifetime hedging portfolio defined here, the following simplifying assumption is made for the remainder of this section.

Assumption 4 Individual k's vector of percentage compensating variations in wealth for changes in the state variables is not a function of k's wealth level.[13,14]

Mathematically, this assumption is that $(\partial/\partial W^k)(\boldsymbol{J}_s^k/W^k J_W^k) = \boldsymbol{0}$, which implies that

$$\boldsymbol{H}_s^k = \frac{-\boldsymbol{J}_{sW}^k}{J_{WW}^k} = W^k(1 - T^{\star k})\boldsymbol{\gamma}_s^k, \tag{21}$$

where $\boldsymbol{\gamma}_s^k$ is k's vector of percentage compensating variations, that is, $\boldsymbol{\gamma}_s^k = -\boldsymbol{J}_s^k/W^k J_W^k$, and $T^{\star k}$ is k's relative risk tolerance, as defined earlier.

Given assumption 4, individual k's portfolio of futures can be rewritten by substituting (21) into (6):

$$\boldsymbol{w}_s^k = (1 - T^{\star k})(\boldsymbol{\gamma}^k - \boldsymbol{\gamma}^M) + \left(1 - \frac{T^{\star k}}{T^{\star M}}\right)\boldsymbol{\gamma}^M + T^{\star k}(\boldsymbol{\gamma}_T^M - \boldsymbol{\gamma}^M), \tag{22}$$

where $\boldsymbol{\gamma}^M = \Sigma_k(W^k/M)\boldsymbol{\gamma}^k$ and $\boldsymbol{\gamma}_T^M = \Sigma_k(T^k/T^M)\boldsymbol{\gamma}^k$ are the wealth and risk tolerance weighted averages respectively of the individual's compensating variations.

From (22), an individual will hedge, in the sense that he will hold futures long for state variables whose increases hurt him more than the average person, if his relative risk tolerance is less than unity (the logarithm). If he is more risk tolerant than the logarithm, then the individual will tend to "reverse hedge," being short in futures for state variables whose increases hurt him more than the "typical" person. This generalizes similar results obtained by Dieffenbach [16] and by Grauer and Litzenberger [19] to investment opportunities, as well as consumption opportunities, and to more general utility functions.[15]

Individuals who have a greater relative risk tolerance than the average will bear more of the social risk of changes in consumption and investment opportunities. The final term in (22) is a residual portfolio that will be the same for all individuals; it represents the difference between the risk tolerance weighted average index weights and the wealth weighted average. If all individuals have identical relative risk tolerance, then this term is a vector of zeros. Of course, an individual who is infinitely risk averse (zero risk tolerance) would perfectly hedge against changes in investment and consumption opportunities, that is, $w_s^k = \gamma^k$, and would hold no other risky assets.

Equations (4) and (5) give the optimal portfolio of all assets for individual k. From (5), the total optimal portfolio consists of market portfolio holdings, futures holdings (6), and holdings of the riskless asset. The futures components of individuals' optimal portfolios have been described and related to individuals' consumption bundles and to their compensating variations in wealth for changes in state variables. An individual's total portfolio (market, futures, and riskless asset) can be viewed as a mean–variance efficient portfolio in his "real wealth," as shown by the following analysis.

An individual's asset portfolio is chosen to maximize his expected change in real wealth for a given variance of real wealth.[16] The individual's real wealth $W^\star$ is defined as nominal wealth deflated by an inverse index of consumption and investment opportunities, that is, $W^{\star k} = W^k / I^k(s, W^k)$. An asset's portfolio weight is an increasing function of its contribution to the individual's expected change in real wealth, and it is a decreasing function of its contribution to the variance of real wealth. With a wealth-invariant wealth deflator, an individual's asset portfolio (4) can be restated as

$$\begin{aligned} w^k &= T^{\star k}\mathbf{V}_{aa}^{-1}(\mu - r) + \mathbf{V}_{aa}^{-1}\mathbf{V}_{as}\gamma^k(1 - T^{\star k}) \\ &= \mathbf{V}_{aa}^{-1}\mathbf{V}_{al_k} + T^{\star k}\mathbf{V}_{aa}^{-1}(\mu - r - V_{al_k}), \end{aligned} \tag{23}$$

where V_{al_k} is the $A \times 1$ vector of covariances of assets' returns with the individual's wealth deflator. If futures contracts exist for all the state variables for the opportunity set, this simplifies to

$$w^k = \begin{pmatrix} \gamma^k \\ 0 \end{pmatrix} + T^{\star k}\left| \mathbf{V}_{aa}^{-1}(\mu - r) - \begin{pmatrix} \gamma^k \\ 0 \end{pmatrix} \right|. \tag{24}$$

The individual's total portfolio demands with incomplete markets (equation (23)) and those with effectively complete markets (equation (24)) can be explained as follows. The portfolio given by $\mathbf{V}_{aa}^{-1}\boldsymbol{V}_{al_k}$ has the maximum correlation of return with the wealth deflator and therefore is the best hedge against shifts in the opportunity set. If futures contracts exist, that portfolio is a futures portfolio with weights $\boldsymbol{\gamma}^k$. These holdings can be viewed as a result of the minimization of the variance of real wealth, that is, they represent normal hedging demands.

As an asset's real value is its nominal value divided by the wealth deflator, $P^\star = \tilde{P}/\tilde{I}$, the expression $\boldsymbol{\mu} - \boldsymbol{r} - \boldsymbol{V}_{al_k}$ is the continuous-time vector of expected real returns on assets in excess of the expected real return on the nominally riskless asset. Assets that have positive covariances with the deflator have lower expected real returns. Thus there are offsetting considerations in the holdings of assets to "hedge" against opportunity set change. Variance minimization considerations result in positive holdings of assets that hedge against opportunity set shifts, while mean maximization considerations result in offsetting negative holdings of the same assets. The net result is ambiguous, depending upon the individual's risk tolerance (as discussed). The reverse hedging possibility of the myopic hedging portfolio $\boldsymbol{H}_s^k$ is due to its juxtaposition of the conflicting effects of the holdings on real wealth's mean and variance.

5 Cobb–Douglas Consumption Preferences: An Example

In this example it is assumed that all consumers have utility functions for goods consumed that are members of the Cobb–Douglas class with homogeneity of unity, that is, $U(\boldsymbol{c}, t) = U(\Pi_{j=1}^{c} c_j^{\alpha_j}, t)$, where $\Sigma_j \alpha_j = 1$.

The optimal budget share for any commodity j is the constant α_j^k, regardless of total expenditures e^k or prices $\boldsymbol{P}$. Demand functions have unitary expenditure elasticities, zero cross-price elasticities, and unitary income elasticities. Budget shares $\boldsymbol{\alpha}^k$ could vary nonstochastically over time without changing the nature of the results, thus allowing consumption preferences to vary with age. However, this complication will be avoided here.

It is well known[17] that an expenditure-invariant price index exists for individuals with these homothetic preferences. The vector of budget shares gives the weights for the price index. If it is further assumed that the only changes in consumption and investment opportunities are changes in consumption goods' prices and that those prices follow a random walk over time, then the same price index would be a valid deflator for nominal wealth; that is, real wealth would simply be nominal wealth deflated by the price index. The vector of percentage compensating variations in wealth for percentage changes in consumption goods' prices would be the individual's vector of budget shares $\boldsymbol{\alpha}^k$; thus the individual's demands for commodity futures are as given in the general equation (22), but with $\boldsymbol{\gamma}^k$ identified as $\boldsymbol{\alpha}^k$.

The analysis of which investors will be long and which will be short proceeds much as in the previous section. To examine the effects of hedging and risk allocation on the supply and demand for futures, two polar cases are instructive: (a) assume that all individuals have the same level of relative risk tolerance but different vectors of budget shares, or (b) assume that all individuals have the same vector of budget shares (or price index) but different levels of risk tolerance. Consider first the case where all investors have the same level of relative risk tolerance, and let it be $T^{\star}$. From (22) and the above discussion, individual k's wealth shares $\boldsymbol{w}_c^k$ in the various commodity futures contracts are

$$\boldsymbol{w}_c^k = (1 - T^{\star})(\boldsymbol{\alpha}^k - \boldsymbol{\alpha}^M) \tag{25}$$

Therefore, when relative risk tolerance is less than unity, if an individual consumes more of a good than the aggregate, he will be long in that good's commodity futures market. Unless the individual's consumption bundle is precisely equal to the average bundle, he will be long in all futures such as those, and short in futures of goods that he consumes less of than the average. Conversely, if $T^{\star}$ is greater than unity, then all individuals would reverse hedge, being long in goods that they consume relatively less of and short in futures for goods of which they consume relatively large amounts. In light of the previous section's analysis, the reverse hedging possibility occurs when the increased real wealth variance effect is offset in the individual's expected utility by the increased expected change in real wealth created by the reverse hedging policy.

Consider now the other polar case – all investors have the same consumption bundles, $\boldsymbol{\alpha}^k = \boldsymbol{\alpha}$, but they have varying degrees of relative risk tolerance. In this case investor k will hold the following portfolio of commodity futures:

$$\boldsymbol{w}_c^k = \boldsymbol{\alpha}\left(1 - \frac{T^{\star k}}{T^{\star M}}\right) \tag{26}$$

This shows that an investor will be long in *all* futures contracts if his relative risk tolerance is less than that of the market, and he will be short in all contracts if his risk tolerance is greater than that of the market. This result arises from the fact that social risks and individual risks coincide for each individual in this case; such social risk and the rewards appropriate in equilibrium are allocated to individuals according to their respective tolerances for risk bearing.

6 Commodity Options

In section 2 it was noted that, while buy and hold portfolios of commodity options spanned a much larger space than that spanned by forward contracts, commodity options did not span the space of efficient allocations. Section 3 demonstrated that continuous trading in futures contracts or forward contracts spanned the space of efficient allocations. Of course, continuous trading in commodity options can span the same space of efficient allocations, but why have options when continuous trading in futures will do the same job? The reason is that transactions cost and heterogeneous beliefs were not considered in the analysis of futures. Desired nonlinear payoffs may require less trading with commodity options than with futures or forwards, making commodity options cost effective in nonlinear risk allocation. In this section we briefly combine some of the results of the recent options literature with this paper's theorems to demonstrate that commodity options and options on portfolios of forward contracts have significant allocational roles in an economy with costly transactions.

Consider an economy where individuals have diverse beliefs about the future price of beef.[18] All agree that the price per pound at date t will be in the set $\{\$1, \$2, \$3, \$4, \$5, \$6\}$ but disagree on probabilities. The current futures price is \$4. Individual k receives information that the price is more likely to be \$3 or \$5 than k previously believed, with \$2 and \$6 being less likely. It is not possible for k to profit from this new information by simply buying or selling a futures contract and, since k is therefore unlikely to trade on the information, the allocation will not be efficient and prices will not "fully reflect all information."[19]

The literature on option pricing has shown that commodity options on the price of beef will allow k to speculate precisely on the new information, making both the allocation and the prices more efficient.[20] For readers unfamiliar with this construction, table 1.1 shows the contingent payoffs on commodity call options with exercise prices of \$2, \$3 and \$4 respectively, and shows how a \$1 payoff contingent upon a \$3 beef price is achieved by a portfolio ("butterfly spread") of these commodity options.[21] Since the method of construction is general, a set of commodity options with all exercise prices lets individuals create general risk-sharing functions of the form $f(\tilde{P}_B)$. In the beef price example, individual k would sell \$2 and \$6 claims (portfolios of call options) and buy commodity option portfolios that pay when the price of beef is \$3 or \$5. Thus marginal rates of substitution of beef in different states would be equated for all individuals with commodity options. Both prices and allocations should be more efficient as a result.

Table 1.1 Payoffs on options, spreads, and butterfly spreads

Price of beef ($)	*Payoffs on call options* C(2)	C(3)	C(4)	*Payoffs on spreads* *Spread A* C(2) – C(3)	*Spread B* C(3) – C(4)	*Butterfly spreads: spread A – spread B* C(2) – 2C(3) + C(4)
1.00	0	0	0	0	0	0
2.00	0	0	0	0	0	0
3.00	1	0	0	1	0	1
4.00	2	1	0	1	1	0
5.00	3	2	1	1	1	0
6.00	4	3	2	1	1	0

Actually, the allocational efficiency problem is more complex than in the example. For allocational efficiency, the marginal rate of substitution of beef in one state of the world for beef in another state must be the same for all individuals. For example, if beef and pork are substitutes, then the marginal utility of beef increases with decreases in pork consumption. Trading in commodity options for beef will ensure that the *expected* marginal rates of substitution of beef in various states, *conditional* upon the price of beef, are the same for all individuals. The problem is that there may be a number of states of the world with the same price of beef but different prices of pork. Commodity options for beef will have the same payoff in all states with the same price of beef; therefore they will not span the space of potential payoff functions across these states. Portfolios of commodity options for pork will span states with different pork prices, but will do so with payoffs that are independent of the price of beef, given the price of pork. Simple holdings of commodity options for beef and pork cannot span the general space of efficient allocations since the optimal holding today of beef options is dependent upon the (uncertain) future price of pork and the optimal holding of pork options is dependent upon the future price of beef.

For general optimal allocations, claims must be available that pay $1 only if the price of beef is $3 per pound and, simultaneously, the price of pork is $2 per pound. Such payoffs are particular mappings of commodity prices and of aggregate consumption into the real line, and are therefore subsets of Ross's [32] multiple options. As was just argued, simple commodity options will not span that space of efficient allocations. However, Ross has shown that options on portfolios of the underlying assets (forward contracts) span the larger space that is spanned by multiple options. Combining Ross's result [32, theorem 5] with theorem 2 gives the following corollary to theorem 2.

Corollary 1 Given assumptions 1 and 3, for each date t there exists a portfolio of forward contracts (maturing at date t) on consumption goods' prices and on aggregate nominal consumption such that call options on the portfolio span the space of efficient allocations of consumption at date t.

To see this result, assume that the prices of beef and pork may be any of {\$1, \$2, \$3, \$4, \$5, \$6}, so that there are 36 "states." A portfolio of ten forward contracts for beef and one forward contract for pork has a payoff that is different in each state. Therefore options on that portfolio of forward contracts will span all 36 states, giving general payoffs of the form $f(\tilde{P}_B, \tilde{P}_p)$. After the options on the portfolio are purchased, no additional trading is required until the options mature. At that time, k uses the proceeds to purchase his desired consumption bundle in the spot market.

Ross's [32] characterization of the portfolio in corollary 1 as an "efficient fund" is apt in the sense that options on that fund's return span the space of efficient allocations. However, as Arditti and John [1] have shown, in general there is a virtual continuum of portfolios that span the same space and are therefore just as "efficient." The sets of weights that can be used for the portfolio of forward contracts depend upon the contingent price and expenditure combinations that are the possible states. As the joint probability distribution of the commodity prices is made more fine (continuous in the limit), the weights in the portfolio of forwards for corollary 1 involve more computations.

An alternative construction of a Pareto-optimal capital market in a multi-good economy will now be presented. It involves more complex financial instruments than Ross's simple options on a portfolio of forwards, but has simple and intuitive portfolio weights and spans the same space of allocations. The technique follows from the following observations.

1 As shown in table 1.1, a \$1 payment contingent upon a beef price of \$3 per pound at time t can be obtained from a portfolio of commodity options for beef; let this be portfolio A. Similarly, let portfolio B be the portfolio of commodity options that pays \$1 if the price of pork is \$2 per pound at time t.
2 The portfolio C that consists of portfolio A plus portfolio B has its maximum payoff when, simultaneously, beef is \$3 per pound and pork is \$2 per pound, and that maximum payoff equals \$2, the number of "contingencies."
3 An option on portfolio C, with an exercise price equal to the number of contingencies minus one, pays \$1 if and only if all contingencies are met, and pays zero otherwise.
4 By similar arguments, the same construction will work for a \$1 payoff contingent upon a number of commodity prices being equal to the

vector $\boldsymbol{P}$. If there are N contingencies, then the exercise price of the option on a portfolio of options is $N-1$.

This analysis demonstrates that if there exist sets of commodity options for a number of different goods, then a financial intermediary could buy those commodity options and issue warrants that would pay off only if commodity prices for the component goods simultaneously equaled prespecified levels. With diverse preferences, each individual has a different price index; since the relation of such warrants' payoffs to the commodity price vector is precise, each individual could construct a personalized index bond from a complete set of those warrants. Potential hedging and speculative uses of these options on portfolios of commodity options are immediate.

In practice, the increased hedging and speculative precision that are attainable with such option portfolios are partially offset by the cost of setting up the portfolios. The finer the partition, the lower will be the probability of a payoff and hence the lower will be the value of the payoff. With a number of tightly defined contingencies, each warrant will be nearly worthless. However, with widespread commodity options trading apparently on the horizon in the United States, more sophisticated construction of payoffs contingent upon the prices of groups of goods is not implausible.

7 Conclusion

In this paper we have described the roles of futures markets and commodity options in the optimal allocation of consumption across time–states. With certain assumptions, it has been shown that contingent futures contracts are not necessary for allocational efficiency, since the same allocations can be attained by options on portfolios of commodity options or by continuous trading in unconditional futures contracts. In the continuous-time model, individuals' optimal holdings of the various futures contracts have been derived and interpreted. Both normal hedging and reverse hedging are possible because of the offsetting effects of futures holdings on the mean and variance of real wealth.

Appendix A

Proof of Theorem 1

Any Pareto-optimal allocation of time–state contingent vectors of consumption goods solves max $\Sigma_k a^k U^k$ for a set of positive constants $\{a_k\}$, where the maximum is taken over all feasible allocations which are subject to resource constraints. A central planner (competitive equilibrium with optimal capital markets) would maximize the Lagrangian

$$\max_{\{c_{ts}^k\}} L = \sum_k a^k \left[\sum_t \sum_{s \in S_t} \pi_{ts}^k u_t^k (\boldsymbol{c}_{ts}^k) \right] + \sum_t \sum_{s \in S_t} \boldsymbol{\lambda}_{ts}' \left(\boldsymbol{C}_{ts} - \sum_k \boldsymbol{c}_{ts}^k \right). \qquad \text{(A1)}$$

With assumption 2, the right-hand side of (A1) can be rewritten as

$$\sum_t \sum_{\boldsymbol{C}_t} \sum_{s \in S_{t\boldsymbol{C}}} \pi_{ts|\boldsymbol{C}} \left[\sum_k a^k \pi_{t\boldsymbol{C}}^k u_t^k (\boldsymbol{c}_{ts}^k) + \frac{\boldsymbol{\lambda}_{ts}'}{\pi_{ts|\boldsymbol{C}}} \left(\boldsymbol{C}_t - \sum_k \boldsymbol{c}_{ts}^k \right) \right], \qquad \text{(A2)}$$

where $S_{t\boldsymbol{C}}$ is the set of all states at t with aggregate consumption vector $\boldsymbol{C}$. Thus, because of the assumption of time additivity of utility functions, the central planner's problem can be solved separately for each time–state, given $\{a^k\}$ and $\{\boldsymbol{C}_{ts}'\}$. As shown by examining expression (A2), the assumptions of state independence of utility and of conditionally homogeneous beliefs as in assumption 2 make the central planner's objective, resource constraint, and hence solution the same for all states with the same aggregate consumption vector (assuming uniqueness of the solutions to these subproblems). The critical element in this proof is that the central planner's objective function and constraint are effectively the same for all states with the same vector of aggregate consumption. The only state-dependent element of the central planner's weights on $\{U_t^k\}$ is $\pi_{ts|\boldsymbol{C}}$, but this is assumed to be the same for all individuals and does not affect the maximum problem.

The necessity of assumption 2, given assumption 1, is easily seen from the first-order conditions to (A1), which imply that if assumption 2 does not hold

$$\frac{\pi_{t\boldsymbol{C}}^k \pi_{ts_1|\boldsymbol{C}}^k \boldsymbol{u}_{ts_1}'^k}{\pi_{t\boldsymbol{C}}^k \pi_{ts_2|\boldsymbol{C}}^k \boldsymbol{u}_{ts_2}'^k} = \frac{\pi_{t\boldsymbol{C}}^j}{\pi_{t\boldsymbol{C}}^j} \frac{\pi_{ts_1|\boldsymbol{C}}^j \boldsymbol{u}_{ts_1}'^j}{\pi_{ts_2|\boldsymbol{C}}^j \boldsymbol{u}_{ts_2}'^j}, \qquad \forall s_1, s_2 \in S_{t\boldsymbol{C}} \qquad \text{(A3)}$$

where $u_{ts_1}'^k$ is individual k's marginal utility in time–state ts_1 of another unit of, say, good 1. Since $\boldsymbol{c}_{ts_1}^k = \boldsymbol{c}_{ts_2}^k$ implies that $u_{ts_1}'^k / u_{ts_2}'^k = 1$, for the theorem to hold

$$\frac{\pi_{ts_1|\boldsymbol{C}}^k}{\pi_{ts_2|\boldsymbol{C}}^k} = \frac{\pi_{ts_1|\boldsymbol{C}}^j}{\pi_{ts_2|\boldsymbol{C}}^j}, \qquad \forall s_1, s_2 \in S_{t\boldsymbol{C}}$$

must be true. Since $\sum_{s \in S_{t\boldsymbol{C}}} \pi_{ts|\boldsymbol{C}}^k = 1$ for all k, this condition implies assumption 2. ■

Proof of Theorem 2

At any given date, an individual k with state-independent consumption preferences has an optimal consumption bundle that depends upon nominal consumption expenditure e_k and consumption good prices $\boldsymbol{P}$ at that date, that is, $\boldsymbol{c}_{ts}^k = \boldsymbol{c}_{ts}^k(e_{ts}^k; \boldsymbol{P}_{ts})$. Any two states in which k has the same nominal expenditure and the same prices result in the same consumption bundle, as the solution to that subproblem is assumed to be unique. Consequently, to prove the first part of the theorem, it is sufficient to show that any two states at the same date with the same $(E, \boldsymbol{P})$ have the same optimal allocation of nominal expenditure $\{e^k\}$, where $E = \sum_k e^k$.

If we consider two states at date t with the same $(E, \boldsymbol{P})$, an optimal allocation of consumption expenditure results in the same MRS of "dollars" in one state for dollars in the other state for all individuals, that is,

$$\frac{\pi_{ts_1|\boldsymbol{E}}\pi^k_{t\boldsymbol{E}}u^k_e(e^k_{s_1};\boldsymbol{P},t)}{\pi_{ts_2|\boldsymbol{E}}\pi^k_{t\boldsymbol{E}}u^k_e(e^k_{s_2};\boldsymbol{P},t)} = \frac{\pi_{ts_1|\boldsymbol{E}}\pi^j_{t\boldsymbol{E}}u^j_e(e^j_{s_1};\boldsymbol{P},t)}{\pi_{ts_2|\boldsymbol{E}}\pi^j_{t\boldsymbol{E}}u^j_e(e^j_{s_2};\boldsymbol{P},t)}$$

$$\Rightarrow \frac{u^k_e(e^k_{s_1};\boldsymbol{P},t)}{u^k_e(e^k_{s_2};\boldsymbol{P},t)} = \frac{u^j_e(e^j_{s_1};\boldsymbol{P},t)}{u^j_e(e^j_{s_2};\boldsymbol{P},t)}, \qquad \forall\, j,k \text{ and } \forall\, s_1, s_2 \in S_{t\boldsymbol{E}}, \tag{A4}$$

where $S_{t\boldsymbol{E}}$ is a set of states with a common vector $(E, \boldsymbol{P})$. Since each individual has a utility function for nominal expenditure that is monotonic with $u_e > 0$ and $u_{ee} < 0$, $u^k_e(e^k_{s_1};\boldsymbol{P},t)/u^k_e(e^k_{s_2};\boldsymbol{P},t) \gtreqless 1$ iff $e^k_{s_1} \lesseqgtr e^k_{s_2}$. Thus, for assumption 4 to be satisfied, $e^k_{s_1} - e^k_{s_2}$ must be of the same sign for all individuals for all states s_1, $s_2 \in S_{t\boldsymbol{C}}$. However, this relation and the conservation equation cannot hold unless $e^k_{s_1} = e^k_{s_2}$, $\forall k$, $\forall s_1, s_2 \in S_{t\boldsymbol{C}}$. Thus the first part of the theorem is proved. The necessity of assumption 3 for the theorem, given assumption 1, is proved in the same way as for theorem 1. ■

Appendix B

The definition of the consumer's indirect utility function is

$$u(e,t;\boldsymbol{P}_c) = \max_{\boldsymbol{P}'\boldsymbol{c}=e} U(\boldsymbol{c},t) = \max_{\boldsymbol{c}}\,[U(\boldsymbol{c},t) + \lambda(e - \boldsymbol{P}'_c\boldsymbol{c})], \tag{B1}$$

and the first-order conditions for a maximum are

$$U_c = \lambda \boldsymbol{P}_c, \qquad \boldsymbol{u}_p = -\lambda \boldsymbol{c}, \qquad \text{and the shadow price } \lambda = u_e. \tag{B2}$$

It is most convenient to deal in changes in the logarithm of price changes. Doing so, from equation (19) we obtain

$$H_{\ln P_j} = \left(\frac{\partial e}{\partial \ln P_j}\bigg|_{u_e} - \frac{\partial e}{\partial \ln P_j}\right)\bigg/\left(\frac{\partial e}{\partial W}\right). \tag{B3}$$

By differentiating the optimality conditions in (B2) we obtain

$$\frac{\partial e}{\partial \ln P_j}\bigg|_{u_e} = \frac{-P_j u_{p_j e}}{u_{ee}} = \frac{u_e}{u_{ee}} P_j \frac{\partial c_j}{\partial e} + P_j c_j \tag{B4}$$

and

$$T = \frac{-J_W}{J_{WW}} = \frac{-u_e/u_{ee}}{\partial e/\partial W}. \tag{B5}$$

By substituting (B4) and (B5) into (B3), we obtain equation (20):

$$H_{\ln P_j} = e\left(\frac{P_j c_j}{e} - \frac{\partial \ln e}{\partial \ln P_j}\right)\bigg/\left(\frac{\partial e}{\partial W}\right) - TP_j \frac{\partial c_j}{\partial e}.$$

Notes

1 As Ross's model assumed that the complete state space must be spanned, it includes a multi-good economy as a special case; however, the number of options necessary for spanning in that model is much greater than in the other more recent papers referenced.

2 Throughout this paper the focus is upon *ex ante* Pareto optimality, rather than upon the *ex post* optimality of Starr [35].

3 Note that assumptions 2 and 3 are equivalent under the conditions of theorems 1 and 2, if the allocation is optimal.

4 The aggregate consumption vector is important information, but it is not a complete state description in the Arrow–Debreu sense. Given an aggregate consumption vector, states may, for example, differ in their descriptions of assets' payoffs, production possibilities, and probabilities of future consumption rates and asset returns.

5 See Merton's [28] equation (16), which can be derived with many commodities in terms of a general state vector $\boldsymbol{X}$.

6 This constant dimension but changing securities market basis is discussed by Cox, Ingersoll, and Ross [11].

7 An important point made by the referee is that if an opportunity set state variable (such as an expected inflation rate) is unobservable, then futures or options cannot be written for it. Theorem 3 demonstrates that if there is not a portfolio perfectly correlated with each state variable, then a reasonable economy can easily be found for which the allocation is not optimal. This is not such a significant problem in theorem 2 since commodity prices and aggregate expenditure are more reasonably assumed to be observable.

8 Breeden [6] demonstrated that $\mathbf{V}_{aa}^{-1}\mathbf{V}_{as}$ has as its columns the portfolios of assets that have maximum correlations of returns with the various state variables, that is, column j gives the portfolio that has the maximum correlation with state variable s_j. Given the "futures contracts" as defined, clearly these maximum correlation portfolios are holdings of only those futures contracts that correspond to the state variables (since they provide perfect correlations). Thus, $\mathbf{V}_{aa}^{-1}\mathbf{V}_{as}$ must be diagonal. With suitable normalizations of state variables, the diagonal elements can all be set to unity.

9 Standard futures contracts require no investment, which makes the vector of wealth fractions w_s^k difficult to interpret. The interpretation of w_s^k is that this is the wealth share that should be invested in the portfolio of (a) the futures contract for s and (b) a number of riskless bonds that pay in the next instant the current futures price multiplied by the "quantity" specified in the futures contract. In any case, the vector w_s^k divided by the vector of futures prices (one by one) gives the number of contracts that are optimally held (assuming each contract is for one unit).

10 If there exists an asset with positive net supply that is perfectly correlated with a state variable, then (from (5)) k would hold $T^k M/T^M$ times its weight in the market portfolio, as well as its demand component in (6). For such assets, the subsequent analysis should be viewed as an analysis of their supplies and demands as deviations from the market portfolio holdings of them by individuals.

11 Actually, Cox, Ingersoll, and Ross [11] showed that the riskless rate equals minus the expected rate of change of marginal utility in an economy with identical individuals. However, their proof can be used to derive that result for any single individual k, and the fact that the riskless rate is the same for all therefore implies that the expected rates of change of all individuals' marginal utilities must be the same.

12 To obtain (18) and (19) note that $e^k = e^k(W^k, s, t)$. Given this, for elements of the

investment opportunity set (that is, not commodity prices in $\boldsymbol{P}$), differentiation of (17) with respect to s_j gives $\mathcal{J}^k_{Ws_j} = u^k_{ee} e^k_{s_j}$. For elements of the consumption goods price vector $\boldsymbol{P}$, which are elements of the state vector $\boldsymbol{s}$, we have $\mathcal{J}^k_{WP_j} = u^k_{ee} e^k_{P_j} + u^k_{eP_j}$. Differentiating (17) with respect to wealth gives $\mathcal{J}^k_{WW} = u^k_{ee} e^k_W$. Substituting these expressions into the definition $H_{s_j} = -\mathcal{J}^k_{Ws_j}/\mathcal{J}^k_{WW}$ gives (18) and (19) for investment opportunity set elements and for consumption opportunity set elements respectively.

13 Assumption 4 will be true with complete (or Pareto-optimal) capital markets for individuals with time-additive isoelastic utility functions. This is easiest to see in a discrete-time multiperiod state preference model, where the individual's subjective probability belief today for the occurrence of time–state ts is π_{ts}, the individual's wealth is W_0, and the price of a \$1 claim for time–state ts is ϕ_{ts}. With those definitions, the individual maximizes the Lagrangian $L = \sum_t \sum_{s \in S_t} \pi_{ts} \rho^t c_{ts}^{1-\gamma} + \lambda(W_0 - \sum_t \sum_s \phi_{ts} c_{ts})$. First-order conditions are the budget constraint and E conditions of the form

$$\pi_{ts} c_{ts}^{-\gamma} \rho^t = \phi_{ts} c_0^{-\gamma}$$

which can be rewritten as $c_{ts} = c_0(\phi_{ts}/\pi_{ts}\rho^t)^{-1/\gamma}$, where E is the number of time–states. In the latter form of the first-order conditions, it is seen that there are E linear equations in the $E+1$ unknowns (c_0, c_{ts}). Combining these and the budget equations into a matrix system, we can write $\mathbf{A}\boldsymbol{c} = W_0\boldsymbol{b}$, where $\mathbf{A}$ is the coefficient matrix, $\boldsymbol{c}$ is the vector of contingent consumption claims purchased, and $\boldsymbol{b}$ is a vector with a one in the first position and zeros elsewhere. Note that the coefficient matrix $\mathbf{A}$ depends on probability beliefs, contingent-claim prices, relative risk aversion, and pure time preference, but not upon initial wealth. The consumption vector can be found by premultiplying by $\mathbf{A}^{-1}$, that is, $\boldsymbol{c} = (\mathbf{A}^{-1}\boldsymbol{b})W_0$. Substituting these optimal consumption claim purchases back into the objective function, we find that the indirect utility function for wealth can be written as $\mathcal{J}(W, \boldsymbol{s}, t) = W^{1-\gamma} f(\boldsymbol{s}, t)$, where $\boldsymbol{s}$ describes the state of the world and $\mathbf{A} = \mathbf{A}(\boldsymbol{s}, t)$. It is easily verified that this utility function satisfies assumption 4.

14 A similar assumption was made by Dieffenbach [15, 16], who also provided some estimates for percentage compensating variations in wealth for changes in consumer prices and Treasury bill rates.

15 The "reverse hedging" possibility was discussed in a 1974 version of the paper by Grauer and Litzenberger [19]. However, their model was quite different, as it was a two-period state preference model with complete markets. Stochastic investment opportunities were not considered by them. Dieffenbach [16] considered hedging against changes in investment opportunities in a multiperiod model and also found the logarithm of utility to be the dividing line between hedging and reverse hedging.

16 See Breeden (Dissertation, Stanford University, 1977) for a definition of real wealth with stochastic opportunities and for a proof of the efficiency result in this model.

17 See Samuelson and Swamy [33].

18 Note that heterogeneous beliefs with respect to commodity prices are possible under assumption 3 and hence in theorem 2.

19 See Fama [17] for a discussion of the efficient market hypothesis.

20 Hart's [24] result that the addition of a new market can make all worse off must be noted as a qualifier to this efficiency statement.

21 The particular technique for constructing elementary claims in table 1.1 was given by Breeden and Litzenberger [8]. Equivalent techniques were presented by Ross [32] and by Banz and Miller [3].

Bibliography and References

1 Arditti, F. and John, K. "Spanning the State Space with Options," *Journal of Financial and Quantitative Analysis*, March 1980, 1–9.

2 Arrow, K. J. "The Role of Securities in the Optimal Allocation of Risk Bearing," *Review of Economic Studies*, 1964, 91–6.

3 Banz, R. W. and Miller, M. "Prices for State-Contingent Claims: Some Estimates and Applications," *Journal of Business*, October 1978, 653–72.

4 Black, F. "The Pricing of Commodity Contracts," *Journal of Financial Economics*, January 1976, 167–79.

5 Black, F. and Scholes, M. S. "The Pricing of Options and Corporate Liabilities," *Journal of Political Economy*, 81, 1973, 637–54.

6 Breeden, D. T. "An Intertemporal Asset Pricing Model with Stochastic Consumption and Investment Opportunities," *Journal of Financial Economics*, September 1979, 265–96.

7 Breeden, D. T. "Consumption Risk in Futures Markets," *Journal of Finance*, May 1980, 503–20.

8 Breeden, D. T. and Litzenberger, R. H. "Prices of State-Contingent Claims Implicit in Option Prices, *Journal of Business*, October 1978, 621–51.

9 Cootner, P. H. "Speculation and Hedging," *Food Research Institute Studies*, 7, Supplement, 1967.

10 Cox, J. C., Ingersoll, J. E. and Ross, S. A. "The Relation Between Forward Prices and Futures Prices," *Journal of Financial Economics*, December 1981, 321–46.

11 Cox, J. C., Ingersoll, J. E. and Ross, S. A. "A Theory of the Term Structure of Interest Rates," *Econometrica*, May 1985.

12 Danthine, J. P. "Information, Futures, and Stabilizing Speculation," *Journal of Economic Theory*, 17, 1978, 79–98.

13 Debreu, G. *The Theory of Value* (New York: Wiley, 1959).

14 Diamond, P. A. "The Role of a Stock Market in a General Equilibrium Model with Technological Uncertainty," *American Economic Review*, 57, 1967, 759–76.

15 Dieffenbach, B. C. "A Quantitative Theory of Risk Premiums on Securities with an Application to the Term Structure of Interest Rates," *Econometrica*, 43, 1975, 431–54.

16 Dieffenbach, B. C. "A Theory of Securities Markets under Uncertainty," *Review of Economic Studies*, 43, 1976, 317–27.

17 Fama, E. F. "Efficient Capital Markets: A Review of Theory and Empirical Work," *Journal of Finance*, March 1970, 309–61.

18 Fischer, S. "The Demand for Index Bonds," *Journal of Political Economy*, 83, 1975, 509–34.

19 Grauer, F. L. A. and Litzenberger, R. H. "The Pricing of Nominal Bonds and Commodity Futures Contracts under Uncertainty," *Journal of Finance*, March 1979, 69–84.

20 Grossman, S. J. "The Existence of Futures Markets, Noisy Rational Expectations and Informational Externalities," *Review of Economic Studies*, 44, 1977, 431–49.

21 Hakansson, N. H. "The Purchasing Power Fund: A New Kind of Financial Intermediary," *Financial Analysts Journal*, 1976, 2–12.

22 Hakansson, N. H. "Efficient Paths Toward Efficient Capital Markets in Large and Small Countries." In *Financial Decision Making Under Uncertainty*, eds H. Levy and M. Sarnat (New York: Academic Press, 1977).

23 Hakansson, N. H. "Welfare Aspects of Options and Supershares," *Journal of Finance*, 33, 1978, 759–76.

24 Hart, O. "On the Optimality of Equilibrium when the Market Structure is Incomplete," *Journal of Economic Theory*, 11, 1975, 418–43.
25 Hoag, J. W. "An Introduction to the Valuation of Commodity Options," *Paper 19*, Columbia Center for the Study of Futures Markets, 1978.
26 Long, J. B. "Stock Prices, Inflation, and the Term Structure of Interest Rates," *Journal of Financial Economics*, 1974, 131–70.
27 Malinvaud, E. "The Allocation of Individual Risks in Large Markets, *Journal of Economic Theory*, 1972, 312–28.
28 Merton, R. C. "An Intertemporal Capital Asset Pricing Model," *Econometrica*, 41, 1973, 867–87.
29 Merton, R. C. "Theory of Rational Option Pricing," *Bell Journal of Economics and Management Science*, 4, 1973, 141–83.
30 Pye, G. "Lifetime Portfolio Selection with Age Dependent Risk Aversion." In *Mathematical Methods in Investment and Finance*, eds G. Szego and K. Shell (New York: North-Holland, 1972), pp. 49–64.
31 Rolfo, J. "Optimal Hedging under Price and Quantity Uncertainty: The Case of a Cocoa Producer," *Journal of Political Economy*, 88: 1, February 1980, 100–16.
32 Ross, S. A. "Options and Efficiency," *Quarterly Journal of Economics*, 90, 1976, 75–89.
33 Samuelson, P. A. and Swamy, S. "Invariant Economic Index Numbers and Canonical Duality: Survey and Synthesis," *American Economic Review*, 64, 1974, 566–93.
34 Schrems, E. L. "The Sufficiency of Existing Financial Instruments for Pareto-Optimal Risk Allocation," Ph.D. Thesis, Stanford University, 1973.
35 Starr, R. M. "Optimal Production and Allocation under Uncertainty," *Quarterly Journal of Economics*, 87, 1973, 81–95.
36 Townsend, R. M. "On the Optimality of Forward Markets," *American Economic Review*, 68, 1978, 54–66.

Chapter 2

Stephen Figlewski

Background and Comments

The following paper by Stephen Figlewski and Thomas Urich is concerned with the information efficiency of securities markets – that is, whether security prices respond promptly and accurately to the arrival of new information. The contributions to this book by Terry Marsh, Kenneth French, and James Poterba (chapters 11, 16, and 17) are likewise concerned with informational efficiency. However, the Figlewski–Urich paper differs from the others in several interesting ways.

First, it is not concerned with the stock market, but with Treasury bills and financial futures. Second, it concentrates on market responses to macroeconomic information – changes in the money supply – and specifically analyzes how a rational investor might use published forecasts of these changes. The other papers examine the statistical behavior of stock prices but do not identify the information that moves prices. (The paper by Terry Marsh and Robert Merton rests on the assumption that changes in stock prices are driven by changes in real earnings. However, their tests concentrate on the behavior of dividends, not changes in earnings. See my comments on their paper.) Third, the Figlewski–Urich paper tests efficiency "the old-fashioned way," by seeing whether profits could have been made by trading on publicly available information. In a fully efficient market, all available information is already incorporated in prices, and therefore no one can successfully predict price changes. If changes can be predicted and superior trading profits can be earned, then the market cannot be fully efficient. Simulations of the profits generated by trades based on the money supply forecasts by Figlewski and Urich are described in section 5 of their paper.

Author's Introduction

The idea that financial markets should be, and largely are, informationally "efficient" occupies a central position in modern finance. Theoretical models of financial markets often assume that investors have homogeneous expectations about asset returns, and so informational efficiency occurs almost automatically. However, real world financial markets are characterized by diversity of information as well as differences among investors in their ability to analyze information that is widely available. The market aggregates investors' diverse beliefs into a single price which, if it is to be fully efficient, must embody the best composite estimate of each asset's true value.

This raises two related questions. First, what is the best way to combine a set of diverse, and subjective, forecasts into a single composite? Second, do financial markets combine information in this way? Examining these questions was a major area of research for me before and during the year I spent as a Batterymarch Fellow.

The most natural choice for forming a composite from a set of diverse forecasts has always been to take a simple average. If the forecasts are unbiased, independent, and identically distributed, the average is the minimum mean squared error composite. However, in survey data on expectations we never find that all three of these conditions hold in practice. In some cases, such as inflation forecasting, there appear to have been systematic biases. Forecasters also have different forecast accuracies, and invariably forecast errors are highly correlated. If we allow for some or all of these factors and focus on the objective of finding a composite forecast whose error has zero mean and minimum variance, we have what amounts to a portfolio problem whose solution is that the optimal forecast is a weighted average of the individual forecasts after correcting for any biases. The weights are derived from the inverse of the covariance matrix of the individuals' forecast errors.

In "Optimal Price Forecasting Using Survey Data" (Figlewski, 1983) I applied the procedure to aggregate inflation expectations drawn from the well-known Livingston survey. One problem with the method is that estimating the error covariance matrix can require a large amount of data on previous forecasts. The paper looks at constrained forms of the matrix that limit data requirements. Earlier researchers had found that the simple average inflation forecast from this survey was not a very accurate predictor and did not seem to incorporate readily available information on the time series behavior of the consumer price index. However, I found that using the aggregation technique to weight the same individual forecasts optimally reduced the mean squared forecast error by more than 40 percent. Adjusting the composite to reduce the effect of correlation among forecast errors proved to be especially important.

In two theoretical papers (Figlewski, 1978, 1982) I had looked at the way that a speculative market combined heterogeneous information. Since investors' expectations enter the market price weighted by the size of their trades, and not by the quality of their information, the market did not achieve full informational efficiency. However, one of the most interesting properties of the models examined in those papers was that an investor whose market weight was less than the weight that his price forecast would have been assigned in an optimal weighting scheme had an expected positive trading profit, while an investor whose expectations were overweighted tended to lose money.

These theoretical results received empirical support in "Optimal Aggregation of Money Supply Forecasts: Accuracy, Profitability, and Market Efficiency," co-authored with Tom Urich. We looked at composite predictions of the weekly money supply announcement, using data from a survey of business economists. The forecasters were much more homogeneous than those in the Livingston sample, and consistent improvement in accuracy was not possible. However, the composite forecasts did capture information from the survey data that had not been accurately discounted in Treasury bill cash and futures prices. A trading rule based on the difference between the optimal composite and the simple average forecast made significant profits. Once again, the success of the weighting scheme appeared to be due to the fact that it reduced the effect of prediction errors that the forecasters made in common.

In addition to work on these issues of information aggregation and market efficiency, the Batterymarch Fellowship allowed me to begin working on stock index futures, which has been one of my major research interests since.

References

Figlewski, S. (1978) "Market 'Efficiency' in a Market with Heterogeneous Information," *Journal of Political Economy*, 86, August, 581–97.
Figlewski, S. (1982) "Investor Diversity and Market Behavior," *Journal of Finance*, 37:1, March, 87–102.
Figlewski, S. (1983) "Optimal Price Forecasting Using Survey Data," *Review of Economics and Statistics*, 65:1, February, 13–21.

Bibliographical Listing

"Money, Government Debt and National Income 1919–75: An Empirical Investigation" (with A. Saunders), *Salomon Brothers Center Working Paper 250*, revised April 1983.

"Optimal Price Forecasting Using Survey Data," *Review of Economics and Statistics*, 65:1, February 1983, 13–21.

"Options on Commodity Futures: Recent Experience in the London Market" (with M. Desmond Fitzgerald), *Option Pricing: Theory and Applications*, ed. Menachem Brenner (Lexington, MA: Lexington Books, 1983), pp. 223–35.

"Investor Diversity and Market Behavior," *Journal of Finance*, 37:1, March 1982, 87–102.

"Portfolio Management with Stock Market Index Futures" (with Stanley Kon), *Financial Analysts Journal*, 38:1, January–February 1982, 52–60.

Optimal Aggregation of Money Supply Forecasts: Accuracy, Profitability, and Market Efficiency

STEPHEN FIGLEWSKI and THOMAS URICH

The adjustment of prices to information in financial markets has been studied at length, mostly from the perspective of the efficient markets hypothesis. Market efficiency tests typically look at the behavior of prices, the end product of a market's information processing, without considering the actual mechanism by which information enters prices. Examining this complex process is difficult because expectations formation is inherently subjective. This is compounded by the fact that much of the information used by market participants is itself subjective, consisting of predictions and opinions of professional analysts and other investors. Many participants rely almost exclusively on this type of "second-hand" information.

For available information to be accurately incorporated into prices three conditions must be satisfied. First, those with access to objective information must use it correctly in making forecasts. Second, traders who rely on forecasts made by others must be able to evaluate the information that they contain accurately. In particular, they must be able to form an accurate composite forecast from a set of diverse individual predictions. Finally, the market must aggregate investors' expectations, as manifested in their demand functions, in such a way that each piece of information receives the appropriate weight in the market clearing price.

This paper deals with the last two aspects of a market's information processing. We begin by examining methods for aggregating individual forecasts into a composite that captures as much information as possible. Then market prices are tested to see whether they reflect all the information that can be obtained in this way. Specifically, we are concerned with whether forecasts of money supply changes made by major

Reproduced from *Journal of Finance*, 28: 3, June 1983, 695–710.

Thomas Urich is currently Vice President, Bankers Trust Corporation. At the time that this paper was originally published, he was Assistant Professor of Finance, Baruch College, City University of New York. We would like to thank Roy Radner and Roger Klein for many helpful discussions and Michael Brennan for excellent editorial suggestions.

securities dealer firms contain information that is not fully incorporated in yields on Treasury bills and Treasury bill futures.

The data are described in section 1. In section 2 we present a general procedure which uses the estimated stochastic structure of the forecast errors to aggregate individual forecasts into an unbiased minimum mean squared forecast error composite. Since this error structure must be estimated from past data, it may be advantageous to impose constraints on its form. Section 3 describes several constrained models and tests their restrictions in our sample. Under the most extensive set of constraints, forecast errors are assumed to have zero mean and to be independent and identically distributed. In this case the optimal forecast is the simple average. However, the hypothesis of independence among forecast errors is overwhelmingly rejected for our data: errors are highly positively correlated with one another.

The forecasting performance of the models is analyzed in section 4. Because the estimated error structure was not completely stable over time, the models which adjusted for correlation did not achieve lower mean squared forecast errors than the simple average in out-of-sample tests. Even so, we find in section 5 that forecasts from these models, while less accurate than the simple mean, do contain information which is not fully reflected in prices in the money market and is therefore economically valuable. The final section contains concluding comments.

1 The Data

Since mid-1977, Money Market Services Inc. has conducted weekly surveys of US Government security dealer firms for their forecasts of the money supply. During the period covered by our sample, the money supply was announced on Thursday afternoon. The 50–60 individual respondents were asked for their forecasts of the change in M1, first on Tuesday morning and then again on Thursday morning. The Thursday data are less complete than the Tuesday data and preliminary tests showed similar results for the two data sets. We therefore focus our attention solely on the Tuesday forecasts. Our sample consists of the responses for the 20 forecasters we are able to identify individually and follow over the sample period. Seventeen of these represented primary US Government security dealer firms. There are 118 weeks in the sample, spanning the period from October 1977 to January 1980.

This survey provides information about the money supply expectations of some of the largest and most sophisticated participants in the money market. Earlier analysis by Urich and Wachtel [9, 10] found that the mean forecast from the survey was clearly superior to the predictions from an autoregressive integrated moving-average (ARIMA) model, in contrast with what has been found in other studies of forecast data, e.g. Pearce [7]. Also, the survey mean appears to be a good measure of the market's expectation of the change in the money supply which is incorporated in short-term interest rates. The monetary surprise, as measured by the difference between the actual change and the mean expectation from the survey, was a significant determinant of the change in Treasury bill yields immediately after the money supply announcement, while the mean expectation itself had no explanatory power. The median forecast (though not the mean) is publicly available on various computerized data systems and is widely followed by the financial community.

2 Aggregating Diverse Forecasts with Limited Information

This section presents a general procedure for aggregating a collection of diverse forecasts into a composite which captures as much information as possible but does not require independent knowledge beyond a past history of forecasts and realizations. [1]

Suppose that an investor regularly has access to point forecasts F_{it} of the weekly change M_t in the money supply at time t, where $i = 1, \ldots, I$ designates the producer of the forecast. The investor's objective in the current period T is to use the vector of forecasts $\boldsymbol{F}_T$ to form an optimal composite prediction $M_T^\star$ of M_T. We shall consider composite forecasts that minimize mean squared forecast error and are linear, that is, of the form $M_T^\star = W_0 + \boldsymbol{W}'\boldsymbol{F}_T$, and unbiased over all realizations of $(M_T, \boldsymbol{F}_T)$.

We assume that the only relevant data available to the investor are the vector of current period forecasts $\boldsymbol{F}_T$ and a set of T observed forecast vectors and actual money supply changes from earlier periods, $\{\boldsymbol{F}_0, \ldots, \boldsymbol{F}_{T-1}, M_0, \ldots, M_{T-1}\}$. Even if investors do have knowledge of fundamental factors beyond present and past expert forecasts, it is reasonable for them to assume that any information that they may have is also known to the experts and has been appropriately included in their forecasts. In that case, the conditional probability distribution of M_T given $\boldsymbol{F}_T$ is the same as the conditional distribution given $\boldsymbol{F}_T$ plus the investor's additional information, so that only the forecasts need be analyzed. We do assume, however, that the experts report personal forecasts based on their own information, rather than composite forecasts. Thus the investor may derive valuable information from the *set* of expert forecasts which has not been accurately impounded in the individual predictions.

Economic time series are in general nonstationary processes. Because seasonal factors, money growth targets, operating procedures, and numerous other factors change over time, the joint probability distribution of M and $\boldsymbol{F}$ for one week cannot be assumed to be exactly the same as that for the previous week. To deal with this problem, we focus instead on the *information generating process*, which will be defined in terms of the probability distribution of forecast errors. It is this process that will be treated as being time invariant. For example, we assume that a forecaster whose good information has led to small forecast errors in the past will continue to be accurate in the future, and that when two experts make similar predictions their positive correlation will persist over time.[2]

We first make an assumption about the properties of individual forecasts which amounts to assuming that forecasters are rational except for a possible additive bias.

Assumption 1

$$M_t = F_{it} + \varepsilon_{it} \qquad E(\varepsilon_{it}) = b_i \quad \text{for all } i.$$

Although full rationality would require that all b_i be zero, since a consistent bias ought to be corrected over time, we prefer to treat unbiasedness as a testable proposition at this stage rather than imposing it *a priori*.

Our second assumption concerns the joint distribution of the errors the forecasters make in predicting the money supply.

Assumption 2 The vector of forecast errors $\boldsymbol{\varepsilon}_t \equiv M_t\boldsymbol{1} - \boldsymbol{F}_t$ is distributed as a multivariate normal with mean vector $\boldsymbol{b}$ and variance–covariance matrix Ω, which has full rank.

The term $\boldsymbol{1}$ denotes a vector of 1s.

From assumption 1 we have

$$E(\boldsymbol{F}_T) = E(M_T)\boldsymbol{1} - \boldsymbol{b}.$$

Imposing the condition of unbiasedness on the composite forecast $M_T^{\star}$ yields

$$E(M_T) = E(M_T^{\star}) = E(W_0 + \boldsymbol{W}'\boldsymbol{F}_T)$$

or

$$(W_0 - \boldsymbol{W}'\boldsymbol{b}) + (\boldsymbol{W}'\boldsymbol{1} - 1)E(M_T) = 0 \tag{1}$$

Since W_0 and $\boldsymbol{W}$ must not depend on the unknown value of $E(M_T)$, this equation yields two constraints:

$$\begin{aligned} \boldsymbol{W}'\boldsymbol{1} &= 1 \\ W_0 &= \boldsymbol{W}'\boldsymbol{b} \end{aligned} \tag{2}$$

The first constraint implies that the optimal predictor will be a weighted average of the forecasts, with weights which sum to unity. The second implies that one can correct the forecasts for bias first and then average, that is, $M_T^\star = \boldsymbol{W}'(\boldsymbol{F}_T + \boldsymbol{b})$.

Since $M_T^\star$ is unbiased, the mean squared forecast error is just the forecast variance of $M_T^\star$ given by

$$\begin{aligned} E[(M_T - M_T^\star)^2] &= E\{[M_T - \boldsymbol{W}'(\boldsymbol{F}_T + \boldsymbol{b})][M_T - \boldsymbol{W}'(\boldsymbol{F}_T + \boldsymbol{b})]'\} \\ &= \boldsymbol{W}'E[(\boldsymbol{\varepsilon}_T - \boldsymbol{b})(\boldsymbol{\varepsilon}_T - \boldsymbol{b})']\boldsymbol{W} \\ &= \boldsymbol{W}'\Omega\boldsymbol{W}, \end{aligned}$$

where the second equality uses the constraint that $\boldsymbol{W}'\boldsymbol{1} = 1$.

Thus the optimal weights $\boldsymbol{W}^\star$ solve the minimization problem

$$\underset{\boldsymbol{W}}{\text{minimize}}\ \boldsymbol{W}'\Omega\boldsymbol{W} \text{ subject to } \boldsymbol{W}'\boldsymbol{1} = 1, \tag{3}$$

which has the solution[3]

$$\boldsymbol{W}^\star = (\boldsymbol{1}'\Omega^{-1}\boldsymbol{1})\Omega^{-1}\boldsymbol{1}. \tag{4}$$

Thus

$$M_T^\star = (\boldsymbol{1}'\Omega^{-1}\boldsymbol{1})^{-1}\boldsymbol{1}'\Omega^{-1}(\boldsymbol{F}_T + \boldsymbol{b}). \tag{5}$$

Because of the stationarity assumption, $\boldsymbol{b}$ and Ω can be estimated using historical data on M and $\boldsymbol{F}$, so that $M_T^\star$ can be computed by the investor from the information he has available.

Equation (5) gives the minimum mean squared error linear predictor for the case of a general error bias vector $\boldsymbol{b}$ and covariance matrix Ω. This expression reduces to one of the more familiar aggregation procedures when $\boldsymbol{b}$ and Ω have certain special forms. Clearly, when all forecasters are assumed to be unbiased, $\boldsymbol{b}$ drops out. If, in addition, all forecasts are independent and identically distributed, Ω is proportional to the identity matrix and (5) reduces to taking a simple average. The more general case of independent errors with different variances leads to a weighted average in which each forecaster's weight is proportional to his precision (the inverse of his error variance). Thus these aggregation methods can be thought of as special cases of (5) when the error structure is constrained to be a specific form. In the following sections, we shall test whether such constraints are valid for our sample of money supply forecasts and examine the effects on forecast performance of relaxing them selectively.

3 The Structure and Stability of Money Supply Forecasts

Equation (5) shows how to construct the minimum variance linear unbiased predictor given a set of forecasts for the current period and the parameters $\boldsymbol{b}$ and Ω of the forecast error distribution. In turning (5) into an operational system, it may be appropriate to impose constraints on these parameters for various reasons. In this section we shall examine several types of constraints and present evidence on their validity for our data sample.

One reason to constrain the error distribution is to impose *a priori* beliefs about forecasting behavior. In particular, we may want to eliminate constant bias terms as being too contrary to rationality. In this case $\boldsymbol{b}$ will be constrained to be zero.

It may also be desirable, and in some cases necessary, to impose constraints in order to reduce the number of parameters to be estimated. Since there are $(I^2 + I)/2$ distinct elements in a general Ω matrix, a large amount of data from earlier periods is needed when I is large. An extreme case is when there are fewer periods in the sample than there are forecasters, and an Ω matrix estimated without constraints will be singular. Even when enough past data are available to fit an unconstrained matrix, the potential gains in forecasting accuracy from allowing a general error structure must be weighed against the increased effect of sampling error when a larger number of parameters are estimated from a limited data sample.

Instability of the error structure may also be mitigated by constraining its form to require fewer parameters. We have assumed that the error distribution was stationary, but at best this will only be approximately true, and the assumption becomes less tenable the longer the span of time that is being considered. Forecasters can change their behavior over time as they refine their techniques. Inaccurate forecasters in particular will try to improve and, failing that, may be replaced. Also, when forecasts are identified by firm and not individually, normal turnover in personnel can induce instability.

The most common and the easiest procedure to aggregate diverse forecasts is to take a simple average. The average will also be the minimum mean squared error composite if all forecasts are unbiased, identically distributed, and independent, that is, under an extensive set of restrictions on the structure of forecast errors.[4] We now examine a series of models in which these restrictions are progressively relaxed.

Unbiasedness is a restriction on the mean of the error distribution and can be imposed independently of the covariance structure. Therefore each covariance model was fitted in both "uncorrected" and "bias corrected" form.

The model in which Ω is assumed to be proportional to the identity matrix will be called the mean model. In moving towards more general cases, the first restriction to be relaxed is that of equal variances. When forecast errors are independent but some forecasts are more accurate than others, Ω becomes a diagonal matrix. We refer to this as the diagonal model.

Of the restrictions implied by the mean model, probably the most likely to be incorrect in practical forecasting applications is that of independence. To a large extent, forecasters share the same information and methods of analysis, and a good portion of every forecaster's error is due to events which were not fully anticipated by any of them. This is especially true in our sample. The 20 money supply forecasters were a very homogeneous group. The smallest (most negative) estimated bias was -0.45 ($-\$450$ million) and the largest was 0.05. The small size of these numbers can be seen in the fact that a bias of -0.45 added only 0.05 to the root mean squared forecast error (RMSE). Differences in individual accuracy were also rather unimportant. The lowest RMSE was 1.64 and the largest was 1.93, which is a considerably smaller range than has been found in other forecast data sets. However, all the forecast errors showed a large degree of positive correlation. Of 190 pairwise correlation coefficients, the smallest was 0.65 while the largest was 0.88.

This suggests that allowing the off-diagonal elements of the Ω matrix to be nonzero may make a substantial difference to the composite forecasts. Estimating the Ω matrix with no constraints (the unconstrained model) is clearly one solution. In this case this involves fitting 210 distinct elements of Ω plus 20 bias terms, and the associated problems of sampling error and instability. We therefore include another constrained model, the single-index model, which represents an intermediate step between the diagonal and the fully unconstrained models.

In the single-index model, each forecaster's error is assumed to be made up of one part which is independent of all other forecasters' errors plus a part which is proportional to a common error. That is, $\varepsilon_{it} = \eta_{it} + \beta_i \delta_t$, where η_{it} is the independent error and δ_t is the common error. If $\text{var}(\delta_t) = \theta^2$, the covariance between ε_i and ε_j is then $\beta_i \beta_j \theta^2$. Letting D be a diagonal matrix with $\text{var}(\eta_i)$ on the diagonal, we can write $\Omega = D + \theta^2 \boldsymbol{\beta}\boldsymbol{\beta}'$. The single-index model allows nonzero covariances among errors but constrains them to arise only from mutual correlation with the single index δ. This reduces the number of distinct parameters in Ω from $(I^2 + I)/2$ to $2I + 1$: I independent variances, I β_is, and θ^2, that is, 41 parameters in the present case. Actually, because of a linear dependence among the β_i and θ^2, only 40 parameters are independent.

The reader may recognize that the single-index model is identical with the "market" model in financial theory, where θ^2 represents market risk, the diagonal elements of D represent nonmarket risk, and β_i measures the sensitivity of the individual security (forecaster) to the common part of the variance. To impose the single-index constraint, we have taken the forecast error of the simple average to represent the common portion of individual errors. Thus each forecaster's error is split up into one part which is perfectly correlated with the average error and one part which is orthogonal. The parameter β_i is given by $\text{cov}(\varepsilon_i, \varepsilon_A)/\text{var}(\varepsilon_A)$, where ε_A is the average error.

The discussion brings out the essential similarity between our procedures for constructing a minimum mean squared error composite forecast, given the probability distribution of forecast errors, and the portfolio problem of constructing a minimum variance asset portfolio, given a distribution of security returns. Although the two problems are not identical, since we make use of characteristics of rationally formed forecasts which need not apply to securities, much of the intuition is the same in both cases.

The validity of the various constraints we have discussed can be tested using a likelihood ratio test. Under the assumption of multivariate normality the log likelihood function is given by

$$\log L = -\frac{IT}{2}\log(2\pi) - \frac{T}{2}\log|\Omega| - \frac{1}{2}\sum_{t=1}^{T}(\boldsymbol{\varepsilon}_t - \boldsymbol{b})'\Omega^{-1}(\boldsymbol{\varepsilon}_t - \boldsymbol{b}) \quad (6)$$

Let L_c be the maximized value of the likelihood function when constraints are imposed on $\boldsymbol{b}$ or Ω, and L_u be the maximized value without the constraints. Under the hypothesis that the constrained model is the true model, the statistic $-2(\log L_c - \log L_u)$ is distributed asymptotically as χ^2 with degrees of freedom equal to the number of constraints, which in this case is the difference between the number of independent parameters estimated in the two models.

Table 2.1 shows the values of the log likelihoods for the various models. Consider first the unconstrained model in its uncorrected and bias corrected form. Minus twice the difference in log likelihoods is 42.0 which is significant at the 0.005 level for a χ^2 distribution with 20 degrees of

Table 2.1 Log likelihood of constrained error structures

	Uncorrected		*Bias corrected*	
	log *L*	*Number of parameters*	log *L*	*Number of parameters*
Unconstrained	−2952.4	210	−2931.4	230
Single-index	−3112.6	41	−3086.7	61
Diagonal	−4722.0	20	−4690.9	40
Mean	−4726.2	1	−4695.4	21

Estimation of the single-index models uses one degree of freedom less than the number of parameters.

freedom. Thus the hypothesis that all b_i are zero is strongly rejected for the unconstrained model and for the others as well.

Testing the constraints on the form of the Ω matrix yields the following results. Estimating 169 additional parameters increases the log likelihood of an unconstrained model over that of a single-index model by an amount which is significant at the 0.001 level. However, the difference is small compared with the increase in log likelihood of the single index over the diagonal model. The latter is not found to be significantly different from a simple average in either uncorrected or bias corrected form. We find that in most cases relaxing a constraint yields a statistically significant increase in log likelihood, but the largest difference occurs when nonindependence among errors is allowed as one goes from the diagonal to the single-index model.

The same test can easily be applied to examine the error structure's stability over time. Each model is fitted over the whole sample period to produce the log likelihood when the parameters are constrained to be the same throughout. Then the sample is split in half and the parameters are estimated separately for the two parts. The unconstrained log likelihood is the sum of the log likelihoods from the subsamples. Under the joint null hypothesis that the specified form of the model represents the true error structure and that its parameters are the same in both periods, the likelihood ratio test becomes a test of stability.

Both the simple average and the diagonal models appear to be stable over time, whether or not they are corrected for bias. The models which fit covariances are not completely stable, however, with the hypothesis of stability being rejected at the 0.05 level for the single index and the 0.001 level for the unconstrained model.

4 Forecasting Accuracy of Composite Forecasts

The fully unconstrained model with bias adjustment explains the data significantly better than any constrained model in tests based on analysis of the whole sample. However, formal stability tests showed that the single-index and unconstrained parameter estimates changed significantly over time. Since the error structure must be estimated from past data, the fitted parameters will generally be somewhat different from the true parameters for the current period. If the difference is substantial, forecasts from the unconstrained model may be less accurate than those from one with more restrictions and greater stability, despite their theoretical superiority.

The true test of a forecasting strategy is how well it performs out of sample. To look at the operational forecasting performance of the various models, we constructed series of post-sample predictions and compared them on the basis of mean forecast error, standard deviation, and RMSE. Beginning in period 59, the model parameters were estimated on data from all earlier periods, the weights were constructed, and composite forecasts were calculated for the next period. The parameters were then refitted adding period 60 to the sample. The process of fitting the models on all previous data and forecasting one period ahead was continued until post-sample forecasts for the whole second half of the data sample had been created.

Table 2.2 shows the summary statistics for the various models. As might be anticipated from previous results, the mean and diagonal models are virtually identical, with an RMSE of about $1.7 billion in both uncorrected and bias corrected form. The single-index model did distinctly less well, and the unconstrained model was the least accurate in the post-sample. Apparently parameter instability was sufficiently great to offset the potential increase in accuracy afforded by allowing a more detailed error structure.

This result contrasts with what was found in tests on the Livingston inflation expectations survey. While unconstrained models could not be estimated on that data set, both the diagonal and single-index models were substantially more accurate than the simple mean (see Figlewski [3]). An important reason for the difference is that the money supply forecasters are an exceptionally homogeneous group. This limits the ability of these techniques to exploit differences in accuracy and correlation within the forecaster population.

Table 2.2 Post-sample forecasting performance of composite predictions

	Mean error	*Standard deviation*	*Root mean squared error*	*Full sample weights*	
				Maximum	*Minimum*
Uncorrected					
Mean	−0.111	1.605	1.595	0.050	0.050
Diagonal	−0.111	1.603	1.594	0.060	0.043
Single-index	−0.078	1.696	1.683	0.345	−0.237
Unconstrained	−0.108	1.804	1.792	0.560	−0.456
Bias corrected					
Mean	0.326	1.598	1.617	0.050	0.050
Diagonal	0.326	1.596	1.616	0.060	0.044
Single-index	0.351	1.695	1.717	0.325	−0.259
Unconstrained	0.305	1.784	1.795	0.490	−0.413

Figures represent performance over 59 post-sample periods. Model parameters were reestimated every period using all previous data. Amounts are in billions of dollars. Full sample weights were calculated from model parameters estimated over all 118 periods.

One possibility for reducing the problem of parameter instability is to eliminate old data in the estimation. We tried this by dropping a sample point each time the models were refitted and using only 59 periods for estimation. The differences in forecast performance were small except for the unconstrained model, for which the RMSE increased to 1.999 and 2.065 in uncorrected and bias corrected form respectively.

Comparing the bias corrected and uncorrected versions of the models shows them to be very similar. It is interesting that in all cases the mean error of the uncorrected model is smaller in magnitude than that of the corrected model, though this does not have much effect on RMSE.

One way to see the differences between the models and to understand why the single-index and unconstrained models are less accurate is to compare the weights that they produce. The last two columns in table 2.2 show the largest and the smallest weights for each model. Since the weights change when a model is refitted, we have chosen to report only those derived from parameters estimated on all sample data. These tend to be less extreme than weights from shorter estimation periods. The simple average naturally gives equal weights of 1/20 to each forecaster, and the diagonal model hardly deviates from this. The two models which fit covariances, however, allow negative weights and show a much wider spread. These models are trying to make use of the small differences in correlation among individuals to reduce the effect of the common portion of their forecast errors. Forecasts from an expert who is highly correlated with others' errors will be assigned a negative weight.[5] However, to the extent that differences in correlations are small and not completely stable over time, the relatively extreme weights produced by the more detailed models can lead to less accurate post-sample forecasts.

5 Composite Forecasts and Interest Rate Movements

In this section we examine whether yields in the Treasury bill and Treasury bill futures markets fully incorporate all the information about money supply changes which can be obtained by our composite forecasting methods. The forecast errors made by individuals in our sample are highly correlated with one another. Even though the error structure is not stable enough over time for the single-index and unconstrained models which attempt to correct for correlation to produce more accurate forecasts than the simple mean, they may still contain economically valuable information that has not been impounded in prices. This is particularly likely if investors concentrate primarily on obtaining the most accurate forecast of money growth and only pay attention to the average forecast.

If our aggregation procedures are able to capture information that the market has not fully discounted, the difference between a forecast from a composite model and the market's expectation of the money supply change should explain changes in yields immediately after the money supply is announced. Such a test is clearly impossible, however, since the market's expectation is unobservable. Instead, we base our tests on the differences between the average forecast and the single-index and unconstrained composites. Recent articles by Urich [8] and Urich and Wachtel [9] have shown that the interest rate movement after the money supply announcement is positively related to the unanticipated change in the money supply, as measured by the difference between the announced figure and the average forecast. The rationale for the direction of response is that market participants take current money growth as an indicator of future Federal Reserve policy. For example, an unanticipated increase in the money supply tends to push interest rates up because investors expect that the Federal Reserve will have to tighten credit conditions in the future to meet its money growth targets.

These results suggest that the mean forecast from the survey may be a reasonable proxy for the market's expectation. However, the validity of our test does not depend on that being true. If market yields before the announcement do accurately discount all the information contained in the set of money supply forecasts, no combination of them will have any power to explain the subsequent movement. However, if the market expectation does not fully adjust for the effect of correlation in forecast errors, by looking at the difference between the mean forecast, which takes no account of correlation, and a composite forecast, which does, we can obtain a proxy for the information that the market price does not contain, regardless of whether the market's expectation is close to the mean forecast.

Information enters prices when investors trade on it in hopes of earning a profit, and information which is not accurately impounded will give rise to profitable trading opportunities. Thus our test of the ability of the composite models to predict interest rate changes takes the form of a trading rule. If the composite forecast predicts smaller money supply growth than the average forecast, Treasury bills or Treasury bill futures are purchased on Thursday afternoon just prior to the announcement and resold at the beginning of trading on Friday. When the composite forecast is above the average forecast, a short position is taken before the announcement and covered on Friday morning. Profits earned by the rule indicate to what extent the composite forecast contains information that is not fully discounted in prices.

We examined the profitability of this strategy over periods 60 through 118 using the post-sample composite forecasts which were analyzed in the previous section. Three maturities of Treasury bills and four futures contracts on 3 month Treasury bills were examined. The Treasury bills were the most recently issued 3 month, 6 month, and year bills. The futures contracts used were the nearest four International Monetary Market contracts. Thus, the first contract, labelled F1, matured within 3 months, the second, F2, in 3–6 months, and so forth. Profits were measured by the change in yield in basis points (bid on discount basis) from 3:30 p.m. on Thursday to 10:30 a.m. on Friday for the cash bills, and from the Thursday settlement price to Friday's opening price for the futures. Weeks in which Thursday or Friday was a holiday were dropped from the sample.

Table 2.3 shows the results of these tests for the single-index and unconstrained models in uncorrected and bias corrected form. In the first panel, a position is assumed to be taken in every period, while in the second and third panels we try to reduce the effects of random noise by requiring that the difference between the composite forecast and the average exceed a threshold of $300 million and $600 million respectively before initiating a trade. As a base to gauge how well these rules capture the interest rate change after a money supply announcement, the first line in each panel shows the profit rate of a "perfect forecast," that is, a rule based on the difference between the actual money supply change and the mean forecast. For example, knowing the figure that would be announced and trading in the nearest futures contract according to the rule that we have specified would have yielded an average of 6.0 basis points per week.

In nearly all cases the composite models successfully predicted interest rate movements, with the largest profits being shown by the uncorrected models in the futures market. For instance, the single-index uncorrected model produced an average return of 3.9 basis points per week in the F1 futures contract (out of a possible 6.0 earned by the perfect forecast). This figure was statistically significant at the 1 percent level in a one-tailed test.

Contrasting the various models, markets, and strategies leads to several general conclusions. In virtually all cases, the uncorrected models were more successful than their corrected counterparts. This provides further evidence that attempting to correct the forecasts for bias is not appropriate. For the uncorrected models, requiring a threshold difference between the composite and the average reduced the number of trades, as expected, and increased their profit rate substantially. It also improved the results for the uncorrected unconstrained model relative to the single-index models, probably because the unconstrained forecasts are noisier.

A useful benchmark for evaluating the attractiveness of these trading rules is to compare them with a buy and hold strategy. With no threshold requirement, our strategies earned higher mean returns in every case. In 21 of 28 cases, the standard deviation of returns was also lower than for buy and hold. In the other seven cases, the largest increase was only 0.1 basis points.

Table 2.3 Average profit per trade of trading rules based on differences between composite and average forecasts

Required difference	*Method*	*No. of trades*	*Treasury bills* 3 month	*Treasury bills* 6 month	*Treasury bills* 1 year	*Treasury bill futures* F1	*Treasury bill futures* F2	*Treasury bill futures* F3	*Treasury bill futures* F4
0	Perfect	54	3.8[a]	4.4[a]	4.6[a]	6.0[a]	6.7[a]	6.6[a]	6.2[a]
	forecast		(2.69)	(3.29)	(3.11)	(3.97)	(3.63)	(3.81)	(4.26)
	Single-index	54	1.5	1.4	1.5	3.9[a]	4.2[a]	3.3[a]	3.1[a]
	uncorrected		(0.98)	(0.98)	(0.92)	(2.42)	(2.11)	(1.74)	(1.93)
	Unconstrained	54	1.0	0.7	0.9	3.1[a]	2.8	2.6	2.2
	uncorrected		(0.68)	(0.48)	(0.57)	(1.88)	(1.40)	(1.36)	(1.31)
	Single-index	54	−0.8	−0.6	−0.1	−0.5	−0.1	0.4	−0.2
	bias corrected		(0.56)	(0.40)	(0.08)	(0.31)	(0.06)	(0.22)	(0.13)
	Unconstrained	54	0.2	0.7	1.2	1.3	2.5	2.4	1.9
	bias corrected		(0.11)	(0.50)	(0.78)	(0.77)	(1.21)	(1.22)	(1.14)
	Median	54	−1.8	−2.6[a]	−1.8	−3.1[a]	−3.6[a]	−3.0	−2.6
			(1.24)	(1.80)	(1.16)	(1.84)	(1.79)	(1.56)	(1.56)
300	Perfect	44	4.6[a]	5.3[a]	5.5[a]	7.2[a]	8.3[a]	8.0[a]	7.3[a]
	forecast		(2.77)	(3.31)	(3.14)	(4.10)	(3.85)	(3.95)	(4.38)
	Single-index	29	1.5	1.3	2.0	4.0	3.7	3.5	2.1
	uncorrected		(0.63)	(0.55)	(0.77)	(1.59)	(1.21)	(1.17)	(0.92)
	Unconstrained	35	2.4	2.1	2.7	4.9[a]	5.1[a]	4.7[a]	3.9[a]
	uncorrected		(1.16)	(1.04)	(1.18)	(2.24)	(2.02)	(1.88)	(2.06)
	Single-index	38	0.3	0.6	1.2	1.5	2.5	2.6	2.1
	bias corrected		(0.17)	(0.32)	(0.53)	(0.67)	(0.93)	(1.00)	(0.97)
	Unconstrained	41	0.1	0.6	1.2	2.1	3.2	2.8	2.4
	bias corrected		(0.05)	(0.31)	(0.60)	(0.96)	(1.23)	(1.11)	(1.18)
600	Perfect	37	5.1[a]	6.0[a]	6.2[a]	7.8[a]	9.0[a]	8.7[a]	8.1[a]
	forecast		(2.65)	(3.25)	(3.06)	(3.84)	(3.58)	(3.65)	(4.14)
	Single-index	20	3.8	3.3	4.0	5.9[a]	5.9	5.8	4.1
	uncorrected		(1.13)	(0.99)	(1.07)	(1.68)	(1.42)	(1.41)	(1.33)
	Unconstrained	26	3.2	2.7	3.6	6.4[a]	7.5[a]	6.7[a]	5.0[a]
	uncorrected		(1.25)	(1.06)	(1.24)	(2.41)	(2.66)	(2.41)	(2.20)
	Single-index	25	−0.3	0.1	0.1	2.0	2.2	2.1	1.2
	bias corrected		(0.10)	(0.03)	(0.17)	(0.64)	(0.64)	(0.59)	(0.47)
	Unconstrained	27	0.5	0.2	0.9	2.2	2.3	2.5	1.6
	bias corrected		(0.06)	(0.06)	(0.31)	(0.77)	(0.72)	(0.78)	(0.64)

Profit figures are changes in yield in basis points. *t* statistics in parentheses.
[a]Statistically significant at the 5 percent level in one-tailed test.

Profits for trades in the futures market were substantially larger than in the cash bills. Looking at the performance of the perfect forecast, we see that money supply changes appear to affect the futures market more than the cash market, but that does not account for all the difference. Reasons for this result could include differences in the way the two markets incorporate money supply expectations from the government bond dealer community, differences in their speed of reaction to new information, or the slight difference in timing between cash and futures quotes in our data.

The trading performance of one other "composite" model, the median, is shown in table 2.3 since the median, not the mean, is the statistic which is reported to the financial community by Money Market Services. The sizeable losses generated by the trading rule suggest that the median may not be the best summary statistic to publish.

Overall, the results in table 2.3 indicate that the information that can be obtained from the set of money supply forecasts by comparing the single-index or unconstrained model forecasts with the mean is not fully incorporated in short-term interest rates.[6] An especially significant result which is not visible in the table is that the composite forecasts exhibited a higher percentage of correct trades in periods when there was a large interest rate movement after the announcement. For example, both the single-index and unconstrained uncorrected methods produced correct decisions in 18 of 27 periods when the F2 futures contract moved 5 basis points or more; they were profitable 12 and 11 times respectively in 13 periods when the rate changed 10 or more basis points. Large price adjustments may well be the result of widely shared expectations errors, which these procedures are designed to correct for.

A final issue which should be raised concerns transactions costs. It is not inconsistent with a fully efficient market for prices to be slightly out of line with available information if the discrepancy is small relative to the transactions cost that would be incurred in trying to exploit it. For the small investor, both the bid–ask spread in cash bills and the commission on a futures transaction are of the order of 2–3 basis points. Costs of this size would substantially reduce the attractiveness of this kind of trade. However, the costs to a securities dealer or a member of the futures exchange for the same trade are negligible. In particular, securities dealers adjust their positions in advance of the money supply announcement anyway. The marginal cost of taking a different position may well be zero. In any case, our objective in this research has not been to uncover evidence of major market inefficiency, but rather to explore how information is aggregated in a financial market. The results suggest that market prices may not accurately discount all available information when investors are subject to widely shared expectations errors.

6 Concluding Comments

The process of price formation in a financial market involves information aggregation at several levels. In forming expectations about future prices, individual investors must combine diverse information in the form of forecasts from well-informed sources. These expectations enter investors' demand functions and are aggregated by the market into a single price which, to some extent, reflects all the information held by the market population. In this paper we have explored statistical procedures for aggregating diverse subjective forecasts optimally, based on the variances, covariances, and biases in the set of forecast errors. Neither individual investors nor the market are likely to combine forecasts in the ways we suggested. Individuals are, if anything, most likely to use a simple average which produces accurate forecasts but does not adjust for correlation among forecast errors. Financial markets aggregate investors' expectations by weighting them according to the size of their transactions. The trading rule results of section 5 indicate that our composite forecasting methods could capture information about the structure of expectations within the market population which was not fully incorporated in short-term interest rates.

Notes

1 The procedure presented here has been applied successfully to aggregating expectations about the consumer price index drawn from the well-known Livingston survey, see Figlewski [3].

2 Clearly, the distribution of forecast errors may also be nonstationary. In that case, further procedures to minimize the effects of changes over time may be appropriate.

3 From the Lagrangian equation, the first-order conditions are

$$\mathbf{0} = 2\Omega \mathbf{W} - \lambda \mathbf{1}$$
$$0 = \mathbf{W}'\mathbf{1} - 1.$$

Premultiplying the first condition by $\frac{1}{2}\mathbf{1}'\Omega^{-1}$ and rearranging gives

$$\mathbf{W}'\mathbf{1} = \frac{\lambda}{2}\,\mathbf{1}'\Omega^{-1}\mathbf{1} = 1$$
$$\lambda = 2(\mathbf{1}'\Omega^{-1}\mathbf{1})^{-1}.$$

Substituting in the first-order condition and premultiplying by Ω^{-1} yields (4).

4 In fact, the simple average is the optimal composite under more general conditions, that is, if $\mathbf{b}'\mathbf{1} = 0$ and $\mathbf{1}$ is an eigenvector of Ω. The first condition implies that the average is unbiased and the second can be used in (4) to yield $\mathbf{W}^{\star} = (1/I)\mathbf{1}$. The intuitive interpretation of these more general conditions is not clear. However, one important case is when $\Omega = \theta^2\mathbf{1}\mathbf{1}' + \sigma^2 I$, that is, all forecasters have both equal forecast variances and equal covariances with every other forecaster.

5 This is like holding short positions in high beta stocks and long positions in low beta stocks to minimize returns variance in an equity portfolio.

6 An alternative test of the ability of the composite forecasts to explain interest rate movements is simply to regress the change in the rate on the difference between the composite and the average forecast. When we do this, of 28 regression coefficients 15 are statistically significant at the 5 percent level in a one-tailed test; 24 are significant at the 10 percent level. These regression results support the results of table 2.3 from a slightly different perspective.

Bibliography and References

1 Fama, E. "Efficient Capital Markets: A Review of Theory and Empirical Work," *Journal of Finance*, 25, May 1970, 333–417.
2 Figlewski, S. "Subjective Information and Market Efficiency in a Betting Market," *Journal of Political Economy*, 87, February 1979, 75–88.
3 Figlewski, S. "Optimal Price Forecasting Using Survey Data," *Review of Economics and Statistics*, 65: 1, February 1983, 13–21.
4 Granger, C. W. J. and Newbold, P. *Forecasting Economic Time Series* (New York: Academic Press, 1977).
5 Jaffe, J. and Winkler, R. "Optimal Speculation Against an Efficient Market," *Journal of Finance*, 31, March 1976, 49–61.
6 Nelson, C. "The Prediction Performance of the FRB–MIT–Penn Model of the U.S. Economy," *American Economic Review*, 62, September 1972, 902–15.
7 Pearce, D. "Comparing Survey and Rational Measures of Expected Inflation: Forecast Performance and Interest Rate Effects," *Journal of Money, Credit and Banking*, 11, November 1979, 447–56.
8 Urich, T. "The Information Content of Weekly Money Supply Announcements," *Journal of Monetary Economics*, 10: 1, July 1982, 73–88.
9 Urich, T. and Wachtel, P. "Market Response to the Weekly Money Supply Announcement in the 1970's," *Journal of Finance*, 36, December 1981, 1063–72.
10 Urich, T. and Wachtel, P. "The Structure of Expectations of the Weekly Money Supply Announcement," unpublished manuscript, 1981.

Chapter 3

Jonathan E. Ingersoll

Background and Comments

Financial economists find options everywhere – not just on the Chicago Board Options Exchange (CBOE) or in callable or convertible securities, but in common shares (which can be regarded as call options on firms' assets) and in real assets (an offshore oil lease can be regarded as an option to drill, for example). They also find options in the tax laws. Unfortunately for the Internal Revenue Service, these tax options are generally held by the taxpayer.

Jonathan Ingersoll, in the following paper written with George Constantinides, considers the tax options open to an investor in bonds. The effective tax rate is drastically reduced if the bondholder rolls over his or her portfolio at the right time and in the right circumstances. In other words, the option to time sale of a bond and reinvestment of the proceeds can offset a substantial part of the government's tax claim on interest payments or capital gains.

Constantinides and Ingersoll were not the first to recognize tax options. Investors have been taking advantage of them for years. However, they were the first to demonstrate how valuable the options really are and to warn against analyses of after-tax yields calculated on the assumption that bonds are purchased and held to maturity. Yields on taxable and tax-exempt debt are often compared in this way. This paper does not offer any easy practical algorithm for optimal bond trading. The analysis is complex even after various simplifying assumptions are made, and in any case tax law has changed since the paper was written.

If this paper sparks interest, I recommend Constantinides's paper on tax options in common stocks (Constantinides, 1984) and Joseph Stiglitz's paper on "A General Theory of Tax Avoidance" (Stiglitz, 1985).

References

Constantinides, G. M. (1984) "Optimal Stock Trading with Personal Taxes: Implications for Pricing and the Abnormal January Returns," *Journal of Financial Economics*, 13, March, 65–90.

Stiglitz, J. E. (1985) "A General Theory of Tax Avoidance," *National Tax Journal*, 37, September, 325–37.

Author's Introduction

Researchers in the physical sciences are blessed with the particular advantage of experimentation denied to us in the social sciences. In chemistry, for example, a theory deduced from observing many reactions can be subjected to verification under various laboratory conditions. Even if the theory is rejected, these experiments will probably refine the scope of what may be considered true. In a social science such as economics, observations also lead to postulated theories, but they can seldom be subjected to experiment because the scientist cannot control the environment.

Following the stock market crash of October 1987, for example, there was much debate about its causes and what course of action, if any, should be taken to ensure that a similar crash would not occur again. Each economist and every stock market participant probably had his or her own ideas but who, if anyone, was right? How much more might we now know about the behavior of the stock market if we could only turn the clocks back to 1987 and prohibit trading, change margin requirements, initiate circuit breakers etc. and try again?

In attempting to answer these and similar questions, the social scientist is forced to resort to models – a kind of social science fiction: "If investors behave in this fashion and if stock market prices react in this way, then the following will happen." Even if the logic is faultless any conclusions are still subject to the reasonableness of the basic assumptions – and models, by necessity, are based on simplified assumptions.

The Black–Scholes option pricing model is certainly one of the most important developments in financial theory in the last quarter century. Numerous papers have been written analyzing various aspects of this theory, and many investment dollars have been managed using its applications. In the context of the discussion above, one of the reasons why the Black–Scholes model has found such widespread support among both the academic and Wall Street communities is the appeal of its simple behavioral assumption: "People prefer more to less." Or, to be a bit less formal, it assumes that no one will leave a $20 bill lying on the sidewalk – professors of finance, as always, excepted.

"Optimal Bond Trading with Personal Taxes," written with George Constantinides, is a particular application of the techniques of the Black–Scholes option pricing model to "what if" speculation. In the paper we analyze a number of simplified versions of the tax code as it applies to bonds and ask what effect it would have on bond prices and optimal portfolio structuring. We find that the tax effects can be dramatic. The right to realize capital gains and losses at a time of the taxpayer's choosing is a valuable option. Under extreme conditions it can be 25 percent as valuable as the bond's direct cash flows.

Failure to recognize the importance of tax options inherent in bonds could easily result in erroneous judgments in many contexts. Just one example will suffice. As shown in the paper the break-even tax rate apparent in prices may be as low as 20 percent even if banks or dealers with a 50 percent marginal tax rate are the marginal (or only) holders of bonds. Investment advice or tax policy decisions which assumed that the marginal investor was in a 20 percent bracket could be quite misleading.

Bibliographical Listing

"Some Results in the Theory of Arbitrage Pricing," *Journal of Finance*, 39: 4, September 1984, 1021–39.

"Exact Pricing in Linear Factor Models with Finitely Many Assets: a Note" (with Nai-Fu Chen), *Journal of Finance*, 38: 3, June 1983, 985–8.

"Is Immunization Feasible? Evidence from the CRSP Data." In *Innovations in Bond Portfolio Management: Duration Analysis and Immunization, Contemporary Studies in Economics and Financial Analysis*, eds George G. Kaufman, G. O. Bierwag and Alden Toeus, vol. 41 (Greenwich, CT: JAI Press, 1983), pp. 163–82.

Optimal Bond Trading with Personal Taxes

GEORGE M. CONSTANTINIDES and JONATHAN E. INGERSOLL

1 Introduction

The yield curve implied by the prices of Treasury notes and bonds and corporate bonds is of interest to economists and practitioners alike: it reflects investors' beliefs about the future course of the short-term interest rate. In calculating the yield curve, the tax bracket of the marginal bondholder either is taken to be some given number or is estimated simultaneously with the yield curve. The implied tax bracket of the marginal investor is of independent interest. It provides a direct (but incomplete) test of Miller's (1977) theory of the optimal capital structure of firms. It may also be useful for determining fair prices for other assets.

There are two major problems in estimating pure discount rates (the yield curve of zero coupon bonds) and the implied marginal tax rate. The first problem is that of differing clienteles, studied in detail by Schaefer (1981, 1982a). For a given investor some bonds of particular maturities and coupon rates may be dominated by combinations of other bonds. In this case tax clienteles naturally arise. If there is no one clientele for which every bond remains undominated, then the concept of the "marginal taxable investor" who "sets" all prices may well be meaningless.

The second problem is that of the assumed investment horizon. This is the focus of the present paper. By necessity we ignore the problem of tax clienteles. Extant estimation procedures assume either that the bond is held to maturity, without intermediate realization of capital gains and losses (the buy and hold policy), or that capital gains and losses are realized

Reproduced from *Journal of Financial Economics*, 13, 1984, 299–335.

George M. Constantinides is Professor of Finance at the University of Chicago. Earlier versions of the paper were presented at the annual AFA meeting in Washington, DC, and at workshops at the Universities of Chicago, Michigan, and Rochester, Massachusetts Institute of Technology, Yale University, and New York University. We would like to thank Mark Wolfson, Steve Schaefer (the referee), Rene Stulz, and the participants at the above meeting and workshops for helpful comments. Additional support was provided by the Sloan Foundation.

every period as they occur (the continuous realization policy). Both the buy and hold policy and the continuous realization policy lead to relatively simple bond pricing formulae. This facilitates the estimation of the yield curve and the implied tax bracket of the marginal investor.

The assumption that bondholders follow either a buy and hold or a continuous realization policy, rather than the optimal trading policy, is at variance with reality and, as we demonstrate, may seriously bias the estimation of the yield curve and the implied tax bracket of the marginal investor. Perusal of the *Wall Street Journal* provides convincing evidence that investment advisors – and presumably their clients – are aware of the optimal trading policies which frequently differ sharply from a buy and hold or continuous realization policy. By definition, the marginal bondholder is an economic agent (or group of agents) of sufficient stature to set bond prices at the margin. It is questionable then to assert that the marginal investor follows a suboptimal trading policy through ignorance.

The present paper unifies two recent strands of research, the pricing of bonds with stochastically varying interest rates and investment opportunity set and the pricing of stocks in the presence of personal taxes. Cox, Ingersoll, and Ross (1981, 1985) present an equilibrium theory of bond pricing and the term structure of interest rates, in particular explaining the valuation of a deterministic stream of cash flows but with a stochastically varying interest rate and investment opportunity set. Constantinides (1983, 1984) and Constantinides and Scholes (1980) discuss the optimal trading of stocks and options in the presence of personal taxes and present an equilibrium theory of stock pricing, in particular explaining the effect of optimal realization of capital gains and losses on the pricing of stocks.

Tax considerations which govern a bondholder's optimal trading policy include the following: realization of capital losses, short term if possible; deferment of the realization of capital gains, especially if they are short term; changing the holding period status from long to short term by sale of the bond and repurchase, so that future capital losses can be realized short term; raising the basis through sale of the bond and repurchase in order to deduct the amortized premium from ordinary income. Because of the interaction of these factors, no simple characterization of the optimal trading policy is possible. We can say, however, that it differs substantially from the buy and hold policy irrespective of whether the bondholder is a bank, a bond dealer, or an individual. We obtain these strong results even when we allow for transactions costs and explicitly consider numerous Internal Revenue Service (IRS) regulations designed to curtail tax avoidance.

The paper is organized as follows. In section 2 we outline the tax provisions in four representative tax scenarios which may apply to the elusive marginal bondholder. The formal model is presented in section 3.

Closed-form solutions for the prices of consol bonds and the value of the timing option are presented in section 4 for a special case. In section 5 we derive the optimal trading policies under more general conditions, and in section 6 we illustrate the effect of taxes on the prices of bonds and on the value of the timing option. The estimation of the yield curve and the tax bracket of the marginal investor is grossly biased if the value of the timing option is ignored. This point is illustrated in section 7. In section 8 we discuss municipal bonds. Concluding remarks are offered in section 9.

2 The Tax Environment

To avoid a profusion of details in our discussion we abstract from many of the nuances of the regulations governing the taxation of income, as defined by the tax code and its interpretation by the IRS and the courts. However, we do emphasize certain important aspects of the code, which, though largely ignored in finance, may materially affect bond prices and the estimation of the yield curve and the marginal tax rate. We also provide some historical perspective to familiarize the reader with major changes in the tax code which may be reflected in a time series of bond yields.

At least four broad classes of potential marginal investors warrant examination: individuals, banks and bond dealers, corporations, and tax-exempt institutions. Consider first the tax rules applicable to individual investors.

Coupon income (net of interest expense) is taxed at the individual's marginal tax rate on ordinary income, the maximum rate currently being 50 percent. Between 1970 and 1980, coupon income was classified as "unearned income" and was taxed at a maximum rate of 72 percent. Prior to the 1970s, the top marginal tax rate varied from a low of 7 percent in 1913 to a high of 95 percent in 1945. In our calculations we assume that the marginal tax rate τ_c on coupon income for an individual is 0.5.[1]

The taxation of capital gains is complex. Unrealized gains and losses remain untaxed. Gains and losses are taxed in the year that they are realized. A realized gain or loss is the difference between the sales price (less cost of sale) and the basis. For most assets the basis is just the purchase price (plus cost of purchase), but for some bonds the purchase price is subject to adjustment.

We consider only original issue par bonds, defined as such by the IRS if the original issue discount does not exceed one-fourth of 1 percent multiplied by the number of full years to maturity. For these bonds, if the purchase price in the secondary market is below par, no adjustment is made and the basis is just the purchase price. If the purchase price is above par, this difference is amortized linearly to the maturity date.[2] The amount amortized in a tax year is allowed as a deduction against ordinary income and the bond's basis is correspondingly reduced. There is no specific limitation on this deduction. In our calculations the amortized amount is (negatively) taxed at the rate $\tau_c = 0.5$.

Realized capital gains and losses are either short term or long term. The required holding period for long-term treatment is currently 1 year. This has varied many times since capital gains were first differentiated from ordinary income in 1922. In the years 1942–77 the holding period was 6 months. Prior to that time there were three or more categories of long-term capital gains with required holding periods as long as 10 years.

Net short-term capital gains are taxed as ordinary income. Net long-term capital gains are currently taxed at 40 percent of the investor's marginal tax rate on ordinary income. This treatment has also been changed. The tax rate on long-term gains has varied from 20 to 80 percent of the tax rate on ordinary income. In addition there have been periods in which alternative treatment could be elected (or was required for large capital gains).

Net short-term capital losses and 50 percent of net long-term capital losses are deducted from ordinary income and may jointly reduce the taxable ordinary income by a maximum of \$3,000 (until 1976, \$1,000). Unused losses are carried forward indefinitely. Short-term losses and long-term gains, incurred in the same year, offset each other dollar for dollar instead of being taxed at their respective rates.

We define τ_S to be the marginal tax rate on short-term capital gains and losses. This rate is not necessarily equal to the marginal tax rate on ordinary income: if the investor has net short-term losses and the deduction limit is binding, $\tau_S = 0$; if the investor has net short-term losses but larger long-term gains, τ_S is 40 percent of the marginal tax rate on ordinary income. Likewise, we define τ_L to be the *marginal* tax rate on long-term capital gains and losses.

If an asset is sold at a loss within 30 days before or after the acquisition of "substantially identical" property, the IRS can disallow the loss deduction under the "wash sale" rule. An investor has a high probability of circumventing this rule by purchasing instead another bond with a slightly different coupon or maturity. In any case, this rule is not applicable to dealers or individual taxpayers who are in the business of trading bonds. Consequently we ignore the wash sale rule throughout this paper.

We consider three representative tax scenarios for an individual bondholder and one scenario for banks or bond dealers, as defined by the marginal rates τ_c, τ_S and τ_L.

1 The marginal investor is an individual. Coupon income is taxed at the rate $\tau_c = 0.5$. Realized short-term and long-term

gains and losses are taxed at the rate $\tau_S = \tau_L = 0.25$. The deduction limit is not binding.

This scenario is plausible if the individual is periodically forced to sell some of his portfolio assets by factors beyond his control (or of more importance than the tax consequences) and, on average, realizes large long-term gains. Then the deduction limit is not binding. Since short-term losses must be used to offset the long-term gains, the marginal tax rate is the long-term gains rate.[3] We take the long-term gains rate to be half the investor's marginal tax rate on ordinary income, as it was between 1942 and 1979. We also assume that the investor can always defer the realization of short-term gains until the holding period exceeds 1 year and then realize the gains long term.

2 The marginal investor is an individual. Coupon income is taxed at the rate $\tau_c = 0.5$. Realized short-term gains and losses are taxed at the rate $\tau_S = 0.5$. Realized long-term gains and losses are taxed at the rate $\tau_L = 0.25$. The deduction limit is not binding.

Scenario 2 is the least plausible because it ignores both the deduction limit and the (unfavorable to the taxpayer) offsetting of long-term gains with short-term losses.[4] Since investors have a tax incentive to realize losses and defer gains (at least short-term gains), the assumption that the deduction limit is not binding may be tenuous and is relaxed in the next scenario.

3 The marginal investor is an individual. Coupon income is taxed at the rate $\tau_c = 0.5$. Short- and long-term gains and losses remain untaxed, that is, $\tau_S = \tau_L = 0$.

One justification for this scenario is to assume that the individual realizes losses and defers gains. At the margin losses can only be carried forward as the deduction limit is binding. The only tax "game" permitted under this scenario is to realize a gain on a bond in order to raise its basis above par and start deducting the premium amortization against ordinary income. As we shall see, this policy is profitable.

Although corporations are taxed differently from individuals, the tax regulations on nonbank corporations that hold bonds for reasons not directly related to their business operations are sufficiently similar to those applying to individuals that the previous scenarios remain at least qualitatively correct. The primary distinction is that a net capital loss (short and long term combined) cannot be deducted in any amount from ordinary income but can be carried back for 3 years and forward for 5 years as a short-term loss to offset gains. Banks and (corporate or individual) bond dealers are taxed differently, however.

For banks and dealers, bond coupons and all realized capital gains and losses are treated as ordinary income or loss without explicit limitation. Net operating losses of banks are carried back for 10 years and forward for 5 years. In the following scenario we effectively assume that the bank has positive net earnings in every 10 year period so that loss benefits are earned immediately. Corporate earnings and losses are taxed at the corporate rate of 50 percent. (The current corporate tax rate is 46 percent on earnings in excess of $100,000. In the past it has been as high as 54 percent.) The same scenario applies to a bond dealer with marginal personal or corporate tax rate on ordinary income equal to 50 percent.

4 The marginal holder is a bank or bond dealer. Coupon income and all capital gains and losses are taxed at the rate $\tau_c = \tau_s = \tau_L = 0.5$. There is no deduction limit.

In each of the scenarios 1–4 the tax rates τ_c, τ_s, and τ_L are assumed to remain constant over time because we wish to focus on the long-run effect of taxes on bond prices. Certain trading policies not examined here would become optimal at the time that tax provisions were about to change. For example, when the effective maximum rate on long-term capital gains was changed from 28 to 20 percent by the 1978 Tax Revenue Act, individuals paying the 28 percent rate should have deferred realizing their capital gains, *ceteris paribus*. Similarly, if an investor's income were to change sufficiently to place him in a different tax bracket, the optimal trading policy might be affected.

We also examine bond prices in each of the four tax scenarios under the assumption that the bondholder is (artificially) constrained to follow a buy and hold policy and compare the bond prices, tax timing option, and yields with the case when the investor follows optimal policies. The buy and hold economy is taken as our primary benchmark in which there are no price effects induced by tax trading.

We do not explicitly examine a scenario in which the marginal bondholder is exempt from all taxes. This might be considered a serious omission because tax-exempt intermediaries currently hold more than a third of all the outstanding government and corporate bonds and account for an even greater proportion of the trading volume. Furthermore, liberalized tax-deferred retirement plans provide growing opportunities for taxable individuals to defer the tax on coupons, dividends, and capital gains until retirement. If the marginal investor is tax exempt, then there are obviously no tax-induced "biases" in bond prices.[5] However, since the no-trading policy is not dominated by any other for a tax-exempt investor (in a perfect market), we can assume the buy and hold policy. Consequently bond prices should equal the benchmark values, and standard estimation techniques, such as that of McCulloch (1975), should verify that the marginal tax bracket is zero.

3 The Model

Our goal is to find the price of a default-free bond with par value unity, continuous coupon rate c, and maturity date T. The bond is perfectly divisible and can be bought or sold with zero transactions costs.[6] The bond price is a function of the state vector Y (defined below) and time t, that is, $P = P(Y, t; c, T)$.

We price the coupon bond relative to short-term (instantaneous) lending via a riskless "single-period" bond with maturity $\mathrm{d}t$ and before-tax yield $r(Y, t)$. The single-period bond is perfectly divisible and can be bought or sold with zero transactions costs. Effectively there is unlimited riskless lending over the time interval $\mathrm{d}t$ at the before-tax interest rate r. If an investor's tax rate on ordinary income is τ_c, his after-tax interest rate is $(1 - \tau_c)r$.

We assume that, throughout the term to this coupon bond's maturity, some investor with marginal tax rates τ_c, τ_s, and τ_L (on coupon income, short-term capital gains and losses, and long-term capital gains and losses respectively) is indifferent between buying the coupon bond or investing in the single-period bond. The assumption that there exists some tax bracket (τ_c, τ_s, τ_L) with the property that an investor in this tax bracket is indifferent between the two investments over a time interval $\mathrm{d}t$ is weak. The strong part of our assumption is that *investors in the same tax bracket are at the margin throughout the bond's term to maturity*. In a richer model (beyond our present scope) we might allow for the possibility that the bond is passed from one tax clientele to another as it approaches maturity or as it becomes a premium or discount bond due to shifts in interest rates. Since we wish to focus on the already complex problem of the optimal realization of capital gains and losses, we abstract from issues related to changing tax clienteles.[7]

At each point of time and for each coupon bond there is a reservation purchase price defined to be such that a (marginal) investor in the given tax bracket (τ_c, τ_s, τ_L) is indifferent between purchasing the coupon bond now or investing in the single-period bond over the time interval $\mathrm{d}t$. This equilibrium condition is formalized below as the after-tax version of the local expectations hypothesis. After purchasing the coupon bond, the investor follows the derived optimal trading policy as opposed to a continuous realization or a buy and hold policy.

Each bondholder also has a reservation sale price which depends on his cost basis and the length of time for which he has held the bond. In general the prevailing reservation purchase and sale prices differ. We assume that the government supplies all maturity and coupon bonds with infinite elasticity at the reservation purchase price of the (marginal) investor and that all trades take place at this price, denoted P.[8] When the reservation sale price exceeds the reservation purchase price, only the government supplies the bond. When the reservation purchase price exceeds the reservation sale price, the seller earns a "producer's" surplus which we attribute to his tax timing option.

The value $V(Y, t; c, T; \hat{P}, \hat{t})$ of the bond to an investor is defined as the present value of the stream of cash flows associated with the bond, assuming that the optimal policy in realizing capital gains and losses is followed. The symbols $\hat{P}$ and $\hat{t}$ denote the current cost basis and the time at which the bond was purchased. Because of amortization of the basis, $\hat{P}$ may differ from the price at which the bond was purchased.

At those "stopping times" at which the investor sells the bond, either by choice or by force, and realizes a capital gain or loss, the value to the investor is simply the after-tax proceeds from its immediate sale. The bond's maturity date is an obvious stopping time for all investors. At maturity, the capital gain or loss is unavoidably realized; hence

$$V(Y, T; c, T; \hat{P}, \hat{t}) = 1 - \tau(t, \hat{t})(1 - \hat{P}), \tag{1}$$

where $\tau(t, \hat{t})$ is the short- or long-term tax rate depending on the bond's status.

A similar result is true at any stopping time prior to maturity when the investor sells his bonds. For the sequence of (possibly random) stopping times, $t = t_1, t_2, \ldots$, at which the investor realizes a capital gain or loss,

$$V(Y, t; c, T, \hat{P}, \hat{t}) = P - \tau(t, \hat{t})(P - \hat{P}) \qquad \text{at } t = t_1, t_2, \ldots. \tag{2}$$

Stopping times may differ across investors. At the stopping times chosen by the investor the "smooth-pasting" (or "high contact") condition also must hold:[9]

$$\frac{\partial V}{\partial Y_n} = [1 - \tau(t, \hat{t})] \frac{\partial P}{\partial Y_n} \qquad \text{for } n = 1, 2, \ldots, N \text{ at } t_1^0, t_2^0, \ldots. \tag{3}$$

The smooth-pasting condition is not imposed at those stopping times where a realization is forced. Forced realizations are assumed to be caused by events exogenous to the model, for example an unanticipated and unavoidable need for consumption or portfolio revision. Forced realizations are formally modeled as Poisson arrivals with constant force λ. The Poisson process is independent of the process which generates the movements of the state variables.

For a marginal investor the time of purchase is also an optimal stopping time since, by definition, he is indifferent to the purchase. Thus

$$V(Y, t; c, T; P, t) = P \tag{4a}$$

$$\frac{\partial V}{\partial Y_n} = (1 - \tau_s)\frac{\partial P}{\partial Y_n}, \qquad n = 1, \ldots, N. \tag{4b}$$

This condition provides the link between the value of the bond and its market price. It can also be interpreted as an alternative description of the marginal investor. Equation (4a) need not hold for nonmarginal investors who either receive a surplus by purchasing the bond at the prevailing price or find buying the bond to be dominated by lending at the short-term rate.

At all other times, the investor's value of the bond exceeds the after-tax proceeds from immediate sale and the investor optimally defers the realization of a capital gain or loss. The set of states and times $\{Y, t\}$ at which this occurs is referred to as the continuation region, that is, in the continuation region

$$V(Y, t; c, T; \hat{P}, \hat{t}) > P - \tau(t, \hat{t})(P - \hat{P}). \tag{5}$$

In the continuation region the investor's after-tax rate of return on his bond is

$$\frac{\mathrm{d}V + (1 - \tau_c)c\ \mathrm{d}t + \max[0, (\hat{P} - 1)\tau_c\ \mathrm{d}t/(T - t)]}{V}. \tag{6}$$

The term $(\hat{P} - 1)\tau_c\ \mathrm{d}t/(T - t)$ is the tax benefit of the linearly amortized premium when the basis is above par.

We assume the after-tax version of the local expectations hypothesis:[10] the after-tax expected rate of return on the coupon bond (measured via the value function) equals the after-tax single-period rate of interest over the period $\{t, t + \mathrm{d}t\}$, that is,

$$E\left\{\frac{\mathrm{d}V + (1 - \tau_c)c\ \mathrm{d}t + \max[0, (\hat{P} - 1)\tau_c\,\mathrm{d}t/(T - t)]}{V}\right\}$$

$$= (1 - \tau_c)r\ \mathrm{d}t \tag{7}$$

for all $Y, t, \hat{P}$, and $\hat{t}$.

We assume that the state of the economy at time t is summarized by a vector $\{Y_n(t)\}_{N\times 1}$. This vector also summarizes the history of the economy $Y(\tau)$, $\tau < t$, to the extent that it is of current economic relevance. The state variables are jointly Markov with movements determined by the system of stochastic differential equations

$$\mathrm{d}Y_n(t) = \mu_n(Y, t)\ \mathrm{d}t + \sigma_n'(Y, t)\ \mathrm{d}w(t), \qquad n = 1, 2, \ldots, N, \tag{8}$$

where μ_n is a scalar, σ_n is a K-dimensional vector, $K \leqslant N$, and $\mathrm{d}w(t)$ is the increment of the Wiener process $w(t)$ in R^k. The variance–covariance matrix $\{\sigma_n'\sigma_m\}$ is positive semidefinite and of rank K (positive definite if $K = N$).

If $\{Y, t\}$ lies in the continuation region, the expected value of $\mathrm{d}V$ due to the movement of the state variables Y, t is given by Itô's lemma as the first three terms of equation (9) below. The expected value of $\mathrm{d}V$ due to a stochastic forced realization is $[P - \tau(t, \hat{t})(P - \hat{P}) - V]\,\lambda\,\mathrm{d}t$. The term in the brackets multiplying λ is the loss incurred when the investor is forced to deviate from his optimal policy. The term $\lambda\,\mathrm{d}t$ is the probability of a forced realization over $[t, t + \mathrm{d}t]$. Also, the expected value of $\mathrm{d}V$ due to the amortization of the premium is $-(\partial V/\partial \hat{P})\max[0, (\hat{P} - 1)\mathrm{d}t/(T - t)]$. Then equation (7) becomes

$$\frac{1}{2}\sum_{n=1}^{N}\sum_{m=1}^{N}\frac{\partial^2 V}{\partial Y_n \partial Y_m}\sigma_n'\sigma_m + \sum_{n=1}^{N}\frac{\partial V}{\partial Y_n}\mu_n + \frac{\partial V}{\partial t}$$
$$+ [P - \tau(t, \hat{t})(P - \hat{P}) - V]\,\lambda + (1 - \tau_c)c$$
$$+ \left(\tau_c - \frac{\partial V}{\partial \hat{P}}\right)\max\left(0, \frac{\hat{P} - 1}{T - t}\right) - (1 - \tau_c)rV = 0. \tag{9}$$

The solution to this differential equation, subject to the boundary conditions (1)–(5), provides the bond price P, the value V of a bond to the investor, and the optimal policy for the realization of capital gains and losses.[11]

For general functions $\sigma_n(Y, t)$ and $\mu_n(Y, t)$, a closed-form solution does not typically exist. In section 4 we illustrate the solution procedure in a simplified version of this problem and discuss the economic implications. In section 5 we provide numerical solutions to the general problem.

4 An Example

In this section we begin to examine the value of the timing option regarding the realization of capital gains and losses on bonds and to analyze the effect of the capital gains tax on their pricing. To discuss these issues in the simplest possible setting and through closed-form solutions, we make a number of simplifying assumptions.

We assume that there is only one state variable, the short-term rate of interest r, with movements determined by the stochastic differential equation

$$\mathrm{d}r = \alpha r^2\,\mathrm{d}t + s r^{3/2}\,\mathrm{d}w(t), \tag{10}$$

where $\mathrm{d}w(t)$ is the increment of the scalar Wiener process $w(t)$.[12] The price $P(r; c)$ of an infinite maturity coupon bond is then a function of the short-term interest rate r but is independent of the current time t because the process generating interest rate movements is stationary.

We also assume that the tax rates on all capital gains and losses are equal, that is, $\tau_s = \tau_L \equiv \tau$. Thus the length of time over which the bond has been held is irrelevant, and the consol's value $V(r; c; \hat{P})$ to an investor is also independent of the current time t. Finally, we assume away forced realizations, that is, $\lambda = 0$.

It is easy to prove that any investor's optimal policy is to realize capital losses immediately and defer capital gains indefinitely.[13] Given the basis $\hat{P}$, the continuation region is defined by the range of interest rates such that $P(r; c) > \hat{P}$. In the continuation region the differential equation (9) becomes

$$\frac{1}{2} s^2 r^3 \frac{\partial^2 V}{\partial r^2} + \alpha r^2 \frac{\partial V}{\partial r} - (1 - \tau_c) r V + (1 - \tau_c) c = 0, \qquad P(r; c) > \hat{P}. \quad (11)$$

The boundary condition (4a) becomes

$$V(r; c; \hat{P}) = \hat{P} \text{ at } P(r; c) = \hat{P}, \quad (12)$$

and the smooth-pasting conditions (3) and (4b) become

$$\frac{\partial V(r; c; \hat{P})}{\partial r} = (1 - \tau) \frac{\partial P(r, c)}{\partial r} \text{ at } P(r; c) = \hat{P}. \quad (13)$$

The bond price $P(r; c)$ is a function of the interest rate r and of the parameters c, α, s, τ and τ_c. Inspection of equation (10) indicates that the parameters α and s are dimensionless as are the parameters τ and τ_c. The units of the coupon yield c are dollars per unit of time, and the unit of the interest rate is the inverse of the time unit. The bond price must be proportional to the coupon rate, and since it is invariant to changes in the unit of time, it must also be inversely proportional to r. Hence

$$P(r; c) = Hc/r, \quad (14)$$

where H is a function of only the parameters α, s, τ, and τ_c.

Since we have determined the functional form of P, we can simplify (11) with the aid of equation (14) to eliminate r and its derivatives, obtaining

$$\frac{s^2}{2} P^2 V_{PP} + (s^2 - \alpha) P V_P - (1 - \tau_c) V + \frac{(1 - \tau_c) P}{H} = 0, \qquad P > \hat{P}. \quad (15)$$

The general solution to equation (15) is given below:[14]

$$V = \frac{(1 - \tau_c) P}{(1 - \tau_c + \alpha - s^2) H} + A \hat{P}^{1-\eta} P^{\eta} + A' \hat{P}^{1-\eta'} P^{\eta'}, \qquad P > \hat{P}, \quad (16)$$

where A and A' are arbitrary constants to be determined and η and

η' $(\eta < 0 < \eta')$ are the roots of the quadratic equation

$$\frac{s^2}{2}\,\eta(\eta - 1) + (s^2 - \alpha)\eta - (1 - \tau_c) = 0. \tag{17}$$

By homogeneity, the coefficients of P^{η} and $P^{\eta'}$ must be proportional to the parameters $\hat{P}^{1-\eta}$ and $\hat{P}^{1-\eta'}$ respectively. Thus A and A' depend only on the parameters α, s, τ, and τ_c.

The following argument determines A'. Since the optimal trading policy involves no sales at any price above the basis, $\hat{P}$ must have a negligible effect on the value function whenever $P \gg \hat{P}$. Formally

$$\lim_{P/\hat{P} \to \infty} \left(\frac{\partial V}{\partial \hat{P}}\right) = 0. \tag{18}$$

This condition is satisfied only if $A' = 0$. The remaining two constants can be determined using (12) and (13). Substituting (16) into (12) and setting $A' = 0$, we obtain

$$\frac{(1 - \tau_c)P}{(1 - \tau_c + \alpha - s^2)H} + AP = P. \tag{19}$$

Similarly, substituting (16) into (13) and setting $A' = 0$, we obtain

$$\frac{1 - \tau_c}{(1 - \tau_c + \alpha - s^2)H} + A\eta = 1 - \tau. \tag{20}$$

We solve for H and A and obtain

$$P(r; c) = \frac{(1 - \tau_c)c}{(1 - \tau_c + \alpha - s^2)[1 - \tau/(1 - \eta)]r} \tag{21}$$

and

$$\begin{aligned} V(r; c; \hat{P}) &= (1 - \tau)P + \tau\hat{P} && P \leqslant \hat{P} \\ &= \left(1 - \frac{\tau}{1 - \eta}\right)P + \frac{\tau}{1 - \eta}\,P^{\eta}\hat{P}^{1-\eta} && P > \hat{P} \end{aligned} \tag{22}$$

where

$$\eta \equiv -\frac{s^2/2 - \alpha + [(s^2/2 - \alpha)^2 + 2s^2(1 - \tau_c)]^{1/2}}{s^2}$$

is the negative root of (17).

Equation (21) shows that the price of a consol bond is increasing in the capital gains tax rate of the marginal investor. A high capital gains rate does not hurt the investor because he is never forced to realize gains and his optimal policy is to defer indefinitely the realization of capital gains. In fact a high capital gains rate is a benefit because it enables him to obtain larger tax rebates by realizing a capital loss whenever such a loss occurs.

Provided that forced realizations are not too frequent, the same conclusion also applies to a finite maturity par bond, as indeed is demonstrated in the numerical solutions of section 6. If the bond currently sells at par, the investor can be neutral to the capital gains tax by following the naive policy of deferring both gains and losses. The intelligent policy of deferring gains and realizing losses can only turn the taxation to his advantage, and he therefore benefits by a high capital gains tax rate.

Using Itô's lemma and equations (10) and (11), we find the consol dynamics to be

$$\frac{\mathrm{d}P}{P} = (s^2 - \alpha)r\ \mathrm{d}t - sr^{1/2}\ \mathrm{d}w \equiv \gamma r\ \mathrm{d}t - sr^{1/2}\ \mathrm{d}w. \tag{23}$$

The expected capital gains rate γr can be either positive or negative. We write the bond price in terms of γ and obtain

$$P(r; c) = \frac{c/r}{[1 - \gamma/(1 - \tau_c)]\ [1 - \tau/(1 - \eta)]}. \tag{21$'$}$$

We observe that the bond price is increasing (decreasing) in the ordinary income tax rate if capital gains (losses) are expected. This indeterminacy is due to the light taxation of capital gains relative to interest and coupon income in this model. If capital gains are expected, the consol's current coupon yield is less than the interest rate, and an increase in τ_c represents a greater loss for potential holdings in the instantaneous bond than in the consol.

We use two benchmarks to measure the value of the tax timing option. The first is the price P_H of the consol in an economy where the marginal investor follows a buy and hold policy. This benchmark is also the consol's price in an economy with zero capital gains tax.[15] Hence we write

$$P_H = \frac{(1 - \tau_c)c}{(1 - \tau_c - \gamma)r}. \tag{24}$$

The second benchmark is the consol price P_C in an economy where the marginal bondholder realizes all gains and losses continuously. Proceeding as before, we find that this consol price satisfies the equation

$$(1 - \tau)\left(\frac{s^2}{2}\ r^3 P_C'' + \alpha r^2 P_C'\right) - (1 - \tau_c)rP_C + (1 - \tau_c)c = 0 \tag{25}$$

with solution

$$P_C = \frac{(1 - \tau_c)c}{[1 - \tau_c - \gamma(1 - \tau)]\, r}. \tag{26}$$

Note that $P_C \gtreqless P_H$ as $\gamma \lesseqgtr 0$: a continuous realization policy dominates the buy and hold policy whenever capital losses are expected.

The tax effect on the consol's price is expressed relative to the two benchmarks as follows:

$$\frac{P - P_{\mathrm{H}}}{P} = \frac{\tau}{1 - \eta} \tag{27a}$$

$$\frac{P - P_{\mathrm{C}}}{P} = \frac{\tau}{1 - \eta}\left[1 + \frac{\gamma(1 - \eta - \tau)}{1 - \tau_{\mathrm{c}} - \gamma(1 - \tau)}\right]. \tag{27b}$$

When the buy and hold benchmark is used, the timing option's value derives from the right to realize capital losses early. When the continuous realization benchmark is used, the timing option measures the value of deferring capital gains.

To measure the magnitude of the timing option we require estimates of the parameters α and s and the marginal tax bracket. When the data from Ibbotson and Sinquefield (1982) are used, the annualized standard deviation of changes in the short rate over the period 1926–81 is 2.2 percent. Using equation (10) and $r = 0.11$ we set $s = 0.022(0.11)^{-3/2} = 0.604$. In the same study the reported standard deviation of annualized returns on long-term US Treasury bonds is 5.7 percent. If we take this number as an estimate of the standard deviation of returns on a consol, then using (23) and $r = 0.11$ we obtain $s = 0.057/(0.11)^{1/2} = 0.172.$[16]

Ibbotson and Sinquefield do not report the average change in the interest rate, and so somewhat arbitrarily we examine the two cases $\alpha = 0$ and $\alpha = s^2$ which correspond to zero expected change in the interest rate and the consol price respectively. If we choose to interpret α as a risk premium measure, then under the assumption of no drift in the interest rate, the expected rate of return on a consol is $r(1 + \alpha)$. Ibbotson and Sinquefield estimate that investors expected on average a premium of 131 basis points on 20 year bonds. This gives an estimate for α of 0.44 based on the average interest rate.

Table 3.1 displays the value of the timing option as a percentage of price

Table 3.1 The value of the timing option as a percentage of the consol price[a]

	$s = 0.604$			$s = 0.172$		
	$\alpha = 0$	$\alpha = s^2$	$\alpha = 0.44$	$\alpha = 0$	$\alpha = s^2$	$\alpha = 0.44$
Buy and hold benchmark	7.7	11.2	11.9	3.4	3.9	11.7
Continuous realization benchmark	44.9	11.2	9.0	4.9	3.9	0.5

[a]Computed for infinitely lived investors. The interest rate follows the risk-adjusted stochastic process $dr = \alpha r^2\, dt + sr^{3/2}\, dw$. Marginal bondholder's tax rates are $\tau_c = 0.5$ on coupon income and $\tau = 0.25$ on all capital gains.

(equations (27a) and (27b)). For the higher variance process the timing option contributes a significant portion of the bond's value as measured against either benchmark. For the lower variance process the timing option remains important except in the case when large capital losses are expected and the continuous realization benchmark is employed. We conclude that the potential effect of tax trading on bond prices cannot be safely ignored in practice.

5 Optimal Bond Trading: The General Case

We examine a discrete-time version of the model outlined in section 3, focusing on the distinction between short- and long-term gains and losses, the effect of the amortization deduction, and transactions costs. Since our primary concern is on how optimal trading affects the bond prices, we confine our attention to the marginal bondholder.

We assume that the trading interval is 1 year.[17] If an asset is sold 1 year after purchase, we assume that the holding period is short term or long term at the investor's discretion. Since the cutoff point is 1 year after purchase, the investor can make the holding period long or short term by delaying or advancing the bond sale by only 1 day. By a simple dominance argument, all capital gains are realized long term. Similarly, whenever the investor realizes a capital loss 1 year after purchasing the bond, he does so short term.

We maintain our assumption that there are no forced realizations. On each trading date the investor either holds his bond, deferring the realization of a capital gain or loss, or sells his bond and immediately repurchases it, thereby realizing a capital gain or loss and reestablishing a short-term status. The following set of factors determines whether the investor holds his bond or executes a wash sale.

1 If the bond price is below the basis, the investor would like to sell the bond and receive the tax deduction immediately. The reason becomes more compelling if the bond was purchased 1 year earlier, so that this is the only chance to realize the capital loss short term.
2 If the bond price is above the basis, the investor would like to defer the realization of the capital gain and thereby defer the tax liability. As stated previously, he never realizes a short-term gain because he can wait one more day. Nevertheless, he may wish to realize a long-term gain as explained in 3 and 4.
3 A short-term holding status is beneficial to the investor. This status helps when he realizes a capital loss, because he realizes it short-term, and it never hurts, even when the investor realizes a capital gain,

because he can always wait one more day and convert to the long-term status. The short-term status turns out to be a very important factor governing the optimal liquidation policy. Under certain realistic conditions, an investor may realize a capital gain solely to convert to the beneficial short-term status.

4 The peculiar amortization rules on bonds introduce another twist to this already complex problem. If the bond's basis is above par, this difference is linearly amortized over its remaining term to maturity with the "loss" applied against the investor's ordinary income. The present value of this tax deduction is high for short maturity bonds, but decreases with longer maturity because of the linearity of the amortization rule. For short maturity bonds the benefit in establishing a basis above par may be sufficiently large to make it optimal to realize a capital gain.

We assume that the short-term rate of interest r is the only state variable and that it follows a driftless binomial random walk with two reflecting barriers. We consider two specifications for the interest rate process. In the low variance process the interest rate takes on the 21 values $0.04, 0.05, 0.06, \ldots, 0.24$. At each point in time the interest rate either increases or decreases by 0.01, each with probability 0.5, unless it is currently at one of the reflecting barriers 0.04 or 0.24. If the interest rate is equal to one of the reflecting barriers, then at the next date it remains unchanged or takes on the value 0.05 or 0.23 respectively with probability 0.5. The reader may verify that the unconditional distribution of r is uniform over the 21 points. The standard deviation of changes in the interest rate is $\sigma_r \equiv \text{std}\,[r(t+1)|\, r(t)] = 0.01$ per year, independent of the state (except in the end-point states).

In the high variance process, the interest rate takes one of the 11 values $0.04, 0.06, \ldots, 0.24$. The probabilities of increase or decrease by 0.02 are as in the low variance process with the same reflecting barriers at 0.04 and 0.24. The standard deviation of the changes in the interest rate in the high variance process is $\sigma_r = 0.02$ per year. From the Ibbotson and Sinquefield (1982) study, the annualized standard deviation of the short-term rate is 0.022. The low variance process then underestimates the interest rate variability, while the high variance process reflects the average variability in the period 1926–81.

As we shall see, the low variance process implies, on average, that the standard deviation of the annual rate of return of 20 year Treasury bonds is 5.66 percent if priced under the buy and hold policy, and 5.82 percent if priced under the optimal policy with $\tau_S = \tau_L = 0.25$ (scenario 1). For the high variance process, the corresponding numbers are 9.47 and 8.73

percent. From the Ibbotson and Sinquefield (1982) study this standard deviation is 5.7 percent for long-term Treasury bonds over the period 1926–81. Therefore the low variance process reflects the actual *initial* variability of long-term bonds over that period.[18] However, the high variance process may be more representative of recent history.

In discrete time the differential equation (9) becomes a difference equation which we can solve numerically subject to the boundary conditions. Equivalently and more directly we obtain the bond price and the value of a bond to the marginal investor at dates $T, T-1, T-2, \ldots$, etc. by dynamic programming.

Equations (28) and (29) establish the bond price and value of a bond to the investor at maturity, that is, at $t = T$. At maturity the ex-coupon bond is priced at par, which we take to be unity:

$$P(r, T; c, T) = 1. \tag{28}$$

The value of the bond to an investor is the after-tax sale proceeds. By the maturity date, the bond basis cannot exceed unity because the excess will have been completely amortized by then. Thus only a gain can be realized at maturity, and the appropriate capital gains tax rate is the long-term rate. Thus

$$V(r, T; c, T; \hat{P}, \hat{t}) = 1 - \tau_L + \tau_L \hat{P}. \tag{29}$$

With the terminal values established, the bond's price and its value to a given investor at points in time prior to maturity can now be obtained through dynamic programming. We distinguish between the cases in which amortization is and is not utilized.

The bond price is what a marginal investor is willing to pay for it. His alternative is investing in the short-term asset over the next year in which case his investment increases at the prevailing after-tax interest rate. He is indifferent to buying the bond, therefore, only if the after-tax coupon and amortization benefit plus the expectation of the value function next period is greater than the current bond price by exactly the after-tax forgone interest. If the bond is selling today for less than par, then its price is the appropriate basis in the value function. If the bond is priced above par, then $(P-1)/(T-t)$ will be amortized in the next year, and the basis in the value function next year is less than the prevailing price by this amount. Thus at time t,

$$\begin{aligned} P = {} & [1 + (1 - \tau_c)r]^{-1}((1 - \tau_c)c \\ & + E_t\{ V[\tilde{r}(t+1), t+1; c, T; P, t] \}) \qquad \text{if } P \leqslant 1 \end{aligned} \tag{30}$$

and

$$P = [1 + (1 - \tau_c)r]^{-1}\left((1 - \tau_c)c + \frac{(P - 1)\tau_c}{T - t}\right.$$

$$\left. + E_t\left\{V\left[\tilde{r}(t+1), t+1; c, T; P - \frac{P-1}{T-t}, t\right]\right\}\right) \quad \text{if } P > 1. \tag{31}$$

The bond price P is the solution to (30) and (31).[19]

The value of a long position in the bond is the greater of the after-tax proceeds from immediate sale and the discounted value of the benefits if the bond is retained. The after-tax proceeds from immediate sale are

$$P - \tau(t, \hat{t})(P - \hat{P}). \tag{32}$$

If the bond is retained, the discounted benefits are

$$[1 + (1 - \tau_c)r]^{-1}((1 - \tau_c)c + E_t\{V[\tilde{r}(t+1), t+1; c, T; \hat{P}, t]\}) \quad \text{if } \hat{P} \leqslant 1 \tag{33}$$

and

$$[1 + (1 - \tau_c)r]^{-1}\left((1 - \tau_c)c + \frac{(\hat{P} - 1)\tau_c}{T - t}\right.$$

$$\left. + E_t\left\{V\left[\tilde{r}(t+1), t+1; c, T; \hat{P} - \frac{\hat{P}-1}{T-t}, \hat{t}\right]\right\}\right) \quad \text{if } \hat{P} > 1. \tag{34}$$

In comparing equations (30) and (33) we note that $P = V(r, t; c, T; P, t)$ and so the relation in (4a) is satisfied.

We illustrate the optimal trading policies for a bond with a 14 percent stated coupon payable annually in the four tax scenarios.

1 Treasury bond held by a high tax bracket individual, with $\tau_c = 0.5$, $\tau_s = \tau_L = 0.25$.

Table 3.2 reports the bond prices and values V for the high variance interest rate process, a range of interest rates and bases, and maturities of 1, 5 and 20 years.[20] If both the basis and the bond price are less than unity, the amortization feature is not in effect and the simple trading rule is to realize a loss and defer a gain as indicated by daggers. If either the basis or the bond price exceeds unity, the amortization feature becomes relevant and complicates the rule. Asterisks and daggers mark the states in which a wash sale is optimal. In these states the value function is equal to the after-tax proceeds from an immediate sale as stated in (32). Asterisks indicate the realization of capital gains establishing a new or higher amortizable basis. Daggers denote the realization of a capital loss. In

Table 3.2 Treasury bond prices and values of a long position under tax scenario 1[a]

Interest rate	*Bond price*	*Basis* 0.7	0.8	0.9	1.0	1.1	1.2	1.3
Maturity, 1 year								
0.06	1.0755	*0.98	*1.01	*1.03	*1.06	1.09	1.14	1.18
0.10	1.0364	*0.95	*0.98	*1.00	*1.03	1.07	1.11	1.16
0.14	1.0000	0.93	0.95	0.98	*1.00	1.05	1.09	1.14
0.18	0.9762	0.91	0.94	0.96	†0.98	1.03	1.07	1.12
0.22	0.9535	0.90	0.92	0.94	†0.97	1.01	1.05	1.10
Maturity, 5 years								
0.06	1.3363	*1.18	*1.20	*1.23	*1.25	*1.28	*1.30	*1.33
0.10	1.1771	*1.06	*1.08	*1.11	*1.13	*1.16	1.18	1.22
0.14	1.0197	0.95	0.97	0.99	*1.01	1.05	1.08	1.12
0.18	0.9110	0.88	0.89	0.91	†0.93	0.96	1.00	1.04
0.22	0.8354	0.81	0.83	†0.85	†0.88	†0.90	0.93	0.97
Maturity, 20 years								
0.06	1.7358	1.48	*1.50	*1.53	*1.55	*1.58	*1.60	*1.63
0.10	1.4187	1.26	1.27	1.29	1.31	1.34	1.36	*1.39
0.14	1.1044	1.03	1.04	1.06	1.08	1.10	†1.13	†1.15
0.18	0.8793	0.85	0.86	†0.88	†0.91	†0.93	†0.96	†0.98
0.22	0.7429	0.74	†0.76	†0.78	†0.81	†0.83	†0.86	†0.88

[a]Tax scenario 1 is characterized by a tax rate on coupon income of $\tau_c = 0.5$ and a tax rate on short- and long-term capital gains of $\tau_S = \tau_L = 0.25$ corresponding to a situation in which the offset rule is binding but the deduction limit is not. The coupon rate on bond is 0.14 paid annually. The interest rate follows the high variance process with a standard deviation of 0.02 per year. The solid line divides the states with capital gains, realized or not, from those with capital losses. Asterisks and daggers mark the states in which the optimal policy is to perform a wash sale. Asterisks indicate the realization of a long-term capital gain establishing a new or higher amortizable basis. Daggers denote the realization of a long-term capital loss.

unmarked states the value of holding exceeds the after-tax proceeds from a sale and no sale is executed. For example, when the interest rate is 14 percent a 5 year bond sells for 1.0197. With a basis of 1.3 a tax rebate of 0.07 could be earned by realizing a capital loss; however, the total value of the wash sale $(1.02 + 0.07 = 1.09)$ is less than that of holding the bond and continuing to amortize the higher basis (1.12).

For 1 year bonds, if the bond sells at a premium, $P > 1$, and the basis is below the bond price, $\hat{P} < P$, the investor realizes a capital gain in order to establish a higher basis and benefit from the amortization of the basis. Conversely, if the bond price drops below the basis, $P < \hat{P}$, the investor defers realization of the loss to continue amortizing the original premium. For 5 year bonds the amortization benefit is reduced and large capital gains may be deferred, or capital losses may be realized even at the expense of forgoing future amortization benefits. For example, if the bond price rises to 1.1097 from a basis of 1.0, the investor realizes a capital gain; however, if $\hat{P} < 1.0$ the investor defers the capital gain. The amortization benefit becomes negligible for 20 year bonds. For example, if $P = 1.42$ and $\hat{P} \leqslant 1.3$, the investor optimally defers the realization of a capital gain and thereby forgoes the amortization benefit of increasing the basis to 1.42. In fact, if $P = 0.88$ and $\hat{P}$ is 1.1, 1.2, or 1.3, the investor forgoes the amortization benefit and realizes the capital loss.

2 Treasury bond held by a high tax bracket individual with $\tau_C = 0.5$, $\tau_S = 0.5$, $\tau_L = 0.25$.

Table 3.3 reports the bond price and values V for the high variance interest rate process, a range of interest rates and bases, and maturities of 1, 5, and 20 years. Asterisks, daggers, and double daggers mark the states where the optimal policy is to perform a wash sale. Panel A reports results when the bond has been held for longer than 1 year, $t - \hat{t} > 1$, while panel B reports results when the bond has been held for just 1 year, $t - \hat{t} = 1$. Note that the value function in the two panels can differ only when a wash sale is executed and a capital loss is realized. When a gain is realized, it is presumed to be long term and so the taxes paid are the same. When no wash sale occurs, the ensuing status must be long term regardless of the current status.

These tables indicate that the investor performs a wash sale of long-term bonds practically every year in order to revert to the short-term status. This is emphasized by the double daggers which mark states in which a wash sale is executed to this end alone. The desirability of the short-term status seems to dominate all other considerations.

3 Treasury bond held by a high tax bracket individual with $\tau_C = 0.5$, $\tau_S = \tau_L = 0$.

The optimal trading policy is quite simple and need not be illustrated in a table. Whenever the bond price is above par and the basis, the investor makes a wash sale to establish a higher basis and deduct from future ordinary income the premium amortization. The investor has no tax incentives to perform any other trades.

Table 3.3 Treasury bond prices and values of a long position under tax scenario 2[a]

Interest rate	*Bond price*	*Basis 0.7*	*0.8*	*0.9*	*1.0*	*1.1*	*1.2*	*1.3*
A Long-term status								
Maturity, 1 year								
0.06	1.0755	★0.98	★1.01	★1.03	★1.06	1.09	1.14	1.18
0.10	1.0364	★0.95	★0.98	★1.00	★1.03	1.07	1.11	1.16
0.14	1.0000	0.93	0.95	0.98	‡1.00	1.05	1.09	1.14
0.18	0.9762	0.91	0.94	0.96	†0.98	1.03	1.07	1.12
0.22	0.9535	0.90	0.92	0.94	†0.97	1.01	1.05	1.10
Maturity, 5 years								
0.06	1.3476	★1.19	★1.21	★1.24	★1.26	★1.29	★1.31	★1.34
0.10	1.1919	★1.07	★1.09	★1.12	★1.14	★1.17	†1.19	1.22
0.14	1.0368	0.95	★0.98	★1.00	★1.03	†1.05	1.08	1.12
0.18	0.9177	0.88	0.89	‡0.91	†0.94	†0.96	1.00	1.04
0.22	0.8357	0.81	0.83	†0.85	†0.88	†0.90	0.93	0.97
Maturity, 20 years								
0.06	1.9200	★1.62	★1.64	★1.67	★1.69	★1.72	★1.74	★1.77
0.10	1.6138	★1.39	★1.41	★1.44	★1.46	★1.49	★1.51	★1.54
0.14	1.2672	★1.13	★1.15	★1.18	★1.20	★1.23	★1.25	†1.28
0.18	0.9791	‡0.91	‡0.93	‡0.96	†0.98	†1.01	†1.03	†1.06
0.22	0.7856	‡0.76	†0.79	†0.81	†0.84	†0.86	†0.89	†0.91
B Short-term status								
Maturity, 1 year								
0.06	1.0755	★0.98	★1.01	★1.03	★1.06	†1.09	†1.14	†1.19
0.10	1.0364	★0.95	★0.98	★1.00	★1.03	†1.07	†1.12	†1.17
0.14	1.0000	0.93	0.95	0.98	‡1.00	†1.05	†1.10	†1.15
0.18	0.9762	0.91	0.94	0.96	†0.99	†1.04	†1.09	†1.14
0.22	0.9535	0.90	0.92	0.94	†0.98	†1.03	†1.08	†1.13
Maturity, 5 years								
0.06	1.3476	★1.19	★1.21	★1.24	★1.26	★1.29	★1.31	★1.34
0.10	1.1919	★1.07	★1.09	★1.12	★1.14	★1.17	†1.20	†1.25
0.14	1.0368	0.95	★0.98	★1.00	★1.03	†1.07	†1.12	†1.17
0.18	0.9177	0.88	0.89	‡0.91	†0.96	†1.01	†1.06	†1.11
0.22	0.8375	0.81	0.83	†0.87	†0.92	†0.97	†1.02	†1.07

Table 3.3 *(Continued)*

Interest rate	*Bond price*	*Basis 0.7*	*0.8*	*0.9*	*1.0*	*1.1*	*1.2*	*1.3*
Maturity, 20 years								
0.06	1.9200	*1.62	*1.64	*1.67	*1.69	*1.72	*1.74	*1.77
0.10	1.6138	*1.39	*1.41	*1.44	*1.46	*1.49	*1.51	*1.54
0.14	1.2672	*1.13	*1.15	*1.18	*1.20	*1.23	*1.25	†1.28
0.18	0.9791	‡0.91	‡0.93	‡0.96	†0.99	†1.04	†1.09	†1.14
0.22	0.7856	‡0.76	†0.79	†0.84	†0.89	†0.94	†0.99	†1.04

[a]Tax scenario 2 is characterized by a tax rate on coupon income and short-term capital gains of $\tau_c = \tau_s = 0.5$ and a tax rate on long-term capital gains of $\tau_L = 0.25$ corresponding to a situation in which neither the offset rule nor the deduction limit is binding. The coupon rate on the bond is $c = 0.14$, paid annually. The interest rate follows the high variance process with a standard deviation of 0.02 per year. The solid line divides the states with capital gains, realized or not, from those with capital losses. Asterisks, daggers, and double daggers mark the states in which the optimal policy is to perform a wash sale. In each case, one of the benefits is reestablishing a short-term holding status. Asterisks and double daggers indicate the realization of a long-term capital gain. The former also denote the establishment of a new or higher amortizable basis. Double daggers also indicate the realization of a long-term capital gain; however, in these cases the only benefit is the reestablishing of a short-term holding period. Daggers indicate the realization of a long- or short-term capital loss in panels A and B respectively.

4 Treasury bond held by a bank or bond dealer with $\tau_c = \tau_s = \tau_L = 0.5$.

Again the optimal policy can be described without a table. The investor optimally realizes all capital losses and defers the realization of capital gains. He never realizes a capital gain in order to establish a higher basis with the benefit of the amortization deduction. The tax rate on ordinary income is the same as that on capital gains and so amortization "losses" at best exactly offset the capital gain and occur later. Neither does he defer the realization of a capital loss in order to maintain the benefit of the amortization deduction.

6 Bond Prices and the Tax Timing Option

Table 3.4 displays simulated Treasury bond prices that would be established by the marginal investor following the optimal trading policy under each of the four tax scenarios. We assume that the current value of

Table 3.4 Treasury bond prices established by optimal trading policies: tax scenarios 1–4[a,b]

	High variance process ($\sigma_r = 0.02$ *per year*)				*Low variance process* ($\sigma_r = 0.01$ *per year*)			
Maturity	*1*	*2*	*3*	*4*	*1*	*2*	*3*	*4*
Coupon rate $c = 0.06$								
5	0.802	0.803	0.837	0.748	0.801	0.801	0.836	0.746
10	0.690	0.706	0.728	0.642	0.681	0.683	0.721	0.628
15	0.624	0.664	0.655	0.592	0.607	0.613	0.641	0.568
20	0.584	0.644	0.605	0.566	0.561	0.578	0.586	0.535
25	0.558	0.633	0.570	0.551	0.531	0.560	0.548	0.516
30	0.540	0.627	0.545	0.542	0.512	0.553	0.523	0.505
Coupon rate $c = 0.10$								
5	0.904	0.912	0.923	0.878	0.901	0.901	0.918	0.874
10	0.861	0.903	0.889	0.840	0.844	0.855	0.864	0.821
15	0.841	0.923	0.874	0.833	0.812	0.842	0.831	0.800
20	0.832	0.947	0.865	0.836	0.796	0.846	0.812	0.792
25	0.828	0.969	0.859	0.841	0.787	0.857	0.801	0.791
30	0.825	0.986	0.853	0.847	0.783	0.869	0.796	0.792
Coupon rate $c = 0.14$								
5	1.020	1.037	1.039	1.010	1.009	1.017	1.018	1.004
10	1.054	1.118	1.103	1.043	1.023	1.054	1.048	1.019
15	1.082	1.199	1.153	1.080	1.035	1.096	1.075	1.037
20	1.104	1.267	1.188	1.113	1.047	1.137	1.097	1.055
25	1.120	1.320	1.209	1.139	1.057	1.172	1.114	1.071
30	1.132	1.359	1.221	1.159	1.067	1.201	1.127	1.085
Coupon rate $c = 0.18$								
5	1.161	1.176	1.184	1.147	1.150	1.157	1.163	1.142
10	1.276	1.344	1.342	1.255	1.244	1.275	1.282	1.231
15	1.350	1.484	1.453	1.339	1.301	1.367	1.365	1.292
20	1.401	1.593	1.527	1.402	1.337	1.440	1.422	1.337
25	1.436	1.676	1.574	1.450	1.363	1.496	1.460	1.370
30	1.460	1.746	1.601	1.485	1.382	1.536	1.484	1.396

1, Offset rule binding, deduction limit not binding, $\tau_s = \tau_L = 0.25$; 2, neither rule binding, $\tau_s = 0.5$, $\tau_L = 0.25$; 3, deduction limit binding, offset rule irrelevant, $\tau_s = \tau_L = 0$; 4, bank or dealer at the margin, $\tau_s = \tau_L = 0.5$.

[a]Computed at the midpoint of the interest rate range, $r = 0.14$. For each process σ_r is the annual standard deviation of changes in the short-term rate of interest.

[b]Tax scenarios are described by their capital gains tax rates τ_s (short term) and τ_L (long term). If the investor is an individual, these depend on whether the short-term loss/long-term gain offset rule and the $3,000 deduction limit are binding. These rules are not applicable for banks and dealers. In each case the ordinary tax rate is $\tau_c = 0.5$.

the short-term interest rate is 14 percent. For comparison, the 14 percent coupon bond would be priced just above par if the marginal investor followed a buy and hold policy. The exact buy and hold prices range from 1.002 to 1.071 for the high variance process and from 1.001 to 1.030 for the low variance process.[21]

The prices which prevail under tax scenario 2 are uniformly higher than those under scenario 1 since investors are not subject to the restrictive offset provision of the tax code but can exploit in full their short-term losses. Furthermore, except for the bonds of 5 year maturity, tax scenario 2 typically results in the highest price. We would expect the second scenario to yield high prices because short-term losses provide valuable rebates and a short-term holding period is relatively cheap to establish. This advantage is least valuable for short maturity bonds because they are the least volatile. Consequently all the 5 year bonds and a few of the other short maturity bonds are priced highest under tax scenario 3. There are two distinct reasons for this.

First, for discount bonds the buy and hold price is highest under tax scenario 3 since the guaranteed capital gain escapes all taxation. Second, with a zero capital gains tax rate, it is costless to establish an above-par amortizable basis. For sufficiently short maturities these two effects dominate.

A comparison of the pricing under scenarios 1, 3, and 4 is also of interest. While their interpretation is radically different, they actually differ in only one respect. The capital gain tax rates, both long and short term, are 0.25, 0, and 0.5 respectively. All other taxes are the same. Scenario 3 with the lowest tax rate has prices which are uniformly highest; nevertheless, the high tax rate in scenario 4 does not always induce the lowest price. Again there is a tradeoff between the value of capital losses and the cost of capital gains. The former is more important for the volatile longer maturity bonds. The latter is more important for the shorter maturity bonds, particularly those selling below par.

Litzenberger and Rolfo (1984b) note that, under the buy and hold policy, the price of a discount bond is linearly increasing in the coupon rate: in comparing three discount bonds with the same maturity, prices P_1, P_2, P_3, and coupon rates c_1, c_2, c_3, where $c_1 < c_2 < c_3$, the after-tax cash flows of the bond P_2 are replicated by a portfolio of bonds P_1 and P_3 with weights α and $1-\alpha$, where $c_2 = \alpha c_1 + (1-\alpha)c_3$. A similar argument also applied to premium bonds, but the rate at which the bond price increases in the coupon rate is higher for premium than for discount bonds, reflecting the tax-advantageous amortization of the premium. Considering discount and premium bonds together, under the buy and hold policy the bond price is piecewise linear, increasing, and convex in the coupon rate.

Examination of table 3.4 reveals that the price–coupon relation is also convex for the bond prices under the various optimal policies. However, now the relation is strictly convex throughout for both premium and discount bonds.[22] The different buy and hold linear relations contribute to this, but the strict convexity is due to the tax timing effect. The basic intuition for this convexity comes from Merton's (1973) study of stock purchase options. The right to realize capital gains and losses optimally and the right to amortize (even under a buy and hold policy) convey a valuable option to the bondholder. If we compare a single bond with a portfolio of bonds with the same total coupons and face value, the latter must be at least as valuable since its "options" can be exercised singly. The convexity is empirically tested by Litzenberger and Rolfo (1984b).

With different tax clienteles each following a buy and hold policy, the linear price–coupon relation may become convex or concave. Thus the tax timing effect discussed in this paper and the buy and hold clientele effect may reinforce or cancel one another and it is difficult to distinguish them empirically. Previous evidence in support of clientele effects could be due, at least in part, to tax trading within a single tax bracket.

It is frequently asserted that discount bond prices are higher than is justified by the term structure of interest rates, reflecting the fact that a portion of the return is realized as a lightly taxed capital gain. Our discussion of table 3.4 demonstrates that this is just one of several tax effects on bond prices. The direction and magnitude of the tax effect depends critically on the tax scenario applicable to the marginal investor and on whether the marginal investor follows a passive or optimal trading policy.

We now turn our attention to the tax timing option, defined as the difference between the bond prices under the optimal and buy and hold policies.[23,24] Table 3.5 reports the value of the timing option as a percentage of the bond price under the optimal policy. In each case the buy and hold price is calculated using the corresponding long-term capital gains tax rate (0.25, 0.25, 0, 0.5). If this price is above par, the amortization is deducted every year. Thus no capital losses (or gains) are earned under the buy and hold policy for premium bonds, and the benchmark price is the same for all scenarios. For discount bonds the buy and hold prices vary across the scenarios and are inversely related to the long-term capital gains tax rate. The timing option varies widely for different coupon rates, maturities, and tax scenarios, but in most cases it represents a substantial fraction of the bond price, just as the example in section 4 illustrates.

The one exception is deep discount bonds under tax scenario 3. Here the timing option is worth little since there is only a small probability of ever amortizing a premium and no other tax trading benefit is possible. For bonds selling near or above par, however, the timing option is more

Table 3.5 Value of the timing option on Treasury bonds measured as the percentage difference between the prices under the optimal and buy and hold policies; tax scenarios 1–4[a,b]

	High variance process ($\sigma_r = 0.02$ *per year*)				*Low variance process* ($\sigma_r = 0.01$ *per year*)			
Maturity	*1*	*2*	*3*	*4*	*1*	*2*	*3*	*4*
Coupon rate $c = 0.06$								
5	0.0	0.1	0.0	0.1	0.0	0.0	0.0	0.0
10	0.5	2.8	0.2	1.6	0.1	0.3	0.0	0.4
15	1.3	7.2	0.4	3.4	0.4	1.4	0.0	1.3
20	2.0	11.1	0.5	5.1	0.9	3.7	0.1	2.4
25	2.6	14.2	0.4	6.3	1.3	6.5	0.2	3.4
30	3.0	16.4	0.4	7.1	1.8	8.9	0.3	4.2
Coupon rate $c = 0.10$								
5	0.2	1.1	0.4	0.4	0.0	0.1	0.0	0.1
10	1.5	6.1	2.5	2.2	0.3	1.6	0.2	0.9
15	2.6	11.2	4.3	4.2	0.8	4.4	0.9	2.0
20	3.4	15.1	5.5	5.8	1.4	7.4	1.6	3.1
25	3.9	17.9	6.9	6.9	2.0	10.0	2.4	4.0
30	4.1	19.7	6.2	7.7	2.4	12.1	3.0	4.7
Coupon rate $c = 0.14$								
5	1.7	3.3	3.5	0.8	0.8	1.6	1.7	0.4
10	3.9	9.4	8.1	2.8	1.9	4.8	4.2	1.5
15	5.0	14.2	10.8	4.7	2.6	8.0	6.1	2.7
20	5.4	17.6	12.0	6.1	3.0	10.7	7.4	3.7
25	5.5	19.8	12.4	7.0	3.3	12.7	8.2	4.5
30	5.4	21.2	12.2	7.6	3.4	14.3	8.6	5.0
Coupon rate $c = 0.18$								
5	1.7	2.9	3.6	0.5	0.9	1.5	2.0	0.2
10	3.5	8.4	8.3	2.0	1.9	4.3	4.8	0.8
15	4.2	12.8	11.0	3.4	2.3	7.0	6.9	1.6
20	4.4	15.9	12.3	4.5	2.3	9.3	8.2	2.3
25	4.4	18.1	12.8	5.3	2.4	11.1	8.9	2.9
30	4.3	20.0	12.7	5.9	2.5	12.2	9.2	3.4

1, Offset rule binding, deduction limit not binding, $\tau_s = \tau_L = 0.25$; 2, neither rule binding, $\tau_s = 0.5$, $\tau_L = 0.25$; 3, deduction limit binding, offset rule irrelevant, $\tau_s = \tau_L = 0$; 4, bank or dealer at the margin, $\tau_s = \tau_L = 0.5$.

[a]Computed at the midpoint of the interest rate range, $r = 0.14$. For each process σ_r is the annual standard deviation of changes in the short-term rate of interest.

[b]Tax scenarios are described by their capital gains tax rates τ_s (short term) and τ_L (long term). If the investor is an individual, these depend on whether the short-term loss/long-term gain offset rule and the $3,000 deduction limit are binding. These rules are not applicable for banks and dealers. In each case the ordinary tax rate is $\tau_c = 0.5$.

important under tax scenario 3 than under scenarios 1 or 4. The binding deduction limit under scenario 3 is a mixed blessing. On the one hand the individual may not obtain tax rebates from the government by realizing capital losses. On the other hand he can costlessly realize capital gains in order to raise the basis and take advantage of the amortization deduction.

For tax scenario 3 the timing option's relative value is increasing in the coupon rate. The only tax trading benefit comes from the establishment of an amortizable basis. For deep discount bonds the probability of ever doing so is low and the timing option has little value. For bonds with higher coupon rates, and therefore higher prices, the timing option is increasingly valuable. For premium bonds, however, the rate of increase of the timing option slackens since the expected capital gains component of the bond's return is negative and there is a decreasing chance of future price rises to create the opportunity for further amortization deductions.

For the other three tax scenarios the option–coupon relation has an inverted U shape. Low coupon, deep discount bonds have large expected capital gains and therefore little chance of future deductible losses. Near-par bonds can benefit from either a deductible decrease in price or an increase in price which is later amortizable. As under scenario 3 premium bonds have reduced changes for future increases in amortization. While they do have the largest expected decreases in price, these are deductible only to the extent that they exceed the amortization and only if future amortization is forgone.

The reported values show that the tax timing option is typically increasing in maturity. This is due to both the increased value of standard options when their maturities are lengthened and the greater volatility of the longer maturity bonds underlying these options. This feature explains why the 25 and 30 year 10 percent coupon bonds are more expensive than those with 10–20 year maturities even though the interest rate is above the coupon rate at 14 percent and the yield curve is essentially flat.

Although longer maturity bonds generally have more valuable timing options, it does not follow that a larger tax subsidy flow is available on long bonds. For example, holding two 15 year bonds in succession may provide greater total tax benefit than that provided by a single 30 year bond. One way to compare the benefits of different maturity bonds is to express the timing option on an annualized basis. The maturity of bonds with the largest annualized benefits would then represent the natural "habitat" of investors particularly concerned with tax benefits. The annualized tax subsidy on a T year bond is approximately $r(1-\tau_c)/\{1-\exp[-r(1-\tau_c)T]\}$ per dollar value of the timing option. Using this approximation we establish that the lowest annual subsidy is on short maturity bonds. On bonds with 10 or more years to maturity the benefits are fairly constant, regardless of the tax scenario.

Annualizing the timing option also permits us to normalize the tax benefits relative to the rate of return earned on the bond. For example, under the four scenarios tax benefits provide on average 7 percent, 32 percent, 18 percent and 10 percent respectively of the total return expected on the 25 year 14 percent coupon bond.

The tax timing effect on bond prices also provides a possible explanation of why discounts are so prevalent in the seasoned bond market. Since Treasury bonds are issued at par and are not callable (except occasionally during their last 5 years before maturity), we should expect, in the absence of tax timing effects, an equal probability of observing seasoned bonds at a premium or discount under a random walk assumption and in the absence of any risk or term premiums. If long-term bonds are riskier and command higher expected returns, then bonds issued at par should later sell at premium prices, at least on average, when these high term premiums are no longer justified by their reduced risk. Only if interest rates rise dramatically should discounts be observed.

The value added to a long-term bond by its tax timing option lets it be issued at par with a coupon rate below what would otherwise be required. For example (see table 3.4) under scenario 2 and with no term premiums, a 30 year bond could be issued at par with a coupon rate just above 10 percent, even though the interest rate was 14 percent and rates were not expected to change. The other prices in this section of table 3.4 show the expected path of this bond's price over its life. With no change in the interest rate, the expected outcome is that the bond would fall in price by about 10 points over a period of 20 years before recovering in value.

We have so far ignored transactions costs. A bid–ask spread or other costs of trading will reduce the value of the timing option since the optimal policies involve substantially more trading than the buy and hold policy. Constantinides has examined the optimal tax trading policy on stocks in the presence of proportional transactions costs.[25] In a simple continuous-time lognormal model he found that investors should not realize losses immediately but should wait until the price falls to a specific fraction of the basis. A similar rule applies to our model in section 4. The modifications to the optimal trading policies of the models here are more complicated, but the basic idea remains the same: trades are deferred until capital gains and losses are larger than in the absence of transactions costs.

Table 3.6 displays the value of the timing option when trading is costly. The round-trip transaction cost is represented by a bid–ask spread of 0.2, 0.5, or 1.0 percent of par.[26] The timing option retains a large fraction of its value even with sizeable transactions costs. Bonds of 10 or more years to maturity retain at least half of the original timing option even with 1 percent transactions costs. The reduction may not be as large as we might have expected because transactions costs are not entirely a deadweight loss.

Table 3.6 Effects of transactions costs on the timing option: tax scenarios 1–4[a,b]

	Value of timing option (%) for k =				*Value of timing option (%) for k =*			
Maturity	*0.0*	*0.2*	*0.5*	*1.0*	*0.0*	*0.2*	*0.5*	*1.0*
	Tax scenario 1				*Tax scenario 2*			
5	1.7	1.4	1.0	0.5	3.3	2.8	2.0	1.2
10	3.9	3.3	2.7	2.0	9.4	8.4	7.0	5.0
15	5.0	4.4	3.8	3.0	14.2	13.1	11.4	8.7
20	5.4	4.8	4.2	3.5	17.6	16.3	14.4	11.4
25	5.5	4.9	4.3	3.7	19.8	18.4	16.5	13.2
30	5.4	4.8	4.2	3.6	21.2	19.9	17.8	14.4
	Tax scenario 3				*Tax scenario 4*			
5	3.5	3.2	2.7	1.9	0.8	0.6	0.4	0.2
10	8.1	7.6	6.9	5.9	2.8	2.6	2.3	1.9
15	10.8	10.1	9.3	8.2	4.7	4.5	4.2	3.7
20	12.0	11.3	10.4	9.2	6.1	5.8	5.5	5.0
25	12.4	11.6	10.7	9.4	7.0	6.7	6.4	5.9
30	12.2	11.4	10.5	9.2	7.6	7.4	7.0	6.6

1, Offset rule binding, $\tau_s = \tau_L = 0.25$; 2, neither rule binding, $\tau_s = 0.5$, $\tau_L = 0.25$; 3, deduction limit binding, offset rule irrelevant, $\tau_s = \tau_L = 0$; 4, bank or dealer at the margin, $\tau_s = \tau_L = 0.5$.

[a]Computed at the midpoint of the interest rate range, $r = 0.14$. Interest rate follows the high variance process with a standard deviation of 0.02 per year. The coupon rate on the bond is $c = 0.14$. k measures the transactions costs (bid–ask spread) as a percentage of par.

[b]Tax scenarios are described by their capital gains tax rates τ_s (short term) and τ_L (long term). If the investor is an individual, these depend on whether the short-term loss/long-term gain offset rule and the \$3,000 deduction limit are binding. These rules are not applicable for banks and dealers. In each case the ordinary tax rate is $\tau_c = 0.5$.

The cost of purchase is added to the basis while the cost of sale is deducted from the sales proceeds. Effectively, the taxing authority subsidizes the costs of trading.

Transactions costs decrease the value of the timing option on short maturity bonds more than they do on long maturity bonds. With a 1 point bid–ask spread, the 5 year bond loses 71, 64, 46, or 75 percent of its timing option under the four tax scenarios, while bonds with at least 15 years to maturity never give up more than 40 percent. At 30 year maturities the bonds examined always retain at least two-thirds of the value of their timing option.

7 The Tax-Adjusted Yield Curve and Implied Tax Rates

We have demonstrated that bond prices set by the marginal investor following the optimal trading policy are markedly different from those set under a buy and hold or continuous realization policy. In this section we explore the implications of these differences when interest rate and tax bracket estimates are inferred from market prices.

Previous authors typically have assumed that a particular marginal investor holds the bond to maturity. Under this assumption the price at time zero of a bond with maturity date T, coupon rate c, and par value 1 is the solution to

$$P = (1 - \tau_c)c \sum_{t=1}^{T} \pi_t + (1 - \tau_L + \tau_L P)\pi_T, \qquad P \leqslant 1 \tag{35a}$$

or

$$P = \left[(1 - \tau_c)c + \frac{\tau_c(P-1)}{T}\right] \sum_{t=1}^{T} \pi_t + \pi_T, \qquad P > 1, \tag{35b}$$

where π_t is the price at time zero of \$1 after tax at time t. Given a set of bond prices, the resulting set of equations (35) can be inverted to solve for the discount factors and the tax rates.[27]

Robichek and Niebuhr (1970) do this by imposing the additional assumption $\tau_L = 0.5\tau_c$ and a flat term structure $\pi_t = (1+y)^{-t}$. They then solve for the remaining unknowns τ_c and y using just two bonds. Their estimates of the marginal tax bracket for the year 1968 range from 37.5 to 50 percent depending on the pair of bonds used (and disregarding the cheapest flower bond).

McCulloch (1975) also assumes $\tau_L = 0.5\tau_c$. He does not require a flat term structure but estimates the tax bracket and a cubic spline for the discount function to minimize a weighted sum of the squared deviations between actual and modeled prices. Using data from 1963 to 1966 he concludes that "the effective tax rate that best explains the prices of U.S. Treasury securities lies somewhere in the range 0.22 to 0.33." For later data from 1973 the best estimate of the tax rate is only 0.19.

Litzenberger and Rolfo (1984a) estimate tax brackets under a variety of assumptions about the capital gains tax rate. When they set $\tau_L = 0.5\tau_c$ ($\tau_L = 0.4\tau_c$ after October 1978), they confirm McCulloch's estimates. For the period 1973–80 their yearly US tax bracket estimates range from 12 percent in 1979 to 45 percent in 1976. The average is 28 percent.

Pye (1969) estimates the tax bracket of the marginal bondholder using various combinations of discount and par, taxable and exempt bonds. The analysis closest to ours compares par and moderately discounted taxable bonds. Pye concludes that the effective tax rate at the margin varies between 10 and 36 percent over the period 1967–8.

Our analysis provides a possible explanation of these findings which is nevertheless consistent with the true marginal tax bracket's being substantially higher as suggested by Miller (1977). If bond prices are set by investors who follow an optimal trading policy, estimates of the yield curve and the marginal tax bracket obtained under the assumption of a naive buy and hold policy may be biased. To test for bias, we generate a sample of simulated bond prices under the assumption of optimal trading policies with known tax rates and yield curves. We then estimate the yield curve and tax rate from this sample by a procedure which is in the spirit of the methods discussed.

Since our "data" are simulated and therefore not subject to measurement error, there is no statistical advantage in using many prices. Thus, like Robichek and Niebuhr, we use an exact "estimation" requiring only a few bonds. We eliminate the need to assume a flat term structure, however, by using four rather than two bonds. In fact with four bonds no smoothness requirement for the yield curve, even of the weak type assumed by McCulloch, is required.

For each estimation we use two different coupon bonds from each of two adjacent maturities. Under an assumed buy and hold policy, the two longer bonds with maturity $T+1$ are priced according to

$$P' = (1-\tau_c)c \sum_{t=1}^{T} \pi_t + [1-\tau_L+\tau_L P' + (1-\tau_c)c]\,\pi_{T+1}, \qquad P' \leqslant 1 \quad \text{(36a)}$$

or

$$P' = \left[(1-\tau_c)c + \frac{\tau_c(P'-1)}{T+1}\right] \sum_{t=1}^{T} \pi_t$$

$$+ \left[(1-\tau_c)c + \frac{\tau_c(P'-1)}{T+1} + 1\right] \pi_{T+1}, \qquad P' > 1, \quad \text{(36b)}$$

while the shorter maturity bonds are priced by (35).

Substituting the four bond prices into (35) and (36) gives four equations in the five unknowns $\Sigma\pi_t$, π_T, π_{T+1}, τ_c, and τ_L. If we assume $\tau_L = \tau_c/2$, the system of equations is now fully specified. We eliminate π_T, π_{T+1}, τ_c, and τ_L to obtain a quadratic equation in the variable $\Sigma\pi_t$. Solving for this unknown and then the others yields two solution sets. Only one of these satisfies the constraints $0 \leqslant \pi_{T+1} \leqslant \pi_T \leqslant 1$ and $\tau_c \leqslant 100$ percent, and this is the one chosen.[28]

Tables 3.7 and 3.8 report the errors in the estimated forward rates and the estimated tax brackets on coupon income (correct tax bracket $\tau_c = 50$ percent in each case) for different maturities, tax scenarios, coupon rates, and interest rate variances.[29] The errors are usually opposite in sign since an increase in the tax rate decreases the effective discount rate and errors of opposite signs have partially offsetting effects. In most cases the interest rate is overestimated while the tax bracket is underestimated. In the extreme, the tax rate is estimated to be negative.

Table 3.7 Errors (basis points) in estimated forward rates under the buy and hold assumption with $\tau_L = 0.5\tau_c$: tax scenarios 1–4[a,b]

		High variance process ($\sigma_r = 0.02$ per year)					*Low variance process ($\sigma_r = 0.01$ per year)*			
Forecast period	*Std dev.*[c]	*1*	*2*	*3*	*4*	*Std dev.*[c]	*1*	*2*	*3*	*4*
Coupon rates $c = 0.08, 0.10$										
5	400	39	203	−136	466	200	5	27	−201	470
10	549	85	266	22	357	300	17	201	−134	350
15	595	98	255	126	287	403	33	243	−64	284
20	620	105	283	243	238	426	42	271	10	246
25	625	98	296	391	198	468	50	292	87	212
30	631	82	338	657	179	497	57	318	175	192
Coupon rates $c = 0.04, 0.06$										
5	400	5	30	−200	467	200	0	0	−201	420
10	549	7	129	−146	328	300	13	45	−167	338
15	595	6	112	−125	260	403	6	65	−138	262
20	620	4	97	−105	211	426	7	141	−114	222
25	625	0	67	−97	151	468	7	149	−94	188
30	631	−23	47	−83	94	497	0	127	−79	138

1, Offset rule binding, deduction limit not binding, $\tau_s = \tau_L = 0.25$; 2, neither rule binding, $\tau_s = 0.5$, $\tau_L = 0.25$; 3, deduction limit binding, offset rule irrelevant, $\tau_s = \tau_L = 0$; 4, bank or dealer at the margin, $\tau_s = \tau_L = 0.5$.

[a]Computed at the midpoint of the interest rate range, $r = 0.14$. Errors reported in basis points. For each process σ_r is the annual standard deviation of changes in the short-term rate of interest.

[b]Tax scenarios are described by their capital gains tax rates τ_s (short term) and τ_L (long term). If the investor is an individual, these depend on whether the short-term loss/long-term gain offset rule and the $3,000 deduction limit are binding. These rules are not applicable for banks and dealers. In each case the ordinary tax rate is $\tau_c = 0.5$.

[c]Standard deviation of single-period interest rate being forecast.

The errors are usually smaller for the low variance process, as we would expect, since the timing option then has less value and buy and hold prices are more accurate. For the same reason, errors are smaller when the deep discount bonds are used in the estimation.

The estimates are generally most accurate under tax scenario 1. Again this corresponds to the case when the timing option has the least value. Tax scenario 2 yields very poor results as does scenario 3 when near-par bonds are used. Tax scenario 4 is interesting because the implied tax bracket is about the same for all maturities. It ranges between 20 and 30 percent, disturbingly reminiscent of the tax rate estimated by McCulloch. (By construction, the actual tax rates in this case are all 50 percent.)

While the errors in the forward rates are often large, the computed numbers are almost invariably within one standard deviation of both the true forward rate and the single-period rate expected to prevail at the

Table 3.8 Estimated tax brackets (percent) under the buy and hold assumption with $\tau_L = 0.5\tau_c$: tax scenarios 1–4[a,b]

	High variance process ($\sigma_r = 0.02$ per year)				*Low variance process ($\sigma_r = 0.01$ per year)*			
Maturity	*1*	*2*	*3*	*4*	*1*	*2*	*3*	*4*
Coupon rates $c = 0.08, 0.10$								
5	44	17	52	20	49	45	63	18
10	36	17	28	23	47	11	53	27
15	35	0	14	25	44	7	42	31
20	35	−17	−6	26	42	−2	30	31
25	38	−26	−36	29	40	−15	16	31
30	44	−48	−108	27	38	−33	−4	30
Coupon rates $c = 0.04, 0.06$								
5	49	44	63	18	50	50	63	26
10	48	20	55	27	47	39	59	28
15	47	20	56	29	48	30	56	32
20	47	18	54	30	47	8	54	32
25	48	24	56	39	47	5	52	33
30	55	27	55	50	49	11	51	43

1, Offset rule binding, deduction limit not binding, $\tau_s = \tau_L = 0.25$; 2, neither rule binding, $\tau_s = 0.5$, $\tau_L = 0.25$; 3, deduction limit binding, offset rule irrelevant, $\tau_s = \tau_L = 0$; 4, bank or dealer at the margin, $\tau_s = \tau_L = 0.5$.

[a]Computed at the midpoint of the interest rate range, $r = 0.14$. For each process σ_r is the annual standard deviation of changes in the short-term rate of interest.

[b]Tax scenarios are described by their capital gains tax rates τ_s (short term) and τ_L (long term). If the investor is an individual, these depend on whether the short-term loss/long-term gain offset rule and the $3,000 deduction limit are binding. These rules are not applicable for banks and dealers. In each case the ordinary tax rate is $\tau_c = 0.5$.

forecast time. Consequently, verifying the induced tax trading bias in the forward rates would require a large data sample. Furthermore, even with large amounts of data available, the errors probably could not be distinguished from liquidity or other term premiums. It is interesting to note that the positive errors are at least qualitatively consistent with the usually claimed upward bias in the yield curve.

We also tried estimation under the buy and hold assumption with $\tau_L = 0$ and $\tau_L = \tau_c$. These rates are correct for tax scenarios 3 and 4 respectively, but the estimates are not noticeably improved, probably because the buy and hold policy is "too far" from optimal.

8 Municipal Bonds

The tax treatment of municipal bonds differs from the tax treatment of Treasury and corporate bonds in two important respects. First, coupon income on municipal bonds is exempt from federal tax. Second, if the purchase price in the secondary market is above par the difference must be amortized, but the amortized amount is not allowed as a deduction even though the bond's tax basis is correspondingly reduced. In effect the taxation of bond coupons and of premium amortization are symmetric: for Treasury bonds, the coupons and premium amortization are taxed at the individual's marginal tax rate on ordinary income; for municipal bonds the coupons and premium amortization remain untaxed.

Coupon income on municipal bonds may be subject to state tax, but in our calculations we ignore state taxes. We consider this a good first approximation for two reasons. Many states exempt from state tax the coupons on bonds issued by municipalities within the state and so the marginal holders of such bonds may well be exempt from taxes. Also, while state tax rates vary widely across states, they are generally very low relative to the federal tax rates of investors who would consider holding municipal bonds.[30]

The main difference between the optimal trading policies for municipal and taxable bonds is that no trades are ever made at a price above par since there is no advantage in establishing an amortizable basis. Since this is the only trading advantage of taxable bonds under tax scenario 3, the value of the timing option on municipal bonds is zero in this scenario. At the opposite extreme is tax scenario 4. In this case it is never optimal to establish an above-par basis on a taxable bond, and so the right to amortize such a basis contributes nothing to the value of the timing option. Thus, under scenario 4, the value of the timing option on a municipal bond is equal to that on a taxable bond with the same after-tax coupons. Under tax scenarios 1 and 2 the timing option on municipal bonds is less valuable than the option on coupon-equivalent taxable bonds.

Table 3.9 presents the value of the timing option on municipal bonds. When municipal bonds are deep discount, the timing option under scenarios 1 and 2 is nearly as valuable as on coupon-equivalent taxable bonds. The same is true on short maturity municipal bonds even if the discount is small. Of course, these are the cases when the right to amortize the basis in the future has negligible value. On premium municipal bonds the timing option is substantially smaller than on coupon-equivalent taxable bonds, especially if the comparison is made with short maturity bonds. For example, under tax scenario 2 the timing option on short maturity municipal bonds is one-third as large as the timing option on short-term taxable bonds; the timing option on long-term municipal bonds is half as large as the timing option on long-term taxable bonds.

Table 3.9 Value of the timing option on municipal bonds measured as the percentage difference between the prices under the optimal and buy and hold policies: tax scenarios 1, 2, and 4[a,b]

	High variance process ($\sigma_r = 0.02$ *per year*)			*Low variance process* ($\sigma_r = 0.01$ *per year*)		
Maturity	*1*	*2*	*4*	*1*	*2*	*4*
Coupon rate $c = 0.03$						
5	0.0	0.1	0.1	0.0	0.0	0.0
10	0.5	2.6	1.6	0.1	0.3	0.4
15	1.2	6.6	3.4	0.4	1.0	1.3
20	1.9	10.5	5.1	0.7	1.9	2.4
25	2.5	13.6	6.3	1.0	3.0	3.4
30	3.0	15.9	7.1	1.2	4.1	4.2
Coupon rate $c = 0.05$						
5	0.1	0.8	0.4	0.0	0.1	0.1
10	0.7	3.8	2.2	0.2	1.2	0.9
15	1.5	7.2	4.2	0.6	2.9	2.0
20	2.2	10.0	5.8	1.0	4.5	3.1
25	2.8	12.2	6.1	1.3	5.8	4.0
30	3.2	13.8	7.7	1.5	6.8	4.7
Coupon rate $c = 0.07$						
5	0.2	1.0	0.8	0.1	0.5	0.4
10	0.9	3.3	2.8	0.5	1.7	1.5
15	1.8	5.7	4.7	0.9	2.9	2.7
20	2.4	7.9	6.1	1.2	3.9	3.7
25	3.0	9.6	7.0	1.5	4.8	4.5
30	3.4	11.1	7.6	1.7	5.4	5.0
Coupon rate $c = 0.09$						
5	0.6	1.2	0.5	0.3	0.6	0.2
10	1.4	3.1	2.0	0.7	1.5	0.8
15	2.1	4.9	3.4	1.0	2.2	1.6
20	2.6	6.6	4.5	1.3	2.7	2.3
25	2.9	8.1	5.3	1.4	3.2	2.9
30	3.2	9.4	5.9	1.5	3.7	3.4

1, Offset rule binding, deduction limit not binding, $\tau_s = \tau_L = 0.25$; 2, neither rule binding, $\tau_s = 0.5$, $\tau_L = 0.25$; 4, bank or dealer at the margin, $\tau_s = \tau_L = 0.5$. The timing option is always zero under tax scenario 3.

[a]Computed at the midpoint of the interest rate range, $r = 0.14$. For each process σ_r is the annual standard deviation of changes in the short-term rate of interest.

[b]Tax scenarios are described by their capital gains tax rates. If the investor is an individual, these depend on whether the short-term loss/long-term gain offset rule and the $3,000 deduction limit are binding. These rules are not applicable for banks and dealers. In each case the ordinary tax rate is $\tau_c = 0.5$.

9 Concluding Remarks

In this paper we extended the work of Cox, Ingersoll, and Ross (1981, 1985) on valuing bonds and combined it with the work of Constantinides (1983, 1984) and Constantinides and Scholes (1980) on optimal trading policies. We determined that the tax timing option is an important fraction of the bond price.

We also discussed how the price distortion affects standard estimation techniques for extracting interest rates and marginal tax brackets from observed bond prices. We found the implied errors to be substantial.

We only examined the case when the tax bracket of the marginal bondholder remains unchanged. That is, an investor may buy and sell the bond in the course of the optimal trading policy, but the bond remains in the hands of investors in the same tax bracket throughout its term to maturity. The next step should be to recognize the existence of tax clienteles as in Schaefer (1981) but, unlike Schaefer, to explore the implications of the bondholders' following optimal trading policies and of the bond being passed from one tax bracket investor to another as its maturity shortens or as it changes from a discount to a premium bond.

Notes

1 Miller (1977) shows that, under simple tax rules, the marginal bondholder is in the corporate tax bracket, providing partial justification for our choice of the tax rate. In any case, our qualitative results are insensitive to the assumed rate.

2 Amortization is optional for Treasury and corporate bonds. Since for practically all individuals the marginal tax rate on ordinary income is no less than the capital gains tax rate, amortization of the basis dominates forgoing this option. The amortization method need not be a straight line, but may be that customarily used by the individual if it is deemed to be reasonable. If the bond is callable, the basis is amortized to the call price at the call date or to par at maturity, whichever yields the smaller amortization. If there are alternative call dates the rule is complex.

3 Similarly the right to deduct half the long-term losses from income, even under the current 40 percent rule for long-term capital gains, could not be used. Losses could only be deducted from other capital gains. Thus the effective tax rate on both long-term gains and long-term losses is the same.

4 The individual can mitigate this offset provision of the tax law by realizing long-term gains and short- and long-term losses in alternate tax years; however, we do not explicitly model this (see Constantinides, 1984). This procedure may also help to avoid the unfavorable long-term gain and loss offset.

5 Even in this case, however, when taxes do not affect bond prices, taxed investors will still benefit from following trading policies different from the buy and hold. The value of trading optimally will of course depend upon what taxes they must pay. Thus the timing option will have the same qualitative properties as it does in one of the scenarios examined.

6 Transactions costs on bonds are small and are of the order of magnitude of the bid–ask spread. In section 6 (table 3.6) we introduce transactions costs and show that the pricing implications and the value of the timing option remain largely unaffected.

7 Tax clienteles for bonds is an important issue extensively discussed by Schaefer (1981, 1982a, b) under the assumption that bonds are held to maturity. As we demonstrate below, under tax laws similar to those in the United States a buy and hold policy is inferior to trading schemes which involve (among other things) early realization of capital losses. Under UK regulations, which imposed no long-term capital gains tax on "gilt" securities prior to 1962 or after 1969, such trading schemes have no direct benefits, and so a buy and hold policy is not necessarily inferior. Neither need it be correct, however. Even in Schaefer's world, future changes in interest rates or the introduction of new bonds may cause an existing bond to become dominated for its current clientele. The anticipation of such events should be reflected in the bond's current price, and this may mask some clientele effects.

8 Alternatively, we could assume that bonds are fixed in supply and some investors are occasionally forced to trade for reasons unrelated to optimal tax trading. "Liquidity purchasers" will never pay above their reservation price because the discount bond is available. "Liquidity sellers," however, may not be able to hold out for their reservation price.

9 Merton (1973) demonstrates that this condition is the result of optimizing behavior in the context of option pricing. It is formally derived by Grigelionis and Shiryaev (1966).

10 See Cox, Ingersoll, and Ross (1981) for a discussion of the different forms of the expectations hypothesis. In another paper (Cox, Ingersoll, and Ross, 1985) they show how this assumption can be weakened by incorporating a risk premium into the drift terms for the state variables. As discussed there, the absence of arbitrage opportunities is insufficient to close the model as it is in option pricing. The difference here is that the state variables need not be prices.

11 The now familiar American put pricing problem provides a useful analogy. Let $G(S, K, T)$ denote the value of a put with striking price K and time to maturity T on a stock with price S. Equation (2) is analogous to the condition at exercise: $G(S^\star, K, T) = K - S^\star$. The smooth-pasting condition analogous to (3) is $G_S(S^\star, K, T) = -1$. Together these relations are sufficient to derive both the pricing function G and the optimal exercise policy $S^\star(T)$. Similarly, we derive here both the value function and the optimal realization policy $Y^\star$ conditional on the bond price function. Equation (4) then provides the closure finally giving all three.

12 Alternatively we can consider (10) as the risk-adjusted interest rate dynamics with $\alpha = \mu + \pi$, where μ measures the expected change in the short rate and π captures the risk premium due on interest-rate-sensitive securities. Cox, Ingersoll, and Ross (1980) discuss this interpretation of the stochastic process in (10).

13 This statement is formally proved by Constantinides (1983). If the tax rates τ_S and τ_L are unequal the optimal policy is a great deal more complex. For these circumstances, the optimal policy for trading stocks is discussed by Constantinides (1984) and the optimal policy for trading bonds is discussed in section 5 of this paper.

14 For a meaningful solution the parameters of the interest rate process must satisfy $s^2 - \alpha < 1 - \tau_c$. From (22) and (23) the expected rate of price appreciation and the limit (as r goes to zero) of the expected rate of appreciation of the value function are both $(s^2 - \alpha)r$. Thus, if the stated condition is violated, the expected rates of return including coupons must exceed the after-tax rate of interest $(1 - \tau_c)r$ and the expectations hypothesis cannot obtain as was assumed. Furthermore, given that the dynamics can be interpreted in a risk-adjusted sense, as discussed in note 12, no other equilibrium is possible either.

15 The buy and hold price is unaffected by the capital gains tax rate of the marginal investor for the simple reason that no capital gains tax is ever paid. This result differs from that reported by Constantinides (1983) for stocks. Although the tax liability is also postponed indefinitely for equities, the expected rate of growth in price, adjusted for risk, equals the discount rate so that the present value of the tax liability is not negligible. In our problem, the expected rate of growth in price γr must be smaller than the discount rate $(1-\tau_c)r$. See note 14.

16 The Ibbotson–Sinquefield estimate based on a portfolio of long-term bonds may be a downwardly biased estimate of the standard deviation of a consol's rate of return for two reasons: (a) they considered a portfolio of bonds with an average maturity of 20 years (not infinite); (b) the variability of a portfolio of bonds generally underestimates the return variability of each bond. For example, a shock in the economy which raises the price of 10 year bonds and lowers the price of 30 year bonds may leave the portfolio's price essentially unchanged and contribute little to the variability of the portfolio's return. The same shock, however, may have a significant impact on the consol's return. Both our estimates of s, particularly the first, may also be negatively biased because the interest rate was substantially less than 11 percent for most of this period.

17 The choice of 1 year is primarily a matter of convenience, coinciding with both the minimum holding period for long-term gains and the length of the tax year. If the holding period were shorter, as it was until recently, and the offset provision were to be considered, then an additional complication would arise. The value of short-term losses in the first part of the year could not be determined until it was known if there were later offsetting long-term capital gains.

18 See, however, the second caveat in note 16. In addition, when the low variance process is used, the simulated volatility of a 20 year bond over its life will be lower than the historic average because the low variance process understates the variance of the short-term rate and hence the variance of short-term bonds.

19 The right-hand side of (30) is positive at $P=0$ since the first term is, and the right-hand side of (31) is less than P for large values (since the maximum benefit of future tax losses is $\tau_c(P-1)$). These expressions are continuous at $P=1$. Therefore a solution to (30) and (31) exists. For the dynamics assumed, the solution is also unique.

20 Some of the entries in this table as well as those in table 3.3 give the value function for states which could never arise along the optimal path. For example, since losses are always realized when the basis is below par, the basis can never be substantially in excess of the current price in this situation. Therefore these entries give the value of changing to the optimal policy from a suboptimal position.

21 Buy and hold prices are computed using formula (35) below. Even though the interest rate is not expected to increase or decrease from 14 percent, the yield curve is slightly downward sloping due to Jensen's inequality and prices are above par. For these and other premium bonds the buy and hold policy assumes that the excess above par is amortized and deducted year by year. Thus no capital losses (or gains) are earned on premium bonds under the buy and hold policy. Therefore this benchmark price is the same for all scenarios.

22 The strict convexity cannot be illustrated in table 3.4 because at least three premium bonds and three discount bonds would be required.

23 An alternative definition of the timing option is the difference between the bond prices under the optimal and continuous realization policies. The assumption of a buy and hold policy is by far the more common in previous research. The two definitions are compared in the example in section 4.

24 Since the interest rate dynamics employed here are without drift, the results are most

similar to the case $\alpha = 0$ in the continuous-time model. The buy and hold benchmark resulted in smaller timing options in that case and so our choice is conservative.

25 In an earlier version of Constantinides (1983).

26 US Treasury bonds are typically quoted with spreads of a quarter to a half of a point in the *Wall Street Journal*. A few have spreads of an eighth of a point. Treasury note spreads are usually an eighth to a quarter of a point.

27 McCulloch (1975) and Litzenberger and Rolfo (1984a) explicitly and Caks (1977) implicitly use equations identical with (35a). Only McCulloch and Litzenberger and Rolfo recognize the premium amortization embodied in (35b). See also Pye (1969), Robichek and Niebuhr (1970), and Schaefer (1981).

28 In some cases the estimated tax rates are negative.

29 The error in the estimated forward rate is the deviation between the estimate and the true forward rate calculated from the binomial model. The true forward rate is not equal to the future expected spot rate, 14 percent in this case, as a result of Jensen's inequality.

30 As of 1980 seven states had no individual income tax on interest. More than half the states had maximum marginal tax rates at or below 7 percent. In only three states was the maximum tax rate above 11 percent. The highest rate was Minnesota at 16 percent.

References

Caks, J. (1977) "The Coupon Effect on Yield to Maturity," *Journal of Finance*, 32, 103–15.

Constantinides, G. M. (1983) "Capital Market Equilibrium with Personal Tax," *Econometrica*, 51, 611–36.

Constantinides, G. M. (1984) "Optimal Stock Trading with Personal Taxes: Implications for Prices and the Abnormal January Returns," *Journal of Financial Economics*, 13, 65–89.

Constantinides, G. M. and Scholes, M. S. (1980) "Optimal Liquidation of Assets in the Presence of Personal Taxes: Implications for Asset Pricing," *Journal of Finance*, 35, 439–49.

Cox, J. C., Ingersoll, J. E., Jr, and Ross, S. A. (1980) "An Analysis of Variable Rate Loan Contracts," *Journal of Finance*, 35, 389–403.

Cox, J. C., Ingersoll, J. E., Jr, and Ross, S. A. (1981) "A Re-examination of Traditional Hypotheses about the Term Structure of Interest Rates," *Journal of Finance*, 36, 769–99.

Cox, J. C., Ingersoll, J. E., Jr, and Ross, S. A. (1985) "A Theory of the Term Structure of Interest Rates," *Econometrica*, 53, 385–407.

Grigelionis, B. I. and Shiryaev, A. N. (1966) "On Stefan's Problem and Optimal Stopping Rules for Markov Processes," *Theory of Probability and Its Applications*, 11, 541–58.

Ibbotson, R. G. and Sinquefield, R. A. (1982) *Stocks, Bonds, Bills and Inflation: The Past and the Future* (Charlottesville, VA: Financial Analysts Research Foundation, University of Virginia).

Litzenberger, R. H. and Rolfo, J. (1984a) "An International Study of Tax Effects on Government Bonds, *Journal of Finance*, 39, 1–22.

Litzenberger, R. H. and Rolfo, J. (1984b) "Arbitrage Pricing, Transaction Costs and Taxation of Capital Gains: A Study of Government Bonds with the Same Maturity Date," *Journal of Financial Economics*, 13, 337–51.

McCulloch, J. H. (1975) "The Tax-Adjusted Yield Curve," *Journal of Finance*, 30, 811–30.

Merton, R. C. (1973) "Theory of Rational Option Pricing," *Bell Journal of Economics and Management Science*, 4, 141–83.

Miller, M. H. (1977) "Debt and Taxes," *Journal of Finance*, 32, 261–75.

Pye, G. (1969) "On the Tax Structure of Interest Rates," *Quarterly Journal of Economics*, 83, 562–79.

Robichek, A. A. and Niebuhr, W. D. (1970) "Tax-Induced Bias in Reported Treasury Yields," *Journal of Finance*, 25, 1081–90.

Schaefer, S. M. (1981) "Measuring a Tax-Specific Term Structure of Interest Rates in the Market for British Government Securities," *Economic Journal*, 91, 415–38.

Schaefer, S. M. (1982a) "Tax Induced Clientele Effects in the Market for British Government Securities: Placing Bounds on Security Values in an Incomplete Market," *Journal of Financial Economics*, 10, 121–59.

Schaefer, S. M. (1982b) "Taxes and Security Market Equilibrium," *Financial Economics: Essays in Honor of Paul H. Cootner*, eds W. F. Sharpe and C. M. Cootner (Englewood Cliffs, NJ: Prentice-Hall), pp. 159–78.

Chapter 4

John C. Cox

Background and Comments

Most theoretical analyses of portfolio theory and asset pricing are now done in continuous time. We may observe a stock price only at the discrete intervals when transactions occur, but in the background the true price is assumed to be changing continuously. The idea of continuous time is not new in finance. For example, continuously compounded interest rates are often used in practice to capture the time value of money. However, thinking of risk in continuous time is not so easy. We have to think of a variable moving along a path that is smooth – no kinks or discontinuities – but also uncertain.

Robert Merton introduced the necessary mathematical tools for describing risk in continuous time in his paper analyzing optimal consumption and investment strategies (Merton, 1971). The following paper by John Cox and Chi-fu Huang is a direct extension of Merton's work.

Many readers will find it difficult (as I did) to extract the message in Cox and Huang's mathematics. One contribution is to solve an important problem left over from Merton's paper. As they explain in example 3, several of Merton's solutions "are not completely appropriate, because they allow the agent to incur negative wealth and may require negative consumption." Humans may consume nothing at all, of course, but nothing is the absolute lower limit.

This "non-negativity" condition has not barred qualitative insights into optimal consumption and investment strategies, but it has made explicit quantitative solutions extremely difficult. Cox and Huang have developed a new procedure which allows explicit solutions for a variety of interesting cases. We are now in a position to *compute* the (theoretically) optimal lifetime consumption and investment strategy for individual investors.

Reference

Merton, R. C. (1971) "Optimum Consumption and Portfolio Rules in a Continuous-Time Model," *Journal of Economic Theory*, 3: 4, December, 373–413.

Author's Introduction

Individuals face many decisions in making their consumption and portfolio plans over time. They must continually choose how much of their wealth to consume and how much to invest. Of the amount invested, they must decide on the proportion that will be placed in each of a variety of investment alternatives. The way in which these decisions should best be made is a classical problem in financial theory, and one which has traditionally been addressed using the technique of dynamic programming.

In this paper we present a new approach to intertemporal consumption and portfolio problems. A key feature of this approach is the use of the correspondence between optimal allocations in a world of complete markets and in a world where markets can effectively be made complete by sequential trading in a set of basic securities. This allows us to reduce the original dynamic problem to an equivalent static problem that can readily be solved. We then use some results from option pricing theory to transform the solution of the static problem into the corresponding optimal decision rules for the dynamic problem. This methodology enables us to derive very easily a number of explicit results that would be quite difficult to obtain in any other way.

Bibliographical Listing

"A Variational Problem Arising in Financial Economics" (with Chi-fu Huang), *Journal of Mathematical Economics*, forthcoming.

"A Continuous Time Portfolio Turnpike Theorem" (with Chi-fu Huang), *Working Paper 3117-88*, Sloan School of Management, Massachusetts Institute of Technology, September 1988.

"On Dynamic Investment Strategies" (with Hayne Leland), *Proceedings of the Seminar on the Analysis of Security Prices*, 27: 2, November 1982, 139–73.

Optimal Consumption and Portfolio Policies when Asset Prices Follow a Diffusion Process

JOHN C. COX and CHI-FU HUANG

1 Introduction

Optimal intertemporal consumption–portfolio policies in continuous time under uncertainty have traditionally been characterized by stochastic dynamic programming. Merton [30] is the pioneering paper in this regard. To show the existence of a solution to the consumption–portfolio problem using dynamic programming, there are two approaches. The first is through application of the existence theorems in the theory of stochastic control. These existence theorems often require an admissible control to take its values in a compact set. This is unsatisfactory, since if we are modeling frictionless financial markets, any compactness assumption on the values of controls is arbitrary. Moreover, many of the existence theorems are limited to cases where the controls affect only the drift term of the controlled processes. Unfortunately, this rules out the portfolio problem under consideration.

The second approach is through construction: construct a control, usually by solving a nonlinear partial differential equation either analytically or numerically, and then use the verification theorem of dynamic programming to verify that it is indeed a solution. Merton's paper uses this second approach. It is in general difficult, however, to construct

Reproduced from *Journal of Economic Theory*, 49: 1, October 1989, 33–83.

The authors would like to thank Hua He, Hayne Leland, Robert Merton, Henri Pagès, Daniel Stroock, and Tong-sheng Sun for comments. Preliminary results of this paper were first reported at Carnegie-Mellon University in 1983, and summary results were given at the Institute of Mathematics and Its Applications at the University of Minnesota in the summer of 1986. The May 1986 version of this paper has been presented at Brown University, Cornell University, Massachusetts Institute of Technology, Northwestern University, the University of California at Berkeley, the University of Chicago, and the University of Pennsylvania. The current version has been presented at the Copenhagen Institute of Economics. We thank the seminar participants for their comments. We are of course solely responsible for any remaining errors.

a solution. Moreover, when there are constraints on controls, such as the nonnegativity constraint on consumption, this approach becomes even more difficult.

Recently, a martingale representation technology has been used in place of the theory of stochastic control to show the existence of optimal consumption–portfolio policies without the requirement of compactness of the values of admissible controls (see Cox and Huang [6] and Pliska [32]). Notably, Cox and Huang show that for a quite general class of utility functions it suffices to check, for the existence of optimal controls, whether the parameters of a system of stochastic differential equations, derived completely from the price system, satisfy a local Lipschitz condition and a uniform growth condition. This approach takes care of the nonnegativity constraint on consumption in a simple and direct way.

The focus of this paper is on the explicit construction of optimal controls using martingale technology, with the nonnegativity constraint on consumption being taken into account. We provide two characterization theorems of optimal policies (theorems 1 and 2) and one verification theorem (theorem 3). Theorem 3 is the counterpart of the verification theorem of dynamic programming. One advantage of our approach is that our verification theorem involves a *linear* partial differential equation unlike the *nonlinear* partial differential equation appearing in dynamic programming. In many specific situations optimal controls can even be directly computed without solving any partial differential equation. For example, we compute in closed form the optimal consumption–portfolio policies for the hyperbolic absolute risk aversion (HARA) utility functions when the asset prices follow a geometric Brownian motion.

In addition to the papers by Cox and Huang [6] and Pliska [32] mentioned above, other related work includes papers by Brennan and Solanki [4], Cox and Leland [7], Duffie and Huang [9], Harrison and Kreps [17], Harrison and Pliska [18], Huang [22], and Kreps [26].[1]

Merton [31, ch. 6] recently utilized the technology developed here to investigate an optimal consumption–portfolio problem with an infinite horizon in the geometric Brownian motion model of Merton [30]. He showed, for example, that in the region where an investor chooses to consume zero, his optimal portfolio policy is a constant-proportion levered combination of the riskless security and the growth-optimal portfolio – the portfolio that maximizes the expected continuously compounded growth rate. Readers interested in applications of the techniques developed here should consult Merton [31].

The rest of this paper is organized as follows. Section 2 contains our general theory. We formulate a dynamic consumption–portfolio problem for an agent in continuous time with general diffusion price processes in section 2.1. The agent's problem is to dynamically manage a portfolio of securities and withdraw funds out of it in order to maximize his expected utility of consumption over time and of final wealth, while facing a nonnegativity constraint on consumption as well as on final wealth. Section 2.2 contains the main results of section 2. In theorems 1 and 2 we give characterizations of optimal consumption–portfolio policies. We show in theorem 3 how candidates for optimal policies can be constructed by solving a *linear* partial differential equation and how candidates can be verified to indeed be optimal. We discuss the relationship between our approach and dynamic programming in section 2.3. We also demonstrate the connection between a solution with the nonnegativity constraint and a solution without the constraint.

In section 3, we specialize the general model of section 2 to a model originally considered by Merton [30], where securities price processes follow a geometric Brownian motion. In this case, optimal consumption–portfolio policies can be computed directly without solving any partial differential equation. Several examples of utility functions are considered. In particular, we solve the consumption–portfolio problem for the family of HARA utility functions. In the unconstrained case given by Merton [30], the optimal policies for HARA utility functions are linear in wealth; when nonnegativity constraints are included, this is no longer true. We also obtain some characterizations of optimal policies that are of independent interest.

Section 4 contains some concluding remarks.

2 The General Case

In this section, a model of securities markets in continuous time with diffusion price processes will be formulated. We shall consider the optimal consumption–portfolio policies of an agent who faces a nonnegativity constraint on consumption and final wealth. The connection between our approach and dynamic programming will be demonstrated and the advantages of our approach will be pointed out. We shall also discuss the relationship between a solution to the agent's problem with the nonnegativity constraint and a solution to his problem without the constraint.

2.1 The formulation

Taken as primitive is a complete probability space[2] $(\Omega, \mathcal{F}, P)$ and a time span $[0, T]$, where T is a strictly positive real number. Let there be an N-dimensional standard Brownian motion defined on the probability space, denoted by $w = \{w_n(t); t \in [0, T], n = 1, 2, \ldots, N\}$. Let

$F = \{ \mathscr{F}_t; t \in [0, T] \}$ be the *filtration* (an increasing family of subsigma fields of $\mathscr{F}$) generated by w.

We assume that $\mathscr{F}_0$ contains all the P-null sets and that $\mathscr{F}_T = \mathscr{F}$. Since for an N-dimensional standard Brownian motion, $w(0) = 0$ almost surely (a.s.), $\mathscr{F}_0$ is almost trivial.[3]

A process $X = \{ X(t); t \in [0, T] \}$ is said to be *adapted* to $\boldsymbol{F}$ if $X(t)$ is measurable with respect to $\mathscr{F}_t$ $\forall t \in [0, T]$. In words, the value of X at time t cannot depend on the realizations of the Brownian motion strictly after time t.

We use $\mathscr{O}$ to denote the optional sigma field and ν to denote the product measure on $\Omega \times [0, T]$ generated by P and the Lebesgue measure. (The optional sigma field is the sigma field on $\Omega \times [0, T]$ generated by $\boldsymbol{F}$-adapted right-continuous processes (e.g. Chung and Williams [5, p.59].) A process measurable with respect to $\mathscr{O}$ is naturally adapted to $\boldsymbol{F}$ and is said to be an optional process. A pair of consumption rate process and final wealth (c, W) is said to be admissible if

$$(c, W) \in L^p_+(\nu) \times L^p_+(P) \equiv L^p_+(\Omega \times [0, T], \mathscr{O}, \nu) \times L^p_+(\Omega, \mathscr{F}, P)$$

for some $p > 1$, where $L^p_+(\nu)$ and $L^p_+(P)$ are the positive orthants of $L^p(\Omega \times [0, T], \mathscr{O}, \nu)$ and $L^p(\Omega, \mathscr{F}, P)$ respectively. As we mentioned above, since an optional process is adapted, all the consumption processes are adapted. Note that using the terminology of general equilibrium theory, we have taken the commodity space to be $L^p(\nu) \times L^p(P)$ and an agent's consumption set to be $L^p_+(\nu) \times L^p_+(P)$. All the processes to appear will be adapted to $\boldsymbol{F}$.

Consider a frictionless securities market with $N + 1$ long-lived securities traded, indexed by $n = 0, 1, 2, \ldots, N$. Security $n \neq 0$ is risky and pays dividends at rate $\iota_n(t)$ and sells for $S_n(t)$ at time t. We shall henceforth use $S(t)$ and $\iota(t)$ to denote $[S_1(t), \ldots, S_N(t)]^{\mathrm{T}}$ and $[\iota_1(t), \ldots, \iota_N(t)]^{\mathrm{T}}$ respectively, where superscript T denotes transpose. Security 0 is (locally) riskless, pays no dividends, and sells for

$$B(t) = B(0) \exp\left[\int_0^t r(s)\, ds\right]$$

at time t, where $B(0)$ is a strictly positive real number. Assume further that $r(t) = r[S(t), t]$ with $r(x, t): \mathbb{R}^N \times [0, T] \to \mathbb{R}_+$ continuous. Note that, since $r(t) \geqslant 0$, $B(t)$ is bounded below away from zero. Henceforth we shall refer to security 0 as the "bond."

We shall use the following notation. If σ is a matrix or a column vector, then $|\sigma|^2$ denotes $\mathrm{tr}(\sigma\sigma^{\mathrm{T}})$ where tr denotes trace. Note also that all terms such as increasing, decreasing, positive, negative, greater than, and smaller than have their weak meaning throughout.

The price processes for risky securities plus their accumulated dividends follow an Itô process satisfying

$$S(t) + \int_0^t \iota[S(s), s]\ \mathrm{d}s = S(0) + \int_0^t \varsigma[S(s), s]\ \mathrm{d}s$$
$$+ \int_0^t \sigma[S(s), s]\ \mathrm{d}w(s), \qquad \forall t \in [0, T] \text{ a.s.}, \quad (1)$$

where $\varsigma(t)$ is an $N \times 1$ vector process and $\sigma(t)$ is an $N \times N$ matrix process. We assume that $\varsigma(x, t)$ and $\sigma(x, t)$ are continuous in $x \in \mathbb{R}^N$ and t, and $\sigma(x, t)$ is nonsingular for all $x \in \mathbb{R}^N$ and t.

A trading strategy is an $(N + 1)$-vector of processes, denoted generically by

$$\{\alpha(t), \theta(t) \equiv (\theta_1(t), \ldots, \theta_N(t))^{\mathrm{T}}; t \in [0, T]\},$$

where $\alpha(t)$ and $\theta_n(t)$ are respectively the numbers of shares of the zeroth and nth securities held at time t. We shall specify the set of admissible trading strategies more fully later. For now, an admissible trading strategy must satisfy the following conditions:

1
$$\int_0^T |\alpha(t)B(t)r(t) + \theta(t)^{\mathrm{T}}\varsigma(t)|\ \mathrm{d}t < \infty \qquad P\text{–a.s.} \qquad (2)$$

2
$$\int_0^T |\theta(t)^{\mathrm{T}}\sigma(t)|^2\ \mathrm{d}t < \infty \qquad P\text{–a.s.} \qquad (3)$$

3 There exists a consumption–final wealth pair $(c, W) \in L_+^p(\nu) \times L_+^p(P)$ such that, almost surely with respect to P (P–a.s.),

$$\alpha(t)B(t) + \theta(t)^{\mathrm{T}}S(t) + \int_0^t c(s)\ \mathrm{d}s$$
$$= \alpha(0)B(0) + \theta(0)^{\mathrm{T}}S(0) + \int_0^t [\alpha(s)B(s)r(s) + \theta(s)^{\mathrm{T}}\varsigma(s)]\ \mathrm{d}s$$
$$+ \int_0^t \theta(s)^{\mathrm{T}}\sigma(s)\ \mathrm{d}w(s) \qquad \forall t \in [0, T]. \qquad (4)$$

4
$$\alpha(T)B(T) + \theta(T)^{\mathrm{T}}S(T) = W \qquad P\text{–a.s.} \qquad (5)$$

Relations (2) and (3) ensure that the stochastic integrals of (4) are well defined (see Liptser and Shiryayev [29, ch. 4]). The left-hand side of (4) is the value of the portfolio at time t plus the accumulated withdrawals of consumption from time zero to time t, while the right-hand side is equal to the initial value of the portfolio plus accumulated capital gains (losses) and dividends from trading from time zero to time t. The fact that the left-hand side is equal to the right-hand side is a natural budget constraint. Relation (5) simply says that the final wealth is equal to the final value of the portfolio. Note that since $W \in L^p_+(P)$ and thus $W \geqslant 0$ P–a.s., (5) also ensures that borrowing to consume without paying back is not admissible. The consumption–final wealth pair (c, W) of (4) and (5) will be said to be *financed* by the trading strategy (α, θ).

Trading strategies satisfying (2) and (3) include all the *simple trading strategies* – a trading strategy (α, θ) is *simple* if there exist a finite number of time points $0 \leqslant t_0 < t_1 < \cdots < t_J = T$ and bounded random variables $\{x_{nj}; n = 0, 1, \ldots, N; j = 0, 1, \ldots, J-1\}$ such that x_{nj} is measurable with respect to $\mathscr{F}_{t_j}$ and

$$\begin{aligned} \alpha(t) &= x_{0j} \qquad P\text{–a.s.} \quad \text{if } t \in (t_j, t_{j+1}] \\ \theta_n(t) &= x_{nj} \qquad P\text{–a.s.} \quad \text{if} \\ &\qquad t \in (t_j, t_{j+1}] \quad \forall n = 1, 2, \ldots, N. \end{aligned}$$

Note that a simple trading strategy is a portfolio policy that changes its composition of assets at a finite number of nonstochastic time points. Simple trading strategies are among the strategies that can actually be implemented in the real world. Their inclusion in the set of admissible strategies is necessary for our model to be reasonable.

Now we shall turn our attention briefly to the price processes before completing our specification of the set of admissible trading strategies. Thus far, we have not put any restriction on the price processes other than certain continuity and nonsingularity conditions on their parameters. For our consumption–portfolio problem to be well posed, we certainly do not want the price processes to allow something to be created from nothing when reasonable strategies are employed. Formally, a *free lunch* is a consumption–final wealth pair $(c, W) \in L^p_+(\nu) \times L^p_+(P)$ financed by an admissible trading strategy (α, θ) such that $\alpha(0)B(0) + \theta(0)^{\mathrm{T}}S(0) = 0$ and either $c > 0$ with a strictly positive ν measure or $W > 0$ with a strictly positive P measure. In words, a free lunch is a consumption–final wealth pair that is nonnegative and nonzero and is financed by an admissible trading strategy with zero initial cost. Harrison and Kreps [17] and Huang [21] have shown that for free lunches not to be available for *simple strategies* it suffices that S is related to martingales after a change of unit and a change of probability, or equivalently that there exists an *equivalent martingale measure*. An equivalent martingale measure Q is a probability measure on $(\Omega, \mathscr{F})$ equivalent to P so that the Radon–Nikodym derivative $\mathrm{d}Q/\mathrm{d}P$ lies in $L^q(\Omega, \mathscr{F}, P)$ with $1/p + 1/q = 1$ and

$$G^\star(t) \equiv \frac{S(t)}{B(t)} - \frac{S(0)}{B(0)} + \int_0^t \frac{\iota(s)}{B(s)}\,\mathrm{d}s,$$

the accumulated capital gains plus accumulated dividends, in units of the bond, is a martingale under Q. The existence of an equivalent martingale measure can be ensured by some regularity conditions on the parameters of the price processes. Since this subject is treated elsewhere, we shall simply assume that there exists an equivalent martingale measure and refer the reader to Cox and Huang [6, proposition 2.1 and section 4] for details.

Assumption 1 There exists an equivalent martingale measure denoted by Q.

Indeed, Cox and Huang [6, proposition 2.1] show that, since $\sigma(x,t)$ is nonsingular for all x and t, Q must be the unique equivalent martingale measure.

Remark 1 Probability measure Q is said to be equivalent to P if P and Q have the same measure zero sets. This definition is symmetric, and thus we say that P and Q are equivalent to each other. A necessary and sufficient condition for this is that the Radon–Nikodym derivative $\mathrm{d}Q/\mathrm{d}P$ is strictly positive. If $\mathrm{d}Q/\mathrm{d}P$ is merely positive, we say that Q is absolutely continuous with respect to P. Since P and Q are equivalent probability measures, all the almost surely statements to appear will be with respect to both. ■

Remark 2 Harrison and Kreps [17] and Kreps [27] show that the existence of an equivalent martingale measure is not only a sufficient but also a necessary condition for free lunches not to be available for simple strategies in the limit. Interested readers should consult their work for details. We should also note that, in the setup of Harrison and Kreps [17], securities do not pay dividends and an individual maximizes his preferences for final wealth. Our model here is more general and uses results of Huang [21]. ■

The unique martingale measure Q has an explicit expression. It follows from Harrison and Kreps [17, theorem 3] and Huang [21, theorem 4.1] that

$$\frac{\mathrm{d}Q}{\mathrm{d}P} = \exp\left\{\int_0^T \varkappa[S(s),s]^{\mathrm{T}}\,\mathrm{d}w(s) - \frac{1}{2}\int_0^T |\varkappa[S(s),s]|^2\,\mathrm{d}s\right\}, \tag{6}$$

where

$$\varkappa[S(t),t] \equiv -\sigma[S(t),t]^{-1}\{\zeta[S(t),t] - r[S(t),t]\,S(t)\}, \tag{7}$$

For future use, we define a martingale under P:

$$\eta(t) \equiv E\left[\frac{\mathrm{d}Q}{\mathrm{d}P}\middle| \mathscr{F}_t\right] \qquad \text{a.s.}$$

$$= \exp\left\{\int_0^t \varkappa[S(s), s]^{\mathrm{T}} \,\mathrm{d}w(s) - \frac{1}{2}\int_0^t |\varkappa[S(s), s]|^2 \,\mathrm{d}s\right\} \qquad \text{a.s.} \quad (8)$$

where $E[\cdot]$ denotes expectation under P. Since $\mathrm{d}Q/\mathrm{d}P$ is strictly positive, $\eta(t)$ is strictly positive. A P martingale $\{X(t); t \in [0, T]\}$ is said to be an $L^p(P)$ martingale if

$$E[|X(t)|^p] < \infty \qquad \forall t \in [0, T].$$

By the fact that $\mathrm{d}Q/\mathrm{d}P \in L^q(P)$, $\{\eta(t); t \in [0, T]\}$ is an $L^q(P)$ martingale. We shall demonstrate later that $\eta(\omega, t)B(0)/B(\omega, t)$ can be interpreted to be the price at time zero, per unit of P probability, of one unit of consumption at time t in state ω.

The following lemma will be useful later.

Lemma 1 Under Q,

$$w^\star(t) \equiv w(t) - \int_0^t \varkappa[S(s), s] \,\mathrm{d}s \qquad (9)$$

is a standard Brownian motion. We can write

$$G^\star(t) = \int_0^t \frac{\sigma[S(s), s]}{B(s)} \,\mathrm{d}w^\star(s) \qquad \text{a.s.,} \qquad (10)$$

which by assumption is a martingale under Q.

PROOF The first assertion follows from the Girsanov theorem (e.g. Liptser and Shiryayev [29, ch. 6]). Next by Itô's lemma,

$$G^\star(t) = \int_0^t \frac{\zeta[S(s), s] - r[S(s), s]S(s)}{B(s)} \,\mathrm{d}s + \int_0^t \frac{\sigma[S(s), s]}{B(s)} \,\mathrm{d}w(s).$$

The second assertion then follows from substituting $w^\star$ into the above relation and using the definition of $\varkappa$ in (7). ■

The existence of an equivalent martingale measure ensures that there are no free lunches for simple strategies. However, free lunches financed by trading strategies satisfying (2)–(5) can still exist. For example, a doubling strategy, named after the strategy of doubling one's bet each time one loses at a roulette, can produce a free lunch, as was pointed out by Harrison and Kreps [17]. Therefore, either we allow only simple strategies or conditions in addition to (2)–(5) must be imposed to rule out free lunches for nonsimple strategies. The former proves mathematically intractable since the set of consumption–final wealth pairs financed by simple strategies is not closed in $L^p(\nu)\times L^p(P)$ and the optimization problem is not well posed. Moreover, the set of simple strategies is not "rich enough" in that it does not include strategies of practical interest such as those that replicate call options on securities.

There are two approaches for the latter. Both are motivated by the observation that, for a doubling strategy to be implementable, it is necessary that an individual can borrow without bound and that there be no limit on the number of shares of risky securities held over time. The first approach is to put a nonnegative wealth constraint on trading strategies. Such a constraint certainly rules out doubling strategies, since it limits the amount of borrowing that can be made. Harrison and Kreps [17] conjectured that this constraint would also rule out all the free lunches. This conjecture was verified by Dybvig [10] in the model due to Black and Scholes [2] and by Dybvig and Huang [11] in a model like ours. The second approach is to put a constraint on θ. Note that a bound on θ also constrains α through the budget constraint of (4) and (5). It turns out that a uniform bound on θ across states of nature is too strong – θ can be allowed to grow unbounded on sets of small Q probability. Formally, the appropriate constraint is the following integrability condition on θ:

$$E^\star\left[\left\{\int_0^T\left|\frac{\theta(t)^\mathrm{T}\sigma(t)}{B(t)}\right|^2\mathrm{d}t\right\}^{p/2}\right]<\infty, \tag{11}$$

where $E^\star[\cdot]$ denotes expectation under Q. Duffie and Huang [9] used this kind of integrability constraint in their general equilibrium model. However, Dybvig and Huang [11] show that the two approaches discussed above are equivalent for individuals with strictly increasing preferences. They show that any trading strategy that satisfies (2)–(5) and (11) must satisfy the nonnegative wealth constraint. The strategies satisfying (2)–(5) and the nonnegative wealth constraint but not (11) are suicidal strategies – strategies that essentially run a free lunch in reverse and throw money away. Any individual with strictly increasing preferences will certainly never employ a suicidal strategy. We note now that the following lemma shows that (11) is sufficient for (3).

Lemma 2 Let θ satisfy (11). Then θ satisfies (3).

PROOF Let θ satisfy (11). Then it is necessary that

$$\int_0^T\left|\frac{\theta(t)\sigma(t)}{B(t)}\right|^2\mathrm{d}t<\infty \qquad \text{a.s.}$$

Since $B(t)$ is a continuous process, a sample path is bounded on $[0, T]$

almost surely. Thus

$$\int_0^T |\theta(t)\sigma(t)|^2 \, dt < \infty \qquad \text{a.s.,}$$

which is (3). ∎

Now we are ready to complete the specification of admissible trading strategies. A trading strategy (α, θ) is admissible if it satisfies (2), (4), (5), and (11). We shall use $H(Q)$ to denote the space of admissible trading strategies, where Q signifies that the expectation of (11) is taken with respect to the unique equivalent martingale measure Q. We can verify that $H(Q)$ is a linear space by the linearity of the stochastic integral.

Now consider an agent with a time-additive utility function $u(y, t)$ for consumption, a utility function $V(y)$ for final wealth, and an initial wealth $W_0 > 0$. We assume that $u(y, t)$ and $V(y)$ are continuous, increasing, and strictly concave in y, and possibly unbounded from below at $y = 0$. The agent wants to solve the following problem:

$$\begin{aligned} &\sup_{(c, W) \in L^p_+(\nu) \times L^p_+(P)} E\left[\int_0^T u\{c(t), t\} \, dt + V(W)\right] \\ &\text{s.t. } (c, W) \text{ is financed by some } (\alpha, \theta) \in H(Q) \\ &\quad \text{with } \alpha(0)B(0) + \theta(0)^{\mathrm{T}} S(0) = W_0, \end{aligned} \tag{12}$$

where s.t. denotes subject to. Our task here is to provide ways to construct an optimal consumption–portfolio policy when one is known to exist and to construct candidate policies to be verified to be optimal when existence cannot be established on prior grounds.

We shall first record a mathematical result and a well-known property of the cost over time of a consumption–final wealth pair financed by some $(\alpha, \theta) \in H(Q)$.

Lemma 3 Let θ satisfy (11). Then

$$\int_0^t \frac{\theta(s)^{\mathrm{T}} \sigma(s)}{B(s)} \, dw^\star(s) \qquad t \in [0, T]$$

is an $L^p(Q)$ martingale.

PROOF See Jacod [23, ch. IV]. ∎

Lemma 4 Let $(c, W) \in L^p_+(\nu) \times L^p_+(P)$ be financed by $(\alpha, \theta) \in H(Q)$.

For all $t \in [0, T]$,

$$E^\star\left[\int_0^T \frac{c(s)}{B(s)}\,\mathrm{d}s + \frac{W}{B(T)}\,\middle|\,\mathscr{F}_t\right]$$

$$= \alpha(0) + \frac{\theta(0)^{\mathrm{T}} S(0)}{B(0)} + \int_0^t \frac{\theta(s)^{\mathrm{T}}\sigma(s)}{B(s)}\,\mathrm{d}w^\star(s)$$

$$= \alpha(t) + \frac{\theta(t)^{\mathrm{T}} S(t)}{B(t)} + \int_0^t \frac{c(s)}{B(s)}\,\mathrm{d}s \qquad \text{a.s.,}$$

and as a consequence the value of (c, W) at time t is

$$\alpha(t)B(t) + \theta(t)^{\mathrm{T}} S(t) = B(t)E^\star\left[\int_t^T \frac{c(s)}{B(s)}\,\mathrm{d}s + \frac{W}{B(T)}\,\middle|\,\mathscr{F}_t\right] \qquad \text{a.s.} \qquad (13)$$

Moreover,

$$\int_0^T \frac{c(s)}{B(s)}\,\mathrm{d}s + \frac{W}{B(T)}$$

is an element of $L^p(Q)$.

PROOF See Cox and Huang [6, proposition 2.2] for the first assertion. The second assertion follows from the first assertion and lemma 3. ■

With the aid of the following lemma, (13) has an intuitive interpretation in the context of Arrow–Debreu economies.

Lemma 5 Let g be an adapted process. Then

$$E^\star\left[\int_t^T g(s)\,\mathrm{d}s\,\middle|\,\mathscr{F}_t\right] = E\left[\int_t^T g(s)\eta(s)\,\mathrm{d}s\,\middle|\,\mathscr{F}_t\right]\Big/\eta(t) \qquad \text{a.s.,}$$

whenever the integrals are well defined. Thus for any $(c, W) \in L^p(\nu) \times L^p(P)$ we can write

$$B(t)E^\star\left[\int_t^T \frac{c(s)}{B(s)}\,\mathrm{d}s + \frac{W}{B(T)}\,\middle|\,\mathscr{F}_t\right]$$

$$= B(t)E\left[\int_t^T \frac{c(s)\eta(s)}{B(s)}\,\mathrm{d}s + \frac{W\eta(T)}{B(T)}\,\middle|\,\mathscr{F}_t\right]\Big/\eta(t) \qquad \text{a.s.} \qquad (14)$$

PROOF The first assertion follows from Dellacharie and Meyer [8, ch. VI, section 57]. The second assertion follows since c and B are adapted processes. ■

From lemma 4, the left-hand side of (14) is the value of (c, W) at time

t. Thus, we can interpret $B(\omega,t)\eta(\omega,s)/[B(\omega,s)\eta(\omega,t)]$ as the price at time t, per unit of P probability, of an Arrow–Debreu security that pays one unit of consumption in state ω at time $s \geqslant t$. That is, there exists an implicit system of Arrow–Debreu prices such that we can compute the value over time of a pair of $(c, W) \in L^p_+(\nu) \times L^p_+(P)$ financed by an admissible trading strategy. Note that since the equivalent martingale measure Q is unique and since $\eta(t)$ is constructed from Q, the system of implicit Arrow–Debreu prices is uniquely determined.

For future reference, we now cite several properties of a concave utility function. At every interior point of the domain of a concave function, the right-hand derivative and the left-hand derivative exist. At the left boundary of its domain, the right-hand derivative exists. The right-hand and left-hand derivatives are decreasing functions and are equal to each other except possibly at a countable number of points. That is, a concave function is differentiable everywhere except possibly at a countable number of points and thus is continuously differentiable at all but a countable number of points. (Note that, for strictly concave functions, the *decreasing* relation above becomes a strict relation.) The right-hand derivative is a right-continuous function. Moreover, at every point, the left-hand derivative is greater than the right-hand derivative.

Now let $u_{y+}(y,t)$, $V'_+(y)$ and $u_{y-}(y,t)$, $V'_-(y)$ denote the right-hand derivatives and left-hand derivatives respectively with respect to y for $u(y,t)$ and $V(y)$. Let $y < y'$; then $V'_-(y) \geqslant V'_+(y) > V'_-(y')$ by the strict concavity of V, and similarly for $u(y,t)$. We assume that

$$\lim_{y\to\infty} u_{y+}(y,\,t) = 0$$

and

$$\lim_{y\to\infty} V'_+(y) = 0.$$

Define inverse functions $\hat{f}(x^{-1},t) = \inf\{y \in \mathbb{R}_+ : u_{y+}(y,t) \leqslant x^{-1}\}$ and $V'^{-1}_+(x^{-1}) = \inf\{y \in \mathbb{R}_+ : V'_+(y) \leqslant x^{-1}\}$. By the right-continuity of the right-hand derivatives, the infima are equal to minima.

Remark 3 Note that the assumption that utility functions are increasing and strictly concave implies that they are strictly increasing. ■

We now state three sets of conditions that will be used in the next subsection. Conditions A and B are concerned with properties of the price system, while condition C is concerned with those of the utility functions.

First define the following two processes:

$$Z(t) = Z(0) + \int_0^t \{r[S(s), s] + |\varkappa[S(s), s]|^2\} Z(s)\ ds - \int_0^t \varkappa[S(s), s]^{\mathrm{T}} Z(s)\ dw(s) \tag{15}$$

for some constant $Z(0) > 0$, and

$$Y(t) = \ln\ Z(0) + \int_0^t \{r[S(s), s] + \tfrac{1}{2}|\varkappa[S(s), s]|^2\}\ ds - \int_0^t \varkappa[S(s), s]^{\mathrm{T}}\ dw(s). \tag{16}$$

Using Itô's lemma, it is easily verified that

$$Z(t) = \frac{Z(0)B(t)}{\eta(t)B(0)} \tag{17}$$

and

$$Y(t) = \ln\ Z(t). \tag{18}$$

Note that $[\ln Z(T) - \ln Z(0)]/T$ is the realized continuously compounded growth rate from time zero to time T of the growth-optimal portfolio – the portfolio that maximizes the expected continuously compounded growth rate.

We adopt the following notation:

$$D_y^m = \frac{\partial^m}{\partial y^m} = \frac{\partial^{m_1 + m_2 + \cdots + m_N}}{\partial y_1^{m_1} \ldots \partial y_N^{m_N}}, \qquad m = m_1 + \cdots + m_N,$$

for positive integers $m_1, m_2, \ldots, m_N$. If $g: \mathbb{R}^N \times [0, T] \mapsto \mathbb{R}$ has partial derivatives with respect to its first N arguments, the vector $(\partial g/\partial y_1, \ldots, \partial g/\partial y_N)^{\mathrm{T}}$ is denoted $D_y g$ or g_y.

Condition A Write (1) and (16) compactly as follows:

$$\begin{pmatrix} S(t) \\ Y(t) \end{pmatrix} = \begin{pmatrix} S(0) \\ \ln\ Z(0) \end{pmatrix} + \int_0^t \hat{\xi}[S(s), s]\ ds + \int_0^t \hat{\sigma}[S(s), s]\ dw(s) \qquad \forall t \in [0, T], \text{ a.s.} \tag{19}$$

Suppose that there exist strictly positive constants K_1, K_2, K_3, and γ such that, for all t,

$$|\hat{\xi}(x, t)| \leqslant K_1(1 + |x|), \qquad |\hat{\sigma}(x, t)| \leqslant K_1(1 + |x|) \qquad \forall x \in \mathbb{R}^N, \tag{20}$$

$$|\hat{\xi}(x, t) - \hat{\xi}(y, t)| \leqslant K_2|x - y|, \qquad |\hat{\sigma}(x, t) - \hat{\sigma}(y, t)| \leqslant K_2|x - y| \qquad \forall x, y \in \mathbb{R}^N, \tag{21}$$

that $D_y^m \hat{\zeta}(y,t)$ and $D_y^m \hat{\sigma}(y,t)$ exist for $m = 1, 2$ and are continuous in y and t, and that

$$|D_y^m \hat{\zeta}(y,t)| + |D_y^m \hat{\sigma}(y,t)| \leqslant K_3(1 + |y|^{\gamma}) \tag{22}$$

for all $y \in \mathbb{R}^N$.

Condition B Consider the system of stochastic integral equations (1) and (15) under P and the martingale measure Q:

$$\begin{aligned}\begin{pmatrix} S(t) \\ Z(t) \end{pmatrix} &= \begin{pmatrix} S(0) \\ Z(0) \end{pmatrix} + \int_0^t \bar{\zeta}[S(s), Z(s), s]\ \mathrm{d}s + \int_0^t \bar{\sigma}[S(s), Z(s), s]\ \mathrm{d}w(s) \\ &= \begin{pmatrix} S(0) \\ Z(0) \end{pmatrix} + \int_0^t \{\bar{\zeta}[S(s), Z(s), s] + \bar{\sigma}[S(s), Z(s), s]\,\varkappa[S(s), s]\}\ \mathrm{d}s \\ &\quad + \int_0^t \bar{\sigma}[S(s), Z(s), s]\ \mathrm{d}w^{\star}(s).\end{aligned} \tag{23}$$

Suppose that there exists a strictly positive constant K such that, for all t and all $x \in \mathbb{R}^{n+1}$,

$$\begin{aligned}|\bar{\zeta}(x,t) + \bar{\sigma}(x)\varkappa(x,t)| &\leqslant K(1 + |x|), \\ |\bar{\sigma}(x,t)| &\leqslant K(1 + |x|), \\ |\bar{\zeta}(x,t)| &\leqslant K(1 + |x|).\end{aligned} \tag{24}$$

Moreover, for any $M > 0$ there is a constant K_M such that, for all y, $z \in \mathbb{R}^{N+1}$, with $|y| \leqslant M$, $|z| \leqslant M$, and $t \in [0, T]$,

$$\begin{aligned}|\bar{\zeta}(y,t) + \bar{\sigma}(y,t)\varkappa(y,t) - \bar{\zeta}(z,t) - \bar{\sigma}(z,t)\varkappa(z,t)| &\leqslant K_M|y - z|, \\ |\bar{\sigma}(y,t) - \bar{\sigma}(z,t)| &\leqslant K_M|y - z|, \\ |\bar{\zeta}(y,t) - \bar{\zeta}(z,t)| &\leqslant K_M|y - z|.\end{aligned} \tag{25}$$

Note that (20) and (24) are linear growth conditions, (21) is a uniform Lipschitz condition, (25) is a local Lipschitz condition, and (22) is a polynomial growth condition.

Condition C $\mathrm{e}^{-x}\hat{f}(\mathrm{e}^{-x}, t)$ and $\mathrm{e}^{-x}V_+^{\prime -1}(\mathrm{e}^{-x})$ are such that, for $m \leqslant 2$, $D_x^m[\mathrm{e}^{-x}\hat{f}(\mathrm{e}^{-x}, t)]$ and $D_x^m[\mathrm{e}^{-x}V_+^{\prime -1}(\mathrm{e}^{-x})]$ are continuous and satisfy a polynomial growth condition in that

$$|D_x^m[\mathrm{e}^{-x}\hat{f}(\mathrm{e}^{-x}, t)]| \leqslant K(1 + |x|^{\gamma}) \tag{26}$$

and

$$|D_x^m[\mathrm{e}^{-x}V_+^{\prime -1}(\mathrm{e}^{-x})]| \leqslant K(1 + |x|^{\gamma}) \tag{27}$$

for some strictly positive constants K and γ.

The purpose of conditions A and C is to guarantee that certain functionals of S and Y have two continuous derivatives. Here we remark that for $D_x^m[\mathrm{e}^{-x}\hat{f}(\mathrm{e}^{-x},t)]$ to exist and be continuous it is not necessary that $u(y,t)$ be continuously differentiable.

Condition B is to ensure that the moments of (Z,S) have certain nice properties under P and Q. To have a feel for the restrictiveness of condition C, we note that, if

$$V(y)=\frac{1}{1-b}\,y^{1-b},$$

then $b \geqslant 1$. In many specific situations, differentiability will obtain under much weaker conditions. For example, in section 3 of this paper, we consider a special case of the general model developed here. All the HARA utility functions give rise to the desired differentiability conditions.

2.2 Main results

We shall give explicit characterizations of an optimal consumption–portfolio policy under the following assumption that the optimal consumption policy is also a solution to a corresponding static maximization problem. Assumption 2 is valid under quite mild regularity conditions, for which we refer the reader to sections 2 and 4 of Cox and Huang [6].

Henceforth we make the following assumption.

Assumption 2 There exists a solution to (12), denoted by (α,θ,c,W), if and only if (c,W) is a solution to

$$\sup_{(\hat{c},\hat{W})\in L_+^p(\nu)\times L_+^p(P)} E\left[\int_0^T u(\hat{c},t)\,\mathrm{d}t+V(\hat{W})\right]$$

s.t.

$$B(0)E\left[\int_0^T \frac{\hat{c}(t)\eta(t)}{B(t)}\,\mathrm{d}t+\frac{\hat{W}\eta(T)}{B(T)}\right]=W_0. \tag{28}$$

Remark 4 The idea behind assumption 2 is as follows. The assumption that the martingale measure is unique, the integrability restriction on the trading strategies of (11), and some regularity conditions imply that any element of $L^p(\nu^\star)\times L^p(Q)$ is financed by an admissible trading strategy, where $\nu^\star$ is the product measure generated by Q and the Lebesgue measure. In such a case, as long as the solution to (28) lies in $L^p(\nu^\star)\times L^p(Q)$, assumption 2 will be valid. ■

It follows from the Lagrangian theory (e.g. Holmes [20], Rockafellar [33]) that, if (c, W) is a solution to (28), there exists a strictly positive real number λ such that

$$u_{c+}[c(\omega,t),t]\begin{cases}\leqslant \dfrac{\lambda\eta(\omega,t)B(0)}{B(\omega,t)} \leqslant u_{c-}[c(\omega,t),t] & \text{for } \nu\text{–a.e. } (\omega,t) \text{ such that } c(\omega,t)>0,\\[2ex] \leqslant \dfrac{\lambda\eta(\omega,t)B(0)}{B(\omega,t)} & \text{for } \nu\text{–a.e. } (\omega,t) \text{ such that } c(\omega,t)=0,\end{cases} \tag{29}$$

$$V'_{+}[W(\omega)]\begin{cases}\leqslant \dfrac{\lambda\eta(\omega,T)B(0)}{B(\omega,T)} \leqslant V'_{-}[W(\omega)] & \text{for } P\text{–a.e. } \omega \text{ such that } W(\omega)>0,\\[2ex] \leqslant \dfrac{\lambda\eta(\omega,T)B(0)}{B(\omega,T)} & \text{for } P\text{–a.e. } \omega \text{ such that } W(\omega)=0,\end{cases}$$

where ν–a.e. (ω, t) means almost every (ω, t) with respect to the measure ν.

Now let $\{Z(t); t \in [0, T]\}$ be defined as in (15) with the initial condition $Z(0) = 1/\lambda$. Then the above first-order conditions become

$$u_{c+}[c(\omega,t),t]\begin{cases}\leqslant Z(\omega,t)^{-1} \leqslant u_{c-}(c(\omega,t),t) & \text{for } \nu\text{–a.e. } (\omega,t) \text{ such that } c(\omega,t)>0,\\[2ex] \leqslant Z(\omega,t)^{-1} & \text{for } \nu\text{–a.e. } (\omega,t) \text{ such that } c(\omega,t)=0,\end{cases} \tag{30}$$

$$V'_{+}[W(\omega)]\begin{cases}\leqslant Z(\omega,T)^{-1} \leqslant V'_{-}[W(\omega)] & \text{for } P\text{–a.e. } \omega \text{ such that } W(\omega)>0,\\[2ex] \leqslant Z(\omega,T)^{-1} & \text{for } P\text{–a.e. } \omega \text{ such that } W(\omega)=0,\end{cases}$$

where we have used (17). Thus we have

$$\begin{aligned} c(t) &= \hat{f}[Z(t)^{-1}, t] = \hat{f}(\mathrm{e}^{-Y(t)}, t) && \nu\text{–a.e.},\\ W &= V'^{-1}_{+}[Z(T)^{-1}] = V'^{-1}_{+}(\mathrm{e}^{-Y(T)}) && \text{a.s.,}\end{aligned} \tag{31}$$

where we have used the fact that $Y(t) = \ln Z(t)$.

Here is our first main result.

Theorem 1 Suppose that there exists a solution to (28) with a Lagrangian multiplier $\lambda > 0$ and that conditions A and C are satisfied. Let $Z(0) = 1/\lambda$

and define the function

$$F[Z(t), S(t), t] = Z(t)E\left[\int_t^T Z(s)^{-1}\hat{f}\{Z(s)^{-1}, s\}\, ds + V_+'^{-1}\{Z(T)^{-1}\}Z(T)^{-1}\,\middle|\, Z(t), S(t)\right], \quad (32)$$

where we have fixed a right-continuous version of the conditional expectation. Then $D_y^m F(y,t)$ and $F_t(y,t)$ exist and are continuous for $m \leqslant 2$, and together with F satisfy the linear partial differential equation

$$\mathscr{L}F + F_t = F_Z Z\varkappa^{\mathrm{T}}\varkappa - F_S^{\mathrm{T}}\sigma\varkappa + rF - \hat{f}(Z^{-1}, t) \quad (33)$$

with boundary conditions

$$\begin{aligned} F(Z, S, T) &= V_+'^{-1}(Z^{-1}) \\ F[Z(0), S(0), 0] &= W_0, \end{aligned} \quad (34)$$

where $\mathscr{L}$ is the differential generator of (Z, S) under P and

$$\mathscr{L}F = \tfrac{1}{2}\operatorname{tr}(F_{SS}\sigma\sigma^{\mathrm{T}}) + \tfrac{1}{2}F_{ZZ}Z^2\varkappa^{\mathrm{T}}\varkappa + F_{SZ}^{\mathrm{T}}\sigma\varkappa + F_S^{\mathrm{T}}(\zeta - \iota) + F_Z Z(r + |\varkappa|^2).$$

The optimal portfolio policy is

$$\begin{aligned} \theta(t) = F_S[Z(t), S(t), t] &+ \{\sigma[S(t), t]\,\sigma[S(t), t]^{\mathrm{T}}\}^{-1} \\ &\times \{\zeta[S(t), t] - r[S(t), t]\,S(t)\}Z(t)F_Z[Z(t), S(t), t] \qquad \nu\text{–a.e.}, \end{aligned} \quad (35)$$

$$\alpha(t) = \frac{F[Z(t), S(t), t] - \theta(t)^{\mathrm{T}}S(t)}{B(t)} \qquad \nu\text{–a.e.},$$

and the optimal consumption–final wealth pair is specified in (31).

PROOF Let (c, W) be the solution to (28). Then (c, W) satisfies (31) and according to assumption 1 is an optimal consumption–final wealth pair to (12). Our task now is to construct an optimal trading strategy that finances (c, W). We first claim that F defined in (32) gives the value over time of (c, W). Moreover, it has continuous $D_y^m F(y,t)$ and $F_t(y,t)$ for $m \leqslant 2$ under conditions A and C. Note that, under condition A, (Y, S) is a diffusion process and thus possesses the strong Markov property. Moreover, since $Z(t) = \mathrm{e}^{Y(t)}$, (Z, S) is also a diffusion process as it has continuous sample paths and possesses the strong Markov property. By lemma 4, the value of (c, W) at time t is

$$B(t)E^{\star}\left[\int_t^T \frac{\hat{f}\{Z(s)^{-1}, s\}}{B(s)}\, ds + \frac{V_+'^{-1}\{Z(T)^{-1}\}}{B(T)}\,\middle|\,\mathscr{F}_t\right]$$

$$= \eta(t)^{-1}B(t)E\left[\int_t^T \frac{\hat{f}\{Z(s)^{-1}, s\}\eta(s)}{B(s)}\, ds + \frac{V_+'^{-1}\{Z(T)^{-1}\}\eta(T)}{B(T)}\,\middle|\,\mathscr{F}_t\right]$$

$$= Z(t)E\left[\int_t^T Z(s)^{-1}\hat{f}\{Z(s)^{-1}, s\}\,\mathrm{d}s + Z(T)^{-1}V_+'^{-1}\{Z(T)^{-1}\}\,\middle|\, Z(t), S(t)\right]$$

$$= F[Z(t), S(t), t],$$

where the first equality follows from (14), the second equality follows from (17) and the above mentioned fact that (Z, S) has the strong Markov property, and the third equality follows from the definition of F. Immediately, we have $F[Z(0), S(0), 0] = W_0$ and $F(Z, S, T) = V_+'^{-1}(Z^{-1})$, which are the boundary conditions of (34).

Now we claim that $D_y^m F(y, t)$ and $F_t(y, t)$ exist and are continuous for $m \leqslant 2$. To see this, we define another function

$$G[Y(t), S(t), t] \equiv \mathrm{e}^{Y(t)}E\left[\int_t^T \mathrm{e}^{-Y(s)}\hat{f}(\mathrm{e}^{-Y(s)}, s)\,\mathrm{d}s + \mathrm{e}^{-Y(T)}V_+'^{-1}(\mathrm{e}^{-Y(T)})\,|\, Y(t), S(t)\right], \tag{36}$$

where we have fixed a right-continuous version of the conditional expectation. It is easily seen that $G[Y(t), S(t), t] = F[Z(t), S(t), t]$. Conditions A and C and a multidimensional version of remark 11.3 of Gihman and Skorohod [16, p.77] show that $D_y^m G(y, t)$ and $G_t(y, t)$ exist and are continuous for $m \leqslant 2$. It then follows that $D_y^m F(y, t)$ and $F_t(y, t)$ exist and are continuous for $m \leqslant 2$. Moreover, we can verify that $F_Z = Z^{-1}G_Y$, $F_S = G_S$, $F_t = G_t$, $F_{ZZ} = Z^{-2}G_{YY} - Z^{-2}G_Y$, $F_{SS} = G_{SS}$, and $F_{ZS} = Z^{-1}G_{YS}$. We have thus proved our claim that $D_y^m F(y, t)$ and $F_t(y, t)$ are continuous for $m \leqslant 2$ under conditions A and C.

Since $D_y^m F(y, t)$ and $F_t(y, t)$ are continuous for $m \leqslant 2$, Itô's lemma implies that

$$\frac{F[Z(t), S(t), t]}{B(t)} + \int_0^t \frac{\hat{f}[Z(s)^{-1}, s]}{B(s)}\,\mathrm{d}s$$

$$= \frac{F(0)}{B(0)} + \int_0^t \frac{F_S(s)^{\mathrm{T}}\sigma(s) - F_Z(s)Z(s)\varkappa(s)^{\mathrm{T}}}{B(s)}\,\mathrm{d}w^\star(s)$$

$$+ \int_0^t \{\mathscr{L}F(s) + F_s(s) - F_Z(s)Z(s)\varkappa(s)^{\mathrm{T}}\varkappa(s) + F_S(s)^{\mathrm{T}}\sigma(s)\varkappa(s) - r(s)F(s) + \hat{f}[Z(s)^{-1}, s]\}\,[B(s)]\,\mathrm{d}s^{-1}, \tag{37}$$

where $\mathscr{L}$ is the differential generator of Z and S under P. By lemmas 3 and 4, the left-hand side of the above relation is an L^p martingale under Q. Now note that the integrand of the Itô integral on the right-hand side is a continuous function of $Z(t)$, $S(t)$, and t, and thus

$$\int_0^T \frac{|F_S(s)^{\mathrm{T}}\sigma(s) - F_Z(s)Z(s)\varkappa(s)^{\mathrm{T}}|^2}{B^2(s)}\,\mathrm{d}s < \infty \qquad \text{a.s.} \tag{38}$$

Let

$$T_n \equiv \inf\left\{t \in [0, T]: \int_0^t \frac{|F_S(s)^{\mathrm{T}}\sigma(s) - F_Z(s)Z(s)\varkappa(s)^{\mathrm{T}}|^2}{B^2(s)}\, \mathrm{d}s \geqslant n\right\},$$

where we have used the convention that if the infimum does not exist it is set to be T. By (38), we know that $T_n \to T$ a.s. as $n \to \infty$. On the stochastic interval $[0, T_n]$, the Itô integral on the right-hand side of (37) is an $L^p(Q)$ martingale by lemma 3. It then follows that the second integral on the right-hand side of (37) must also be a martingale on $[0, T_n]$. Indeed, it is a martingale with absolutely continuous sample paths. It is known that any continuous martingale must be a constant or have unbounded variation sample paths (see Fisk [12]). Hence the integrand of the second integral on the right-hand side of (37) must vanish on $[0, T_n]$. Since the integrand of the Lebesgue integral of the right-hand side of (37) is continuous and $T_n \to T$ a.s., we have, a.s.,

$$\mathscr{L}F + F_t = F_Z Z \varkappa^{\mathrm{T}} \varkappa - F_S^{\mathrm{T}} \sigma \varkappa + rF - \hat{f}(Z^{-1}, t)$$

which is (33).

Now we are ready to provide ways to compute an optimal trading strategy. Let (α, θ) be an optimal trading strategy that finances (c, W). From lemma 4 we know that

$$\frac{W}{B(T)} + \int_0^T \frac{\hat{f}[Z(s)^{-1}, s]}{B(s)}\, \mathrm{d}s = \frac{F[Z(0), S(0), 0]}{B(0)} + \int_0^T \frac{\theta(s)^{\mathrm{T}}\sigma(s)}{B(s)}\, \mathrm{d}w^\star(s) \quad (39)$$

lies in $L^p(Q)$. We can thus subtract (37) evaluated at $t = T$ from (39) and take the expectation under Q of the pth power of the difference to obtain

$$E^\star\left[\left(\int_0^T (\theta(t) - [F_S + (\sigma\sigma^{\mathrm{T}})^{-1}(\zeta - rS)ZF_Z])^{\mathrm{T}}\sigma\sigma^{\mathrm{T}} \times \frac{(\theta(t) - [F_S + (\sigma\sigma^{\mathrm{T}})^{-1}(\zeta - rS)ZF_Z])}{B^2(t)}\, \mathrm{d}t\right)^{p/2}\right] = 0.$$

By assumption, $\sigma\sigma^{\mathrm{T}}$ is positive definite. We therefore have

$$\theta(t) = F_S[Z(t), S(t), t] + \{\sigma[S(t), t]\sigma[S(t), t]^{\mathrm{T}}\}^{-1} \times\{\zeta[S(t), t] - r[S(t), t]S(t)\}Z(t)F_Z[Z(t), S(t), t] \qquad \nu\text{–a.e.}$$

The rest of the assertion follows immediately. ■

Note that in theorem 1 we used condition A, which involves the process Y rather than Z. This is because the parameters of the process Z fail to satisfy a uniform Lipschitz condition which is needed for the differentiability of the function F. Thus we transformed Z into Y. Condition A together with condition C then ensures that the G function has the desired derivatives and so does F.

Theorem 1 is most useful when it is used together with Cox and Huang [6] where sufficient conditions for the existence of an optimal policy are given. Then, provided that conditions A and C are satisfied, the optimal policy can be computed by taking derivatives of the function F, which gives the value of the optimally invested wealth over time. However, conditions A and C may not be satisfied in applications. From the proof of theorem 1, it should be clear that the sole function of conditions A and C is to ensure that the F have the desired derivatives for Itô's lemma to apply. Thus, if we can verify that F has the desired derivatives through other means, say through direct computation, then the conclusion of theorem 1 follows. Theorem 2 states this fact.

Theorem 2 Let F be defined as in theorem 1. Suppose that there exists a solution to (28) with a Lagrangian multiplier $\lambda > 0$ or equivalently that there exists $Z_0 > 0$ such that $F[Z_0, S(0), 0] = W_0$ and that (31) lies in $L^p(\nu) \times L^p(P)$ when $Z(0) = Z_0$. If $D_y^m F(y, t)$ and $F_t(y, t)$ exist and are continuous for $m \leqslant 2$, then the optimal policy is specified in (31) and (35). Moreover, F satisfies (33) and (34).

PROOF Note that if there exists $Z_0 > 0$ such that $F[Z_0, S(0), 0] = W_0$ and (31) lies in $L^p(\nu) \times L^p(P)$ with $Z(0) = Z_0$, then there exists a solution to (28) by the Lagrangian theory and thus there is a solution to (12). The rest of the proof is then identical with that of theorem 1. ■

Note that, consistent with results using stochastic dynamic programming (e.g. Breeden [3]), (35) indicates that the optimal risky asset portfolio is composed of two parts: N portfolios most highly correlated with "state variables" S and an instantaneous mean–variance efficient portfolio, which are the first term and the second term respectively on the right-hand side of the first equation of (35). The mean–variance-efficient portfolio here is just the growth-optimal portfolio discussed earlier. The portfolio having the maximum correlation with respect to S_n is just S_n itself.

Theorems 1 and 2 are characterization theorems – if an optimal policy exists and F has the desired derivatives, then the optimal policy can be computed by taking derivatives of F. In many instances, we can verify neither the existence of a solution to (28) by citing an existence theorem nor the desired differentiability of F. However, we may be able to construct a candidate policy and then verify that it is indeed an optimal policy. This procedure is termed the *verification procedure*. The following theorem gives a verification procedure and will be termed the verification theorem, which is the counterpart of the verification theorem in dynamic programming with one distinct aspect – in dynamic programming we work with processes under P, while here we work mostly with processes under the equivalent martingale measure Q.

Theorem 3 Let condition B be satisfied. Suppose that there exists $Z_0 > 0$ and $F:(0,\infty)\times\mathbb{R}^N\times[0,T]\mapsto\mathbb{R}_+$ such that $DF_y^m(y,t)$ and $F_t(y,t)$ are continuous for $m \leqslant 2$ and that F is a solution to the partial differential equation of (33) with boundary conditions (34) by taking $Z(0)=Z_0$ and $F(Z,S,t)\rightarrow F(Z,S,T)$ as $t\rightarrow T$. Suppose also that, for all t,

$$|F(y,t)| \leqslant K(1+|y|^{\gamma}) \qquad \forall y \in (0,\infty)\times\mathbb{R}^N$$

for some strictly positive constants K and γ, and that there exist strictly positive constants K_1 and γ_1 such that

$$|\hat{f}(x^{-1},t)| \leqslant K_1(1+|x|^{\gamma_1}), \qquad |V_+'^{-1}(x^{-1})| \leqslant K_1(1+|x|^{\gamma_1})$$

for all $x \in (0,\infty)$. Then there exists a solution to (12) with optimal policies described in (31) and (35) and with $Z(0)=Z_0$.

PROOF Define Z according to (15) with $Z(0)=Z_0$. Let $F:(0,\infty)\times\mathbb{R}^n\mapsto\mathbb{R}$ be the solution to (33) with boundary conditions (34). Since F has continuous partial derivatives, Itô's lemma implies that (37) is valid. Substituting (33) into (37) and evaluating (37) at $t=T$ gives

$$\frac{F[Z(T),S(T),T]}{B(T)}+\int_0^T\frac{\hat{f}[Z(s)^{-1},s]}{B(s)}\,ds$$
$$=\frac{F(0)}{B(0)}+\int_0^T\frac{F_S(s)^{\mathrm{T}}\sigma(s)-F_Z(s)Z(s)\varkappa(s)^{\mathrm{T}}}{B(s)}\,dw^{\star}(s). \qquad (40)$$

Suppose for the time being that the Itô integral on the right-hand side of (40) is a martingale under Q. We take the expectation under Q of both sides of (40) and use the boundary conditions of (34) to obtain

$$E^{\star}\left[\frac{V_+'^{-1}\{Z(T)^{-1}\}}{B(T)}+\int_0^T\frac{\hat{f}[Z(t)^{-1},t\}}{B(t)}\,dt\right]=\frac{F[Z(0),S(0),0]}{B(0)}=\frac{W_0}{B(0)} \qquad (41)$$

That is, $(\hat{f}[Z(t)^{-1},t],V_+'^{-1}[Z(T)^{-1}])$ exhausts the initial wealth (recall lemma 4). If we can verify that $(\hat{f}[Z(t)^{-1},t],\ V_+'^{-1}[Z(T)^{-1}])$ lies in $L^p(\nu)\times L^p(P)$ then we are done, since it will be a solution to (28) and a solution to (12) by assumption 2. The optimal trading strategy is then (35) by theorem 2.

We shall first show that $(\hat{f}[Z(t)^{-1},t],V_+'^{-1}[Z(T)^{-1}])$ lies in $L^p(\nu)\times L^p(P)$. Under condition B, we know that $\bar{\xi}$ and $\bar{\sigma}$ satisfy a linear growth condition and a local Lipschitz condition. Theorem 5.2.3 of Friedman [14] then implies that, for all strictly positive integers m, there exist constants L_m such that

$$E[|Z(t)|^{2m}] \leqslant [1+|Z(0)|^{2m}]\,\exp(L_m t)$$

This and the growth condition on $\hat{f}$ imply that

$$E[|\hat{f}\{Z(t)^{-1},t\}|^p] < K_3 \exp(Lt)$$

for some strictly positive constants K_3 and L. The Fubini theorem then implies that $\{\hat{f}[Z(t)^{-1},t]\} \in L^p(\nu)$. Similar arguments show that $V'^{-1}_{+}[Z(T)^{-1}] \in L^p(P)$.

Next we want to show that (41) holds generally. First note that the linear growth condition and local Lipschitz condition on $\bar{\zeta} + \bar{\sigma}\varkappa$ and $\bar{\sigma}$ in condition B imply that, for all strictly positive integers m, there exist constants L_m such that

$$E^\star[|Z(t)|^{2m}] \leqslant [1 + |Z(0)|^{2m}] \exp(L_m t). \tag{42}$$

This and the growth condition on $\hat{f}$ and V'^{-1}_{+} immediately imply

$$E^\star\left[\frac{V'^{-1}_{+}\{Z(T)^{-1}\}}{B(T)} + \int_0^T \frac{\hat{f}\{Z(t)^{-1},t\}}{B(t)}\,\mathrm{d}t\right] < \infty.$$

For convenience, we shall write $\psi(t) = (S(t), Z(t))$ and $\hat{\psi}(t) = (S(t), \ln Z(t))$. Now let

$$T_n \equiv \inf\{t \in [0, T] : |\hat{\psi}(t)| \geqslant n\},$$

where we have used the convention that if $\{t \in [0,1] : |\hat{\psi}(t)| \geqslant n\}$ is empty, then $T_n = 1$. On the stochastic interval $[0, T_n]$, $|S(t)|$ and $|\ln Z(t)|$ are bounded by n. Since F_S, F_Z, σ, and $\varkappa$ are continuous functions of S, Z, and t, the integrand of the Itô integral on the right-hand side of (40) is bounded on $[0, T_n]$ and hence the Itô integral is an L^p martingale under Q by lemma 3. (Here we note that the stopping time is defined with respect to the process $\hat{\psi}$ rather than ψ, since F_Z and F_S can become unbounded when Z approaches zero.) It follows that

$$E^\star\left[\frac{F\{Z(T_n), S(T_n), T_n\}}{B(T_n)} + \int_0^{T_n} \frac{\hat{f}[Z(s)^{-1},s]}{B(s)}\,\mathrm{d}s\right] = \frac{F[Z(0), S(0), 0]}{B(0)} \tag{43}$$

By the continuity of F_Z, F_S, $\varkappa$, and B, we know that $T_n \rightarrow T$ a.s. Thus, as $n \rightarrow \infty$,

$$\int_0^{T_n} \frac{\hat{f}[Z(s)^{-1},s]}{B(s)}\,\mathrm{d}s \rightarrow \int_0^T \frac{\hat{f}[Z(s)^{-1},s]}{B(s)}\,\mathrm{d}s \qquad \text{a.s.}$$

The Lebesgue convergence theorem implies that, as $n \rightarrow \infty$,

$$E^\star\left[\int_0^{T_n} \frac{\hat{f}\{Z(s)^{-1},s\}}{B(s)}\,\mathrm{d}s\right] \rightarrow E^\star\left[\int_0^T \frac{\hat{f}\{Z(s)^{-1},s\}}{B(s)}\,\mathrm{d}s\right].$$

If we can show that

$$E^\star\left[\frac{F\{Z(T_n), S(T_n), T_n\}}{B(T_n)}\right] \rightarrow E^\star\left[\frac{F\{Z(T), S(T), T\}}{B(T)}\right]$$

as $n \to \infty$ then we are done, since we can let $n \to \infty$ in (43), and (41) follows. The arguments for this use condition B and the growth condition on F and are contained in theorem V.4.2 of Fleming and Rishel [13]. For completeness of the proof, we shall repeat their arguments. Note that we shall be working with the process ψ in the remainder of the proof.

Put

$$H(x) \equiv Q\left[\sup_{0 \leqslant t \leqslant T} |\psi(t)| > x\right].$$

Condition B implies that there exists $x_0 > 0$ such that for all positive integers m there is an $M_1 > 0$ with

$$H(x) \leqslant M_1 x^{-2m} \qquad \forall x \geqslant x_0. \tag{44}$$

Now $F[Z(T_n), S(T_n), T_n] \to F[Z(T), S(T), T]$ a.s. since F is continuous in Z and S and by the hypothesis $F(Z, S, t) \to F(Z, S, T)$ as $t \to T$. For $R > 0$, let

$$\chi_R = \begin{cases} 1 & \text{if } \sup_{0 \leqslant t \leqslant T} |\psi(t)| \leqslant R \\ 0 & \text{if } \sup_{0 \leqslant t \leqslant T} |\psi(t)| > R. \end{cases}$$

By the dominated convergence theorem

$$\lim_{n \to \infty} E^\star[F\{Z(T_n), S(T_n), T_n\}\chi_R] \to E^\star[F\{Z(T), S(T), T\}\chi_R]$$

for each $R > 0$. Since $F(Z, S, t)$ satisfies a polynomial growth condition

$$|F(y, t)| \leqslant K(1 + |y|^\gamma),$$

we can write

$$|F[Z(T_n), S(T_n), T_n]| \leqslant K(1 + \sup_{0 \leqslant t \leqslant T} |\psi(t)|^\gamma).$$

Take $2m > \gamma$ in (44). Then

$$\int^\infty x^{\gamma - 1} H(x)\, \mathrm{d}x < \infty,$$

which implies that, upon integration by parts on (R, ∞),

$$\lim_{R \to \infty} \int_R^\infty (1 + x^\gamma)\, \mathrm{d}H(x) = 0.$$

Thus

$$E^\star[|F\{Z(T_n), S(T_n), T_n\}|(1 - \chi_R)] \leqslant -K \int_R^\infty (1 + x^\gamma)\, \mathrm{d}H(x),$$

and the right-hand side tends to zero as $R \to \infty$. This shows that

$$E^\star[F\{Z(T_n), S(T_n), T_n\}] \to E^\star[F\{Z(T), S(T), T\}]$$

as $n \to \infty$, which was to be proved. ∎

Note that, unlike the verification theorem of dynamic programming, the verification procedure in theorem 3 involves a *linear* partial differential equation. Note also that in deriving (43) we have made a logarithmic transformation of Z into Y. This is because Z is strictly positive with probability one and F_Z and F_S may be unbounded as Z approaches zero. There is no need to perform the same transformation on S since, by assumption, S takes its values in the whole of $\mathbb{R}^N$. When some of the price processes are strictly positive with probability one, they can similarly be handled by a logarithmic transformation.

For the rest of this section, we shall assume that there exists a solution to (28) and conditions A and C are satisfied.

We use $\{W(t); t \in [0, T]\}$ to denote the process of the optimally invested wealth:

$$W(t) = F[Z(t), S(t), t].$$

It is clear that $W(T) = W$ a.s. The following proposition shows that after the optimally invested wealth reaches zero, the optimal consumption–portfolio policies are zeros.

Define an optional time $\mathscr{T} = \inf\{t \in [0, T) : W(t) \leqslant 0\}$, which is the first time the optimally invested wealth reaches zero. As a convention, when the infimum does not exist, it is set to be T.

Proposition 1 On the stochastic interval $[\mathscr{T}, T]$,

$$\begin{aligned} \theta[Z(t), S(t), t] &= 0 \qquad \nu\text{–a.e.} \\ \alpha[Z(t), S(t), t] &= 0 \qquad \nu\text{–a.e.} \\ c(t) &= 0 \qquad \nu\text{–a.e.} \\ W &= 0 \qquad \text{a.s.} \end{aligned}$$

PROOF From the definition of F, it is clear that it is equal to zero at $\mathscr{T}$ if and only if on $[\mathscr{T}, T]$ the optimal consumption and final wealth are zeros. Arguments similar to the second half of the proof of Theorem 1 prove the rest of the assertion. ■

Note that if we consider the agent's problem in the context of the theory of stochastic control, given the setup of the securities markets, we would like the optimal controls such as (α, θ, c, W) to be feedback controls. That is, the optimal controls at each time t depend only upon time t, the values of $S(t)$, and the agent's optimally invested wealth at that time. In the above theorem, the optimal controls are functions of $S(t)$, $Z(t)$, and t. However, Z is determined in part by the agent's initial wealth through the initial condition $Z(0) = 1/\lambda$. The following proposition shows that, given $S(t)$ and t, the agent's optimally invested wealth at time t is an invertible function of Z if $u(y,t)$ and $V(y)$ are differentiable in y. Hence the optimal controls are indeed feedback controls.

Proposition 2 $F_Z \geqslant 0$. Furthermore, if $u(y,t)$ and $V(y)$ are differentiable in y, then $F_Z > 0$ if $F > 0$, and there exists a function $F^{-1}[W(t), S(t), t] = Z(t)$ if $W(t) > 0$. In addition, F^{-1}_{WW}, F^{-1}_{W}, F^{-1}_{SS}, F^{-1}_{S}, and F^{-1}_{t} exist and are continuous. Thus we have

$$\theta[Z(t), S(t), t] = \begin{cases} \theta\{F^{-1}[W(t), S(t), t], S(t), t\} & \nu\text{–a.e. if } W(t) > 0, \\ 0 & \text{if } W(t) = 0, \end{cases}$$

$$\alpha[Z(t), S(t), t] = \begin{cases} \theta\{F^{-1}[W(t), S(t), t], S(t), t\} & \nu\text{–a.e. if } W(t) > 0, \\ 0 & \text{if } W(t) = 0, \end{cases}$$

$$c(t) = \begin{cases} \hat{f}\{1/F^{-1}[W(t)\ , S(t), t], t\} & \nu\text{–a.e. if } W(t) > 0, \\ 0 & \text{if } W(t) = 0, \end{cases}$$

$$W = W(T) \qquad \text{a.s.} \tag{45}$$

PROOF It follows from Friedman [14, theorem 5.5.5] and the fact that $\partial Z(s)/\partial Z(t) = Z(s)/Z(t)$ if $s \geqslant t$ that

$$F_Z[Z(t), S(t), t]$$

$$= -E\left[\int_t^T \frac{\hat{f}'\{Z(s)^{-1}, s\}}{Z^2(s)}\,ds + \frac{V'^{-1\prime}_{+}\{Z(T)^{-1}\}}{Z^2(T)} \,\Big|\, Z(t), S(t)\right],$$

where $\hat{f}'$ denotes the derivative of $\hat{f}$ with respect to its first argument and $V'^{-1\prime}_{+}$ denotes the derivative of V'^{-1}_{+}. Thus $F_Z \geqslant 0$ since $\hat{f}(y,t)$ and $V'^{-1}_{+}(y)$ are decreasing in y. Note that if $u(y,t)$ is differentiable in y then $\hat{f}$ is strictly decreasing when $\hat{f}(y,t) > 0$, and similarly V'^{-1}_{+} is strictly decreasing if V is differentiable and $V'^{-1}_{+}(y) > 0$. If $F_Z = 0$, we must have $F[Z(t), S(t), t] = 0$, and proposition 1 gives the optimal consumption and portfolio policies. If $F[Z(t), S(t), t] > 0$, then $F_Z[Z(t), S(t), t] > 0$. Therefore, given $S(t)$ and t, $Z(t)$ is an invertible function of $W(t)$ if $W(t) > 0$. Let this function be denoted by $F^{-1}[W(t), S(t), t]$. The differentiability of F^{-1} follows from the implicit function theorem (e.g. Hestenes [19, p.172]). The rest of the assertion then follows from theorem 1 and substitution. ■

Remark 5 For $F_Z > 0$ when $F > 0$, it is certainly not necessary that $u(y,t)$ and $V(y)$ be differentiable in y. In the special case of our current general model to be dealt with in section 3, many utility functions that are concave and nonlinear yield $F_Z > 0$ for $F > 0$. ■

When utility functions have a finite marginal utility at zero, the optimal consumption policy may involve zero consumption. The following proposition identifies the circumstances in which optimal consumption is zero.

Proposition 3 Suppose that $u_{c+}(0,t) < \infty$. Consumption at time t is zero only if $W(t) \leqslant F[u_{c+}(0,t)^{-1}, S(t), t]$. Suppose in addition that $u(y,t)$ and $V(y)$ are differentiable in y. Then an optimal policy has the property that consumption will be zero if and only if $W(t) \leqslant F[u_{c+}(0,t)^{-1}, S(t), t]$.

PROOF From (30) we know that $c(t) \leqslant 0$ if and only if $u_{c+}(0,t) \leqslant Z(t)^{-1}$. It then follows from proposition 2 that $u_{c+}(0,t) \leqslant Z(t)^{-1}$ only if

$$F[u_{c+}(0,t)^{-1}, S(t), t] \geqslant F[Z(t), S(t), t] = W(t).$$

This is the first assertion. Next suppose that both $u(y,t)$ and $V(y)$ are differentiable. We want to show that if $W(t) \leqslant F[u_{c+}(0,t)^{-1}, S(t), t]$, then $c(t) = 0$. We take two cases.

Case 1: $W(t) = 0$. Then proposition 1 shows that $c(t) = 0$.
Case 2: $W(t) > 0$. Proposition 1 also shows that when $W(t) > 0$, $F_Z > 0$. Thus $u_{c+}(0,t) \leqslant Z(t)^{-1}$ if and only if

$$F[u_{c+}(0,t)^{-1}, S(t), t] \geqslant F[Z(t), S(t), t] = W(t). \qquad \blacksquare$$

By inspection of (35) and (45) we can easily see that, when $F_Z > 0$, the feedback controls are differentiable functions of $W(t)$ and $S(t)$ (recall that condition A is imposed). In particular, the optimal consumption policy is twice continuously differentiable in $W(t)$ and $S(t)$, which follows directly from the assumption that $\hat{f}(y,t)$ is twice continuously differentiable with respect to y (see condition C).

The following proposition gives a complete characterization of utility functions such that $\hat{f}(y,t)$ is twice continuously differentiable with respect to y, given that $u(y,t)$ is differentiable in y.

Proposition 4 Suppose that $u(y,t)$ is differentiable with respect to y. $D_y^m \hat{f}(y,t)$ exists and is continuous for $m \leqslant 2$ if and only if $D_y^m u(y,t)$ exists and is continuous for $m \leqslant 3$, and, for $u_{y+}(0,t) < \infty$,

$$\lim_{y \downarrow 0} -\frac{u_y(y,t)}{u_{yy}(y,t)} = 0 \tag{46}$$

and

$$\lim_{y \downarrow 0} -\frac{u_{yyy}(y,t)}{u_{yy}(y,t)} \left[\frac{u_y(y,t)}{u_{yy}(y,t)}\right]^2 = 0. \tag{47}$$

Similar conclusions also hold for $V(y)$.

PROOF On the interval $(0, \infty)$, u_y is continuous and strictly decreasing. Hence $D_y^m \hat{f}(y, t)$ exists and is continuous for $m \leqslant 2$ in $(0, u_y(0, t))$ if and only if $D_y^m u(y, t)$ exists and is continuous for $m \leqslant 3$. When $u_y(0, t) < \infty$ on $(u_y(0, t), \infty)$, $D_y^m \hat{f}(y, t)$ is equal to zero for $m \leqslant 2$. This implies (46) and (47).

The proof for $V(y)$ is identical. ■

2.3 Relation to dynamic programming

Traditionally, the agent's optimal consumption–portfolio policy has been computed by stochastic dynamic programming (e.g. Merton [30]). We shall now demonstrate the connection between our approach and stochastic dynamic programming.

The usual formulation of the consumption–portfolio problem uses a consumption policy and a vector of dollar amounts invested in risky assets to be the controls. The former is denoted by $c[W(t), S(t), t]$, and the latter will be called an *investment policy* and be denoted by $A[W(t), S(t), t]$. Given a pair of controls (c, A), the dynamic behavior of the agent's wealth is

$$W(t) = W_0 + \int_0^t \{W(s)r(s) - c(s) + A(s)I_{S^{-1}}(t)[\zeta(s) - r(s)S(s)]\}\, ds$$

$$+ \int_0^t A(s)I_{S^{-1}}(s)\sigma(s)\, dw(s) \qquad \forall t \in [0, T] \text{ a.s.}$$

where $I_{S^{-1}}(t)$ is a diagonal matrix with diagonal elements $S_n(t)^{-1}$. Define

$$\mathcal{J}[W(t), S(t), t] = \sup_{c,A} E\left[\int_t^T u\{c(s), s\}\, ds + V\{W(T)\} \middle| W(t), S(t)\right]$$

subject to the constraints that the wealth follows the above dynamics, that consumption cannot be negative, and that

$$\mathcal{J}[0, S(t), t] = \int_t^T u(0, s)\, ds + V(0). \tag{48}$$

The last constraint is basically a nonnegative wealth constraint that rules out free lunches.

The existence of a pair of optimal controls is a nontrivial problem. We shall refer readers to Krylov [28], for example, for an extensive treatment using the theory of stochastic controls. For a much easier approach specific to the consumption–portfolio problem, we refer readers to Cox and Huang [6] and the references cited therein.

We assume that there exists a pair of optimal controls (c, A) and that $\mathcal{J}$

has two continuous derivatives with respect to its first two arguments and a continuous derivative with respect to t. The Bellman equation is then

$$0 = \max_{\hat{c}(t),\hat{A}(t)} \{u[\hat{c}(t), t] + \mathscr{L}\mathcal{J}[W(t), S(t), t] + \mathcal{J}_t[W(t), S(t), t]\}, \tag{49}$$

where $\mathscr{L}$ is the differential generator of (W, S). The optimal controls satisfy the first-order necessary conditions

$$\begin{aligned} u_{c+}[c(t), t] &\begin{cases} \leqslant \mathcal{J}_W(t) \leqslant u_{c-}[c(t), t] & \text{if } c(t) > 0, \\ \leqslant \mathcal{J}_W(t) & \text{if } c(t) = 0, \end{cases} \\ V'_{+}(W) &\begin{cases} \leqslant \mathcal{J}_W(T) \leqslant V'_{-}(W) & \text{if } W > 0, \\ \leqslant \mathcal{J}_W(T) & \text{if } W = 0, \end{cases} \end{aligned} \tag{50}$$

$$A(t) = I_S(t)\left\{\left[-\frac{\mathcal{J}_{WS}(t)}{\mathcal{J}_{WW}(t)}\right] + [\sigma(t)\sigma(t)^{\mathrm{T}}]^{-1}[\zeta(t) - r(t)S(t)]\left[-\frac{\mathcal{J}_W(t)}{\mathcal{J}_{WW}(t)}\right]\right\}, \tag{51}$$

where $I_S(t)$ is a diagonal matrix with diagonal elements $S_n(t)$. Substituting (50) and (51) into (49), we have a nonlinear partial differential equation for $\mathcal{J}$. To compute the optimal controls, we need to solve this nonlinear partial differential equation with two boundary conditions: equation (48) and $\mathcal{J}(W, S, T) = V(W)$. Once we solve this partial differential equation, the optimal controls can be obtained by simply substituting the solution into (50) and (51). Note that, in solving the nonlinear partial differential equation, the nonnegativity constraint on consumption usually makes this nontrivial problem even more difficult when $\hat{f}$ is not differentiable at the boundary (see Karatzas et al. [25], for example, for a special case of our general model).

To see that dynamic programming is consistent with our approach, note that at each time t the dynamic strategy corresponds to the allocation that would be chosen in a newly initiated static problem of the form of (12) and that $Z(t)^{-1}$ is the marginal utility of wealth. Hence

$$u_{c+}[c(\omega, t), t] \begin{cases} \leqslant Z(\omega, t)^{-1} \leqslant u_{c-}[c(\omega, t), t] \\ \qquad \text{for } \nu\text{–a.e. } (\omega, t) \text{ such that } c(\omega, t) > 0, \\ \leqslant Z(\omega, t)^{-1} \\ \qquad \text{for } \nu\text{–a.e. } (\omega, t) \text{ such that } c(\omega, t) = 0, \end{cases} \tag{52}$$

$$V'_{+}[W(\omega)]\begin{cases}\leqslant Z(\omega,T)^{-1}\leqslant V'_{-}[W(\omega)] & \text{for } P\text{–a.e. } \omega \text{ such that } W(\omega)>0,\\ \leqslant Z(\omega,T)^{-1} & \text{for } P\text{–a.e. } \omega \text{ such that } W(\omega)=0,\end{cases}$$

$$\mathcal{J}_W(t)=Z(t)^{-1}=\frac{1}{F^{-1}[W(t),S(t),t]}\qquad \nu\text{–a.e.,}\tag{53}$$

and

$$\mathcal{J}_{WW}(t)=-\frac{F_W^{-1}(t)}{[F^{-1}(t)]^2}\qquad \mathcal{J}_{WS}(t)=\frac{F_S^{-1}(t)}{[F^{-1}(t)]^2}.\tag{54}$$

Recall that

$$Z(t)=F^{-1}[W(t),S(t),t]\qquad \nu\text{–a.e.}$$

Therefore

$$F_Z F_W^{-1}=1\tag{55}$$

and

$$F_Z F_S^{-1}+F_S=0.\tag{56}$$

Relations (55) and (56) imply that

$$-\frac{\mathcal{J}_{WS}}{\mathcal{J}_{WW}}=F_S$$

and

$$-\frac{\mathcal{J}_W}{\mathcal{J}_{WW}}=\frac{F^{-1}}{F_W^{-1}}=F_Z Z.$$

Hence it follows from (51) that

$$A(t)=I_s(t)\{F_S(t)+[\sigma(t)\sigma(t)^{\mathrm{T}}]^{-1}[\varsigma(t)-r(t)S(t)]\,F_Z(t)Z(t)\}\qquad \nu\text{–a.e.}\tag{57}$$

Relations (52) and (57) are consistent with (30) and (35).

Although our approach and stochastic dynamic programming are essentially consistent, there are several advantages to our approach.

First, as mentioned above, the problem of the existence of optimal consumption–portfolio policies can be dealt with very easily using our approach. This issue has been extensively discussed in the paper by Cox and Huang [6], to which we refer interested readers.

Second, in the verification theorem of dynamic programming, we need to solve a nonlinear partial differential equation. However, theorems 3 and 4 require only the solution of a linear partial differential equation.

Third, our approach yields optimal policies without having to find the indirect utility function. The indirect utility function will be a byproduct of our analysis even when it does not have the desired derivatives to satisfy Bellman's equation. To see this, we put

$$\hat{\mathcal{J}}[Z(t), S(t), t] \equiv$$
$$E\left[\int_t^T u\{\hat{f}[Z(s)^{-1}, s], s\} \, ds + V\{V_+'^{-1}[Z(T)^{-1}]\} \middle| Z(t), S(t)\right].$$

Once we have $F_Z > 0$, the indirect utility function is

$$\mathcal{J}[W(t), S(t), t] = \begin{cases} \hat{\mathcal{J}}\{F^{-1}[W(t), S(t), t], S(t), t\} & \text{if } W(t) > 0, \\ \int_t^T u(0, s) \, ds + V(0) & \text{if } W(t) = 0. \end{cases}$$

The indirect utility function $\mathcal{J}$ may not be twice continuously differentiable in $W(t)$ and $S(t)$ and continuously differentiable in t. In such an event, the optimal policies cannot be determined by solving a nonlinear partial differential equation.

2.4 *The relationship between the constrained and the unconstrained solutions*

The optimization problem of (12) has nonnegativity constraints on consumption as well as on final wealth. For utility functions that exhibit infinite marginal utilities at zero consumption and zero wealth, the nonnegativity constraints are not binding at the optimal solution. For problems for which the nonnegativity constraints are binding, there is an intuitive way to interpret the optimal solution. To illustrate this, we shall consider utility functions that are defined on the whole of the real line. If the consumption–portfolio problems for these utility functions have optimal solutions without the nonnegativity constraint, it is possible to obtain the optimal constrained solutions in a simple and direct way. In effect, the market informs an agent that he or she can follow an unconstrained consumption–portfolio policy only if he or she simultaneously buys an insurance package that will pay off the negative consumption and wealth as they are incurred. An optimal constrained policy will be one that allocates the initial wealth between an unconstrained policy and the insurance package on the unconstrained policy and exhausts all the initial wealth.

Formally, consider an agent with a utility function for consumption $u: \mathbb{R} \times [0, T] \mapsto \mathbb{R}$ and a utility function for final wealth $V: \mathbb{R} \mapsto \mathbb{R}$. Assume that $u(y, t)$ and $V(y)$ are increasing and strictly concave in y. Consider the following program:

$$\sup_{(\hat{c}, \hat{W}) \in L^p(\nu) \times L^p(P)} E\left[\int_0^T u(\hat{c}, t) \, dt + V(\hat{W})\right]$$
$$\text{s.t.} \quad B(0)E\left[\int_0^T \frac{\hat{c}(t)\eta(t)}{B(t)} \, dt + \frac{\hat{W}\eta(T)}{B(T)}\right] = W_\lambda(0). \tag{58}$$

Note that there is no nonnegativity constraint on consumption and on final wealth in (58). If there exists a solution to (58), by the strict concavity of the utility functions it is unique and is denoted by $(\hat{c}_\lambda, \hat{W}_\lambda)$. By the Lagrangian theory, there exists a unique $\lambda > 0$ such that

$$\begin{aligned} u_{c+}[c_\lambda(t), t] &\leqslant \frac{\lambda \eta(t) B(0)}{B(t)} \leqslant u_{c-}[c_\lambda(t), t] \qquad \nu\text{–a.e.,} \\ V'_+(W_\lambda) &\leqslant \frac{\lambda \eta(T) B(0)}{B(T)} \leqslant V'_-(W_\lambda) \qquad \text{a.s.} \end{aligned} \tag{59}$$

We shall use the following notation. Let $(\hat{c}, \hat{W}) \in L^p(\nu) \times L^p(P)$. Then $\hat{c}^+ \equiv \{\max[\hat{c}(t), 0]; t \in [0, T]\}$ and $\hat{W}^+ \equiv \max[\hat{W}, 0]$. Similarly, $\hat{c}^- \equiv \{\max[-c(t), 0]; t \in [0, T]\}$ and $\hat{W}^- \equiv \max[-\hat{W}, 0]$. By definition, we have $\hat{c} = \hat{c}^+ - \hat{c}^-$ and $\hat{W} = \hat{W}^+ - \hat{W}^-$. Moreover, by the fact that $L^p(\nu)$ and $L^p(P)$ are lattices, we know that $\hat{c}^+$, $\hat{c}^-$ are elements of $L^p(\nu)$ and $\hat{W}^+$, $\hat{W}^-$ are elements of $L^p(P)$.

The following theorem is the main result of this subsection.

Theorem 4 Suppose that $W_0 > 0$, (c_λ, W_λ) is the solution to (58) with an initial wealth $W_\lambda(0) \in (0, W_0]$, and

$$B(0)E\left[\int_0^T \frac{c_\lambda^-(t)\eta(t)}{B(t)}\, dt + \frac{W_\lambda^- \eta(T)}{B(T)}\right] = W_0 - W_\lambda(0). \tag{60}$$

Then $(c_\lambda^+, W_\lambda^+)$ is the solution to (58) with the additional nonnegativity constraints $\hat{c} \geqslant 0$ and $\hat{W} \geqslant 0$ and with an initial wealth $W_0 > 0$. Conversely, suppose that there exists a solution to (58) with the additional nonnegativity constraints on consumption and final wealth. Denote this solution by (c, W). Let λ be the Lagrangian multiplier associated with (c, W). Suppose that there exists $(c_\lambda, W_\lambda) \in L^p(\nu) \times L^p(P)$ such that (59) holds. Then there exists $W_\lambda(0) \in (0, W_0]$ such that (c_λ, W_λ) is a solution to (58) with $(c_\lambda^+, W_\lambda^+) = (c, W)$ and (60).

PROOF By concavity of the utility functions and (59) we have

$$u_{c+}[c(\omega, t), t] \begin{cases} \leqslant \dfrac{\lambda \eta(\omega, t) B(0)}{B(\omega, t)} \leqslant u_{c-}[c_\lambda^+(\omega, t), t] \\ \qquad \text{for } \nu\text{–a.e. } (\omega, t) \text{ such that } c_\lambda^+(\omega, t) > 0, \\ \leqslant \dfrac{\lambda \eta(\omega, t) B(0)}{B(\omega, t)} \\ \qquad \text{for } \nu\text{–a.e. } (\omega, t) \text{ such that } c_\lambda^+(\omega, t) = 0, \end{cases} \tag{61}$$

$$V'_+[W(\omega)] \begin{cases} \leqslant \dfrac{\lambda\eta(\omega,T)B(0)}{B(\omega,T)} \leqslant V'_-(W) & \text{for } P\text{–a.e. } \omega \text{ such that } W_\lambda^+(\omega) > 0, \\ \leqslant \dfrac{\lambda\eta(\omega,T)B(0)}{B(\omega,T)} & \text{for } P\text{–a.e. } \omega \text{ such that } W_\lambda^+(\omega) = 0, \end{cases}$$

Next we claim that $(c_\lambda^+, W_\lambda^+)$ has an initial value W_0. To see this, we recall that $c_\lambda = c_\lambda^+ - c_\lambda^-$ and $W_\lambda = W_\lambda^+ - W_\lambda^-$. Therefore

$$\begin{aligned} B(0)E\left[\int_0^T \frac{c_\lambda^+(t)\eta(t)}{B(t)}\,dt + \frac{W_\lambda^+\eta(T)}{B(T)}\right] \\ = B(0)E\left[\int_0^T \frac{\{c_\lambda(t)+c_\lambda^-(t)\}\eta(t)}{B(t)}\,dt + \frac{(W_\lambda + W_\lambda^-)\eta(T)}{B(T)}\right] \\ = W_\lambda(0) + W_0 - W_\lambda(0) = W_0, \end{aligned} \tag{62}$$

where the second equality follows from (60). Finally, $(c_\lambda^+, W_\lambda^+) \in L_+^p(\nu) \times L_+^p(P)$, the concavity of the utility functions, (61), and (62) imply that $(c_\lambda^+, W_\lambda^+)$ is the solution to (58) with the nonnegativity constraints and an initial wealth W_0.

Conversely, let (c, W) be the solution to (58) with the additional nonnegativity constraints and let $\lambda > 0$ be the Lagrangian multiplier associated with it. By the hypothesis, there exists $(c_\lambda, W_\lambda) \in L^p(\nu) \times L^p(P)$ such that (59) holds. By the definition of (c_λ, W_λ), it is obvious that $(c_\lambda^+, W_\lambda^+) = (c, W)$. Now define

$$W_\lambda(0) \equiv B(0)E\left[\int_0^T \frac{c_\lambda(t)\eta(t)}{B(t)}\,dt + \frac{W_\lambda\eta(T)}{B(T)}\right].$$

The rest of the assertion then follows from direct verification. ■

The agent invests $W_\lambda(0)$ in the unconstrained policy and then spends $W_0 - W_\lambda(0)$ on an insurance package that pays $(c_\lambda^-, W_\lambda^-)$. The combination of the unconstrained policy and the insurance package gives precisely the constrained policy. Note that the insurance package can be thought of as consisting of a continuum of put options with zero exercise price. To see this, we observe that $c_\lambda^-(t) = \max[-c_\lambda(t), 0]$ is the payoff of a European put option written on the unconstrained consumption policy at time t with a zero exercise price, and $W_\lambda^- = \max[-W_\lambda, 0]$ is the payoff of a European put option written on the unconstrained policy for final wealth with a zero exercise price. The price at time zero for the former is $B(0)E[c_\lambda^-(t)\eta(t)/B(t)]$ and for the latter is $B(0)E[W_\lambda^-\eta(T)/B(T)]$. Consider buying a continuum of these put options on consumption according to the Lebesgue measure on $[0, T]$ and the put option on the final wealth. The payoff of this package is just $(c_\lambda^-, W_\lambda^-)$ and its price at time zero is

$$\int_0^T B(0)E\left[\frac{c_\lambda^-(t)\eta(t)}{B(t)}\right] \mathrm{d}t + B(0)E\left[\frac{W_\lambda^-\eta(T)}{B(T)}\right]$$

$$= B(0)E\left[\int_0^T \frac{c_\lambda^-(t)\eta(t)}{B(t)} \mathrm{d}t + \frac{W_\lambda^-\eta(T)}{B(T)}\right]$$

$$= W_0 - W_\lambda(0),$$

where the first equality follows from the Fubini theorem.

Once we solve the static problem, then we can use the methodology developed in section 2.2 to compute the optimal portfolio strategy. In many specific situations, the optimal consumption–portfolio policies for the unconstrained problem are well known. We can thus simply find the optimal allocation of the initial wealth between the unconstrained policy and its associated insurance package, and then compute the portfolio strategy for the insurance package. The optimal consumption policy is then the positive part of the unconstrained consumption policy, and the optimal portfolio policy is the sum of the known portfolio policy for the unconstrained problem and the portfolio policy for the insurance policy. This procedure will be demonstrated in the next section in the context of the model of Merton [30].

3 A Special Case

We now specialize our general model of uncertainty developed in section 2 to the model considered by Merton [30] and revisited recently by Karatzas et al. [25]. We shall employ the general method developed in the previous section in place of the dynamic programming used by Karatzas et al. and Merton. The optimal consumption–portfolio policies for a class of utility functions will be explicitly computed. For many of the HARA utility functions for which the nonnegativity constraints are binding, the optimal policies fail to be linear policies. Note that the fact that the optimal policies fail to be linear policies has been pointed out by Sethi and Taksar [35]. However, they do not provide closed-form solutions for the complete family of HARA utility functions.

3.1 Formulation

We take the model of uncertainty of section 2 with the following specialization. Assume that risky security gain processes follow a geometric

Brownian motion:

$$S(t) + \int_0^t \iota[S(s), s]\ ds = S(0) + \int_0^t I_S(s)\mu\ ds$$
$$+ \int_0^t I_S(s)\sigma\ dw(s) \qquad \forall t \in [0, T]\ \text{a.s.}$$

where μ is an $N \times 1$ vector of constants, σ is an $N \times N$ nonsingular matrix of constants, and $I_S(t)$ is a diagonal matrix with elements $S_n(t)$. Assume further that $r(t) = r$ is a constant.

Given $Z(0) > 0$, the process Z becomes

$$Z(t) = Z(0) + \int_0^t [r + (\mu - r\boldsymbol{1})^{\mathrm{T}}(\sigma\sigma^{\mathrm{T}})^{-1}(\mu - r\boldsymbol{1})]\, Z(s)\ ds$$
$$+ \int_0^t (\mu - r\boldsymbol{1})^{\mathrm{T}}\sigma^{-1\mathrm{T}} Z(s)\ dw(s)$$
$$= Z(0)\ \exp\{(\mu - r\boldsymbol{1})^{\mathrm{T}}\sigma^{-1\mathrm{T}} w(t) + [r + \tfrac{1}{2}(\mu - r\boldsymbol{1})^{\mathrm{T}}(\sigma\sigma^{\mathrm{T}})^{-1}(\mu - r\boldsymbol{1})]t\}$$
$$= Z(0)\ \exp\{[r - \tfrac{1}{2}(\mu - r\boldsymbol{1})^{\mathrm{T}}(\sigma\sigma^{\mathrm{T}})^{-1}(\mu - r\boldsymbol{1})]t + (\mu - r\boldsymbol{1})^{\mathrm{T}}\sigma^{-1\mathrm{T}} w^{\star}(t)\}$$

where $\boldsymbol{1}$ is an N-vector of ones. Thus, $\ln Z(t)$ is normally distributed with mean

$$\ln Z(0) + [r + \tfrac{1}{2}(\mu - r\boldsymbol{1})^{\mathrm{T}}(\sigma\sigma^{\mathrm{T}})^{-1}(\mu - r\boldsymbol{1})]t$$

and variance

$$(\mu - r\boldsymbol{1})^{\mathrm{T}}(\sigma\sigma^{\mathrm{T}})^{-1}(\mu - r\boldsymbol{1})t$$

under P and is normally distributed with mean

$$\ln Z(0) + [r - \tfrac{1}{2}(\mu - r\boldsymbol{1})^{\mathrm{T}}(\sigma\sigma^{\mathrm{T}})^{-1}(\mu - r\boldsymbol{1})]t$$

and variance

$$(\mu - r\boldsymbol{1})^{\mathrm{T}}(\sigma\sigma^{\mathrm{T}})^{-1}(\mu - r\boldsymbol{1})t$$

under Q. To simplify notation, we note that

$$\frac{(\sigma\sigma^{\mathrm{T}})^{-1}(\mu - r\boldsymbol{1})}{(\mu - r\boldsymbol{1})^{\mathrm{T}}(\sigma\sigma^{\mathrm{T}})^{-1}\boldsymbol{1}}$$

is an N-vector of constants that sum to unity and therefore can be thought of as a vector of portfolio weights on the N risky securities. The mean $\hat{\mu}$ and the variance $\hat{\sigma}^2$ of the rate of return of this portfolio are

$$\hat{\mu} = \frac{(\mu - r\boldsymbol{1})^{\mathrm{T}}(\sigma\sigma^{\mathrm{T}})^{-1}\mu}{(\mu - r\boldsymbol{1})^{\mathrm{T}}(\sigma\sigma^{\mathrm{T}})^{-1}\boldsymbol{1}}$$

$$\hat{\sigma}^2 = \frac{(\mu - r\boldsymbol{1})^{\mathrm{T}}(\sigma\sigma^{\mathrm{T}})^{-1}(\mu - r\boldsymbol{1})}{[(\mu - r\boldsymbol{1})^{\mathrm{T}}(\sigma\sigma^{\mathrm{T}})^{-1}\boldsymbol{1}]^2}.$$

To avoid the degenerate case, we assume that $\hat{\mu} \neq r$. Now put

$$\rho^2 \equiv (\mu - r\mathbf{1})^{\mathrm{T}}(\sigma\sigma^{\mathrm{T}})^{-1}(\mu - r\mathbf{1}) = \frac{(\hat{\mu} - r)^2}{\hat{\sigma}^2}$$

and we can write the mean and variance of $\ln Z(t)$ under P as $\ln Z(0) + (r + \frac{1}{2}\rho^2)t$ and $\rho^2 t$, and under Q as $\ln Z(0) + (r - \frac{1}{2}\rho^2)t$ and $\rho^2 t$.

For this special case of uncertainty, we shall be able to consider a class of utility functions that is larger than that specified in condition C. We assume that the utility function for consumption is continuous, increasing, and concave. It is either defined on the positive real line with a value at zero level of consumption possibly equal to minus infinity or defined on the whole of the real line. The utility function for the final wealth has the same characteristics. Note that we do not require utility functions to be strictly concave, and thus an optimal consumption–portfolio policy may not be unique when it exists. As in section 2, we use $u(y, t)$ and $V(y)$ to denote the utility function for consumption at time t and the utility function for final wealth. We also assume that one of $u(y, t)$ and $V(y)$ is nonlinear. We still maintain that

$$\lim_{y \to \infty} u_{y+}(y, t) = 0$$

and

$$\lim_{y \to \infty} V'_+(y) = 0,$$

and define $\hat{f}(y, t)$ and $V'^{-1}_+(y)$ as in section 2. We further assume that $u_t(y, t)$ is continuous in t.

3.2 *Explicit formulae for optimal consumption and portfolio policies*

We shall continue to impose assumption 2. Note that since $u(y, t)$ and $V(y)$ may not be strictly increasing in y, satiation may be attained. In such an event, investing completely in the riskless security while withdrawing minimum satiation levels of consumption over time is an optimal consumption–portfolio policy. Note that whenever

$$W(t) \geqslant \int_t^T \exp[-r(s-t)]\, \hat{f}(0, s)\, \mathrm{d}s + \exp[-r(T-t)]\, V'^{-1}_+(0)$$

satiation occurs at time t.

When satiation has not occurred, define

$$F[Z(t),t]=E^{\star}\Bigg[\int_t^T \exp\{-r(s-t)\}\hat{f}\{Z(s)^{-1},s\}\,\mathrm{d}s + \exp\{-r(T-t)\}\,V'^{-1}_{+}\{Z(T)^{-1}\}\Bigg|\,Z(t)\Bigg]$$

$$=\int_0^{T-t}\exp(-rs)\,\frac{1}{\rho s^{1/2}} \times\int_{-\infty}^{+\infty}\hat{f}[\exp(-x),t+s]\;n\left[\frac{x-\ln Z(t)-(r-\frac{1}{2}\rho^2)s}{\rho s^{1/2}}\right]\mathrm{d}x\,\mathrm{d}s$$

$$+\exp[-r(T-t)]\,\frac{1}{\rho(T-t)^{1/2}} \times\int_{-\infty}^{+\infty}V'^{-1}_{+}[\exp(-x)]\;n\left[\frac{x-\ln Z(t)-(r-\frac{1}{2}\rho^2)(T-t)}{\rho(T-t)^{1/2}}\right]\mathrm{d}x, \tag{63}$$

where

$$n(y)=\frac{1}{(2\pi)^{1/2}}\exp\left(-\frac{y^2}{2}\right)$$

is the standard normal density function. This function is just the F defined in theorem 1. In our present setup, F is independent of $S(t)$.

For future reference, we shall use $N(\cdot)$ to denote the distribution function for a standard normal random variable.

The following proposition shows that the optimally invested wealth will never become zero before time T.

Proposition 5 Suppose that there exists a solution to (28) with a Lagrangian multiplier λ. The optimally invested wealth will never reach zero before time T.

PROOF If the agent reaches satiation, the assertion is obvious. Now suppose that satiation does not occur and thus $\lambda > 0$. Define Z by taking $Z(0)$ to be $1/\lambda$. Since either $u(y,t)$ or $V(y)$ is nontrivial, nonlinear, and concave, and since the support of a normally distributed random variable is the whole real line, the right-hand side of (63) is strictly positive for all $Z(t)$ and all $t \in [0,T)$. When there is no satiation, $F[Z(t),t]$ is equal to the optimally invested wealth at time t and the assertion follows. ■

The following proposition shows that in this special case we are currently considering, there is a one-to-one correspondence between $W(t)$ and $Z(t)$, where $W(t) \equiv F[Z(t), t]$, when satiation has not occurred.

Proposition 6 Suppose that there exists a solution to (28). When satiation has not occurred, $F[Z(t), t]$ is strictly increasing in $Z(t)$ and thus $Z(t) = F^{-1}[W(t), t]$, ν–a.e.

PROOF When satiation has not occurred, an increase in $Z(t)$ implies an increase in the mean for $\ln Z(s)$, $s > t$, while the variance stays the same. The assertion then follows from the hypothesis that either $u(y, t)$ or $V(y)$ is nontrivial, nonlinear, and concave. ∎

The following proposition is a specialization of proposition 3.

Proposition 7 Suppose that $u(y, t)$ is nontrivial, that $u_{c+}(0, t) < \infty$, and that satiation has not occurred. An optimal consumption policy has the property that consumption will be zero if and only if wealth is less than the nonstochastic time-dependent boundary given by

$$\underline{W}(t) = \int_0^{T-t} \frac{\exp(-rs)}{\rho s^{1/2}} \times \int_{-\infty}^{+\infty} \hat{f}[\exp(-x), t+s]\, n\left[\frac{x + \ln u_{c+}(0,t) - (r - \frac{1}{2}\rho^2)s}{\rho s^{1/2}}\right] \mathrm{d}x\, \mathrm{d}s$$
$$+ \frac{\exp[-r(T-t)]}{\rho(T-t)^{1/2}} \times \int_{-\infty}^{+\infty} V_+'^{-1}[\exp(-x)]\; n\left[\frac{x + \ln u_{c+}(0,t) - (r - \frac{1}{2}\rho^2)(T-t)}{\rho(T-t)^{1/2}}\right] \mathrm{d}x.$$

PROOF Note that $c(t) = 0$ if and only if $u_{c+}(0, t) \leqslant Z(t)^{-1}$. The assertion then follows from proposition 6. ∎

The following proposition gives a set of sufficient conditions for $D_y^m F(y, T)$ and $F_t(y, t)$ to exist and to be continuous.

Proposition 8 Suppose that (63) is finite for all $Z(t)$. Suppose further that for every subinterval $[a, b]$ of $\mathbb{R}$ and for every subinterval $[a', b')$ of $[0, T)$ there exist functions $G^m(x, s)$, $m = 1, 2$, such that for all $t \in [a', b')$

$$\frac{1}{\rho s^{1/2}} \hat{f}[\exp(-x), s+t] \left| \frac{\partial^m}{\partial y^m}\, n\left[\frac{x - y - (r - \frac{1}{2}\rho^2)s}{\rho s^{1/2}}\right] \right| \leqslant G^m(x, s)$$
$$\forall y \in (a, b) \;\; \forall s \in (0, T-t)$$

and

$$\int_0^{T-t}\int_{-\infty}^{+\infty} G^m(x,s)\,\mathrm{d}x\,\mathrm{d}s < \infty \qquad \forall t \in [0,T)$$

and for every subinterval $[a,b]$ of $\mathbb{R}$ there exists a function $H(x,s)$ such that $\forall s \in (0, T-t)$, $y \in (a,b)$, and x

$$\left|\frac{1}{\rho s^{1/2}}\hat{f}_t[\exp(-x), t+s]\,n\left[\frac{x-y-(r-\frac{1}{2}\rho^2)s}{\rho s^{1/2}}\right]\right| \leqslant H(x,s)$$

and

$$\int_0^{T-t}\int_{-\infty}^{+\infty} H(x,s)\,\mathrm{d}x\,\mathrm{d}s < \infty.$$

Then $D_y^m F(y,t)$, $m \leqslant 2$, and $F_t(y,t)$ exist and are continuous. In particular,

$$\begin{aligned} F_Z[Z(t),t] = {} & \int_0^{T-t}\frac{\exp(-rs)}{\rho s^{1/2}}\int_{-\infty}^{+\infty}\hat{f}[\exp(-x),t+s] \\ & \times\frac{\partial}{\partial Z(t)}\,n\left[\frac{x-\ln Z(t)-(r-\frac{1}{2}\rho^2)s}{\rho s^{1/2}}\right]\mathrm{d}x\,\mathrm{d}s \\ & + \frac{\exp[-r(T-t)]}{\rho(T-t)^{1/2}}\int_{-\infty}^{+\infty} V_+'^{-1}[\exp(-x)] \\ & \times\frac{\partial}{\partial Z(t)}\,n\left[\frac{x-\ln Z(t)-(r-\frac{1}{2}\rho^2)(T-t)}{\rho(T-t)^{1/2}}\right]\mathrm{d}x. \end{aligned}$$

PROOF The assertions follow from repeated application of the Lebesgue convergence theorem, the fact that $u_{y+}(y,t)$ is continuous in t for every y, and the fact that the normal distribution density function is an exponential function (see theorems 10.38 and 10.39 of Apostol [1] for example). ■

Note that the conditions in proposition 8 do not involve the differentiability of $\hat{f}[\exp(-x),t]$ with respect to x, in contrast with Theorem 1. They do involve differentiability with respect to t, however. The proposition below is a direct consequence of theorem 2, with the difference that now there exists a possibility of satiation.

Proposition 9 Suppose that $D^m F(y,t)$ and F_t exist and are continuous for $m \leqslant 2$, and that differentiation of F can be carried out under the integral sign. If

$$W_0 < \int_0^T \exp(-rt)\hat{f}(0,t)\,\mathrm{d}t + \exp(-rT)V_+'^{-1}(0)$$

and if there exists $Z_0 > 0$ such that $F(Z_0, 0) = W_0$ and (31) lies in $L^p(\nu) \times L^p(P)$ with $Z(0) = Z_0$, a solution to (12) exists. If we define Z by taking $Z(0) = Z_0$, an optimal consumption–portfolio policy and its corresponding indirect utility function, before satiation occurs, are

$$c[W(t), t] = \hat{f}(\exp\{-\ln F^{-1}[W(t), t]\}, t)$$

$$\begin{aligned}
A[W(t), t] &= (\sigma\sigma^{\mathrm{T}})^{-1}(\mu - r\mathbf{1}) \\
&\quad \times \left[\int_0^{T-t} \frac{\exp(-rs)}{(\rho^2 s)^{3/2}} \left(\int_{-\infty}^{+\infty} \hat{f}[\exp(-x), t+s] \right.\right. \\
&\quad \times \{x - \ln F^{-1}[W(t), t] - (r - \tfrac{1}{2}\rho^2)s\} \\
&\quad \left. \times n\left\{ \frac{x - \ln F^{-1}[W(t), t] - (r - \frac{1}{2}\rho^2)s}{\rho s^{1/2}} \right\} \mathrm{d}x \right) \mathrm{d}s \\
&\quad + \frac{\exp[-r(T-t)]}{[\rho^2(T-t)]^{3/2}} \int_{-\infty}^{+\infty} V_+'^{-1}[\exp(-x)] \\
&\quad \times \{x - \ln F^{-1}[W(t), t] - (r - \tfrac{1}{2}\rho^2)(T-t)\} \\
&\quad \left. \times n\left\{ \frac{x - \ln F^{-1}[W(t), t] - (r - \frac{1}{2}\rho^2)(T-t)}{\rho (T-t)^{1/2}} \right\} \mathrm{d}x \right]
\end{aligned}$$

$$\begin{aligned}
\mathcal{J}[W(t), t] &= \int_0^{T-t} \frac{1}{\rho s^{1/2}} \int_{-\infty}^{+\infty} u[\hat{f}[\exp(-x), t+s], t+s] \\
&\quad \times n\left\{ \frac{x - \ln F^{-1}[W(t), t] - (r + \frac{1}{2}\rho)s}{\rho s^{1/2}} \right\} \mathrm{d}x\, \mathrm{d}s \\
&\quad + \frac{1}{\rho (T-t)^{1/2}} \int_{-\infty}^{+\infty} V\{V_+'^{-1}[\exp(-x)]\} \\
&\quad \times n\left\{ \frac{x - \ln F^{-1}[W(t), t] - (r + \frac{1}{2}\rho)(T-t)}{\rho (T-t)^{1/2}} \right\} \mathrm{d}x.
\end{aligned}$$

When

$$W(t) \geqslant \int_t^T \exp[-r(s-t)]\, \hat{f}(0, s)\, \mathrm{d}s + \exp[-r(T-t)]\, V_+'^{-1}(0),$$

there is satiation, and therefore investing completely in the riskless security and consuming $c(s) = \hat{f}(0, s)$ at time $s \geqslant t$ is an optimal strategy.

PROOF The first assertion is a consequence of theorem 2. The second assertion is obvious. ■

Note that, with exponential discounting, the utility function has the form $u(y,t)=\exp(-\rho t)\,u(y)$. For this important special case, $\hat{f}[\exp(-x),t]=u'^{-1}_{+}[\exp(-x+\rho t)]$.

We shall now illustrate our results with several examples. Using proposition 9 or Cox and Huang [6], we can verify that assumption 2 is valid and that there exists an optimal consumption–portfolio policy for all the examples. We shall demonstrate our proposed method by computing explicit optimal consumption–portfolio policies. In particular, example 4 solves the optimal consumption–portfolio problem for the complete family of HARA utility functions while taking into account the nonnegativity constraints on consumption and final wealth.

Example 1 Let $u(y,t)=0$ and

$$V(y)=\begin{cases} y & \text{for } 0\leqslant y<\bar{y} \\ \bar{y} & \text{for } y\geqslant \bar{y}. \end{cases}$$

In this case $V'_{+}(y)$ equals unity for $0\leqslant y<\bar{y}$ and zero for $y>\bar{y}$. Hence, $V'^{-1}_{+}[\exp(-x)]=\bar{y}$ for $x>0$ and $V'^{-1}_{+}[\exp(-x)]=0$ for $x\leqslant 0$. Computation yields

$$F[Z(t),t]=\bar{y}\exp[-r(T-t)]\;N\left[\frac{\ln Z(t)+(r-\frac{1}{2}\rho^2)(T-t)}{\rho(T-t)^{1/2}}\right].$$

Note that if $W_0>\exp(-rT)\,\bar{y}$ there is no $Z(0)<\infty$ such that $F[Z(0),0]=W_0$. This is so because, by investing W_0 completely in the riskless asset, the agent will reach satiation at time T with probability one and this riskless strategy is an optimal strategy. For $W_0<\exp(-rT)\,\bar{y}$, an optimal investment strategy and its corresponding indirect utility function, before satiation occurs, are

$$A[W(t),t]=\bar{y}\exp[-r(T-t)](\sigma\sigma^{\mathrm{T}})^{-1}(\mu-r\mathbf{1})\,\frac{1}{\rho(T-t)^{1/2}}$$

$$\times\, n\left\{\frac{\ln F^{-1}[W(t),t]+(r-\frac{1}{2}\rho^2)(T-t)}{\rho(T-t)^{1/2}}\right\},$$

$$J[W(t),t]=\bar{y}N\left\{\frac{\ln F^{-1}[W(t),t]+(r+\frac{1}{2}\rho^2)(T-t)}{\rho(T-t)^{1/2}}\right\}.$$

Note that, for any given time t, the optimal amount invested in the risky assets is the largest when $F^{-1}[W(t),t]=\exp[-(r-\frac{1}{2}\rho^2)(T-t)]$, which occurs when $W(t)=\frac{1}{2}\bar{y}\exp[-r(T-t)]$. ■

Example 2 Let $u(y,t)=0$ and $V(y)=-(1/a)\exp(-ay)$, where $a>0$ is the coefficient of absolute risk aversion. Then $V'_{+}(y)=\exp(-ay)$ and

$V_+'^{-1}[\exp(-x)] = (x/a)^+$. Hence we have

$$F[Z(t),t]$$
$$= \exp[-r(T-t)] \frac{1}{a\rho(T-t)^{1/2}}$$
$$\times \int_0^\infty xn\left[\frac{x - \ln Z(t) - (r - \frac{1}{2}\rho^2)(T-t)}{\rho(T-t)^{1/2}}\right] dx$$
$$= \exp[-r(T-t)] \frac{\rho(T-t)^{1/2}}{a} \left\{\left[\frac{\ln Z(t) + (r - \frac{1}{2}\rho^2)(T-t)}{\rho(T-t)^{1/2}}\right]\right.$$
$$\left. \times N\left[\frac{\ln Z(t) + (r - \frac{1}{2}\rho^2)(T-t)}{\rho(T-t)^{1/2}}\right] + n\left[\frac{\ln Z(t) + (r - \frac{1}{2}\rho^2)(T-t)}{\rho(T-t)^{1/2}}\right]\right\},$$

$$A[W(t),t] = \exp[-r(T-t)] \frac{1}{a} (\sigma\sigma^{\mathrm{T}})^{-1}(\mu - r\mathbf{1})$$
$$\times N\left\{\frac{\ln F^{-1}[W(t),t] + (r - \frac{1}{2}\rho^2)(T-t)}{\rho(T-t)^{1/2}}\right\}.$$

Note that the optimal amount invested in the risky assets is not independent of the wealth level. This is a consequence of the nonnegativity constraint. However, note the following:

$$\lim_{W(t)\to\infty} A[W(t),t] = \exp[-r(T-t)] \frac{1}{a} (\sigma\sigma^{\mathrm{T}})^{-1}(\mu - r\mathbf{1}),$$

which is a constant policy. ■

Recall from section 2.4 that there exists a relationship between constrained solutions and unconstrained solutions. The following example illustrates this connection.

Example 3 Consider the utility function for wealth of example 2. First assume that there is no nonnegativity constraint. Then $V_+'^{-1}[\exp(-x)] = x/a$. Since x is normally distributed, x/a lies in $L^p(P)$. Let

$$\hat{F}[Z_\lambda(t),t] \equiv \exp[-r(T-t)] \frac{1}{a\rho(T-t)^{1/2}}$$
$$\times \int_{-\infty}^{+\infty} xn\left[\frac{x - \ln Z_\lambda(t) - (r - \frac{1}{2}\rho^2)(T-t)}{\rho(T-t)^{1/2}}\right] dx$$
$$= \exp[-r(T-t)] \frac{1}{a\rho(T-t)^{1/2}} \ln Z_\lambda(t) + (r - \tfrac{1}{2}\rho^2)(T-t),$$

where Z_λ denotes the process Z with $Z(0) = 1/\lambda$. $\hat{F}$ is the value, at time t, of the optimally invested wealth given that the initial wealth $W_\lambda(0)$ gives rise to the Lagrangian multiplier λ. Independent of the initial wealth, the optimal amounts invested in risky assets are

$$\hat{A}[W_\lambda(t), t] = \exp[-r(T-t)]\ \frac{1}{a}\ (\sigma\sigma^{\mathrm{T}})^{-1}(\mu - r\boldsymbol{1}).$$

Following this strategy, the final wealth will be

$$W_\lambda(T) = \frac{1}{a}\ \{\ln\ Z_\lambda(0) + [(r - \tfrac{1}{2}\rho^2)T - (\mu - r\boldsymbol{1})^{\mathrm{T}}\sigma^{-1\mathrm{T}}w^\star(T)]\}.$$

The value at t of the European put option $p[Z_\lambda(t), T]$ written on $W_\lambda(T)$ is

$$\hat{\hat{W}}_\lambda(t) = p[Z_\lambda(t), t] = \exp[-r(T-t)]\ \frac{1}{a\rho(T-t)^{1/2}}$$

$$\times \int_{-\infty}^{0} xn\left[\frac{x - \ln\ Z_\lambda(t) - (r - \frac{1}{2}\rho^2)(T-t)}{\rho(T-t)^{1/2}}\right] \mathrm{d}x$$

$$= \exp[-r(T-t)]\ \frac{\rho(T-t)^{1/2}}{a}\ \left\{n\left[\frac{-\ln\ Z_\lambda(t) - (r - \frac{1}{2}\rho^2)(T-t)}{\rho(T-t)^{1/2}}\right]\right.$$

$$\left. - \frac{\ln\ Z_\lambda(t) + (r - \frac{1}{2}\rho^2)(T-t)}{\rho(T-t)^{1/2}}\ N\left[\frac{-\ln\ Z_\lambda(t) - (r - \frac{1}{2}\rho^2)(T-t)}{\rho(T-t)^{1/2}}\right]\right\}.$$

The investment strategy in the risky assets that replicates this put option is

$$\hat{A}[\hat{\hat{W}}_\lambda(t), t] = -\exp[-r(T-t)]\ \frac{1}{a}\ (\sigma\sigma^{\mathrm{T}})^{-1}(\mu - r\boldsymbol{1})$$

$$\times N\left\{\frac{-\ln\ p^{-1}[\hat{\hat{W}}_\lambda(t), t] - (r - \frac{1}{2}\rho^2)(T-t)}{\rho(T-t)^{1/2}}\right\}.$$

Now we want to find $Z_\lambda(0)$ such that

$$\hat{F}[Z_\lambda(0), 0] + p[Z_\lambda(0), 0] = W_0.$$

Note that $\hat{F}(t) + p(t) = F(t)$, where $F(t)$ is the value of the constrained policy at time t. Hence

$$\frac{1}{\lambda} = Z_\lambda(0) = F^{-1}(W_0, t),$$

which is what we anticipated. Now the process Z_λ is well defined, and the optimal investment strategy for the constrained problem is

$$A[W(t),t] = \hat{A}[W_\lambda(t),t] + \hat{\hat{A}}[\hat{\hat{W}}_\lambda(t),t]$$

$$= \exp[-r(T-t)] \frac{1}{a} (\sigma\sigma^{\mathrm{T}})^{-1}(\mu - r\mathbf{1})$$

$$\times N\left\{\frac{\ln F^{-1}[W(t),t] + (r - \frac{1}{2}\rho^2)(T-t)}{\rho(T-t)^{1/2}}\right\},$$

which is identical with that of example 2. ∎

Among many other results in his pioneering paper, Merton [30] derived optimal consumption and portfolio rules for HARA utility functions when securities prices follow a geometric Brownian motion and the interest rate is constant. However, as Merton noted, the solutions given for some members of the HARA family are not completely appropriate, since they allow the agent to incur negative wealth and may require negative consumption. We might hope that this difficulty could easily be remedied by setting consumption equal to zero whenever negative consumption would have been required and by following the designated rules only as long as wealth remains positive. Unfortunately, this is not the case. The optimal solution with nonnegativity constraints on consumption and wealth will have a completely different form, as shown already by example 2. In the following example, we shall derive explicit solutions that satisfy these constraints.

Example 4 Let

$$u(y,t) = \exp(-\phi t) \frac{1-\gamma}{\gamma} \left(\frac{\beta y}{1-\gamma} + \xi\right)^{\gamma}$$

$$V(y) = u(y,T)$$

with $\beta > 0$, $\gamma \neq 0$ or 1. It is understood that, if $\gamma > 1$, then $u(y,t) = 0$ for all $y \geqslant (\gamma - 1)\xi/\beta$. With $\gamma < 1$ and $\xi < 0$, the agent's problem is not completely specified because the utility function does not state the consequence of consuming less than $|\xi|(1-\gamma)/\beta$. Furthermore, for sufficiently low initial wealth,

$$W_0 < |\xi|(1-\gamma) \frac{1-\exp(-rT)}{\beta r},$$

there is no policy that can guarantee $c(t) \geqslant |\xi|(1-\gamma)/\beta$ for all t with probability one. Consequently, we only consider the case $\xi \geqslant 0$.

By evaluating the integrals of (63), we obtain the following results for the

HARA functions:

$$F[Z(t),t] = \frac{1-\gamma}{\beta}\int_0^{T-t}\Bigg([\beta Z(t)]^{1/(1-\gamma)}\exp(-\delta s)$$

$$\times N\left\{\frac{\ln[\beta Z(t)]^{1/(1-\gamma)} - \ln\xi + (r-\delta+\tfrac{1}{2}\bar{\sigma}^2)s}{[\operatorname{sgn}(1-\gamma)]\bar{\sigma}s^{1/2}}\right\}$$

$$-\xi\exp(-rs)N\left\{\frac{\ln[\beta Z(t)]^{1/(1-\gamma)} - \ln\xi + (r-\delta-\tfrac{1}{2}\bar{\sigma}^2)s}{[\operatorname{sgn}(1-\gamma)]\bar{\sigma}s^{1/2}}\right\}\Bigg)\,\mathrm{d}s$$

$$+\frac{1-\gamma}{\beta}\Bigg([\beta Z(t)]^{1/(1-\gamma)}\exp[-\delta(T-t)]$$

$$\times N\left\{\frac{\ln[\beta Z(t)]^{1/(1-\gamma)} - \ln\xi + (r-\delta+\tfrac{1}{2}\bar{\sigma}^2)(T-t)}{[\operatorname{sgn}(1-\gamma)]\bar{\sigma}(T-t)^{1/2}}\right\}$$

$$-\xi\exp[-r(T-t)]$$

$$\times N\left\{\frac{\ln[\beta Z(t)]^{1/(1-\gamma)} - \ln\xi + (r-\delta-\tfrac{1}{2}\bar{\sigma}^2)(T-t)}{[\operatorname{sgn}(1-\gamma)]\bar{\sigma}(T-t)^{1/2}}\right\}\Bigg)$$

where

$$\delta = \frac{1}{1-\gamma}\left\{\phi - \gamma\left[r + \frac{\rho^2}{2(1-\gamma)}\right]\right\}$$

and

$$\bar{\sigma}^2 = \left(\frac{1}{1-\gamma}\right)^2\rho^2.$$

Using the properties of $n(\cdot)$ and $N(\cdot)$, it can be verified that $D_y^m F(y,t)$, $m \leqslant 2$, and $F_t(y,t)$ exist and are continuous. In particular, $F_Z[Z(t),t]$ can be computed by differentiating under the integral sign. When $\gamma > 1$, satiation occurs at t if

$$W(t) \geqslant \frac{1-(1-r)\exp[-r(T-t)]}{r}\,\frac{(\gamma-1)\xi}{\beta}.$$

When satiation has not occurred, an optimal policy and its corresponding indirect utility function are

$$c[W(t),t] = \left[\frac{1-\gamma}{\beta}\left(\{\beta F^{-1}[W(t),t]\}^{1/(1-\gamma)} - \xi\right)\right]^+$$

$$A[W(t),t]$$

$$= (\sigma\sigma^{\mathrm{T}})^{-1}(\mu - r\mathbf{1})\,\frac{\{\beta F^{-1}[W(t),t]\}^{1/(1-\gamma)}}{\beta}$$

$$\times\Bigg[\int_0^{T-t}\exp(-\delta s)$$

$$\times N\left(\frac{\ln\{\beta F^{-1}[W(t),t]\}^{1/(1-\gamma)} - \ln\xi + (r-\delta-\frac{1}{2}\bar{\sigma}^2)s}{[\operatorname{sgn}(1-\gamma)]\bar{\sigma}s^{1/2}}\right) ds$$

$$+\exp[-\delta(T-t)]$$

$$\times N\left(\frac{\ln\{\beta F^{-1}[W(t),t]\}^{1/(1-\gamma)} - \ln\xi + (r-\delta-\frac{1}{2}\bar{\sigma}^2)(T-t)}{[\operatorname{sgn}(1-\gamma)]\bar{\sigma}(T-t)^{1/2}}\right)\Bigg]$$

$\mathcal{J}[W(t),t]$

$$=\frac{1-\gamma}{\gamma}\exp(-\phi t)\left\{\int_0^{T-t}\Bigg[\{\beta F^{-1}[W(t),t]\}^{\gamma/(1-\gamma)}\exp(-\delta s)\right.$$

$$\times N\left(\frac{\ln\{\beta F^{-1}[W(t),t]\}^{\gamma/(1-\gamma)} - \ln\xi^\gamma + (\rho-\delta+\frac{1}{2}\gamma^2\bar{\sigma}^2)}{[\operatorname{sgn}(1-\gamma)]\gamma\bar{\sigma}s^{1/2}}\right)$$

$$+\xi^\gamma\exp(-\phi s)$$

$$\times N\left(\frac{-\ln\{\beta F^{-1}[W(t),t]\}^{\gamma/(1-\gamma)} + \ln\xi^\gamma - (\rho-\delta-\frac{1}{2}\gamma^2\bar{\sigma}^2)s}{[\operatorname{sgn}(1-\gamma)]\gamma\bar{\sigma}s^{1/2}}\right)\Bigg] ds$$

$$+\{\beta F^{-1}[W(t),t]\}^{\gamma/(1-\gamma)}\exp[-\delta(T-t)]$$

$$\times N\left(\frac{\ln\{\beta F^{-1}[W(t),t]\}^{\gamma/(1-\gamma)} - \ln\xi^\gamma + (\rho-\delta+\frac{1}{2}\gamma^2\bar{\sigma}^2)(T-t)}{[\operatorname{sgn}(1-\gamma)]\gamma\bar{\sigma}(T-t)^{1/2}}\right)$$

$$+\xi^\gamma\exp[-\phi(T-t)]$$

$$\left.\times N\left(\frac{-\ln\{\beta F^{-1}[W(t),t]\}^{\gamma/(1-\gamma)} + \ln\xi^\gamma - (\rho-\delta-\frac{1}{2}\gamma^2\bar{\sigma}^2)(T-t)}{[\operatorname{sgn}(1-\gamma)]\gamma\bar{\sigma}(T-t)^{1/2}}\right)\right\}.$$

As $W(t)$ becomes large, the optimal consumption and investment policies approach the linear functions of wealth given by Merton [30]. ■

Remark 6 Example 4 can easily be generalized to allow the utility function for final wealth to be a HARA function with a different coefficient from that of the utility function for consumption. No substantial changes need to be made in the solution; only trivial changes in notation are required. ■

For many utility functions, the optimal consumption policy will not be differentiable and may not even be continuous in wealth. A specific example is given below.

Example 5 Let

$$u(y,t)=\begin{cases} y & \text{for } 0 \leqslant y < \bar{y} \\ \bar{y} & \text{for } y \geqslant \bar{y} \end{cases}$$

and let $V(y) = 0$. Suppose that satiation does not occur. We know that

$$\hat{f}[\exp(-x), t] = \begin{cases} \bar{y} & \text{for } x > 0 \\ 0 & \text{for } x \leqslant 0. \end{cases}$$

Direct computation yields

$$F[Z(t), t] = \bar{y} \int_0^{T-t} \exp(-rs)\ N\left[\frac{\ln Z(t) + (r - \frac{1}{2}\rho^2)s}{\rho s^{1/2}}\right] \mathrm{d}s.$$

The optimal time t consumption is zero if and only if $Z(t) < 1$. By the strict monotonicity of $F(y, t)$ in y, we know that $Z(t) < 1$ if and only if $F[Z(t), t] < F(1, t)$. Thus we have

$$c(t) = \begin{cases} 0 & \text{if } W(t) < F(1, t), \\ \bar{y} & \text{if } W(t) \geqslant F(1, t). \end{cases}$$

The optimal consumption is not a continuous function of the wealth and fails to be differentiable at a single point. ■

We conclude this section by giving, in the two propositions below, necessary and sufficient conditions for the consumption policy prescribed by $\hat{f}$ to have certain derivatives.

Proposition 10 Suppose that the utility function for consumption has a possibly time-dependent satiation level $\bar{c}(t)$ and yields an F such that $D_y^m F(y, t)$ and F_t exist and are continuous. Suppose also that satiation has not occurred. Let y' be a point of discontinuity of $u_{c+}(c, t)$. A necessary and sufficient condition for $c[W(t), t]$ to be a differentiable function of $W(t)$ and t is that for all $t \in [0, T]$ and for all y' the following hold:

1 $u(y, t)$ is strictly concave for all $y < \bar{c}(t)$;
2 $u(y, t)$ is twice differentiable with respect to y for all $y < \bar{c}(t)$ except at y';
3

$$\lim_{y \to y'} -\frac{u_y(y, t)}{u_{yy}(y, t)} = 0;$$

4 for $u_{y+}(0, t) < \infty$,

$$\lim_{y \downarrow 0} -\frac{u_y(y, t)}{u_{yy}(y, t)} = 0;$$

5 for $\bar{c}(t) < \infty$,

$$\lim_{y \uparrow \bar{c}(t)} -\frac{u_y(y, t)}{u_{yy}(y, t)} = 0.$$

$c[W(t), t]$ is a continuously differentiable function of $W(t)$ and t if and only if, in addition, $u(y, t)$ is twice continuously differentiable with respect to y for all $y < \bar{c}(t)$ except at y' and continuously differentiable with respect to t.

PROOF Suppose first that $\bar{c}(t) = \infty$. $c[W(t), t]$ is differentiable in $W(t)$ if and only if $\hat{f}(y, t)$ is differentiable in y. For every subinterval (a, b) on which $u_{y+}(y, t)$ is continuous, $\hat{f}(y, t)$ is differentiable if and only if $u_{y+}(y, t)$ is strictly decreasing and differentiable in y, which is 1 and 2. On the interval $(u_{y+}(y', t), u_{y-}(y', t))$, $\hat{f}$ is flat. Hence $\hat{f}(y, t)$ is differentiable in y at y' if and only if 3. When $u_{y+}(0, t) < \infty$, $\hat{f}$ is flat on the interval $(u_{y+}(0, t), \infty)$. Thus $\hat{f}(y, t)$ is differentiable at zero if and only if 4. Similar arguments prove 5. ■

The following proposition gives circumstances in which c_{WW} exists and is continuous.

Proposition 11 Suppose that the utility function for consumption has a possibly time-dependent satiation level $\bar{c}(t)$ and yields an F such that $D_y^m F(y, t)$ and F_t exist and are continuous. Suppose also that satiation has not occurred. Let y' be a point of discontinuity of $u_{c+}(c, t)$ and suppose that $u(y, t)$ is three times differentiable with respect to y except at y'. A necessary and sufficient condition for $c[W(t), t]$ to be twice differentiable with respect to $W(t)$ is that, for all t and for all y', 1–4 of proposition 8 are satisfied and the following hold:

6
$$\lim_{y \to y'} \left[\frac{u_y(y, t)}{u_{yy}(y, t)}\right]^2 \frac{u_{yyy}(y, t)}{u_{yy}(y, t)} = 0;$$

7 for $u_{y+}(0, t) < \infty$,

$$\lim_{y \downarrow 0} \left[\frac{u_y(y, t)}{u_{yy}(y, t)}\right]^2 \frac{u_{yyy}(y, t)}{u_{yy}(y, t)} = 0;$$

8 for $\bar{c}(t) < \infty$,

$$\lim_{y \uparrow \bar{c}(t)} \left[\frac{u_y(y, t)}{u_{yy}(y, t)}\right]^2 \frac{u_{yyy}(y, t)}{u_{yy}(y, t)} = 0.$$

$c[W(t), t]$ is a twice continuously differentiable function of $W(t)$ if and only if, in addition, $u(y, t)$ is three times continuously differentiable with respect to y for all $y < \bar{c}(t)$ except at y'.

PROOF The arguments are similar to those of propositions 4 and 10, and so we omit them. ■

4 Concluding Remarks

The focus of our paper is on the characterization and computation of optimal consumption–portfolio policies. It is a companion paper to Cox and Huang [6], in which the existence of optimal policies was examined. Several questions remain for future research. First, we have assumed that markets are dynamically complete or, equivalently, that there are as many linearly independent risky securities as the dimension of the uncertainty. It would be interesting to generalize our approach to situations where markets are not dynamically complete. Second, we have shown how nonnegativity constraints on consumption and final wealth can be easily accommodated using our approach. An important question is the extent to which constraints on trading strategies, such as restrictions on borrowing, can also be included. Finally, we have used only time-additive utility functions in our analysis. An issue for further study is the extension of the methods developed here to the case of non-time-additive utility functions.

Notes

1 Karatzas, Lehoczky, and Shreve [24], working independently and concurrently with the May 1986 version of this paper, develop ideas similar to ours.
2 A probability space $(\Omega, \mathcal{F}, P)$ is complete if any subset of a P-null set is contained in $\mathcal{F}$.
3 A sigma field is *almost trivial* if it contains only sets of probability zero or unity.

References

1 Apostol, T. *Mathematical Analysis*, 2nd edn (Reading, MA: Addison-Wesley, 1974).
2 Black, F. and Scholes, M. "The Pricing of Options and Corporate Liabilities," *Journal of Political Economy*, 81, 1973, 637–54.
3 Breeden, D. "An Intertemporal Capital Asset Pricing Model with Stochastic Investment Opportunities," *Journal of Financial Economics*, 7, 1979, 265–96.
4 Brennan, M. and Solanki, R. "Optimal Portfolio Insurance," *Journal of Financial and Quantitative Analysis*, 16, 1981, 279–300.
5 Chung, K. and Williams, R. *Introduction to Stochastic Integration* (Boston, MA: Birkhauser, 1983).
6 Cox, J. and Huang, C. "A Variational Problem Arising in Financial Economics," *Journal of Mathematical Economics*, forthcoming.
7 Cox, J. and Leland, H. "Notes on Intertemporal Investment Policies," Mimeo, Graduate School of Business, Stanford University, 1982.
8 Dellacherie, C. and Meyer, P. *Probabilities and Potential B: Theory of Martingales* (Amsterdam: North-Holland, 1982).
9 Duffie, D. and Huang, C. "Implementing Arrow–Debreu Equilibria by Continuous Trading of Few Long-Lived Securities," *Econometrica*, 53, 1985, 1337–56.
10 Dybvig, P. "A Positive Wealth Constraint Precludes Arbitrage in the Black–Scholes Model," Mimeo, Princeton Economics Department, 1980.

11 Dybvig, P. and Huang, C. "Nonnegative Wealth, Absence of Arbitrage, and Feasible Consumption Plans," *Review of Financial Studies*, 1, 1988, 377–401.
12 Fisk, D. "Quasi-Martingales," *Transactions of the American Mathematical Society*, 120, 1965, 369–89.
13 Fleming, W. and Rishel, R. *Deterministic and Stochastic Optimal Control* (New York: Springer, 1975).
14 Friedman, A. *Stochastic Differential Equations and Applications*, vol. 1 (New York: Academic Press, 1975).
15 Gihman, I. and Skorohod, A. *Stochastic Differential Equations* (New York: Springer, 1972).
16 Gihman, I. and Skorohod, A. *Controlled Stochastic Processes* (New York: Springer, 1979).
17 Harrison, M. and Kreps, D. "Martingales and Multiperiod Securities Markets," *Journal of Economic Theory*, 20, 1979, 381–408.
18 Harrison, M. and Pliska, S. "Martingales and Stochastic Integrals in the Theory of Continuous Trading," *Stochastic Processes and Applications*, 11, 1981, 215–60.
19 Hestenes, M. *Optimization Theory: The Finite Dimensional Case* (New York: Wiley, 1975).
20 Holmes, R. *Geometric Functional Analysis and its Applications* (New York: Springer, 1975).
21 Huang, C. "Information Structures and Viable Price Systems," *Journal of Mathematical Economics*, 14, 1985, 215–40.
22 Huang, C. "An Intertemporal General Equilibrium Asset Pricing Model: The Case of Diffusion Information," *Econometrica*, 55, 1987, 117–42.
23 Jacod, J. *Calcul Stochastique et Problèmes de Martingales*, Lecture Notes in Mathematics 714 (New York: Springer, 1979).
24 Karatzas, I., Lehoczky, J. and Shreve, S. "Optimal Portfolio and Consumption Decisions for a 'Small Investor' on a Finite Horizon," *SIAM Journal of Control and Optimization*, 25, 1987, 1557–86.
25 Karatzas, I., Lehoczky, J., Sethi, S. and Shreve, S. Explicit Solution of a General Consumption/Investment Problem, *Mathematics of Operations Research*, 11, 1986, 613–36.
26 Kreps, D. "Three Essays on Capital Markets," Technical Report 298, Institute for Mathematical Studies in the Social Sciences, Stanford University, 1979.
27 Kreps, D. "Arbitrage and Equilibrium in Economies with Infinitely Many Commodities," *Journal of Mathematical Economics*, 8, 1981, 15–35.
28 Krylov, N. *Controlled Diffusion Processes* (New York: Springer, 1980).
29 Liptser, R. and Shiryayev, A. *Statistics of Random Processes I: General Theory* (New York: Springer, 1977).
30 Merton, R. "Optimum Consumption and Portfolio Rules in a Continuous Time Model," *Journal of Economic Theory*, 3, 1971, 373–413.
31 Merton, R. *Continuous-Time Finance* (Cambridge, MA: Basil Blackwell, 1990).
32 Pliska, S. "A Stochastic Calculus Model of Continuous Time Trading: Optimal Portfolios," *Mathematics of Operations Research*, 11, 1986, 371–82.
33 Rockafellar, R. "Integral Functionals, Normal Integrands, and Measurable Selections," In *Nonlinear Operators and the Calculus of Variations*, eds J. Gossez et al. (New York: Springer, 1975).
34 Royden, H. *Real Analysis* (New York: Macmillan, 1968).
35 Sethi, S. and Taksar, M. "A Note on Merton's Optimum Consumption and Portfolio Rules in a Continuous-Time Model," *Journal of Economic Theory*, 46, 1988, 395–401.

Chapter 5

Philip H. Dybvig

Background and Comments

Portfolio insurance schemes are the best known examples of the dynamic trading strategies popular with some portfolio managers. Philip Dybvig's paper shows that portfolio insurance is probably, perhaps generally, *not* a good investment strategy for a rational risk-averse individual. Why then has this strategy attracted institutional investors?

Perhaps the objectives of institutional money managers are not well aligned with the objectives of the individuals whose money they are managing. For example, my accumulated stake in the MIT retirement plan is not invested by me, but by MIT, which parcels the money out to institutions, who in turn delegate portfolio selection to various employees. These decision makers do not know my utility function, and even if they did I doubt they would always be perfect agents for my interests.

It is often said that the business of managing money is the business of getting other people's money to manage. Success in this business depends as much on relative as on absolute performance. It may take a generation to separate the truly superior from the average but lucky portfolio managers. In this sense long-run absolute performance is extremely difficult to measure. Institutional money managers frequently find themselves judged instead on performance relative to competing managers. Therefore it may not be too surprising to find money managers following tactical strategies that may not match up with the ultimate client's interests. Looking good may be just as important as performing well in the long run.

Of course these are my conjectures, not Dybvig's. He concentrates on exposing the shortcomings of certain intuitively appealing rules in a simple model of individual portfolio choice. He does not offer any cookbook for optimal dynamic portfolio strategies. He does offer healthy skepticism about certain currently popular techniques.

Author's Introduction

One of my goals for my Batterymarch Fellowship year, as expressed in my proposal, was to develop a strategy-proof method of evaluating portfolio managers. This goal was motivated in part by my developing work with Ross that pointed out some deficiencies in existing performance measures (Dybvig and Ross, 1985a,b), and in part by my concern about the use by practitioners of performance measures that are relatively easy to manipulate. For example, a strategy resembling a doubling strategy at roulette can beat a performance scheme that rewards a manager for beating the market by at least 1 percent over a year. During the year, riskier and riskier policies are taken until the point at which the market is beaten by more than 1 percent, at which time the fund is indexed to the market, or until the account is exhausted. At the end of the year, the manager gets the bonus almost all the time. However, the manager is fired if the account is exhausted. For the manager, it is worth taking a small chance of being fired in exchange for getting a bonus the rest of the time.

One of the papers I wrote in my Batterymarch Fellowship year (Dybvig, 1982) did in fact develop a strategy-proof method of evaluating portfolio managers, based on a model I call the payoff-distribution pricing model. Unfortunately, on reflection I decided that neither this measure nor any of the other popular measures could measure performance over the relevant time interval (say 1 year), because we cannot accurately estimate a mean return over a year let alone some more sophisticated measure. I now believe that effective oversight of portfolio managers involves judgment about whether the manager's plan makes sense and analysis of trades to monitor adherence to the plan. This is in contrast with the traditional view in academic finance which focuses on mechanical measures based primarily or entirely on realized returns. However, as is often the case, the tools developed for one purpose found more interesting application in another context. "Inefficient Dynamic Portfolio Strategies, or How to Throw Away a Million Dollars in the Stock Market" uses the analysis originally intended to aid in performance measurement to measure the degree of efficiency loss from following some types of strategies used on Wall Street. The size of the efficiency loss is a striking reminder that capital market efficiency rules out superior performance but not inferior performance.

References

Dybvig, P. (1982) "Some New Tools for Testing Market Efficiency and Measuring Mutual Fund Performance," *Working Paper*, Yale University.

Dybvig, P. and Ross, S. (1985a) "Differential Information and Performance Measurement Using a Security Market Line," *Journal of Finance*, 40: 2, June, 383–99.

Dybvig, P. and Ross, S. (1985b) "The Analytics of Performance Measurement Using a Security Market Line," *Journal of Finance*, 40: 2, June, 401–16.

Bibliographical Listing

"Distributional Analysis of Portfolio Choice," *Journal of Business*, 61: 3, July 1988, 369–93.

"Banking Theory, Deposit Insurance and Bank Regulation" (with Douglas W. Diamond), *Journal of Business*, 59: 1, January 1986, 55–68.

"Yes, the APT is Testable" (with Stephen Ross), *Journal of Finance*, 40: 4, September, 1985, 1173–88.

"The Analytics of Performance Measurement Using a Security Market Line" (with Stephen Ross), *Journal of Finance*, 40: 2, June 1985, 401–16.

"Differential Information and Performance Measurement Using a Security Market Line" (with Stephen Ross), *Journal of Finance*, 40: 2, June 1985, 383–99.

"An Explicit Bound on Individual Assets' Deviations from APT Pricing in a Finite Economy," *Journal of Financial Economics*, 12: 4, December 1983, 483–96.

"Agency and the Market for Portfolio Managers: The Principle of Preference Similarity" (with Chester Spatt), *Working Paper*, Yale University, 1983.

"Some New Tools for Testing Market Efficiency and Measuring Mutual Fund Performance," *Working Paper*, Yale University, 1982.

Inefficient Dynamic Portfolio Strategies or How to Throw Away a Million Dollars in the Stock Market

PHILIP H. DYBVIG

Portfolio managers regularly use a number of dynamic portfolio strategies that have not received careful theoretical analysis; some examples are lock-in strategies, stop-loss strategies, rolling over portfolio insurance, and contingent immunization. The lack of analysis has been due largely to the inadequacy of the traditional theoretical tools. Specifically, mean–variance analysis is not valid when the portfolio return is nonlinearly related to market returns, as it will be under these strategies.[1] Cox and Leland (1982) have shown that when the riskless rate is constant and the risky asset follows geometric Brownian motion or a geometric binomial process, strategies such as these are inefficient; unfortunately, the Cox–Leland approach, while elegant and insightful, does not tell us the *magnitude* of the inefficiency. The purpose of this article is to use the payoff distribution pricing model (Dybvig, 1982, 1988) to compute the cost of the inefficiency directly. As a result, we can now compare the cost of a failure to diversify over time with nonmodeled costs, such as trading commissions. The results indicate that the inefficiency costs of the strategies are substantial and should not be ignored by practitioners.

A common misconception among students first learning about the efficient markets hypothesis is that portfolio managers can do no damage. Of course, this is not true, because managers choosing random or poorly diversified portfolios throw away investors' money by obtaining less return for them than is justified by the amount of risk taken on. For example, in the mean–variance world an efficient portfolio choice could have given the investors the same mean and variance of terminal wealth at a lower cost. In an intertemporal context, things become a little more complicated. Besides the importance of diversification across assets, an efficient portfolio

Reproduced from *Review of Financial Studies*, 1: 1, 1988, 67–88.

I am grateful for helpful discussions with Michael Brennan, Stephen Brown, Kent Dybvig, David Feldman, Mike Granito, Roger Ibbotson, Jon Ingersoll, Alan Kraus, Steve Ross, Eduardo Schwartz, and participants in various seminars. I am also grateful for financial support from the Sloan Research Fellowship Program.

choice must also be diversified across time. Furthermore, a nonconstant portfolio choice over time may be optimal, but such a portfolio choice must react appropriately to information arrival.

Fortunately, there is a simpler way of viewing the multiperiod problem. As Ross (1978) has emphasized, the space of feasible consumption bundles is quite generally a linear space. Therefore, if all consumption takes place at the end, we can replace the original dynamic problem with an equivalent one-period problem that has the appropriate terminal state prices.[2] The use of state prices to reduce a multiperiod problem to a one-period problem is the basis of Cox and Leland (1982) and has been emphasized by many others, starting perhaps with Ross (1976) and Rubinstein (1976).[3]

Once we assume that all consumption takes place at the end, we apply the payoff distribution pricing model (PDPM), which allows us to calculate a lower bound on the cost of the efficiency loss. The assumptions of the PDPM are as follows (see Dybvig (1988) for a formal development of the PDPM).

1 Agents' preferences depend only on the probability distribution of terminal wealth.
2 Agents prefer more to less; that is, given a choice between two ordered random terminal wealths, an agent will always choose the larger.
3 The market faced by an individual comes from our standard model of a perfect market (no taxes, transaction costs, or information asymmetries) that is complete over finitely many equally probable terminal states or over some atomless continuum of states. Such a market allows short sales without penalty.

Informally, the assumptions are (a) state independence of preferences, (b) preference of more to less, and (c) completeness of frictionless complete markets with equally probable states.[4]

The first assumption says that preferences depend only on the probability distribution of terminal consumption. This assumption allows von Neumann–Morgenstern preferences over wealth, or more generally Machina (1982) preferences over wealth, but it precludes state-dependent preferences (including those induced by nontraded wealth). The second assumption – preference of more to less – would not be reasonable for ice cream but is certainly reasonable for wealth. The third assumption – completeness of markets over equally probable or continuous terminal states – is a natural assumption in the presence of continuous trading or a complete set of options. The assumption of equally probable terminal states is for convenience; it allows us to use first-order stochastic dominance. If we allow terminal state probabilities to be unequal and assume concavity of preferences, the analysis is messier, but exactly the same numerical results are valid (see Dybvig, 1988, appendix I).

These assumptions imply that any optimal strategy purchases more consumption in terminal states in which consumption is cheaper. What is new to the PDPM is the idea of computing how much the cheapest portfolio generating a given *distribution function* of consumption should cost, and the development of simple machinery for doing so. This cost is given by the change in price in response to swapping consumption across terminal states to make the consumption a decreasing function of the state price density while maintaining the same marginal distribution.

Section 1 contains simple numerical examples. Section 2 presents some computer-generated numerical results for reasonable parameter values. Section 3 discusses generalizations, particularly to term structure models. The article is intended to be self-contained in the sense that it does not require any prior knowledge of the PDPM.

1 Some Numerical Examples

We now present some simple examples designed to illustrate the principle behind applying the PDPM to measuring inefficiency. These examples use the binomial model of stock returns introduced by Cox, Ross, and Rubinstein (1979). For convenience, numerically simple parameters are chosen: the initial wealth level and initial stock price are both 16, the riskless rate is always zero, and in each period the stock doubles in price or halves in price, each with probability $\frac{1}{2}$. A four-period model is required since, given the other assumptions, this is the shortest time span over which the analysis does not degenerate.[5] Obviously, these examples are for illustration only; more realistic examples will be analyzed in section 3 using the general form of the PDPM.

Before moving to the examples, let us review some important properties of the binomial model (all these properties have appeared in the literature in one form or another) and a few PDPM concepts and results.

1.1 The binomial model and the PDPM

Stock and bond returns in the binomial model are shown graphically in table 5.1. For binomial models, it is most common to represent the stock price movements by an *ingrown tree*. An expanded tree in which all possible stock price paths are distinguished will also be useful, since we shall be studying portfolio strategies for which the terminal portfolio value will depend on the whole path of stock prices and not just on the final stock price. The bond price is constant over time and in all states, and is represented by a line segment.

Table 5.1 Security returns, state probabilities, and state prices

Bond:
16 — 16 — 16 — 16 — 16

Stock:

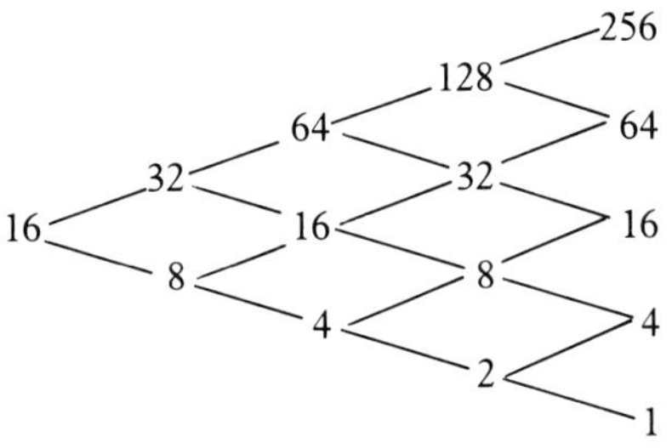

State probability	*State price*	*State price density*
1/16	1/81	16/81
4/16	8/81	32/81
6/16	24/81	64/81
4/16	32/81	128/81
1/16	16/81	256/81

Stock (expanded):

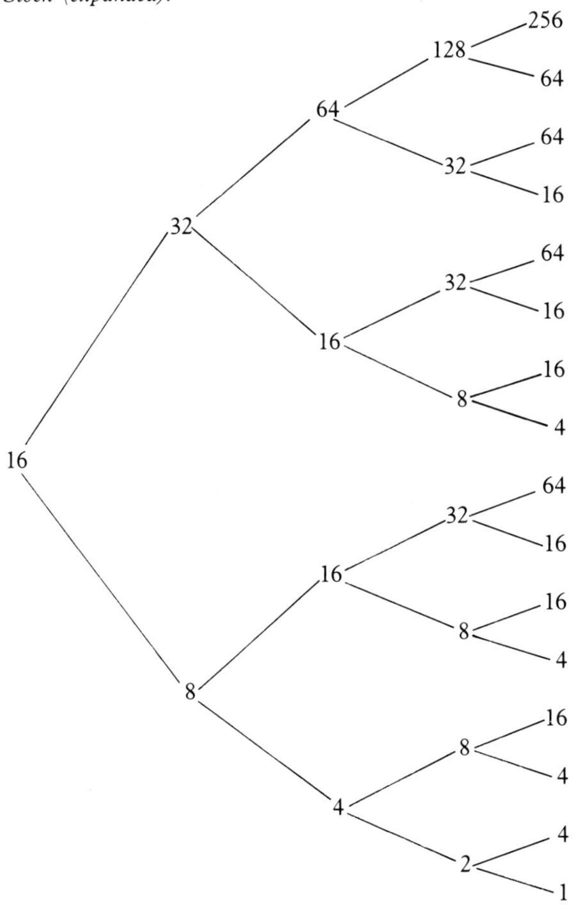

State probability	*State price*	*State price density*
1/16	1/81	16/81
1/16	2/81	32/81
1/16	2/81	32/81
1/16	4/81	64/81
1/16	2/81	32/81
1/16	4/81	64/81
1/16	4/81	64/81
1/16	8/81	128/81
1/16	2/81	32/81
1/16	4/81	64/81
1/16	4/81	64/81
1/16	8/81	128/81
1/16	4/81	64/81
1/16	8/81	128/81
1/16	8/81	128/81
1/16	16/81	256/81

We can see from table 5.1 that the usual convention of representing the stock price in terms of an ingrown tree is simply a shorthand that combines all the states in which the stock price is the same. In the expanded tree each state has the same probability, $\frac{1}{16} = (\frac{1}{2})^4$, because at each node the up and down probabilities are both $\frac{1}{2}$. We could write the bond in an expanded tree in the same way, but the result would be a boring tree with 16 at each node.

From option pricing theory (and explicitly Cox, Ross, and Rubinstein (1979)) we know that every contingent claim paying off various amounts in the last period can be priced, because each contingent claim can be duplicated by some hedging strategy. In particular, we can price a claim that pays 1 in a given state and 0 in all other states. By definition, the price of this claim is called the *state price* of the given state. State prices are useful because the value of any security can be written as the sum across states of the state price times the value of the security in the state.

To compute the state price for the binomial model, look first to a single period. Suppose that the value of an asset next period is v_1 if the stock goes up and v_2 if the stock goes down. We want to duplicate holding the asset. If we invest an amount v_S in stock and an amount v_B in bond, tomorrow we shall have $2v_S + v_B$ if the stock goes up and $v_S/2 + v_B$ if the stock goes down. If this investment duplicates the asset's value, then we have

$$v_1 = 2v_S + v_B \qquad \text{and} \qquad v_2 = v_S/2 + v_B$$

Solving for v_S and v_B, we obtain $v_S = 2(v_1 - v_2)/3$ and $v_B = (4v_2 - v_1)/3$, which is the hedging strategy. Note that $v_S + v_B = v_1/3 + 2v_2/3$, which is the one-period pricing relation. In other words, the up state has price $\frac{1}{3}$ and the down state has price $\frac{2}{3}$.

Of course, we can use this procedure to obtain the state price of any node and, by extension, the value of any claim. In particular, the state price of any node equals the price of a claim that pays 1 in that state at that time and 0 otherwise. By folding back, we conclude that the state price of any node is $(\frac{1}{3})^u(\frac{2}{3})^d$, where u is the number of times the stock price goes up and d is the number of times the stock price goes down. This formula applies to all time intervals. For example, the value of a security at any point is equal to $\frac{1}{3}$ times the value one period later if the stock goes up plus $\frac{2}{3}$ times the value one period later if the stock goes down. Working backward a period at a time using state prices is analogous to solving the Black and Scholes (1973) differential equation, while valuing a claim directly by summing over the four-period state prices is analogous to using the Rubinstein (1976) integral approach to option pricing. From now on we shall focus on the approach using state prices. Keep in mind, however, that the derivation of the state prices tells us explicitly how to compute the amounts of stock and bond held at each point in time in the dominating strategy.

The one aspect of table 5.1 that remains to be discussed is the *state price density* (or state price per unit probability), which is simply the state price divided by the probability.[6] It is useful to think in terms of this ratio, which plays a central role in the PDPM. For one thing, maximizing a von Neumann–Morgenstern utility function gives the first-order condition that the marginal utility is proportional to the terminal state price density. Suppose that an agent solves the following problem:

$$\begin{aligned}&\text{choose } c_i\text{s to}\\&\text{maximize } \textstyle\sum \pi_i u(c_i)\\&\text{subject to } \textstyle\sum p_i c_i = w_0,\end{aligned}$$

where c_i is consumption in terminal state i, π_i is the probability of terminal state i, $u(\cdot)$ is the agent's utility function, and p_i is the state price of terminal state i. If $u(\cdot)$ is differentiable, then the first-order condition is that, for some λ,

$$\pi_i u'(c_i) = \lambda p_i$$

or

$$u'(c_i) = \lambda \frac{p_i}{\pi_i} \equiv \lambda \rho_i, \tag{1}$$

which is to say that the agent's marginal utility of wealth in terminal state i is proportional to the terminal state price density $\rho_i \equiv p_i/\pi_i$.[7] A second important feature of the state price density is that, if we combine states with the same state price density, the combined aggregate state will also have the same state price density. Perhaps more importantly, we can define the state price density even if there is a nonatomic continuum of states (in which case both the state price and the probability are zero), as in the diffusion models. The state price density is defined at each node as the ratio of the state price to the probability of the node. The state price density follows a multiplicative process whose movements locally price all assets correctly. In our specialized binomial model, the state price density at a node following u ups and d downs is given by $\rho_n = p_n/\pi_n = [(\frac{1}{3})^u(\frac{2}{3})^d]/[(\frac{1}{2})^u(\frac{1}{2})^d] = (\frac{2}{3})^u(\frac{4}{3})^d$.

We shall need a few concepts and results of the payoff distribution pricing model (PDPM). An asset pricing model (such as the capital asset pricing model (CAPM), the arbitrage pricing theory (APT), or the Black–Scholes model) gives us the price of a random cash flow, as in the budget constraint to the agent's maximization problem above. For discrete models with complete markets, the asset pricing model is $P_A(c) = \Sigma_i p_i c_i$.

The PDPM assigns a price to a distribution function of consumption by assigning to it the price of the least expensive consumption pattern having that payoff. In other words, we can write the distributional pricing function as $P_D(F) = \min\{P_A(c) \mid c \sim F\}$, where $\sim$ means "is distributed as." For the extensions in section 3, we shall refer to a general formula for this minimum cost in terms of the distribution functions of c and ρ, but for now all we need is the following theorem which combines several results from Dybvig (1988).

Theorem 1 The following are equivalent:

1 the consumption pattern c is chosen by some agent who has strictly increasing von Neumann–Morgenstern preferences over terminal wealth;
2 the consumption pattern has an asset price equal to the distributional price of its distribution function, that is, $P_A(c) = P_D(F_c)$;
3 consumption is nondecreasing in the terminal state price density.

PROOF See theorems 1 and 2 of Dybvig (1988). ■

This theorem is useful to us for two different reasons. First, it says that $P_A(c) - P_D(F_c)$ is a tight lower bound on the amount of initial wealth an agent would pay to switch from c to an optimal strategy, given that we do not know the agent's actual preferences. (This is a bound because all agents are indifferent between c and the strategy underlying $P_D(c)$, and the bound is tight because the theorem tells us that there is some agent who would follow that underlying strategy, implying that the bound is achieved for this agent.) Second, it tells us how to compute the bound: namely, by swapping consumption across terminal states, leaving the distribution function unchanged, until consumption is nondecreasing in the terminal state price density.

Now that the binomial model and the PDPM have been reviewed, we are ready to proceed to the examples. All the examples use the concepts and tools of the PDPM to quantify the amount of damage done by following an inefficient policy, that is, a policy for which consumption is not nonincreasing in the terminal state price density. The first example examines a policy of holding stock initially but limiting potential losses by switching from the stock to the bond if ever the portfolio value falls too much. Let us call this policy a stop-loss strategy.

Example 1: Stop-loss strategy The rule under this strategy is to invest in the stock until the portfolio value falls to 8 and to stay in the bond from then on. The value of the portfolio under this strategy is given in the ingrown tree in table 5.2. The probabilities are computed by adding up the number of paths to the terminal node and multiplying by $\frac{1}{16}$. For example, there are three paths (UUUD, UUDU and UDUU) with a terminal wealth of 64 and two paths (UUDD and UDUD) with a terminal wealth of 16. Horizontal paths corresponding to holding the bond have to be counted twice *per period the bond is held*, since the horizontal line captures both states. Therefore, there are ten paths with a terminal wealth of 8

> (UDDU, UDDD, DUUU, DUUD, DUDU, DUDD, DDUU, DDUD, DDDU, and DDDD).

The second strategy in table 5.2 was chosen to obtain the same distribution of terminal wealth (allocated differently across states) but with consumption ordered the opposite of the terminal state price density, which, from table 5.1, is ordered the opposite of the stock price. To do this, we walk down the two probability distributions together. First, we assign the $\frac{1}{16}$ probability of 256 to the terminal state in which the stock reaches 256. Next, we assign the $\frac{3}{16}$ probability of 64 to three of the four terminal states in which the stock price reaches 64. Now, we assign $\frac{1}{16}$ of the $\frac{2}{16}$ probability of obtaining 16 to the remaining terminal state in which the stock is 64, and the remaining $\frac{1}{16}$ to one of the terminal states in which the stock is 16. In all the remaining terminal states (ten of them) the amount we obtain is 8. Because this selection makes consumption nonincreasing in the terminal state price density, by theorem 1 the resulting portfolio strategy is efficient. The values earlier on in the tree are computed by walking back period by period using the $\frac{1}{3}$, $\frac{2}{3}$ weighting rule. We find that this portfolio strategy, while giving exactly the same probability distribution of terminal wealth as the stop-loss strategy, costs only $15\frac{65}{81}$ (compared with 16).

What is really going on here? If we compare the terminal wealth of the two strategies state by state, we find that they differ only in the two marked states, UDUD and DUUU. Since the latter state has more ups and fewer downs, the terminal state price density is lower. The efficient dominating strategy has its higher consumption in that state (16 versus 8), while the reverse is true for the stop-loss strategy (8 versus 16). The saving is the difference in cost of the two strategies ($16-\frac{1280}{81}=\frac{16}{81}$), which is the probability ($\frac{1}{16}$) times the difference in terminal state price density ($\frac{64}{81}-\frac{32}{81}=\frac{32}{81}$) times the amount of consumption moved ($16-8=8$). In richer examples with more periods or more elaborate strategies, there would be more terminal states in which the inefficient and dominating strategies disagree. Nonetheless, the concept would be the same: the dominating strategy would move consumption from expensive terminal states to cheaper states.

Table 5.2 The stop-loss strategy (limit 8) and a dominating strategy

Stop-loss strategy:

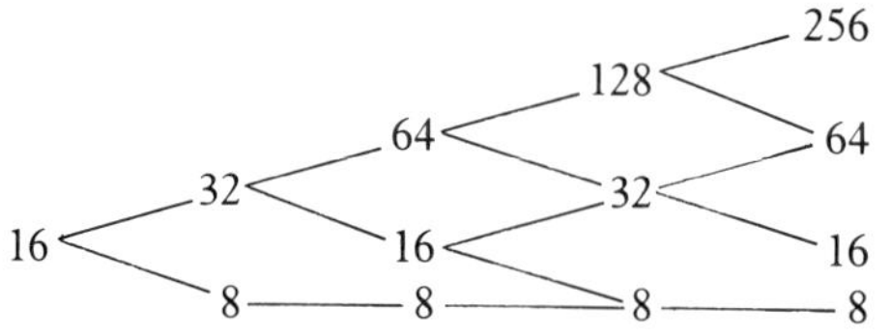

Probability
1/16
3/16
2/16
10/16

Dominating strategy, which is itself undominated. This strategy costs only $15\frac{65}{81}$ (= 1280/81) but gives the same terminal probability distribution of wealth (in different states).

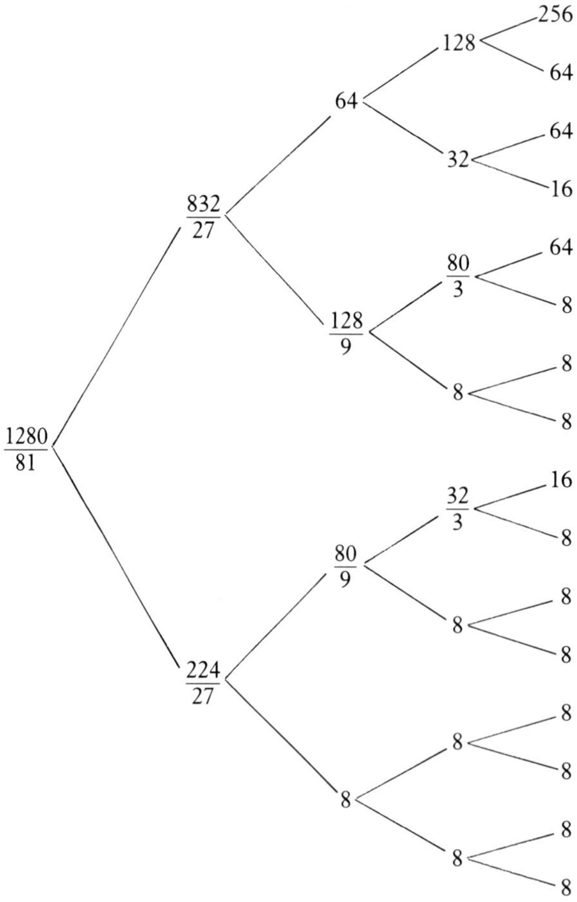

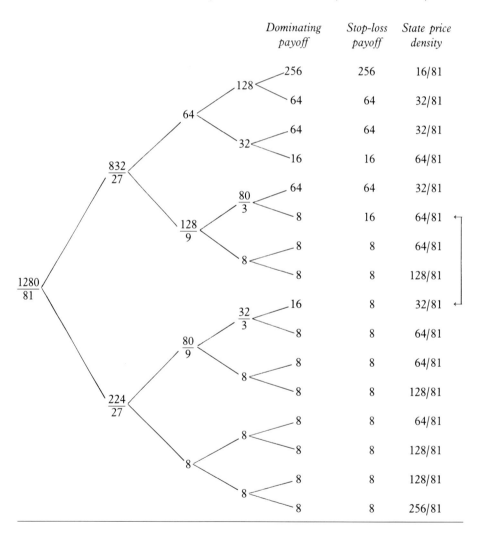

Dominating payoff	*Stop-loss payoff*	*State price density*
256	256	16/81
64	64	32/81
64	64	32/81
16	16	64/81
64	64	32/81
8	16	64/81
8	8	64/81
8	8	128/81
16	8	32/81
8	8	64/81
8	8	64/81
8	8	128/81
8	8	64/81
8	8	128/81
8	8	128/81
8	8	256/81

Table 5.3 The lock-in strategy (limit 32) and a dominating strategy

Lock-in strategy:

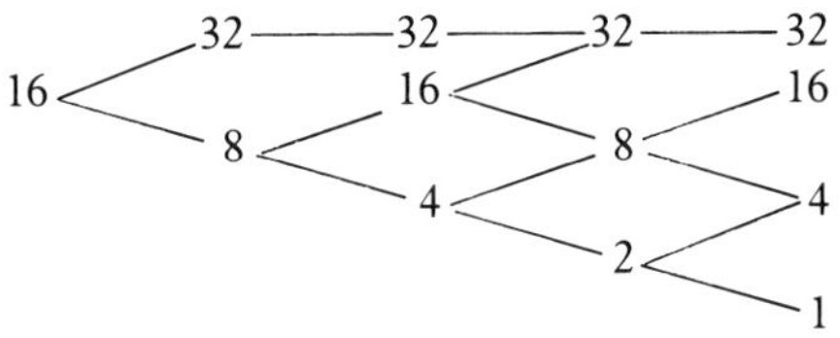

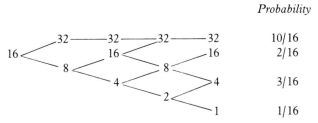

	Probability
32	10/16
16	2/16
4	3/16
1	1/16

Dominating strategy, which is itself undominated. This strategy costs only $15\frac{17}{81}$ ($=1232/81$) but gives the same terminal probability distribution of wealth (in different states).

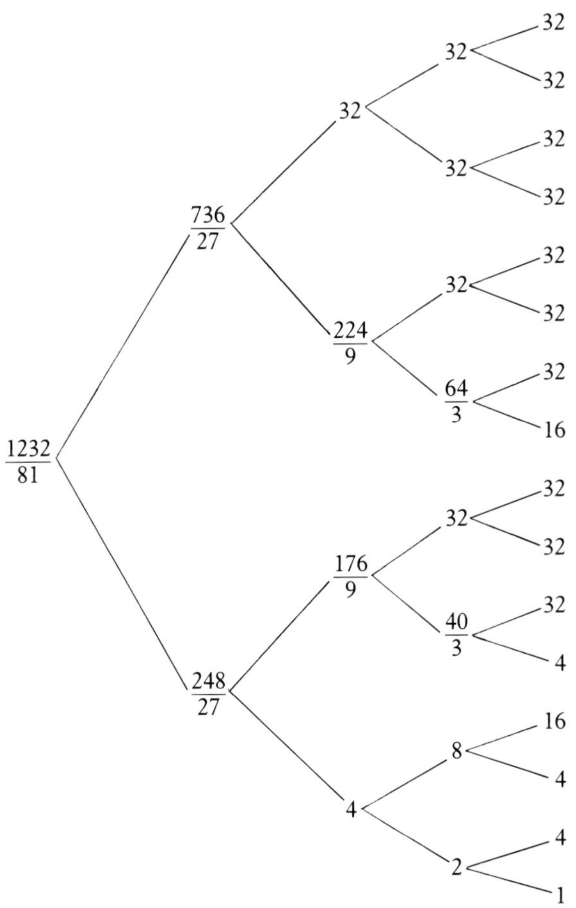

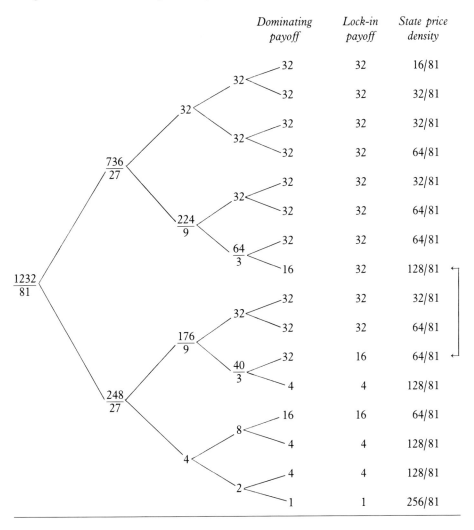

Dominating payoff	*Lock-in payoff*	*State price density*
32	32	16/81
32	32	32/81
32	32	32/81
32	32	64/81
32	32	32/81
32	32	64/81
32	32	64/81
16	32	128/81 ←
32	32	32/81
32	32	64/81
32	16	64/81 ←
4	4	128/81
16	16	64/81
4	4	128/81
4	4	128/81
1	1	256/81

The second example is in the same spirit as the first, but in reverse. The policy is to hold stock initially but to switch into bonds (to lock in the gain) if there is sufficient improvement in the portfolio value. Let us refer to this policy as a lock-in strategy.

Example 2: Lock-in strategy The rule under this strategy is to invest in the stock until the portfolio value rises to 32 and to stay in the bond from then on. The value of the portfolio is given by the ingrown tree in table 5.3. In terms of which paths can occur (and therefore the probabilities of the outcomes), the ingrown tree is just the same as the stop-loss tree of example 1 shown in table 5.2, only upside down. The efficiency loss is different, however, since the quantities and terminal state prices are different when we turn the tree upside down.

The second strategy in table 5.3 was chosen to obtain the same terminal distribution of terminal wealth as the lock-in strategy but with consumption ordered the opposite of the terminal state price density. This process is just as in example 1, except that it starts from the opposite side. Computing the initial investment required for this strategy, we find that it costs only $15\frac{17}{81}$ (compared with 16).

As in example 1, if we compare the terminal wealth of the lock-in strategy with its dominating strategy state by state, we find that the two differ only in the two marked states (UDDD and DUDU). The

Table 5.4 Random market timing strategy (50 percent stock) and a dominating strategy

Random market timing strategy A:

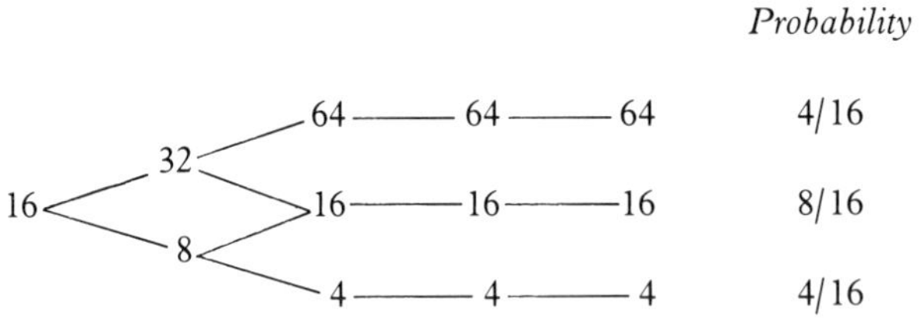

Random market timing strategy B:

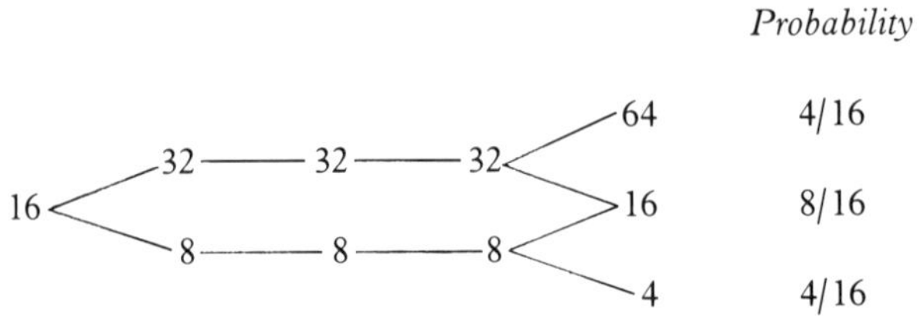

Table 5.4 (*Continued*)

Dominating strategy, which is itself undominated. This strategy costs only $14\frac{2}{9}$ ($=129/9$) but gives the same terminal probability distribution of wealth (in different states).

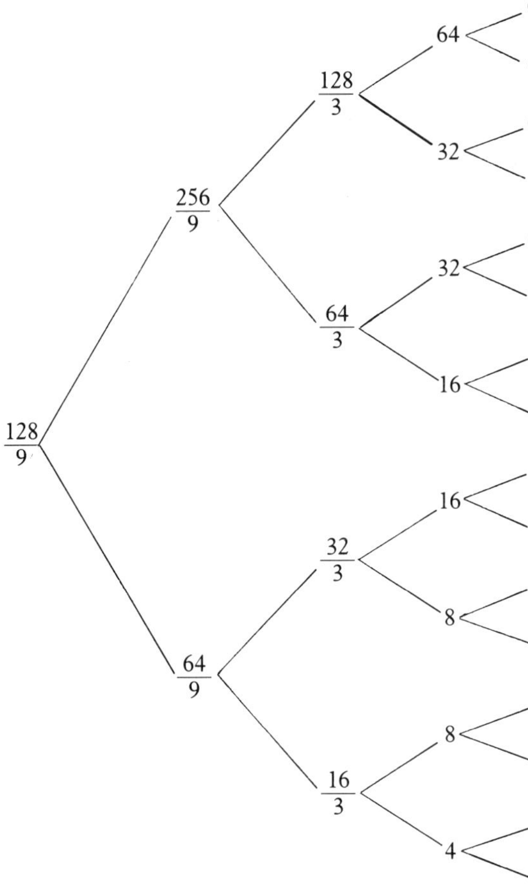

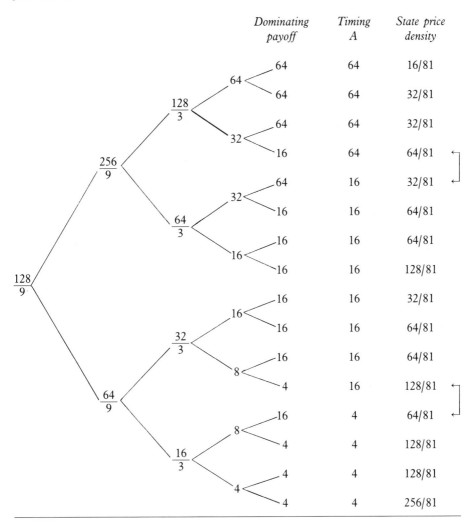

Dominating payoff	*Timing A*	*State price density*
64	64	16/81
64	64	32/81
64	64	32/81
16	64	64/81
64	16	32/81
16	16	64/81
16	16	64/81
16	16	128/81
16	16	32/81
16	16	64/81
16	16	64/81
4	16	128/81
16	4	64/81
4	4	128/81
4	4	128/81
4	4	256/81

improvement made by the dominating strategy is to move the larger consumption from the more expensive of the two states to the cheaper one.

In the third example, we compute the potential cost of hiring someone who claims to have timing ability but actually may not.

Example 3: Random market timing strategy (market timer who cannot) The rule under this strategy is to invest in the stock in some two of the four periods (half the time) and to invest in the bond in the other two. The timing is based on any random rule that is independent of market returns. The distribution of terminal wealth is the same whatever the timing; two examples (A and B) are illustrated in table 5.4. Strategy A has the stock investment in the first two periods. Strategy B has the stock investment in the first and last periods. Since the terminal distribution is the same independent of the random choice, the unconditional distribution is the same under each choice.

As before, the way to dominate the strategy is to move the large amounts of consumption to terminal states in which consumption is cheaper. From table 5.4, we can see that the move to the dominating strategy requires two switches (both marked), one between UUDD and UDUU, and the other between DUDD and DDUU. The first switch reduces the cost by the product of the probability $\frac{1}{16}$, the amount 48 $(=64-16)$ of consumption moved, and the difference $\frac{32}{81}$ $(=\frac{64}{81}-\frac{32}{81})$ in terminal state price density, for a cost reduction $1\frac{5}{27}$ $(=\frac{32}{27})$. The second switch reduces the cost by the product of the probability $\frac{1}{16}$, the amount 12 $(=16-4)$ of consumption moved, and the difference $\frac{64}{81}$ $(=\frac{128}{81}-\frac{64}{81})$ in terminal state price density, for a cost reduction of $\frac{16}{27}$. Combining these two changes, we have a total cost reduction of $1\frac{7}{9}$ $(1\frac{21}{27})$, which reduces the initial cost from 16 to $14\frac{2}{9}$.

This concludes the simple numerical examples. In section 2 we report computer-based calculations of the loss under more reasonable parameter values.

2 Realistically, How Large Is the Cost?

In section 1 we examined three numerical examples that showed the theoretical principle behind measuring the cost of following a dominated strategy. Now we compute the cost in more realistic situations. The calculations approximate continuous lognormal stock movements using a binomial process with a daily grid. To approximate current conditions with a round number, the short riskless rate is assumed to be 8 percent. To approximate historical returns on well-diversified portfolios, the stock is assumed to have an expected return of 16 percent (that is, an excess return of 8 percent annually) and an annual standard deviation of about 20 percent (in logarithms).

Table 5.5 summarizes how these parameter assumptions map into per period returns. As the time increment Δt becomes smaller and smaller, the stochastic process described in table 5.5 and the corresponding pricing converge to a standard lognormal diffusion model for the stock price (as is consistent with Black and Scholes (1973) with a constant mean return).

Table 5.5 One-period returns in terms of the underlying parameters[a]

One-period bond return:

$$1 \text{———} 1 + r\,\Delta t \approx 1.0002222$$

One-period stock return:

	Probability
$1 \nearrow 1 + \mu\,\Delta t + \sigma(\Delta t)^{1/2} \approx 1.0109854$	0.5
$1 \searrow 1 + \mu\,\Delta t - \sigma(\Delta t)^{1/2} \approx 0.9899035$	0.5

State price density:

$$1 \nearrow \frac{1}{1 + r\,\Delta t}\left[1 - \frac{(\mu - r)\,\Delta t}{\sigma(\Delta t)^{1/2}}\right] \approx 0.9787007$$

$$1 \searrow \frac{1}{1 + r\,\Delta t}\left[1 + \frac{(\mu - r)\Delta t}{\sigma(\Delta t)^{1/2}}\right] \approx 1.0208550$$

[a]Parameters used in numerical work: $r = 0.08$ (annual interest rate is 8%, continuous compounding); $\mu = 0.16$ (annual expected return is 16%, for an 8% risk premium); $\sigma = 0.2$ (annual proportional standard deviation is 20%); $\Delta t = 1/360 \approx 0.0027778$ (daily); $(\Delta t)^{1/2} \approx 0.0527046$.

(For related analyses, see Garman (1976), Ross (1976), Rubinstein (1976), Banz and Miller (1978), Cox, Ross, and Rubinstein (1979), Brennan and Solanki (1981), and Cox and Leland (1982).) Therefore the numerical results can be considered an approximation to what would be obtained in continuous time.

Now we are ready to look at some numerical results. Figures 5.1, 5.2, and 5.3 are plots of numerical estimates of the cost of following the three inefficient strategies described in section 1. The estimates were made by using a set of routines for analyzing probability distributions. These routines were written in the SCHEME programming language, which is a dialect of LISP (R. K. Dybvig, 1987). The program computes the minimum cost by matching consumption levels in reverse order of the terminal state price density as described in section 1. In computing the terminal distribution, the routines manage the size of the problem by combining indistinguishable states along the way.

Figure 5.1 shows the cost of following a stop-loss strategy, as a function of the limit value. (The "jaggedness" of the plot comes from the coarseness of the daily binomial approximation to the diffusion; the plot became smoother when the computations were repeated for a half-day interval.) For example, assume that the current portfolio value is \$2 billion and that we plan to switch into stock if the value falls to \$1.8 billion or below; then the limit value is 90 percent (=1.8/2.0). Figure 5.1 says that we shall be

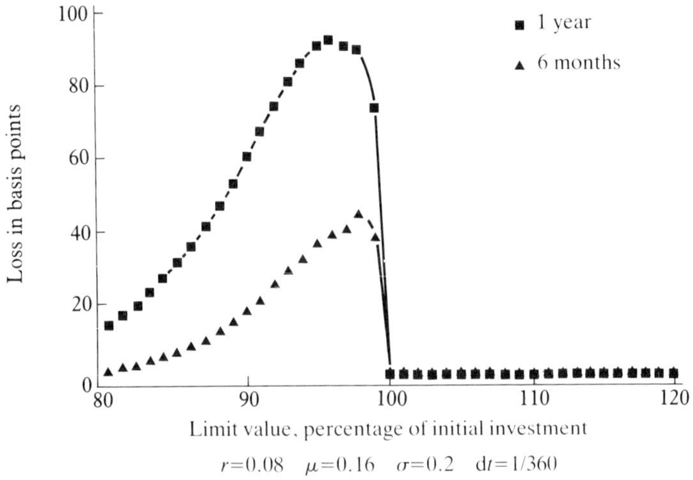

Figure 5.1 Efficiency loss of a stop-loss strategy. The efficiency loss is shown in basis points (0.01 percent of the initial investment). Under the stop-loss strategy, the manager invests the entire portfolio in stocks until the portfolio value reaches or falls below the limit value. When the limit value is at or above 100 percent of the initial wealth, the switch takes place immediately and the strategy is the same as just holding the bond (and is therefore efficient). The size of the efficiency loss can be dramatic: at its worst it is nearly 1 percent of the portfolio value in only a year!

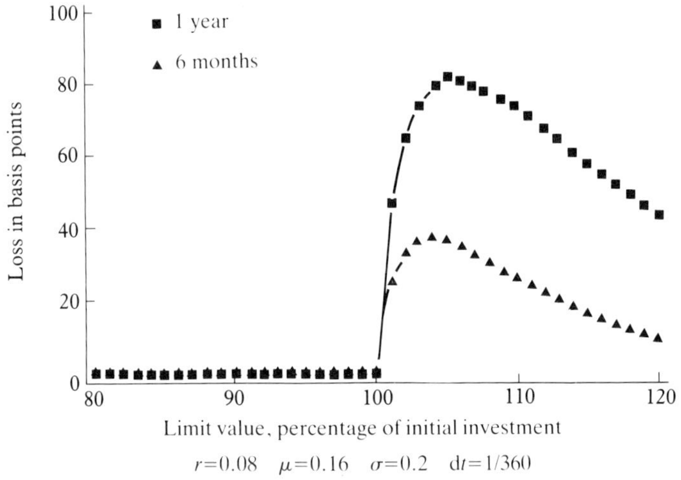

Figure 5.2 Efficiency loss of a lock-in strategy. The efficiency loss is shown in basis points (0.01 percent of the initial investment). Under the lock-in strategy, the manager invests the entire portfolio in stocks until the portfolio value reaches or exceeds the limit value. When the limit value is at or below 100 percent of the initial wealth, the switch takes place immediately and the strategy is the same as just holding the bond (and is therefore efficient). Again, the size of the efficiency loss can be dramatic: at its worst it is roughly 0.8 percent of the portfolio value in only a year. (It is not exactly the same as for the very similar stop-loss strategy, since the state prices are not symmetric for increases and decreases.)

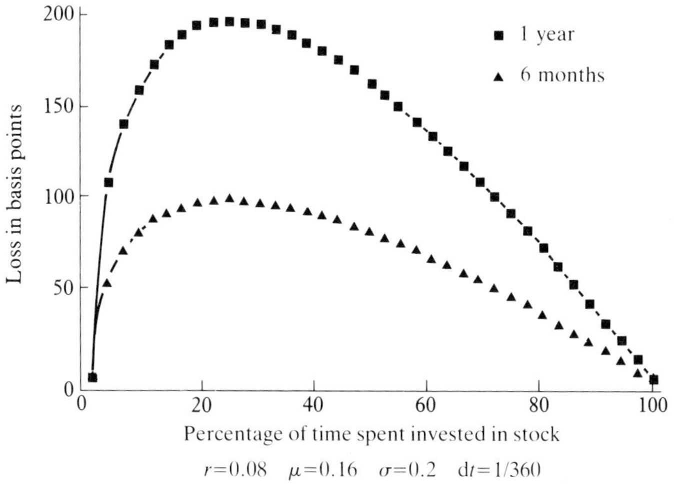

Figure 5.3 Efficiency loss of a random timing strategy. A random timing strategy is a strategy followed by an agent who claims to have market timing ability but really does not. By assumption, such a manager spends a fixed fraction of the time fully invested in the stock and a fixed fraction of the time fully invested in the bond, using a rule that is independent of security returns. For the limits with 0 percent or 100 percent of the time spent invested in the stock, the strategy is efficient because these limits correspond to buying and holding the bond or the stock respectively. For other cases, the efficiency loss is even larger than for the stop-loss and lock-in strategies: at its worst it is nearly 2 percent of the portfolio value in only a year!

throwing away about 60 basis points, or $12 million, by following the stop-loss strategy for a year, compared with following the efficient strategy giving the same distribution of terminal wealth. While this ignores transaction costs for the two strategies, 60 basis points over a year is a large number, and we can surely do better than a stop-loss strategy. When the limit value is small, the efficiency loss is small, since the limit is rarely achieved and the portfolio strategy is nearly the same as holding the stock (which is efficient). Similarly, as the limit value approaches 100 percent from below, the probability of hitting the limit close to the starting time increases to 1 and the strategy looks more and more like holding the bond (which is also efficient). When the limit value is 100 percent or more, the strategy switches immediately to the bond and the strategy is precisely holding the bond (which is efficient). Intuitively, the loss is largest when there is a large chance both of hitting and of missing the limit soon after the start. This is consistent with figure 5.1, which shows the largest loss at a limit of about 96 percent (with a 1 year horizon), which is one-fourth of the 1 year standard deviation of the stock.

Figure 5.2 shows the efficiency loss of a lock-in strategy, which is in some sense a mirror image of a stop-loss strategy. The loss is not exactly symmetric, since the terminal state price density is higher for lower stock prices. This means that the damage done by the stop-loss strategy (which usually occurs when the stock has gone down) is more costly than the damage done by the lock-in strategy; nonetheless, the cost of following a lock-in strategy is substantial and should not be ignored by practitioners.

Figure 5.3 shows the efficiency loss of a random timing strategy (a "timer who cannot") as a function of the fraction of time that the timer holds the stock. The efficiency loss of this strategy can be as high as 200 basis points over a year, or \$40 million for a \$2 billion portfolio! While figure 5.3 contains numerical results, this is one of the few cases that we can actually solve analytically for the diffusion model. The random timer follows a strategy which holds the stock a fixed fraction f of the time and which holds the bond a fraction $1-f$ of the time. (Because there are assumed to be no transaction costs, the exact allocation does not matter – it only matters that the stock is held exactly a fraction f of the time.) If w_0 is the initial wealth, then the wealth $\tilde{w}_T$ at the end (time T) is lognormally distributed as

$$\log \tilde{w}_T \sim N[\log w_0 + \mu f T + r(1-f)T - \sigma^2 fT/2, \sigma^2 fT]. \tag{2}$$

An alternative strategy with initial wealth x_0 and a fixed portfolio weight α is also lognormally distributed and is efficient for $\alpha > 0$. Its terminal distribution is

$$\log \tilde{x}_T \sim N[\log x_0 + \mu\alpha T + r(1-\alpha)T - \sigma^2\alpha^2 T/2, \sigma^2\alpha^2 T]. \tag{3}$$

To give these two the same distribution (for $\alpha > 0$), we must choose $\alpha = f^{1/2}$ to match variances and then choose

$$\log x_0 = \log w_0 - (f^{1/2} - f)(\mu - r)T \tag{4}$$

to match means. In logarithms $(f^{1/2} - f)(\mu - r)T$ is the loss, and up to scaling this is essentially what is plotted in figure 5.3.[8]

Figure 5.4 shows the efficiency loss of a strategy, not analyzed in section 1, that uses portfolio insurance repeatedly. (Because of the technical limitations of the computer program, we have chosen slightly different parameters and weekly rebalancing for this example; both choices reduce the number of terminal nodes and help keep the size manageable despite exponential growth.) Since many managers create synthetic portfolio insurance with a 1 year horizon repeated annually, the large size of the efficiency loss shown in figure 5.4 (over 5 percent in 10 years) is particularly troubling.

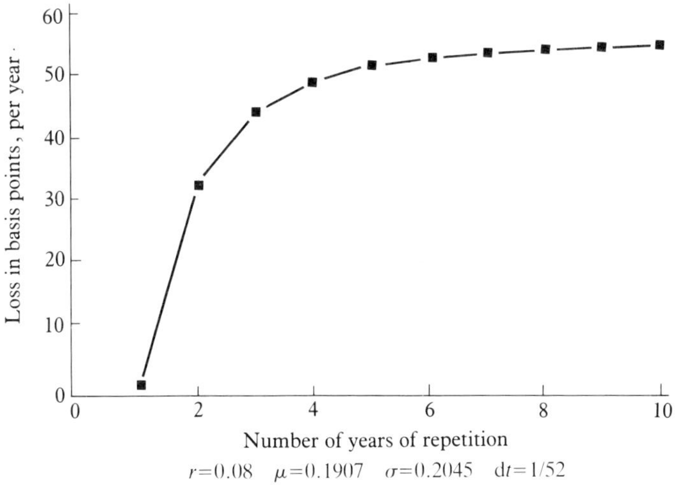

Figure 5.4 Efficiency loss of repeated portfolio insurance. Under portfolio insurance, a dynamic strategy based on option pricing theory varies the portfolio mix between stocks and bonds to create a payoff at the end of the insurance horizon that is the larger of the initial investment and a proportion of the terminal stock price. This plot shows that while following this strategy for 1 year is efficient, following it repeatedly with a 1 year horizon is poorly diversified over time and is very costly: in 10 years, the strategy throws away over 5 percent of the initial investment.

3 Generalizations

In this section we derive a formula for the state price density in the general case when asset prices follow general Itô processes. The main economic assumptions we need are completeness of markets and the absence of arbitrage.[9] We then turn to applications involving the term structure of interest rates. While numerical analysis like that in section 2 has not been performed for the term structure applications, performing such computations is a promising avenue for future research.

3.1 State price density in continuous-time models

The state price density ρ gives a representation of the linear pricing rule of Ross (1978). If we let P be the vector of reinvested price series, then in terms of ρ and the price at a later time t, the price at time s is

$$\rho_s P_s \equiv E_s(\tilde{\rho}_t \tilde{P}_t) \tag{5}$$

or, in particular, if we take $\rho = 1$ at $s = 0$, we have

$$P_0 \equiv E_0(\tilde{\rho}_t \tilde{P}_t). \tag{6}$$

Equation (5) says that ρP is a martingale, which implies that ρP has no drift.

Assume that prices follow an Itô process. Specifically, the n-vector of risky asset price changes is given by

$$\frac{\mathrm{d}\tilde{P}}{P} = \mu \ \mathrm{d}t + \sigma \ \mathrm{d}\tilde{Z} \tag{7}$$

where the division is componentwise, μ is the n-vector of expected returns, $\tilde{Z}$ is a k-dimensional Wiener process, and σ is an $n \times k$ matrix of risk exposures. Under reasonable assumptions, ρ itself follows an Itô process involving only $\tilde{Z}$; taking this as given, we have

$$\frac{\mathrm{d}\tilde{\rho}}{\rho} = a \ \mathrm{d}t + b' \ \mathrm{d}\tilde{Z}, \tag{8}$$

where $\rho_0 = 1$, or equivalently

$$\tilde{\rho}_t = \exp\left(\int_{s=0}^{t} a \ \mathrm{d}s + \int_{s=0}^{t} b' \ \mathrm{d}\tilde{Z}_s - \frac{1}{2} \int_{s=0}^{t} b'b \ \mathrm{d}s \right) \tag{9}$$

for some random one-dimensional process a and some k-dimensional process b. Since equation (5) holds for all assets,

$$\frac{\mathrm{d}(\tilde{\rho}\tilde{P})}{\rho P} = \frac{\mathrm{d}\tilde{\rho}}{\rho} + \frac{\mathrm{d}\tilde{P}}{P} + \frac{\mathrm{d}\tilde{\rho}}{\rho}\frac{\mathrm{d}\tilde{P}}{P} \tag{10}$$

has no drift, or by Itô's lemma this implies that

$$0 = \mathrm{drift}\left[\frac{\mathrm{d}(\tilde{\rho}\tilde{P})}{\rho P}\right] = ae + \mu + \sigma b \tag{11}$$

where e is an n-vector of 1s. If we eliminate locally redundant assets, completeness implies that σ is square and nonsingular, and therefore

$$a = -r \tag{12}$$

and

$$b = -\sigma^{-1}(\mu - re) \tag{13}$$

where r is the local riskless rate. Generally, a and b are solutions to equation (10) even if we have not eliminated locally redundant assets. Of course, completeness of markets implies that there is a locally riskless portfolio.

To use equations (8), (11), and (12) with the payoff distribution pricing model, we have to use the continuous state space analog of valuation using consumption ordered in reverse of the terminal state price density. This analog implies that the cost of the dominating portfolio (the distributional price) is

$$P_{\mathrm{D}} = \int_{\gamma=0}^{1} F_{\rho}^{-1}(\gamma) F_{c}^{-1}(1-\gamma)\, \mathrm{d}\gamma \tag{14}$$

which is equation (3) of Dybvig (1988). This is a general expression for the expectation of the product of two variables ρ and c that are perfectly inversely related. F_{ρ}^{-1} has the same units as ρ (state price over probability), F_{c}^{-1} has units of consumption, and γ has units of probability. The arguments γ and $1-\gamma$ signify inverse ordering, and the integral corresponds to summing across states in the finite model.[10]

3.2 Term structure models

To illustrate the evolution of the state price density in continuous-time models, in this section we compute the state price density in closed form for a class of models with interest rate uncertainty. Because interest rates can move randomly, there is a nontrivial term structure of interest rates in these models. Throughout the rest of this section, it will be assumed either that preferences are over nominal payoffs or that we are expressing all returns in real terms (which is formally equivalent).

To illustrate the computation of ρ, let us assume that the vector b of asset risk premiums is constant. Then we can write the state price density (9) as

$$\tilde{\rho}_t = \exp\left(-\int_{s=0}^{t} r_s \, \mathrm{d}s + \int_{s=0}^{t} b' \, \mathrm{d}\tilde{Z}_s - \frac{t}{2} b'b \right) \tag{15}$$

In particular, if $b=0$, we have the local expectations hypothesis (Cox, Ingersoll, and Ross, 1981), which is a reasonable assumption if all the assets in our list are bonds or derivatives of bonds. In this case, every efficient portfolio has a terminal value that is a nondecreasing function of the compounded return on rolling over shorts. One interesting implication of this result is that contingent immunization is not an efficient strategy.[11] This is formally true from equation (15) whenever the local expectations hypothesis holds; more generally, equations (9) and (12) tell us that we would have to make a bizarre assumption about the movement of the vector b of risk premiums to make contingent immunization efficient.

To apply our analysis to a term structure model, we would want to use equation (14), for which we need to know the distribution of the state price density. The state price density's process is given by equation (15). In general, we can compute the density numerically, and in this article we shall consider a special case in which the distribution can be computed analytically. We shall use a special case of Vasicek (1977). Loosely speaking, Vasicek showed that, if interest rates follow a Gaussian process, then we can compute bond prices. (We have to make an assumption about risk premiums as well; the assumption that the vector b of risk premiums is a constant is sufficient.) Vasicek's model is attractive analytically because the normality makes it tractable. (Unfortunately, however, it is not a good approximation to the actual movement of interest rates, except perhaps over very short periods of time.[12]) From equations (6) and (15), we can see how to compute bond prices in the Vasicek model. By equation (6), the price at time zero of a bond paying 1 at t is $E_0(\tilde{\rho}_t/\rho_0)=E_0(\tilde{\rho}_t)$. If r nd Z are jointly normal (as they are in Vasicek's model), we can compute this expectation using the normal moment generating function.

For our extended example, assume that r follows the following simple mean-reverting process:

$$\mathrm{d}r = \varkappa(\bar{r}-r)\,\mathrm{d}t + \Sigma'\,\mathrm{d}\tilde{Z} \tag{16}$$

where $\varkappa$, $\bar{r}$, and Σ are known and constant and where $\tilde{Z}$ is the k-dimensional Wiener process that drives security prices. Then we have

$$r_t = \bar{r} + (r_0-\bar{r})\exp(-\varkappa t) + \int_{\tau=0}^{t} \exp[-\varkappa(t-\tau)]\ \Sigma'\,\mathrm{d}\tilde{Z}_\tau \tag{17}$$

and

$$\int_{\tau=0}^{t} r_\tau\,\mathrm{d}\tau = \bar{r}t + (r_0-\bar{r})\frac{1-\exp(-\varkappa t)}{\varkappa} + \int_{\tau=0}^{t}\frac{1-\exp[-\varkappa(t-\tau)]}{\varkappa}\ \Sigma'\,\mathrm{d}\tilde{Z}_\tau \tag{18}$$

From equations (15) and (18), we have

$$\begin{aligned}\log \rho_t = &-\left(\frac{b'b}{2}+\bar{r}\right)t - (r_0-\bar{r})\frac{1-\exp(-\varkappa t)}{\varkappa}\\ &+\int_{\tau=0}^{t}\left\{b' - \frac{1-\exp[-\varkappa(t-\tau)]}{\varkappa}\ \Sigma'\right\}\mathrm{d}\tilde{Z}_\tau\end{aligned} \tag{19}$$

Therefore ρ_t is normally distributed with mean

$$M = -\left(\frac{b'b}{2}+\bar{r}\right)t - (r_0-\bar{r})\frac{1-\exp(-\varkappa t)}{\varkappa} \tag{20}$$

and variance

$$\begin{aligned}V &= \int_{\tau=0}^{t}\left(b - \frac{1-\exp[-\varkappa(t-\tau)]}{\varkappa}\ \Sigma\right\}'\left\{b - \frac{1-\exp[-\varkappa(t-\tau)]}{\varkappa}\ \Sigma\right\}\mathrm{d}\tau\\ &= \left(b'b - \frac{2b'\Sigma}{\varkappa} + \frac{\Sigma'\Sigma}{\varkappa^2}\right)t + \frac{2}{\varkappa}\left(b'\Sigma - \frac{\Sigma'\Sigma}{\varkappa}\right)\frac{1-\exp(-\varkappa t)}{\varkappa}\\ &\quad + \frac{\Sigma'\Sigma}{\varkappa^2}\,\frac{1-\exp(-2\varkappa t)}{2\varkappa}\end{aligned} \tag{21}$$

Therefore ρ_t is distributed lognormally, and $\log\rho_t$ has mean M and variance V. By the normal moment generating function, then, the bond price is given by $\exp(M + \frac{1}{2}V)$.

The lognormality of ρ_t implies that it is possible (although not done here) to compute analytically the cost of some types of random timing strategies. Of course, more numerical work is required in order to compute the cost of following other dominated strategies. In numerical work, having a closed-form expression for the distribution of the state price density is very useful, because computing it numerically requires us to keep track of two state variables r and ρ. In some sense, this is why term structure models are difficult to solve analytically: the state price density is not a function of the natural state variable (the interest rate).

4 Conclusion

The numerical results reported in this article show that the efficiency loss to inefficient strategies may in fact be very large, even given very realistic assumptions. The strategies that we have considered – stop-loss, lock-in, random timer, and repeated portfolio insurance – are very similar to strategies used in practice. It is interesting to note that the efficiency loss is the same whether or not the strategy was "planned" in advance; in other words, a manager deciding to lock in the gains at the time a boundary is reached has the same terminal distribution of wealth as a manager who planned from the start to follow this strategy.

Much work remains. In one direction, it would be nice to extend the analysis to include transaction costs explicitly. Short of that, we can add the transaction cost to the cost described here to obtain an overall measure of the cost of a given policy, and it would be useful to have a collection of examples of this sort to aid our understanding. Along other lines, it is possible to measure the efficiency loss of other strategies. For example, it would be nice to know the magnitude of loss from contingent immunization and other fixed income strategies.

Notes

1 See Dybvig and Ingersoll (1982) for a discussion of the difficulty of using mean–variance analysis for evaluating options and other nonlinear claims, and Dybvig and Ross (1985a,b) for a general discussion of why mean–variance performance measures may not be valid even in the absence of measurement error.

2 Consumption will always be assumed to occur at the end. More generally, if preferences are time separable, the analysis is unchanged if we treat consumption at each date separately.

3 Other papers emphasizing state prices and the reduction of a multiperiod problem to

one period include those by Banz and Miller (1978), Cox, Ross, and Rubinstein (1979), Brennan and Solanki (1981), Cox and Leland (1982), Pliska (1986), and Cox and Huang (forthcoming).

4 By definition, any atomless distribution has equally probable states each having probability zero. (An *atom* is an indivisible state with positive probability.) *Continuum* will be taken to mean a nonatomic continuum.

5 Readers who are familiar with the path independence results of Cox and Leland (1982) may find this confusing, since the strategies we shall consider have path-dependent strategies in three or even two periods. However, these strategies will not be inefficient for agents who have concave preferences that are not necessarily strictly concave. To obtain inefficiency for these general agents, we need something slightly stronger than path independence, which is that a path with strictly higher state price should have strictly higher consumption. For a general discussion of the relation between the amount of regularity assumed for utility functions and the first-order conditions in terms of the state price density, see Dybvig and Ross (1982), especially table 1 and the related discussion.

6 One special feature of table 5.1 is that the terminal state price density is a function only of the terminal stock price. This is a very special feature of this particular example and of certain other examples, including economies with geometric independent identically distributed (i.i.d.) stock price movements (see Cox and Leland, 1982). In models of the term structure (with random interest rate movements) in particular, it is not reasonable to assume that the state price density is a function only of the natural state variables. Fortunately, as we shall see in section 3, the approach in this article does not require the state price to be a function only of the state variables driving asset returns.

7 If $u(\cdot)$ is concave but not everywhere differentiable, $u'(\cdot)$ should be interpreted as some element of the marginal utility correspondence, which is the closed interval bounded by the right and left derivatives (see Dybvig and Ross, 1982).

8 The formula for the loss in the random timer case is linear in T. Another way of saying this is that, if you split the time interval into two parts, the value as a percentage of the potential on the whole period is the product of the value as a percentage of the potential on each half. This is a special case of a general result. Suppose that security returns are independent over time and that the return on the inefficient portfolio strategy in the two subperiods is independent; then the value as a percentage of the potential on the whole period is less than or equal to the product of the values as a percentage of the potential on the subperiods. To prove this, consider making the dominated strategies on the subperiods your strategy over the whole period. This may not be optimal over the whole period, but it achieves a value that proves the bound. This result says that when stock returns are independent you cannot recover from past inefficient policies. As an example of applying this result, rolling over portfolio insurance each year is efficient in each period but inefficient over 2 years (an example of inequality). The result implies that rolling over portfolio insurance each year over 4 years is at least twice as bad (measured in logarithms) as rolling over portfolio insurance each year for 2 years (and in fact it is even worse).

9 There are some additional technical assumptions that would be required in a more formal analysis. See, for example, Harrison and Pliska (1981), Cox and Huang (forthcoming), or Dybvig and Huang (1988) for related results. In these papers the emphasis is on the risk-neutral probabilities (called martingale probabilities). The state price density is equal to a discount factor times the Radon–Nikodyn derivative of the risk-neutral probabilities applied to indicator sets with respect to the probability measure.

10 For details, see Dybvig (1988). To define the inverse distribution function for discrete

variables (or more generally at mass points), we put "risers" on the step function. For example, suppose that a random variable is either 1 or 2, each with probability $\frac{1}{2}$; then the inverse distribution function is defined to be 1 on $(0, \frac{1}{2})$ and 2 on $(\frac{1}{2}, 1)$. The values assigned to the end-points 0 and 1 do not matter because they do not affect the integral in equation (14).

11 Intuitively, a contingent immunization strategy switches from one risky portfolio into an immunized portfolio using a cutoff rule that is qualitatively similar to the stop-loss strategy, if we consider the initial portfolio as the stock and the immunized portfolio as the bond. (Using the immunized portfolio as numeraire makes the analogy almost exact.) Therefore, while the qualitative properties of the efficiency loss should be as in figure 5.1, without further analysis we cannot be sure of the magnitude of the loss. It does seem, however, that if the size of the loss we are insuring is significant, the efficiency loss will also be significant.

12 For example, interest rates can be arbitrarily negative in Vasicek's model, and they will go negative frequently under reasonable variance assumptions. Also, it has been shown empirically that the variance of interest rates changes over time in a way that can be predicted by looking at yield curves, contradicting the assumption of constant variance (Brown and Dybvig, 1986).

References

Banz, R. and Miller, M. (1978) "Prices for State-Contingent Claims: Some Estimates and Applications," *Journal of Business*, 51, 653–72.

Black, F. and Scholes, M. (1973) "The Pricing of Options and Corporate Liabilities," *Journal of Political Economy*, 81, 637–54.

Brennan, M. and Solanki, R. (1981) "Optimal Portfolio Insurance," *Journal of Financial and Quantitative Analysis*, 16, 279–300.

Brown, S. J. and Dybvig, P. H. (1986) "The Empirical Implications of the Cox, Ingersoll, Ross Theory of the Term Structure of Interest Rates," *Journal of Finance*, 41, 617–32.

Cox, J. C. and Huang, C. (forthcoming) "A Variational Problem Arising in Financial Economics," *Journal of Mathematical Economics*.

Cox, J. C. and Leland, H. (1982) "On Dynamic Investment Strategies," *Proceedings of the Seminar on the Analysis of Security Prices*, 26 (2), Center for Research in Security Prices, University of Chicago.

Cox, J. C., Ingersoll, J. E., Jr, and Ross, S. A. (1981) "A Re-examination of Traditional Hypotheses about the Term Structure of Interest Rates," *Journal of Finance*, 36, 769–99.

Cox, J. C., Ross, S. A. and Rubinstein, M. (1979) "Option Pricing: A Simplified Approach," *Journal of Financial Economics*, 7, 229–63.

Dybvig, P. H. (1982) "Some New Tools for Testing Market Efficiency and Measuring Mutual Fund Performance," *Working Paper*, Yale University.

Dybvig, P. H. (1988) "Distributional Analysis of Portfolio Choice," *Journal of Business*, 61: 3, July, 369–93.

Dybvig, P. H. and Huang, C. (1988) "Nonnegative Wealth, Absence of Arbitrage, and Feasible Consumption Plans," *Review of Financial Studies*, 1: 4, 377–401.

Dybvig, P. H. and Ingersoll, J. E., Jr (1982) "Mean–Variance Theory in Complete Markets," *Journal of Business*, 55, 233–51.

Dybvig, P. H. and Ross, S. A. (1982) "Portfolio Efficient Sets," *Econometrica*, 50, 1525–46.

Dybvig, P. H. and Ross, S. A. (1985a) "The Analytics of Performance Measurement Using a Security Market Line," *Journal of Finance*, 40: 2, June, 401–16.

Dybvig, P. H. and Ross, S. A. (1985b) "Differential Information and Performance Measurement Using a Security Market Line," *Journal of Finance*, 40: 2, June, 383–99.

Dybvig, R. K. (1987) *The Scheme Programming Language* (Englewood Cliffs, NJ: Prentice-Hall).

Garman, M. (1976) "A General Theory of Asset Valuation Under Diffusion State Processes," *Working Paper*, University of California, Berkeley.

Harrison, J. M. and Pliska, S. (1981) "Martingales and Stochastic Integrals in the Theory of Continuous Trading," *Stochastic Processes and Their Applications*, 11, 215–60.

Machina, M. (1982) "'Expected Utility' Analysis without the Independence Axiom," *Econometrica*, 50, 277–323.

Pliska, S. (1986) "A Stochastic Calculus Model of Continuous Time Trading: Optimal Portfolios," *Mathematics of Operations Research*, 11, 371–82.

Ross, S. A. (1976) "Options and Efficiency," *Quarterly Journal of Economics*, 90, 75–89.

Ross, S. A. (1978) "A Simple Approach to the Valuation of Risky Streams," *Journal of Business*, 51, 453–75.

Rubinstein, M. (1976) "The Valuation of Uncertain Income Streams and the Pricing of Options," *Bell Journal of Economics*, 7, 407–25.

Vasicek, O. (1977) "An Equilibrium Characterization of the Term Structure," *Journal of Financial Economics*, 5, 177–88.

Chapter 6

G. William Schwert

Background and Comments

The leading practical rule of thumb for calculating hurdle rates for capital outlays is the capital asset pricing model:

$$r = r_f + \beta(r_m - r_f).$$

Here r is the expected rate of return used as the hurdle rate, r_f is a risk-free (Treasury) interest rate, β is the risk measure relative to the market portfolio, and $r_m - r_f$ is the expected risk premium on the market portfolio. The following numbers would be plugged for an average risk ($\beta = 1$) asset in mid-October 1989:

$$r = 8.2 + 1.0(8.4) = 16.6 \text{ percent.}$$

The 8.4 percent risk premium is the average risk premium on Standard & Poor's Composite Index for the 63 years from 1926 through 1988 (*Stocks, Bonds, Bills and Inflation*: *1989 Yearbook*, p. 83, Exhibit 86).

Why rely on so much ancient history to estimate the market risk premium? There is no law of finance that says it should be constant.

The standard reply? There is no alternative because stock returns are so noisy that mean returns over shorter periods are statistically untrustworthy. You can generate any number you like – just pick the right decade. Even 20 year averages are disturbingly imprecise estimates of the true underlying mean.

Good estimates of mean returns or risk premiums require long periods of calendar time. Volatility of return, however, can be measured over shorter periods, and common sense says that investors ought to demand higher expected rates of return when volatility increases. If this relationship can be accurately measured, then managers could escape the assumption that today's expected rate of return exactly matches long-run historical experience. Hurdle rates could be updated to reflect current measures of market risk.

The following paper takes us part way to that goal. Kenneth French, William Schwert, and Robert Stambaugh confirm that higher volatility means higher expected return. Although they are unable to pin down the form of the relationship, their paper is nevertheless a significant empirical advance.

I have used the example of setting project hurdle rates to show the importance of this topic. The relationship between volatility and expected return is obviously also crucially important to individual and institutional investors.

Reference

Stocks, Bonds, Bills and Inflation: 1989 Yearbook (Chicago, IL: Ibbotson Associates).

Author's Introduction

This paper is unusual in many ways, not least of which is that it took so long to complete that three different Batterymarch Fellows worked on it during three different Fellowship years. Not being a fan of the labor theory of value, however, I do not want to confuse the time required to finish the paper with its contribution to financial research.

In this paper we investigate the empirical relation between stock returns and return volatility. Two basic issues arise. First, if predictions of volatility increase, do expected returns (above Treasury bill yields) increase to reflect the greater risk? Second, if there is an unexpected increase in volatility, what happens to stock prices? Using daily returns to Standard & Poor's composite portfolio from 1928 to 1984, we calculate a time series of monthly estimates of return standard deviations. We then use Box–Jenkins time series models to decompose volatility into predictable and unpredictable components. When this technique is used, there is only weak evidence that returns are related to the predictable component of volatility. There is strong evidence, however, of a negative relation between shocks to volatility and returns. Stock prices drop when volatility increases. We show that this effect is too large to be explained by financial leverage. Therefore we conclude that it is indirect evidence of a positive relation between expected returns and expected volatility.

We also use generalized autoregressive conditional heteroskedasticity (GARCH) models to represent the relation between expected returns and volatility. These models show a much stronger effect of predicted volatility on expected returns. We investigate why the Box–Jenkins and the GARCH models yield different answers and conclude that probably neither is completely adequate.

There have been many papers that have documented the fact that excess returns on stocks can be predicted using information available at the beginning of the investment period. There have also been several papers that show that the volatility (standard deviation or variance of returns) varies through time. This paper is among the first to apply modern time series econometric techniques to test whether predictable movements in excess returns are related to predictable movements in risk. There are many interesting questions that remain unresolved, and several subsequent papers have continued this line of research.

As a byproduct of the research for this paper, I became very interested in the behavior of stock market volatility. I have written the following papers that explore different aspects to time-varying volatility since Ken, Rob and I finished "Expected Stock Returns and Volatility": "Heteroskedasticity in Stock Returns" (with Paul Seguin), "Stock Volatility and the Crash of '87," "Alternative Models for Conditional Stock Volatility" (with Adrian R. Pagan), "Indexes of United States Stock Prices from 1802 to 1987," "Why Does Stock Market Volatility Change Over Time?", and "Business Cycles, Financial Crises and Stock Volatility." Details are given in the Bibliographical Listing below.

Among other things, these papers document the behavior of stock market volatility using monthly data from 1802 to 1987 and daily data from 1885 to 1987. They relate stock volatility to financial crises such as banking panics, to margin regulation, and to the behavior of macroeconomic volatility. Some of these papers also explore new econometric methods for modeling volatility. I have found this research program to be both interesting and challenging, and I want to take this opportunity to thank Batterymarch for their support.

Bibliographical Listing

"Heteroskedasticity in Stock Returns" (with Paul J. Seguin), *Journal of Finance*, 45: 4, September 1990.

"Alternative Models for Conditional Stock Volatility" (with Adrian R. Pagan), *Journal of Econometrics*, 45: 1–2, July–August 1990, 267–90.

"Indexes of United States Stock Prices from 1802–1987," *Journal of Business*, 63: 3, July 1990, 399–426.

"Stock Market Volatility," *Financial Analysts Journal*, 46: 3, May–June 1990, 23–34.

"Testing for Covariance Stationarity in Stock Market Data" (with Adrian R. Pagan), *Economics Letters*, 33: 2, May 1990, 165–70.

"Stock Volatility and the Crash of '87," *Review of Financial Studies*, 3: 1, 1990, 77–102.

"Margin Regulation and Stock Volatility," *Journal of Financial Services Research*, 3: 2–3, December 1989, 153–64.

"Why Does Stock Market Volatility Change Over Time?" *Journal of Finance*, 44: 5, December 1989, 1115–53.

"Business Cycles, Financial Crises and Stock Volatility," *Carnegie–Rochester Conference Series on Public Policy*, 31, Autumn 1989, 83–125. Reprinted in the *Proceedings of the Seminar on the Analysis of Security Prices*, 33: 2, November 1988, 207–43.

"Information Aggregation, Inflation, and the Pricing of Indexed Bonds" (with Gur Huberman), *Journal of Political Economy*, 93: 1, February 1985, 92–114.

"Size and Stock Returns, and Other Empirical Regularities," *Journal of Financial Economics*, 12: 1, June 1983, 3–12.

Expected Stock Returns and Volatility

KENNETH R. FRENCH, G. WILLIAM SCHWERT and ROBERT F. STAMBAUGH

1 Introduction

Many studies document cross-sectional relations between risk and expected returns on common stocks. These studies generally measure a stock's risk as the covariance between its return and one or more variables. For example, the expected return on a stock is found to be related to covariances between its return and (a) the return on a market portfolio (Black, Jensen, and Scholes, 1972; Fama and MacBeth, 1973), (b) factors extracted from a multivariate time series of returns (Roll and Ross, 1980), (c) macroeconomic variables such as industrial production and changes in interest rates (Chen, Roll, and Ross, 1986), and (d) aggregate consumption (Breeden, Gibbons, and Litzenberger, 1989).

We examine the intertemporal relation between risk and expected returns. In particular, we ask whether the expected market risk premium, defined as the expected return on a stock market portfolio minus the risk-free interest rate, is positively related to risk as measured by the volatility of the stock market.

Some argue that the relation between expected returns and volatility is strong. For example, Pindyck (1984) attributes much of the decline in stock prices during the 1970s to increases in risk premiums arising from increases in volatility. Poterba and Summers (1986), however, argue that the time series properties of volatility make this scenario unlikely. Neither study provides a direct test of the relation between expected risk premiums and volatility.

We investigate relations of the form

$$E(R_{mt} - R_{ft} \mid \hat{\sigma}_{mt}) = \alpha + \beta \hat{\sigma}^{p}_{mt}, \qquad p = 1, 2, \tag{1}$$

Reproduced from *Journal of Financial Economics*, 19: 1, 1987, 3–29.

We have received helpful comments from Joel Hasbrouck, Donald Keim, John Long, Charles Plosser, Jay Shanken, Lawrence Summers, Jerold Warner, Larry Weiss, Jerold Zimmerman, an anonymous referee, and especially Eugene Fama. The Center for Research in Security Prices, the Foundation for Research in Economics and Education, and the Managerial Economics Research Center provided additional support for this project.

where R_{mt} is the return on a stock market portfolio, R_{ft} is the risk-free interest rate, $\hat{\sigma}_{mt}$ is an *ex ante* measure of the portfolio's standard deviation, and $\hat{\sigma}^2_{mt}$ is an *ex ante* measure of the variance. If $\beta = 0$ in (1), the expected risk premium is unrelated to the *ex ante* volatility. If $\alpha = 0$ and $\beta > 0$, the expected risk premium is proportional to the standard deviation ($p = 1$) or variance ($p = 2$) of stock market returns.

Merton (1980) estimates the relation between the market risk premium and volatility with a model similar to (1). Because his study is exploratory, he does not test hypotheses about (1), such as whether $\beta = 0$. Merton also uses contemporaneous, rather than *ex ante*, measures of volatility, so his measures include both *ex ante* volatility and the unexpected change in volatility. We argue below that a positive relation between the expected risk premium and *ex ante* volatility will induce a negative relation between the excess holding period return $R_{mt} - R_{ft}$ and the unexpected change in volatility. Therefore combining the two components of volatility obscures the *ex ante* relation.

This study uses two statistical approaches to investigate the relation between expected stock returns and volatility. In the first, we use daily returns to compute estimates of monthly volatility. We decompose these estimates into predictable and unpredictable components using univariate autoregressive integrated moving-average (ARIMA) models. Regressions of monthly excess holding period returns on the predictable component provide little evidence of a positive relation between *ex ante* volatility and expected risk premiums. There is a strong negative relation, however, between excess holding period returns and the unpredictable component of volatility. We interpret this as indirect evidence of a positive *ex ante* relation.

We also use daily returns to estimate *ex ante* measures of volatility with a generalized autoregressive conditional heteroskedasticity (GARCH) model (Engle, 1982; Bollerslev, 1986). The GARCH-in-mean model of Engle, Lilien, and Robins (1987) is used to estimate the *ex ante* relation between risk premiums and volatility. These results support our interpretation of the ARIMA results by indicating a reliable positive relation between expected risk premiums and volatility.

2 Time Series Properties of the Data

2.1 Standard deviations of stock market returns

We use daily values of Standard & Poor's (S&P) composite portfolio to estimate the monthly standard deviation of stock market returns from January 1928 through December 1984. This estimator has three advantages over the rolling 12 month standard deviation used by Officer (1973) and by Merton (1980) over his full 1926–78 sample period. (Merton uses daily returns to estimate monthly standard deviations for 1962–78.) First, by sampling the return process more frequently, we increase the accuracy of the standard deviation estimate for any particular interval. Second, the volatility of stock returns is not constant. We obtain a more precise estimate of the standard deviation for any month by using only returns within that month. Finally, our monthly standard deviation estimates use nonoverlapping samples of returns, whereas adjacent rolling 12 month estimators share 11 returns.

Nonsynchronous trading of securities causes daily portfolio returns to be autocorrelated, particularly at lag 1 (Fisher, 1966; Scholes and Williams, 1977). Because of this autocorrelation, we estimate the variance of the monthly return to the S&P portfolio as the sum of the squared daily returns plus twice the sum of the products of adjacent returns:

$$\sigma_{mt}^2 = \sum_{i=1}^{N_t} r_{it}^2 + 2 \sum_{i=1}^{N_t - 1} r_{it} r_{i+1,t}, \tag{2}$$

where there are N_t daily returns r_{it} in month t. We do not subtract the sample mean from each daily return in calculating the variance because this adjustment is very small. [1]

Figure 6.1 contains a plot of the monthly standard deviation estimates for 1928–84. As Officer (1973) notes, stock returns are more volatile in the period 1929–40 than either before or after. The plot in figure 6.1 is not as smooth as plots of 12 month rolling estimates in Officer (1973) because each point is based on a nonoverlapping sample of returns. This plot highlights the variation in estimated volatility.

As suggested by figure 6.1 the mean and standard deviation of the stock market standard deviation estimates in table 6.1, panel A, are higher in 1928–52 than in 1953–84. The autocorrelations of σ_{mt} in table 6.1, panel A, are large and decay slowly beyond lag 3. This behavior is typical of a nonstationary integrated moving-average process (Wichern, 1973). The standard deviation estimates are positively skewed. To adjust for this skewness we examine the logarithm of σ_{mt}. Because nonstationarity is suggested by the autocorrelations in table 6.1, panel A, we examine the changes in the logarithm of the standard deviation estimates in table 6.1, panel B. The autocorrelations in table 6.1, panel B, are close to zero beyond lag 3. These autocorrelations suggest that the first differences of $\ln \sigma_{mt}$ follow a third-order moving average process

$$(1 - L) \ln \sigma_{mt} = \theta_0 + (1 - \theta_1 L - \theta_2 L^2 - \theta_3 L^3) u_t \tag{3}$$

for 1928–84, 1928–52, and 1953–84. The estimates of the constant term θ_0 are small in relation to their standard errors, suggesting that there is no

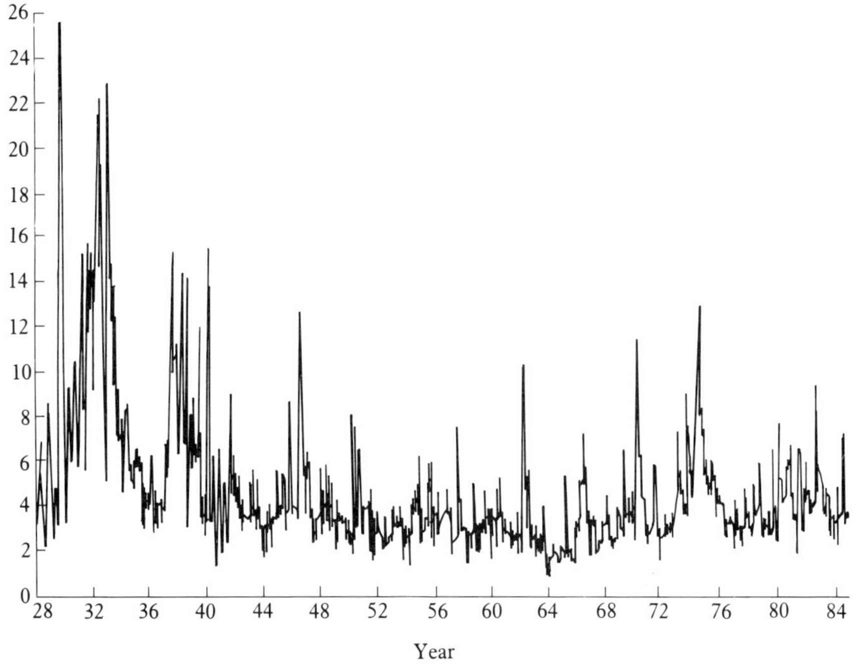

Figure 6.1 Monthly percentage standard deviations of the returns to the Standard & Poor's composite portfolio σ_{mt} estimated from returns r_{it} for days i within the month t, 1928–84 (equation (2)).

deterministic drift in the standard deviation of the stock market return. The moving average estimate at lag 1 is large in all periods, whereas the estimate at lag 2 is largest in the first subperiod and the estimate at lag 3 is largest in the second. Nevertheless, the F statistic testing the hypothesis that the model parameters are the same in 1928–52 and 1953–84 is below the critical value of 0.10. The small Box–Pierce statistics $Q(12)$ support the hypothesis that the forecast errors from these models are random.

The skewness coefficients are small (table 6.1, panels B and C) indicating that the logarithmic transformation has removed most of the positive skewness in σ_{mt}. The Studentized range statistics in table 6.1, panel C, are large in the overall sample period and in the first subperiod, but not in the second subperiod. The standard deviation $S(u_t)$ of the errors is about a third larger in 1928–52 than in 1953–84, which accounts for part of the large Studentized range statistic for the combined sample.

We construct conditional forecasts of the standard deviation and variance of S&P returns using the formulae

$$\hat{\sigma}_{mt} = \exp[\widehat{\ln\ \sigma_{mt}} + 0.5V(u_t)] \tag{4a}$$

Table 6.1 Time series properties of estimates of the standard deviation of the return to Standard & Poor's composite portfolio[a]

Period	Mean	Std dev.	Skewness	Autocorrelation at lags 1	2	3	4	5	6	7	8	9	10	11	12	Std error	Q(12)
A Monthly standard deviation of S&P composite returns estimated from daily data																	
1928–84	0.0474	0.0325	2.80[b]	0.71	0.59	0.55	0.54	0.50	0.51	0.54	0.54	0.49	0.51	0.49	0.45	0.04	2409.2[b]
1928–52	0.0607	0.0417	2.08[b]	0.68	0.53	0.50	0.49	0.43	0.46	0.51	0.51	0.44	0.46	0.44	0.40	0.06	893.4[b]
1953–84	0.0371	0.0168	1.70[b]	0.62	0.49	0.38	0.34	0.31	0.27	0.24	0.23	0.25	0.25	0.21	0.17	0.05	533.6[b]
B Percent changes of monthly standard deviation of S&P composite returns estimated from daily data																	
2/28–12/84	0.0000	0.3995	0.18	−0.33	−0.08	−0.09	0.07	−0.04	−0.04	0.00	0.06	−0.04	0.02	−0.01	0.07	0.04	96.6[b]
2/28–12/52	−0.0014	0.4473	0.27[b]	−0.32	−0.14	−0.08	0.12	−0.09	−0.06	0.01	0.15	−0.09	0.02	0.00	0.12	0.06	59.5[b]
1/53–12/84	0.0011	0.3585	0.04	−0.35	−0.02	−0.10	0.00	0.02	−0.01	−0.01	−0.06	0.02	0.02	−0.01	0.00	0.05	52.3[b]

C ARIMA models for the logarithm of the monthly standard deviation of S&P composite returns estimated from daily data (equation (3))[c]

	θ_0	θ_1	θ_2	θ_3	$S(u_t)$	R^2	Q(12)	Skewness[d]	SR(u_t)	F test for stability[e]
2/28–12/84	0.0000	0.524	0.158	0.090	0.350	0.238	8.2	0.31[b]	9.58[b]	0.64
	(0.0031)	(0.038)	(0.043)	(0.038)						(0.62)
2/28–12/52	−0.0012	0.552	0.193	0.031	0.387	0.261	17.9	0.33[b]	8.76[b]	
	(0.0051)	(0.058)	(0.066)	(0.058)						
1/53–12/84	0.0010	0.506	0.097	0.161	0.319	0.216	3.3	0.27[b]	6.31	
	(0.0039)	(0.051)	(0.057)	(0.051)						

[a]The monthly standard deviation estimator σ_{mt} is calculated from the daily rates of return to the S&P composite portfolio for each day in the month:

$$\sigma^2_{mt} = \sum_{i=1}^{N_t} r^2_{it} + 2\sum_{i=1}^{N_t-1} r_{it}r_{i+1,t}$$

where r_{it} is the return on day i within month t, and there are N_t days in the month. Q(12) is the Box–Pierce (1970) statistic for 12 lags of the autocorrelation function, and SR(u_t) is the studentized range, that is, the sample range divided by the standard deviation. See Fama (1976, ch. 1) for a discussion and fractiles of SR under the hypothesis of a stationary normal distribution.

[b]Greater than the 0.95 fractile of the sampling distribution under the hypothesis of a stationary serially uncorrelated normal distribution.

[c]Standard errors are in parentheses.

[d]The asymptotic standard error for the sample skewness coefficient is $2.45/T^{1/2}$ under the hypothesis of a stationary normal distribution. This standard error equals 0.142, 0.125, and 0.094 for $T = 299$, 384, and 683.

[e]The F test for stability of the time series models is based on the residual sums of squares from the subperiods and for the overall sample period, and so the F statistic would have k and $T-2k$ degrees of freedom in large samples, where $T = 683$ is the overall sample size and $k = 4$ is the number of parameters including the constant. The value in parentheses adjusts the F statistic for the fact that the residual variances are unequal in the two subperiods.

and

$$\hat{\sigma}^2_{mt} = \exp[2\,\widehat{\ln\,\sigma_{mt}} + 2V(u_t)]\,, \tag{4b}$$

where $\widehat{\ln\,\sigma_{mt}}$ is the fitted value for $\ln\,\sigma_{mt}$ from (3) and $V(u_t)$ is the variance of the prediction errors from (3) for 1928–84. If the errors u_t are normally distributed, σ_{mt} is lognormal and the corrections in (4a) and (4b) are exact. Figure 6.2 contains a plot of the predictions $\hat{\sigma}_{mt}$ from (4a). The predicted standard deviations track the actual standard deviations closely, although the predicted series is smoother.

The evidence in table 6.1 indicates that there is substantial variation in stock market volatility. The time series models are stable over time, and the residuals appear to be random. In the subsequent tests, we interpret the transformed fitted value $\hat{\sigma}^p_{mt}$ from these models as the predictable volatility of stock returns and the unexpected volatility $\sigma^{pu}_{mt} = \sigma^p_{mt} - \hat{\sigma}^p_{mt}$ as proportional to the change in predicted volatility. The models seem to be stable, and so we treat the parameters as if they were known to investors and estimate them using all the data.[2] Conditional on the parameters, the forecasts depend only on past data.

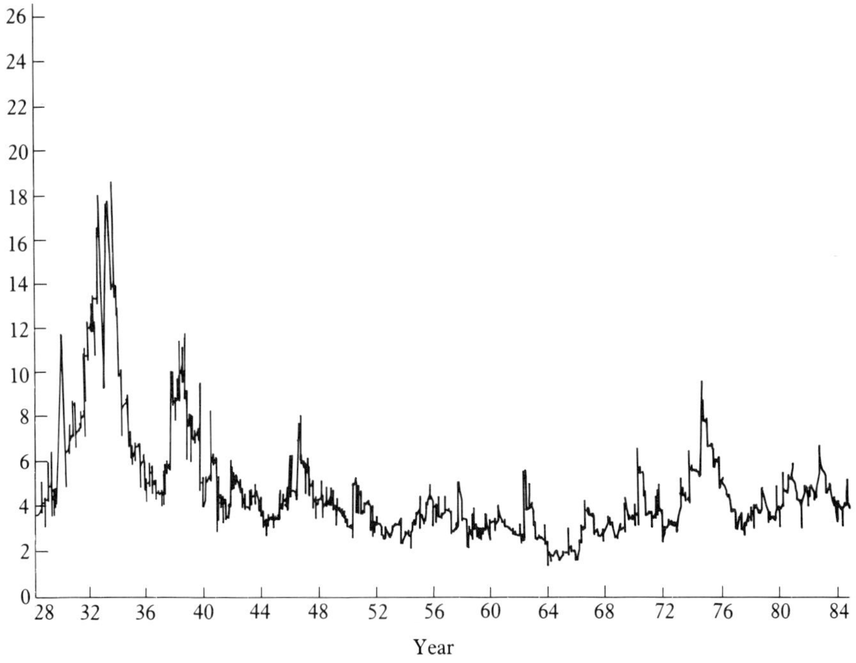

Figure 6.2 Predicted monthly percentage standard deviations of the returns to the Standard & Poor's composite portfolio $\hat{\sigma}_{mt}$ estimated from the ARIMA model in table 6.1, panel C, 1928–84 (equations (3) and (4a)).

2.2 ARCH models

Engle (1982) proposed the autoregressive conditional heteroskedasticity (ARCH) model

$$r_t = \alpha + \varepsilon_t, \qquad \varepsilon_t \sim \mathrm{N}(0, \sigma_t^2), \tag{5a}$$

$$\sigma_t^2 = a + b\varepsilon_{t-1}^2, \tag{5b}$$

to represent a series with changing volatility. The assumption in (5b) that volatility is a deterministic function of past returns is restrictive. For example, conditional on the shock ε_{t-1} at time $t-1$, there is no unpredictable component of volatility at time t. The ARCH model is attractive, however, because the return and variance processes are estimated jointly.

We compute maximum likelihood estimates of the ARCH model using daily risk premiums, defined as the percentage change in the S&P index minus the daily yield on a 1 month Treasury bill: $r_t = R_{mt} - R_{ft}$.[3] To account for the positive first-order serial correlation in the returns to portfolios of stocks induced by nonsynchronous trading (Fisher, 1966; Scholes and Williams, 1977), we generalize the model for daily risk premiums in (5a) by including a first-order moving-average process for the errors:

$$R_{mt} - R_{ft} = \alpha + \varepsilon_t - \theta\varepsilon_{t-1}, \tag{5c}$$

where the moving average coefficient θ will be negative. The autocorrelations of the squared risk premiums $(R_{mt} - R_{ft})^2$ decay slowly (from 0.27 at lag 1 to 0.10 at lag 60), suggesting that σ_t^2 is related to many lags of ε_t^2. Therefore we generalize (5b) in two ways. First, we use the average of the previous 22 squared errors to predict the variance of ε_t:

$$\sigma_t^2 = a + b\left(\sum_{i=1}^{22} \frac{\varepsilon_{t-i}^2}{22}\right). \tag{5d}$$

This is comparable to using the monthly variance estimates in table 6.1, since there are about 22 trading days per month. Second, we use a generalized autoregressive conditional heteroskedasticity (GARCH) model (Bollerslev, 1986) of the form

$$\sigma_t^2 = a + b\sigma_{t-1}^2 + c_1\varepsilon_{t-1}^2 + c_2\varepsilon_{t-2}^2. \tag{5e}$$

Table 6.2 contains estimates of the ARCH model (5d) and the GARCH model (5e) for 1928–84, 1928–52, and 1953–84. The 1928–84 estimate of b for the ARCH model is 0.94, with a standard error of 0.01, and so there is a strong relation between recent squared errors and the estimate of volatility. The χ^2 test in table 6.2 implies that the parameters of the ARCH model are not equal in 1928–52 and 1953–84.

Table 6.2 ARCH models for daily excess holding period returns to Standard & Poor's composite portfolio[a]

$$R_{mt} - R_{ft} = \alpha + \varepsilon_t - \theta\varepsilon_{t-1} \qquad (5c)$$

$$\sigma_t^2 = a + b\left(\sum_{i=1}^{22} \frac{\varepsilon_{t-1}^2}{22}\right) \qquad (5d)$$

$$\sigma_t^2 = a + b\sigma_{t-1}^2 + c_1\varepsilon_{t-1}^2 + c_2\varepsilon_{t-2}^2 \qquad (5e)$$

ARCH model equations	$\alpha \times 10^3$	$a \times 10^5$	b	c_1	c_2	θ	χ^2 *test for stability*
A January 1928 to December 1984, T = 15,369							
ARCH	0.265	1.006	0.938			−0.142	92.7
(5c), (5d)	(0.061)	(0.048)	(0.012)			(0.007)	
GARCH	0.324	0.062	0.919	0.121	−0.044	−0.157	86.7
(5c), (5e)	(0.063)	(0.005)	(0.002)	(0.007)	(0.007)	(0.007)	
B January 1928 to December 1952, T = 7,326							
ARCH	0.405	1.678	0.924			−0.080	
(5c), (5d)	(0.111)	(0.094)	(0.015)			(0.010)	
GARCH	0.496	0.149	0.898	0.106	−0.012	−0.090	
(5c), (5e)	(0.111)	(0.013)	(0.004)	(0.009)	(0.009)	(0.012)	
C January 1953 to December 1984, T = 8,043							
ARCH	0.218	0.947	0.856			−0.194	
(5c), (5d)	(0.076)	(0.069)	(0.023)			(0.010)	
GARCH	0.257	0.052	0.922	0.130	−0.060	−0.211	
(5c), (5e)	(0.080)	(0.008)	(0.004)	(0.010)	(0.010)	(0.012)	

[a] $R_{mt} - R_{ft}$ is the daily excess holding period return to the S&P composite portfolio (the percentage price change minus the yield on a short-term default-free government bond). Nonlinear optimization techniques are used to calculate maximum likelihood estimates. Asymptotic standard errors are in parentheses under the coefficient estimates. The χ^2 test statistic is distributed χ_4^2 for the ARCH model (5d) and χ_6^2 for the generalized ARCH or GARCH model (5e) under the hypothesis that the parameters are equal in the subperiods.

The estimates of the GARCH model (5c) and (5e) in table 6.2 also indicate that the variance of daily risk premiums is highly autocorrelated. To compare the persistence implied by the GARCH model with the ARCH model (5d) it is useful to consider the sum $b + c_1 + c_2$, which must be less than 1.0 for the volatility process to be stationary (Bollerslev, 1986, theorem 1). This sum equals 0.996, 0.992, and 0.992 for the 1928–84, 1928–52, and 1953–84 sample periods respectively. The comparable estimates of b for the ARCH model are 0.938, 0.924, and 0.856. The χ^2 test implies that the GARCH model parameters are not equal across the two subperiods.

2.3 Stock market risk premiums

We use the value-weighted portfolio of all New York Stock Exchange (NYSE) stocks from the Center for Research in Security Prices (CRSP) at the University of Chicago to measure monthly stock market returns. We use the NYSE portfolio because its returns include dividends. We use the S&P returns to estimate monthly variances because the CRSP portfolio is not available on a daily basis before July 1962. The fact that the S&P returns do not include dividends should have little effect on the estimates of monthly volatility.[4] The returns on the NYSE portfolio are highly correlated with the returns on the S&P composite portfolio. For example, the correlation between these portfolios is 0.993 for 1928–84. The yield on a 1 month Treasury bill is subtracted from the NYSE value-weighted return to compute the excess holding period return.

Table 6.3 contains estimates of the means, standard deviations, and skewness coefficients of the monthly excess holding period returns. The mean excess holding period return is an estimate of the average expected risk premium. The mean is estimated in three ways: (a) using ordinary least squares (OLS), (b) using weighted least squares (WLS) where the weight for each observation is the reciprocal $1/\sigma_{mt}$ of the monthly standard deviation estimated from daily S&P returns, and (c) using weighted least squares where the weight is the reciprocal $1/\hat{\sigma}_{mt}$ of the predicted standard deviation from the ARIMA model in table 6.1, panel C. The WLS

Table 6.3 Means, standard deviations, and skewness of the monthly CRSP value-weighted market excess holding period returns (t statistics in parentheses)[a]

Period	*Mean*	*WLS mean*[b]	*WLS mean*[c]	*Std dev.*	*Skewness*
1928–84	0.0061	0.0116	0.0055	0.0579	0.44[d]
	(2.73)	(9.42)	(3.51)		
1928–52	0.0074	0.0151	0.0083	0.0742	0.45[d]
	(1.74)	(6.68)	(2.76)		
1953–84	0.0050	0.0102	0.0044	0.0410	−0.05
	(2.38)	(6.91)	(2.42)		

[a]The 1 month Treasury bill yield is subtracted from the CRSP value-weighted stock market return to create an excess holding period return.

[b]Sample mean estimated by weighted least squares, where the standard deviation σ_{mt} of the S&P composite portfolio estimated from the days within the month is used to weight the observations.

[c]Sample mean estimated by weighted least squares, where the predicted standard deviation of the S&P composite portfolio estimated from the ARIMA model in table 6.1, panel C, is used to weight the observations.

[d]Greater than the 0.95 fractile of the sampling distribution under the hypothesis of a stationary serially uncorrelated normal distribution.

estimator using the actual standard deviation σ_{mt} gives larger estimates of the expected risk premium and larger t statistics than either of the other estimates. This foreshadows a result in the regression tests below: in periods of unexpectedly high volatility (so that σ_{mt} is larger than $\hat{\sigma}_{mt}$), realized stock returns are lower than average. These lower returns receive less weight when $1/\sigma_{mt}$ is used to estimate the average risk premium.

As Merton (1980) stresses, variances of realized stock returns are large in relation to the likely variance of expected returns. This low "signal to noise" ratio makes it difficult to detect variation in expected stock returns. For example, consider the average risk premiums for 1928–52 and 1953–84. The sample standard deviations are much higher in the first subperiod, and the mean risk premiums are also higher in that period. The standard errors of the sample means are so large, however, that neither the hypothesis that the subperiod expected premiums are equal nor the hypothesis that expected risk premiums in 1928–52 are twice the expected premiums in 1953–84 can be rejected at conventional significance levels. The tests below provide more structured ways to assess the relation between expected risk premiums and volatility.

3 Estimating Relations between Risk Premiums and Volatility

3.1 Regressions of excess holding period returns on ARIMA forecasts of volatility

In an efficient capital market, investors use best conditional forecasts of variables, such as the standard deviation of stock returns, that affect equilibrium expected returns. Thus we can estimate the relation between expected risk premiums and volatility by regressing excess holding period returns on the predictable components of the stock market standard deviation or variance:

$$R_{mt} - R_{ft} = \alpha + \beta \hat{\sigma}^{p}_{mt} + \varepsilon_t. \tag{6}$$

If $\beta = 0$ in (6), the expected risk premium is unrelated to the variability of stock returns. If $\alpha = 0$ and $\beta > 0$, the expected risk premium is proportional to the standard deviation ($p = 1$) or variance ($p = 2$) of stock returns.

Table 6.4 contains WLS estimates of regression (6). Each observation is weighted by the predicted standard deviation $\hat{\sigma}_{mt}$ from the ARIMA model in table 6.1, panel C, to correct for heteroskedasticity. Two sets of standard errors are calculated for each regression. The first (in parentheses) is based on the usual least squares formula. The second (in

Table 6.4 Weighted least squares regressions of monthly CRSP value-weighted excess holding period returns against the predictable and unpredictable components of the standard deviations or variances of stock market returns[a]

$$R_{mt} - R_{ft} = \alpha + \beta\hat{\sigma}^{p}_{mt} + \varepsilon_t \quad (6)$$

$$R_{mt} - R_{ft} = \alpha + \beta\hat{\sigma}^{p}_{mt} + \gamma\sigma^{pu}_{mt} + \varepsilon_t \quad (7)$$

Volatility	Equation (6)		Equation (7)						
measure	α	β	α	β	γ	$S(\varepsilon)$	R^2	$Q(12)$	$SR(\varepsilon)$
A February 1928 to December 1984, T = 683									
σ_{mt}	0.0047	0.023	0.0077	−0.050	−1.010	0.0562	0.152	17.4	6.90
	(0.0043)	(0.116)	(0.0039)	(0.107)	(0.092)				
	[0.0041]	[0.109]	[0.0039]	[0.105]	[0.111]				
σ^2_{mt}	0.0050	0.335	0.0057	0.088	−4.438	0.0573	0.107	16.1	6.44
	(0.0021)	(0.939)	(0.0020)	(0.889)	(0.496)				
	[0.0021]	[0.897]	[0.0021]	[0.930]	[0.886]				
B February 1928 to December 1952, T = 299									
σ_{mt}	0.0142	−0.133	0.0199	−0.230	−1.007	0.0728	0.213	10.5	6.52
	(0.0085)	(0.182)	(0.0076)	(0.163)	(0.115)				
	[0.0086]	[0.177]	[0.0081]	[0.175]	[0.131]				
σ^2_{mt}	0.0092	−0.324	0.0114	−0.671	−3.985	0.0736	0.175	9.8	6.65
	(0.0041)	(1.139)	(0.0038)	(1.042)	(0.515)				
	[0.0043]	[1.105]	[0.0039]	[1.140]	[0.707]				
C January 1953 to December 1984, T = 384									
σ_{mt}	0.0027	0.055	0.0068	−0.071	−1.045	0.0399	0.111	13.8	6.12
	(0.0059)	(0.182)	(0.0056)	(0.172)	(0.152)				
	[0.0055]	[0.164]	[0.0051]	[0.161]	[0.205]				
σ^2_{mt}	0.0031	1.058	0.0046	−0.349	−9.075	0.0407	0.081	11.7	6.41
	(0.0032)	(2.192)	(0.0031)	(2.118)	(1.571)				
	[0.0031]	[1.991]	[0.0031]	[2.186]	[2.382]				

[a] σ_{mt} is the prediction and σ^{u}_{mt} is the prediction error for the estimate of the monthly stock market standard deviation from the ARIMA model in table 6.1, panel C $\hat{\sigma}^2_{mt}$ and σ^{2u}_{mt} are the prediction and the prediction error for the variance of stock returns. The estimated time series model for σ_{mt} is reported in table 6.1, panel C. Standard errors are in parentheses below the coefficient estimates. The numbers in square brackets are standard errors based on White's (1980) consistent heteroskedasticity correction. $S(\varepsilon)$ is the standard deviation of the residuals, R^2 is the coefficient of determination, $Q(12)$ is the Box–Pierce statistic for 12 lags of the residual autocorrelation function which should be distributed as χ^2_{12}, and $SR(\varepsilon)$ is the Studentized range of the residuals. These regressions are estimated using WLS, where the predicted standard deviation $\hat{\sigma}_{mt}$ of the S&P composite portfolio is used to standardize each observation. R^2, $Q(12)$ and $SR(\varepsilon)$ are based on the weighted residuals, but the standard deviation of the residuals is based on the unweighted residuals (in the same units as the original data).

square brackets) is based on White's (1980) consistent correction for heteroskedasticity.[5]

The estimates of regression (6) provide little evidence of a relation between expected risk premiums and predictable volatility. For example, the 1928–84 estimate of β is 0.02, with a standard error of 0.12, in the standard deviation specification ($p = 1$), and 0.34, with a standard error of 0.94, in the variance specification ($p = 2$). All the estimates of β are within one standard error of zero.

Regressions measuring the relation between excess holding period returns and contemporaneous unexpected changes in market volatility

$$R_{mt} - R_{ft} = \alpha + \beta\hat{\sigma}^p_{mt} + \gamma\sigma^{pu}_{mt} + \varepsilon_t \tag{7}$$

provide more reliable evidence. In this regression, $\sigma^{pu}_{mt} = \sigma^p_{mt} - \hat{\sigma}^p_{mt}$ is the unpredicted standard deviation ($p = 1$) or variance ($p = 2$) of returns from the ARIMA model in table 6.1, panel C. The unpredicted components of volatility are essentially uncorrelated with the predicted components, and so including them in the regression should not affect the estimates of β. Including σ^{pu}_{mt}, however, improves the tests in two ways. First, because more of the excess holding period returns are explained, the standard errors of the regression coefficients are reduced. More important, the coefficient on the unpredicted component of volatility γ provides indirect evidence about the effects of predictable volatility on *ex ante* risk premiums.

Suppose that this month's standard deviation is larger than predicted. Then the model in table 6.1, panel C, implies that predicted standard deviations will be revised upward for all future time periods. If the risk premium is positively related to the predicted standard deviation, the discount rate for future cash flows will increase. If the cash flows are unaffected, the higher discount rate reduces both their present value and the current stock price.[6] Thus a positive relation between the predicted stock market volatility and the expected risk premium induces a negative relation between the unpredicted component of volatility and excess holding period returns.

Table 6.4 contains WLS estimates of (7). There is a reliably negative relation between excess holding period returns and unpredicted changes in the volatility of stock returns. The estimated coefficients of the unexpected change in the standard deviation γ range from -1.01 to -1.04, with t statistics between -6.88 and -10.98. The estimates of γ in the variance specification vary from -3.99 to -9.08, with t statistics between -5.78 and -8.95.

Again, regression (7) provides little direct evidence of a relation between the expected risk premium and volatility. Five of the six estimates of β are negative, and only one is more than one standard error from zero.[7]

Many of the estimates of α are reliably positive in (7). For example, the estimate for 1928–84 is 0.0077, with a standard error of 0.0039, when $p = 1$, and 0.0057, with a standard error of 0.0020, when $p = 2$. This implies that the expected risk premium is not proportional to either the predicted standard deviation or the predicted variance of stock market return. It also implies that the expected slope $E_{t-1}[(R_{mt} - R_{ft})/\hat{\sigma}_{mt}]$ of the capital market line conditional on $\hat{\sigma}_{mt}$ is not constant.

The evidence in table 6.4 provides little basis to choose between the standard deviation and variance specifications of the relation between volatility and expected risk premiums. The residual variances $S(\varepsilon)$ are smaller for the estimates of the standard deviation specification in (7) and the R^2 statistics based on weighted residuals are larger (except for 1928–52). These differences favoring the standard deviation specification are not large, however.[8]

3.2 GARCH-in-mean models

Engle, Lilien, and Robins (1987) and Bollerslev, Engle, and Wooldridge (1985) propose generalizations of the ARCH model that allow the conditional mean return to be a function of volatility, and they refer to these as GARCH-in-mean models. Table 6.5 contains estimates of the GARCH-in-mean model in two forms:

$$R_{mt} - R_{ft} = \alpha + \beta\sigma_t + \varepsilon_t - \theta\varepsilon_{t-1} \tag{8a}$$

and

$$R_{mt} - R_{ft} = \alpha + \beta\sigma_t^2 + \varepsilon_t - \theta\varepsilon_{t-1}, \tag{8b}$$

where $R_{mt} - R_{ft}$ is the daily excess holding period return on the S&P composite portfolio and the variance σ_t^2 of the unexpected excess holding period return ε_t follows the process in (5e). As before (cf. (5c)), the moving average term $\theta\varepsilon_{t-1}$ is included to capture the effect of nonsynchronous trading. The slope has the same interpretation in (8b) that it has in the monthly ARIMA regression (6) with $p = 2$ because both the risk premium and the variance σ_t^2 should be approximately proportional to the length of the measurement interval.[9] Since the standard deviation σ_t should be proportional to the square root of the measurement interval, the estimate of β in (8a) should be about 4.5 times smaller than the comparable monthly estimate in (6) with $p = 1$. The intercept α has the dimension of an average daily risk premium in (8a) and (8b), and so it should be about a factor of 22 times smaller than the monthly estimates in (6).

The results in table 6.5 indicate that there is a reliably positive relation between expected risk premiums and predicted volatility. The estimated coefficient of predicted volatility β for 1928–84 is 0.073, with a standard

Table 6.5 GARCH-in-mean models for daily excess holding period returns to Standard & Poor's composite portfolio[a]

$$R_{mt} - R_{ft} = \alpha + \beta\sigma_t + \varepsilon_t - \theta\varepsilon_{t-1} \qquad (8a)$$

$$R_{mt} - R_{ft} = \alpha + \beta\sigma_t^2 + \varepsilon_t - \theta\varepsilon_{t-1} \qquad (8b)$$

$$\sigma_t^2 = a + b\sigma_{t-1}^2 + c_1\varepsilon_{t-1}^2 + c_2\varepsilon_{t-2}^2 \qquad (5e)$$

GARCH-in-mean equations	$\alpha \times 10^3$	β	$a \times 10^5$	b	c_1	c_2	θ	χ^2 *test for stability*
A January 1928 to December 1984, T = 15,369								
Std dev.	−0.159	0.073	0.063	0.918	0.121	−0.043	−0.157	86.6
(8a), (5e)	(0.170)	(0.023)	(0.006)	(0.003)	(0.007)	(0.007)	(0.008)	
Variance	0.201	2.410	0.063	0.918	0.121	−0.043	−0.157	89.3
(8b), (5e)	(0.079)	(0.934)	(0.006)	(0.003)	(0.007)	(0.007)	(0.008)	
B January 1928 to December 1952, T = 7,326								
Std dev.	0.100	0.048	0.151	0.897	0.107	−0.011	−0.090	
(8a), (5e)	(0.272)	(0.030)	(0.014)	(0.004)	(0.009)	(0.009)	(0.012)	
Variance	0.377	1.510	0.151	0.897	0.107	−0.012	−0.090	
(8b), (5e)	(0.138)	(1.009)	(0.014)	(0.004)	(0.009)	(0.009)	(0.012)	
C January 1953 to December 1984, T = 8,043								
Std dev.	−0.406	0.112	0.052	0.922	0.131	−0.061	−0.211	
(8a), (5e)	(0.277)	(0.044)	(0.008)	(0.004)	(0.010)	(0.011)	(0.012)	
Variance	−0.019	7.220	0.052	0.922	0.131	−0.061	−0.211	
(8b), (5e)	(0.134)	(2.809)	(0.008)	(0.004)	(0.010)	(0.010)	(0.012)	

[a] $R_{mt} - R_{ft}$ is the daily excess holding period return to the S&P composite portfolio (the percentage price change minus the yield on a short-term default-free government bond). Nonlinear optimization techniques are used to calculate maximum likelihood estimates. Asymptotic standard errors are in parentheses under the coefficient estimates. The χ^2 test statistic is distributed χ_7^2 under the hypothesis that the parameters are equal in the two subperiods.

error of 0.023, in the standard deviation specification (8a), and 2.41, with a standard error of 0.934, in the variance specification (8b). This evidence supports our interpretation of the negative relation between realized risk premiums and the unexpected change in volatility in table 6.4.

As with the results in table 6.4, the standard deviation specification (8a) of the GARCH model fits the data slightly better than the variance specification (8b). The log likelihoods from the GARCH model are larger for the standard deviation specification in 1928–84 and 1928–52. Also, if the power of the standard deviation p is estimated as a parameter in the model

$$R_{mt} - R_{ft} = \alpha + \beta\sigma_t^p + \varepsilon_t - \theta\varepsilon_{t-1}, \qquad (9)$$

the estimates of p are closer to 1.0 than 2.0. The standard errors of the estimates are large, however. The evidence in favor of the standard deviation specification is not strong.

3.3 Comparisons of ARIMA and GARCH models

The ARIMA models in table 6.4, which use monthly excess holding period returns, and the GARCH-in-mean models in table 6.5, which use daily data, yield sufficiently different results that it is worth exploring the relation between these models. Table 6.6 contains estimates of the GARCH-in-mean models in (8a) and (8b) using monthly excess holding period returns. The estimates in table 6.6 do not use daily return data to predict the volatility of risk premiums, and so we would expect the volatility estimates to be less precise. Nevertheless, the estimates of β, the coefficient of predicted volatility, are quite large in comparison with the regression model estimates in table 6.4. In particular, these estimates of β for 1928–84 and 1953–84 in table 6.6 are closer to the estimates from the comparable daily GARCH-in-mean models in table 6.5 than to the

Table 6.6 Comparison of ARIMA with GARCH predictions of stock market volatility and their relations with monthly CRSP value-weighted excess holding period returns: GARCH-in-mean estimates using monthly excess holding period returns[a]

$$R_{mt} - R_{ft} = \alpha + \beta\sigma_t + \varepsilon_t - \theta\varepsilon_{t-1} \quad (8a)$$

$$R_{mt} - R_{ft} = \alpha + \beta\sigma_t^2 + \varepsilon_t - \theta\varepsilon_{t-1} \quad (8b)$$

$$\sigma_t^2 = a + b\sigma_{t-1}^2 + c_1\varepsilon_{t-1}^2 + c_2\varepsilon_{t-2}^2 \quad (5e)$$

GARCH-in-mean equations	α	β	$a \times 10^3$	b	c_1	c_2	θ	χ^2 *test for stability*[b]
A February 1928 to December 1984, T = 683								
Std dev.	−0.0020	0.224	0.083	0.814	0.058	0.104	−0.073	9.6
(8a), (5e)	(0.0056)	(0.132)	(0.031)	(0.027)	(0.044)	(0.054)	(0.038)	
Variance	0.0041	1.693	0.085	0.813	0.061	0.101	−0.072	9.7
(8b), (5e)	(0.0023)	(0.873)	(0.031)	(0.027)	(0.044)	(0.054)	(0.037)	
B February 1928 to December 1952, T = 299								
Std dev.	0.0109	0.005	0.070	0.847	0.121	0.017	−0.077	
(8a), (5e)	(0.0085)	(0.171)	(0.063)	(0.032)	(0.079)	(0.087)	(0.054)	
Variance	0.0097	0.598	0.073	0.845	0.124	0.015	−0.080	
(8b), (5e)	(0.0041)	(1.077)	(0.065)	(0.033)	(0.081)	(0.089)	(0.053)	
C January 1953 to December 1984, T = 384								
Std dev.	−0.0209	0.686	0.172	0.746	−0.021	0.172	−0.053	
(8a), (5e)	(0.0132)	(0.353)	(0.090)	(0.076)	(0.045)	(0.070)	(0.049)	
Variance	−0.0064	7.809	0.167	0.751	−0.019	0.168	−0.053	
(8b), (5e)	(0.0062)	(4.198)	(0.089)	(0.075)	(0.044)	(0.068)	(0.049)	

[a]The statistical procedure is the same as in table 6.5 except that monthly excess holding period returns to the CRSP value-weighted portfolio are used instead of the daily excess holding period returns to the S&P composite portfolio.

[b]The χ^2 statistic is distributed χ_7^2 under the hypothesis that the parameters are equal in the two subperiods.

regression estimates in table 6.4, and several are more than two standard errors above zero.[10]

Table 6.7 contains estimates of the regression on the monthly excess holding period return on the prediction of the monthly standard deviation or variance from the monthly GARCH-in-mean model in table 6.6:

$$R_{mt} - R_{ft} = \alpha + \beta\sigma_t + \varepsilon_t \tag{10a}$$

and

$$R_{mt} - R_{ft} = \alpha + \beta\sigma_t^2 + \varepsilon_t. \tag{10b}$$

Each observation in these regressions is weighted by the predicted monthly

Table 6.7 Comparison of ARIMA with GARCH predictions of stock market volatility and their relations to monthly CRSP value-weighted excess holding period returns: weighted least squares regressions of monthly CRSP value-weighted excess holding period returns against the predicted standard deviation or variance of stock returns from the monthly GARCH-in-mean model[a]

$$R_{mt} - R_{ft} = \alpha - \beta\sigma_t + \varepsilon_t \quad (10a)$$

$$R_{mt} - R_{ft} = \alpha - \beta\sigma_t^2 + \varepsilon_t \quad (10b)$$

Volatility measure	α	β	$S(\varepsilon)$	R^2	$Q(12)$	$SR(\varepsilon)$
A February 1928 to December 1984, T = 683						
Monthly GARCH	0.0035	0.049	0.0580	0.0005	20.9	6.83
Std dev.	(0.0057)	(0.133)				
	[0.0057]	[0.133]				
Monthly GARCH	0.0049	0.349	0.0580	0.0005	20.8	6.81
Variance	(0.0025)	(0.989)				
	[0.0024]	[0.973]				
B February 1928 to December 1952, T = 299						
Monthly GARCH	0.0209	−0.233	0.0750	0.0180	12.9	6.75
Std dev.	(0.0090)	(0.179)				
	[0.0089]	[0.179]				
Monthly GARCH	0.0121	−0.884	0.0749	0.0144	13.4	6.71
Variance	(0.0042)	(1.152)				
	[0.0041]	[1.107]				
C January 1953 to December 1984, T = 384						
Monthly GARCH	−0.0108	0.372	0.0408	0.0035	16.5	5.99
Std dev.	(0.0093)	(0.237)				
	[0.0087]	[0.218]				
Monthly GARCH	−0.0034	4.423	0.0408	0.0044	16.6	5.99
Variance	(0.0045)	(2.655)				
	[0.0043]	[2.381]				

[a]The statistical procedure is the same as in table 6.4 except that the predicted standard deviation of the CRSP value-weighted return σ_t estimated in table 6.6 is used to standardize each observation, instead of the prediction $\hat{\sigma}_{mt}$ from the ARIMA model in table 6.1, panel C. See the footnotes to tables 6.4 and 6.5 for more detailed descriptions of the statistical procedures.

standard deviation σ_t from table 6.6. Table 6.7 contains estimates of (10a) and (10b) that are comparable with the estimates of regression (6) in table 6.4. The estimates of the coefficient of predicted volatility β are small in relation to their standard errors in the sample period 1928–84. In the period 1928–52 the estimates of β are negative, and in the period 1953–84 they are positive, although none of the estimates is more than two standard errors from zero. Although these regressions use the GARCH-in-mean estimates of predicted volatilities, they provide no evidence of a relation between expected risk premiums and predictable volatility.

As a final comparison of the regression and GARCH-in-mean models, we create a series of monthly predicted standard deviations from the daily GARCH-in-mean model in table 6.5 by using the fitted GARCH process (5e) to forecast σ_t^2 for each of the N_t trading days in the month, conditional on data available on the first day in the month. We compute the implied monthly standard deviation by summing the predicted variances within the month and taking the square root of the sum. We estimate the expected monthly risk premium from the GARCH-in-mean model by inserting the predicted standard deviations for the days in the month into (8a) and summing the predicted daily expected risk premiums.

The GARCH-in-mean prediction of the monthly standard deviation is similar to the ARIMA prediction $\hat{\sigma}_{mt}$ (the correlation for 1928–84 is 0.89 and the means are virtually identical). The GARCH-in-mean and ARIMA predictions have essentially the same correlation with the actual monthly standard deviation σ_{mt} (0.755 and 0.744), although the sample variance of the GARCH prediction is about a third larger. Thus the two models have similar abilities to predict future volatility.[11]

In contrast, the behavior of the expected risk premiums implied by the regression and GARCH-in-mean models is quite different. Figure 6.3 shows a plot of the monthly expected risk premium from regression (6) with $p = 1$ for 1928–84 from table 6.4, and figure 6.4 shows a plot of the monthly expected risk premium from the daily GARCH-in-mean model (8a). The correlation between the two measures is 0.88 over the full sample period. However, the predicted risk premiums from the daily GARCH model have a much higher mean and variance than the predictions from regression (6). (The scale in figure 6.3 is from 0 to 1.0 percent per month, and the scale in figure 6.4 is from 0 to 10.0 percent per month.) The higher variability of predicted risk premiums in figure 6.4 is caused by two factors: (a) the greater variability of the predicted standard deviation from the GARCH-in-mean model and (b) the larger coefficient of the predicted standard deviation β in the GARCH-in-mean model. The sensitivity of the monthly expected risk premium to a change in the predicted monthly standard deviation is about 15 times greater in the GARCH-in-mean model than in the ARIMA regression model.[12] Thus, although the ARIMA and

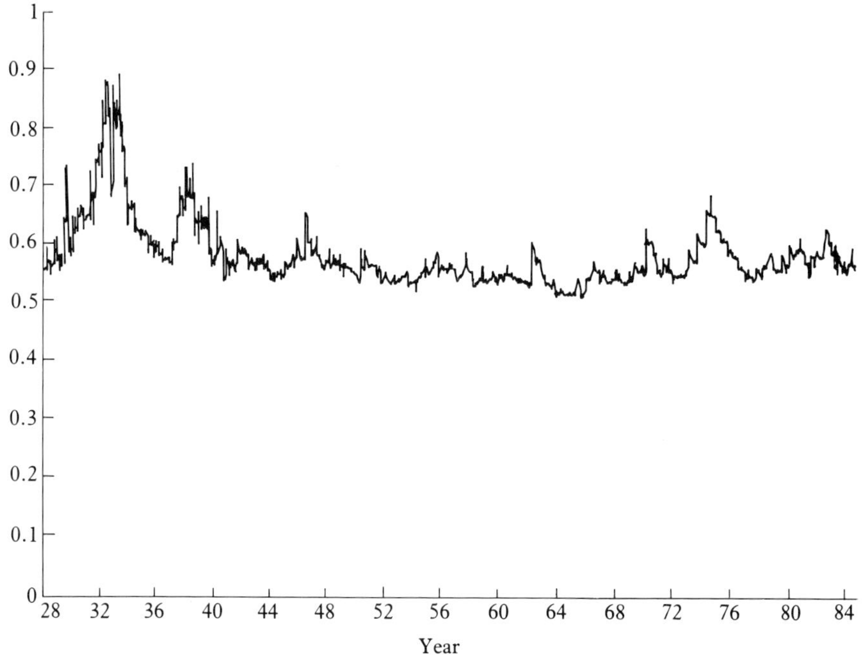

Figure 6.3 Predicted percentage monthly risk premium to the Standard & Poor's composite portfolio from the regression on ARIMA predictions of the standard deviation $\hat{\sigma}_{mt}$ in table 6.4, 1928–84: $R_{mt} - R_{ft} = \alpha + \beta\hat{\sigma}_{mt}$.

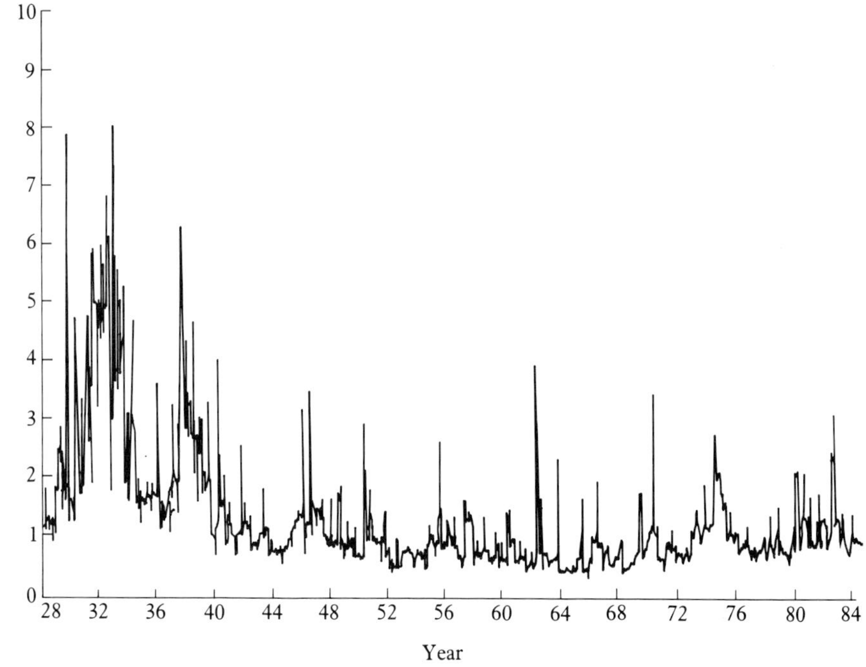

Figure 6.4 Predicted percentage monthly risk premium to the Standard & Poor's composite portfolio from the daily GARCH-in-mean model for the standard deviation σ_t in table 6.5, 1928–84 (equations (8a) and (5e)).

GARCH-in-mean models have a similar ability to predict volatility, the GARCH-in-mean model implies greater variability of expected risk premiums.[13] More puzzling, however, is the fact that the average of the expected risk premiums is much higher for the GARCH-in-mean model (1.34 percent per month in figure 6.4 versus 0.58 percent per month for the regression model on ARIMA predictions of the standard deviation in figure 6.3). The GARCH-in-mean predictions seem too high, since they are almost twice the average realized premium (see table 6.3).

The high GARCH-in-mean predictions probably reflect the negative relation between the unexpected component of volatility and the unexpected return observed in table 6.4. The likelihood function used to estimate the GARCH model assumes that the standardized residuals ε_t/σ_t have a unit normal distribution. The daily standardized residuals from the standard deviation specification (8a) and (5e) for the sample period 1928–84 in table 6.5 have a mean of -0.038, a standard deviation of 0.999, and a skewness coefficient of -0.37. The mean and skewness coefficients are reliably different from zero, implying that the normality assumption underlying the GARCH-in-mean model is violated. Since σ_t is predetermined in the GARCH model, the negative skewness of the standardized residuals reflects the negative relation between the unexpected component of volatility and the unexpected excess holding period return.[14] This negative skewness probably causes the negative mean of the standardized residuals, which in turn causes the GARCH-in-mean predictions of the risk premiums to be too high (for example, the average monthly error from the GARCH-in-mean model is -0.90 percent per month, which is greater than the difference between the average predicted risk premiums in figures 6.3 and 6.4). Of course, this argument says that the level of the predictions in figure 6.4 is too high because α is too large; it is also possible that the sensitivity β of expected risk premiums to changes in predictable volatility is biased.

It is well known in the econometrics literature that full information maximum likelihood (FIML) estimators such as the GARCH models are more efficient than instrumental variables estimators such as the two-step regression procedures, although both estimators are consistent if the model is correctly specified. However, FIML estimators are generally more sensitive than instrumental variables estimators to model misspecification. Hausman (1978) proposes a class of model specification tests based on this observation. Thus one interpretation of the apparent differences between the GARCH-in-mean and the regression results is that the statistical specification underlying these models is not adequate. A formal test such as that of Hausman is difficult because the GARCH and ARIMA models for volatility are not nested. It is likely that neither model is entirely adequate for predicting expected risk premiums.

4 Analysis of the Results

4.1 Interpreting the estimated coefficients

Merton (1980) notes that in a model of capital market equilibrium where a "representative investor" has constant relative risk aversion, there are conditions under which the expected market risk premium will be approximately proportional to the *ex ante* variance of the market return:[15]

$$E_{t-1}(R_{mt} - R_{ft}) = C\hat{\sigma}^2_{mt}. \tag{11}$$

The parameter C in (11) is the representative investor's coefficient of relative risk aversion. For example, the logarithmic utility function for wealth $U(W) = \log W$ implies $C = 1$. If we ignore the intercepts α, the coefficient of relative risk aversion equals β in both the regression model (6) for $p = 2$ and the GARCH-in-mean model (8b).

The estimate of relative risk aversion β from the regression model in table 6.4 is 0.34 for the overall period, but the large standard error (0.90) does not allow us reliably to distinguish the coefficient from zero. The corresponding GARCH-in-mean estimate of β in table 6.5 is 2.41, which is about 2.75 times its estimated standard error. Both these point estimates appear economically reasonable, however, and they are well within the range of estimates produced by other studies using different approaches. For example, Friend and Blume (1975) estimate relative risk aversion to be about 2.0, Hansen and Singleton (1982) obtain estimates between −1.6 and 1.6, and Brown and Gibbons (1985) obtain estimates between 0.1 and 7.3. Estimates of relative risk aversion can also be obtained from the standard deviation specifications in (6) for $p = 1$ and in (8a) by dividing the β estimates by an average value of σ_m. The estimates obtained in this fashion are similar to those obtained from the variance specifications.

As noted above, a negative *ex post* relation between excess holding period returns and the unexpected component of volatility is consistent with a positive *ex ante* relation between risk premiums and volatility. The negative coefficient in the *ex post* relation is also likely to be larger in absolute value than the positive coefficient in the *ex ante* relation, especially when volatilities, and thus expected future risk premiums, are highly autocorrelated. This can be seen using a model developed by Poterba and Summers (1986). They model volatility as a first-order autoregressive process to illustrate this effect. Let ρ denote the first-order autocorrelation of the variance. Assume that expected real dividends grow at a constant rate g, that the real risk-free rate is a constant r_f and that the expected risk premium in period $t + \tau$, conditional σ_t^2, equals $\beta E(\sigma^2_{t+\tau} \mid \sigma_t^2)$. Then, as Poterba and Summers show, the percentage change in stock price arising from a change in volatility is approximately

$$\frac{\mathrm{d}\log P}{\mathrm{d}\sigma^2} = -\left[\frac{1}{1 + r_{\mathrm{f}} + \beta\sigma_t^2 - \rho(1+g)}\right]\beta. \tag{12}$$

The quantity in square brackets in (12) exceeds unity and is increasing in ρ. The value of the derivative is sensitive to the choice of ρ, but an example can illustrate the potential magnitude of the *ex post* relation between returns and volatility in comparison with the *ex ante* relation. Assume that (a) the monthly variance σ_t^2 equals 0.002, (b) the real risk-free rate equals 0.035 percent per month, and (c) real dividends are expected to grow at 0.087 percent per month. (The last two values are the same as those used by Poterba and Summers.) The estimate of the coefficient of the unpredicted component of volatility for 1928–84 in table 6.4 is -4.438, which implies that $\beta = 2.05$ if $\rho = 0.5$ and $\beta = 1.07$ if $\rho = 0.7$. Given these hypothetical magnitudes and the estimated standard errors in table 6.4, it is not surprising that an *ex post* negative relation is detected more strongly in the data than is an *ex ante* positive relation.[16]

4.2 *The effect of leverage*

Many of the firms whose common stocks constitute the indexes used in computing the market risk premiums are levered. Although the observed strong negative relation between excess holding period returns and unexpected volatility is consistent with a positive *ex ante* relation between risk premiums and volatility at the firm level, Black (1976) and Christie (1982) suggest another interpretation. They note that leverage can induce a negative *ex post* relation between returns and volatility for common stocks, even if the volatility and the expected return for the total firm are constant.

Suppose that a firm's volatility and expected return are constant. A decline in stock prices (in relation to bond prices) increases leverage, increases the expected return on the stock, and increases the variance of the stock's return. As Black (1976) and Christie (1982) demonstrate, however, if this is the sole reason for the relation between stock returns and volatility, then a regression of the percentage change in standard deviation on the percentage change in stock price should have a coefficient (elasticity) greater than -1.0.

An elasticity of -1.0 is an extreme lower bound. Consider a firm with riskless debt. The elasticity of the stock return standard deviation with respect to the stock price is $-D/V$, where D is the value of the debt and V is the value of the firm. The lower bound of -1.0 occurs only when the stock has no value. Evidence in Taggart (1986) suggests that the fraction of debt in the capital structure of large US corporations was below 45 percent throughout 1926–79, and so the leverage hypothesis should not generate an elasticity below -0.45.

To test the hypothesis that the relation between realized risk premiums and unexpected volatility is caused only by leverage, we regress the percentage change in the estimated standard deviation of the S&P composite portfolio against the continuously compounded return on that portfolio:

$$\ln\left(\frac{\sigma_{mt}}{\sigma_{mt-1}}\right) = \alpha_0 + \alpha_1 \ln(1 + R_{mt}) + \varepsilon_t. \qquad (13)$$

The estimated elasticity α_1 is -1.69, with a standard error of 0.25, for 1928–84. The estimates for 1928–52 and 1953–84 are -1.63 and -1.89, with standard errors of 0.32 and 0.45. The estimated elasticity is reliably less than -1.0. Black (1976) obtains a similar result using a sample of 30 stocks from May 1964 to December 1975. Our longer sample period and more inclusive market index support Black's conclusion: leverage is probably not the sole explanation for the negative relation between stock returns and volatility.

4.3 *Extensions*

In this paper we have examined the time series relation between the risk of a stock market portfolio and the portfolio's expected risk premium. The tests above use the predicted volatility of stock returns as the measure of risk. We have also tried to estimate this relation using several other measures of risk, including the predicted variability of the real interest rate, the predicted covariance between the stock market return and consumption, and the predicted variability of decile portfolios formed on the basis of firm size. All these variables involve monthly data, and so none is estimated as precisely as our measure of volatility that uses daily data. Perhaps because of this estimation problem, none of these risk measures produces a stronger relation between risk and return than we observe using the volatility of stock returns based on daily data.

We have also tried to improve the tests by including other predictive variables in the models. Fama and Schwert (1977) show that the nominal interest rate can be used to predict stock returns. Keim and Stambaugh (1986) use (a) the yield spread between long-term low grade corporate bonds and short-term Treasury bills, (b) the level of the S&P composite index in relation to its average level over the previous 45 years, and (c) the average share price of the firms in the smallest quintile of NYSE firms to predict stock returns. Including these variables in the models does not have much impact on our estimates of the time series relation between risk and return.

5 Conclusions

We find evidence of a positive relation between the expected risk premium on common stocks and the predictable level of volatility. The variability of realized stock returns is so large, however, that it is difficult to discriminate among alternative specifications of this relation. We present several estimates of the relation between the expected risk premium and the predicted volatility of NYSE common stocks over the period 1928–84.

There is also a strong negative relation between the unpredictable component of stock market volatility and excess holding period returns. If expected risk premiums are positively related to predictable volatility, then a positive unexpected change in volatility (and an upward revision in predicted volatility) increases future expected risk premiums and lowers current stock prices. The magnitude of the negative relation between contemporaneous returns and changes in volatility is too large to be attributed solely to the effects of leverage discussed by Black (1976) and Christie (1982), and so we interpret this negative relation as evidence of a positive relation between expected risk premiums and *ex ante* volatility.

The estimates of volatility and expected risk premiums in this paper suggest that these variables have fluctuated widely over the past 60 years. Although we are unwilling to choose a particular model for the relation between expected risk premiums and predictable movements in volatility, it seems obvious that future work in this area is called for. Other variables that could affect expected risk premiums should be integrated into this analysis, as well as different measures of time-varying risk. We have done some work along these lines, but the results are so ambiguous – probably because the measures of risk and other factors that might affect expected risk premiums are less precise than the volatility measures reported above – that they are not worth reporting in detail.

Notes

1 See Merton (1980). We tried several modifications of (2), including (a) subtracting the within-month mean return from each observation and (b) ignoring the cross-products. These modifications had little effect on our results.

2 We also conducted many of our tests with one-step-ahead predictions of $\hat{\sigma}^2_{mt}$ from (3) where the parameters were estimated using the previous 60 months of data. Other variables were also used to model $\hat{\sigma}^2_{mt}$. The only variables that seem to have reliable predictive power are two lags of the return to a market portfolio, such as the Center for Research in Security Prices (CRSP) value or equal-weighted portfolio. Results using these alternative models are similar to the results we report.

3 Yields are calculated from the average of bid and ask prices for the US government

security that matures closest to the end of the month. Daily yields are calculated by dividing the monthly yield by the number of trading days in the month. These data are from the CRSP US Government Securities File. We are grateful to David Hsieh for providing the computer program used to estimate the ARCH models.

4 Since the ex-dividend days are different for different stocks in the S&P composite portfolio, there are no large changes due to dividend payments in the daily index. We compared the estimates of monthly volatility computed from daily data for the CRSP value-weighted portfolio of NYSE and American Stock Exchange stocks with the estimates for the S&P composite portfolio from July 1962 through December 1984, and they are very similar.

5 The importance of correcting for heteroskedasticity is illustrated by results in Gennotte and Marsh (1985). They estimate a model like (6), except that the prediction of this month's variance is the square of last month's risk premium. Their estimate of β is more than five standard errors from zero for 1926–78 using the CRSP equal-weighted portfolio. We replicated their estimates for 1928–84, and the OLS estimate of β is 0.69 with a standard error of 0.11. The regression errors are heteroskedastic, however, much like the behavior of the standard deviation of market returns in figure 6.1. The OLS standard errors are too small since White's (1980) corrected standard error is 0.42. The WLS estimate of β is 0.75, with a standard error of 0.25 (0.29 with White's correction). Thus the reliability of the relation reported by Gennotte and Marsh (1985) is overstated because of heteroskedasticity.

6 This volatility-induced change in the stock price in turn contributes to the volatility estimated for that month, but this effect is likely to be a negligible fraction of the month's total unexpected volatility.

7 The correlation between the predicted standard deviation $\hat{\sigma}_{mt}$ from the ARIMA model and the prediction error σ^{u}_{mt} is -0.07 for the sample period 1928–84. This small negative correlation and the highly significant negative coefficient on the prediction error cause a number of the estimates of β to change sign relative to the simple regression (6).

8 Pagan (1984) and Murphy and Topel (1985) argue that regressions with generated regressors (such as (6) or (7)) produce understated standard errors because the randomness in the predictions is ignored. Following Pagan, we estimated (6) using several lags of σ_{mt} as instrumental variables, and the estimates of β and their standard errors were similar to the estimates in table 6.4. We also calculated the adjustment suggested by Murphy and Topel (1985). The results in table 6.4 were unaffected, and so they are not reported. Pagan and Ullah (1985) discuss other estimation strategies, including ARCH models, for models like (6) or (7).

9 If the errors in (8a) are serially independent, the variance of the N_t-step-ahead forecast error (ignoring parameter estimation error) is $N_t\sigma_t^2$. Since the variance process in (5e) is almost a random walk, the sum of the one-step-ahead through N_t-step-ahead forecasts of the risk premium is approximately $N_tE(R_{mt} - R_{ft} \mid \sigma_t)$.

10 The daily estimate of β for the standard deviation specification (10a) in table 6.5 should be multiplied by the square root of the number of days in the month, $N_t^{1/2} = 4.5$, to be comparable with the monthly estimates in table 6.6. Thus, the values of β for (10a) implied by table 6.5 are 0.30, 0.25, and 0.39 for 1928–84, 1928–52, and 1953–84 respectively.

11 The monthly GARCH-in-mean predictor of the standard deviation has a correlation of 0.702 with σ_{mt}.

12 The estimate of β for equation (6) is 0.023 for the sample period 1928–84 in table 6.4; the comparable estimate of β is 0.073 for the standard deviation specification of the daily GARCH-in-mean model in table 6.5. As discussed in note 10, the daily estimate

of β in table 6.5 must be multiplied by $N_t^{1/2} = 4.5$ to make it comparable with the monthly estimate in table 6.4, and so $(4.5)(0.073)/(0.023) = 15$.

13 The greater variability of the expected risk premiums from the GARCH-in-mean model does not arise solely because we use forecasts conditional on information for the first day in the month to construct each month's forecast. We also constructed monthly "forecasts" by cumulating all the one-step-ahead daily forecasts within each month. The variance of these forecasts is 0.000 872; the variance of the monthly forecasts constructed from first-of-the-month estimates is 0.000 867.

14 Indeed, a WLS regression of the daily errors ε_t from (8a) on the "unexpected" standard deviation yields a coefficient of -0.375 with a t statistic of -34.1. This regression is similar to the multiple regression estimates of equation (7) in table 6.4.

15 This approximation will hold in Merton's (1973) intertemporal model if (a) the partial derivative of the representative investor's consumption with respect to wealth is much larger than the partial derivative with respect to any state variable or (b) the variance of the change in wealth is much larger than the variance of the change in any state variable.

16 Poterba and Summers estimate that the elasticity of the stock price with respect to the variance σ_t^2 is about ten times higher for the IMA(1, 3) model in table 6.1, panel C, than for their AR(1) model. This means that the implied values of β would be correspondingly smaller, given our estimates of γ. In an earlier version of this paper we presented estimates of β that used a constraint similar to (12). The constrained estimates of β were small, but several standard errors from zero, reflecting the precision of the estimates of γ.

References

Black, F. (1976) "Studies of Stock Price Volatility Changes," *Proceedings of the 1976 Meetings of the Business and Economics Statistics Section, American Statistical Association*, pp. 177–81.

Black, F., Jensen, M. C. and Scholes, M. (1972) "The Capital Asset Pricing Model: Some Empirical Tests." In *Studies in the Theory of Capital Markets*, ed. M. C. Jensen (New York: Praeger).

Bollerslev, T. (1986) "Generalized Autoregressive Conditional Heteroskedasticity," *Journal of Econometrics*, 31, 307–28.

Bollerslev, T., Engle, R. F. and Wooldridge, J. M. (1985) "A Capital Asset Pricing Model with Time Varying Covariances," Unpublished Manuscript, University of California, San Diego, CA.

Breeden, D. T., Gibbons, M. R. and Litzenberger, R. H. (1989) "Empirical Tests of the Consumption-Oriented CAPM," *Journal of Finance*, 44: 2, June, 231–62.

Brown, D. P. and Gibbons, M. R. (1985) "A Simple Econometric Approach for Utility-Based Asset Pricing Models, *Journal of Finance*, 40, 359–81.

Chen, N.-F., Roll, R. and Ross, S. A. (1986) "Economic Forces and the Stock Market: Testing the APT and Alternative Asset Pricing Theories," *Journal of Business*, 59, 383–403.

Christie, A. A. (1982) "The Stochastic Behavior of Common Stock Variances: Value, Leverage and Interest Rate Effects," *Journal of Financial Economics*, 10, 407–32.

Engle, R. F. (1982) "Autoregressive Conditional Heteroskedasticity with Estimates of the Variance of United Kingdom Inflation," *Econometrica*, 50, 987–1007.

Engle, R. F., Lilien, D. M. and Robins, R. P. (1987) Estimating Time Varying Risk Premia in the Term Structure: The ARCH-M Model, *Econometrica*, 55, 391–407.

Fama, E. F. (1976) *Foundations of Finance* (New York: Basic Books).

Fama, E. F. and MacBeth, J. D. (1973) "Risk, Return, and Equilibrium: Empirical Tests," *Journal of Political Economy*, 81, 607–36.

Fama, E. F. and Schwert, G. W. (1977) "Asset Returns and Inflation," *Journal of Financial Economics*, 5, 115–46.

Fisher, L. (1966) "Some New Stock Market Indices," *Journal of Business*, 29, 191–225.

Friend, I. and Blume, M. (1975) "The Demand for Risky Assets," *American Economic Review*, 65, 900–22.

Gennotte, G. and Marsh, T. A. (1985) "Variations in Ex-ante Risk Premiums on Capital Assets," Unpublished Manuscript, Massachusetts Institute of Technology, Cambridge, MA.

Hansen, L. P. and Singleton, K. J. (1982) "Generalized Instrumental Variables Estimation of Nonlinear Rational Expectations Models," *Econometrica*, 50, 1269–86; corrected tables in *Econometrica*, 52, 1984, 267–68.

Hausman, J. A. (1978) "Specification Tests in Econometrics," *Econometrica*, 46, 1251–72.

Keim, D. B. and Stambaugh, R. F. (1986) "Predicting Returns in the Stock and Bond Markets," *Journal of Financial Economics*, 17: 2, 357–90.

Merton, R. C. (1973) "An Intertemporal Asset Pricing Model," *Econometrica*, 41, 867–87.

Merton, R. C. (1980) "On Estimating the Expected Return on the Market: An Exploratory Investigation," *Journal of Financial Economics*, 8, 323–61.

Murphy, K. M. and Topel, R. H. (1985) "Estimation and Inference in Two-step Econometric Models," *Journal of Business and Economics Statistics*, 3, 370–9.

Officer, R. R. (1973) "The Variability of the Market Factor of New York Stock Exchange," *Journal of Business*, 46, 434–53.

Pagan, A. (1984) "Econometric Issues in the Analysis of Regressions with Generated Regressors," *International Economic Review*, 25, 221–47.

Pagan, A. and Ullah, A. (1985) "The Econometric Analysis of Models with Risk Terms," Unpublished Manuscript, University of Rochester, Rochester, NY.

Pindyck, R. S. (1984) "Risk, Inflation, and the Stock Market," *American Economic Review*, 74, 335–51.

Poterba, J. M. and Summers, L. H. (1986) "The Persistence of Volatility and Stock Market Fluctuations," *American Economic Review*, 76, 1142–51.

Roll, R. and Ross, S. A. (1980) "An Empirical Investigation of the Arbitrage Pricing Theory," *Journal of Finance*, 20, 1073–103.

Scholes, M. and Williams, J. (1977) Estimating Betas from Non-Synchronous Data," *Journal of Financial Economics*, 5, 309–27.

Taggart, R. A. (1986) "Secular Patterns in the Financing of U.S. Corporations." In *The Changing Roles of Debt and Equity in Financing U.S. Capital Formation*, ed. B. M. Friedman (Chicago, IL: University of Chicago Press), pp. 13–75.

White, H. (1980) "A Heteroskedasticity-Consistent Covariance Matrix Estimator and a Direct Test for Heteroskedasticity," *Econometrica*, 48, 817–38.

Wichern, D. W. (1973) The Behavior of the Sample Autocorrelation Function for an Integrated Moving Average Process," *Biometrika*, 60, 235–9.

Chapter 7

Sudipto Bhattacharya

Background and Comments

Money managers can excel in two ways: by picking good stocks or by picking good times to be in all stocks. The paper by Sudipto Bhattacharya and his colleagues considers how an outside analyst might evaluate a manager's performance on these two dimensions of selectivity and timing. The paper also gives an appreciation of how difficult the separation of selectivity and timing really is.

Bhattacharya et al. assume that the analyst can only observe rates of return measured every month, say, or every quarter. It is a little easier when the analyst can track changes in portfolio composition. If a manager is 80 percent invested in stocks in January, for example, but 95 percent invested in February, he is presumably making a bullish bet on the market. But suppose the manager instead sells out of certain industries at the end of January and buys into others. Stocks in the January industries have low betas, and stocks in February industries have high betas. The portfolio stays 80 percent invested. Is this an attempt to profit from fundamental good news about the new industries? Or is it simply a shift to high beta stocks in order to make a bullish bet?

There would be no easy way to distinguish timing from selectivity based on this one observation. However, as the following paper shows, it is possible in principle to draw the distinction statistically, given a time series of portfolio returns. Distinguishing skill from luck is even more difficult. The statistical "noise" in returns on stocks and portfolios is enormous. Identifying the manager who can generate superior long-run average performance may not be possible until the long run is nearly over.

Obviously the analyst facing all these difficulties requires precise and powerful econometrics. That is why papers such as the following are valuable as well as interesting.

Author's Introduction

I spent a productive and enjoyable academic year in 1983–84 as a Batterymarch Fellow, carrying out research on financial economics at the University of California, Berkeley, and also at Harvard University. My work during this period focused primarily on the design of statistical evaluation and performance incentive schemes for managers of portfolios, who may have private information regarding the future market returns on individual securities and/or the stock market as a whole. Two published papers, the one following and one with Paul Pfleiderer (see Bibliographical Listing), resulted from these efforts.

In designing statistical portfolio performance evaluation schemes, my co-authors and I were concerned with estimating managers' accuracy of forecasts of returns – on the "market factor" and idiosyncratic security-specific shocks – as well as managers' responsiveness in changing portfolio compositions to correspond to forecasted returns. To this end Admati, Pfleiderer, Ross, and I analyzed and extended an earlier "quadratic regression" procedure due to Treynor and Mazuy

(1966) – which is predicated on normal distributions of unconditional and conditional (forecast) returns – in a well-specified decision-theoretic and econometric context. We showed that the precision and responsiveness of managerial forecasts and portfolio revision rules could *both* be separately estimated, without knowledge of the portfolio compositions or the unconditional expected return on the market portfolio, under some assumptions that included linearity of portfolio response with respect to mean return forecasts. This was a major advance on earlier work, which had either claimed that such estimates of managerial attributes could not be obtained or used much stronger assumptions only to obtain weaker results on estimating the product of precision and responsiveness coefficients.

In economic terms, earlier evaluation procedures based on results of portfolio performance measurement left the investing community vulnerable to *manipulation* of evaluation schemes by managers, who could simply exaggerate their portfolio responsiveness to mask low precision forecasting ability. In my companion paper with Pfleiderer, we considered a related problem of negating manipulation of performance evaluation schemes by managers when long-horizon estimation using portfolio and market returns is not feasible, by using managerial *self-selection* among multiple incentive schemes differing in their magnitudes of fixed salaries versus penalties for forecast inaccuracies. Much further work remains to be done on integrating these approaches, using evaluation schemes based on explicit multiperiod incentive contracts, and on considering issues relating to questions of infrequent observability of managerial portfolio revisions and fund returns by evaluators. A fuller menu of asset choices by managers, which includes derivative securities such as options and futures as well as stocks and bonds, also needs to be incorporated into the design of performance evaluation schemes.

Reference

Treynor, J. L. and Mazuy, F. (1966) "Can Mutual Funds Outguess the Market," *Harvard Business Review*, 44, July–August, 131–6.

Bibliographical Listing

"Delegated Portfolio Management" (with Paul Pfleiderer), *Journal of Economic Theory*, 36: 1, June 1985, 1–25.

On Timing and Selectivity

ANAT R. ADMATI, SUDIPTO BHATTACHARYA,
PAUL PFLEIDERER and STEPHEN A. ROSS

The study of investment performance has long sought to draw the distinction between the ability to "time" the market and the ability to forecast the returns on individual assets.[1] This distinction has been viewed as a useful device for attributing a manager's performance, that is, superior performance is due to either timing or selection ability or some combination of the two. Indeed, portfolio managers often characterize themselves as market timers or stock pickers. An ability to distinguish between these two sources of superior performance may allow more accurate measures of the value of the services provided by managers. At the same time, the distinction between these two types of performance may have intrinsic interest. The distribution of prices and observed trades may be very different depending on whether private information in the economy is predominantly about market aggregates or is predominantly firm specific.

The active nature of portfolio management is often based on the claim of superior information. If this is so, then the main problem in performance evaluation is inferring the *quality* of private information possessed by a portfolio manager. Many tests do not successfully separate measures of quality from measures of aggressiveness. By trading aggressively, a manager with little information may be able to mimic certain aspects of the performance of a manager having more precise information. Since a client can always alter the aggressiveness of a managed portfolio on his own account, aside from possible savings in transactions costs that may make mutual funds superior to individual investment, the value added by a portfolio manager is a function solely of the precision of his information. Empirical tests of timing and selectivity should be designed to recover some measure of the quality of the information a

Reproduced from *Journal of Finance*, 41: 3, July 1986, 715–30.

Paul Pfleiderer is Associate Professor of Finance at Stanford University and Stephen A. Ross is Sterling Professor of Economics and Finance, School of Organization and Management at Yale University. We would like to acknowledge the useful comments of Mike Gibbons, Mark Grinblatt, David Modest, and Robert Verrecchia. PP received support from the Stanford Program in Finance.

manager has, as distinct from measuring his investment strategies (such as the level of changes in the beta of his portfolio). We show that this can be done for a number of interesting specifications. Related work can be found in Admati and Ross [2].

Our focus in this paper is mainly on the conceptual and econometric problems involved in distinguishing timing and selection ability. Although the terms timing and selectivity have been used quite often, providing satisfactory definitions is not an easy task. Timing is often characterized (e.g. Jensen [8]) by the *response* of the informed manager to the private information he or she obtains. In the language we shall use, there is a small set of portfolios, called *timing portfolios*, which essentially provide separating funds for the managed portfolio – the change in the portfolio's composition in response to timing information always involves only shifting funds among the timing portfolios. Selectivity is usually thought of as the ability of a manager to pick individual assets. Two intuitive characterizations of this notion are (a) as distinct from timing, selectivity information is *statistically independent* of the returns on the timing portfolios,[2] and (b) different types or coordinates of selectivity information pertain to different assets. We first observe that these two characterizations may be inconsistent with each other. Indeed, they are, strictly speaking, inconsistent with each other if asset returns are normally distributed, as we assume for most of our analysis.[3]

In the next section we discuss two approaches to defining selectivity, which are motivated by the observation above. We call the first the *portfolio approach* and the second the *factor approach*. In the portfolio approach we use the first characterization of selectivity. Specifically, for a given set of timing portfolios, selectivity information pertains to the residuals in the regression of asset returns on the returns of the timing portfolios. For example, if timing portfolios are the riskless asset and the market portfolio of risky assets, then selectivity information pertains to the residuals from the standard market model regression. This definition is consistent with many of the empirical studies in the literature, but it is somewhat awkward and not easily motivated. In particular, it is difficult to reconcile the information structures that arise in this formulation with the information acquisition technology that gives rise to the existence of this information.

In what we call the *factor approach*, a factor-generating process is postulated for asset returns, and timing and selectivity information are interpreted in terms of their statistical relation to the factors and to the idiosyncratic terms in the generating process. This approach is consistent with the above definition of timing, that is, if information pertains to a set of K factors, then there are (at least) K timing portfolios. But now the selectivity information, which pertains to the idiosyncratic terms in the factor model, is truly information about individual assets that is statistically independent (given the factors) of returns on other assets and, further, is independent of the factor information that gives rise to the timing portfolios. What is not true any more is that selectivity information is distinct from timing in the sense that this information is independent of the returns on the timing portfolios. Thus this definition captures the second characterization of selectivity mentioned above, but not the first. It is, in our opinion, more natural and easier to motivate.

One result we derive, which is important to the ability to study timing and selectivity empirically, is that, surprisingly, the composition of the timing portfolios obtained in the factor approach is independent of the quality of the private information. For example, if two managers each have timing information (information that pertains to some K factors of the distribution of returns), then no matter what the precision of the private information is, the two managers have the same timing portfolios, that is, they shift the composition of their portfolios within the same set of separating portfolios. However, this result depends on the manager's possessing no selectivity information. Information about the idiosyncratic terms affects the composition of the timing portfolios, so that although the response to the timing information is such that L timing portfolios are used, these portfolios would be different for two managers possessing selectivity information where the quality of information is different. In particular, if the quality and nature of private information are unknown, then it is not possible to identify *ex ante* the timing portfolios and use them in a market type regression. Instead we must use the data to infer the identity of the timing portfolios.

The above conceptual distinctions between timing and selectivity are discussed in section 1. We then examine the possibilities for attributing the performance of a managed fund to one activity or the other when only *ex post* returns are observed. Contrary to Jensen [8], we can show that it is possible to disentangle timing and selectivity empirically. In section 2 we discuss the statistical properties that are special to the factor approach with regard to measuring performance. In section 3 we focus on the portfolio approach, where statistical methods for measuring performance may be different. The tests are essentially extensions of the approach first suggested by Treynor and Mazuy [13] and developed further by Jensen [8]. Essentially it is assumed that the manager's optimal portfolio position is linearly related to his expectations of the returns to be earned on assets and timing portfolios. This gives rise to an estimable relation between the returns earned on the managed fund and a quadratic function of observables. Although the factor approach seems to be superior to the portfolio approach on conceptual grounds, we find that it presents more difficulties in testing. Section 4 provides concluding remarks.

1 The Distinction Between Timing and Selectivity

In this section we present a general definition of timing and then discuss two approaches to the definition of selectivity. The first approach, which we call the *portfolio approach*, is implicit in much of the previous literature but suffers from some conceptual problems. The second, the *factor approach*, is not subject to these problems and seems to us to be more in the spirit of the intuitive interpretation of these terms. In both approaches, the distinctions are ultimately statements about the type of information which managers receive.

For most of our analysis, we assume that information signals and asset returns are distributed multivariate normal.[4] The information signals that managers receive are, if they are informative, correlated with some or all of the returns to be realized on the individual assets. Under what conditions can a signal be called a timing signal? In the approach taken here, a signal is a timing signal if the appropriate response to *any* realization of the signal involves only the shifting of funds among timing portfolios. Timing information is therefore characterized by the limited nature of the response it produces.

To make this precise, assume that there are $N+1$ assets in the economy and that the return on the ith asset is $\tilde{R}_i$. Assume also that a riskless asset exists, which is labeled as the zeroth asset. (All the concepts we present here are easily extended to settings in which no riskless asset exists.) A portfolio α is an $(N+1)$-vector with α_i equal to the weight placed on asset i and $\Sigma_{i=0}^{N} \alpha_i = 1$. We assume that the portfolio manager receives a signal $\tilde{Y}$ that is informative about the returns to be earned on some or all of the $N+1$ assets, and that this information is used to construct his or her optimal portfolio $\alpha^{\star}(\tilde{Y})$. Let $\{\alpha_0^0, \alpha_1^0, \ldots, \alpha_N^0\}$ be a set of $N+1$ linearly independent portfolios. The set $\{\alpha_0^0, \alpha_1^0, \ldots, \alpha_N^0\}$ is a basis for $\mathscr{R}^{N+1}$, and any portfolio α can be constructed by combining portfolios in the basis, that is, $\alpha = \Sigma_{n=0}^{N} \gamma_n \alpha_n^0$ for some γ_n, $\Sigma_{n=0}^{N} \gamma_n = 1$. Thus, when the portfolio is chosen in response to the information signal $\tilde{Y}$, we can write, without loss of generality, $\alpha^{\star}(\tilde{Y}) = \Sigma_{n=0}^{N} \gamma_n(\tilde{Y})\alpha_n^0$. Let us consider a particular set of basis portfolios and call the first $L+1$ portfolios timing portfolios. Then, if the signal $\tilde{Y}$ is a timing signal, the optimal portfolio $\alpha^{\star}(\tilde{Y})$ can be constructed as a combination of the timing portfolios $\{\alpha_0^0, \alpha_1^0, \ldots, \alpha_L^0\}$:

$$\alpha^{\star}(\tilde{Y}) = \sum_{l=0}^{L} \gamma_l(\tilde{Y})\alpha_l^0. \tag{1}$$

Upon receiving timing signals, a manager shifts his funds among the first $L+1$ portfolios and never needs to choose portfolios that are not spanned by these $L+1$ funds. A simple example is *market timing*, where only two portfolios are used, the riskless asset and the market portfolio of risky assets; that is,

$$\alpha_1^0 = \begin{pmatrix} 1 \\ 0 \\ \vdots \\ 0 \end{pmatrix} \qquad \alpha_2^0 = \begin{pmatrix} 0 \\ \alpha_1^{\mathrm{m}} \\ \vdots \\ \alpha_N^{\mathrm{m}} \end{pmatrix}, \tag{2}$$

where α_i^{m} is the value weight of the ith risky asset in the portfolio of all risky assets. More generally, we might have timing defined over industry portfolios. In this case a portfolio in $\{\alpha_1^0, \alpha_2^0, \ldots, \alpha_L^0\}$ would be the value-weighted portfolio of risky assets corresponding to firms in a particular industry. There clearly are as many ways to define specific timing abilities as there are ways to identify timing portfolios. Presumably, the timing distinction is meaningful only when the number $L+1$ of timing portfolios is substantially less than the number $N+1$ of assets. Note also that once the timing portfolios are specified, there are still many different signals that are timing signals, that is, that produce a timing response with regard to these portfolios.

Now consider a manager whose information is exclusively timing information. Let $\tilde{R}$ be the vector of returns on the $N+1$ assets. Then the return on the manager's portfolio is

$$[\alpha(\tilde{Y})]'\tilde{R} = \sum_{l=0}^{L} \gamma_l(\tilde{Y})(\alpha_l^0)'\tilde{R} = \sum_{l=0}^{L} \gamma_l(\tilde{Y})\tilde{R}_l^0, \tag{3}$$

where $\tilde{R}_l^0$ is the return on the lth timing portfolio. The timing information $\tilde{Y}$ is valuable if the $\gamma_l(\tilde{Y})$ and the $\tilde{R}_l^0$ are correlated. If a time series of the $\gamma_l(\tilde{Y})$ and the $\tilde{R}_l^0$ is observable, we can in principle detect timing information by looking at the joint distribution between $\gamma_l(\tilde{Y})$ and $\tilde{R}_l^0$. Under the assumption that the vector of returns $\tilde{R}$ is (unconditional on any private information) independently and identically distributed over time, only an informed manager could choose $\gamma_l, l=0, \ldots, L$, to be correlated with $\tilde{R}_l^0, l=0, \ldots, L$. In general we would like not only to detect timing information but also to measure its precision. To do this requires that we specify in some detail the manner in which the manager reacts to his information, that is, the functional form of $\gamma_l(\tilde{Y})$. Examples are found in the next two sections.

In contrast with timing information, which pertains to portfolios or aggregates, selectivity information is usually considered to be information about individual assets. This implies that no restrictions can be placed on the space spanned by the optimal portfolios of a manager receiving selectivity information. Indeed, for a manager who receives selectivity information about each individual asset, the set of all possible portfolio responses $\{\alpha^\star(\tilde{Y})\}$ spans $\mathbf{R}^N$. Thus it appears that we cannot easily define selectivity in terms of the portfolio space in which the manager reacts to his information. In the end, signals about the $L+1$ timing portfolios and the $N+1$ assets are melded together to produce at most an $(N+1)$-dimensional response.

How then do we define selectivity information once we have specified what we mean by timing? We discuss two approaches to this problem here. To illustrate these two we consider a very simple example. Assume that there are three assets $(N=2)$ with asset 0 being riskless. Let asset 1 and asset 2 be risky with identically and normally distributed returns (unconditional on any private information). The following three portfolios span the portfolio space:

$$\alpha_0^0 = \begin{pmatrix} 1 \\ 0 \\ 0 \end{pmatrix} \qquad \alpha_1^0 = \begin{pmatrix} 0 \\ \frac{1}{2} \\ \frac{1}{2} \end{pmatrix} \qquad \alpha_2^0 = \begin{pmatrix} 0 \\ 0 \\ 1 \end{pmatrix}. \tag{4}$$

Let us define timing in terms of the first two portfolios in the basis (that is, the riskless asset and the equally weighted portfolio of risky assets). Thus a manager who receives only timing information has an optimal portfolio of the form

$$\alpha^\star(\tilde{Y}) = \begin{pmatrix} 1-\gamma(\tilde{Y}) \\ \frac{1}{2}\gamma(\tilde{Y}) \\ \frac{1}{2}\gamma(\tilde{Y}) \end{pmatrix}. \tag{5}$$

In the portfolio approach to distinguishing selectivity from timing we define a selectivity signal to be one that is (potentially) informative about the returns on some of the assets but uninformative about the returns on the timing portfolios. If $\tilde{Y}^S$ is selectivity information, then $\mathscr{E}(\tilde{R}_l^0 \mid \tilde{Y}^S) = \mathscr{E}(\tilde{R}_l^0)$ for $l=0,1,2,\ldots,L$ or, in the context of our particular example, $\mathscr{E}[\frac{1}{2}(\tilde{R}_1+\tilde{R}_2) \mid \tilde{Y}^S] = \mathscr{E}[\frac{1}{2}(\tilde{R}_1+\tilde{R}_2)]$. To see what form such a signal might take, consider our example. We can imagine regressing the returns of the second and third assets on the returns of the second portfolio in the basis. We have

$$\begin{aligned} \tilde{R}_1 &= \mathscr{E}(\tilde{R}_1) - \frac{\operatorname{cov}(\tilde{R}_1, \tilde{R}_1^0)}{\operatorname{var}(\tilde{R}_1^0)}\,\mathscr{E}(\tilde{R}_1^0) + \frac{\operatorname{cov}(\tilde{R}_1, \tilde{R}_1^0)}{\operatorname{var}(\tilde{R}_1^0)}\,\tilde{R}_1^0 + \tilde{\nu}_1 \\ \tilde{R}_2 &= \mathscr{E}(\tilde{R}_2) - \frac{\operatorname{cov}(\tilde{R}_2, \tilde{R}_1^0)}{\operatorname{var}(\tilde{R}_1^0)}\,\mathscr{E}(\tilde{R}_1^0) + \frac{\operatorname{cov}(\tilde{R}_2, \tilde{R}_1^0)}{\operatorname{var}(\tilde{R}_1^0)}\,\tilde{R}_1^0 + \tilde{\nu}_2 \end{aligned} \tag{6}$$

where $\tilde{\nu}_1$ and $\tilde{\nu}_2$ are independent of $\tilde{R}_1^0$. Information about the realizations of $\tilde{\nu}_1$ or $\tilde{\nu}_2$ is therefore informative about the returns on the individual assets but reveals nothing about the return $\tilde{R}_1^0$ to be earned on the timing portfolio. Note, however, that since $\frac{1}{2}(\tilde{R}_1+\tilde{R}_2) = \tilde{R}_1^0, \frac{1}{2}(\tilde{\nu}_1+\tilde{\nu}_2)$ must equal zero for all realizations of $\tilde{\nu}_1$ and $\tilde{\nu}_2$. This means that $\tilde{\nu}_1$ and $\tilde{\nu}_2$ must be perfectly correlated. Clearly it is impossible to have independent information about $\tilde{R}_1$, $\tilde{R}_2$, and $\tilde{R}_1^0$. Selectivity information, when it is defined in this way, cannot be information exclusively about each of the N individual risky assets. It must also be noted that the random variables $\tilde{\nu}_1$ and $\tilde{\nu}_2$ do not have a natural interpretation in this approach. That is, what does it mean for a manager to gather information about $\tilde{R}_1$ and $\tilde{R}_2$ which happens to be uninformative about the return $\frac{1}{2}(\tilde{R}_1 + \tilde{R}_2)$ on the portfolio. We do not have an appealing story about the source of this information. Thus the approach seems to be artificial. Nevertheless, this approach to defining selectivity is consistent with much of the literature about timing and selectivity. For example, in many empirical tests designed to detect and distinguish timing and selectivity, portfolio returns are regressed on a constant term and terms which control for timing, that is, which are a proxy for the interaction of $\gamma_l(\tilde{Y})$ and $\tilde{R}_l^0$. It is claimed that the constant term in these regressions is related to the selectivity performance of the portfolio manager. This will be true if we define selectivity in the manner just proposed, as will be shown in section 3. The optimal portfolio $\alpha^\star(\tilde{Y})$ of a manager having only selectivity information is independent of the returns $\tilde{R}_l^0$ on the timing portfolios. Thus, in the regression described, only the constant term can be affected by the manager's actions.

The second approach to defining selectivity is, we believe, more in the spirit of the intuitive interpretation of this term and the concept of timing. We call this the factor approach. The terms macroforecasting and microforecasting are often used in place of timing and selectivity. These suggest that timing involves predicting those factors that affect the aggregate, while selectivity is based on forecasting firm-specific determinants of asset returns. Assume that in our example the returns on assets 1 and 2 can be represented in terms of the following very simple factor model:[5]

$$\begin{aligned} \tilde{R}_1 &= E + \tilde{\delta} + \tilde{\varepsilon}_1 \\ \tilde{R}_2 &= E + \tilde{\delta} + \tilde{\varepsilon}_2, \end{aligned} \tag{7}$$

where $\tilde{\varepsilon}_1$ and $\tilde{\varepsilon}_2$ are independently and identically distributed. In this factor model, it is natural to consider information about $\tilde{\delta}$ to be timing information and information about $\tilde{\varepsilon}_1$ and $\tilde{\varepsilon}_2$ to be stock-specific or selectivity information. Note that a manager observing only information about $\tilde{\delta}$ will indeed form portfolios spanned by α_0^0 and α_1^0 in (4). The manager will engage only in timing. In contrast with the first approach, however, a manager observing selectivity information, that is, information about either $\tilde{\varepsilon}_1$ or $\tilde{\varepsilon}_2$, does learn something about the return $\tilde{R}_1^0$ on the timing portfolio. Thus the portfolio selections of a manager receiving only selectivity information may be weakly correlated with the return $\tilde{R}_1^0$ on the timing portfolio. However, they are independent of the realization of the factor $\tilde{\delta}$. Empirical tests designed to detect timing ability as defined in the factor approach will therefore look for evidence of correlation between a manager's portfolio positions and the factor realizations (rather than with returns on timing portfolios).

In a model with more than one factor, it is natural to define several timing portfolios, one for each factor. A manager with only timing information will shift his funds only among these factor-timing portfolios. Even when there are several factors, it is still possible to define N distinct selectivity signals corresponding to the N asset-specific disturbances $\tilde{\varepsilon}_i, i = 1, 2, \ldots, N$.

The factor model resolves several conceptual problems inherent in the portfolio approach. First, selectivity information can be truly asset specific. In the factor approach, there are as many degrees of freedom to define selectivity signals as there are risky assets. This is not so in the portfolio definition. Second, and more importantly, in the factor approach the information signals potentially correspond to economically meaningful sources of uncertainty. As argued above, there is no satisfactory way to give such an interpretation to the selectivity signals in the portfolio definition.

Note that, under joint normality, with N risky assets there always exists a sufficient statistic whose dimension is at most N. A manager may observe (under the factor definition) K timing signals and N asset-specific selectivity signals, but these can be collapsed into N signals. The same is true for managers receiving timing and selectivity signals under the portfolio interpretation. In other words, any jointly normal signal can be written as $\tilde{Y} = C\tilde{R} + \tilde{\eta}$ for some matrix C. It thus seems that the only distinctions we can make between different types of information signals can concern either the matrix C or the variance–covariance matrix of the errors $\tilde{\eta}$. Nevertheless, the two approaches discussed above are distinct in some important ways. First, the distinction on the individual level comes in when we consider statistical tests of performance, since the set of observables and the statistical hypotheses that are tested would be different in the two formulations. Second, the portfolio and factor specifications are different on the equilibrium level. If, for example, we postulate that a large number of investors collect timing and selectivity signals of some specific nature, and that the private information is diverse in the sense that individual signals are conditionally independent of each other (given some sufficient statistic), then the aggregation of these diverse pieces of information in asset equilibrium prices may give rise to observationally distinct economies.[6]

2 A Factor Model of Timing and Selectivity

In this section we develop an explicit model of timing and selectivity under the factor approach. This requires that we specify the nature of the information received by a portfolio manager. We are mainly interested in determining whether it is possible to identify empirically the quality of a particular manager's timing and selectivity information from a time series of the returns earned on a managed portfolio. We show that in principle this is always possible but in practice it may not be feasible.[7] This leads us to consider in the next section a simpler case in which the problem is to determine the quality of only the timing information. Rather than measuring the quality of the selectivity information, we simply test to see whether such information is present. These more modest goals seem to be achievable with the limited data on mutual fund returns that are usually available.

Assume that the N risky asset returns are generated by a factor model. The returns earned in period t are given by

$$\tilde{R}_t = \hat{E} + B\tilde{\delta}_t + \tilde{\varepsilon}_t, \tag{8}$$

where $\tilde{R}_t$ is the vector of the N risky asset returns, $\tilde{\delta}_t$ is a K-dimensional random vector, $\tilde{\varepsilon}_t$ is an N-dimensional random vector, and B is an $N \times K$ dimensional matrix of the factor loadings. We can normalize the factors so that $\text{var}(\tilde{\delta}_t) = I$ where I is the K-dimensional identity matrix. Let D be the variance of $\tilde{\varepsilon}_t$ and assume that $\tilde{\delta}_t$ and $\tilde{\varepsilon}_t$ are uncorrelated and distributed multivariate normal. Since we do not require that D be diagonal, (8) is completely general. Of course, if we want to think of the $\tilde{\delta}_t$ as being meaningful factors, then we shall want to assume that D is nearly diagonal so that most sources of common variation are due to the $\tilde{\delta}_t$ terms.

There are two types of signals in our model. Each signal is assumed to be jointly normally distributed with $\tilde{\delta}_t$ and $\tilde{\varepsilon}_t$. Timing signals have the form $\tilde{Y}_t^{\mathrm{T}} = \tilde{\delta}_t + \tilde{\eta}_t$; correspondingly, selectivity signals are written as $\tilde{Y}_t^{\mathrm{S}} = \tilde{\varepsilon}_t + \tilde{\theta}_t$. It is assumed that the vectors $\tilde{\eta}_t$ and $\tilde{\theta}_t$ are uncorrelated and that each is independent of $\tilde{\delta}_t$ and $\tilde{\varepsilon}_t$. The assumption that $\tilde{\eta}_t$ and $\tilde{\theta}_t$ are independent is made to simplify the analysis. Since $\tilde{\eta}_t$ corresponds to the errors made in forecasting the factors and $\tilde{\theta}_t$ is related to the errors made in forecasting the firm-specific disturbances, it seems sensible to assume that they are independent. We let $\text{var}(\tilde{\eta}_t) = \Sigma$ and $\text{var}(\tilde{\theta}_t) = \Omega$ and assume that these are both positive definite. The quality of a manager's information is completely determined by Σ and Ω and it is these two variance matrices that we wish to identify.

It is clearly not possible to recover Σ and Ω from a time series of portfolio returns unless some restrictions are placed on the way that the manager responds to his information. One of the simplest assumptions specifies a linear response to forecasts. This is consistent with the manager's acting as if he were maximizing the expected utility of someone with constant absolute risk tolerance. With this assumption, the optimal portfolio of risky assets is

$$\alpha^\star(\tilde{Y}_t^{\mathrm{T}}, \tilde{Y}_t^{\mathrm{S}}) = \rho\,[\mathrm{var}(\tilde{R}_t \mid \tilde{Y}_t^{\mathrm{T}}, \tilde{Y}_t^{\mathrm{S}})]^{-1}[\mathscr{E}(\tilde{R}_t \mid \tilde{Y}_t^{\mathrm{T}}, \tilde{Y}_t^{\mathrm{S}}) - R_0\boldsymbol{e}], \tag{9}$$

where ρ is a measure at risk tolerance, $\mathscr{E}(\tilde{R}_t \mid \tilde{Y}_t^{\mathrm{T}}, \tilde{Y}_t^{\mathrm{S}})$ is the vector of conditional expected returns given the manager's information, and $\boldsymbol{e}$ is the vector of 1s. It is easily shown, using the theory of normal variables, that

$$\mathscr{E}(\tilde{R}_t \mid \tilde{Y}_t^{\mathrm{T}}, \tilde{Y}_t^{\mathrm{S}}) = \hat{E} + B(I+\Sigma)^{-1}(\tilde{\delta}_t + \tilde{\eta}_t) + (D+\Omega)^{-1}D(\tilde{\varepsilon}_t + \tilde{\theta}_t) \tag{10}$$

and

$$\mathrm{var}(\tilde{R}_t \mid \tilde{Y}_t^{\mathrm{T}}, \tilde{Y}_t^{\mathrm{S}}) = B(I+\Sigma^{-1})^{-1}B' + (D^{-1}+\Omega^{-1})^{-1}. \tag{11}$$

Let $E = \hat{E} - R_0\boldsymbol{e}$ be the expected excess return vector. Then the optimal portfolio $\alpha^\star(\tilde{Y}_t^{\mathrm{T}}, \tilde{Y}_t^{\mathrm{S}})$ is

$$\rho\,[B(I+\Sigma^{-1})^{-1}B' + (D^{-1}+\Omega^{-1})^{-1}]^{-1}[E + B(I+\Sigma)^{-1}(\tilde{\delta}_t + \tilde{\eta}_t) + (D+\Omega)^{-1}D(\tilde{\varepsilon}_t + \tilde{\theta}_t)] \tag{12}$$

First note that the information signal $\tilde{Y}_t^{\mathrm{T}}$ is truly a timing signal. The portfolio position of a manager receiving only timing information is

$$\alpha^\star(\tilde{Y}_t^{\mathrm{T}}) = \rho\,[B(I+\Sigma^{-1})^{-1}B' + D]^{-1}[E + B(I+\Sigma)^{-1}(\tilde{\delta}_t + \tilde{\eta}_t)]. \tag{13}$$

Thus the response to the information signal $\tilde{\delta}_t + \tilde{\eta}_t$ is simply to shift funds among K timing portfolios in the span of

$$[B(I+\Sigma^{-1})^{-1}B' + D]^{-1}B(I+\Sigma)^{-1}. \tag{14}$$

From (14) it might appear that the set of timing portfolios depends upon Σ, the nature of the timing information received. This is not true. It is shown in the appendix that the span of $[B(I+\Sigma^{-1})^{-1}B' + D]^{-1}B(I+\Sigma)^{-1}$ is independent of Σ. Thus all managers who receive only timing information shift funds among the same set of timing portfolios.

If a fund manager receives both timing and selectivity information, it is still true that the responses to timing information are restricted to a set of K portfolios. However, unlike the situation when only timing information is received, it is not true that this set of portfolios is independent of the quality of the information received. The timing response portfolios now lie in the span of

$$[B(I+\Sigma^{-1})^{-1}B' + (D^{-1}+\Omega^{-1})^{-1}]^{-1}B(I+\Sigma)^{-1}, \tag{15}$$

which does depend on the value of Ω, the quality of the selectivity information. Thus two managers who receive the same timing signals but selectivity information of differing qualities will respond to the timing signals in different fashions. This makes the disentanglement of timing and selectivity much more cumbersome than it would otherwise be.

Despite the fact that the timing portfolios depend upon the quality of the selectivity information, it is in principle possible to identify both Σ and Ω, even if the parameter ρ, which measures the aggressiveness of the manager's response to information, is unknown. Using (12) it can be shown that the realized excess return on the managed portfolio

$$\begin{aligned}\tilde{R}_t^{\mathrm{P}} &= \alpha^{\star}(\tilde{Y}_t^{\mathrm{T}}, \tilde{Y}_t^{\mathrm{S}})'(\tilde{R}_t - R_0 \boldsymbol{e}) \\ &= \rho\,[E'\Psi^{-1}E + E'\Psi^{-1}B(I+\Sigma)^{-1}(\tilde{\delta}_t + \tilde{\eta}_t) \\ &\quad + E'\Psi^{-1}(D+\Omega)^{-1}D(\tilde{\varepsilon}_t + \tilde{\theta}_t) \\ &\quad + \tilde{\delta}_t' B'\Psi^{-1}E + \tilde{\delta}_t' B'\Psi^{-1}B(I+\Sigma)^{-1}(\tilde{\delta}_t + \tilde{\eta}_t) \\ &\quad + \tilde{\delta}_t' B'\Psi^{-1}(D+\Omega)^{-1}D(\tilde{\varepsilon}_t + \tilde{\theta}_t) \\ &\quad + \tilde{\varepsilon}_t'\Psi^{-1}E + \tilde{\varepsilon}_t'\Psi^{-1}B(I+\Sigma)^{-1}(\tilde{\delta}_t + \tilde{\eta}_t) \\ &\quad + \tilde{\varepsilon}_t'\Psi^{-1}(D+\Omega)^{-1}D(\tilde{\varepsilon}_t + \tilde{\theta}_t)]\,, \end{aligned} \tag{16}$$

where $\Psi = \mathrm{var}(\tilde{R}_t \mid \tilde{Y}_t^{\mathrm{T}}, \tilde{Y}_t^{\mathrm{S}}) = B(I+\Sigma^{-1})^{-1}B' + (D^{-1}+\Omega^{-1})^{-1}$. If we assume that E, B, and D are known parameters of the generating process, then it is possible to determine (*ex post*) the realizations of $\tilde{\delta}_t$ and $\tilde{\varepsilon}_t$. The factor realizations can be obtained by the cross-sectional regression of $\tilde{R}_t - \hat{E}$ on B. If N is sufficiently large (and the elements of D are bounded), $\tilde{\delta}_t$ can be recovered with negligible error. The idiosyncratic terms are then recovered: $\tilde{\varepsilon}_t = \tilde{R}_t - B\tilde{\delta}_t$.

Consider now the time series regression of $\tilde{R}_t^{\mathrm{P}}$ on a constant, $\tilde{\delta}_t$, $\tilde{\varepsilon}_t$, and the distinct terms in the matrices $\tilde{\delta}_t\tilde{\delta}_t'$ ($K(K+1)/2$ terms), $\tilde{\varepsilon}_t\tilde{\varepsilon}_t'$ ($N(N+1)/2$ terms), and $\tilde{\varepsilon}_t\tilde{\delta}_t'$ (NK terms). The constant term is easily shown to be a consistent estimator of $\rho E'\Psi^{-1}E$. For the other terms we have

$$\mathrm{plim}(\text{coefficients on } \tilde{\delta}_t) = \rho E'\Psi^{-1}B[I + (I+\Sigma)^{-1}] \tag{17}$$

$$\mathrm{plim}(\text{coefficients on } \tilde{\varepsilon}_t) = \rho E'\Psi^{-1}[I + (D+\Omega)^{-1}D] \tag{18}$$

$$\mathrm{plim}(\text{coefficients on } \tilde{\delta}_t\tilde{\delta}_t') = \rho\{\mathrm{sym}[B'\Psi^{-1}B(I+\Sigma)^{-1}]\} \tag{19}$$

$$\mathrm{plim}(\text{coefficients on } \tilde{\varepsilon}_t\tilde{\varepsilon}_t') = \rho\{\mathrm{sym}[\Psi^{-1}(D+\Omega)^{-1}D]\} \tag{20}$$

$$\mathrm{plim}(\text{coefficients on } \tilde{\varepsilon}_t\tilde{\delta}_t') = \rho[\Psi^{-1}B(I+\Sigma)^{-1} + D(D+\Omega)^{-1}\Psi^{-1}B]\,, \tag{21}$$

where sym(A) refers to the $M(M+1)/2$ distinct terms in the symmetric version[8] of the $M \times M$ matrix A.

If we include the constant term, we have a total of $(K^2+3K)/2 + (N^2+3N)/2 + NK + 1$ estimated coefficients. The number of unknown parameters in Σ, Ω, and ρ is $(K^2+K)/2 + (N^2+N)/2 + 1$. It appears that we potentially have $K + N + NK$ over-identifying restrictions. In fact there are many more than this. First there are the restrictions required for Σ and Ω to be positive definite. Added to these are restrictions related to the information contained in the disturbance terms in the proposed regression. These terms are heteroskedastic with the variance related in a known way to ρ, Σ, and Ω.[9] Given the nonlinearities involved and the distributional assumptions made, an attractive estimation procedure would be the maximum likelihood approach which explicitly accounts for these additional restrictions. Whether this procedure is used or not, it is possible to recover the appropriate measures of the quality of both the timing information and the selectivity information. Note also that to identify the information quality of a manager using the procedure just discussed, it is not necessary to assume that any particular model of asset pricing holds.

Although both Σ and Ω (as well as ρ) can in principle be recovered, in practice this may generally prove too difficult or impossible. The reason is that the number of regressors in (17)–(21) is extremely large and most likely exceeds the number of time series observations obtainable for any fund. In the next section we look at a much simpler problem based on the portfolio approach and show that recovery of at least the quality of timing information will generally be feasible.

3 A Portfolio Model of Timing and Selectivity

In the last section it was shown that when the factor approach is used to define timing and selectivity it is possible to identify both the quality of timing information and the quality of selectivity information. This can be done even if the only observable effect of the manager's information in each period is the total return earned on the managed fund; for identification of the quality of information it is not, for example, necessary to observe portfolio positions. Unfortunately, because of the large number of interactions between information signals and asset returns, it was necessary to include an extremely large number of regressors in the regression proposed in the last section. For this reason, estimation of the quality parameters of the timing and selectivity information seems to be possible under the assumptions of the last section only when the number of time series observations is impractically large.

In this section we pursue the more modest goal of estimating the quality of only the timing information. The testing procedure proposed will only be capable of determining whether selectivity information is or is not present; the quality of the selectivity information will not be identified. By reducing the number of parameters to be estimated, we obviously simplify the estimation problem. It should be noted, however, that the complexity of the estimation procedure discussed in the last section is due to more than just the large number of parameters that must be estimated. Much of the difficulty can be attributed to the fact that under the factor definition the timing response portfolios cannot be identified without knowing the quality of the selectivity information. Although managers receiving only timing information respond to their information using the same set of timing portfolios, this is not the case for managers who receive both timing and selectivity information. (The span of (15) is not independent of Ω.) Because the set of portfolios used to respond to factor information cannot be defined without knowledge of the quality of selectivity information, the estimation of information quality becomes much more complex than it would otherwise be.

In contrast with the factor approach, the portfolio approach to defining timing and selectivity does allow the timing response portfolios to be specified without knowing the quality of the selectivity information. This is because selectivity information under the portfolio approach is by definition completely uninformative about the returns to be earned on the timing portfolios. The estimation problem is thus simplified if selectivity information is assumed to be independent of the return earned on the timing portfolios. Despite the conceptual problems inherent in the portfolio approach, or perhaps because of them, identification of information quality, given certain assumptions, is easier under this approach than it is under the factor approach.

To show how estimation of the quality of timing information can be accomplished under the portfolio approach we consider a simple case where there is only one timing portfolio. Let there be N risky assets and let the variance of their returns be $\hat{V}$. The timing portfolio can in principle be any portfolio of the N risky assets. In almost all the previous discussions of timing in the literature, the timing portfolio is assumed to be the market portfolio. We shall not make this particular assumption here but the reader is free to think of the timing being discussed as market timing. Let the timing portfolio be α^{T} and let its variance be $\sigma^2 = (\alpha^{\mathrm{T}})'\hat{V}\alpha^{\mathrm{T}}$. It is possible to define $N-1$ portfolios, $\alpha_j^{\mathrm{S}}, j = 1, \ldots, N-1$, such that

$$\begin{aligned}(\alpha_j^{\mathrm{S}})'\boldsymbol{e} &= 1\\ (\alpha^{\mathrm{T}})'\hat{V}\alpha_j^{\mathrm{S}} &= 0\end{aligned} \tag{22}$$

for each j. We can define N new assets with the first being the timing portfolio and the remaining $N-1$ being a set of portfolios which satisfy (22). In other words we can rotate assets so that the first is the timing portfolio and all the other portfolios are uncorrelated with the first. Let $\tilde{R}_t^{\mathrm{T}}$ be the return on the timing portfolio and $\tilde{R}_{i,t}^{\mathrm{S}}$ be the return on the portfolio with weights α_j^{S}. Then

$$\operatorname{var}\begin{pmatrix} \tilde{R}_t^{T} \\ \tilde{R}_{1,t}^{S} \\ \vdots \\ \tilde{R}_{N-1,t}^{S} \end{pmatrix} = \begin{pmatrix} \sigma^2 & O'_{N-1} \\ O_{N-1} & V \end{pmatrix}, \tag{23}$$

where O_{N-1} is the $N-1$ vector of zeros and V is the variance–covariance matrix of the $N-1$ portfolios that have returns orthogonal to the return of the timing portfolio. In the portfolio approach we define the timing signal to be $\tilde{Y}_t^{T} = \tilde{R}_t^{T} + \tilde{\eta}_t$ and the $N-1$ possible selectivity signals to be of the form $\tilde{Y}_{i,t}^{S} = \tilde{R}_{i,t}^{S} + \tilde{\theta}_{i,t}$. We assume as before that returns and the information errors $\tilde{\eta}_t$ and $\tilde{\theta}_t$ are jointly normally distributed and that $\tilde{\eta}_t$ and $\tilde{\theta}_t$ are independent. The parameters of interest are again $\operatorname{var}(\tilde{\eta}_t) = \sigma_\eta^2$ and $\operatorname{var}(\theta_t) = \Omega$. We shall be able to estimate σ_η^2, but given our more limited goals we shall only test whether Ω is finite or not, that is, whether selectivity information exists or not.

As in the previous section it is necessary to specify how the manager reacts to his information. Again we make the assumption that the response is linear and therefore consistent with maximization of utility with constant absolute risk aversion. The position taken in the N portfolios by the manager is given by

$$\rho \begin{bmatrix} \left(\frac{1}{\sigma^2} + \frac{1}{\sigma_\eta^2}\right) & O'_{N-1} \\ O_{N-1} & (V^{-1} + \Omega^{-1})^{-1} \end{bmatrix}^{-1} \begin{bmatrix} \frac{\sigma_\eta^2}{\sigma^2 + \sigma_\eta^2}\,\mathscr{E}(\tilde{R}_t^{T}) + \frac{\sigma^2}{\sigma^2 + \sigma_\eta^2}\tilde{Y}_t^{T} - R_0 \\ [I_{N-1} - (V+\Omega)^{-1}V]\,\mathscr{E}(\tilde{R}_t^{S}) \\ + (V+\Omega)^{-1}V\tilde{Y}_t^{S} - R_0 e \end{bmatrix} \tag{24}$$

where R_0 is the riskless rate.

The return $\tilde{R}_t^{P}$ realized on the managed portfolio in period t is consequently equal to

$$\rho\left[\frac{\mathscr{E}(\tilde{R}_t^{T}) - R_0}{\sigma^2} - \frac{R_0}{\sigma_\eta^2}\right]\tilde{R}_t^{T} + \frac{\rho}{\sigma_\eta^2}(\tilde{R}_t^{T})^2 + \frac{\rho}{\sigma_\eta^2}\tilde{\eta}_t\tilde{R}_t^{T} + \tilde{u}_t \tag{25}$$

where

$$\begin{aligned}\tilde{u}_t = \rho(\tilde{R}_t^{S})'(V^{-1} + \Omega^{-1})\{[I_{N-1} - (V+\Omega)^{-1}V]\,\mathscr{E}(\tilde{R}_t^{S}) \\ + (V+\Omega)^{-1}V\tilde{Y}_t^{S} - R_0\}\end{aligned} \tag{26}$$

and $(\tilde{R}_t^{S})' = (\tilde{R}_{1,t}^{S}, \tilde{R}_{2,t}^{S}, \ldots, \tilde{R}_{N-1,t}^{S})$.

Now consider the regression of the managed portfolio's return on a constant term, the return on the timing portfolio, and the squared return on the timing portfolio:

$$\tilde{R}_t^{P} = \Gamma_0 + \Gamma_1\tilde{R}_t^{T} + \Gamma_2(\tilde{R}_t^{T})^2 + \tilde{\omega}_t. \tag{27}$$

Since $\tilde{u}_t$ and $\tilde{\eta}_t$ are by assumption independent of $\tilde{R}_t^{\mathrm{T}}$, Γ_2 is a consistent estimator of ρ/σ_η^2. As we argued above, the parameter of interest is σ_η^2. Therefore we need to obtain an estimate of ρ. This can be done using the residuals of the regression. The true disturbance terms are heteroskedastic and equal to $(\rho/\sigma_\eta^2)\tilde{\eta}_t\tilde{R}_t^{\mathrm{T}} + \tilde{u}_t - \mathscr{E}(\tilde{u}_t)$. Consider regressing $\tilde{\omega}_t^2$ on a constant and the square of $\tilde{R}_t^{\mathrm{T}}$:

$$\tilde{\omega}_t^2 = \Lambda_0 + \Lambda_1(\tilde{R}_t^{\mathrm{T}})^2 + \tilde{\xi}_t. \tag{28}$$

Under the distributional assumptions we have made, $\mathrm{plim}(\Lambda_1) = \rho^2/\sigma_\eta^2$. Since we have estimates of ρ/σ_η^2 and ρ^2/σ_η^2, we can recover both σ_η^2 and ρ.

The two-step procedure just discussed clearly does not produce the most efficient estimates of the information quality parameter σ_η^2. More efficient estimates can be obtained by taking into account the heteroskedasticity of the disturbance terms. One possible approach would use the estimates of ρ and σ_η^2 obtained in the inefficient manner just described to predict the variance of the residuals. A generalized least squares procedure could then be used to obtain better estimates of the coefficients in the two regressions. As before, a maximum likelihood approach which completely accounts for the structure of the model is probably most appropriate. It is beyond the scope of this paper to discuss such refinements in detail.

Having shown that the quality of timing information can be identified, we now turn to the detection of selectivity information. Responses to selectivity information affect only the distribution of $\tilde{u}_t$ in (25) and Γ_0 can be shown to be a consistent estimator of $\mathscr{E}(\tilde{u}_t)$. It is not possible, however, to infer anything from the value of $\mathscr{E}(\tilde{u}_t)$ unless further assumptions are made about asset pricing. Assume, for example, that the capital asset pricing model holds and $\tilde{R}_t^{\mathrm{T}}$ is the return on the market portfolio. The portfolios α_i^{S} are constructed to have returns orthogonal to $\tilde{R}_t^{\mathrm{T}}$. This means that $\mathscr{E}(\tilde{R}_{i,t}^{\mathrm{S}}) = R_0$, the riskless rate, for all i. A manager who does not have any selectivity information will not be able (in expectation) to earn more than the riskless rate by shifting funds among the portfolios α_i^{S}. If a manager does have valuable selectivity information (finite Ω) and if he responds linearly to this information as is assumed in (26), then he will earn (in expectation) more than the riskless rate and this will be reflected in a higher value of $\mathscr{E}(\tilde{u}_t)$. It is clear that we cannot learn from $\mathscr{E}(\tilde{u}_t)$ all that we need to know to value the manager's selectivity information. The value of the selectivity information depends on the matrix Ω and is not summarized in the scalar $\mathscr{E}(\tilde{u}_t)$. Nevertheless, it is still encouraging that the simple regression procedure described above can be used to identify fully the quality of timing information and to detect the existence of selectivity information.

4 Conclusions

The important problem in performance evaluation is the measurement of the quality of the information possessed by a portfolio manager. Many tests proposed in the literature do not successfully separate the aggressiveness of a manager from the quality of the information he possesses. To measure the quality of information it is necessary to specify both the nature of the information received and the nature of the manager's reaction to it. For this the distinction between timing information and selectivity information may be useful. We have argued that the distinction between timing and selectivity is not straightforward, and we have examined two approaches that can be used to make the distinction precise. Under the factor approach timing information is information about the realizations of factors which affect the returns of many assets. Selectivity information is then defined to be information about the asset-specific determinants of asset returns. Under the portfolio approach, timing information is information about the returns to be earned on a prespecified set of timing portfolios. Selectivity information under this definition is any information that is uninformative about the timing portfolio returns but informative about some asset returns.

These two approaches to defining timing and selectivity are not equivalent. They are observationally distinct both in their implications for the joint distribution of returns on assets and managed funds and in their implications for asset pricing. We have shown that under each interpretation it is possible to identify empirically some measure of the quality of information possessed by a fund manager. This is possible even when all that is observed is the *ex post* returns earned on the managed fund. It is important to note, however, that the specification of these tests depends in critical ways on the approach taken to define timing and selectivity. Although the factor approach has conceptual advantages over the portfolio approach, testing may be more feasible if the information received by managers is consistent with the portfolio approach.

It should be noted finally that our discussion has abstracted from an equilibrium model explaining asset returns. In discussing empirical tests we have made assumptions of independence (and normal distributions) that are consistent with most of the empirical literature. However, such assumptions have not been justified by a theoretical intertemporal asset pricing model which explicitly admits asymmetric information. If returns are determined in a world of homogeneous beliefs, only an insignificant portion of the market can possess any superior information. The importance of measuring performance in such a world is questionable.

Appendix

In this appendix we show that in the factor model developed in section 2 the factor timing portfolios used by managers receiving timing information do not depend upon the quality or nature of that information. This requires that we show that the span of the matrix

$$[B(I+\Sigma^{-1})^{-1}B'+D]^{-1}B(I+\Sigma)^{-1} \tag{A1}$$

does not depend on Σ. To do this we shall show that

$$\text{span}\{[B(I+\Sigma^{-1})^{-1}B'+D]^{-1}B(I+\Sigma)^{-1}\}=\text{span}[(BB'+D)^{-1}B] \tag{A2}$$

for all Σ. Let F and G be two $N\times K$ matrices with $N>K$. Then $\text{span}(F)=\text{span}(G)$ if and only if there exists a $K\times K$ matrix H such that $F=GH$. Since $I+\Sigma$ is invertible, (A2) is established if it is shown that there exists H that solves

$$[B(I+\Sigma^{-1})^{-1}B'+D]^{-1}BH=(BB'+D)^{-1}B. \tag{A3}$$

Let $Q=(BB'+D)^{-1}B$. Then $B=(BB'+D)Q$ or $B-BB'Q=DQ$. Substituting Q into (A3) and rearranging gives us $BH-B(I+\Sigma^{-1})^{-1}B'Q=DQ$. Combining these two we obtain

$$B(I-B'Q)=B[H-(I+\Sigma^{-1})^{-1}B'Q], \tag{A4}$$

which means that H must satisfy

$$I-B'Q=H-(I+\Sigma^{-1})^{-1}B'Q. \tag{A5}$$

A matrix H which solves (A3) therefore exists and is given by

$$\begin{aligned} H&=I-[I-(I+\Sigma^{-1})^{-1}]B'Q\\ &=I-[I-(I+\Sigma^{-1})^{-1}]B'(BB'+D)^{-1}B. \end{aligned} \tag{A6}$$

Since all matrices $[B(I+\Sigma^{-1})^{-1}B'+D]^{-1}B$ have the same span as $(BB'+D)^{-1}B$ and the spanning relation defines equivalence classes, we have proved the result. ■

Notes

1 A partial list of references includes Treynor and Mazuy [13], Fama [6], Jensen [8], Kon [9], Kon and Jen [10], Merton [12], Henriksson and Merton [7], and Connor and Korajczyk [3].

2 This characterization has been important in the recent controversy with regard to the use of the securities market line to measure performance (see Mayers and Rice [11] and Dybvig and Ross [4, 5]). It was argued that using the securities market line is justified if there is no timing information. Private information is assumed to be independent of the returns on the index. This is the main motivation behind the portfolio approach developed below.

3 To see this most clearly, note that in this case, if there are L timing portfolios and N assets, and if selectivity information is independent of the returns on the timing portfolios, then it can be summarized by an $(N-L)$-dimensional sufficient statistic. It

follows that, if selectivity information satisfies (a) above, then it is impossible that there are N independent selectivity signals, one for each asset.

4 This makes the calculation of the optimal response to information and the econometric analysis in the next section more tractable.

5 We choose here a particularly simple representation of a factor model to illustrate the approach. Obviously the definition can be applied to any factor model. This is done in the next section.

6 To see this, we need to examine the measurability requirement of prices. When the aggregate of private information is observationally distinct, then the equilibrium results will also be distinct. This argument is similar to that in Admati [1, section 6].

7 See Admati and Ross [2] for related results on the identifiability of performance parameters in a similar model.

8 The symmetric version of a square matrix A is $(A + A')/2$.

9 The error term is $\rho[\tilde{\varepsilon}_t' \Psi^{-1} B(I+\Sigma)^{-1}\tilde{\eta}_t + \tilde{\varepsilon}_t' \Psi^{-1}(D+\Omega)^{-1} D\tilde{\theta}_t + \tilde{\delta}_t' B' \Psi^{-1} B(I+\Sigma)^{-1}\tilde{\eta}_t + \tilde{\delta}_t' B' \Psi^{-1}(D+\Omega)^{-1} D\tilde{\theta}_t + \tilde{\varepsilon}_t' \Psi^{-1} B(I+\Sigma)^{-1}\tilde{\eta}_t + \tilde{\varepsilon}_t' \Psi^{-1}(D+\Omega)^{-1} D\tilde{\theta}_t]$.

References

1 Admati, A. R. "A Noisy Rational Expectations Equilibrium for Multi-Asset Securities Markets," *Econometrica*, 53, May 1985, 629–57.

2 Admati, A. R. and Ross, S. A. "Measuring Investment Performance in a Rational Expectations Equilibrium Model," *Journal of Business*, 58, January 1985, 1–26.

3 Connor, G. and Korajczyk, R. A. "Performance Measurement with the Arbitrage Pricing Theory: A New Framework for Analysis," Unpublished Manuscript, Northwestern University, July 1984.

4 Dybvig, P. H. and Ross, S. A. "Differential Information and Performance Measurement Using a Security Market Line," *Journal of Finance*, 40: 2, June 1985, 383–99.

5 Dybvig, P. H. and Ross, S. A. "The Analytics of Performance Measurement Using a Security Market Line," *Journal of Finance*, 40: 2, June 1985, 401–16.

6 Fama, E. "Components of Investment Performance," *Journal of Finance*, 27, June 1972, 551–68.

7 Henriksson, R. D. and Merton, R. C. "On Market Timing and Investment Performance II: Statistical Procedures for Evaluating Forecasting Skills," *Journal of Business*, 54, October 1981, 513–33.

8 Jensen, M. "Optimal Utilization of Market Forecasts and the Evaluation of Investment Performance." In *Mathematical Methods in Investment and Finance*, eds G. Szego and K. Shell (Amsterdam: North-Holland, 1972).

9 Kon, S. "The Market Timing Performance of Mutual Fund Managers," *Journal of Business*, 56, July 1983, 323–47.

10 Kon, S. and Jen, F. "The Investment Performance of Mutual Funds: An Empirical Investigation of Timing, Selectivity and Market Efficiency," *Journal of Business*, 52, April 1979, 263–89.

11 Mayers, D. and Rice, E. "Measuring Portfolio Performance and the Empirical Content of Asset Pricing Models," *Journal of Financial Economics*, 7, March 1979, 3–28.

12 Merton, R. C. "On Market Timing and Investment Performance Part I: An Equilibrium Theory of Value for Market Forecasts," *Journal of Business*, 54, July 1981, 363–406.

13 Treynor, J. L. and Mazuy, F. "Can Mutual Funds Outguess the Market," *Harvard Business Review*, 44, July–August 1966, 131–6.

Chapter 8

Michael R. Gibbons

Background and Comments

Each new cohort of financial economists acquires or develops a still more abstract and powerful analytical tool kit, but effective application of the tools requires a well-posed problem. There is no point aiming the heaviest mathematical or econometric artillery at leveraged buyouts (LBOs), for example, because we have too few facts and too many theories about how LBOs might or might not work.

The analysis of investor behavior and capital asset pricing provides plenty of well-posed problems. On the theory front, look to John Cox's and Chi-fu Huang's paper (this volume, chapter 4) for an example of use of heavy artillery. On the empirical front, see the contributions by Shmuel Kandel and Robert Stambaugh (this volume, chapter 13), Jay Shanken (this volume, chapter 18), as well as the following paper by David Brown and Michael Gibbons. The Brown–Gibbons paper is particularly welcome because it offers relatively simple explanations of several recently developed empirical techniques.

It is interesting to contrast these three empirical papers. The paper by Kandel and Stambaugh explores one of the most serious problems in testing traditional single-period capital asset pricing models, that is, the identification of the proper proxy for the ideal "market portfolio" of all the economy's assets. (The problem is that tests based on a particular proxy may support the theory, but use of another plausible and apparently closely related proxy may reject it.) Shanken's paper was motivated by development of *intertemporal* capital asset pricing models, which stress how investors may adapt portfolios to protect against unfavorable shifts in future investment opportunities. Among other things he investigates how risk–return tradeoffs in the stock market respond to unexpected shifts in short-term interest rates.

Brown and Gibbons explain and explore "utility-based" models, which connect risk and return in securities markets directly to the portfolio rules that ought to guide rational investors. Thus it may be possible to explain risk premiums earned in the stock market by reference to the risk aversion of a representative investor, or alternatively to infer the degree of risk aversion from observed risk premiums.

Author's Introduction

Since the publication of "A Simple Econometric Approach for Utility-Based Asset Pricing Models," there has been an increased interest in both utility-based paradigms and the use of the generalized method of moments first developed by Lars Hansen. Hopefully, my joint paper with David Brown has had some influence in directing research toward these topics.

The papers by Hansen (1982) and Hansen and Singleton (1982) develop the relevant econometric theory which provides a foundation for later empirical research by various people. When David and I found these two papers, I have to admit to a feeling of frustration, for we had invested considerable time in deriving similar results only to discover that our work was less general than existing research. Since we could no longer claim that our methodology was innovative, we turned our attention to explaining the econometric procedures to others. At the time we were convinced that the methodology had great importance and deserved further elaboration. We chose to explain the method by means of a simple example, which allowed us to highlight the underlying intuition for the general case. The illustration is rather special, for it is both tractable (although nonlinear) and interesting to financial economists. Economic models with a single parameter can rarely make this claim.

In teaching graduate courses on empirical methods in financial economics, I rely heavily on the generalized method of moments. In fact, this methodology provides one unifying theme throughout the whole quarter since many econometric procedures can be viewed as special cases of this approach. However, I find graduate students internalize the methodology better after working through the illustration that David and I developed in this paper. As further applications of the generalized method of moments are developed in finance, researchers may find that this paper serves as a useful pedagogical introduction to the approach.

References

Hansen, L. (1982) "Large Sample Properties of Generalized Method of Moments Estimators," *Econometrica*, 50, July, 1029–84.

Hansen, L. and Singleton, K. (1982) "Generalized Instrumental Variables Estimation of Nonlinear Rational Expectations Models," *Econometrica*, 50, September, 1269–86; corrections in *Econometrica*, 52, January 1984, 267–8.

Bibliographical Listing

"On the Volatility of Bond Prices." In *IMF Policy Advice, Market Volatility, Commodity Price Rules and Other Essays*, eds Karl Brunner and Allan H. Meltzer, The Carnegie–Rochester Conference Series on Public Policy, vol. 31 (Amsterdam: North-Holland, 1989), pp. 139–75.

"Empirical Tests of the Consumption-Oriented CAPM" (with Douglas T. Breeden and Robert H. Litzenberger), *Journal of Finance*, 44: 2, June 1989, 231–62.

"The Term Structure of Interest Rates: Empirical Evidence" (with Krishna Ramaswamy), *Working Paper*, The Wharton School of the University of Pennsylvania, November 1986.

"Testing Asset Pricing Models with Changing Expectations and an Unobservable Market Portfolio" (with Wayne Ferson), *Journal of Financial Economics*, 14: 2, June 1985, 217–36.

A Simple Econometric Approach for Utility-Based Asset Pricing Models

DAVID P. BROWN and MICHAEL R. GIBBONS

The distribution of asset returns is a fundamental quantity to be explained by financial economics. Consequently, utility-based models of asset pricing are of special interest since they allow the distributions of returns to be explained rather than assumed as in distribution-based models.

Despite this attractive feature, preference-based theories have received little empirical attention in financial economics. Perhaps there is a belief that a rigorous econometric investigation of these models requires distributional assumptions about asset returns. As a result, empiricists may view utility-based paradigms as unattractive, for the appropriate econometric models are burdened by assumptions not only about distributions but also about preferences.

In the hope of stimulating empirical interest in utility-based models of asset pricing, we present a statistical methodology that is appropriate for this class of theories. Since the suggested approach does not rely on strong distributional assumptions, it preserves the inherent attractiveness of preference-based models. To develop the intuition for the suggested methodology, we focus on a particular equilibrium model for asset pricing that was developed in the seminal paper by Rubinstein [34]. This model provides a simple economic environment that is characterized by a power (isoelastic) aggregate utility function and a constant investment opportunity set. Once this situation is analyzed, extensions to more general, and admittedly more interesting, frameworks are reasonably straightforward.

However, the specific case under study has importance beyond its pedagogical value. Since the unknown parameter of isoelastic preferences

Reproduced from *Journal of Finance*, 40: 2, June 1985, 359–81.

David P. Brown is Assistant Professor of Finance at the School of Business, Indiana University. This research has benefited from the helpful comments made by our friends at Dartmouth, Harvard, Stanford, UBC, Wharton, and Yale where this paper was presented. We also thank Wayne Ferson, Allan Kleidon, Paul Pfleiderer, Peter Reiss, Mark Rubinstein, and Ken Singleton for many useful discussions. Of course, all remaining errors are our responsibility. Financial support was provided in part by the Stanford Program in Finance.

is relative risk aversion (RRA), analyzing this utility function provides valuable information for several reasons. First, some theoretical results rely on log utility (e.g. Cox, Ingersoll, and Ross [4]; Hakansson [14]; Kraus and Litzenberger [23]; Merton [27]; Rubinstein [35]; Samuelson [36]); by estimating the difference between RRA and unity, the appropriateness of these results can be judged. Second, the effects of changes in risk on the demand for risky assets and the savings decision depend on the magnitude of RRA (e.g. Rothschild and Stiglitz [31]). Third, some of the current debate as to whether or not stock prices have excessive volatility relates to the degree of aggregate risk aversion (e.g. Grossman and Shiller [12]). Indeed, the importance of RRA in financial economics can be judged by the number of papers which have attempted to determine its value. A sample of such papers includes Ferson [7], Friend and Blume [8], Grossman and Shiller [12], and Hansen and Singleton [19, 20].

In fact, Hansen and Singleton [20] develop a methodology which also relies on very weak assumptions about the distribution of returns. They consider a general economic environment which includes the economic model of this paper as a special case.[1] The generality that they achieve is important, but the intuition underlying their methods is more easily seen by focusing on a simpler setting as in this paper. Thus, one of the contributions of this work is that it may serve as a useful pedagogical introduction to Hansen and Singleton [20].

The next section provides the theoretical underpinnings of the econometric analysis, and a structural relation between RRA and certain moments of asset returns is established. Two alternative estimators of RRA are developed in sections 2 and 3. The first estimator is parametric and has the advantage of tractability. Unfortunately, it depends critically on the distributional assumption (made in earlier studies of RRA) which is neither an implication of the theory nor consistent with the data. The second estimator is nonparametric. While it requires nonlinear estimation, the approach is intuitive and easy to implement. In section 4, these two alternative approaches are applied to estimate RRA using monthly stock return data from 1926 to 1981. The relation between the nonparametric estimator and the approach developed by Hansen and Singleton [20] is discussed in section 5. Section 6 concludes the paper.

1 The Relation Between Preferences and the Moments of Security Returns

The well-known Euler condition for the dynamic consumption–portfolio problem faced by a representative individual under uncertainty is used to derive a relationship between RRA and the moments of security returns.

This first-order necessary condition for optimality with a time-additive von Neumann–Morgenstern utility function is

$$E\left[\frac{1}{1+r}\frac{U'(\tilde{C}_t)}{U'(C_{t-1})}(1+\tilde{R}_{it}) \mid Z^{\star}_{t-1}\right]=1 \qquad \forall i=1,\ldots,N \quad \forall t=1,\ldots,T, \tag{1}$$

where $U'(\tilde{C}_t)$ is the marginal utility in period t from consumption $\tilde{C}_t$, r is the rate of pure time discount, $\tilde{R}_{it}$ is the return on asset i in period t, and $Z^{\star}_{t-1}$ is the information set available to the market in period $t-1$. This first-order condition reflects the loss of marginal utility of consumption today if one additional share of a security is purchased versus the gain in expected marginal utility tomorrow when the share is sold and the return is consumed. Among others, Lucas [25] discusses this equation in the discrete-time case and Grossman and Shiller [13] provide a derivation in the continuous-time setting. Hansen, Richard, and Singleton [18] have also emphasized the importance of equation (1) for econometric analyses of asset pricing models. One feature of (1) is that the equality holds for all time horizons. If agents make decisions daily, (1) is still relevant to the econometrician who has data sampled at monthly intervals; thus, by working with (1) temporal aggregation bias may be avoided.[2]

Without additional assumptions, equation (1) provides little guidance for empirical research. In the work that follows, power (or isoelastic) utility is specified; that is,

$$U(C_t)=\frac{C_t^{1-B}-1}{1-B}, \tag{2}$$

where $B=-U''(C_t)C_t/U'(C_t)$ is the RRA. By assuming isoelastic utility, equation (2) can be restated as

$$E\left[\frac{1}{1+r}\left(\frac{\tilde{C}_t}{C_{t-1}}\right)^{-B}(1+\tilde{R}_{it}) \mid Z^{\star}_{t-1}\right]=1. \tag{3}$$

Power utility is a natural choice because of its desirable theoretical properties. As a member of the hyperbolic absolute risk aversion (HARA) class of utility functions, its aggregation properties over individuals in the economy have been established by Rubinstein [33]. Further, log utility is a special case of isoelastic utility as B approaches unity. Given the theoretical attractiveness of log utility (e.g. Rubinstein [35]) as well as its use in theoretical work (see the introductory section for examples), its empirical relevance needs investigation. Since B is estimated, its distance from unity can be determined. Finally, Arrow [2], among others, has emphasized that absolute risk aversion should be decreasing, and power utility displays this characteristic.

If appropriate measures of consumption were available,[3] equation (3) could be transformed to yield empirical implications. However, much of the early research on utility-based asset pricing models replaced aggregate consumption with the return on some proxy for the market portfolio; this substitution is also employed here to avoid measurement problems with consumption as well as to relate to these earlier studies. With additional assumptions equation (3) can be rewritten as

$$E\left[\frac{1}{1+r}(1-k)^{-B}(1+\tilde{R}_{mt})^{-B}(1+\tilde{R}_{it}) \mid Z^{\star}_{t-1}\right] = 1, \tag{4}$$

where R_{mt} is the return on the market portfolio and k is the proportion of wealth consumed in every period (that is, if C is consumption and W is wealth, then $C = kW$). Hakansson [14] points out that consumption is a constant proportion of wealth if individuals with infinite horizons have isoelastic utility functions and the distribution of real production opportunities is constant and characterized by constant stochastic returns to scale.[4] Alternatively, in a pure exchange economy, Rubinstein [34] demonstrates that if aggregate consumption growth rates are independently and identically distributed over time or if $B = 1$ then (4) results with the return on the market index also being independently and identically distributed.[5] In fact, (4) is consistent with an equilibrium in *any* production economy in which aggregate consumption growth rates are independently and identically distributed.

Substituting $\tilde{R}_{mt}$ and R_{ft} (the return on the one-period riskless bond) for $\tilde{R}_{it}$ in (4) and equating the left-hand sides of the resulting relations, it is evident after a simple rearrangement that

$$\begin{aligned} E[(1+\tilde{R}_{mt})^{1-B} \mid Z^{\star}_{t-1}] &= (1+r)(1-k)^{B} \\ &= E[(1+\tilde{R}_{mt})^{-B}(1+R_{ft}) \mid Z^{\star}_{t-1}] \end{aligned}$$

$$E[(1+\tilde{R}_{mt})^{1-B} \mid Z^{\star}_{t-1}] - E[(1+\tilde{R}_{mt})^{-B}(1+R_{ft}) \mid Z^{\star}_{t-1}] = 0. \tag{5}$$

Since a riskless asset has a nonstochastic return conditional on $Z^{\star}_{t-1}$, R_{ft} can be brought outside the expectation operator. With a little algebraic manipulation

$$E[(\tilde{x}_t - 1)\tilde{x}_t^{-B} \mid Z^{\star}_{t-1}] = 0, \tag{6}$$

where $\tilde{x}_t = (1+\tilde{R}_{mt})/(1+R_{ft})$ is a discrete-time "excess return." Equation (6) has implications for moments not only conditional on complete information but also conditional on coarser information. If the relevant moments exist, the law of iterated expectations applied to (6) implies

$$E[(\tilde{x}_t - 1)\tilde{x}_t^{-B}] = 0. \tag{7}$$

Even if individuals have changing conditional expectations through time, the econometrician, by relying on (7), can still construct a valid test of the theory based on unconditional and fixed moments. There is no need to specify a model for the conditional expectations or even the variables which affect these conditional expectations. The significance of the law of iterated expectations for asset pricing models has been emphasized by Gibbons and Ferson [9], Grossman and Shiller [13], and Hansen and Singleton [19, 20].

Equation (7), which will be used throughout the paper, follows from replacing consumption in equation (3) with the market index and from assuming the existence of an observable return on a riskless asset. While the estimators which follow can easily be extended to situations not relying on these two assumptions, the cost of such an extension is the loss of intuition, for in that case we must analyze a relation involving two or more random variables whereas equation (7) has only a single random variable.[6] Of course, there is one interesting case where (7) applies even if the investment opportunity set changes through time. In the case of log utility (that is, $B = 1$), the market index can be substituted for consumption without strong restrictions on the temporal characteristics of asset returns. This particular case deserves emphasis, for log utility is an important null hypothesis to examine given the attention that it has received in theoretical work. Thus, this null hypothesis is testable in this framework with only weak assumptions concerning the time series on returns.

The next section develops the relevant econometrics assuming a lognormal distribution for the excess return on the market; this analysis simplifies equation (7). The third section then discusses the case of the method of moments solution which works directly with equation (7).

2 A Parametric Estimator of Relative Risk Aversion

For a transformed version of equation (7), Rubinstein [34] suggested a parametric estimator for B which assumes that the total return on the market portfolio has a lognormal distribution. Similarly, if we assume that the excess return on the market $\tilde{x}_t$ has a lognormal distribution, then

$$B = \frac{E(\ln \tilde{x}_t)}{\operatorname{var}(\ln \tilde{x}_t)} + 0.5. \tag{8}$$

The derivation of (8) is provided by Rubinstein [34].

Given that the excess return on the market portfolio has a lognormal distribution, equation (8) provides a relationship between RRA and the first two moments of this log excess return. Since $\ln x_t$ has a normal distribution, the maximum likelihood estimators for $E(\ln x_t)$ and $\operatorname{var}(\ln x_t)$ are their sample equivalents[7] ($\overline{\ln x}$ and s^2 respectively). Since a function of maximum likelihood estimators is also a maximum likelihood estimator (Zehna [39]), the following has all the well-known properties of maximum likelihood (that is, consistency, asymptotic efficiency, and asymptotic normality):

$$\hat{b} = \frac{\overline{\ln x}}{s^2} + 0.5. \tag{9}$$

Determining the variance of the asymptotic distribution of $\hat{b}$ is straightforward given the variances of the asymptotic distributions of $\overline{\ln x}$ and s^2. The normality of $\ln x_t$ implies that these two sample moments are independent with small sample variances:

$$\operatorname{var}[T^{1/2}(\overline{\ln x_t})] = \operatorname{var}(\ln \tilde{x}_t)$$

Table 8.1 Inconsistency of the parametric estimator when the lognormal distribution is violated

Parameters of the underlying distribution				
Probability of first outcome	*Value of first outcome* ($\ln x_1$)	*Value of second outcome* ($\ln x_2$)	$E\{[\ln x_t - E(\ln x_t)]^3\}$	*True RRA*
0.000	−5.311	0.005	−0.01771	0.706
0.331	−0.078	0.045	−0.00014	1.779
0.661	−0.037	0.085	0.00013	1.852
0.814	−0.023	0.125	0.00031	1.907
0.886	−0.016	0.165	0.00047	1.959
0.924	−0.012	0.205	0.00061	2.013
0.946	−0.009	0.245	0.00076	2.071
0.959	−0.008	0.285	0.00090	2.134
0.969	−0.006	0.325	0.00103	2.203
0.975	−0.005	0.365	0.00117	2.280
0.980	−0.004	0.405	0.00131	2.367
0.983	−0.003	0.445	0.00144	2.466
0.986	−0.003	0.485	0.00158	2.581
0.988	−0.002	0.525	0.00171	2.718
0.990	−0.002	0.565	0.00185	2.885
0.991	−0.001	0.605	0.00198	3.096
0.992	−0.001	0.645	0.00212	3.380
0.993	−0.001	0.685	0.00225	3.798
0.994	−0.000	0.725	0.00239	4.550
0.994	−0.000	0.765	0.00252	8.633

These values are based on a discrete distribution with only two outcomes for the excess return on the market index. In all cases, the outcomes and the probabilities are changed so that the first two moments are constant across all rows. These moments were set so that $E(\ln x_t) = 0.0044$ and $\mathrm{SD}(\ln x_t) = 0.0577$ which corresponds to the Center for Research in Security Prices (CRSP) value-weighted index for the period 1926–81. Since the first two moments are constant, the lognormal estimator for RRA would converge to 1.81 for all rows even though this is not the true value of RRA.

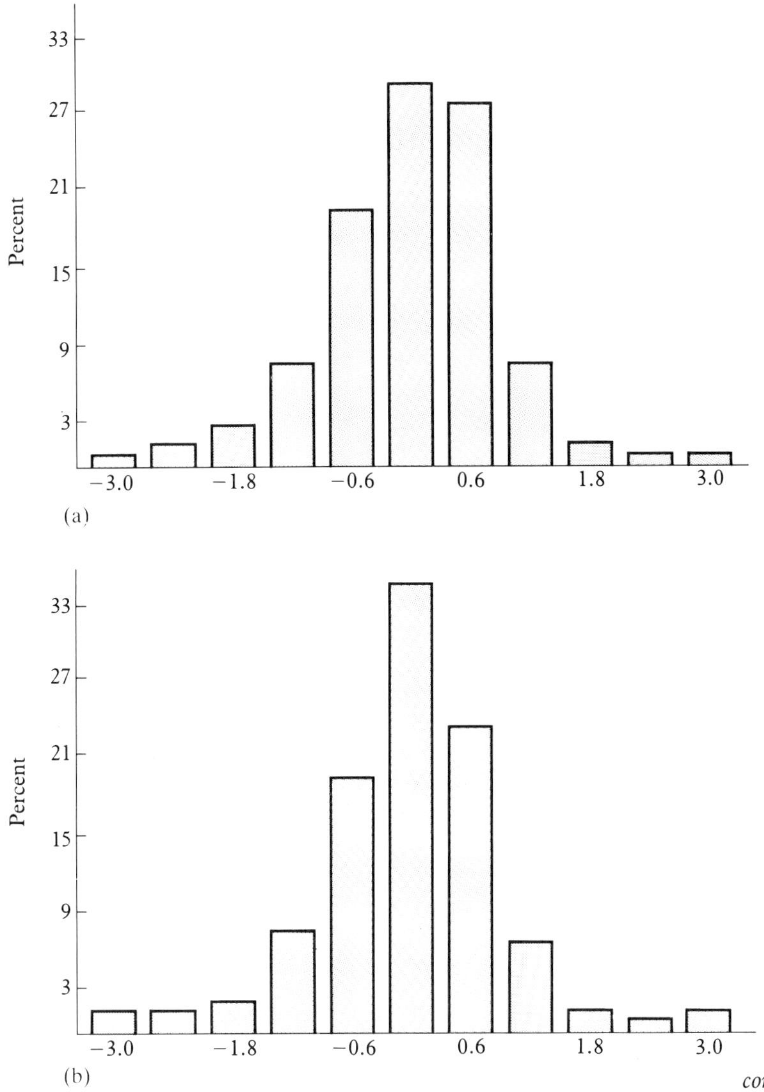

continued

Figure 8.1 Histograms of standardized monthly excess returns on stock market indices (the left-hand tail of each histogram has been truncated): (a) CRSP value-weighted index, January 1926 to December 1981; (b) CRSP equal-weighted index, January 1926 to December 1981; (c) CRSP value-weighted index, July 1939 to December 1952; (d) standardized normal distribution.

and

$$\text{var}(T^{1/2}s^2) = \frac{2T}{T-1}\,[\text{var}(\ln\,\tilde{x}_t)]^2,$$

where T is the number of observations. Combining the above with

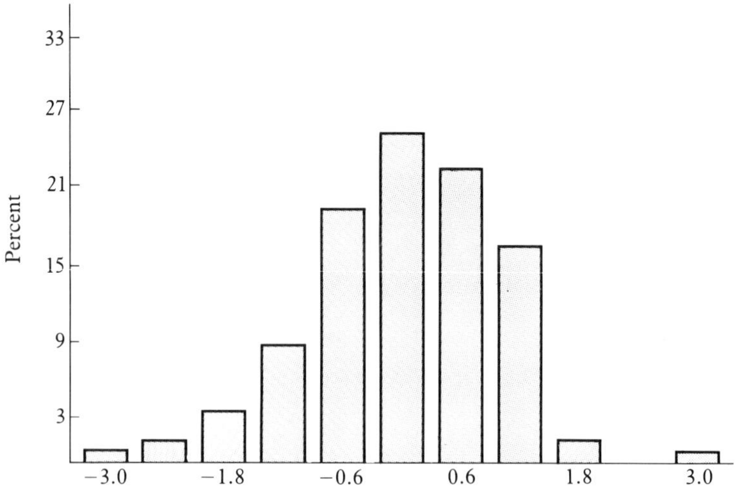

(c)

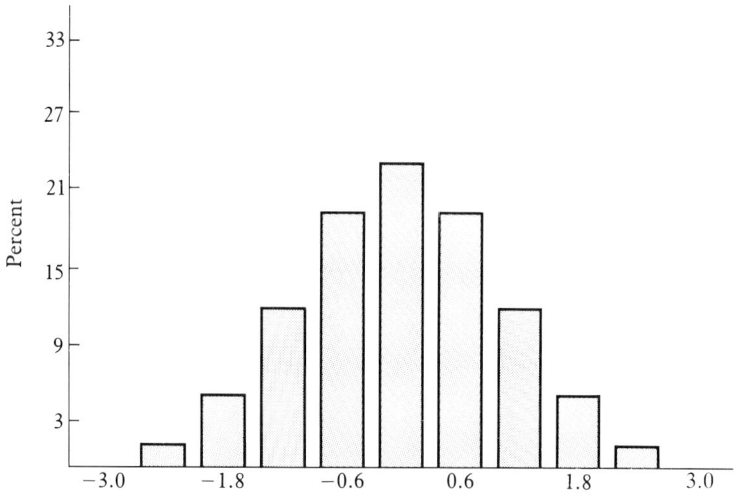

(d)

Figure 8.1 *(Continued)*

standard asymptotic theory[8] yields

$$\mathrm{var}(T^{1/2}\hat{b}) = \frac{2\,[E(\ln\ \tilde{x}_t)]^{2} + \mathrm{var}(\ln\ \tilde{x}_t)}{[\mathrm{var}(\ln\ \tilde{x}_t)]^{2}}. \tag{10}$$

The parametric approach has a shortcoming: the estimator (9) can be inconsistent if the lognormal assumption is violated. This lack of robustness is not surprising, for the functional form of (9) depends on the simplifications achieved by this distributional assumption.

A simple example demonstrates that the parametric estimator is

Table 8.2 Summary statistics on the logarithm of the monthly excess returns on the value-weighted and equal-weighted indices (1926–1981)

	Value-weighted index				*Equal-weighted index*			
Subperiod (no. of observations)	*Sample mean*	*Sample std dev.*	*Sample skewness*[a]	*D statistic for normality*[b] *(p value)*	*Sample mean*	*Sample std dev.*	*Sample skewness*	*D statistic for normality (p value)*
1/1926–12/1981 (672)	0.0044	0.0577	−0.360	0.081 (<0.01)	0.0071	0.0769	0.551	0.098 (<0.01)
1/1926–12/1952 (324)	0.0053	0.0716	−0.353	0.099 (<0.01)	0.0086	0.0975	0.551	0.111 (<0.01)
1/1953–12/1981 (348)	0.0035	0.0409	−0.339	0.054 (0.01)	0.0057	0.0506	−0.154	0.059 (0.01)
1/1926–6/1939 (162)	0.0010	0.0909	−0.085	0.094 (<0.01)	0.0032	0.1228	0.681	0.101 (<0.01)
7/1939–12/1952 (162)	0.0097	0.0446	−1.298	0.070 (0.05)	0.0140	0.0629	0.185	0.082 (<0.01)
1/1953–6/1967 (174)	0.0078	0.0339	−0.450	0.067 (0.05)	0.0090	0.0377	−0.264	0.075 (0.02)
7/1967–12/1981 (174)	−0.0009	0.0465	−0.157	0.062 (0.10)	0.0021	0.0608	−0.006	0.047 (>0.15)

[a] The sample skewness is calculated as the third sample moment *after* the random variable has been standardized so that its sample mean is zero and sample standard deviation is unity. Under normality, this measure of skewness should equal approximately zero.

[b] The D statistic is the usual Kolmogorov test for normality.

inconsistent if the normality assumption is violated. If $\ln x_t$ is actually generated from a discrete distribution with only two outcomes, then this distribution can be characterized by three parameters – the value of each outcome and the probability of any one outcome.[9] These parameters can be varied in such a way that the mean and the variance of the $\ln x_t$ are constant and yet the skewness of the distribution changes. If the mean and the variance remain constant, then the estimator given in (9) will always converge to the same value. However, true RRA as given by (7) is not a function of just the first two moments, and so RRA may change as the skewness changes. Table 8.1 provides a range of values for RRA when the mean and the variance have typical values for the log excess return on the value-weighted New York Stock Exchange (NYSE) index. Clearly, the parametric estimator is not robust to this departure from normality of the log excess return.[10]

Since the distributional assumption is critical in deriving (9), figures 8.1(a) and 8.1(b) provide histograms of the log excess return on the value-weighted NYSE index and the equal-weighted NYSE index for monthly data from 1926 to 1981. (A more detailed data description is provided in section 4.) Table 8.2 quantifies the graphical presentations by providing summary statistics for the overall period and several subperiods. The negative sample skewness of the value-weighted index, which is apparent in the histogram, is confirmed in table 8.2. Further, the Kolmogorov D statistic, which is also reported in table 8.2, rejects a normality assumption for either index. An alternative estimation scheme is proposed in the next section.

3 A Method of Moments Estimator of Relative Risk Aversion

An advantage of utility-based pricing theories is the lack of strong distributional assumptions regarding asset returns. If statistical inference concerning such theories necessitates additional distributional assumptions, then these theoretical models are burdened by assumptions concerning both preferences and the probability distributions for returns. Thus we attempt to estimate B directly from equation (7) with a minimal amount of additional distributional assumptions; we refer to such a solution as a method of moments.

An obvious estimator of RRA follows directly from equation (7). Replacing the population moment in (7) with its sample equivalent, we could estimate RRA by finding that value of b such that

$$f(b) = \frac{1}{T} \sum_t (x_t - 1) x_t^{-b} = 0 \qquad (11)$$

where $b \in (0, +\infty)$. Under reasonable assumptions a unique value of b which satisfies (11) always exists.[11] Various search procedures are available to find the appropriate value of b; a simple gradient search algorithm which was quite satisfactory in all the data analysis is employed in section 4.

The only difficulty with this method of moments estimator is the determination of the appropriate measure of its precision. Under the assumption that $\tilde{x}_t$ is independently and identically distributed,[12] the following equation for the variance of the asymptotic distribution of b is derived in appendix A:

$$\operatorname{var}(T^{1/2}b) = \frac{E\{[(\tilde{x}_t - 1)\tilde{x}_t^{-B}]^2\}}{\{E[(\tilde{x}_t - 1)\tilde{x}_t^{-B} \ln \tilde{x}_t]\}^2}. \tag{12}$$

Fortunately, equation (12) has a nice intuitive interpretation. In solving (11) for b, we could draw a graph with $f(b)$ on the vertical axis and b on the horizontal axis. When the curve for $f(b)$ crosses the horizontal axis, this point is b. Figure 8.2 illustrates a typical graph of $f(b)$. The denominator of (12) is the square of the slope of $f(b)$ at B while the numerator equals the variability of the line at B. As the variance of the line increases or as the absolute value of the slope of the line decreases, the asymptotic variance increases. Such behavior in the variance of b is to be expected. If the line in figure 8.2 has more *ex ante* variability at the crossing point on the horizontal axis or if the line flattens out near the crossing point, then selecting a point estimate (or finding the crossing point) becomes more difficult.

Since the method of moments estimator does not rely on assumptions about the exact distribution of $\tilde{x}_t$, (11) is robust to departures from lognormality of $\tilde{x}_t$, unlike its parametric counterpart. The price of this robustness is the potential loss of statistical efficiency if the distributional assumption is appropriate. This disadvantage is analyzed by studying the relative asymptotic efficiency, the ratio of the asymptotic variances of the parametric estimator (given in (10)) divided by that of the method of moments approach (see (12)). This relative efficiency RE is defined in appendix B for assumed lognormality:

$$\begin{aligned}\mathrm{RE} &= \frac{\operatorname{var}(\hat{b})}{\operatorname{var}(b)} \\ &= \frac{2\mu^2 + \sigma^2}{\exp(\mu^2/\sigma^2 + \mu + \sigma^2/4)[1 + \exp(-2\mu) - 2\exp(-\mu - \tfrac{1}{2}\sigma^2)]}\end{aligned}$$

where $\mu = E(\ln \tilde{x}_t)$ and $\sigma^2 = \operatorname{var}(\ln \tilde{x}_t)$.

Figure 8.3 summarizes the inefficiency of the nonparametric estimator versus its parametric counterpart. Each curve represents various combinations of $E(\ln \tilde{x}_t)$ and $\operatorname{var}(\ln x_t)$ which yield the same relative efficiency when x_t is lognormal. The points on the plot represent estimated means

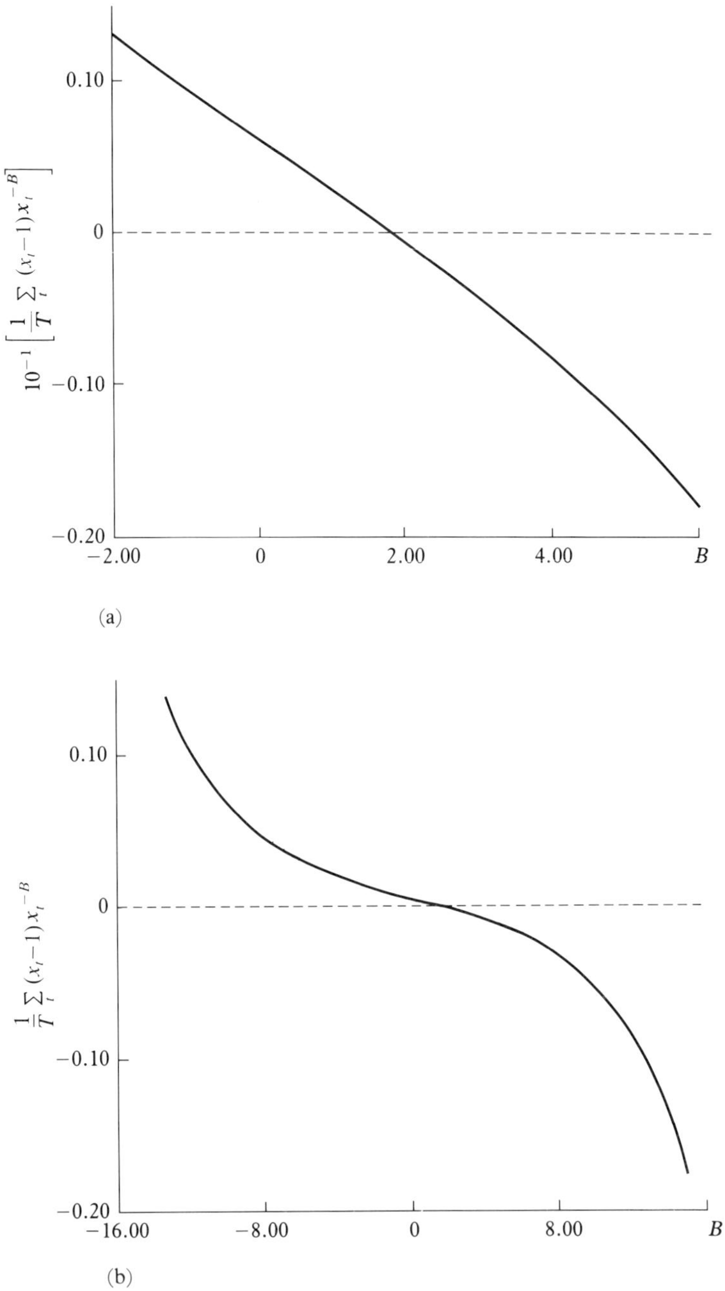

Figure 8.2 Graphical determination of the value B of RRA for which the equilibrium condition is satisfied, i.e. the left-hand side of equation (7) must equal zero (x_t is the excess return on the CRSP value-weighted index, and the monthly observations are from January 1926 to December 1981).

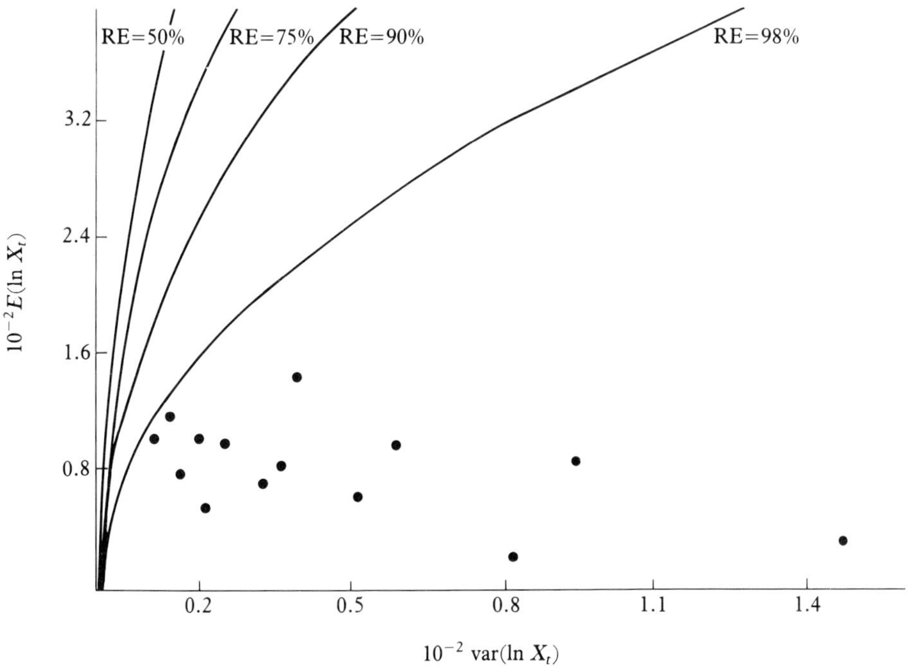

Figure 8.3 The relative efficiency RE $=\text{var}(\hat{b})/\text{var}(b)$ of the parametric versus nonparametric estimators of RRA for different pairs of $\{E(\ln X_t), \text{var}(\ln X_t)\}$. Each curve represents all pairs which yield a particular value of RE. The points represent sample means and variances for CRSP indices over different subperiods.

and variances for the market index over different subperiods from 1926 to 1981. As is clear from the figure, typical values for the mean and variance suggest that 99 percent of the precision obtained by the parametric estimator $\hat{b}$ is obtained by the nonparametric alternative b. Given the robustness of the latter estimator, this small drop in precision makes the method of moments approach very attractive.

4 Some Empirical Results

Other studies have attempted to estimate aggregate RRA. One class of studies has utilized cross-sectional surveys of the portfolio holdings of individuals to measure RRA using wealth, not consumption.[13] For example, Friend and Blume [8] estimate RRA to be 2 and roughly constant across different levels of wealth.

The other class of research uses time series data on asset returns and aggregate consumption. Grossman and Shiller [12] claim that RRA is close to 4 on the basis of a graphical examination of the data. However, there was no attempt to estimate this value precisely or to determine confidence intervals about the estimate.[14] Hansen and Singleton [20] develop a clever approach involving instrumental variables. Using monthly consumption data and stock returns since 1959, they determine RRA to be somewhere between −1.6 and 1.6.

RRA has been estimated by three groups of researchers using a dynamic model for expectations and a lognormal distribution assumption. With stock return data, Hansen and Singleton [19] estimate a range of values for RRA from 0.07 to 0.62 while Ferson [7], using bond data, reports a range from −1.4 to 5.4. Both studies involve nonlinear techniques on postwar consumption data. With a similar methodology, but in a Bayesian framework, Hall [16] concludes that RRA is in a range from −26.3 to 25.6, depending on whether stock returns or interest rates are employed with annual sampling intervals.

The empirical results in this section are based on monthly data from 1926 to 1981. Two proxies for the market portfolio are examined – the value-weighted and equal-weighted indices of the NYSE from the Center for Research in Security Prices (CRSP) at the University of Chicago. Interest rates are needed to form the "excess returns" on these market proxies. Prior to 1953, monthly returns[15] on US Treasury bills are from Ibbotson and Sinquefield [22]. From 1953 to 1981, yields on 30 day (approximately) bills are from the CRSP Government Bond File. While all returns are nominal, the transformation to "excess returns" may still satisfy the theoretical underpinnings given in section 1; a sufficient, but not necessary, condition is that inflation over the sampling interval is known with certainty.

Using the value-weighted index, figure 8.2 illustrates the nonlinear search for the method of moments estimate. In all subperiods and for both indices, convergence to the estimate occurred within three iterations.[16] Using both the method of moments and the parametric alternative, table 8.3 summarizes the estimates of RRA for both indices across various subperiods.

In all but two subperiods (that is, July 1939 to December 1952 and January 1953 to June 1967) the estimated RRA is within two standard errors of unity; that is, the data cannot reject log utility as the appropriate specification for the aggregate utility function. As was noted above, the formula for the standard error remains valid even if returns are not independent and identically distributed, and so the acceptance of the null hypothesis that $B = 1$ holds for economic environments where the conditional investment opportunity set is not constant. Furthermore, the results for the subperiod 1939–52 are not clearly rejecting log utility, for the method of moments estimate is within the usual confidence intervals. Since the parametric estimator is not robust, the method of moments

Table 8.3 Estimates of relative risk aversion (1926–1981)

	RRA using value-weighted index			*RRA using equal-weighted index*		
Subperiod (no. of observations)	*Method of moments (std error)*	*Parametric with lognormal distribution (std error)*	*Hausman's specification test*[a] *(p value)*	*Method of moments (std error)*	*Parametric with lognormal distribution (std error)*	*Hausman's specification test (p value)*
1/1926–12/1981	1.79	1.81	26.57	1.71	1.70	14.23
(672)	(0.68)	(0.67)	(<0.0001)	(0.52)	(0.51)	(0.0002)
1/1926–12/1952	1.52	1.54	5.43	1.42	1.40	8.42
(324)	(0.79)	(0.78)	(0.0198)	(0.59)	(0.57)	(0.0037)
1/1953–12/1981	2.55	2.58	18.46	2.68	2.70	6.05
(348)	(1.33)	(1.32)	(<0.0001)	(1.09)	(1.07)	(0.0139)
1/1926–6/1939	0.62	0.62	0.00	0.72	0.71	1.86
(162)	(0.87)	(0.86)	(1.00)	(0.64)	(0.64)	(0.1726)
7/1939–12/1952	4.69	5.35	103.92	3.81	4.03	15.66
(162)	(2.02)	(1.84)	(<0.0001)	(1.49)	(1.31)	(<0.0001)
1/1953–6/1967	7.00	7.29	−1256.88[b]	6.77	6.99	51.05
(174)	(2.35)	(2.35)	(0.00)	(2.17)	(2.13)	(<0.0001)
7/1967–12/1981	0.09	0.09	0.11	1.06	1.06	0.11
(174)	(1.64)	(1.63)	(0.7401)	(1.25)	(1.25)	(0.7401)

[a]Hausman's [21] specification test is distributed asymptotically as χ^2 with one degree of freedom in this application.

[b]The χ^2 statistic is negative because the *estimated* asymptotic variance of the nonparametric estimator is less than that of its parametric counterpart. Under the null hypothesis, the precision of the two approaches should be reversed since the parametric estimator is a maximum likelihood estimator. Thus the p value is set equal to zero.

estimate for 1939–52 deserves the primary attention. Figure 8.1(c) visually confirms the departure from normality for the value-weighted index for this subperiod, and table 8.2 quantifies the inadequacy of this distributional assumption.

The results from the overall period suggest no *statistically* significant departure from log utility. The *economic* distinction between RRA = 1 versus (say) RRA = 2 may not be very important given the behavior of an individual to a timeless gamble (see Ferson [7] and Pratt [29]). An individual with log utility will pay a half basis point of wealth to avoid a fair coin toss which risks 1 percent of current wealth. When RRA = 2, the individual will pay one basis point of wealth to avoid the same gamble.

Three final observations are based on table 8.3. First, the results are not sensitive to the index except for the last subperiod (July 1967 to December 1981). Such results are comforting, given the arbitrariness in selecting an index.[17] Second, the standard errors confirm the analysis in section 3 of the relative asymptotic efficiency of the two alternative estimation schemes. While the precision of the lognormal estimator is greater than that of the method of moments, the difference is insignificant. Finally, table 8.3 provides a test of the distributional assumption underlying the parametric estimator. Rather than compare the fit of log excess returns with a normal distribution (as was done in table 8.2 with the Kolmogorov D statistic), Hausman's [21] specification test can be used.[18] This statistic compares the parametric and nonparametric estimates which should be equal in large samples if log excess returns are normally distributed. However, under the alternative hypothesis of nonnormality, the parametric estimator is not necessarily consistent, and the difference between the estimates may be nonzero. The advantage of the Hausman test is that it measures departures from normality with an interesting metric. Nonnormality is only important here to the extent that the parametric estimator is inconsistent, and the asymptotic χ^2 test reported in table 8.3 directly examines this issue. Table 8.3 confirms the results in table 8.2, for log excess returns do violate normality in all but two subperiods for each index. However, despite the rejection of lognormality by the Hausman test, the most striking feature of table 8.3 is the strong similarity between the method of moments and the parametric approach. For most subperiods, the difference between the two point estimates is economically insignificant. Thus, the potential problems with the parametric approach are not important in this application.

Time preference cannot be estimated because we are working with the market index and not consumption. Since portfolio allocation is not affected by time preference with isoelastic utility, consumption as well as wealth must be known to identify the time preference parameter. However, given the proportion of wealth that is consumed, time preference can be uncovered from the data. From (5) when RRA is not equal to unity, pure time preference r is given by

$$r = \frac{E[(1+R_{mt})^{1-B}]}{(1-k)^B} - 1 \tag{13}$$

where k is the proportion of wealth consumed.

If $B = 1.79$, then the numerator in (13) is 0.9974 for the value-weighted index from 1926 to 1981. Ando and Modigliani [1] suggest that the proportion k of wealth consumed is between 4 and 8 percent (annualized). This suggests a range of 4–11 percent for time preference. In contrast with Mehra and Prescott [26] and Nordhaus and Dulant [28], these parameter estimates for both time preference and RRA are within the range of economically acceptable bounds.

5 Applying the Hansen and Singleton Methodology to the Case of Many Assets

Until now, this research has focused on estimating RRA using two assets – the market portfolio and the riskless security. The econometric analysis for the case of many assets is outlined in this section.

In most of the empirical work on utility-based asset pricing models, a specific utility function (usually logarithmic) was assumed, and then the appropriate risk measures and the risk premium were estimated. Fama and MacBeth [6], Kraus and Litzenberger [23], and Roll [30] use log utility and then test the implied risk–return relation across assets. Grauer [10] examines the specification for a range of specific aggregate utility functions. Few have estimated the appropriate specification of RRA from the data and then tested the cross-sectional implications of such a value.[19]

Equation (5) implies that

$$E[(1+\tilde{R}_{mt})^{-B}(1+\tilde{R}_{it}) - (1+\tilde{R}_{mt})^{-B}(1+R_{ft})] = 0 \qquad \forall i = 1, 2, \ldots, N.$$

As in the derivation of equation (7), the above result can be transformed as

$$E[\tilde{x}_t^{-B}(\tilde{x}_{it} - 1)] = 0 \qquad \forall i = 1, 2, \ldots, N \tag{14}$$

where $\tilde{x}_t = (1+\tilde{R}_{mt})/(1+R_{ft})$ and $\tilde{x}_{it} = (1+\tilde{R}_{it})/(1+R_{ft})$. A nonparametric estimator[20] for B using individual securities would replace (14) with its sample equivalent and search for the appropriate value of RRA. Unlike the case where only the excess return on the market is utilized, a single estimate of B which simultaneously satisfies (14) for all N nonlinear equations is not expected. In other words, when many assets are observed, RRA is over-identified.

Fortunately, Hansen and Singleton [20] have developed a very general econometric approach which could be adapted to this problem and which would select a single estimate for B. Their procedure begins by replacing the population expectations in (14) with their sample counterparts for all N equations. B would then be estimated by choosing that value which minimizes the weighted squared deviations of these N sample moments from zero. In other words,[21]

$$\min_{b}\left[\frac{1}{T}\sum_{t} x_{mt}^{-b}(\boldsymbol{x}_t - \boldsymbol{1})\right]' S^{-1}\left[\frac{1}{T}\sum_{t} x_{mt}^{-b}(\boldsymbol{x}_t - \boldsymbol{1})\right] \quad (15)$$

where $\boldsymbol{x}_t' = (x_{1t} x_{2t} \ldots x_{Nt})$, $\boldsymbol{1}' = (1, 1, \ldots, 1)$, and S^{-1} is an $N \times N$ weighting matrix which reflects the asymptotic variance–covariance matrix of the sample counterparts to (14).

If the theory underlying (14) is correct, then the sample counterparts to (14) should be close to zero in large samples when evaluated at true RRA. This observation provides the basis for a test of the theory by measuring the distance of the objective function (15) from zero. The asymptotic distribution of such a test statistic is intuitive. The objective function (15) is just the sum of squared asymptotically normal random variables which have means equal to zero and which are weighted by S^{-1} so as to transform them into uncorrelated random variables. Not surprisingly, Hansen and Singleton [20] have demonstrated that the objective function evaluated at the optimal value b does have an asymptotic χ^2 distribution.

The estimator developed in section 3 can be viewed as a special case of the Hansen and Singleton [20] approach when there are no over-identifying restrictions to test. In this particular case, the squared deviation on the left-hand side of (11) from zero is zero when b is selected in the appropriate fashion.

6 Conclusions

Utility-based models of asset pricing can be estimated and tested without strong distributional assumptions concerning asset returns. By selecting a general parameterization for an aggregate utility function, the appropriateness of certain specializations can be determined from available data. Here an isoelastic utility function was selected, and log utility, which is a special case of the isoelastic class, is consistent with the data from 1926 to 1981.

Although distributional assumptions can simplify the estimation of utility-based asset pricing models, such an approach may not be robust to departures from the assumed distribution. The suggested nonparametric estimator, although nonlinear, is easy to compute and provides reasonably precise estimates – at least for the data analyzed here.

Given the limited amount of statistical analyses of utility-based paradigms of asset pricing, the empirical usefulness of such models was open to question. While this paper has relied on a simple and special case to highlight the conceptual issues, it is clear that preference-based theories can yield tractable econometric models. Future empirical work should further investigate the implications of such theories.

Appendix A A derivation of the asymptotic standard error for the method of moments estimator

The following provides a derivation of the asymptotic standard error for the methods of moments estimator. An exact first-order Taylor series expansion of (11) around the population value of B yields

$$f(B) - f'(b^\star)(b - B) = 0,$$

where $b^\star \in (b, B)$, and $f'(b^\star)$ is the first derivative of $f(b)$ evaluated at $b^\star$, or

$$b - B = [f'(b^\star)]^{-1} f(B).$$

If $\tilde{x}_t$ is independently and identically distributed through time, then $(\tilde{x}_t - 1)\tilde{x}_t^{-b}$ is also. Thus equation (7) and the Lindeberg–Levy central limit theorem imply that $T^{1/2} f(b)$ is distributed asymptotically as normal with mean zero and variance equal to the var$[(\tilde{x}_t - 1)\tilde{x}_t^{-B}]$, which can be estimated by

$$\frac{1}{T} \sum_t [(x_t - 1)x_t^{-b}]^2.$$

Since $T^{1/2} f(B)$ converges to a random variable with a known distribution and $[f'(b^\star)]^{-1}$ converges in probability to a constant, the product $[f'(b^\star)]^{-1} T^{1/2} f(B)$ converges in distribution to the distribution of $T^{1/2} f(b)$ scaled up by this constant (Serfling [37, p. 19]). Thus, for large samples, b is normally distributed about B with variance given by equation (12).

Appendix B The relative asymptotic efficiency of the parametric estimator versus the method of moments approach assuming a lognormal distribution

From equation (12),

$$\text{var}(T^{1/2} b) = \frac{E\{[(x_t - 1)x_t^{-B}]^2\}}{\{E[(x_t - 1)x_t^{-B} \ln x_t]\}^2}.$$

Based on note 11, the above can be written as

$$\text{var}(T^{1/2} b) = \frac{E\{[(x_t - 1)x_t^{-B}]^2\}}{\lim_{\lambda \to 0} (E\{(x_t - 1)x_t^{-B}[(x_t^{\lambda} - 1)/\lambda]\})^2}.$$

Under the assumption that x_t has a lognormal distribution with $E(\ln x_t) = \mu$ and

$\text{var}(\ln x_t) = \sigma^2$, the above equation can be rewritten as

$$\text{var}(T^{1/2}b) = \frac{\exp(-2B\mu + 2B^2\sigma^2)}{[\exp(-B\mu + \frac{1}{2}B^2\sigma^2)]^2} \frac{A_1 + A_2}{\lim\limits_{\lambda \to 0} \{[A_3(\lambda) + A_4(\lambda)]^2/\lambda\}}$$

where

$$A_1 = \exp[2\mu + 2(1 - 2B)\sigma^2]$$

$$A_2 = 1 - 2\exp[\mu + \tfrac{1}{2}(1 - 4B)\sigma^2]$$

$$A_3(\lambda) = \exp\{(1+\lambda)\mu + \tfrac{1}{2}[(1+\lambda)^2 - 2B(1+\lambda)]\sigma^2\}$$

$$A_4(\lambda) = 1 - \exp[\lambda\mu + \tfrac{1}{2}(\lambda^2 - 2\lambda B)\sigma^2] - \exp[\mu + \tfrac{1}{2}(1 - 2B)\sigma^2].$$

Taking the limit using l'Hôpital's rule,

$$\text{var}(T^{1/2}b) = \exp(B^2\sigma^2) \times \frac{\exp[2\mu + 2(1-2B)\sigma^2] - 2\exp[\mu + \frac{1}{2}(1-4B)\sigma^2] + 1}{\{\exp[\mu + \frac{1}{2}(1-2B)\sigma^2][\mu + (1-B)\sigma^2] - (\mu - B\sigma^2)\}^2}.$$

Under the lognormal assumption, $B = (\mu/\sigma^2) + 0.5$, and so the above can be rewritten as

$$\text{var}(T^{1/2}b) = \frac{1}{\sigma^4}\exp\left(\frac{\mu^2}{\sigma^2} + \mu + \frac{\sigma^2}{4}\right)\left[\exp(-2\mu) - 2\exp\left(-\mu - \frac{\sigma^2}{2}\right) + 1\right].$$

Recalling from the text that the relative efficiency RE is defined as $\text{var}(T^{1/2}\hat{b})/\text{var}(T^{1/2}b)$, the above equation can be combined with (10) to yield the equation for RE at the end of section 3.

Notes

1 However, this application was derived independently of Hansen and Singleton [20].

2 As Singleton has emphasized to us, temporal aggregation bias is avoided as long as the econometrician has access to instantaneous consumption sampled at discrete intervals. Since equation (1) is transformed into a statement involving the return on the market index, rather than consumption, temporal aggregation bias is avoided in this paper even without data on instantaneous consumption.

3 Breeden, Gibbons, and Litzenberger [3] discuss some of the problems with measuring aggregate consumption over discrete time intervals. These problems include not only pure measurement error which arises from the necessity to sample aggregate consumption but also problems with the distinction between expenditures on goods and services versus actual consumption as well as temporal aggregation issues (see note 2).

4 While a constant real investment opportunity set is an extreme and unrealistic assumption, the advantages of generalizing this assumption to estimate RRA are by no means clear. Indeed, there is limited empirical evidence to support constant investment opportunities. For example, Hall [15] found consumption growth rates to be uncorrelated over time, and Fama [5] found that a constant expected real rate of interest was a plausible assumption for some research objectives. Of course, the theoretical assumptions leading to equation (5) have the unfortunate implication that

aggregate consumption growth will be perfectly correlated with growth in aggregate wealth.

5 Rubinstein [34] derives the more general result that the proportion k of wealth consumed changes in a deterministic fashion if the time preference r is not constant and/or if investors have a finite time horizon. Rubinstein's [34] terminology differs from that in the text, for he assumes that the growth in consumption is a "stationary random walk" which is used to imply that the growth rate is serially uncorrelated with identically distributed innovations. Of course, Rubinstein [34] does not assume that all asset returns (for example, options) have stationary distributions – just the two "basic" portfolios (the riskless asset and the market portfolio).

6 For example, for any two assets (one asset may be the market index) an alternative to equation (7) is

$$E\left[\left(\frac{\tilde{C}_t}{\tilde{C}_{t-1}}\right)^{-B}(\tilde{R}_{1t}-\tilde{R}_{2t})\right]=0.$$

7 Throughout this paper, the sample variance refers to the unbiased estimator using a degrees of freedom adjustment, and not the true maximum likelihood estimator. This has no effect on the asymptotic properties.

8 The interested reader should consult Serfling [37, pp. 118–25] for theorems which provide the asymptotic distribution of a random variable given the asymptotic distribution of the random variables of which it is a function.

9 Obviously, this distribution was not selected for its realism. Rather, a two-outcome distribution allows for an easy analytic solution to equation (7). Alternative distributions can be used, but these could require extensive numerical integration. Since the purpose here is only to illustrate the concept, more realistic distributions were not analyzed.

10 Interestingly, this example suggests that negative sample skewness results in the parametric estimator's overstating RRA and conversely. The empirical evidence in table 8.3 is consistent with the relationship observed in this illustration.

11 In solving (11) for b, we could draw a graph with $f(b)$ on the vertical axis and b on the horizontal axis. If investors are risk averse (that is, $B>0$), then $E(\tilde{x}_t)>1$, and to solve (11) for b it is assumed that $f(b=0)=(1/T)\,\Sigma_t\,(x_t-1)>0$. Furthermore, as long as the sample contains at least one observation on x_t different from unity, then $f'(b)$ is strictly negative. Thus, the graph of $f(b)$ starts above the horizontal axis at $b=0$ and monotonically declines towards that axis. To guarantee a solution for (11) requires that the graph of $f(b)$ eventually crosses the horizontal axis. If the sample contains one observation on x_t less than unity, then it is easy to verify that $\lim_{b\to\infty}f(b)=-\infty$. Figure 8.2 illustrates a typical graph of $f(b)$. Using a similar line of argument, we can establish the existence of a unique solution to (7), the population counterpart to (11), as long as (a) $E[x_t^{-B}(x_t-1)\ln x_t]$ and (b) $E[x_t^{-B}(x_t-1)(x_t^{\lambda}-1)/\lambda]$, for some $\lambda>0$, are finite. These conditions assure that the derivative of (7), the limit of (b) as λ declines toward zero, exists and is equal to (a). See theorems 6 and 15 in Royden [32, pp. 81, 88].

12 While a specific distributional assumption about returns has been avoided, the requirement of independent and identical draws for $\tilde{x}_t$ is still quite strong. However, the approach can be extended using a generalization of the Lindeberg–Levy central limit theorem (Hansen [17] and Hansen and Singleton [20]), and the formula (12) is *exactly* the same. Since the theoretical justification in section 1 for replacing consumption with the market return is more consistent with the simple version of the central limit theorem, this generalization has not been emphasized. Of course, if the null hypothesis is that of log utility (that is, $B=1$), then allowing for dependent and

nonidentical draws for $\tilde{x}_t$ is an important extension since such time series properties are consistent with the theory used to derive (7). Fortunately, equation (12) is general enough to handle such a situation. Equation (12) still obtains when the conditional investment opportunity set changes through time as long as $\tilde{x}_t$ is a stationary and ergodic stochastic process. (For example, the economic model of Cox, Ingersoll, and Ross [4] implies a changing conditional investment opportunity set with returns which follow a stationary and ergodic stochastic process.)

13 In these studies, RRA is derived through a Taylor series approximation of the utility function. However, in the case where RRA is a constant through time (that is, isoelastic utility), this approximation is not necessarily accurate for power utility functions with discrete time periods (Loistl [24]). The approximation may also break down in continuous time models if the stochastic process for security returns contains jump components.

14 Grossman and Shiller [11] provide a more rigorous estimation scheme for RRA. Their main focus is on working with consumption data which have been time averaged.

15 The economic theory underlying (7) calls for interest rates on one-period bonds, and not an uncertain return series which includes capital gains and losses. However, a reliable monthly interest rate prior to 1953 is difficult to construct. This deficiency in the data motivated the subperiod breakdown in the work that follows.

16 The starting point for the nonlinear solution to (11) was the parametric estimator given in (8). The convergence criterion was to continue to search for b until $[(1/T)\,\Sigma_t\,(x_t - 1)x_t^{-b}] < 0.000\,000\,1$.

17 For the period February 1953 to December 1977, RRA was estimated using an even broader index constructed by Stambaugh [38]. Both the nonparametric estimate of 2.76 and the parametric estimate of 2.75 correspond closely to the values that we obtained for the CRSP indices over this same subperiod. We thank Rob Stambaugh for providing us with this index.

18 We thank Richard Startz for suggesting this test to us.

19 Hansen and Singleton [19, 20] are two exceptions to this statement, and both papers rely on consumption data, not a market index. Hansen and Singleton [19] use a lognormal distribution and conditional expectations while Hansen and Singleton [20] use unconditional expectations, as in this paper, but emphasize instrumental variables for the estimation.

20 Naturally, a distributional assumption can be added to simplify the estimation of RRA. A bivariate lognormal distribution for $\tilde{x}_t$ and $\tilde{x}_{it}$ provides a very tractable estimator for B.

21 In the notation of Hansen and Singleton [20], $h(b) = f(b) = x_{mt}^{-b}(x_t - 1)$. Hansen and Singleton [20] distinguish between $h(b)$ and $f(b)$ because their procedure also incorporates the use of instrumental variables. Since (7) holds for both unconditional expectations and conditional expectations given any predetermined variables (or instruments), it must be the case that $\tilde{x}_t^{-B}(\tilde{x}_t - 1)$ is uncorrelated with these instruments. That is, the unconditional covariance between $\tilde{x}_t^{-B}(\tilde{x}_t - 1)$ and any instrument must be zero. The knowledge that these unconditional covariances must equal zero provides additional equations from which to estimate b. Throughout this paper, we have relied only on an instrument equal to unity for all t.

References

1 Ando, A. and Modigliani, F. "The 'Life Cycle' Hypothesis of Saving: Aggregate Implications and Tests," *American Economic Review*, 53, March 1963, 55–84.

2 Arrow, K. *Essays in the Theory of Risk Bearing* (Chicago, IL: Markham, 1971).

3 Breeden, D., Gibbons, M. and Litzenberger, R. "The Consumption-Oriented CAPM: Some Empirical Tests," *Working Paper*, Graduate School of Business, Stanford University, 1982.

4 Cox, J., Ingersoll, J. and Ross, S. "A Theory of the Term Structure of Interest Rates," *Econometrica*, 53, 385–407.

5 Fama, E. "Short-Term Interest Rates as Predictors of Inflation," *American Economic Review*, 65, June 1975, 269–82.

6 Fama, E. and MacBeth, J. "Long-Term Growth in a Short-Term Market," *Journal of Finance*, 29, June 1974, 857–85.

7 Ferson, W. "Expected Real Interest Rates and Consumption in Efficient Financial Markets: Theory and Tests," Ph.D. Dissertation, Graduate School of Business, Stanford University, 1982.

8 Friend, I. and Blume, M. "The Demand for Risky Assets," *American Economic Review*, 65, December 1975, 900–22.

9 Gibbons, M. and Ferson, W. "Testing Asset Pricing Models with Changing Expectations and an Unobservable Market Portfolio," *Journal of Financial Economics*, 14: 2, June 1985, 217–36.

10 Grauer, R. "Generalized Two Parameter Asset Pricing Models: Some Empirical Evidence," *Journal of Financial Economics*, 6, March 1978, 11–32.

11 Grossman, S. and Shiller, R. "Capital Asset Returns and Consumption," *Working Paper*, The Wharton School, University of Pennsylvania, 1980

12 Grossman, S. and Shiller, R. "The Determinants of Variability of Stock Market Prices," *American Economic Review*, 71, May 1981, 222–7.

13 Grossman, S. and Shiller, R. "Consumption Correlatedness and Risk Measurement in Economies with Non-Traded Assets and Heterogeneous Information," *Journal of Financial Economics*, 10, July 1982, 195–210.

14 Hakansson, N. "Optimal Investment and Consumption under Risk for a Class of Utility Functions," *Econometrica*, 38, September 1970, 587–607.

15 Hall, R. "Stochastic Implications of the Life Cycle Permanent Income Hypothesis: Theory and Empirical Evidence," *Journal of Political Economy*, 86, December 1978, 971–88.

16 Hall, R. "Intertemporal Substitution in Consumption," *Working Paper*, Department of Economics, Stanford University, 1981.

17 Hansen, L. "Large Sample Properties of Generalized Method of Moments Estimators," *Econometrica*, 50, July 1982, 1029–84.

18 Hansen, L., Richard, S. and Singleton, K. "Econometric Implications of the Intertemporal Capital Asset Pricing Model," *Working Paper*, Graduate School of Industrial Administration, Carnegie-Mellon University, 1981.

19 Hansen, L. and Singleton, K. "Stochastic Consumption, Risk Aversion, and the Temporal Behavior of Asset Returns," *Journal of Political Economy*, 91, April 1983, 249–65.

20 Hansen, L. and Singleton, K. "Generalized Instrumental Variables Estimation of Nonlinear Rational Expectations Models," *Econometrica*, 50, September 1982, 1269–86; corrections to the tables appear in *Econometrica*, 52, January 1984, 267–8.

21 Hausman, J. "Specification Tests in Econometrics," *Econometrica*, 46, November 1978, 1251–72.

22 Ibbotson, R. and Sinquefield, R. *Stocks, Bonds, Bills and Inflation: Historical Returns (1926–1978)* (Charlottesville, VA: The Financial Analysts Research Foundation, 1979).

23 Kraus, A. and Litzenberger, R. "Market Equilibrium in a Multiperiod State Preference Model with Logarithmic Utility," *Journal of Finance*, 30, December 1975, 1213–27.

24 Loistl, O. "The Erroneous Approximation of Expected Utility by Means of a Taylor's Series Expansion: Analytical and Computational Results," *American Economic Review*, 66, December 1976, 904–10.

25 Lucas, R., Jr "Asset Prices in an Exchange Economy," *Econometrica*, 46, November 1978, 1429–45.

26 Mehra, R. and Prescott, E. "A Test of the Intertemporal Asset Pricing Model," *Working Paper*, Graduate School of Business, Columbia University, 1982.

27 Merton, R. "Optimum Consumption and Portfolio Rules in a Continuous-Time Model," *Journal of Economic Theory*, 3, December 1971, 373–413.

28 Nordhaus, W. and Dulant, S. "The Structure of Social Risk," *Discussion Paper 648*, Cowles Foundation for Research in Economics, Yale University, 1982.

29 Pratt, J. "Risk Aversion in the Small and in the Large," *Econometrica*, 32, January 1964, 122–36.

30 Roll, R. "Evidence on the Growth Optimum Model," *Journal of Finance*, 28, June 1973, 551–66.

31 Rothschild, M. and Stiglitz, J. "Increasing Risk II: Its Economic Consequences," *Journal of Economic Theory*, 3, March 1971, 66–84.

32 Royden, H. *Real Analysis* (New York: Macmillan, 1968).

33 Rubinstein, M. "An Aggregation Theorem for Securities Markets," *Journal of Financial Economics*, 1, September 1974, 225–44.

34 Rubinstein, M. "The Valuation of Uncertain Income Streams and the Pricing of Options," *Bell Journal of Economics*, 7, Autumn 1976, 407–25.

35 Rubinstein, M. "The Strong Case for the Generalized Logarithmic Utility Model as the Premier Model of Financial Markets." In *Financial Decision-Making under Uncertainty*, eds H. Levy and M. Sarnat (New York: Academic Press, 1977).

36 Samuelson, P. "Lifetime Portfolio Selection by Dynamic Stochastic Programming," *Review of Economics and Statistics*, 51, August 1969, 239–46.

37 Serfling, R. *Approximation Theorems of Mathematical Statistics* (New York: Wiley, 1980).

38 Stambaugh, R. "On the Exclusion of Assets from Tests of the Two-Parameter Model: A Sensitivity Analysis," *Journal of Financial Economics*, 10, November 1982, 237–68.

39 Zehna, P. "Invariance of Maximum Likelihood Estimation," *Annals of Mathematical Statistics*, 37, December 1966, 744.

Chapter 9

Kose John

Background and Comments

Modern corporate finance theory explains much of the boilerplate in debt contracts as cost-efficient rules designed to control opportunistic behavior on the part of managers, who are assumed to have better information than lenders and who are tempted to act to transfer value from lenders to themselves or to their shareholders. For example, in the paper by Kose John and David Nachman managers are tempted to pay out cash to shareholders that really should be plowed back into the business. Payout restrictions in the debt contract may make both sides better off by supporting sensible investment decisions by the firm.

I wonder how effective boilerplate really is. As recent events in the leveraged buyout (LBO) business show, apparently well-protected lenders can be painfully undercut if managers decide on an abrupt change of course. Boilerplate can never cover all contingencies.

In practice managers voluntarily forbear from many kinds of opportunistic actions. They do so because the reputation for forbearance is valuable to them and their firms. Yet explaining how reputation is created and maintained is not easy. Reputation cannot be analyzed in one-period models. (If there is no "tomorrow," only "today," the models predict that any reputation will be run down immediately.)

John and Nachman were among the first to show formally how a concern for reputation would help align the interests of lenders and stockholders. In their model, firms with relatively good future investment opportunities expand real investment today in order to establish their reputation as "good" firms. This is a very interesting contrast to the acquisition of reputation in Douglas Diamond's paper in this volume (chapter 10).

Author's Introduction

What follows is a brief discussion of dynamic modeling of financial markets (under imperfect information) and reputation effects, in the context of my papers with Nachman. In these papers, originally part of John and Nachman (1984), we study how endogenously obtained reputation effects ameliorate incentive problems between borrowers and lenders. The underinvestment problem of risky debt (Myers, 1977; John and Kalay, 1982) is embedded in a multiperiod scenario where the firm *may* have to return to the debt market for future financing. Important differences from previous work include the following: (a) the debt market is modeled as a competitive (anonymous) capital market rather than a financial institution or a lender with monopoly powers; (b) firms may finance their future projects optimally from retained earnings and from additional borrowing; (c) lenders cannot commit themselves to take actions in the future that are not in their *ex post* interest, even when this would be beneficial *ex ante*. We show that reputation effects which arise endogenously in a "sequential equilibrium" of the game (our extension, in the same spirit, of the Kreps and Wilson (1982) concept to our continuum strategy set) lead to a partial resolution of the underinvestment problem. Reputation effects on private decisions (here, investment choices) by corporate insiders arise when they adjust their investment behavior to influence data (repayment history and extent of borrowing) that the capital market uses to learn about the *quality* of the firm's investment opportunities (which is private information to corporate insiders). Here the joint influence of adverse selection and moral hazard brings about the reputation effects reducing agency conflicts (see also John and Kalay, 1985; John, 1987).

Although the focus of this paper is on debt and the underinvestment problem, its framework can be used to study reputation effects in other settings. In my own related work, I have examined intertemporal patterns in dividend payouts, the value of reputation in investment banking, and stage-of-life-cycle patterns in payout policies, financing strategies, and restrictiveness of bond covenants of firms. Other applications include reputation effects in labor markets (Holmstrom, 1982) and corporate takeovers (Leach, 1988). Diamond (1989; this volume, chapter 10) gives an alternative analysis of reputation in debt markets where debt induces risk-shifting incentives and the firm has private information about the riskiness of its project menu; it is an excellent analysis of the horizon effects of the value of reputation and its evolution over time. In a similar model, Maksimovic and Titman (1989) study how financial policy affects incentives to maintain its reputation for producing a high quality product.

My own related work over the last five years has focused on financial and dividend policies in static and dynamic settings under asymmetric information between the corporate insiders and the market. In John and Williams (1985) we provide a motivation for firms (a) paying cash dividends despite the personal tax disadvantage and (b) raising equity and paying dividends in the same planning horizon. Ambarish, John, and Williams (1987) allowed multiple signals and examined the mix of signals chosen in the least cost ("efficient") signaling equilibrium as a function of firm technology. The model yields several testable implications including those for stock price behavior when dividend, investment, and new issue announcements are made by growth firms and mature firms. In John and Nachman (1986) we study the optimal dynamic financing strategies of firms under asymmetric information. The optimization over signaling costs (dividends and extent of outside financing are signals) yields "intertemporal smoothing of dividends" as part of optimal policy. In John (1987) and John and Ronen (forthcoming) we study optimal managerial and financing contracts for different patterns of temporal evolution of information structures (who knows what, when) of the managers, corporate insiders, and the market. The investment technology and the monitoring technology available determine the different patterns optimally generated. John and Mishra (1990) and John and Lang (1987) examine strategic insider trading around corporate announcement of dividend changes, dividend initiations, and capital expenditures. Using insider trading as one of the signals, the equilibrium yields a rich harvest of testable implications. The evidence we present seems to support the predictions of these models.

References

Ambarish, R., John, K. and Williams, J. (1987) "Efficient Signalling with Dividends and Investments," *Journal of Finance*, 42: 2, June, 321–43.

Diamond, D. (1989) "Reputation Acquisition in Debt Markets," *Journal of Political Economy*, 97: 4, 828–62.

Holmstrom, B. (1982) "Managerial Incentive Problems – A Dynamic Perspective." In *Essays in Honour of Lars Wahlbeck* (Helsinki: Swedish School of Economics).

John, K. (1987) "Risk-Shifting Incentives and Signalling Through Corporate Capital Structure," *Journal of Finance*, 42: 3, July, 623–41.

John, K. and Kalay, A. (1982) "Costly Contracting and Optimal Payout Constraints," *Journal of Finance*, 37, May, 457–70.

John, K. and Kalay, A. (1985) "Informational Content of Optimal Debt Contracts." In *Recent Advances in Corporate Finance*, eds E. I. Altman and M. G. Subrahmanyam (Homewood, IL: Irwin).

John, K. and Lang, L. (1987) "Insider Trading around Dividend Announcements: Theory and Evidence," *Working Paper*, New York University.

John, K. and Mishra, B. (1990) "Information Content of Insider Trading around Corporate Announcements: The Case of Capital Expenditures," *Journal of Finance*, 45: 3, 835–55.

John, K. and Nachman, D. (1984) "Reputation and Investment Incentives," *Working Paper*, New York University.

John, K. and Nachman, D. (1986) "On the Optimality of Intertemporal Smoothing of Dividends," *Working Paper*, New York University.

John, K. and Ronen, J. (forthcoming) "Evolution of Information Structures, Optimal Contracts and the Theory of the Firm," *Journal of Accounting, Auditing and Finance*.

John, K. and Williams, J. (1985) "Dividends, Dilutions and Taxes: A Signalling Equilibrium," *Journal of Finance*, 40: 4, September, 1053–70.

Kreps, D. M. and Wilson, R. (1982) "Sequential Equilibria," *Econometrica*, 50, July, 863–94.

Leach, C. (1988) "Reputation and Takeovers," *Working Paper*, University of Pennsylvania.

Maksimovic, V. and Titman, S. (1989) "Financial Policy and a Firm's Reputation for Product Quality," *Working Paper*, University of California at Los Angeles.

Myers, S. (1977) "Determinants of Corporate Borrowing," *Journal of Financial Economics*, 5, November, 147–75.

Bibliographical Listing

"Evolution of Information Structures, Optimal Contracts and the Theory of the Firm" (with Joshua Ronen), *Journal of Accounting, Auditing and Finance*, forthcoming.

"Information Content of Insider Trading around Corporate Announcements: The Case of Capital Expenditures" (with B. Mishra), *Journal of Finance*, 45: 3, 1990, 835–55.

"Managerial Incentives and Strategies in Production Decisions Under Uncertainty: A Game-Theoretic Approach" (with Ari Ovadia and Joshua Ronen). In *Advances in Mathematical Programming and Financial Planning*, vol. 2, ed. J. Guerard (Greenwich, CT: JAI Press, 1990).

"Risk-Shifting Incentives and Signalling Through Corporate Capital Structure," *Journal of Finance*, 42: 3, July 1987, 623–41.

"Efficient Signalling with Dividends and Investments" (with R. Ambarish and J. Williams), *Journal of Finance*, 42: 2, June 1987, 321–43.

"Dividends, Dilution and Taxes: A Signalling Equilibrium" (with Joseph Williams), *Journal of Finance*, 40: 4, September 1985, 1053–70.

"Informational Content of Optimal Debt Contracts," *Recent Advances in Corporate Finance*, eds Edward I. Altman and Marti G. Subrahmanyam (Homewood, IL: Irwin, 1985).

"Parametric Fixed Point Algorithms with Applications to Economic Policy Analysis," *Computers and Operations Research*, 11: 2, 1984, 157–78.

"Collective Fineness of Stock Prices and Efficiency of Financial Markets," *European Economic Review*, 23: 2, November 1983, 223–30.

Risky Debt, Investment Incentives, and Reputation in a Sequential Equilibrium

KOSE JOHN and DAVID C. NACHMAN

In this paper we study the agency relationship between corporate insiders and external claimholders in a dynamic setting. In particular, we examine the investment incentives of a firm with risky debt outstanding when (it is common knowledge that) the firm has to return to the debt market for future financing. A "reputation" effect which arises endogenously as a part of the equilibrium is shown to involve the curtailment of the underinvestment incentives of the levered firm. Although the focus of this paper is on the underinvestment problem, it is hoped that its framework will be useful for studying reputation in financial models of other phenomena in a multiperiod setting such as patterns of corporate dividend payments, ratings of corporate bonds, disciplining of managers by labor markets, strategies in the market for corporate control, and reputation capital in investment banking.[1]

The adverse incentive effects of risky debt on the investment policy of a levered firm in a one-period model are well known.[2] One of these incentive problems is that of underinvestment, that is, of passing up positive net present value projects. Jensen and Meckling [7] and Myers [19] have shown that a firm with risky debt outstanding will underinvest. Of course, with the proper pricing of bonds by a debt market which rationally anticipates the incentive effect, the insiders of the firm bear all the costs of their own distorted investment policy. Mechanisms which have been studied to resolve or ameliorate the problem include the role of debt covenants and optimal monitoring and auditing.[3]

Although it has been conjectured that a multiperiod horizon with repeated entry into the market will somehow ameliorate the incentive problems, such a situation has not been analyzed. We model the agency relationship of insiders and bondholders as a dynamic game with asymmetric information in a framework consistent with sequentially

Reproduced from *Journal of Finance*, 40: 3, July 1985, 863–78. Appendices A and B appeared in the original working paper but were not printed in the journal because of space constraints.

David C. Nachman is Professor of Finance at Georgia Institute of Technology.

We are grateful for helpful discussions with Avner Kalay, Roy Radner, and Chester Spatt. Our work was partially supported by a research grant from the Graduate School of Business Administration, New York University.

rational and competitive behavior. We establish the existence of a sequential equilibrium and examine its properties and the nature of the optimal strategies of insiders and bondholders. For the prescribed investment opportunity sets, it is shown that the concept of "reputation" can be endogenized (and related to the availability of good investment opportunity sets) in an equilibrium where the "reputable" firms optimally curtail their incentives to underinvest in response to anticipated (and realized) higher rating in the pricing of their bonds by the market. It should be emphasized that the bond market is given no monopoly or bargaining power at any point in time. Its favorable pricing of the bonds of the "reputable" firm is entirely consistent with rational expectations pricing in a competitive market. The equilibrium concept that we use is sequential equilibrium (see Kreps and Wilson [15]).

Our basic model consists of an agency relationship between the insiders of the firm and the outside claimants (here, debt holders). The investment decision is modeled as "private" action on the part of the insiders, that is, outside claimants would find it too costly to monitor the investment policy. In such an environment, it is well known that there will be underinvestment (that is, insiders will invest less than the full-information Pareto-optimal levels). It is easy to show that a simple repeating of this relationship a finite number of times does not ameliorate the agency costs of the relationship.[4] In other words, if the multiperiod relationship simply involves replication of otherwise independent situations with no intertemporal linkage, full agency costs of the one-period setting will persist. Asymmetry of information between insiders and the market about the evolution of the firm's investment opportunities introduces in a natural way the required intertemporal link. The insiders of different firms are assumed to know more about the quality of their investment opportunity set than do the market participants (including the bond market).

The equilibrium in the resulting dynamic game is interesting. In the equilibrium which obtains, the insiders' current optimal investment policy (and resulting ability to repay) is influenced by the quality of the investment opportunities that they will have in the future. Firms expecting better investment opportunities optimally curtail the degree of underinvestment, moving closer toward the Pareto-optimal levels and anticipating higher pricing of their bonds in the debt market. The bond market would find it rational to price the new issue of bonds conditional on what they know about the past investment policy of the firms. The equilibrium is such that the beliefs of the insiders and the market and their optimal actions (investment policy by insiders and pricing of bonds by the markets) are mutually rational and consistent. Since the market is modeled as competitive, it cannot impose any deliberate punishment to discipline past deviations from optimal investment. Thus the results are driven by sequential optimality and informational consistency of the equilibrium rather than by any monopoly power on the part of the bond market. In other words, the pricing by the market, given its information set (including the investment policies of firms), is such that issuing debt is a zero net present value transaction. The equilibrium is characterized by less underinvestment and agency costs than that in the equilibrium of the single-period game. In addition, firms with better investment and repayment records obtain gains to maintaining reputation and higher pricing of their bonds. The higher the quality differential between the low and high quality technologies, the better is the resolution of the underinvestment problem.

This research is closely related to several strands in the literature. The literature on reputation effects in repeated games with incomplete information is now fairly extensive (Wilson [29]). The endogenous incentive to maintain reputation has been studied in finitely repeated games (e.g. Kreps and Wilson [16], Kreps et al. [14], Milgrom and Roberts [17], Rogerson [21], and Sobel [24]) or in infinite horizon models (e.g. Dybvig and Spatt [1] and Holmstrom [6]). The paper which is probably the closest to our investigation is Spatt [25]. Spatt studies the bank–borrower relationship in a setting of asymmetry of information about the current realized return. This enables the borrower to misreport the realized cash flows and repay only if he chooses to. In the equilibrium obtained, firms with good draws voluntarily repay, demonstrating their future creditworthiness, while firms with low current returns default (despite adequate liquidity). However, Spatt [25] does not study the underinvestment problem and its resolution through reputation effects.[5]

John and Nachman [10] study the effect of endogenous reputation considerations on the investment incentives of firms when they are allowed to use the optimal mix of external and internal funds (retained earnings from the past) to finance their investments. With reduced dependence on external markets, the need to maintain reputation is less. The repayment behavior, as well as the new amount borrowed, conveys information to the bond market. The equilibrium here is also characterized by reputation effects on underinvestment incentives, leading to reduced agency costs. The rating of the bonds is higher with better investment (and repayment) record and lower with the amount borrowed. See Appendix B for details.

In the next section, we present the basic model of the agency relationship and the resulting incentives to underinvest. In section 2 we establish the existence of an equilibrium and its properties in the context of the multiperiod model where there is asymmetry of information about the quality of the future technology of the firm between the insiders and the bond market. Conclusions, extensions, and empirical implications are discussed in section 3.

1 The Basic Model

In this section we shall characterize the features of the basic model for the one-period (two-date) setting. We shall use it to illustrate the incentive effects of risky debt which we show will not be ameliorated in finite repetitions of the game. Augmented versions of the basic model presented here will be used as components of the dynamic game studied in section 2.

Since the characterizations of equilibria in these dynamic games are complex and tend to become intractable, one of the main considerations in the choice of the technology is its simplicity and tractability. In the related literature, researchers have used two-state discrete probability models (Spatt [25], Kreps and Wilson [16]), mainly motivated by simplicity. Our framework is also selected for its simplicity, while retaining the essential features which give rise to the agency costs of underinvestment: (a) discretionary investment choices on the part of corporate insiders and (b) the agency relationship between creditors and insiders (in general, external claimants and insiders who control investment choices). The salient features of the model (in its one-period version) are given below in the context of a representative firm. To a great extent, we have preserved and extended Myers' [19] original model of the underinvestment problem.

In this two-date ($t = 0$ and $t = 1$) model, insiders of each firm control the investment, financing and dividend decisions of the firm, and act in the interests of current shareholders.[6] The eventual states of the world to be realized at $t = 1$ are indexed by $s_1 \in [0, \bar{s}]$. A pair $\{R(s_1), I\}$ denotes investment opportunities available to the representative firm at $t = 1$. These technologies are the only asset the firm possesses, and they have the following interpretation. The insiders of the firm observe the realized state s_1 at $t = 1$ and choose to invest either zero or an amount I in the technology. If zero is invested, the investment opportunity lapses and the firm is worthless; if I is invested, $R(s_1)$ is the total realized cash flow. For convenience, let the states be ordered such that $R(s_1)$ is monotonically increasing in s_1 (figure 9.1). At $t = 0$, the insiders issue a pure discount bond with a payment F_1 promised at maturity $t = 1$. The usual priority rule applies such that $\min\{F_1, C(s_1)\}$ is pledged to the bondholders, where $C(s_1)$ is the total cash flow resulting from the investment decision. (Here, $C(s_1) = R(s_1)$ if investment I is made; otherwise, $C(s_1) = 0$.)

A crucial feature of the model is that the external claimants cannot write forcing contracts on the investment decision of the insiders. A sufficient condition for this to be true is that the outsiders would find it prohibitively costly to verify the realized $s_1 \in [0, \bar{s}]$ so that mutually verifiable state-contingent contracts cannot be written or enforced. Once the debt is issued, the insiders take the investment decisions which maximize the value of equity.

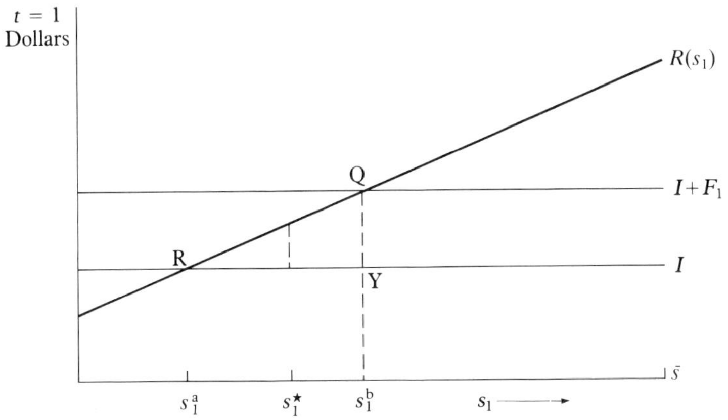

Figure 9.1 Agency costs of risky debt: s_1^b, cutoff investment state in a one-shot game; $s_1^\star$ cutoff investment state in sequential equilibrium.

The pricing of claims will be done, as is customary, by taking conditional expectations of the random cash flow with respect to the appropriate unique state price density function, say $q(s_1)$. For simplicity, we shall assume that $q(s_1)$ is a uniform density function over $[0, \bar{s}]$. This enables claim values to be related to areas in the figures used. All taxes (corporate and personal) are zero; similarly, the bankruptcy costs are assumed to be zero.

The insider's overall objective is to maximize the value accruing to equity holders from the available investment opportunity. If the firm were all-equity financed, their optimal investment rule would be simple: observe the realized state s_1 and invest I if $R(s_1) \geqslant I$; in other words, invest in nonnegative net present value projects. Define s_1^a such that $R(s_1^a) = I$. Then the all-equity investment rule can be equivalently stated as follows: invest I if $s_1 \geqslant s_1^a$.

The incentive of the insiders (who take investment decisions on behalf of the shareholders) changes when the firm has risky debt outstanding. At $t = 0$, the insiders have collected a price B_1 from the bondholders, promising to pay the minimum of F_1 or the available cash flow $C(s_1)(= 0$ or $R(s_1))$ at $t = 1$. After observing the realized state s_1 at $t = 1$, the insiders will invest I or zero depending on which results in a higher (net) return to equity holders. It is easy to see that they will invest I only in states s_1 such that $R(s_1) - I - F_1 \geqslant 0$. Define s_1^b such that $R(s_1^b) = I + F_1$. Then the investment is only undertaken in the levered firm for $s_1 \geqslant s_1^b$. Positive net present value projects are forgone in states $s_1 \in (s_1^a, s_1^b)$. The resulting loss in value is given by

$$A = \int_{s_1^a}^{s_1^b} [R(s_1) - I] q(s_1) \, ds_1 \tag{1}$$

where A is proportional to the area of triangle QRY in figure 9.1. This loss in value, called the agency cost of risky debt, results from the incentives of the insiders to underinvest in the technology when risky debt is outstanding.

1.1 Agency costs of equity

In the above discussion, we are only considering risky debt as the means of raising the required external funds for investment. This is done for ease of modeling and exposition. It should not leave the reader with the impression that the whole problem can be solved by issuing external equity as the means of raising funds. With external equity outstanding, the resulting fractional ownership of the technology by insiders gives rise to distortion in investment similar to the case of risky debt (John and Williams [11]).[7] Figure 9.2 shows this claim in the framework of this section. Here, the insiders have issued external equity equal to a fraction $1-\alpha$ of the value of the firm, with corresponding claim to $1-\alpha$ of all cash flows, $R(s_1)$ or zero. As in the case of risky debt, assume that outside claimants do not perfectly monitor the state s_1 realized or the amount I which is invested in the productive assets of the firm; that is, out of total investable funds I, the insiders have the discretionary choice of investing either the amount I (as before) or the amount zero and consuming the remainder as perquisites. In this setting, it is easy to show that insiders will invest only in states such that $-I+\alpha R(s_1) \geqslant 0$. Let s_1^e be defined as the value of s_1 such that $-I+\alpha R(s_1^e)=0$. Insiders will only invest when $s_1 \geqslant s_1^e$, leading to loss in value (agency costs of external equity) denoted by area LMN in figure 9.2.[8]

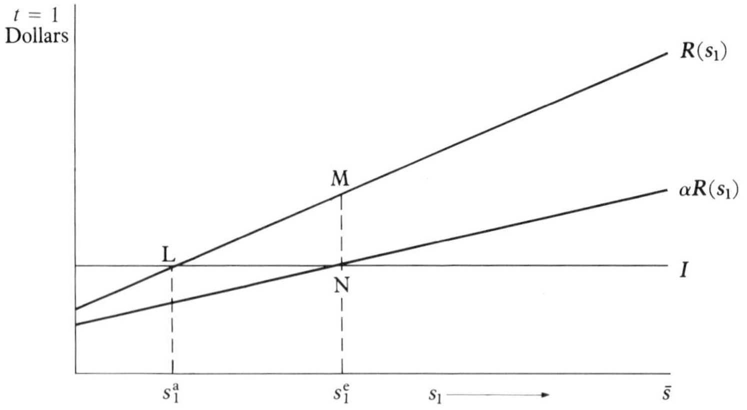

Figure 9.2 Agency cost of external equity: s_1^e, cutoff investment state in a one-shot game.

Even when the firm has issued an optimal mix of risky debt and external equity, there are distortions in investment policy and resulting agency costs. We expect reputation effects to be an important determinant of the tradeoff between debt and equity. Interesting issues of optimal capital structure in the presence of reputation effects will be pursued in future work (John and Nachman [10]). In this paper, however, our focus is limited to the existence and character of an endogenous reputation in the context of underinvestment incentives.

1.2 Finite repetitions

Several researchers (e.g. Fama [3], Jensen and Meckling [7], Myers [19]) suggest that the agency problems would be ameliorated in a multiperiod setting where the agency relationship is repeated. Although such an argument is intuitively appealing, its fine structure has to be examined closely. As noted earlier (see also note 4), if the repeated agency relationship involves simply replicating independent one-period relationships with no intertemporal linkage, there is no mitigation of agency costs in the repeated scenario. In other words, in each time period i the firm invests only in states $s_i \geqslant s_i^b$ and the market prices the bonds appropriately. The full agency costs of underinvestment persist in each time period.

One way out of this deadlock is to introduce some exogenous uncertainty as to the identity ("type") of one of the players (see Kreps and Wilson [16] and Milgrom and Roberts [17]). The resulting asymmetry of information gives rise to equilibria in which the component subgame strategies of players might take on a cooperative flavor. In the context of our model, an assymmetry of information between insiders of the representative firm and the bond market arises in a natural way. The agency problem of underinvestment exists because of insiders' private information. This private information could quite naturally include more precise probabilistic information about the future investment opportunities of the firm. Given this private information about their future technology, the insiders might find it optimal to curtail underinvestment, which results in better repayment behavior. In the equilibrium, the market, which prices future bond issues at favorable terms, would find their conjectured beliefs to be verified. In other words, we shall show that in the equilibrium of our model firms with better future investments underinvest less in the current period, resulting in a reduction in the agency costs. Interestingly, introduction of asymmetry of information about the future technologies results in a partial solution to the original agency problem.[9] The properties of the equilibrium will be examined in detail in section 2.

1.3 Role of debt covenants

It has been suggested that debt covenants could provide another solution to the underinvestment problem (John and Kalay [8,9], Myers [19], Smith and Warner [23]). The idea is that it would pay insiders to self-impose constraints on their own future investment decisions. Bondholders who price their claims incorporating the rationally anticipated effect of these constraints pass on to the insiders the value of any saving in agency costs. We have chosen not to include the debt covenants in our model for the following reasons. As John and Kalay [8] demonstrate based on the information structures of insiders and the market, there is an optimal set of such constraints. However, even under the best possible set of contracts, there are some residual agency costs of suboptimal investments. It is this residual problem that we are addressing. Clearly the only contract which is enforceable in our model (given that outsiders do not observe the realized state s_1) is to pledge to invest in all states. Such a contract involves large agency costs of overinvestment. Our mechanism can be viewed as a self-enforcing implicit contract. The details of the equilibrium will make this interpretation clearer.

In the next section we study the nature of the equilibrium and its properties in the context of a two-period three-date model.

2 The Equilibrium with Reputation

In this section we shall set up a simple version of the sequential game of two periods with incomplete information which underlies our arguments. We shall also study the equilibrium of the game which endogenizes a form of "reputation" in the debt markets. The mathematical construct, roughly interpretable as reputation, arises naturally as a part of the specification of the equilibrium of our sequential game.

As we discussed earlier, simply repeating the game (agency relationship) of the basic model twice does not change the behavior of either the firm (its investment policy) or the bond market (its beliefs used in pricing the bonds). In this section, we shall introduce some informational asymmetry between the firm's insiders and the bond market about the probability of obtaining a superior quality investment opportunity set. This in turn brings about a role for "reputation" which will account for intertemporal linkages between the first and the second play of the game. Moreover, such a linkage can produce strategic and market behavior that is different from that predicted from analysis of a sequence of independent games.

In a sequential game, a player's strategy is a function that assigns the action to be taken in each situation (that is, each possible information condition) in which he might make a choice. If the player has some private information (for example his technology), then the choices of actions may depend on this information. In this case, the other player can interpret his past actions as signals about what his private information might have been. More specifically, observers can use Bayes's rule to infer from the history of his observed actions, and from a supposition about what his strategy is, a conditional probability assessment about what it is that he knows. These inferences about the private information can be used to improve predictions of the player's future behavior. This type of argument brings about the role of reputation in sequential games.

We now describe the sequential game with the basic features of each component subgame described in section 1. The additional feature is that, in the second period, the technology which becomes available to firms is of two types – high quality and low quality. Private observation of the realized state in period 1 will give the insiders "better" probabilistic information about their future technology. This private information will influence their investment decisions in a manner which will be characterized by the equilibrium.

2.1 Some notation

The essential features of the model and the timing of the crucial events and decisions are as follows: the model is a three-date ($t=0, t=1$, and $t=2$) two-period model. $s_1 \in S_1 = [0, \bar{s}]$ indexes the state of the world to be realized at $t=1$. This realization is privately observed by insiders. $s_2 = (s_{21}, s_{22})$ where s_{21} is $+1$ or -1 as the firm's cash flow is of the high or low type and s_{22} is the state realized at $t=2$. Clearly, $s_2 \in S_{21} \times S_{22}$, where $S_{21} = \{+1, -1\}$, $S_{22} = [0, \bar{s}]$.

$R(s) = b + cs, s \in [0, \bar{s}]$ is the basic cash flow technology specifying the cash flows obtained if a fixed amount $I > 0$ is invested. More specifically, $R_1(s_1) = R(s_1)$ is the cash flow obtained at time $t=1$ if the realized state is s_1 and the firm invests. Similarly, $R_2(s_2) = R_2(s_{21}, s_{22}) = (1 + s_{21}\,\delta)R(s_{22})$ is the cash flow at time $t=2$ if the firm invests at $t=2$ when s_{21} is the quality of the technology, where $0 < \delta < 1$ is a given parameter. Assume that the firm has an initial capital Q at $t=0$, where $0 < Q < I$.

B_1 is the amount borrowed by the firm at $t=0$ to finance its investment at the end of the period $t=1$. The firm raises this amount by issuing a pure discount bond of promised payment F_1 to be paid at $t=1$ from the cash flows obtained from the technology. I_1 is the amount invested in period 1 technology at $t=1$ by the insiders after observing state s_1. The invested amount is equal to zero or I, where $I > 0$ is the amount required to undertake the firm's period 1 investment opportunities. D_1 is the dividend paid at $t=1$, a decision made contemporaneously with I_1. If $I_1=0$, then $D_1=B_1+Q$, and if $I_1=I$, then $D_1=B_1+Q-I+R(s_1)-F_1$; that is, all the uninvested funds are paid out as well as the cash flow from the technology after debt service. Here we are making a "no retention" assumption, that is, cash from the current period cannot be carried over to finance the investment in the next period. Clearly, retention (if allowed) would reduce the dependence of the firm on the external market. This "no retention" assumption is made purely for ease of exposition. The main results are not dependent on this assumption (see John and Nachman [10] and appendix B).

B_2 is the amount borrowed at $t=1$ (and is allowed to depend on s_1 but not s_2) by promising an amount F_2 due to be paid at $t=2$. I_2 is the amount invested at $t=2$ after the insiders have observed both s_1 and s_2. I_2 can be zero or I, with the same interpretation as that for I_1. The required investment for undertaking period 2 technology can be different than that for period 1 technology without changing anything. We assume equality for convenience. D_2 is the dividend paid at $t=2$ contemporaneously with I_2. If $I_2=0$, then $D_2=B_2$. If $I_2=I$, then $D_2=B_2-I+R_2(s_2)-F_2$. D_1 and D_2 are required to be nonnegative, since we do not allow financing with outside equity. Further, for period 1, we shall assume that if the firm invests they are able to repay the promised payment, that is, $R_1(s_1^a) > F_1$ (there exists $\beta < 1$, determined exogenously, such that $Q > \beta I$ implies that this condition holds). The risk-free interest rates are assumed to be zero in both time periods for convenience.

Distributional assumptions s_1 and s_{21} are distributed independently of s_{22}. s_1 and s_{22} are uniformly distributed over $[0,\bar{s}]$. $P_0(s_1)=1/\bar{s}$ and $P_0(s_{22})=1/\bar{s}$ denote the density functions of s_1 and s_{22} respectively. Moreover, $P_0(s_{21}=+1 \mid s_1)=s_1/\bar{s}$ gives the conditional probability of $s_{21}=+1$ given s_1. This information about the distributions of s_1 and s_2 is common knowledge.

2.2 *Strategies and beliefs*

The firm makes its borrowing decisions B_1 and B_2 and its investment decisions I_1 and I_2 (which in turn specify dividends D_1 and D_2). At $t=0$, the firm's insiders have the same information as the market. At $t=1$, the insiders privately observe the state realization s_1 which gives them some probabilistic information about their future investment opportunities. The investment decision that they take knowing s_1 and the resulting (observed) repayment behavior is used by the market to compute $P_1(s_{21}=+1 \mid I_1) \equiv P_1(+ \mid I_1)$, that is, the posterior probability of a superior technology based on their observed repayment behavior. Let

$P_1(+ \mid I)$ ($P_1(+ \mid 0)$) denote this posterior probability given that the firm does (does not) repay its period 1 loan. These posterior probabilities are used, in turn, to price the debt issued in period 2. More precisely, for the same amount B_2 borrowed, the promised payment F_2 would be set such that the market price of a promise F_2 would be B_2. We shall use $F_2(I)$ (and $F_2(0)$) to denote the promised payment for the repaying firm (and for the defaulting firm). It will be shown that $F_2(0) > F_2(I)$, which would give the firms incentive to invest and repay. This incentive was not there in the one-shot game or in the complete information, finite repetitions game discussed in section 1.

The following lemma will simplify the characterization of strategies.

Lemma Under the assumptions of our model, the optimal borrowing by the representative firm in each time period is the minimum required for the investment, that is, $B_1 = I - Q$ and $B_2 = I$.

The proof of the lemma is given in appendix A.

Given the lemma we can characterize the firm's strategies simply in terms of the investment decisions I_1 and I_2, and the market's strategies as simply setting the promised payments F_1 and F_2 based on their beliefs and given all available information in a sequentially rational competitive manner. The market values the bonds of the representative firm by taking the expected value of the promised payment conditional on their information. Intuitively, the bond market values the securities of the representative firm as if investors were risk neutral because the firm is negligible relative to aggregate output and uncorrelated with aggregate output. Such an argument for risk-neutral valuation has been made in several contexts in the literature. See Harris and Raviv ([5], pp. 37–9) for a recent example where this valuation mechanism is formally derived (see also Ross [22]).

Before formalizing the equilibrium, it would be useful to go through the underlying recursive argument. When the investment decision for period 2 is made at $t = 2$, the firm's insiders will know the values of s_{21} and s_{22}. Given a promised payment of F_2, they will invest I if and only if $R_2(s_2) - F_2 \geqslant I$. Define

$$s_{22}^{b}(s_{21}, F_2) = \frac{I + F_2 - (1 + s_{21}\,\delta)b}{(1 + s_{21}\,\delta)c}. \tag{2}$$

The optimal investment policy for period 2 is

$$\begin{aligned} I_2(s_2, F_2) &= I \qquad \text{if } s_{22} \geqslant s_{22}^{b}(s_{21}, F_2) \\ &= 0 \qquad \text{if } s_{22} < s_{22}^{b}(s_{21}, F_2). \end{aligned} \tag{3}$$

Now, let us consider the optimal investment decision by insiders at $t=1$ after they have privately observed the realization of s_1. They will undertake the investment $I_1=I$ or $I_1=0$ to maximize the expected value of the cash flows to the shareholders. Let us use $E[D(F_2)\mid s_1]$ to denote the expected value of $D\equiv D_1+D_2$ when the promised payment is F_2, given that state s_1 has occurred. Clearly, the valuation of the period 2 debt borrowed by the firm at $t=1$ is done by the market's incorporating its beliefs at $t=1$ about the probability of the firm's having a high quality investment opportunity. In the given environment of asymmetric information, the market uses the past actions of the firm (the investment and the resulting observable repayment behavior) to form these beliefs. Then the value of $E\{D[F_2(I_1)]\mid s_1\}$ is a function of the investment policy $I_1(=0$ or $I)$ of the firm at $t=1$. Now, for each $s_1\in[0,\bar{s}]$, the insiders will choose that investment which maximizes the value of dividends $E\{D[F_2(I_1)]\,|s_1\}$.

Let $I_1(s_1)$ be the optimal investment policy taken at $t=1$. Outsiders (the market) will use their anticipation of this investment policy to price the debt borrowed at $t=0$ (that is, for the amount B_1 borrowed at $t=0$, the promised payment F_1 will be set incorporating their anticipation of $I_1(s_1)$). Recall that in the one-period game or in the complete information repetition of the game, the optimal investment policy is $I_1(s_1)=0$ for $s_1<s_1^{\mathrm{b}}$ and $I_1(s_1)=I$ for $s_1\geqslant s_1^{\mathrm{b}}$. In the equilibrium of this paper, specified formally below, the optimal investment policy will be $I_1(s_1)=0$ for $s_1<s_1^{\star}$ and $I_1(s_1)=I$ for $s_1\geqslant s_1^{\star}$, where $s_1^{\star}<s_1^{\mathrm{b}}$. That is, the firm will optimally invest in more states than was the case in the one-period game in order to develop a reputation and obtain favorable pricing for future issues of debt. This pricing by the debt market will be based on beliefs which are verified in equilibrium.[10]

Equilibrium An equilibrium of the game described above is as follows: (a) a set of strategies $\sigma_1(I_1\mid s_1)$ and $\sigma_2(I_2\mid s_1,s_2)$ for the firm which define the probabilities of investing given the realized states and decisions, and (b) a set of beliefs P_1 by the market which give the posterior probabilities assigned by investors to s_{21}, given the observed investment-induced repayment behavior, such that the following hold.

1 Beliefs of investors are consistent with Bayes's rule, given strategies σ_1 and σ_2 and past decisions I_1 and I_2. That is

$$P_1(s_1,s_{21}\mid I_1)=\frac{\sigma_1(I_1\mid s_1)P_0(s_{21}\mid s_1)P_0(s_1)}{\int_{S_1}\sigma_1(I_1\mid s_1')P_0(s_1')\,\mathrm{d}s_1'}. \tag{4}$$

$P_1(s_{21}\mid I_1)$ is computed from (4) and used by the bond market in setting $F_2(I_1)$, the relevant promised payment for the borrowing B_2 at $t=1$.

2 Firm's insiders maximize the market value of dividends at each stage, given that $F_2(I_1)$ is determined using (4), and given future investment policies of the firm. That is, for any s_1, s_2, $x = \sigma_2(I_2 = I \mid s_1, s_2)$ is chosen to maximize

$$x\{-I + R_2(s_2) - \min[R_2(s_2), F_2]\} + (1-x)[0], \tag{5}$$

and for any $s_1 \in [0, \bar{s}]$, $y = \sigma_1(I_1 = I \mid s_1)$ is chosen to maximize

$$yE\{D[F_2(I)] \mid s_1\} + (1-y)E\{D[F_2(0)] \mid s_1\}, \tag{6}$$

where $F_2(I_1)$ is computed using market beliefs in (4) to yield a $(t = 1)$ value equal to B_2, and where $D(F_2)$ results from using the solution to equation (5).

The equilibrium concept used here is the sequential equilibrium (Kreps and Wilson [15]). As seen from the definition above, sequential equilibria invoke the criterion of sequential rationality: in each circumstance, a player chooses an action that is part of an optimal strategy for the remainder of the game, given the strategies and beliefs of the other players. Thus optimality is checked repeatedly as the game proceeds or, in reverse, the strategy is computed by backward recursion using dynamic programming. Players' beliefs are both rational and consistent in that they are calculated according to the assumed strategies of others and the resulting conditional probability satisfying Bayes's rule (whenever the conditioning event has nonzero probability according to the supposed strategies of the other players).[11]

Theorem There is a pure strategy sequential equilibrium in which

$$I_1(s_1) = \begin{cases} I & \text{for } s_1 \geqslant s_1^{\star} \\ 0 & \text{for } s_1 < s_1^{\star} \end{cases}$$

and $I_2(s_1, s_2)$ satisfies (3) and $P_1(s_1, s_{21} \mid I_1)$ satisfies (4).[12] Moreover, $s_1^{\star} < s_1^{b}$.

The proof of this theorem is given in appendix A.

The sequential equilibrium in the theorem has the following interpretation. Since the insiders have private information about their future investment technology at $t = 1$ through their observation of s_1, then their investment choices I_1 may depend on their private information. The market interprets investment decisions through the observed repayment behavior as signals about what the private information might have been. The market uses Bayes's rule to infer a conditional probability assessment of the insiders' private information from the insiders' repayment behavior and from a supposition of what the insiders' investment strategy might be. The firm's insiders, who are cognizant of the market's belief formation process, would find it optimal to curtail their underinvestment (that is, $s_1^\star < s_1^b$) in order to build a reputation which commands favorable pricing in the market. In equilibrium, the market perceptions are verified by the optimal investment strategies of the insiders. An implication of the theorem is that firms with better future investment opportunities invest larger amounts on their own discretion. An indirect implication could be that investment levels could act as signals of the quality of future investment opportunities. Consequently, investment announcements could elicit a price response by corporate bonds. Empirical evidence in support of these implications has been documented (see section 3).

The bond market prices the period 1 bonds incorporating the effects of reputation and improved investment incentives; that is, for any amount B_1 borrowed, F_1 will be computed such that $B_1 = F_1(\bar{s} - s_1^\star)/\bar{s}$ instead of the single-period version $B_1 = F_1(\bar{s} - s_1^b)/\bar{s}$ (see figure 9.1). This, in turn, implies that there is a saving in the first period 1 agency costs equal to

$$\frac{1}{\bar{s}} \int_{s_1^\star}^{s_1^b} [R_1(s_1) - I] \ \mathrm{d}s_1.$$

The basic model assumes that firms will have to return to *debt* markets for financing their future investments. Such an assumption is commonly made in models of reputation in debt markets. A realistic and important extension would be to consider equity financing as well, in particular equity retained from the cash flows from earlier projects. In appendix B, entitled "Equilibrium with Retention" we extend the basic model to allow firms to retain funds from one period and use them to finance investments in a subsequent period. Firms' dependence on external markets is thereby reduced. In this scenario the market not only observes the repayment behavior of firms but also the amount borrowed for subsequent investments. In the resulting equilibrium, it is shown that reputation effects curtail underinvestment incentives. For details, see appendix B.

The method of proof employed for the theorem suggests the following conjecture: $s_1^\star$ is decreasing in δ, that is, the larger is the difference between the superior and inferior technologies, the less is the underinvestment at $t = 1$. This is a comparative statics result with an appealing interpretation. As the difference between the qualities of the two technologies (parameterized by δ) increases, the stakes in building a reputation increase, providing better incentives for investment at $t = 1$. $s_1^b - s_1^\star$, which can be taken to be a measure of the reduction in underinvestment, increases with δ. There is some empirical evidence which is consistent with the implications of this conjecture (see section 3).

3 Empirical Implications and Extensions

The model, although simple, has some interesting empirical implications. Like the model due to Spatt [25], our model has implications regarding the impact of the credit history of the firm in determining the terms and the interest rate on debt, even in a competitive bond market. Some indirect implications for the investment behavior of firms with different degrees of "growth potential" are perhaps even more interesting. John and Kalay [8] analyze the optimal maximum dividend constraints (and their role to act as minimum investment restrictions) which are self-imposed by stockholders in covenants of risky debt. Kalay [12] has documented that firms invest on their own initiative more than they have to under these constraints. Moreover, the extent to which they do so is increasing in a measure of the "growth potential" of the firm's technology. Such a result is consistent with the implications of our theorem.

In the equilibrium of our paper, the firms with superior future investment opportunities will curtail current underinvestment without an explicit contract. The mechanism described by our equilibrium acts as an implicit contract for the more reputable firms. Consistent with this implication is the observation that the higher rated debt (bonds of reputable firms) carries less restrictive constraints in the bond covenants on maximal payouts or minimum investment than those of lower rated debt. Another indirect implication of our model is that the current investment decisions of firms lead to a revision of beliefs in the bond market and consequently elicit an appropriate response in bond prices. Mishra [18] documents empirical evidence of bond price reaction to announcements of investments (capital expenditure outlays) consistent with this implication of our model.

This research is at a very preliminary stage and the work can be extended in several directions. In this model, we had only risky debt as the allowed form of external financing. Although external equity has similar incentive problems with regard to underinvestment, it would be useful to model external equity as an alternate source of external financing and examine issues of optimal capital structure in a model with reputation. John and Nachman [10] study some aspects of reputation effects allowing internal as well as external financing. The analysis should also be extended to n periods $n \gg 2$. This would allow examination of the dynamics of building a reputation in the debt markets and possibly milking a reputation with respect to investment strategies. Extensions of such a framework might be useful for studying reputation in financial models of other phenomena in a dynamic setting. For example, stable patterns of corporate dividend payments seem to be inconsistent with one-period signaling models – a multiperiod model with reputation effects might provide some explanation. Similarly, issues of agency and managerial labor markets, market for corporate control, rating of corporate bonds, and reputation in investment banking might be better understood in a multiperiod setting with reputation effects.

Appendix A Proof of the theorem

It will be shown that creditors' beliefs about the strategies of insiders given in the theorem for a parameter $s_1^\star$ are consistent with the equilibrium optimal behavior of firms given this parameter. We shall show that there exists such a value of the parameter and that it is strictly less than s_1^{b}. Given the conjectures of outsiders about the strategy of insiders, that for some s_1^0

$$\sigma_1(I_1 \mid s_1) = \begin{cases} 0 & s_1 < s_1^0 \\ I & s_1 \geqslant s_1^0, \end{cases}$$

and given the distributional assumptions of section 2.1, the posterior probabilities $P_1(s_{21} \mid I_1)$ are computed from equation (4). For notational simplicity we shall denote $P_1(s_{21} = +1 \mid I_1 = I)$ as $P_1(+ \mid I)$ etc. The posterior probabilities are

$$P_1(+ \mid 0) = s_1^0/2\bar{s}, \qquad P_1(- \mid 0) = 1 - P_1(+ \mid 0)$$

and

$$P_1(+ \mid I) = (\bar{s} + s_1^0)/2\bar{s}, \qquad P_1(- \mid I) = 1 - P_1(+ \mid I).$$

For simplicity, we shall also assume that the parameters of the technology $R(s)$ satisfy $b = \alpha I$ for some $\alpha, 0 \leqslant \alpha \leqslant 1$, and that $R(\bar{s}) = \lambda I$ for some $\lambda > 1$.

For any promised payment F_2 and technology realization s_{21}, the firm's optimal period 2 investment policy I_2 will be given by equations (2) and (3). The bond market anticipates such future investment policy and uses its posterior beliefs about the future technology (conditioned on the current investment and repayment observation) in pricing the bonds and determining the appropriate promised payment F_2. If the firm invests zero and defaults in period 1, the bond market will determine the promised payment $F_2(0)$ according to posterior probabilities $P_1(+ \mid 0)$ and $P_1(- \mid 0)$. Denote $s_{22}^{\mathrm{b}}(s_{21}, F_2)$ (defined in equation (2)) for convenience as $s_+^{\mathrm{b}}(F_2)$ or $s_-^{\mathrm{b}}(F_2)$ depending on whether $s_{21} = +1$ or $s_{21} = -1$. Then, $F_2(0)$ will have to satisfy

$$F_2\left[\frac{\bar{s} - s_+^{\mathrm{b}}(F_2)}{\bar{s}}\, P_1(+ \mid 0) + \frac{\bar{s} - s_-^{\mathrm{b}}(F_2)}{\bar{s}}\, P_1(- \mid 0)\right] = I. \tag{A1}$$

Substituting for $P_1(+ \mid 0)$, $P_1(- \mid 0)$, $s_+^{\mathrm{b}}(F_2)$, and $s_-^{\mathrm{b}}(F_2)$ and simplifying, we have

$$F_2\left(1 - \frac{I + F_2 - bK_1}{\bar{s}cK_1}\right) = I \tag{A2}$$

where

$$K_1 = \frac{1-\delta^2}{1+(\delta/\bar{s})(\bar{s}-s_1^0)}. \tag{A3}$$

Similarly, if the firm invests I and repays the bondholders in period 1, the bond market will determine the promised payment $F_2(I)$ for period 2 debt using posterior probabilities $P_1(+\mid I)$ and $P_1(-\mid I)$. As before, simplifying we find that $F_2(I)$ satisfies

$$F_2\left(1-\frac{I+F_2-bK_2}{\bar{s}cK_2}\right)=I, \tag{A4}$$

where K_2 is given by

$$K_2 = \frac{1-\delta^2}{1-\delta s_1^0/\bar{s}}, \tag{A5}$$

and

$$\text{for } \delta < 1 \text{ we have } K_1 < K_2. \tag{A6}$$

It can be shown that (A2) and (A4) have two solutions. The lower of the two is the relevant value in each case. (It is better from the point of view of the insiders and the bondholders are indifferent.) We take the smaller root for each equation. With some algebra and analysis it can be shown that

$$F_2(0) > F_2(I). \tag{A7}$$

Now we focus on the optimal investment strategies of the insiders given the pricing of the bonds indicated above. For any state s_1, the insiders will choose optimal investment decision $I_1 = I$ or $I_1 = 0$ to maximize their expected cash flows. Their optimal decision will be based on their private information s_1, the probabilistic information $P(s_{21} = +1 \mid s_1) \equiv P(+\mid s_1)$ about future technology, and the anticipated pricing of bonds by the market (which determines $F_2(I)$ or $F_2(0)$ depending on their investment choice and subsequent repayment behavior).

If the firm does not invest in period 1 (and consequently does not repay its period 1 debt), the promised payment will be set at $F_2(0)$ in period 2. The resulting expected total cash flow will be

$$I + E\{D_2[F_2(0)] \mid s_1\} \tag{A8}$$

$$= I + \frac{1}{\bar{s}}\left\{[(1-\delta)b - F_2(0)]\bar{s} + \frac{[I+F_2(0)-(1-\delta)b]^2}{2c(1-\delta)} + \frac{c(1-\delta)\bar{s}^2}{2}\right\}P(-\mid s_1)$$

$$+ \frac{1}{\bar{s}}\left\{[(1+\delta)b - F_2(0)]\bar{s} + \frac{[I+F_2(0)-(1+\delta)b]^2}{2c(1+\delta)} + \frac{c(1+\delta)\bar{s}^2}{2}\right\}P(+\mid s_1). \tag{A9}$$

Similarly, if the firm invests I and repays its period 1 loan, the total expected cash flow will be

$$R(s_1) - F_1 + E\{D_2[F_2(I)] \mid s_1\}. \tag{A10}$$

Clearly, given s_1, the firm will invest in period 1 if and only if (A10) is greater than (A8). Let $\hat{s}_1$ be a point where (A8) and (A10) are equal – that is, for $s_1 \geqslant \hat{s}_1$, (A10) is larger than (A8), and for $s_1 < \hat{s}_1$, (A8) is larger. Equating (A9) and the corresponding version of (A10) and simplifying yields

$$\hat{s}_1\left(1+\frac{1}{c\bar{s}^2}\left\{\frac{[I+F_2(0)-(1-\delta)b]^2-[I+F_2(I)-(1-\delta)b]^2}{2c(1-\delta)}\right.\right.$$
$$\left.\left.-\frac{[I+F_2(0)-(1+\delta)b]^2-[I+F_2(I)-(1+\delta)b]^2}{2c(1+\delta)}\right\}\right)$$
$$=s_1^{\mathrm{b}}+\frac{1}{c\bar{s}}\left\{[F_2(I)-F_2(0)]\bar{s}+\frac{[1+F_2(0)-(1-\delta)b]^2-[I+F_2(I)-(1-\delta)b]^2}{2c(1-\delta)}\right\}. \tag{A11}$$

Denote by

$$g(K)=\frac{[I+F_2(0)-Kb]^2-[I+F_2(I)-Kb]^2}{2cK}.$$

Using (A3) and (A5), and (A2) and (A4), let

$$f(K_1,K_2)=[F_2(I)-F_2(0)]\bar{s}+\frac{[I+F_2(0)-(1-\delta)b]^2-[I+F_2(I)-(I-\delta)b]^2}{2c(1-\delta)}. \tag{A12}$$

Rewrite (A11) as

$$\hat{s}_1\left[1+\frac{g(1-\delta)-g(1+\delta)}{c\bar{s}^2}\right]=s_1^{\mathrm{b}}+\frac{f(K_1,K_2)}{c\bar{s}}. \tag{A13}$$

Now, $g'(K)<0$ for $K<1/\alpha+F_2(I)/b$. If

$$I+\delta<\frac{1}{\alpha}+\frac{F_2(I)}{b}, \tag{A14}$$

we have $g'(K)<0$ for $1-\delta\leqslant K\leqslant 1+\delta$.

Expression (A14) is equivalent to the condition that the debt is risky and therefore satisfied. This implies that the term on the left-hand side of (A13) is positive. Moreover, we have $f(K_1,K_2)<0$.

Suppose that

$$s_1^{\mathrm{b}}+\frac{f(K_1,K_2)}{s\bar{c}}<0. \tag{A15}$$

Then it is easy to see that (A10) is greater than (A8) at $s_1=0$ and it would be optimal for the firm to invest and repay in all states $s_1\in[0,\bar{s}]$. Therefore define

$$\hat{s}_1=\begin{cases}0 & \text{if (A15) holds}\\ \dfrac{s_1^{\mathrm{b}}+f(K_1,K_2)/\bar{s}c}{1+[g(1-\delta)-g(1+\delta)]/c\bar{s}^2} & \text{otherwise.}\end{cases} \tag{A16}$$

It can be seen that $\hat{s}_1$ is a function of the parameter s_1^0 that maps $[0, \bar{s}]$ continuously into $[0, s_1^b)$. By Brouwer's fixed point theorem, there exists a fixed point $s_1^\star$ which characterizes an equilibrium specified in the theorem where $s_1^\star < s_1^b$.

Appendix B Equilibrium with retention

The model in this appendix generalizes that given in the main text along some important dimensions. The firms are allowed to retain funds from one period and use them to finance investments in the subsequent period. The firms' dependence on external markets is thereby reduced. Moreover, in this scenario the market observes not only the repayment behavior of firms but also the amount borrowed (for subsequent investment) and incorporates this information to infer posterior probabilities about the realized state s_1 and therefore the future technology. It is also shown in this model that the underinvestment incentives are curtailed in an equilibrium with reputations.

The model

All the features of the model in section 2 are carried forward with two generalizations. The major new feature is the possibility for firms to retain funds from one period and use them for financing projects in the next. In other words only the required amount, if any, has to be borrowed in the debt market. With this possibility for raising different amounts in the debt market the amount of funds borrowed by firms could provide additional useful information for the bond market. In fact a major burden of the analysis of this section is to characterize the sequential equilibrium where the amount of funds borrowed as well as the observed repayment behavior at $t = 1$ are used in the formation of investor beliefs which will be verified by the optimal investment and borrowing decisions of insiders.

An additional (nonessential) change in the model is to allow the possibility of positive (risk-free) interest rates in each time period.

To reflect the above changes we specify some notation additional to that in section 2.1.

C_0 initial cash flow available at the beginning of period 1 (that is, at $t = 0$)
$C_0 + B_1 = I_1 + D_1$ cash balance equation for period 1
C_1 cash flow available from operations in period 1 after debt service

$$C_1 = \begin{cases} 0 & \text{if } I_1 = 0 \\ R_1(s_1) - F_1 & \text{if } I_1 = I \end{cases}$$

r_1 risk-free rate (exogenously given) of interest for period 1
$C_1 + B_1 = I_2 + D_2$ cash balance equation for period 2
r_2 risk-free rate (exogenously given) of interest for period 2

It is important to specify precisely the information that the debt market obtains from the amount of funds borrowed. To keep matters simple, we assume as before that creditors do not directly observe the firm's cash flows in period 1. An audit mechanism tells them only whether there is enough cash flow for the firm to repay its period 1 loan, that is, the creditors are told whether the firm's cash flow is zero or at least F_1. To make this reasonable we rule out partial repayments; that is, if the firm invests, its cash flow is at least F_1. This will be true if $b \geqslant F_1$.

The distributional assumptions of section 2.1 will also be made in this extended model.

Strategies and beliefs

Going through a recursive argument similar to that in the earlier section we obtain the optimal investment decision of the firm in period 2. The firm will know the realization of s_{21} and s_{22} before the investment is made. Given a promised payment of F_2 and assuming $C_1 + B_2 \geqslant I$, the firm will invest I if and only if

$$s_{22} \geqslant \frac{I(1+r_2) + F_2 - (1+s_{21}\ \delta)b}{(1+s_{21}\ \delta)c}. \tag{B1}$$

Define $\hat{s}_{22}(s_{21}, F_2)$ to be the term on the right-hand side of (B1). For $s_2 = (s_{21}, s_{22})$ let

$$I_2(s_2, F_2) = \begin{cases} I & \text{if } s_{22} \geqslant \hat{s}_{22}(s_{21}, F_2) \\ 0 & \text{if } s_{22} < \hat{s}_{22}(s_{21}, F_2). \end{cases} \tag{B2}$$

For notational convenience, set

$$\hat{s}_{22}^{+}(F_2) = \hat{s}_{22}(+1, F_2), \qquad \hat{s}_{22}^{-}(F_2) = \hat{s}_{22}(-1, F_2).$$

It is shown in theorem B1 that it is optimal for the firm always to borrow enough at the beginning of period 2 to make the required investment in period 2; that is, regardless of the value of $C_1, B_2 \geqslant I - C_1$. The bond market realizes this as well as the optimal investment policy specified in (B2).

We are now ready to specify the beliefs of the bond market. We still model the bond market as having a simple model of the firm's investment behavior in period 1. There is a parameter s_1^d such that the market believes that the firm will invest in period 1 if and only if $s_1 \geqslant s_1^d$, and hence they associate the event of investment and subsequent repayment of F_1, to be denoted D^c, with the event $\{s_1 \geqslant s_1^d\}$, and the event D (nonrepayment of F_1) with the event $\{s_1 < s_1^d\}$. The beliefs of the bond market play an integral part in the pricing of the firm's debt. At the end of period 1 the market observes whether or not the firm has paid F_1, and hence they infer whether or not $s_1 \geqslant s_1^d$ or $s_1 < s_1^d$. In addition, at the beginning of period 2 they observe the amount B_2 that the firm borrows. We make the following assumptions in specifying market beliefs.

1 When the firm borrows more (less) than is needed to raise I and this result can be inferred by the market, then the market assumes that the worst (best) possible state has occurred that is consistent with this inference.
2 The bond market, in equilibrium, will know the optimal borrowing policy of the firm. Rational expectations consistency requires that their beliefs are the probabilities conditional on this optimal policy.

Table 9.B1 Market beliefs

Range of B_2	*Period 1 repayment behavior*	*Inference*
$0 \leqslant B_2 < I$	D	$s_1 = s_1^d$
$B_2 = I$	D	$s_1 < s_1^d$
$I < B_2$	D	$s_1 = 0$
$B_2 = 0$	D^c	$s_1 \geqslant s_1^b \vee s_1^d$
$0 < B_2 \leqslant (s_1^b - s_1^d)^+ c$	D^c	$s_1 = s_1^b - B_2/c$
$(s_1^b - s_1^d)^+ c < B_2$	D^c	$s_1 = s_1^d$

State s_1^b is as defined in section 1. Denote by $P_1(s_{21} = +1 \mid D, B_2) \equiv P_+^d(D, B_2)$ the conditional probability of a superior technology given no investment (observed default) and borrowing amount B_2.

The above assumptions lead to the specifications given in table 9.B1. Given the inferences in table 9.B1, the specifications below follow from the probability calculus:[13]

$$P_+^d(D, B_2) = \begin{cases} P(s_{21} = +1 \mid s_1 = s_1^d) = \dfrac{s_1^d}{\bar{s}} & \text{for } 0 \leqslant B_2 < I \\[2ex] P(s_{21} = +1 \mid 0 \leqslant s_1 < s_1^d) = \dfrac{s_1^d}{2\bar{s}} & \text{for } B_2 = I \\[2ex] P(s_{21} = +1 \mid s_1 = 0) = 0 & \text{for } B_2 > I \end{cases} \tag{B3}$$

$$P_+^d(D^c, B_2) = \begin{cases} P(s_{21} = +1 \mid s_1 \geqslant s_1^b \vee s_1^d) = \dfrac{\bar{s} + s_1^b \vee s_1^d}{2\bar{s}} & \text{for } B_2 = 0 \\[2ex] P\left(s_{21} = +1 \mid s_1 = s_1^b - \dfrac{B_2}{c}\right) = \dfrac{s_1^b - B_2/c}{\bar{s}} & \text{for } 0 < B_2 \leqslant (s_1^b - s_1^d)^+ c \\[2ex] P(s_{21} = +1 \mid s_1 = s_1^d) = \dfrac{s_1^d}{\bar{s}} & \text{for } (s_1^b - s_1^d)^+ c < B_2. \end{cases} \tag{B4}$$

Creditors use these conditional probabilities in determining the appropriate promised payment for the amount borrowed by the firm. Let $F_2(D, B_2)$ denote this payment. It follows from (B1) and (B2) that the firm will make this payment at the end of period 2 if and only if it invests in period 2, and hence $F_2(D, B_2)$ must satisfy the equation

$$B_2 = \frac{F_2(D, B_2)}{1 + r_2} \big(P\{s_{22} \geqslant \hat{s}_{22}^+[F_2(D, B_2)]\} P_+^d(D, B_2)$$
$$+ P\{s_{22} \geqslant \hat{s}_{22}^-[F_2(D, B_2)]\}[1 - P_+^d(D, B_2)]\big). \tag{B5}$$

After simplifying,

$$B_2 = \frac{F_2(D, B_2)}{1 + r_2} \left[1 - \frac{I(1 + r_2) + F_2(D, B_2) - bK(D, B_2)}{\bar{s}cK(D, B_2)} \right] \tag{B6}$$

where

$$K(D, B_2) = \frac{1 - \delta^2}{1 + \delta[1 - 2P_+^{\rm d}(D, B_2)]}$$

as in appendix A, equations (A3) and (A5). Clearly

$$1 - \delta \leqslant K(D, B_2) \leqslant 1 + \delta,$$

with equality holding on the left (right) only if $P_+^{\rm d}(D, B_2) = 0$ (1). Arguments similar to that in appendix A can be used to determine the value of $F_2(D, B_2)$ and $F_2(D^{\rm c}, B_2)$.

The equilibrium

The characterization of the equilibrium is as in section 2.2. Define

$$\hat{s}_1^{\rm b} = \frac{I(1 + r_1) + F_1 - b}{c}. \tag{B7}$$

Theorem B1 There is a pure-strategy sequential equilibrium characterized by the parameter value $s_1^{\rm d\star}$ such that

$$I_1(s_1) = \begin{cases} I & \text{for } s_1 \geqslant s_1^{\rm d\star} \\ 0 & \text{for } s_1 < s_1^{\rm d\star} \end{cases}$$

$$B_2(s_1) = \begin{cases} I & \text{for } s_1 < s_1^{\rm d\star} \\ [I - R(s_1) - F_1]^+ & \text{for } s_1 \geqslant s_1^{\rm d\star} \end{cases}$$

and $I_2(s_1, s_2)$ satisfies (B1) and (B2) and the beliefs of the bond market satisfy (B3) and (B4). Moreover, $s_1^{\rm d\star} < \hat{s}_1^{\rm b}$.

In this equilibrium, although the reliance on debt markets has been reduced, firms optimally curtail their underinvestment incentives. Firms invest more than is short term optimal to build a reputation and elicit favorable pricing for future issues of bonds. It is our conjecture that when $r_1 = r_2 = 0$, such that $s_1^{\rm b} = \hat{s}_1^{\rm b}$ and the equilibria in section 2.2 can be compared with the equilibrium in theorem B1, we shall have $s_1^{\rm d\star} > s_1^\star$; that is, with less reliance on the debt market in the future, the improvement in investment incentives is less.

Proof of Theorem B1

The intent here is to sketch some of the crucial steps in the proof of theorem B1. The lengthy and tedious parts that are left out are identified. Those interested in the omitted parts are referred to the complete proof that is available from the authors on request.

Suppose that C_1 is such that $C_1 + B_2 < I$. For $B_2^! = (I - C_1)^+$,

$$C_1 + B_2 < I \leqslant C_1 + B_2^! \leqslant C_1 + B_2^! + E\left[-I_2(F_2^!) + \frac{R_2(F_2^!)}{1+r_2} \middle| s_1 \right], \tag{B8}$$

where $F_2^!$ is any promised payment associated with borrowing of $B_2^!$, $I_2(F_2^!)$ is given in (B2), and $R_2(F_2^!)(s_2) = R_2(s_2) - F_2^!$. The conditional expectation on the right in (B8) is nonnegative because of the discretionary nature of investment spelled out in (B1). Hence it is in the firm's interest to at least raise I even if all of I (or more) must be borrowed.

A major portion of the remainder of the proof involves modeling the firm's period 1 investment decision by a parameter s_1^d as indicated earlier and verifying that the corresponding beliefs given in table 9.B1 result in the optimal borrowing policy B_2^d given s_1^d specified as follows:

$$B_2^d(s_1) = \begin{cases} I & \text{for all } s_1 \text{ such that the firm does not invest in period 1} \\ [I - R(s_1) + F_1]^+ & \text{for all } s_1 \text{ such that the firm does invest in period 1.} \end{cases}$$

The difficulty here is proving that it is never in the firm's interest to borrow more than is needed given its investment policies for period 1 and period 2. This is done in lengthy detail in the complete proof, and establishes the sequential rationality of the assumed form of beliefs and strategies.

The corresponding constrained optimal period 1 investment policy will depend on s_1^d. It remains to show that there is an s_1^d such that the firm invests in period 1 if and only if $s_1 \geqslant s_1^d$. Comparing total expected discounted cash flows from investing and not investing when that decision must be made in period 1 yields that the crucial cutoff level of the state is

$$h(s_1^d, s_1) = \frac{\hat{s}_1^b + y(s_1)/c - \{\bar{s}(F_2(D, I) - F_2(D^c, [I - R(s_1) + F_1]^+)) + g(1-\delta, s_1)\}/\bar{s}c(1+r_2)}{1 + [g(1+\delta, s_1) - g(1-\delta, s_1)]/\bar{s}^2 c(1+r_2)}, \tag{B9}$$

where $y(s_1) = I$ if $s_1 \geqslant s_1^b$, and $y(s_1) = R(s_1) - F_1$ if $s_1 < s_1^b$. This expression is similar to (A13) in appendix A and serves the same purpose here. Note, however, that it is not possible to separate out s_1^d in (B9) to make a straightforward fixed point argument. This is a result of the complicated nature of the borrowing strategy and market beliefs when cash flow can be retained. The remainder of this sketch is devoted to the more complicated fixed point argument required by (B9).

The function g in (B9) is given by

$$g(K, s_1) = \frac{[I(1+r_2) + F_2(D^c, [I - R(s_1) + F_1]^+) - Kb]^2 - [I(1+r_2) + F_2(D, I) - Kb]^2}{2cK},$$

and is like the negative of the function g after (A11). It is easy to check that

$\partial g / \partial K > 0$ as long as $1 + \delta \leqslant \alpha^{-1}$, which we have assumed. It follows that the denominator of h is at least unity and hence that the firm will invest in period 1, given s_1^d, if and only if $s_1 \geqslant h(s_1^d, s_1)$. It also follows from a tedious evaluation of h for $s_1^d \leqslant \hat{s}_1^b$ that

$$s_1^d \leqslant \hat{s}_1^b \text{ and } s_1 \geqslant \hat{s}_1^b \Rightarrow \hat{s}_1^b > h(s_1^d, s_1). \tag{B10}$$

Let

$$h^+(s_1^d, s_1) = \max[0, h(s_1^d, s_1)] \tag{B11}$$

$$h^b(s_1^d, s_1) = \begin{cases} h^+(s_1^d, s_1) & 0 \leqslant s_1^d \leqslant \hat{s}_1^b, \quad 0 \leqslant s_1 \leqslant \bar{s} & \text{(B12)} \\ h^+(\hat{s}_1^b, s_1) & \hat{s}_1^b < s_1^d \leqslant \bar{s}, \quad 0 \leqslant s_1 \leqslant \bar{s} & \text{(B13)} \end{cases}$$

$$h^\star(s_1^d, s_1) = \min[\bar{s}, h^b(s_1^d, s_1)] \qquad 0 \leqslant s_1^d,\ s_1 \leqslant \bar{s}. \tag{B14}$$

Then $h^\star$: $[0, \bar{s}]^2 \to [0, \bar{s}]$, and h^+, h^b, and $h^\star$ are continuous in (s_1^d, s_1) if h is.

An examination of (B4) indicates that $P_+^d(D^c, B_2)$ is jointly continuous in s_1^d and B_2 for all $B_2 > 0$. Thus $F_2(D^c, [I - R(s_1) + F_1]^+)$ is continuous in $(s_1^d, s_1) \in [0, \bar{s}]^2$ since $F_2(D^c, B_2)$ is continuous at $B_2 = 0$ and $F_2(D^c, 0) = 0$ for all s_1^d. By (B3), $P_+^d(D, I)$ is continuous in s_1^d and hence so is $F_2(D, I)$. Since the function y is continuous (by definition of s_1^b), it follows that g is continuous on $[1 - \delta, 1 + \delta] \times [0, \bar{s}]$ and hence h is continuous on $[0, \bar{s}]^2$. Define the map T by

$$T(s_1^d, s_1) = (h^\star(s_1^d, s_1), s_1^d). \tag{B15}$$

It follows from (B11)–(B14) that T: $[0, \bar{s}]^2 \to [0, \bar{s}]^2$ and that T is continuous since each coordinate map is. By Brouwer's theorem, T has a fixed point $(s_1^{d\star}, s_1^\star)$. It follows by the definition of T in (B15) that $s_1^\star = s_1^{d\star} = h^\star(s_1^{d\star}, s_1^{d\star})$. It also follows from (B11)–(B14) and (B10) that

$$h^b(s_1^{d\star}, s_1^{d\star}) = h^+(\hat{s}_1^b, s_1^{d\star}) = h(\hat{s}_1^b, s_1^{d\star}) < \hat{s}_1^b. \tag{B16}$$

Hence we must have

$$s_1^{d\star} < \hat{s}_1^b, \tag{B17}$$

for if not then $h^b(s_1^{d\star}, s_1^{d\star}) \geqslant h^\star(s_1^{d\star}, s_1^{d\star}) = s_1^{d\star} \geqslant \hat{s}_1^b$, contradicting (B16). Finally, the fixed point $s_1^{d\star}$ is the desired point if it is an equilibrium, that is, if it satisfies

$$s_1 < s_1^{d\star} \Rightarrow s_1 < h(s_1^{d\star}, s_1) \tag{B18}$$

and

$$s_1 \geqslant s_1^{d\star} \Rightarrow s_1 \geqslant h(s_1^{d\star}, s_1). \tag{B19}$$

These conditions follow from the fact that the function $s_1 - h^+(s_1^{d\star}, s_1)$ is strictly increasing in s_1, which is established by a tedious and lengthy argument relying on the properties of the promised payments described in (B5) and (B6) and the function $K(D, B_2)$ given after (B6). The existence of $s_1^{d\star}$ with the properties (B17)–(B19) is what was to be proved. ■

Notes

1 Models of reputation effects in repeated games with asymmetric information have been very useful in economics for studying issues such as predatory pricing below cost and incentives for high product quality. For an introduction and discussion of reputations in finitely repeated games, see the first three papers in *Journal of Economic Theory*, 27, August 1982, 245–312.

2 The distortion in the investment incentives of a firm when there are external outstanding claims (equity or debt claims) has been the subject of many studies (Green [4], Jensen and Meckling [7], John and Kalay [8, 9], John and Williams [11], and Myers [19] are a few examples). When some aspect of investment (for example its level, its riskiness, the split between risky and safe investments) is a discretionary private decision by the insiders of the firm which is not observed or perfectly monitored by outside claimants, it has been shown that insiders have incentives to deviate from investment policies which maximize the total value of the firm.

3 John and Kalay [8] examine the role of debt covenants where stockholders precommit minimum future investment levels by self-imposing optimally specified payout constraints. Bondholders price the debt incorporating the effects of these constraints on the *ex post* investment choices of the insiders, thereby passing on the "saved" agency costs to the insiders. Other related solutions have been for the insiders to undertake optimal levels of monitoring and auditing so as to minimize the deviation of their *ex post* actions from total-value-maximizing levels.

4 This is consistent with the results of recent literature on finitely repeated versions of the prisoner's dilemma (Kreps et al. [14]) and Selten's chain store paradox (Kreps and Wilson [16] and Milgrom and Roberts [17]). The intuition is that in the last game the insiders will underinvest since their incentives are no different from those in a one-shot game. Then a process of backward induction repeats the same strategies for the insiders as being optimal with appropriate pricing by the market. Thus, with no intertemporal linkage, the Nash equilibrium of the overall game involves the same strategies in each of the component games as in a one-shot game. Clearly, the full agency costs persist.

5 Adverse selection and moral hazard issues in credit markets have been explored extensively (e.g. Stiglitz and Weiss [26, 27]). Eaton and Gersovitz [2] examine credit reputation in international borrowing, but exogenously assume that those who default are indefinitely denied credit.

6 For simplicity, no distinction is made between inside equity and outside equity. However, as argued in section 1, outside equity induces underinvestment incentives similar to that of risky debt. See also note 8.

7 Jensen and Meckling [7] also model agency costs of equity. Their argument is related, but the focus is not on underinvestment. Their insiders consume perquisites from the realized value of the firm which is private information. Myers and Majluf [20] also model costs associated with external equity in an environment of asymmetry of information about the realized value of the new and old assets of the firm. They show that firms' insiders might choose to underinvest (pass up positive net present value projects) rather than issue external equity to finance them.

8 This is simply to show that the problems of underinvestment are general to external claims, risky debt, or external equity. More importantly, by comparing figures 9.1 and 9.2 the astute reader can see that the partial resolution of the underinvestment problem in the equilibrium of this paper can be made to apply to the case of external equity as well as that of risky debt. However, for expositional ease, we shall explicitly model only risky debt.

9 Another way of viewing this feature of our model is that it seems to integrate the paradigms of agency and signaling (see John and Williams [11] for another example). First we have a model of agency resulting from investment's being a "private" action. When we introduce additional asymmetry of information about the technology, the optimal strategy of insiders involves deviating from agency levels of investment because investment (and the observable repayment behavior) acts as a credible signaling device in equilibrium. In other words, investment also plays the role of a signaling mechanism. This, in turn, has a favorable effect on their underinvestment incentives. Thus, when we have asymmetry of information about both the private action of insiders and the quality of the technology, the underinvestment incentives resulting from the first effect (agency effect) are partially offset by the second effect (signaling effect).

10 We can specify the exact relationship among the beliefs of the market and strategies of the firm's insiders such that each is rational, given the other. Such a relationship is characterized by the equilibrium of this paper which is a sequential equilibrium in the sense of Kreps and Wilson [15].

11 When the conditioning events have zero probability according to the strategies of other players the consistency requirement is more technical (Kreps and Wilson [15]). This becomes crucial in the model due to John and Nachman [10] and is discussed further there. No serious consistency problems arise in the model in this paper.

12 The equilibrium described here is interesting and natural from a finance perspective, but there may be other equilibria. In particular we have not studied mixed strategy equilibria in general nor have we been able to prove uniqueness in the pure strategy case. The multiplicity of (even sequential) equilibria is a common difficulty in games of this type. Approaches to this problem have been suggested by Kreps [13] (and references therein) in the context of signaling games and Dybvig and Spatt [1] in the context of an infinite horizon model of product quality.

13 These specifications are also consistent in the same spirit as the consistency requirement in Kreps and Wilson [15], which is specified only for finite action, finite state games. A proof of this claim is available from the authors upon request.

References

1 Dybvig, P. H. and Spatt, C. S. "Does it Pay to Maintain a Reputation? Consumer Information and Product Quality," Technical Report 32, Financial Research Center, Princeton University, May 1980.

2 Eaton, J. and Gersovitz, M. "Debt with Potential Repudiation: Theoretical and Empirical Analysis," *Review of Economic Studies*, 48, March 1981, 289–309.

3 Fama, E. F. "Agency Problems and the Theory of the Firm," *Journal of Political Economy*, April 1980, 288–307.

4 Green, R. C. "Investment Incentives, Debt and Warrants," *Journal of Financial Economics*, 13, March 1984, 115–36.

5 Harris, M. and Raviv, A. "A Sequential Signalling Model of Convertible Debt Call Policy," *Working Paper*, Northwestern University, July 1983.

6 Holmstrom, B. "Managerial Incentive Problems – A Dynamic Perspective." In *Essays in Honour of Lars Wahlbeck* (Helsinki: Swedish School of Economics, 1982).

7 Jensen, M. and Meckling, W. "Theory of the Firm: Managerial Behavior, Agency Costs and Ownership Structure," *Journal of Financial Economics*, 3, October 1976, 305–60.

8 John, K. and Kalay, A. "Costly Contracting and Optimal Payout Constraints," *Journal of Finance*, 37, May 1982, 457–70.
9 John, K. and Kalay, A. "Signalling Via Optimal Contracts," *Working Paper*, New York University, August 1982.
10 John, K. and Nachman, D. C. "Reputation and Investment Incentives," *Working Paper*, New York University, November 1984.
11 John, K. and Williams, J. "Financial Signalling with Agency Costs," *Working Paper*, New York University, November 1982.
12 Kalay, A. "Towards a Theory of Corporate Dividend Policy," *Working Paper*, New York University, November 1979.
13 Kreps, D. M. "Signalling Games and Stable Equilibria," Research Paper 758, Stanford University, July 1984.
14 Kreps, D. M., Milgrom, P., Roberts, J. and Wilson, R. "Rational Cooperation in the Finitely Repeated Prisoner's Dilemma," *Journal of Economic Theory*, 27, August 1982, 245–52.
15 Kreps, D. M. and Wilson, R. "Sequential Equilibria," *Econometrica*, 50, July 1982, 863–94.
16 Kreps, D. M. and Wilson, R. "Reputation and Imperfect Information," *Journal of Economic Theory*, 27, August 1982, 253–79.
17 Milgrom, P. and Roberts, J. "Predation, Reputation and Entry Deterrence," *Journal of Economic Theory*, 27, August 1982, 280–312.
18 Mishra, B. "Informational Asymmetry in Finance: Three Related Essays," Unpublished Dissertation, New York University, December 1984.
19 Myers, S. "Determinants of Corporate Borrowing," *Journal of Financial Economics*, 5, November 1977, 147–75.
20 Myers, S. and Majluf, N. "Corporate Finance and Investment Decisions When Firms Have Information that Investors Do Not Have," *Journal of Financial Economics*, 13, June 1984, 187–221.
21 Rogerson, W. P. "The Role of Reputation in a Repeated Agency Problem Involving Information Transmission," IMSSS Technical Report 377, Stanford University, May 1982.
22 Ross, S. "A Simple Approach to the Valuation of Risky Streams," *Journal of Business*, 51, July 1978, 453–76.
23 Smith, C. and Warner, J. "On Financial Contracting: An Analysis of Bond Covenants," *Journal of Financial Economics*, 7, June 1979, 117–61.
24 Sobel J. "A Theory of Credibility," Technical Report 82-33, University of California at San Diego, September 1982.
25 Spatt, C. S. "Credit Reputation Equilibrium and the Theory of Credit Markets," *Working Paper*, Carnegie-Mellon University, May 1983.
26 Stiglitz, J. E. and Weiss, A. "Credit Rationing in Markets with Imperfect Information," *American Economic Review*, 71, June 1981, 393–411.
27 Stiglitz, J. E. and Weiss, A. "Incentive Effects of Terminations," *American Economic Review*, 73, December 1983, 912–27.
28 Wilson, R. "Reputation in Games and Markets," IMSSS Technical Report 434, Stanford University, November 1983.

Chapter 10

Douglas W. Diamond

Background and Comments

Corporate managers obviously know more than outsiders about their firms' operations and prospects. A temptation to act opportunistically naturally follows. A manager acting on behalf of shareholders may take advantage of lenders by shifting to higher risk assets, for example.

These temptations are presumably less for a going concern than in a one-shot transaction. A reputation for not undercutting the bank is a valuable asset if your firm will be back next year asking for another loan.

The problem is to understand how the reputational assets are created in the first place. A concern for reputation may reflect personal ethics and social standards. However, it may also arise endogenously from the economic system. That is how it works in Douglas Diamond's paper and also in the preceding paper by Kose John and David Nachman (chapter 9).

Diamond's model has an especially interesting twist. He suggests that a "young" firm does not really care about reputation at first: it takes advantage of lenders by shifting their money to risky investments. But if it is lucky and the risky projects pay off, lenders begin to treat it as a "good" firm and favor it with lower interest rates. (If the risky projects fail, the young firm defaults and is out of the game.) Eventually, if the firm survives, its *undeserved* reputation for being a "good" firm becomes too valuable to risk. The firm is born again and reforms its behavior.

It is like the case of a reckless driver who breaks the speed limit every day but by chance goes for 10 years without receiving a ticket and is awarded a "safe driver discount" on auto insurance. If the discount is large enough, this person may become a careful driver rather than risk losing it.

Author's Introduction

In my paper I examine how reputation effects (the fear of loss of one's credit rating) lead to cross-sectional differences in incentive problems with debt, and study the process by which a young firm can acquire a reputation with sufficient value to provide beneficial incentives. The motivation for this line of research is to identify the types of firms for which the incentive effects of high leverage are not likely to be severe, and to contrast their financing choices with those made by firms facing more severe incentive problems. The intent is to understand the choice of the type of debt financing selected by various borrowers. The recent movement to increased use of debt financing and management control of equity due to leveraged buyouts suggests important applications of this broadening of financial structure theory beyond the traditional study of debt versus equity. More recent work of mine explores related models of the choice of form of debt financing by firms with various credit ratings.

Diamond (1989a) examines the determinants of which firms choose to borrow from banks that can monitor their actions. The interaction between bank monitoring and reputation implies that bank borrowers have "middle market" credit ratings: there is a minimum credit rating needed to receive a bank loan, but with a sufficiently high rating firms choose instead to use directly placed commercial paper that does not involve the monitoring. This paper also develops a theory to aggregate fluctuations in the quantity of bank loans relative to the quantity of new commercial paper issues.

Diamond (1989b) analyzes debt maturity structure. Borrowers need a sufficiently good credit rating to find short-term debt desirable. The optimal maturity structure trades off high quality borrowers' preference for short maturity, because they possess private information that leads them to expect their credit ratings to improve, versus liquidity risk. Liquidity risk is the risk that a borrower will lose control rents in a default workout or liquidation. Lenders choose *ex post* value maximizing debt workouts, but these differ from the *ex ante* optimum if an inappropriate maturity structure is selected. This notion of liquidity risk is distinct from that in Diamond and Dybvig (1983), which results from lenders not coordinating their actions, but the two notions of liquidity risk are compatible.

References

Diamond, D. W. (1989a) "Monitoring and Reputation: The Choice Between Bank Loans and Directly Placed Debt," presented at Garn Institute of Finance Symposium, Snowbird, UT, August 1988; *Working Paper*, University of Chicago, January.

Diamond, D. W. (1989b) "Debt Maturity Structure and Liquidity Risk," *Working Paper*, University of Chicago, July; incorporates the results in "Information and Debt Markets: Reputation, Financial Intermediation and Optimal Maturity Structure," January 1987.

Diamond, D. W. and Dybvig, P. H. (1983) "Bank Runs, Deposit Insurance, and Liquidity," *Journal of Political Economy*, 91, June, 401–19.

Bibliographical Listing

"Asset Services and Financial Intermediation," *Financial Markets and Incomplete Information: Frontiers of Modern Financial Theory*, eds Sudipto Bhattacharya and George M. Constantinides, vol. 2 (Totowa, NJ: Rowman and Littlefield, 1989), pp. 272–83.

"Monitoring and Reputation: The Choice Between Bank Loans and Directly Placed Debt," *Working Paper 254*, Center for Research in Security Prices, University of Chicago, July 1988, revised January 1989.

"Constraints on Short-selling and Asset Price Adjustment to Private Information" (with Robert Verrecchia), *Journal of Financial Economics*, 18: 2, June 1987, 277–311.

"Banking Theory, Deposit Insurance and Bank Regulation" (with Philip H. Dybvig), *Journal of Business*, 59: 1, January 1986, 55–68.

Reputation Acquisition in Debt Markets

DOUGLAS W. DIAMOND

1 Introduction

In this paper we analyze the dynamics of an incentive problem between borrowers and lenders. The main result is that incentive problems can be most severe for borrowers with very short track records and become less severe for borrowers who manage to acquire a "good reputation." This explicit prediction about the evolution of incentives over time extends the existing work on reputation that focuses on the beneficial effect of a long horizon in the future.

We follow Kreps and Wilson (1982a) and Milgrom and Roberts (1982) in viewing a reputation as arising from learning over time from observed behavior about some exogenous characteristics of agents. Reputation effects on decisions arise when an agent adjusts his or her behavior to influence data that others use in learning about him.

Reputation is important when there is a diverse pool of relevant exogenous characteristics in an observationally equivalent group of agents because this implies that there is a substantial amount to learn about an agent. In our model we analyze the joint influence of adverse selection and moral hazard on the ability of reputation to eliminate the conflict of interest between borrowers and lenders about the choice of risk in investment decisions. If, initially, there is widespread adverse selection (a large proportion of borrowers with undesirable characteristics), reputation effects will be too weak to eliminate the conflict of interest for borrowers with short track records. Adverse selection becomes less severe as time

Reproduced from *Journal of Political Economy*, 97: 4, 1989, 828–62.

I am grateful for useful comments from Elizabeth Cammack, Bengt Holmstrom, Tommy Tan, Robert Vishny, Andrew Weiss, an anonymous referee, and workshop participants at Chicago, Columbia, Massachusetts Institute of Technology, the National Bureau Conference on Game Theory and Finance, Princeton, Stanford, University of British Columbia, University of California at Los Angeles, Wharton, and Yale. Additional financial support for this research was provided by the University of Bonn, Department of Economics, the Center for Research in Security Prices at the University of Chicago, and National Science Foundation grant SES-8709250. Some of the work was completed when I was on the faculty of the Yale School of Management.

produces a longer track record, and a good reputation can eventually become strong enough to eliminate the conflict of interest for borrowers with a long record of repayment without a default. Alternatively, if there is not substantial initial adverse selection, reputation can begin to work immediately. Two examples in section 6 illustrate these points explicitly.

A reputation that takes time to begin to work implies that new borrowers (with short track records) will face more severe incentive problems and would be the ones most likely to utilize costly technologies for dealing with such problems, such as restrictive covenants in bond indentures (Smith and Warner, 1979) and additional monitoring by a financial intermediary (Diamond, 1984, 1988). The model focuses on the study of debt markets but has implications about the dynamics of reputation formation in general.[1] The general characteristics of markets in which reputation takes time to begin to work are discussed in the conclusion.

An implication of most existing models of reputation, especially Holmstrom (1982), is that the effect of reputation is strongest at the start of an agent's "career" and does not take time to begin to work. This occurs because the amount of information that an action can reveal about one's type is highest in the beginning when there are few previous data about actions (and because the horizon can only become shorter).[2] This implies that a strong effort would be put into having a good beginning to one's track record. This previous work focuses on the incentive effects of the prospect of having a reputation in the future rather than the effects of one's current reputation. Other models of reputation, such as Fama (1980) and Klein and Leffler (1981), are silent on the dynamics of the strength of reputation effects.

Our model begins with an observationally equivalent cohort of risk-neutral borrowers with no track record. One type of borrower has two projects available (which arrive each period): a safe project with a high expected return and a negative net present value risky project with a low expected return (but a high maximum return). The incentive problem is that the debt contract might provide incentives to choose the risky less valuable project. There are two other indistinguishable types of borrowers: those who have access only to a risky project and those who have access only to a safe project.

Imperfect information about borrowers leads to different types being lumped together and initially treated identically: all will be charged the same initial interest rate.[3] Interest rates charged in the future and the prospects for borrowing in the future will depend on the information that later becomes available; a borrower's repayment record (the "track record") will provide this information. Apart from information that is unrelated to repayment history (such as accounting information), all situations in which there is no default are indistinguishable. The investment project chosen by a borrower is not observed by lenders. The most favorable message that a repayment history can provide is a lack of default. Because many borrowers who select risky projects do not default, it takes a long time to indicate that safe projects have been selected.

Ex post project returns are borrowers' private information: outsiders cannot observe the *ex post* profitability because the entrepreneur can appropriate some of the returns to himself. This implies that financial contracts cannot depend directly on this information, ruling out equity contracts. Lenders know the proportion of each borrower type. The interest rate charged in the initial period (for one-period zero-coupon bonds) is set such that, given the proportions, lenders receive a competitive expected return. The higher is the proportion of borrowers who choose the risky project, the higher is the rate. After one period, some borrowers default and some do not. The class of nondefaulters is now a more select group: the proportion of those with only risky projects has declined. The second-period interest rate charged to this group will be less than the initial rate, and this decline continues over time for the class of nondefaulters. With a long time horizon, these reduced rates for a borrower who does not default imply that the present value of the borrower's rents for any constant investment decision rises over time: the reputation itself becomes a valuable asset, and a single default causes a large decline in its value. This loss of value arises because default leads to a cutoff of credit (or, more generally, to an increase in the interest rate charged).

The value of a good reputation rises over time, as does the cost of a default. Therefore, over time, the relative payoff of the risky project (a very large payoff when it has a favorable outcome) declines relative to a safe but profitable project. If there is a sufficient adverse selection, then a typical equilibrium path for a borrower with access to both types of projects is to choose risky projects when "young" and, if able to survive long enough without a default, to switch to safe projects. In this formulation, reputation is important because it becomes a valuable asset worth protecting.[4]

The balance of the paper is organized as follows. The setup of the model is described in section 2. The borrowing and lending arrangements each period are outlined and the one-period horizon is studied in section 3. Analysis of the details of the model's equilibrium is provided in sections 4 and 5. An optimal project choice for given interest rates and interest rates for a given project choice are derived in section 4. The endgame (the periods near the horizon) is analyzed in section 5. A special case of the model to make the main points about what determines the evolution of reputation effects over time is presented in section 6. The characterization is generalized to the general model in section 7 and some conclusions are given in section 8.

2 The Basic Model: Technology, Endowments, and Preferences

All borrowers and lenders are risk neutral. Lenders receive an endowment of inputs each period, and each has access to a constant returns to scale technology for storing endowment within a period, converting it to a consumption good at the end of a period. This technology returns r units of output at the end of a period per unit of input at the beginning of the period. Inputs must be stored (or used as an input in a project described below) within a period before it is possible to consume them. In an attempt to model lenders as an anonymous capital market rather than a financial institution, we assume that a given lender exists for only one period, implying that borrowers face a new set of lenders each period. The implication of this assumption is that reputation in the form of a borrower's credit history is the only intertemporal linkage. There is an infinite number of potential lenders each period. There is no commitment technology available to lenders. Lenders cannot commit themselves to take actions in the future (or at the end of a given period) that are not then in their *ex post* interest, even if this would be beneficial *ex ante*.

Borrowers receive no endowment but have access to indivisible investment projects each period (and do not have storage technology). They are indistinguishable from lenders (but contracts for borrowers turn out to be unattractive to lenders, and vice versa, so that this is an unnecessary assumption). There are three sorts of projects, and the set of projects available to each borrower is his private information. Borrowers can commit to some degree by writing contracts each period that depend on publicly observed variables.

There are three types of borrowers. Type G borrowers have one safe project each period. They can invest 1 (dollar) and receive $G > r$ at the end of the period. Type B borrowers have one risky low-expected-return project each period. They can invest 1, and with probability $\Pi_{\mathrm{B}} < 1$, the project returns B (where $\Pi_{\mathrm{B}}B < r$ and $B > G$); with probability $1 - \Pi_B$, it returns zero. Type BG borrowers have their choice each period between either one of two projects, but not both. One project is identical with that of type G and the other is similar to that of type B, except that the probability of its returning B is $\Pi \leqslant \Pi_{\mathrm{B}}$.[5]

Let the initial population of borrowers contain a fraction f_{G} of type G, f_{B} of type B, and f_{BG} of type BG. These fractions are public information. The returns on the risky projects are all independently distributed. A borrower's type is private information, and all borrowers initially appear identical. In addition, the realized output of a project is private information observed only by the borrower. This makes it difficult to make a borrower's payments depend on a project's realized return. However, there is a costly liquidation technology that borrowers can commit to use in financial contracts contingent on any publicly observed action or outcome. This technology allows the output of the project to be seized before the borrower can consume it. It is extremely costly to do this: it destroys the output, and so the value then observed by the public is always zero if the project is liquidated. This limits the liquidation and bankruptcy process to working as a contract enforcement device that is costly to utilize. This corresponds to the role of liquidation in the world; it is used as a threat rather than a universally used information service. If an alternative assumption were made that costly liquidation made the realized value of project output observable to the public, liquidation would be useful in determining the type of the borrower. In particular, it would then allow those with successful risky projects to be distinguished from those with safe projects. Even without such an informational role, liquidation is useful in providing incentives for repayment. It serves to prevent the borrower from following a policy of "take the money and run."

Lenders in each period observe each borrower's history of defaults. They know the dates on which a borrower has borrowed and on which there was liquidation. This is assumed to be the only information available about the past; the series of past interest rates paid is not observed. In an earlier version of this paper (Diamond, 1986) we use the more general assumption that all past interest rates are observed and obtain identical outcomes to those found under this assumption.[6]

Borrowers maximize discounted expected consumption over T periods, where T is finite but very large (we take the limit as $T \to \infty$). Assume finite T because infinite T introduces many equilibria that are not limits as $T \to \infty$ (Dybvig and Spatt, 1980). Borrowers make decisions to maximize discounted expected consumption, given by $\Sigma_{t=1}^{T} E(\tilde{c}_t) d^t$, where c_t is the realization of the consumption random variable $\tilde{c}_t$ in period t, and d is the discount factor that discounts end of period expected consumption to its beginning of period value. Assume $d < 1$, implying that borrowers discount the future.

To focus on the importance of a long time horizon in providing incentives, assume that with a one-period horizon (with $T = 1$) type BG borrowers would select risky projects. The restriction on parameter values that yield this result is discussed in section 3.1.

The total inputs that can be utilized by all available projects (the sum of all three types) is less than the aggregate endowment of capital goods each period. The storage process is in use at the margin in any equilibrium, and competition among lenders in selecting debt contracts implies that a borrower can borrow by offering lenders a contract that provides an expected return of r per unit loaned. The projects are in economic scarcity, and any rents that they generate in equilibrium will go to the agents endowed with the projects.

Consumption of each agent must be nonnegative ($c_t \geqslant 0$ for all t). This bit of realism is important. If this assumption were dropped, one might never need outside financing; one could simply consume a negative amount in early periods (producing goods) and consume positive amounts later (repaying one's "borrowed utility"). Alternatively, one could always issue riskless debt in that case, by producing enough goods through negative consumption to pay off any claim. In addition, no stronger punishment or nonpecuniary penalty can be imposed that is more severe than zero consumption. This is a form of limited liability, ruling out debtors' prisons, physical punishment, and similar phenomena.

The equilibrium concept used in this repeated game of incomplete information is sequential Nash equilibrium, defined by Kreps and Wilson (1982b). At each stage and for all possible actions, beliefs about the implied type of borrower are specified and all actions are a best response to these beliefs and the actions of all other players in the game. In addition, beliefs about all equilibrium actions are self-fulfilling.

Review of assumptions

1 There are four types of agents: lenders and three type of borrowers. All agents are risk neutral. A borrower's type is private information.
2 Inputs are endowed to each lender at the beginning of each period, and none to borrowers. The endowment must be used as an input to storage or a project during a period to become a consumption good. Each lender lives only one period. The amount of each loan is 1 (dollar), the scale of a borrower's indivisible project.
3 There is no commitment technology for lenders. Borrowers can commit to use the liquidation technology conditional on some payments to lenders and not to use it given other payments.
4 There are T time periods; T is finite, but limiting behavior $T \rightarrow \infty$ is used for most results.
5 Projects are in short supply, and as a result the storage technology is in use. Borrowers can borrow with any contract that offers an expected return of the return r of storage.
6 Project selection and outcomes are private information observed only by the borrower. Each borrower's track record of repayment or default for all past periods is observed by all current lenders.
7 Consumption must be nonnegative, and nonpecuniary penalties are not feasible.
8 With a single-period horizon, $T = 1$, type BG borrowers choose risky projects.

3 Borrowing and Lending with Debt Contracts

The contract between borrowers and lenders is assumed to be a debt contract. At the cost of longer arguments, debt can be shown to be the optimal contract given the private information and unobservability of project returns that makes equity contracts (where lenders receive a share of realized returns) infeasible. Work on single-period contract design by Townsend (1979), Diamond (1984), and Gale and Hellwig (1985) shows that this unobservability implies that contracts are optimally of the debt form.

There are four stages in each period. First borrowers offer contracts to lenders, then lenders decide which loan contracts to accept, then borrowers who receive loans choose their projects, and then they observe the return on their projects and decide how much to pay to lenders (facing liquidation for some possible payments). In the sequential equilibrium established below, the face value r_t (1 plus the interest rate) on debt in a given period is the same for all types. If r_t is such that lenders receive an expected return below r, given the proportion of types in a period, the contract is rejected in the second stage. If r_t provides an expected return of at least r, it is accepted. A debt contract at date t is parameterized by r_t and involves commitment to liquidation for all payments less than r_t. It will turn out that all borrowers who can pay r_t or more will pay r_t, and all others will be liquidated. Although r_t is a face value of a loan of 1 dollar, at times r_t will be referred to as the "interest rate," and parameters that result in higher or lower interest rates will be discussed. This will not lead to ambiguity because the interest rate on a loan is $r_t - 1$, which is a one-to-one function of the face value.

3.1 One-period horizon: $T = 1$ (or the final period for $T > 1$)

The one-period horizon case is the case that has been analyzed previously by Fama and Miller (1972) and Jensen and Meckling (1976). The one-period model here is different because of the imperfect information about borrowers, but it is similar to that of Stiglitz and Weiss (1981). This is a necessary input to the multiperiod model because at the final period there will remain just one period.

Project outcomes are unobservable to lenders and cannot be used to specify debt repayments directly. Use of the liquidation technology can provide incentives for repayment by specifying a face value r_T for each loan of one unit, such that there is liquidation if less is repaid and liquidation is avoided if at least r_T is paid. Because liquidation implies the destruction of all output from the project, it also implies zero consumption by a borrower. If a project returns more than r_T, a borrower can repay r_T and consume the remainder of the project's return. No borrower would ever pay less than face value (and consume zero) if he could pay face value (and consume the excess of his project's return over the face value of debt). No borrower would pay more than r_T because this reduces the borrower's consumption (compared with paying r_T) and has no other benefit since liquidation is avoided by paying r_T. This implies that borrowers with projects returning r_T or more pay r_T, and all others are liquidated. In addition, if loans are made, r_T must be less than or equal to G, the maximum amount that type G borrowers can pay. A higher r_T would lead to liquidation for all borrowers with projects with an expected return greater than the opportunity cost r, implying that lenders would not lend.

The choice of project by type BG borrowers facing a given face value of debt r_T needs to be analyzed to determine the equilibrium value of r_T. Facing an exogenous face value r_T implies that if BGs choose safe projects, their expected utility at the end of the period is $G - r_T$. If they choose risky projects, the expected utility is $\Pi(B - r_T)$.[7] The optimal selection is the one with the larger expected utility, implying that safe projects are best if and only if $r_T \leqslant (G - \Pi B)/(1 - \Pi)$, and risky projects are best if and only if the reverse inequality holds. This means that the level of interest rates can influence the optimal choice. Lower values of r_T improve the relative position of safe projects (because interest costs are paid only with probability Π with a risky project, but with certainty with a safe project). Figure 10.1 plots the beginning of period values $d(G - r_T)$ and $d\Pi(B - r_T)$ as functions of r_T.

The equilibrium face value r_T is set such that risk-neutral lenders receive an expected return of at least r, the riskless return on storage. The face value that will deliver an expected return of r depends on the investment decision that the type BGs are expected to make because more loans default if they select risky projects. Let r_T^{g} denote the face value that makes a lender's expected return equal to r if type BGs are assumed to select safe projects, and r_T^{b} the face value that provides that expected return if BGs are assumed to select risky projects. If safe projects are selected, then only type Bs default, and this implies that r_T^{g} is given by $r_T^{\mathrm{g}} = r(f_{\mathrm{B}}\Pi_{\mathrm{B}} + f_{\mathrm{BG}} + f_{\mathrm{G}})^{-1}$ because type Bs repay with probability Π_{B}, all type Gs and BGs will repay, and the probability of repayment is then $f_{\mathrm{B}}\Pi_{\mathrm{B}} + f_{\mathrm{BG}} + f_{\mathrm{G}}$. If risky projects are selected by all type BGs, then the face value r_T^{b} is given by $r_T^{\mathrm{b}} = r(f_{\mathrm{B}}\Pi_{\mathrm{B}} + f_{\mathrm{BG}}\Pi + f_{\mathrm{G}})^{-1}$.

The rate offered by borrowers depends on the policy that they anticipate that lenders will use to grant loans. The following policy is an equilibrium, supported by lenders' beliefs specified below. If

$$r_T^{\mathrm{g}} \leqslant (G - \Pi B)/(1 - \Pi),$$

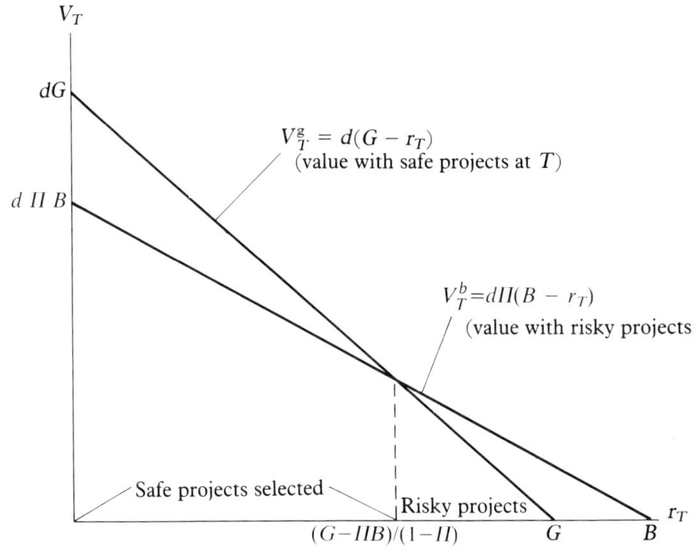

Figure 10.1 Value of safe and risky projects at the final date T as a function of the face value r_T.

then make loans if $r_T \in [r_T^g, G]$. If

$$r_T^g \geqslant (G - \Pi B)/(1 - \Pi)$$

(so that it is not self-fulfilling for lenders to believe that BGs will select safe projects at r_T^g), make loans if $r_T \in [r_T^b, G]$; in this case if r_T^b exceeds G, no loans are made. In any case, if $r_T^g > G$, no loans are made. Given this policy, all borrowers offer the lowest interest rate that lenders will accept. Lenders' belief about borrower type as a function of the interest rate r_T offered is that, for all feasible rates, the type is not a function of the rate. This is self-fulfilling because, given this belief, all borrowers offer the lowest rate that will lead to a loan: r_T^g is the equilibrium rate if it offers lenders an expected return of r.[8] The equilibrium rate in the final period is the lowest one that gives lenders an expected return of exactly r.

To focus on the role of a long horizon (as distinct from just imperfect information), we assume that the risky projects are sufficiently close to being profitable (have expected values $\Pi B < r$, but not close to zero), such that even if financed at the lowest possible rate (the riskless interest rate r) the optimal one-period choice for a type BG is to choose risky projects. That is, we know $r_T \geqslant r$ and we assume

$$r > \frac{G - \Pi B}{1 - \Pi}. \tag{1}$$

Thus for *all* values of f_B, f_{BG}, and f_G for which the market does not fail, the type BG borrowers will select risky projects and the interest rate r_T^b will prevail if there is a one-period horizon. The market is open at T if and only if $r_T^b < G$ or, equivalently, $f_G > [(r/G) - (\Pi f_{BG} + \Pi_B f_B)] > 0$. One interpretation of this condition is that only a borrower with a track record that implies a strictly positive probability of being of type G will have a chance of borrowing at the final date T. Lemma 1 summarizes the results for a one-period horizon.

Lemma 1 At the final period T (a) all borrowers offer the debt contract with the lowest interest rate that provides an expected return of r, (b) all borrowers who can repay their debt do so and all others default, and (c) only those borrowers with track records that imply a sufficiently high (and strictly positive) probability of being of type G are able to borrow.

3.2 *Lending and repayment decisions with multiple periods*

The three properties of equilibrium at T in lemma 1 turn out to be properties of equilibrium at all previous dates. The stage that is of most interest in this study is the decision of borrowers about the choice of project. To focus on this decision, the policies followed at the other stages are briefly studied first, and analysis of the project selection decision is deferred to section 4. Let us begin with the final strategic stage in a period: the decision of borrowers on how much to repay. This can be studied without a full analysis of the previous stages by establishing two useful properties of the second stage in which lenders decide whether to grant credit in a period. Given the characterization of the final (repayment) stage and the two properties of the second (loan-granting) stage, we show in section 3.3 that at the first stage all borrowers offer the lowest possible interest rate, as in the one-period analysis.

Lenders observe the previous default record of each borrower. Borrowers face lenders who live for a single period, but lenders know that borrowers will want to continue borrowing in the future. Both take these anticipated future actions into account. One implication of this forecast of future actions is that lenders will not lend to a borrower unless they think that there is some chance that he is of type G. We saw that no one would lend at T unless there was a strictly positive probability that a borrower was of type G. No one known to be of type B would receive a loan because a type B borrower's project has a total expected return below r. No one would lend to a known type BG by a familiar argument using backward induction: no one would lend in the final period (because risky projects with expected return below r would be selected), and successively earlier periods become the "last" borrowing opportunity, implying that no one would ever lend. This establishes the following lemma.

Lemma 2 If a borrower is revealed at time t to be of either type B or type BG, no one will lend to him thereafter.

This cutoff of credit to those known not to be of type G requires no commitment by lenders; such lending is simply unprofitable.

Lemma 3 states a property of the face value of any loan that lenders would accept. It follows from the requirement that lenders receive an expected return of at least r per dollar lent.

Lemma 3 If a loan is made at date t, then the face value $r_t \in [r, G]$.

PROOF If $r_t < r$, then even if repaid with certainty it provides a return below r. If $r_t > G$, then all borrowers with projects returning G default and are liquidated. All other borrowers have projects with expected returns below r, implying that lenders would receive an expected return below r. ■

These properties of the loan-granting stage are almost enough to characterize the repayment policy of borrowers. Lemma 4 states the equilibrium repayment in each period by each type of borrower.

Lemma 4 Borrowers repay face value r_t (and avoid liquidation) if their project returns at least r_t, and borrowers with projects that return less than r_t are liquidated.

The proof of lemma 4 is given in the appendix.

The proof of the optimal repayment policy is almost the same as that in the one-period case. Suppose that credit is cut off on a single default. Then all borrowers who could avoid default and liquidation would do so, and because all situations in which there is no default are indistinguishable, no borrower would pay more than the minimum necessary to avoid default. Given this repayment policy, only those who cannot repay $r_t \in [r, G]$ default, and such borrowers are not of type G. A default then does indeed cut off credit, by lemma 2, and the beliefs about the implications of a default are self-fulfilling.[9]

An immediate consequence of this lemma is a rule that lenders use in deciding whether a loan should be made. This is lemma 5.

Lemma 5 Any default (payment of less than r_t) by a borrower at a date t leads to no lending for all future dates.

Because default will reveal that a borrower is not of type G, it will influence his future treatment by lenders: no more credit will be advanced.[10] This learning from observed behavior is key to the incentive value of reputation. One might actively avoid default (by choosing safe projects) to avoid the premature cutoff of one's credit, even though one will later choose risky projects (for example in the final period). This incentive effect is analyzed in section 4.

3.3 Rates offered at the beginning of each period

Borrowers who can repay and avoid liquidation will pay the minimum payment that avoids liquidation: this payment is r_t. This first stage is for borrowers to offer the debt contracts, and this is a choice of r_t. We saw in section 3.1 that in the final period all borrowers offer the lowest rate that provides lenders with an expected return of r. Borrowers offer the lowest possible rate in all periods. The supporting beliefs and actions of lenders are that they believe that the rate offered at $T-1$ reveals nothing new about a borrower's type, and they will lend at the lowest rate that gives an expected return of r given the belief that each borrower is a random draw from the pool of all borrowers who have not yet defaulted. Under this belief there is no current benefit from offering a rate that is higher than needed. The only possible motivation for such a higher current rate is a possible future benefit: for example, a borrower's attempt to signal his type by offering an interest rate that is higher than needed. If any borrower deviated and offered a rate higher than the minimum, he would be indistinguishable in the future from those who offered the lower rate and would achieve no future benefit.[11] This implies that all borrowers pool and offer the lowest rate that provides lenders with an expected return of r at $T-1$. The argument extends recursively to all previous $t < T$.[12] We have established the following lemma.

Lemma 6 At all dates all borrowers offer the lowest interest rate that provides lenders with an expected return of r.

Within each period we have established some properties of a sequential equilibrium in which the interest rate offered at the beginning correctly takes into account a part of the rule that lenders use to grant loans and the rule that each borrower will use to repay at the end of each period. Given these properties, the project decisions of type BG borrowers can be analyzed. Only given that analysis can the "lowest interest rate that provides lenders with an expected return of r" in lemma 6 be precisely defined. Section 4 provides this analysis for given interest rates and an analysis of interest rates for given project decisions.

4 Project Choice and Interest Rates

4.1 Project decisions for given interest rates

At the final period, type BG borrowers will select risky projects. The $T-1$ present value of continuing to borrow until period T (by not defaulting at $T-1$ because a default cuts off credit by lemma 5) is thus the value of choosing a risky project. Let V_t be the maximized value as of t of making optimal project decisions from t to T. At T this is given by $V_T = d\Pi(B - r_T)$.

Define V_t^{b} and V_t^{g} to be the value as of t of choosing respectively a risky and a safe project at t and making optimal decisions thereafter. Clearly, $V_t = \max\{V_t^{\mathrm{b}}, V_t^{\mathrm{g}}\}$, where $V_t^{\mathrm{b}} = d\Pi(B - r_t + V_{t+1})$ and $V_t^{\mathrm{g}} = d(G - r_t + V_{t+1})$. A type BG borrower chooses safe projects if and only if $V_t^{\mathrm{g}} - V_t^{\mathrm{b}} \geqslant 0$ or $d\{G - \Pi B - [(1-\Pi)(r_t - V_{t+1})]\} \geqslant 0$, implying $r_t - V_{t+1} \leqslant (G - \Pi B)/(1-\Pi)$. If and only if this condition holds, $V_t = V_t^{\mathrm{g}}$, and this is then equivalent to $V_t \geqslant d\{G - [(G - \Pi B)/(1-\Pi)]\}$. This establishes lemma 7.

Lemma 7 Safe projects are the optimal choice at date t if and only if

$$r_t - V_{t+1} \leqslant \frac{G - \Pi B}{1 - \Pi}$$

or equivalently

$$V_t \geqslant d\left(G - \frac{G - \Pi B}{1 - \Pi}\right).$$

Risky projects are the optimal choice if and only if the reverse inequalities hold.

The implication of lemma 7 is that repaying a loan has the short-run cost of r_t and the long-run benefit of V_{t+1}, and the term $r_t - V_{t+1}$ plays an identical role to r_t in the single-period case because a default cuts off a borrower's credit. Figure 10.2 shows V_t^{b} and V_t^{g} as a function of $r_t - V_{t+1}$. Risky projects are selected when $r_t - V_{t+1}$ is high. The optimality of risky projects also implies that V_t is low, and so type BGs always prefer to have reason to select the safe project. When type BGs are indifferent between safe and risky projects,

$$V_t = d\left(G - \frac{G - \Pi B}{1 - \Pi}\right).$$

Further results on periods of indifference by type BGs are presented below in lemmas 11 and 12.

Reducing the interest rate charged to a borrower at any date makes safe

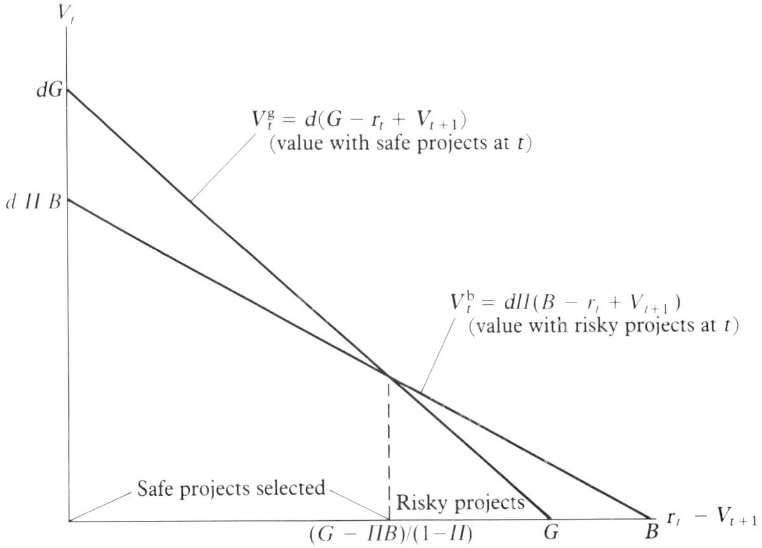

Figure 10.2 Value of safe and risky projects at date t as a function of $r_t - V_{t+1}$.

projects become relatively more attractive on that date. Reduced interest rates at date t also increase V_t^b and V_t^g, implying that $V_t = \max\{V_t^b, V_t^g\}$ is increased. This makes safe projects more attractive at $t-1$. By a similar argument, V_{t-1} is increasing in V_t, implying that a reduction in r_t increases V_{t-1}, which makes safe projects relatively more attractive on date $t-2$ and, by recursion, on all dates before t.

The most favorable situation for the selecton of safe projects is one in which "interest rates" are at their minimum possible value, $r_t = r$. This provides a necessary condition for reputation effects to have value and induce type BGs to select safe projects on some date. It will later be shown to be a sufficient condition when $T \to \infty$. This is a necessary condition for there to exist a date t on which $V_t^g \geqslant V_t^b$.

Lemma 8 Type BG borrowers will select safe projects on some date only if $d(G-r)/(1-d) > d\Pi(B-r)/(1-d\Pi)$, implying that the present value of financing the safe project at the riskless rate of interest for an infinite number of periods exceeds the present value of selecting the risky project for an infinite number of periods (until the first default).

PROOF From (1), risky projects are optimal at T. From lemma 7, safe projects are best if and only if $r_t - V_{t-1} \leqslant (G - \Pi B)/(1-\Pi)$. Because risky projects are selected at T and if safe projects are ever optimal, there will be a date $\hat{t}$ when safe projects are selected, followed by risky ones until T.

On such a date $\hat{t}$, we know

$$V_{\hat{t}+1} < \frac{d\Pi(B-r)}{1-d\Pi} = \lim_{T\to\infty} \sum_{t=1}^{T} (B-r)(d\Pi)^t$$

because this is the upper bound on the value of selecting risky projects until the first default for an infinite number of periods and $r_t \geqslant r$. Thus safe project optimality at t requires

$$d\left[G-r+\frac{d\Pi(B-r)}{1-d\Pi}\right] \leqslant d\Pi\left[B-r+\frac{d\Pi(B-r)}{1-d\Pi}\right]$$

or

$$r-\frac{d\Pi(B-r)}{1-d\Pi} \leqslant \frac{G-\Pi B}{1-\Pi}.$$

Rearranging terms produces the following equivalent conditions that are necessary for reputation ever to have value:

$$\frac{d\Pi(B-r)}{1-d\Pi} > r-\frac{G-\Pi B}{1-\Pi} \quad (2)$$

$$\frac{d(G-r)}{1-d} > \frac{d\Pi(B-r)}{1-d\Pi} \quad (3)$$

$$\frac{d\Pi(B-G)}{1-\Pi} > r-\frac{G-\Pi B}{1-\Pi}. \quad (4)$$

■

Lemma 8 makes sense because the loss of reputation from a default at worst results in a cutoff of credit, and if the rents on the safe project are low enough for them to be exceeded by those of choosing risky projects at the low rate r (and conditions (2)–(4) fail), loss of reputation is not a potent enough weapon to induce cooperative behavior. This condition is also sufficient if $T\to\infty$, but proof of this is deferred to section 5.

Lemma 9 provides a sufficient condition for the selection of safe projects at a date if the horizon is long. It states that if future interest rates are below a given level at all dates in the future, then safe projects are currently optimal. This level of future interest rates will specify feasible future rates (that is, rates greater than the riskless rate) only if conditions in lemma 8 hold.

Lemma 9 If, for all $t \in [\hat{t}, T]$,

$$r_t < dG + \frac{(1-d)(G-\Pi B)}{1-\Pi},$$

then there exists $T < \infty$ such that safe projects are the optimal choice at date $\hat{t}$: T such that

$$r_{\hat{t}} - V_{\hat{t}+1} \geqslant \frac{G - \Pi B}{1 - \Pi}.$$

This bound on future interest rates specifies feasible rates, that is,

$$dG + \frac{(1-d)(G - \Pi B)}{1 - \Pi} > r,$$

if and only if the necessary conditions (in lemma 8) for reputation to have value are true.

The proof of lemma 9 is given in the appendix.

The conditions for safe projects to be selected at some date in lemmas 8 and 9 are stated in terms of interest rates, which are endogenous. Equilibrium interest rates for given project decisions are described in section 4.2. These results are used in section 5 to provide general necessary and sufficient conditions for reputation effects to be strong enough on some date to imply the selection of safe projects on some date. The remainder of the characterization in the general case is deferred to section 7.

4.2 *Interest rates for given project decisions*

For any equilibrium there is a range that bounds the equilibrium interest rate (face value) r_t. The lowest value that it can attain is the value that provides a normal expected return r to lenders under the assumption that type BG borrowers choose safe projects. As in our discussion in section 3.1, we call this rate r_t^{g}. The largest possible value of the interest rate is r_t^{b}, the one that gives lenders a normal expected return if all type BGs choose risky projects. At $t = 1$, these rates are given by

$$r_1^{\mathrm{g}} = \frac{r}{f_{\mathrm{G}} + f_{\mathrm{BG}} + \Pi_{\mathrm{B}} f_{\mathrm{B}}}$$

and

$$r_1^{\mathrm{b}} = \frac{r}{f_{\mathrm{G}} + \Pi f_{\mathrm{BG}} + \Pi_{\mathrm{B}} f_{\mathrm{B}}}.$$

The bounds on the rates in periods after $t = 1$ depend on the population of borrowers with a given track record. Because those who default are denied future credit, all those who continue to borrow have perfect records of no default. Define $f_{\Theta t}$ as the fraction of the original pool of all borrowers who are of type Θ and have not yet defaulted by the beginning of period t. For example, $f_{\mathrm{B}1} = f_{\mathrm{B}}$. Because type B borrowers always select risky projects, $f_{\mathrm{B}t} = \Pi_{\mathrm{B}}^{t-1} f_{\mathrm{B}}$.[13] Type G borrowers always select safe projects, implying $f_{Gt} = f_G$ for all t. The fraction of type BG borrowers in the pool of those with a reputation of no default depends on the decisions made in each period: if safe projects are selected at date $t-1$ by all BGs, then $f_{BGt} = f_{BGt-1}$. If all BGs select risky projects at $t-1$, then $f_{BGt} = \Pi f_{BGt-1}$. At date t, the pool of borrowers is a fraction of $f_G + f_{Bt} + f_{BGt}$ of the original pool of borrowers, and out of the original pool, the fraction of loans repaid at t is $f_G + \Pi_B f_{Bt} + \Pi f_{BGt}$. The bounds on r_t at date t that give lenders an expected return of r are therefore given by

$$r_t^g = r \frac{f_G + f_{BGt} + f_{Bt}}{f_G + f_{BGt} + \Pi_B f_{Bt}}$$

and

$$r_t^b = r \frac{f_G + f_{BGt} + f_{Bt}}{f_G + \Pi f_{BGt} + \Pi_B f_{Bt}}.$$

Note that, if $f_{BG} = 0$, then $r_t^b = r_t^g$. In the case of $f_{BG} = 0$ the interest rates can be specified without knowing the equilibrium actions of the finite number of type BGs (because there are an infinite number of borrowers).

Characterization of the choice between r_t^g and r_t^b for all t is presented in section 5. This choice is first analyzed for the periods near the horizon T.

5 The Endgame: Analysis of Decisions near the Horizon T

Lemmas 8 and 9 provide necessary and sufficient conditions, in terms of interest rates, for the selection of safe projects at some date if $T \to \infty$. In this section we extend these to conditions in terms of exogenous parameters.

Define the "endgame" as the period until T that begins when a type BG switches to (or back to) risky projects. Formally, the endgame begins on date τ, where τ is the smallest t with $V_t^g \leqslant V_t^b$ that occurs after some date $\hat{t}$ where $V_{\hat{t}}^g > V_{\hat{t}}^b$. If no date $\hat{t}$ exists, then $V_t^g \leqslant V_t^b$ for all t, and we define the endgame as the entire game from $t = 1$ to $t = T$.

The endgame is *bounded* if there exists $K < \infty$ such that $T - \tau < K$ as $T \to \infty$. A bounded endgame implies that $\tau \to \infty$ as $T \to \infty$.

5.1 A low fraction of type BGs

To develop the basic points about the endgame, consider the case in which, of the infinite number of borrowers, a fraction f_B are of type B, a fraction $f_G = 1 - f_B$ are of type G, and a finite number (representing a zero fraction)

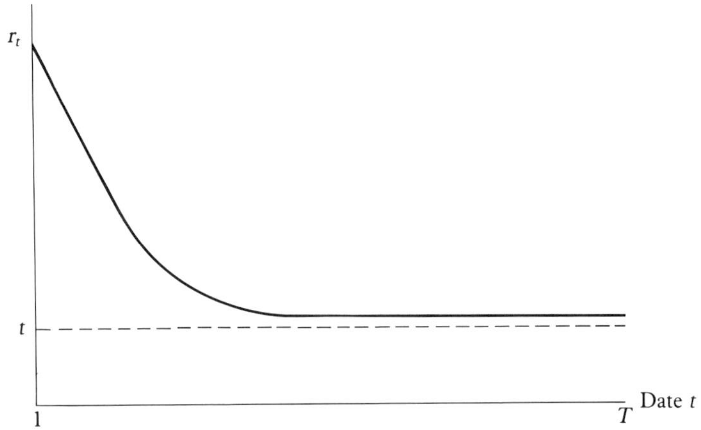

Figure 10.3 Face values r_t, given no default up to date t. It is assumed that $f_B > 0$ and $f_{BG} = 0$.

of borrowers are of type BG. The series of the lowest interest rate that provides lenders an expected return of r (given the current population of borrowers with a given track record) is exogenous, and $r_t^g = r_t^b$. By lemma 6, the face value series r_t is given by (and shown in figure 10.3)

$$r_t = r \, \frac{\Pi_B^{t-1} f_B + 1 - f_B}{\Pi_B^t f_B + 1 - f_B}. \tag{5}$$

Provided that $r_1 \leqslant G$, (5) states the interest rate charged over time to those who do not default up to time t. All those who default are revealed to be types other than G and thus have their credit cut off from that point forward. If $r_1 > G$, then the capital market fails and no one can borrow at any interest rate.

Note that r_t strictly falls over time and converges to r (the riskless rate) as $t \to \infty$. This occurs because the class of borrowers who have not yet defaulted contains a decreasing proportion of borrowers with risky projects (and $f_{Bt} \to 0$ as $t \to \infty$). The decision facing the finite number of type BG borrowers is to choose between the two projects available to them given the anticipated time path of interest rates available to them specified in (5).

Because $r_t \to r$ as $t \to \infty$, if the horizon $T \to \infty$, there will be an arbitrarily large number of periods in which, for all $\varepsilon > 0$, $r_t < r + \varepsilon$. Lemma 9 then implies that the necessary conditions for the selection of safe projects on some t (for example condition (2)) are necessary and sufficient for the selection of safe projects at some date and for the endgame to have bounded length as $T \to \infty$. This is lemma 10.

Lemma 10 If $f_{BG} = 0$, then the necessary conditions stated in lemma 8 for selection of safe projects on some t as $T \to \infty$ are necessary and sufficient for a bounded endgame as $T \to \infty$.

This result can be directly extended to $f_{\mathrm{BG}} > 0$ but not too large. On any date, $r_t \leqslant r_t^{\mathrm{b}}$. Suppose that f_{BG} is low enough so that, if $f_{\mathrm{B}t} = 0$, then

$$r_t^{\mathrm{b}} < dG + \frac{(1-d)(G - \Pi B)}{1 - \Pi}.$$

As $t \to \infty$, $f_{\mathrm{B}t} \to 0$, implying that there is a $t < \infty$ such that

$$r_t^{\mathrm{b}} < dG + \frac{(1-d)(G - \Pi B)}{1 - \Pi}.$$

If the horizon $T \to \infty$, then an immediate application of lemma 9 implies that the conditions in lemma 8 are necessary and sufficient for a bounded length endgame if f_{BG} is not too large.

If f_{BG} is large, implying that r_t^{b} might exceed

$$dG + \frac{(1-d)(G - \Pi B)}{1 - \Pi}$$

even with a low $f_{\mathrm{B}t}$, the direct application of lemma 9 to an upper bound on future interest rates cannot be made. In section 5.2 we analyze the case of large f_{BG}.

5.2 *A bounded endgame as $T \to \infty$ with $f_{\mathrm{BG}} > 0$*

To establish that (2) and $r_1 \leqslant G$ are necessary and sufficient for a bounded length endgame (that is, $\tau \to \infty$ as $T \to \infty$), we proceed in two steps. First, an interest rate path r_t that provides lenders with an expected return of r each period and yields a bounded length endgame is established. Then it is shown that borrowers will offer interest rates that result in a bounded length endgame.

For $f_{\mathrm{BG}} > 0$, the possible increase in interest rates on a date τ when a switch is made to risky projects implies that there may need to be some periods in which some type BGs select safe projects and others select risky projects. The interest rate r_τ^{b} that prevails if all BGs select risky projects could be too high if the fraction $f_{\mathrm{BG}\tau}$ of the original pool of borrowers who are of type BG and who have not defaulted by date τ is too high. For example, r_τ^{b} could exceed G (and be inconsistent with an open market) or it could be less than G but be high enough to imply such a low V_τ that it would be inconsistent with selection of safe projects at $\tau - 1$. In either case a period of time is needed in which some type BGs select safe projects and others select risky projects. This would require that they be indifferent between the two projects on those dates.

If f_{BG} is large, r_t^b might exceed the level specified in lemma 9, even if $f_{Bt}=0$. The following lemmas show that a bounded period of mixed strategy project selection will allow f_{BGt} to be reduced sufficiently to guarantee that, after the mixed strategy period,

$$r_t^b \leqslant dG + \frac{(1-d)(G-\Pi B)}{1-\Pi},$$

allowing application of lemma 9 and the result that the period after the mixed strategy period is bounded. In addition we show that, directly before the mixed strategy period, type BGs select safe projects in pure strategy.

A period of mixed strategy indifference obviously requires that on all its dates, including the final date of indifference, BGs are willing to select safe projects. Lemma 11 gives a bound on V_{t+1} that is required for indifference at t. At some period $t=t'$ after an indifference period, risky projects will be selected in pure strategy (for example at $t=T$), and the interest rates $r_{t'}^b$ will prevail. At any date t', we know that $r_t \leqslant r_{t'}^b$ for $t>t'$. Lemmas 12 and 13 show that a bounded period of mixed strategy before t' can reduce $f_{BGt'}$ sufficiently to allow $r_{t'}^b$ to be less than or equal to the level (given in lemma 9) that implies that safe projects will be selected at t'. The result (proposition 1) is that, if the market does not fail, then the necessary conditions (in lemma 8) for reputation to have value are necessary and sufficient for a bounded length endgame.

Lemma 11 There exists an interest rate $r_t \in [r, G]$ such that type BGs are indifferent between safe and risky projects, implying that $V_t^g = V_t^b$ if and only if $V_{t+1} \in [L, H]$, where $L \equiv r-(G-\Pi B)/(1-\Pi)$ and $H \equiv G-(G-\Pi B)/(1-\Pi)$.

PROOF $V_t^g = V_t^b$ implies (by lemma 7) $V_{t+1} = r_t - (G-\Pi B)/(1-\Pi)$, and replacing r_t by r and by G provides the bounds L and H. ■

Lemma 11 implies that, if $V_t \in [L, H]$, indifference between projects is feasible (as is strict preference for either type of project in the open interval (L, H)) as long as f_{Bt} is low enough to allow a low r_t^g and f_{BGt} is not too low for an r_t^g sufficiently above r. Lemma 12 provides a characterization of repeated periods of mixed strategy indifference between projects.

Lemma 12 If $V_t^g = V_t^b$, with $r_t \in [r, G]$, implying indifference between safe and risky projects at t, then the following hold:

$$V_t = d\left(G - \frac{G-\Pi B}{1-\Pi}\right);$$

$$V_t \in [L, H];$$

there exists $r_{t-1} \in [r, G]$ such that $V^{g}_{t-1} = V^{b}_{t-1}$ and

$$r_{t-1} = dG + \frac{(1-B)(G-\Pi B)}{1-\Pi}.$$

PROOF $V^{g}_{t} = V^{b}_{t}$ implies, by lemma 7,

$$V_t = d\left(G - \frac{G-\Pi B}{1-\Pi}\right) = dH < H$$

$$V_t = d\left(G - \frac{G-\Pi B}{1-\Pi}\right) = \frac{1}{1-\Pi}\,[d\Pi(B-G)] > L$$

by (4). By lemma 11, $V_t \in (L, H)$ implies that there exists $r_{t-1} \in (r, G)$ with $V^{g}_{t-1} = V^{b}_{t-1}$ and substitution of V_t into

$$r_{t-1} = V_t + \frac{G-\Pi B}{1-\Pi}$$

produces

$$r_{t-1} = dG + \frac{(1-d)(G-\Pi B)}{1-\Pi}.$$ ■

Lemma 12 shows that repeated periods of mixed strategy indifference are possible as long as f_{Bt} and f_{BGt} are such that

$$r_t = dG + \frac{(1-d)(G-\Pi B)}{1-\Pi}$$

is feasible, implying that

$$r^{b}_{t} \geqslant dG + \frac{(1-d)(G-\Pi B)}{1-\Pi} \geqslant r^{g}_{t}.$$

Note that the same interest rate,

$$dG + (1-d)\,\frac{G-\Pi B}{1-\Pi}$$

is also the bound specified in lemma 9 such that, if there is the ability to borrow at future rates less than the bound, then a finite number of remaining periods before T guarantees that safe projects are optimal at the current date. A mixed strategy period ending at date t' can thus reduce f_{BGt} sufficiently to imply $V_{t'+1} > L$, to use the notation of lemma 11. To support a preceding repeated mixed strategy period, lemma 11 implies that we need $V_{t'+1} \in [L, H]$. Lemma 13 provides this stronger result.

Lemma 13 If the necessary conditions for reputation to have value in lemma 8 are true, then there exists a bounded mixed strategy period ending on a date t' such that $V_{t'} \in [L, H)$.

The proof of lemma 13 is given in the appendix.

The previous results imply that there exists an interest rate path such that the length of the endgame has an upper bound as $T \to \infty$: a mixed strategy period of bounded length can guarantee that thereafter

$$r_t^{\mathrm{b}} \leqslant dG + \frac{(1-d)(G - \Pi B)}{1 - \Pi},$$

and there exists a bounded length period thereafter that begins with $V_t \in [L, H)$; this supports the mixed strategy period. This implies that there exists an interest rate path that leads to a bounded endgame. The result of lemma 6, that borrowers offer the lowest feasible rates each period, implies the stronger result that the interest rates actually offered by borrowers imply a bounded length endgame. This is because, at any date before the shortest feasible endgame, it is feasible for all borrowers to offer the interest rate r_t^{g}, and by lemma 6 this is the rate that is offered. During the endgame, rates above r_t^{g} will be offered, but these are the lowest feasible rates on those dates.

Overall, we have established the following proposition.

Proposition 1 If the loan market is active, then the endgame is of bounded length as $T \to \infty$ if and only if (2) is true.

With this result that the endgame comprises a bounded number of periods near T, the focus on the few periods near the end is complete.

6 The Dynamics of Reputation with a Long Horizon

Far enough from the horizon, T, safe projects will be selected if and only if (2) holds. If (2) is false, there is never an incentive effect of reputation. We now focus on the case in which (2) is true and reputation eventually has value. To see how the incentive value of reputation evolves over time and develop intuition into how it evolves, two special cases of the model are developed. The contrast between the two cases will develop the relevant ideas, and section 7 shows that these intuitive ideas are true in the general model. There are two special cases: (a) near absence of adverse selection ($f_{\mathrm{B}} = 0$), with near absence of moral hazard ($f_{\mathrm{BG}} = 0$), and (b) significant adverse selection ($f_{\mathrm{B}} > 0$), with near absence of moral hazard ($f_{\mathrm{BG}} = 0$).

In both cases, $f_{\mathrm{BG}} = 0$ is assumed to allow the simple determination of interest rates to ease exposition. The two cases illustrate the importance of adverse selection in the dynamics of reputation by a comparison of $f_B = 0$ with $f_B > 0$.

6.1 Near absence of adverse selection ($f_B = 0$), with $f_{BG} = 0$

With $f_G = 1$ and a finite number of other types, (5) shows that $r_t = r$ for all t. At T, risky projects will be selected, and thus $V_T = d\Pi(B - r)$ while $r_{T-1} - V_T = r - d\Pi(B - r)$. By lemma 7, safe projects are selected at t if and only if $r - V_{t+1}$ is greater than $(G - \Pi B)/(1 - \Pi)$, and for t' sufficiently near T

$$V_{t'} = \sum_{t=t'}^{T} (B - r) d\Pi^{1 - t' + t},$$

which is a strictly decreasing function of t'. On some date $t' < T$, safe projects will be selected because the sum will exceed the critical value $r - (G - \Pi B)/(1 - \Pi)$ and will exceed this value for all $t < t'$. This implies that on all dates $t < t'$ safe projects will be selected because at any date t' the value of continuing to borrow is at least the value of borrowing and choosing the risky project each period. Figure 10.4 shows $r - V_{t+1}$ when interest rates are constant at the riskless rate r.

The implication of this special case is that if there is no significant adverse selection, so that interest rates do not change as a function of one's reputation, then reputation works immediately if it ever works: safe

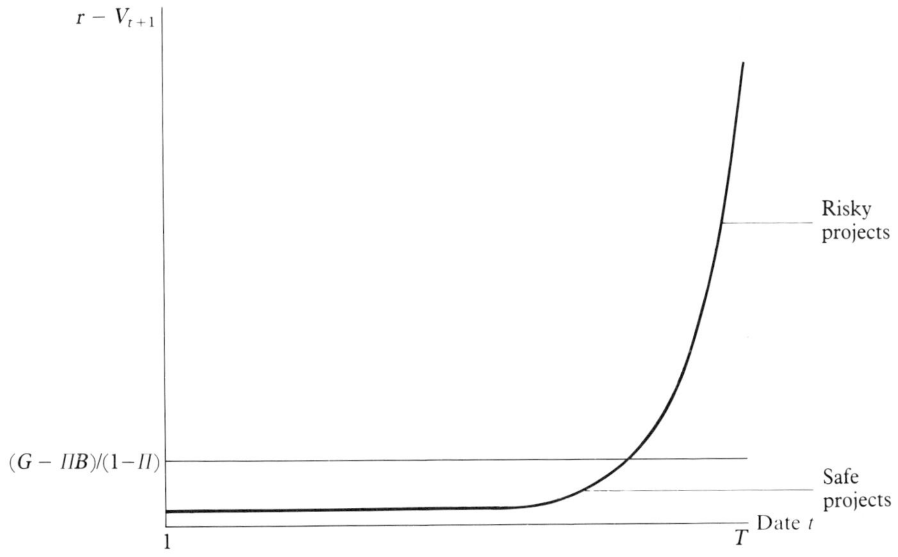

Figure 10.4 The time series of $r_t - V_{t+1}$ assuming $f_B = 0$. Assuming that $f_B = 0$ implies that interest rates are constant at the riskless rate, that is, $r_t = r$.

projects are selected at $t = 1$ unless risky projects are selected for all t. This is consistent with the basic intuition from previous models of reputations.

6.2 *Significant adverse selection ($f_B > 0$) with $f_{BG} = 0$*

With $f_{BG} = 0$, r_t is given by (5). For large t, $r_t \to r$, so that if $T \to \infty$, then near T the analysis is similar to the section 6.1 where $r_t = r$. However, for borrowers with short track records (small t), the higher rates $r_t > r$ have two effects because the decision between safe and risky projects depends only on $r_t - V_{t+1}$. Higher rates make safe projects relatively less attractive for given $V_{t'+1}$, and higher current rates reduce $V_{t'}$, making safe projects less attractive for $t < t'$. This implies that, if f_B is high enough (initial interest rates are high enough), then the finite number of type BGs will select risky projects at some early dates, even though those who do not default will later select safe projects. In principle they might switch back and forth between the two projects. Proposition 2 provides a characterization of the scope for project switching assuming only that r_t falls over time. Under the assumption that $f_{BG} = 0$, (5) shows that r_t does fall over time. In section 7, proposition 2 will be shown to apply with $f_{BG} > 0$ if the remaining time before the horizon is sufficiently long.

Proposition 2 If r_t falls over time and a type BG borrower optimally selects safe projects at t^+ and selects risky projects at some $t' < t^+$, then risky projects are optimal for all $t < t'$. This implies that, if safe projects are best on two dates t_1 and t^+ ($t_1 < t^+$), then the optimal project selection is safe projects for all $t \in [t_1, t^+]$.

PROOF Let date $\hat{t} \geqslant t'$ be the largest date that is less than t^+ on which risky projects are selected. Safe projects are best at $\hat{t} + 1$ and, by lemma 7,

$$V_{\hat{t}+1} \geqslant d\left(G - \frac{G - \Pi B}{1 - \Pi}\right).$$

Because risky projects are best at $\hat{t}$,

$$V_{\hat{t}} < d\left(G - \frac{G - \Pi B}{1 - \Pi}\right) \leqslant V_{\hat{t}+1},$$

and

$$r_{\hat{t}} - V_{\hat{t}+1} > \frac{G - \Pi B}{1 - \Pi}.$$

Interest rates fall, implying $r_{\hat{t}} \leqslant r_{\hat{t}-1}$, and combined with $V_{\hat{t}} < V_{\hat{t}+1}$ we have

$$r_{\hat{t}-1} - V_{\hat{t}} > r_{\hat{t}} - V_{\hat{t}+1}$$
$$> \frac{G - \Pi B}{1 - \Pi}.$$

This implies that risky projects are best at $\hat{t} - 1$, and because $r_{t'} \leqslant r_{\hat{t}}$ for all $t' < \hat{t}$, recursion implies that, because

$$V_{\hat{t}-1} < d\left(G - \frac{G - \Pi B}{1 - \Pi}\right) \leqslant V_{\hat{t}+1},$$

risky projects are best for all $t < t'$. ■

Proposition 2 makes no use of the length of the time horizon. There are only two reasons for choosing risky projects: a short horizon or high current interest rates. Because interest rates fall over time conditional on not defaulting, the only reason for switching to risky projects once rates are low enough to justify safe projects is a short horizon. If there is a date on which safe projects are selected, then on such a date, or any earlier date, a short horizon is not the problem. If risky projects are selected on such an earlier date, the problem is high interest rates. If one goes back further in time, rates are higher, and so risky projects are again best. Figure 10.5

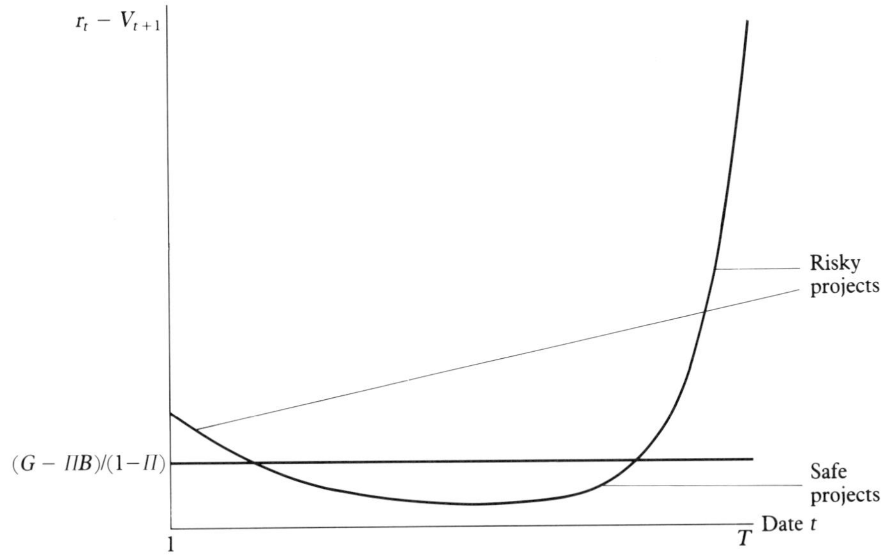

Figure 10.5 The time series of $r_t - V_{t+1}$ assuming $f_B > 0$; $f_B > 0$ implies that interest rates fall as a longer track record is acquired. Sufficiently high f_B implies that risky projects are best at $t = 1$.

shows the time path of $r_t - V_{t+1}$, computed using the interest rates in figure 10.3 (rates that decline over time). Proposition 2 implies that if rates decline with longer periods of lack of default, then $r_t - V_{t+1}$ plotted as a function of t can cross the threshold $(G - \Pi B)/(1 - \Pi)$ for choice of safe projects at most twice. If the rates in the early periods are sufficiently above r because of a large fraction of type Bs (but are less than G), then the optimal choice on those dates will be risky projects, again by the reasoning of lemma 7. If the horizon is long, the reason is simpler. If the horizon is long enough, $V_{t+1} \geqslant V_t$ because rates fall while the horizon is not significantly reduced (the proof is left to the reader).

The result of this example is that when there is significant adverse selection (a heterogeneous pool of borrower qualities) in the initial pool of borrowers with no track record, then reputation initially will not deal with moral hazard problems, but instead a period of "reputation acquisition" will be required. If the adverse selection is severe enough, so that there are high interest rates (from (5)) in early periods for those with short track records and resulting low V_t for low t, reputation will not work in early periods and risky projects will be selected for $t = 1, \ldots, \bar{t}$ until rates fall enough for $r_t - V_{t+1}$ to be less than $(G - \Pi B)/(1 - \Pi)$. Borrowers without track records will select risky projects. Only some of those who select risky projects will default, and the others will acquire a good reputation. This will eventually lead to such a good credit rating and such low interest rates that type BG borrowers who have not defaulted will want to avoid loss of this valuable credit rating and will switch to safe projects for an unbounded number of periods until the endgame. That is, there will be a period of reputation acquisition, but eventually reputation will work to provide incentives. The next section shows that this result applies in general, with $f_{\mathrm{BG}} > 0$, and provides a full characterization of equilibrium.

7 Equilibrium Path of Project Choices with $f_{\mathrm{BG}} > 0$

Under the assumption $f_{\mathrm{BG}} = 0$, characterization of equilibrium for any horizon length was a matter of computing the functions V_t^{b} and V_t^{g} using the interest rates in (5). With $f_{\mathrm{BG}} > 0$, we need to determine whether the appropriate rate in each period is r_t^{g} or r_t^{b}. The result of proposition 1, that all borrowers offer the lowest feasible interest rate, suggests the following characterization, which is established below. First, try a conjecture in which, from $t = 1$ until the endgame, type BGs choose safe projects (and face interest rates $r_t = r_t^{\mathrm{g}}$ every period until the endgame). If this leads to interest rates that imply the conjectured behavior by type BGs, it is the equilibrium rate path, by proposition 1. However, if the interest rate series conditioned on the assumption that type BGs select safe projects leads type

BGs to find risky projects more profitable (because there are many type Bs and thus high rates), then the equilibrium at $t = 1$ involves their selecting risky projects (and paying higher rates that reflect this). If $r_1 < G$ and (2) holds, eventually the fraction of type Bs who have not defaulted becomes low enough, and BGs will switch to safe projects for an unbounded number of periods ($\tau \to \infty$ as $T \to \infty$). If (2) is false and $r_1 < G$ so that the market does not fail, then reputation never has value and BGs select risky projects every period.

Consider more precisely the case in which markets do not fail and the necessary conditions for reputation to have value (for example equation (2)) are true. If $T \to \infty$, then both t and $T - t$ can be made arbitrarily large. On such a date $t^\star$, proposition 1 states that safe projects are best and $r_{t^\star} = r^{g}_{t^\star}$. Because safe projects are best at $t^\star$, by lemma 7,

$$V_{t^\star} \geqslant d\left(G - \frac{G - \Pi B}{1 - \Pi}\right).$$

Note that r^g_t is a strictly decreasing function of t because f_{Bt} is strictly decreasing in t. When one moves back in time, if r^g_t becomes sufficiently high that risky projects are best at some date t', then on that date $r_{t'} = r^b_{t'}$. In addition, at any date $t < t'$, $r_t \geqslant r^g_{t'+1}$, and so safe projects will not be selected at $t < t'$. This implies that interest rates fall over time until the endgame and that the result of proposition 2 applies: if $T \to \infty$ and one considers dates away from the bounded endgame, then if safe projects are selected at $t^\star$ and risky projects at $t' < t^\star$, risky projects are selected for all $t \leqslant t'$.

To compute the values of V_t, values for r^g_t and r^b_t are needed, and these depend on decisions by type BGs at earlier periods. Because proposition 2 applies, the only information needed to calculate these interest rates is the single date $\bar{t}$, near $t = 1$, where BGs switch from risky to safe projects. Define the face value $R^g_t[\bar{t}]$ to be the one that gives lenders an expected return of r at date t if BGs choose safe projects at t, and the projects selected for dates less than t are risky projects from dates 1 to $\bar{t} - 1$ and safe projects for $t \in [\bar{t}, t-1]$ (if $t < \bar{t} - 1$, obviously there are no past dates on which safe projects were selected). The term $R^b_t[\bar{t}]$ is the face value that provides an expected return of r if risky projects are selected at t, and the projects selected at dates less than t are as described in the previous sentence. These rates are easily computed using the definitions of r^b_t and r^g_t because $f_{Bt} = \Pi_B^{t-1}$ and $f_{BGt} = \Pi^{t-1}$ if $t \leqslant \bar{t}$, with $f_{BGt} = \Pi^{\bar{t}-1}$ for $t > \bar{t}$.

The face values $R^b_t[\bar{t}]$ are given by

$$R^b_t[\bar{t}] = \frac{\Pi^{t-1} f_{BG} + \Pi_B^{t-1} f_B + f_G}{\Pi^t f_{BG} + \Pi_B^t f_B + f_G} r \qquad \text{if } t < \bar{t}$$

$$R^b_t[\bar{t}] = \frac{\Pi^{\bar{t}-1} f_{BG} + \Pi_B^{t-1} f_B + f_G}{\Pi^{\bar{t}} f_{BG} + \Pi^t f_B + f_G} r \qquad \text{if } t \in [\bar{t}, \tau]. \tag{6}$$

The face values $R_t^g[\bar{t}]$ are given by

$$R_t^g[\bar{t}] = \frac{\Pi^{t-1} f_{BG} + \Pi_B^{t-1} f_B + f_G}{\Pi^{t-1} f_{BG} + \Pi_B^t f_B + f_G} r \qquad \text{if } t < \bar{t}$$

$$R_t^g[\bar{t}] = \frac{\Pi^{\bar{t}-1} f_{BG} + \Pi_B^{t-1} f_B + f_G}{\Pi^{\bar{t}-1} f_{BG} + \Pi_B^t f_B + f_G} r \qquad \text{if } t \in [\bar{t}, \tau]. \tag{7}$$

Define the τ element vector $\boldsymbol{R}[\bar{t}]$ to be the face value series from 1 to τ, where the first $\bar{t}-1$ elements (for $t = 1, \ldots, \bar{t}-1$) are given by $R_t^b[\bar{t}]$ and the final elements (from $\bar{t}$ to τ) are given by $R_t^g[\bar{t}]$. This is the interest rate series anticipated given the definition of $\bar{t}$. The equilibrium value of $\bar{t}$ is the smallest self-fulfilling value of $\bar{t}$: if $\bar{t} = 1$ is self-fulfilling in the sense that safe projects are best if $\boldsymbol{R}[1]$ (that is, $r_t = R_t^g[1]$ for $t = 1, \ldots, \tau$) is anticipated, then no period of reputation acquisition is required and $\bar{t} = 1$.

Denote the present value of choosing safe projects from $\hat{t}$ to τ facing rates $\boldsymbol{R}[\bar{t}]$ as $W_{\hat{t}}[\bar{t}]$, given by

$$W_{\hat{t}}[\bar{t}] = \sum_{t=\hat{t}}^{\tau} (G - R_t^g[\bar{t}])d^{1+t-\hat{t}} + (V_\tau d^{1+\tau-\hat{t}}).$$

As $\tau \to \infty$, the final term approaches zero, and we can approximate $W_{\hat{t}}[\bar{t}]$ arbitrarily closely by $\overline{W}_{\hat{t}}[\bar{t}]$:

$$\overline{W}_{\hat{t}}[\bar{t}] \equiv \sum_{t=\hat{t}}^{\infty} (G - R_t^g[\bar{t}])d^{1+t-\hat{t}}.$$

If

$$R_1^g[1] - \overline{W}_2[1] \leqslant \frac{G - \Pi B}{1 - \Pi},$$

then $r_t = R_t^g[1]$ for all $t \in [1, \tau]$, and $\tau \to \infty$ as $T \to \infty$. In this case, reputation works immediately. Alternatively, if

$$R_1^g[1] - \overline{W}_2[1] > \frac{G - \Pi B}{1 - \Pi},$$

then risky projects will be selected at $t = 1$. Under the assumption that markets do not fail and that (2) holds, then eventually safe projects will be selected. This will occur on the smallest $\hat{t}$ such that

$$R_t^g[\hat{t}] - \overline{W}_{\hat{t}} + 1[\hat{t}] \leqslant \frac{G - \Pi B}{1 - \Pi}.$$

Safe projects will be selected from that date for an unbounded number of periods until τ, as $T \to \infty$.

This provides a characterization of interest rates and project decisions of type BGs up to any fixed $\tau < \infty$ as $T \to \infty$, under the assumption that (2) holds and that markets do not fail. If (2) is false, then risky projects are selected in each period if markets do not fail. The condition for markets not to fail is $r_1 \leqslant G$. If safe projects are best at $t = 1$, there are open markets if and only if $R_1^g[1] \leqslant G$. If risky projects are best at $t = 1$, there are open markets if and only if $R_1^b[1] \leqslant G$.

It is straightforward to show that the condition that determines the optimal project at $t = 1$ for type BGs, $R_1^g[1] - \overline{W}_2[1]$, is a strictly increasing function of f_B because higher f_B implies higher interest rates at all dates. Because $R_1^g[1] - \overline{W}_2[1]$ is computed using the interest rates r_t^g, the condition does not depend on f_{BG}. There are two conditions for open markets. The first, $R_1^g[1] \leqslant G$, does not depend on f_{BG} but requires f_B to be below some positive level. The second condition, $R_1^b[1] \leqslant G$, requires an upper bound on f_B and $f_B + f_{BG}$. These results are used to add conditions on f_B and f_{BG} to the characterization of equilibrium. Further comparative statics properties of $R_1^g[1] - \overline{W}_2[1]$ are presented in section 7.1. Proposition 3 summarizes our characterization.

Proposition 3 For any fixed date $\tau < \infty$, there exists a horizon $T < \infty$ such that, for all $t < \tau$, the following conditions hold.

1 If $R_1^g[1] - \overline{W}_2[1] \leqslant (G - \Pi B)/(1 - \Pi)$ and $R_1^g[1] \leqslant G$ (that is, f_B is sufficiently low and (2) holds), then there is an *immediate reputation equilibrium* in which safe projects are selected for all $t \leqslant \tau$ and interest rates are $\boldsymbol{R}[1]$.
2 If $R_1^g[1] - \overline{W}_2[1] > (G - \Pi B)/(1 - \Pi)$ and $R_1^b[1] \leqslant G$ (that is, f_B is above a positive critical level and $f_B + f_{BG}$ is not too high) and (2) holds, then there is a *reputation acquisition equilibrium*: BGs choose risky projects on dates $t < \bar{t}$ and safe projects on $t \in [\bar{t}, \tau)$, where $\bar{t}$ is the smallest t such that $R_{\bar{t}}^g[\bar{t}] - \overline{W}_{\bar{t}+1}[\bar{t}] \leqslant (G - \Pi B)/(1 - \Pi)$. The equilibrium r_t is $\boldsymbol{R}[\bar{t}]$.
3 If $R_1^g[1] - \overline{W}_2[1] > (G - \Pi B)/(1 - \Pi)$ and $R_1^g[1] \leqslant G$ (that is, f_B and $f_B + f_{BG}$ are each not too high) and (2) is false, then there is *no reputation effect* and BGs select risky projects for all $t \leqslant T$ with interest rates given by $\boldsymbol{R}[\tau]$.
4 If either $R_1^g[1] - \overline{W}_2[1] \leqslant (G - \Pi B)/(1 - \Pi)$ and $R_1^g[1] > G$ (that is, f_B is too high) or $R_1^g[1] - \overline{W}_2[1] > (G - \Pi B)/(1 - \Pi)$ and $R_1^b[1] > G$ (that is, f_B and $f_B + f_{BG}$ are each too high and (2) is false), then *markets fail* on all $t \leqslant T$.

The reason that a period of reputation acquisition in which risky projects are selected may be necessary is the same as with $f_{BG} = 0$: type BGs are pooled together with type Bs, which leads to high initial interest rates. If there were very few type Bs, then the initial interest rates would be low, near r, because rates are low under the conjecture that type BGs choose safe projects. The many type Bs lead to high initial rates for all borrowers that imply a lower present value of rents in the future, weakening the cementing force of a valuable reputation.

It is the type Bs in the initial pool of borrowers that cause reputation initially to be too weak: adverse selection prevents immediate reputation effects. The consequences of a weak initial reputation depend on the large number of type BGs. The larger is f_{BG}, the larger is the difference between the interest rate r_t^g that occurs if type BGs choose safe projects and the rate r_t^b, that occurs when they choose risky projects.

7.1 *A summary of comparative statics*

Simple calculations show that each of the following comparative statics changes decreases $R_1^g[1] - \overline{W}_2[1]$, improving the relative payoff of the risky project at $t = 1$ and making it less likely that reputation will provide incentives to those with short track records: (a) increase the fraction f_B of type Bs; (b) decrease the payment G of the safe project; (c) increase the payment B of the risky project when successful; (d) increase the riskless interest rate r; (e) decrease the discount factor d.

The first four changes increase $R_1^g[1]$ and (weakly) decrease $\overline{W}_2[1]$, both of which improve the current relative payoff of the risky project (lemma 7). A decrease in the discount factor d makes the present value of any fixed decision in the future lower and decreases $\overline{W}_2[1]$, and this improves the relative payoff to selecting the risky project.

There is not an unambiguous comparative statics effect on $R_1^g[1] - \overline{W}_2[1]$ from reducing the probability Π_B of type B's project succeeding, because a lower Π_B implies both that the initial face value $R_1^g[1]$ is higher and that $R_t^g[1]$ falls at a more rapid rate. These two effects are weighted by the discount factor d. Depending on the value of d, the net effect can go in either direction. One simple result is that, given pairs of f_B and Π_B that imply the same value of $R_1^g[1]$, higher f_B combined with higher Π_B improves the value of beginning with the risky project because the rate then falls less rapidly. This decreases the value $\overline{W}_2[1]$ of going into period 2 without a default. All the comparative statics results above, except those dealing with f_B and Π_B, influence not only $R_1^g[1] - \overline{W}_2[1]$ but also condition (2), the condition for reputation to have value at some date. Reputation acquisition requires $R_1^g[1] - \overline{W}_2[1] > (G - \Pi B)/(1 - \Pi)$ and (2). The simplest explanation of when this is likely to be the case relates to the "amount of inequality" in (2), that is, by how much safe projects dominate risky projects when financed forever at the riskless rate of interest. If (2) is close to an equality, then values of $f_B > 0$ and $\Pi_B < 1$ that imply even a small increase in interest rates $R_1^g[1]$ above r in early periods will tip the balance to risky projects because $\overline{W}_2[1]$ needs to be near its maximum possible value $d(G-r)/(1-d)$ for safe projects to be best. If, instead, (2) is far from being an equality, then reputation acquisition will not be the equilibrium. This is because very large values of $R_1^g[1]$ are necessary to tip the balance toward risky projects, implying high f_B and low Π_B that also imply rapidly falling rates. The value of $R_1^g[1]$ necessary to make risky projects best at $t=1$ would exceed G and result instead in market failure.

In summary, if the maximal value of future rents is too small, (2) is also false and there will be no reputation effect. If there are sufficient rents so that (2) is true and is far enough from being an equality, then an active loan market implies immediate reputation. If the rents on safe projects are positive but not exceedingly large (and (2) is not too far from an equality), then there will be reputation acquisition in early periods with risky projects dominating if there is sufficient adverse selection: if f_B and Π_B imply that the face value $R_t^g[1]$ is significantly above r for small t.

8 Conclusion

The analysis of incentive problems in debt markets shows that it is likely that these problems will be most severe in early periods when new firms have short track records. If there is sufficiently widespread adverse selection, the initial pool of borrowers will be of low average quality and the interest rates for borrowers with short track records will be high. As a result, the present value of rents in the future from establishing a good reputation will start out very low. Rents can be sufficiently low that those with a choice of projects choose the short-run optimum, the risky low value project. A fraction of those who select the risky project achieve success and are able to repay their loans continually, achieving a good reputation. As a borrower achieves a good reputation, the interest rate falls, and the present value of rents in the future from a good reputation rises. Eventually these rents become high enough for the borrower to switch to the long-run optimum, the safe high value project, for an arbitrarily large number of periods until the endgame. Only if there is little adverse selection will reputation instead work to provide incentives to new borrowers immediately. The model specifies the reputation in terms of the credit rating, which is public information. Observable implications of the model then have empirical content.

A number of the model's conclusions are quite general and apply to the general study of reputation in markets. The key assumptions that differ from the reputation model in Kreps and Wilson (1982a) are that, in our model, actions are not observed and there is a nontrivial fraction of all agent types. If actions (project choices) are directly observable, then unless there are incentives in the first period to take an action that is beneficial to one's reputation, there is never any incentive to take that action. In terms of our model, once observed selecting a risky project, a borrower can never credibly claim to be of type G. In terms of the chain store in Kreps and Wilson (1982a), once it gives in to an entrant, it can never credibly claim to be "tough." The existence of nontrivial fractions of all types, that is, significant adverse selection, is important because otherwise the incentive effect of a reputation would be near its maximal value in the initial period. In our model, borrowing would begin at essentially the riskless rate of interest. In a more general setting, for example a market for goods or services of unobservable quality, if there is significant adverse selection the market will have low expectations of initial quality, and the market will not pay very high prices for the output of agents without a long record. This implies that agents with short track records will have a low initial present value of rents in the future, and those with a choice will supply low quality. Only over time, with an acquired good record, will there be a large present value of rents in the future from maintaining a good reputation by providing high quality. In addition, although we have not modeled entry, the low initial present value of rents is an appealing notion in a free-entry setting.

The model has direct applications to examinations of differential new project acceptance decisions: firms with certain reputations will turn down a given profitable project that others would accept. This can be interpreted as a well-defined cost of capital that is firm specific rather than project specific because of the private information about project decisions. In addition, the model can be used to explain, on the basis of public information, some determinants of which firms choose to borrow through financial intermediaries and use their delegated monitoring services (Diamond, 1988). If the intermediary (at a cost) can help control project decisions, then the model suggests that firms with short histories will acquire their reputation by borrowing from intermediaries. Firms with a long standing high credit rating will borrow directly in the open market. These are just a few examples of what we hope will be a large harvest of extensions with strong empirical implications.

Appendix

Proof of lemma 4

Lenders observe the past record of default/liquidation. Lenders believe the following. If there was a past liquidation, the project was assumed to return less than G in that period, and type is assumed to be either B or BG with probabilities specified by Bayes's law. If there were no liquidations in any previous period when credit was granted, a borrower's project returned at least r each past period (this is implied by lemma 3), and Bayes's law specifies conditional probabilities across the types that could produce such a record. The actions supported by these beliefs are that a default implies no future loans (this action is the important one) and a lack of past default leads to future loans if they are at rates that offer an expected return of at least r. It turns out that the repayment decision does not depend on the specification of the action taken when there is no previous default.

Let $V_t \geqslant 0$ be the beginning of period t present value of expected consumption of a borrower making optimal project selection and loan repayment decisions from t to T. If a borrower repays less than r_t, then $V_{t+1} = 0$ because those who default are not believed to be type Gs. For all payments that avoid liquidation, V_{t+1} is a nonnegative constant. Let θ_t be the realization of the project return of the borrower in period t (that is, $\theta_t \in \{0, B, G\}$). The repayment selected at the end of period t by a borrower is Z_t; it is subject to the constraints $Z_t \leqslant \theta_t$ and $Z_t \geqslant 0$. The constraints imply that if $\theta_t = 0$ then $Z_t = 0$.

Discounted expected consumption of the borrower with $\theta_t \geqslant G \geqslant r$ at date t for each of the three actions $Z_t = r_t$, $Z_t > r_t$, and $Z_t < r_t$ is given by

$$\underbrace{\theta_t - r_t + V_{t+1}}_{\text{payoff from } Z_t = r_t} \quad > \quad \underbrace{\theta_t - Z_t + V_{t+1}}_{\text{payoff from } Z_t > r_t} \quad \geqslant \quad \underbrace{0.}_{\text{payoff from } Z_t < r_t}$$

All borrowers with $\theta_t \geqslant r_t$ select $Z_t = r_t$. Only borrowers with project returns less than r_t default, and they pay $Z_t = 0$. This implies that the beliefs above are self-fulfilling when $r_t \leqslant G$.

For completeness, consider the case $r_t \geqslant G$. It might appear that lenders' beliefs would be contradicted by the necessity of type G's defaulting if $r_t > G$. However, future lenders condition on the fact that a loan was made in a past period, and lemma 3 shows that lenders would not lend at date t if $r_t > G$. ■

Proof of lemma 9

It is always feasible to select safe projects each period, and we know, for $t \geqslant \hat{t}$, that $r_t < dG + (1-d)(G - \Pi B)/(1-\Pi)$, implying

$$V_{\hat{t}} \geqslant \sum_{t=\hat{t}}^{T} (G - r_t) d^{t+1-\hat{t}} > \sum_{t=\hat{t}}^{T} \left\{ G - \left[dG + (1-d) \frac{G - \Pi B}{1 - \Pi} \right] \right\} d^{t+1-\hat{t}}.$$

Taking the limit of the final expression as $T \to \infty$ yields

$$\frac{d}{1-d} \left\{ G - \left[dG + (1-d) \frac{G - \Pi B}{1 - \Pi} \right] \right\}$$

$$= \frac{d}{(1-d)(1-\Pi)} \{ [G(1-d)(1-\Pi)] + [(1-d)(G - \Pi B)] \}$$

$$= d\left(G - \frac{G - \Pi B}{1 - \Pi} \right).$$

This implies that we can find $T < \infty$ such that

$$V_{\hat{t}} > d\left(G - \frac{G - \Pi B}{1 - \Pi}\right).$$

By lemma 7, we can then conclude that safe projects are optimal at date $\hat{t}$. We now prove that $dG + (1 - d)(G - \Pi B)/(1 - \Pi) > r$ if and only if (4) holds:

$$\begin{aligned} dG + (1 - d)\frac{G - \Pi B}{1 - \Pi} &= d\left(G - \frac{G - \Pi B}{1 - \Pi}\right) + \frac{G - \Pi B}{1 - \Pi} \\ &= \frac{d\Pi(B - G)}{1 - \Pi} + \frac{G - \Pi B}{1 - \Pi} \\ &> r \end{aligned}$$

if and only if (4) holds. ■

Proof of lemma 13

A mixed strategy period can be continued on a date on which f_{Bt} is close to zero if

$$r_t^{\mathrm{b}} > dG + \frac{(1 - d)(G - \Pi B)}{1 - \Pi},$$

and continuing the mixed strategy period reduces f_{BGt} at an increasing rate. This implies that a finite number of indifference periods, ending on date t^0, will reduce f_{BGt} sufficiently, and so, for $t \in [t^0, T]$,

$$r_t \leqslant r_t^{\mathrm{b}} < dG + \frac{(1 - d)(G - \Pi B)}{1 - \Pi}.$$

By lemma 9, there exists $T < \infty$ such that

$$V_{t^0} \geqslant d\left(G - \frac{G - \Pi B}{1 - \Pi}\right) = H,$$

implying that safe projects can be best at t^0. For such a fixed T, there exists $t^1 \leqslant T$ such that $V_{t^1} < L$ because $V_T < L$ by (1). This implies that the mixed strategy period could end on date t^0 such that $V_{t^0} \geqslant H$ or on date t^1 such that $V_{t^1} \leqslant L$. There then exists an ending date for mixed strategy period $t' \in [t^0, t^1]$ such that $V_{t'} \in [L, H]$: choose the largest ending date t such that $V_t < L$, implying that $V_{t-1} \geqslant L$. If $V_t \leqslant L$, then risky projects are selected at $t - 1$, and by lemma 7,

$$V_{t-1} \leqslant d\left(G - \frac{G - \Pi B}{1 - \Pi}\right) = dH < H.$$

Thus $V_{t-1} \in [L, H)$. ■

Notes

1 For some early studies of reputation in debt markets see Spatt (1983) and Stiglitz and Weiss (1983).

2 There has been some previous analysis of reputation building. In the two-sided uncertainty version of Kreps and Wilson (1982a) "weak" types follow a mixed strategy between playing tough or weak, and enough repeated realizations of tough behavior convince others that one is probably not weak, building one's reputation. Milgrom and Roberts (1982) also allow a type that cannot play tough, and this can cause reputation building in the initial period of their model. Neither paper focuses on reputation acquisition, and because actions are assumed to be observable, neither is consistent with a given agent choosing the weak action in the beginning and then switching to the strong action later.

3 In the model, *ex ante* separation by choice of contract before any borrowing takes place is not viable.

4 This feature of the collateral-like incentive value of an asset that depreciates in case of default is also present in Merton (1978), where it arises in the case of a bank that prepays for many years of deposit insurance and failure implies that it can issue insured deposits for only a few of those years. The difference is that it arises endogenously in this formulation and is not necessarily present in the initial time periods.

5 It is simplest to think about the case in which $\Pi = \Pi_B$, and the risky project is identical with that of type B borrowers. The extra generality is stated simply because all our results hold for $\Pi \leqslant \Pi_B$ as well.

6 Diamond (1986) found that the identical outcomes are a sequential equilibrium supported by the belief that for any interest rate offered in a period there is no information about a borrower's type.

7 Beginning of period expected utility is obtained by multiplying each end of period expected utility by $d < 1$.

8 This belief – that the implication of any rate offered is the pool of all current borrowers – satisfies various refinements of sequential Nash equilibrium (for example, the Cho–Kreps (1987) intuitive criterion that disallows inferences from off-equilibrium actions that imply belief that some type took an action dominated by the proposed equilibrium payoff). This is true because all types prefer lower interest rates, and the only types that want to distinguish themselves are the type Gs, who never default and therefore face a cost of higher rates that is weakly higher than the cost for other types. There is no consistent interpretation of a deviation from all types offering the same rate, and this is true in any sequential equilibrium. This also implies that the pooling on the lowest rate is the unique equilibrium that satisfies the definition given by Grossman and Perry (1986).

9 The belief that those who have defaulted are those who were constrained to default and that those who did not are the pool of all who could avoid default satisfies the refinements to equilibrium mentioned in note 8. This is because default is feasible for all types and has the lowest cost for the types who must default, implying that it is not self-fulfilling to believe that default conveys news that default could have been avoided. There can be no future favorable inference from current default and there is a current benefit from avoiding liquidation, and so all who can do so avoid default. This is the unique self-fulfilling belief about repayment and default of a loan actually granted in the past.

10 It is not essential to our basic approach that credit be cut off. A similar effect occurs in a version of this model in which all projects have positive net present value but safe

projects have higher net present value. This implies that the best response to a default is an increase in the interest rate.

11 One more general implication of lemma 1 is that contract choice cannot separate the various types of borrowers, no matter how the beliefs are specified. Any contract that only a type other than G would offer would lead to no lending now or in the future and zero consumption for the borrower offering the contract. A contract that specifies a payment feasible for type Gs (who can pay at most G) would allow the other types to have positive expected consumption, dominating the zero consumption implied by a separating contract that would be offered only by a type other than G.

12 The belief that the rate offered reveals nothing new about type satisfies the refinements mentioned in note 8, and pooling of rates at this rate is the only outcome that fulfills the equilibrium defined by Grossman and Perry (1986). The reason is the same as at the final period T: offering rates above the minimum needed has no differentially lower cost for type G (the only type that would want to differentiate itself), and the new wrinkle is that in later periods those who offer rates deviating from the proposed equilibrium rates are treated identically to those who offer the proposed equilibrium rates. Therefore there is no consistent interpretation of a deviation from the proposed rates.

13 We use a version of the law of large numbers here by equating the fraction of type Bs who actually repay with its expected value. This can be made rigorous (Feldman and Gilles, 1985).

References

Cho, I.-K. and Kreps, D. M. (1987) "Signaling Games and Stable Equilibria," *Quarterly Journal of Economics*, 102, May, 179–221.

Diamond, D. W. (1984) "Financial Intermediation and Delegated Monitoring," *Review of Economic Studies*, 51, July, 393–414.

Diamond, D. W. (1986) "Reputation Acquisition in Debt Markets," Manuscript, Graduate School of Business, University of Chicago, February.

Diamond, D. W. (1988) "Monitoring and Reputation: The Choice between Bank Loans and Directly Placed Debt," *Working Paper*, Graduate School of Business, University of Chicago, July.

Dybvig, P. H. and Spatt, C. (1980), "Does It Pay to Maintain a Reputation?" Manuscript, Princeton University, Princeton, NJ.

Fama, E. F. (1980) "Agency Problems and the Theory of the Firm," *Journal of Political Economy*, 88, April, 288–307.

Fama, E. F. and Miller, M. H. (1972) *The Theory of Finance* (New York: Holt, Rinehart and Winston).

Feldman, M. and Gilles, C. (1985) "A Expository Note on Individual Risk without Aggregate Uncertainty," *Journal of Economic Theory*, 35, February, 26–32.

Gale, D. and Hellwig, M. (1985) "Incentive-Compatible Debt Contracts: The One-Period Problem," *Review of Economic Studies*, 52, October, 647–63.

Grossman, S. J. and Perry, M. (1986) "Perfect Sequential Equilibrium," *Journal of Economic Theory*, 39, June, 97–119.

Holmstrom, B. (1982) "Managerial Incentive Problems: A Dynamic Perspective." In *Essays in Economics and Management in Honour of Lars Wahlbeck* (Helsinki: Swedish School of Economics).

Jensen, M. C. and Meckling, W. H. (1976) "Theory of the Firm: Managerial Behavior, Agency Costs and Ownership Structure," *Journal of Financial Economics*, 3, October, 305–60.

Klein, B. and Leffler, K. B. (1981) "The Role of Market Forces in Assuring Contractual Performance," *Journal of Political Economy*, 89, August, 615–41.

Kreps, D. M. and Wilson, R. (1982a) "Reputation and Imperfect Information," *Journal of Economic Theory*, 27, August, 253–79.

Kreps, D. M. and Wilson, R. (1982b) "Sequential Equilibria," *Econometrica*, 50, July, 863–94.

Merton, R. C. (1978) "On the Cost of Deposit Insurance When There Are Surveillance Costs," *Journal of Business*, 51, July, 439–52.

Milgrom, P. and Roberts, J. (1982) "Predation, Reputation, and Entry Deterrence," *Journal of Economic Theory*, 27, August, 280–312.

Smith, C. W., Jr, and Warner, J. B. (1979) "On Financial Contracting: An Analysis of Bond Covenants," *Journal of Financial Economics*, 7, June, 117–61.

Spatt, C. (1983) "Credit Reputation Equilibrium and the Theory of Credit Markets," Manuscript, Carnegie-Mellon University, May.

Stiglitz, J. E. and Weiss, A. (1981) "Credit Rationing in Markets with Imperfect Information," *American Economic Review*, 71, June, 393–410.

Stiglitz, J. E. and Weiss, A. (1983) "Incentive Effects of Terminations: Applications to the Credit and Labor Markets," *American Economic Review*, 73, December, 912–27.

Townsend, R. M. (1979) "Optimal Contracts and Competitive Markets with Costly State Verification," *Journal of Economic Theory*, 21, October, 265–93.

Chapter 11

Terry A. Marsh

Background and Comments

The paper by Terry Marsh and Robert Merton is an exhaustive and authoritative treatment of the behavior of aggregate dividends. It is fully consistent with managers' practical sense of dividend policy (as first expressed by Lintner (1956)). However, their statistical expression of these ideas is new.

The problem is to capture the hypothesized relationship between changes in cash dividends and changes in true economic income – a variable which is not observable and very difficult to approximate by adjusting reported book earnings. In Marsh and Merton's specification, changes in stock prices are used as an indirect measure for changes in economic income. If the stock market is rational and efficient, stock prices will anticipate changes in economic income and therefore will also anticipate changes in dividends. The good performance of Marsh and Merton's model therefore supports market efficiency.

In fact a controversy about market efficiency was one original motivation for their work. Robert Shiller had argued that the stock market's volatility was much too large to be explained by rational valuation models. Such models basically state that stock price should equal the present value of future dividends. Yet Shiller observed that stock prices have been much more volatile than dividends. He argued that prices must be disconnected from dividends and therefore from fundamentals.

Marsh and Merton show that Shiller's conclusion depends on a critical assumption about how dividends evolve over time. If they behave as this paper says they do, the high volatility of stock prices can be explained in a fully rational market. The interested reader should pay particular attention to section 6 of this paper and also look into other work by Shiller (1981) and Marsh and Merton (1986) on this topic. They should also turn to the papers in this volume by Eugene Fama and Kenneth French (chapter 16) and by James Poterba and Lawrence Summers (chapter 17).

References

Lintner, J. (1956) "Distribution of Incomes of Corporations Among Dividends, Retained Earnings, and Taxes," *American Economic Review*, 61: 2, May, 97–113.

Marsh, T. A. and Merton, R. C. (1986) "Dividend Variability and Variance Bounds Tests for the Rationality of Stock Market Prices," *American Economic Review*, 76: 3, June, 483–98.

Shiller, R. J. (1981) "Do Stock Prices Move Too Much to be Justified by Subsequent Changes in Dividends?" *American Economic Review*, 71, June, 421–36.

Author's Introduction

The model in the paper was developed in the course of our attempt to understand the behavior of stock prices relative to firm fundamentals. The building blocks of our dividend model are the stylized facts established by John Lintner in his survey of corporate dividend decisions in the mid-1950s. Specifically, Lintner's evidence suggests that, on average, managers base their dividend decisions on shifts in permanent earnings, and that they try to maintain some steady state dividend payout ratio. Our model, in which aggregate annual corporate dividends move systematically with stock prices and regress toward a long-run ratio of aggregate stock prices, is consistent with Lintner when changes in stock prices are a good indicator of changes in firms' permanent earnings.

If investors hold portfolios of securities, their dividend demands will be couched in terms of some aggregate of corporate dividends. Our finding that the simple sum of corporations' dividends displays systematic behavior raises interesting questions that in part concern the supply side. Are the micro-level mechanics of supply indeterminate, or is some corporate objective function being maximized in dividend decisions? If there is smoothing of dividends relative to permanent earnings changes, is it supply side or demand side driven? Dividend decisions are, with some constraints, under the control of corporate management, so perhaps compensation contexts and arrangements will yield insights – indeed, the agency approach explains dividends as a broad brush means of aligning corporate and management objectives. The asymmetric information models of dividends also ultimately involve investor objective functions or, more precisely, the question of how to combine the demand functions of disparately informed or heterogeneous investors and construct appropriate management incentive contracts. The stability of the behavior of aggregate dividends, for which announcement dates are not meaningful, gives us an additional piece of information on how these problems are solved if asymmetric information is the driving force behind dividend behavior.

Of course it is possible that the breakdown in supply of dividends is determinate but reasonably unimportant. After all, Merton Miller and Franco Modigliani made it clear that dividends are not *per se* a first-order determinant of firm value. Minor transactions costs, desired "management style," historical precedent, and the like may be essentially the neutral mutations discussed by Miller in a related context. In our own preliminary empirical work at the firm level, we have not so far found any meaningful cross-sectional explanation of different firms' dividend dynamics.

However, the paucity of time series data on dividends and firm life-cycle characteristics severely limits our ability to study cross-sectional consistencies in the micro-level time series behavior of annual corporate dividends. We plan to supplement available data with our own survey of corporate dividend decisions. A "follow-up Lintner survey" should itself prove useful. It will take advantage of the substantial improvement in sample survey statistical methods and our understanding of the relevant questions about dividend behavior which has taken place in the 30 years since Lintner's study.

With the opportunity to collect survey evidence, we plan to broaden the scope of the analysis to net dividends. It is perhaps above all the combination of dividend payments and simultaneous new equity issues which makes dividend payments "a puzzle." At the general level of sources and uses of funds, we hope to gain insight into what is currently one of the larger dividend substitutes – the leveraged buyout.

Bibliographical Listing

"Trading Activity and Price Behavior in the Stock and Stock Index Futures Markets in October 1987" (with James E. Gammill Jr), *Journal of Economic Perspectives*, 2: 3, Summer 1988, 25–44.

"Dividend Variability and Variance Bounds Tests for the Rationality of Stock Market Prices" (with Robert C. Merton), *American Economic Review*, 76: 3, June 1986, 483–98.

"Nontrading, Market Making, and Estimates of Stock Price Volatility" (with Eric R. Rosenfeld), *Journal of Financial Economics*, 15: 3, March 1986, 359–72.

"Exchange Listing and Liquidity: A Comparison of the American Stock Exchange with the NASDAQ National Market System" (with Kevin Rock), American Stock Exchange Transactions Data Research Project Report No. 2, January 1986.

"On Nonlinear Temporal Dependencies in Stock Returns," *Journal of Econometrics*, 30: 1–2, October–November 1985, 289–96.

Dividend Behavior for the Aggregate Stock Market

TERRY A. MARSH and ROBERT C. MERTON

1 Introduction

In this paper, we develop a model of the dividend process for the aggregate stock market. Previous research has focused almost exclusively on dividend behavior at the micro-level of the individual firm. Hence to motivate the focus here on aggregate dividend behavior, we begin with a brief review of these earlier micro studies, which is followed by a discussion that locates the place of our aggregate analysis within this body of research. In sections 2–5, we derive and fit our econometric model of the dividend process. In section 6, we compare the performance of the model with other models in the literature.

Although long a staple of financial management textbooks, corporate dividend policy remains a topic on which the field has failed to arrive at even a local sense of closure.[1] Black (1976) has aptly described this lack of closure as the "dividend puzzle." The pivotal point in this puzzle is the classic work of Miller and Modigliani (1961), which demonstrated the irrelevance of dividend policy for determining the firm's cost of capital.

Miller and Modigliani showed that, when investors can create any payout pattern they want by selling and purchasing shares, the expected return required to induce them to hold these shares will be invariant to the way in which firms "package" gross dividend payments and new issues of stock (and/or other zero-net-present-value transactions). Since neither the firm's expected future net cash flows nor its discount rate is affected by the choice of dividend policy *per se*, its current market value cannot be changed by a change in that policy. Thus dividend policy "does not matter." Although, under Miller and Modigliani's proposition, there are no *a priori* reasons for firms to follow any systematic dividend policy, there are also no penalties if they choose to do so.

Reproduced from *Journal of Business*, 60: 1 (1987) 1–40.

Robert C. Merton is George Fisher Baker Professor of Business Administration at Harvard University. This work was done while he was at Massachusetts Institute of Technology. We dedicate this paper to the scientific contributions and the memory of John V. Lintner Jr. We are grateful to J. Hausman, M. Miller, S. Myers, R. Ruback, and especially F. Black for helpful comments and to the Institute for Quantitative Research in Finance for partial funding.

Exceptions to Miller and Modigliani's view are, of course, to be found in the literature. Gordon (1959, 1962) and Lintner (1962) claim that dividend policy does affect the firm's cost of capital, and they provide some early evidence to support the view that a higher dividend payout reduces the cost of capital (that is, investors prefer dividends). Others argue that personal and corporate taxes cause dividend policy to affect the firm's cost of capital, but in the direction that a higher payout raises the cost of capital (that is, investors prefer capital gains). Litzenberger and Ramaswamy (1979) and Poterba and Summers (1984, 1985) offer empirical support for this view. In contrast Black and Scholes (1974), Miller and Scholes (1978, 1982), Hess (1983), and Eades, Hess, and Kim (1984) present analysis and evidence suggesting that, as an empirical matter, tax effects *per se* do not appear to affect the cost of capital. Easterbrook (1984) proposes an agency theory explanation for dividends. Along different lines from these studies, Shefrin and Statman (1984) have used behavioral theories of individual choice to argue that investors will prefer cash dividends even if they are tax disadvantaged. Although some of these analyses might provide reasons to believe that investors are not indifferent between cash dividends and capital gains, the empirical evidence to date is still inconclusive for rejecting Miller and Modigliani's proposition.

Even with their view of investor indifference for dividends, Miller and Modigliani (1961, p. 431) point out that dividend policy can matter if dividend changes are used by firms to convey information not otherwise known to the market. Bhattacharya (1979), John and Williams (1985), and Miller and Rock (1985) use a signaling model approach to formalize this notion. Hakansson (1982) derives the additional general equilibrium conditions required for dividend signals to improve investor welfare. Aharony and Swary (1980) provide some empirical evidence on the informational content of dividends in their study of dividend announcement events for 149 New York Stock Exchange (NYSE) industrials, in which they find that, on average, unexpected dividend and unexpected price changes are positively correlated around announcement dates. Asquith and Mullins (1983) find similar results for firms that initiate dividend payments for the first time. The evidence, however, is that the correlations, while statistically significant, are rather small, a conclusion also reached in empirical work by Watts (1973) and Gonedes (1978).

In summary, there are a number of conflicting theories of dividend behavior, and the empirical studies to date provide little compelling evidence for one over the others. The management of a firm is free to choose a dividend policy with virtually any time pattern it wants, subject only to the overall constraint that the present value of expected future distributions net of new stock offerings cannot exceed the present value of the firm's expected net cash flows generated by its investments. Indeed, except for certain debt indenture restrictions and accumulated earnings tax penalties, there do not appear to be any significant legal, accounting convention, or corporate tax factors to exert pressures on managers of publicly traded and widely held corporations to follow any particular dividend policy.

With so much controversy surrounding the various normative theories of the dividend process, it is perhaps not surprising that empirical researchers have relied heavily on positive theories of dividend behavior to specify their models. The prototype for these models is that of Lintner (1956), which is based on stylized facts first established by him in a classic set of interviews with managers about their dividend policies. A similar model, motivated by Friedman's permanent income hypothesis, is proposed by Fisher (1957). From Lintner's interviews, it was readily apparent that dividend policies across firms were hardly uniform. However, Lintner did identify some common characteristics: namely, managers tend to change dividends primarily in response to an unanticipated and nontransitory change in their firm's earnings, and they are guided by target payout ratios in making those changes. Using an econometric model based on these perceived patterns, Lintner found that he could explain a significant portion of annual dividend changes for a sample of companies over the period 1918–41. Using similar types of models, subsequent empirical work by Fama and Babiak (1968), Petit (1972), and Watts (1973) supports Lintner's original findings.

With few exceptions, notably Brittain (1966) and Shiller (1981a,b), research on both normative and positive models of dividends has focused on the microbehavior of individual firms. The relative lack of research on aggregate dividend behavior is perhaps not surprising since many of the more interesting issues surrounding dividend policy are likely to be firm specific. For example, clientele effects and indenture restrictions that could in principle affect an individual firm's dividend policy are likely to "wash out" in any aggregate dividend analysis. Similarly, issues involving the informational content of an individual firm's dividends are likely to be considerably less important for the stock market as a whole than for an individual firm. It is, indeed, difficult to see how one could identify meaningful announcement dates for aggregate dividends to perform event studies along the lines of those by Gonedes (1978) and Aharony and Swary (1980).

If firms only changed their dividends to signal information, and if the only information worth signaling is specific to the firm, then changes in aggregate dividends would be random and their magnitudes small. If, however, firms change their dividends for reasons other than signaling, then the very fact that aggregate dividend changes are unlikely to contain much signaling information may make them an especially useful series for measuring the informational content of an individual firm's dividend announcements. To identify the signals or abnormal changes in a firm's dividends, it is, of course, necessary to have a model of its "normal" dividend behavior. Watts (1973), for example, uses Lintner's model for this purpose. However, Lintner's model does not take account of the cross-sectional dependences among firms' dividend policies. It is reasonable to expect that, in addition to its own economic circumstances, the firm would use the dividend behavior of other firms to calibrate its dividend policy – as, for example, observing industry practice in the selection of its target payout ratio. Moreover, these dependences may be of considerable empirical significance in the light of the already documented strong correlations among different firms' contemporaneous stock price changes. Removal of the aggregate market component of a stock's return to obtain a better estimate of its abnormal price change is commonplace. Just so, use of an aggregate dividend model to remove the "systematic" component of an individual firm's dividend policy would appear to provide a better estimate of its abnormal dividend changes.[2]

If individual firms follow reasonably stable dividend policies over time, then the aforementioned cross-sectional dependences will induce systematic behavior in the time series of aggregate dividends. It is possible, however, for aggregate dividends to exhibit stable and consistent time series properties even if no such stability were found for individual firms. For example, in a purely demand driven model for dividends, the demand for dividends is not firm specific because investors care only about the dividend–capital gain mix at the portfolio level. Hence, as in Miller's (1977) theory of corporate debt, there will be, in general, many different allocations of dividend policies to individual firms that will support an equilibrium in the dividend market. Thus equilibrium aggregate dividends may be determinate, but which firms service this demand and the quantity each chooses to supply may not.[3]

In the next section, we motivate the specification of our econometric model with a discussion of the descriptive facts established in Lintner's interviews.[4] This is followed in sections 3, 4, and 5 by the estimation and testing of the model.

Although sharing Lintner's stylized facts with the previously cited empirical studies of micro dividend behavior, our model, in addition to being applied at the aggregate level, differs significantly from these earlier studies because it assumes that economic earnings, not accounting earnings, are the primary determinant of dividends. The analysis in section 6 compares the performance of our model with one that uses accounting earnings. Because the Brittain (1966) study of aggregate dividends relies on the relations between dividends and accounting variables, our analysis sheds light on his findings as well. In this same section, we also compare the relative performance of our model with the univariate trend autoregressive model associated with Shiller's (1981a,b) model of aggregate dividends.

2 Model of Aggregate Dividend Dynamics

Lintner found considerable heterogeneity among firms' dividend policies in his interviews with corporate managers. However, he also found some characteristics to be common to many of these firms' dividend policies. These stylized facts are summarized as follows: (a) managers believe that firms should have some long-term target payout ratio; (b) in setting dividends, they focus on the change in existing payouts, not on the level; (c) a major unanticipated and nontransitory change in earnings would be an important reason to change dividends; (d) most managers try to avoid making changes in dividends that stand a good chance of having to be reversed within the near future.

Most textbook discussions seem to agree with the interpretation of these stylized facts to the effect that it is changes in some measure of long-run sustainable or "permanent" earnings, rather than current earnings, that drive dividend decisions. That is, a change in current earnings flow that is viewed by management as essentially transitory would not be likely to give rise to a noticeable change in dividends. Unfortunately, except for the special case of a firm whose future earnings are certain and generated without further net new investment, the textbooks are not specific in defining permanent earnings. Our interpretation (which is consistent with this special case) defines the permanent earnings per share of a firm at time t as equal to the expectation as of time t of that level of uniform payments that could be made by the firm to a single share in perpetuity. For an all-equity-financed firm, permanent earnings are determined as follows. Let $\Pi(s)$ denote the real after-tax cash flow from the physical and financial assets of the firm at time s and $I(s)$ denote the real net new investment by the firm at time s, where $I(s)$ is the gross new physical investment plus purchases of financial assets minus sales of physical and financial assets. If α denotes the firm's real cost of capital, then the discounted value of the expected cash flows available for distribution to each share outstanding at time t is given by

$$V(t) \equiv \frac{\varepsilon_t\{\int_t^\infty [\Pi(s) - I(s)] \exp[-\alpha(s-t)] \, ds\}}{N(t)}, \qquad (1)$$

where ε_t denotes the expectation operator, conditional on information available as of time t, and $N(t)$ denotes the number of shares outstanding. The variable $V(t)$ is sometimes called the "intrinsic value" (per share) of the firm, and permanent earnings per share are determined by creating a perpetual annuity from this intrinsic value.[5] That is, if $E(t)$ denotes permanent earnings per share of the firm at time t, then

$$E(t) = \alpha V(t). \tag{2}$$

Since corporate managers set dividends for their firms, it is their assessments of permanent earnings that are relevant for the evolution of aggregate dividends. For this purpose, we denote managers' determination of permanent earnings by $E^{\mathrm{m}}(t) = \alpha V^{\mathrm{m}}(t)$, where $V^{\mathrm{m}}(t)$ is given by (1) with the expectation operator $\varepsilon_t = \varepsilon_t^{\mathrm{m}}$ based on the probability distribution for future $\Pi(s)$ and $I(s)$ generated by the managers' information sets as of time t.

Although Lintner's stylized facts suggest that dividend changes are related to changes in permanent earnings, the interview data on which they are based contain little information about the detailed functional form of that relation.[6] In the absence of a specific structural model of that relation, we posit that logarithmic dividends can be expressed as the sum of a rational distributed lag of logarithmic permanent earnings, a drift term $a(t)$ that is conditional on information known at time t, and a disturbance term $\eta(t)$. That is, we represent the aggregate dividend process as

$$(1 - \phi_1 L) \log[D(t)] = a(t) + (\lambda - \theta_1 L) \log[E^{\mathrm{m}}(t-1)] + \eta(t), \tag{3}$$

where $D(t)$ is the integral $\int_{t-1}^{t} D(s)\, ds$ of aggregate dividends paid per share of the market portfolio over the interval from time $t-1$ to time t, $E^{\mathrm{m}}(t)$ is permanent earnings as defined in (2) per share of the market portfolio at time t, and the roots of the first-order polynomials in the lag operator L are outside the unit circle.

As specified, (3) is consistent with the "short-run" dividend dynamics of Lintner's model. It does not, however, capture his stylized fact (a) that firms typically set a long-run target for the dividend payout ratio. In line with the discussion concerning the steady state properties of long-run equilibrium dividend payout, we take account of this long-run objective in our model by requiring that dividend payouts converge to a constant target ratio, that is, as $t \to \infty$ (and in the absence of any disturbances)

$$\lim_{t \to \infty} \log\left[\frac{D(t)}{E^{\mathrm{m}}(t-1)}\right] = \beta. \tag{4}$$

This special assumption that the long-run target be literally constant is more stringent than necessary.[7] Moreover, this assumption does not, of course, imply that dividends and permanent earnings follow (trend) stationary processes.[8]

As shown in the appendix, if the long-run steady state condition (4) is imposed on the short-run dynamics (3), then (3) can be rewritten as

$$\log[D(t+1)] - \log[D(t)]$$
$$= g(t) + \lambda\{\log[E^{\mathrm{m}}(t)] - \log[E^{\mathrm{m}}(t-1)] - m(t-1)\}$$
$$+ \gamma(\beta - \{\log[D(t)] - \log[E^{\mathrm{m}}(t-1)]\}) + \eta(t+1), \quad (5)$$

where $m(t-1)$ is the time $t-1$ expectation $\log[E^{\mathrm{m}}(t)] - \log[E^{\mathrm{m}}(t-1)]$ of the logarithmic change in permanent earnings and $g(t)$ is the expected logarithmic change $\log[D(t)] - \log[D(t-1)]$ in dividends if the time $t-1$ logarithmic payout ratio $\log[D(t)/E^{\mathrm{m}}(t-1)]$ is equal to its long-run target β and the unexpected change in logarithmic permanent earnings $\log[E^{\mathrm{m}}(t)] - \log[E^{\mathrm{m}}(t-1)] - m(t-1)$ is zero.

The model described by (5) takes the form of the well-known "error correction" model, which has been studied and applied by Sargan (1964), Davidson et al. (1978), Nickell (1980), Salmon (1982), and Ericsson and Hendry (1984). It obviously satisfies the condition for a long-run steady state distribution for D/E^{m} because, if $\eta(t+1) = 0$, then $\Delta \log[E^{\mathrm{m}}(t)] = m(t-1)$ implies $\log[D(t)] - \log[E^{\mathrm{m}}(t-1)] = \beta$ as required. Given specification (4) of the long-run equilibrium, the model's potential for describing the short-run dynamics of aggregate dividends depends on the appropriateness of the rational distributed lag in (3). Since the error correction model is applicable to a wide range of stochastic processes governing $E^{\mathrm{m}}(t)$, including the geometric random walk (cf. Nickell, 1980), the major assumptions imbedded in (3) are those of symmetry in the responsiveness of dividend changes to changes in permanent earnings and, empirically, the constancy of coefficients.[9]

In economic terms, the "normal" or unconditional growth rate for dividends $g(t)$ equals $\alpha r(t)$, which is the usual expression for the deterministic growth rate of dividends, where $r(t) \equiv 1 - D(t)/E^{\mathrm{m}}(t-1)$ is the retention rate (in terms of permanent earnings) at time t and α is defined as the aggregate cost of capital. That is, specification of the deterministic component $g(t)$ reflects the standard textbook proposition that, if the current payout is high relative to permanent earnings and therefore the retention rate $r(t)$ is low, then dividends per share will be expected to grow more slowly than if the current payout were lower and the retention rate were correspondingly higher. The rest of the terms on the right-hand side of (5) describe the deviation of the growth in dividends from this normal rate.

The second term in (5), which is multiplied by λ, captures Lintner's stylized fact (c) that managers will change dividends away from the anticipated path in response to an unanticipated change in permanent earnings $\log[E^{\mathrm{m}}(t)/E^{\mathrm{m}}(t-1)] - m(t-1)$. The third term, which is multiplied by γ, is the error correction component that drags short-run dividends toward their long-run steady state payout ratio, thus capturing Lintner's stylized fact (a). The value of γ, which should be positive, measures the average speed of convergence of the payout ratio to its target.

The *a priori* reasons for choosing the lag specification in (3) and (5), in which an unanticipated change in permanent earnings from time $t-1$ to time t causes a dividend change in the interval $(t, t+1)$, are as follows. First, an unanticipated change in permanent earnings, by definition, cannot be known until it happens, and so any reaction in dividends to such a change must occur at the same time or later. Unlike delays in the reaction of speculative prices to new information, no arbitrage opportunities are created by managers if they delay changing dividends in response to new information. Second, although firms usually declare dividends once a quarter, many firms make significant changes only at the end of their fiscal year. Third, even if individual firms' managers did react instantaneously, the reaction in aggregate dividends will appear to be lagged because of different announcement dates and different speeds of reaction across firms.

In responding to an unanticipated change in permanent earnings, managers will change dividends in the same direction, which implies that λ in (5) should be positive. From stylized fact (d), managers prefer to avoid reversals in dividends, and it can be established that a partial adjustment policy with $\lambda < 1$ is optimal if reversals or changes are costly.

3 The Dividend Model Expressed as a Regression Equation

In the empirical studies of both Lintner's model and subsequent dividend models based on his original formulation, the equations corresponding to our (5) are treated as regression equations. We also assume that equation (5) is both a structural equation and a causal equation because our view of the economic process is that an unanticipated change in permanent earnings causes a predictable change in the next-period dividends, not the reverse.

Of course, in a complete general equilibrium model, dividend changes and intrinsic value changes, along with other quantities and prices, are jointly endogenous. However, insofar as the bivariate series of dividend changes and intrinsic value changes is concerned, there are persuasive grounds for treating the latter as a proper predetermined endogenous variable, particularly when the discount rate α is assumed constant.

As already noted, there are no important legal or accounting constraints on dividend policy; hence managers have almost complete discretion and control over the choice of dividend policy. If, however, managers are not irrational, then they will at least choose a dividend policy that is feasible in both the short and the long run. Such "feasible" policies must satisfy the constraint that the discounted value of expected future dividends per share is equal to the discounted value of expected future net cash flows as given by (1). Because managers set dividend policy, this constraint is properly specified in terms of their probability assessments. Hence, from (2), it follows that a rational dividend policy must satisfy[10]

$$\varepsilon_t^{\mathrm{m}}\left\{\int_t^{\infty} D(s)\exp[-\alpha(s-t)]\,\mathrm{d}s\right\}=\frac{E^{\mathrm{m}}(t)}{\alpha}. \tag{6}$$

As discussed by Marsh and Merton (1986), this constraint on dividend choice is very much analogous to the intertemporal budget constraint on consumption choice in the basic lifetime consumption decision problem for an individual. Like consumers in selecting their planned intertemporal expenditures for a given amount of wealth, managers, facing a given level of permanent earnings, have a great deal of latitude in their choice of dividend policy.[11] The fact that individual firms pursue dividend policies that are vastly different from one another is empirical evidence consistent with this view.

It does not follow from (6) that a change in dividend policy by managers will cause a change in their current assessments of permanent earnings.[12] However, for a fixed discount rate α it does follow from (6) that an unanticipated change in permanent earnings must necessarily cause a change in expected future dividends. The direction of causation between unanticipated changes in permanent earnings and changes in subsequent dividends posited in our model is thus consistent with the direction of causation between changes in current wealth and changes in future consumption that is normally assumed for the life-cycle model in a fixed-discount-rate world.[13]

In making the case for causality in equation (5), we are not unaware of the possibility that there are other exogenous variables that may cause managers to change dividends. If this is the case, and if, further, these variables are correlated with unanticipated changes in current permanent earnings, then, of course, equation (5) is flawed as a causal equation. If, however, managers are rational predictors of permanent earnings, then an unanticipated change in permanent earnings this period will be uncorrelated with all variables that are observable prior to this period (including both past dividends and permanent earnings). Therefore it must also be uncorrelated with all future unanticipated changes in permanent earnings. Thus, if there are other exogenous variables that explain the next-period change in dividends, it seems unlikely that they would be correlated with this period's unanticipated change in permanent earnings. Hence the assumption that equation (5) is a proper regression equation is likely to be robust with respect to other "missing" explanatory variables.

This property of rationally predicted permanent earnings together with the lagged structure of equation (5) may perhaps at first suggest that the causality issue can be resolved empirically by applying an appropriate version of the Granger–Sims test of causality. A careful review of this possibility, however, will lead to the well-known identification problem that statistical tests alone are not sufficient to establish causality and that, ultimately, this issue can be resolved only by *a priori* economic reasoning (cf. Zellner, 1979).

4 A Reduced Form for the Dynamic Model

Although we have proposed equation (5) for aggregate dividend dynamics as both a structural and a regression equation, it cannot be estimated in its current form because management assessments of changes in firms' permanent earnings are not observable. In this section we add the necessary further specification to estimate the model.

If managers are rational forecasters and if the market is reasonably efficient, then the market's estimate of a firm's intrinsic value should on average be equal to the intrinsic value estimate made by that firm's management. We therefore assume that the discounted value $V^{M}(t)$ of the expected future aggregate net cash flows of all firms per market share, as estimated from the market's information set, is equal to the aggregate sum of the intrinsic values, where the intrinsic value of each firm is estimated from the information set of that firm's management.[14] This market efficiency condition can be written as

$$V^{M}(t) = V^{m}(t), \qquad \text{for all } t \tag{7}$$

where $V^{M}(t)$ is given by (1) with $\varepsilon_t = \varepsilon_t^{M}$.

We further assume that the stock market price is equal to its intrinsic value, that is, that there are no speculative bubbles. From this assumption and (7), we can write the *cum* dividend price of a share of the market portfolio at time t:[15]

$$P_c(t) = \varepsilon_t^{M} \frac{\int_t^{\infty} \exp[-\alpha(s-t)]\,[\Pi(s) - I(s)]\,\mathrm{d}s}{N(t)}. \tag{8}$$

Using the market efficiency condition (7) and the definition of permanent earnings in (2), we can rewrite (8) as

$$P_c(t) = \frac{E^{m}(t)}{\alpha}. \tag{9}$$

If, as we have assumed, the expected real rate of return α on the market is a positive constant, it follows from (9) that the percentage change in stock market price is equal to the percentage change in manager's assessment of permanent earnings. Substituting for $E^m(t)$ from (9) and splitting the *cum* dividend stock price change $P_c(t)/P_c(t-1)$ into its two component parts – the ex dividend change $P(t)/P(t-1)$ and the dividend yield $D(t)/P(t-1)$ – we rewrite (5) as

$$\log\left[\frac{D(t+1)}{D(t)}\right] = \left[\alpha - \frac{D(t)}{P(t-1)}\right] + \lambda\left\{\log\left[\frac{P(t)+D(t)}{P(t-1)}\right] - \alpha\right\}$$

$$+\gamma\left\{\rho - \log\left[\frac{D(t)}{P(t-1)}\right]\right\} + u(t+1) \qquad (10)$$

where $\rho \equiv \beta + \log\alpha$. By rearranging terms, we can rewrite (10) as

$$\log\left[\frac{D(t+1)}{D(t)}\right] + \frac{D(t)}{P(t-1)} = a_0 + a_1 \log\left[\frac{P(t)+D(t)}{P(t-1)}\right]$$

$$+ a_2 \log\left[\frac{D(t)}{P(t-1)}\right] + u(t+1), \qquad (11)$$

where $a_1 = \lambda$, $a_2 = -\gamma$, and $a_0 = (1-\lambda)\alpha + \gamma\rho$.

Note that (9) is not an identity. It is a specification that is valid under the hypothesis that market prices are rational predictors of firms' future net cash flows. Thus (11) is a reduced form equation and, as such, can be consistent with more than one set of structural hypotheses. If market price provides a good estimate of managements' assessments of permanent earnings, then (11) should be a good predictor of the dividend process. Such would be the case if managers are rational predictors of future cash flows and the market is efficient. But it would also be the case if the market is inefficient because it is moved by waves of optimism and pessimism and managers either rely on market prices for their estimates of permanent earnings or are influenced by the same irrational waves as investors in making their assessments of intrinsic values.

To investigate this identification matter further, consider the following model first suggested to us by Zvi Griliches. Managers are rational forecasters of permanent earnings, and they fully adjust dividends in response to changes in these earnings, that is, $\lambda = 1$ in (5) and

$$\log\left[\frac{D(t+1)}{D(t)}\right] = \log\left[\frac{E^m(t)}{E^m(t-1)}\right].$$

The market is assumed to be inefficient both because of random "animal spirits" and because investors tend to overreact to new information about the fundamentals. That is, replace (9) with the alternative hypothesis

$$\log\left[\frac{P_c(t)}{P_c(t-1)}\right] = \psi \log\left[\frac{E^m(t)}{E^m(t-1)}\right] + \varepsilon(t)$$

where $\psi > 1$. If equation (11) is fitted under these assumptions, then the predicted value for a_1 is given by $a_1 = \psi / (\psi^2 + q)$, where q is the ratio of the variance of animal-spirits-induced price changes to the variance of rational permanent earnings changes.

As in our model, the Griliches model predicts that $0 < a_1 < 1$. If market price is a very noisy estimator of permanent earnings principally because of animal spirits (that is, $q/\psi \gg 1$), then (11) should be a poor predictor of the evolution of dividends. Alternatively, the market could be efficient and (11) could be a poor predictor because management dividend decisions in the aggregate are not well described by behavioral equation (5). If (11) exhibits strong explanatory power, it is still possible for the Griliches model to hold if overreaction is the primary source of market inefficiency (that is, $q/\psi \ll 1$). It thus appears that the empirical properties of equation (11) are inadequate alone to distinguish between our model and Griliches' alternative.

The focus of our study is not to test the hypothesis of stock market inefficiency but instead to develop a model of aggregate dividend behavior that is consistent with that hypothesis.[16] Nevertheless, we digress briefly from that focus to point out some ancillary conditions to equation (11) that do provide some discriminatory power between our model and that of Griliches.

As already noted, unanticipated changes in rationally forecast permanent earnings should have no serial dependences. In Griliches' model, this implies that successive changes in dividends should be uncorrelated. As shown in section 6, the empirical time series of dividend changes exhibits rather strong positive serial correlation. In contrast, such serial correlations have little effect on the robustness of our model.

If we assume that even inefficient stock prices cannot wander arbitrarily far from their intrinsic values for an indefinite period of time, then with a constant discount rate the regressivity of price toward intrinsic value will induce negative serial dependence in stock price changes. If this regression takes place in a series of small adjustments systematically over time, then we would expect to find significant negative serial correlation in the stock return series. As is well known, the empirical evidence does not support this prediction.[17] If the regression takes place in the form of large adjustments at random and relatively infrequent points in time, then the standard estimates of serial correlation may not detect this dependence. However, these "outliers" would tend to cause the empirical distribution of stock price changes to exhibit higher kurtosis than the distribution of rational permanent earnings changes. In the context of the Griliches model, stock price changes should have higher kurtosis than dividend changes. As shown in section 6, quite the opposite seems to be the case as an empirical matter. As discussed there, this finding is consistent with our model. Although hardly a complete analysis, these ancillary findings appear to support our model over Griliches' alternative. With this, we end the digression and return to the development of our model of dividend behavior in an environment with a rational stock market.

For (11) to be a proper reduced form equation, its right-hand-side variables must be predetermined relative to its left-hand-side variables. As discussed at length in section 3, an unanticipated change in this-period permanent earnings, over which managers have no control, is an exogenous variable relative to the change in the next-period dividends, which managers control almost completely. From (7) and structural equation (9), it therefore follows that an unanticipated change in this-period price is exogenous relative to the next-period dividend change; hence (11) is a proper reduced form equation. In this limited sense of a reduced form, an unanticipated change in this-period price "causes" a (predictable) change in the next-period dividends.

In specifying (11), our intent is to construct a simple model of the dividend process that nevertheless captures the basic stylized facts of management behavior. We have therefore assumed a simple one-period lagged adjustment. It is possible that the dividend process may involve higher order lags with different speeds of adjustment and, as already noted, there may be other "missing" variables that enter into the process. As we shall show, the empirical conclusions derived from this simple model are likely to be robust with respect to refinements that include such additional variables.

5 Model Estimation

To estimate the reduced form equation (11), we use annual data constructed from monthly dividend and price series for the value weighted NYSE index contained in the Center for Research in Security Prices (CRSP) data set over the period 1926–81.[18] Over the period 1927–80, the discrete-time version of (11) estimated by ordinary least squares (OLS) is given by

$$\log\left[\frac{D(t+1)}{D(t)}\right] + \frac{D(t)}{P(t-1)} = \underset{(0.157)}{-0.101} + \underset{(0.064)}{0.437} \log\left[\frac{P(t)+D(t)}{P(t-1)}\right]$$

$$\underset{(0.050)}{-0.042} \log\left[\frac{D(t)}{P(t-1)}\right] + u(t+1) \qquad (12)$$

$$\bar{R}^2 = 0.47, \quad \text{DW} = 1.53$$

In (12), $D(t)$ refers to aggregate NYSE dividends totaled over year t and $P(t)$ refers to price at the end of year t. The numbers in parentheses under the coefficients are standard errors, not t statistics. For example, the coefficient of the lagged logarithmic change in price has a standard error of 0.064 and a t statistic of 6.83. The coefficient point estimates in (12) indicate that the deviations of real dividend changes from their normal growth rate covary positively and strongly with the previous-year unexpected *cum* dividend price changes and negatively with the previous-year dividend yield. The Durbin–Watson (DW) statistic suggests that there is positive autocorrelation in the residuals of the OLS fit of (12). Disturbance correlation can arise in various ways. As already noted, our simple model assumes one-period adjustment in dividends by management, whereas longer lags are entirely possible. Further, as we noted earlier, it is possible that the target dividend yield is not literally constant. For example, yield might change if tax rates, the technology of communications and trading, or the mix of institutional and individual ownership change. It is highly likely that any yield changes induced by such factors, which will show up in the residuals in (12), are serially correlated. Indeed, any omitted variables that are serially correlated could be a potential source of residual autocorrelation.[19]

In light of the autocorrelation in the residuals of (12) we reestimated (11) using generalized least squares (GLS), and the results are

$$\log\left[\frac{D(t+1)}{D(t)}\right]+\frac{D(t)}{P(t-1)}=\underset{(0.198)}{-0.234}+\underset{(0.061)}{0.444}\log\left[\frac{P(t)+D(t)}{P(t-1)}\right]$$

$$\underset{(0.082)}{-0.085}\log\left[\frac{D(t)}{P(t-1)}\right]+u'(t+1) \qquad (13)$$

$$\bar{R}^2=0.53,\ \mathrm{DW}=1.83$$

Although the GLS estimate, which takes into account the positive autocorrelation, appears to have slightly more explanatory power, the results from either the OLS or the GLS fits are essentially the same in that they explain about 50 percent of aggregate NYSE real dividend changes. As will be shown in section 6, the explanatory power of our single-equation aggregate time series model[20] is considerably higher than that of univariate trend autoregressive models such as the one fitted by Shiller (1981a).

The point estimate of 0.44 for the coefficient on the lagged percentage price change is positive, of substantial magnitude, and highly significant. This finding is consistent with the hypothesis that the market price is a good indicator of permanent earnings and that managers systematically change dividends in response to an unanticipated change in permanent earnings.[21]

Because the coefficient on percentage price changes is both significantly greater than zero and significantly less than unity, this finding is also consistent with Lintner's stylized fact that managers smooth dividends by responding in a partial adjustment fashion to an unanticipated change in permanent earnings. The well-established empirical fact that the variation in the percentage change in dividends is significantly less than the variation in the percentage change in prices might suggest to some that prices are too volatile. However, the empirical verification in (12) and (13) of the partial adjustment mechanism posited in our model provides an explanation of this well-established fact that is entirely consistent with market price's being a rational predictor of future dividends.

The estimated coefficient of the dividend-to-price ratio is negative in both (12) and (13), which is consistent with the hypothesis that this ratio converges to a long-run stationary distribution. The point estimates for the speed of adjustment, however, are rather small, which at best suggests that a substantial period of time is required for the dividend-to-price ratio to converge to its steady state distribution. Thus using the estimate of -0.085 from (13), a conventional "half-life" calculation shows that it takes more than 8 years for the expected value of this ratio to move halfway from its initial value to its expected steady state value.[22]

To investigate further the extent of synchronization between dividend changes and price changes, we computed the leads and lags of the percentage changes in dividends regressed on percentage changes in prices estimated by the Hannan-efficient procedure, and these are plotted in figure 11.1. By inspection, the cross-correlation at the lag in price change of 1 year specified in our model dominates that at all other leads and lags. In even a reasonably efficient market, we would not expect lagged variables of any sort to have meaningful predictive power for future price changes. It is therefore not surprising that changes in dividends are not significantly correlated with subsequent changes in price. The modest positive correlation between contemporaneous dividend and price changes is, of course, consistent with an efficient market and is perhaps suggestive of a mild information or announcement effect for dividend and price changes at the aggregate level. Indeed, we do find about an 8 percent correlation between contemporaneous (that is, year $t+1$) unanticipated price changes and the residuals from our regression (13). As noted in the discussion in the introduction of the informational content of dividends, it is difficult to identify an announcement date for aggregate dividends in a meaningful way. Moreover, what is perceived to be contemporaneous correlation between dividend and price changes over the coarse grid of annual data may simply turn out to be lagged price changes explaining subsequent dividend changes when examined under the finer grids of quarterly or monthly data. Thus an 8 percent correlation is likely to be a significant overstatement of the announcement effect of aggregate dividends.

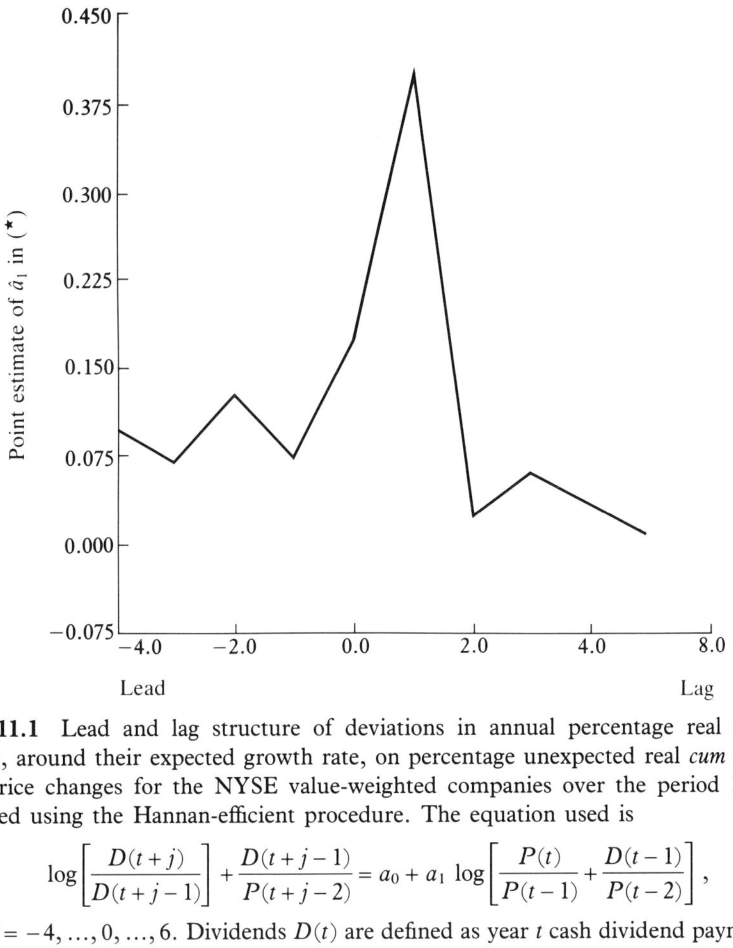

Figure 11.1 Lead and lag structure of deviations in annual percentage real dividend changes, around their expected growth rate, on percentage unexpected real *cum* dividend stock price changes for the NYSE value-weighted companies over the period 1927–80, computed using the Hannan-efficient procedure. The equation used is

$$\log\left[\frac{D(t+j)}{D(t+j-1)}\right] + \frac{D(t+j-1)}{P(t+j-2)} = a_0 + a_1 \log\left[\frac{P(t)}{P(t-1)} + \frac{D(t-1)}{P(t-2)}\right], \qquad (\star)$$

where $j = -4, \ldots, 0, \ldots, 6$. Dividends $D(t)$ are defined as year t cash dividend payments for all NYSE companies, and the index "price" $P(t)$ is the end-of-year t value weighted index. The dividend-to-price ratio $D(t+j-1)/P(t+j-2)$ is, up to a constant, the expected rate of growth of dividends and prices in year $t+j$.

The efficient market hypothesis does not rule out the change in this-period dividends being predicted by variables that are observable prior to this period, as it does for speculative price changes. Nevertheless, if the posited economic process underlying the specification of (11) is a reasonably accurate description of reality, then lagged price changes much beyond the 1 year lag specified in (11) might be expected to exhibit relatively little explanatory power in forecasting the dividend change this period. If an unanticipated change in permanent earnings causes managers to change dividends, then strict rational forecasting would seem to dictate that their decision be based on their most recent assessment of permanent earnings; hence earlier revisions in those assessments should have relatively little effect on the change in dividends. In attempting to smooth the time path of dividends, it is possible that managers would choose to change dividends in response to changes in a moving-average or distributed lag of unanticipated permanent earnings changes over an extended past history. Such behavior would create a dependence between the current change in dividends and lagged price changes of all orders. Because these averaging techniques embody much "stale" information, it appears that this approach to dividend smoothing leads to an inefficient use of the available information. If, instead, managers change the dividend in a partial adjustment response to the most recent unanticipated change in permanent earnings, they can use the most up to date information. The partial dividend adjustment will be appropriate in a wide variety of contexts in which the policy problem facing managers does not admit a certainty equivalence solution.

Even if managers forecast this rationally, there will still be some lag between a change in permanent earnings and the change it induces in subsequent dividends. As indicated in the discussion surrounding the specification of equation (5), it is unlikely that the lag between a change in permanent earnings and the change it induces in subsequent aggregate dividends could be much shorter than a year.[23] The correlations between the change in dividends and lagged price changes displayed in figure 11.1 are therefore consistent with this view of rational forecasting by managers. As a further more quantitative test, (11) was reestimated with 5 years of lagged unexpected price changes as additional variables. None of these additional lagged variables had a coefficient point estimate more than one standard error from zero, and the F statistic for their inclusion is 0.361, which has a p value of 0.872.

If these empirical results had turned out differently, they would imply neither an arbitrage opportunity in the stock market nor an inefficiency in the allocation of capital. We need hardly mention again that managers have great latitude in their selection of dividend policies, including the option to choose ones that are not based on the most up to date information. It is reassuring, however, for the overall credibility of our model that the data tend to support such "super-rational" forecasting behavior by managers even in the relatively unimportant area of dividend policy.

With the exception of contemporaneous changes in other speculative prices, it is a well-established empirical fact that there are few, if any, observable variables that exhibit high contemporaneous correlation with changes in aggregate stock prices. It is therefore rather unlikely that the change in stock price is merely serving in (11) as a proxy for some other observable variables that, if included, would cause the significance of the coefficient on the price change to disappear.

We have investigated whether the dividend response to stock price changes is symmetric with respect to negative and positive price changes. The point estimate of this elasticity with respect to the 20 annual negative price change observations in our sample is 0.597, while it is 0.271 with respect to the positive price changes. Although an asymmetry of dividend response to negative and positive price changes could be readily explained in a more complete dividend model, the small number of negative price change observations causes the standard error for the difference in point estimates to be so large that equality of the elasticity coefficients cannot be rejected. In addition, two of the negative price change observations are the 1929 and 1974 market "crashes" in which the constant discount rate assumption is surely strained.

In his discussion of the stability of Lintner's original regression results, Tarshis (1959) writes, "Everything else in the economy changed in those years: it seems unreasonable that these many changes exerted no influence upon dividend policy." More recently, Brittain (1966) and Miller (1985) document apparent shifts in dividend payout policies in the late 1930s and the 1940s, which they attribute to tax changes. As we have already discussed, the factors that historically could have caused dividend policy to be important may themselves have diminished in significance over the sample period and thereby induced secular changes in the dividend response function. With these observations in mind, we examine the temporal stability of the coefficients in our regression model (11).

A plot of the elasticity coefficient a_1 in (11), estimated recursively forward and recursively backward, is presented in figure 11.2. The plot suggests a downward shift in the coefficient in the 1940s. This suggestion is confirmed by formal squared CUSUM, Quandt (1958, 1960), and Chow tests (not reported here).[24] The absolute value of the coefficient of reversion of the dividend-to-price ratio a_2 decreases steadily from approximately -0.49 at the beginning of the period to -0.03 for the full period up to 1979. When (11) is estimated using robust regression and the tests of coefficient stability are repeated (see Kuh, Samarov, and Shell, 1986), the change in the model coefficients appears to have begun as early as 1938. That instability might be attributed to the undistributed profits tax in the years 1936 and 1937.[25] A shift in dividend policy in the late 1930s and the 1940s is, of course, not necessarily attributable to taxes. For example, Officer (1971) shows that stock market volatility also shifts towards the end of the 1930s. We do find that if the elasticity coefficient a_1 in (11) is allowed to depend linearly on a naive measure of the market's volatility – the square of the cum dividend stock price change $\log\{[P(t)+D(t)]/P(t-1)\}$ – the fit is marginally, but significantly, improved. However, the apparent shift in dividend policy remains.[26] We consider and reject the hypothesis that variations in the discount rate are the reason for the shift in dividend policy in the 1930s and 1940s.[27]

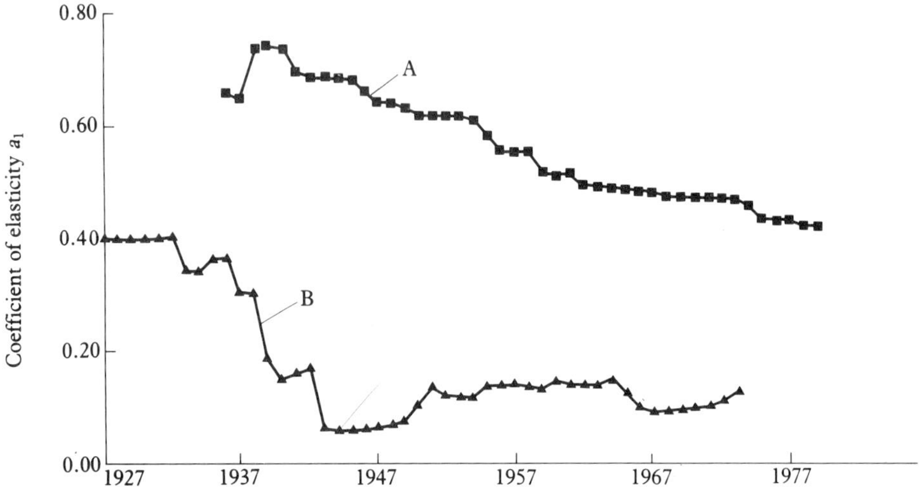

Figure 11.2 Plot of the recursively estimated coefficient of elasticity of the deviation in annual percentage real dividend change around its expected growth rate with respect to *cum* dividend prior-year stock price change for the value-weighted NYSE companies over the period 1927–79. The plot is of the point estimate of the coefficient a_1, where

$$\log\left[\frac{D(t+1)}{D(t)}\right] + \frac{D(t)}{P(t-1)} = a_0 + a_1 \log\left[\frac{P(t)+D(t)}{P(t-1)}\right] + a_2 \log\left[\frac{D(t)}{P(t-1)}\right] + u(t+1)$$

and a_1 is estimated recursively forward (curve A) and recursively backward (curve B). Here dividends $D(t)$ are defined as year t cash dividend payments for all NYSE companies, and the index "price" $P(t)$ is the end-of-year t value weighted NYSE index. The dividend-to-price ratio $D(t)/P(t-1)$ is, up to a constant, the expected rate of growth of dividends in year $t+1$.

As Miller and Modigliani (1961) make clear, the determination of gross dividends is the principal issue to be explained in resolving the dividend puzzle. As an empirical matter, we find that both the explanatory power and the coefficient estimates of our model remain virtually unchanged whether it is fitted to gross dividends or to aggregate net dividends (measured by gross dividends less net new stock issues). This finding may be surprising in the light of the recent 5 year wave of mergers and acquisitions financed by cash and debt, which has been large enough to cause net dividends actually to exceed gross dividends by significant amounts. It does not appear, however, that such large additional "distributions" to equity holders were typical during our earlier sample period, although the CRSP data from which we constructed our net dividend series may not account completely for all such transactions.

For an all-equity-financed firm, net operating cash flow minus investment equals the net dividend, as a cash flow identity. Because net operating cash flow is largely uncontrollable by managers in the short run, it would appear from the cash flow identity that a model of net dividend policy cannot be distinguished from a model of investment choice. Thus the empirical invariance of our model to gross versus net dividends raises the question of whether it describes dividend policy or corporate investment behavior.

We believe that the aggregate net dividend series is not a reliable indicator of investment policy and therefore that our model should not be interpreted as one of investment behavior. As noted in note 5, an important source of spillage in the empirical application of the identity is the cash inflow and outflow of the firm from financing sources not accounted for in the standard measure of net dividends. These sources would include changes in publicly issued and privately placed corporate debt, bank loans, trade credit and other short-term accruals, lease contracts, and other legal liabilities such as pensions and customer warranties.

New stock issues that figure in the difference between gross and net dividend calculations are small by comparison with these sources and uses of funds. For example, a 5 percent shift in the approximately $120 billion of outstanding nonfinancial corporate net trade credit would alone amount to more than half the $8 billion to $10 billion level of average annual common stock offerings. Public offerings of corporate debt typically exceed annual new equity issues; hence changes in debt offerings could easily offset changes in equity financing without affecting investment flows. Changes in the level of interest rates on floating rate debt will also cause changes in cash flow without a change in investment. Thus it seems to us that dividends net of new equity issues cannot be used reliably to infer variations in investment policy.

In summary, our main empirical results are (a) that past (or possibly contemporaneous) changes in stock market prices explain a significant portion of the change in aggregate dividends and (b) that the (partial) elasticity of the dividend response to a change in price is positive and significantly less than unity. Further, there are reasonable grounds for believing that these results will be robust to more refined versions of this dividend model. If, for example, log price and log dividend levels follow integrated stochastic processes, as they seem to do empirically (cf. Kleidon, 1986), the target-to-payout ratio can satisfy the steady state properties assumed in the reduced form of our error correction model (11).

6 Further Discussion and Comparison of Our Model with Others in the Literature

In this section we compare the fit of the model of aggregate dividends that has been developed in previous sections with that of the "final form" trend autoregressive model employed by Shiller (1981a) to describe aggregate dividends. We show that our model fits considerably better than does the trend autoregressive model and that lagged dividends explain little, if any, of the variation in aggregate dividends once prior-period stock price changes are taken into account. We also claim that the characteristics of the observed distributions of dividend and stock price changes reported by Shiller can readily be interpreted within the context of our model.

In section 6.3 the explanatory power of our model of aggregate dividend behavior, in which stock price changes are used to measure changes in firms' permanent earnings, is also compared with models such as those fitted by Lintner (1956), Brittain (1966), and Fama and Babiak (1968), in which dividend movements are explained by accounting earnings changes. We find that our model, using only prior-period stock price changes, fits at least as well as models based on accounting earnings, which use contemporaneous accounting earnings data. Moreover, our model significantly outperforms models that use lagged accounting earnings only, as would be required if these models were used to forecast future dividend changes.

6.1 A trend autoregressive model for aggregate dividends?

Shiller (1983, p. 237) reports that "if log $D(t)$ is regressed on log $D(t-1)$, a constant and a linear time trend for 1872 to 1978, the coefficient of log $D(t-1)$ is 0.807, with an estimated standard error of 0.058," implying that "log dividends would always be expected to return half way to the trend line in three years." We repeat essentially the same OLS regression on our data set, and the results are

$$\Delta \log[D(t)] = \underset{(0.890)}{2.492} - \underset{(0.089)}{0.249} \log[D(t)] + \underset{(0.002)}{0.004t} + u(t) \tag{14}$$

$$\bar{R}^2 = 0.130, \ \mathrm{DW} = 1.495.$$

Because the left-hand-side of (14) is the change in $\log[D(t)]$, the comparable autoregressive coefficient is $1 - 0.249 = 0.751$, which is rather close to Shiller's estimate of 0.807. By the standards of a conventional t test, the coefficients in both samples are significantly less than unity with a t statistic of -2.80 in our sample versus a t statistic of -3.33 in Shiller's. The t statistic for the trend coefficient in (14) is 2.00. This finding serves to confirm our belief that the important empirical results derived from our 1926–81 data set are not likely to be significantly altered if fitted to the longer 1871–1979 data set used by Shiller in his analysis of aggregate dividend and stock price behavior.

Because the Durbin–Watson statistic suggests positively autocorrelated residuals, the lagged endogenous variable in (14) may cause the OLS coefficients to be biased. We therefore reestimated the reported Shiller equation (14) using a GLS iterative technique,[28] and the results are

$$\Delta \log[D(t)] = \underset{(1.211)}{5.225} - \underset{(0.121)}{0.524} \log[D(t)] + \underset{(0.003)}{0.009t} + u(t) \qquad (15)$$

$$\bar{R}^2 = 0.243, \ \mathrm{DW} = 1.85.$$

Hence, when the OLS specification of Shiller's autoregressive model for dividends is correctly adjusted for autocorrelation, its measured explanatory power almost doubles. That is, only about half of the total 24 percent explanation of the variation in dividend changes can be attributed to the lagged dividend and time trend variables. The other half is attributable to the time series model of the disturbances or "unknown variables" in the regression.[29]

Given the apparent statistical significance of the coefficients in (14) and (15), it is perhaps tempting to some to conclude that dividends follow an autoregressive process that approaches a steady state distribution (possibly around a positive trend). Such a conclusion, if true, has far-reaching implications for the whole of financial economics. For example, if (14) were to describe fully the "true" dividend process (that is, $\bar{R}^2 = 1$), then this result, along with even a casual inspection of the stock return time series, would surely imply that stock prices are "too volatile." If, as implied by (15), dividends were to regress over 90 percent of the way to their deterministic trend line within one presidential term, then uncertainty about the future path of dividends would be rather unimportant and therefore rational stock prices should exhibit trivial fluctuations. Because equities are the residual claims of the private sector, variations in their returns are "blown up" reflections of the uncertainties about the whole economy. If rational stock returns should have small variations, then the fluctuations in the economy should be even smaller. It therefore seems that in such an environment we economists could safely neglect such uncertainties in the specification of our macroeconomic models. While this is perhaps an appealing hypothesis, the real world is not this way, as further analysis of (14) and (15) will clearly indicate.

The fit of the autoregressive model (14) and (15) is rather poor, with half the explanatory power of (15) represented by unspecified variables. With respect to a different regression on similar data, Shiller (1981a, p. 433) gives one possible explanation for low $\bar{R}^2$: "regression tests are not insensitive to data misalignment. Such low R^2 might be the result of dividend or commodity price index data errors." Although we agree that such data errors can be a source for lower R^2, our alternative explanation is simply that the autoregressive process posited in (14) and (15) is not an accurate specification of the dividend process.

Motivated by the analysis of our model of the dividend process, we add the 1 year lagged unanticipated change in the logarithm of stock price to the specification of (15). By the same iterative GLS procedure used in (15), the results are

$$\Delta \log[D(t)] = \underset{(0.918)}{2.107} + \underset{(0.064)}{0.347} \log\left[\frac{P(t)}{P(t-1)} + \frac{D(t)}{P(t-1)}\right]$$

$$- \underset{(0.092)}{0.213} \log[D(t)] + \underset{(0.002)}{0.004t} + u(t) \qquad (16)$$

$$\bar{R}^2 = 0.473, \ \mathrm{DW} = 1.755.$$

By inspection, the addition in (16) of the unexpected price change in the previous year doubles the explanatory power of (15). This measured increase in $\bar{R}^2$ greatly understates the effect of this added variable because, in addition to increasing $\bar{R}^2$ by 100 percent, it also virtually eliminates the explanatory power of the remaining unspecified variables whose effects are captured by the GLS procedure.[30] We would also note that, by adding the log price change variable, the absolute magnitudes of both the $\log[D(t)]$ and time trend coefficients are cut in half.

To explore the relative importance of the specified variables further, equation (16) was reestimated – first, with the time trend deleted and, second, with both the time trend and $\log[D(t)]$ removed. The results are

$$\Delta \log[D(t)] = \underset{(0.564)}{0.566} + \underset{(0.064)}{0.388} \log\left[\frac{P(t)}{P(t-1)} + \frac{D(t)}{P(t-1)}\right]$$

$$- \underset{(0.053)}{0.055} \log[D(t)] + u(t) \qquad (17a)$$

$$\bar{R}^2 = 0.437, \ \mathrm{DW} = 1.814$$

and

$$\Delta \log[D(t)] = \underset{(0.016)}{-0.014} + \underset{(0.063)}{0.402} \log\left[\frac{P(t)}{P(t-1)} + \frac{D(t)}{P(t-1)}\right] + u(t) \qquad (17b)$$

$$\bar{R}^2 = 0.435, \ \mathrm{DW} = 1.82.$$

Comparing (16) with (17a), the elimination of the time trend variable causes only a modest reduction in $\bar{R}^2$, and it has little effect on the estimated coefficient of the log price change. However, by eliminating the time trend variable, the magnitude of the regressive coefficient on $\log[D(t)]$ falls by 75 percent, and, with a p value equal to 0.309, it is not statistically significant. It appears that there is a strong interaction between $\log[D(t)]$ and the time trend, which together with the GLS iterative procedure is responsible for the significant coefficients in (15). If either variable is removed, then the magnitude and the statistical significance of the coefficient of the remaining variable are both zero. In this light, it is not surprising that the elimination of $\log[D(t)]$ as a variable in (17b) has no effect on either the $\bar{R}^2$ of that equation or the coefficient of log price change.

Unless the log price change can be "explained" by some distributed lag of past dividends (which, as an empirical matter, it cannot), then surely it belongs in the specification of the dividend process. Because it alone accounts for over 90 percent of the explanatory power of (16), its omission from (14) and (15) is rather important. In sharp contrast, the elimination of either the time trend or the $\log[D(t)]$ variables has no significant effect on the fit. Hence, unless there are strong *a priori* economic reasons to believe that these variables belong in the specification of the dividend process, there appears to be no valid empirical reason for their inclusion.

In our model of the dividend process, there is no role for a time trend. Its inclusion produces an insignificant coefficient and actually causes the corrected OLS and GLS values for $\bar{R}^2$ in (12) and (13) to fall. Our model would, however, predict that changes in log dividends are related to $\log[D(t)]$ through the dividend-to-price ratio $\log[D(t)/P(t-1)]$. Although not explicit in our simple model, it is entirely consistent with the spirit of the model that lagged changes in log dividends explain part of the adjustment process used by managers to decide on subsequent dividend changes. If this were the case, then $\log[D(t)]$ may be a proxy for these lagged changes. The inclusion of such lagged dividend changes would in no substantive way change the conclusions derived for the dividend and rational stock price processes in section 5. To investigate this possibility, we reestimate equation (13) with the addition of $\log[D(t)]$, and the fitted results are given by

$$\log\left[\frac{D(t+1)}{D(t)}\right]+\frac{D(t)}{P(t-1)}$$

$$\begin{aligned}&= \underset{(1.923)}{1.550} + \underset{(0.061)}{0.441} \log\left[\frac{P(t)}{P(t-1)}+\frac{D(t)}{P(t-1)}\right]\\ &\quad - \underset{(0.267)}{0.247} \log\left[\frac{D(t)}{P(t-1)}\right] - \underset{(0.256)}{0.220} \log D(t) + u(t+1) \qquad (18)\\ &\qquad \bar{R}^2 = 0.532, \quad \mathrm{DW} = 1.88.\end{aligned}$$

The F statistic for $\log[D(t)]$ in (18) is 3.23, which is insignificant at the 5 percent level. If $\log[D(t-1)]$ is added to (18), its estimated coefficient is -0.135, while that of $\log[D(t)]$ becomes 0.064. Although this result suggests that $\log[D(t)]$ in (22) may be a proxy for $\log[D(t)/D(t-1)]$, the coefficient of $\log[D(t-1)]$ is also statistically insignificant. As expected, the addition of these lagged dividend variables in (18) had no effect on the point estimate of the coefficient of lagged log price change.[31]

In summary, adding the trend and lagged dividend variables of Shiller's autoregressive model to our specification does little to improve the explanatory power of our model in terms of $\bar{R}^2$. Moreover, the estimated coefficients of these "added" variables are statistically insignificant. The other side of this result is that the addition of the variables from our model to the autoregressive specification (14) substantially increases the explanatory power of that model. As these variables are added, however, the statistical significance of the autoregressive variables is reduced. This result is perhaps surprising because it is a common belief that the dividend time series is quite smooth by comparison with the price series. Thus a distributed lag of past dividends together with a time trend might have been expected to do a better job than stock price changes in explaining subsequent dividend changes, almost independently of the "true" economic specification.[32]

Although there appears to be no significant empirical evidence for regressivity in the time series of dividends, the lack of such evidence does not disprove the hypothesis that dividends have a stationary distribution around a deterministic trend. As discussed at length in section 3, the resolution of such issues must ultimately come from economic reasoning. As Shiller (1983, p. 236) notes on the specification issue, "Of course, we do not literally believe with certainty all the assumptions in the model which are the basis of testing. I did not intend to assert in the paper that I knew dividends were indeed stationary around the historical trend." We surely echo this view with respect to the theoretical assumptions underlying our own empirical model. Nevertheless, unlike our model's assumptions, there appears to be little theoretical structure to support the assumption that dividends follow a stationary process with a trend. In particular, there is neither an oral nor a written tradition in the financial economics literature that assumes that dividends and rational stock prices have stationary distributions.[33]

We could, of course, revive Malthus, or the more contemporary "limits to growth" view of economics, to justify the assumption of a steady state distribution for the levels of real dividends and prices. However, this theory also rules out an exponential growth trend in these levels. When we refit equation (14) without the trend, the OLS estimate is given by

$$\Delta \log[D(t)] = \underset{(0.576)}{0.802} - \underset{(0.055)}{0.076} \log[D(t-1)] + u(t) \qquad (19)$$

$$\bar{R}^2 = 0.017, \ \mathrm{DW} = 1.576.$$

By inspection of (19), it appears that, at least in the dividend series, there is no evidence at all to support this "zero growth" model.

Perhaps notable by its absence from this section is any discussion of tests of stationarity of stock price levels. We have not directly tested the time series of price changes for evidence of regressivity because the literature is almost uniform in failing to find any lagged variables that have much power in forecasting future stock price changes. Moreover, using autocorrelation and Dickey–Fuller (1979, 1981) tests, Kleidon (1986) finds that neither the arithmetic nor the geometric Brownian motion models can be rejected against the trend model for the Standard & Poor's 500 annual composite index over the period 1926–79. We would expect that these same results would obtain for our data set.

Shiller (1981a, pp. 432–3) does report that the dividend-to-price ratio appears to forecast next-period holding-period returns. We replicated this result on our data set and found, as did he, that the $\bar{R}^2$ is about 0.06. As Shiller himself stresses, such regression tests are sensitive to data problems, and such problems could explain the positive relation between stock returns and lagged dividend yield.[34] In addition, Miller and Scholes (1982) show that holding-period returns for individual firms can be forecast just as accurately using the reciprocal of stock price as they can using dividend yield, which suggests that the numerator of the dividend-to-price ratio does not play an important role in its predictive power for future stock price changes. Of course, forecastability of discrete-period returns is compatible with market efficiency if it reflects no more than forecastable variations in expectations of those returns. However, as the size of Shiller's R^2 estimate would seem to indicate, forecastable changes in expected returns probably account for only a small amount of the variation in 1 year holding-period returns.

6.2 *The distribution of rational stock prices and dividends in our model*

In our dividend model, the dividend-to-price ratio has a stationary distribution with a finite variance. It follows that, for large T, $\text{var}\{\log[P(T)/P(0)]\}$ will be proportional to T. Hence, for large T, the cumulative dynamics for P can be well approximated as having come from a geometric Brownian motion with an instantaneous expected rate of growth equal to $\alpha - \rho$, where ρ is the expected "long-run" dividend-to-price ratio computed from the steady state distribution for D/P. In this same sense, the asymptotic process for dividends will also be a geometric Brownian motion with $\text{var}\{\log[D(T)/D(0)]\}$ proportional to T.

In a reply to a comment on his work by Copeland (1983), Shiller (1983, p. 237) notes: "Even if we assumed log dividends were a random walk with trend with independent increments, stock prices still would show too much volatility." As he correctly points out, if $D(t+1)/D(t)$ is independent of $D(t'+1)/D(t')$ for $t \neq t'$, then the current dividend will be proportional to the current price, that is (in our notation), $D(t) = \rho P(t)$. Hence, in such a model, the variance of logarithmic dividend changes will equal the variance of logarithmic price changes. Shiller goes on to report that, for his Standard & Poor's data set from 1871 to 1979, the sample standard deviation for log dividend changes is 0.127, whereas the sample standard deviation for log price changes is 0.176. Because the ratio of sample variances of 1.93 is significant at the 1 percent level, he concludes that prices are too volatile to be consistent with this model. In our much shorter 1926–81 sample period, the standard deviation of dividend changes is virtually the same as in his sample (0.124), but the standard deviation of price changes is higher (0.203), which leads to a larger sample variance ratio of 2.64. We therefore agree with Shiller's conclusion, although our description would be that the sample variations in dividend changes are too small to be consistent with this model.

The extreme polar case of our model is $D(t) = \rho P(t)$, where managers do not attempt to smooth dividends at all and fully and immediately adjust dividends to reflect unanticipated changes in permanent earnings. If the "short-run" instantaneous variance rate for logarithmic price changes is σ^2, then in our model the corresponding short-run variance rate for dividends is $\lambda^2\sigma^2$. If managers fully adjust dividends in response to unanticipated changes in permanent earnings, then $\lambda = 1$, and the variance of dividend changes and price changes will be the same for all observation intervals. If, as empirically appears to be the case, managers smooth the dividend time path by making partial adjustment responses, then $\lambda < 1$, and the variance of dividend changes will be strictly smaller than the variance of price changes. If, indeed, our model completely explained the process for dividend changes, then the coefficient estimate in (13) of 0.44 for λ would imply that the ratio of the variances of annual log price changes to log dividend changes would exceed 5. Because the model explains only about 50 percent of the variation in dividends, the actual ratio is reduced to 2.64.

As is generally true of "smoothed" processes that are constrained to converge to a more variable process, the variance rate of the percentage change in dividends increases as the interval over which it is computed is increased. However, it is also the case that, for $\lambda < 1$,

$$\frac{\operatorname{var}\{\log[D(T)/D(0)]\}}{T} \leqslant \frac{\operatorname{var}\{\log[P(T)/P(0)]\}}{T},$$

for any interval T, with equality holding only in the limit as $T \to \infty$. Our model of rationally determined prices and rationally determined dividends therefore predicts that the variance rate of logarithmic dividend changes will always be smaller (and, at least for annual or shorter intervals, considerably smaller) than the variance rate of logarithmic price changes. Hence, it is reassuring to find this prediction confirmed by Shiller's statistics, which are based on a considerably longer sample period than our own.

Shiller (1981a, p. 428) also discusses the higher order moment properties of the stock price and dividend processes, with a focus on the relation between infrequent arrivals of important information and the often observed high kurtosis (or "fat tail") sample characteristic of stock price changes. He demonstrates this relation by an illustrative example in which dividends are taken to be independently and identically distributed. To capture the effect on stock price of infrequent arrivals of important information, he assumes that at each time t, with probability $1/n$, the market is told the current dividend level and, with probability $(n-1)/n$, the market has no information about current or future dividends. In this example, the kurtosis of the stock price change is shown to be n times greater than the kurtosis of the normal distribution posited for dividends. Our model, however, predicts exactly the opposite result: namely, dividend changes should exhibit relatively higher kurtosis than stock price changes. That is, although the variance of dividend changes is smaller than that for stock price changes, the time series of dividends should contain more relatively small changes and more relatively large changes than the corresponding time series of stock prices.

The "lumpy" arrival of information (which may, in fact, cause the sample distribution of log stock price changes to have fatter tails than a normal distribution) is not the source of this prediction about dividend changes. Instead, it comes as a result of managers smoothing the time path of dividends. To illustrate this point, we use an example that is very much like Shiller's information example.

Suppose that unanticipated logarithmic changes in stock price are serially independent and identically distributed. Suppose further that managers smooth the time path of dividends according to the following rule. At each time t, with probability $1/n$, they change the dividend to reflect fully the unanticipated change in stock price, that is,

$$\log\left[\frac{D(t)}{D(t-1)}\right] = \log\left[\frac{P(t)}{P(t-1)}\right],$$

and, with probability $(n-1)/n$, they change the dividend to equal its expected long-run normal growth rate, that is,

$$\log\left[\frac{D(t)}{D(t-1)}\right] = g\,.$$

As expected for smoothed processes generally, in this example the variance σ^2/n of dividend changes is smaller than the variance σ^2 of stock price changes around the trend. If m_4 denotes the fourth central moment of the stock price change distribution, then the fourth moment of the dividend change distribution is m_4/n. Hence the kurtosis $(m_4/n)/(\sigma^2/n)^2$ of the dividend change process is simply n times the kurtosis m_4/σ^4 of the stock price process. Thus, unless managers do not attempt to smooth dividends at all (that is, $n = 1$), the kurtosis of the controlled dividend process will always exceed the kurtosis of the (uncontrolled) stock price process. Indeed, the more strongly that managers attempt to smooth dividends (that is, the larger is n), the greater is the relative kurtosis of the dividend process.

The basic reasoning underlying our claim that a large kurtosis of dividend changes relative to stock price changes is evidence in support of dividend changes being a (short-run) controlled process is hardly new. Over half a century ago, Means (1935) used it to contend that many product prices are "administered." By comparing the frequency of product price changes in "administered" and competitive markets, he found that administered market price changes were much less frequent and that, when they did occur, the changes were much larger in magnitude than they were in competitive markets. That is, the distribution of administered price changes has fatter tails than the distribution for competitive prices. Quandt and Ramsey (1978), among others, have developed techniques that take account of other information in addition to kurtosis to estimate the parameters of the mixed distributions that arise from such administered price processes.

In the light of these results, we estimate the kurtosis of each of the time series as a further empirical check on our model. As predicted, the estimated kurtosis for the annual logarithmic dividend changes, 7.377, is 2.79 times the estimate of 2.648 for the kurtosis of the logarithmic changes in stock prices.[35] As it happens, the sample kurtosis for stock prices is not much different than the kurtosis of 3 for a normal distribution, whereas the sample kurtosis for dividend changes is more than twice as large.

6.3 *Stock price versus accounting earnings as a measure of permanent earnings*

In deriving our reduced form dividend model (11), we adopted the specification (9) that stock prices embody rational predictions of firms' future net cash flows and thus permanent earnings. In past empirical work based on Lintner's model, the practice is to use accounting earnings, modified accounting earnings, or cash flow data to measure firms' permanent earnings. Hence we compare the performance of our model with these alternative measures of permanent earnings.

Since the readily available data on aggregate earnings are for the

Standard & Poor's 500 companies, the results reported in this section pertain to this index. The fit of our model (11) for the Standard & Poor's index is virtually identical with that reported in (12) or (13) for the NYSE. The GLS fit for the period 1928–80 is given by

$$\log\left[\frac{D(t+1)}{D(t)}\right]+\frac{D(t)}{P(t-1)}=\underset{(0.178)}{-0.140}+\underset{(0.069)}{0.426}\log\left[\frac{P(t)+D(t)}{P(t-1)}\right]$$

$$\underset{(0.061)}{-0.056}\log\left[\frac{D(t)}{P(t-1)}\right]+u'(t+1) \qquad (20)$$

$$\bar{R}^2=0.41,\ \mathrm{DW}=1.94.$$

If the change in accounting earnings from year t to year $t+1$ is used to explain (not predict) the dividend change from year t to year $t+1$, and if $\alpha - D/P$ is used to account for the expected growth in accounting earnings, then the GLS fit of this contemporaneous accounting earnings model can be expressed as

$$\log\left[\frac{D(t+1)}{D(t)}\right]+\frac{D(t)}{P(t-1)}=\underset{(0.158)}{0.146}+\underset{(0.081)}{0.518}\log\left[\frac{E(t+1)}{E(t)}+\frac{D(t)}{P(t-1)}\right]$$

$$\underset{(0.051)}{+0.039}\log\left[\frac{D(t)}{P(t-1)}\right]+u'(t+1) \qquad (21)$$

$$\bar{R}^2=0.44,\ \mathrm{DW}=2.06,$$

where $E(t)$ refers to the aggregate accounting earnings for the Standard & Poor's companies over year t. These results suggest that data on year $t+1$ accounting earnings, which only become available at the end of year $t+1$, explain no larger a percentage of aggregate dividend changes in year $t+1$ than is explained by using price data available at the beginning of year $t+1$. Moreover, the coefficient on the dividend-to-price ratio (that is, the dividend-to-permanent earnings ratio) has the wrong sign for regressivity, although that coefficient is imprecisely measured with only 50 years of data. Except for the regressivity coefficient, the contemporaneous accounting earnings model has roughly the same fitted characteristics as the lagged stock price model.

We examined the temporal stability of the coefficients in regression model (21) and found a pattern of secular decline in their magnitudes quite similar to that reported for our model in section 5. When backward recursion is used over the period 1926–80, the full sample estimate of the coefficient of the earnings change variable declines by about 75 percent by the end of the sample period. The point estimate for the sign on the dividend price variable decreases in magnitude but continues to have the "wrong" sign. As Brittain (1966) found, the standard diagnostic tests (Chow, Quandt likelihood, CUSUM squared) indicate that the instability occurs around the years 1939–42.

Empirical analysis of the elasticity of response in accounting earnings to lagged stock price changes shows that it remains reasonably stable over the sample period. Thus it appears that the secularly reduced responsiveness of dividend changes to permanent earnings changes is essentially the same whether permanent earnings are measured by stock price or by accounting earnings. Therefore it would seem unlikely that this seemingly secular change in dividend behavior is the result of a temporal pattern of increasing disparity between managements' assessments of permanent earnings and those implied by stock prices.

If the accounting earnings change from period $t-1$ to t is substituted for the period t to $t+1$ change, the accounting model's explanatory power drops to about 20 percent (and to only 10 percent if OLS is used). An examination of the distributed leads and lags of dividend changes and accounting earnings changes confirms that the substantial portion of their association is, in fact, contemporaneous. This result is consistent with Fama and Babiak's (1968) finding that their "best" accounting-earnings-based model of dividend changes includes contemporaneous and lagged earnings levels since our accounting earnings change variable involves both contemporaneous and lagged accounting earnings levels.

Contemporaneous accounting earnings are roughly on a par with lagged stock price changes in explaining aggregate dividend changes, in part because lagged stock price changes themselves provide reasonably good forecasts of the subsequent earnings changes. If the component of contemporaneous accounting earnings changes that could have been predicted from the lagged stock price change is removed, then the unpredictable component of contemporaneous earnings, which we denote by $UE(t)$, does add significantly (at the 95 percent level) to past price changes in explaining aggregate dividend movements. Using GLS over the period 1929–79,

$$\log\left[\frac{D(t+1)}{D(t)}\right] + \frac{D(t)}{P(t-1)} = \underset{(0.166)}{-0.069} + \underset{(0.069)}{0.426} \log\left[\frac{P(t)+D(t)}{P(t-1)}\right] + \underset{(0.085)}{0.246} UE(t) - \underset{(0.053)}{0.032} \log\left[\frac{D(t)}{P(t-1)}\right] + u'(t+1) \tag{22}$$

$$\bar{R}^2 = 0.47, \quad \text{DW} = 1.88.$$

The F statistic for inclusion of the earnings forecast error $UE(t)$ is about 7.96, which is significant at the 5 percent level. The OLS and GLS estimates of (22) are virtually identical, which is consistent with the earnings forecast error eliminating part of the serial dependence in the disturbances. The measured correlation between the variable $\log[P(t+1)/P(t)+D(t+1)/P(t)]$, which, up to a constant, is the unexpected price change from the end of period t to the end of period $t+1$, and the (GLS) residual $u(t+1)$ in (19) is about 10 percent. By including contemporaneous unanticipated earnings, this contemporaneous correlation between unexpected price changes and the (GLS) residual $u(t+1)$ in (22) is reduced to about 3.3 percent. Thus the previously noted small amount of "information content" in aggregate dividends is further reduced by taking account of earnings changes. We pursue this no further because, as we noted earlier, the information content of dividends and earnings is probably not well defined for an aggregate of corporations over a coarse annual grid.

7 Conclusion

In this paper we have shown that aggregate dividends exhibit a systematic time series behavior that can be well described by an error correction model in which aggregate real dividend changes are driven by the one-period lagged real changes in stock prices. Although the time series of aggregate dividends is considerably less volatile than the stock price series, this model significantly outperforms the trend autoregressive model in which a distributed lag of past dividends together with a time trend is used to explain subsequent dividend changes.

The stock price model performs on a par with dividend models that use contemporaneous and lagged accounting earnings variables, as in previous studies of Lintner's (1956) model by Brittain (1966), Fama and Babiak (1968), and Watts (1973). However, because the stock price model uses only lagged prices, it can be used to forecast future dividend changes, whereas the accounting earnings model that employs contemporaneous earnings cannot be used to forecast. The version of the accounting earnings model that uses only lagged accounting earnings to forecast dividends significantly underperforms the stock price model.

As noted at the outset, a wide range of possible micro theories of dividend behavior could be consistent with the observed systematic behavior of aggregate dividends. However, our finding that aggregate dividends do exhibit systematic time series behavior provides evidence that strictly firm-specific theories of dividends such as signaling cannot by themselves explain the dividend puzzle.

Appendix

The long-run steady state (4) in the text can be imposed on the short-run dynamics (3) by the further coefficient restrictions

$$\lambda - \theta_1 = 1 - \phi_1 \equiv \gamma, \tag{A1}$$

that is,

$$\lambda - \theta_1 = 1 - \phi_1,$$

and by setting the constant in the deterministic function $a(t)$ in (3) equal to $\gamma\beta$. Denoting the function $a(t)$ without the constant by $a'(t)$ and incorporating (A1), we can rewrite (3) as follows:

$$\begin{aligned}\log[D(t+1)] - \log[D(t)] &= \gamma\beta + a'(t) + \lambda\{\log[E^{\mathrm{m}}(t)] - \log[E^{\mathrm{m}}(t-1)]\}\\ &\quad - \gamma\{\log[D(t)] - \log[E^{\mathrm{m}}(t-1)]\} + \eta(t+1)\end{aligned} \tag{A2}$$

or, by rearrangement,

$$\begin{aligned}\log[D(t+1)] - \log[D(t)] &= a'(t) + \lambda\{\log[E^{\mathrm{m}}(t)] - \log[E^{\mathrm{m}}(t-1)]\}\\ &\quad + \gamma(\beta - \{\log[D(t)] - \log[E^{\mathrm{m}}(t-1)]\})\\ &\quad + \eta(t+1).\end{aligned} \tag{A3}$$

To derive (5), define the expected logarithmic change in permanent earnings

$$\log[E^{\mathrm{m}}(t)] - \log[E^{\mathrm{m}}(t-1)]$$

as $m(t-1)$. Then (A3) can be rewritten as

$$\begin{aligned}\log[D(t+1)] - \log[D(t)] &= a'(t) + \lambda m(t-1)\\ &\quad + \lambda\{\log[E^{\mathrm{m}}(t)] - \log[E^{\mathrm{m}}(t-1)] - m(t-1)\}\\ &\quad + \gamma(\beta - \{\log[D(t)] - \log[E^{\mathrm{m}}(t-1)]\}) + \eta(t+1).\end{aligned} \tag{A4}$$

Substituting $g(t) \equiv a'(t) + \lambda m(t)$ gives (5) in the text.

Notes

1 For a more complete summary of the dividend controversy, see Brealey and Myers (1984, ch. 16). The degree to which this controversy is unresolved is exemplified by its inclusion in their list of ten important unsolved problems in finance that "seem ripe for productive research" (Brealey and Myers, 1984, p. 790).

2 In fact, in their events study of the dividend behavior of split stocks, Fama et al. (1969) did adjust individual firm dividend changes for market-wide dividend changes before classifying the former as increases or decreases. Fama et al. did this to be internally consistent in associating security return residuals with dividend changes. Note that, as would be the case for our model at the micro-level, an added variable might well be required to account for dividend increases or decreases associated with a firm's "normal" secular progression through its "life cycle."

3 Note, however, that with only slight embellishment to include transactions costs for either issuers or investors even this extreme demand-driven model would predict systematic micro dividend behavior. With issuing costs, for example, firms in mature or declining industries with large cash flows relative to their new investment needs would be marginally lower cost producers of dividends than firms in growth industries. Since the position of a firm or an industry within its "life cycle" is hardly random from year to year, both individual firm and industry payout patterns are likely to exhibit serial dependences. The empirical evidence for microstability in dividends is explored by Marsh and Merton (1985a).

4 The stylized facts distilled by Lintner from his interviews can be interpreted as a description of "average" or "systematic" dividend behavior. In this sense, these facts are macro rather than micro.

5 Although $V(t)$ is the present value per share of the future cash flows available for distribution to the shares outstanding at time t, it does not follow that the dividend per share paid at time s must equal $[\Pi(s) - I(s)]/N(s)$. By the accounting identity

$$\Pi(s) - I(s) \equiv N(s)D(s) - [N(s+1) - N(s)]\,P(s),$$

where $[N(s+1) - N(s)]\,P(s)$ is the cash flow received from the issue of new shares of stock at time s, and therefore

$$D(s) = \frac{\Pi(s) - I(s) + [N(s+1) - N(s)]\,P(s)}{N(s)}$$

If issues or purchases of shares are made at "fair" market prices, then such future transactions have a zero net present value and therefore have no effect on the current intrinsic value per share of the firm. If the firm has debt in its capital structure, then interest payments must be subtracted and net proceeds of new debt issues added to the cash flows of the firm. As with stock issued, if the debt is issued or retired at fair market prices, then such future debt transactions will also have no effect on the current intrinsic value of the firm. Although the additional future cash flows from new share and debt issues do not affect current permanent earnings (for a given value of permanent earnings), such financial transactions provide management with considerable flexibility to control the time path of dividends per share.

6 At least at the time of his survey 30 years ago, Lintner's (1956) evidence indicated that dividend policy was not viewed by management as simply a balancing item in the flow of funds account: "Dividends [rather than retained earnings and savings] represent the primary and active decision variable in most situations" (p. 97). "In general, management's standards with respect to its current liquidity position appeared to be very much more flexible than its standards with respect to dividend policy, and this flexibility frequently provided the buffer between reasonably definite dividend requirements in line with established policy and especially rich current investment opportunities" (p. 105). Other statements could be interpreted as hints regarding the loss function underlying dividend rules, but they are not very specific; for example, by "stabilizing" dividends, managers can "minimize adverse shareholder reactions," and "management can live more comfortably with its unavoidable uncertainties regarding future developments" (p. 100).

7 It can be verified that only trivial modifications in the dynamic equation developed below are required to account explicitly for any steady state variation in the ratio. For example, if it is hypothesized that the equilibrium ratio depends on a vector of

stationary stochastic variables $\boldsymbol{Z}(t)$, (4) is replaced by

$$\log\left[\frac{D(t)}{E^{\mathrm{m}}(t-1)}\right] = \beta_0 + \beta' \boldsymbol{Z}(t),$$

with the only effect being a change in the regressivity term in (5).

8 For example, if the dynamics of the firm's intrinsic value follow a geometric Brownian motion, and if management pays out a constant proportion of permanent earnings as dividends, then the dividend dynamics will also be described by a geometric Brownian motion. No amount of time detrending will make either of these processes stationary. Nevertheless, the ratio of dividends to permanent earnings is (trivially) a stationary process. For further discussion, see Rubinstein (1976, pp. 409–11) and Marsh and Merton (1985b, appendix A).

9 The interpretation of the parameter γ in (5) suffers from the absence of a more precise underlying structural model that leads to (3). To see this, suppose for simplicity that $\Delta \log[E^{\mathrm{m}}(t)] = m(t-1)$ and $\eta(t) = 0$ in (5) but that the current dividend yield is out of equilibrium. Salmon (1982, p. 622) shows that a "proportional, integral, derivative" (PID) control rule

$$\begin{aligned}\Delta \log[D(t)] = \beta - k_{\mathrm{i}}\{\log[D(t)] - \log[E^{\mathrm{m}}(t-1)]\} - k_{\mathrm{p}}\Delta\{\log[D(t)] - \log[E^{\mathrm{m}}(t-1)]\} \\ - k_{\mathrm{d}}\Delta^2\{\log[D(t)] - \log[E^{\mathrm{m}}(t-1)]\}\end{aligned}$$

leads to the following error correction term:

$$\begin{aligned}\Delta \log[D(t)] &= [(k_{\mathrm{p}} + k_{\mathrm{i}} + k_{\mathrm{d}}) - (k_{\mathrm{p}} + 2k_{\mathrm{d}})L - k_{\mathrm{d}}^2 L]\{\log[D(t)] - \log[E^{\mathrm{m}}(t-1)]\} \\ &\equiv \beta - A(L)\{\log[D(t)] - \log[E^{\mathrm{m}}(t-1)]\}.\end{aligned}$$

In the absence of a more explicit model, we can only speculate about the need to include a term like $\Delta^2\{\log[D(t)] - \log[E^{\mathrm{m}}(t-1)]\}$ in (5). For example, in Salmon's general discussion, he argues that an error correction rule might be appropriate when a decision maker faces an uncertain environment in which the control problem is itself changing over time. Terms like $\Delta^2\{\log[D(t)] - \log[E^{\mathrm{m}}(t-1)]\}$ may pick up such changes, especially if the type of model changes that occur result in a non-time-additive "control problem" to be solved for the short-run dynamics of dividends. Insofar as changes in the long-run equilibrium dividend-to-price ratio are concerned, many can be accommodated in the formulations in the text. Given these formulations, if uncertainties about the "short-run" dividend control problem cannot be completely described by a linear quadratic problem, a nonlinear model will generally be needed in place of (5) – the certainty equivalence principle will no longer hold and $\eta(t)$ will not be an additive error.

10 Strictly, feasibility requires only the weaker "less than or equal to." If, however, dividends include all distributions to stockholders, and if managers do not throw cash away, then strict equality is required. In contrast with the actual dividend payments made, the term "dividend policy" refers to the contingent schedule or plan for future dividend payments. A dividend policy is thus much like the state-contingent functions for optimal control variables, which are derived from the solution of a stochastic dynamic programming problem.

11 Indeed, even in the restrictive context of our simple behavioral model, any values for λ and γ in (5) such that $0 \leqslant \lambda \leqslant 1$ and $\gamma > 0$ are more than sufficient to ensure satisfaction of the rationality constraint.

12 Even the strongest supporters of the view that dividend policy matters would agree that the only effect of a change in dividend policy on investment policy is through its effect on the firm's cost of capital α. Although a change in dividend policy may "signal" a

change in investment policy, one could hardly argue that such a dividend policy change "caused" the subsequent change in investment policy that it signaled.

13 See, for example, Hall (1978). We note further that, if consumer behavior is to smooth the time path of changes in consumption, then the dynamics for a change in the next-period consumption in response to an unanticipated change in this-period wealth may well be described by a partial adjustment process analogous to our equation (5).

14 Note that the degree of market efficiency posited here is much weaker than would be implied by assuming that the market information set contains all the relevant information included in managers' aggregated information sets. Under our assumption, a manager may have information relevant to the estimation of his or her firm's intrinsic value that is not available to the market. If, as would seem reasonable, such nonpublic information is firm specific, then differences between the market's and the manager's assessments of the individual firm's intrinsic value that arise from this source are likely to disappear (statistically) when these individual assessments are averaged over all firms. It is, of course, possible that the market's information set is richer than the individual manager's, even with respect to estimates of his or her own firm's intrinsic value. However, rationally behaving managers would, presumably, take this possibility into account when making their dividend decisions.

15 As discussed in note 5, because of transactions by the firm in its own liabilities, it is not the case that $[\Pi(s) - I(s)]/N(s) \equiv D(s)$ in (8). Even without such transactions, managers can still implement virtually any change in dividends per share by the purchase or sale of financial assets held by the firm or by marginal changes in the amount of investment in any other "zero-net-present-value" asset (for example, inventories). While the latter transactions will change the time pattern of $\Pi(s) - I(s)$, they will not affect the present value of these future cash flows and therefore will not affect the current level of permanent earnings. The presence of such significant nonequity sources of cash flow causes practical difficulties in testing theories that make fine distinctions between the behavior of gross and net dividends.

16 The joint hypothesis implied by the assumption used to derive equation (11) includes the dividend behavioral equation (5) and a constant real discount rate in addition to stock market rationality. Thus the goodness of fit of (11) is hardly a meaningful test of stock market rationality. This is, indeed, the central point in Marsh and Merton (1986), made there with respect to the joint hypothesis of Shiller's (1981a) variance bound tests and their interpretation as tests of stock market rationality. If the model of dividend behavior posited here is substituted for the Shiller assumption of a stationary process for dividends, then these variance bounds will be systematically violated even if stock prices are rationally determined. If, as the theoretical and empirical evidence presented here suggests, this model of dividends is a plausible alternative to the one posited by Shiller, then his variance bounds are not a reliable test of stock market rationality. This is so whether or not stock prices are, in fact, rationally determined. See Merton (1987) for a related discussion of other variance bound tests for this hypothesis.

17 Although the majority of studies using serial correlation, filtering, and spectral analysis tests support this view, Summers (1986) shows that their power is low in detecting long-wave serial dependences in stock returns. Moreover, Fama and French (1988) find evidence of a regressive or temporary component in 3–5 year stock returns. Such findings are consistent with the view that stock prices deviate significantly from fundamental values with a slow speed of adjustment toward these values. They are also consistent, however, with rational stock prices and time-varying equilibrium expected returns.

18 Our data set is different from those used by Shiller (1981a). However, our data set produces essentially the same empirical findings as reported by Shiller for his data sets. We therefore expect that the results reported here for our model will also obtain if our model were fit to his data sets. Equation (17) was also fitted using quarterly data. Although it might at first appear that the use of quarterly rather than annual data would quadruple the number of observations available, there are good reasons for doubting this. There is a distinct yearly (and half yearly) seasonal in real quarterly dividends. If, as this suggests, managers wait until the fourth (fiscal) quarter to take a look at the year's performance before deciding to raise or lower that year's dividend relative to the previous year's, then the last quarter's dividend contains effectively the same information as the annual dividend. Further, any "seasonal adjustment" of quarterly dividends not only runs the risk of smoothing away the very innovations in dividends in which we are interested but also is doubly hazardous when autocorrelated disturbances or lagged dependent variables might be present, as in (11). Therefore only the results for annual data are reported.

19 Any of the above-mentioned ways in which the adjustment lags could arise are also potential explanations for disturbance autocorrelation because, in dynamic regression models, lag structure and disturbance autocorrelation can act as proxies for each other.

20 Our $\bar{R}^2$ is below the 85 percent figure given by Lintner (1956). However, Lintner, who stressed that his results were preliminary, pooled his time series observations from 1918 to 1941 for his 28 companies to estimate his model. Fama and Babiak (1968), who reestimated Lintner's model separately for each firm over the years 1946–64, report (for example, in their table 2) average $\bar{R}^2$ figures of (roughly) 40–45 percent, which are comparable with ours.

21 By inspection of (12) and (13), the OLS and GLS estimates of the coefficient on percentage price changes are negligibly different. If the GLS transformation is interpreted as a quasi-differencing operator, and if a logic similar to that of Plosser, Schwert, and White (1982) is applied, then the invariance of the coefficient estimate to GLS suggests, in terms of Hausman's (1978) specification test, that there is no simultaneity bias in regressions (12) and (13).

22 The point estimate of the dividend yield coefficient is sensitive to how the autocorrelation is taken into account. The half-life calculation in the text uses the GLS rather than the OLS estimate because the positive autocorrelation in the OLS residuals reduces the absolute magnitude of the (negative) dividend yield coefficient. Dynamic regression models with autocorrelated disturbances cannot be easily distinguished from ones with lagged dependent variables, and the dividend yield will be correlated with the lagged dependent variable if, as both our model and Shiller's posit, the dividend-to-price ratio is autoregressive. There is evidence that the residual autocorrelation estimate is somewhat sensitive to an outlier in 1951, but this outlier apparently has no effect on the estimates of the coefficients in our model. We therefore omit a more detailed analysis of the disturbance autocorrelation.

23 In their classic events study of stock splits and the cash dividend changes that often accompany them, Fama et al. (1969) report a result similar to ours: stock splits, and the increased dividends that typically accompany them, were on the average preceded by abnormal price increases. In their study, some of the average "run-up" in prices took place earlier than 12 months before the stock split event, but Fama et al. deliberately select the individual companies that, *ex post*, split their stocks. The early small run-up in prices could easily wash out in our aggregate data, and in any case Fama et al.'s study does not provide information on changes in cash dividends other than those associated with the stock split.

24 Both these tests and the recursive estimation were performed using the Troll program Recur. Details of all results cited but not reported are available on request.

25 The usual problems of identifying the point of shift in the regression regime are exacerbated when the shift occurs at the beginning (or end) of the sample period, where the tax change explanation would place it (e.g. Quandt 1958, pp. 877–8). Moreover, an advocate of Tarshis's position might argue that it is at best only "half naive" to search for a single discrete shift in regimes over our long sample period.

26 The significance of stock price volatility changes in explaining dividend movements has implications for the stock price rationality debate. If managers "smooth out" what they consider to be irrational fluctuations in stock prices as measures of permanent earnings, then it seems rather implausible that the magnitude of the response coefficient to stock price changes would decrease, rather than increase, when stock price volatility decreases.

27 Tests for the effects of a nonconstant discount rate were performed using the program Adapt, written by Craig F. Ansley.

28 In previous estimations, we used a "one-step" GLS procedure. Because Maddala (1971) has shown that "iteration pays" in GLS estimation when a lagged dependent variable is present, we use the iterative approach for the equations in this section.

29 Comparing the OLS and GLS values of $\bar{R}^2$ provides only a heuristic measure of the incremental explanatory power afforded by the GLS regression because the OLS $\bar{R}^2$ is not a proper benchmark in light of autocorrelation in the residuals. The $\bar{R}^2$ for the GLS regression, which, in this case and all others in the paper, we compute as (geometrically) the square of the cosine of the angle between the (centered) dependent variable and the (centered) fitted dependent variable, is also well known not to be uniquely defined for GLS and nonlinear regression models. However, we believe that our statements in this paper concerning model fit are not sensitive to our $\bar{R}^2$ measure, especially since the OLS and GLS fits of our model are essentially the same. Further, it is hard to think of a more "natural" way of generally measuring the tightness between the fitted and the actual dependent variables.

30 As was the case for the OLS and GLS fits (12) and (13) of our model, the GLS fit of (16) is not a significant improvement on its OLS fit. The F statistic for the autoregressive correction in (16) is 2.85, which is not significant at the conventional 5 percent level. Thus the addition of log price change to (15) substantially increases its explanatory power and improves the autoregressive model's specification (14) by eliminating the requirement that it be supplemented by more structure on the stochastic process for the "unknown" variables before it is a proper regression equation.

31 This regression is almost the equivalent of the Granger–Sims causality test referred to in the discussion of causality in section 3.

32 It is all the more surprising because the model does not use contemporaneous price changes. Because all the variables in our model are lagged, equation (18) is a "true" forecast equation in the sense that, at time t, it provides an unconditional forecast for $D(t+1)$. The relatively high $\bar{R}^2$ suggests that aggregate dividends may be forecast rather successfully.

33 There is, of course, ample precedent in the economics literature for assuming that relative values such as the dividend-to-price and earnings-to-price ratios have steady state or stationary distributions. As exemplified by our model, the existence of steady state distributions for such relative values surely does not justify the assumption of stationarity distributions for the levels (or absolute values) of dividends, earnings, or prices. Further, unless investors are risk neutral and the riskless rate of interest is

constant, the assumption of a constant expected return on the market, made by Shiller (1981a,b) and in much of the finance literature, is inconsistent with the trend autoregressive process for dividends and stock prices. For proofs and further discussion, see Fama (1977) and Myers and Turnbull (1977).

34 Study of our sample using blunt interocular analysis suggests that there are a few influential "outliers" in the annual data that cause the correlation, and the correlation disappears completely with monthly data.

35 Although not presented here, the sample distributions of dividend and stock price changes were plotted using Tukey's (1970) robust statistics. These plots are consistent with the relatively fat tails of the dividend process implied by our reported kurtosis statistics.

References

Aharony, J. and Swary, I. (1980) "Quarterly Dividend and Earnings Announcements and Stockholders' Returns: An Empirical Analysis," *Journal of Finance*, 35: 1, 1–11.

Asquith, P. and Mullins, D. W., Jr (1983) "The Impact of Initiating Dividend Payments on Shareholders' Wealth," *Journal of Business*, 56: 1, 77–95.

Bhattacharya, S. (1979) "Imperfect Information, Dividend Policy, and 'the Bird in the Hand' Fallacy," *Bell Journal of Economics*, 10: 1, Spring, 259–70.

Black, F. (1976) "The Dividend Puzzle." In *Modern Developments in Financial Management*, ed. S. C. Myers (Hinsdale, IL: Dryden).

Black, F. and Scholes, M. S. (1974) "The Effects of Dividend Yield and Dividend Policy on Common Stock Prices and Returns," *Journal of Financial Economics*, 1, May, 1–22.

Brealey, R. A. and Myers, S. C. (1984) *Principles of Corporate Finance*, 2nd edn (New York: McGraw-Hill).

Brittain, J. A. (1966) *Corporate Dividend Policy* (Washington, DC: Brookings Institution).

Copeland, B. L., Jr (1983) "Do Stock Prices Move Too Much To Be Justified by Subsequent Changes in Dividends? Comment," *American Economic Review*, 73: 2, 234–5.

Davidson, J. E. H., Hendry, D. F., Srba, D. and Yeo, S. (1978) "Econometric Modelling of the Aggregate Time-Series Relationship Between Consumers' Expenditure and Income in the United Kingdom," *Economic Journal*, 88, December, 661–92.

Dickey, D. A. and Fuller, W. A. (1979) "Distribution of the Estimators for Autoregressive Time Series with a Unit Root," *Journal of the American Statistical Association*, 74: 366, June, 427–31.

Dickey, D. A. and Fuller, W. A. (1981) "Likelihood Ratio Statistics for Autoregressive Time Series with a Unit Root," *Econometrica*, 49: 4, July, 1057–72.

Eades, K. M., Hess, P. J. and Kim, E. H. (1984) "On Interpreting Security Returns During the Ex-Dividend Period," *Journal of Financial Economics*, 13: 1, 3–34.

Easterbrook, F. H. (1984) "Two Agency Cost Explanations of Dividends," *American Economic Review*, 74: 1, 650–9.

Ericsson, N. R. and Hendry, D. F. (1984) "Assertion Without Empirical Basis: An Econometric Appraisal of *Monetary trends in ... the United Kingdom* by Milton Friedman and Anna J. Schwartz," Presented to the Macro Conference of the NBER Research Program on Economic Fluctuations, July 12–13, Cambridge, MA.

Fama, E. F. (1977) "Risk-Adjusted Discount Rates and Capital Budgeting under Uncertainty," *Journal of Financial Economics*, 5, 3–24.

Fama, E.F . and Babiak, H. (1968) Dividend Policy: An Empirical Analysis," *Journal of the American Statistical Association*, 63: 324, December, 1132–61.

Fama, E. F. and French, K. R. (1988) "Permanent and Temporary Components of Stock Prices," *Journal of Political Economy*, 96: 2, April, 246–73.

Fama, E. F., Fisher, L., Jensen, F. and Roll, R. (1969) "The Adjustment of Stock Prices to New Information," *International Economic Review*, 10, February, 1–21.

Fisher, M. R. (1957) "L'Epargne et les Profits des Enterprises dans l'Hypothèse du 'Revenu permanent'," *Economie Appliqué*, 10, October–December, 539–62.

Gonedes, N. J. (1978) "Corporate Signalling, External Accounting, and Capital Market Equilibrium: Evidence on Dividends, Income, and Extraordinary Items," *Journal of Accounting Research*, 16: 1, Spring, 16–79.

Gordon, M. J. (1959) "Dividends, Earnings and Stock Prices," *Review of Economics and Statistics*, 41, May, 99–105.

Gordon, M. J. (1962) "The Savings, Investment and Valuation of a Corporation," *Review of Economics and Statistics*, 44: 1, February, 37–51.

Hakansson, N. H. (1982) "To Pay or Not to Pay Dividends," *Journal of Finance*, 37: 2, May, 415–28.

Hall, R. E. (1978) "Stochastic Implications of the Life-Cycle–Permanent Income Hypothesis: Theory and Evidence," *Journal of Political Economy*, 86: 6, 971–87.

Hausman, J. A. (1978) "Specification Tests in Econometrics," *Econometrica*, 46: 6, 1251–71.

Hess, P. J. (1983) "Tests for Tax Effects in the Pricing of Financial Assets," *Journal of Business*, 56: 4, October, 537–54.

John, K. and Williams, J. (1985) "Dividends, Dilution, and Taxes: A Signalling Equilibrium," *Journal of Finance*, 40: 4, September, 1053–70.

Kleidon, A. W. (1986) "Variance Bounds Tests and Stock Price Valuation Models," *Journal of Political Economy*, 94: 5, October, 953–1001.

Kuh, E., Samarov, A. and Shell, M. 1986, "Troll Program: Recur," Technical Report TR-62, Center for Computational Research in Economics and Management Science, Massachusetts Institute of Technology.

Lintner, J. (1956) "Distribution of Incomes of Corporations Among Dividends, Retained Earnings, and Taxes," *American Economic Review*, 61: 2, May, 97–113.

Lintner, J. (1962) "Dividends, Earnings, Leverage, Stock Prices and the Supply of Capital to Corporations," *Review of Economics and Statistics*, 64: 3, August, 243–69.

Litzenberger, R. H. and Ramaswamy, K. (1979) "The Effect of Personal Taxes and Dividends on Capital Asset Prices," *Journal of Financial Economics*, 7, 163–95.

Maddala, G. S. (1971) "Generalized Least Squares with an Estimated Variance–Covariance Matrix," *Econometrica*, 39: 1, January, 23–33.

Marsh, T. A. and Merton, R. C. (1985a) "Corporate Dividend Dynamics at the Firm Level," Mimeo, Sloan School of Management, Massachusetts Institute of Technology.

Marsh, T. A. and Merton, R. C. (1985b) "Dividend Behavior for the Aggregate Stock Market," *Working Paper 1670-85*, Sloan School of Management, Massachusetts Institute of Technology.

Marsh, T. A. and Merton, R. C. (1986) "Dividend Variability and Variance Bounds Tests for the Rationality of Stock Market Prices," *American Economic Review*, 76: 3, June, 483–98.

Means, G. C. (1935) "Industrial Prices and their Relative Inflexibility," Senate Document 13, 74th Congress, 1st Session (Washington, DC: US Government Printing Office).

Merton, R. C. (1987) "On the Current State of the Stock Market Rationality Hypothesis." In *Macroeconomics and Finance: Essays in Honor of Franco Modigliani*, eds R. Dornbusch, S. Fischer, and J. Bossons (Cambridge, MA: MIT Press).

Miller, M. H. (1977) "Debt and Taxes," *Journal of Finance*, 32: 2, May, 261–75.
Miller, M. H. (1985) "Behavioral Rationality in Finance: The Case of Dividends," Presented to the Conference on Behavioral Foundations of Theory, October 14–15, Chicago, IL.
Miller, M. H. and Modigliani, F. (1961) "Dividend Policy, Growth and the Valuation of Shares," *Journal of Business*, 34: 4, October, 411–33.
Miller, M. H. and Rock, K. (1985) "Dividend Policy under Asymmetric Information," *Journal of Finance*, 40, September, 103–51.
Miller, M. H. and Scholes, M. S. (1978) "Dividends and Taxes," *Journal of Financial Economics*, 6, 333–64.
Miller, M. H. and Scholes, M. S. (1982) "Dividends and Taxes: Some Empirical Evidence," *Journal of Political Economy*, 90, 1118–42.
Myers, S. C. and Turnbull, S. M. (1977) "Capital Budgeting and the Capital Asset Pricing Model: Good News and Bad News," *Journal of Finance*, 32: 2, 321–33.
Nickell, S. (1980) "Error Correction, Partial Adjustment and All That: An Expository Note," *C.L.E. Working Paper 255*, London School of Economics, May.
Officer, R. R. (1971) "A Time Series Examination of the Market Factor of the New York Stock Exchange," Ph.D. Dissertation, University of Chicago.
Petit, R. R. (1972) "Dividend Announcements, Security Performance, and Capital Market Efficiency," *Journal of Finance*, 27: 5, December, 993–1007.
Plosser, C. I., Schwert, G. H. and White, H. (1982) "Differencing as a Test of Specification," *International Economic Review*, 23: 3, October, 535–52.
Poterba, J. M. and Summers, L. H. (1984) "New Evidence that Taxes Affect the Valuation of Dividends," *Journal of Finance*, 39: 5, December, 1397–415.
Poterba, J. M. and Summers, L. H. (1985) "The Economic Effects of Dividend Taxation." In *Recent Advances in Corporate Finance*, eds E. Altman and M. Subrahmanyam (Homewood, IL: Irwin).
Quandt, R. E. (1958) "Tests of the Hypothesis that a Linear Regression System Obeys Two Separate Regimes," *Journal of the American Statistical Association*, 53: 290, June, 324–30.
Quandt, R. E. (1960) "The Estimation of the Parameters of a Linear Regression System Obeying Two Separate Regimes," *Journal of the American Statistical Association*, 55: 284, December, 873–80.
Quandt, R. E. and Ramsey, J. B. (1978) "Estimating Mixtures of Normal Distributions and Switching Regressions," *Journal of the American Statistical Association*, 73: 364, December, 730–52.
Rubinstein, M. (1976) "The Valuation of Uncertain Income Streams and the Pricing of Options," *Bell Journal of Economics*, 7: 2, Autumn, 407–25.
Salmon, M. (1982) "Error Correction Mechanisms," *Economic Journal*, 92, September, 615–29.
Sargan, J. D. (1964) "Wages and Prices in the United Kingdom: A Study in Econometric Methodology." In *Econometric Analysis for National Economic Planning*, eds P. E. Hart, G. Mills, and J. K. Whitaker (London: Butterworths).
Shefrin, H. M. and Statman, M. (1984) "Explaining Investor Preference for Cash Dividends," *Journal of Financial Economics*, 13: 2, 253–82.
Shiller, R. J. (1981a) "Do Stock Prices Move Too Much To Be Justified by Subsequent Changes in Dividends?" *American Economic Review*, 71: 3, June, 421–36.
Shiller, R. J. (1981b) "The Use of Volatility Measures in Assessing Market Efficiency," *Journal of Finance*, 34: 2, May, 291–311.
Shiller, R. J. (1983) "Do Stock Prices Move Too Much To Be Justified by Subsequent Changes in Dividends? Reply," *American Economic Review*, 73: 1, 236–7.

Summers, L. H. (1986) "Does the Stock Market Reflect Fundamental Values?" *Journal of Finance*, 41, July, 591–600.

Tarshis, L. (1959) "Discussion of J. Lintner, Distribution of Incomes of Corporations Among Dividends, Retained Earnings, and Taxes," *American Economic Review*, 66: 2, May, 118.

Tukey, J. W. (1970) *Explanatory Data Analysis* (Reading, MA: Addison-Wesley).

Watts, R. (1973) "The Information Content of Dividends," *Journal of Business*, 46: 2, April, 191–211.

Zellner, A. (1979) "Causality and Econometrics." In *Three Aspects of Policy and Policy Making*, eds K. Brunner and A. H. Meltzer, Carnegie–Rochester Conference Series, vol. 10 (Amsterdam: North-Holland).

Chapter 12

Richard S. Ruback

Background and Comments

Old-timers in corporate finance often hark back to the days when academic corporate finance was descriptive and institutional – the days before Modigliani and Miller, discounted cash flow, and the capital asset pricing model. This is misleading because the "descriptive" and "institutional" tradition is still alive and well, though in a much more sophisticated form.

Wayne Mikkelson and Richard Ruback's paper is a leading example. They give us a descriptive treatment of the process of investment by one firm in another, with special attention to investments leading to greenmail. However, they are less interested in case studies of *how* the process unfolds than in what happens *in general* and why. Rates of return to investors in the companies involved are given very careful statistical attention; they reveal the stock market's assessments of relevant events, allowing the authors to measure their economic impact and to interpret the motives of the managers involved.

This paper is a first-class example of modern empirical applied corporate finance. However, one of the chief findings still leaves me uncomfortable. Mikkelson and Ruback show that target firm shareholders end up ahead when an aggressive suitor is bought off by greenmail. The stock price fall at the point of greenmail does not offset the run-up of price beforehand. However, the target shareholders would apparently be even better off if their management had not paid greenmail but had given in and accepted a takeover on the best terms attainable. Mikkelson and Ruback's results still leave the impression that managers' interests override shareholders' in greenmail transctions.

Author's Introduction

Most empirical studies of corporate control changes analyze events individually. This study – which was written with Wayne H. Mikkelson – takes a different approach. It uses the concept of a corporate control process to emphasize that many control contests are preceded by toehold positions in which acquiring firms purchase 5 percent or more of the target firm. We treat the toehold accumulation and subsequent announcements as a sequence of events that comprise the corporate control process. Our measure of the profitability of the outcome includes the valuation consequences of these events.

The process approach provides a more accurate measure of the valuation consequences of an event. Major corporate control events are often not complete surprises, and some of the valuation change associated with the events are impounded into stock prices as the events are anticipated. As my studies of the Conoco and Cities Service acquisitions illustrate, the market reacts to a variety of announcements that precede formal corporate control announcements (Ruback, 1982, 1983). Yet most empirical studies of control changes examine events in isolation and do not examine the stock price response to the sequence of events that precede the formal announcement (e.g. Dodd and Ruback, 1977). In contrast, the process approach includes the stock price changes associated with the sequence of events that precede formal control contests, and thereby captures the evolution of control changes.

The paper reprinted here is the first systematic study of toehold positions and their outcomes. Based on stock price changes throughout the corporate control process, the order of the profitability of the four outcomes (lowest to highest) for acquiring firms is completed takeover, third party takeover, shares sold, and targeted repurchase. For target firms, the ordering is just the opposite: targeted repurchase, shares sold, third party takeover, and completed takeover. Among toeholds with major corporate control events, the four outcomes were equally likely. About half the toehold positions were not followed by a major control event during the 3 years after the announcement of the toehold.

Mikkelson and I further emphasize the process approach in our paper on targeted repurchases (popularly called "greenmail") (Mikkelson and Ruback, 1988). Our primary evidence includes the stock price effects on repurchasing firms from the initial accumulation of the block through its repurchase. Stock prices rise at the initial block accumulation and fall at the targeted repurchase announcement. The stock price increases while the block is being accumulated more than offset the decreases at the repurchase. The average total return is 7.4 percent throughout the process, from the initial blockholding through the repurchase.

When the targeted repurchase is treated as an isolated event, the stock price fall at the repurchase implies that repurchasing managers harm shareholders through, for example, entrenchment. In contrast, when the targeted repurchase is viewed as the outcome of an ongoing corporate control process, the price fall at the repurchase may simply reflect the market's unmet expectations instead of managerial entrenchment. Overall, the positive total returns suggest that the entire transaction – from the initial purchase through the repurchase – helps shareholders of the repurchasing firm.

In summary, this research documents the evolution and valuation consequences of major corporate control events. From a conceptual viewpoint, it emphasizes that examining major corporate control events in isolation can be misleading when these events are the outcome of an ongoing process.

References

Dodd, P. R. and Ruback, R. S. (1977) "Tender Offers and Stockholder Returns: An Empirical Analysis," *Journal of Financial Economics*, 5: 3, December, 351–73.

Mikkelson, W. H. and Ruback, R. S. (1988) "Targeted Repurchases and Common Stock Returns," *Working Paper 89-019*, Harvard Business School, December.

Ruback, R. S. (1982) "The Conoco Takeover and Stockholder Returns," *Sloan Management Review*, 23: 2, Winter, 13–33.

Ruback, R. S. (1983) "The Cities Service Takeover: A Case Study," *Journal of Finance*, 38: 2, May, 319–30.

Bibliographical Listing

"Targeted Repurchases and Common Stock Returns" (with Wayne Mikkelson), *Working Paper 89-019*, Harvard Business School, December 1988.

"Calculating the Market Value of Riskless Cash Flows," *Journal of Financial Economics*, 15: 3, March 1986, 323–39.

An Empirical Analysis of the Interfirm Equity Investment Process

WAYNE H. MIKKELSON and RICHARD S. RUBACK

1 Introduction

A great deal of research has focused on valuation consequences of corporate takeovers for acquiring and target firms. These studies typically examine the stock prices of the participating firms at the time of takeover announcements.[1] However, many of these takeover attempts are preceded by the purchase of 5 percent or more of the common stock of the target firms. This study expands the investigation of transactions in the market for corporate control by measuring security valuation effects of corporate investments in the equity securities of other firms. Valuation effects are measured from the time a 5 percent or greater investment position is first disclosed to the outcome of the investment.

Our sample consists of corporate acquisitions of another company's common stock, securities convertible into common stock, and options to buy common stock that were reported in a filing of Schedule 13D with the Securities and Exchange Commission (SEC) during the years 1978–80. Common stock returns of both the acquiring and target firms are analyzed around the date of the earliest report that an ownership position of 5 percent or more of the target firm's equity securities has been or will be taken. In addition, common stock returns are examined at related events subsequent to the initial announcement date and at the outcome of the investment. The abnormal stock returns at the initial announcement, the

Reproduced from *Journal of Financial Economics*, 14, 1985, 523–53.

Wayne H. Mikkelson is Associate Professor of Finance at the University of Oregon. We would like to thank the participants of seminars at Boston College, Massachusetts Institute of Technology, Tulane University, University of Chicago, University of Michigan, University of Oregon, University of Pittsburgh, and University of Rochester. We would also like to thank J. Brickley, P. Healy, R. Holthausen, M. Jensen, R. Leftwich, K. Palepu, M. Partch, J. Poterba, K. Schipper, D. Sheehan, R. Watts, J. Zimmerman, and D. Mayers (the referee) for comments on previous versions of this paper. We are also grateful to M. Ahearn, G. Maffei, R. McLaughlin, A. Morrisette, B. Rider-Martin, and D. Swanson for their research assistance. This research was partially supported by National Science Foundation Grant SES-8420677.

outcome announcement, and the intervening events are used to estimate the total valuation effect of the investment activity on the acquiring and target firm's common stock.

One objective of this study is to determine whether and how the acquiring and target firms' stock prices respond to different types of corporate investments in common stock. The sizes of the initial investments range from a 5 percent ownership position to a block of shares that transfers voting control. Most of the investments examined in this study initially represent a minority ownership stake in the target firm and are not part of a publicly announced takeover attempt by the acquiring firm. In some cases the acquiring firm discloses that the purchase of shares is solely for investment purposes, while in other cases the acquiring firm indicates that an attempt to acquire control of the target firm is under consideration. However, all the investments represent a potentially important change in the security ownership structure of the target firm. In general, we find that the share prices of both the acquiring and target firms increase in response to the initial disclosure of the investment position.

A second objective is to measure and compare the total valuation effects of investments with different outcomes. That is, we measure the combined value changes at the initial announcement, the outcome, and the intervening events for various categories of outcomes. The possible outcomes of the investment positions include a completed takeover, a completed takeover by another firm, a repurchase of the investment position by the target firm (targeted repurchase), and a sale of shares in the market or to a third party. In some cases, none of these outcome events follows the initial investment. Several of the outcome events, such as completed takeovers and targeted repurchases, have been examined individually in previous studies. In this study we analyze these events as the outcomes of an investment process that begins with the purchase of 5 percent or more of the common stock of the target firm. This provides a consistent framework for comparing the total abnormal returns associated with various outcomes and investment strategies.

Our evidence uncovers differences in the average total stock returns of both acquiring and target firms across the different outcomes. When the outcome is a completed takeover, the total abnormal return is zero for acquiring firms and is large and positive for target firms. Of the outcomes we examine, a completed takeover has the smallest total valuation effect for the acquiring firms and the largest total valuation effect for the target firms. When the outcome is a completed takeover attempt by a third party, the total valuation effect is positive for both the acquiring and the target firms. The outcomes with the most favorable total valuation effect for the acquiring firms are a sale of shares in the market or to a third party and a targeted repurchase. Target firms realize a statistically significant, positive total abnormal return for investments that conclude with a sale of shares or a targeted repurchase. We find that the negative price effect of the targeted repurchase announcement is more than offset on average by the positive price effects of preceding events.

The third objective of the study is to investigate whether firms that frequently purchase shares of other companies earn profits on this activity, and how the stockholders of the firms in which they invest fare relative to the stockholders of firms that are targets of other acquiring firms. The subset of frequent acquiring firms, defined to be firms that appear six or more times in our sample of investments, includes firms that are sometimes characterized as "corporate raiders." We find that frequent acquiring firms differ from other acquiring firms in that a greater proportion of their investments terminate with a targeted repurchase or in the sale of shares. Also, frequent purchasers of common stock rarely attempt to acquire control of a target firm. Somewhat surprisingly, frequent acquiring firms do not on average experience a larger total return than other acquiring firms. The evidence also indicates that the target firm's shareholders experience a positive valuation effect when the acquiring firm is a frequent purchaser of other companies' shares.

In the next section we describe the sample of corporate investments, the characteristics of the sample, and our method of estimating abnormal stock returns. In section 3 we present average abnormal common stock returns of the acquiring and target firms around the initial announcement date, the outcome announcement, and intermediate announcements for 13D filings that are not associated with an outstanding takeover proposal. Average returns are also presented for subsamples grouped by the type of investment plans disclosed at the initial announcement and by the outcome of the investment. Investments by frequent acquiring firms and by infrequent acquiring firms are also compared. In section 4 we examine the abnormal returns for Schedule 13D filings associated with outstanding takeover proposals. Our conclusions are presented in section 5.

2 Sample and Methodology

2.1 Schedule 13D filings

The sample of corporate acquisitions of equity securities is drawn from filings of Schedule 13D required by the Williams Act, a set of amendments to the Securities and Exchange Act of 1934. According to the provisions of the Williams Act that became effective in July 1968, an individual, group of individuals, or a corporation is required to report to the SEC the accumulated acquisition of more than 10 percent of any class of a company's voting equity securities. Effective December 1970, the Act was amended so that the ownership of more than 5 percent of a class of securities must be reported. The Act requires that a Schedule 13D must be filed within 10 days of the purchase of shares that increase holdings beyond the 5 percent level. An amended Schedule 13D must be filed within 10 days of any subsequent material change in the investment position.

Our sample includes all initial 13D filings for the years 1978–80 filed by corporations listed on either the New York or the American Stock Exchange. These filings are reported in the *SEC News Digest*, which is our primary source for the filing date and the number of shares acquired. These data are supplemented with information on selected 13D filings published in the *Insider's Chronicle*. The sample consists of 473 Schedule 13D filings by listed corporations. For 299 of these filings, the target firm is also listed on the New York or the American Stock Exchange.

For each Schedule 13D filing, the *Wall Street Journal Index* was examined to identify any news reports related to the investment in the target firm's common stock. The period covered by our examination begins 12 months before the date of the initial 13D filing and terminates at the end of the third full calendar year that follows the year of the initial 13D filing. *Wall Street Journal* articles related to the investment were read, and from these articles we recorded the specific actions taken by the acquiring or target firm. The publication dates of selected articles represent the dates we designate as the initial announcement date, the outcome date, or an intermediate event date.

The initial announcement date of the investment position is defined as the publication date of a *Wall Street Journal* report of the initial 13D filing or of a report preceding the filing that reveals plans to acquire shares of the target firm. When no such report is found, the date of the initial 13D filing is defined as the initial announcement date. Subsequent to the initial announcement date, we identified *Wall Street Journal* reports of the following events: (a) the purchase of additional shares, (b) the sale of shares in the market or to a third party, (c) the initial report of opposition by the target firm to the filing firm's investment or stated intentions, (d) legal rulings issued in connection with the investment position, (e) the announcement of a takeover offer by the filing firm or by another firm, (f) the announcement of a targeted repurchase or standstill agreement, (g) the cancellation or withdrawal of a takeover offer, and (h) stockholder approval or completion of a takeover. An event is classified as having an outcome if, subsequent to the initial announcement of the investment position, one of the following events occurs: stockholder approval or completion of a takeover with either the filing firm or another firm, failure or withdrawal of a takeover offer by the filing firm, a targeted repurchase, or a sale of shares by the filing firm. The last occurrence of any of these four events is defined as the outcome and all other preceding events are classified as intermediate events.

Row A of table 12.1 classifies the initial announcements of the 13D filings by the information contained in the *Wall Street Journal* articles. When no report of the initial 13D filing was found, the investment is classified as having no *Wall Street Journal* report. There are two qualitatively different types of initial announcements: 13D filings associated with a previously or simultaneously announced takeover proposal, and 13D filings that are not associated with an outstanding takeover proposal. For the 136 13D filings that are associated with an outstanding takeover proposal (row A, column 7 of table 12.1), the intended outcome of the investment in the target firm is known at the time of the initial announcement. In contrast, the intended actions of the filing firm are less clear for the remaining 337 13D filings. Since the focus of this paper is on investments that do not begin as a publicly announced takeover attempt, we separate the 13D filings associated with an outstanding takeover proposal from the filings that are not associated with a takeover proposal.[2]

Among the 13D filings that are not associated with a takeover announcement and are reported in the *Wall Street Journal*, the acquiring firm disclosed that an attempt to acquire control of the target firm is being considered in 41 cases. In 50 cases the transaction resulted from direct negotiation between the acquiring firm and either the target firm or another firm. For the 131 filings classified as investments, the *Wall Street Journal* disclosed no information about the acquiring firm's investment plans or it was reported that the shares were acquired only for investment purposes. In 126 cases no report of the initial 13D filing appeared in the *Wall Street Journal*.

Outcome events were reported for 177 of the 337 initial filings that were not associated with an outstanding takeover proposal. The frequency of outcomes is presented in column 2 of table 12.1. The investment process concludes with a completed takeover (merger or tender offer) by the filing firm in 43 cases. A completed takeover by another firm is the outcome of the investment process in 45 observations. In 39 cases the investment terminates with a targeted repurchase. The targeted repurchase category also includes three transactions that concluded with a standstill agreement but did not involve a targeted purchase.[3] The acquired shares are sold in the market or to a third party in 47 cases. Three investments conclude with an unsuccessful takeover attempt. Thus the reported outcomes of the investment process are roughly evenly divided among completed takeovers, third party takeovers, targeted repurchases, and shares sold. The 160 investments classified as having "no outcome" represent an undetermined combination of cases where either no outcome event took

Table 12.1 Number of 13D filings in the period 1978–1980 classified by the type of information at the initial announcement of the investment and by the outcome

	1	2	3	4	5	6	7
	Type of initial announcement for filings not associated with an outstanding takeover proposal						Filings associated with an outstanding takeover proposal
Outcome	*Total sample*	*Total*[a]	*Considering takeover*	*Negotiated transaction*	*Investment*	*No Wall Street Journal report*	*Total*
A Total sample	473	337	41	50	131	126	136
B Completed takeover	157	43	20	14	11	5	114
C Third party takeover	49	45	4	0	18	23	4
D Unsuccessful takeover	15	3	1	1	0	1	12
E Targeted repurchase	40	39	3	3	28	5	1
F Shares sold	52	47	5	8	30	6	5
G No outcome within 3 years[b]	160	160	8	24	44	86	0

[a]The entries in columns 3, 4, 5, and 6 do not sum to the total in column 2 because 11 filings are included in both the considering takeover and negotiated transaction categories.

[b]No outcome means that none of the outcome events listed above were reported between the initial announcement and the end of the third full calendar year following the initial investment.

place prior to the end of the third full calendar year following the initial investment or the *Wall Street Journal* did not report an outcome event. Over half the investments classified as having no outcome were not reported in the *Wall Street Journal* at the initial announcement.

The size of the initially reported investment in the target firms' shares

Table 12.2 Average percentage of the target firm's shares held and the dollar value of the investment at the initial 13D filing

	Percentage of target held[a]	*Dollar value of investment*[a] *(million)*
A Classified by the type of initial announcement		
Considering takeover	21.0 (20.5, 38)	17.3 (24.5, 38)
Negotiated transaction	21.8 (12.2, 36)	20.7 (26.8, 36)
Investment	9.8 (13.0, 115)	13.0 (28.7, 115)
No *Wall Street Journal* report	14.8 (17.4, 98)	11.9 (41.1, 98)
Takeover	37.0 (28.7, 120)	54.3 (104.2, 120)
B Classified by type of outcome		
Takeovers (following filings associated with an outstanding takeover proposal)	40.9 (29.1, 102)	62.0 (111.1, 102)
Takeovers (following filings not associated with an outstanding takeover proposal)	30.0 (26.3, 37)	34.7 (68.8, 37)
Targeted repurchase	7.6 (3.3, 36)	10.2 (19.0, 36)
Shares sold	12.8 (14.5, 46)	9.5 (9.6, 46)
Third party takover	7.0 (4.1, 39)	7.0 (6.8, 39)
Unsuccessful takeover	14.7 (13.2, 11)	11.8 (20.2, 11)
No outcome	13.7 (13.9, 126)	11.4 (26.0, 126)
Average	20.9 (23.3, 397)	25.8 (66.0, 397)

The sample period for 13D filings is 1978–80. The sample excludes filings associated with securities other than common stock (74 of the total sample of 473 13D filings are excluded because the filings involved securities other than common stock; two additional observations are excluded because of insufficient data).

[a]Standard deviation and sample size are in parentheses.

varies across the different types of initial announcements and outcomes. Table 12.2 presents the average percentage of the target firms' shares held and the average market value of the holdings at the time of the initial 13D filing.[4] The 74 filings that involve securities other than common stock are excluded from table 12.2. For the classifications of filings by types of initial announcement (panel A), the largest average ownership position is 37 percent, or $54 million, for filings that are associated with an outstanding takeover proposal. The smallest average percentage ownership stake is 9.8 percent when the initial announcement is classified as an investment. The smallest average dollar position is $11.9 million for filings not reported in the *Wall Street Journal*. The classification by outcomes reveals that the largest average ownership position reported in the intial 13D filing is 40.9 percent, or $62 million, for completed takeovers in which the initial filing is associated with an outstanding takeover proposal. The average ownership initial level is approximately 30 percent for other 13D filings that conclude with completed takeovers. The average initial positions are considerably smaller for the other outcome categories.[5]

The sample of 473 events represents Schedule 13D filings by 275 firms. About 87 percent of the filing firms appear only once or twice in the final sample, but several firms invested frequently in other companies' common stock between 1978 and 1980. To explore possible differences between investments by frequent and other acquiring firms, we examine investments by the subsample of firms that appear six or more times in the sample as an acquiring firm.[6] This subsample represents 95 of the 473 Schedule 13D filings.

2.2 *Method of measuring abnormal returns*

The event study method pioneered by Fama et al. (1969) is used to measure the price effects of the initial purchase, intermediate and outcome announcements. Since most stocks tend to move up or down with the market, the realized stock returns are adjusted for market-wide movements to isolate the component of the returns due to events related to the investment. This adjustment is accomplished using linear regression to estimate the following market model:[7]

$$R_{jt} = \alpha_j + \beta_j R_{\mathrm{m}t} + \varepsilon_{jt}. \qquad (1)$$

The parameter β_j measures the sensitivity of the jth firm's return R_{jt} to movements in the market index $R_{\mathrm{m}t}$. The term $\beta_j R_{\mathrm{m}t}$ in equation (1) is the portion of the return to security j that is due to market-wide factors. The parameter α_j measures that part of the average return of the stock which is not due to market movements. Lastly, ε_t measures that part of the return to the firm which is not due to movements in the market or the firm's average return.

Two sets of coefficients are estimated for each firm to incorporate potential changes in the market model parameters. Coefficients α^{B} and β^{B} before the initial announcement are estimated using daily returns beginning 260 trading days before the initial announcement and ending 61 days before the initial announcement. Similarly, coefficients after the outcome announcement are estimated over the period beginning 61 days after the outcome announcement (if returns are available) and ending 260 days after the outcome. In those cases in which 100 days of data are not available to estimate either the before or the after coefficients, returns before the initial announcement and after the outcome announcement are combined to estimate the coefficients. In all cases, returns for the 60 days preceding the initial announcement through 60 days following the outcome announcement are excluded from the estimation period.

Prediction errors are calculated for each firm for 60 days prior to the initial announcement through 60 days after the outcome announcement according to the following expression:

$$\begin{aligned} \mathrm{PE}_{jt} &= R_{jt} - (\hat{\alpha}_j^{\mathrm{B}} + \hat{\beta}_j^{\mathrm{B}} R_{\mathrm{m}t}) && \text{for } t < \text{initial announcement} \\ &= R_{jt} - (\hat{\alpha}_j^{\mathrm{A}} + \hat{\beta}_j^{\mathrm{A}} R_{\mathrm{m}t}) && \text{for } t \geqslant \text{initial announcement.} \end{aligned} \tag{2}$$

The prediction errors equal the deviation of the daily returns from their estimated normal relation with the market and represent abnormal returns. The average abnormal return over an interval of days defined relative to an event date for a sample of firms is calculated by summing the prediction errors over the holding period for each firm and then averaging across firms.[8]

To test the statistical significance of the abnormal returns, we compute the following t statistic:

$$t = \frac{1}{\mathcal{J}} \sum_{j=1}^{J} \left\{ \sum_{t=\tau_1}^{\tau_2} \mathrm{PE}_{jt} \Big/ \left[\sum_{t=\tau_1}^{\tau_2} \mathrm{var}(\mathrm{PE}_{jt}) \right]^{1/2} \right\} \tag{3}$$

where τ_1 and τ_2 are the first and last days of the interval, $\mathcal{J}$ is the number of observations, and $\mathrm{var}(\mathrm{PE}_{jt})$ is the variance of the prediction error of firm j on day t. The variance of the prediction errors is

$$\mathrm{var}(\mathrm{PE}_{jt}) = S_j^2 \left[1 + \frac{1}{N} + \frac{(R_{\mathrm{m}t} - \bar{R}_{\mathrm{m}j})^2}{(N-1)\ \mathrm{var}(R_{\mathrm{m}})} \right]. \tag{4}$$

In (4), S_j^2 is the residual variance from the market model regression, $\bar{R}_{\mathrm{m}j}$ is the average market return over the estimation interval, and N is the number of days used to estimate the market model.[9] The t statistic adjusts for heteroskedasticity in the prediction errors by standardizing the cumulative prediction error for each firm by its standard deviation. This standardization gives less weight to the prediction errors with more volatility, which are measured less precisely.[10]

3 Common Stock Returns for Filings Not Associated with Outstanding Takeover Proposals

3.1 Returns of acquiring and target firms around the initial announcement date

Table 12.3 presents the average prediction errors for acquiring and target firms at the initial announcement date (AD) and over selected holding periods prior to the initial announcement date for the 13D filings that are not associated with an outstanding takeover proposal. The announcements of these filings appear to increase the stock price of both acquiring and target firms. The average prediction error for the day before and day of the initial announcement is 1.17 percent for acquiring firms. This is statistically significant with a *t* statistic of 7.15. The average 2 day period

Table 12.3 Average prediction errors before and at the initial 13D announcement

Interval of trading days[a]	*Acquiring firms*[b] *(%)*	*Target firms*[b] *(%)*
2 day announcement period AD − 1 to AD	1.17 (7.15, 61, 337)	2.88 (16.56, 66, 230)
AD − 60 to AD − 41	0.46 (0.94, 48, 337)	2.48 (4.07, 57, 229)
AD − 40 to AD − 21	−1.37 (−2.23, 43, 337)	3.39 (5.00, 59, 229)
AD − 20 to BD − 1	0.32 (0.85, 46, 337)	3.45 (6.25, 60, 230)
BD to AD − 2[c]	−0.12 (0.60, 45, 251)	3.40 (6.15, 57, 175)
AD − 1	0.60 (4.63, 54, 335)	2.64 (17.37, 67, 222)
AD	0.58 (5.34, 54, 337)	0.34 (6.45, 49, 230)

The sample period for 13D filings is 1978–80. The sample excludes 13D filings associated with outstanding takeover proposals.

[a]AD is the initial announcement date, which is the date of either a *Wall Street Journal* report or a Schedule 13D filing with the SEC. BD is the buy date, which is the date that a 5 percent position in the target firm was attained. When the exact buy date cannot be determined, BD is defined to be 10 days prior to the date of the 13D filing.

[b]The *t* statistic, percentage positive, and sample size are in parentheses.

[c]The sample size is smaller in this interval because in several cases the *Wall Street Journal* reported plans to purchase shares more than 8 days before the filing date of Schedule 13D. Thus, the interval BD to AD − 2 contains zero days for these observations.

prediction error for targets is 2.88 percent with a t statistic of 16.56. Furthermore, 61 percent of the 2 day prediction errors are positive for acquiring firms and 66 percent of the 2 day prediction errors are positive for target firms.

Table 12.3 also presents abnormal returns for selected holding periods

Table 12.4 Average 2 day initial announcement prediction errors for 13D filings in the period 1978–1980, classified by type of announcement and by type of acquiring firm[a]

Category	*Acquiring firms*[b] *(%)*	*Target firms*[b] *(%)*
A Types of initial announcements		
Considering acquisition	2.46	7.74
	(4.06, 71, 41)	(12.80, 81, 26)
Negotiated transaction	1.28	5.91
	(2.93, 56, 50)	(11.40, 60, 30)
Investment	1.27	3.24
	(4.77, 59, 131)	(12.26, 77, 106)
No *Wall Street Journal* report	0.64	−0.40
	(3.04, 60, 126)	(0.45, 45, 76)
B Types of purchaser[c]		
Frequent purchasers[d]	1.54	3.81
	(4.18, 59, 90)	(13.40, 77, 75)
Infrequent purchasers	1.04	2.44
	(5.84, 61, 247)	(10.85, 60, 155)
C Investment category by types of purchaser		
Frequent purchasers[d]	1.75	3.49
	(4.06, 56, 63)	(9.27, 82, 56)
Infrequent purchasers	0.83	2.96
	(2.72, 62, 68)	(8.04, 72, 50)
D Filings not reported in the Wall Street Journal *by types of purchaser*		
Frequent purchasers[d]	0.91	0.17
	(0.93, 67, 21)	(0.56, 53, 15)
Infrequent purchasers	0.58	−0.54
	(2.91, 59, 105)	(0.23, 43, 61)

The sample excludes 13D filings associated with outstanding takeover proposals.

[a]The average 2 day initial announcement prediction errors are the average of the sum of the prediction errors for each observation on the day before and day of the initial announcement.

[b]The t statistic, percentage positive, and sample size are in parentheses.

[c]The total number of observations reported in panel B is less than the total number of observations in panel A because 11 filings are included in both the considering takeover and negotiated transaction categories.

[d]Frequent purchasers are defined as acquiring firms that appear in our sample six or more times.

prior to the initial announcement of 13D filings. For acquiring firms, the only statistically significant abnormal return is −1.37 percent (*t* statistic, −2.23) in the period AD − 40 through AD − 21. In contrast, there are statistically significant positive abnormal returns for target firms in each holding period prior to the initial announcement.

The pre-announcement abnormal returns may reflect the leakage of information about a sizeable investment in the target firm's shares. This leakage is likely because a 13D filing can occur up to 10 days following the attainment of the 5 percent stake and the acquiring firm can add to its holdings during this period. To measure the abnormal returns associated with this lag in reporting, the abnormal returns are cumulated from the date on which the 5 percent position was attained, which is defined as the "buy date" (BD), to 2 days prior to the initial announcement (AD − 2). The abnormal return over this interval for the target firms is 3.40 percent with a *t* statistic of 6.15.[11] The average prediction error of −0.12 percent for the acquiring firms in the interval BD to AD − 2 suggests that the market learns the identity of the target firm in advance of the announcement date but not the identity of the acquiring firm. This is consistent with the interpretation that the market reacts to increased trading activity in the target firm's shares prior to the disclosure of the filing firm's identity in the 13D filing.

The significant positive abnormal returns for target firms that precede the buy date may also reflect leakage of information. The acquiring firm may have spread its purchases over several weeks prior to obtaining a 5 percent position. Additionally, corporate purchases of common stock may tend to follow a period of positive abnormal returns for target firms.

Table 12.4 reports the 2 day average prediction errors at the initial announcement date for subsamples of 13D filings grouped by the type of information disclosed in the initial report and by the type of acquiring firm. The abnormal returns for each subsample are discussed below.

Considering acquisition

Acquiring firms that disclosed that they are considering additional investments in the target firm's shares and acquiring control realize a positive average abnormal return of 2.46 percent (*t* statistic, 4.06), and 71 percent of the prediction errors are positive. The average abnormal return for target firms in this subsample is 7.74 percent with a *t* statistic of 12.80. The abnormal returns for both acquiring and target firms are higher for this type of initial announcement than for the other three categories in panel A of table 12.4.

Negotiated transactions

We classify common stock purchases as negotiated transactions when the *Wall Street Journal* reports that the acquiring firm and seller(s) transacted directly. The seller may be either the target firm or a third party. The average 2 day announcement period prediction error for the 50 acquiring firms in this subsample is 1.28 percent with a t statistic of 2.93. The corresponding abnormal return for 30 target firms is 5.91 percent with a t statistic of 11.40.

One reason for the similar average stock price reactions to the "considering acquisition" announcements and the "negotiated transaction" announcements is that 11 filings are common to these two samples. Another possible reason for the similar announcement period prediction errors is that negotiated transactions which involve a substantial ownership stake may convey that the acquiring firm is considering acquiring control of the target firm.

Investments

This sample represents 131 filings reported in the *Wall Street Journal* where the report disclosed that the purchase is only for investment purposes or the report contained no information about the acquiring firm's intentions. The 2 day event period abnormal return for both target and acquiring firms is positive and statistically significant for 13D filings in the investment category. The average abnormal return is 1.27 percent (t statistic, 4.77) for acquiring firms and 3.24 percent (t statistic, 12.26) for target firms. Thus, even for the announcements that do not indicate the possibility of a takeover by the acquiring firm and that represent on average an ownership stake of 9.8 percent, the stock prices of both acquiring and target firms respond favorably.

No Wall Street Journal report

When there is no report of the 13D filing in the *Wall Street Journal*, the average 2 day return at the filing date for acquiring firms is 0.64 percent with a t statistic of 3.04. However, the average 2 day prediction error for the target firms is -0.40 percent, which is not significant at the 0.10 level. One possible explanation for the smaller stock price effects is that the *Wall Street Journal* selectively reports events that tend to have greater valuation consequences. For example, 54 of the unreported filings are by investment companies, investment banking firms, and insurance companies, which in many cases represent investments that are part of the companies' normal business activity.

Another potential explanation for the smaller average abnormal return for filings that are not reported in the *Wall Street Journal* is that information about these filings takes longer to be disseminated. However, two pieces of evidence do not support this explanation. First, the average abnormal return from the buy date through 2 days prior to the announcement, which should be unaffected by whether the filing is reported later, is larger for the filings that are reported. For target firms, the abnormal return over this interval is 4.65 percent (*t* statistic, 6.98) for filings in the investment category and −0.42 percent (*t* statistic, 0.11) for filings that are not reported in the *Wall Street Journal*. Second, the average abnormal return is not significant for target firms on the days that immediately follow filings not reported in the *Wall Street Journal*: the abnormal return in the 10 days following the filing is 1.10 percent with a *t* statistic of 1.22.

Panel B of table 12.4 contains the 2 day average prediction errors for filings by frequent and infrequent firms. These data seem to suggest that the purchases by the two types of acquiring firms have similar valuation effects for both themselves and the target firms. However, this comparison is potentially misleading since the purchases by the two types of acquiring firms are not evenly divided among the four types of initial announcements. Of the 90 purchases by frequent acquiring firms that are not associated with outstanding takeover attempts, 63 are in the investment category and 21 are in the no *Wall Street Journal* report category. Panel C presents the abnormal returns for 13D filings by frequent and infrequent acquiring firms that are classified as an investment. The abnormal returns for the acquiring and target firms are similar for investments by frequent and infrequent acquiring firms. Furthermore, panel D shows that the abnormal returns for investments that are not reported in the *Wall Street Journal* are also similar for frequent and infrequent acquiring firms and for the targets of frequent and infrequent acquiring firms.

The abnormal returns for acquiring firms and their targets appear to depend on the type of initial announcement and not the type of purchasing firm. To test this hypothesis, we regress the 2 day adjusted prediction errors on four binary variables:

$$\mathrm{PE}_j = \alpha_0 + \alpha_1 D_{1j} + \alpha_2 D_{2j} + \alpha_3 D_{3j} + \alpha_4 D_{4j} + \varepsilon_j,$$

where D_{1j} is unity if the acquiring firm is a frequent purchaser and zero otherwise, D_{2j} is unity if the initial announcement is in the considering acquisition category and zero otherwise, D_{3j} is unity if the initial announcement is in the negotiated transaction category and zero otherwise, and D_{4j} is unity if the filing is in the no *Wall Street Journal* report category and zero otherwise. Table 12.5 presents the estimated regression equations. For both target and acquiring firms, the coefficient on D_{1j} is insignificantly different from zero. The coefficients for the three binary variables that represent the type of initial announcement are statistically significant for target firms, but are statistically insignificant for acquiring firms. These regressions indicate that there are statistically significant differences between the abnormal returns for target firms in different initial

Table 12.5 Relation between the percentage prediction errors at the initial 13D announcement and the type of purchaser and the type of announcement[a]

$$PE_j = \alpha_0 + \alpha_1 D_{1j} + \alpha_2 D_{2j} + \alpha_3 D_{3j} + \alpha_4 D_{4j} + \varepsilon_j$$

	α_0[b]	α_1[b]	α_2[b]	α_3[b]	α_4[b]	R^2
Target firms	2.86	1.63	3.96	5.59	−2.71	0.11
(N = 230)	(2.96)	(1.46)	(2.15)	(3.12)	(−2.30)	
Acquiring firms	1.06	0.19	0.13	−0.41	−0.56	−0.01
(N = 337)	(3.02)	(0.42)	(0.22)	(−0.81)	(−1.39)	

The sample period for 13D filing is 1978–80.

[a] PE_j is the 2 day prediction error in percent. D_1 is a binary variable which equals 1.0 if the acquiring firm is a frequent purchaser and 0.0 if the acquiring firm is an infrequent purchaser; D_{2j} equals 1.0 if the initial announcement is in the considering acquistion category and zero otherwise; D_{3j} equals 1.0 if the initial announcement is in the negotiated transaction category and zero otherwise; and D_{4j} equals 1.0 if the filing is in the no *Wall Street Journal* report category and zero otherwise. The regressions are estimated using weighted least squares where the weights equal the inverse of the standard deviation of the 2 day prediction errors. R^2 is computed using the unweighted data and the coefficients from the weighted regressions.

[b] t statistics are in parentheses.

announcement categories. There is no statistically significant difference between the abnormal returns of frequent and infrequent acquiring firms or their targets.

Summary

The equity values of acquiring and target firms increase in response to the *Wall Street Journal* report of 13D filings that are not associated with an outstanding takeover proposal. The valuation effects appear to depend on the type of information disclosed in the initial report. The 2 day initial announcement abnormal returns for both acquiring and target firms are largest for filings in which the acquiring firm indicates that it is considering a takeover of the target firm, next largest for negotiated transactions, and smallest for filings in the investment category. The average valuation effect for target firms is not significantly different from zero when the 13D filing is not reported in the *Wall Street Journal*. After controlling for the type of initial announcement, there is no statistically significant difference between the abnormal returns for frequent and infrequent acquiring firms or for their respective targets.

3.2 *Returns at selected intermediate announcements*

Table 12.6 presents 2 day average adjusted prediction errors at the disclosure of selected intermediate announcements that occur between the initial announcement date and the outcome date. The average abnormal

Table 12.6 Average 2 day prediction errors at the announcement of selected events that occur between the initial announcement and the outcome[a]

Intermediate event	*Acquiring firms*[b] *(%)*	*Target firms*[b] *(%)*
Acquiring firm announces a takeover proposal	−0.45 (−1.82, 45, 44)	10.38 (19.84, 81, 26)
Third party announces a takeover proposal	0.55 (1.50, 52, 44)	10.30 (21.46, 76, 29)
Acquiring firm purchases more shares	0.30 (1.42, 47, 136)	1.07 (6.26, 61, 126)
Target firm discloses opposition to investment	0.32 (0.66, 55, 29)	−1.36 (−2.33, 39, 23)

The sample period for 13D filings is 1978–80. The sample excludes filings associated with outstanding takeover proposals.

[a]The average 2 day prediction errors are the average of the sum of the prediction errors for each observation on the day before and day of the announcement.

[b]The t statistic, percentage positive, and sample size are in parentheses.

return for target firms is about 10 percent when a takeover offer by either the initial filing firm or another firm is disclosed. Target firms on average also realize a significant return of 1.07 percent when the acquiring firm purchases additional shares of the target firm. The announcement that the management of the target firm objected to the investment is associated with a significant negative average return for target firms of −1.36 percent with a t statistic of −2.33. These announcements range from active opposition, such as filing a legal action, to statements that the target management is not interested in being acquired. In contrast, no significant abnormal returns are associated with any of these intermediate announcements for acquiring firms.

3.3 *Returns of acquiring and target firms at the announcement of the outcome and total returns*

Table 12.7 presents the 2 day abnormal returns associated with the initial, intermediate, and outcome announcements grouped by outcome categories for acquiring (panel A) and target (panel B) firms. The outcome date is the date of the *Wall Street Journal* report of the last occurrence of an event in one of the outcome categories. The intermediate announcements include events occurring between the initial announcement and the outcome announcement that are related to the investment position and are reported in the *Wall Street Journal*. These events include the announcements examined in section 3.2 (acquiring firm takeover announcements, third party takeover announcements, purchases of additional shares, and the

Table 12.7 Average total and 2 day adjusted prediction errors associated with initial, intermediate, and outcome announcements grouped by type of outcome[a]

Announcement	*Completed takeover*[b] *(%)*	*Targeted repurchase*[b] *(%)*	*Shares sold*[b] *(%)*	*Third party takeover*[b] *(%)*
A Acquiring firms				
Initial	2.04 (4.45, 70, 43)	1.50 (2.82, 51, 39)	1.48 (2.98, 60, 47)	0.87 (1.97, 60, 45)
Intermediate	−2.10 (−2.12, 43, 37)	3.66 (2.66, 57, 21)	3.61 (2.84, 52, 25)	1.46 (2.21, 62, 34)
Outcome	0.83 (0.45, 47, 43)	2.13 (3.45, 68, 38)	1.62 (2.16, 52, 46)	0.07 (0.34, 53, 40)
Total[a]	1.07 (0.96, 53, 43)	5.69 (4.99, 68, 38)	5.10 (3.76, 59, 46)	2.25 (2.59, 65, 40)
B Target firms				
Initial	6.34 (12.32, 72, 25)	4.64 (9.46, 80, 30)	3.65 (9.01, 76, 38)	2.46 (5.58, 60, 30)
Intermediate	16.36 (14.60, 76, 21)	−1.40 (−0.51, 56, 18)	3.11 (3.78, 65, 23)	13.87 (13.89, 70, 23)
Outcome	3.97 (3.22, 68, 19)	−2.29 (−4.86, 39, 31)	0.83 (−0.54, 43, 37)	1.47 (0.77, 42, 19)
Total	21.10 (10.09, 79, 19)	1.69 (3.08, 57, 30)	6.32 (5.70, 70, 37)	15.98 (10.99, 58, 19)

The sample period for 13D filings is 1978–80. The sample excludes 13D filings associated with outstanding takeover proposals.

[a]Prediction errors are adjusted for changes in the price of the firm's common stock and equal the abnormal change in stock price divided by the stock price on the day before the initial announcement. The 2 day average adjusted prediction errors are the average of the sum of the adjusted prediction errors for each observation on the day before and day of the announcement. The total average adjusted prediction error is the average of the sum of the 2 day adjusted prediction errors at the initial, intermediate, and outcome announcements for each observation. Observations without initial or outcome announcement returns are excluded from these calculations.

[b]The t statistic, percentage positive, and sample size are in parentheses.

disclosure of opposition to the investment by the target firm's management) as well as other intermediate announcements.[12]

Table 12.7 also contains our measure of the total abnormal return from the initial announcement through the outcome. One possible estimate of the total valuation effect of the investment is the abnormal holding-period return over the interval that encompasses the initial disclosure of the investment activity through the outcome. An important difficulty with such a measure, however, is that the time interval from initial announcement through outcome is sufficiently long that the power of tests of significance is low; the average number of trading days between the initial and outcome announcements is 308. Instead, we aggregate the 2 day prediction errors for the initial, intermediate, and outcome announcements to calculate a total abnormal return. The advantage of this method is that we exclude extraneous events and their effects on stock price. This approach increases the power of our tests by substantially reducing the variance of the total abnormal returns.

To compute the total valuation effect of the series of events associated with a particular investment, we do not simply sum the series of 2 day prediction errors. Instead, we first compute the 2 day abnormal *price* changes at the initial announcement, the intermediate events, and the outcome event, and then sum these abnormal price changes. That is, we compute ΔP_j for all events associated with investment j as

$$\Delta P_j = \sum_{k=1}^{K} P_{jt_k-2}(\mathrm{PE}_{jt_k-1}) + P_{jt_k-1}(\mathrm{PE}_{jt_k}), \tag{5}$$

where t_k is the announcement date for event k, P_{jt} is share price on day t, and PE_{jt} is the prediction error for day t. The sum ΔP_j represents the total dollar effect per share of the initial, intermediate, and outcome announcements. The total abnormal price change ΔP_j is divided by the firm's share price 2 days before the initial announcement date to obtain a measure in return form. Unlike the sum of prediction errors, our measure of total abnormal return or total adjusted prediction error represents the cumulative dollar effect of a series of events measured relative to the value of shares at the initial announcement. Each column of table 12.7 presents average adjusted prediction errors for a subsample of investments grouped by type of outcome.[13,14]

Our measure of total abnormal returns only includes event days. It therefore possibly misses important relevant changes in stock prices following generally positive average abnormal returns at the initial announcement. For example, nonevent days may be associated with negative abnormal returns as the market reduces its assessment of the probability of a favorable outcome. To check this source of bias, we compute the average holding-period return for targets with outcomes by summing the adjusted prediction errors for each observation from the day before the initial announcement through the outcome announcement and averaging these holding-period returns cross-sectionally. The average holding-period return for 126 targets with an outcome is 12.10 percent with a t statistic of 3.67. To determine the stock price behavior on nonevent days, we compute average holding-period returns for event days only (2 day initial, intermediate, and outcome announcements) and the average holding-period return for nonevent days. The average holding-period return for event days is 10.45 percent with a t statistic of 17.89 and the average holding-period return for nonevent days is 1.65 percent with a *t* statistic of 0.36 percent. Therefore, virtually all the positive average holding-period return for targets is due to event days and there is no indication of significant abnormal returns on nonevent days.

Completed takeover

Both acquiring and target firms realize a positive 2 day abnormal return at the initial announcement of investment positions that are not initially disclosed as part of a takeover attempt but later result in a completed takeover by the acquiring firm. However, the average sum of the valuation effects of the intermediate events, which includes the initial takeover announcement, is negative for acquiring firms and positive for target firms. At the announcement of the outcome of a completed takeover, which is the earlier of a report of stockholder approval or consummation of a merger or the report of a successful tender offer, the average return is statistically insignificant for acquiring firms and positive for target firms.

The average total abnormal return is 1.07 percent for the acquiring firms that successfully acquired the target firm, which is not statistically significant at the 0.10 level. The corresponding average total prediction error for target firms is 21.10 percent with a *t* statistic of 10.09. The insignificant average total prediction error for acquiring firms is consistent with the findings of previous corporate takeover studies and with the notion that the average net present value of takeovers is zero. A new finding uncovered by this study is that the positive average prediction error for acquiring firms at the initial announcement for a 5 percent or greater investment position is offset by a negative average price effect during the subsequent period in which a takeover attempt materializes. The average abnormal return for target firms of about 20 percent is also generally consistent with the findings of other studies of takeovers. However, we show that an important part of the total valuation effect occurs at the initial announcement of the 13D filing, which precedes the earliest report of a takeover offer.

Targeted repurchases

At the announcement that the target firm has or will repurchase the shares held by the acquiring firm, the acquiring firms experience a significant average abnormal return of 2.13 percent. Target firms on average incur a significant loss of −2.29 percent in the 2 day announcement period of a targeted repurchase. These findings are similar to the stock price effects around the announcements of targeted repurchases that are reported by Bradley and Wakeman (1983) and Dann and DeAngelo (1983).

The 2 day outcome abnormal returns are not a measure of the total effect of the investment for either target or acquiring firm since they exclude the abnormal returns associated with the initial and intermediate announcements. For acquiring firms, the average abnormal returns at the initial announcement and at the intermediate events are both positive and statistically significant. Thus the average prediction error is positive at all three stages of the investment process. The average total abnormal return for acquiring firms is 5.69 percent with a *t* statistic of 4.99.

For target firms the initial announcement average abnormal return for transactions that conclude with a targeted repurchase is 4.64 percent with a *t* statistic of 9.46. This positive average initial return at the announcement more than offsets the negative 2 day abnormal return at the announcement of the targeted repurchase. The average total abnormal return for target firms is 1.69 percent which is significant at the 0.01 level. Our measures indicate that on average stockholders of target firms *benefit* from investments that result in a targeted repurchase. Additionally, Mikkelson and Ruback (1988) report similar results for a much larger sample of transactions that conclude with a targeted repurchase.

One interpretation of the returns for target firms is that the stock price of target firms rises at the time of the initial announcement of the investment position in anticipation of a favorable outcome, such as a takeover. Therefore the negative average return at the announcement of the targeted repurchase is due, at least in part, to the reversal of expectations formed at the initial announcement date. In addition, a portion of the negative price effect of a targeted repurchase reflects any premium paid to the selling stockholder. Since the total abnormal return is positive and statistically significant, the increase in stock price associated with expectations formed at the initial announcement of the investment more than offsets the stock price effects of the targeted repurchase. Based on our measure of total abnormal return, we conclude that investments that end in a targeted repurchase on average do not harm the target firm's stockholders. Of course, the total average returns reported in table 12.7 indicate that the target firm's stockholders prefer a completed takeover to a targeted repurchase. However, we cannot determine whether the targeted repurchase thwarted a potential takeover bid or whether the targeted repurchase was the best course of action for the remaining stockholders of these firms.

Shares sold

The average abnormal return for acquiring firms is 1.62 percent (*t* statistic, 2.16) at the announcement that the acquiring firm sold shares of the target firm in the market or to a third party. The corresponding target firms on average realize an insignificant abnormal return of 0.83 percent. Between the initial announcement of the investment position and the announcement that shares were sold, the average valuation effect of related events is positive and significant for both the acquiring and target firms. Thus, when the investment concludes with the sale of shares in the market or directly to a third party, the positive valuation effect of the initial disclosure of the investment is reinforced, rather than reversed, by the valuation effects of subsequent events. The average total return for acquiring firms that sell shares is 5.10 percent with a t statistic of 3.76, which is comparable with the gains associated with investments that conclude with a targeted repurchase. The average total return for the target firms is statistically significant and equals 6.32 percent.

Third party takeover

When the outcome is a takeover of the target by a firm other than the firm filing Schedule 13D, the average total return for the filing firms is 2.25 percent with a t statistic of 2.59. Part of this return can be explained by the gains from selling shares of the target firm at a premium to the bidding firm. In addition, based on the returns of filing firms when the outcome is a completed takeover (column 1, table 12.7), the positive average total return may reflect a favorable response to news that another firm, and not the filing firm, acquired control of the target firm. For target firms, the average 2 day outcome return of 1.47 percent and the average total return of 15.98 percent are comparable with the returns for target firms when the outcome is a completed takeover by the firm filing Schedule 13D.

Summary

The average total adjusted prediction errors indicate that the shareholders of the filing firms and target firms generally benefit from the 5 percent or greater investment positions that result in one of the four outcomes represented in table 12.7.[15] Only the average total return for filing firms that acquire control of the target firm is not significantly greater than zero.

All the investments represented in table 12.7 began with a filing of Schedule 13D and were not disclosed as part of an attempt to acquire control of the target firm. The average 2 day prediction error at the initial announcement of the investment position is generally positive across the categories of outcomes. The similar average prediction errors at the initial announcement across the four types of outcomes indicate that market participants do not accurately predict the type of outcome.

Following the initial announcement of the investment position, the valuation effects of subsequent events depend on the outcome of the investment. When the outcome is a targeted repurchase, a sale of shares, or a completed takeover of the target by another firm, the average valuation effect of the subsequent events is positive for the firms filing Schedule 13D. However, when the outcome is a completed takeover by the filing firm, the average valuation effect of the subsequent events is negative for the acquiring firm. However, the target firms experience a positive valuation effect following the initial investment when the outcome is a completed takeover by the filing firm or another firm. The valuation effect of the subsequent events is also positive for target firms when the outcome is the sale of shares, but when the outcome is a targeted repurchase, the average return following the initial announcement is negative.

The pattern of average prediction errors associated with the four outcomes illustrates that the valuation effects of intermediate and outcome announcements reflect the resolution of uncertainty about the outcome. Therefore the average total prediction errors represent the most complete measures of the valuation effects of the investments. Based on the total abnormal returns, the ordering of the profitability of the outcomes (lowest to highest) for acquiring firms is completed takeover, third party takeover, shares sold, and targeted repurchase. For target firms, the ordering is targeted repurchase, shares sold, third party takeover, and completed takeover.

3.4 Comparison of total returns for investments by frequent and infrequent acquiring firms

Frequent and infrequent acquiring firms appear to have different relative frequencies of investment outcomes. As shown in table 12.8, only four, or 7 percent, of the investments by frequent acquiring firms with outcomes end as a completed takeover, which is the least favorable outcome for acquiring firms and the most favorable outcome for target firms. In contrast, the outcome of 35 percent of investments by infrequent acquiring firms is a completed takeover. The smaller proportion of takeovers by frequent acquiring firms means that these firms have a higher proportion of investments that conclude with the more favorable outcomes for the acquiring firms, such as targeted repurchases, shares sold, or third party takeovers. For example, 35 percent of the investments with an outcome by frequent acquiring firms conclude with a targeted repurchase, whereas 17 percent of the outcomes for investments by infrequent acquiring firms are in this category.[16]

Despite the differences in relative frequencies of types of outcomes, the last row of table 12.8 reports that the average total abnormal returns for all investments with an outcome are virtually equal for frequent and infrequent acquiring firms: 3.67 percent for frequent acquiring firms and 3.44 percent for infrequent acquiring firms. Furthermore, as the t statistics presented in table 12.8 indicate, the differences between the total abnormal returns for the two samples of acquiring firms are insignificant in each outcome classification.[17]

The average total abnormal return across all outcomes for targets of frequent acquiring firms is 6.84 percent and it is 11.21 percent for targets

Table 12.8 Average total adjusted prediction errors for frequent and infrequent acquiring firms and the associated target firms classified by outcome[a,b]

Outcome	*Infrequent acquiring firms*[c]	*Frequent acquiring firms*[c]	*t statistic for the difference*[d]	*Targets of infrequent acquiring firms*[c]	*Targets of frequent acquiring firms*[c]	*t statistic for the difference*[d]
Completed takeover	1.53 (1.39, 54, 39)	−3.42 (−1.19, 50, 4)	−1.08	22.57 (10.19, 81, 16)	13.22 (1.86, 67, 3)	−0.26
Targeted repurchase	7.58 (4.10, 68, 19)	3.80 (2.95, 68, 19)	−0.68	−0.14 (1.56, 46, 13)	3.08 (2.73, 65, 17)	−0.32
Shares sold	5.26 (2.22, 58, 26)	4.89 (3.17, 60, 20)	0.84	4.71 (3.10, 68, 19)	8.02 (4.99, 72, 18)	0.71
Third party takeover	1.60 (1.71, 64, 28)	3.77 (2.13, 67, 12)	0.94	17.58 (11.35, 64, 14)	11.51 (2.44, 40, 5)	−2.03
All outcomes	3.44 (4.43, 60, 112)	3.67 (4.32, 64, 55)	1.19	11.21 (13.00, 66, 62)	6.84 (6.26, 65, 43)	−2.00

The sample period for 13D filings is 1978–80. The sample excludes filings associated with outstanding takeover proposals.

[a] Prediction errors are adjusted for changes in the price of the firm's common stock and equal the abnormal change in stock price divided by the stock price on the day before the initial announcement. The total average adjusted prediction error is the average of the sum of the 2 day adjusted prediction errors at the initial, intermediate, and outcome announcements for each observation. Observations without initial or outcome announcements are excluded from these calculations.

[b] Frequent acquiring firms are defined as acquiring firms that appear in our sample six or more times.

[c] The t statistic, percentage positive, and sample size are in parentheses.

[d] The t statistic for the difference between the total abnormal returns for investments involving frequent and infrequent acquiring firms is calculated by estimating the following regression on the appropriate subsample: $\mathrm{PE}_j = C_0 + C_1 D_{1j} + \varepsilon_j$, where PE_j is the total abnormal return and D_{1j} is a binary variable that equals unity if the transaction involves a frequent acquiring firm and zero otherwise. The regressions are estimated using weighted least squares where the weights equal the inverse of the standard deviation of the total abnormal returns. The t statistic on the coefficient C_1 is reported in the table.

of infrequent acquiring firms. The t statistic for the difference between these total abnormal returns is -2.00. However, the t statistics indicate that the difference between the total abnormal returns is insignificant for each outcome category except third party takeovers. Therefore the difference between the total abnormal returns across all outcomes for the targets of the two types of purchasing firms appears to reflect the lower relative frequency of completed takeovers by frequent acquiring firms.

The significant positive total abnormal returns indicate that the stockholders of frequent and infrequent acquiring firms and the stockholders of the targets of these two types of acquiring firms generally benefit from the investment activity. Our findings do not support the view that frequent investors systematically benefit at the expense of the target firm's shareholders. In fact, when the outcome is a targeted repurchase from a frequent acquiring firm, the average total prediction error for the target firms is positive. Holderness and Sheehan (1984) reach a similar conclusion in their study of six investors who have been portrayed as corporate raiders.

3.5 Returns of target firms for investments without an outcome

No outcome event was reported in the *Wall Street Journal* prior to the end of the third complete calendar year following the initial announcement for 160 of the 337 filings that were not associated with an outstanding takeover attempt. Since there is no outcome date, the total abnormal return for these investments cannot be measured by aggregating the abnormal returns at the initial, intermediate and outcome announcements. Instead, we measure the average total abnormal return for investments without an outcome by computing the average cumulative prediction errors from the day before the initial announcement through the last trading day in the third calendar year following the initial announcement. For comparison, we also compute the average cumulative prediction error for observations with an outcome from the day before the initial announcement through the outcome date.

The average cumulative prediction errors of target firms for investments with and without an outcome on days following the initial announcement are plotted in figure 12.1. The average cumulative prediction errors are positive for investments with outcomes and negative for investments without outcomes over the entire period following the initial announcement. The average cumulative prediction error from the day before the initial announcement through the last trading day of the third calendar year following the initial announcement is -44.14 percent (t statistic, -4.22) for the 105 targets without an outcome. In contrast, the average cumulative prediction error for the 126 targets with an outcome is 12.10

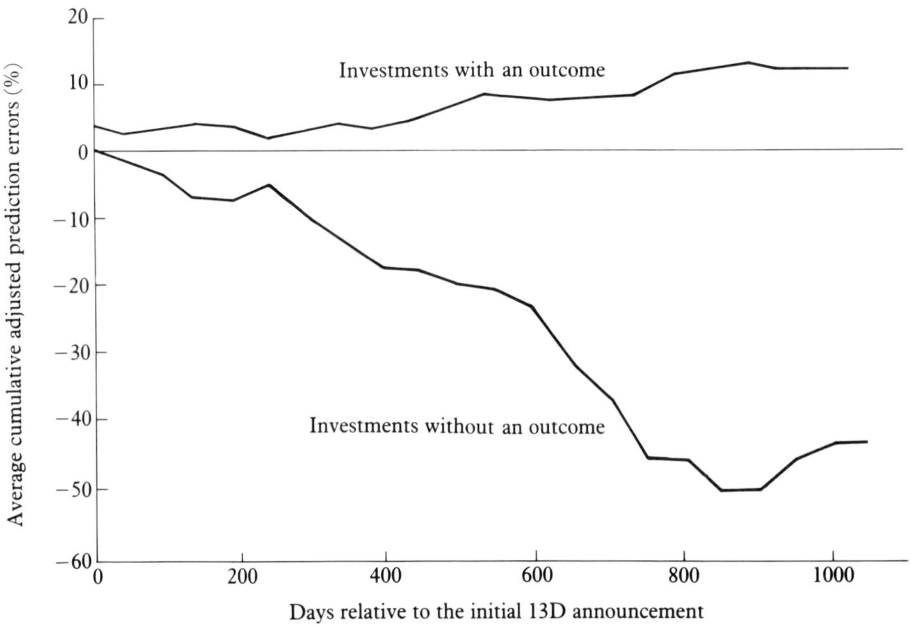

Figure 12.1 Average cumulative prediction errors for target firms. The sample period for 13D filings is 1978–80. The sample excludes filings associated with outstanding takeover proposals. (Prediction errors are adjusted for changes in the price of the firm's common stock and equal the abnormal change in stock price divided by the stock price on the day before the initial announcement. Adjusted prediction errors for each observation are summed from the day before the initial announcement through the outcome date for observations with outcomes and through the last trading day of the third calendar year following the initial announcement for observations without outcomes. The first average cumulative adjusted predictions shown on the figure are for the initial announcement date, day 0.)

percent (*t* statistic, 3.67) over the entire holding period from the day before the initial announcement through the outcome. This evidence, combined with the results in table 12.7, suggests that the least favorable outcome of the investment process for the stockholders of target firms is no outcome.[18]

The long cumulation period makes it difficult to apply the average cumulative prediction error technique to acquiring firms. Many acquiring firms appear in the sample more than once and these observations overlap. Additionally, some of the overlapping observations have outcomes and others have no outcomes. Therefore we limit our analysis of investments without outcomes to target firms. The valuation effects for the target firms without outcomes, however, provide some insight into the profitability of these investments for the acquiring firms. In the absence of an outcome, the return to the acquiring firm depends on the stock price performance of the target firms. Thus the evidence of negative average cumulative prediction errors for target firms suggests that these investments also have negative valuation effects for the acquiring firms.

4 Common Stock Returns for 13D Filings Associated With Outstanding Takeovers

A substantial portion of 13D filings took place concurrently or after the announcement of a takeover proposal by the filing firm. These 13D filings are qualitatively different from the filings examined in section 3 in that a takeover attempt was announced at the time of or before a 5 percent ownership position was acquired.

Table 12.9 presents average prediction errors at the initial announcement, intermediate events, and outcome of 13D filings where the initial announcement disclosed a takeover proposal. Acquiring firms realize a statistically significant negative return of −0.59 percent in the 2 day initial announcement period (AD − 1 and AD), and 64 percent of the 2 day prediction errors are negative. The average abnormal return for target firms is 14.90 percent in the 2 day announcement period and 87 percent of the 2 day prediction errors are positive.

Compared with the average 2 day returns at the initial announcement of the 13D filings not associated with a takeover (table 12.4), the average initial announcement return of a 13D filing associated with a takeover attempt is greater for the target firms and smaller for acquiring firms. This ordering of initial announcement returns is consistent with two other findings of this study. First, the average total returns reported in table 12.7 are lowest for acquiring firms and highest for target firms when the outcome is a completed takeover by the filing firm. Second, the ordering is consistent with the relative frequencies of completed takeovers for different types of initial announcements. Table 12.1 shows that the relative frequency of a completed takeover is highest (114 of 136 13D filings) when the initial announcement discloses a takeover attempt. Thus the average 2 day initial announcement returns reported in table 12.9 reflect the relatively high likelihood of a completed takeover by the filing firm, which is the least favorable outcome for the filing firm and the most favorable outcome for the target firm.

The last row of table 12.9 reports the total abnormal returns for 13D filings associated with outstanding takeovers. For completed takeover attempts, the average total return for the acquiring firms is −0.72 percent with a t statistic of −2.16. In contrast, the average total return is 1.07 percent with a t statistic of 0.96 (table 12.7) for the 43 completed takeovers that are not initially disclosed as part of a takeover attempt. The t statistic for the difference between the total abnormal returns is 1.10. When the

Table 12.9 Average total and 2 day adjusted errors for acquiring and target firms for 13D filings associated with outstanding takeover proposals[a]

	All filings[b] *(%)*		*Completed takeovers attempts*[b] *(%)*		*Failed takeover attempts*[b] *(%)*	
Announcements	*Acquiring firms*	*Target firms*	*Acquiring firms*	*Target firms*	*Acquiring firms*	*Target firms*
Initial	−0.59	14.90	−0.62	15.55	−0.45	10.56
	(−2.34, 36, 136)	(41.59, 87, 69)	(−2.36, 38, 114)	(40.84, 92, 60)	(−0.45, 27, 22)	(9.72, 56, 9)
Intermediate	−0.24	2.95	−1.04	1.25	2.54	11.11
	(−1.04, 39, 54)	(2.40, 52, 29)	(−1.92, 33, 42)	(0.25, 46, 24)	(1.42, 58, 12)	(5.25, 80, 5)
Outcome	0.38	−1.21	0.29	0.23	0.89	−8.96
	(1.92, 58, 136)	(−3.14, 57, 51)	(1.16, 57, 114)	(0.74, 60, 43)	(2.15, 64, 22)	(−9.64, 38, 8)
Total	−0.30	16.35	−0.72	17.69	1.83	9.16
	(−1.50, 41, 136)	(22.58, 88, 51)	(−2.16, 37, 114)	(22.94, 95, 43)	(1.18, 64, 22)	(3.85, 50, 8)

The sample period for 13D filings is 1978–80.

[a]Prediction errors are adjusted for changes in the price of the firm's common stock and equal the abnormal change in stock price divided by the stock price on the day before the initial announcement. The 2 day average adjusted prediction errors are the average of the sum of the adjusted prediction errors for each observation on the day before and the day of the announcement. The total average adjusted prediction error is the average of the sum of the 2 day adjusted prediction errors at the initial, intermediate, and outcome announcements for each observation. Observations without initial or outcome announcement returns are excluded from these calculations.

[b]The t statistic, percentage positive, and sample size are in parentheses.

takeover attempt does not succeed, the average total return is 1.83 percent, which is not significant at the 0.10 level.

For acquiring firms, it is tempting to conclude that the positive average total abnormal return for completed takeovers that begin with a toehold position is greater than the average return for completed takeovers that do not begin with a toehold position, even though the difference is not statistically significant. Since a purchasing firm intent on acquiring the target presumably announces its intention at the time of the initial 13D filing, the appropriate comparison is between filings in the considering acquisition category of initial announcements and the completed takeovers in table 12.9. For the 20 observations in which the initial announcement is in the considering acquisition category and the outcome is a completed takeover, the average total abnormal return is only 0.08 percent, which is not significant at the 0.10 level. This evidence therefore does *not* imply that a more desirable takeover strategy for acquiring firms is to purchase a toehold position before announcing a takeover.

The total abnormal return for target firms in completed takeovers is 17.69 percent. This is similar to the total abnormal return of 20 percent reported in table 12.7 for target firms that are acquired by a company that does not initially disclose a takeover attempt at the time of a 13D filing.

5 Conclusion

This investigation of investments in equity securities that are reported in a filing of Schedule 13D reveals that an attempt to acquire control of another firm represents only a minority of interfirm investments. Among the 473 filings of Schedule 13D in the sample, 337 are not associated with outstanding takeover proposals. We also document the events that occur in the three calendar years that follow the initial 13D filings and classify investments according to one of four outcomes when an outcome event takes place. The investments that do not begin as a takeover attempt and are classified as having an outcome are roughly evenly divided among four outcomes: completed takeover, targeted repurchase, third party takeover, and the sale of the purchased shares.

At the initial announcement of 13D filings that are not part of a takeover attempt, the average price response is positive and statistically significant for both the filing and target firms. These positive average stock price changes imply that investments representing 5 percent or more of a company's shares are expected to benefit both the acquiring and the target firm's shareholders.

We also measure the total valuation effect of each investment by combining the 2 day abnormal stock returns at the initial announcement of the 13D filing, at the outcome, and at any intervening related events. This procedure provides a set of comparable measures of the total stock price effect of investments that result in different outcomes. We find that the average total return of acquiring and target firms depends on whether a takeover is the outcome of the investment. On average, completed takeovers appear to be zero net present value investments for acquiring firms, regardless of whether the takeover attempt is preceded by a 5 percent or greater investment in the target firm's shares. In contrast, the average total return is positive and statistically significant for the acquiring firms for investments that end with a targeted repurchase, a sale of shares, or a third party takeover.

The target firm's shareholders benefit the most from a completed takeover by either the filing firm or another firm. However, the average total valuation effect for investments that terminate in the sale of shares or a targeted repurchase is also positive and statistically significant for target firms. The stock price of the repurchasing firm falls when a targeted repurchase is announced, but the average total valuation effect of these investments on target firms is positive. Therefore, regardless of the investment outcome including a targeted repurchase, we find that the investments typically increase stockholder wealth for the target firm. The average total valuation effect appears to be negative when no outcome occurs in the three years following the initial announcement.

The total valuation effect of investments is also examined for a subsample of acquiring firms that made six or more 13D filings during our sample period. Investments by the frequent investing firms are represented by a relatively high proportion of targeted repurchase outcomes and a relatively low proportion of completed takeover outcomes. In addition, this sample is of interest because it includes investors who are claimed by some to take actions that benefit the acquiring firm at the expense of the other shareholders of the target firm. We find, however, that the average total valuation effect for both acquiring and target firms does not depend on whether the acquiring firm is classified as a frequent investor. In addition, shareholders of target firms experience positive average total returns for all types of outcomes, including targeted repurchases, when the acquiring firm is a frequent investor.

Notes

1 See Jensen and Ruback (1983) for a summary of this evidence.

2 Of the 337 investments not associated with a takeover proposal at the initial announcement, 279 investments involved the purchase of only common stock. We have rerun our computations of average prediction errors that are presented in this paper excluding the subsample of 58 investments that involved convertible securities,

warrants, or options. None of the principal findings change when only the subsample of pure common stock investments is examined. In addition, the distribution across types of announcement and outcomes for this subsample of 279 investments is virtually identical with those for the full sample.

3 We include the three transactions that conclude with pure standstill agreements in the targeted repurchase category because Dann and DeAngelo (1983) show that these two outcomes have similar stock price effects.

4 In most cases the *SEC News Digest* reports the ownership stake, that is, the percentage of the target firms' shares held. For the selected filings reported in the *Insiders' Chronicle*, the percentage stake held as well as the dollar amount paid for the stake is reported. In some cases, this information is given in the *Wall Street Journal* report of the filing. When no report of the percentage stake held or dollar amount paid could be found, we computed the percentage stake as the number of shares held divided by the number of shares outstanding at the time of filing and the dollar amount as the number of shares held multiplied by the closing stock price at the end of the filing month.

5 We did not collect data on the number of shares held or percentage ownership stake attained for dates following the initial filing of Schedule 13D.

6 This subsample includes five corporations (DWG, NVF, Pennsylvania Engineering, Sharon Steel, and Southeastern Public Service) that are ostensibly controlled by Victor Posner and seven other firms (American General, Baldwin United, Gulf and Western, Merrill Lynch, Reliance Group, Teledyne, and Walco National).

7 Fama (1976) describes the market model in detail.

8 When there are missing stock returns within a holding period, the normal return is cumulated over the days in which there are missing stock returns. This cumulative normal return is subtracted from the next observed stock return to calculate the abnormal return.

9 The formula for the variance of PE_{jt} assumes that prediction errors are independent across firms. We calculate the variance of the cumulative prediction errors over event time as the sum of the individual variances. This is only an approximation since it ignores the covariances between prediction errors.

10 The average abnormal return and the t statistic can differ in sign because the former assigns uniform weights to each observation whereas the latter assigns nonuniform weights (equal to the inverse of the standard deviation) to each observation. A difference in sign is most likely to occur when the average abnormal returns are close to zero.

11 In many cases we identified the filing date of Schedule 13D, but not the date that the 5 percent ownership position was attained. Since regulations require a filing of Schedule 13D within 10 days after reaching the 5 percent level, we chose to define the buy date as 10 days before the filing date. In a few cases there is no buy date in advance of the earliest public disclosure, because the *Wall Street Journal* reported plans to purchase shares prior to acquisition of a 5 percent position more than 10 days in advance of a filing with the SEC.

12 The other intermediate events include three standstill agreements, two targeted repurchases, four sale of shares, one successful tender offer, six unsuccessful takeover attempts, one successful takeover by a third party, seven unsuccessful takeover attempts by a third party, and ten miscellaneous announcements.

13 For ease of computation, we do not use the actual stock prices of the firm. Instead, we define a price index which equals unity 2 days before the initial announcement date and on each succeeding day equals the compound value of $1 that was invested in the

stock 2 days before the initial announcement date. That is

$$P_{\tau-1} = \prod_{t=-1}^{\tau-1} (1 + R_{jt}).$$

where $P_{\tau-1}$ is the price index on day τ and R_{jt} is the stock return of firm j on day t.

14 The t statistics for these adjusted abnormal returns are calculated by substituting the adjusted prediction errors and their variance in equation (3). The adjusted prediction errors are $P_{jt-1}(\mathrm{PE}_{jt-1})$, where P_{jt-1} is the price index defined in note 13. The variance associated with the adjusted prediction error is $P_{jt}^2\,\mathrm{var}(\mathrm{PE}_{jt})$.

15 Table 12.7 excludes the three investments that conclude as an unsuccessful takeover. The total abnormal return for the three acquiring firms is 22.70 percent with a t statistic of 0.96. For the two listed targets involved in these transactions, the total abnormal return is 13.69 percent with a t statistic of 2.60.

16 Among the frequent investors, there is a concentration of firms with investments that end in a targeted repurchase. The 19 targeted repurchases from frequent investors include six from Gulf and Western, five from firms controlled by Victor Posner, and four from Walco National.

17 Two caveats about a comparison of the average prediction errors for frequent and infrequent acquiring firms should be noted. First, we have not controlled for a possible difference between the sizes of frequent and infrequent acquiring firms. Second, investments by frequent acquiring firms are probably anticipated to a greater degree and thus the price effects of announcements of investments by frequent acquiring firms reflect a smaller degree of surprise. Shipper and Thompson (1983) discuss this issue with respect to the price reactions for mergers that involve bidder firms that previously announced a program of acquiring control of other firms.

18 A t statistic for the difference between the average cumulative prediction errors for investments with and without outcomes is calculated by estimating the following regression equation:

$$\mathrm{CPE}_j = C_0 + C_1 D_j + \varepsilon_j,$$

where CPE_j is the cumulative prediction error over the entire holding period for observations j, D_j is a binary variable which equals unity if the observation has an outcome and zero otherwise. The t statistic on the coefficient C_1 is the test statistic for the difference in average cumulative prediction errors. When the regression is estimated using ordinary least squares, the t statistic for the coefficient C_1 is 2.98. When the regression is estimated using weighted least squares (where the weights equal the inverse of the standard deviation of the cumulative prediction errors), the t statistic for the coefficient C_1 is 1.98.

References

Bradley, M. and Wakeman, L. M. (1983) "The Wealth Effects of Targeted Share Repurchases," *Journal of Financial Economics*, 11, 301–28.

Dann, L. Y. and DeAngelo, H. (1983) "Standstill Agreements, Privately Negotiated Stock Repurchases, and the Market for Corporate Control," *Journal of Financial Economics*, 11, 275–300.

Fama, E. (1976) *Foundations of Finance* (New York: Basic Books).

Fama, E., Fisher, L., Jensen, M. and Roll, R. (1969) "The Adjustment of Stock Prices to New Information," *International Economic Review*, 10: 1, 1–21.

Holderness, C. G. and Sheehan, D. P. (1984) "Raiders or Saviors? The Evidence on Six Controversial Investors," *Journal of Financial Economics*, 14, 555–79.
Jensen, M. C. and Ruback, R. S. (1983) "The Market for Corporate Control: The Scientific Evidence," *Journal of Financial Economics*, 11, 5–50.
Mikkelson, W. H. and Ruback, R. S. (1988) "Targeted Repurchases and Common Stock Returns," *Working Paper 89-019*, Harvard Business School, December.
Shipper, K. and Thompson, R. (1983) "Evidence on the Capitalized Value of Merger Activity for Acquiring Firms," *Journal of Financial Economics*, 11, 85–119.

Chapter 13

Robert F. Stambaugh

Background and Comments

The standard capital asset pricing model (CAPM) is usually expressed as a relationship between expected return r and risk measured by beta:

$$r = r_{\mathrm{f}} + \beta(r_{\mathrm{m}} - r_{\mathrm{f}}).$$

Here r_{f} is the risk-free (Treasury) interest rate and $r_{\mathrm{m}} - r_{\mathrm{f}}$ is the expected risk premium on the market portfolio of all assets. The CAPM is widely used in this form in corporate finance (see my comments on William Schwert's contribution to this book, chapter 6).

In portfolio theory the same CAPM often finds a different expression. It says that investors who are concerned solely with the mean and variance of portfolio return cannot "beat the market" because the market portfolio offers the highest expected return per unit of risk.

Of course it is easy to beat the market with hindsight, but that does not disprove the CAPM, which speaks only about expectations. The CAPM specifies *ex ante* relationships, but we can observe only *ex post* results.

The CAPM could be rejected by finding a portfolio strategy with the same risk as the market but a higher *average* return. Of course the tester would also have to prove statistical significance, which is not so easy given the amount of noise in common stock returns.

The difficulty of testing any theory about expected returns in the stock market is obvious. However, there is another more subtle and serious problem, first stressed by Richard Roll (1977). The Roll critique can be put several ways. Perhaps the easiest is to ask: "What do we mean by the market?" In principle it should include all assets. In practice we usually look to a small subset, a proxy such as Standard & Poor's 500.

Now suppose that the tester finds portfolios that "beat" this proxy for the true market portfolio. Suppose that there is no problem with statistical significance. Does that disprove the CAPM? No, because if the true market portfolio were observed, it might have won the race. Moreover, it is usually possible with hindsight to identify a plausible alternative proxy for which the CAPM seems to work out just fine.

Rejecting the CAPM is not easy. Unfortunately a theory which cannot be rejected is not credible either.

I have sketched the difficulties in testing the CAPM to give a context for reading the following paper by Shmuel Kandel and Robert Stambaugh. Readers with special interests in these topics may wish to refer to Roll's paper and also to the contributions to this volume by Jay Shanken (chapter 18) and David Brown and Michael Gibbons (chapter 8).

Reference

Roll, R. (1977) "A Critique of the Asset Theory's Tests; Part I: On Past and Potential Testability of the Theory," *Journal of Financial Economics*, 4, March, 129–76.

Author's Introduction

This paper was my first collaboration with Shmuel Kandel in the area of testing asset pricing models in a mean–variance framework. (Shmuel also became a Batterymarch Fellow in 1988.) The central problem addressed, one whose recognized importance stems in large part from Roll's classic paper of 1977, is the unobservability of the appropriate market benchmark portfolio in tests of the capital asset pricing model (CAPM).

Shmuel and I combine two lines of analysis in addressing the issue of sensitivity of tests to specification of the benchmark portfolio. The first line of analysis represents a likelihood ratio test of a pricing model in terms of the position of one or more benchmark portfolios in sample mean–standard deviation space. The second line of analysis uses results that Shmuel and I derived regarding the maximum correlation between two portfolios with given positions in mean–standard deviation space. By combining these two separate lines of analysis, we are able to calibrate the sensitivity of inferences provided by any asset pricing test that can be characterized in terms of the position of one or more benchmark portfolios in sample mean–standard deviation space.

In this paper, in which we investigate the sensitivity of inferences about the Sharpe–Lintner version of the model (with a riskless asset), the first line of analysis uses a previously known result for representing the likelihood ratio test of that model in sample mean–standard deviation space. In the three years or so since completing "On Correlations and Inferences...," Shmuel and I have done more work in this area. In a paper entitled, "A Mean–Variance Framework for Tests of Asset Pricing Models" (Kandel and Stambaugh, 1989), we analyze likelihood ratio tests of additional asset pricing models and provide their representations in terms of the positions of benchmark portfolios in sample mean–standard deviation space. Our more recent work expands the first line of analysis and thereby increases the number of pricing models that can be analyzed in the manner presented in this paper.

A brief example can illustrate the sort of additional analysis that is now possible. In this paper, we report (table 13.3) that the data reject the Sharpe–Lintner CAPM using the value-weighted New York and American Stock Exchange (NYSE–AMEX) index as the market benchmark. In the first subperiod, for example, the maximum correlation between this market benchmark and an alternative benchmark giving the opposite inference at, say, the 0.05 significance level is 0.763. Our more recent results allow the same analysis for other pricing models. If the zero-beta version of the CAPM (no riskless asset) is tested instead using the same market benchmark, the data again reject the model, but the maximum correlation between the benchmark used and one giving the opposite inference becomes 0.95. We see the extent to which the rejection of the zero-beta version of the model appears to be more sensitive to specification of the benchmark. *Some* alternative portfolios highly correlated with the original benchmark, if used in place of the original, would give the opposite inference about the validity of the zero-beta version of the model.

Reference

Kandel, S. and Stambaugh, R. F. (1989) "A Mean–Variance Framework for Tests of Asset Pricing Models," *Review of Financial Studies*, 2, 125–56.

Bibliographical Listing

"A Mean–Variance Framework for Tests of Asset Pricing Models" (with Shmuel Kandel), *Review of Financial Studies*, 2, 1989, 125–56.

"The Information in Forward Rates: Implications for Models of the Term Structure," *Journal of Financial Economics*, 21: 1, May 1988, 41–70.

"Expected Stock Returns and Volatility" (with Kenneth French and G. William Schwert), *Journal of Financial Economics*, 19: 1, September 1987, 3–29.

"Tests of Asset Pricing with Time-Varying Expected Risk Premiums and Market Betas" (with Wayne Ferson and Shmuel Kandel), *Journal of Finance*, 42: 2, June 1987, 201–20.

"Mimicking Portfolios and Exact Arbitrage Pricing" (with Gur Huberman and Shmuel Kandel), *Journal of Finance*, 42: 1, March 1987, 1–9.

"Predicting Returns in the Stock and Bond Markets" (with Donald Keim), *Journal of Financial Economics*, 17: 2, December 1986, 357–90.

On Correlations and Inferences about Mean–Variance Efficiency

SHMUEL KANDEL and ROBERT F. STAMBAUGH

1 Introduction

Many asset pricing models imply the mean–variance efficiency of one or more benchmark portfolios. Models for which the benchmarks have been identified include the capital asset pricing model (CAPM), the intertemporal consumption-based model, and the arbitrage pricing theory.[1] Researchers concerned with testing asset pricing models have faced at least two important questions in recent years. First, how does one test the mean–variance efficiency of a given portfolio in a finite sample? Second, how can one make inferences about the mean–variance efficiency of a benchmark when its exact rate of return is unobservable?

In addressing the problem of testing a given portfolio's efficiency, researchers have sought to apply methods that account for finite-sample variability. Various tests have been developed and applied by Gibbons (1982), Jobson and Korkie (1982), Stambaugh (1982), and Shanken (1985). Ross (1983) and Kandel (1984a) obtain analytical solutions for computing one such test, the likelihood ratio. The distributions of the tests in finite samples have been investigated analytically (Ross, 1983; Gibbons, Ross, and Shanken, 1989; Shanken, 1985) and through simulations (Gibbons, 1980; Stambaugh, 1981; Jobson and Korkie, 1982; MacKinlay, 1987).

Precise measurement of the relevant benchmark return can be difficult. Roll (1977) discusses how unobservability of the market portfolio's return presents problems in testing the CAPM. When the benchmark portfolio is measured imprecisely by a proxy, the researcher may wish to investigate the sensitivity of inferences to alternative specifications of the proxy. One approach is to repeat tests using various proxies (Stambaugh, 1982). Another approach, pursued in this study, is to ask whether any portfolio

Reproduced from *Journal of Financial Economics*, 18, 1987, 61–90.

Shmuel Kandel is Associate Professor of Finance at the University of Chicago. We are grateful to Eugene Fama, Wayne Ferson, Richard Green, participants in workshops at the Ohio State University and the University of Chicago, an anonymous referee, and especially John Long (the editor) for helpful comments and discussions.

in a class of portfolios would provide a different inference, where the class includes all portfolios satisfying some specified relation (for example correlation) with the original proxy.

We characterize an alternative proxy portfolio in terms of the correlation between its return and the return on the original proxy. This characterization allows us to define a class of alternative proxies as all portfolios having a sample correlation of at least, say, 0.9 with the original proxy. We then ask whether any portfolio in that class gives an inference about mean–variance efficiency that differs from the inference about the original proxy. This question is examined in a finite-sample context. We also test whether the *ex ante* correlation between the proxy and the Sharpe–Lintner tangent portfolio of the global asset universe exceeds a given value. Thus our study integrates the problems of finite-sample tests and benchmark portfolio measurement.

A brief example can illustrate the type of information provided by the approach developed here. Using weekly data from July 1969 through October 1975, the second of three subperiods, a likelihood ratio test can reject at the 0.05 significance level the hypothesis that the value-weighted portfolio of all New York and American Stock Exchange (NYSE–AMEX) stocks is the Sharpe–Lintner tangent portfolio. We find that no alternative index portfolio whose sample (*ex post*) correlation with that original proxy exceeds 0.50 could have provided a different inference. In addition to conducting this *ex post* sensitivity analysis, we also reject in the same subperiod the hypothesis that the original proxy has an *ex ante* correlation of at least 0.70 with the Sharpe–Lintner tangent portfolio of the global universe of assets. If the market portfolio has a correlation of at least 0.70 with the NYSE–AMEX value-weighted proxy, then the latter result also rejects the CAPM.

The paper proceeds as follows. In section 2 we first analyze the above problem when all parameter values are given. This framework allows us to introduce the relevant mean–variance mathematics before turning to the complications of finite-sample variability. The starting point is Roll's (1977) well-known example, in which he shows that the market proxy used by Black, Jensen, and Scholes (1972) has a correlation of 0.9 with the sample Sharpe–Lintner tangent portfolio. We show that the correlation between the tangent portfolio and the proxy is sensitive to how the efficient set is constructed. This applies for both the population and the sample. For example, if the set is constructed from 16 portfolios of stocks and bonds, the sample correlation between the tangency and the proxy of Black, Jensen, and Scholes drops to 0.48. If still more assets are used to construct the set, the correlation can only decrease. The last statement follows from the result that the correlation between a proxy and the tangent portfolio is simply the ratio of their Sharpe measures.

In section 2 we also discuss a more general question examined by Kandel and Stambaugh (1986): where, in mean–variance space, are the portfolios having correlations with a given proxy of at least, say, 0.9? Do such portfolios include points on the minimum variance boundary? Do they include the Sharpe–Lintner tangency? Do they exist at all levels of mean return? A complete analytical characterization of this set of portfolios is provided by Kandel and Stambaugh (1986). In section 2 we illustrate graphically the properties of this set that are useful in deriving the sensitivity analysis and the tests in sections 3 and 4.

In section 3 we expand the analysis to include finite-sample inference. We analyze the sensitivity of inferences based on the likelihood ratio test of tangency in the presence of a riskless asset. As Ross (1983) demonstrates, this test has a known finite-sample distribution and, conveniently for our purposes, can be constructed easily from parameters of the sample efficient set. The latter feature allows us to extend the analytical results in section 2 and to compute the highest sample correlation between the proxy and a portfolio that, in the same sample, reverses the inference about the proxy's tangency. Using stock and bond returns data, we compute that correlation for various proxies and sets of assets. In many cases the correlation is quite high. In other cases there are no portfolios that would reverse inferences, whatever the correlation. The latter cases occur when, for that sample, there is no rejection region for the likelihood ratio test for standard test sizes.

In section 4 we present a new test of the hypothesis that a given proxy is correlated *ex ante* at least ρ_0 with the *ex ante* tangent portfolio. The null hypothesis is, in fact, a joint hypothesis that some portfolio whose exact return is unobservable, for example the market portfolio, is both (a), the *ex ante* tangent portfolio of the global universe of all assets and (b) correlated *ex ante* at least ρ_0 with the given observable proxy. The null hypothesis is rejected if the proxy itself is inferred to be nontangent for the econometrician's observed asset universe by Ross's test and if the highest sample correlation between the proxy and a portfolio that is inferred to be tangent is too low. The latter sample statistic is derived in section 3, and it is used there for sensitivity analysis within the same sample. In section 4 the same statistic is used in a formal test whose significance level is bounded from above.

In a recent paper, Shanken (1987) suggests an approach for testing the hypothesis that the correlation between an observable proxy and the *ex ante* tangent portfolio of the econometrician's observed asset universe exceeds a given level. His approach gives a test statistic whose distribution depends on an unknown parameter. Given that parameter, which can be estimated, the approach provides exact significance levels for a test of this hypothesis. The second part of section 4 generalizes Shanken's approach slightly to consider instead the *ex ante* tangent portfolio of the global asset universe, and we obtain a test whose significance level is bounded from above, conditional on the unknown parameter. We then apply this test and obtain inferences similar to those produced by the first approach. Both approaches indicate that the above hypothesis is typically rejected at conventional significance levels for ρ_0 equal to 0.9, and often for ρ_0 equal to 0.8 or 0.7, when the market proxy is either the equally weighted or the value-weighted portfolio of NYSE–AMEX stocks.

The paper's conclusions are reviewed in section 5.

2 Correlations Between a Given Portfolio and Alternative Portfolios

In this section we explore the relations that govern the correlations between the returns on a given proxy portfolio and the returns on (a) the Sharpe–Lintner tangent portfolio, (b) other portfolios on the minimum variance boundary, and (c) arbitrary feasible portfolios, given only the locations of the latter in mean–variance space. We also note that these relations give a simple implication about the relevant benchmark portfolio of a subset of assets. The relations in this section are stated in terms of *ex ante* values, but they hold (and are subsequently used) for both *ex ante* and sample values.

2.1 The correlation between the proxy and the tangent portfolio

Given a universe of n risky assets and a riskless asset, define the mean return $\mu(p)$ on portfolio p, the standard deviation $\sigma(p)$ of the return on portfolio p, the correlation $\rho(p,q)$ between returns on portfolios p and q, and the riskless return r.

The Sharpe measure of a portfolio is the ratio of its mean excess return to its standard deviation of return. That is, the Sharpe measure of p is given by

$$S(p) = \frac{\mu(p) - r}{\sigma(p)}. \tag{1}$$

The Sharpe–Lintner *tangent* portfolio is the portfolio of the n risky assets with the maximum Sharpe measure.[2]

The term "minimum variance portfolio" will be used throughout the paper to denote a portfolio on the minimum variance boundary of the risky assets. A circumflex will denote a sample value. The following notation is used to denote various portfolios of the n risky assets in the universe: α, proxy portfolio; γ, *ex ante* tangent portfolio; $\hat{\gamma}$, sample tangent portfolio; p_z, minimum variance portfolio whose return is uncorrelated with the minimum variance portfolio p, that is, p_z is a "zero-beta" portfolio with respect to p; $p^\star$, minimum variance portfolio with the same mean return as portfolio p.

As established in the following proposition, Sharpe measures provide a convenient way to compute the correlation between the proxy and the tangent portfolio.

Proposition 1[3]

$$\rho(\alpha, \gamma) = \frac{S(\alpha)}{S(\gamma)}. \tag{2}$$

PROOF The linear mean–beta relation implied by the tangency of γ gives

$$\mu(\alpha) - r = \frac{\mathrm{cov}(\alpha, \gamma)}{\sigma^2(\gamma)} [\mu(\gamma) - r] = \frac{\sigma(\alpha)}{\sigma(\gamma)} \rho(\alpha, \gamma)[\mu(\gamma) - r]. \tag{3}$$

Solving (3) for $\rho(\alpha, \gamma)$ gives

$$\rho(\alpha, \gamma) = \frac{[\mu(\alpha) - r]/\sigma(\alpha)}{[\mu(\gamma) - r]/\sigma(\gamma)} = \frac{S(\alpha)}{S(\gamma)}. \tag{4}$$

■

In his critique of tests of the CAPM, Roll (1977) constructs efficient sets from sample parameters and then computes the correlation between a market proxy and the sample tangent portfolio. In Roll's examples, the correlations are high, 0.9 or more, which leads Roll to suggest that rejections of the CAPM can be reversed easily with an alternative proxy that is highly correlated with the original. Proposition 1 is useful in analyzing such examples. As we demonstrate, the correlation between the proxy and the sample tangent portfolio is sensitive to how the efficient set is constructed.

We construct several sample minimum variance boundaries using monthly returns on various assets for the overall period January 1926 through November 1978 and for two subperiods. All returns are in excess of the 1 month Treasury bill rate (from Ibbotson and Sinquefield, 1982). Our market proxy is the equally weighted New York Stock Exchange (NYSE) index, following Black, Jensen, and Scholes (1972), one of the studies from which Roll (1977) generates his examples. The second column of table 13.1 displays the correlation between the equally weighted NYSE index and the tangent portfolio for three minimum variance boundaries. (The tangent emanates from the origin, since we use excess returns.) The first minimum variance boundary is essentially the same as that constructed by Roll. That is, we form a zero-beta portfolio in the manner of Black, Jensen, and Scholes and compute a series of monthly returns on

Table 13.1 Sample correlations between the equally weighted NYSE index (EW) and portfolios on the minimum variance boundary

Assets used to construct the minimum variance boundary		*Correlation between EW and the Sharpe–Lintner tangent portfolio*	*Maximum correlation between EW and a portfolio on the boundary*
Number	*Description*		
Jan 1926 to Nov 1978			
2	EW plus the BJS zero-beta portfolio[a]	0.994	1.000
11	EW plus ten size-ranked portfolios of common stocks[b]	0.596	0.783
16	EW, the size-ranked portfolios, the value-weighted NYSE, and four bond portfolios[c]	0.484	0.484
Jan 1926 to Dec 1952			
2	EW plus the BJS zero-beta portfolio	0.920	1.000
11	EW plus ten size-ranked portfolios of common stocks	0.440	0.650
16	EW, the size-ranked portfolios, the value-weighted NYSE, and four bond portfolios	0.269	0.328
Jan 1953 to Nov 1978			
2	EW plus the BJS zero-beta portfolio	0.902	1.000
11	EW plus ten size-ranked portfolios of common stocks	0.528	0.883
16	EW, the size-ranked portfolios, the value-weighted NYSE, and four bond portfolios	0.438	0.550

[a]The zero-beta portfolio is formed in essentially the same manner as in Black, Jensen, and Scholes (1972) (BJS).

[b]All firms on the NYSE are assigned to deciles based on the market value of equity at the end of the previous year. Portfolios are equally weighted.

[c]The four bond portfolios consist of long-term US Government bonds, long-term high grade corporate bonds, BAA-rated corporate bonds, and below-BAA-rated corporate bonds.

that portfolio. The boundary is then generated as all possible combinations of the NYSE index and the zero-beta portfolio, using the return series to estimate the necessary parameters. Consistent with Roll's finding, the correlations between the NYSE proxy and the sample tangent portfolio are 0.9 or more in this case.

The other two boundaries constructed here, unlike the first, are not assumed to include the equally weighted NYSE index. Rather, that portfolio now lies somewhere inside the sample boundary. We construct the first of these alternative boundaries from a universe containing the equally weighted NYSE index plus ten equally weighted common stock portfolios formed by ranking firms into deciles of market value of equity at the end of the previous year.[4] The correlations between the sample tangent portfolio of this boundary and the NYSE proxy are considerably lower than in the original example: 0.60 for the overall period.

The decline in the correlation from the first boundary to the second is easily understood given the following corollary.

Corollary 1 For a given proxy α, $\rho(\alpha, \gamma)$ cannot increase as risky assets are added to the universe (and γ changes).

PROOF Use proposition 1 and the fact that $S(\gamma)$ cannot decrease as the universe expands. ∎

This corollary is illustrated further with the third boundary, which is constructed by adding the value-weighted NYSE index and four bond portfolios to the previous universe of 11 stock portfolios. The bond portfolios consist of long-term US Government bonds, long-term high grade corporate bonds, BAA-rated corporate bonds, and below-BAA-rated corporate bonds.[5] The correlations between the sample tangent portfolio and the NYSE proxy are, as they must be, lower than in the previous case: 0.48 for the overall period. Adding more assets can only decrease the correlation still further.

2.2 *The correlation between the proxy and portfolios on the minimum variance boundary*

When a riskless asset exists, the above examples illustrate the difference, in terms of correlation, between the proxy and the portfolio that, *ex post*, supports the Sharpe–Lintner pricing theory. A similar analysis is possible when no riskless asset exists. In this case, however, there is no longer a unique boundary portfolio of the risky assets. Rather, many portfolios on the positively sloped minimum variance boundary could in principle support the more general Black (1972) version of the two-parameter model.[6]

The following propositions are useful in understanding the correlation between the proxy and portfolios on the minimum variance boundary.

Proposition 2 For any minimum variance portfolio p,

$$\rho(\alpha, p) = \frac{[\mu(\alpha) - \mu(p_z)]/\sigma(\alpha)}{[\mu(p) - \mu(p_z)]/\sigma(p)}. \tag{5}$$

PROOF Replace r with $\mu(p_z)$ in the proof of proposition 1. ■

Proposition 3 The minimum variance portfolio having the highest correlation with α is $\alpha^\star$, the minimum variance portfolio having the same mean return as α. The maximum correlation is

$$\rho(\alpha, \alpha^\star) = \frac{\sigma(\alpha^\star)}{\sigma(\alpha)}. \tag{6}$$

PROOF Consider an arbitrary minimum variance portfolio p. Let (μ_a, σ_a) be the point in mean–standard deviation space on the line tangent to the minimum standard deviation boundary at p with $\mu_a = \mu(\alpha)$. Then (from proposition 2)

$$\rho(\alpha, p) = \frac{[\mu(\alpha) - \mu(p_z)]/\sigma(\alpha)}{[\mu(p) - \mu(p_z)]/\sigma(p)}$$

$$= \frac{[\mu(\alpha) - \mu(p_z)]/\sigma(\alpha)}{[\mu_a - \mu(p_z)]/\sigma_a} = \frac{\sigma_a}{\sigma(\alpha)}.$$

Since, for all choices of p, $\sigma_a \leqslant \sigma(\alpha^\star)$, $\rho(\alpha, p)$ is maximized at $\sigma_a = \sigma(\alpha^\star)$, which is accomplished by choosing $p = \alpha^\star$.[7] ■

If the question of primary interest is the sensitivity of inferences to choosing alternative proxies, then an important boundary portfolio is the one having the highest correlation with the original proxy. That portfolio, in a sense, is the one that most easily reverses a violation of the pricing theory. From proposition 3, that boundary portfolio is the one with the same mean return as the original proxy.

The third column of table 13.1 displays the maximum sample correlation between the equally weighted NYSE index and portfolios on the sample minimum variance boundaries described earlier. For the first boundary, the maximum correlation equals unity, since the proxy lies on the boundary by construction. The maximum correlations for the other boundaries are, as in the previous examples, considerably lower. In fact, for the overall period and for the most inclusive boundary, the boundary portfolio having maximum correlation with the proxy happens to be the sample tangent portfolio. In other words, the sample tangent portfolio in that case has the same mean return as the NYSE proxy (by proposition 3).

As in the previous examples, the decline in correlations as assets are added to the universe is easily understood given the following corollary.

Corollary 2 For a given proxy α, the maximum correlation between α and a portfolio on the minimum variance boundary cannot increase as risky assets are added to the universe.

PROOF Use proposition 3 and the fact that $\sigma(\alpha^\star)$ cannot increase as the opportunity set expands. ■

2.3 *The correlation between the proxy and an arbitrary portfolio*

We have examined the correlation between a proxy portfolio and portfolios on the minimum variance boundary, but a more complete characterization

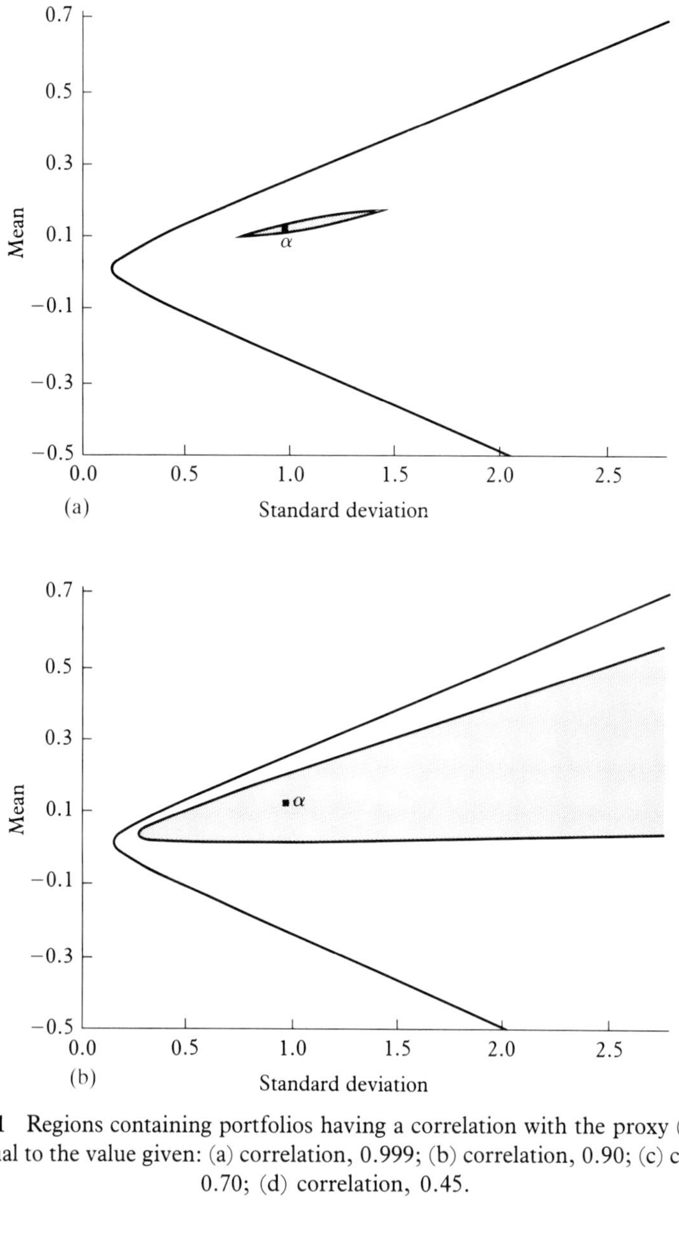

Figure 13.1 Regions containing portfolios having a correlation with the proxy (α) greater than or equal to the value given: (a) correlation, 0.999; (b) correlation, 0.90; (c) correlation, 0.70; (d) correlation, 0.45.

is possible. Where in mean–variance space are the portfolios correlated at least ρ_0 with the proxy? Kandel and Stambaugh (1986) provide a complete analytical characterization, in mean–variance space, of the set of portfolios having a correlation of at least ρ_0 with a given proxy. Here we illustrate graphically the properties of this set that are useful in developing the sensitivity analysis in section 3.

We restrict attention to a universe of risky assets having a nonsingular variance–covariance matrix, and we assume that the proxy does not lie on

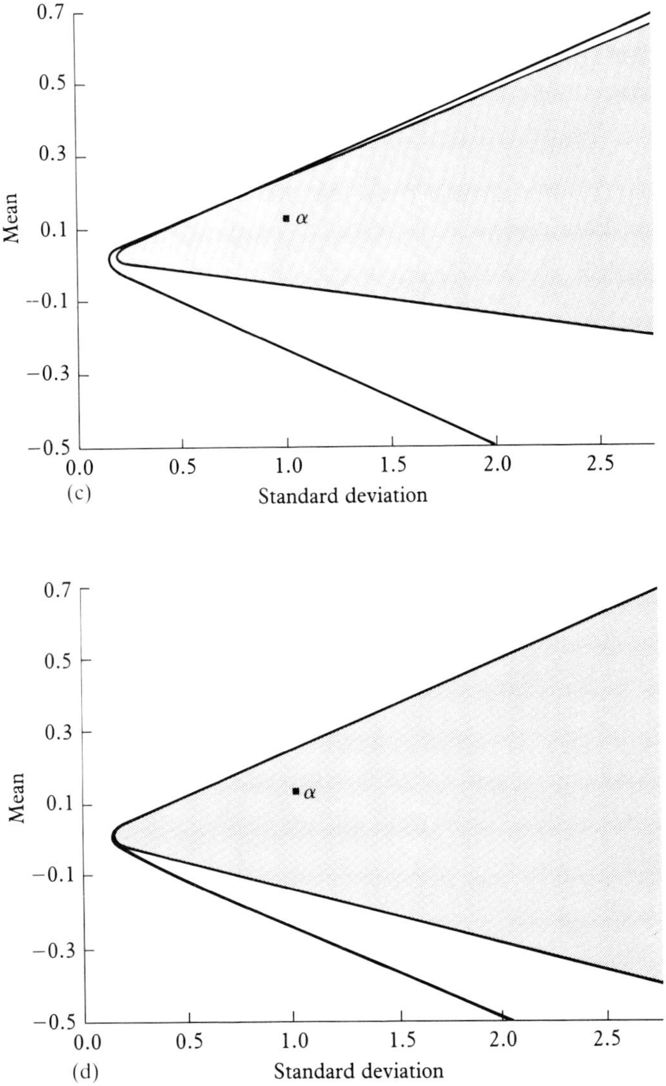

Figure 13.1 (*Continued*)

the minimum variance boundary. Consider the set of portfolios whose correlation with the proxy is at least ρ_0. For $\rho_0 = 1$, the set contains only the proxy itself. The set expands as ρ_0 declines. For sufficiently low values of ρ_0, the set contains portfolios at all levels of mean return. Roll (1980) shows, for example, that portfolios uncorrelated with an inefficient proxy exist at all levels of mean return. For intermediate values of ρ_0, the set contains portfolios only at certain levels of mean return.

Just as the set of portfolios correlated at least ρ_0 with the proxy expands as ρ_0 declines, the region of mean–variance space that this set of portfolios can occupy also expands as ρ_0 declines. Figure 13.1 displays some examples of these regions for various values of ρ_0. We plot the regions in mean–standard deviation space, given that most readers are probably more familiar with graphs in those dimensions. The minimum standard deviation boundary is constructed from the 16 stock and bond portfolios used in the earlier examples, where parameters are estimated over the period 1926–78. We again use the equally weighted NYSE index as the proxy. Thus the graphs represent the same proxy and asset universe used to compute the third row of table 13.1. The parameter values are annualized, and the returns are stated in excess of the Treasury bill rate.

All portfolios having a correlation of at least ρ_0 with the proxy lie in a convex region in mean–standard deviation space, although that region can also contain portfolios whose correlation with the proxy is less than ρ_0. The region may or may not be bounded in various directions, depending on ρ_0. The four cases displayed in figure 13.1 illustrate some of the possibilities. For a sufficiently high ρ_0, as in the first case where $\rho_0 = 0.999$, the region is bounded in all directions. When $\rho_0 = 0.9$, portfolios having the required minimum correlation exist at all mean returns greater than a critical level, but for a given mean the variance of such portfolios is bounded. When $\rho_0 = 0.7$, the portfolios exist at all mean returns and the variance has no upper bound. The same is true when $\rho_0 = 0.45$, except that the region of portfolios then extends to include points on the minimum standard deviation boundary. Given the earlier discussion of table 13.1, recall that, when $\rho_0 = 0.48$, the region touches the boundary at one point – the point with the same mean return as the proxy.

2.4 *Benchmark portfolios for subsets*

Investigations of asset pricing models must use subsets of the global universe of assets. The above relations also provide a relevant benchmark portfolio formed from a subset of assets. Let b denote the benchmark portfolio of the global universe, which is identified by the pricing theory, and let p' be the portfolio from the subset of assets that is most highly correlated with b. The following corollaries, easily shown given propositions 1 and 2, establish p' as a relevant benchmark for testing the pricing theory with the subset of assets.

Corollary 3 If b is the Sharpe–Lintner tangent portfolio for the global universe of assets and p' is the portfolio from a subset of assets that is most highly correlated with b, then p' is the tangent portfolio for the subset of assets.

PROOF For any portfolio p of the subset, propostion 1 gives $\rho(b, p) = S(p)/S(b)$. Since this correlation is maximized for $p = p'$, $S(p')$ is the maximum Sharpe measure for any portfolio of the subset, and thus p' is the tangent portfolio for the subset. ■

Corollary 4 If b is on the minimum variance boundary of all assets and p' is the portfolio from a subset of assets that is most highly correlated with b, then p' is on the minimum variance boundary of the subset of assets.

PROOF The proof is identical with that of corollary 3 except that, using proposition 2, Sharpe measures are defined with respect to $\mu(b_z)$ instead of r. ■

Corollary 3 implies, for example, that if the tangency of p' is rejected on a subset of assets, then the tangency of b for the global universe is also rejected. It is important to note that the exact construction of p' is not likely to be known by the researcher. In the discussions that follow, however, it is sufficient to view the observable portfolio α as a proxy for the unobservable p'.

3 The Sensitivity of Finite-Sample Inferences

The previous section addresses the question of how similar, in terms of correlation, the proxy portfolio is to a sample *efficient* portfolio that supports the pricing theory exactly. In a finite sample, however, there will also be sample *inefficient* portfolios for which the hypothesis of *ex ante* efficiency cannot be rejected. Those portfolios are not sufficiently "far" from sample efficiency to rule out parameter estimation error as the cause of their sample inefficiency. The correlations in table 13.1 essentially provide information about inference sensitivity in infinite samples. In this section we address the issue of inference sensitivity in finite samples.

We continue to pose the question raised originally by Roll (1977) and pursued in the previous section: how highly correlated with the original proxy can an alternative proxy be and still provide a different inference about *ex ante* mean–variance efficiency? In an infinite sample this question is interesting only if the original proxy is inefficient – if the proxy happens to be efficient, there are clearly inefficient portfolios "close by" whose correlations with the proxy are arbitrarily close to unity. In a finite sample, however, the question of inference reversal becomes interesting whether or not the proxy is inferred to be inefficient, since a *sample* inefficient portfolio is not necessarily inferred to be *ex ante* inefficient.

3.1 *The statistical framework*

The sensitivity of finite-sample inferences obviously depends, *inter alia*, on the type of test performed. We investigate here the sensitivity of the likelihood ratio test of whether a given portfolio is the Sharpe–Lintner tangent portfolio. A transformation of the test statistic has a finite-sample F distribution, as shown by Ross (1983). Another convenient feature of the test for our purposes is that it can be characterized completely in terms of the sample mean–standard deviation space. A portfolio's tangency is accepted or rejected by comparing its estimated Sharpe measure with that of the sample tangent portfolio. If the difference in squared Sharpe measures is large enough, tangency is rejected. Specifically,

$$F = \frac{T-n}{n-1}\left[\frac{\hat{S}(\hat{\gamma})^2 - \hat{S}(p)^2}{1+\hat{S}(p)^2}\right] \tag{7}$$

has an F distribution with $n-1$ and $T-n$ degrees of freedom if p is the *ex ante* tangent portfolio, where n is the number of assets and $T\ (\geqslant n)$ is the number of time series observations (Ross, 1983).[8]

Our objective is to describe, in terms of sample correlation with the original proxy α, the portfolios that are inferred (a) tangent if α is inferred nontangent or (b) nontangent if α is inferred tangent. The first step is to observe that, in some cases, no such reversal of inferences is possible for any correlation. For a given sample of assets, F has a maximum

$$\bar{F} = \frac{T-n}{n-1}\hat{S}(\hat{\gamma})^2 \tag{8}$$

which is attained when $\hat{S}(p)=0$. Note that $\bar{F}$ could still be less than F_θ, the critical F value for significance level θ. In such a case, which is more likely to occur in samples where n is large relative to T, there are no feasible portfolios whose tangency is rejected at significance level θ.

When $\bar{F}$ in (8) exceeds F_θ, then the *ex post* rejection region is nonempty and can be characterized in terms of critical Sharpe measures. In such a case the likelihood ratio test rejects tangency of p if $|\hat{S}(p)| < S_{\text{crit}}$, where

$$S_{\text{crit}} = \left[\frac{\hat{S}(\hat{\gamma})^2 - \nu F_\theta}{1+\nu F_\theta}\right]^{1/2} \tag{9}$$

and $\nu = (n-1)/(T-n)$. (Set $F = F_\theta$ in (7) and solve for $\hat{S}(p)$.) Tangency is accepted for portfolios with sample Sharpe measures that are either high enough ($> S_{\text{crit}}$) or low enough ($< -S_{\text{crit}}$). Given the symmetric treatment of positive and negative Sharpe measures, the test's power is clearly greatest against a zero Sharpe measure and diminishes as the Sharpe measure moves either up or down. The test ignores the restriction that the mean excess return of the tangent portfolio is strictly positive.

Combined with our earlier analysis in section 2.3, the critical Sharpe measures provide a simple way of addressing the issue of inference sensitivity. For a given ρ_0 first construct the region Φ in sample mean–standard deviation space containing portfolios having sample correlation of at least ρ_0 with the proxy α. (Recall that examples of such a region are displayed in figure 13.1.) Next construct the lines representing the critical Sharpe measures S_{crit} and $-S_{\text{crit}}$. If either line passes through Φ, then whatever the inference about α's tangency, some portfolio having a sample correlation of at least ρ_0 with α gives a different inference.

As described earlier, the region Φ expands as ρ_0 decreases. Figure 13.2 illustrates two cases where the universe contains the same 16 risky assets used in the previous section, parameters are estimated for the subperiod 1926–52, and the proxy α is the equally weighted NYSE index. The critical Sharpe measure S_{crit} reflects a 0.05 significance level, and α lies in the rejection region. In figure 13.2(a) Φ is constructed with $\rho_0 = 0.95$, and no points in Φ lie in the acceptance region. When ρ_0 is lowered to 0.70 in figure 13.2(b), Φ then crosses S_{crit}, and so some portfolios in Φ lie in the acceptance region. We compute the highest ρ_0 for which the region Φ is tangent to one of the critical Sharpe measures, that is, the highest ρ_0 for which a reversal of inferences is possible.

Proposition 4 Assume $\bar{F} > F_\theta$ (nonempty rejection region). The maximum correlation between α and a portfolio that is inferred (a) tangent if α is inferred nontangent or (b) nontangent if α is inferred tangent at significance level θ is given by

$$\bar{\rho}_\theta(\alpha) = \frac{S_{\text{crit}}\,|\hat{S}(\alpha)| + c(\alpha)}{\hat{S}(\hat{\gamma})^2}, \tag{10}$$

where

$$c(\alpha) = \{[\hat{S}(\hat{\gamma})^2 - S_{\text{crit}}^2]\,[\hat{S}(\hat{\gamma})^2 - \hat{S}(\alpha)^2]\}^{1/2}.$$

PROOF By proposition 6 in Kandel and Stambaugh (1986), the maximum sample correlation between α and a portfolio with sample Sharpe measure S is

$$\rho(S) = \frac{S \cdot \hat{S}(\alpha) + c(\alpha)}{\hat{S}(\hat{\gamma})^2}, \tag{11}$$

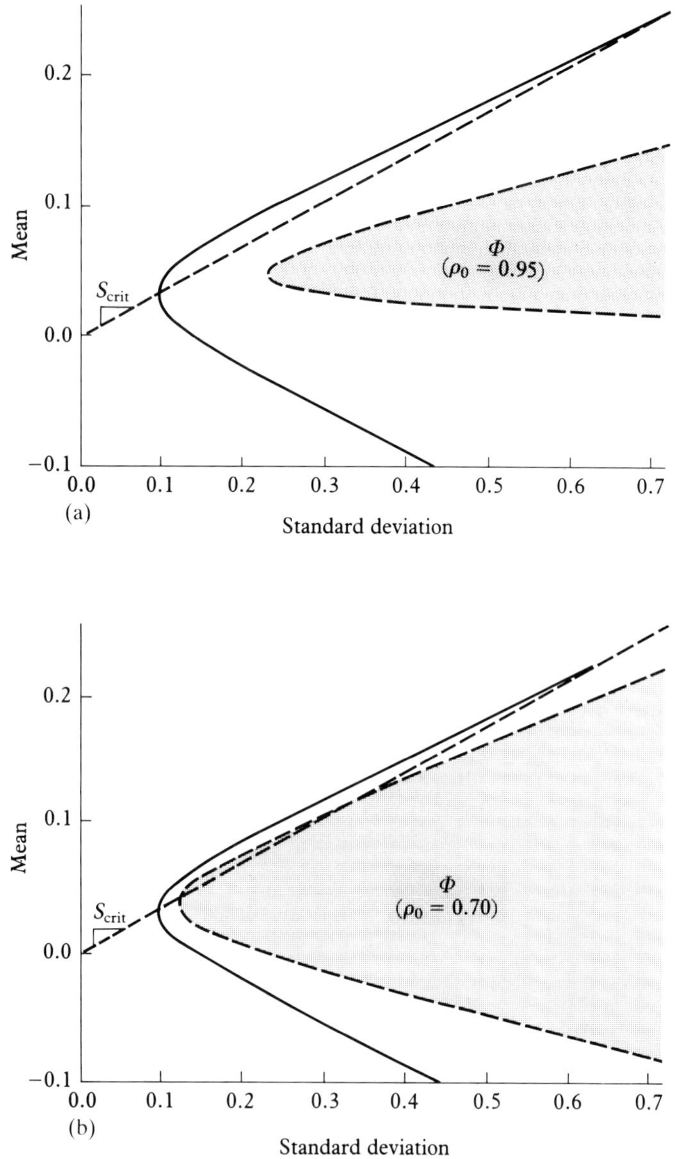

Figure 13.2 Portfolios that plot above the broken line whose slope is S_{crit} are inferred to be the *ex ante* tangent portfolio at a significance level of 0.05: (a) tangency is rejected for the original proxy as well as for all portfolios correlated at least 0.95 with the proxy (no reversal); (b) some portfolios correlated at least 0.70 with the proxy are inferred to be the *ex ante* tangent portfolio (reversal).

with $c(\alpha)$ defined as above except that S replaces S_{crit}. It is easily verified that $\rho'(S) < 0$ (>0) if $\hat{S}(\alpha) < S$ ($>S$), which implies that a portfolio satisfying the conditions of the proposition will lie on a critical Sharpe measure. (A portfolio beyond the boundary of the critical region cannot produce a higher correlation.) Therefore S can be either S_{crit} or $-S_{\text{crit}}$, whichever produces the higher correlation. From (11), the higher correlation occurs for $S = S_{\text{crit}}$ when $\hat{S}(\alpha) > 0$ and for $S = -S_{\text{crit}}$ when $\hat{S}(\alpha) < 0$, and this choice is accomplished in (10). ∎

We note here that the alternative portfolios considered in proposition 4 consist of different combinations of the original n assets used in the test. We do not investigate empirically the sensitivity of inferences when assets are added (n increases). With an infinite number of time series observations, such sensitivity can be discussed easily. In that case the only portfolio that will reverse an inference of nontangency is the tangent portfolio itself. As discussed in section 2, the correlation between the original proxy α and the tangent portfolio cannot increase as more assets are added to the universe (and to the tangent portfolio). With a finite number of time series observations, however, the problem of inference sensitivity when the number of assets is increased becomes less straightforward. In fact, it is difficult to pose a question in a way that could elicit an interesting answer.

The major problem in finite samples stems from how one handles the number T of time series observations. Holding T fixed presents one problem, but letting T increase presents another. For example, if T is held fixed as assets are added, the size of the rejection region can decrease. Unless the maximum absolute sample Sharpe measure $|\hat{S}(\hat{\gamma})|$ increases sufficiently, S_{crit} in (9) will decrease as the number of assets n increases. In fact, the *ex post* rejection region can disappear if $\bar{F}$ in (8) falls below the critical F value, F_θ. Therefore an inference of nontangency of the original proxy α could be reversed by a portfolio highly correlated with α, after adding enough assets to reduce the rejection region of the test sufficiently. However, if time series observations are added in order to overcome the above problem, then a reversal of inferences could again occur for a portfolio highly correlated with the original proxy α, but the reversal could arise solely from the additional time series observations. Indeed, we could in principle reverse the original inference by testing the *same* proxy using the longer time series. For these reasons, we confine our attention to alternative portfolios of the original n assets. Given the preceding discussion of benchmarks for subsets of assets (section 2.4), such an investigation is relevant for testing asset pricing theories.

3.2 Results with the monthly data

Table 13.2 displays values of the maximum sample correlation $\bar{\rho}_\theta(\alpha)$ that allows reversal of inferences about tangency in tests using the monthly returns data. The proxies are the equally weighted NYSE index (EW) and the value-weighted NYSE index (VW), and tangency is tested with respect to the 16 risky assets examined earlier. In addition to the absolute sample Sharpe measure $|\hat{S}(\alpha)|$ of the proxy, $\bar{\rho}_\theta(\alpha)$ depends on the maximum absolute sample Sharpe measure $|\hat{S}(\hat{\gamma})|$, the number of assets n, the number of observations T, and the significance level θ of the test. Thus, table 13.2 provides only a few examples of the analyses that could be conducted for various proxies and collections of assets. Nevertheless, some interesting observations emerge.

When reversals of inferences are possible, the correlations with alternative portfolios that allow such reversals are often higher than table 13.1 might lead us to suspect. For example, the equally weighted NYSE index is correlated only 0.48 with the sample tangent portfolio in the

Table 13.2 Sensitivity of the F test of Sharpe–Lintner tangency using monthly returns[a]

Market proxy[b]	*Absolute sample Sharpe measure of proxy*	*Sample correlation of the proxy with the sample tangent portfolio*	*P value of the test of tangency of the proxy*	*Maximum correlation between the proxy and a portfolio that gives the opposite inference at significance level*		
				0.10	*0.05*	*0.01*
Jan 1926 to Nov 1978 ($T = 635$, $\lvert\hat{S}(\hat{\gamma})\rvert = 0.262$)[c]						
EW	0.127	0.483	0.008	0.972	0.986	0.999
VW	0.109	0.416	0.004	0.952	0.970	0.995
Jan 1926 to Dec 1952 ($T = 324$, $\lvert\hat{S}(\hat{\gamma})\rvert = 0.487$)						
EW	0.131	0.269	0.000	0.791	0.817	0.863
VW	0.110	0.226	0.000	0.764	0.791	0.840
Jan 1953 to Nov 1978 ($T = 311$, $\lvert\hat{S}(\hat{\gamma})\rvert = 0.320$)						
EW	0.140	0.438	0.089	0.999	0.999	None[d]
VW	0.120	0.372	0.059	0.992	0.999	None

[a]The set of risky assets consists of 16 portfolios: ten portfolios of common stocks of the NYSE, the equally weighted and the value-weighted NYSE portfolios, and four bond portfolios, The ten stock portfolios are based on market value deciles at the end of the previous year and they are equally weighted portfolios.

[b]EW, equally weighted NYSE; VW; value-weighted NYSE.

[c]$|\hat{S}(\hat{\gamma})|$ is the sample's maximum absolute Sharpe measure.

[d]"None" indicates that there is no rejection region *ex post*.

overall period (table 13.1), but there exists a portfolio correlated as high as 0.99 with that proxy that would reverse the inference of *ex ante* nontangency at the 0.05 significance level. In this case, the proxy lies very close to the critical Sharpe measure. Although such a result need not always occur, this example illustrates the often dramatic effect of allowing for finite-sample variability. A similar comparison can be made in the first subperiod, except that each of the correlations is lower than in the overall period (0.48 becomes 0.27; 0.99 becomes 0.82).

A rather different phenomenon occurs in the second subperiod. No portfolios would have been inferred to be nontangent at significance levels of 0.01 or less. This illustrates the possibility discussed earlier, where the maximum of the test statistics ($\bar{F}$ in (8)) is less than the critical F value. Here again, however, observe the contrast between infinite and finite samples. In an infinite sample, all portfolios would be inferred nontangent except one – the tangency. In the finite sample, no portfolios would be inferred nontangent. Thus any other portfolio would reverse an original inference of tangency in an infinite sample, whereas no portfolio could reverse such an inference in this finite sample.

3.3 Results with weekly data

Although the above discussion illustrates well a range of outcomes that can occur when investigating the sensitivity of inferences, the implied stationarity assumptions are fairly strong. The overall period of 53 years and the subperiods of 27 and 26 years are long by usual standards. Shorter subperiods, while relaxing the assumed stationarity, result in fairly small numbers of time series observations when using monthly data, and the power of the test is thereby reduced (the rejection region is often empty *ex post* in such cases). In order to illustrate the above sensitivity analysis without imposing such strong stationarity assumptions, we conduct additional tests using weekly data.

Weekly returns are computed for ten value-weighted portfolios formed by ranking all firms on the NYSE–AMEX by market value at the end of the previous year. We use as two market proxies both the equally weighted and the value-weighted portfolios of stocks on the NYSE–AMEX. The riskless rate is the return on a US Treasury bill with 1 week to maturity.[9] We test the tangency of each proxy with respect to a universe of 12 risky assets consisting of the ten size portfolios and both market proxies. Table 13.3 reports the results of the same sensitivity analysis as conducted in table 13.2, except that now the analysis is performed on three periods, each about 6 years (324 weeks) in length. Thus, the number T of time series observations is the same as in the first subperiod in table 13.3, but the period is only one-fourth as long. Tangency of both proxies is rejected strongly in all three subperiods. At a 0.05 significance level, the maximum sample correlation $\bar{\rho}_\theta(\alpha)$ between the proxy and a portfolio inferred to be tangent ranges from 0.76 to 0.48 for the value-weighted NYSE–AMEX index and from 0.90 to 0.46 for the equally weighted index.

If $\bar{\rho}_\theta(\alpha)$ is high, as occurs for some cases in tables 13.2 and 13.3, then the researcher knows that there exists a portfolio highly correlated (in his sample) with the original proxy that will give a different inference about the pricing theory. This does not mean that any highly correlated portfolio will reverse inferences. For example, Stambaugh (1982) obtains the same inferences from several highly correlated market proxies. Rather, a high $\bar{\rho}_\theta(\theta)$ means that, without specifying additional characteristics of reasonable alternative proxies, the researcher is unable to conclude that his inferences *cannot* be easily reversed by another portfolio. Additional characteristics could include, for example, the condition that the alternative proxies resemble portfolios of aggregate wealth or the condition that all asset weights be positive. Such conditions are not imposed in computing $\bar{\rho}_\theta(\alpha)$ in tables 13.2 and 13.3.

Table 13.3 Sensitivity of the F test of Sharpe–Lintner tangency using weekly returns[a]

Market proxy[b]	*Absolute sample Sharpe measure of proxy*	*Sample correlation of the proxy with the sample tangent portfolio*	*P value of the test of tangency of the proxy*	*Maximum correlation between the proxy and a portfolio that gives the opposite inference at significance level* 0.10	0.05	0.01
Jan 2, 1963, to Jun 25, 1969 ($T=324$, $\lvert\hat{S}(\hat{\gamma})\rvert=0.445$)[c]						
EW	0.200	0.449	0.000	0.876	0.897	0.934
VW	0.097	0.218	0.000	0.733	0.763	0.819
Jan 2, 1969, to Oct 1, 1975 ($T=324$, $\lvert\hat{S}(\hat{\gamma})\rvert=0.681$)						
EW	0.018	0.026	0.000	0.433	0.459	0.510
VW	0.034	0.051	0.000	0.455	0.481	0.531
Oct 8, 1975, to Dec 23, 1981 ($T=324$, $\lvert\hat{S}(\hat{\gamma})\rvert=0.608$)						
EW	0.178	0.292	0.000	0.686	0.709	0.753
VW	0.047	0.077	0.000	0.511	0.539	0.591

[a]The set of risky assets consists of 12 portfolios: ten portfolios of NYSE–AMEX stocks and their value-weighted and equally weighted portfolios. The ten portfolios are based on market value deciles at the end of the previous year and are value-weighted portfolios.

[b]EW, equally weighted NYSE–AMEX index; VW, value-weighted NYSE–AMEX index.

[c]$\lvert\hat{S}(\hat{\gamma})\rvert$ is the sample's maximum absolute Sharpe measure.

4 Testing the Efficiency of an Unobservable Portfolio Using Partial Information

The approach outlined in the previous section allows the researcher to investigate the *ex post* sensitivity of inferences to alternative specifications of the proxy portfolio. This approach is potentially useful if, for example, the researcher believes that the returns on an observable proxy have a sample correlation of at least ρ_0 with the unobservable portfolio of interest. Such partial information about the unobservable portfolio can also be included in the test itself, in the form of the *ex ante* correlation between the proxy and the unobservable portfolio.

Other studies discuss the value of partial information in evaluating the efficiency of an unobservable portfolio. Examples of such partial information include the nonnegativity of market portfolio weights (Roll, 1979; Green, 1986) and upper bounds on the relative value and return variance of a missing asset (Kandel, 1984b; Shanken, 1986). Shanken (1984) derives an inequality relation that contains the (multiple) correlation between the unobservable portfolio and a set of observable instruments, and he suggests that this relation could be useful in formulating tests of asset pricing theories.

We assume that the researcher summarizes his partial information about the unobservable portfolio by specifying a lower bound on the *ex ante* correlation between that portfolio and an observable proxy α. We also distinguish between the global universe of all assets and the *observed* universe consisting of the subset of n assets used by the econometrician. The unobservable portfolio can contain any assets in the global universe. Let $\gamma^\star$ denote the *ex ante* tangent portfolio of the global universe (as distinct from γ, the *ex ante* tangent portfolio for the observed universe of n assets). The null hypothesis is a joint hypothesis that the unobservable portfolio is (a) the *ex ante* tangent portfolio of the global universe and (b) *ex ante* correlated at least ρ_0 with the proxy. In other words,

$$\mathrm{H}_0: \qquad \rho(\alpha, \gamma^\star) \geqslant \rho_0. \tag{12}$$

Special cases of H_0 include those where the global universe is identical with the observed universe and where $\rho_0 = 1$. Thus, H_0 is a generalization of the hypothesis tested in previous investigations of the CAPM, wherein the tangency of a given proxy was tested.

In this section we discuss two alternative approaches to testing H_0. Both approaches, in general, give tests whose significance levels can be bounded above. We first develop in section 4.1 an approach that uses the preceding sensitivity analysis. We then examine in section 4.2 an alternative approach, similar to that of Shanken (1987), which uses the distribution of the statistic in (7) under nontangency of the tested portfolio p. The latter distribution includes an unknown nuisance parameter, but, given that parameter, the approach gives an exact significance level when the global universe is identical with the observed universe.

4.1 A test based on the sensitivity analysis

Before proceeding to the formal development of the test, we first provide a brief informal description. Consider two sets of portfolios consisting of assets in the observed universe: (a) the portfolios inferred, at significance level θ, to be the *ex ante* tangent portfolio γ of the observed universe, and (b) the portfolios inferred, at significance level ψ, to have a correlation of at least ρ_0 with the proxy α. Note that both these sets of portfolios can be observed by the researcher. The probability that γ lies outside the first set is θ, and, if H_0 is true, the probability that γ lies outside the second set is at most ψ (since H_0 implies that $\rho(\alpha, \gamma) \geqslant \rho_0$, by corollary 1). If H_0 is true, then the probability that the two sets are disjoint is at most $\theta + \psi$, and this provides us with the test developed below.

Let $S_{\text{crit}}(\theta)$ be the critical Sharpe measure (in (9)) for testing the tangency of a given portfolio at significance level θ. The portfolio α is inferred nontangent if $|\hat{S}(\alpha)| < S_{\text{crit}}(\theta)$. In the previous section we derived $\bar{\rho}_\theta(\alpha)$, the maximum sample correlation between α and any portfolio that is inferred tangent at significance level θ when α is inferred nontangent. Using the distribution of the sample correlation $\hat{\rho}$ of bivariate normal random variables, given the true population value ρ, define the critical value $\rho_1(\rho_0, \psi)$ such that

$$\Pr[\hat{\rho} \leqslant \rho_1(\rho_0, \psi) | \rho = \rho_0] = \psi. \tag{13}$$

Reject H_0 if (a) $|\hat{S}(\alpha)| < S_{\text{crit}}(\theta)$ and (b) $\bar{\rho}_\theta(\alpha) < \rho_1(\rho_0, \psi)$. In other words, reject H_0 if the tangency of α is rejected at significance level θ and the maximum correlation between α and a portfolio inferred tangent is less than $\rho_1(\rho_0, \psi)$. As proved in the following proposition, the significance level (size) of this test is at most $\theta + \psi$.

Proposition 5

$$\Pr[|\hat{S}(\alpha)| < S_{\text{crit}}(\theta) \qquad \bar{\rho}_\theta(\alpha) < \rho_1(\rho_0, \psi) | H_0] \leqslant \theta + \psi. \tag{14}$$

PROOF Consider the sample correlation between the proxy α and the *ex ante* tangent portfolio of the observed universe γ, denoted $\hat{\rho}(\alpha, \gamma)$. The weights in γ, and therefore the returns on γ, are not observed by the researcher, and so $\hat{\rho}(\alpha, \gamma)$ cannot be computed. Nevertheless, this hypothetical sample correlation is useful in proving the proposition.

Define the events

A_1	$\lvert \hat{S}(\alpha) \rvert < S_{crit}(\theta)$
A_2	$\bar{\rho}_\theta(\alpha) < \rho_1(\rho_0, \psi)$
B	$\hat{\rho}(\alpha, \gamma) \geqslant \rho_1(\rho_0, \psi)$
C	$\hat{\rho}(\alpha, \gamma) \geqslant \bar{\rho}_\theta(\alpha)$
D	$\lvert \hat{S}(\gamma) \rvert < S_{crit}(\theta)$.

First observe that $[A_2 \cap B] \Rightarrow C$ by transitivity. Next observe that $[A_1 \cap C] \Rightarrow D$, since the tangency of α is rejected (by A_1) and γ gives the same inference (by C). (Note that $\hat{S}(\gamma)$ is the hypothetical sample Sharpe measure of the *ex ante* tangent portfolio of the observed universe.) Therefore

$$\begin{aligned} \Pr[A_1 \cap A_2 \cap B \mid H_0] &\leqslant \Pr[A_1 \cap C \mid H_0] \\ &\leqslant \Pr[D \mid H_0] = \Pr[D] = \theta. \end{aligned} \tag{15}$$

Next observe that

$$\begin{aligned} \Pr[A_1 \cap A_2 \cap (\sim B) \mid H_0] &\leqslant \Pr[\sim B \mid H_0] \\ &\leqslant \Pr[\sim B \mid \rho(\alpha, \gamma) \geqslant \rho_0] \leqslant \psi. \end{aligned} \tag{16}$$

The second inequality follows from corollary 1 and the implication that H_0 implies $\rho(\alpha, \gamma) \geqslant \rho_0$. The third inequality follows from (13) and the fact that, for a fixed $\rho_1(\rho_0, \psi)$, the probability on the left-hand side of (13) is decreasing in ρ. The probability in (14), $\Pr[A_1 \cap A_2 \mid H_0]$, can be written as

$$\Pr[A_1 \cap A_2 \mid H_0] = \Pr[A_1 \cap A_2 \cap B \mid H_0] + \Pr[A_1 \cap A_2 \cap (\sim B) \mid H_0],$$

and combining this with (15) and (16) gives the desired result. ■

The choice of θ and ψ in the above test is arbitrary. Together both parameters determine the maximum significance level of the test, but we do not know which combination of θ and ψ gives the highest power. In order to give a simple illustration of the test, we specify $\theta = \psi$. In addition, the exact sampling distribution of the correlation coefficient is rather complicated, and so in computing $\rho_1(\rho_0, \psi)$ we use Fisher's z transformation, in which

$$z = \frac{1}{2} \log\left(\frac{1+\hat{\rho}}{1-\hat{\rho}}\right) \tag{17}$$

has an approximately normal distribution (see Kendall and Stewart (1977, equation 16.77) for the moments of the distribution).

In table 13.4, we apply the test to the same weekly return data that we analyzed in table 13.3. Consider the first row of table 13.4, where the above hypothesis is tested in the first subperiod with ρ_0 equal to 0.9, a maximum significance level of 0.10 $(= \theta + \psi)$, and the value-weighted

Table 13.4 Test of H_0: $\rho(\alpha, \gamma^\star) \geqslant \rho_0$[a]

			$\rho_0 = 0.9$		$\rho_0 = 0.8$		$\rho_0 = 0.7$	
Market proxy α[b]	$\theta + \psi$[c]	$\bar{\rho}_\theta(\alpha)$[d]	*Critical value* $\rho_1(\rho_0, \psi)$[e]	*Inference about* H_0	*Critical value* $\rho_1(\rho_0, \psi)$	*Inference about* H_0	*Critical value* $\rho_1(\rho_0, \psi)$	*Inference about* H_0
Jan 2, 1963, to Jun 25, 1969 ($T = 324$)								
VW	0.10	0.763	0.881	Reject	0.765	Reject	0.651	Accept
VW	0.05	0.789	0.877	Reject	0.758	Accept	0.641	Accept
VW	0.01	0.839	0.869	Reject	0.743	Accept	0.620	Accept
EW	0.10	0.897	0.881	Accept	0.765	Accept	0.651	Accept
EW	0.05	0.915	0.877	Accept	0.758	Accept	0.641	Accept
EW	0.01	0.946	0.869	Accept	0.743	Accept	0.620	Accept
July 2, 1969, to Oct 1, 1975 ($T = 324$)								
VW	0.10	0.481	0.881	Reject	0.765	Reject	0.651	Reject
VW	0.05	0.504	0.877	Reject	0.758	Reject	0.641	Reject
VW	0.01	0.549	0.869	Reject	0.743	Reject	0.620	Reject
EW	0.10	0.459	0.881	Reject	0.765	Reject	0.651	Reject
EW	0.05	0.483	0.877	Reject	0.758	Reject	0.641	Reject
EW	0.01	0.528	0.869	Reject	0.743	Reject	0.620	Reject
Oct 8, 1975, to Dec 23, 1981 ($T = 324$)								
VW	0.10	0.539	0.881	Reject	0.765	Reject	0.651	Reject
VW	0.05	0.563	0.877	Reject	0.758	Reject	0.641	Reject
VW	0.01	0.611	0.869	Reject	0.743	Reject	0.620	Reject
EW	0.10	0.709	0.881	Reject	0.765	Reject	0.651	Accept
EW	0.05	0.729	0.877	Reject	0.758	Reject	0.641	Accept
EW	0.01	0.768	0.869	Reject	0.743	Accept	0.620	Accept

[a] The null hypothesis H_0 states that the proxy portfolio α has an *ex ante* correlation of at least ρ_0 with the Sharpe–Lintner tangent portfolio $\gamma^\star$ of the global universe. The tests are based on weekly returns. The set of 12 risky assets consists of ten value-weighted portfolios based on market-value deciles at the end of the previous year, the value-weighted NYSE–AMEX portfolio and the equally weighted NYSE–AMEX portfolio.

[b] VW, value-weighted NYSE–AMEX portfolio; EW, equally weighted NYSE–AMEX portfolio.

[c] Upper bound on the significance level ($\theta = \psi$).

[d] Maximum correlation between α and a portfolio inferred tangent in the observed universe at significance level θ.

[e] The critical value $\rho_1(\rho_0, \psi)$ is chosen so that $\Pr[\hat{\rho} \leqslant \rho_1(\rho_0, \psi) | \rho = \rho_0] = \psi$, where $\hat{\rho}$ is the sample correlation between bivariate normal variables.

NYSE–AMEX index as the proxy. The test proceeds as follows. First, the tangency of the proxy itself is rejected at a significance level of 0.05 ($=\theta$). The maximum sample correlation between the proxy and a portfolio inferred tangent $\bar{\rho}_\theta(\alpha)$ equals 0.763 (third column). Up to this point, we have simply repeated the procedure in table 13.3. Next compute $\rho_1(\rho_0, \psi)$ for $\rho_0 = 0.9$ and $\psi = 0.05$; this value is 0.881 (fourth column). Since this value exceeds $\bar{\rho}_\theta(\alpha)$, we reject H_0. The same procedure is repeated in table 13.4 for maximum significance levels of 0.05 and 0.01, for ρ_0 equal to 0.8 and 0.7, and with the equally weighted NYSE–AMEX index as an alternative proxy.

For the value-weighted index, H_0 is rejected in the last two subperiods for $\rho_0 = 0.7$ at a significance level of at most 0.01. In the first subperiod, H_0 is rejected at the 0.01 level with $\rho_0 = 0.9$ and at the 0.10 level for $\rho_0 = 0.8$, but H_0 is not rejected for $\rho_0 = 0.7$ in that subperiod. The results for the equally weighted index are similar, the primary exceptions being that H_0 with $\rho_0 = 0.7$ is rejected only in the second subperiod and H_0 is not rejected at all in the first subperiod. In general, these results suggest that if the correlation between either of these proxies and the market portfolio exceeds 0.9, or even a lower value, then the CAPM is rejected.

4.2 A test based on the power function of Ross's statistic

As described in section 3, Ross's test statistic is distributed central F when the tested portfolio is the *ex ante* tangent portfolio of the observed universe. When the tested portfolio is not the tangent portfolio, the same test statistic is distributed, conditional on $\hat{S}(\alpha)$, as noncentral F, with noncentrality parameter

$$\lambda = \frac{T}{1 + \hat{S}(\alpha)^2} [S(\gamma)^2 - S(\alpha)^2], \tag{18}$$

as shown by Gibbons, Ross, and Shanken (1989) (see also MacKinlay, 1987). This result is useful for understanding the power function of Ross's test of tangency against various alternatives, but, as Shanken (1987) demonstrates in a slightly different fashion, the same result can be used to test the hypothesis $\rho(\alpha, \gamma) \geqslant \rho_0$.

Using proposition 1, we can rewrite (18) as

$$\lambda = \frac{T}{1 + \hat{S}(\alpha)^2} S(\gamma)^2 [1 - \rho^2(\alpha, \gamma)]. \tag{19}$$

In addition to T and $\hat{S}(\alpha)$, which are known to the researcher, the noncentrality parameter depends on the unknown parameters $\rho(\alpha, \gamma)$ and $|S(\gamma)|$ (the maximum absolute *ex ante* Sharpe measure of the observed universe). Given a value of $|S(\gamma)|$, however, a test of H_0 is straightforward. Note that the noncentrality parameter λ is decreasing in $\rho(\alpha, \gamma)$, so that a test of the hypothesis $\rho(\alpha, \gamma) \geqslant \rho_0$ can be based on the noncentral F distribution with λ evaluated at $\rho(\alpha, \gamma) = \rho_0$. The (exact) significance level of this test gives an upper bound for the significance level of a test of H_0, since H_0 implies that $\rho(\alpha, \gamma) \geqslant \rho_0$, given corollary 1. The significance levels for both tests are identical if the global and observed universes coincide ($\gamma^\star = \gamma$).

Table 13.5 displays results of the above test for values of ρ_0 equal to 0.9, 0.8, and 0.7, using the same subperiods and weekly return data as in tables

Table 13.5 Test of H_0: $\rho(\alpha, \gamma^\star) \geqslant \rho_0$, conditional on the maximum absolute Sharpe measure $|S(\gamma)|$[a]

	Upper bounds on the p values for the test of H_0					
	Proxy α: VW[b]			*Proxy α: EW*[b]		
$S(\gamma)$	$\rho_0 = 0.9$	$\rho_0 = 0.8$	$\rho_0 = 0.7$	$\rho_0 = 0.9$	$\rho_0 = 0.8$	$\rho_0 = 0.7$
Jan 2, 1963, to Jun 25, 1969 ($T = 324$, $\lvert\hat{S}(\hat{\gamma})\rvert = 0.445$)[c]						
0.3	0.000	0.001	0.004	0.001	0.006	0.022
0.4	0.001	0.011	0.056	0.005	0.053	0.181
0.5	0.004	0.087	0.328	0.026	0.246	0.586
0.6	0.025	0.345	0.763	0.099	0.604	0.914
0.7	0.100	0.719	0.970	0.272	0.890	0.994
0.8	0.281	0.941	0.999	0.533	0.986	0.999
Jul 2, 1969, to Oct 1, 1975 ($T = 324$, $\lvert\hat{S}(\hat{\gamma})\rvert = 0.681$)						
0.3	0.000	0.000	0.000	0.000	0.000	0.000
0.4	0.000	0.000	0.000	0.000	0.000	0.000
0.5	0.000	0.000	0.000	0.000	0.000	0.000
0.6	0.000	0.000	0.000	0.000	0.000	0.000
0.7	0.000	0.000	0.014	0.000	0.000	0.014
0.8	0.000	0.006	0.143	0.000	0.006	0.140
Oct 8, 1975, to Dec 23, 1981 ($T = 324$, $\lvert\hat{S}(\hat{\gamma})\rvert = 0.608$)						
0.3	0.000	0.000	0.000	0.000	0.000	0.000
0.4	0.000	0.000	0.000	0.000	0.000	0.000
0.5	0.000	0.000	0.000	0.000	0.000	0.002
0.6	0.000	0.001	0.015	0.000	0.002	0.041
0.7	0.000	0.011	0.151	0.000	0.031	0.272
0.8	0.000	0.088	0.546	0.001	0.178	0.703

[a] The null hypothesis H_0 states that the proxy portfolio α has an *ex ante* correlation of at least ρ_0 with the Sharpe–Lintner tangent portfolio of the global universe $\gamma^\star$. $|S(\gamma)|$ is the maximum absolute *ex ante* Sharpe measure of the observed universe of assets. The tests are based on weekly returns. The set of 12 risky assets consists of ten value-weighted portfolios based on market-value deciles at the end of the previous year, the value-weighted NYSE–AMEX portfolio, and the equally weighted NYSE–AMEX portfolio.

[b] VW, value-weighted NYSE–AMEX portfolio; EW, equally weighted NYSE–AMEX portfolio.

[c] $|\hat{S}(\hat{\gamma})|$ is the sample's maximum absolute Sharpe measure.

13.3 and 13.4. We show results for values of the maximum absolute Sharpe measure of the observed universe $|S(\gamma)|$ ranging from 0.3 to 0.8. The *ex post* values of $|\hat{S}(\hat{\gamma})|$, which are also shown, range from 0.445 to 0.681. The noncentrality parameter λ, and thus the p value as well, increases with $|S(\gamma)|$, and the increases in the p values can be large in table 13.5 as $|S(\gamma)|$ increases to 0.7 and 0.8. Such apparent sensitivity to the larger values of $|S(\gamma)|$ suggests caution in interpreting the results. Nevertheless, for values of $|S(\gamma)|$ near or slightly larger than the *ex post* values, the inferences provided by this method are similar to those obtained in table 13.4.

5 Summary and Conclusions

This paper presents a framework for investigating the mean–variance efficiency of an unobservable portfolio based on its correlation with an observable proxy portfolio. We first analyze some useful mean–variance relations based on the correlation between a given proxy portfolio and other portfolios in both the observed and global universes. We then develop a sensitivity analysis that provides the highest sample correlation between the proxy and a portfolio that reverses the inference of a test of Sharpe–Lintner tangency. Extending that analysis, we formally test whether an observable proxy is *ex ante* highly correlated with the *ex ante* tangent portfolio.

We conclude that the correlation between the tangent portfolio and the market proxy is sensitive to how the efficient set is constructed, both *ex ante* and in the sample. In his critique of tests of the CAPM, Roll (1977) shows that the sample inefficient market proxy used by Black, Jensen, and Scholes (1972) is correlated 0.9 with the estimated Sharpe–Lintner tangent portfolio. He concludes that inferences about the CAPM can be reversed easily with an alternative market proxy whose return is highly correlated with the return on the original proxy. Starting with the same minimum variance boundary constructed by Roll, we show that the correlation between the sample tangent portfolio and the proxy of Black, Jensen, and Scholes decreases as additional assets are added to the observed universe. For example, the correlation drops to 0.48 when the universe consists of 16 portfolios of stocks and bonds. The decline in correlation is easily understood when it is realized that the correlation between the proxy and the tangent is the ratio of the Sharpe measures of the two portfolios.

The relation between correlations and Sharpe measures also implies that the mean–variance efficiency of a "true" benchmark portfolio, possibly containing all assets, is rejected if the efficiency of a particular alternative benchmark portfolio in an observed universe consisting of a subset of assets is rejected. The relevant alternative benchmark in the observed universe is the portfolio from the observed universe that is most highly correlated with the true benchmark.

In a finite sample we analyze the sensitivity of inferences using a likelihood ratio test of Sharpe–Lintner tangency. Ross (1983) demonstrates that the test statistic has a known finite sample distribution, and he derives a representation of the test statistic in mean–variance space. Combining Ross's geometric representation with the mean–variance analysis described in section 2 (and derived in Kandel and Stambaugh (1986)), we obtain the highest sample correlation between the proxy and a portfolio that reverses the inference about the proxy's tangency.

When monthly data over long periods (26–52 years) are used to test the tangency of the equally weighted or value-weighted NYSE portfolio, there are some cases where no rejection region exists at standard test sizes and other cases where the correlation that reverses the inference about the tangency of the NYSE portfolio is quite high. When weekly data over shorter periods (about 6 years) are used, the tangency of both the equally weighted and the value-weighted NYSE–AMEX portfolios is rejected. The maximum sample correlation between the NYSE–AMEX proxy and a portfolio inferred to be tangent at the 0.05 level ranges from 0.76 to 0.48 for the value-weighted portfolio and from 0.90 to 0.46 for the equally weighted portfolio.

We extend the preceding sensitivity analysis to test whether a given observable proxy portfolio is correlated at least ρ_0 with the *ex ante* tangent portfolio of the global universe. We apply the test to weekly returns data for common stocks, with both the equally weighted and the value-weighted NYSE–AMEX indexes as the observable proxies. The null hypothesis is in fact a joint hypothesis that the unobservable benchmark portfolio is (a) the *ex ante* tangent portfolio and (b) highly correlated (at least ρ_0) with the NYSE–AMEX index. This hypothesis is almost always rejected for ρ_0 equal to 0.9 and is often rejected for ρ_0 equal to 0.8 and even 0.7.

Notes

1 The CAPM is due to Sharpe (1964), Linter (1965), and Black (1972); the consumption-based intertemporal model is due to Breeden (1979); the arbitrage pricing theory is due to Ross (1976). Benchmark portfolio efficiency is discussed by Fama (1976), Roll (1977), and Ross (1977) for the CAPM, by Breeden (1979) for the consumption model, and by Chamberlain (1983), Grinblatt and Titman (1987), and Huberman, Kandel, and Stambaugh (1987) for the arbitrage pricing theory.

2 We assume throughout that such a portfolio exists for both the population and the sample, which is equivalent to assuming that the riskless return is less than the mean return on the portfolio of risky assets having the smallest variance.

3 See also Jensen (1969) and Long (1977) for related results.
4 The ten size-ranked portfolios exclude firms for which market values cannot be computed at the end of the previous calendar year. Thus the equally weighted NYSE index, which includes all stocks on the Exchange in any month, is not a redundant asset here.
5 The first two series are from Ibbotson and Sinquefield (1982); the last two are from Ibbotson (1979).
6 We say "many" rather than "any" because, as Ehrbar (1984) notes, portfolios on the positively sloped boundary but below the point of tangency of a ray emanating from −100 percent are inefficient for investors not constrained to invest all their money.
7 We are grateful to John Long for suggesting this method of proof.
8 See also Gibbons, Ross, and Shanken (1989) and MacKinlay (1987).
9 We thank Richard Rogalski for providing the Treasury bill data.

References

Black, F. (1972) "Capital Market Equilibrium with Restricted Borrowing," *Journal of Business*, 45, 444–54.

Black, F., Jensen, M. C. and Scholes, M. (1972) "The Capital Asset Pricing Model: Some Empirical Tests." In *Studies in the Theory of Capital Markets*, ed. M. C. Jensen (New York: Praeger).

Breeden, D. T. (1979) "An Intertemporal Asset Pricing Model with Stochastic Consumption and Investment Opportunities," *Journal of Financial Economics*, 7, 265–96.

Chamberlain, G. (1983) "Funds, Factors, and Diversification in Arbitrage Pricing Models," *Econometrica*, 51, 1305–23.

Ehrbar, H. (1984) "Mean–Variance Efficiency if Investors Are Not Required to Invest All Their Money," *Working Paper*, University of Michigan.

Fama, E. F. (1976) *Foundations of Finance* (New York: Basic Books).

Gibbons, M. R. (1980) "Econometric Methods for Testing a Class of Financial Models: An Application of the Nonlinear Multivariate Regression Model," Ph.D. Dissertation, University of Chicago.

Gibbons, M. R. (1982) "Multivariate Tests of Financial Models: A New Approach," *Journal of Financial Economics*, 10, 3–27.

Gibbons, M. R., Ross, S. A. and Shanken, J. (1989) "A Test of the Efficiency of a Given Portfolio," *Econometrica*, 57: 5, September, 1121–52.

Green, R. C. (1986) "Positively Weighted Portfolios on the Minimum-Variance Frontier," *Journal of Finance*, 41, 1051–68.

Grinblatt, M. and Titman, S. (1987) "The Relation Between Mean–Variance Efficiency and Arbitrage Pricing," *Journal of Business*, 60, 97–112.

Huberman, G., Kandel, S. and Stambaugh, R. F. (1987) "Mimicking Portfolios and Exact Arbitrage Pricing," *Journal of Finance*, 42: 1, March, 1–9.

Ibbotson, R. G. (1979) "The Corporate Bond Market: Structure and Returns," *Working Paper*, University of Chicago.

Ibbotson, R. G. and Sinquefield, R. A. (1982) *Stocks, Bonds, Bills and Inflation: The Past and the Future* (Charlottesville, VA: Financial Analysts Research Foundation).

Jensen, M. C. (1969) "Risk, the Pricing of Capital Assets and the Evaluation of Investment Portfolios," *Journal of Business*, 42, 167–247.

Jobson, J. D. and Korkie, B. (1982) "Potential Performance and Tests of Portfolio Efficiency," *Journal of Financial Economics*, 10, 433–66.

Kandel, S. (1984a) "The Likelihood Ratio Test Statistic of Mean–Variance Efficiency Without a Riskless Asset," *Journal of Financial Economics*, 13, 575–92.
Kandel, S. (1984b) "On the Exclusion of Assets from Tests of the Mean–Variance Efficiency of the Market Portfolio," *Journal of Finance*, 39, 63–75.
Kandel, S. and Stambaugh, R. F. (1986) "Correlation and Mean–Variance Analysis," *Working Paper*, University of Chicago.
Kendall, M. and Stuart, A. (1977) *The Advanced Theory of Statistics*, vol. 1 (New York: Macmillan).
Lintner, J. (1965) "The Valuation of Risk Assets and the Selection of Risky Investments in Stock Portfolios and Capital Budgets," *Review of Economics and Statistics*, 47, 13–27.
Long, J. B., Jr (1977) "Efficient Portfolio Choice with Differential Taxation of Dividends and Capital Gains," *Journal of Financial Economics*, 5, 25–53.
MacKinlay, A. C. (1987) "On Multivariate Tests of the CAPM," *Journal of Financial Economics*, 18, 341–71.
Roll, R. (1977) "A Critique of the Asset Pricing Theory's Tests. Part I: On Past and Potential Testability of the Theory," *Journal of Financial Economics*, 4, 129–76.
Roll, R. (1979) "Testing a Portfolio for *ex ante* Mean/Variance Efficiency," *TIMS Studies in the Management Sciences*, 11, 135–49.
Roll, R. (1980) "Orthogonal Portfolios," *Journal of Financial and Quantitative Analysis*, 15, 1005–23.
Ross, S. A. (1976) "The Arbitrage Theory of Capital Asset Pricing," *Journal of Economic Theory*, 13, 341–60.
Ross, S. A. (1977) "The Capital Asset Pricing Model (CAPM), Short Sale Restrictions and Related Issues," *Journal of Finance*, 32, 177–83.
Ross, S. A. (1983) "A Test of the Efficiency of a Given Portfolio," *Working Paper*, Yale University.
Shanken, J. (1984) "Equilibrium, Factors, and Arbitrage Pricing," *Working Paper*, University of California at Berkeley.
Shanken, J. (1985) "Multivariate Tests of the Zero-Beta CAPM," *Journal of Financial Economics*, 14, 327–48.
Shanken, J. (1986) "On the Exclusion of Assets from Tests of the Mean Variance Efficiency of the Market Portfolio: An Extension," *Journal of Finance*, 41, 331–7.
Shanken, J. (1987) "Mulitivariate Proxies and Asset Pricing Relations: Living with the Roll Critique," *Journal of Financial Economics*, 18, 91–110.
Sharpe, W. F. (1964) "Capital Asset Prices: A Theory of Market Equilibrium under Conditions of Risk," *Journal of Finance*, 19, 425–42.
Stambaugh, R. F. (1981) "Missing Assets, Measuring the Market, and Testing the Capital Asset Pricing Model," Ph.D. Dissertation, University of Chicago.
Stambaugh, R. F. (1982) "On the Exclusion of Assets from Tests of the Two-Parameter Model: A Sensitivity Analysis," *Journal of Financial Economics*, 10, 273–68.

Chapter 14

Meir Statman

Background and Comments

How many stocks make a diversified portfolio? I am one of the embarrassed textbook writers who have implied that, say, 15 stocks are enough (Brealey and Myers, 1988, p. 132). As Meir Statman shows, 30 or 40 are really needed. His paper makes the lack of diversification by many individual investors all the more puzzling.

This paper is one of several written by Statman applying concepts from psychology to finance. Most of finance theory assumes standards of rationality which are not observed in experiments in individual decision making. Recent work in behavioral decision theory attempts to describe how individuals really behave when faced with complex decisions and uncertain outcomes. Statman and his colleague, Hersh Shefrin, were the first to apply these ideas in finance; their work is perhaps controversial, but always interesting. Their paper on "Explaining Investor Preference for Cash Dividends" (Statman and Shefrin, 1984) is an excellent example. I also recommend Merton Miller's discussion of "Behavioral Rationality in Finance: The Case of Dividends" (Miller, 1986) which appeared in a special issue of *The Journal of Business* addressing the behavioral foundations of economic and financial theory.

References

Brealey, R. A. and Myers, S. C. (1988) *Principles of Corporate Finance*, 3rd edn (New York: McGraw-Hill).

Miller, M. (1986) "Behavioral Rationality in Finance: The Case of Dividends," *Journal of Business*, 59: 2, October, S451–68.

Statman, M. and Shefrin, H. (1984) "Explaining Investor Preference for Cash Dividends," *Journal of Financial Economics*, 13, June, 253–82.

Author's Introduction

Investors lacking inside information know that insiders trade in the stock market. Why do they trade? How do investors structure their portfolios? And why do they prefer particular positions such as covered call options? These are some of the questions that I tried to answer in work supported by the Batterymarch Fellowship. Much of this work was done in collaboration with Hersh Shefrin.

Standard financial theory is built on the assumption of "rational man" who attempts to maximize expected utility as he chooses among alternatives. However, standard finance offers no compelling answers to the preceding questions and to many more. We think that knowledge about human behavior, gained by psychologists, can augment standard financial theory and provide a clearer picture of individual and market behavior. We focus on errors in cognition, regret, and framing of choices, and offer tests which might support or refute our hypotheses.

Portfolio construction provides one example. Surveys found that investors do not make full use of diversification. However, if investors do not construct their portfolios by Markowitz's prescription, how do they construct them? Hersh Shefrin and I present a model of portfolio construction in "A Mental Accounting-Based Portfolio Theory." A sketch of that model appears in "How Many Stocks Make a Diversified Portfolio?" Investors in our model frame their portfolios as collections of mental accounts. They might be risk averse in the retirement mental account while they are risk seeking in the mental account that they hope will move them into the upper class. However, unlike Markowitz's model, investors in our model do not integrate mental accounts into an overall portfolio, and so they ignore covariances that underlie the risk reduction benefits of diversification.

The use of the Bearish Sentiment Index to forecast the direction of the stock market provides another example. The Index is the ratio of investment advisers who are bearish to advisers who are bullish or bearish. In "How Useful Is the Sentiment Index?" Michael Solt and I show that the index has been useless as a forecasting tool; it provided as many bad forecasts as good ones. We suggest that investors fail to see that the Index is no better than a coin toss because they are subject to the cognitive error of "illusion of validity." Specifically, they place too much weight on evidence favoring the Index and neglect evidence against it. In "A Behavioral Finance Solution to the Noise Trader Puzzle," Hersh Shefrin and I present models where noise traders, who are subject to a number of cognitive errors, interact in a market place with information traders who are free from cognitive errors. We show that such interaction can lead to a high volume of trading and high volatility.

While not entirely consistent, the weight of the evidence still supports the hypothesis that, on average, investment advisers are not able to beat the market. So why do investors hire them? In "Equilibrium Implications of Regret Theory: Applications to Pricing Regularities, Investment Advisers and Money Management," Hersh Shefrin and I present a model where investors hire investment advisers to bear the regret that comes with investment choices that turn out badly. We also suggest that aversion to regret might explain the existence of return regularities such as those associated with small firms and companies with low price-to-earnings ratios.

These are only a few of the many areas where insights from psychology can be used to build on the foundation of standard finance; I continue my work.

Bibliographical Listing

"Applying Behavioral Finance to the Use of Options" (with Hersh Shefrin), *Working Paper*, Santa Clara University, 1990.

"Equilibrium Implications of Regret Theory: Applications to Pricing Regularities, Investment Advisers and Money Management" (with Hersh Shefrin), *Working Paper*, Santa Clara University, 1990.

"Introducing Prospect Theory Preferences into General Equilibrium: Implications for CAPM and Portfolio Insurance" (with Hersh Shefrin), *Working Paper*, Santa Clara University, 1990.

"A Mental Accounting-Based Portfolio Theory" (with Hersh Shefrin), *Working Paper*, Santa Clara University, 1990.

"Noise Trading and Efficiency in Behavioral Finance" (with Hersh Shefrin), *Working Paper*, Santa Clara University, 1990.

"Project Termination Announcements and the Market Value of the Firm" (with James F. Sepe), *Financial Management*, 18: 4, Winter 1989, 74–81.

"Event Studies and Model Misspecification: Another Look at the Benefits to Outsiders from Public Information about Insider Trading" (with Ivan E. Brick and Daniel G. Weaver), *Journal of Business Finance and Accounting*, 16: 3, Summer 1989, 399–424.

"Good Companies, Bad Stocks" (with Michael E. Solt), *Journal of Portfolio Management*, 15: 4, Summer 1989, 39–44.

"How Useful is the Sentiment Index?" (with Michael E. Solt), *Financial Analysts Journal*, 44: 5, September–October 1988, 45–55.

"Investor Psychology and Market Inefficiencies." In *Equity Markets and Valuation Methods*, ed. Katrina F. Sherrerd (Charlottesville, VA: Institute of Chartered Financial Analysts, 1988), pp. 29–33.

"Applying Behavioral Finance to Capital Budgeting: Project Terminations" (with David Caldwell), *Financial Management*, 16: 4, Winter 1987, 7–15.

"Bonds Versus Stocks: Another Look" (with Neal Ushman), *Journal of Portfolio Management*, 13: 2, Winter 1987, 33–8.

"The Benefits of Insured Stocks for Corporate Cash Management" (with Keith Brown). In *Advances in Futures and Options Research*, vol. 2, ed. Frank J. Fabozzi (Greenwich, CT: JAI Press, 1987), pp. 243–61.

"How Not to Make Money in the Stock Market" (with Hersh Shefrin), *Psychology Today*, 20: 2, February 1986, 52–7.

How Many Stocks Make a Diversified Portfolio?

MEIR STATMAN

1 Introduction

How many stocks make a diversified portfolio? Evans and Archer [9] concluded that approximately ten stocks will do. They stated that their results "raise doubts concerning the economic justification of increasing portfolio sizes beyond 10 or so securities" (p. 767). Evans and Archer's conclusion has been widely adopted and cited in many current textbooks, but is it correct? No. The primary purpose of this paper is to show that no less than 30 stocks are needed for a well-diversifed portfolio. A secondary purpose is to compare this finding with the levels of diversification observed in studies of individual investors' portfolios.

2 Portfolios and Risk

The risk of a stock portfolio depends on the proportions of the individual stocks, their variances, and their covariances. A change in any of these variables will change the risk of the portfolio. Still, it is generally true that when stocks are randomly selected and combined in equal proportions into a portfolio, the risk of a portfolio declines as the number of different stocks in it increases. Evans and Archer observed that the risk reduction effect diminishes rapidly as the number of stocks increases. They concluded that the economic benefits of diversification are virtually exhausted when a portfolio contains ten or so stocks.

Evans and Archer's conclusion has been cited in many textbooks. For example, Francis ([10], p. 749) wrote:

[P]ortfolio managers should not become overzealous and spread their assets over

Reproduced from *Journal of Financial and Quantitative Analysis*, 22: 3, September 1987, 353–63.

The author thanks Melanie Austin, Ivan Brick, Wayne Lee, and especially an anonymous referee for helpful comments, but retains full responsibility for all errors.

too many assets. If 10 or 15 different assets are selected for the portfolio, the maximum benefits from naive diversification most likely have been attained. Further spreading of the portfolio's assets is *superfluous diversification* and should be avoided. (Emphasis in the original.)

Stevenson and Jennings ([22], pp. 532–3) wrote:

The results of the Evans and Archer study indicate that a portfolio of approximately eight to sixteen randomly-selected stocks will closely resemble the market portfolio in terms of fluctuations in the rate of return. Other studies have shown similar results and an unusual consistency using different time periods, different groups of stocks, and different research techniques. Consequently, while the CAP model requires the purchase of the market portfolio, essentially the same result can be achieved from a practical standpoint with a much smaller portfolio.

Gup ([11], pp. 363–4) wrote:

Proper diversification does not require investing in a large number of different industries or securities .... [T]he diversifiable risk is reduced as the number of stocks increases from one to about eight or nine .... [W]hen the number of securities is increased to about nine, almost all of the diversifiable risk is eliminated.

Reilly ([18], p. 101) wrote:

In terms of overdiversification, several studies have shown that it is possible to derive most of the benefits of diversification with a portfolio consisting of from 12 to 18 stocks. To be adequately diversified does *not* require 200 stocks in a portfolio. (Emphasis in the original.)

Early studies, including that by Evans and Archer, reached their conclusions by simulating the relationship between risk and the number of stocks. Elton and Gruber [7] investigated this relationship further and provided an analytical solution. [1] Elton and Gruber's results, presented in table 14.1, imply that 51 percent of a portfolio standard deviation is eliminated as diversification increases from one to ten securities. Adding ten more securities eliminates an additional 5 percent of the standard deviation. Increasing the number of securities to 30 eliminates only an additional 2 percent of the standard deviation.

3 The Costs and Benefits of Diversification

The principle that marginal costs should be compared with marginal benefits in determining the optimal levels of production or consumption is

Table 14.1 Expected standard deviations of annual portfolio returns

No. of stocks in portfolio	*Expected standard deviation of annual portfolio returns*	*Ratio of portfolio standard deviation to standard deviation of a single stock*
1	49.236	1.00
2	37.358	0.76
4	29.687	0.60
6	26.643	0.54
8	24.983	0.51
10	23.932	0.49
12	23.204	0.47
14	22.670	0.46
16	22.261	0.45
18	21.939	0.45
20	21.677	0.44
25	21.196	0.43
30	20.870	0.42
35	20.634	0.42
40	20.456	0.42
45	20.316	0.41
50	20.203	0.41
75	19.860	0.40
100	19.686	0.40
200	19.423	0.39
300	19.336	0.39
400	19.292	0.39
450	19.277	0.39
500	19.265	0.39
600	19.247	0.39
700	19.233	0.39
800	19.224	0.39
900	19.217	0.39
1000	19.211	0.39
Infinity	19.158	0.39

Portfolios are equally weighted. Elton and Gruber reported variances of weekly returns. We have converted these to standard deviations of annual returns.

Source: Elton and Gruber ([8], p. 35)

fundamental to economic theory. The fact that "almost all" of the portfolio's unsystematic risk is eliminated when it contains ten or 100 stocks is meaningless when presented by itself.

Diversification should be increased as long as the marginal benefits exceed the marginal costs. The benefits of diversification are in risk reduction. The costs are transaction costs. The usual argument for limited diversification is that marginal costs increase faster than marginal benefits as diversification increases. For example, Mayshar [17] developed a model that shows that it is optimal to limit diversification in the presence of transaction costs.

Comparison of benefits and costs requires a common measure. We use returns as our measure. The risk reduction benefits of diversification, in units of expected return, can be determined through a simple comparison of any two portfolios. The analysis is similar to that by Blume and Friend ([5], pp. 52–8).

We use a 500 stock portfolio as our benchmark portfolio and compare other less diversified portfolios with it. We use a 500 stock portfolio as an example of an attainable fairly diversified portfolio, but we claim neither that a 500 stock portfolio is a proxy for the market portfolio nor that we cannot obtain better diversified portfolios.

The 500 stock portfolio can be levered, through borrowing or lending, to form portfolios $P(n)$ with combinations of expected returns and standard deviations according to the equation

$$E(R_{P(n)}) = (R_{\mathrm{F}} + \alpha) + \left[\frac{E(R_{P(500)}) - (R_{\mathrm{F}} + \alpha)}{\sigma_{P(500)}}\right]\sigma_{P(n)}, \tag{1}$$

where $E(R_{P(n)})$ is the expected return of portfolio $P(n)$, R_{F} is the risk-free rate, α is the excess of the borrowing rate over the lending or risk-free rate for a borrowing investor, and is zero for a lending investor, $E(R_{P(500)})$ is the expected return of the 500 stock portfolio, $\sigma_{P(n)}$ is the standard deviation of portfolio $P(n)$, and $\sigma_{P(500)}$ is the standard deviation of the 500 stock portfolio.

Equation (1) defines what we shall call the 500 stock line and all portfolios $P(n)$ lie on it (figure 14.1). The 500 stock line is composed of two segments. The first, from R_{F} to $P(500)$, represents the portfolio combinations for a lending investor. The lending rate is the risk-free rate R_{F}. The second, from $P(500)$ through $P(10)$, represents the portfolio combination for a borrowing investor. The borrowing rate is $R_{\mathrm{F}} + \alpha$, where α is the excess of the borrowing rate over the lending rate.

Markowitz [16] developed a formula for the expected variance of a portfolio on n securities. That formula has been used by Elton and Gruber. We assume, as in Elton and Gruber, that an investor draws randomly from all stocks to form portfolios that differ in the number of stocks but have identical expected returns. We use the findings of Ibbotson Associates [12] about the risk premium on a particular 500 stock portfolio, Standard & Poor's (S&P) 500 Index. Note that the S&P 500 Index is one attainable 500 stock portfolio. While Elton and Gruber use equally weighted portfolios, the S&P 500 Index is value weighted. We assume, for now, that the cost

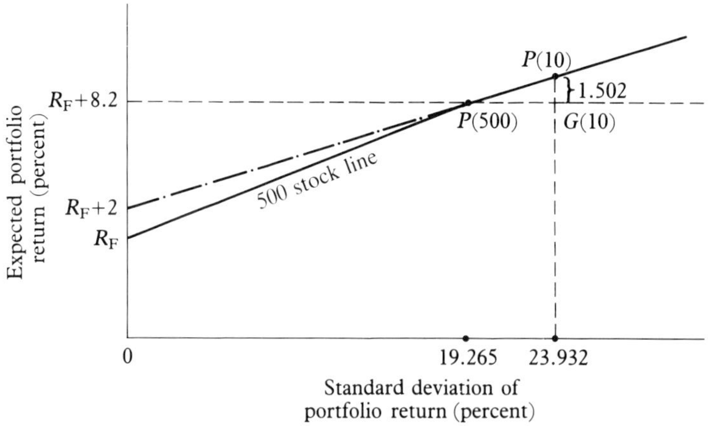

Figure 14.1 An expected return 1.502 percent higher than that of a 500 stock portfolio $P(500)$ is necessary to offset the higher risk, due to limited diversification, of the ten stock portfolio $G(10)$. A portfolio $P(10)$ can be constructed by leveraging $P(500)$ where the expected return of $P(10)$ is 1.502 percent higher than that of $G(10)$, while the two have identical risks. Data on standard deviations of portfolio returns are from table 14.1. An estimate of 2 percent was used for α, the excess of the borrowing rate over the lending rate. An estimate of 8.2 percent was used for the risk premium.

of maintaining an equally weighted 500 stock portfolio is identical with the cost of maintaining a value-weighted 500 stock portfolio.

We use an Ibbotson Associates ([12], p. 42) estimate of the risk premium $E(R_{P(500)}) - R_F$ on the 500 stock portfolio. The arithmetic mean of the risk premium over the period 1926–84 is 8.2 percent per year. We use 2.0 percent per year as an estimate of α, the excess of the borrowing rate over the risk-free or lending rate. The estimate is based on a comparison between the Treasury bill rate, a proxy for the lending rate, and the call money rate. The call money rate is the rate charged on loans to brokers on stock exchange collateral (that is, margin loans), and it provides a starting point for the estimate of the borrowing rate. The call money rate is less than 2 percent higher than the Treasury bill rate (table 14.2). However, brokers typically charge their borrowing customers somewhat more than the call money rate. An estimate of 2 percent for α seems reasonable.

To calculate the risk reduction benefits of diversification, compare, for example, a portfolio $G(10)$ of ten randomly selected stocks with a portfolio $P(10)$ that lies on the 500 stock line and has a standard deviation identical with that of portfolio $G(10)$. We know from Elton and Gruber (table 14.1) that portfolio $G(10)$ has an expected standard deviation $\sigma_{G(10)}$ of 23.932 percent, and that the expected standard deviation $\sigma_{P(500)}$ of the 500 stock

Table 14.2 Difference between the call money rate and the Treasury bill rate

Date	*1 Call money rate (%)*	*2 Treasury bill rate (%)*		*Difference, column 1 minus column 2*
Jan 15, 1985	9.25	7.74		1.50
Feb 15, 1985	9.38	8.20		1.18
Mar 15, 1985	9.75	8.48		1.27
Apr 15, 1985	9.50	8.14		1.36
May 15, 1985	9.00	7.69		1.31
Jun 14, 1985	8.63	7.21		1.42
Jul 15, 1985	8.63	6.92		1.71
Aug 15, 1985	9.25	7.14		2.11
Sep 15, 1985	8.75	7.22		1.53
Oct 17, 1985	8.88	7.20		1.68
Nov 15, 1985	9.13	7.21		1.92
Dec 16, 1985	9.00	7.05		1.95
			Mean	1.58

Data are from the money rate tables of the *Wall Street Journal* on the specified dates. We used data from the *Wall Street Journal* for the 15th of each month during 1985, or a date close to the 15th if data for the 15th were not available. The call money rate is the mean of the range of rates provided. The Treasury bill rate is the rate for the most recent auction of 13 week bills.

portfolio is 19.265 percent. The standard deviation $\sigma_{G(10)}$ exceeds $\sigma_{P(500)}$ as portfolio $G(10)$ contains more diversifiable risk than portfolio $P(500)$.

If stocks are chosen randomly, every stock and every portfolio has an expected return of $R_F + 8.2$ percent, composed of the risk-free rate and an 8.2 percent risk premium. Thus the expected returns of both the ten stock portfolio $G(10)$ and the 500 stock portfolio $P(500)$ are equal to $R_F + 8.2$ percent.

How much would a portfolio $P(10)$ that levers the 500 stock portfolio $P(500)$ be expected to yield if $P(500)$ were levered so that the standard deviation of the returns on portfolio $P(10)$ is 23.932 percent? Using equation (1) we find that

$$E(R_{P(10)}) = (R_F + 2) + \left[\frac{(R_F + 8.2) - (R_F + 2)}{19.265}\right] 23.932 = R_F + 9.702.$$

An investor obtains the expected return of $R_F + 9.702$ percent on portfolio $P(10)$ by borrowing 0.242 of his or her wealth and investing 1.242 of his or her wealth in the 500 stock portfolio (see figure 14.1).

The return differential between the levered 500 stock portfolio $P(10)$ and the ten stock portfolio $G(10)$ is

$$E(R_{P(10)}) - E(R_{G(10)}) = (R_F + 9.702) - (R_F + 8.2) = 1.502.$$

The 1.502 percent differential in the expected return between the levered 500 stock portfolio $P(10)$ and the ten stock portfolio $G(10)$ can be interpreted as the benefit that an investor derives from increasing the number of stocks in the portfolio from ten to 500. In general, the benefit from increasing the number of stocks in a portfolio from n to 500 is

$$E(R_{P(n)}) - E(R_{G(n)}) = \left(\frac{\sigma_{P(n)}}{\sigma_{P(500)}} - 1\right)[E(R_{G(n)}) - (R_F + \alpha)]. \tag{2}$$

For the ten stock portfolio discussed earlier we have

$$E(R_{P(10)}) - E(R_{G(10)}) = \left(\frac{23.932}{19.265} - 1\right)[(R_F + 8.2) - (R_F + 2)] = 1.502.$$

Benefits, in terms of expected returns, of increasing the number of stocks in various portfolios to 500 are presented in table 14.3.

We turn now from the measurement of the benefits of diversification to the measurement of its costs. Assume for now that no costs are incurred in buying, selling, and holding portfolios $G(n)$ composed of less than 500 stocks. A leveraged 500 stock portfolio $P(n)$ is preferable to a portfolio $G(n)$ if the costs of $P(n)$ are lower than the benefits that come with increased diversification.

A 500 stock portfolio is available to all investors in the form of the Vanguard Index Trust, a no-load index fund that mimics the S&P 500 Index. The fund provides a return that is lower than that of the S&P 500

Table 14.3 Difference between the expected annual return of a portfolio of n stocks $G(n)$ and the expected annual return of a portfolio $p(n)$ that levers a 500 stock portfolio such that standard deviations of returns of portfolios $G(n)$ and $P(n)$ are equal[a]

No. n of stocks in portfolio	*Return differences for borrowing and lending investors*	
	Borrowing investor	*Lending investor*
10	1.502	1.986
20	0.776	1.027
30	0.517	0.683
40	0.383	0.507
50	0.302	0.399
100	0.135	0.179

[a]The figures in this table were calculated using equation (2) with data from table 14.1. The risk premium is estimated as 8.2 percent, the arithmetic mean risk premium. Risk premium data are from Ibbotson Associates ([12], p. 42). The value of the excess α of the borrowing rate over the lending rate was estimated as 2 percent.

Table 14.4 Comparison of returns to investors in the S&P 500 Index and Vanguard Index Trust, 1979–1984

Year	*1* *Rate of return on S&P 500 Index (%)*	*2* *Rate of return on Vanguard Index Trust (%)*		*Difference, column 1 minus column 2*
1979	18.44	18.04		0.40
1980	32.42	31.92		0.50
1981	−4.91	−5.21		0.30
1982	21.41	20.98		0.43
1983	22.51	21.29		1.22
1984	6.27	6.21		0.06
			Mean	0.49

Source: Vanguard Index Trust returns data are from Wiesenberger Financial Services [23]; S&P 500 Index returns data are from Ibbotson Associates [12]

Index because investors pay transaction costs and administrative expenses. The mean annual return differential for the years 1979–84 is 0.49 percent (table 14.4). Of course, 0.49 is less than 1.502, and so the Vanguard portfolio dominates a ten stock portfolio even when the cost of buying, selling, and holding these ten securities is zero.

Note that the Vanguard Index Trust serves only as an example of an attainable, well-diversified, and unmanaged mutual fund. Similar funds with various combinations of securities would be offered, if investors demand them.

A comparison of the 0.49 percent figure with the figures in table 14.3 makes it clear that the Vanguard Index Trust dominates a 30 stock portfolio $G(30)$ for a borrowing investor and a 40 stock portfolio $G(40)$ for a lending investor, even if we assume that no costs exist for buying, selling, and holding stocks in portfolios $G(30)$ and $G(40)$ while the Vanguard Index Trust costs are paid.

The figures quoted above were obtained under a set of particular assumptions, and they may increase or decrease as the assumptions change. We shall consider some prominent cases here.

First is the issue of transaction costs. So far we have assumed that investors pay the costs of the Vanguard Index Trust, but they pay nothing for buying and selling and holding stocks of less diversified portfolios $G(n)$. This assumption leads to an underestimation of the advantage of the Vanguard Index Trust over portfolios $G(n)$. For example, consider the case where costs associated with portfolios $G(n)$ amount to 0.1 percent per year of the value of the portfolio. The effect of these costs on the relative positions of portfolios $G(n)$ and the Vanguard Index Trust is equal to the effect of reducing the Vanguard Index Trust annual costs by 0.1 percent, from 0.49 to 0.39. Such a change makes the Vanguard Index Trust superior to a portfolio of 35 stocks, rather than 30 stocks, for the case of a borrowing investor, and 50 stocks, rather than 40 stocks, for the case of a lending investor.

The estimation of annual costs associated with portfolios $G(n)$ is difficult because they depend on the interval between stock trades; costs are higher for those who trade frequently. However, the earlier example probably underestimates the advantages of the Vanguard Index Trust. The cost of a round trip stock trade is probably not lower than 1 percent, and the mean holding period of a stock is probably not much higher than 1 year ([20], p. 306).

Second, the reliability of the standard deviation estimate for returns of portfolios consisting of few stocks is low relative to that of portfolios of many stocks. Elton and Gruber ([7], table 8) reported that the standard deviation of the estimate of the standard deviation of the portfolio return is 1.8 percent for a portfolio of ten stocks, and 0.3 percent for a portfolio of 50 stocks, but it drops to virtually zero for a portfolio of 500 stocks. We do not know how to measure the loss that is due to the inherent unreliability of the estimate of the standard deviation of portfolio returns in portfolios of few stocks. However, it is another disadvantage of low levels of diversification.

The case for the Vanguard Index Trust may have been overstated for two reasons. First, investors may be able to choose superior stocks and use the returns on these stocks to compensate for the additional risk due to lack of diversification. Indeed, there is some evidence that investors are able to choose stocks that offer return advantages sufficient to eliminate some of the negative effects of transaction costs. For example, Schlarbaum, Lewellen, and Lease ([20], Table 14) found that individual investors had mean returns, after transaction costs, that were identical with the mean returns of mutual funds. However, Schlarbaum, Lewellen, and Lease adjusted only for the systematic risk of stocks in both individuals' portfolios and mutual funds. The lack of diversification in individuals' portfolios relative to that of mutual funds implies that individuals may do worse than mutual funds when proper consideration is given to both systematic and unsystematic risk.

Second, stocks in the Vanguard Index Trust are value weighted while the analysis here is based on equally weighted portfolios. It is possible that the cost of the Vanguard Index Trust underestimates the costs of an equally weighted 500 stock portfolio, since transaction costs per dollar investment are generally higher for small company stocks than for large company stocks.

4 Do Individuals Follow Markowitz's Prescription on Diversification?

The framework in which individuals construct portfolios by choosing combinations of expected return and risk, measured as the standard deviation of the return, is a crucial building block for much work in finance. Markowitz developed the prescriptive (normative) framework.

An important prediction of the capital asset pricing model (CAPM), a descriptive (positive) model based on Markowitz's idea, is that every investor would hold a portfolio of all securities available in the market (given efficient markets, perfectly divisible securities, and no transaction costs).

Evidence suggests, however, that the typical investor's stock portfolio contains only a small fraction of the available securities. Blume, Crockett, and Friend [3] found that, in 1971, 34.1 percent of investors in their sample held only one dividend-paying stock, 50 percent held no more than two stocks, and only 10.7 percent held more than ten stocks. A 1967 Federal Reserve Board Survey of Financial Characteristics of Consumers showed that the average number of stocks in a portfolio was 3.41 [4]. A survey of investors who held accounts with a major brokerage company revealed that the average number of stocks in a portfolio ranged from 9.4 to 12.1 depending on the demographic group [15].

Of course, the number of securities in the portfolio is not the sole determinant of the degree of diversification. Studies by Jacob [13] and others have shown that an investor can reduce unsystematic risk significantly with few securities if he or she chooses securities judiciously. However, there is no evidence that investors follow the suggested rules on optimal diversification with few securities. Blume and Friend ([5], p. 49) reported that the actual degree of diversification in 70 percent of the investors in their study *was lower* than suggested by the number of securities in the portfolios. Blume and Friend (p. 58) concluded that

> The empirical results show, however, that many investors, particularly those of limited means, do not hold well-diversified portfolios. The analysis of the returns realized by them confirms that these investors have exposed themselves to far greater risks than necessary.

Observing individuals' stock portfolios provides only limited information about the level of diversification in their overall portfolios. While we know that there are only a few stocks in the typical portfolio, it is possible that diversification is accomplished through bonds, real estate, and other assets. However, recent evidence by King and Leape [14] strongly suggests that limited diversification is observed even where assets other than stocks are included. Their study was based on a detailed survey of 6,010 US households conducted in 1978. The survey oversampled high income families and therefore provides a rich source of information on the composition of portfolios. One conclusion of King and Leape (pp. 33–4) was that

> the differences in portfolio composition across households cannot be fully explained within the framework of the conventional portfolio choice model. The households in our sample, though wealthy, own a surprisingly small number of assets and liabilities, and this lack of diversification was found to be important when estimating asset demand equations. Given that the mean net worth of the sample was almost a quarter of a million dollars in 1978, it is hard to imagine that transactions costs, as traditionally defined, played a decisive role in producing incomplete portfolios.

It seems that a descriptive theory of portfolio construction, based on Markowitz, does not hold. People forgo available opportunities for diversification, and transaction costs are not likely to provide a complete explanation for it.

5 Conclusion

We have shown that a well-diversified stock portfolio must include, at the very least, 30 stocks for a borrowing investor and 40 stocks for a lending investor. This conclusion contradicts earlier results, quoted in many current textbooks, that the benefits of diversification for stock portfolios are exhausted when the number of stocks reaches ten or 15. Moreover, observation of individuals' portfolios suggests that people do not hold portfolios that are well diversified.

Why do people forgo the benefits of diversification? Maybe investors are simply ignorant about the benefits of diversification. If ignorance is the problem, education may be the solution. However, existing evidence does not warrant a claim that investors should indeed be educated to increase diversification.

Alternative approaches to portfolio construction exist. One is the framework in which investors are concerned about the skewness of the return distribution as well as the mean and variance (e.g. [6]). The other is the "safety first" framework [19]. However, we are not sanguine about the ability of either of these two theories to provide an adequate description of the way portfolios are built because neither is consistent with the following two common observations.

First, people do not seem to treat their assets as parts in an integrated portfolio. For example, some people borrow at 15 percent interest to finance a car rather than "borrow" from the college education fund that they have set for their young children that pays only 10 percent interest. As Black [2] wrote, people "keep their money in separate pockets." Second, people display risk seeking and risk aversion that varies with the various "pockets." Many people seek risk by buying lottery tickets, while they are extremely risk averse with assets in retirement accounts. (For a discussion of these issues in the context of portfolio construction, see Shefrin and Statman [21].)

We have to know much more about investors' goals and preferences to develop a framework that describes how they form portfolios. Meanwhile, we should not rush to conclude that investors should be educated to hold fully diversified portfolios.

Note

1 Bird and Tippett [1] have shown that studies using the simulation methodology are deficient. In particular, simulation studies tend to exaggerate the rate of decline in portfolio risk as the number of stocks in the portfolio increases.

References

1 Bird, R. and Tippett, M. "Naive Diversification and Portfolio Risk: A Note," *Management Science*, 32, February 1986, 244–51.
2 Black, F. "The Future for Financial Services," *Working Paper*, Massachusetts Institute of Technology, October 1982.
3 Blume, M. E., Crockett, J. and Friend, I. "Stock Ownership in the United States: Characteristics and Trends," *Survey of Current Business*, 54, November 1974, 16–40.
4 Blume, M. E. and Friend, I. "The Asset Structure of Individual Portfolios and Some Implications for Utility Functions," *Journal of Finance*, 30, May 1975, 585–603.
5 Blume, M. E. and Friend, I. *The Changing Role of the Individual Investor: A Twentieth Century Fund Report* (New York: Wiley, 1978).
6 Conine, T. E. and Tamarkin, M. J. "On Diversification Given Asymmetry in Returns," *Journal of Finance*, 36, December 1981, 1143–55.
7 Elton, E. J. and Gruber, M. J. "Risk Reduction and Portfolio Size: An Analytical Solution," *Journal of Business*, 50, October 1977, 415–37.
8 Elton, E. J. and Gruber, M. J. *Modern Portfolio Theory and Investment Analysis*, 2nd edn (New York: Wiley, 1984).
9 Evans, J. L. and Archer, S. H. "Diversification and the Reduction of Dispersion: An Empirical Analysis," *Journal of Finance*, 23, December 1968, 761–7.
10 Francis, J. C. *Investments: Analysis and Management*, 4th edn (New York: McGraw-Hill, 1986).
11 Gup, B. E. *The Basics of Investing*, 2nd edn (New York: Wiley, 1983).

12 Ibbotson Associates, *Stocks, Bonds, Bills, and Inflation: 1985 Yearbook* (Chicago, IL: Ibbotson Associates, 1985).
13 Jacob, N. L. "A Limited-Diversification Portfolio Selection Model for the Small Investor," *Journal of Finance*, 29, June 1974, 837–57.
14 King, M. A. and Leape, J. I. "Wealth and Portfolio Composition: Theory and Evidence," *NBER Working Paper 1468*, National Bureau of Economic Research, Cambridge, MA, September 1984.
15 Lease, R. C., Lewellen, W. G. and Schlarbaum, G. G. "Market Segmentation: Evidence on the Individual Investor," *Financial Analysts Journal*, 32, September 1976, 53–60.
16 Markowitz, H. *Portfolio Selection: Efficient Diversification of Investments* (New York: Wiley, 1959).
17 Mayshar, J. "Transaction Cost in a Model of Capital Market Equilibrium," *Journal of Political Economy*, 87, August 1979, 673–700.
18 Reilly, F. K. *Investment Analysis and Portfolio Management*, 2nd edn (San Francisco, CA: Dryden, 1985).
19 Roy, A. D. "Safety-First and the Holding of Assets," *Econometrica*, 20, July 1952, 431–49.
20 Schlarbaum, G. G., Lewellen, W. G. and Lease, R. C. "Realized Returns on Common Stock Investments: The Experience of Individual Investors," *Journal of Business*, 51, April 1978, 299–325.
21 Shefrin, H. M. and Statman, M. "A Mental Accounting-Based Portfolio Theory," *Working Paper*, Santa Clara University, November 1985.
22 Stevenson, R. A. and Jennings, E. H. *Fundamentals of Investments*, 3rd edn (San Francisco, CA: West, 1984).
23 *Wiesenberger Investment Companies Service: Investment Companies 1985* (New York: Wiesenberger Financial Services, 1985).

Chapter 15

Sheridan Titman

Background and Comments

Corporate capital structure is another area of corporate finance where theories outnumber hard facts (see my comments on the paper by Espen Eckbo and Herwig Langohr, chapter 20, in this volume). The theories tend to be judged less on their ability to predict financing decisions than on their inherent plausibility and on unstructured practical observations.

Sheridan Titman (1984) has advanced one highly plausible story, that firms producing "unique" products should be conservatively financed. For example, think of products whose long run usefulness and value depend on continued support from the manufacturer. A manufacturer of such products which borrows aggressively undermines potential customers' confidence in its own future and thus constrains its sales. The solution for such companies is *not* to borrow aggressively. (Who would want to buy a personal computer from a small company financed with junk debt?)

Titman and Wessels' proxies for uniqueness work well in the empirical tests described in the following paper. However, these same variables could have been used as proxies for other theories of capital structure choice. For example, one of their measures of uniqueness, the ratio of research and development expenditures to sales, is probably also a proxy for the intangible values that investors would see in a business, and thus might be used to test the relationship between the "collateral value of assets" and capital structure choice.

My point is not to criticize Titman and Wessels' paper, but to stress the difficulty of establishing one-to-one correspondences between the variables they are using and the theories they are testing.

Reference

Titman, S. (1984) "The Effect of Capital Structure on a Firm's Liquidation Decision," *Journal of Financial Economics*, 13, March, 137–51.

Author's Introduction

The determinants of a firm's optimal capital structure have been one of the more traditional areas of research in financial economics. Spurred by the high levels of debt used to finance recent takeovers and leveraged buyouts (LBOs) policy makers have joined this debate, questioning the economic consequences of so much leverage. One of the principal concerns of these policy makers relates to the economic impact of the increase in financial distress and bankruptcies that they expect to follow from the high levels of debt.

In my earlier research (Titman, 1984) I examined the impact of debt financing on firms with nonfinancial stakeholders (for example, customers, workers, and suppliers) who incur costs if the firm goes out of business. The model explains why these stakeholders might be reluctant to do business with a firm in financial distress, and how this reluctance can in turn exacerbate the firm's difficulties, creating a cost associated with debt financing. These costs would be particularly important for a manufacturer of specialized durable goods whose customers may rely on the firm for future services and which requires that employees and suppliers develop very specific skills. My more recent work (Maksimovic and Titman, forthcoming) demonstrates that such costs are also relevant for manufacturers of nondurable goods if the quality of their products is difficult to assess before purchase.

Although these theories indicate that there are costs associated with high leverage, they also suggest that those firms which experience the highest costs will have the lowest levels of debt. The following paper provides evidence that supports this claim. We found that not only did producers of machinery and equipment have lower debt levels than other firms but that, the more specialized the firm's line of business, the lower is its debt ratio.

Although there has not been a systematic analysis of the types of firms that have carried out LBOs, the evidence seems to be consistent with these results. For the most part, LBOs occur in industries with less specialized nondurable products which are expected to have relatively low costs associated with financial distress. However, given the increased interest in the economic impact of high debt levels, a study that applied the methodology of this paper to analyze which firms choose to carry out LBOs would be of interest.

References

Maksimovic, V. and Titman, S. (forthcoming) "Financial Policy and a Firm's Reputation for Product Quality," *Review of Financial Studies*.

Titman, S. (1984) "The Effect of Capital Structure on a Firm's Liquidation Decision," *Journal of Financial Economics*, 13, March, 137–51.

Bibliographical Listing

"Financial Policy and a Firm's Reputation for Product Quality" (with Vojislav Maksimovic), *Review of Financial Studies*, forthcoming.

"Portfolio Performance Evaluation: Old Issues and New Insights" (with Mark Grinblatt), *Review of Financial Studies*, 2: 3, 1989, 393–421.

"Adverse Risk Incentives and the Design of Performance-Based Contracts" (with Mark Grinblatt), *Management Science*, 35: 7, July 1989, 807–22.

"Mutual Fund Performance: An Analysis of Quarterly Portfolio Holdings" (with Mark Grinblatt), *Journal of Business*, 62: 3, July 1989, 393–416.

"Stock Returns as Predictors of Interest Rates and Inflation" (with Arthur Warga), *Journal of Financial and Quantitative Analysis*, 24: 1, March 1989, 47–58.

"How to Avoid Games Portfolio Managers Play" (with Mark Grinblatt), *Institutional Investor Money Management Forum*, 23: 14, 1989, 35–6.

"Mutual Fund Performance: An Analysis of Monthly Returns" (with Mark Grinblatt), *Working Paper*, University of California at Los Angeles, July 1988.

"An Explanation of Accounting Income Smoothing" (with Brett Trueman), *Journal of Accounting Research*, 26 (Supplement), 1988, 127–39.

"How Clients Can Win the Gaming Game" (with Mark Grinblatt), *Journal of Portfolio Management*, 13: 4, Summer 1987, 14–20.

"Risk and the Performance of Real Estate Investment Trusts: A Multiple Index Approach" (with Arthur Warga), *AREUEA Journal*, 14: 3, Fall 1986, 414–31.

The Determinants of Capital Structure Choice

SHERIDAN TITMAN and ROBERTO WESSELS

In recent years, a number of theories have been proposed to explain the variation in debt ratios across firms. The theories suggest that firms select capital structures depending on attributes that determine the various costs and benefits associated with debt and equity financing. Empirical work in this area has lagged behind the theoretical research, perhaps because the relevant firm attributes are expressed in terms of fairly abstract concepts that are not directly observable.

The basic approach taken in previous empirical work has been to estimate regression equations with proxies for the unobservable theoretical attributes. This approach has a number of problems. First, there may be no unique representation of the attributes we wish to measure. There are often many possible proxies for a particular attribute and researchers, lacking theoretical guidelines, may be tempted to select those variables that work best in terms of statistical goodness of fit criteria, thereby biasing their interpretation of the significance levels of their tests. Second, it is often difficult to find measures of particular attributes that are unrelated to other attributes that are of interest. Thus, selected proxy variables may be measuring the effects of several different attributes. Third, since the observed variables are imperfect representations of the attributes they are supposed to measure, their use in regression analysis introduces an errors-in-variable problem. Finally, measurement errors in the proxy variables may be correlated with measurement errors in the dependent variables,

Reproduced from *Journal of Finance*, 43: 1, March 1988, 1–19.

Professor Roberto Wessels is at Erasmus University, Rotterdam. This work was done while he was visiting at the University of California at Los Angeles. We gratefully acknowledge the research assistance provided by Jim Brandon, Won Lee, and Erik Sirri and helpful comments from our UCLA colleagues, especially Julian Franks, David Mayers, Ron Masulis, and Walter Torous. We also received helpful comments from seminar participants at UCLA and the University of Rochester. Titman received partial financial support from the UCLA Foundation for Research in Financial Markets and Institutions. Wessels received financial support from the Netherlands Organization for the Advancement of Pure Research (ZWO).

creating spurious correlations even when the unobserved attribute being measured is unrelated to the dependent variable.

In this study we extend empirical work on capital structure theory in three ways.[1] First, we extend the range of theoretical determinants of capital structure by examining some recently developed theories that have not, as yet, been analyzed empirically. Second, since some of these theories have different empirical implications with regard to different types of debt instruments, we analyze separate measures of short-term, long-term, and convertible debt rather than an aggregate measure of total debt. Third, a technique is used that explicitly recognizes and mitigates the measurement problems discussed above.

This technique, which is an extension of the factor analytic approach to measuring unobserved or latent variables, is known as linear structural modeling.[2] Very briefly, the method assumes that, although the relevant attributes are not directly observable, we can observe a number of indicator variables that are linear functions of one or more attributes and a random error term. In this specification there is a direct analogy with the return-generating process assumed to hold in the arbitrage pricing theory (APT). While the identifying restrictions imposed on our model are different, the technique for estimating it is very similar to the procedure used by Roll and Ross [29] to test the APT.

Our results suggest that firms with unique or specialized products have relatively low debt ratios. Uniqueness is categorized by the firms' expenditures on research and development, selling expenses, and the rate at which employees voluntarily leave their jobs. We also find that smaller firms tend to use significantly more short-term debt than larger firms. Our model explains virtually none of the variation in convertible debt ratios across firms and finds no evidence to support theoretical work that predicts that debt ratios are related to a firm's expected growth, nondebt tax shields, volatility, or the collateral value of its assets. We do find some support, however, for the proposition that profitable firms have relatively less debt relative to the market value of their equity.

1 Determinants of Capital Structure

In this section we present a brief discussion of the attributes that different theories of capital structure suggest may affect the firm's debt–equity choice. These attributes are denoted asset structure, nondebt tax shields, growth, uniqueness, industry classification, size, earnings volatility, and profitability. The attributes, their relation to the optimal capital structure choice, and their observable indicators are discussed below.

1.1 Collateral value of assets

Most capital structure theories argue that the type of assets owned by a firm in some way affects its capital structure choice. Scott [33] suggests that, by selling secured debt, firms increase the value of their equity by expropriating wealth from their existing unsecured creditors. [3] Arguments put forth by Myers and Majluf [28] also suggest that firms may find it advantageous to sell secured debt. Their model demonstrates that there may be costs associated with issuing securities about which the firm's managers have better information than outside shareholders. Issuing debt secured by property with known values avoids these costs. For this reason, firms with assets that can be used as collateral may be expected to issue more debt to take advantage of this opportunity.

Work by Galai and Masulis [16], Jensen and Meckling [20], and Myers [26] suggests that stockholders of leveraged firms have an incentive to invest suboptimally to expropriate wealth from the firm's bondholders. This incentive may also induce a positive relation between debt ratios and the capacity of firms to collateralize their debt. If the debt can be collateralized, the borrower is restricted to use the funds for a specified project. Since no such guarantee can be used for projects that cannot be collateralized, creditors may require more favorable terms, which in turn may lead such firms to use equity rather than debt financing.

The tendency of managers to consume more than the optimal level of perquisites may produce the opposite relation between collateralizable capital and debt levels. Grossman and Hart [18] suggest that higher debt levels diminish this tendency because of the increased threat of bankruptcy. Managers of highly levered firms will also be less able to consume excessive perquisites since bondholders (or bankers) are inclined to monitor such firms closely. The costs associated with this agency relation may be higher for firms with assets that are less collateralizable since monitoring the capital outlays of such firms is probably more difficult. For this reason, firms with less collateralizable assets may choose higher debt levels to limit their managers' consumption of perquisites.

The estimated model incorporates two indicators for the collateral value attribute. They include the ratio of intangible assets to total assets (INT/TA) and the ratio of inventory plus gross plant and equipment to total assets (IGP/TA). The first indicator is negatively related to the collateral value attribute, while the second is positively related to collateral value.

1.2 Nondebt tax shields

DeAngelo and Masulis [12] present a model of optimal capital structure that incorporates the impact of corporate taxes, personal taxes, and nondebt-related corporate tax shields. They argue that tax deductions for depreciation and investment tax credits are substitutes for the tax benefits of debt financing. As a result, firms with large nondebt tax shields relative to their expected cash flow include less debt in their capital structures.

Indicators of nondebt tax shields include the ratios of investment tax credits over total assets (ITC/TA), depreciation over total assets (D/TA), and a direct estimate of nondebt tax shields over total assets (NDT/TA). The latter measure is calculated from observed federal income tax payments T, operating income OI, interest payments i, and the corporate tax rate during our sample period (48 percent) using the following equation:

$$\mathrm{NDT} = \mathrm{OI} - i - \frac{T}{0.48},$$

which follows from the equality

$$T = 0.48(\mathrm{OI} - i - \mathrm{NDT}).$$

These indicators measure the current tax deductions associated with capital equipment and hence only partially capture the nondebt tax shield variable suggested by DeAngelo and Masulis. First, this attribute excludes tax deductions that are not associated with capital equipment, such as research and development and selling expenses. (These variables, used as indicators of another attribute, are discussed later.) More important, our nondebt tax shield attribute represents tax deductions rather than tax deductions net of true economic depreciation and expenses, which is the economic attribute suggested by theory. Unfortunately, this preferable attribute would be very difficult to measure.

1.3 Growth

As we mentioned previously, equity-controlled firms have a tendency to invest suboptimally to expropriate wealth from the firm's bondholders. The cost associated with this agency relationship is likely to be higher for firms in growing industries, which have more flexibility in their choice of future investments. Expected future growth should thus be negatively related to long-term debt levels. Myers, however, noted that this agency problem is mitigated if the firm issues short-term rather than long-term debt. This suggests that short-term debt ratios might actually be positively related to growth rates if growing firms substitute short-term financing for long-term financing. Jensen and Meckling [20], Smith and Warner [36], and Green [17] argued that the agency costs will be reduced if firms issue convertible debt. This suggests that convertible debt ratios may be positively related to growth opportunities.

It should also be noted that growth opportunities are capital assets that add value to a firm but cannot be collateralized and do not generate current taxable income. For this reason, the arguments put forth in the previous subsections also suggest a negative relation between debt and growth opportunities.

Indicators of growth include capital expenditures over total assets (CE/TA) and the growth of total assets measured by the percentage change in total assets (GTA). Since firms generally engage in research and development to generate future investments, research and development over sales (RD/S) also serves as an indicator of the growth attribute.[4]

1.4 Uniqueness

Titman [39] presents a model in which a firm's liquidation decision is causally linked to its bankruptcy status. As a result, the costs that firms can potentially impose on their customers, suppliers, and workers by liquidating are relevant to their capital structure decisions. Customers, workers, and suppliers of firms that produce unique or specialized products probably suffer relatively high costs in the event that they liquidate. Their workers and suppliers probably have job-specific skills and capital, and their customers may find it difficult to find alternative servicing for their relatively unique products. For these reasons, uniqueness is expected to be negatively related to debt ratios.

Indicators of uniqueness include expenditures on research and development over sales (RD/S), selling expenses over sales (SE/S), and quit rates (QR), that is, the percentage of the industry's total work force that voluntarily left their jobs in the sample years. It is postulated that RD/S measures uniqueness because firms that sell products with close substitutes are likely to do less reserch and development since their innovations can be more easily duplicated. In addition, successful research and development projects lead to new products that differ from those existing in the market. Firms with relatively unique products are expected to advertise more and, in general, spend more in promoting and selling their products. Hence, SE/S is expected to be positively related to uniqueness. However, it is expected that firms in industries with high quit rates are probably relatively less unique since firms that produce relatively unique products tend to employ workers with high levels of job-specific human capital who will thus find it costly to leave their jobs.

It is apparent from two of the indicators of uniqueness, RD/S and SE/S, that this attribute may also be related to nondebt tax shields and collateral value. Research and development and some selling expenses (such as advertising) can be considered capital goods that are immediately expensed and cannot be used as collateral. Given that our estimation technique can only imperfectly control for these other attributes, the uniqueness attribute may be negatively related to the observed debt ratio because of its positive correlation with nondebt tax shields and its negative correlation with collateral value.

1.5 Industry classification

Titman [39] suggests that firms that make products requiring the availability of specialized servicing and spare parts will find liquidation particularly costly. This indicates that firms manufacturing machines and equipment should be financed with relatively less debt. To measure this, we include a dummy variable equal to unity for firms with Standard Industrial Classification (SIC) codes between 3400 and 4000 (firms producing machines and equipment) and zero otherwise as a separate attribute affecting the debt ratios.

1.6 Size

A number of authors have suggested that leverage ratios may be related to firm size. Warner [41] and Ang, Chua, and McConnell [1] provide evidence that suggests that direct bankruptcy costs appear to constitute a larger proportion of a firm's value as that value decreases. It is also the case that relatively large firms tend to be more diversified and less prone to bankruptcy. These arguments suggest that large firms should be more highly leveraged.

The cost of issuing debt and equity securities is also related to firm size. In particular, small firms pay much more than large firms to issue new equity (see Smith [34]) and also somewhat more to issue long-term debt. This suggests that small firms may be more leveraged than large firms and may prefer to borrow short term (through bank loans) rather than issue long-term debt because of the lower fixed costs associated with this alternative.

We use the natural logarithm of sales (LnS) and quit rates (QR) as indicators of size.[5] The logarithmic transformation of sales reflects our view that a size effect, if it exists, affects mainly the very small firms. The inclusion of quit rates as an indicator of size reflects the phenomenon that large firms, which often offer wider career opportunities to their employees, have lower quit rates.

1.7 Volatility

Many authors have also suggested a firm's optimal debt level is a decreasing function of the volatility of earnings.[6] We were only able to include one indicator of volatility that cannot be directly affected by the firm's debt level.[7] It is the standard deviation of the percentage change in operating income (SIGOI). Since it is the only indicator of volatility, we must assume that it measures this attribute without error.

1.8 Profitability

Myers [27] cites evidence from Donaldson [13] and Brealey and Myers [7] that suggests that firms prefer raising capital first from retained earnings, second from debt, and third from issuing new equity. He suggests that this behavior may be due to the costs of issuing new equity. These can be the costs discussed by Myers and Majluf [28] that arise because of asymmetric information, or they can be transaction costs. In either case, the past profitability of a firm, and hence the amount of earnings available to be retained, should be an important determinant of its current capital structure. We use the ratios of operating income over sales (OI/S) and operating income over total assets (OI/TA) as indicators of profitability.

2 Measures of Capital Structure

Six measures of financial leverage are used in this study. They are long-term, short-term, and convertible debt divided by market and by book values of equity.[8] Although these variables could have been combined to extract a common "debt ratio" attribute, which could in turn be regressed against the independent attributes, there is good reason for not doing this. Some of the theories of capital structure have different implications for the different types of debt, and, for the reasons discussed below, the predicted coefficients in the structural model may differ according to whether debt ratios are measured in terms of book or market values. Moreover, measurement errors in the dependent variables are subsumed in the disturbance term and do not bias the regression coefficients.

Data limitations force us to measure debt in terms of book values rather than market values. It would perhaps have been better if market value data were available for debt. However, Bowman [5] demonstrated that the cross-sectional correlation between the book value and market value of debt is very large, and so the misspecification due to using book value measures is probably fairly small. Furthermore, we have no reason to suspect that the cross-sectional differences between market values and book values of debt should be correlated with any of the determinants of capital structure suggested by theory, and so no obvious bias will result because of this misspecification.

There are some other important sources of spurious correlation, however. The dependent variables used in this study can potentially be correlated with the explanatory variables even if debt levels are set randomly. Consider first the case where managers set their debt levels according to some randomly selected target ratio measured at book value.[9] This would not be irrational if capital structure were in fact irrelevant. If managers set debt levels in terms of book value rather than market value ratios, then differences in market values across firms that arise for reasons other than differences in their book values (such as different growth opportunities) will not necessarily affect the total amount of debt that they issue. Since these differences do, of course, affect the market value of their equity, this will have the effect of causing firms with higher market-to-book value ratios to have lower debt-to-market value ratios. Since firms with growth opportunities and relatively low amounts of collateralizable assets tend to have relatively high market value-to-book value ratios, a spurious relation might exist between debt-to-market value and these variables, creating statistically significant coefficient estimates even if the book value debt ratios are selected randomly.[10]

Similar spurious relations will be induced between debt ratios measured at book value and the explanatory variables if firms select debt levels in accordance with market value target ratios. If some firms use book value targets while others use market value targets, both dependent variables will be spuriously correlated with the independent variables. Fortunately, the book and market value debt ratios induce spurious correlation in opposite directions. Using dependent variables scaled by both book and market values may then make it possible to separate the effects of capital structure suggested by theory, which predicts coefficient estimates of the same sign for both dependent variable groups, from these spurious effects.

3 Data

The variables discussed in the previous sections were analyzed over the period 1974–82. The source of all data except the quit rates is the Annual Compustat Industrial Files. The quit rate data are from "Employment and Earnings" published by the Bureau of Labor Statistics, US Department of Labor. These data are available only at the four-digit (SIC code) industry level for manufacturing firms.

From the total sample, we deleted all the observations that did not have a complete record on the variables included in our analysis. Furthermore, since many of the indicator variables are scaled by total assets or average operating income, we were forced to delete a small number of observations that included negative values for one of these variables. These requirements may bias our sample toward relatively large firms. In total, 469 firms were available.

The sampling period was divided into three subperiods of 3 years each, over which sample averages of the variables were calculated. Averaging over 3 years reduces the measurement error due to random year to year fluctuations in the variables. The dependent variables were measured during the subperiod 1977–9. Two of the indicators of expected future growth, the growth rate of total assets (GTA) and capital expenditures over total assets (CE/TA), were measured over the period 1980–2. By doing this, we are using the realized values as (imperfect) proxies of the values expected when the capital structure decision was made. The variables used to measure uniqueness, nondebt tax shields, asset structure, and the industry classification were measured contemporaneously with the dependent variables, that is, during the period of 1977–9. The variables used as indicators of size and profitability were taken from the period 1974–6. Measuring the profitability attribute during the earlier period allows us to determine whether profitability has more than just a short-term effect on observed leverage ratios. Measuring size in the earlier periods avoids creating a spurious relation between size and debt ratios that arises because of the relation between size and past profitability (profitable firms become larger) and the short-term relation between profitability and leverage (profitable firms increase their net worth). Finally, the standard deviation of the change in operating income was measured using all 9 years in the sample in order to obtain as efficient a measure as possible.

In comparing our results with results from previous research, it should be noted that our sample is somewhat more restricted than others. It reflects the fact that most of the theories were developed with the knowledge that regulated and unregulated firms have very different capital structures. Given this and other well-known capital structure differences between broad industry groups, we think that it is more appropriate to test the capital structure theories on a sample restricted only to those firms in the manufacturing sector of the economy. Of course, the drawback to limiting the sample is the loss in power associated with reducing the variation in the independent variables.

4 The Model Specification

In section 2 we discussed a number of attributes and their indicators that may in theory affect a firm's capital structure choice. Unfortunately, the theories do not specify the functional forms describing how the attributes relate to the indicators and the debt ratios. The statistical procedures used to estimate the model require that these relations be linear.

The model we estimate is an application of the LISREL system developed by Jöreskog and Sörbom.[11] It can be conveniently thought of as a factor analytic model consisting of two parts – a measurement model and a structural model – that are estimated simultaneously. In the measurement model, unobservable firm-specific attributes are measured by relating them to observable variables, for example accounting data. In the structural model, measured debt ratios are specified as functions of the attributes defined in the measurement model.

The measurement model can be specified as follows:

$$x = \Lambda\xi + \delta \tag{1}$$

where x is a $q \times 1$ vector of observable indicators, ξ is an $m \times 1$ vector of unobservable attributes, and Λ is a $q \times m$ matrix of regression coefficients of x on ξ. Errors of measurement are represented by the vector δ. In our model we have 15 indicator variables for eight attributes – thus, x is 15×1 and Λ is 15×8.

The structural model can be specified as the following system of equations:

$$y = \Gamma\xi + \varepsilon \tag{2}$$

where y is a $p \times 1$ vector of debt ratios, Γ is a $p \times m$ matrix of factor loadings, and ε is a $p \times 1$ vector of disturbance terms. The model is estimated for two separate 3×1 vectors of debt: short-term, long-term, and convertible debt scaled by book value and market value of equity.

Equation (1) simply states that, although the firm-specific attributes that supposedly determine capital structures cannot be observed, a number of other variables denoted as indicators, that are imperfect measures of the attributes, are observable. These indicator variables can be expressed as linear functions of one or more of the unobservable attributes and a random measurement error.

The principal advantage of this estimation procedure over standard regression models is that it explictly specifies the relation between the unobservable attributes and the observable variables. However, in order to identify the estimated equations, additional structure must be added. In most factor analytic models, the common factors are constrained to be orthogonal and scaled to have unit variances, and the residuals are assumed to be uncorrelated. However, since the common factors in this study are given definite interpretations by identifying them with specific attributes, the assumption that the common factors are uncorrelated is untenable since many firm-specific attributes are likely to be related (for example size and growth). For this reason, the correlations among the unobservable attributes (the matrix Ψ) are estimated within the model. Of course, in order to achieve identification, additional restrictions on the parameters of the model must be imposed.

Table 15.1 The structure of the measurement model

$$
\begin{bmatrix} \mathrm{NDT/TA} \\ \mathrm{ITC/TA} \\ \mathrm{D/TA} \\ \mathrm{RD/S} \\ \mathrm{SE/S} \\ \mathrm{CE/TA} \\ \mathrm{INT/TA} \\ \mathrm{IGP/TA} \\ \mathrm{LnS} \\ \mathrm{GTA} \\ \mathrm{QR} \\ \mathrm{OI/TA} \\ \mathrm{OI/S} \\ \mathrm{SIGOI} \\ \mathrm{IDUM} \end{bmatrix}
=
\begin{bmatrix}
0 & 0 & \lambda_{1.3} & 0 & 0 & 0 & 0 & 0 \\
0 & 0 & \lambda_{2.3} & 0 & 0 & 0 & 0 & 0 \\
0 & 0 & \lambda_{3.3} & 0 & 0 & 0 & 0 & 0 \\
\lambda_{4.1} & \lambda_{4.2} & 0 & 0 & 0 & 0 & 0 & 0 \\
0 & \lambda_{5.2} & 0 & 0 & 0 & 0 & 0 & 0 \\
\lambda_{6.1} & 0 & 0 & 0 & 0 & 0 & 0 & 0 \\
0 & 0 & 0 & \lambda_{7.4} & 0 & 0 & 0 & 0 \\
0 & 0 & 0 & \lambda_{8.4} & 0 & 0 & 0 & 0 \\
0 & 0 & 0 & 0 & \lambda_{9.5} & 0 & 0 & 0 \\
\lambda_{10.1} & 0 & 0 & 0 & 0 & 0 & 0 & 0 \\
0 & \lambda_{11.2} & 0 & 0 & \lambda_{11.5} & 0 & 0 & 0 \\
0 & 0 & 0 & 0 & 0 & \lambda_{12.6} & 0 & 0 \\
0 & 0 & 0 & 0 & 0 & \lambda_{13.6} & 0 & 0 \\
0 & 0 & 0 & 0 & 0 & 0 & 1 & 0 \\
0 & 0 & 0 & 0 & 0 & 0 & 0 & 1
\end{bmatrix}
\times
\begin{bmatrix} \xi_1 \\ \xi_2 \\ \xi_3 \\ \xi_4 \\ \xi_5 \\ \xi_6 \\ \xi_7 \\ \xi_8 \end{bmatrix}
+
\begin{bmatrix} \delta_1 \\ \delta_2 \\ \delta_3 \\ \delta_4 \\ \delta_5 \\ \delta_6 \\ \delta_7 \\ \delta_8 \\ \delta_9 \\ \delta_{10} \\ \delta_{11} \\ \delta_{12} \\ \delta_{13} \\ 0 \\ 0 \end{bmatrix}
$$

In total, we have imposed 105 restrictions on the matrix Λ of factor loadings. These are shown in table 15.1 as the factor loadings that are exogenously specified to equal either unity or zero. For example, since RD/S is not assumed to be an indicator of size, its factor loading on the size attribute is set to zero and is not estimated within the model. In addition, we have constrained the measurement error in the equation of indicator variables SIGOI and IDUM to be zero, implying that the factor loadings of these variables on their respective attributes are constrained to equal unity. Also, we have assumed that the measurement errors δ are uncorrelated with each other, with the attributes, or with the errors in the structural equations.

Since the restrictions may not all be appropriate, interpretations of the estimates should be made with caution. It is quite likely, for example, that some of the measurement errors may in fact be correlated. It is unfortunate that there is an arbitrary element in the choice of identifying restrictions; however, similar restrictions must be made implicitly in order to interpret a standard regression model that uses proxy variables.

In contrast with the measurement model, the structural model is totally unrestricted. The model estimates the impact of each of the attributes on each of the different debt ratios. In other words, none of the factor loadings in the structural equations is fixed exogenously. In addition, the correlations between the residual errors in the structural equations are estimated within the model. This allows for the possibility that there exist additional attributes, not considered in the model, that are determinants of each of the debt ratios.

5 Estimates of the Parameters

The parameters of our model can be estimated by fitting the covariance matrix of observable variables implied by the specification of the model Σ to the covariance matrix S of these variables observed from the sample. In the LISREL system, this is done by minimizing the function

$$F = \log(\det \Sigma) + \mathrm{tr}(S\Sigma^{-1}) - \log(\det S) - (p + q) \tag{3}$$

with respect to the vector of parameters of the matrices referred to above. This fitting function is derived from maximum likelihood procedures and assumes that the observed variables are conditionally multinormally distributed.

Our estimates of the parameters of the measurement model are presented in tables 15.2 and 15.3. The estimates are generally in accord with our *a priori* ideas about how well the indicator variables measure the unobserved attributes. Both the direction and the magnitude, as well as the statistical significance, of the estimates suggest that these indicators capture the concepts we wish to consider as determinants of capital structure choice.[12]

The estimates of the structural coefficients are presented in table 15.4. These coefficients specify the estimated impact of the unobserved attributes on the observed debt ratios. For the most part, the coefficient estimates for the long-term and short-term debt ratios were of the predicted sign. However, many of the estimated coefficients are fairly small in magnitude and are statistically insignificant. In particular, the attributes representing nondebt tax shields, asset structure, and volatility do not appear to be related to the various measures of leverage. Moreover, the estimated models explain virtually none of the cross-sectional variation in the convertible debt ratios.

Some of the coefficient estimates are both large in magnitude and statistically significant. The large negative coefficient estimate for the uniqueness attribute (ξ_2) indicates that firms characterized as having relatively large research and development expenditures and high selling expenses, and that have employees with relatively low quit rates, tend to have low debt ratios. The coefficient estimate of -0.263 in the equation with LT/MVE indicates that firms that differ in "uniqueness" by 1 variance are expected to have long-term debt ratios that differ by 0.263 variances. This evidence, along with the estimated coefficients of the industry dummy variable, are consistent with the implications of Titman [39]. As mentioned previously, a negative relation between uniqueness and the debt ratios could also be due to the relation between this attribute and nondebt tax shields and collateral values.

Although the reported t statistics for the coefficients of the uniqueness

Table 15.2 Measurement model: factor loadings for independent variables[a]

	Attributes[a]								
Variable	ξ_1 *(growth)*	ξ_2 *(uniqueness)*	ξ_3 *(nondebt tax shields)*	ξ_4 *(collateral value)*	ξ_5 *(size)*	ξ_6 *(profitability)*	ξ_7 *(volatility)*	ξ_8 *(IDUM)*	σ_δ^2
NDT/TA			0.779 (26.7)						0.393
ITC/TA			0.606 (19.2)						0.744
D/TA			0.848 (30.1)						0.280
RD/S	0.246 (6.6)	0.781 (21.6)							0.401
SE/S		0.681 (19.7)							0.536
CE/TA	0.951 (26.4)								0.095
INT/TA				−0.331 (−8.7)					0.891
IGP/TA				1.180 (15.7)					−0.392
LnS					0.938 (7.9)				0.120
GTA	0.471 (13.9)								0.778
QR		−0.228 (−5.6)			−0.273 (−5.5)				0.896
OI/TA						0.641 (18.8)			0.589
OI/S						0.998 (27.8)			0.005
SIGOI							1.000		0.000
IDUM								1.000	0.000

[a]Reported t statistics are in parentheses.

Table 15.3 Estimated correlations between attributes

Attribute	ξ_1	ξ_2	ξ_3	ξ_4	ξ_5	ξ_6	ξ_7	ξ_8
ξ_1 (growth)	1.00							
ξ_2 (uniqueness)	−0.18	1.00						
ξ_3 (nondebt tax shields)	0.72	−0.04	1.00					
ξ_4 (asset structure)	0.27	−0.39	0.47	1.00				
ξ_5 (size)	0.15	−0.18	0.19	0.28	1.00			
ξ_6 (profitability)	0.53	0.12	0.46	0.12	−0.02	1.00		
ξ_7 (volatility)	−0.08	−0.01	−0.02	0.03	−0.11	−0.04	1.00	
ξ_8 (industry dummy)	−0.14	0.38	−0.13	−0.22	−0.24	−0.05	−0.05	1.00

attribute are quite high, we feel that their statistical significance should be interpreted cautiously. The reported *t* statistics are based on the assumptions of independent, identical, and normally distributed error terms – assumptions that are surely violated by our data. To provide further evidence about the statistical significance of the relation between uniqueness, the industry dummy, and the measured debt ratios, we compared the estimated likelihood function for the reported model with the likelihood function of the model with the coefficients of uniqueness and the industry dummy constrained to equal zero. The difference in these likelihood functions has a χ^2 distribution with six degrees of freedom. The estimated χ^2 for the debt ratios scaled by market values is 40 which is statistically significant at well beyond the 0.005 level. With the debt ratios scaled by book value of equity, this statistic is 17, which is significant at the 0.01 level. Given these results, we feel comfortable in asserting that the evidence supports the implication of Titman [39] that firms that can potentially impose high costs on their customers, workers, and suppliers in the event of liquidation tend to choose lower debt ratios.

The evidence also indicates that small firms tend to use significantly more short-term financing than large firms. This difference in financing practice probably reflects the high transaction costs that small firms face when they issue long-term debt or equity. Our finding that small firms use more short-term financing may also provide some insights about possible risk factors underlying the "small firm effect." By borrowing more short term, these firms are particularly sensitive to temporary economic downturns that have less of an effect on larger firms that are less leveraged and use longer-term financing (see Chan, Chen, and Hsieh [10] for a similar argument and evidence relating to this).

The results also suggest that size is related to LTD/BVE but not LTD/MVE. This finding may be due to the positive relation between our size attribute and the total market value of the firm. Firms with high

Table 15.4 Estimates of structural coefficients[a]

	Attributes							
Debt measures	ξ_1 (*growth*)	ξ_2 (*uniqueness*)	ξ_3 (*nondebt tax shields*)	ξ_4 (*asset structure*)	ξ_5 (*size*)	ξ_6 (*profitability*)	ξ_7 (*volatility*)	ξ_8 (*industry dummy*)
1 LT/MVE	−0.068	−0.263	−0.058	0.041	−0.033	−0.213	−0.031	−0.106
	(−0.7)	(−3.7)	(−0.6)	(0.8)	(−0.6)	(−3.7)	(−0.7)	(−2.1)
ST/MVE	−0.112	−0.260	−0.041	−0.046	−0.183	−0.179	−0.017	−0.063
	(−1.2)	(−3.7)	(−0.4)	(−0.9)	(−3.2)	(−3.1)	(−0.4)	(−1.2)
C/MVE	−0.067	−0.076	−0.050	0.004	0.055	−0.108	−0.027	0.026
	(−0.7)	(−1.0)	(−0.5)	(0.1)	(1.0)	(−1.8)	(−0.6)	(0.5)
2 LT/BVE	0.230	−0.281	−0.113	−0.076	−0.132	−0.052	−0.043	−0.066
	(2.4)	(−3.6)	(−1.1)	(−1.4)	(−2.3)	(−0.9)	(−0.9)	(−1.2)
ST/BVE	0.140	−0.185	−0.079	−0.096	−0.284	−0.044	−0.038	−0.051
	(1.5)	(−2.4)	(−0.8)	(−1.7)	(−4.1)	(−0.7)	(−0.8)	(−0.9)
C/BVE	0.028	−0.065	−0.156	−0.019	0.050	0.026	−0.016	0.074
	(0.3)	(−0.8)	(−1.5)	(−0.3)	(0.9)	(0.4)	(0.3)	(1.3)

[a]The coefficient estimates are scaled to represent the estimated change in the dependent variable, relative to its variance, with respect to a change in an attribute, relative to its variance. Reported t statistics are in parentheses.

market values relative to their book values have higher borrowing capacities and hence have higher debt levels relative to their book values. Thus, rather than indicating a size effect, we think that this evidence suggests that many firms are guided by the market value of their equity when selecting their long-term debt levels.

Coefficient estimates for the "profitability" attribute are large and have high *t* statistics in the equations with debt over market value of equity-dependent variables, but they are not statistically significant in the equations with the debt measures scaled by book value of equity. This suggests that increases in the market value of equity, due to an increase in operating income, are not completely offset by an increase in the firm's borrowing. This provides additional evidence supporting the importance of transaction costs and is consistent with the observation of Myers [27] regarding what he calls "the pecking order theory" that firms prefer internal to external financing. However, the evidence suggests that borrowing is increased to the extent that the higher operating income leads to an increase in the book value of equity (through increases in retained earnings). This suggests that many firms do in fact use book value target debt-to-equity ratios.

It should be emphasized that the significant coefficient estimates for profitability and size are not necessarily inconsistent with the hypothesis of capital structure irrelevance. As we mentioned in section 3, significant coefficient estimates for either (but not both) the market value or book value equations are consistent with random choice of debt ratios. Similarly, we should not view the positive coefficient estimate of the growth attribute in the long-term debt over book value of the equity equation as necessarily being inconsistent with the agency- and tax-based theories that predict a negative coefficient for this attribute. The observed positive coefficient simply implies that, since growth opportunities add value to a firm, they increase the firm's debt capacity and hence the ratio of debt to book value, since this additional value is not reflected in the firm's book value.

6 Robustness

An examination of the correlation matrix of the sample data (table 15.5) provides some insights about the robustness of our results. Particularly noteworthy is the high negative simple correlation between OI/TA and the various debt ratios. This relation can potentially create a problem in interpreting the correlation between variables scaled by either OI or TA and the debt ratio measures.

The best examples of this are the indicators of nondebt tax shields. For instance, the simple correlation between NDT/TA and the different

Table 15.5 Correlation matrix

	LT/MVE	ST/MVE	C/MVE	LT/BVE	ST/BVE	C/BVE	NDT/TA	ITC/TA	D/TA	RD/S	SE/S	CE/TA	INT/TA	IGP/TA	LnS	GTA	QR	OI/TA	OI/S	SIGOI	IDUM
LT/MVE	1																				
ST/MVE	0.66	1																			
C/MVE	0.29	0.19	1																		
LT/BVE	0.73	0.47	0.15	1																	
ST/BVE	0.43	0.75	0.10	0.66	1																
C/BVE	0.15	0.10	0.89	0.14	0.11	1															
NDT/TA	−0.25	−0.32	−0.15	−0.11	−0.17	0.14	1														
ITC/TA	−0.06	−0.14	−0.06	0.09	−0.02	−0.07	0.46	1													
D/TA	−0.08	−0.12	−0.10	0.02	−0.02	−0.09	0.66	0.52	1												
RD/S	−0.27	−0.24	−0.07	−0.19	−0.12	−0.03	0.30	−0.04	0.11	1											
SE/S	−0.25	−0.14	−0.08	−0.20	−0.06	−0.04	0.06	−0.24	−0.10	0.50	1										
CE/TA	−0.14	−0.20	−0.13	0.14	0.04	−0.06	0.51	0.47	0.58	0.09	−0.13	1									
INT/TA	0.03	0.02	0.13	0.00	−0.01	0.12	−0.13	−0.11	−0.17	−0.03	0.23	−0.09	1								
IGP/TA	0.09	0.06	0.03	0.01	0.11	0.08	0.37	0.39	0.51	−0.22	−0.43	0.31	−0.39	1							
LnS	0.04	−0.14	0.05	−0.07	−0.24	0.01	0.18	−0.01	0.17	−0.01	−0.25	0.14	−0.09	0.31	1						
GTA	−0.20	−0.22	−0.17	0.04	−0.01	−0.10	0.24	0.26	0.27	0.18	0.07	0.45	−0.03	−0.01	−0.18	1					
QR	0.11	0.19	0.06	0.10	0.14	0.02	−0.13	0.03	−0.01	−0.23	−0.01	−0.04	0.07	−0.13	−0.22	0.07	1				
OI/TA	−0.38	−0.34	−0.23	−0.24	−0.19	−0.17	0.31	0.18	0.29	0.03	0.07	0.25	−0.04	0.09	−0.01	0.20	−0.06	1			
OI/S	−0.29	−0.28	−0.18	−0.02	−0.03	−0.05	0.41	0.20	0.39	0.19	0.12	0.50	−0.06	0.14	−0.02	0.29	−0.13	0.64	1		
SIGOI	0.00	0.03	−0.02	−0.04	−0.01	−0.02	−0.02	−0.02	−0.01	0.02	−0.05	−0.07	0.04	−0.04	−0.10	−0.09	−0.04	−0.02	−0.04	1	
IDUM	−0.17	−0.07	0.01	−0.13	−0.04	0.06	−0.08	−0.16	−0.11	0.32	0.16	−0.14	−0.04	−0.25	0.23	−0.03	−0.18	−0.11	−0.10	−0.06	1

measures of leverage is strongly negative. While this correlation is predicted by the DeAngelo–Masulis [12] model, it should be noted that the large negative correlation may be due to the large positive correlation between OI/TA and NDT/TA caused by their common denominators. In the estimated structural model, where we control for the profitability attribute that is measured by OI/TA and OI/S, the coefficient estimate for the nondebt tax shield attribute is not statistically significant. Moreover, if we replace the denominators of the nondebt tax shield indicators with OI, the simple correlations are still just as strong but are reversed. For example, NDT/OI is strongly negatively correlated with OI/TA and strongly positively correlated with the measures of leverage. Using indicators scaled by OI for the nondebt tax shield attribute leads to positive coefficient estimates that are sometimes marginally statistically significant in the structural equations. While this result is inconsistent with the DeAngelo–Masulis model, it is most probably caused by the way that the variables used as indicators are scaled.

We expect that similar changes in coefficient estimates caused by scaling indicator variables by OI rather than TA would be found for other attributes. For example, IGP/OI is very highly correlated with the inverse of OI/TA and is therefore probably strongly positively correlated with leverage. This positive correlation could be put forth as evidence in support of the hypothesis that firms with assets that have high collateral value choose high debt levels. However, we feel that such a variable would actually be measuring profitability and therefore thought it more appropriate to scale the variable by TA.

The above discussion suggests that one should be cautious when interpreting variables scaled by OI that are positively correlated with debt ratios and to a lesser extent variables scaled by TA that are negatively related to the debt ratios. Fortunately, the indicators of "uniqueness," the attribute that appears to do the best job of explaining debt ratios, are not scaled by either TA or OI. Research and development expenditures could conceivably have been scaled by OI or TA; however, the correlation between debt and this variable is not nearly as sensitive to its scaling as, for example, NDT. The other indicators of "uniqueness," SE/S and QR, suggest no alternative scaling variable; hence the robustness of the correlation between these variables and the debt ratios is not a serious issue.

7 Summary and Conclusion

In this paper we introduced a factor analytic technique for estimating the impact of unobservable attributes on the choice of corporate debt ratios.

While our results are not conclusive, they serve to document empirical regularities that are consistent with existing theory. In particular, we find that debt levels are negatively related to the "uniqueness" of a firm's line of business. This evidence is consistent with the implications of Titman [39] that firms that can potentially impose high costs on their customers, workers, and suppliers in the event of liquidation have lower debt ratios.

The results also indicate that transaction costs may be an important determinant of capital structure choice. Short-term debt ratios were shown to be negatively related to firm size, possibly reflecting the relatively high transaction costs that small firms face when issuing long-term financial instruments. Since transaction costs are generally assumed to be small relative to other determinants of capital structure, their importance in this study suggests that the various leverage-related costs and benefits may not be particularly significant. In this sense, although the results suggest that capital structures are chosen systematically, they are in line with Miller's [25] argument that the costs and benefits associated with this decision are small. Additional evidence relating to the importance of transaction costs is provided by the negative relation between measures of past profitability and current debt levels scaled by the market value of equity. This evidence also supports some of the implications of Myers and Majluf [28] and Myers [27].

Our results do not provide support for an effect on debt ratios arising from nondebt tax shields, volatility, collateral value, or future growth. However, it remains an open question whether our measurement model does indeed capture the relevant aspects of the attributes suggested by these theories. One could argue that the predicted effects were not uncovered because the indicators used in this study do not adequately reflect the nature of the attributes suggested by theory. If stronger linkages between observable indicator variables and the relevant attributes can be developed, then the method suggested here can be used to test more precisely the extant theories of optimal capital structure.

Notes

1 Recent cross-sectional studies include Toy et al. [40], Ferri and Jones [14], Flath and Knoeber [15], Marsh [24], Chaplinsky [11], Titman [38], Castanias [8], Bradley, Jarrell, and Kim [6], Auerbach [2], and Long and Malitz [23]. Titman [38], Bradley, Jarrell, and Kim [6], Auerbach [2], and Long and Malitz [23] examine variables that are similar to some of those examined here. The studies find a negative relation between both research and development and advertising and leverage but have mixed findings relating to the different measures of nondebt tax shields and leverage and volatility and leverage. Also see Schwartz and Aronson [30], Scott [31], and Scott and Martin [32] for evidence of industry effects in capital structure choice.

2 References to linear structural modeling can also be found in the literature under the headings of analysis-of-covariance structures, path analysis, causal models, and content-variables models. A nontechnical introduction to the subject providing many references is Bentler and Bonett [4].

3 See Smith and Warner [35] for a comment on Scott's model.

4 We also considered using price-to-earnings ratios as an indicator of growth. However, this variable is determined in part by the firm's leverage ratio and hence is subject to bias due to reverse causality.

5 An unreported model was estimated that included the natural logarithm of total assets (LnTA) as a third indicator of size. The very high correlation between LnTA and LnS (about 0.98) created a near singularity in the covariance matrix, causing problems in estimating the model. However, parameter estimates of the structural model are not sensitive to the choice between LnS or LnTA as an indicator for size.

6 Counter-examples to this basic hypothesis have been demonstrated (e.g. Castanias and DeAngelo [9]; Jaffe and Westerfield [19]; Bradley, Jarrell, and Kim [6]).

7 Other possible indicators, such as a firm's stock beta or total volatility, are of course partially determined by the firm's debt ratio. Calculating "unlevered betas" and "unlevered volatilities" requires accurate measurements of the market value of the firm's debt ratio as it evolves over time and of the tax gain to leverage. The potential for spurious correlation arises if the impact of leverage and taxes is not completely purged from these volatility estimates.

8 We also examined these debt levels divided by total assets and market value of equity plus book value of debt and preferred stock. The results using these dependent variables were very similar to those reported here.

9 There is evidence that managers do think in terms of book values. See, for example, the survey evidence presented by Stonehill et al. [37].

10 It may be easier to understand how this spurious correlation arises in the case where all firms have the same book debt ratios. In this case, the cross-sectional variation in debt-to-market value will be determined entirely by the variation in the difference between book and market values across firms. Variables that are related to this difference will therefore also be related to debt-to-market value. It should be noted that the previously cited empirical work shares this potential for spurious results. Clearly, the different measures of firm size and industry classifications used in past studies are correlated with their market-to-book value ratios.

11 For a lucid introduction to the system and its many applications, see Jöreskog and Sörbom [22]; for a critical review see Bentler [3]. A detailed description of the technical procedures of LISREL is given by Jöreskog [21].

12 The goodness of fit of the measurement model was evaluated by testing the model against two alternatives (see Bentler and Bonett [4]). The first alternative model is one in which the observed variables are assumed to be mutually uncorrelated – the χ^2 statistic is 1893 with 42 degrees of freedom, which for this test is highly significant. The second alternative model specifies that the covariance matrix is totally unrestricted. The χ^2 statistic is 378 with 63 degrees of freedom; this result is also highly significant, indicating that, although our model captures a significant part of the information in the sample covariance matrix, relaxing one or more of the imposed restrictions could improve its fit.

References

1 Ang, J., Chua, J. and McConnell, J. "The Administrative Costs of Corporate Bankruptcy: A Note," *Journal of Finance*, 37, March 1982, 219–26.

2 Auerbach, A. "Real Determinants of Corporate Leverage." In *Corporate Capital Structures in the United States*, ed. B. Friedman (Chicago, IL: University of Chicago Press, 1985).

3 Bentler, P. M. "Simultaneous Equation Systems as Moment Structure Models. With an Introduction to Latent Variable Models," *Journal of Econometrics*, 22 (Issue of the the *Annals of Applied Econometrics*), March 1983, 13–42.

4 Bentler, P. M. and Bonett, D. G. "Significance Tests and Goodness of Fit in the Analysis of Covariance Structures," *Psychological Bulletin*, 88, September 1980, 588–606.

5 Bowman, J. "The Importance of a Market Value Measurement of Debt in Assessing Leverage," *Journal of Accounting Research*, 18, Spring 1980, 242–54.

6 Bradley, M., Jarrell, G. and Kim, E. H. "On the Existence of an Optimal Capital Structure: Theory and Evidence," *Journal of Finance*, 39, July 1984, 857–78.

7 Brealey, R. and Myers, S. *Principles of Corporate Finance* (New York: McGraw-Hill, 1984).

8 Castanias, R. "Bankruptcy Risk and Optimal Capital Structure," *Journal of Finance*, 38, December 1983, 1617–35.

9 Castanias, R. and DeAngelo, H. "Business Risk and Optimal Capital Structure," *Working Paper*, University of Washington, 1981.

10 Chan, K. C., Chen, N. F. and Hsieh, D. "An Exploratory Investigation of the Firm Size Effect," *Journal of Financial Economics*, 14, March 1985, 451–71.

11 Chaplinsky, S. "The Economic Determinants of Leverage: Theories and Evidence," Ph.D. Dissertation, University of Chicago, 1983.

12 DeAngelo, H. and Masulis, R. "Optimal Capital Structure under Corporate and Personal Taxation," *Journal of Financial Economics*, 8, March 1980, 3–29.

13 Donaldson, G. "Corporate Debt Capacity: A Study of Corporate Debt Policy and the Determination of Corporate Debt Capacity," Division of Research, Harvard School of Business Administration, Boston, MA, 1961.

14 Ferri, M. and Jones, W. "Determinants of Financial Structure: A New Methodological Approach," *Journal of Finance*, 34, June 1979, 631–44.

15 Flath, D. and Knoeber, C. "Taxes, Failure Costs, and Optimal Industry Capital Structure: An Empirical Test," *Journal of Finance*, 35, March 1980, 99–117.

16 Galai, D. and Masulis, R. "The Option Pricing Model and the Risk Factor of Stock," *Journal of Financial Economics*, 3, January–March 1976, 53–81.

17 Green, R. "Investment Incentives, Debt, and Warrants," *Journal of Financial Economics*, 13, March 1984, 115–35.

18 Grossman, S. and Hart, O. "Corporate Financial Structure and Managerial Incentives." In *The Economics of Information and Uncertainty*, ed. J. McCall (Chicago, IL: University of Chicago Press, 1982).

19 Jaffe, J. and Westerfield, R. "Risk and Optimal Debt Level," *Working Paper*, University of Pennsylvania, Philadelphia, PA, 1984.

20 Jensen, M. and Meckling, W. "Theory of the Firm: Managerial Behavior, Agency Costs and Ownership Structure," *Journal of Financial Economics*, 3, October 1976, 305–60.

21 Jöreskog, K. G. "Structural Equation Models in the Social Sciences: Specification

Estimation and Testing." In *Applications of Statistics*, ed. P. R. Krishnaiah (Amsterdam: North-Holland, 1977), pp. 265–87.
22 Jöreskog, K. G. and Sörbon, D. "LISREL V, Analysis of Linear Structural Relationships by the Method of Maximum Likelihood," National Educational Resources, Chicago, IL, 1981.
23 Long, M. S. and Malitz, E. B. "Investment Patterns and Financial Leverage." In *Corporate Capital Structures in the United States*, ed. B. Friedman (Chicago, IL: University of Chicago Press, 1985).
24 Marsh, P. "The Choice between Equity and Debt: An Empirical Study," *Journal of Finance*, 37, March 1982, 121–44.
25 Miller, M. "Debt and Taxes," *Journal of Finance*, 32, May 1977, 261–75.
26 Myers, S. "Determinants of Corporate Borrowing," *Journal of Financial Economics*, 9, November 1977, 147–76.
27 Myers, S. "The Capital Structure Puzzle," *Journal of Finance*, 39, July 1984, 575–92.
28 Myers, S. and Majluf, N. "Corporate Financing and Investment Decisions When Firms Have Information Investors Do Not Have," *Journal of Financial Economics*, 13, June 1984, 187–221.
29 Roll, R. and Ross, S. "An Empirical Investigation of the Arbitrage Pricing Theory," *Journal of Finance*, 35, December 1980, 1073–103.
30 Schwartz, E. and Aronson, J. "Some Surrogate Evidence in Support of the Concept of Optimal Financial Structure," *Journal of Finance*, 22, March 1967, 10–19.
31 Scott, D. "Evidence on the Importance of Financial Structure," *Financial Management*, 1, Summer 1972, 45–50.
32 Scott, D. and Martin, J. "Industry Influence on Financial Structure," *Financial Management*, 4, Spring 1975, 67–73.
33 Scott, J. "Bankruptcy, Secured Debt, and Optimal Capital Structure," *Journal of Finance*, 32, March 1977, 1–20.
34 Smith, C. "Alternative Methods for Raising Capital: Rights versus Underwritten Offerings," *Journal of Financial Economics*, 5, December 1977, 273–307.
35 Smith, C. and Warner, J. "Bankruptcy, Secured Debt, and Optimal Capital Structure: Comments," *Journal of Finance*, 34, March 1979, 247–52.
36 Smith, C. "On Financial Contracting: An Analysis of Bond Covenants," *Journal of Financial Economics*, 7, June 1979, 117–61.
37 Stonehill, A., Beekhuisen, T., Wright, R., Remmers, L., Toy, N., Pares, A., Shapiro, A., Egan, D. and Bates, T. "Determinants of Corporate Financial Structure: A Survey of Practice in Five Countries," Unpublished Paper, 1973.
38 Titman, S. "Determinants of Capital Structure: An Empirical Analysis," *Working Paper*, University of California at Los Angeles, 1982.
39 Titman, S. "The Effect of Capital Structure on a Firm's Liquidation Decision," *Journal of Financial Economics*, 13, March 1984, 137–51.
40 Toy, N., Stonehill, A., Remmers, L., Wright, R. and Beekhuisen, T. "A Comparative International Study of Growth, Profitability, and Risk as Determinants of Corporate Debt Ratios in the Manufacturing Sector," *Journal of Financial and Quantitative Analysis*, November 1974, 875–86.
41 Warner, J. "Bankruptcy Costs: Some Evidence," *Journal of Finance*, 32, May 1977, 337–47.

Chapter 16

Kenneth R. French

Background and Comments

The idea of efficient capital markets is popularly identified with the random walk hypothesis, which states that a series of daily, weekly, monthly, or yearly rates of return are uncorrelated in the same sense that the heads and tails of a series of coin flips are uncorrelated. This is still a good approximation for individual stocks over short time periods. However, there is increasing evidence of "mean reversion" over periods of, say, 2–4 years.

Few economists now believe that stock prices follow a strict random walk. This does not require them to give up on market efficiency (although some have given up). *Rational* investors may accept relatively low expected rates of return after a run-up of stock prices and demand higher expected returns after market lows. If so, a tendency for relatively low returns after bull markets and high returns after bear markets would not be surprising.

This behavior might reflect changes in investors' aggregate risk aversion – note that a bull market rewards the risk-tolerant more than the conservative investor and reduces the conservative investors' weight in the subsequent pricing of shares. Conversely a bear market should give more influence to the high rates of return demanded by more conservative and relatively risk-averse investors. This is just one of the ideas that financial economists are now exploring.

The evidence for medium-term mean reversion in stock returns is not universally accepted, however. Stock prices are extremely noisy, and there are not that many nonoverlapping 4 year periods. Some tests of statistical significance depend on the inclusion of evidence from the depression years of the 1930s (Kim, Nelson, and Startz, 1988).

These issues are addressed in the following paper by Eugene Fama and Kenneth French, and also in the paper by James Poterba and Lawrence Summers (chapter 17). Fama and French have taken a step toward understanding the causes of mean reversion by investigating the implications of changing dividend yields for subsequent returns.

Reference

Kim, M. J., Nelson, C. R. and Startz, R. (1988) "Mean Reversion in Stock Prices? A Reappraisal of the Empirical Evidence," *Working Paper 2795*, National Bureau of Economic Research, Cambridge, MA.

Author's Introduction

Until recently, most financial economists agreed that stock returns are essentially unpredictable. Using daily and monthly returns, researchers typically concluded that the predictable component of returns accounts for a small fraction (usually less than 3 percent) of return variances. Prompted by the evidence in Fama and French (1987) and Poterba and Summers (1988; this volume, chapter 17), we explore the forecastability of longer-horizon returns.

We find that dividend yields often explain more than 25 percent of the variance of 2–4 year returns. Two factors contribute to this predictability. First, the persistence of expected returns makes them more apparent in long-horizon returns. Because expected returns are autocorrelated, their variance tends to grow more than in proportion to the return horizon. Second, unexpected changes in expected returns are associated with opposite changes in current prices. For example, an increase in future expected returns is usually associated with a decrease in the current price. Because of this discount rate effect, the variance of the unexpected component of returns grows less than in proportion to the return horizon. By looking at longer-horizon returns, we increase the relative importance of the expected component of returns.

The predictability of returns in our dividend yield regressions, and in similar long-horizon regressions by Cutler, Poterba, and Summers (1988) and Campbell and Shiller (1988), among others, is striking. A number of researchers are currently exploring the implications of this predictability for economic models and financial applications.

References

Campbell, J. Y. and Shiller, R. (1988) "Stock Prices, Earnings, and Expected Dividends," *Journal of Finance*, 43, July, 661–76.

Cutler, D., Poterba, J. M. and Summers, L. (1988) "International Evidence on the Predictability of Stock Returns," *Seminar on the Analysis of Security Prices*, Center for Research in Security Prices, November, pp. 97–126.

Fama, E. F. and French, K. R. (1988) "Permanent and Temporary Components of Stock Prices," *Journal of Political Economy*, 96: 2, April, 246–73.

Poterba, J. M. and Summers, L. (1988) "Mean Reversion in Stock Prices: Evidence and Implications," *Journal of Financial Economics*, 22, October, 27–59.

Bibliographical Listing

"Business Cycles and the Behavior of Metals Prices" (with Eugene Fama), *Journal of Finance*, 43: 5, December 1988, 1075–93.

"Permanent and Temporary Components of Stock Prices" (with Eugene Fama), *Journal of Political Economy*, 96: 2, April 1988, 246–73.

"Common Factors in the Serial Correlation of Stock Returns" (with Eugene Fama), *Working Paper 200*, Center for Research in Security Prices, University of Chicago, October 1986.

Dividend Yields and Expected Stock Returns

EUGENE F. FAMA and KENNETH R. FRENCH

1 Introduction

There is much evidence that stock returns are predictable. The common conclusion, usually from tests on monthly data, is that the predictable component of returns, or, equivalently, the variation through time of expected returns, is a small fraction (usually less than 3 percent) of return variances (e.g. Fama and Schwert, 1977; Fama, 1981; Keim and Stambaugh, 1986; French, Schwert, and Stambaugh, 1987). Recently, however, Fama and French (1988) find that portfolio returns for holding periods beyond a year have strong negative autocorrelation. They show that under some assumptions about the nature of the price process the autocorrelations imply that time-varying expected returns explain 25–40 percent of 3–5 year return variances. Using variance ratio tests, Poterba and Summers (1987) also estimate that long-horizon stock returns have large predictable components.

Univariate tests on long-horizon returns are imprecise. Although their point estimates suggest strong predictability, Poterba and Summers (1987) cannot reject the hypothesis that stock prices are random walks, even with variance ratios estimated on returns from 1871 to 1985. Fama and French (1988) find reliable negative autocorrelation in tests on long-horizon returns for the period 1926–85, but subperiod results suggest that the autocorrelation is largely due to the period 1926–40. Because sample sizes for long-horizon returns are small, however, it is impossible to make reliable inferences about changes in their time series properties.

We use dividend-to-price ratios D/P, henceforth called dividend yields,

Reproduced from *Journal of Financial Economics*, 22, 1988, 3–25.

Eugene F. Fama is the Theodore O. Yntema Distinguished Service Professor at the University of Chicago. This research is supported by the National Science Foundation (EFF) and the Center for Research in Security Prices (KRF). We have had helpful comments from David Booth, Nai-fu Chen, John Cochrane, Bradford Cornell, Michael Hemler, Merton Miller, Kevin Murphy, Rex Sinquefield, Robert Stambaugh, and especially the editor, G. William Schwert, and the referee, James Poterba.

to forecast returns on the value-weighted and equally weighted portfolios of New York Stock Exchange (NYSE) stocks for return horizons (holding periods) from 1 month to 4 years. Our tests confirm existing evidence that the predictable (expected) component of returns is a small fraction of short-horizon return variances. Regressions of returns on yields typically explain less than 5 percent of monthly or quarterly return variances. More interesting, our results add statistical power to the evidence that the predictable component of returns is a larger fraction of the variation of long-horizon returns. Regressions of returns on D/P often explain more than 25 percent of the variances of 2–4 year returns. In contrast with the univariate tests of Fama and French (1988) and Poterba and Summers (1987), regressions of returns on yields provide reliable evidence of forecast power for subperiods as well as for the sample period 1927–86.

The hypothesis that D/P forecasts returns has a long tradition among practitioners and academics (e.g. Dow, 1920; Ball, 1978). The intuition of the "efficient markets" version of the hypothesis is that stock prices are low relative to dividends when discount rates and expected returns are high, and vice versa, so that D/P varies with expected returns. There is also evidence, primarily for annual returns, that supports the hypothesis (e.g. Rozeff, 1984; Shiller, 1984; Flood, Hodrick, and Kaplan, 1986; Campbell and Shiller, 1987). Thus, neither the hypothesis nor the evidence that D/P forecasts returns is new. What we offer are (a) evidence that forecast power increases with the return horizon, (b) an economic story to explain this result, and (c) evidence consistent with the explanation.

Part of the story of why the predictable component of returns becomes more important for longer return horizons is easy to document. If expected returns have strong positive autocorrelation, rational forecasts of 1 year returns 1–4 years ahead are highly correlated. As a consequence, the variance of expected returns grows faster with the return horizon than the variance of unexpected returns – the variation of expected returns becomes a larger fraction of the variation of returns. Our results, like those of others, indicate that expected returns are highly autocorrelated.

The second part of the story for forecast power that increases with the return horizon is more interesting. It starts from the observation that residual variances for regressions of returns on yields (the unexpected returns estimated from the regressions) increase less than in proportion to the return horizon. Our explanation centers on what we call the discount rate effect, that is, the offsetting adjustment of current prices triggered by shocks to discount rates and expected returns. We find that estimated shocks to expected returns are indeed associated with opposite shocks to prices. The cumulative price effect of these shocks is roughly zero; on average, the expected future price increases implied by higher expected returns are offset by the immediate decline in the current price.

These results are consistent with models (e.g. Summers, 1986) in which time-varying expected returns generate mean-reverting components of prices. The interesting economic question, motivated but unresolved by our results, is whether the predictability of returns implied by such temporary price components is driven by rational economic behavior (the investment opportunities of firms and the tastes of investors for current versus risky future consumption) or by animal spirits.

2 Dividend Yields

Consider a discrete-time perfect certainty model in which $D(t)$, the dividend per share for the time period from $t-1$ to t, grows at a constant rate g, and the market interest rate that relates the stream of future dividends to the stock price $P(t-1)$ at time $t-1$ is the constant r. In this model, the price $P(t-1)$ is

$$P(t-1)=\frac{D(t)}{1+r}\left[1+\frac{1+g}{1+r}+\frac{(1+g)^2}{(1+r)^2}+\cdots\right]=\frac{D(t)}{r-g}. \quad (1)$$

The dividend yield is the interest rate less the dividend growth rate:

$$\frac{D(t)}{P(t-1)}=r-g. \quad (2)$$

In the certainty model, the interest rate r is the discount rate for dividends and the period by period return on the stock. The transition from certainty to a model that (a) accommodates uncertain future dividends and discount rates and (b) shows the correspondence between discount rates and time-varying expected returns is difficult (Campbell and Shiller, 1987; Poterba and Summers, 1987). The direct relation between the dividend yield and the interest rate in the certainty model (2) suffices, however, to illustrate that yields are likely to capture variation in expected returns.

3 Variables for the Basic Regressions

3.1 Returns and dividend yields

Fama and French (1988) find that the predictability of long-horizon returns implied by negative autocorrelation is stronger for portfolios of small firms. They also find that the return behavior of large and small firm portfolios is typified by the value-weighted and equally weighted portfolios of NYSE stocks constructed by the Center for Research in Security Prices

(CRSP). Our tests use continuously compounded returns $r(t, t+T)$ on the two market portfolios for return horizons T of 1 month, one quarter, and 1–4 years. The monthly, quarterly, and annual returns are nonoverlapping. The 2–4 year returns are overlapping annual (end of year) observations. The sample period for the returns is 1927–86.

The tests center on regressions of the future return $r(t, t+T)$ on two measures of the time t dividend yield $Y(t)$:

$$r(t, t+T) = \alpha(T) + \beta(T)Y(t) + \varepsilon(t, t+T). \tag{3}$$

The yields are constructed from returns, with and without dividends, provided by CRSP. Consider a 1 dollar investment in either the value-weighted or equally weighted market portfolio at the end of December 1925. If dividends are not reinvested, the value of the portfolio at the end of the month m is

$$P(m) = \exp[r_0(1) + r_0(2) + r_0(3) + \cdots + r_0(m)], \tag{4}$$

where $r_0(m)$ is the continuously compounded without-dividend return for month m. If the continuously compounded with-dividend return is $r(m)$, the dividend on the portfolio in month m is

$$D(m) = P(m-1)\exp[r(m)] - P(m). \tag{5}$$

Two dividend yields, $D(t)/P(t-1)$ and $D(t)/P(t)$, are computed by summing the monthly dividends, from (5), for the year preceding time t and dividing by the value of the portfolio at the beginning or end of the year, from (4). We use annual yields to avoid seasonal differences in dividend payments. The annual yields are used in the estimates of (3) for all return horizons.

3.2 *Estimation problems and the definition of the yield*

The certainty model (2) shows that the dividend yield is a noisy proxy for expected returns because it also reflects expected dividend growth. Variation in the dividend yield $Y(t)$ due to changes in the expected growth of dividends can cloud the information in the yield about time-varying expected returns. More generally, any variation in $Y(t)$ that is unrelated to variation in the time t expected return $E_t r(t, t+T)$ is noise that tends to cause the regression of $r(t, t+T)$ on $Y(t)$ to miss some of the variation in expected returns – it shows up in the regression residuals.

On the other hand, when expected returns vary through time, the discount rate effect tends to cause estimates of (3) to overstate the variation in expected returns. Suppose that an expected return shock at t increases discount rates. If the discount rate increases are not offset by increases in expected dividends, the expected return shock causes an unexpected decline in $P(t)$. If dividend yields forecast returns, the expected return shock also causes an unexpected increase in $Y(t)$. Thus, because of the discount rate effect, expected return shocks produce a negative correlation between unexpected returns and contemporaneous yield shocks that tends to produce upward-biased slopes in regressions of returns on yields (Stambaugh, 1986). This bias arises only when yields track time-varying expected returns. It does not bias the tests toward false conclusions that yields have forecast power.

Upward bias of the estimated slope in (3) due to the discount rate effect and downward bias due to variation in $Y(t)$ unrelated to $E_t r(t, t+T)$ can arise for any definition of the yield. Other problems in estimating (3) are specific to the definition of $Y(t)$ as $D(t)/P(t)$ or $D(t)/P(t-1)$. For example, because we would like a yield with up-to-date but known information about expected returns for periods forward from t, $D(t)/P(t)$ is a natural choice. Because stock prices are forward looking, however, $D(t)$ is old relative to the dividend forecasts in $P(t)$. Good news about future dividends produces a high price $P(t)$ relative to the current dividend $D(t)$ and a low dividend yield $D(t)/P(t)$. Good news about dividends also produces a high return $r(t-T, t)$. The result is a negative correlation between the disturbance $\varepsilon(t-T, t)$ and the time t shock to $D(t)/P(t)$ that again tends to produce upward-biased slopes in regressions of $r(t, t+T)$ on $D(t)/P(t)$.

Table 16.1 shows that the cross-correlations between 1 year stock returns and dividend changes more than a year ahead are close to 0.0. These results suggest that stock prices do not forecast dividend changes more than a year ahead. Thus variation in the dividend yield due to a denominator price that looks beyond the dividend in the numerator is substantially reduced when $Y(t)$ is defined as $D(t)/P(t-1)$, where $P(t-1)$ is the price at the beginning of the year covered by $D(t)$. If stock prices do not forecast dividend changes more than a year ahead, the dividend forecasts in $P(t-1)$ will not produce variation in $D(t)/P(t-1)$, and they will not produce upward-biased slopes in regressions of $r(t, t+T)$ on $D(t)/P(t-1)$.

Confident conclusions that $D(t)/P(t)$ or $D(t)/P(t-1)$ produces regressions that overstate or understate the variation of expected returns cannot be made on *a priori* grounds. $D(t)/P(t-1)$ is more conservative. Any upward bias in the slopes it produces occurs only when expected returns vary through time (the discount rate effect). Thus regressions that use $D(t)/P(t-1)$ are more likely to avoid a false positive conclusion that yields track expected returns. However, they are also more likely to be too conservative. The deviation of $D(t)$ from its expected value at $t-1$ is noise that tends to cause regressions of $r(t, t+T)$ on $D(t)/P(t-1)$ to understate the variation in expected returns. Moreover, because $P(t-1)$ can only

Table 16.1 Cross-correlations between 1 year continuously compounded returns and current and future 1 year changes in the logarithm of annual dividends for the CRSP value-weighted and equally weighted NYSE portfolios

$\mathrm{cor}[r(t-1,t), \ln D(t+i) - \ln D(t+i-1)]$

	Lead i					
Period	*0*	*1*	*2*	*3*	*4*	$s(0)$[a]
Value-weighted nominal returns						
1927–86	0.10	0.68	0.22	0.03	−0.16	0.13
1927–56	0.13	0.78	0.26	0.08	−0.18	0.18
1957–86	−0.09	0.37	0.05	−0.29	−0.10	0.18
1941–86	−0.12	0.26	0.00	−0.16	−0.05	0.15
Equally weighted nominal returns						
1927–86	0.17	0.72	0.21	0.04	−0.20	0.13
1927–56	0.19	0.80	0.23	0.08	−0.22	0.18
1957–86	0.09	0.46	0.13	−0.11	−0.10	0.18
1941–86	0.03	0.46	0.11	−0.01	−0.12	0.15

[a] $s(0)$ is the asymptotic standard error of the contemporaneous cross-correlation, that is, $n^{-0.5}$, where n is the sample size. Real returns produce correlations similar to those shown for nominal returns.

reflect information about expected returns available at $t-1$, $D(t)/P(t-1)$ is about a year out of date with respect to expected returns measured forward from t. If current shocks have a decaying effect on expected returns, using an "old" yield to track expected returns is likely to understate the variation of expected returns. We present results for the more timely measure $D(t)/P(t)$ as well as for $D(t)/P(t-1)$.

4 Summary Statistics

Table 16.2 shows summary statistics for 1 year nominal and real returns on the value-weighted and equally weighted portfolios. Standard deviations of returns are about 50 percent higher during the period 1927–56 than during the period 1957–86. As in Blume (1968), the high variability of returns for 1927–56 is largely due to the period 1927–40. The standard deviations of returns are similar for 1957–86 and 1941–86. We shall find that the regression results are also similar for these periods.

Like stock returns, dividend changes are more variable toward the beginning of the sample. The standard deviations of year to year changes in the logarithms of annual dividends on the value-weighted and equally weighted portfolios for 1957–86 are about 25 percent of those for 1927–56. Dividend variability declines relative to that of returns. During the period

Table 16.2 Summary statistics for 1 year nominal and real returns, dividend yields, and changes in the logarithms of annual dividends for the CRSP value-weighted and equally weighted NYSE portfolios[a]

			Autocorrelations							Autocorrelations				
Period	*Mean*	*SD*	*1*	*2*	*3*	*4*	*5*	*Mean*	*SD*	*1*	*2*	*3*	*4*	*5*
	Value-weighted nominal returns							*Equally weighted nominal returns*						
1927–86	0.092	0.206	0.10	−0.20	−0.07	−0.15	−0.02	0.125	0.280	0.13	−0.18	−0.14	−0.23	−0.11
1927–56	0.088	0.244	0.21	−0.10	−0.18	−0.44	−0.03	0.124	0.336	0.19	−0.11	−0.23	−0.51	−0.12
1957–86	0.096	0.163	−0.16	−0.39	0.19	0.30	0.06	0.125	0.216	−0.04	−0.36	0.13	0.26	−0.07
1941–86	0.112	0.155	−0.08	−0.33	0.03	0.27	0.10	0.143	0.210	0.04	−0.28	−0.07	0.17	−0.01
	Value-weighted real returns							*Equally weighted real returns*						
1927–86	0.062	0.208	0.04	−0.24	−0.08	−0.09	0.05	0.094	0.282	0.08	−0.22	−0.15	−0.19	−0.04
1927–56	0.074	0.239	0.11	−0.17	−0.22	−0.40	0.06	0.109	0.334	0.13	−0.15	−0.26	−0.47	−0.04
1957–86	0.050	0.174	−0.10	−0.38	0.18	0.29	0.06	0.079	0.224	−0.03	−0.39	0.11	0.26	−0.05
1941–86	0.068	0.173	−0.01	−0.29	−0.01	0.24	0.16	0.099	0.223	0.04	−0.31	−0.12	0.15	0.05
	Value-weighted $\ln D(t+1) - \ln D(t)$							*Equally weighted* $\ln D(t+1) - \ln D(t)$						
1927–86	0.041	0.133	0.30	−0.10	−0.17	−0.20	−0.00	0.079	0.220	0.31	−0.15	−0.16	−0.28	−0.20
1927–56	0.028	0.184	0.28	−0.13	−0.21	−0.23	−0.00	0.083	0.304	0.30	−0.18	−0.17	−0.30	−0.21
1957–86	0.055	0.041	0.54	0.30	0.22	0.08	−0.19	0.075	0.077	0.55	0.37	0.12	−0.09	−0.22
1941–86	0.058	0.058	0.25	0.10	0.11	−0.21	−0.34	0.089	0.087	0.33	0.21	0.14	0.12	0.02
	Value-weighted $D(t)/P(t-1)$							*Equally weighted* $D(t)/P(t-1)$						
1926–85	0.047	0.012	0.81	0.59	0.48	0.44	0.39	0.044	0.013	0.78	0.51	0.36	0.30	0.28
1926–55	0.053	0.009	0.64	0.18	−0.14	−0.25	−0.10	0.048	0.015	0.79	0.50	0.26	0.18	0.28
1956–85	0.040	0.010	0.79	0.65	0.64	0.58	0.41	0.040	0.010	0.65	0.34	0.32	0.30	0.10
1940–85	0.046	0.013	0.84	0.67	0.57	0.50	0.41	0.046	0.014	0.78	0.51	0.39	0.40	0.38

[a]The 1 year value-weighted and equally weighted portfolio returns are continuously compounded. Real returns are calculated by summing the differences between monthly continuously compounded nominal returns and the 1 month inflation rate, calculated from the US Consumer Price Index (CPI). $D(t)/P(t-1)$ is the ratio of dividends for year t to the value of the portfolio at the end of year $t-1$. The time periods for $D(t)/P(t-1)$ are those for $D(t)$. The periods for $D(t)/P(t-1)$ match the periods to be used in the regressions of 1 year returns on the yields. For example, the returns for 1927–86 are regressed on the yields for 1926–85.

1927–56, dividend changes are almost as variable as returns. After 1940 returns are more than 2.4 times as variable as dividend changes.

Dividend variability also declines relative to the variability of earnings. For the period 1927–56, the standard deviation of annual changes in the logarithm of annual earnings on the Standard & Poor's (S&P) Composite Index (0.259) is about 43 percent greater than that of changes in annual Index dividends (0.181). For 1957–86, the standard deviation of changes in earnings (0.113) is more than three times that of dividend changes (0.037).

The estimated speed of adjustment of dividends to target dividends in Lintner's (1956) dividend model also declines over the sample period. Lintner postulates that a firm's target dividend $D^\star(t)$ for year t is a constant fraction of earnings $E(t)$:

$$D^\star(t) = kE(t). \tag{6}$$

The change in the actual dividends from $t-1$ to t is assumed to follow a partial adjustment model

$$D(t) - D(t-1) = a + s[D^\star(t) - D(t-1)] + u(t). \tag{7}$$

When this model is fitted to the annual S&P earnings and dividends, the estimated speed of adjustment s drops from 49 percent per year for 1927–56 to 12 percent per year for 1941–86, and 11 percent for 1957–86.

In short, the data suggest systematic changes in the dividend policies of firms (toward dividends that are smoother relative to earnings) during the sample period. For our purposes, changes in dividend policy are important because they can produce variation in yields that obscures information about expected returns or causes the relation between the yield and expected returns to change through time.

Finally, table 16.2 shows summary statistics for end of year observations on the yield $D(t)/P(t-1)$, the explanatory variable in regressions of $r(t,t+T)$ on $D(t)/P(t-1)$ for 1–4 year returns. The first-order autocorrelations of $D(t)/P(t-1)$ are large, but the autocorrelations decay across longer lags. If yields track expected returns, high first-order autocorrelation implies persistence in expected returns. The decay of the autocorrelations across longer lags then suggests the appealing conclusion that, though highly autocorrelated, expected returns have a mean-reverting tendency.

5 Regressions for Nominal and Real Returns

The change in return variability around 1940 suggests that a weighted least squares (WLS) approach that deflates the observations by estimates of return variability will produce more efficient estimates of regressions of returns on dividend yields. Some of our more interesting analysis, however, involves explaining why the expected return variation tracked by yields is a larger fraction of the variation of returns for longer return horizons. WLS estimates would complicate the analysis by changing the meaning of what is being explained. Thus the text uses ordinary least squares (OLS) estimates. WLS regressions produce slopes that are similar to OLS slopes, however, and so produce similar estimates of the variation in expected returns. In fact, for periods that overlap the shift in return variances around 1940 (for example, 1927–86 and 1927–56), WLS estimates actually give a stronger view of the statistical reliability of return forecasts from yields. The WLS estimates are available on request.

Tables 16.3 and 16.4 summarize the OLS regressions of the value-weighted and equally weighted portfolio returns $r(t, t+T)$ on their *ex ante* yields $D(t)/P(t-1)$ and $D(t)/P(t)$. Because the regressions are the central evidence on the variation of expected returns, the results are shown in some detail. Each table splits the 1927–86 sample into 30 year periods (1927–56 and 1957–86). Results for the period 1941–86 of roughly constant return variances are also shown. Estimates of regression slopes and their t statistics for 1946–86 and 1936–86 (not shown) are close to those for 1941–86. Finally, to illustrate that the results are similar for different definitions of returns, regressions for nominal and real returns are shown.

5.1 Nominal returns

All the regression slopes in tables 16.3 and 16.4 are positive. For value-weighted nominal returns, regressions that use the less timely $D(t)/P(t-1)$ as the explanatory variable produce only one slope less than 1.8 standard errors from 0.0. Slopes for value-weighted nominal returns more than 2.0 standard errors from 0.0 are the rule, and slopes more than 2.5 standard errors from 0.0 are common. For 1941–86, the longest period of roughly constant return variances, all the slopes for value-weighted nominal returns are more than 2.4 standard errors from 0.0.

Except for the period 1927–56, the regressions of equally weighted nominal returns on $D(t)/P(t-1)$ are also strong evidence that expected returns vary through time. For the sample period 1927–86 and the subperiods 1941–86 and 1957–86, the regression slopes for equally weighted nominal returns are typically more than 2.0 standard errors from 0.0. Moreover, the weak results for equally weighted returns for 1927–56 are a consequence of the high variability of returns in the early years of the sample. The slopes for 1927–56 are similar to those for the period 1941–86 of lower return variances, and the 1941–86 slopes are all more than 2.6 standard errors from 0.0.

Table 16.3 Regressions of nominal and real CRSP value-weighted NYSE portfolio returns on dividend yields[a]

$$r(t, t+T) = a + bY(t) + e(t, t+T)$$

Return horizon		Nominal returns								Real returns							
		$Y(t)=D(t)/P(t-1)$				$Y(t)=D(t)/P(t)$				$Y(t)=D(t)/P(t-1)$				$Y(t)=D(t)/P(t)$			
T	N	b	$t(b)$	R^2	$s(e)$	b	$t(b)$	R^2	$s(e)$	b	$t(b)$	R^2	$s(e)$	b	$t(b)$	R^2	$s(e)$
1927–86																	
M	720	0.53	2.99	0.01	0.06	0.21	1.40	0.00	0.06	0.49	2.76	0.01	0.06	0.28	1.83	0.00	0.06
Q	240	1.12	1.87	0.01	0.11	1.07	2.10	0.01	0.11	1.04	1.71	0.01	0.11	1.26	2.48	0.02	0.11
1	60	5.37	2.40	0.07	0.20	2.47	1.27	0.01	0.20	5.32	2.35	0.07	0.20	3.35	1.72	0.03	0.20
2	59	9.10	2.18	0.10	0.29	7.38	2.04	0.09	0.29	9.08	2.31	0.11	0.28	8.77	2.59	0.15	0.28
3	58	11.56	2.14	0.13	0.33	9.94	2.21	0.13	0.33	11.73	2.51	0.15	0.31	11.53	2.93	0.21	0.30
4	57	12.68	1.93	0.13	0.37	12.86	2.43	0.19	0.36	13.44	2.46	0.17	0.33	14.43	3.25	0.29	0.31
1927–56																	
M	360	0.93	2.77	0.02	0.07	0.17	0.69	−0.00	0.07	0.78	2.33	0.01	0.07	0.27	1.08	0.00	0.07
Q	120	1.79	1.55	0.01	0.14	1.16	1.41	0.01	0.14	1.38	1.20	0.00	0.14	1.42	1.75	0.02	0.13
1	30	11.04	2.49	0.15	0.22	1.50	0.46	−0.03	0.25	9.61	2.16	0.11	0.23	2.62	0.83	−0.01	0.24
2	29	22.49	2.88	0.28	0.33	8.92	1.49	0.07	0.37	19.43	2.65	0.23	0.32	10.16	1.89	0.13	0.34
3	28	29.24	2.86	0.33	0.39	15.27	2.21	0.18	0.43	24.73	2.74	0.29	0.36	15.94	2.73	0.26	0.36
4	27	28.16	2.25	0.24	0.46	20.86	3.14	0.30	0.44	23.00	2.21	0.22	0.40	20.39	3.70	0.40	0.35
1957–86																	
M	360	0.53	2.31	0.01	0.04	0.68	2.66	0.02	0.04	0.42	1.79	0.01	0.04	0.51	1.95	0.01	0.04
Q	120	1.40	1.82	0.02	0.08	2.33	2.78	0.05	0.08	1.11	1.40	0.01	0.08	1.87	2.14	0.03	0.08
1	30	5.60	1.86	0.08	0.16	9.32	3.02	0.22	0.14	4.58	1.39	0.03	0.17	7.74	2.21	0.12	0.16
2	29	7.51	1.89	0.09	0.20	16.40	4.04	0.45	0.16	5.68	1.10	0.02	0.23	14.06	2.53	0.25	0.20
3	28	10.41	3.01	0.21	0.19	17.12	4.12	0.51	0.15	8.16	1.38	0.08	0.23	14.03	2.05	0.24	0.21
4	27	15.05	3.37	0.38	0.18	19.69	3.87	0.57	0.15	12.48	1.57	0.17	0.24	16.21	1.83	0.26	0.23

1941–86																	
M	552	0.39	2.95	0.01	0.04	0.36	2.59	0.01	0.04	0.37	2.73	0.01	0.04	0.32	2.20	0.01	0.04
Q	184	1.07	2.47	0.03	0.08	1.20	2.64	0.03	0.08	1.04	2.28	0.02	0.08	1.07	2.23	0.02	0.08
1	46	4.46	2.62	0.12	0.15	5.09	2.88	0.14	0.14	4.40	2.29	0.09	0.17	4.82	2.38	0.09	0.16
2	45	7.15	3.04	0.17	0.19	10.34	4.18	0.35	0.17	7.21	2.36	0.13	0.23	10.26	3.15	0.25	0.21
3	44	9.42	4.77	0.29	0.19	12.94	5.68	0.51	0.15	9.66	2.91	0.21	0.24	13.10	3.53	0.36	0.21
4	43	12.75	5.49	0.49	0.17	15.35	5.62	0.64	0.14	13.34	3.18	0.36	0.23	15.71	3.31	0.45	0.22

[a] N is the number of observations. $P(t)$ is the time t price. $D(t)$ is the dividend for the year preceding t. $r(t, t+T)$ is the continuously compounded return from t to $t+T$. The regressions for $T = 1$ month (M), one quarter (Q), and 1 year use nonoverlapping returns. The regressions for 2–4 year returns use overlapping annual observations. The standard errors in the t statistic $t(b)$ for the 2–4 year slopes are adjusted for the sample autocorrelation of overlapping residuals using the method of Hansen and Hodrick (1980). Regression slopes and t statistics for 1946–86 and 1936–86 (not shown) are close to those for 1941–86.

Table 16.4 Regressions of nominal and real CRSP equallyweighted NYSE portfolio returns on dividend yields[a]

$$r(t, t+T) = a + bY(t) + e(t, t+T)$$

Return horizon		*Nominal returns*								*Real returns*							
		$Y(t) = D(t)/P(t-1)$				$Y(t) = D(t)/P(t)$				$Y(t) = D(t)/P(t-1)$				$Y(t) = D(t)/P(t)$			
T	N	b	$t(b)$	R^2	$s(e)$	b	$t(b)$	R^2	$s(e)$	b	$t(b)$	R^2	$s(e)$	b	$t(b)$	R^2	$s(e)$
1927–86																	
M	720	0.52	2.40	0.01	0.07	0.21	0.97	−0.00	0.07	0.45	2.10	0.00	0.07	0.24	1.15	0.00	0.08
Q	240	1.07	1.41	0.00	0.15	1.28	1.74	0.01	0.15	0.91	1.19	0.00	0.16	1.40	1.90	0.01	0.15
1	60	5.87	2.21	0.06	0.27	2.69	1.06	0.00	0.28	5.48	2.04	0.05	0.27	3.38	1.33	0.01	0.28
2	59	10.75	2.14	0.10	0.40	9.91	2.15	0.10	0.40	10.06	2.05	0.09	0.40	11.23	2.54	0.14	0.39
3	58	13.60	2.09	0.12	0.47	14.68	2.63	0.17	0.46	12.38	2.02	0.10	0.46	16.08	3.14	0.22	0.43
4	57	14.28	1.96	0.11	0.53	17.96	2.95	0.21	0.49	12.64	1.86	0.09	0.50	18.91	3.47	0.27	0.45

continued

Table 16.4 (*Continued*)

$$r(t, t+T) = a + bY(t) + e(t, t+T)$$

Return horizon		Nominal returns								Real returns							
		$Y(t)=D(t)/P(t-1)$				$Y(t)=D(t)/P(t)$				$Y(t)=D(t)/P(t-1)$				$Y(t)=D(t)/P(t)$			
T	N	b	$t(b)$	R^2	$s(e)$	b	$t(b)$	R^2	$s(e)$	b	$t(b)$	R^2	$s(e)$	b	$t(b)$	R^2	$s(e)$
1927–56																	
M	360	0.49	1.50	0.00	0.09	0.06	0.20	−0.00	0.09	0.38	1.18	0.00	0.09	0.10	0.34	−0.00	0.09
Q	120	0.85	0.73	−0.00	0.19	0.91	0.83	−0.00	0.19	0.56	0.48	−0.01	0.19	1.03	0.95	−0.00	0.19
1	30	5.14	1.25	0.02	0.33	0.38	0.10	−0.04	0.34	4.21	1.02	0.00	0.33	1.13	0.31	−0.03	0.34
2	29	11.97	1.45	0.09	0.50	7.86	1.11	0.03	0.52	10.18	1.28	0.06	0.49	8.97	1.35	0.06	0.49
3	28	16.05	1.44	0.11	0.61	14.92	1.73	0.13	0.61	12.92	1.23	0.07	0.59	15.65	2.00	0.17	0.56
4	27	13.92	1.11	0.05	0.71	19.35	2.03	0.19	0.65	9.58	0.84	0.01	0.66	18.93	2.23	0.22	0.59
1957–86																	
M	360	0.87	2.76	0.02	0.05	0.99	2.80	0.02	0.05	0.76	2.37	0.01	0.05	0.82	2.30	0.01	0.05
Q	120	2.24	2.08	0.03	0.10	3.68	3.18	0.07	0.10	1.97	1.78	0.02	0.11	3.28	2.75	0.05	0.10
1	30	10.01	2.68	0.18	0.20	12.58	3.28	0.25	0.19	9.31	2.35	0.13	0.21	11.56	2.79	0.19	0.20
2	29	13.02	2.39	0.16	0.28	23.85	4.59	0.51	0.21	11.82	1.93	0.11	0.30	22.86	3.83	0.42	0.24
3	28	16.22	2.66	0.22	0.29	23.87	3.84	0.45	0.24	14.77	2.14	0.17	0.31	22.84	3.30	0.38	0.26
4	27	21.99	3.01	0.35	0.30	25.98	3.39	0.42	0.28	20.26	2.47	0.28	0.32	24.85	3.00	0.37	0.30
1941–86																	
M	552	0.51	3.21	0.02	0.05	0.45	2.57	0.01	0.05	0.51	3.18	0.02	0.05	0.44	2.49	0.01	0.05
Q	184	1.42	2.64	0.03	0.10	1.64	2.78	0.04	0.10	1.47	2.64	0.03	0.10	1.63	2.67	0.03	0.10
1	46	6.75	3.35	0.19	0.19	7.05	3.15	0.17	0.19	6.99	3.24	0.17	0.20	7.27	3.03	0.15	0.21
2	45	10.38	3.15	0.22	0.27	14.64	4.02	0.37	0.24	10.89	3.07	0.21	0.29	15.51	4.00	0.36	0.26
3	44	11.90	2.94	0.23	0.30	17.71	4.02	0.43	0.26	12.37	2.96	0.22	0.32	18.99	4.25	0.45	0.27
4	43	13.68	2.76	0.26	0.32	19.00	3.60	0.43	0.28	14.19	2.90	0.27	0.33	20.50	3.97	0.47	0.28

[a] N is the number of observations. $P(t)$ is the time t price. $D(t)$ is the dividend for the year preceding t. $r(t, t+T)$ is the continuously compounded return from t to $t+T$. The regressions for $T=$ 1 month (M), one quarter (Q), and 1 year use nonoverlapping returns. The regressions for 2–4 year returns use overlapping annual observations. The standard errors in the t statistic $t(b)$ for the 2–4 year slopes are adjusted for the sample autocorrelation of overlapping residuals using the method of Hansen and Hodrick (1980). Regression slopes and t statistics for 1946–86 and 1936–86 (not shown) are close to those for 1941–86.

Regressions that use the more timely $D(t)/P(t)$ to explain nominal returns also produce strong evidence of forecast power for the period 1927–86 and especially for the subperiods 1941–86 and 1957–86. For the two post-1940 periods, the slopes for $D(t)/P(t)$ are more than 2.5 standard errors from 0.0 for both market portfolios and for all return horizons. Slopes more than 4.0 standard errors from 0.0 are common.

5.2 *Real returns*

The slopes for real returns in tables 16.3 and 16.4 are typically close to those for nominal returns. Because the real and nominal regressions have the same explanatory variable, similar slopes indicate that variation in expected nominal returns translates into similar variation in expected real returns. If the market is efficient, the results indicate that dividend yields signal variation in equilibrium expected real returns.

Fama and French (1987) show regressions of excess stock returns on dividend yields. Excess returns for horizons beyond 1 month are calculated by cumulating the differences between monthly nominal stock returns and the 1 month US Treasury bill rate. The results for excess returns are similar to those for real returns in tables 16.3 and 16.4. Thus the variation in expected real stock returns tracked by dividend yields is also present in the expected premiums of stock returns over 1 month bill returns.

5.3 *The behavior of the regression slopes*

The slopes in the regressions of real or nominal returns $r(t, t+T)$ on $Y(t)$ increase with the return horizon T. When the explanatory variable is $D(t)/P(t-1)$, the increase in the slopes is roughly proportional to T for horizons to 1 year, but less than proportional to T for 2–4 year returns. For the more timely $D(t)/P(t)$ and for periods after 1940, the slopes increase roughly in proportion to T for return horizons to 4 years, but more slowly thereafter.

This behavior of the slopes has an appealing explanation. The slope in the regression of the T-period return $r(t, t+T)$ on $Y(t)$ is the sum of the slopes in the T regressions of the one-period returns $r(t, t+1), \ldots,$ $r(t+T-1, t+T)$ on $Y(t)$. Slopes in regressions of $r(t, t+T)$ on $Y(t)$ that increase in proportion to T for horizons of 1 or 2 years thus imply that variation in $Y(t)$ signals similar variation in one-period expected returns out to 1 or 2 years. Slopes that increase less than in proportion to T for longer return horizons suggest that $Y(t)$ signals less variation in more distant one-period expected returns. This behavior of the slopes suggests that expected returns are highly autocorrelated but slowly mean reverting.

The decay of the autocorrelations of $D(t)/P(t-1)$ in table 16.2 also suggests slow mean reversion.

5.4 Other tests

The intuition of the hypothesis that dividend yields forecast returns is that stock prices are low relative to dividends when discount rates and expected returns are high, and vice versa, so that yields capture variation in expected returns. There is a similar intuition for earnings-to-price ratios E/P.

We have estimated regressions (available on request) of value-weighted and equally weighted NYSE returns $r(t, t+T)$ on $E(t)/P(t-1)$ and $E(t)/P(t)$. $E(t)$ is earnings per share on the S&P Composite Index for calendar year t, as reported by S&P. $P(t)$ is the value of the index at the end of the year. In many ways the E/P results are similar to the D/P results. For example, the regression slopes and R^2 produced by E/P increase with the return horizon. The t values for the slopes suggest that E/P has reliable forecast power. E/P tends, however, to have less explanatory power than D/P.

Earnings are more variable than dividends (see section 4). If this higher variability is unrelated to the variation in expected returns, E/P is a noisier measure of expected returns than D/P. This "numerator noise" argument may also explain why the forecast power of dividend yields is higher in the periods after 1940 when the variability of dividends declines substantially relative to the variability of returns.

It would seem that a solution to problems caused by noise in the numerator of E/P or D/P is to use $1/P$ as the forecast variable. Miller and Scholes (1982) show that the cross-section of $1/P$ for common stocks helps explain the cross-section of expected returns. Suppose, however, that reinvestment of earnings causes stock prices to have an upward-drifting nonstationary component. Then $1/P$ is nonstationary (it tends to drift downward), and it is not a good variable for tracking expected returns in time series tests. In fact, for the value-weighted and equally weighted NYSE portfolios, regressions (not shown) of $r(t, t+T)$ on $1/P(t)$, where $P(t)$ is the value of the portfolio at t, produce slopes and R^2 close to 0.0.

6 Out-of-Sample Forecasts

The slopes in tables 16.3 and 16.4 are apparently strong evidence that yields signal variation in expected returns. Given the uncertainty about the bias of the slopes, however, further testing is in order. One approach is to use the regressions to forecast out-of-sample returns. We forecast returns for the 20 year period 1967–86. Each forecast is from a regression of $r(t, t+T)$ on $Y(t)$ estimated with returns that begin and end in the preceding 30 year period. For example, to forecast the first 1 year return (1967), we use coefficients estimated with the 30 1 year returns for 1937–66. To forecast the first 4 year return (1967–70), we use coefficients estimated with the 27 overlapping annual observations on the 4 year returns that begin and end in the period 1937–66. For monthly and quarterly returns, the 30 year estimation period rolls forward in monthly or quarterly steps. For 1–4 year returns, the estimation period rolls forward in annual increments.

We start the estimation periods in 1937 because of the evidence that returns and yields behave differently during the first 10 years of the sample. Because the overlap of annual observations on multi-year returns reduces effective sample sizes, we judge that estimation periods shorter than 30 years would not produce meaningful forecasts of 2–4 year returns. The 1937 starting date and the choice of 30 year estimation periods then limit the forecast period to 1967–86. For this 20 year forecast period, there are only five nonoverlapping forecasts of 4 year returns.

6.1 Perspective

With respect to possible bias of the regression slopes, the out-of-sample tests are conservative. They correct for bias that causes the in-sample slopes to overstate the variation of expected returns, but they leave the estimation problems that cause the regressions to understate the variation of expected returns.

Thus in section 3 we argue that negative correlation between shocks to returns and yields (because of the discount rate effect or because yields and returns respond to dividend forecasts) produces positive bias in the slope estimates for dividend yields, with possibly more bias in the slopes for $D(t)/P(t)$ than in the slopes for $D(t)/P(t-1)$. The bias means that in-sample R^2 tends to overstate explanatory power. The bias decreases out-of-sample forecast power, however, so that out-of-sample tests are appropriately punitive.

On the other hand, yields contain noise (variation unrelated to expected returns) that tends to cause estimates of (3) to understate the variation in expected returns. Since the noise reduces both in-sample and out-of-sample forecast power, out-of-sample tests do not correct for this source of error. Likewise, if regressions of $r(t, t+T)$ on the less timely $D(t)/P(t-1)$ understate the variation of expected returns, the understatement remains in out-of-sample forecasts.

6.2 Results

Table 16.5 summarizes the mean squared errors (MSE) of the out-of-sample forecasts. To compare the forecasts with the in-sample fit of the

Table 16.5 Mean squared error R^2 for out-of-sample forecasts for NYSE portfolio returns for 1967–1986 and R^2 for in-sample forecasts for 1957–1986[a]

Return horizon T	$D(t)/P(t-1)$		$D(t)/P(t)$		$D(t)/P(t-1)$		$D(t)/P(t)$	
	Out	*In*	*Out*	*In*	*Out*	*In*	*Out*	*In*
	Value-weighted nominal returns				*Value-weighted real returns*			
M	0.01	0.01	0.02	0.02	0.01	0.01	0.01	0.01
Q	0.03	0.02	0.06	0.05	0.01	0.01	0.03	0.03
1	0.13	0.08	0.23	0.22	0.07	0.03	0.13	0.12
2	0.20	0.09	0.43	0.45	0.05	0.02	0.22	0.25
3	0.24	0.21	0.48	0.51	−0.18	0.08	0.00	0.24
4	0.35	0.38	0.50	0.57	−0.38	0.17	−0.26	0.26
	Equally weighted nominal returns				*Equally weighted real returns*			
M	0.01	0.02	0.01	0.02	0.01	0.01	0.01	0.01
Q	0.02	0.03	0.04	0.07	0.02	0.02	0.04	0.05
1	0.17	0.18	0.16	0.25	0.17	0.13	0.15	0.19
2	0.18	0.16	0.34	0.51	0.18	0.11	0.35	0.42
3	0.16	0.22	0.35	0.45	0.10	0.17	0.36	0.38
4	0.23	0.35	0.36	0.42	0.09	0.28	0.36	0.37

[a]The out-of-sample (Out) MSE R^2 is $1 - \{\mathrm{MSE}/s^2[r(t, t+T)]\}$. Each out-of-sample forecast is made with coefficients estimated using the previous 30 years of returns and yields. Monthly (M), quarterly (Q), and 1-year forecasts are for nonoverlapping periods. The 2–4 year forecasts are overlapping annual observations. The in-sample regressions are given in tables 16.3 and 16.4.

regressions, the MSE are reported as R^2. Specifically, the MSE R^2 in table 16.5 is

$$1 - \frac{\mathrm{MSE}}{s^2[r(t, t+T)]},$$

where $s^2[r(t, t+T)]$ is the out-of-sample variance of the forecasted return. The out-of-sample forecasts cover 1967–86. The in-sample R^2 values for 1957–86, the most comparable period in tables 16.3 and 16.4, are also shown in table 16.5.

For horizons out to 2 years, the MSE R^2 for the 1967–86 out-of-sample return forecasts from $D(t)/P(t-1)$ and $D(t)/P(t)$ are close to the in-sample R^2 for 1957–86. The signs of the differences between the in-sample R^2 and the out-of-sample MSE R^2 are random. The MSE R^2 for forecasts of 3 and 4 year value-weighted nominal returns from $D(t)/P(t-1)$ are also similar to the in-sample R^2. Otherwise, the MSE R^2 values produced by $D(t)/P(t-1)$ deteriorate relative to the in-sample R^2 in 3 and 4 year forecasts. (The obvious worst cases are the negative MSE R^2 for forecasts of value-weighted 3 and 4 year real returns.) The results for longer return horizons are less reliable, however, because they involve fewer independent returns during the 20 year forecast period. The uniform similarity of in-sample and out-of-sample forecast power for horizons to 2 years suggests that regressions of $r(t, t+T)$ on either $D(t)/P(t-1)$ or $D(t)/P(t)$ do not produce strongly biased slopes and thus biased estimates of explanatory power.

The out-of-sample forecasts do not confirm that $D(t)/P(t)$ slopes are more biased than $D(t)/P(t-1)$ slopes. The out-of-sample forecast power of $D(t)/P(t)$ actually matches in-sample explanatory power better than $D(t)/P(t-1)$. Only the out-of-sample MSE R^2 for forecasts of 3 and 4 year value-weighted real returns from $D(t)/P(t)$ are much less than the in-sample R^2. Thus there is no evidence in the out-of-sample tests that slope estimates for the more timely $D(t)/P(t)$ exaggerate the variation in expected returns.

On the other hand, like the in-sample R^2, the MSE R^2 for out-of-sample forecasts from $D(t)/P(t)$ are higher, often much higher, than those for forecasts from $D(t)/P(t-1)$. For example, the MSE R^2 for forecasts of 2–4 year returns from $D(t)/P(t)$ commonly exceed 0.35, while those for forecasts from $D(t)/P(t-1)$ are typically less than 0.20. The out-of-sample forecasts thus confirm that using the less timely $D(t)/P(t-1)$ to avoid false positive conclusions about forecast power produces regressions that understate the variation of expected returns.

7 Why Does Forecast Power Increase with the Return Horizon?

The out-of-sample MSE R^2 values tend to confirm the more extensive evidence from the in-sample R^2 in tables 16.3 and 16.4 that the explanatory power of the regressions increases with the return horizon. The in-sample R^2 in tables 16.3 and 16.4 and the out-of-sample MSE R^2 in table 16.5 are 0.07 or less for monthly and quarterly returns, but they are often greater than 0.25 for 2–4 year returns. That the same yields capture more return variance for longer forecast horizons is an interesting and challenging result.

Algebraically, the regression R^2 increases with the return horizon because the variance of the fitted values grows more quickly than the horizon, whereas the variance of the residuals generally grows less quickly than the horizon. Our goal is to explain why.

7.1 The regression fitted values and residuals

In the regressions of returns on dividend yields, the explanatory variable is the same for all return horizons. Thus, as return horizon increases, the variance of the fitted values grows in proportion to the square of the regression slopes. The slopes in tables 16.3 and 16.4 increase roughly in proportion to the return horizon out to 1 or 2 years, and then more slowly. As noted earlier, this behavior suggests that short-horizon expected returns are autocorrelated but slowly mean reverting. The persistence of short-horizon expected returns implied by slow mean reversion causes the variances of multiperiod expected returns to grow more than in proportion to the return horizon.

On the other hand, tables 16.3 and 16.4 show that for periods after 1940 the residual variances in regressions of $r(t, t+T)$ on $Y(t)$ grow less than in proportion to the return horizon, at least for 1–4 year returns. For example, the residual standard errors for 4 year returns never come close to twice the 1 year standard errors. The residual in the regression of the multi-year return $r(t, t+T)$ on $Y(t)$ is the sum of the residuals from regressions of the 1 year returns $r(t, t+1), \ldots, r(t+T-1, t+T)$ on $Y(t)$. If multi-year residual variances grow less than in proportion to the return horizon, the correlations of the residuals from the 1 year regressions must on average be negative. The negative correlation is documented in table 16.6. It has an economic explanation that, along with the persistence of expected returns, completes the story for the predictability of long-horizon returns.

Table 16.6 Correlations of residuals from regressions of 1 year real CRSP value-weighted and equally weighted NYSE returns on the dividend yield $D(t)/P(t-1)$[a]

$$r(t+i-1, t+i) = \alpha + bD(t)/P(t-1) + e(t+i-1, t+i)$$

$$\text{cor}[e(t+i-1, t+i),\ e(t+j-1, t+j)], \qquad i = 2, 3, 4, \quad j = 1, 2, 3$$

Lead	*Value-weighted returns, lead j*			*Equally weighted returns, lead j*		
i	*1*	*2*	*3*	*1*	*2*	*3*
1927–86						
2	−0.05			−0.00		
3	−0.30	−0.05		−0.29	−0.00	
4	−0.14	−0.31	0.1	−0.20	−0.26	0.09
1941–86						
2	−0.15			−0.18		
3	−0.39	−0.09		−0.43	−0.00	
4	−0.08	−0.39	−0.05	−0.17	−0.35	0.02

$\text{cor}[e(t+i-1, t+i), e(t+j-1, t+j)]$ is the correlation between the residual for the regression forecast of the 1 year return i years ahead and the residual for the regression forecast of the 1 year return j years ahead. The correlations for nominal returns and for the other subperiods in tables 16.3 and 16.4 are similar to those shown. Using $D(t)/P(t)$ as the forecast variable produces similar results.

[a] The residuals are from regressions that use $D(t)/P(t-1)$ to forecast 1 year returns 1, 2, 3, and 4 years ahead.

7.2 *Stock prices and expected return shocks*

Suppose that there is a shock at $t+1$ that increases expected returns. Since the shock occurs after the yield $Y(t)$ is set, fitted values from regressions of $r(t+1, t+2), \ldots, r(t+T-1, t+T)$ on $Y(t)$ will tend to underestimate returns after $t+1$, and the residuals will tend to be positive. On the other hand, if expected return shocks generate opposite unexpected changes in prices (the discount rate effect), the positive shock to expected returns at $t+1$ will tend to produce a negative residual in the regression of the 1 year return $r(t, t+1)$ on $Y(t)$. Thus, because of the discount rate effect, the residual from the regression of $r(t, t+1)$ on $Y(t)$ is negatively correlated with the residuals from regressions of $r(t+1, t+2), \ldots, r(t+T-1, t+T)$ on $Y(t)$. A similar argument implies that the residuals from the regression of $r(t+k-1, t+k)$ on $Y(t)$ tend to be negatively correlated with the residuals from regressions of 1 year returns after $t+k$ on $Y(t)$.

In the next section we present further tests for the discount rate effect, based on estimates of the relation between contemporaneous return and dividend yield shocks.

8 Yields and Temporary Components of Stock Prices

8.1 *Yield shocks, price shocks, and future expected returns*

Table 16.1 suggests that 1 year returns are uncorrelated with dividend changes more than 1 year ahead. This suggests that $D(t+1)$ is an unbiased (but noisy) measure of the information in $P(t)$ about future dividends, so that $D(t+1)/P(t)$ is relatively free of variation due to dividend forecasts. Thus the unexpected component of $D(t+1)/P(t)$ can be interpreted as a (noisy) measure of the shock to expected returns at t.

Preliminary tests (not shown) indicated that the highly autocorrelated yields on the value-weighted and equally weighted portfolios are approximated well as first-order autoregressions (AR1s), with AR1 parameters close to the first-order autocorrelations in table 16.2. We use residuals from AR1s estimated on end of year yields to measure yield shocks:

$$\frac{D(t+1)}{P(t)} = \alpha + \phi \frac{D(t)}{P(t-1)} + v(t-1, t). \tag{8}$$

We use the yield shock $v(t-1, t)$ as a proxy for the expected return shock from $t-1$ to t.

The discount-rate effect implies a negative relation between expected return shocks and contemporaneous returns; an unexpected increase in expected returns drives the current price down. We measure this relation with the slope δ in the regression of $r(t-1,t)$ on $v(t-1,t)$:

$$r(t-1,t) = \gamma + \delta v(t-1,t) + u(t-1,t). \tag{9}$$

We interpret δ as the response of $P(t)$ per unit of the time t yield shock. The slope $\beta(T)$ in the regression of $r(t,t+T)$ on $D(t)/P(t-1)$ then measures the T-period expected future price change due to the changes in expected returns implied by a yield shock. A comparison of estimates of δ and $\beta(T)$ allows us to judge the relative magnitudes of the current and expected future price responses to yield shocks. The logic of this approach is that we want estimates of $\beta(T)$ for a long return horizon (we use $T=4$ years), since the autocorrelation of expected returns implies that a yield shock has a slowly decaying effect on one-period expected future price changes.

Estimates of δ in (9) must be interpreted cautiously. The lack of correlation between returns and dividend changes more than a year ahead suggests that $D(t+1)/P(t)$ is relatively free from variation due to dividend forecasts. But this does not mean that all variation in $D(t+1)/P(t)$ is due to expected returns. Moreover, whatever its source, variation in $P(t)$ that results in variation in $D(t+1)/P(t)$ tends to produce a negative correlation between $r(t-1,t)$ and the yield shock $v(t-1,t)$. Thus negative estimates of δ are not *per se* evidence of a discount rate effect. To infer that negative estimates of δ reflect offsetting changes in current prices related to changes in expected future returns, we need the complementary evidence from estimates of $\beta(T)$ that yields track expected returns so that yield shocks imply expected future price changes of the same sign.

8.2 *The estimates*

Table 16.7 shows estimates of δ for real returns on the NYSE value-weighted and equally weighted portfolios. The estimates are always negative, less than -17.0, and more than 2.9 standard errors from 0.0. Table 16.7 also shows estimates of $\beta(T)$ for $T=4$ years. Despite large standard errors, the estimates are usually more than 2.0 standard errors above 0.0. We conclude from the estimates of δ and $\beta(4)$ that dividend yield shocks are associated with (a) contemporaneous price changes of the opposite sign and (b) expected future price changes of the same sign.

The positive estimates of $\beta(4)$ from regressions of $r(t,t+T)$ on $D(t)/P(t-1)$ are large but typically smaller in magnitude than the negative estimates of δ. The out-of-sample forecasts in table 16.5 suggest, however, that the $D(t)/P(t-1)$ slopes understate the variation of expected returns because the information in $D(t)/P(t-1)$ is about a year out of date for expected returns measured forward from t. The estimates of $\beta(4)$ for

Table 16.7 Tests for a discount rate effect in stock returns: comparisons of the relation δ between contemporaneous real returns and dividend yield shocks and the relation b between future returns and current dividend yields[a]

$$D(t+1)/P(t) = \alpha + \phi D(t)/P(t-1) + v(t-1,t)$$
$$r(t-1,t) = \gamma + \delta v(t-1,t) + u(t-1,t)$$
$$r(t,t+4) = a + bY(t) + e(t,t+4)$$

			$Y(t) = D(t)/P(t-1)$		$Y(t) = D(t)/P(t)$	
Period	δ	$s(\delta)$	$b(4)$	$s[b(4)]$	$b(4)$	$s[b(4)]$
Value-weighted real returns						
1927–86	−22.27	2.71	13.44	5.47	14.43	4.44
1927–56	−20.42	4.69	23.00	10.40	20.39	5.51
1957–86	−25.72	2.44	12.48	7.94	16.21	8.88
1941–86	−20.10	2.15	13.34	4.19	15.71	4.75
Equally weighted real returns						
1927–86	−20.42	3.48	12.64	6.81	18.91	5.45
1927–56	−17.80	5.95	9.58	11.45	18.93	8.47
1957–86	−24.73	3.17	20.26	8.22	24.85	8.29
1941–86	−20.37	2.23	14.19	4.90	20.50	5.16

[a]The contemporaneous response δ of the return $r(t-1,t)$ to the yield shock $v(t-1,t)$ is estimated with regressions of annual observations on 1 year returns on the residuals from a first-order autoregression for the yield. The estimates of $b(4)$, interpreted as the response of future 1 year returns to a current yield shock, are from tables 16.3 and 16.4. $s(\delta)$ and $s[b(4)]$ are standard errors. The results for nominal returns are similar.

regressions of $r(t,t+4)$ on the more timely $D(t)/P(t)$ are closer in magnitude to (usually within 1.0 standard error of) the estimates of δ.

We interpret the estimates of δ and $\beta(4)$ as suggesting that, on average, the expected future price increases implied by higher expected returns are just offset by the immediate price decline due to the discount rate effect. Thus, as postulated by Summers (1986) and Fama and French (1988), positively autocorrelated expected returns generate mean-reverting components of prices. We next consider competing scenarios for such temporary price components.

8.3 *Temporary price components*

Temporary components of prices and the forecast power of yields are consistent with an efficient market. Suppose that investor tastes for current versus risky future consumption and the stochastic evolution of firms' investment opportunities result in equilibrium expected returns that are highly autocorrelated but mean reverting. Suppose that shocks to expected returns and shocks to rational forecasts of dividends are independent.

Then a shock to expected returns has no effect on expected dividends or expected returns in the distant future. Thus, the shock has no long-term effect on expected prices. The cumulative effect of a shock on expected returns must be exactly offset by an opposite adjustment in the current price. It follows that mean-reverting equilibrium expected returns can give rise to mean-reverting (temporary) components of stock prices (see Poterba and Summers (1987) for a formal analysis).

On the other hand, temporary components of prices and the forecast power of yields are also consistent with common models of an inefficient market, such as those of Keynes (1936), Shiller (1984), DeBondt and Thaler (1985), and Summers (1986), in which stock prices take long temporary swings away from fundamental values. In this view, high D/P ratios signal that future returns will be high because stock prices are temporarily irrationally low. Conversely, low D/P ratios signal irrationally high prices and low future returns.

As always, market efficiency *per se* is not testable. It must be tested jointly with restrictions on the behavior of equilibrium expected returns (Fama, 1970). One reasonable restriction is that equilibrium in an efficient market never implies predictable price declines (negative expected nominal returns) for the value-weighted and equally weighted NYSE portfolios. The behavior of the fitted values for the regressions in tables 16.3 and 16.4 supports this hypothesis.

The fitted values from the regressions of nominal returns on dividend yields are rarely negative. For example, when the explanatory variable is the more timely $D(t)/P(t)$, the regressions for equally weighted returns for all horizons produce a total of six negative fitted values during the period 1927–86 and no negative fitted values during the period 1941–86. The regressions of value-weighted nominal returns on $D(t)/P(t)$ produce no negative fitted values in either period. In both the $D(t)/P(t)$ and the $D(t)/P(t-1)$ regressions, no negative fitted value is close to 2.0 standard errors from 0.0. As a rule at least two-thirds of the return forecasts are more than 2.0 standard errors above 0.0.

A stronger hypothesis is that equilibrium in an efficient market never implies negative expected real returns for the value-weighted and equally weighted NYSE portfolios. The regression fitted values are more often negative for real returns than for nominal returns, but again no negative forecast of real returns is more than 2.0 standard errors from 0.0, whereas typically more than half of the forecasts are more than 2.0 standard errors above 0.0.

In short, low dividend yields forecast that nominal returns will be relatively low, but they do not forecast that prices will decline. Likewise, the strong forecast power of yields does not imply that expected real returns are ever reliably negative.

8.4 Dividend yields and the autocorrelation of returns

Autocorrelated expected returns and the opposite response of prices to expected return shocks (the discount rate effect) can combine to produce mean-reverting components of stock prices. Fama and French (1988) show that mean-reverting price components tend to induce negative autocorrelation in long-horizon returns. Thus, the negative autocorrelation of long-horizon returns in the earlier work is consistent with the positive autocorrelation of expected returns documented here.

But a mean-reverting positively autocorrelated expected return does not necessarily imply negative autocorrelated returns or a mean-reverting component of prices. If shocks to expected returns and expected dividends are positively correlated, the opposite response of prices to expected return shocks can disappear. In this case, the positive autocorrelation of expected returns will imply positively autocorrelated returns, and time-varying expected returns will not generate mean-reverting price components. Moreover, changes through time in the autocorrelation of expected returns, or in the relation between shocks to expected returns and expected dividends, can change the time series properties of returns and obscure tests of forecast power based on autocorrelation.

In contrast, as long as yields move with expected returns, regressions of returns on yields can document time-varying expected returns irrespective of changes in the autocorrelation of returns. This may explain why yields have strong forecast power in post-1940 periods, when the autocorrelations of returns in Fama and French (1988) give weak indications of time-varying expected returns.

Does the variation of expected returns tracked by yields subsume the predictability of long-horizon returns implied by the negative autocorrelation in Fama and French (1988)? We have estimated multiple regressions of $r(t, t+T)$ on $D(t)/P(t)$ and the lagged return $r(t-T, t)$. The lagged return rarely has marginal explanatory power. Negative slopes for the lagged return are typically less than 1.0 standard error from 0.0. In contrast, as in the univariate regressions, the slopes for the dividend yield in the multiple regressions increase with the return horizon and are typically more than 2.0 standard errors from 0.0 for the period 1927–86 and for all periods after 1935. Thus including the lagged return in the regressions has no effect on the conclusion that dividend yields have systematic forecast power across different time periods and return horizons.

9 Conclusions

Like previous work, our regressions of returns on dividend yields indicate that time variation in expected returns account for small fractions of the variances of short-horizon returns. Dividend yields typically explain less than 5 percent of the variances of monthly or quarterly returns. An interesting and challenging feature of our evidence is that time variation in expected returns accounts for more of the variation of long-horizon returns. Dividend yields often explain more than 25 percent of the variances of 2–4 year returns. We offer a simple explanation.

The persistence (high positive autocorrelation) of expected returns causes the variance of expected returns, measured by the fitted values in the regressions of returns on dividend yields, to grow more than in proportion to the return horizon. On the other hand, the growth of the variance of the regression residuals is attenuated by a discount rate effect: shocks to expected returns are associated with opposite shocks to current prices.

The cumulative price effect of an expected return shock and the associated price shock is roughly zero. On average, the expected future price increases implied by higher expected returns are just offset by the immediate decline in the current price. Thus the time variation of expected returns gives rise to mean-reverting or temporary components of prices.

References

Ball, R. (1978) "Anomalies in Relationships Between Securities' Yields and Yield-Surrogates," *Journal of Financial Economics*, 6, 103–26.

Blume, M. E. (1968) "The Assessment of Portfolio Performance: An Application of Portfolio Theory," Ph.D. Dissertation, University of Chicago.

Campbell, J. Y. and Shiller, R. (1987) "The Dividend–Price Ratio and Expectations of Future Dividends and Discount Factors," Unpublished Manuscript, Princeton University.

DeBondt, W. F. M. and Thaler, R. (1985) "Does the Stock Market Overreact?" *Journal of Finance*, 40, 793–805.

Dow, C. H. (1920) "Scientific Stock Speculation," *The Magazine of Wall Street (New York)*.

Fama, E. F. (1970) "Efficient Capital Markets: A Review of Theory and Empirical Work," *Journal of Finance*, 25: 2, May, 383–417.

Fama, E. F. (1981) "Stock Returns, Real Activity, Inflation, and Money," *American Economic Review*, 71, 545–65.

Fama, E. F. and French, K. R. (1987) "Business Conditions and Expected Returns on Stocks and Bonds," *Working Paper*, Center for Research in Security Prices, Graduate School of Business, University of Chicago.

Fama, E. F. and French, K. R. (1988) "Permanent and Temporary Components of Stock Prices," *Journal of Political Economy*, 96: 2, April, 246–73.

Fama, E. F. and Schwert, G. W. (1977) "Asset Returns and Inflation," *Journal of Financial Economics*, 5, 115–46.

Flood, R. P., Hodrick, R. J. and Kaplan, P. (1986) "An Evaluation of Recent Evidence on Stock Market Bubbles," Unpublished Manuscript, National Bureau of Economic Research, Cambridge, MA.

French, K. R., Schwert, G. W. and Stambaugh, R. (1987) "Expected Stock Returns and Volatility," *Journal of Financial Economics*, 19: 1, September, 3–29.

Hansen, L. P. and Hodrick, R. J. (1980) "Forward Exchange Rates as Optimal Predictors of Future Spot Rates: An Econometric Analysis," *Journal of Political Economy*, 88, 829–53.

Keim, D. B. and Stambaugh, R. F. (1986) "Predicting Returns in the Stock and Bond Markets," *Journal of Financial Economics*, 17: 2, December, 357–90.

Keynes, J. M. (1936) *The General Theory of Employment, Interest, and Money* (New York: Harcourt, Brace).

Lintner, J. (1956) "Distribution of Incomes of Corporations Among Dividends, Retained Earnings and Taxes," *American Economic Review*, 46, 97–113.

Miller, M. H. and Scholes, M. S. (1982) "Dividends and Taxes: Some Empirical Evidence," *Journal of Political Economy*, 90, 1118–41.

Poterba, J. M. and Summers, L. (1987) "Mean Reversion in Stock Returns: Evidence and Implications," Unpublished Manuscript, National Bureau of Economic Research, Cambridge, MA.

Rozeff, M. (1984) "Dividend Yields are Equity Risk Premiums," *Journal of Portfolio Management*, 11: 1, 68–75.

Shiller, R. J. (1984) "Stock Prices and Social Dynamics," *Brookings Papers on Economic Activity*, 2, 457–98.

Stambaugh, R. F. (1986) "Bias in Regressions with Lagged Stochastic Regressors," Unpublished Manuscript, University of Chicago.

Summers, L. H. (1986) "Does the Stock Market Rationally Reflect Fundamental Values?" *Journal of Finance*, 41, 591–601.

Chapter 17

James M. Poterba

Background and Comments

Many economists – even those intellectually convinced by the evidence for market efficiency – retain a gut belief that common stocks are not too risky if one can invest for the long run. Many individual investors feel the same way.

This intuition is fallacious if successive stock returns are independent, so that stock prices follow a random walk. In this case, short-run ups and downs of the market do not cancel out; they accumulate. The variance of return increases steadily as the holding period increases.

James Poterba and Lawrence Summers have turned this point around: if variance of return does *not* increase in proportion to the holding period, then stock prices cannot be described by a random walk. In fact they find that variance increases less rapidly than the random walk model would predict, apparently confirming gut intuition. Stock returns appear to be mean reverting.

Poterba and Summers have accumulated an impressive amount of evidence for mean reversion, although in the end, even after showing results for 18 different countries, absolutely bulletproof statistical significance eludes them. The noise in our database of stock returns is enormous. Sixty years of returns are *not* adequate data for many statistical tests.

The preceding paper by Eugene Fama and Kenneth French (chapter 16) takes a different approach to many of these issues.

Author's Introduction

In this paper we challenge the traditional wisdom that stock prices follow random walks. Using data from the US stock market for the period 1871–1986, and data from 17 other stock markets for shorter periods, we find a common pattern in the autocorrelation of stock returns. Over time horizons shorter than 1 year, returns exhibit positive autocorrelation. This implies that annual returns, for example, are more than 12 times as variable as monthly stock returns. Over longer horizons, however, returns exhibit negative serial correlation. Returns over an 8 year time interval, for example, are roughly four times as variable as annual returns. This is in contrast with the random walk model, which implies that 8 year returns should be eight times as variable as annual returns.

These results have potentially important implications for financial practice. If stock prices are mean reverting over long horizons, then for long-horizon investors the stock market is less risky than it appears to be when the variance of single-period returns is extrapolated using the random walk model. For investors with relative risk aversion of greater than unity, recognizing the transitory component in prices will translate into larger portfolio shares invested in equities.

Finding transitory components in stock prices does not necessarily provide evidence against the efficient market hypothesis. Such transitory components could be the result of variation over time in *ex ante* returns as a result of changing risk factors. For simple models of the evolution of required returns, we calibrate the amount of variation in required returns that would be needed to account for the observed degree of mean reversion in prices. The requisite changes in *ex ante* returns appear large by comparison with the variation in *ex post* returns, and may be difficult to explain on the basis of traditional risk considerations.

Since the publication of this paper, numerous other studies have documented substantial predictable components in stock returns. The dividend-to-price ratio, for example, can explain as much as a third of the historical variation in US stock returns. The outstanding question is whether these findings can be attributed to time-varying required returns or whether they indicate the presence of fads or other transitory components in stock prices.

Bibliographical Listing

"Finite Lifetimes and the Effects of Budget Deficits on National Saving" (with Lawrence H. Summers), *Journal of Monetary Economics*, 20: 2, September 1987, 369–91.

"Household Behavior and the Tax Reform Act of 1986" (with Jerry A. Hausman), *Journal of Economic Perspectives*, 1: 1, Summer 1987, 101–19.

"Tax Evasion and Capital Gains Taxation," *American Economic Review, Papers and Proceedings*, 77: 2, May 1987, 234–9.

"Tax Reform and Residential Investment Incentives," *Proceedings of the 79th Annual Meeting of the National Tax Association–Tax Institute of America*, May 1987, pp. 112–18.

"Tax Policy and Corporate Saving," *Brookings Papers on Economic Activity*, 2, 1987, 455–503.

"Why Have Corporate Tax Revenues Declined?" (with A. Auerbach), *Tax Policy and the Economy*, ed. Lawrence H. Summers (Cambridge, MA: MIT Press, 1987), pp. 1–28.

Mean Reversion in Stock Prices

Evidence and Implications

JAMES M. POTERBA and LAWRENCE H. SUMMERS

1 Introduction

The extent to which stock prices exhibit mean-reverting behavior is crucial in assessing assertions such as Keynes's (1936, p. 152) statement that "all sorts of considerations enter into market valuation which are in no way relevant to the prospective yield." If market and fundamental values diverge but beyond some range the differences are eliminated by speculative forces, then stock prices will revert to their mean. Returns must be negatively serially correlated at some frequency if "erroneous" market moves are eventually corrected.[1] Merton (1987) notes that reasoning of this type has been used to draw conclusions about market valuation from failure to reject the absence of negative serial correlation in returns. Conversely, the presence of negative autocorrelation may signal departures from fundamental values, although it could also arise from variation in risk factors over time.

Our investigation of mean reversion in stock prices is organized as follows. In section 2 we evaluate alternative statistical tests for transitory price components. We find that variance ratio tests of the type used by Fama and French (1986a) and Lo and MacKinlay (1988) are close to the most powerful tests of the null hypothesis of market efficiency with constant required returns against plausible alternative hypotheses such as the fads model suggested by Shiller (1984) and Summers (1986).

Reproduced from *Journal of Financial Economics*, 22, 1988, 27–59.

Lawrence H. Summers is Professor of Economics at Harvard University. We are grateful to Changyong Rhee, Jeff Zweibel, and especially David Cutler for excellent research assistance, to Ben Bernanke, Fischer Black, Olivier Blanchard, John Campbell, Robert Engle, Eugene Fama, Terence Gorman, Pete Kyle, Andrew Lo, Greg Mankiw, Robert Merton, Julio Rotemberg, Kenneth Singleton, Mark Watson, an anonymous referee, and the editor, William Schwert, for helpful comments, and to James Darcel and Matthew Shapiro for data assistance. This research was partially supported by the National Science Foundation and is part of the NBER Programs in Economic Fluctuations and Financial Markets. A data appendix is on file with the ICPSR in Ann Arbor, Michigan.

Nevertheless these tests have little power, even with monthly data for a 60 year period. We conclude that a sensible balancing of type I and type II errors suggests using critical values above the conventional 0.05 level.

In section 3 we examine the extent of mean reversion in stock prices. For the United States we analyze monthly data on real and excess New York Stock Exchange (NYSE) returns since 1926, as well as annual returns data for the period 1871–1985. We also analyze 17 other equity markets and study the mean-reverting behavior of individual corporate securities in the United States. The results consistently suggest the presence of transitory components in stock prices, with returns showing positive autocorrelation over short periods but negative autocorrelation over longer periods.

In section 4 we use our variance ratio estimates to gauge the significance of transitory price components. For the United States we find that the standard deviation of the transitory price component varies between 15 and 25 percent of value, depending on our assumption about its persistence. The point estimates imply that transitory components account for more than half the monthly return variance, a finding confirmed by international evidence.

In section 5 we investigate whether observed patterns of mean reversion and the associated movements in *ex ante* returns are better explained by shifts in required returns due to changes in interest rates or market volatility or as byproducts of noise trading.[2] We argue that it is difficult to account for observed transitory components on the basis of changes in discount rates. Some implications of our results and directions for future research are discussed in the conclusion.

2 Methodological Issues Involved in Testing for Transitory Components

A vast literature dating at least to Kendall (1953) has tested the efficient markets–constant required returns model by examining individual autocorrelations in security returns. The early literature, surveyed by Fama (1970), found little evidence of patterns in security returns and is frequently adduced in support of the efficient markets hypothesis. Recent work by Shiller and Perron (1985) and Summers (1986) has shown that such tests have relatively little power against interesting alternatives to the null hypothesis of market efficiency with constant required returns. Several recent studies using new tests for serial dependence have nonetheless rejected the random walk model.[3]

In this section we begin by describing several possible tests for the presence of stationary stock price components, including those used in recent studies. We then present Monte Carlo evidence on each test's power against plausible alternatives to the null hypothesis of serially independent returns. Even the most powerful tests have little power against these alternatives to the random walk when we specify the conventional size of 0.05. We conclude with a discussion of test design when the data can only weakly differentiate alternative hypotheses, addressing in particular the degree of presumption that should be accorded to our null hypothesis of serially independent returns.

2.1 Test methods

Recent studies use different but related tests for mean reversion. Fama and French (1986a) and Lo and MacKinlay (1988) compare the relative variability of returns over different horizons using variance ratio tests. Fama and French (1988b) use regression tests that also involve studying the serial correlation in multiperiod returns. Campbell and Mankiw (1987) study the importance of transitory components in real output using parametric autoregressive moving-average (ARMA) models. Each of these approaches involves using a particular function of the sample autocorrelations to test the hypothesis that all autocorrelations are zero.

The variance ratio test exploits the fact that, if the logarithm of the stock price, including cumulated dividends, follows a random walk, the return variance should be proportional to the return horizon.[4] We study the variability of returns at different horizons in relation to the variation over a 1 year period.[5] For monthly returns, the variance ratio statistic is therefore

$$\mathrm{VR}(k) = \frac{\mathrm{var}(R_t^k)/k}{\mathrm{var}(R_t^{12})/12}, \tag{1}$$

where

$$R_t^k = \sum_{i=0}^{k-1} R_{t-i}$$

and R_t denotes the total return in month t. This statistic converges to unity if returns are uncorrelated through time. If some of the price variation is due to transitory factors, however, autocorrelations at some lags will be negative and the variance ratio will fall below unity. The statistics reported below are corrected for small-sample bias by dividing by $E[\mathrm{VR}(k)]$.[6]

The variance ratio is closely related to earlier tests based on estimated autocorrelations. Using Cochrane's (1988) result that the ratio of the k month return variance to k times the 1 month return variance is approximately equal to a linear combination of sample autocorrelations, (1) can be written

$$\mathrm{VR}(k) \approx 1 + 2 \sum_{j=1}^{k-1} \left(\frac{k-j}{k}\right)\hat{\rho}_j - 2 \sum_{j=1}^{11} \left(\frac{12-j}{12}\right)\hat{\rho}_j . \tag{2}$$

The variance ratio places increasing positive weight on autocorrelations up to and including lag 11, with declining positive weight thereafter. Our variance ratios for k period annual returns place declining weight on all autocorrelations up to order k.

A second test for mean reversion, used by Fama and French (1988b), regresses multiperiod returns on lagged multiperiod returns. If $\tilde{R}_t^k$ denotes the de-meaned k period return, the regression coefficient is

$$\hat{\beta}_k = \sum_{t=2k}^{T} (\tilde{R}_t^k \tilde{R}_{t-k}^k) \bigg/ \sum_{t=2k}^{T} (\tilde{R}_{t-k}^k)^2 . \tag{3}$$

This statistic applies negative weight to autocorrelations up to order $2k/3$, followed by increasing positive weight up to lag k, followed by decaying positive weights.[7] Fama and French (1988b) report regression tests because they reject the null hypothesis of serially independent returns more strongly than the variance ratio test. This is the result of the actual properties of the returns data, and not a general rule about the relative power of the two tests. We show below that returns display positive, and then negative, serial correlation as the horizon lengthens. In this case the regression test, by virtue of its negative, then positive, weights on sample autocorrelations will reject the null hypothesis of serial independence more often than the variance ratio test.

A third method of detecting mean reversion involves estimating parametric time series models for returns, or computing likelihood ratio tests of the null hypothesis of serial independence against particular parametric alternatives. Because returns are nearly white noise under both the null hypothesis and the alternatives we consider, standard ARMA techniques often fail.[8] When they are feasible, however, the Neyman–Pearson lemma dictates that the likelihood ratio test is the most powerful test of the null of serial independence against the particular alternative that generated the data, and so its type II error rate is a lower bound on the error rates that other tests with the same size could achieve. In practice, this bound is unlikely to be achieved, since we do not know the precise data generation process.

2.2 *Power calculations*

We analyze the power of tests for transitory components against the alternative hypotheses that Summers (1986) suggests, where the logarithm of stock prices p_t embodies both a permanent ($p_t^{\star}$) and a transitory (u_t)

component. We assume that $p_t = p_t^\star + u_t$. If the stationary component is an AR(1) process

$$u_t = \rho_1 u_{t-1} + \nu_t \tag{4}$$

and $\varepsilon_t = p_t^\star - p_{t-1}^\star$ denotes the innovation to the nonstationary component, then

$$\Delta p_t = \varepsilon_t + (1 - L)(1 - \rho_1 L)^{-1} \nu_t . \tag{5}$$

If ν_t and ε_t are independent, Δp_t follows an ARMA(1, 1) process.[9] This description of returns allows us to capture in a simple way the possibility that stock prices contain transitory, but persistent, components. The parameter ρ_1 determines the persistence of the transitory component, and the share of return variation due to transitory factors is determined by the relative size of σ_ε^2 and σ_ν^2.

We perform Monte Carlo experiments by generating 25,000 sequences of 720 returns, the number of monthly observations in the Center for Research in Securities Prices (CRSP) database.[10] We set $\sigma_\varepsilon^2 = 1$ so that the variance of returns Δp_t equals $1 + 2\sigma_\nu^2/(1 + \rho_1)$ and set parameters for the return-generating process by choosing ρ_1 and $\delta = 2\sigma_\nu^2/(1 + \rho_1 + 2\sigma_\nu^2)$. The parameter δ denotes the share of return variance accounted for by the stationary component; δ and ρ_1 determine σ_ν^2. We consider cases where δ equals 0.25 and 0.75. We set ρ_1 equal to 0.98 for both cases, implying that innovations in the transitory price component have a half-life of 2.9 years.

In evaluating type II error rates – the probability of failing to reject the null hypothesis when it is false – we use the empirical distribution of the test statistic generated with $\delta = 0$ to determine the critical region for a one-sided 0.05 test of the random walk null against the mean-reverting alternative. The panels of table 17.1 report type II error rates for each test when the data are generated by the process indicated at the column head. The mean value of the test statistic under the alternative hypothesis is also reported.

The first row in table 17.1 analyzes a test based on the first-order autocorrelation coefficient. As Shiller and Perron (1985) and Summers (1986) observe, this test has minimal power against the alternative hypotheses we consider. The type II error rate for a size 0.05 test is 0.941 (0.924) when a quarter (three-quarters) of the variation in returns is from the stationary component (that is, $\delta = 0.25$ and $\delta = 0.75$).

The next panel in table 17.1 considers variance ratio tests comparing return variances for several different horizons, indexed by k, with one-period return variances. The variance ratio tests are more powerful than tests based on first-order autocorrelation coefficients, but they still have little power to detect persistent, but transitory, return components. When a quarter of the return variation is due to transitory factors ($\delta = 0.25$), the

Table 17.1 Simulated type II error rates of alternative tests for transitory components in security returns

	Parameters of return-generating process			
	$\rho_1 = 0.98$ $\delta = 0.25$		$\rho_1 = 0.98$ $\delta = 0.75$	
Test statistic and return measurement interval	*Type II error rate*	*Mean value of test statistic*	*Type II error rate*	*Mean value of test statistic*
First-order autocorrelation	0.941	−0.002	0.924	−0.007
Variance ratio				
24 months	0.933	0.973	0.863	0.927
36 months	0.931	0.952	0.844	0.867
48 months	0.929	0.935	0.839	0.815
60 months	0.927	0.920	0.820	0.771
72 months	0.925	0.906	0.814	0.733
84 months	0.927	0.894	0.814	0.700
96 months	0.929	0.884	0.813	0.670
Return regression				
12 months	0.933	−0.044	0.863	−0.089
24 months	0.929	−0.080	0.842	−0.158
36 months	0.929	−0.112	0.841	−0.210
48 months	0.934	−0.141	0.856	−0.250
60 months	0.934	−0.167	0.868	−0.282
72 months	0.941	−0.194	0.887	−0.308
84 months	0.941	−0.221	0.903	−0.332
96 months	0.943	−0.250	0.914	−0.354
LR test	0.924	1.244	0.760	4.497

Each row describes the statistical properties of a particular test for mean reversion. All tabulations are based on one set of 25,000 Monte Carlo experiments using 720 monthly returns generated by the process described at the column heading. Both underlying processes are ARMA (1,1), with parameters set by δ, the share of return variation due to transitory components, and ρ_1, the monthly serial correlation of the transitory component. Each test we analyze has size 0.05.

type II error rate never falls below 0.81. It is useful in considering the empirical results below to note that when the transitory component in prices has a half-life of less than 3 years and accounts for three-quarters of the variation in returns ($\delta = 0.75$), the variance ratio at 96 months is 0.67.

The next panel in table 17.1 shows type II error rates for the long-horizon regression tests. The results are similar to those for variance ratios, although the regression tests appear to be somewhat less powerful against our alternative hypotheses. For example, the best variance ratio test against the $\delta = 0.25$ case has a type II error rate of 0.925, compared with 0.929 for the most powerful regression test.

The final panel of the table presents results on likelihood ratio tests.[11] Although these are more powerful than the variance ratio tests, with type II error rates of 0.922 in the $\delta = 0.25$ case and 0.760 in the $\delta = 0.75$ case, the error rates are still high. Even the best possible tests therefore have little power to distinguish the random walk model of stock prices from alternatives that imply highly persistent, yet transitory, price components.

One potential shortcoming of our Monte Carlo analysis is our assumption of homoskedasticity in the return-generating process. To investigate its importance, we fit a first-order autoregressive model to monthly data on the logarithm of volatility.[12] We expand our Monte Carlo experiments to allow σ_ε^2 to vary through time according to this process. The type II error calculations from the resulting simulations are similar to those in table 17.1. Figure 17.1 illustrates this, showing the empirical distribution function for the 96 month variance ratio in both the homoskedastic and heteroskedastic cases.

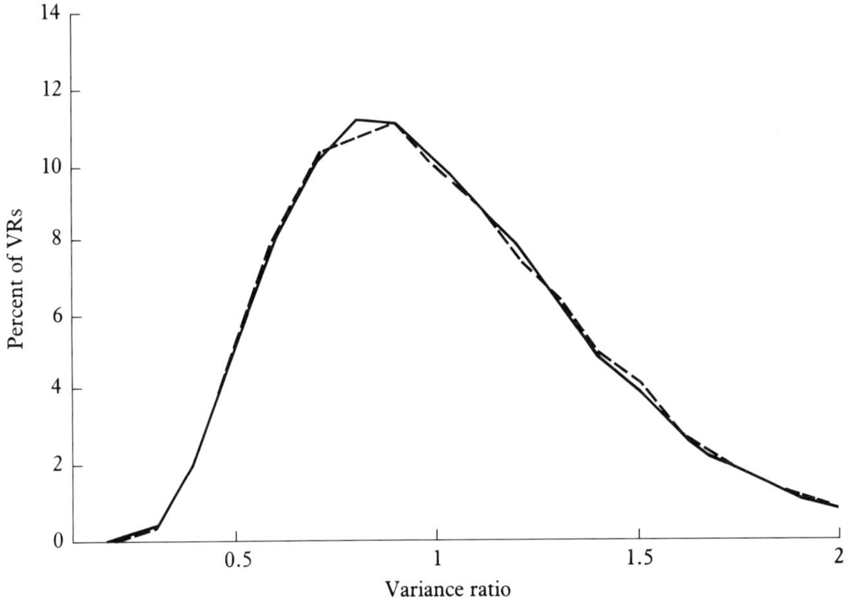

Figure 17.1 Empirical distribution of the 96 month variance ratio statistic (VR) with homoskedastic and heteroskedastic returns: —, the empirical distribution of the 96 month variance ratio statistics calculated from 25,000 replications of 720-observation time series under the null hypothesis of serially independent draws from an identical distribution; ---, a similar empirical distribution calculated from the same number of Monte Carlo draws, but allowing for heteroskedasticity in the simulated returns. The logarithm of the simulated return variance evolves through time as noted in note 12.

2.3 Evaluating statistical significance

For most of the tests described above, the type II error rate would be between 0.85 and 0.95 if the type I error rate were set at the conventional 0.05 level. Leamer (1978, p. 92) echoes a point made in most statistics courses when he writes that "the [popular] rule of thumb, setting the significance level arbitrarily at 0.05, is ... deficient in the sense that from every reasonable viewpoint the significance level should be a decreasing function of sample size." For the case where three-quarters of the return variation is due to transitory factors, figure 17.2 depicts the attainable tradeoff between type I and type II errors for the most powerful variance ratio and regression tests, as well as for the likelihood ratio test. The type

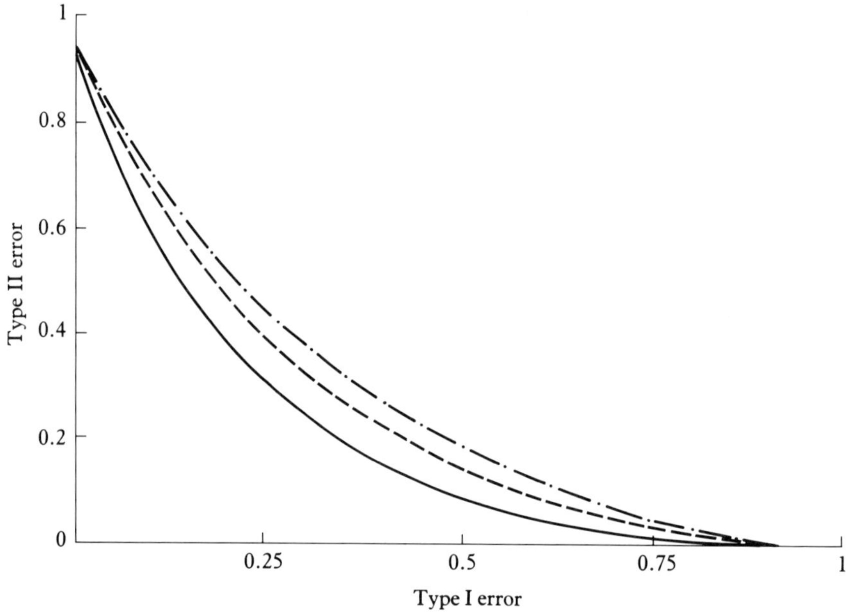

Figure 17.2 Type II versus type I error rates for three alternative tests of mean reversion. Each curve displays the tradeoff between type I and type II error rates for a particular test of mean reversion in stock returns. Critical regions for each test are found using simulated empirical distributions for the variance ratio (---), regression beta (—·—) and likelihood ratio (—) tests under the null hypothesis of serially independent homoskedastic returns. The type II error rate for each test under the alternative hypothesis of $\delta = 0.75$, $\rho_1 = 0.98$ is calculated using another set of simulated empirical distributions. Under both the null and the alternative hypothesis, the empirical distributions are calculated using 25,000 replications of 720-observation time series for synthetic returns. For variance ratio, regression beta, and likelihood ratio tests with given type I error rates shown along the horizontal axis, the figure shows the associated type II error rate against the alternative hypothesis.

II error curve for the variance ratio test lies between the frontiers attainable using regression and likelihood ratio tests. For the variance ratio test, a 0.40 significance level is appropriate if the goal is to minimize the sum of type I and type II errors. To justify using the conventional 0.05 test, we would have to assign three times as great a cost to type I as to type II errors.

Since there is little theoretical basis for strong attachment to the null hypothesis that stock prices follow a random walk, significance levels in excess of 0.05 seem appropriate in evaluating the importance of transitory components in stock prices. Many asset-pricing models, involving rational and irrational behavior, suggest the presence of transitory components and time-varying returns. Furthermore, the same problems of statistical power that plague our search for transitory components complicate investors' lives, and so it may be difficult for speculative behavior to eliminate these components. The only solution to the problem of low power is the collection of more data. In the next section, we bring to bear as much data as possible in evaluating the importance of transitory components.

3 Statistical Evidence on Mean Reversion

This section uses variance ratio tests to analyze the importance of stationary components in stock prices. We analyze excess and real returns using four major data sets: monthly returns on the NYSE for the period since 1926, annual returns on the Standard & Poor's–Cowles stock price indices for the period since 1871, post-Second World War monthly stock returns for 17 stock markets outside the United States, and returns on individual firms in the United States for the post-1926 period.

3.1 Monthly NYSE returns, 1926–1985

We begin by analyzing monthly returns on both the value-weighted and equally weighted NYSE indices from the CRSP database for the period 1926–85. We consider excess returns with the risk-free rate measured as the Treasury bill yield, as well as real returns measured using the consumer price index (CPI) inflation rate. The variance ratio statistics for these series are shown in table 17.2. We confirm the Fama and French (1988b) finding that both real and excess returns at long horizons show negative serial correlation. Eight year returns are about four times rather than eight times as variable as 1 year returns. Despite the low power of our tests, the null hypothesis of serial independence is rejected at the 0.08 level for value-

Table 17.2 Variance ratios for US monthly data, 1926–1985

Data series	Annual return standard deviation (%)	Return measurement interval							
		1 month	*24 months*	*36 months*	*48 months*	*60 months*	*72 months*	*84 months*	*96 months*
Value-weighted real returns	20.6	0.797 (0.150)	0.973 (0.108)	0.873 (0.177)	0.747 (0.232)	0.667 (0.278)	0.610 (0.320)	0.565 (0.358)	0.575 (0.394)
Value-weighted excess returns	20.7	0.764 (0.150)	1.036 (0.108)	0.989 (0.177)	0.917 (0.232)	0.855 (0.278)	0.781 (0.320)	0.689 (0.358)	0.677 (0.394)
Equally weighted real returns	29.6	0.809 (0.150)	0.963 (0.108)	0.835 (0.177)	0.745 (0.232)	0.642 (0.278)	0.522 (0.320)	0.400 (0.358)	0.353 (0.394)
Equally weighted excess returns	29.6	0.785 (0.150)	1.010 (0.108)	0.925 (0.177)	0.878 (0.232)	0.786 (0.278)	0.649 (0.320)	0.487 (0.358)	0.425 (0.394)

Calculations are based on the monthly returns for the value-weighted and equally weighted NYSE portfolios, as reported in the CRSP monthly returns file. The variance ratio statistic is defined as $VR(k) = (12/k)\,\mathrm{var}(R^k)/\mathrm{var}(R^{12})$, where R^j denotes returns over a j-period measurement interval. Values in parentheses are Monte Carlo estimates of the standard error of the variance ratio, based on 25,000 replications under the null hypothesis of serially independent returns. Each variance ratio is corrected for small-sample bias by dividing by the mean value from Monte Carlo experiments under the null hypothesis of no serial correlation.

weighted excess returns and at the 0.005 level for equally weighted excess returns.[13] Mean reversion is more pronounced for the equally weighted returns than for the value-weighted returns, but the variance ratios at long horizons are well below unity for both.

The variance ratios also suggest positive return autocorrelation at horizons shorter than 1 year. The variance of the 1 month return on the equally weighted index is only 0.79 times as large as the variability of 12 month returns implies it should be. A similiar conclusion applies to the value-weighted index. This finding of first positive and then negative serial correlation parallels Lo and MacKinlay's (1988) result that variance ratios exceed unity in their weekly data, whereas variance ratios fall below unity in other studies concerned with longer horizons.[14]

One potential difficulty in interpreting our finding of positive serial correlation at short horizons concerns nontrading effects. If some of the securities in the market index trade infrequently, returns will show positive serial correlation. We doubt this explanation of our results since we are analyzing monthly returns. Nontrading at this frequency is likely to affect only a small fraction of securities, whereas accounting for the degree of positive correlation we observe would require that one security in ten typically did not trade in a given month. We also investigated the incidence of nontrading in a portfolio similar to the value-weighted index by analyzing daily returns on the Standard & Poor's (S&P) Index (Poterba and Summers, 1986) for the period 1928–86. The first-order autocorrelation coefficient for daily returns is only 0.064, and grouping returns into nonoverlapping 5 day periods yields a first-order autocorrelation coefficient of −0.009. This suggests that autocorrelation patterns in monthly returns are not likely to be due to infrequent trading.

A second issue that arises in analyzing the post-1926 data is the sensitivity of the findings to inclusion or exclusion of the Depression years. A number of previous studies, such as that of Officer (1973), have documented the unusual behavior of stock price volatility during the early 1930s. We could argue for excluding these years from analyses designed to shed light on current conditions, although the sharp increase in market volatility in the last quarter of 1987 undercuts this view. The counter-argument suggesting inclusion of this period is that the 1930s, by virtue of the large movements in prices, contain a great deal of information about the persistence of price shocks. We explored the robustness of our findings by truncating the sample period at both the beginning and the end. Excluding the first 10 years weakens the evidence for mean reversion at long horizons. The results for both equally weighted real and excess returns are robust to the sample choice, with variance ratios of 0.587 and 0.736 at the 96 month horizon, but the long-horizon variance ratios on the value-weighted index rise to 0.97 and 1.10 respectively. The 1 month variance ratios are not substantially changed by treatment of the early years. For the post-1936 period, the 1 month variance ratios are 0.782 and 0.825 for value-weighted and equally weighted real returns and 0.833 and 0.851 for value-weighted and equally weighted excess returns.[15] Truncating the sample to exclude the last 10 years of data strengthens the evidence for mean reversion.

3.2 *Historical data for the United States*

The CRSP data are the best available for analyzing recent US experience, but the low power of available statistical tests and the data-mining risks stressed by Merton (1987) suggest the value of examining other data as well. We therefore consider real and excess returns based on the S&P–Cowles Commission stock price indices, revised by Wilson and Jones (1987), which are available beginning in 1871. These data have rarely been used in studies of the serial correlation properties of stock returns, although they have been used in some studies of stock market volatility such as that of Shiller (1981).

The results are presented in table 17.3. For the pre-1925 period, excess returns display negative serial correlation at long horizons. For real returns, however, the pattern is weaker. Although the explanation for this

Table 17.3 Variance ratios for US data, 1871–1985

Data series	Annual return standard deviation (%)	*Return measurement interval*						
		24 months	*36 months*	*48 months*	*60 months*	*72 months*	*84 months*	*96 months*
Excess returns 1871–1925	16.2	0.915 (0.140)	0.612 (0.210)	0.591 (0.265)	0.601 (0.313)	0.464 (0.358)	0.425 (0.398)	0.441 (0.436)
Real returns 1871–1925	17.2	0.996 (0.140)	0.767 (0.210)	0.806 (0.265)	0.847 (0.313)	0.737 (0.358)	0.737 (0.398)	0.807 (0.436)
Excess returns 1871–1985	18.9	1.047 (0.095)	0.922 (0.143)	0.929 (0.179)	0.913 (0.211)	0.856 (0.240)	0.821 (0.266)	0.833 (0.290)
Real returns 1871–1985	19.0	1.035 (0.095)	0.880 (0.143)	0.876 (0.179)	0.855 (0.211)	0.797 (0.240)	0.769 (0.266)	0.781 (0.290)

Each entry is a bias-adjusted variance ratio with a mean of unity under the null hypothesis. The variance ratio statistic is defined as $\mathrm{VR}(k) = (12/k)\ \mathrm{var}(R^k)/\mathrm{var}(R^{12})$, where R^j denotes the return measured over a j month interval. Values in parentheses are Monte Carlo standard deviations of the variance ratio, based on 25,000 replications under the null hypothesis of serial independence. The underlying data are annual returns on the S&P composite stock index, backdated to 1871 using the Cowles data as reported by Wilson and Jones (1987).

phenomenon is unclear, it appears to result from the volatility of the CPI inflation rate in the years before 1900. This may make the *ex post* inflation rate an unreliable measure of expected inflation during this period. The two lower rows in table 17.3 present results for the full 1871–1985 sample period. Both series show negative serial correlation at long lags, but real and excess returns provide less evidence of mean reversion than the monthly post-1925 CRSP data.[16]

3.3 *Equity markets outside the United States*

Additional evidence on mean reversion can be obtained by analyzing the behavior of equity markets outside the United States. We analyze returns in Canada for the period since 1919, in the United Kingdom since 1939, and in 15 other nations for a shorter postwar period.

The Canadian data consist of monthly capital gains on the Toronto Stock Exchange. The UK data are monthly returns, inclusive of dividends, on the *Financial Times*–Actuaries Share Price Index. The first two rows of table 17.4 show that both markets display mean reversion at long horizons. The 96 month variance ratio for the Canadian data is 0.585, while for the UK data it is 0.794. Both markets also display statistically significant positive serial correlation at lags of less than 12 months. For Canada, the

1 month variance is 0.718 times the value that would be predicted on the basis of the 12 month variance. For the United Kingdom, the comparable value is 0.832.

The variance ratios for the 15 other stock markets are calculated from monthly returns based on stock price indices in the International Monetary Fund's (IMF's) *International Financial Statistics*. The IMF does not tabulate dividend yields, and so the reported returns correspond to capital gains alone. To assess the importance of this omission, we reestimated the variance ratios for dividend-exclusive CRSP and UK stock market returns. The results, available from the authors on request, show only minor differences as a result of dividend omission. For example, the 96 month variance ratio for real value-weighted CRSP returns inclusive of dividends is 0.575, and that for dividend-exclusive returns is 0.545. We suspect that yield-inclusive data, although superior to the returns we use, would affect our results in only minor ways.[17]

Table 17.4 presents the variance ratios for individual countries, based typically on data starting in 1957. Most of the countries display negative serial correlation at long horizons. In the Federal Republic of Germany, for example, the 96 month variance ratio is 0.462; in France it is 0.438. Only three of the 15 countries have 96 month variance ratios that exceed unity, and many are substantially below unity. Evidence of positive serial correlation at short horizons is also pervasive. Only one country, Colombia, has a 1 month variance ratio greater than unity. The short data samples, and associated large standard errors, make it difficult to reject the null hypothesis of serial independence for any individual country. The similarity of the results across nations nevertheless supports our earlier finding of substantial transitory price components.

Average variance ratios are shown in the last three rows of the table for all countries, all countries except the United States, and all countries except the United States and Spain. The mean 96 month variance ratio is 0.754 when all countries are aggregated and 0.653 when we exclude Spain, which is an outlier because of the unusual pattern of hyperinflation followed by deflation that it experienced during our sample period. By averaging across many countries, we also obtain a more precise estimate of the long-horizon variance ratio, although the efficiency gain is attenuated because the results for different countries are not independent.[18]

3.4 *Individual firm data*

Arbitrageurs should be better at trading in individual securities to correct mispricing than at taking positions in the entire market to offset persistent misvaluations. Although we expect transitory components to be less likely in the relative prices of individual stocks than in the market as a whole,

Table 17.4 Variance ratios for international data on real monthly returns

Return series (country/sample)	Annual return standard deviation (%)	*Return measurement interval*							
		1 month	*24 months*	*36 months*	*48 months*	*60 months*	*72 months*	*84 months*	*96 months*
Canada/1919–86,	20.1	0.711*	1.055	0.998	0.912	0.799	0.692	0.617	0.575
capital gains only		(0.141)	(0.102)	(0.166)	(0.218)	(0.261)	(0.301)	(0.336)	(0.370)
UK/1939–86	20.9	0.832	0.987	0.868	0.740	0.752	0.807	0.806	0.794
		(0.167)	(0.125)	(0.198)	(0.259)	(0.317)	(0.358)	(0.400)	(0.440)
Austria/1957–86,	21.4	0.663	1.205	1.206	1.132	0.864	0.666	0.582	0.502
capital gains only		(0.214)	(0.156)	(0.254)	(0.334)	(0.403)	(0.464)	(0.518)	(0.566)
Belgium/1957–86,	17.0	0.718*	1.054	1.137	1.121	1.060	0.876	0.807	0.776
capital gains only		(0.214)	(0.156)	(0.254)	(0.334)	(0.403)	(0.464)	(0.518)	(0.566)
Colombia/1959–83,	21.4	1.223	0.822	0.743	0.724	0.583	0.477	0.386	0.180
capital gains only		(0.214)	(0.156)	(0.254)	(0.334)	(0.403)	(0.464)	(0.518)	(0.566)
Germany/1957–86,	23.8	0.610	1.309	1.251	0.987	0.747	0.687	0.581	0.462
capital gains only		(0.214)	(0.156)	(0.254)	(0.334)	(0.403)	(0.464)	(0.518)	(0.566)
Finland/1957–86,	22.1	0.504	1.141	1.262	1.396	1.463	1.381	1.215	1.014
capital gains only		(0.214)	(0.156)	(0.254)	(0.334)	(0.403)	(0.464)	(0.518)	(0.566)
France/1957–86,	23.6	0.874*	0.961	0.914	0.865	0.607	0.460	0.433	0.438
capital gains only		(0.214)	(0.156)	(0.254)	(0.334)	(0.403)	(0.464)	(0.518)	(0.566)
India/1957–86,	15.6	0.752	0.985	0.974	0.942	0.823	0.767	0.619	0.596
capital gains only		(0.214)	(0.156)	(0.254)	(0.334)	(0.403)	(0.464)	(0.518)	(0.566)
Japan/1957–86,	20.0	0.870	1.135	1.015	0.927	0.803	0.691	0.595	0.538
capital gains only		(0.214)	(0.155)	(0.254)	(0.334)	(0.403)	(0.464)	(0.518)	(0.567)
Netherlands/1957–86,	20.0	0.710	1.238	1.263	1.217	1.083	1.047	0.894	0.741
capital gains only		(0.214)	(0.155)	(0.254)	(0.334)	(0.403)	(0.464)	(0.518)	(0.567)

Norway/1957–86,	24.2	0.601	1.033	0.961	0.926	0.844	0.825	0.840	0.784
capital gains only		(0.214)	(0.155)	(0.254)	(0.334)	(0.403)	(0.464)	(0.518)	(0.567)
Philippines/1957–86,	29.7	0.910	0.908	0.749	0.707	0.703	0.839	0.898	0.887
capital gains only		(0.214)	(0.155)	(0.254)	(0.334)	(0.403)	(0.464)	(0.518)	(0.567)
South Africa/1957–86,	23.2	0.767	1.515	1.063	0.963	0.980	1.090	1.131	1.151
capital gains only		(0.214)	(0.155)	(0.254)	(0.334)	(0.403)	(0.464)	(0.518)	(0.567)
Spain/1961–86,	27.7	0.603	1.289	1.584	1.831	2.008	2.246	2.347	2.373
capital gains only		(0.230)	(0.166)	(0.273)	(0.359)	(0.433)	(0.498)	(0.5556)	(0.609)
Sweden/1957–86,	21.1	0.728	0.898	0.822	0.901	0.885	0.916	0.760	0.629
capital gains only		(0.214)	(0.155)	(0.254)	(0.334)	(0.403)	(0.464)	(0.518)	(0.567)
Switzerland/1957–86,	21.5	0.789	1.343	1.395	1.300	1.034	0.749	0.489	0.382
capital gains only		(0.214)	(0.155)	(0.254)	(0.334)	(0.403)	(0.464)	(0.518)	(0.567)
USA/1957–86,	16.6	0.813	0.814	0.653	0.656	0.696	0.804	0.803	0.800
capital gains only		(0.214)	(0.155)	(0.254)	(0.334)	(0.403)	(0.464)	(0.518)	(0.567)
Average value		0.760	1.074	1.048	1.014	0.930	0.890	0.822	0.757
		(0.140)	(0.036)	(0.062)	(0.164)	(0.212)	(0.228)	(0.266)	(0.312)
Average value,		0.757	1.089	1.071	1.035	0.943	0.895	0.824	0.754
excluding USA		(0.135)	(0.024)	(0.100)	(0.173)	(0.204)	(0.207)	(0.243)	(0.290)
Average value,		0.766	1.077	1.039	0.985	0.877	0.811	0.728	0.653
excluding USA, Spain		(0.135)	(0.042)	(0.155)	(0.259)	(0.331)	(0.392)	(0.447)	(0.494)

Each entry reports the variance ratio statistic (or, in the bottom panel, the average of the variance ratio statistics) for a particular nation and return horizon. The variance ratio is defined by $VR(k) = (12/k)\ \mathrm{var}(R^k)/\mathrm{var}(R^{12})$, where R^j denotes the real return over a j month measurement interval. Data underlying the variance ratios are real dividend-exclusive returns, calculated from share price indices in the IMF's *International Financial Statistics*. For most countries the monthly IMF data span the period Jan 1957 to Dec 1986; other data ranges are noted. Values in parentheses are Monte Carlo standard deviations of the variance ratio statistics (and standard deviations for the averages in the last three rows). For the averages, these are computed allowing for a constant correlation across countries. If this correlation was estimated to be negative, we assume that it is zero. In all cases except those marked with an asterisk the data are monthly averages of daily or weekly values. The UK data are point-sampled, but only at the end of each year. The variance ratios are corrected for the time aggregation induced by averaging closing values of the index within each month.

Table 17.5 Average variance ratios for individual company monthly returns, 1926–1985

	Return measurement interval							
Return concept	*1 month*	*24 months*	*36 months*	*48 months*	*60 months*	*72 months*	*84 months*	*96 months*
Excess returns in relation to risk-free rate	0.942 (0.063)	1.035 (0.063)	1.000 (0.100)	0.950 (0.135)	0.888 (0.166)	0.820 (0.198)	0.755 (0.236)	0.739 (0.258)
Excess returns in relation to value-weighted NYSE	1.088 (0.017)	1.034 (0.012)	1.019 (0.020)	1.002 (0.026)	0.968 (0.031)	0.928 (0.035)	0.898 (0.040)	0.886 (0.044)
Residuals from market model	1.107 (0.017)	1.055 (0.012)	1.065 (0.020)	1.057 (0.026)	1.034 (0.031)	1.008 (0.035)	0.995 (0.040)	0.985 (0.044)

Each entry reports the average of variance ratios calculated for the 82 firms on the monthly CRSP returns file with continuous data between 1926 and 1985. The variance ratio statistic is defined as $\mathrm{VR}(k) = (12/k)\ \mathrm{var}(R_k)/\mathrm{var}(R^{12})$, where R^j denotes returns over a j-period measurement interval. Values in parentheses are Monte Carlo estimates of the standard error on the variance ratio, based on 25,000 replications under the null hypothesis of serially independent returns. Each variance ratio is correlated for small-sample bias by dividing the average Monte Carlo value under the null hypothesis of no serial correlation. For the returns in relation to the risk-free rate the standard errors take account of estimated contemporaneous correlation among variance ratios, using the techniques described in note 18.

some previous work has suggested that individual stock returns may show negative serial correlation over some horizons (DeBondt and Thaler, 1985; Lehmann, 1987). We examine the 82 firms in the CRSP monthly master file that have no missing return information between 1926 and 1985. This is a biased sample, weighted toward large firms that have been traded actively over the entire period. Firms that went bankrupt or began trading during the sample period are necessarily excluded.

We compute variance ratios using both real and excess returns for these 82 firms. Because the returns for different firms are not independent, we also examine the returns on portfolios formed by buying $1 of each firm and short selling $82 of the aggregate market. That is, we examine properties of the time series $R_{it} - R_{mt}$ where R_{mt} is the value-weighted NYSE return. Table 17.5 reports the mean values of the individual firm variance ratios along with standard errors that take account of cross-firm correlation. The results suggest some long-horizon mean reversion for individual stock prices in relation to the overall market or a risk-free asset. The point estimates suggest that 12 percent of the 8 year variance in excess returns is due to stationary factors, and the increased precision gained by studying returns for many independent firms enables us to reject the null hypothesis that all the price variation arises from nonstationary factors. The last row, which reports variance ratio calculations using the residuals from market model equations estimated for each firm (assuming a constant beta for the entire period), shows less evidence of serial correlation than the results that subtract the market return. These results suggest that transitory factors account for a smaller share of the variance in relative returns for individual stocks than for the market as a whole.

3.5 *Summary*

Our point estimates generally suggest that over long horizons return variance increases less than proportionally with time, and in many cases they imply more mean reversion than our examples in the last section, where transitory factors accounted for three-fourths of the variation in returns. Many of the results reject the null hypothesis of serial independence at the 0.15 level, a level that may be appropriate given our previous discussion of size versus power tradeoffs. Furthermore, each of the different types of data that we analyze provides evidence of departure from serial independence in stock returns. Taken together, the results are stronger than any individual finding, although not by as much as they would be if the various data sets were independent.

There is some tendency for more mean reversion in less broad-based and sophisticated equity markets. The US data before 1925 show greater evidence of mean reversion than the post-1926 data. The equally weighted portfolio of NYSE stocks shows more mean reversion than the value-weighted portfolio.[19] In recent years, mean reversion is more pronounced in smaller foreign equity markets than in the United States.

4 The Substantive Importance of Transitory Components in Stock Prices

In this section we assess the substantive importance of mean reversion in stock prices. One possible approach would involve calibrating models of the class considered in the first section. We do not follow this strategy because our finding of positive autocorrelation over short intervals implies that the AR(1) specification of the transitory component is inappropriate and because of our difficulties in estimating the ARMA(1, 1) models implied by this approach. Instead, we use an approach that does not require us to specify a process for the transitory component, but nevertheless allows us to focus on its standard deviation and the fraction of the one-period return variance that can be attributed to it.

We treat the logarithm of the stock price as the sum of a permanent and a transitory component. The permanent component evolves as a random walk and the transitory component follows a stationary process. This decomposition may be given two (not necessarily exclusive) interpretations. The transitory component may reflect fads – speculation-induced deviations of prices from fundamental values – or it may be a consequence of changes in required returns. In either case, describing the stochastic properties of the stationary price component is a way of characterizing the part of stock price movements that cannot be explained by changing expectations about future cash flows.

Given our assumptions, the variance of T-period returns is

$$\sigma_T^2 = T\sigma_\varepsilon^2 + 2(1-\rho_T)\sigma_u^2, \tag{6}$$

where σ_ε^2 is the variance of innovations to the permanent price component, σ_u^2 is the variance of the stationary component, and ρ_T is the T-period autocorrelation of the stationary component. Given data on the variance of returns over two horizons T and T' and assumptions about ρ_T and $\rho_{T'}$, a pair of equations with the form (6) can be solved to yield estimates of σ_ε^2 and σ_u^2. Using σ_R^2 for the variance of one-period returns and VR(T) for the T-period variance ratio in relation to one-period returns, estimates of σ_ε^2 and σ_u^2 are given by

$$\sigma_\varepsilon^2 = \frac{\sigma_R^2[\mathrm{VR}(T)(1-\rho_{T'})T - \mathrm{VR}(T')(1-\rho_T)T']}{(1-\rho_{T'})T-(1-\rho_T)T'} \tag{7a}$$

$$\sigma_u^2 = \frac{\sigma_R^2 T'[\mathrm{VR}(T)-\mathrm{VR}(T')]\,T}{2[(1-\rho_T)T'-(1-\rho_{T'})T]}\,. \tag{7b}$$

Many pairs of variance ratios and assumptions about the serial correlation properties of u_t could be analyzed by using (7a) and (7b). We begin by postulating that u_t is serially uncorrelated at the horizon of 96 months. For various degrees of serial correlation at other horizons, we can then estimate the variance σ_u^2 of the transitory component and the share $1-\sigma_\varepsilon^2/\sigma_R^2$ of the return variation due to transitory components. We present estimates based on values of 0, 0.35, and 0.70 for ρ_{12}, the 12 month autocorrelation in u_t. The findings are insensitive to our choice of ρ_{96}; we report values of 0, 0.15, and 0.30.

Table 17.6 presents estimates of the standard deviation of the transitory component in stock prices for the value-weighted and equally weighted NYSE portfolios over the period 1926–85 for various values of ρ_{12}, assuming $\rho_{96}=0$. For the equally weighted portfolio, the transitory component accounts for between 43 and 99 percent of the variance in equally weighted monthly returns, depending on our serial correlation assumption, and it has a standard deviation of between 14 and 37 percent. Results for value-weighted returns also suggest a substantial, though smaller, transitory component. Since other nations and historical periods show patterns of variance ratio decline similar to those in US data, we do not present parallel calculations for them. As we would expect, nations with 96 month variance ratios lower than those for the United States have larger transitory components.

Table 17.6 indicates that increasing the assumed persistence of the transitory component raises both its standard deviation and its contribution to the return variance. More persistent transitory components

Table 17.6 Permanent and transitory return components (US monthly data)

	$\rho_{12}=0.0$		$\rho_{12}=0.35$		$\rho_{12}=0.70$	
ρ_{96}	σ_u (%)	$1-\sigma_\varepsilon^2/\sigma_R^2$	σ_u (%)	$1-\sigma_\varepsilon^2/\sigma_R^2$	σ_u (%)	$1-\sigma_\varepsilon^2/\sigma_R^2$
Value-weighted excess returns						
0.00	9.7	0.369	12.5	0.400	21.6	0.554
0.15	–	–	12.3	0.386	20.5	0.500
0.30	–	–	12.1	0.373	19.6	0.456
Equally weighted excess returns						
0.00	16.8	0.657	21.7	0.712	37.7	0.986
0.15	–	–	21.4	0.687	35.8	0.890
0.30	–	–	21.0	0.664	34.2	0.812

Each entry reports the standard deviation σ_u of the transitory component of prices, measured at annual rates, as well as the share of return variation due to transitory factors, calculated from equations (7a) and (7b) to match the observed pattern of variances in long- and short-horizon returns. The variance ratio estimates that underlie this table are drawn from the entires for 96 month variance ratios for excess returns in table 17.2. The different cases of ρ_{12} (ρ_{96}) correspond to different assumptions about the 12 month (96 month) autocorrelation in the transitory price component.

are less able to account for declining variance ratios at long horizons. To rationalize a given long-horizon variance ratio, increasing the transitory component's persistence requires increasing the weight on the transitory component in relation to the permanent component. Sufficiently persistent transitory components will be unable to account for low long-horizon variance ratios, even if they account for all the return variation. A transitory component that is almost as persistent as a random walk, for example, will be unable to explain very much long-horizon mean reversion.

Which cases in table 17.6 are most relevant? As an *a priori* matter, it is difficult to argue for assuming that transitory components should die out rapidly. Previous claims that there are fads in stock prices have typically suggested half-lives of several years, implying that the elements in the table corresponding to $\rho_{12}=0.70$ are most relevant. With geometric decay, this suggests a half-life of 2 years. One other consideration supports large values for ρ_{12}. For given values of σ_ε^2 and σ_u^2, equation (6) permits us to calculate ρ_T over any horizon. A reasonable restriction, that ρ_T not be very negative over periods of up to 96 months, is satisfied only for cases where ρ_{12} is large. For example, with $\rho_{96}=0$, imposing $\rho_{12}=0.35$ yields an implied autocorrelation for the stationary component of -0.744 at 36 months, -1.27 at 60 months, and -0.274 at 84 months. In contrast, when $\rho_{12}=0.70$ and $\rho_{96}=0$, the implied values of ρ_{36} and ρ_{60} are 0.168 and -0.173 respectively. Similar results obtain for other large values of ρ_{12}. This is because actual variance ratios decline between long and longer horizons, and, as equation (6) demonstrates, rationalizing this requires declining values of ρ_T. If ρ_T starts small, it must become negative to account for the observed pattern. Larger autocorrelations at short horizons do not necessitate such patterns.

Insofar as the evidence in the last section and in Fama and French (1988b) is persuasive in suggesting the presence of transitory components in stock prices, this section's results confirm Shiller's (1981) conclusion that models assuming constant *ex ante* returns cannot account for all the variance in stock market returns. Since our analysis does not rely on the present-value relation between stock prices and expected future dividends, it does not suffer from some of the problems that have been highlighted in the volatility test debate.[20]

5 The Source of the Transitory Component in Stock Prices

Transitory components in stock prices imply variation in *ex ante* returns.[21] Any stochastic process for the transitory price component can be mapped into a stochastic process for *ex ante* returns, and any pattern for *ex ante* returns can be represented by describing the associated transitory price component. The central issue is whether variations in *ex ante* returns are better explained by changes in interest rates and volatility, or instead as byproducts of price deviations caused by noise traders.[22] In this section we note two considerations that incline us toward the latter view.

First, we calibrate the variation in expected returns that risk factors would have to generate to account for the observed transitory components in stock prices. We assume for simplicity that the transitory component follows an AR(1) process as postulated by Summers (1986). This has the virtue of tractability, although it is inconsistent with the observation that actual returns show positive and then negative serial correlation. If required returns show positive autocorrelation, then an innovation that raises required returns will reduce share prices. This will induce a holding-period loss, followed by higher returns. The appendix shows that when required returns follow an AR(1) process,[23] *ex post* returns R_t are given by

$$R_t - \bar{R} \approx \frac{1+\bar{g}}{1+\bar{r}-\rho_1(1+\bar{g})}(r_t - \bar{r}) - \frac{(1+\bar{r})^{-1}(1+\bar{g})^2}{1+\bar{r}-\rho_1(1+\bar{g})}(r_{t+1}-\bar{r}) + \zeta_t \qquad (8)$$

where ζ_t, a serially uncorrelated innovation that is orthogonal to innovations about the future path of required returns ξ_t, reflects revisions in expected future dividends. The average dividend yield and dividend growth rate are $\bar{d}$ and $\bar{g}$, respectively; in steady state, $\bar{r} = \bar{d} + \bar{g}$.

If changes in required returns and profits are positively correlated, then the assumption that ξ_t and ζ_t are orthogonal will *understate* the variance in *ex ante* returns needed to rationalize mean reversion in stock prices. It is possible to construct theoretical examples in which profits and interest rates are negatively related, as in Campbell (1986), but the empirical finding of weak positive correlation between bond and stock returns suggests either positive or weak negative correlation between shocks to cash flows and required returns.[24]

Our assumption that required returns are given by $r_t - \bar{r} = (1-\rho_1 L)^{-1}\xi_t$ enables us to rewrite (8), defining

$$\tilde{\xi}_t \equiv \frac{-\xi_{t+1}(1+\bar{r})^{-1}(1+\bar{g})^2}{1+\bar{r}-\rho_1(1+\bar{g})},$$

as

$$(1-\rho_1 L)(R_t - \bar{R}) \approx \tilde{\xi}_t + \zeta_t - (1+\bar{d})\tilde{\xi}_{t-1} - \rho_1\zeta_{t-1}. \qquad (9)$$

The first-order autocovariance of the expression on the right-hand side of (9) is nonzero, but all higher-order autocovariances equal zero.[25] Provided that $\sigma_\xi^2 > 0$, returns follow an ARMA(1, 1) process; if $\sigma_\xi^2 = 0$, then returns are white noise.

The simple model of stationary and nonstationary price components summarized in equation (5) also yields an ARMA(1, 1) representation for returns. This allows us to calculate the variation in required returns that is needed to generate the same time series process for observed returns as fads of various sizes. In the appendix we show that the required return variance corresponding to a given fad variance is

$$\sigma_r^2 = \frac{[1+\bar{r}-\rho_1(1+\bar{g})]^2(1-\rho_1)^2(1+\bar{r})^2}{\{(1+\bar{d})(1+\rho_1^2)-\rho_1[1+(1+\bar{d})^2]\}(1+\bar{g})^2}\,\sigma_u^2. \tag{10}$$

Table 17.7 reports calculations based on (10). It shows the standard deviation of required excess returns, measured on an annual basis, implied by a variety of fad models. We calibrate the calculations using the average excess return (8.9 percent per year) on the NYSE equally weighted share price index over the period 1926–85. The dividend yield on these shares averages 4.5 percent, implying an average dividend growth rate of 4.4 percent. We use estimates of the variance ratio at 96 months to calibrate the degree of mean reversion.

Substantial variability in required returns is needed to explain mean reversion in prices. For example, if we postulate that the standard deviation of the transitory price component is 20 percent, then even when required return shocks have a half-life of 2.9 years, the standard deviation of *ex ante* returns must be 5.8 percent per annum. Even larger amounts of required return variation are needed to explain the same size price fads when required return shocks are less persistent. These estimates of the

Table 17.7 Amount of variation in required returns needed to account for mean reversion in stock prices

	Standard deviation of transitory component (%)			
Half-life (years)	*15.0%*	*20.0%*	*25.0%*	*30.0%*
1.4	7.9	10.6	13.2	15.8
1.9	6.1	8.2	10.2	12.3
2.9	4.4	5.8	7.3	8.7

Each entry answers the question: "If both required returns and price fads follow first-order autoregressions with half-lives indicated in the row margin, and the amount of mean reversion in observed returns is consistent with a price fad with a standard deviation σ_u given in the column heading, what would the standard deviation of required returns need to be to generate the same time series process for *ex post* returns?" Our calculations employ the fact that, with AR(1) required returns, the *ex post* returns process is given by equation (8). Similarly the price fad is assumed to follow an AR(1) that yields a process like (5) for *ex post* returns. We then ask what value of σ_r (or implicitly σ_ξ) is needed to generate a given size transitory price pattern implied by σ_u. The calculations are calibrated using data on excess returns for the equally weighted NYSE index over the period 1926–85 and are based on equation (10) in the text. The average excess return for this period is 8.9 percent per year, with a dividend yield of 4.5 percent.

standard deviation of required returns are large in relation to the mean of *ex post* excess returns and imply that if *ex ante* returns are never negative they must frequently exceed 20 percent.

It is difficult to think of risk factors that could account for such variation in required returns. Campbell and Shiller (1987), using data on real interest rates and market volatilities, find no evidence that stock prices help to forecast future movements in discount rates, as they should if stock price movements are caused by fluctuations in these factors.[26] Although they show that stock prices do forecast consumption fluctuations, the sign is counter to the theory's prediction. However, if the transitory components are viewed as a reflection of mispricing, they are also large in relation to traditional views of market efficiency.

The second difficulty in explaining the observed correlation patterns with models of time-varying returns arises from our finding of positive followed by negative serial correlation. Models with first-order autoregressive transitory components can rationalize the second but not the first of these observations. It is instructive to consider what type of expected returns behavior is necessary to account for both observations.

There are two potential explanations for the positive autocorrelation in observed returns at short lags. First, contrary to our maintained specification, shocks to required returns and to prospective dividends may be positively correlated. This could lead to positive autocorrelation at short horizons because increases in expected dividends, which would raise share prices, would be followed by higher *ex ante* returns. We explored this possibility by forming monthly "dividend innovations" ($IDIV_t$) for the period 1926–85 as the residuals from a regression of real dividends (on the value-weighted NYSE portfolio) on 12 lagged values of real dividends, a time trend, and a set of monthly dummy variables. We then regressed real returns on the value-weighted index on lagged values of $IDIV_t$. A representative equation, including six lagged values, is shown below. R_t is measured in percentage points and standard errors are given in parentheses:

$$\begin{aligned} R_t = {} & \underset{(0.040)}{1.568} + \underset{(1.380)}{0.844}\ IDIV_{t-1} - \underset{(1.380)}{0.109}\ IDIV_{t-2} - \underset{(1.380)}{3.667}\ IDIV_{t-3} \\ & - \underset{(1.380)}{0.904}\ IDIV_{t-4} - \underset{(1.377)}{1.061}\ IDIV_{t-5} - \underset{(1.374)}{1.769}\ IDIV_{t-6} \\ & R^2 = 0.037, \qquad \text{July 1927 to Dec 1985} \end{aligned}$$

The coefficients on lagged values of IDIV should be positive if required returns and prospective dividends are positively correlated, but the results provide no support for this view. If anything, they suggest a negative but statistically insignificant relationship between dividend innovations and subsequent returns. This would suggest that positive dividend news is followed by lower required returns, a pattern that should be reflected in negative autocorrelation of *ex post* returns over short horizons.

The second potential explanation for positive serial correlation is that the autocorrelogram of *ex post* returns reflects the dynamics of required returns. Some required-return processes could generate positive, followed by negative, return autocorrelation. The required-return processes with this feature that we have identified all show increasing coefficients in some part of their moving-average representation.[27] We are unaware of evidence suggesting that observable proxies for required returns display such stochastic properties. Studies of volatility such as those of French, Schwert, and Stambaugh (1987) or Poterba and Summers (1986) suggest that shocks are persistent but that their moving-average representations show declining coefficients. An alternative possibility is that movements in required returns are due to changes in the equity demands of noise traders. For example, assume that the required return of sophisticated traders is equal to $\alpha + \beta S_t$, where S_t is the fraction of the outstanding common stock that these investors must hold. Equity demands of noise traders (which in equilibrium must equal $1 - S_t$) that follow a moving-average process similar to one of those for required returns that generate positive and then negative autocorrelation in *ex post* returns will also generate this pattern in *ex post* returns. The notion that noise trading impulses intensify and then decline comports with qualitative discussions of fads, but further work is clearly necessary to evaluate this conjecture.

6 Conclusions

Our results suggest that stock returns show positive serial correlation over short periods and negative correlation over longer intervals. This conclusion emerges from data on equally weighted and value-weighted NYSE returns over the period 1926–85, and is corroborated by data from other nations and time periods. Although individual data sets do not consistently permit rejection of the random walk hypothesis at high significance levels, the various data sets together strengthen the case against its validity. Our point estimates suggest that transitory price components account for a substantial part of the variance in returns.

Our finding of significant transitory price components has potentially important implications for financial practice. If stock price movements contain large transitory components, then for long-horizon investors the stock market may be less risky than it appears to be when the variance of single-period returns is extrapolated using the random walk model. Samuelson (1988) demonstrates that in the presence of mean reversion an investor's horizon will influence his portfolio decisions. If the investor's relative risk aversion is greater (less) than unity, as his horizon lengthens he will invest more (less) in equities than he would with serially independent returns. The presence of transitory price components also suggests the desirability of investment strategies, such as those considered by DeBondt and Thaler (1985), involving the purchase of securities that have recently declined in value. It may also justify some institutions' practice of spending on the basis of a weighted average of their past endowment values rather than current market value.

Although the temptation to apply more sophisticated statistical techniques to stock return data in an effort to extract more information about the magnitude and structure of transitory components is ever present, we doubt that a great deal can be learned in this way. Even the broad characteristics of the data examined in this paper cannot be estimated precisely. As the debate over volatility tests has illustrated, sophisticated statistical results are often very sensitive to maintained assumptions that are difficult to evaluate. We have validated the statistical procedures in this paper by applying them to pseudo-data conforming to the random walk model. Our suspicion, supported by Kleidon's (1986) results, is that such Monte Carlo analysis of much of the more elaborate work on stock price volatility would reveal poor statistical properties.

We suggest in the paper's final section that noise trading, that is, trading by investors whose demand for shares is determined by factors other than their expected return, provides a plausible explanation for the transitory components in stock prices.[28] Pursuing this will involve constructing and testing theories of noise trading, as well as theories of changing risk factors, that could account for the characteristic stock return autocorrelogram documented here. Evaluating such theories is likely to require information other than stock returns, such as data on fundamental values, proxies for noise trading such as the net purchases by odd-lot traders, turnover, or the level of participation in investment clubs, and indicators of risk factors such as *ex ante* volatilities implied by stock options. Only by comparing models based on the presence of noise traders with models based on changing risk factors can we judge whether financial markets are efficient in the sense of rationally valuing assets, as well as precluding the generation of excess profits.

Appendix Derivation of *ex post* return process when required returns are AR(1)

The price P_t of a common stock is

$$P_t = E_t\left\{ \sum_{j=0}^{\infty} \left[\prod_{i=0}^{j-1} (1 + r_{t+i})^{-1}(1 + g_{t+i}) \right] D_t \right\}, \tag{A1}$$

where r_{t+i} denotes the required real return in period $t+i, D_t$ is the dividend paid in period t, g_{t+i} is the real dividend growth rate between periods $t+i$ and $t+i+1$, and $E_t\{\ \}$ designates expectations formed using information available as of period t. We linearize inside the expectation operator in r_{t+i} and g_{t+i}:

$$P_t \approx E_t\left\{ \sum_{j=1}^{\infty} \left(\frac{1+\bar{g}}{1+\bar{r}}\right)^{j-1} D_t + \sum_{j=0}^{\infty} \frac{\partial P_t}{\partial r_{t+j}} (r_{t+j}-\bar{r}) + \sum_{j=0}^{\infty} \frac{\partial P_t}{\partial g_{t+j}} (g_{t+j}-\bar{g}) \right\}$$

$$= \frac{D_t(1+\bar{r})}{\bar{r}-\bar{g}} - \frac{D_t(1+\bar{g})}{(1+\bar{r})(\bar{r}-\bar{g})} E_t\left\{ \sum_{j=0}^{\infty} \beta^j (r_{t+j}-\bar{r}) \right\}$$

$$+ \frac{D_t}{\bar{r}-\bar{g}} E_t\left\{ \sum_{j=0}^{\infty} \beta^j (g_{t+j}-\bar{g}) \right\} \tag{A2}$$

where $\beta = (1+\bar{g})/(1+\bar{r})$. We denote $D_t(1+\bar{r})/(\bar{r}-\bar{g})$ as $\bar{P}_t$. In the special case of

$$(r_t-\bar{r}) = \rho_1(r_{t-1}-\bar{r}) + \xi_t \tag{A3}$$

we can simplify the second term in (A2) to obtain

$$P_t - \bar{P}_t \approx \frac{-D_t(1+\bar{g})}{(1+\bar{r})(\bar{r}-\bar{g})} \sum_{j=0}^{\infty} \beta^j \rho_1^j (r_t-\bar{r}) + \frac{D_t}{\bar{r}-\bar{g}} E_t\left\{ \sum_{j=0}^{\infty} \beta^j (g_{t+j}-\bar{g}) \right\}$$

$$= \frac{-D_t(1+\bar{g})(r_t-\bar{r})}{(\bar{r}-\bar{g})[1+\bar{r}-\rho_1(1+g)]} + \frac{D_t}{\bar{r}-\bar{g}} E_t\left\{ \sum_{j=0}^{\infty} \beta^j (g_{t+j}-\bar{g}) \right\}. \tag{A4}$$

Now recall that the holding period return R_t is given by

$$R_t = \frac{P_{t+1}+D_t}{P_t} - 1. \tag{A5}$$

It can be linearized around P_t and P_{t+1} as follows:

$$R_t \approx \bar{R} + \frac{P_{t+1}-\bar{P}_{t+1}}{\bar{P}_t} - \frac{\bar{P}_{t+1}+D_t}{\bar{P}_t^2} (P_t - \bar{P}_t) \tag{A6}$$

where $\bar{P}_{t+1} = (1+\bar{g})\bar{P}_t$ and $\bar{R} = \bar{r}(1+\bar{g})/(1+\bar{r})$. Substituting (A4) into (A6) yields

$$R_t - \bar{R} \approx \frac{-D_{t+1}(1+\bar{g})}{\bar{P}_t(\bar{r}-\bar{g})[1+\bar{r}-\rho_1(1+\bar{g})]} (r_{t+1}-\bar{r})$$

$$+ \frac{D_{t+1}}{\bar{P}(\bar{r}-\bar{g})} \sum_{j=0}^{\infty} \beta^j E_{t+1}\{g_{t+1+j}-\bar{g}\}$$

$$+ \frac{D_t(1+\bar{r})(1+\bar{g})}{\bar{P}_t(\bar{r}-\bar{g})[1+\bar{r}-\rho_1(1+\bar{g})]} (r_t-\bar{r})$$

$$- \frac{D_t(1+\bar{r})}{\bar{P}_t(\bar{r}-\bar{g})} \sum_{j=0}^{\infty} \beta^j E_t\{g_{t+j}-\bar{g}\}. \tag{A7}$$

This can be rewritten as

$$R_t - \bar{R} \approx -\frac{D_t(1+\bar{g})^2}{\bar{P}_t(\bar{r}-\bar{g})[1+\bar{r}-\rho_1(1+\bar{g})]} \times [(r_{t+1}-\bar{r}) - \beta^{-1}(r_t - \bar{r})] + \zeta_t$$

$$= -\frac{\beta(1+\bar{g})}{1+\bar{r}-\rho_1(1+g)} \times [(1-\rho_1 L)^{-1}\xi_{t+1} - \beta(1-\rho_1 L)^{-1}\xi_t] + \zeta_t, \qquad \text{(A8)}$$

where ζ_t reflects changes in expected future dividend growth rates between t and $t+1$, and the last expression exploits the fact that $(1-\rho_1 L)(r_t - \bar{r}) = \xi_t$. Now defining

$$\frac{\beta(1+\bar{g})}{1+\bar{r}-\rho_1(1+\bar{g})}\ \xi_{t+1} = \tilde{\xi}_t,$$

we can multiply through by $1-\rho_1 L$ so that

$$(1-\rho_1 L)(R_t - \bar{R}) \approx \tilde{\xi}_t - \frac{1+\bar{r}}{1+\bar{g}}\ \tilde{\xi}_{t-1} + \zeta_t - \rho_1\zeta_{t-1}. \qquad \text{(A9)}$$

This yields an ARMA(1, 1) representation of returns. Since $(1+\bar{r})/(1+\bar{g}) \approx (1+\bar{d})$, this is equation (8) in the text.

We now explore the parallel between the time-varying returns model and the fad model, which postulates that returns evolve according to

$$(1-\rho_1 L)(R_t - \bar{R}) \approx \varepsilon_t - \rho_1\varepsilon_{t-1} + \nu_t - \nu_{t-1}. \qquad \text{(A10)}$$

For this ARMA(1, 1) process to be the same as (A9), two restrictions must be satisfied. We find them by equating the variances and first-order autocovariance of the right-hand sides of (A9) and (A10):

$$[1+(1+\bar{d})^2]\sigma_{\tilde{\xi}}^2 + (1+\rho_1^2)\sigma_\zeta^2 = 2\sigma_\nu^2 + (1+\rho_1^2)\sigma_\varepsilon^2 \qquad \text{(A11)}$$

$$(1+\bar{d})\sigma_{\tilde{\xi}}^2 + \rho_1\sigma_\zeta^2 = \sigma_\nu^2 + \rho_1\sigma_\varepsilon^2. \qquad \text{(A12)}$$

Using (A12) to eliminate σ_ζ^2 from (A11) we find

$$\sigma_{\tilde{\xi}}^2 = \frac{(1-\rho_1)^2}{(1+\bar{d})(1+\rho_1^2) - \rho_1[1+(1+\bar{d})^2]}\ \sigma_\nu^2. \qquad \text{(A13)}$$

Recall that the variance σ_u^2 of the fad, equals $\sigma_\nu^2/(1-\rho_1^2)$. Using this and the definition of $\tilde{\xi}_t$, we find from (A13) that the variance of required returns corresponding to a given fad variance is

$$\sigma_r^2 = \frac{[1+\bar{r}-\rho_1(1+\bar{g})]^2(1-\rho_1)^2(1+r)^2}{\{(1+\bar{d})(1+\rho_1^2) - \rho_1[1+(1+\bar{d})^2]\}(1+\bar{g})^2}\ \sigma_u^2. \qquad \text{(A14)}$$

This leads immediately to (10) in the text.

Notes

1 Stochastic speculative bubbles, considered by Blanchard and Watson (1982), could create deviations between market prices and fundamental values without negative serial

correlation in returns. In the presence of any limits on valuation errors set by speculators or real investment opportunities, however, such bubbles could not exist.

2 Noise traders are investors whose demands for securities are best treated as exogenous rather than the result of maximizing a conventional utility function using rational expectations of the return distribution. Shiller (1984), Black (1986), Campbell and Kyle (1986), and DeLong et al. (1987) discuss a variety of possible models for noise trader behavior.

3 Fama (1976) acknowledges the difficulty of distinguishing the random walk model from some alternative specifications. In addition to the recent work of Fama and French (1988b) and Lo and MacKinlay (1988), O'Brien (1987) demonstrates the presence of negative serial correlation at very long (up to 20 year) horizons. Huizinga (1987) provides a spectral interpretation of the variance ratio estimator and reports evidence that exchange rates also show long-horizon deviations from random walk behavior.

4 Testing the relationship between the variability of returns at different horizons has a long tradition; see Osborne (1959) and Alexander (1961).

5 We use 12 month returns in the denominator of the variance ratio to permit comparability with our results using annual returns data. With annual data, the variance ratio denominator is $\text{var}(R_t)$.

6 Kendall and Stuart (1976) show that under weak restrictions the expected value of the jth sample autocorrelation is $-1/(T-j)$. Using this result, we compute $E[\text{VR}(k)]$. When the horizon of the variance ratio is large in relation to the sample size, this can be substantially less than unity. For example, with $T=720$ and $k=60$, the bias is -0.069. It rises to -0.160 if $k=120$. Detailed Monte Carlo analysis of the variance ratio statistic can be found in Lo and MacKinlay (1988).

7 Further details on the relationship between regression tests and the sample autocorrelogram are presented in an earlier draft, available on request.

8 We tried estimating ARMA models for the pseudo-returns generated in our Monte Carlo study. Although these data were generated by an ARMA(1, 1) model with first-order autoregressive and moving-average coefficients of roughly equal but opposite signs, standard ARMA estimation packages (that is, RATS) had difficulty recovering this process. For example, with three-quarters of the variation in returns due to transitory factors, the estimation package encountered noninvertibilities in the moving-average polynomial and therefore broke down in more than a third of all Monte Carlo runs. Less than 10 percent of the cases led to well-estimated parameters that were close to those from the data generation process.

9 The parameters of the ARMA(1, 1) model $(1-\phi L)\Delta p_t = (1+\theta L)w_t$ are

$$\phi = \rho_1$$

$$\theta = \frac{-(1+\rho_1^2) - 2\sigma_\nu^2 + (1-\rho_1)[4\sigma_\nu^2 + (1+\rho_1)^2]^{1/2}}{2\sigma_\nu^2 + 2\rho_1}$$

$$\sigma_w^2 = \frac{\rho_1 + \sigma_\nu^2}{\theta}.$$

10 In practice we draw 720 *pairs* of random variables, associate them with (ε_t, ν_t), and then construct Δp_t.

11 The likelihood value under each hypothesis is evaluated using Harvey's (1981) exact maximum likelihood method. Because estimating the mean induces a small-sample bias toward negative autocorrelations, even under the null hypothesis of serial independence the mean likelihood ratios for each alternative hypothesis are above unity.

12 The estimated volatility process that we use for our simulations is

$$\log \sigma_t^2 = -2.243 + 0.7689 \log \sigma_{t-1}^2 + \omega_t,$$

where ω_t has a normal distribution with zero mean and standard deviation 0.691. The monthly volatility data are described by French, Schwert, and Stambaugh (1987).

13 These p values are calculated from the empirical distribution of our test statistic, based on Monte Carlo results. They permit rejection at lower levels than would be possible using the normal approximation to the distribution of the variance ratio, along with the Monte Carlo estimates of the standard deviation of the variance ratio. Further details are available on request.

14 French and Roll (1986) apply variance ratio tests to daily returns for a sample of NYSE and AMEX stocks for the period 1963–82. They find evidence of negative serial correlation, especially among smaller securities. The divergence between their findings and those of Lo and MacKinlay (1988) is presumably due to differences in the two data sets.

15 We also experimented with crude techniques for accounting for time-varying stock market volatility in estimating variance ratios. Estimating sample autocorrelations with a heteroskedasticity correction based on French, Schwert, and Stambaugh's (1987) estimate of the previous month's return volatility effectively reduces the weight of the early Depression years, yielding variance ratio estimates closer to unity.

16 The variance ratio for the full sample period (1871–1985) is not a simple weighted average of the variance ratios for the two subperiods, pre- and post-1926. The 96 month variance ratios for the post-1926 period excess and real S&P data, for example, are 0.463 and 0.731 respectively.

17 In some cases, the monthly stock index data from the *International Financial Statistics* are time averages of daily or weekly index values. Working (1960) showed that the first difference of a time-averaged random walk would exhibit positive serial correlation, with a first-order autocorrelation coefficient of 0.25 as the number of observations in the average becomes large. This will bias our estimated variance ratios. For the countries with time-aggregated data we therefore modify our small-sample bias correction. Instead of taking the expected value of the first-order autocorrelation to be $-1/(T-1)$ when evaluating $E[\mathrm{VR}(k)]$ we use $0.25 - 1/(T-1)$. The reported variance ratios have been bias adjusted by dividing by the resulting expected value.

18 The standard errors for the cross-country averages allow for correlation between the variance ratios for different countries. If all nations have a constant pairwise correlation τ between their variance ratios and these variance ratios have constant variance σ_x^2, then the expected value of the sample variance of the variance ratio statistics is $E(s_n^2) = \sigma_x^2(1-\tau)$. Replacing the expected sample variance with the actual value, we estimated τ as $1 - s_n^2/\sigma_x^2$. The variance of the sample mean for N observations, each with the same variance σ_x^2 but constant cross-correlation τ, is $\sigma_x^2[1+(N-1)\tau]/N$. We use our estimate of τ to evaluate this expression, generalized to allow for different sampling variances for different variance ratios on the basis of our Monte Carlo standard errors from table 17.4.

19 We conjectured that the greater mean reversion in the equally weighted portfolio than in the value-weighted portfolio might be because the less heavily traded equally weighted portfolio experienced larger swings in required returns or fluctuated more in relation to fundamental values than the value-weighted portfolio. Assuming similar sized movements in the permanent component of the two indices, this conjecture can be tested by analyzing the degree of mean reversion in the *relative* returns on the two indices. These returns show positive serial correlation at all lags, contrary to our conjecture.

20 Shiller's conclusion that market returns are too volatile to be reconciled with valuation models assuming constant required returns is controversial; see West (1988) for a survey of recent work.

21 Several recent studies have considered the extent to which equity returns can be predicted using various information sets. Keim and Stambaugh (1986) find that between 8 and 13 percent of the variation in returns for a portfolio of stocks in the bottom quintile of the NYSE can be predicted using lagged information. A much smaller share of the variation in returns to larger companies can be accounted for in this way. Campbell (1987) finds that approximately 11 percent of the variation in excess returns can be explained on the basis of lagged information derived from the term structure. Fama and French (1988a) find that lagged dividend yields can predict a much higher fraction of returns over longer horizons.

22 Lucas (1978) and Cox, Ingersoll, and Ross (1985) study the pricing of assets with time-varying required returns. Several recent papers, including Shiller (1984), Black (1986), Campbell and Kyle (1986), and DeLong et al. (1987), have discussed the possible influence of noise traders on security prices and required returns. Fama and French (1986b) show that the negative serial correlation in different stocks may be attributable to a common factor, and interpret this finding as support for the time-varying returns view of mean reversion.

23 The possibility of negative expected excess returns is an unattractive feature of the simple model we have analyzed. In principle the analysis could be repeated using Merton's (1980) model, which requires the expected excess return to be positive. The exact parallel between the time-varying returns model and the fads model would not hold in this case, however.

24 Campbell (1987) estimates that the correlation between excess returns on long-term bonds and corporate equities was 0.22 for the period 1959–79 and 0.36 for the more recent period 1979–83.

25 Ansley, Spivey, and Wrobleski (1977) prove that an autocorrelogram with zero entries beyond order k implies an MA(k) process.

26 Contrary evidence suggesting that stock returns do predict future volatility patterns is provided by French, Schwert, and Stambaugh (1987).

27 Two examples of required return processes are twelfth-order moving-average processes with the following coefficients: 1, −1.5, −0.75, −0.5, −0.5, 0.75, 0.75, 0.75, 0.75, 0.75, 0.75, 0.75, 0.75 and 1, 1.5, 2, 2.5, 3, 3.5, 4, 4.5, 5, 4, 3, 2, 1. The autocorrelogram of the former process displays positive and then negative correlation in required returns, while the second process exhibits positive autocorrelation at all lags. Both processes generate positive, then negative, autocorrelation in *ex post* returns.

28 Cutler, Poterba, and Summers (1989) document the difficulty of explaining a significant fraction of return variation on the basis of observable news about future cash flows or discount rates.

References

Alexander, S. S. (1961) "Price Movements in Speculative Markets: Trends or Random Walks," *Industrial Management Review*, 2, 7–26.

Ansley, C. Spivey, W. A. and Wrobleski, W. (1977) "On the Structure of Moving Average Processes," *Journal of Econometrics*, 6, 121–34.

Black, F. (1986) "Noise," *Journal of Finance*, 41, 529–43.

Blanchard, O. I. and Watson, M. (1982) "Bubbles, Crashes, and Rational Expectations." In *Crises in the Economic and Financial Structure*, ed. P. Wachtel (Lexington, MA: Lexington Books), pp. 295–315.

Campbell, J. Y. (1986) "Bond and Stock Returns in a Simple Exchange Model," *Quarterly Journal of Economics*, 102, 785–803.

Campbell, J. Y. (1987) "Stock Returns and the Term Structure," *Journal of Financial Economics*, 18, 373–400.

Campbell, J. Y. and Kyle, A. S. (1986) "Smart Money, Noise Trading, and Stock Price Behavior," Unpublished Manuscript, Princeton University, Princeton, NJ.

Campbell, J. Y. and Mankiw, N. G. (1987) "Are Output Fluctuations Transitory?" *Quarterly Journal of Economics*, 102, 857–80.

Campbell, J. Y. and Shiller, R. J. (1987) "The Dividend–Price Ratio and Expectations of Future Dividends and Discount Factors," Mimeo, Yale University.

Cochrane, J. H. (1988) "How Big is the Random Walk in GNP?" *Journal of Political Economy*, 96, October, 893–920.

Cox, J. C., Ingersoll, J. and Ross, S. (1985) "An Intertemporal General Equilibrium Model of Asset Prices," *Econometrica*, 53, 363–84.

Cutler, D. C., Poterba, J. M. and Summers, L. H. (1989) "What Moves Stock Prices?" *Journal of Portfolio Management*, 15, Spring, 4–12.

DeBondt, W. and Thaler, R. (1985) "Does the Stock Market Overreact," *Journal of Finance*, 40, 793–805.

DeLong, J. B., Shleifer, A., Summers, L. and Waldman, R. (1987) "The Economic Consequences of Noise Traders," *Working Paper 2395*, National Bureau of Economic Research, Cambridge, MA.

Fama, E. F. (1970) "Efficient Capital Markets: A Review of Theory and Empirical Work," *Journal of Finance*, 25, 383–417.

Fama, E. F. (1976) *Foundations of Finance* (New York: Basic Books).

Fama, E. F. and French, K. R. (1986a) "Permanent and Temporary Components of Stock Prices," *Working Paper 178*, Center for Research in Security Prices, University of Chicago.

Fama, E. F. and French, K. R. (1986b) "Common Factors in the Serial Correlation of Stock Returns," *Working Paper 200*, Center for Research in Security Prices, University of Chicago.

Fama, E. F. and French, K. R. (1988a) "Dividend Yields and Expected Stock Returns," *Journal of Financial Economics*, 22, 3–26.

Fama, E. F. and French, K. R. (1988b) "Permanent and Temporary Components of Stock Prices," *Journal of Political Economy*, 96: 2, April, 246–73.

French, K. R. and Roll, R. (1986) "Stock Return Variances: The Arrival of Information and the Reaction of Traders," *Journal of Financial Economics*, 17, 5–26.

French, K. R., Schwert, W. and Stambaugh, R. (1987) "Expected Stock Returns and Volatility," *Journal of Financial Economics*, 19: 1, September, 3–29.

Harvey, A. (1981) *Time Series Models* (Oxford: Philip Allan).

Huizinga, J. (1987) "An Empirical Investigation of the Long Run Behavior of Real Exchange Rates," *Carnegie–Rochester Conference Series on Public Policy*, 27, 149–214.

Keim, D. B. and Stambaugh, R. F. (1986) "Predicting Returns in the Stock and Bond Markets," *Journal of Financial Economics*, 17: 2, December, 357–90.

Kendall, M. G. (1953) "The Analysis of Economic Time Series – Part I: Prices," *Journal of the Royal Statistical Society A*, 96, 11–25.

Kendall, M. G. and Stuart, A. (1976) *The Advanced Theory of Statistics*, 3rd edn, vol. 3 (London: Griffin).

Keynes, J. M. (1936) *The General Theory of Employment, Interest, and Money* (New York: Harcourt, Brace).
Kleidon, A. (1986) "Variance Bounds Tests and Stock Price Valuation Models," *Journal of Political Economy*, 94, 953–1001.
Leamer, E. (1978) *Specification Searches: Ad Hoc Inferences with Nonexperimental Data* (New York: Wiley).
Lehmann, B. N. (1987) "Fads, martingales, and market efficiency," Mimeo, Graduate School of Business, Columbia University, New York.
Lo, A. W. and MacKinlay, A. C. (1988) "Stock Market Prices do not Follow Random Walks: Evidence from a Simple Specification Test," *Review of Financial Studies*, 1, 41–66.
Lucas, R. (1978) "Asset Prices in an Exchange Economy," *Econometrica*, 66, 1429–45.
Merton, R. C. (1980) "On Estimating the Expected Return on the Market," *Journal of Financial Economics*, 8, 323–61.
Merton, R. C. (1987) "On the State of the Efficient Market Hypothesis in Financial Economics." In *Macroeconomics and Finance: Essays in Honor of Franco Modigliani*, eds R. Dornbusch, S. Fischer, and J. Bossons (Cambridge, MA: MIT Press), pp. 93–124.
O'Brien, J. M. (1987) "Testing for Transitory Elements in Stock Prices," Mimeo, Board of Governors of the Federal Reserve, Washington, DC.
Officer, R. R. (1973) "The Variability of the Market Factor of the New York Stock Exchange," *Journal of Business*, 46, 434–53.
Osborne, M. F. (1959) "Brownian Motion in the Stock Market," *Operations Research*, 7, 145–73.
Poterba, J. M. and Summers, L. H. (1986) "The Persistence of Volatility and Stock Market Returns," *American Economic Review*, 76, 1142–51.
Samuelson, P. A. (1988) "Longrun Risk Tolerance When Equity Returns are Mean Regressing: Pseudoparadoxes and Vindication of 'Business Man's Risk'," Mimeo, Massachusetts Institute of Technology, Cambridge, MA.
Shiller, R. J. (1981) "Do Stock Prices Move Too Much To Be Justified by Subsequent Changes in Dividends?" *American Economic Review*, 71, 421–36.
Shiller, R. J. (1984) "Stock Prices and Social Dynamics," *Brookings Papers on Economic Activity*, 2, 457–98.
Shiller, R. J. and Perron, P. (1985) "Testing the Random Walk Hypothesis: Power Versus Frequency of Observation," *Economics Letters*, 18, 381–6.
Summers, L. H. (1986) "Does the Stock Market Rationally Reflect Fundamental Values?" *Journal of Finance*, 41, 591–601.
West, K. (1988) "Bubbles, Fads, and Stock Price Volatility: A Partial Evaluation," *Journal of Finance*, 43, 639–55.
Wilson, J. W. and Jones, C. (1987) "A Comparison of Annual Common Stock Returns: 1871–1925 with 1926–1985," *Journal of Business*, 60, 239–58.
Working, H. (1960) "Note on the Correlation of First Differences of Averages in a Random Chain," *Econometrica*, 28, 916–18.

Chapter 18

Jay A. Shanken

Background and Comments

In basic portfolio theory the investor is assumed to consider only expected portfolio return and risk over a single short period, say 1 month. You construct an optimal portfolio on January 1 and do not worry about February's portfolio until February 1.

This short-horizon approach is perfectly adequate for the long run if enough things are held constant. The long run is covered by a series of short steps. If each short step is independent of the last, then the best policy for the short run is also the best policy for the long run.

This approach breaks down if certain key parameters change unpredictably. Suppose that interest rates at the start of February may be unexpectedly higher or lower. Then the investor has two things to worry about on January 1 – not only about possible low returns in January, but also about possible lower interest rates starting in February. Lower interest rates mean less favorable returns when January's proceeds are reinvested.

Such an investor would judge risk on two dimensions. First, he would ask how much each security contributes to uncertainty about January's portfolio return. Second, he would favor securities that helped hedge against unfavorable shifts in interest rates; securities that tended to give low returns in times of falling interest rates would be viewed as especially risky.

Robert Merton stressed these points in a classic paper (Merton, 1973). Nevertheless, many tests of models based on portfolio theory assume that investment opportunities are constant over time. Only a few financial economists have attempted to find out how the expected returns and risks of common stocks change in response to shifts in interest rates. Jay Shanken's paper is a prominent example.

Reference

Merton, R. C. (1973) "An Intertemporal Capital Asset Pricing Model," *Econometrica*, 41: 5, September, 867–87.

Author's Introduction

All my work in finance has been concerned in one way or another with the estimation or testing of asset pricing models. Although the emphasis has been on statistical issues, I have also tried, in several papers dealing with the arbitrage pricing theory (APT) and "Roll's critique," to clarify precisely what economic hypotheses can be tested and to highlight the "hidden" assumptions in these tests. Having come to finance by way of mathematics, I found the asset pricing area to be a source of many interesting statistical/mathematical challenges. However, these abstract problems are grounded in practical questions, providing just the sort of intellectual balance that I was seeking.

My early papers on testing portfolio efficiency focused on the small-sample distributions of multivariate test statistics in situations where conventional asymptotic statistical analysis fails to provide satisfactory results. The mathematical bounds which I derived on the distribution of the test statistic for the "zero-beta problem" indicated that earlier interpretations of the data needed to be significantly revised. Subsequent joint work with Mike Gibbons and Steve Ross exploited the simplifications afforded by the availability of a riskless investment. Several intuitive economic perspectives on the multivariate tests were developed in that work and the power function was analyzed in detail. My interest in applying Bayesian statistics to problems in finance grew out of this attention to the "alternative hypothesis."

Although the Gibbons–Ross–Shanken analysis was originally formulated in the traditional framework of independent (over time) and identically normally distributed excess returns, it is more general. In particular, the expected return and volatility of the market index can change over time without invalidating the statistical inferences. "Market model" regression parameters – alphas, betas, and idiosyncratic risks – must be constant, however. The following paper is a natural extension of this work and reflects my desire to pursue some statistical analysis of a more exploratory nature. When I began developing this project, there were a few studies around documenting interest-rate-related shifts in the (conditional) distribution of stock and bond index returns. I thought it would be interesting to investigate whether other aspects of the joint return distribution vary as well, and to accommodate these changes in tests of risk–return relations.

In recent years, a number of papers have appeared with similar aims. While each of these papers makes a unique contribution, in most cases some parameters of the returns process are permitted to evolve over time while other plausible candidates for time variation are held fixed. Using a simple idea from the stochastic parameter regression literature and standard econometric methods for dealing with heteroskedasticity, the intertemporal paper allows for (and finds) simultaneous variation in expected returns, betas, marketwide and residual risks, and the "price" of market risk. The combination of richness of specification and simplicity of methodology is, I believe, appealing and enables quite a lot of interesting descriptive information to be extracted from the data whether the equilibrium asset pricing restriction holds or not. The results of my particular application add to the growing body of empirical observations concerning patterns of risk return behavior across firms of different sizes and in different industries. My current work continues to evolve in the asset pricing area but is less concerned with equilibrium restrictions and more with the practical investment decisions of individual investors.

Bibliographical Listing

"Macroeconomic Variables and Asset Pricing: Estimation and Tests" (with Mark Weinstein), *Working Paper*, University of Rochester, 1989.

"On the Estimation of Beta-Pricing Models," *Working Paper*, University of Rochester, 1989.

"A Test of the Efficiency of a Given Portfolio" (with Michael Gibbons and Stephen Ross), *Econometrica*, 57: 5, September 1989, 1121–52.

"A Bayesian Approach to Testing Portfolio Efficiency," *Journal of Financial Economics*, 19: 2, December 1987, 195–215.

"Subperiod Aggregation and the Power of Multivariate Tests of Portfolio Efficiency" (with Michael Gibbons), *Journal of Financial Economics*, 19: 2, December 1987, 389–94.

Intertemporal Asset Pricing: An Empirical Investigation

JAY A. SHANKEN

1 Introduction

In a fundamental contribution to the asset pricing literature, Merton (1973) derives the equilibrium relations among expected returns in an intertemporal asset pricing model, where investors' demands for assets are affected by the possibility of uncertain changes in the investment opportunity set.[1] He shows that investors must be compensated, in terms of expected return, for bearing the risk of unfavorable shifts in opportunities as well as for taking on systematic market risk. Although economic theory provides some guidance, identification of the state variables that characterize the opportunity set is essentially an empirical matter. Merton focuses on the interest rate, noting that (p. 879)

> It [the interest rate] is observable, satisfies the condition of being stochastic over time, and while it is surely not the sole determinant of yields on other assets, it is an important factor. Hence, one should interpret the effects of a changing interest rate... in the way economists have generally done in the past: namely, as a single [instrumental] variable representation of shifts in the investment opportunity set.

Empirically, Fama and Schwert (1977) find a strong negative relation between the Treasury bill rate and expected stock index return over the period 1953–71. They also observe a negative relation between changes in the Treasury bill rate and contemporaneous realized returns on government bonds. Christie (1982) documents a positive association between interest rates and the variance of individual equity returns for the

Reproduced from *Journal of Econometrics*, 45: 1–2, July–August 1990, 99–120.
This paper was presented at the NBER Conference on Risk and Financial Markets. Thanks are due to M. Puffer for substantial computational assistance and to J. Bodurtha, J. Campbell, D. Chapman, J. Long, C. MacKinlay, S. Ross, B. Schwert, and an anonymous referee for helpful comments. Seminars at Yale University and the Universities of Rochester, Toronto, Michigan, and Southern California were valuable in formulating these ideas.

period 1962–78. In addition to these studies that relate characteristics of the opportunity set to the level of the Treasury bill rate, Fama (1976) examines the impact of rate volatility on the expected excess returns of Treasury bills with 2–6 months to maturity. He finds positive relations, with regression coefficients that are larger the longer the maturity of the bill.

In this paper we present further evidence on the role of the short-term rate and its volatility as state variables in the financial markets. Our measure of rate volatility TBV_t is

$$0.139\,|TB_t - TB_{t-1}| + 0.125\,|TB_{t-1} - TB_{t-2}| + \cdots + 0.044\,|TB_{t-11} - TB_{t-12}|,$$

where TB_t is the 1 month bill rate for month t. Thus TBV_t is a moving average of the last 12 absolute changes in rates. The weights sum to unity and decline by 10 percent at each step so that recent changes have more of an impact than distant ones. This variation on Fama's measure seemed reasonable *ex ante* and was not based on an analysis of the data. Hence, both TB_t and TBV_t are elements of the information set available to investors at the beginning of month t.[2]

After some descriptive statistics for TB and TBV are presented in section 2, in section 3 we look at the conditional joint distribution of the excess return r_m on the Center for Research in Security Prices (CRSP) value-weighted stock index and the excess return r_g on Ibbotson and Sinquefield's (1982) long-term government bond index. The conditioning state variables are TB, TBV, and a January dummy. Inclusion of the latter variable is motivated by previous evidence which suggests that the distribution of returns in January is different from that in the rest of the year.[3]

In section 4 we explore a two-factor version of the familiar market model with r_m and r_g serving as the factors. The conditional regression coefficients and residual covariance matrix, as well as the joint distribution of r_m and r_g, are allowed to vary over time with the levels of the state variables. Tests of conditional multi-beta pricing relations for size and industry portfolios are also presented in this section.

Tests of conditional beta pricing relations in terms of observable factors or latent variables have been developed in several previous papers. The econometric specifications employed in these papers vary. For example, Hansen and Hodrick (1983) and Gibbons and Ferson (1985) allow for changing conditional expected returns while assuming constant betas. Ferson, Kandel, and Stambaugh (1987) incorporate both time-varying expected risk premiums and betas but assume that the conditional covariance matrix of returns is constant. The approaches adopted by

Bollerslev, Engle, and Wooldridge (1988), Campbell (1987), and Engel (1987) are fairly general but require that the market price of covariance risk be constant over time.[4] One contribution of the present paper is the development of a simple econometric framework in which all these restrictions can be relaxed simultaneously.

The main results of the study are summarized in section 5.

2 Treasury Bill Rates and Volatility: 1953–1982

Plots of the monthly series TB_t and TBV_t, as well as the residuals from a regression of TBV on TB, are shown in figure 18.1 for the 30 year period from 1953 to 1982. All variables are in units of percent per month. The mean values of TB and TBV are 0.41 and 0.05 respectively. The sample distributions are positively skewed, with TB ranging from 0.03 to 1.35 and TBV from 0.01 to 0.19. Although autocorrelations of interest rates are close to unity at short lags, recent work by Fama and Bliss (1987) indicates that rates are slowly mean reverting.

The R^2 from the regression of TBV on TB is 0.44 and the slope coefficient is 0.09. As expected, absolute rate changes tend to be greater when rates are high. There is a fair amount of residual variation in rate volatility, however, particularly in the post-1973 period and, to a lesser extent, in the late 1950s and early 1960s. Such variation is needed, of course, if we are to estimate the separate effects of TB and TBV with any precision.

To a large extent, the high sample correlation between rate level and volatility reflects the fact that both variables generally take on greater values in the last 10 years of the sample than in the first 20 years. The relation between TB and TBV is fairly weak in the earlier period ($R^2 = 0.08$ for 1953–72). It is stronger in the period 1973–82, with a regression R^2 of 0.28.

To facilitate interpretation of the intercepts in the regressions below, from now on TB and TBV will be measured as deviations from their means. The slope coefficients and their standard errors are unaffected by the use of deviations.

3 The Conditional Distribution of Factor Portfolio Returns

The conditional distributions of r_{mt} and r_{gt} are investigated in this section. In addition to the stochastic interest rate TB_t and the rate volatility

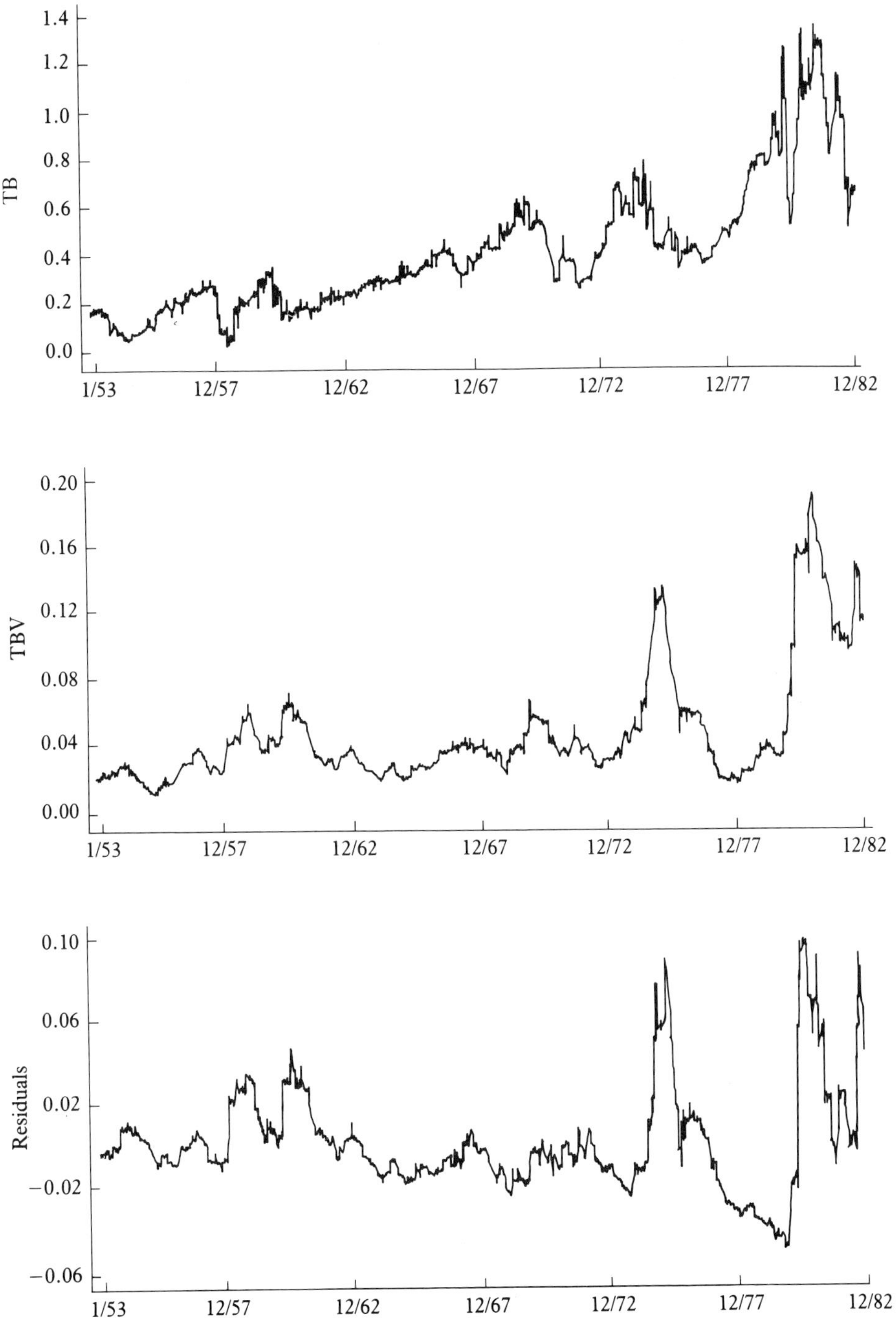

Figure 18.1 Monthly time series of 1 month Treasury bill rates (TB), a measure (TBV) of rate volatility, and the residuals from a regression of TBV on TB. Rates are measured in percent.

measure TBV_t (both measured in percent), we condition on a dummy variable JAN which equals unity if the given month is January and zero otherwise. Both linear and quadratic specifications for conditional moments have been explored. The squared variables (TB2 and TBV2) improve the fit of the variance relations but have a negligible impact on the mean relations. Thus, we report results for the following regressions:

$$r_{\mathrm{m}} = c_{0\mathrm{m}} + c_{1\mathrm{m}}\mathrm{TB} + c_{2\mathrm{m}}\mathrm{TBV} + c_{3\mathrm{m}}\mathrm{JAN} + \varepsilon_{\mathrm{m}} \tag{1}$$

$$r_{\mathrm{g}} = c_{0\mathrm{g}} + c_{1\mathrm{g}}\mathrm{TB} + c_{2\mathrm{g}}\mathrm{TBV} + c_{3\mathrm{g}}\mathrm{JAN} + \varepsilon_{\mathrm{g}} \tag{2}$$

$$\varepsilon_{\mathrm{m}}^2 = d_{0\mathrm{m}} + d_{1\mathrm{m}}\mathrm{TB} + d_{2\mathrm{m}}\mathrm{TBV} + d_{3\mathrm{m}}\mathrm{JAN} + d_{4\mathrm{m}}\mathrm{TB2} + d_{5\mathrm{m}}\mathrm{TBV2} + \eta_{\mathrm{m}} \tag{3}$$

$$\varepsilon_{\mathrm{g}}^2 = d_{0\mathrm{g}} + d_{1\mathrm{g}}\mathrm{TB} + d_{2\mathrm{g}}\mathrm{TBV} + d_{3\mathrm{g}}\mathrm{JAN} + d_{4\mathrm{g}}\mathrm{TB2} + d_{5\mathrm{g}}\mathrm{TBV2} + \eta_{\mathrm{g}} \tag{4}$$

with all disturbances on the right-hand side of (1)–(4) assumed to have zero mean conditional on current and past values of TB, TBV, and JAN. Note that

$$E(\varepsilon_{\mathrm{m}}^2 \mid \mathrm{TB}, \mathrm{TBV}, \mathrm{JAN}) = \mathrm{var}(r_{\mathrm{m}} \mid \mathrm{TB}, \mathrm{TBV}, \mathrm{JAN})$$

and

$$E(\varepsilon_{\mathrm{g}}^2 \mid \mathrm{TB}, \mathrm{TBV}, \mathrm{JAN}) = \mathrm{var}(r_{\mathrm{g}} \mid \mathrm{TB}, \mathrm{TBV}, \mathrm{JAN}).$$

Henceforth, the conditioning variables are omitted but all references to distributions and moments are implicitly conditioned on TB, TBV, and JAN unless noted otherwise.

Estimates of the parameters in (1) are obtained by regressing the monthly excess returns r_{m} on TB, TBV, JAN, and a constant over the period 1953–82. The disturbance term ε_{m} in the regression is conditionally heteroskedastic if any of the slope coefficients in (3) is nonzero. Therefore, standard errors for this regression, as well as all other regressions reported in this paper, are based on methods that are consistent in the presence of conditional heteroskedasticity.[5] In many cases, these standard errors are a good deal larger than the usual ordinary least squares (OLS) standard errors which are not reported.

To estimate the parameters in (3), squared residuals from the time series regression for (1) are regressed on TB, TBV, JAN, TB2, TBV2, and a constant. Under fairly general conditions, these estimates are consistent and have the same asymptotic distribution as estimates based on the (unobserved) squared disturbances $\varepsilon_{\mathrm{m}}^2$.[6] The parameters in (2) and (4) are estimated similarly. Since TB and TBV are measured as deviations from means, the intercepts in regressions (1)–(4) can be interpreted as values of the corresponding conditional moments (for February–December) when rate level and volatility are at their means.

While we would expect the level of the interest rate and a measure of uncertainty about future rates to jointly capture important aspects of the state of the economy, the partial effects of these two positively correlated variables on financial assets may be different. As seen in table 18.1, $E(r_m)$ is positively related to TBV but negatively related to TB. Although not given in the table, the coefficient -2.68 from the simple regression of r_m on TB is also significantly negative ($t = -3.05$).[7] This coefficient implictly reflects the *net* effects of both interest rate level and volatility and is thus smaller in magnitude than the partial coefficient in table 18.1.

Interestingly, the negative relations between $E(r_m)$ and TB are highly significant in the subperiod 1953–72 studied by Fama and Schwert (1977), as well as in the subperiod 1973–82 in which interest rate behavior is more extreme.[8] The $E(r_m)$ coefficient on TBV is positive in both subperiods, but is more than two standard deviations from zero only in the later period.[9] The finding of a significant relation between $E(r_m)$ and TBV for the overall period is rather surprising given the insignificance of (predictable) equity volatility in similar regressions reported by French, Schwert, and Stambaugh (1987).[10] On the other hand, it complements the related result in Fama (1976) for longer term Treasury bills.

The coefficients on TB in the variance relations are both positive and

Table 18.1 Conditional distribution of factor portfolio returns

	Coefficient on							
Moment[a]	*Constant*[b]	*TB*	*TBV*	*JAN*	*TB2*	*TBV2*	R^2	ρ[c]
$E(r_m)$	0.45*[d]	−5.06*	27.9*	0.35			0.05	0.02
	(0.21)	(1.26)	(10.1)	(0.97)				
$E(r_g)$	−0.06	0.43	4.4	−0.50			0.00	0.04
	(0.14)	(1.05)	(7.0)	(0.45)				
var(r_m)	18.2*	21.0*	199*	12.8*	−24.5	−1309	0.08	0.10
	(2.2)	(6.5)	(97.9)	(5.6)	(16.3)	(972)		
var(r_g)	5.9*	12.5*	136*	0.4	29.7	−1607	0.21	0.15
	(1.0)	(3.7)	(46.6)	(2.1)	(20.9)	(842)		

Conditional means and variances of monthly excess returns on the hedge portfolios as a function of observable state variables. The state variables are the 1 month Treasury bill rate TB, a measure TBV of rate volatility, and a dummy variable JAN which equals unity in January and zero otherwise. TB2 and TBV2 are the squared values of TB and TBV respectively. r_m is the excess return on the CRSP value-weighted stock index and r_g is the excess return on the Ibbotson–Sinquefield long-term US government bond index. All returns are computed in excess of TB and are measured in percent. Estimates are for the period 1953–82 with heteroskedasticity-consistent standard errors in parentheses.

[a] All moments are conditioned on TB, TBV, and JAN.

[b] Conditional moment for February–December when rate level and volatility are at their means, since TB and TBV are measured as deviations from means.

[c] First-order residual autocorrelation from time series regressions on the state variables. The dependent variables consist of excess returns for the mean relations and squared residuals from these regressions for the variance relations.

[d] An asterisk indicates that the estimate is more than two standard deviations from zero.

more than three standard errors from zero. The TBV coefficients are also positive and more than two standard errors from zero. Subperiod estimates for TB and TBV are uniformly positive although their statistical significance is reduced. While the estimated quadratic relations are not strictly increasing in TB and TBV, we cannot reject monotonicity of the true variance relations when the estimation error is considered. One other noteworthy observation from table 18.1 is the significant increase in equity volatility in January.[11]

The adjusted R^2 values in table 18.1 are generally low, particularly for the excess return regressions. This reflects the fact that movements in conditional moments are small compared with the total variation in realized returns. Nonetheless, these movements are economically important; in particular, the implied equity risk premium, which averages over 5 percent per year, is negative when rates are relatively high. It is also interesting that more than a fifth of the variation in squared (residual) government bond return is related to the state variables, even though the mean excess return is apparently independent of these variables.

4 Tests of the Multi-Beta Pricing Relation

In the previous section we have established that significant shifts in the investment opportunity set are associated with the levels of our state variables. Following Shanken (1987, 1989), in this section we assume that the factor portfolio returns r_m and r_g span or proxy for variation in the equilibrium benchmark that is correlated with the given asset returns.[12] Equivalently, the residual components of asset returns (see equation (5) below) are assumed to be (conditionally) uncorrelated with the benchmark. In this case, the conditional expected returns of assets are linearly related to their conditional factor-portfolio betas. Since the 1 month Treasury bill has betas equal to zero, the intercept in the relation must equal the Treasury bill rate. Alternatively, the analysis below can be viewed as an evaluation of the conditional mean–variance efficiency of some (unspecified) portfolio of m and g.

Campbell (1987) approaches a single-factor version of this problem by modeling expected excess returns and variances/covariances as linear functions of the state variables. He then imposes the cross-sectional constraint that the expected returns of assets are linear in their covariances with a given benchmark return, while assuming that the ratio of expected excess return to variance is constant for the benchmark. Here we adopt an alternative specification that exploits the fact that the multi-beta pricing relation amounts to an intercept restriction on a multivariate linear regression model; that is, $\varepsilon_j = 0$ for all j, where[13]

$$r_j = a_j + b_{j\mathrm{m}} r_\mathrm{m} + b_{j\mathrm{g}} r_\mathrm{g} + e_j. \tag{5}$$

r_j is the excess return on asset j, a_j is the risk-adjusted mean return, and e_j is a zero-mean residual disturbance. We refer to $b_{j\mathrm{m}}$ and $b_{j\mathrm{g}}$ as "market betas" and "bond betas" respectively.

An advantage of this approach is that it does not impose any structure on the joint distribution of r_m and r_g, apart from some relatively weak conditions that ensure asymptotic convergence of the estimators.[14] Thus developments in the economy that influence market and interest rate factors, but do not affect the conditional relation between asset and factor portfolio returns, are implicitly accommodated. The "prices" of market and interest rate risk, in particular, can vary over time and their evolution need not conform to the simple process posited in section 3. Serial correlation and conditional heteroskedasticity in the factor portfolio returns are also permitted. It *is* necessary to specify the relation between the conditional regression coefficients in (5) and the levels of the state variables, however. For simplicity, we postulate the linear relations[15,16]

$$a_j = h_{j0} + h_{j1}\mathrm{TB} + h_{j2}\mathrm{TBV} + h_{j3}\mathrm{JAN} \tag{6}$$

$$b_{j\mathrm{m}} = c_{j0} + c_{j1}\mathrm{TB} + c_{j2}\mathrm{TBV} + c_{j3}\mathrm{JAN} \tag{7}$$

$$b_{j\mathrm{g}} = d_{j0} + d_{j1}\mathrm{TB} + d_{j2}\mathrm{TBV} + d_{j3}\mathrm{JAN}. \tag{8}$$

Substituting these expressions in (5) yields a regression equation with 12 independent variables:[17]

$$\begin{aligned} r_j = {} & h_{j0} + h_{j1}\mathrm{TB} + h_{j2}\mathrm{TBV} + h_{j3}\mathrm{JAN} \\ & + c_{j0} r_\mathrm{m} + c_{j1}(\mathrm{TB}r_\mathrm{m}) + c_{j2}(\mathrm{TBV}r_\mathrm{m}) + c_{j3}(\mathrm{JAN}r_\mathrm{m}) \\ & + d_{j0} r_\mathrm{g} + d_{j1}(\mathrm{TB}r_\mathrm{g}) + d_{j2}(\mathrm{TBV}r_\mathrm{g}) + d_{j3}(\mathrm{JAN}r_\mathrm{g}) + e_j. \end{aligned} \tag{9}$$

Under the null hypothesis that the a_j equal zero, $h_{j0} = h_{j1} = h_{j2} = h_{j3} = 0$ for all j.

In some applications it may be reasonable to assume that the conditional covariance matrix of the e_j is constant over time. In this case, heteroskedasticity in r_j is solely a function of heteroskedasticity in the joint distribution of factor portfolio returns and/or variation in the conditional betas. If so, exact versions of our asymptotic joint significance tests are feasible, assuming joint normality of the e_j.[18]

We test for heteroskedasticity of the e_j by estimating a conditional linear relation for residual variance. Squared residuals from the regression (9) serve as the dependent variable in this context. The null hypothesis that residual variance is constant over time is rejected if any of the slope coefficients is significantly different from zero. It deserves emphasis that our subsequent pricing tests, unlike this test for residual heteroskedasticity, do not assume any particular specification for the conditional residual variance relation.[19]

4.1 Empirical evidence – size portfolios

This section presents empirical evidence for ten size portfolios. The first size portfolio consists of the decile of smallest firms and the tenth consists of the decile of largest firms on the New York Stock Exchange (NYSE), based on the total market value of equity outstanding. All portfolios are value weighted.[20]

Estimates of the size portfolio residual variance relations are given in table 18.2. Average residual variance for February–December decreases monotonically with size. The coefficients on TB also tend to fall with size and are positive for all portfolios. Two tests of joint significance, with p values in parentheses, are provided at the bottom of table 18.2 for each set of coefficients. The first test statistic is the maximum squared t statistic for a given variable over all portfolio combinations of the ten size portfolios. This is a heteroskedasticity-consistent version of Hotelling's T^2 test and is asymptotically distributed as χ^2 with ten degrees of freedom.[21] The second test statistic is similar except that the maximum is just taken over the size portfolios themselves. The p value given is an upper bound on the true p value and is computed using the Bonferroni method.[22] Since this test is biased toward acceptance, we focus on the χ^2 test and use the Bonferroni test as a supplementary source of information.[23] Since TB and JAN are jointly significant at conventional levels, we shall continue to rely on heteroskedasticity-consistent methods below.

There are distinctive patterns in the market beta relations of table 18.3. The market betas of size portfolios 1–9 are positively related to TB and negatively related to TBV. The coefficient magnitudes are inversely related to size, with the signs reversed in the portfolio of the largest firms.[24] The coefficients are large in economic terms and most of the estimates are more than three standard deviations from zero. Since the average market betas tend to decline with size, the spread in market risk widens with increases in TB or decreases in TBV.

Table 18.3 also presents evidence of a significant January seasonal in the bond betas of several size portfolios. The increases in January for the portfolios of smaller firms represent a reversal of interest rate risk from negative in February–December to positive in January. The effect is strongest, both in estimated magnitude and statistical significance, in portfolio 1, with b_{jg} shifting from -0.26 to 0.87 $(-0.26+1.13)$. Unfortunately, since the JAN coefficient for $E(r_g)$ in table 18.1 is negative, this documentation of increased interest rate risk does not help to explain the large mean return of small firms in January.

Table 18.2 Size portfolio residual variances

	Residual variance coefficient on					
Asset j	*Constant*[a]	*TB*	*TBV*	*JAN*	*Adjusted* R^2[b]	*Residual autocorrelation*[b]
1 Smallest	12.6*[c]	8.2	103.6	1.6	0.03	0.05
	(1.5)	(5.9)	(65.7)	(4.0)		
2	7.0*	5.3	4.2	5.6	0.02	0.02
	(0.6)	(3.3)	(26.9)	(3.2)		
3	5.9*	1.5	−4.0	1.3	0.00	−0.02
	(0.5)	(2.3)	(19.0)	(2.4)		
4	4.5*	3.0	2.1	1.8	0.01	−0.01
	(0.4)	(1.7)	(13.2)	(1.5)		
5	3.4*	3.3*	−12.4	0.0	0.01	0.00
	(0.3)	(1.3)	(10.6)	(1.0)		
6	2.6*	3.5*	−1.5	1.7	0.04	0.03
	(0.2)	(1.2)	(10.1)	(1.3)		
7	2.2*	2.3*	−3.8	−0.7	0.01	0.01
	(0.2)	(1.0)	(9.0)	(0.5)		
8	1.2*	0.8	5.2	1.5	0.05	0.21
	(0.1)	(0.7)	(7.0)	(0.9)		
9	0.8*	0.4	6.2*	−0.3	0.05	0.02
	(0.1)	(0.4)	(3.1)	(0.2)		
10 Largest	0.4*	0.6*	1.1	0.0	0.06	0.01
	(0.0)	(0.2)	(1.6)	(0.2)		
$\chi^2(10)$[d]	337.8	20.5	14.2	25.8		
	(0.00)	(0.03)	(0.17)	(0.00)		
Bonferroni[e]	158.2	9.3	3.9	3.1		
	(0.00)	(0.03)	(0.57)	(0.97)		

The excess return for each asset j is $r_j = a_j + b_{jm}r_m + b_{jg}r_g + e_j$, where r_m is the excess return on the CRSP value-weighted stock index and r_g is the excess return on the Ibbotson–Sinquefield long term government bond index. The regression coefficients and var(e_j) are linear in the 1 month Treasury bill rate TB, a measure TBV of rate volatility, and a dummy variable JAN which equals unity in January and zero otherwise. All returns are measured in percent and are in excess of TB. Estimates are for the period 1953–82 with heteroskedasticity-consistent standard errors in parentheses.

[a]Residual variance for February–December when rate level and volatility are at their means, since TB and TBV are measured as deviations from means.

[b]From the time series regression of squared residuals for asset j on a constant, TB, TBV, and JAN.

[c]An asterisk indicates that the estimate is more than two standard deviations from zero.

[d]Maximum squared heteroskedasticity-consistent t statistic on a given variable over all portfolios of the ten assets; p value in parentheses.

[e]Maximum squared heteroskedasticity-consistent t statistic on a given variable over the ten assets; upper bound on p value in parentheses.

Table 18.3 Size portfolio betas

	Market beta coefficient on				*Bond beta coefficient on*			
Asset j	*Constant*[a]	*TB*	*TBV*	*JAN*	*Constant*[a]	*TB*	*TBV*	*JAN*
1 Smallest	1.26*[b]	1.42*	−8.4*	0.14	−0.26*	0.11	−2.7	1.13*
	(0.06)	(0.24)	(1.9)	(0.14)	(0.10)	(0.24)	(2.8)	(0.25)
2	1.19*	0.89*	−6.0*	0.15	−0.16*	0.30	−1.5	0.63*
	(0.04)	(0.21)	(1.7)	(0.14)	(0.08)	(0.21)	(2.0)	(0.22)
3	1.21*	0.86*	−6.2*	0.12	−0.10	0.13	−0.5	0.50*
	(0.04)	(0.17)	(1.4)	(0.10)	(0.07)	(0.17)	(1.7)	(0.22)
4	1.17*	0.73*	−5.0*	0.10	−0.07	0.03	−0.3	0.47*
	(0.04)	(0.16)	(1.2)	(0.10)	(0.06)	(0.16)	(1.4)	(0.19)
5	1.17*	0.62*	−3.7*	0.02	−0.05	0.07	−1.3	0.25
	(0.03)	(0.13)	(0.9)	(0.05)	(0.05)	(0.13)	(1.2)	(0.16)
6	1.08*	0.49*	−3.0*	0.08	−0.05	0.09	−0.4	0.33*
	(0.03)	(0.12)	(0.9)	(0.08)	(0.05)	(0.11)	(0.9)	(0.14)
7	1.09*	0.34*	−2.3*	0.03	−0.02	−0.04	0.6	0.19
	(0.03)	(0.10)	(0.7)	(0.05)	(0.05)	(0.13)	(1.0)	(0.10)
8	1.05*	0.32*	−2.2*	0.11	0.03	0.04	−0.4	0.27*
	(0.02)	(0.08)	(0.7)	(0.07)	(0.03)	(0.09)	(0.6)	(0.11)
9	1.01*	0.12	−0.4	−0.03	0.10*	−0.13	−0.3	−0.06
	(0.01)	(0.07)	(0.5)	(0.03)	(0.03)	(0.09)	(0.8)	(0.06)
10 Largest	0.95*	−0.23*	1.4*	−0.01	−0.01	0.00	0.2	−0.11*
	(0.01)	(0.05)	(0.4)	(0.02)	(0.02)	(0.05)	(0.5)	(0.05)
$\chi^2(10)$[c]	460,508	46.9	33.2	19.8	28.7	17.5	8.4	65.4
	(0.00)	(0.00)	(0.00)	(0.03)	(0.00)	(0.06)	(0.59)	(0.00)
Bonferroni[d]	7,371	34.2	20.4	2.4	10.7	2.0	1.3	20.0
	(0.00)	(0.00)	(0.00)	(1.00)	(0.01)	(1.00)	(1.00)	(0.00)

The excess return for each asset j is $r_j = a_j + b_{jm}r_m + b_{jg}r_g + e_j$, where r_m is the excess return on the CRSP value-weighted stock index and r_g is the excess return on the Ibbotson–Sinquefield long-term government bond index. The regression coefficients are linear in the 1 month Treasury bill rate TB, a measure of rate volatility TBV, and a dummy variable JAN which equals unity in January and zero otherwise. All returns are measured in percent and are in excess of TB. Estimates are for the period 1953–82 with heteroskedasticity-consistent standard errors in parentheses.

[a]Beta for February–December when rate level and volatility are at their means, since TB and TBV are measured as deviations from means.

[b]An asterisk indicates that the estimate is more than two standard deviations from zero.

[c]Maximum squared heteroskedasticity-consistent t statistic on a given variable over all portfolios of the ten assets; p value in parentheses.

[d]Maximum squared heteroskedasticity-consistent t statistic on a given variable over the ten assets; upper bound on p value in parentheses.

Table 18.4 Size portfolio risk-adjusted returns

	Intercept coefficient on					
Asset j	*Constant*[a]	*TB*	*TBV*	*JAN*	*Adjusted* R^{2}[b]	*Residual autocorrelation*[b]
1 Smallest	0.13	−0.09	23.6*[c]	6.77*	0.71	0.12
	(0.21)	(0.99)	(9.6)	(0.66)		
2	0.43*	−0.67	19.8*	4.70*	0.79	0.06
	(0.15)	(0.79)	(6.9)	(0.63)		
3	0.23	0.11	14.4*	3.97*	0.82	0.11
	(0.13)	(0.65)	(5.8)	(0.48)		
4	0.23	−0.21	14.4*	2.99*	0.84	0.14
	(0.12)	(0.60)	(5.0)	(0.44)		
5	0.23*	−0.04	11.6*	2.64*	0.87	0.12
	(0.10)	(0.54)	(4.2)	(0.33)		
6	0.15	0.01	11.8*	2.30*	0.88	0.11
	(0.09)	(0.46)	(4.1)	(0.36)		
7	0.14	−0.48	10.5*	1.13*	0.90	0.01
	(0.08)	(0.41)	(3.1)	(0.24)		
8	0.10	−0.09	8.8*	1.16*	0.94	0.05
	(0.06)	(0.30)	(2.6)	(0.28)		
9	0.06	−0.04	3.0	0.18	0.96	0.00
	(0.05)	(0.27)	(2.2)	(0.14)		
10 Largest	−0.06	0.09	−5.7*	−0.66*	0.97	0.09
	(0.04)	(0.19)	(1.6)	(0.12)		
$\chi^2(10)$[d]	17.8	6.1	17.0	155.5		
	(0.06)	(0.81)	(0.07)	(0.00)		
Bonferroni[e]	8.5	1.4	13.0	104.5		
	(0.04)	(1.00)	(0.00)	(0.00)		

The excess return for each asset j is $r_j = a_j + b_{jm}r_m + b_{jg}r_g + e_j$, where r_m is the excess return on the CRSP value-weighted stock index and r_g is the excess return on the Ibbotson–Sinquefield long-term government bond index. The regression coefficients are linear in the 1 month Treasury bill rate TB, a measure TBV of rate volatility, and a dummy variable JAN which equals unity in January and zero otherwise. All returns are measured in percent and are in excess of TB. Estimates are for the period 1953–82 with heteroskedasticity-consistent standard errors in parentheses.

[a]Intercept for February–December when rate level and volatility are at their means, since TB and TBV are measured as deviations from means.

[b]From the time series regression of r_j on r_m, r_g, and a constant, and products of these variables with TB, TBV, and JAN.

[c]An asterisk indicates that the estimate is more than two standard deviations from zero.

[d]Maximum squared heteroskedasticity-consistent t statistic on a given variable over all portfolios of the ten assets; p value in parentheses.

[e]Maximum squared heteroskedasticity-consistent t statistic on a given variable over the ten assets; upper bound on p value in parentheses.

Recall that $E(r_m)$ is negatively related to TB and positively related to TBV. TB is not significant in the risk-adjusted intercept relations of table 18.4, however. Apparently, the influence of TB is fully captured by the stock index. TBV is significant, though, with coefficients inversely related to size. The coefficients are positive for all but the largest firms. The average (February–December) risk-adjusted returns are also jointly significant.

The observations above imply rejection of the hypothesis that all a_j equal zero. An alternative interpretation of these statistics, in terms of joint confidence intervals, may convey a clearer sense of the extent of economic deviations from the null hypothesis. Consider, for example, a family of confidence intervals for the ten coefficients on JAN in table 18.4. Suppose that a joint confidence level of at least 0.95 is desired. Using the Bonferroni method, this is achieved by taking each interval to be of the form $\hat{h}_{j3} \mp 2.81s(\hat{h}_{j3})$, where $\hat{h}_{j3}$ is the JAN coefficient estimate and $s(\hat{h}_{j3})$ is its standard error.[25] The confidence interval for the small firm portfolio is (4.92, 8.62). Thus, even after taking into account the fact that we are focusing on the most extreme sample observation, the lower bound of nearly 5 percent per month is still huge.[26]

Many of the patterns observed in this section, for example the relation between market betas and TB, the January risk-adjusted return effects, and the jump in the small firm bond beta in January, are found in both subperiods 1953–72 and 1973–82 of our sample and are statistically significant in each period. The TBV market beta and risk-adjusted return relations are driven by outcomes in the later period, however.

4.2 *Empirical evidence – industry portfolios*

This section presents empirical results for 12 value-weighted industry portfolios.[27] Evidence of industry portfolio residual heteroskedasticity is found in table 18.5, with TBV and JAN both statistically significant.

The TB coefficients and, to a lesser extent, those on TBV are jointly significant in the market beta relations of table 18.6. Traditional "defensive" industries like utilities and food and tobacco live up to their reputations, with average (February–December) market betas of 0.62 and 0.81 respectively. The average services beta is not much greater than unity, but the large coefficient on TB implies considerable variation in the conditional beta, given the range of Treasury bill rates shown in figure 18.1. The lower bound on the confidence interval for the services TB coefficient, in the Bonferroni family with joint confidence of at least 0.95, is only 0.11, however, which rules out any strong conclusions. In general, strong inferences about individual coefficients are not possible unless the

Table 18.5 Industry portfolio residual variances

	Residual variance coefficient on				*Adjusted*	*Residual*
Asset j	*Constant*[a]	*TB*	*TBV*	*JAN*	R^{2}[b]	*autocorrelation*[b]
Petroleum	9.7★[c]	7.9	117.4★	2.8	0.11	−0.01
	(0.8)	(4.7)	(39.1)	(3.2)		
Financial	3.7★	−0.2	33.4	0.0	0.02	0.15
	(0.4)	(2.4)	(25.1)	(1.0)		
Consumer durables	3.8★	−1.5	59.6	0.7	0.05	0.00
	(0.4)	(2.7)	(31.7)	(1.3)		
Basic industries	1.8★	−0.2	24.5★	1.0	0.07	0.11
	(0.2)	(0.7)	(8.8)	(0.8)		
Food and tobacco	3.2★	−0.8	51.0★	0.5	0.06	0.05
	(0.3)	(1.4)	(18.5)	(0.9)		
Construction	5.5★	−0.8	51.7	2.0	0.03	−0.01
	(0.5)	(3.1)	(26.2)	(1.1)		
Capital goods	4.1★	2.5	−2.6	−0.2	0.00	0.02
	(0.4)	(2.0)	(17.2)	(1.1)		
Transportation	8.7★	5.4	7.8	1.6	0.01	−0.03
	(0.8)	(3.1)	(27.3)	(2.5)		
Utilities	3.5★	1.3	1.1	0.4	0.00	−0.02
	(0.3)	(1.5)	(11.9)	(1.0)		
Trade and textiles	7.1★	−3.5	153.1★	6.7	0.13	−0.06
	(0.6)	(3.5)	(44.4)	(3.9)		
Services	13.1★	−0.7	31.9	2.5	0.00	0.11
	(1.2)	(5.9)	(37.8)	(2.4)		
Recreation	9.7★	−2.9	104.2★	−1.5	0.03	0.14
	(0.8)	(4.6)	(48.2)	(3.0)		
$\chi^2(10)$[d]	678.5	10.0	21.0	27.3		
	(0.00)	(0.61)	(0.05)	(0.01)		
Bonferroni[e]	141.0	3.1	11.9	3.5		
	(0.00)	(0.96)	(0.01)	(0.72)		

The excess return for each asset j is $r_j = a_j + b_{jm}r_m + b_{jg}r_g + e_j$, where r_m is the excess return on the CRSP value-weighted stock index and r_g is the excess return on the Ibbotson–Sinquefield long-term government bond index. The regression coefficients and var(e_j) are linear in the 1 month Treasury bill rate TB, a measure TBV of rate volatility, and a dummy variable JAN which equals unity in January and zero otherwise. All returns are measured in percent and are in excess of TB. Estimates are for the period 1953–82 with heteroskedasticity-consistent standard errors in parentheses.

[a]Residual variance for February–December when rate level and volatility are at their means, since TB and TBV are measured as deviations from means.

[b]From the time series regression of squared residuals for asset j on a constant, TB, TBV, and JAN.

[c]An asterisk indicates that the estimate is more than two standard deviations from zero.

[d]Maximum squared heteroskedasticity-consistent t statistic on a given variable over all portfolios of the 12 assets; p value in parentheses.

[e]Maximum squared heteroskedasticity-consistent t statistic on a given variable over the 12 assets; upper bound on p value in parentheses.

Table 18.6 Industry portfolio betas

Asset *j*	Market beta coefficient on				Bond beta coefficient on			
	Constant[a]	*TB*	*TBV*	*JAN*	*Constant*[a]	*TB*	*TBV*	*JAN*
Petroleum	0.97*[b]	0.49*	0.4	−0.14	−0.09	−0.42	2.3	−0.58*
	(0.05)	(0.24)	(1.8)	(0.14)	(0.10)	(0.29)	(2.4)	(0.25)
Financial	1.03*	0.02	−1.1	0.00	0.29*	−0.38*	2.6*	0.29
	(0.03)	(0.15)	(1.2)	(0.08)	(0.06)	(0.14)	(1.2)	(0.19)
Consumer	1.12*	0.14	−2.0	0.21*	−0.12*	0.08	−0.8	−0.08
durables	(0.03)	(0.21)	(2.0)	(0.09)	(0.06)	(0.25)	(1.8)	(0.13)
Basic	1.11*	−0.35*	0.5	−0.09	0.11*	0.21	−0.1	−0.01
industries	(0.02)	(0.12)	(1.0)	(0.09)	(0.04)	(0.12)	(1.0)	(0.13)
Food and	0.81*	−0.07	−0.3	−0.03	0.13*	0.03	0.3	0.24
tobacco	(0.03)	(0.15)	(1.3)	(0.10)	(0.05)	(0.15)	(1.2)	(0.13)
Construction	1.15*	0.31	−1.0	0.12	−0.02	−0.17	−0.4	0.17
	(0.04)	(0.19)	(1.6)	(0.08)	(0.07)	(0.24)	(2.0)	(0.15)
Capital	1.09*	−0.28*	1.4	0.04	−0.16*	0.27	−1.5	0.11
goods	(0.03)	(0.12)	(1.0)	(0.07)	(0.06)	(0.17)	(1.3)	(0.14)
Transportation	1.21*	0.39	−1.5	−0.04	−0.05	0.03	−1.7	0.14
	(0.05)	(0.20)	(1.4)	(0.11)	(0.10)	(0.33)	(2.6)	(0.29)
Utilities	0.62*	−0.28*	0.2	0.00	0.41*	0.01	−1.8	0.07
	(0.03)	(0.12)	(1.0)	(0.09)	(0.07)	(0.18)	(1.5)	(0.14)
Trade and	0.97*	0.18	−2.4	0.08	0.03	−0.04	0.3	0.72*
textiles	(0.05)	(0.26)	(2.4)	(0.19)	(0.09)	(0.25)	(2.3)	(0.20)
Services	1.08*	0.92*	−2.3	0.05	0.00	−0.02	−0.4	0.64*
	(0.06)	(0.28)	(1.7)	(0.12)	(0.10)	(0.28)	(2.5)	(0.26)
Recreation	1.23*	0.54	−4.4	0.19	−0.11	−0.02	0.4	0.82*
	(0.06)	(0.28)	(2.3)	(0.17)	(0.10)	(0.23)	(2.0)	(0.22)
$\chi^2(10)$[c]	99,842	62.3	20.8	10.8	71.6	25.9	16.6	48.7
	(0.00)	(0.00)	(0.05)	(0.54)	(0.00)	(0.01)	(0.17)	(0.00)
Bonferroni[d]	2,782	10.4	3.7	5.7	40.1	7.9	4.9	14.5
	(0.00)	(0.02)	(0.67)	(0.20)	(0.00)	(0.06)	(0.32)	(0.00)

The excess return for each asset j is $r_j = a_j + b_{jm}r_m + b_{jg}r_g + e_j$, where r_m is the excess return on the CRSP value-weighted stock index and r_g is the excess return on the Ibbotson–Sinquefield long-term government bond index. The regression coefficients are linear in the 1 month Treasury bill rate TB, a measure TBV of rate volatility, and a dummy variable JAN which equals unity in January and zero otherwise. All returns are measured in percent and are in excess of TB. Beta estimates are for the period 1953–82 with heteroskedasticity-consistent standard errors in parentheses.

[a]Beta for February–December when rate level and volatility are at their means, since TB and TBV are measured as deviations from means.

[b]An asterisk indicates that the estimate is more than two standard deviations from zero.

[c]Maximum squared heteroskedasticity-consistent t statistic on a given variable over all portfolios of the 12 assets; p value in parentheses.

[d]Maximum squared heteroskedasticity-consistent t statistic on a given variable over the 12 assets; upper bound on p value in parentheses.

Table 18.7 Industry portfolio risk-adjusted returns

Asset j	Intercept coefficient on: Constant[a]	TB	TBV	JAN	Adjusted R^{2}[b]	Residual autocorrelation[b]
Petroleum	0.34	1.39	−16.2★[c]	−1.70★	0.61	0.16
	(0.18)	(0.96)	(7.9)	(0.68)		
Financial	−0.01	0.40	3.4	0.47	0.84	0.09
	(0.10)	(0.55)	(4.5)	(0.40)		
Consumer durables	0.01	−1.01	10.7★	0.03	0.85	0.01
	(0.10)	(0.60)	(4.3)	(0.39)		
Basic industries	−0.17★	0.30	−3.6	−0.09	0.91	0.05
	(0.07)	(0.40)	(3.8)	(0.30)		
Food and tobacco	0.07	−0.19	9.1★	0.97★	0.78	0.17
	(0.10)	(0.52)	(4.2)	(0.37)		
Construction	−0.13	−0.50	6.1	0.47	0.81	0.11
	(0.13)	(0.69)	(4.7)	(0.40)		
Capital goods	0.11	−1.18★	0.8	−0.05	0.83	0.12
	(0.11)	(0.56)	(4.5)	(0.41)		
Transportation	−0.23	−0.01	6.5	2.34★	0.74	0.04
	(0.16)	(0.79)	(7.1)	(0.66)		
Utilities	−0.01	−0.38	4.5	1.29★	0.69	0.09
	(0.10)	(0.49)	(3.7)	(0.36)		
Trade and textiles	0.01	−0.93	18.9★	1.08	0.68	0.11
	(0.15)	(0.80)	(7.7)	(0.64)		
Services	0.32	−0.11	17.4★	1.67★	0.63	0.09
	(0.21)	(1.04)	(7.1)	(0.66)		
Recreation	0.23	−1.01	20.4★	1.15★	0.73	0.17
	(0.17)	(0.91)	(7.5)	(0.54)		
$\chi^2(10)$[d]	33.8	16.5	21.9	47.7		
	(0.00)	(0.17)	(0.04)	(0.00)		
Bonferroni[e]	5.0	4.5	7.5	12.9		
	(0.30)	(0.42)	(0.07)	(0.00)		

The excess return for each asset j is $r_j = a_j + b_{jm}r_m + b_{jg}r_g + e_j$, where r_m is the excess return on the CRSP value-weighted stock index and r_g is the excess return on the Ibbotson–Sinquefield long-term government bond index. The regression coefficients are linear in the 1 month Treasury bill rate TB, a measure TBV of rate volatility, and a dummy variable JAN which equals unity in January and zero otherwise. All returns are measured in percent and are in excess of TB. Estimates are for the period 1953–82 with heteroskedasticity-consistent standard errors in parentheses.

[a]Intercept for February–December when rate level and volatility are at their means, since TB and TBV are measured as deviations from means.

[b]From the time series regression of r_j on r_m, r_g, and a constant, and products of these variables with TB, TBV, and JAN.

[c]An asterisk indicates that the estimate is more than two standard deviations from zero.

[d]Maximum squared heteroskedasticity-consistent t statistic on a given variable over all portfolios of the 12 assets; p value in parentheses.

[e]Maximum squared heteroskedasticity-consistent t statistic on a given variable over the 12 assets; upper bound on p value in parentheses.

Bonferroni p value at the bottom of the associated column is "much" smaller than one minus the desired joint confidence level.

The results in table 18.6 also indicate that several industries are sensitive to interest rate risk. In particular, the February–December average bond betas for the utilities and financial industries are more than four standard deviations above zero.[28] The financial bond beta appears to vary with both TB and TBV, although the latter variable is not jointly significant across industries. Several industries experience increases in interest rate risk in January, as we found earlier for the smaller firm portfolios. The lower bound on the confidence interval for the recreation JAN coefficient is 0.20 (joint confidence at least 0.95). None of the industries with large JAN coefficients has average February–December bond betas that are more than a standard deviation above zero.

There is considerable evidence in table 18.7 against the null hypothesis that a_j equals zero for all industries.[29] Positive January effects show up in several industries, most notably transportation. The lower bound on the confidence interval for the transportation JAN coefficient is nearly 0.5 percent per month (joint confidence at least 0.95). Petroleum has a negative JAN coefficient that is several standard deviations below zero, probably owing to the presence of some very large firms in this industry. In addition to these January effects, the constant and TBV coefficients are both jointly significant, implying rejection of the pricing relation for February–December as well.

5 Summary and Conclusions

A number of interesting empirical regularities have emerged in this study of the conditional distribution of returns. Over the period 1953–82, expected stock return is negatively related to the 1 month Treasury bill rate TB and positively related to a measure TBV of rate volatility. These relations are observed for every size category and industry grouping as well as the CRSP value-weighted market index.[30] Sensitivity to TB varies across industries, with the coefficient for capital goods nearly twice that of petroleum, but there is little variation associated with firm size.

Variance of return is directly related to TB for every portfolio examined, with coefficients that are inversely related to size. Although less significant, systematic relations between variance and TBV are also observed for many portfolios. The variance of the CRSP value-weighted index jumps by 70 percent in January and several other equity portfolios show similar increases. Since the long-term government bond variance rises only slightly in January, however, the variance increases are probably not driven by information about interest rates.

Multiple regressions of portfolio excess returns on the excess returns of our stock and bond indexes are used to examine intertemporal asset pricing restrictions. The (conditional) regression parameters are allowed to vary with TB, TBV, and a January dummy. The smaller firm portfolios exhibit greater sensitivity to market movements than the large firm portfolio. This spread in market risk (beta) increases with TB and decreases with TBV.

Abnormally large risk-adjusted January returns are apparent for several industry portfolios as well as the portfolios of smaller firms. More surprising, given the previous literature, is the increase in interest rate risk for a number of portfolios in January. Once again, the impact is most pronounced in the notorious small firm portfolio, whose bond beta shifts from negative to positive in January. Adjustment for this source of risk does not reduce the small firm mean effect, however, since the average bond return for January is negative.

In addition to the January effect, there is some evidence of "abnormal return" during the rest of the year. Risk-adjusted return increases with rate volatility for all but the largest firms, the effect declining with size. Such deviations from the multi-beta pricing relation may reflect a failure of our stock and bond indexes to proxy adequately for the relevant components of systematic risk, as discussed by Shanken (1987). In any event, these results rule out the existence of a portfolio of the stock and bond indexes that is conditionally efficient with respect to the state variables considered.[31]

Many other reasonable candidates for state variables or factor portfolios are suggested by the existing literature, much of which is cited in the references. The heteroskedasticity-consistent linear regression methods adopted in this exploratory study should prove useful in further investigating the role of these variables in a dynamic asset pricing context. While computationally and conceptually simple, the approach allows for a fairly rich specification of the return process. In contrast with most work in this area, conditional expected returns, betas, variances/covariances, and factor portfolio prices of risk are all permitted to vary over time.

An appealing idea for future research is to combine the "market model" regression orientation of this paper with a multivariate generalized autoregressive conditional heteroskedasticity (GARCH) process for the regression residuals.[32] Simultaneous estimation of regression parameters and residual variance processes might yield more efficient estimates, and the associated pricing tests, like the regression tests above, would impose few restrictions on the stochastic process governing the factor portfolios and their associated prices of risk.[33] On a theoretical level, the development of models to explain the differential behavior of small and large firms, observed here and elsewhere, would be most welcome.

Notes

1 See also related work by Long (1974), Rubinstein (1976), Breeden (1979), Grossman and Shiller (1982), and Cox, Ingersoll, and Ross (1985).
2 Fama (1976) uses equal weights and includes 12 future changes as well as 12 past changes in his volatility measure.
3 See Rozeff and Kinney (1976) and Keim (1983). Keim and Stambaugh (1986) find evidence of seasonality in some conditional measures of risk.
4 Several of the papers cited build on earlier work by Frankel (1982). A recent paper by Bodurtha and Mark (1987) is quite general in its approach. Hansen and Singleton (1982) develop a procedure for simultaneously estimating utility parameters and testing nonlinear asset pricing restrictions.
5 The White (1980) estimator of the standard error is employed.
6 A proof of this result is contained in an appendix that is available on request. See Hasbrouck (1988) for related results.
7 Ferson (1988) provides an interesting interpretation of such regressions.
8 The (multiple) regression estimates of the TB coefficients are -5.97 and -5.41, with t statistics of -3.03 and -2.63 for the earlier and later periods respectively.
9 Subperiod results are not given in the tables but are available from the author on request.
10 These authors do document a positive relation between equity volatility and expected excess stock return in the context of a GARCH-in-mean model.
11 Morgan and Morgan (1987) note an increase in the variance of small firm/large firm return differences in January.
12 The weights in the spanning combination can vary with TB, TBV, and JAN, since we are conditioning the analysis on these variables. We also implicitly assume that the benchmark portfolio is conditionally efficient with respect to an arbitrary subset of the information set. Hansen, Richard, and Singleton (1981) show that this is the case for a class of equilibrium models with a representative investor. In this context, our use of nominal excess returns implies that the appropriate benchmark portfolio should be defined in terms of the marginal utility of real consumption divided by one plus the inflation rate. This follows from the usual first-order condition for utility maximization and the observation that excess real return equals excess nominal return divided by one plus the inflation rate, where the latter divisor is the same for all assets. Additional details are available on request.
13 Campbell takes a similar approach in an early working paper version of his published paper.
14 Shanken (1985) makes a similar point in the context of testing the zero-beta capital asset pricing model (CAPM).
15 Since the intercepts are zero under the null hypothesis we need not let a_j vary with the state variables. If the null hypothesis is false, however, we may learn more by letting the a_j vary as in (6).
16 The specification of this section allows for nonlinear relations between asset expected returns or variances and the state variables since the joint distribution of the factor portfolio returns is quite general. Clearly, more complicated relations could be specified in (6)–(9) by including, say, squared values of TB and TBV as additional independent variables. However, the results become more difficult to communicate and interpret as the number of variables in the corresponding version of (9) increases.

17 Rosenberg and Marathe (1979) adopt a similar specification in terms of firm-specific "descriptors" rather than economy-wide state variables.

18 Gibbons, Ross, and Shanken (1989) and MacKinlay (1987) analyze such tests of efficiency with the excess return regression parameters assumed constant. Joint F tests of the hypothesis that two sets of coefficients equal zero are also possible under the assumptions above (see Rao, 1973, p. 555). Thus a_j could be modeled as a linear combination of two state variables or a single state variable and a constant in such a test.

19 Although not our original concern, the tests conducted below also allow for heteroskedasticity in the e_j conditional on the contemporaneous variables r_{m} and r_{g}. This could be relevant even in the absence of state variable considerations.

20 A more detailed description of the portfolios can be found in Gibbons, Ross, and Shanken (1989).

21 The test statistic is a quadratic form in the vector of OLS coefficient estimates for a given variable. The matrix is the inverse of the heteroskedasticity-consistent covariance matrix of these estimates based on the analysis in White (1984).

22 Following the Bonferroni approach, the reported p value equals the number of parameters in the joint test (in this case ten) times the p value for the maximum statistic that would be computed ignoring the joint nature of the test (see Neter, Wasserman, and Kutner, 1985, pp. 150–4).

23 One test or the other may be more powerful depending on the alternative hypothesis. Of course, we should keep in mind that the reported p values do not reflect the fact that two tests of the same null hypothesis are being considered simultaneously. A simple conservative approach to this inference problem would be to focus on twice the minimum of the χ^2 and Bonferroni p values. This idea could also be used to assess the joint significance of more than one set of coefficients.

24 Since the size portfolios and m are value weighted, a weighted average of the coefficients should equal unity for the constant and zero for the state variables. Similarly, weighted averages of all bond beta and intercept coefficients should equal zero. These relations need not be exact, however, as the value weights change over time.

25 The probability that a standard normal variate exceeds 2.81 in absolute value is 0.005.

26 The family of confidence intervals with joint confidence level 0.95, for all linear combinations of the ten JAN coefficients, consists of points within 4.28 standard errors of each estimate, where $4.28^2 = 18.3$ is the 0.95 fractile of the χ^2 distribution with ten degrees of freedom.

27 A detailed description of these portfolios can be found in Breeden, Gibbons, and Litzenberger (1986).

28 See related results in Sweeney and Warga (1986).

29 Carleton and Lakonishok (1986) provide evidence of pervasive intra-industry size effects.

30 Tables for industry and size portfolios results, with information similar to that in table 18.1, are available on request.

31 Another obvious source of misspecification is the assumed linearity of the conditional beta relations. The deviations from the model appear far too large to be explained in this manner, however. Additional results, not reported here, based on quadratic beta relations confirm this informal observation.

32 See Bollerslev, Engle, and Wooldrige (1988) for an application of the multivariate GARCH process.

33 Attempts to incorporate the estimated residual variance relations in potentially more efficient weighted least squares regressions were unsuccessful and appeared to induce spurious associations that I do not fully understand.

References

Bodurtha, J. and Mark, N. (1987) "Testing the CAPM with Time-Varying Risks and Returns," *Working Paper*, Ohio State University.

Bollerslev, T., Engle, R. and Wooldridge, J. (1988) "A Capital Asset Pricing Model with Time Varying Covariances," *Journal of Political Economy*, 96, 116–31.

Breeden, D. (1979) "An Intertemporal Asset Pricing Model with Stochastic Consumption and Investment Opportunities," *Journal of Financial Economics*, 7: 3, 265–96.

Breeden, D., Gibbons, M. and Litzenberger, R. (1986) "Empirical Tests of the Consumption-Oriented CAPM," *Journal of Finance*, 44: 2, June, 231–62.

Carleton, W. and Lakonishok, J. (1986) "The Size Anomaly: Does Industry Group Matter?" *Journal of Portfolio Management*, 12, 36–40.

Campbell, J. (1987) "Stock Returns and the Term Structure," *Journal of Financial Economics*, 18, 373–99.

Christie, A. (1982) "The Stochastic Behavior of Common Stock Variances: Value, Leverage and Interest Rate Effects," *Journal of Financial Economics*, 10, 407–32.

Cox, J. C., Ingersoll, J. and Ross, S. (1985) "An Intertemporal General Equilibrium Model of Asset Prices," *Econometrica*, 53, 363–84.

Engel, C. (1987) "Tests of International CAPM with Time-Varying Covariances," *Working Paper 2303*, National Bureau of Economic Research, Cambridge, MA.

Fama, E. (1976) "Inflation Uncertainty and Expected Returns on Treasury Bills," *Journal of Political Economy*, 84, 427–48.

Fama, E. and Bliss, R. (1987) "The Information in Long-Maturity Forward Rates," *American Economic Review*, 77, 680–92.

Fama, E. and Schwert, G. W. (1977) "Asset Returns and Inflation," *Journal of Financial Economics*, 5, 115–46.

Ferson, W. (1988) "Changes in Expected Security Returns, Risk and the Level of Interest Rates," *Working Paper*, Stanford University.

Ferson, W., Kandel, S. and Stambaugh, R. (1986) "Tests of Asset Pricing with Time-Varying Expected Risk Premiums and Market Betas," *Journal of Finance*, 42: 2, June, 201–20.

Frankel, J. (1982) "In Search of the Exchange Risk Premium: A Six Currency Test Assuming Mean–Variance Optimization," *Journal of International Money and Finance*, 5, 853–75.

French, K., Schwert, G. W. and Stambaugh, R. (1987) "Expected Stock Returns and Volatility," *Journal of Financial Economics*, 19: 1, September, 3–29.

Gibbons, M. R. and Ferson, W. (1985) "Testing Asset Pricing Models with Changing Expectation and an Unobservable Market Portfolio," *Journal of Financial Economics*, 14, 217–36.

Gibbons, M., Ross, S. and Shanken, J. (1989) "A Test of the Efficiency of a Given Portfolio," *Econometrica*, 57: 5, September, 1121–52.

Grossman, S. and Shiller, R. (1982) "Consumption Correlatedness and Risk Measurement in Economies with Non-Traded Assets and Heterogeneous Information," *Journal of Financial Economics*, 10, 195–210.

Hansen, L. P. and Hodrick, R. (1983) "Risk Averse Speculation in the Foward Foreign Exchange Market: An Econometric Analysis of Linear Models. In *Exchange Rates and International Macroeconomics*, ed. J. Frankel (Chicago, IL: University of Chicago Press).

Hansen, L. P., Richard, S. and Singleton, K. (1981) "Econometric Implications of the Intertemporal Capital Asset Pricing Model," Unpublished Paper, Carnegie Mellon University.

Hansen, L. P. and Singleton, K. (1982) "Generalized Instrumental Variables Estimation of Nonlinear Rational Expectations Models," *Econometrica*, 50, 1269–86.

Hasbrouck, J. (1988) "Estimating Linear Models of Expectations and Uncertainty," *Studies in Banking and Finance*, 5, 99–112.

Ibbotson, R. and Sinquefield, R. (1982) *Stocks, Bonds, Bills, and Inflation: The Past and the Future* (Charlottesville, VA: The Financial Analysts Research Foundation, 1982).

Keim, D. (1983) "Size Related Anomalies and Stock Return Seasonality: Further Empirical Evidence," *Journal of Financial Economics*, 12, 13–32.

Keim, D. and Stambaugh, R. (1986) "Predicting Returns in the Stock and Bond Markets," *Journal of Financial Economics*, 17: 2, December, 357–90.

Long, J. (1974) "Stock Prices, Inflation, and the Term Structure of Interest Rates," *Journal of Financial Economics*, 1: 2, 131–70.

MacKinlay, C. (1987) "On Multivariate Tests of the CAPM," *Journal of Financial Economics*, 18, 341–71.

Merton, R. (1973) "An Intertemporal Capital Asset Pricing Model," *Econometrica*, 44, 867–87.

Morgan, A. and Morgan, I. (1987) "Measurement of Abnormal Returns from Small Firms," *Journal of Business and Economic Statistics*, 5, 121–9.

Neter, J., Wasserman, W. and Kutner, M. (1985) *Applied Linear Statistical Models* (Homewood, IL: Irwin).

Rao, R. (1973) *Linear Statistical Inference and its Applications* (New York: Wiley).

Rosenberg, B. and Marathe, V. (1979) "Tests of Capital Asset Pricing Hypotheses." In *Research in Finance* (Greenwich, CT: JAI Press).

Rozeff, M. and Kinney, W. (1976) "Capital Market Seasonality: The Case of Stock Returns," *Journal of Financial Economics*, 3, 379–402.

Rubinstein, M. (1976) "The Valuation of Uncertain Income Streams and the Pricing of Options," *Bell Journal of Economics*, 7: 2, Autumn, 407–25.

Shanken, J. (1985) "Multivariate Tests of the Zero-Beta CAPM," *Journal of Financial Economics*, 14, 327–48.

Shanken, J. (1987) "Multivariate Proxies and Asset Pricing Relations: Living with the Roll Critique," *Journal of Financial Economics*, 18, 91–110.

Shanken, J. (1989) "On the Estimation of Beta-Pricing Models," *Working Paper*, University of Rochester.

Sweeney, R. and Warga, A. (1986) "The Pricing of Interest-Rate Risk: Evidence from the Stock Market," *Journal of Finance*, 41, 393–410.

White, H. (1980) "A Heteroskedasticity-Consistent Covariance Matrix Estimator and a Direct Test for Heteroskedasticity," *Econometrica*, 48, 817–38.

White, H. (1984) *Asymptotic Theory for Econometricians* (Orlando, FL: Academic Press).

Chapter 19

Anat R. Admati

Background and Comments

In an efficient securities market, all information that becomes available to investors is rationally and instantaneously reflected in prices. (There are different versions of efficiency depending on the definition of "available.") Thus there are no profits to be made by trading on available information. But if there are no profits, who will collect the information? And if the information is not collected, how can the market be efficient in the first place?

Financial economists typically resolve this puzzle by positing "noise" or "liquidity" traders, who come to the market *without* information and take whatever price the market hands them. Liquidity traders lose when there is an informed trader on the other side of the transaction. The informed traders in turn depend on the existence of liquidity traders to justify their investment in acquiring information.

Of course no one can know what type of trader is on the other side of the transaction. Liquidity traders would like to trade only with other liquidity traders. But if they could do that, the informed traders would have to trade among themselves, and there would be little or no reason to become informed – special information is no help to the buyer if the seller has it too.

A large part of observed volume is presumably accounted for by liquidity traders. If so, I have never understood their motives. If you have no special information, why not just buy and hold? Perhaps the liquidity traders think that they are informed but really are not. Perhaps they know that they are not informed but nevertheless put on a show to impress clients – why admit ignorance by indexing?

This simple two-way classification of traders has nevertheless helped us to understand how markets actually work. The following paper by Anat Admati and Paul Pfleiderer is a particularly nice example. They give liquidity traders some discretion in timing their trades and show that trades will then cluster in time. Liquidity traders will move their trades to popular times to increase the probability of transacting with one of their own kind. Naturally the informed traders follow.

In other words, the sheep cluster on the field for mutual protection, and the wolves put on their sheep costumes and join the flock.

Author's Introduction

The general theme in my research, mostly undertaken with Paul Pfleiderer, is the notion that market participants are not equally endowed with information and that the production, dissemination, and usage of information are important to the understanding of financial markets. For example, prior to the paper reprinted here we had explored the endogenous acquisition of information and the economics of markets where information itself is traded (such as markets for newsletters and for managed active funds). The paper reprinted here fits into this overall theme in that it provides a theory based on information issues. At the same time, the paper contributes to the rapidly growing area of market microstructure, which is concerned with trading mechanisms and price formation.

The availability of transactions data in recent years has raised a number of empirical issues and puzzles. In particular, the data show a number of systematic patterns in volume, expected returns, and price variability over the trading day, week, and year. It is possible that exogenous reasons, originating outside the financial market and not related to the interaction between traders, can explain some of these findings. The question that aroused our interest in this topic, however, was whether there are any *endogenous* market forces, possibly in addition to exogenous reasons, that can account for the uneven patterns. The theory discussed in this chapter is based on the idea that the terms of trade might be better for liquidity traders if they can congregate and trade at the same time rather than at different times. If some of these traders have discretion over when they trade, uneven trading patterns would emerge in equilibrium.

It should be noted that the model in this paper is completely general with respect to the length of the time interval it covers. In particular, it does not rely directly on any specific features of the trading day, and so in principle it can explain intraday as well as interday or monthly patterns. However, for many liquidity traders the time interval over which they might have discretion is likely to be rather short, measured in hours or a few days rather than in weeks or months. This suggests that the model may be most appropriate when applied to relatively short time intervals such as the trading day.

While this paper yields patterns in volume and price variability which seem, at least casually, consistent with the data, it does not explain patterns in expected returns or expected price changes. These mean effects are the main focus of a subsequent paper (Admati and Pfleiderer, 1989). That model distinguishes between buy and sell volume and leads to patterns in buy and sell volume, order imbalances, and expected price changes.

Reference

Admati, A. and Pfleiderer, P. (1989) "Divide and Conquer: A Theory of Intraday and Day-of-the-Week Mean Effects," *Review of Financial Studies*, 2: 2, 189–223.

Bibliographical Listing

"Joint Projects Without Commitment" (with Motty Perry), *Review of Economic Studies*, forthcoming.

"Direct and Indirect Sale of Information" (with Paul Pfleiderer), *Econometrica*, 58: 4, July 1990, 901–28.

"Divide and Conquer: A Theory of Intraday and Day-of-the-Week Mean Effects" (with Paul Pfleiderer), *Review of Financial Studies*, 2: 2, 1989, 189–223.

"Selling and Trading on Information in Financial Markets" (with Paul Pfleiderer), *American Economic Review, Papers and Proceedings*, 78: 2, May 1988, 96–103.

A Theory of Intraday Patterns: Volume and Price Variability

ANAT R. ADMATI and PAUL PFLEIDERER

In the last few years, intraday trading data for a number of securities have become available. These data have been used in several empirical studies to identify various patterns in trading volume and in the daily behavior of security prices. In this paper we focus on two of these patterns: trading volume and the variability of returns.

Consider, for example, the data in table 19.1 concerning shares of Exxon traded during 1981.[1] The U-shaped pattern of the average volume of shares traded – namely, the heavy trading at the beginning and the end of the trading day and the relatively light trading in the middle of the day – is very typical and has been documented in a number of studies. (For example, Jain and Joh (1986) examine hourly data for the aggregate volume on the New York Stock Exchange (NYSE), which is reported in the *Wall Street Journal*, and find the same pattern.) Both the variance of price changes and the variance of returns follow a similar U-shaped pattern (e.g. Wood, McInish, and Ord, 1985). These empirical findings raise three questions that we attempt to answer in this paper:

1. Why does trading tend to be concentrated in particular time periods within the trading day?
2. Why are returns (or price changes) more variable in some periods and less variable in others?
3. Why do the periods of higher trading volume also tend to be the periods of higher return variability?

To answer these questions, we develop models in which traders determine

Reproduced from *Review of Financial Studies*, 1: 1, 1988, 3–40.

Paul Pfleiderer is Associate Professor of Finance at Stanford University. We would like to thank Michihiro Kandori, Allan Kleidon, David Kreps, Pete Kyle, Myron Scholes, Ken Singleton, Mark Wolfson, a referee, and especially Mike Gibbons and Chester Spatt for helpful suggestions and comments. We are also grateful to Douglas Foster and S. Viswanathan for pointing out an error in a previous draft. Kobi Boudoukh and Matt Richardson provided valuable research assistance. The financial support of the Stanford Program in Finance is gratefully acknowledged.

Table 19.1 The intraday trading pattern of Exxon shares in 1981

	10 a.m. to 12 noon	*12 noon to 2 p.m.*	*2 p.m. to 4 p.m.*
Average volume	179,349	103,024	122,670
SD(price changes)	0.34959	0.28371	0.37984

The first row gives the average volume of Exxon shares traded in 1981 in each of the three time periods. The second row gives the standard deviation (SD) of price changes, based on the transaction prices closest to the beginning and the end of the period.

when to trade and whether to become privately informed about assets' future returns. We show that the patterns that have been observed empirically can be explained in terms of the optimizing decisions made by these traders.[2]

Two motives for trade in financial markets are widely recognized as important: information and liquidity. Informed traders trade on the basis of private information that is not known to all other traders when trade takes place. Liquidity traders, in contrast, trade for reasons that are not related directly to the future payoffs of financial assets – their needs arise outside the financial market. Included in this category are large traders, such as some financial institutions, whose trades reflect the liquidity needs of their clients or who trade for portfolio-balancing reasons.

Most models that involve liquidity (or "noise") trading assume that liquidity traders have no discretion with regard to the timing of their trades. (Of course, the timing issue does not arise in models with only one trading period and is therefore only relevant in multiperiod models, such as those of Glosten and Milgrom (1985) and Kyle (1985).) This is a strong assumption, particularly if liquidity trades are executed by large institutional traders. A more reasonable assumption is that at least some liquidity traders can choose the timing of their transactions strategically, subject to the constraint of trading a particular number of shares within a given period of time. The models developed in this paper include such discretionary liquidity traders, and the actions of these traders play an important role in determining the types of patterns that will be identified. We believe that the inclusion of these traders captures an important element of actual trading in financial markets. We shall demonstrate that the behavior of liquidity traders, together with that of potentially informed speculators who may trade on the basis of private information that they acquire, can explain some of the empirical observations mentioned above as well as suggest some new testable predictions.

It is intuitive that, to the extent that liquidity traders have discretion over when they trade, they prefer to trade when the market is "thick," that is, when their trading has little effect on prices. This creates strong incentives for liquidity traders to trade together and for trading to be concentrated. When informed traders can also decide when to collect information and when to trade, the story becomes more complicated. Clearly, informed traders also want to trade when the market is thick. If many informed traders trade at the same time that liquidity traders concentrate their trading, then the terms of trade will reflect the increased level of informed trading as well, and this may conceivably drive out the liquidity traders. It is not clear, therefore, what patterns may actually emerge.

In fact, we show in our model that as long as there is at least one informed trader, the introduction of more informed traders generally *intensifies* the forces leading to the concentration of trading by discretionary liquidity traders. This is because informed traders compete with each other, and this typically improves the welfare of liquidity traders. We show that liquidity traders always benefit from more entry by informed traders when informed traders have the same information. However, when the information of each informed trader is different (that is, when information is diverse among informed traders), then this may not be true. As more diversely informed traders enter the market, the amount of information that is available to the market as a whole increases, and this may worsen the terms of trade for everyone. Despite this possibility, we show that with diversely informed traders the patterns that generally emerge involve a concentration of trading.

The trading model used in our analysis is in the spirit of Glosten and Milgrom (1985), and especially Kyle (1984, 1985). Informed traders and liquidity traders submit market orders to a market maker who sets prices so that his expected profits are zero given the total order flow. The information structure in our model is simpler than in those of Kyle (1985) and Glosten and Milgrom (1985) in that private information is only useful for one period. Like Kyle (1984, 1985) and unlike Glosten and Milgrom (1985), orders are not constrained to be of a fixed size such as one share. Indeed, the size of the order is a choice variable for traders.

What distinguishes our analysis from these other papers is that we examine, in a simple dynamic context, the interaction between strategic informed traders and strategic liquidity traders. Specifically, our models include two types of liquidity traders. *Nondiscretionary liquidity traders* must trade a particular number of shares at a particular time (for reasons that are not modeled). In addition, we assume that there are some *discretionary liquidity traders* who also have liquidity demands but who can be strategic in choosing when to execute these trades within a given period of time, for example within 24 hours or by the end of the trading day. It is assumed that discretionary liquidity traders time their trades so as to minimize the (expected) cost of their transactions.

Kyle (1984) discusses a single-period version of the model we use and derives some comparative statics results that are relevant to our discussion. In his model there are multiple informed traders who have diverse information. There are also multiple market makers, so that the model we use is a limit of his model as the number of market makers grows. Kyle (1984) discusses what happens to the informativeness of the price as the variance of liquidity demands changes. He shows that with a fixed number of informed traders the informativeness of the price does not depend on the variance of liquidity demand. However, if information acquisition is endogenous, then price informativeness is increasing in the variance of the liquidity demands. These properties of the single-period model play an important role in our analysis, where the variance of liquidity demands in different periods is determined in equilibrium by the decisions of the discretionary liquidity traders.

We begin by analyzing a simple model that involves a fixed number of informed traders, all of whom observe the same information. Discretionary liquidity traders can determine the timing of their trade, but they can trade only once during the time period within which they must satisfy their liquidity demand. (Such a restriction may be motivated by per-trade transaction costs.) We show that in this model there will be patterns in the volume of trade, namely trade will tend to be concentrated. If the number and precision of the information of informed traders is constant over time, however, then the information content and variability of equilibrium prices will also be constant over time.

We then discuss the effects of endogenous information acquisition and of diverse private information. It is assumed that traders can become informed at a cost, and we examine the equilibrium in which no more traders wish to become informed. We show that the patterns of trading volume that exist in the model with a fixed number of informed traders become more pronounced if the number of informed traders is endogenous. The increased level of liquidity trading induces more informed trading. Moreover, with endogenous information acquisition we obtain patterns in the informativeness of prices and in price variability.

Another layer is added to the model by allowing discretionary liquidity traders to satisfy their liquidity needs by trading more than once if they choose. The trading patterns that emerge in this case are more subtle. This is because the market maker can partially predict the liquidity trading component of the order flow in later periods by observing previous order flows.

This paper is organized as follows. In section 1 we discuss the model with a fixed number of (identically) informed traders. In section 2 we consider endogenous information acquisition, and in section 3 we extend the results to the case of diversely informed traders. In section 4 we relax the assumption that discretionary liquidity traders trade only once. In section 5 we explore some additional extensions to the model and show that our results hold in a number of different settings. In section 6 we discuss some empirically testable predictions of our model, and in section 7 we provide concluding remarks.

1 A Simple Model of Trading Patterns

1.1 Model description

We consider a single asset traded over a span of time that we divide into T periods. It is assumed that the value of the asset in period T is exogenously given by

$$\tilde{F} = \bar{F} + \sum_{t=1}^{T} \tilde{\delta}_t \tag{1}$$

where $\tilde{\delta}_t, t = 1, 2, \ldots, T$, are independently distributed random variables, each having zero mean. The payoff $\tilde{F}$ can be thought of as the liquidation value of the asset: any trader holding a share of the asset in period T receives a liquidating dividend of $\tilde{F}$ dollars. Alternatively, period T can be viewed as a period in which all traders have the same information about the value of the asset and $\tilde{F}$ is the common value that each assigns to it. For example, an earnings report may be released in period T. If this report reveals all those quantities about which traders might be privately informed, then all traders will be symmetrically informed in this period.

In periods prior to T, information about $\tilde{F}$ is revealed through both public and private sources. In each period t the innovation $\tilde{\delta}_t$ becomes public knowledge. In addition, some traders also have access to private information, as described below. In subsequent sections of this paper we shall make the decision to become informed endogenously; in this section we assume that, in period t, n_t traders are endowed with private information. A privately informed trader observes a signal that is informative about $\tilde{\delta}_{t+1}$. Specifically, we assume that at time t an informed trader observes $\tilde{\delta}_{t+1} + \tilde{\varepsilon}_t$, where $\mathrm{var}(\tilde{\varepsilon}_t) = \phi_t$. Thus, privately informed traders observe something about the piece of public information that will be revealed one period later to all traders. Another interpretation of this structure of private information is that privately informed traders are able to process public information faster or more efficiently than others. (Note that it is assumed here that all informed traders observe the same signal. An alternative formulation is considered in section 3.) Since the private information becomes useless one period after it is observed, informed traders only need to determine their trade in the period in which they are informed. Issues related to the timing of informed trading, which are important in Kyle (1985), do not arise here. We assume throughout this paper that in each period there is at least one privately informed trader.

All traders in the model are risk neutral. (However, as discussed in section 5.2, our basic results do not change if some traders are risk averse.) We also assume for simplicity and ease of exposition that there is no discounting by traders.[3] Thus, if $\tilde{\Phi}_t$ summarizes all the information observed by a particular trader in period t, then the value of a share of the asset to that trader in period t is $E(\tilde{F} \mid \tilde{\Phi}_t)$, where $E(\cdot \mid \cdot)$ is the conditional expectation operator.

In this section we are mainly concerned with the behavior of the liquidity traders and its effect on prices and trading volume. We postulate that there are two types of liquidity traders. In each period there exists a group of *nondiscretionary liquidity traders* who must trade a given number of shares in that period. The other class of liquidity traders is composed of traders who have liquidity demands that need not be satisfied immediately. We call these *discretionary liquidity traders* and assume that their demand for shares is determined in some period T' and needs to be satisfied before period T'', where $T' < T'' < T$.[4] Assume that there are m discretionary liquidity traders and let $\tilde{Y}^j$ be the total demand of the jth discretionary liquidity trader (revealed to that trader in period T'). Since each discretionary liquidity trader is risk neutral, he determines his trading policy so as to minimize his expected cost of trading, subject to the condition that he trades a total of $\tilde{Y}^j$ shares by period T''. Until section 4 we assume that each discretionary liquidity trader only trades once between time T' and time T''; that is, a liquidity trader cannot divide his trades among different periods.

Prices for the asset are established in each period by a market maker who stands prepared to take a position in the asset to balance the total demand of the remainder of the market. The market maker is also assumed to be risk neutral, and competition forces him to set prices so that he earns zero expected profits in each period. This follows the approach in Kyle (1985) and in Glosten and Milgrom (1985).[5]

Let $\tilde{x}_t^i$ be the ith informed trader's order in period t, $\tilde{y}_t^j$ be the order of the jth discretionary liquidity trader in that period, and $\tilde{z}_t$ be the *total* demand for shares by the nondiscretionary liquidity traders in period t. Then the market maker must purchase $\tilde{\omega}_t = \sum_{i=1}^{n} \tilde{x}_t^i + \sum_{j=1}^{m} \tilde{y}_t^j + \tilde{z}_t$ shares in period t. The market maker determines a price in period t based on the history of public information, $\tilde{\delta}_1, \tilde{\delta}_2, \ldots, \tilde{\delta}_t$, and on the history of order flows, $\tilde{\omega}_1, \tilde{\omega}_2, \ldots, \tilde{\omega}_t$.[6] Let $\tilde{\Delta}_t = (\tilde{\delta}_1, \tilde{\delta}_2, \ldots, \tilde{\delta}_t)$ and let $\tilde{\Omega}_t = (\tilde{\omega}_1, \tilde{\omega}_2, \ldots, \tilde{\omega}_t)$. The zero expected profit condition implies that the price $\tilde{P}_t$ set in period t by the market maker satisfies

$$\tilde{P}_t = E(\tilde{F} \mid \tilde{\Delta}_t, \tilde{\Omega}_t). \tag{2}$$

Finally, we assume that the random variables

$$(\tilde{Y}^1, \tilde{Y}^2, \ldots, \tilde{Y}^m, \tilde{z}_1, \tilde{z}_2, \ldots, \tilde{z}_{T-1}, \tilde{\delta}_1, \tilde{\delta}_2, \ldots, \tilde{\delta}_T, \tilde{\varepsilon}_1, \tilde{\varepsilon}_2, \ldots, \tilde{\varepsilon}_{T-1})$$

are mutually independent and distributed multivariate normal, with each variable having zero mean.

1.2 Equilibrium

We shall be concerned with the (Nash) equilibria of the trading game that our model defines among traders. Under our assumptions, the market maker has a passive role in the model.[7] Two types of traders do make strategic decisions in our model. Informed traders must determine the size of their market order in each period. At time t, this decision is made knowing the history $\tilde{\Omega}_{t-1}$ of order flows up to period $t-1$, the innovations $\tilde{\Delta}_t$ up to t, and the signal $\tilde{\delta}_{t+1} + \tilde{\varepsilon}_t$. The discretionary liquidity traders must choose a period in $[T', T'']$ in which to trade. Each trader takes the strategies of all other traders, as well as the terms of trade (summarized by the market maker's price setting strategy), as given.

The market maker, who only observes the total order flow, sets prices to satisfy the zero expected profit condition. We assume that the market maker's pricing response is a linear function of $\tilde{\Omega}_t$ and $\tilde{\Delta}_t$. In the equilibrium that emerges, this will be consistent with the zero profit condition. Given our assumptions, the market maker learns nothing in period t from past order flows $\tilde{\Omega}_{t-1}$ that cannot be inferred from the public information $\tilde{\Delta}_t$. This is because past trades of the informed traders are independent of $\tilde{\delta}_{t+1}, \tilde{\delta}_{t+2}, \ldots, \tilde{\delta}_T$ and because the liquidity trading in any period is independent of that in any other period. This means that the price set in period t is equal to the expectation of $\tilde{F}$ conditional on all public information observed in that period plus an adjustment that reflects the information contained in the current order flow $\tilde{\omega}_t$:

$$\begin{aligned} \tilde{P}_t(\tilde{\Delta}_t, \tilde{\Omega}_t) &= E(\tilde{F} \mid \tilde{\Delta}_t) + \lambda_t \tilde{\omega}_t \\ &= \bar{F} + \sum_{\tau=1}^{t} \tilde{\delta}_\tau + \lambda_t \tilde{\omega}_t. \end{aligned} \tag{3}$$

Our notation conforms with that in Kyle (1984, 1985). The reciprocal of λ_t is Kyle's market depth parameter, and it plays an important role in our analysis.

The main result of this section shows that in equilibrium there is a tendency for trading to be concentrated in the same period. Specifically, we shall show that equilibria where all discretionary liquidity traders trade in the same period always exist and that only such equilibria are robust to slight changes in the parameters.

Our analysis begins with a few simple results that characterize the equilibria of the model. Suppose that the total amount of discretionary liquidity demands in period t is $\Sigma_{j=1}^{m} \tilde{y}_t^j$, where $\tilde{y}_t^j = \tilde{Y}^j$ if the jth discretionary liquidity trader trades in period t and where $\tilde{y}_t^j = 0$ otherwise. Define $\Psi_t \equiv \text{var}(\Sigma_{j=1}^{m} \tilde{y}_t^j + \tilde{z}_t)$; that is, Ψ_t is the total variance of the liquidity trading in period t. (Note that Ψ_t must be determined in equilibrium since it depends on the trading positions of the discretionary liquidity traders.) The following lemma is proved in the appendix.

Lemma 1 If the market maker follows a linear pricing strategy, then in equilibrium each informed trader i submits at time t a market order of $\tilde{x}_t^i = \beta_t^i(\tilde{\delta}_{t+1} + \tilde{\varepsilon}_t)$, where

$$\beta_t^i = \left\{\frac{\Psi_t}{n_t[\text{var}(\tilde{\delta}_{t+1}) + \phi_t]}\right\}^{1/2}. \tag{4}$$

The equilibrium value of λ_t is given by

$$\lambda_t = \frac{\text{var}(\tilde{\delta}_{t+1})}{n_t + 1}\left\{\frac{n_t}{\Psi_t[\text{var}(\tilde{\delta}_{t+1}) + \phi_t]}\right\}^{1/2}. \tag{5}$$

This lemma gives the equilibrium values of λ_t and β_t for a given number of informed traders and a given level of liquidity trading. Most of the comparative statics associated with the solution are straightforward and intuitive. Two facts are important for our results. First, λ_t is decreasing in the total variance Ψ_t of liquidity trades; that is, the more variable are the liquidity trades, the deeper is the market. Less intuitive is the fact that λ_t is decreasing in the number n_t of informed traders. This appears surprising since it would seem that with more informed traders the adverse selection problem faced by the market maker is more severe. However, informed traders, all of whom observe the same signal, compete with each other, and this leads to a smaller λ_t. This is a key observation in the next section, where we introduce endogenous entry by informed traders.[8]

When some of the liquidity trading is discretionary, Ψ_t is an endogenous parameter. In equilibrium each discretionary liquidity trader follows the trading policy that minimizes his expected transaction costs, subject to meeting his liquidity demand $\tilde{Y}^j$. We now turn to the determination of this equilibrium behavior. Recall that each trader takes the value of λ_t (as well as the actions of other traders) as given and assumes that he cannot influence it. The cost of trading is measured as the difference between what the liquidity trader pays for the security and the security's expected value. Specifically, the expected cost to the jth liquidity trader of trading at time $t \in [T', T'']$ is

$$E\{[P_t(\tilde{\Delta}_t, \tilde{\Omega}_t) - \tilde{F}]\,\tilde{Y}^j \mid \tilde{\Delta}_t, \tilde{\Omega}_{t-1}, \tilde{Y}^j\}. \tag{6}$$

Substituting for $P_t(\tilde{\Delta}_t, \tilde{\Omega}_t)$ – and using the fact that $\tilde{z}_t, \tilde{y}_t^i, i \neq j$, and $\tilde{\delta}_\tau$, where $\tau = t+1, t+2, \ldots, T$, are independent of $\tilde{\Delta}_t$, $\tilde{\Omega}_{t-1}$, and $\tilde{Y}^j$ (which is the information of discretionary liquidity trader j) – the cost simplifies to $\lambda_t(\tilde{Y}^j)^2$. Thus, for a given set of $\lambda_t, t \in [T', T'']$, the expected cost of liquidity trading is minimized by trading in that period $t^\star \in [T', T'']$ in which λ_t is the smallest. This is very intuitive, since λ_t measures the effect of each unit of order flow on the price and, by assumption, liquidity traders trade only once.

Recall that, from lemma 1, λ_t is decreasing in Ψ_t. This means that if in equilibrium the discretionary liquidity trading is particularly heavy in a particular period t, then λ_t will be set lower, which in turn makes discretionary liquidity traders concentrate their trading in that period. In sum, we obtain the following result.

Proposition 1 There always exist equilibria in which all discretionary liquidity trading occurs in the same period. Moreover, only these equilibria are robust in the sense that, if for some set of parameters there exists an equilibrium in which discretionary liquidity traders do not trade in the same period, then for an aribitrarily close set of parameters (for example by perturbing the vector of variances of the liquidity demands $\tilde{Y}^j$), the only possible equilibria involve concentrated trading by the discretionary liquidity traders.

PROOF Define $h \equiv \text{var}(\Sigma_{j=1}^m \tilde{Y}^j)$, that is, the total variance of discretionary liquidity demands. Suppose that all discretionary liquidity traders trade in period t and that the market maker adjusts λ_t and informed traders set β_t accordingly. Then the total trading cost incurred by the discretionary traders is $\lambda_t(h)h$, where $\lambda_t(h)$ is given in lemma 1 with $\Psi_t = h + \text{var}(\tilde{z}_t)$.

Consider the period $t^\star \in [T', T'']$ for which $\lambda_t(h)$ is the smallest. (If there are several periods in which the smallest value is achieved, choose the first.) It is then an equilibrium for all discretionary traders to trade in $t^\star$. This follows since $\lambda_t(h)$ is decreasing in h, so that, by the definition of $t^\star$, we must have $\lambda_t(0) \geqslant \lambda_{t^\star}(h)$ for all $t \in [T', T'']$. Thus, discretionary liquidity traders prefer to trade in period $t^\star$.

The above argument shows that there exist equilibria in which all discretionary liquidity trading is concentrated in one period. If there is an equilibrium in which trading is not concentrated, then the smallest value of λ_t must be attained in at least two periods. It is easy to see that any small change in var$(\tilde{Y}^j)$ for some j would make the λ_t different in different periods, upsetting the equilibrium. ■

Proposition 1 states that concentrated-trading patterns are always viable and that they are generically the only possible equilibria (given that the market maker uses a linear strategy). Note that in our model all traders take the values of λ_t as given. That is, when a trader considers deviating from the equilibrium strategy, he assumes that the trading strategies of other traders and the pricing strategy of the market maker (that is, λ_t) do not change.[9] We can assume instead that liquidity traders first announce the timing of their trading and then trading takes place (anonymously), so that informed traders and the market maker can adjust their strategies according to the announced timing of liquidity trades. In this case the only possible equilibria are those where trading is concentrated. This follows because if trading is not concentrated, then some liquidity traders can benefit by deviating and trading in another period, which would lower the value of λ_t in that period.

We now illustrate proposition 1 by an example. This example will be used and developed further in the remainder of this paper.

Example Assume that $T = 5$ and that discretionary liquidity traders learn of their demands in period 2 and must trade in or before period 4 (that is, $T' = 2$ and $T'' = 4$). In each of the first four periods, three informed traders trade, and we assume that each has perfect information. Thus each observes in period t the realization of $\tilde{\delta}_{t+1}$. We assume that public information arrives at a constant rate, with $\text{var}(\tilde{\delta}_t) = 1$ for all t. Finally, the variance of the nondiscretionary liquidity trading occurring in each period is set equal to unity. We are interested in the behavior of the discretionary liquidity traders. Assume that there are two of these traders, A and B, and let $\text{var}(\tilde{Y}^A) = 4$ and $\text{var}(\tilde{Y}^B) = 1$. First assume that A trades in period 2 and B trades in period 3. Then $\lambda_1 = \lambda_4 = 0.4330$, $\lambda_2 = 0.1936$, and $\lambda_3 = 0.3061$. This cannot be an equilibrium since $\lambda_2 < \lambda_3$, and so B will want to trade in period 2 rather than in period 3. The discretionary liquidity traders take the λ_t as fixed and B perceives that his trading costs can be reduced if he trades earlier. Now assume that both discretionary liquidity traders trade in period 3. In this case $\lambda_1 = \lambda_2 = \lambda_4 = 0.4330$ and $\lambda_3 = 0.1767$. This is clearly a stable trading pattern. Both traders want to trade in period 3 since λ_3 is the minimal λ_t.

1.3 *Implications for volume and price behavior*

In this section we show that the concentration of trading that results when some liquidity traders choose the timing of their trades has a pronounced effect on the volume of trading. Specifically, the volume is higher in the period in which trading is concentrated both because of the increased liquidity trading volume and because of the induced informed trading volume. The concentration of discretionary liquidity traders does not affect the amount of information revealed by prices or the variance of price changes, however, as long as the number of informed traders is held fixed and is specified exogenously. As we show in the next section, the results on price informativeness and on the variance of price changes are altered if the number of informed traders in the market is determined endogenously.

It is clear that the behavior of prices and of trading volume is determined in part by the rate of public information release and the magnitude of the nondiscretionary liquidity trading in each period. Various patterns can easily be obtained by making the appropriate assumptions about these exogenous variables. Since our main interest in this paper is to examine the effects of traders' *strategic* behavior on prices and volume, we wish to abstract from these other determinants. If the rate at which information becomes public is constant and the magnitude of nondiscretionary liquidity trading is the same in all periods, then any patterns that emerge are due solely to the strategic behavior of traders. We therefore assume in this section that $\mathrm{var}(\tilde{z}_t) = g$, $\mathrm{var}(\tilde{\delta}_t) = 1$, and $\mathrm{var}(\tilde{\varepsilon}_t) = \phi$ for all t. Setting $\mathrm{var}(\tilde{\delta}_t)$ to be constant over time guarantees that public information arrives at a constant rate. (The normalization of $\mathrm{var}\,(\tilde{\delta}_t)$ to unity does not result in a loss of generality.)

Before presenting our results on the behavior of prices and trading volume, it is important to discuss how volume should be measured. Suppose that there are k traders with market orders given by $\tilde{s}_1, \tilde{s}_2, \ldots, \tilde{s}_k$. Assume that the $\tilde{s}_i$ are independently and normally distributed, each with zero mean. Let $\tilde{s}_i^+ = \max(\tilde{s}_i, 0)$ and $\tilde{s}_i^- = \max(-\tilde{s}_i, 0)$. The total volume of trade (including trades that are "crossed" between traders) is $\max(\tilde{S}^+, \tilde{S}^-)$, where $\tilde{S}^+ = \Sigma_{i=1}^k \tilde{s}_i^+$ and $\tilde{S}^- = \Sigma_{i=1}^k \tilde{s}_i^-$. The expected volume is

$$E[\max(\tilde{S}^+, \tilde{S}^-)] = \frac{1}{2}\sum_{i=1}^{k} E\,|\tilde{s}_i| + \frac{1}{2} E\left|\sum_{i=1}^{k} \tilde{s}_i\right|$$

$$= \frac{1}{(2\pi)^{1/2}}\left[\sum_{i=1}^{k} \sigma_i + \left(\sum_{i=1}^{k} \sigma_i^2\right)^{1/2}\right] \tag{7}$$

where σ_i is the standard deviation of $\tilde{s}_i$.

One may think that the variance $\mathrm{var}(\tilde{\omega}_t)$ of the total order flow is appropriate for measuring the expected volume of trading. This is not correct. Since $\tilde{\omega}_t$ is the net demand presented to the market maker, it does not include trades that are crossed between traders and are therefore not met by the market maker. For example, suppose that there are two traders in period t and that their market orders are 10 and -16 respectively (that is, the first trader wants to purchase ten shares and the second trader wants to sell 16 shares). Then the total amount of trading in this period is 16 shares, ten crossed between the two traders and six supplied by the market maker ($\tilde{\omega}_t = 6$ in this case). The parameter var($\tilde{\omega}_t$), which is represented by the last term in equation (7), only considers the trading done with the market maker. The other terms measure the expected volume of trade across traders. In light of the above discussion, we shall focus on the following measures of trading volume, which identify the contribution of each group of traders to the total trading volume:

$$V_t^{\mathrm{I}} \equiv \left[\mathrm{var}\left(\sum_{i=1}^{n} \tilde{x}_t^i\right)\right]^{1/2} = \{\mathrm{var}\,[n_t\beta_t(\tilde{\delta}_{t+1} + \tilde{\varepsilon}_t)]\}^{1/2} \tag{8}$$

$$V_t^{\mathrm{L}} \equiv \sum_{j=1}^{m} [\mathrm{var}(\tilde{y}_t^i)]^{1/2} + [\mathrm{var}(\tilde{z}_t)]^{1/2} \tag{9}$$

$$V_t^{\mathrm{M}} \equiv [\mathrm{var}(\tilde{\omega}_t)]^{1/2} \tag{10}$$

$$V_t \equiv V_t^{\mathrm{I}} + V_t^{\mathrm{L}} + V_t^{\mathrm{M}}. \tag{11}$$

In words, V_t^{I} and V_t^{L} measure the expected volume of trading of the informed traders and the liquidity traders respectively, and V_t^{M} measures the expected trading done by the market maker. The total expected volume V_t is the sum of the individual components. These measures are closely related to the true expectation of the actual measured volume.[10]

Proposition 1 asserts that a typical equilibrium for our model involves the concentration of all discretionary liquidity trading in one period. Let this period be denoted $t^\star$. Note that if we assume that n_t, var($\tilde{\delta}_t$), var($\tilde{\varepsilon}_t$), and var($\tilde{z}_t$) are independent of t, then $t^\star$ can be any period in $[T', T'']$.

The following result summarizes the equilibrium patterns of trading volume in our model.

Proposition 2 In an equilibrium in which all discretionary liquidity trading occurs in period $t^\star$

1 $V_{t^\star}^{\mathrm{L}} > V_t^{\mathrm{L}}$ for $t \neq t^\star$,
2 $V_{t^\star}^{\mathrm{I}} > V_t^{\mathrm{I}}$ for $t \neq t^\star$,
3 $V_{t^\star}^{\mathrm{M}} > V_t^{\mathrm{M}}$ for $t \neq t^\star$.

PROOF Part 1 is trivial, since there is more liquidity trading in $t^\star$ than in other periods. To prove part 2, note that

$$V_t^{\mathrm{I}} = \{\mathrm{var}\,[n_t\beta_t(\tilde{\delta}_{t+1} + \tilde{\varepsilon}_t)]\}^{1/2} = (n_t\Psi_t)^{1/2}. \tag{12}$$

Thus, an increase in the total variance Ψ_t of liquidity trading decreases λ_t and increases the informed component of trading. Part 3 follows immediately from parts 1 and 2. ■

This result shows that the concentration of liquidity trading increases the volume in the period in which it occurs not only directly through the actual liquidity trading (an increase in V_t^L) but also indirectly through the additional informed trading it induces (an increase in V_t^I). This is an example of trading generating trading. A numerical example that illustrates this phenomenon is presented following the next result.[11]

We now turn to examine two endogenous parameters related to the price process. The first parameter measures the extent to which prices reveal private information, and is defined by

$$Q_t \equiv \operatorname{var}(\tilde{\delta}_{t+1} \mid \tilde{P}_t). \tag{13}$$

The second is simply the variance of the price change:

$$R_t \equiv \operatorname{var}(\tilde{P}_t - \tilde{P}_{t-1}). \tag{14}$$

Proposition 3 Assume that $n_t = n$ for every t. Then

1 $Q_t{}^\star = Q_t$ for every t,
2 $R_t{}^\star = R_t = 1$ for every t.

PROOF It is straightforward to show that in general

$$Q_t = \left(1 + \frac{n_t}{1 + \phi + n_t\phi}\right)^{-1} \tag{15}$$

and

$$R_t = \frac{1}{1+\phi}\left(\frac{n_t}{1+n_t} + \frac{1}{1+n_{t-1}} + \phi\right). \tag{16}$$

The result follows since both R_t and Q_t are independent of Ψ_t, and $n_t = n$. ■

As observed by Kyle (1984, 1985), the amount of private information revealed by the price is *independent* of the total variance of liquidity trading. Thus, despite the concentration of trading in $t^\star$, $Q_t{}^\star = Q_t$ for all t. The intuition behind this is that, although there is more liquidity trading in period $t^\star$, there is also more informed trading, as we saw in proposition 2. The additional informed trading is just sufficient to keep the information content of the total order flow constant.

Proposition 3 also says that the variance of price changes is the same when n informed traders trade in each period as it is when there is no informed trading. (When there is no informed trading, $\tilde{P}_t - \tilde{P}_{t-1} = \tilde{\delta}_t$, so that $R_t = \operatorname{var}(\tilde{\delta}_t) = 1$ for all t.) With some informed traders, the market receives information earlier than it would otherwise, but the overall rate at which information comes to the market is unchanged. Moreover, the variance of price changes is independent of the variance of liquidity trading in period t. As will be shown in the next section, these results change if the number of informed traders is determined endogenously. Before turning to this analysis, we illustrate the results of this section with an example.

Example (continued) Consider again the example introduced in section 1.2. Recall that, in the equilibrium we discussed, both the discretionary liquidity traders trade in period 3. Table 19.2 shows the effects of this trading on volume and price behavior. The volume of trading measured in period 3 is $V_3 = 13.14$, while that in the other periods is only 4.73. The difference is only partly due to the actual trading of the liquidity traders. Increased trading by the three informed traders in period 3 also contributes to higher volume. As the table shows, both Q_t and R_t are unaffected by the increased liquidity trading. With three informed traders, three-quarters of the private information is revealed through prices no matter what the magnitude of liquidity demand.

Table 19.2 Effects of discretionary liquidity trading on volume and price behavior when the number of informed traders is constant over time

t	n_t	λ_t	V_t	V_t^{I}	V_t^{L}	V_t^{M}	Q_t	R_t
1	3	0.43	4.73	1.73	1.00	2.00	0.25	
2	3	0.43	4.73	1.73	1.00	2.00	0.25	1.00
3	3	0.18	13.14	4.24	4.00	4.90	0.25	1.00
4	3	0.43	4.73	1.73	1.00	2.00	0.25	1.00

A four period example with $n_t = 3$ informed traders in each period. For $t = 1, 2, 3, 4$, the table gives the market depth parameter, λ_t, a measure V_t of total trading volume, a measure V_t^{I} of the informed trading volume, a measure V_t^{L} of liquidity trading volume, a measure V_t^{M} of the trading volume of the market maker, a measure Q_t of the amount of private information revealed in the price, and the variance R_t of the price change from period $t-1$ to period t.

2 Endogenous Information Acquisition

In section 1 the number of informed traders in each period was taken as fixed. We now assume instead that private information is acquired at some cost in each period and that traders acquire this information if and only if their expected profit exceeds this cost. The number of informed traders is therefore determined as part of the equilibrium. It will be shown that endogenous information acquisition intensifies the result that trading is concentrated in equilibrium and that it alters the results on the distribution and informativeness of prices.

Let us continue to assume that public information arrives at a constant rate and that $\text{var}(\tilde{\delta}_t) = 1$ and $\text{var}(\tilde{z}_t) = g$ for all t. Let c be the cost of observing $\tilde{\delta}_{t+1} + \tilde{\varepsilon}_t$ in period t, where $\text{var}(\tilde{\varepsilon}_t) = \phi$. We assume that $c < 0.5[g/(1+\phi)]^{1/2}$. This will guarantee that in equilibrium at least one trader is informed in each period. We need to determine the equilibrium number n_t of informed traders in period t.[12]

Define $\pi(n_t, \Psi_t)$ to be the expected trading profits of an informed trader (over one period) when there are n_t informed traders in the market and the total variance of all liquidity trading is Ψ_t. Let $\lambda(n_t, \Psi_t)$ be the equilibrium value of λ_t under these conditions. (Note that these functions are the same in all periods.)

The total expected cost of the liquidity traders is $\lambda(n_t, \Psi_t)\Psi_t$. Since each of the n_t informed traders submits the same market order, they divide this amount equally. Thus, from lemma 1 we have

$$\pi(n_t, \Psi_t) = \frac{1}{n_t}\lambda(n_t, \Psi_t)\Psi_t = \frac{1}{n_t + 1}\left[\frac{\Psi_t}{n_t(1+\phi)}\right]^{1/2}. \tag{17}$$

It is clear that a necessary condition for an equilibrium with n informed traders is $\pi(n_t, \Psi_t) \geqslant c$; otherwise, the trading profits of informed traders do not cover the cost of acquiring the information. Another condition for an equilibrium with n_t informed traders is that no additional trader has incentives to become informed.

We shall discuss two models of entry. One approach is to assume that a potential entrant cannot make his presence known (that is, he cannot credibly announce his presence to the rest of the market). Under this assumption, a potential entrant takes the strategies of all other traders and the market maker as given and assumes that they will continue to behave as if n_t traders are informed. Thus we still have $\lambda = \lambda(n_t, \Psi_t)$. The following lemma gives the optimal market order for an entrant and his expected trading profits under this assumption. (The proof is in the appendix.)

Lemma 2 An entrant into a market with n_t informed traders will trade exactly half the number of shares as the other n_t traders for any realization of the signal, and his expected profits will be $\pi(n_t, \Psi_t)/4$.

It follows that with this approach n_t is an equilibrium number of informed traders in period t if and only if n_t satisfies $\pi(n_t, \Psi_t)/4 \leqslant c \leqslant \pi(n_t, \Psi_t)$. If c is large enough, there may be no positive integer n_t satisfying this condition, so that the only equilibrium number of informed traders is zero. However, the assumption that $c \leqslant 0.5[g/(1+\phi)]^{1/2}$ guarantees that this is never the case. In general, there may be several values of n_t that are consistent with equilibrium according to this model.

An alternative model of entry by informed traders is to assume that, if an additional trader becomes informed, other traders and the market maker change their strategies so that a new equilibrium, with $n_t + 1$ informed traders, is reached. If liquidity traders do not change their behavior, the profits of each informed trader would now become $\pi(n_t + 1, \Psi_t)$.[13] The largest n_t satisfying $\pi(n_t, \Psi_t)/4 \leqslant c \leqslant \pi(n_t, \Psi_t)$ is the (unique) n satisfying $\pi(n_t + 1, \Psi_t) < c \leqslant \pi(n_t, \Psi_t)$, which is the condition for equilibrium under the alternative approach. This is illustrated in the example below.

Example (continued) Consider again the example introduced in section 1.2 (and developed further in section 1.3). In period 3, when both the discretionary liquidity traders trade, the total variance of liquidity trading is $\Psi_3 = 6$. Assume that the cost of perfect information is $c = 0.13$. Table 19.3 gives $\pi(n, 6)$ and $\pi(n, 6)/4$ as a function of some possible values for n.

With $c = 0.13$, it is not an equilibrium to have only one or two informed traders for in each of these cases a potential entrant will find it profitable to acquire information. It is also not possible to have seven traders acquiring information since each will find that his equilibrium expected profits are less than $c = 0.13$. Equilibria involving three to six informed

Table 19.3 Expected trading profits of informed traders when the variance of liquidity demand is 6

n	$\pi(n, 6)$	$\pi(n, 6)/4$
1	1.225	0.306
2	0.577	0.144
3	0.354	0.088
4	0.245	0.061
5	0.183	0.046
6	0.143	0.038
7	0.116	0.029

For some possible number n of informed traders the table gives the expected profits $\pi(n, 6)$ of each of the informed traders, assuming that the variance of total liquidity trading is 6; and the profits $\pi(n, 6)/4$ of an entrant who assumes that all other traders will use the same equilibrium strategies after he enters as an informed trader. If the cost of information is 0.13, then the equilibrium number of informed traders is $n \in \{3, 4, 5, 6\}$ in the first approach and $n = 6$ in the second.

Table 19.4 Expected trading profits of informed traders when the variance of liquidity demand is 3

n	$\pi(n, 1)$	$\pi(n, 1)/4$
1	0.500	0.125
2	0.236	0.059
3	0.144	0.036
4	0.100	0.025

For some possible number n of informed traders the table gives $\pi(n, 1)$, the expected profits of each of the informed traders, assuming that the variance of total liquidity trading is unity, and the profits $\pi(n, 1)/4$ of an entrant who assumes that all other traders will use the same equilibrium strategies after he enters as an informed trader. If the cost of information is 0.13, then the equilibrium number of informed traders is $n \in \{1, 2, 3\}$ in the first approach and $n = 3$ in the second.

traders are clearly supportable under the first model of entry. Note that $n_3 = 6$ also has the property that $\pi(7, 6) < 0.13 < \pi(6, 6)$, so that, if informed traders and the market maker (as well as the entrant) change their strategies to account for the actual number of informed traders, each informed trader makes positive profits and no additional trader wishes to become informed.

As is intuitive, a lower level of liquidity trading generally supports fewer informed traders. In period 2 in our example no discretionary liquidity traders trade, and therefore $\Psi_2 = g = 1$. Table 19.4 shows that, if the cost of becoming informed is equal to 0.13, there will be no more than three informed traders. Moreover, assuming the first model of entry, the lower level of liquidity trading makes equilibria with one or two informed traders viable.

To focus our discussion below, we shall assume that the number of informed traders in any period is equal to the maximum number that can be supported. With $c = 0.13$ and $\Psi_t = 6$, this means that $n_t = 6$, and with the same level of cost and $\Psi_t = 1$, we have $n_t = 3$. As noted above, this determination of the equilibrium number of informed traders is consistent with the assumption that an entrant can credibly make his presence known to informed traders and to the market maker.

Does endogenous information acquisition change the conclusion of proposition 1 that trading is concentrated in a typical equilibrium? We know that with an increased level of liquidity trading, more informed traders will generally be trading. If the presence of more informed traders in the market raises the liquidity traders' cost of trading, then discretionary liquidity traders may not want to trade in the same period.

It turns out that in this model the presence of more informed traders actually *lowers* the liquidity traders' cost of trading, intensifying the forces toward concentration of trading. As long as there is some informed trading in every period, liquidity traders prefer that there are more rather than fewer informed traders trading along with them. Of course, the best situation for liquidity traders is for there to be no informed traders, but for $n_t > 0$ the cost of trading is a decreasing function of n_t. The total cost of trading for the liquidity traders was shown to be $\lambda(n_t, \Psi_t)\Psi_t$. That this cost is decreasing in n follows from the fact that $\lambda(n_t, \Psi_t)$ is decreasing in n_t.

Thus endogenous information acquisition intensifies the effects that bring about the concentration of trading. With more liquidity trading in a given period, more informed traders trade, and this makes it even more attractive for liquidity traders to trade in that period. As already noted, the intuition behind this result is that competition among the privately informed traders reduces their total profit, which benefits the liquidity traders.

The following proposition describes the effect of endogenous information acquisition on the trading volume and price process.[14]

Proposition 4 Suppose that the number of informed traders in period t is the unique n_t satisfying $\pi(n_t + 1, \Psi_t) < c \leqslant \pi(n_t, \Psi_t)$, that is, determined by the second model of entry. Consider an equilibrium in which all discretionary liquidity traders trade in period $t^\star$. Then

1. $V_{t^\star} > V_t$ for $t \neq t^\star$,
2. $V^{\mathrm{I}}_{t^\star} > V^{\mathrm{I}}_t$ for $t \neq t^\star$,
3. $Q_{t^\star} < Q_t$ for $t \neq t^\star$,
4. $R_{t^\star} > R_{t^\star-1} > R_{t^\star+1}$.

PROOF The first three statements follow simply from the fact that V_t and V^{I}_t are increasing in n_t and that Q_t is decreasing in n_t. The last follows from equation (16). ■

Example (continued) We again consider our example, but now with endogenous information acquisition. Suppose that the cost of acquiring perfect information is 0.13. In periods 1, 2, and 4, when no discretionary liquidity traders trade, there will continue to be three informed traders trading, as seen in table 19.4. In period 3, when both the discretionary liquidity traders trade, the number of informed traders will now be 6, as seen in table 19.3. Table 19.5 shows what occurs with the increased number of informed traders in period 3.

Table 19.5 Effects of discretionary liquidity trading on volume and price behavior when the number of informed traders is endogenous

t	n_t	λ_t	V_t	V_t^{I}	V_t^{L}	V_t^{M}	Q_t	R_t
1	3	0.43	4.73	1.73	1.00	2.00	0.25	
2	3	0.43	4.73	1.73	1.00	2.00	0.25	1.00
3	6	0.14	16.48	6.00	4.00	6.48	0.14	1.11
4	3	0.43	4.73	1.73	1.00	2.00	0.25	0.90

A four-period example in which the number n_t of informed traders is determined endogenously, assuming that the cost of information is 0.13. For $t = 1, 2, 3, 4$, the table gives the market depth parameter λ_t, a measure V_t of total trading volume, a measure V_t^{I} of the informed trading volume, a measure V_t^{L} of liquidity trading volume, a measure V_t^{M} of the trading volume of the market maker, a measure Q_t of the amount of private information revealed in the price, and the variance R_t of the price change from period $t-1$ to period t.

With the higher number of informed traders, the value of λ_3 is reduced even further, to the benefit of the liquidity traders. It is therefore still an equilibrium for the two discretionary liquidity traders to trade in period 3. Because three more informed traders are present in the market in this period, the total trading cost of the liquidity traders (discretionary and nondiscretionary) is reduced by 0.204, or 19 percent.

The addition of the three informed traders affects the equilibrium in significant ways. First note that the volume in period 3 is even higher now relative to the other periods. With the increase in the number of informed traders, the amount of informed trading has increased. Increased liquidity trading generates trade because (a) it leads to more informed trading by a given group of informed traders and (b) it tends to increase the number of informed traders.

More importantly, the change in the number of informed traders in response to the increased liquidity trading in period 3 has altered the behavior of prices. The price in period 3 is more informative about the future public information release than are the prices in the other periods. Because of the increased competition among the informed traders in period 3, more private information is revealed and $Q_3 < Q_t$ for $t \neq 3$. With endogenous information acquisition, prices will generally be more informative in periods with high levels of liquidity trading than they are in other periods.

The variance of price changes is also altered around the period of higher liquidity trading. From equation (16) we see that, if $n_t = n_{t-1}$, then $R_t = 1$. When the number of informed traders is greater in the later period, $R_t > 1$. This is because more information is revealed in the later period than in the earlier period. When the number of informed traders decreases from one period to the next, $R_t < 1$ since more information is revealed in the earlier period.

It is interesting to contrast our results in this section with those of Clark (1973), who also considers the relation between volume and the rate of information arrival. Clark takes the flow of information to the market as exogenous and shows that patterns in this process can lead to patterns in volume. In our model, however, the increased volume of trading due to discretionary trading leads to changes in the process of private information arrival.

3 A Model with Diverse Information

So far we have assumed that all the informed traders observe the same piece of information. In this section we discuss an alternative formulation of the model in which informed traders observe different signals as in Kyle (1984). The basic results about trading and volume patterns or price behavior do not change. However, the analysis of endogenous information acquisition is somewhat different.

Assume that the *i*th informed trader observes in period t the signal $\tilde{\delta}_{t+1} + \tilde{\varepsilon}_t^i$ and assume that the $\tilde{\varepsilon}_t^i$ are independently and identically distributed with variance ϕ. Note that, as n increases, the total amount of private information increases as long as $\phi > 0$. The next result, which is analogous to lemma 1 for the case of identical private signals, gives the equilibrium parameters for a given level of liquidity trading and a given number of informed traders. (The proof is a simple modification of the proof of lemma 1 and is therefore omitted.)

Lemma 3 Assume that n_t informed traders trade in period t and that each observes an independent signal $\tilde{\delta}_{t+1} + \tilde{\varepsilon}_t^i$, where $\mathrm{var}(\tilde{\delta}_{t+1}) = 1$ and $\mathrm{var}(\tilde{\varepsilon}_t^i) = \phi_t$ for all i. Let Ψ_t be the total variance of the liquidity trading in period t. Then

$$\lambda_t = \frac{1}{1 + n_t + 2\phi_t} = \left[\frac{n_t(1 + \phi_t)}{\Psi_t}\right]^{1/2}. \tag{18}$$

The *i*th informed trader submits market order $\beta_t^i(\tilde{\delta}_{t+1} + \tilde{\varepsilon}_t^i)$ in each period t with

$$\beta_t^i = \frac{1}{\lambda_t(1 + n_t + 2\phi_t)} = \left[\frac{\Psi_t}{n_t(1 + \phi_t)}\right]^{1/2}. \tag{19}$$

Note that, as in the case of identical signals, λ_t is decreasing in Ψ_t. This immediately implies that proposition 1 still holds in the model with diverse signals. Thus, if the number of informed traders is exogenously specified, the only robust equilibria are those in which trading by all discretionary liquidity traders is concentrated in one period.

Recall that the results when information acquisition is endogenous were based on the observation that when there are more informed traders they compete more aggressively with each other. This is favorable to the liquidity traders in that λ_t is reduced, intensifying the effects that lead to concentrated trading. However, when informed traders observe different pieces of information, an increase in their number also means that more private information is actually generated in the market as a whole. Indeed, unlike the case of identical signals, an increase in n_t can now lead to an increase in λ_t. It is straightforward to show that (with $\phi_t = \phi$ for all t as before)

$$\operatorname{sgn}\left[\frac{\partial\lambda(n_t, \Psi_t)}{\partial n_t}\right] = \operatorname{sgn}(1 - n_t + 2\phi). \tag{20}$$

If the information gathered by informed traders is sufficiently imprecise, an increase in n_t will increase λ_t. An increase in n_t has two effects. First it increases the degree of competition among the informed traders and this tends to reduce λ_t. Second it increases the amount of private information represented in the order flow. This generally tends to increase λ_t. For large values of ϕ and small values of n_t, an increase in n_t has a substantial effect on the amount of information embodied in the order flow and this dominates the effect of an increase in competition. As a result, λ_t increases.

The discussion above has implications for equilibrium with endogenous information acquisition. In general, since the profits of each informed trader are increasing in Ψ, there would be more informed traders in periods in which discretionary liquidity traders trade more heavily. When signals are identical, this strengthens the incentives of discretionary liquidity traders to trade in these periods, since it lowers the relevant λ_t further. Since in the diverse information case λ_t can actually increase with an increase in n_t, the argument for concentrated trading must be modified.

Assume for a moment that n_t is a continuous rather than a discrete parameter. Consider two periods, denoted H and L. In period H, the variance of liquidity trading is high and equal to Ψ_{H}; in period L, the variance of liquidity trading is low and equal to Ψ_{L}. Let n_{H} (or n_{L}) be the number of traders acquiring information in period H (or L). To establish the viability of the concentrated-trading equilibrium, we need to show that, with endogenous information acquisition, $\lambda(n_{\mathrm{H}}, \Psi_{\mathrm{H}}) \leqslant \lambda(n_{\mathrm{L}}, \Psi_{\mathrm{L}})$. If n is continuous, then endogenous information acquisition implies that profits must be equal across periods:

$$\pi(n_{\mathrm{H}}, \Psi_{\mathrm{H}}) = \frac{1}{1 + n_{\mathrm{H}} + 2\phi} \left[\frac{\Psi_{\mathrm{H}}(1+\phi)}{n_{\mathrm{H}}}\right]^{1/2}$$
$$= \pi(n_{\mathrm{L}}, \Psi_{\mathrm{L}})$$
$$= \frac{1}{1 + n_{\mathrm{L}} + 2\phi} \left[\frac{\Psi_{\mathrm{L}}(1+\phi)}{n_{\mathrm{L}}}\right]^{1/2}. \tag{21}$$

Since $\Psi_{\mathrm{H}} > \Psi_{\mathrm{L}}$, it follows that $n_{\mathrm{H}} > n_{\mathrm{L}}$. To maintain equality between the profits with $n_{\mathrm{H}} > n_{\mathrm{L}}$, it is necessary that $\Psi_{\mathrm{H}}/n_{\mathrm{H}} > \Psi_{\mathrm{L}}/n_{\mathrm{L}}$. Since $\lambda(n, \Psi) = n\pi(n, \Psi)/\Psi$, it follows that $\lambda(n_{\mathrm{H}}, \Psi_{\mathrm{H}}) < \lambda(n_{\mathrm{L}}, \Psi_{\mathrm{L}})$. Thus, if n were continuous, the value of λ would always be lower in periods with more liquidity trading and the concentrated-trading equilibria would always be viable. These equilibria would also be generic as in proposition 1.

The above is only a heuristic argument, establishing the existence of concentrated-trading equilibria with endogenous information acquisition in the model with diverse information. Since n_t is discrete, we cannot assert that in equilibrium the profits of informed traders are equal across periods. This may lead to the nonexistence of an equilibrium for some parameter values, as we show in the appendix. However, the following can be shown.

1 An equilibrium always exists if the variance of the discretionary liquidity demand is sufficiently high.
2 If an equilibrium exists, then an equilibrium in which trading is concentrated exists. Moreover, for almost all parameters for which an equilibrium exists, only such concentrated-trading equilibria exist.

We now show that, when an equilibrium exists, the basic nature of the results that we derived in the previous sections do not change when informed traders have diverse information. We continue to assume that $\phi_t = \phi$ for all t. Consider first the trading volume. It is easy to show that the variance of the total order flow of the informed traders is given by

$$\mathrm{var}\left(\sum_{i=1}^{n} \beta_i(\tilde{\delta}_{t+1} + \tilde{\varepsilon}_t^i)\right) = \frac{\Psi_t(n_t + \phi)}{1+\phi}. \tag{22}$$

This is clearly increasing in Ψ_t and in n_t. Since informed traders are diversely informed, there will generally be some trading within the group of informed traders. (For example, if a particular informed trader draws an extreme signal, his position may have an opposite sign to that of the aggregate position of informed traders.) Thus the measure V_t^I of trading volume by informed traders will be greater than the expression in equation (22). The amount of trading within the group of informed traders is clearly an increasing function of n_t. Thus this strengthens the effect of concentrated trading on the volume measures: more liquidity trading leads to more informed traders, which in turn implies an even greater trading volume.

The basic characteristics of the price process are also essentially unchanged in this model. First consider the informativeness of the price, as measured by $Q_t = \text{var}(\tilde{\delta}_{t+1} | \tilde{P}_t)$. With diverse information it can be shown that

$$Q_t = \left(1 + \frac{n_t}{1 + 2\phi}\right)^{-1}. \tag{23}$$

As in Kyle (1984), an increase in the number of informed traders increases the informativeness of prices. This is due in part to the increased competition among the informed traders. It is also due to the fact that more information is gathered when more traders become informed. This second effect was not present in the model with common private information. The implications of the model remain the same as before: with endogenous information acquisition, prices will be more informative in periods with higher liquidity trading (that is, periods in which the discretionary liquidity traders trade).

In the model with diverse private information, the behavior of R_t (the variance of price changes) is very similar to what we saw in the model with common information. It can be shown that

$$R_t = \frac{n_t}{1 + n_t + 2\phi} + \frac{1 + 2\phi}{1 + n_{t-1} + 2\phi}. \tag{24}$$

As before, if $n_t = n$ for all t, then $R_t = 1$, and $R_t > 1$ if and only if $n_t > n_{t-1}$.

4 The Allocation of Liquidity Trading

In the analysis so far we have assumed that the discretionary liquidity traders can only trade once, so that their only decision was the timing of their single trade. We now allow discretionary liquidity traders to allocate their trading among the periods in the interval $[T', T'']$, that is, between the time that their liquidity demand is determined and the time by which it must be satisfied. Since the model becomes more complicated, we shall illustrate what happens in this case with a simple structure and by numerical examples.

Suppose that $T' = 1$ and $T'' = 2$, so that discretionary liquidity traders can allocate their trades over two trading periods. Suppose that there are n_1 informed traders in period 1 and n_2 informed traders in period 2 and that the informed traders obtain perfect information (that is, they observe $\tilde{\delta}_{t+1}$ at time t). Each discretionary liquidity trader must choose the proportion α of the liquidity demand $\tilde{Y}^j$ that is satisfied in period 1. The remainder will be satisfied in period 2. Discretionary liquidity trader j therefore trades $\alpha\tilde{Y}^j$ shares in period 1 and $(1-\alpha)\tilde{Y}^j$ shares in period 2.

To obtain some intuition, suppose that the price function is as given in the previous sections, that is,

$$\tilde{P}_t = \bar{F} + \sum_{\tau=1}^{t} \tilde{\delta}_\tau + \lambda_t \tilde{\omega}_t \tag{25}$$

where λ_t is given by lemma 1. Note that the price in period t depends only on the order flow in period t. In this case the discretionary liquidity trader's problem is to minimize the cost of liquidity trading, which is given by

$$[\alpha^2\lambda_1 + (1-\alpha)^2\lambda_2]\,(\tilde{Y}^j)^2. \tag{26}$$

It is easy to see that this is minimized by setting $\alpha = \lambda_2/(\lambda_1+\lambda_2)$. For example, if $\lambda_1 = \lambda_2$, then the optimal value of α is $\frac{1}{2}$. Thus, if each price is independent of previous order flows, the cost function for a liquidity trader is convex, and so discretionary liquidity traders divide their trades among different periods. It is important to note that the optimal α is independent of $\tilde{Y}^j$. This means that all liquidity traders will choose the same α.

If the above argument were correct, it would seem to upset our results on the concentration of trade. However, the argument is flawed, since the assumption that each price is independent of past order flows is no longer appropriate. Recall that the market maker sets the price in each period equal to the conditional expectation of $\tilde{F}$, given all the information available to him at the time. This includes the history of past order flows. In the models of the previous sections, there is no payoff-relevant information in past order flows $\tilde{\Omega}_{t-1}$ that is not revealed by the public information $\tilde{\Delta}_t$ in period t. This is no longer true here, since past order flows enable the market maker to forecast the liquidity component of current order flows. This improves the precision of his prediction of the informed trading component, which is relevant to future payoffs. Specifically, since the information that informed traders have in period 1 is revealed to the market maker in period 2, the market maker can subtract $n_1\beta_1\delta_2$ from the total order flow in period 1. This reveals $\alpha\Sigma_j Y^j + \tilde{z}_1$, which is informative about the discretionary liquidity demand $(1-\alpha)\,\Sigma_j Y^j$ in period 2.

Since the terms of trade in period 2 depend on the order flow in period 1, a trader who is informed in both periods will take into account the effect that his trading in the first period will have on the profits he can earn in the second period. This complicates the analysis considerably. To avoid these complications and to focus on the behavior of discretionary liquidity traders, we assume that no trader is informed in more than one period.

Suppose that the price in period 1 is given by

$$\tilde{P}_1 = P_0 + \tilde{\delta}_1 + \lambda_1 \tilde{\omega}_1, \tag{27}$$

where

$$\tilde{\omega}_1 = n_1 \beta_1 \tilde{\delta}_2 + \alpha \sum_j \tilde{Y}^j + \tilde{z}_1, \tag{28}$$

and that the price in period 2 is given by

$$\tilde{P}_2 = P_0 + \tilde{\delta}_1 + \tilde{\delta}_2 + \lambda_2 \tilde{\omega}_2^{\mathrm{p}}, \tag{29}$$

where

$$\tilde{\omega}_2^{\mathrm{p}} = n_2 \beta_2 \tilde{\delta}_3 + (1 - \alpha) \sum_j \tilde{Y}^j + \tilde{z}_2 - (1 - \alpha) E\left(\sum_j \tilde{Y}^j \middle| \tilde{\omega}_1, \tilde{\delta}_2 \right). \tag{30}$$

Note that the form of the price is the same in the two periods, but that the order flow in the second period has been modified to reflect the prediction of the discretionary liquidity trading component based on the order flow in the first period and the realization of $\tilde{\delta}_2$. Let γ be the coefficient in the regression of $\Sigma_j \tilde{Y}^j$ on $\alpha \Sigma_j \tilde{Y}^j + \tilde{z}_1$. Then it can be shown that the problem that each discretionary liquidity trader faces, taking the strategies of all other traders and the market maker as given, is to choose α to minimize

$$\alpha^2 \lambda_1 + (1 - \alpha)^2 \lambda_2 - \alpha(1 - \alpha) \lambda_2 \gamma.$$

The solution to this problem is to set

$$\alpha = \frac{\lambda_2(\gamma + 2)}{2[\lambda_1 + \lambda_2(\gamma + 1)]}. \tag{31}$$

Given that discretionary liquidity traders allocate their trades in this fashion, the market maker sets λ_1 and λ_2 so that his expected profit in each period (given all the information available to him) is zero. It is easy to show that in equilibrium λ_t and β_t are given by lemma 1, with

$$\Psi_1 = g + \alpha^2 h \tag{32}$$

and

$$\Psi_2 = g + (1 - \alpha)^2 \left(\frac{1}{h} + \frac{\alpha^2}{g} \right)^{-1}. \tag{33}$$

While it can be shown that this model has an equilibrium, it is generally impossible to find the equilibrium in closed form. We now discuss two limiting cases, one in which the nondiscretionary liquidity component vanishes and one in which it is infinitely noisy; we then provide examples in which the equilibrium is calculated numerically.

Consider first the case in which most of the liquidity trading is nondiscretionary. This can be thought of as a situation in which $g \to \infty$. In this situation the market maker cannot infer anything from the information available in the second period about the liquidity demand in that period. It can then be shown that $\gamma \to 0$, so that past order flows are uninformative to the market maker. Moreover,

$$\alpha \to \left[1 + \left(\frac{n_1}{n_2}\right)^{1/2}\left(\frac{1+n_2}{1+n_1}\right)\right]^{-1}. \tag{34}$$

For example, if $n_1 = n_2$, then $\alpha \to \frac{1}{2}$. Not surprisingly, this is the solution we would obtain if we assumed that the price in each period is independent of the previous order flow. When discretionary liquidity trading is a small part of the total liquidity trading, we do not obtain a concentrated-trading equilibrium.

Now consider the other extreme case, in which $g = \text{var}(\tilde{z}_t) \to 0$. In this case almost all the liquidity trading is discretionary, and therefore the market maker can predict with great precision the liquidity component of the order flow in the second period, given his information. It can be shown that in the limit we obtain $\alpha = 1$, so that all liquidity trading is concentrated in the first period. Note that, since there is no liquidity trading in the second period, $\lambda_2 \to \infty$; thus in a model with endogenous information acquisition we shall obtain $n_2 = 0$ and there will be no trade in the second period.[15]

In general, discretionary liquidity traders have to take into account the fact that the market maker can infer their demands as time goes on. This causes their trades to be more concentrated in the earlier periods, as is illustrated by the two examples below. Note that, unlike the concentration result in proposition 1, it now matters whether trading occurs at time T' or later; the different trading periods are not equivalent from the point of view of the discretionary liquidity traders. This will have implications when information acquisition is endogenous. Consider the following two examples.

In the first example we make all the parametric assumptions made in our previous examples, except that now we allow the discretionary liquidity traders A and B to allocate their trades across period 2, 3, and 4. If information acquisition is endogenous and if the cost of perfect information is $c = 0.13$, then we obtain the equilibrium parameters given in table 19.6. In this example, each discretionary liquidity trader j trades about $0.4\tilde{Y}^j$ in period 2, $0.31\tilde{Y}^j$ in period 3, and $0.29\tilde{Y}^j$ in period 4. Note that the measure of liquidity trading volume is highest in period 2 and then

Table 19.6 Volume and price behavior when discretionary liquidity traders allocate trading across several periods

t	n_t	λ_t	V_t	V_t^{I}	V_t^{L}	V_t^{M}	Q_t	R_t
1	3	0.43	4.73	1.73	1.00	2.00	0.25	
2	4	0.30	7.84	2.67	2.19	2.99	0.20	1.05
3	3	0.38	6.51	2.12	1.95	2.45	0.25	0.95
4	3	0.40	6.31	2.06	1.87	2.38	0.25	1.00

A four-period example in which the number n_t of informed traders is determined endogenously, assuming that the cost of information is 0.13 and that liquidity traders can allocate their trade in different periods between 2.00 p.m. and 4.00 p.m. For $t = 1, 2, 3, 4$, the table gives the market depth parameter λ_t a measure V_t of total trading volume, a measure V_t^{I} of the informed trading volume, a measure V_t^{L} of liquidity trading volume, a measure V_t^{M} of the trading volume of the market maker, a measure Q_t of the amount of private information revealed in the price, and the variance R_t of the price change from period $t-1$ to period t.

falls off in periods 3 and 4. Three informed traders are present in each of the periods except period 2, when it is profitable for a fourth to enter. The behavior of prices is therefore similar to that when traders could only time their trades.

In the second example, illustrated in table 19.7, we assume that there is less nondiscretionary liquidity trading. Specifically, we set the variance of nondiscretionary liquidity trading to be 0.1. With the cost of information at $c = 0.04$ and with endogenous information acquisition, we obtain pronounced patterns. For example, there are 11 informed traders in period 2 and three informed traders in each of the other periods. Liquidity trading is much heavier in period 2 as well, and the patterns of the volume and price behavior are very pronounced. In this example, each discretionary liquidity trader j trades $0.74\tilde{Y}^j$ in period 2, $0.14\tilde{Y}^j$ in period 3, and $0.12\tilde{Y}_j$ in period 4.

Table 19.7 An example of pronounced patterns of volume and price behavior when discretionary liquidity traders allocate trading across several periods

t	n_t	λ_t	V_t	V_t^{I}	V_t^{L}	V_t^{M}	Q_t	R_t
1	3	1.37	1.50	0.55	0.32	0.63	0.25	
2	11	0.16	13.95	5.59	2.54	5.83	0.08	1.17
3	3	1.35	2.40	0.77	0.74	0.89	0.25	0.83
4	3	1.35	2.23	0.72	0.68	0.83	0.25	1.00

The same example as in table 19.6 except that the variance of nondiscretionary liquidity trading is lower (0.1). The cost of information is assumed to be $c = 0.04$.

5 Extensions

In this section we discuss a number of additional extensions of our basic model. We show that the main conclusions of the model do not change in more general settings. This indicates that our results are robust to a variety of models.

5.1 Different timing constraints for liquidity traders

For simplicity, we have assumed so far that the demands of all the discretionary liquidity traders are determined at the same time and must be satisfied within the same time span. In reality, of course, different traders may realize their liquidity demands at different times, and the time that can elapse before these demands must be satisfied may also be different for different traders. Our results can be extended to this more general case, and their basic nature remains unchanged.

For example, suppose that there are three discretionary liquidity traders A, B, and C whose demands have the variances 5, 1, and 7 respectively. Suppose that trader A realizes his liquidity demand at 9:00 a.m. and must satisfy it by 2:00 p.m. that day. Trader B realizes his demand at 11:00 a.m. and must satisfy it by 4:00 p.m., and trader C realizes his demand at 2:30 p.m. and must satisfy it by 10:00 a.m. on the following day. If each of these traders trades only once to satisfy his liquidity demands, then it is an equilibrium that traders A and C trade at the same time between 9:00 a.m. and 10:00 a.m. (for example 9:30 a.m.) and that trader B trades some time between 11:00 a.m. and 4:00 p.m.

Now suppose that the variance of B's demand is 9 instead of 1. Then the equilibrium described above is possible only if trader B trades before 2:30 p.m.; otherwise, trader C would prefer to trade at the same time that B trades rather than at the same time that A trades, and the equilibrium would break down. Two other equilibrium patterns exist in this situation. In one, traders B and C trade at the same time between 2:30 p.m. and 4:00 p.m. (for example 3:00 p.m.), and trader A trades some time between 9:00 a.m. and 2:00 p.m. In another equilibrium, traders A and B trade at the same time between 11:00 a.m. and 2:00 p.m. (for example 11:30 a.m.), and trader C trades some time between 4:00 p.m. and 10:00 a.m. the next morning. All these equilibria involve trading patterns in which two of the traders trade at the same time. If informed traders can enter the market, then their trading would also be concentrated in the periods with heavier liquidity trading. Thus, we obtain trading patterns similar to those discussed in the simple model.

5.2 *Risk-averse liquidity traders*

We now ask whether our results change if, instead of assuming that all traders are risk neutral, it is assumed that some traders are risk averse. We focus on the discretionary liquidity traders, since their actions are the prime determinants of the equilibrium trading patterns that we have identified. In the discussion below we continue to assume that informed traders and the market maker are risk neutral. (A model in which these traders are also risk averse is much more complicated and is therefore beyond the scope of this paper.)

A risk-averse liquidity trader, say trader j, is concerned with more than the conditional expectation of $\tilde{Y}^j(\tilde{P}_t - \tilde{F})$ given his own demand $\tilde{Y}^j$. Since he submits market orders, the price at which he trades is uncertain. In those periods in which a large amount of liquidity trading takes place, the variance of the order flow is higher. One may think that, since this will make the price more variable, it will discourage risk-averse liquidity traders from trading together. In fact, the reverse occurs: risk-averse liquidity traders have an even greater incentive to trade together than do risk-neutral traders.

The following heuristic discussion uses the basic model of sections 1–3. Given our assumptions, the conditional distribution of $\tilde{P}_t - \tilde{F}$ is normal, given $\tilde{Y}^j$ and the public information available at time t. Thus liquidity trader j is concerned only with the first two moments of this conditional distribution. Consider first the unconditional variance of $\tilde{P}_t - \tilde{F}$. Since $\tilde{P}_t$ is the expectation of $\tilde{F}$, given the order flow at time t (and public information), the variance of $\tilde{P}_t - \tilde{F}$ is the variance of the prediction error. Suppose that all liquidity traders trade in period $t^\star$. Recall from section 1 that, because of the more intense trading by informed traders at $t^\star$, the prediction variance (which is related to Q_t) is *independent* of the variance Ψ_t of liquidity trading. Thus, as long as the number of informed traders is constant over time, the concentration of liquidity trading in period $t^\star$ does not increase the variance of $\tilde{P}_{t^\star} - \tilde{F}$ relative to other periods. We have also seen that the prediction variance is *decreasing* in the number n_t of informed traders. This implies that with endogenous information acquisition, since more informed traders trade in period $t^\star$, the prediction variance is even lower.

Now, liquidity trader j also knows his own demand $\tilde{Y}^j$, and so we must consider the conditional variance of $\tilde{P}_t - \tilde{F}$, given $\tilde{Y}^j$. If $f_t(n_t)$ is the unconditional variance discussed above, then the conditional variance is equal to $f_t(n_t) - \lambda_t^2 \operatorname{var}(\tilde{Y}^j)$ if trader j trades in period t and to $f_t(n_t)$ if he trades in a different period. It is clear now that the fact that trader j knows $\tilde{Y}^j$ does not change the direction of the results outlined in the preceding paragraph; if all discretionary liquid traders trade in period $t^\star \in [T', T'']$, then $f_{t^\star}(n_{t^\star}^\star) - \lambda_{t^\star}^2 \operatorname{var}(\tilde{Y}^j) < f_t(n_t)$ for all $t \in [T', T'']$ and $t \neq t^\star$ and for all j. Thus the equilibrium in which discretionary liquidity traders concentrate their trading in one period is still viable even if these traders are risk averse.

5.3 *Correlated demands of liquidity traders*

We have assumed that the demands of discretionary liquidity traders are independent of each other. This assumption seems to be reasonable if liquidity demands are driven by completely idiosyncratic life-cycle motives that are specific to individual traders. If liquidity demands are correlated across traders because of some common factors affecting these demands, and if these factors are observed by the market maker before he forms prices, then our analysis is still valid, with the interpretation that liquidity trading corresponds to the unpredictable part of these demands.

It is possible to extend our analysis to the case where common factors in liquidity demands are not observable (or, in general, to the case of correlated liquidity demands). Two considerations arise in this case. First, if liquidity traders trade in different periods, then past order flows may provide information to the market maker concerning the liquidity component in the current order flow. Second, if more than one liquidity trader trades in a given period, then the cost of trading in this period, which is proportional to the correlation of his demands with the total order flow, involves an additional term that reflects the correlation of the trader's demand with the other liquidity demands.

If liquidity demands are negatively correlated, then it can be shown that concentrated-trading equilibria always exist, and so our results are still valid. The same is true if the variance of nondiscretionary liquidity demands is small enough, that is, if there is very little nondiscretionary liquidity trading. The results may be different if liquidity demands are positively correlated. In this case it is possible that an equilibrium in which trading is completely concentrated does not exist, or that equilibria in which different traders trade in different periods also exist, in addition to the concentrated-trading equilibria (and they are robust to slight perturbations in the parameters). Examples are not difficult to construct.

6 Empirical Implications

The result that trading is concentrated in particular periods during the day and that the variability of price changes is higher in periods of concentrated trading is clearly consistent with empirical observations of financial markets, as discussed in the introduction and in the following section. Our models also provide a number of more specific predictions, examples of which we shall discuss below. For simplicity, we shall generally use the model of sections 1–3, where discretionary liquidity traders trade only once within the period in which they have to satisfy their liquidity demands.

In the context of our model, it seems reasonable to treat prices $\tilde{P}_t$ and order flows $\tilde{\omega}_t$ as observables. Specifically, if we define the periods to be, say, 30 min long, then the relevant price would be the last transaction price of the interval, and the order flow would be the net change in the position of the market maker during the interval. (It should be noted, however, that in practice the order flow data may not be easily available from market makers.)

Suppose for simplicity that trading periods are divided into two types, those with high trading volume and those with low trading volume. We shall use H and L to denote the set of periods with high and low trading volumes respectively. (We also use superscript parameters accordingly.) The basic pricing equation in our model is

$$\tilde{P}_t = \sum_{\tau=1}^{t} \tilde{\delta}_\tau + \lambda^{\mathrm{H}} \tilde{\omega}_t \tag{35}$$

for periods with high volume ($t \in \mathrm{H}$) and

$$\tilde{P}_t = \sum_{\tau=1}^{t} \tilde{\delta}_\tau + \lambda^{\mathrm{L}} \tilde{\omega}_t \tag{36}$$

for periods with low volume ($t \in \mathrm{L}$).

Three hypotheses follow directly from our results in sections 1–3.

Hypothesis 1 $\lambda^{\mathrm{H}} < \lambda^{\mathrm{L}}$.

In other words, our model predicts that the market depth coefficient (defined by $1/\lambda_t$) is higher when the volume is lower. This hypothesis can easily be tested by using standard statistical procedures, as long as we can estimate λ^{H} and λ^{L} from price and order flow observations. To see how this can be done, define

$$\tilde{m}_t \equiv \tilde{P}_{t+1} - \tilde{P}_{t-1} = \tilde{\delta}_{t+1} + \tilde{\delta}_t + \lambda_{t+1}\tilde{\omega}_{t+1} - \lambda_{t-1}\tilde{\omega}_{t-1}. \tag{37}$$

An estimate of λ^{H} can be obtained by regressing the observations of $\tilde{m}_t$ for $t \in \mathrm{H}$ on the order flow observations $\tilde{\omega}_t$. This follows because all the terms in the above expression, except $\tilde{\delta}_{t+1}$, are independent of $\tilde{\omega}_t$ and because, by construction, λ_t is set by the market maker as the regression coefficient in the prediction of $\tilde{\delta}_{t+1}$, given $\tilde{\omega}_t$. Similarly, a regression of the observations of $\tilde{m}_t$ for $t \in \mathrm{L}$ on $\tilde{\omega}_t$ would give an estimate of λ^{L}.[16]

Hypothesis 2 If $t \in \mathrm{H}$ and $t' \in \mathrm{L}$, then $Q_t < Q_{t'}$, that is, $\mathrm{var}(\tilde{\delta}_{t+1} | \tilde{P}_t) < \mathrm{var}(\tilde{\delta}_{t'+1} | \tilde{P}_{t'})$.

This simply says that prices are more informative in periods in which the trading volume is heavier. Although it is less transparent to see, hypothesis 2 can also be tested empirically using price and order flow observations. This is shown in the appendix.

Hypothesis 3 The variance of the price change from $t \in \mathrm{L}$ to $(t+1) \in \mathrm{H}$ is larger than the variance of the price change from $t \in \mathrm{L}$ to $(t+1) \in \mathrm{L}$, and this exceeds the variance of the price change from $t \in \mathrm{H}$ to $(t+1) \in \mathrm{L}$.

It is straightforward to test this hypothesis, given price and volume observations.

Cross-sectional implications can also be derived from our analysis. For example, it is reasonable to assume that a typical discretionary liquidity trader is a large institutional trader. Our models predict that trading patterns will be more pronounced for stocks that are widely held by these institutional traders.

7 Concluding Remarks

In this paper we have presented a theory of trading patterns in financial markets. Some of the conclusions of our theory are as follows.

1 In equilibrium, discretionary liquidity trading is typically concentrated.
2 If discretionary liquidity traders can allocate their trades across different periods, then in equilibrium their trading is relatively more concentrated in periods closer to the realization of their demands.
3 Informed traders trade more actively in periods when liquidity trading is concentrated.
4 If information acquisition is endogenous, then in equilibrium more traders become privately informed in periods of concentrated liquidity trading, and prices are more informative in those periods.

We have obtained our results in models in which the information process and the amount of nondiscretionary liquidity trading are completely stationary over time. All the patterns we have identified in volume and price variability emerge as consequences of the interacting strategic decisions of informed and liquidity traders. The main innovation in our theory is the explicit inclusion of *discretionary liquidity* traders who can time their trading. As discussed in the introduction, observations similar to the last two points above have been made as comparative statics results in Kyle (1984), where the variance of liquidity trading is parametrically varied in a single-period model. We have shown that these results continue to hold in equilibrium when the timing of liquidity trading is endogenized. As we have seen, it is a delicate matter whether the strategic interaction between liquidity traders and informed traders actually leads to pronounced patterns of trading over time. Among other things, what is important in this regard is the degree of competition among informed traders. When informed traders observe highly correlated signals, competition between them is intense, and this improves the terms of trade for liquidity traders, promoting concentration of trading. If private signals are weakly correlated, however, then competition among informed traders is less intense, and an increase in the number of informed traders can actually worsen the terms of trade. This may lead to the nonexistence of an equilibrium. However, despite the complexity of the strategic interaction among traders, our analysis shows that, whenever an equilibrium exists, it is characterized by the concentration of liquidity and informed trading and by the resulting patterns in volume and price behavior.

The actual timing and shape of trading patterns in financial markets are determined by a number of factors and parameters that are exogenous to the model, such as the rate of arrival of public information, the amount of nondiscretionary liquidity trading, and the length of the interval within which each discretionary liquidity trader trades. As we noted, empirical observations suggest that the *daily* patterns in trading volume and returns are quite profound. In particular, there is heavier trading at the beginning and end of the trading day than there is in the middle of the day, and the returns and price changes are more variable.

There are a few hypotheses that, combined with our results, may explain the concentration of trading at the open and the close. The open and close are distinguished by the fact that they fall just after and just before the exchange is closed, that is, after and before a period of time in which it is difficult or impossible to trade. This may cause an increase in (nondiscretionary) liquidity trading at the open and close. As a result, discretionary liquidity trading (as well as informed trading) will also be concentrated in these periods, as implied by our results. In this case the forces we have identified for concentration would be intensified.

The concentration of trading at the end of the trading day may also be due to the settlement rules that are followed by many exchanges. Under these rules all trades undertaken on a particular day are actually settled by the close several days later. While delivery depends on the day in which the transaction takes place, the exact time within a day in which the trade occurs has no effect on delivery. This suggests that the interval within which many discretionary liquidity traders must trade terminates at the close of a trading day (that is, that for many liquidity traders T'' is the close of a trading day). Since the time T' at which liquidity demands are realized may vary across traders, there will be a tendency for trading to be concentrated at the close, when there is the most overlap among the intervals available to different liquidity traders (see section 5.1 for an intuitive discussion of this in the context of a related example).

Note that the model of section 4, in which discretionary liquidity traders can allocate their trades over different periods, predicts that trading will be concentrated in "earlier" trading periods (that is, in periods closer to the time in which the liquidity demand is realized). For example, if many discretionary liquidity traders realize their liquidity demands after the market closes, then our model predicts that they will satisfy them as soon as the market opens the next day. If, however, liquidity demands are realized late in the trading day, then we shall observe heavy trading by discretionary liquidity traders and informed traders near the close of the market.

Our analysis may also shed some light on the finding discussed by French and Roll (1986) that the variance of returns over nontrading periods is much lower than the variance of returns over trading periods. If the liquidity trading volume is higher at the end of the trading day, then more informed traders will trade at this time. As a result, the prices quoted at the end of the trading day will reflect more of the information that will be released publicly during the following nontrading hours (see hypothesis 2 in section 6). While this effect may explain some of these findings, it is probably not sufficiently strong to account for the striking differences in variance reported by French and Roll (1986).

It is interesting to ask whether our results can account for the actual magnitudes of the observed patterns. A satisfactory answer to this question requires a serious empirical investigation, something we shall not attempt here. However, casual calculations suggest that the predictions from the model may accord well with the observed magnitudes. For example, consider again the Exxon data presented in table 19.1. Suppose that there are four informed traders in period 1 (10 a.m. to 12 noon), one informed trader in period 2 (12 noon to 2 p.m.), and three informed traders in period 3 (2 p.m. to 4 p.m.). These values are roughly consistent with the pattern of trading volume. Suppose also that $\phi = 0$, that is, informed traders in period t have perfect information about $\tilde{\delta}_{t+1}$. Finally, let the average σ_δ^2 of the variance of the price changes in the three periods be 0.115 661. Then we can calculate the variance of the price change in each period as predicted by our model using equation (16), modified to include σ_δ (in performing this calculation we ignore the overnight period and assume that the third period of one day immediately precedes the first period of the next):

$$R_1^{1/2} = \left(\frac{n_1}{1+n_1} + \frac{1}{1+n_3}\right)^{1/2} \sigma_\delta = 0.34849$$

$$R_2^{1/2} = \left(\frac{n_2}{1+n_2} + \frac{1}{1+n_1}\right)^{1/2} \sigma_\delta = 0.28454$$

$$R_3^{1/2} = \left(\frac{n_3}{1+n_3} + \frac{1}{1+n_2}\right)^{1/2} \sigma_\delta = 0.38023.$$

These values are quite close to to observed values (0.34959, 0.28371, 0.37984).[17] The foregoing should in no way be construed as a test of the model. We simply conclude that the effects that the model predicts can be of the same magnitude as those seen in the data.

In closing, we note that many intraday phenomena remain unexplained. For example, a number of studies have shown that mean returns also vary through the day (e.g. Wood, McInish, and Ord, 1985; Harris, 1986; Jain and Joh, 1986; Marsh and Rock, 1986). In our model, prices are a martingale, and so patterns in means do not arise. This is due in part to the assumption of risk neutrality. (Williams (1987) analyzes a model that is related to ours in which risk aversion plays an important role and mean effects do arise.) Developing additional models that produce testable predictions for transaction data is an important task for future research.

Appendix

Proof of Lemma 1

Consider the informed traders' decisions. The ith informed trader chooses the amount x_t^i to trade in period t, to maximize the expected profits, which are given by

$$E\{x_t^i[\tilde{F} - P_t(\tilde{\Delta}_t, \tilde{\Omega}_t)] \,|\, \tilde{\Delta}_t, \tilde{\Omega}_{t-1}, \tilde{\delta}_{t+1} + \varepsilon_t\}. \tag{A1}$$

Given the form of the price function in equation (3), this can be written as

$$E[x_t^i(\tilde{\delta}_{t+1} - \lambda_t\tilde{\omega}_t) | \tilde{\delta}_{t+1} + \varepsilon_t] \tag{A2}$$

Suppose that informed trader i conjectures that the market order of the other $n-1$ informed traders is equal to $\beta_t(\tilde{\delta}_{t+1} + \tilde{\varepsilon}_t)$. Then the total order flow is

$$\tilde{\omega}_t = x_t^i + (n_t - 1)\beta(\tilde{\delta}_{t+1} + \tilde{\varepsilon}_t) + \sum_{j=1}^{m} \tilde{y}_t^j + \tilde{x}_t,$$

and the ith informed trader chooses x_t^i to maximize

$$E\left\{x_t^i\tilde{\delta}_{t+1} - x_t^i\lambda_t\left[x_t^i + (n_t - 1)\beta_t(\tilde{\delta}_{t+1} + \tilde{\varepsilon}_t) + \sum_{j=1}^{m} \tilde{y}_t^j + \tilde{z}_t\right] \middle| \tilde{\delta}_{t+1} + \tilde{\varepsilon}_t\right\} \tag{A3}$$

which is equal to

$$\frac{x_t^i \operatorname{var}(\tilde{\delta}_{t+1})}{\operatorname{var}(\tilde{\delta}_{t+1}) + \phi_t} (\tilde{\delta}_{t+1} + \tilde{\varepsilon}_t) - x_t^i \lambda_t [x_t^i + (n_t - 1)\beta_t(\tilde{\delta}_{t+1} + \tilde{\varepsilon}_t)]. \tag{A4}$$

It is easily seen that the expected profits of the *i*th informed trader in period t are maximized if x_t^i is set equal to

$$\left\{\frac{\operatorname{var}(\tilde{\delta}_{t+1})}{2\lambda_t[\operatorname{var}(\tilde{\delta}_{t+1}) + \phi_t]} - \frac{(n_t - 1)\beta_t}{2}\right\}(\tilde{\delta}_{t+1} + \tilde{\varepsilon}_t). \tag{A5}$$

The Nash equilibrium is found by setting the above equal to $\beta_t(\tilde{\delta}_{t+1} + \tilde{\varepsilon}_t)$ and solving for β_t.[18] We obtain

$$\beta_t = \frac{\operatorname{var}(\tilde{\delta}_{t+1})}{(n_t + 1)\lambda_t[\operatorname{var}(\tilde{\delta}_{t+1}) + \phi_t]}. \tag{A6}$$

We now determine the value of λ_t for a given set of strategies by all traders. Recall that the total amount of discretionary liquidity demands in period t is $\sum_{j=1}^{m} \tilde{y}_t^j$, where $\tilde{y}_t^j = \tilde{Y}^j$ if the jth discretionary liquidity trader trades in period t and is zero otherwise. The zero profit condition for the market maker implies that

$$\lambda_t = \frac{\operatorname{cov}(\tilde{\delta}_{t+1}, \tilde{\omega}_t)}{\operatorname{var}(\tilde{\omega}_t)} = \frac{n_t\beta_t \operatorname{var}(\tilde{\delta}_{t+1})}{n_t^2\beta_t^2[\operatorname{var}(\tilde{\delta}_{t+1}) + \phi_t] + \Psi_t}. \tag{A7}$$

Substituting equation (A6) for β_t, we obtain a cubic equation for λ_t. The unique positive root gives the equilibrium value for the assumed level of liquidity trading. This is the value given in equation (5). ■

Proof of Lemma 2

As shown in the proof of lemma 1, when n_t traders are informed, in period t each places a market order of $\beta_t(\tilde{\delta}_{t+1} + \tilde{\varepsilon}_t)$ shares, where

$$\beta_t = \frac{1}{(n_t + 1)\lambda(n_t, \Psi_t)(1 + \phi)}. \tag{A8}$$

(We assume here that $\operatorname{var}(\tilde{\delta}_{t+1}) = 1$ and $\phi_t = \phi$.) Now consider a deviant trader who acquires information in addition to the other n traders. He will demand x_t shares, where x_t maximizes

$$E(x_t\{\tilde{\delta}_{t+1} - \lambda(n_t, \Psi_t)[x_t + n_t\beta_t(\tilde{\delta}_{t+1} + \tilde{\varepsilon}_t) + \tilde{u}_t]\} \mid \tilde{\delta}_{t+1} + \tilde{\varepsilon}_t) \tag{A9}$$

where $\tilde{u}_t$ is the total liquidity demand in period t. This is maximized at

$$x_t = \left[\frac{1}{2\lambda(n_t, \Psi_t)(1 + \phi)} - \frac{n_t\beta_t}{2}\right](\tilde{\delta}_{t+1} + \tilde{\varepsilon}_t) \tag{A10}$$

or, substituting for β_t,

$$\begin{aligned} x_t &= \left[\frac{1}{2\lambda(n_t, \Psi_t)(1 + \phi)} - \frac{n_t}{2(n_t + 1)\lambda(n_t, \Psi_t)(1 + \phi)}\right](\tilde{\delta}_{t+1} + \tilde{\varepsilon}_t) \\ &= \frac{1}{2(n_t + 1)\lambda(n_t, \Psi_t)(1 + \phi)} (\tilde{\delta}_{t+1} + \tilde{\varepsilon}_t) \\ &= \frac{\beta_t}{2} (\tilde{\delta}_{t+1} + \tilde{\varepsilon}_t). \end{aligned} \tag{A11}$$

The expected profits $\pi^{\mathrm{d}}(n_t, \Psi_t)$ earned by the deviant trader will be

$$E\left(\frac{\beta_t}{2}(\tilde{\delta}_{t+1}+\tilde{\varepsilon}_t)\left\{\tilde{\delta}_{t+1}-\lambda(n_t,\Psi_t)\left[\frac{(2n_t+1)\beta_t(\tilde{\delta}_{t+1}+\tilde{\varepsilon}_t)}{2}+\tilde{u}_t\right]\right\}\right) \tag{A12}$$

which is

$$\frac{\beta_t}{2}\left[1-\frac{\lambda(n_t,\Psi_t)}{2}(2n_t+1)\beta_t(+\phi)\right]. \tag{A13}$$

Substituting for β_t and $\lambda(n_t, \Psi_t)$, we can simplify this to

$$\pi^{\mathrm{d}}(n_t,\Psi_t)=\frac{1}{4(n_t+1)}\left[\frac{\Psi_t}{n_t(1+\phi)}\right]^{1/2}=\frac{\pi(n_t,\Psi_t)}{4} \tag{A14}$$

This completes the proof. ■

An example of the nonexistence of an equilibrium

Assume that there are two discretionary liquidity traders A and B with var($\tilde{Y}^{\mathrm{A}}$) = 0.6 and var(Y^{R}) = 0.4. Assume that the cost of trader i observing the signal $\tilde{\delta}_{t+1}+\tilde{\varepsilon}_t^i$ in period t is 0.11 for all i and that var($\tilde{\varepsilon}_t^i$) $=\phi=10$, again for all i. Finally, assume that the variance of the nondiscretionary liquidity trading is 1. Is it an equilibrium for both discretionary liquidity traders to trade in the same period? If they do, the total variance of liquidity trading in that period will be 2, and in all other periods it will be 1. Table 19.A1 shows the profits earned by informed traders as a function of the number informed and of the variance of the liquidity trading. It also shows the value of λ in each case.

From the first two columns of the table it follows that in equilibrium there will be one informed trader in the market if $\Psi = 1$ and $c = 0.11$, and three informed traders when $\Psi = 2$. This creates a problem, since $\lambda(3,2) = 0.169 > \lambda(1,1) = 0.151$. Taking λ_t as given, neither of the two discretionary liquidity traders will

Table 19.A1 An example of the nonexistence of an equilibrium

n	$\pi(n,1)$	$\pi(n,2)$	$\pi(n,1.4)$	$\pi(n,1.6)$	$\lambda(n,1)$	$\lambda(n,2)$	$\lambda(n,1.4)$	$\lambda(n,1.6)$
1	0.151	0.213	0.178	0.191	0.151	0.107	0.127	0.119
2	0.102	0.144	0.121	0.129	0.204	0.144	0.172	0.161
3	0.080	0.113	0.094	0.101	0.239	0.169	0.202	0.189
4	0.066	0.094	0.078	0.084	0.265	0.188	0.224	0.210
5	0.057	0.081	0.067	0.072	0.285	0.202	0.241	0.226
6	0.050	0.071	0.059	0.063	0.301	0.213	0.254	0.238
7	0.045	0.063	0.053	0.057	0.313	0.222	0.265	0.248

For each number n of informed traders this table gives the profits $\pi(n,1)$ of each informed trader if no discretionary liquidity trader trades in that period, the profits $\pi(n,2)$ of each informed trader if both discretionary liquidity traders trade in that period, the profits $\pi(n,1.4)$ of each informed trader if only discretionary liquidity trader B trades in that period, and the profits $\pi(n,1.6)$ of each informed trader if only discretionary liquidity trader A trades in that period. Similarly, for each n and each of these four values of Ψ, the table gives the equilibrium value of λ_t, which measures the cost of liquidity trading under the assumed traders' composition.

be content to trade in the period that they are assumed to trade in. If each assumes that he can move to another period without affecting other traders' strategies, then each will want to move to one of the periods with $\lambda = 0.151$.

Having shown that it is not an equilibrium for both A and B to trade in the same period, we now show that it is also not an equilibrium for each discretionary liquidity trader to trade in a different period. From the third and fourth columns of the table it follows that if each discretionary liquidity trader trades in a different period, then there will be two informed traders in each period. However, in the period in which A trades, $\lambda = \lambda(2, 1.6) = 0.161$, while in the period in which B trades, $\lambda = \lambda(2, 1.4) = 0.172$. If B takes the strategies of all other traders and λ_t as given, he will want to trade in the period in which A is trading.

A statistical test of hypothesis 2

Note first that $Q_t = \text{var}\,[\hat{\delta}_{t+1} - E(\tilde{\delta}_{t+1}|\tilde{\omega}_t)] = \text{var}(\tilde{\delta}_{t+1} - \lambda_t\tilde{\omega}_t)$. Thus, hypothesis 2 is equivalent to the hypothesis that, if $t \in \text{H}$ and $t' \in \text{L}$, then

$$\text{var}(\tilde{\delta}_{t+1} - \lambda_t\tilde{\omega}_t) < \text{var}(\tilde{\delta}_{t'+1} - \lambda_{t'}\tilde{\omega}_{t'}). \tag{A15}$$

Since $\tilde{\delta}_t = \tilde{P}_{t+1} - \tilde{P}_t - \lambda_{t+1}\tilde{\omega}_{t+1} + \lambda_t\tilde{\omega}_t$, equation (A15) is equivalent to

$$\text{var}(\tilde{P}_{t+1} - \tilde{P}_t - \lambda_{t+1}\tilde{\omega}_{t+1}) < \text{var}(\tilde{P}_{t'+1} - \tilde{P}_{t'} - \lambda_{t'+1}\tilde{\omega}_{t'+1}). \tag{A16}$$

Denote the estimates of λ^{H} and λ^{L}, obtained by the regression described after hypothesis 1, by $\hat{\lambda}^{\text{H}}$ and $\hat{\lambda}^{\text{L}}$. Suppose that these are estimated out of sample. Also assume for simplicity that both $t+1$ and $t'+1$ are periods with low trading volume.[19] Then hypothesis 2 can be tested by comparing $\text{var}(\tilde{P}_{t+1} - \tilde{P}_t - \hat{\lambda}^{\text{L}}\tilde{\omega}_{t+1})$ with $\text{var}(\tilde{P}_{t'+1} - \tilde{P}_{t'} - \hat{\lambda}^{\text{L}}\tilde{\omega}_{t'+1})$. To see this, note that

$$\begin{aligned}\text{var}(\tilde{P}_{t+1} - \tilde{P}_t - \hat{\lambda}^{\text{L}}\tilde{\omega}_{t+1}) &= \text{var}(\tilde{P}_{t+1} - \tilde{P}_t - \lambda^{\text{L}}\tilde{\omega}_{t+1}) + \text{var}(\lambda^{\text{L}} - \hat{\lambda}^{\text{L}})\ \text{var}(\tilde{\omega}_{t+1}) \\ &\quad + 2\ \text{cov}\,[(\lambda^{\text{L}} - \hat{\lambda}^{\text{L}})\tilde{\omega}_{t+1}, \tilde{P}_{t+1} - \tilde{P}_t - \lambda^{\text{L}}\tilde{\omega}_{t+1}].\end{aligned} \tag{A17}$$

The covariance term is zero (since $\hat{\lambda}^{\text{L}}$ is estimated out of sample), and the second term on the right-hand side is the same whether the trading volume is high or low at time t, as long as the trading volume is low in period $t+1$. Thus equation (A16) can be tested by comparing $\text{var}(\tilde{P}_{t+1} - \tilde{P}_t - \hat{\lambda}^{\text{L}}\tilde{\omega}_{t+1})$ with $\text{var}(\tilde{P}_{t'+1} - \tilde{P}_{t'} - \hat{\lambda}^{\text{L}}\tilde{\omega}_{t'+1})$.

Notes

1 We have looked at data for companies in the Dow Jones 30, and the patterns are similar. The transaction data were obtained from Francis Emory Fitch Inc. We chose Exxon here since it is the most heavily traded stock in the sample.

2 Another paper which focuses on the strategic timing of trades and their effect on volume and price behavior is Foster and Viswanathan (1987). In contrast with our paper, however, their paper is mainly concerned with the timing of informed trading when information is long lived.

3 This assumption is reasonable since the span of time covered by the T periods in this model is to be taken as relatively short and since our main interests concern the volume of trading and the variability of prices. The nature of our results does not change if a positive discount rate is assumed.

4 In reality, of course, different traders may realize their liquidity demands at different times, and the time that can elapse before these demands must be satisfied may also be different for different traders. The nature of our results will not change if the model is complicated in order to capture this. See the discussion in section 5.1.

5 The model here can be viewed as the limit of a model with a finite number of market makers as the number of market makers grows to infinity. However, our results do not depend in any important way on the assumption of perfect competition among market makers. The same basic results would obtain in an analogous model with a finite number of market makers, where each market maker announces a (linear) pricing schedule as a function of his own order flow and traders can allocate their trade among different market makers. In such a model, market makers earn positive expected profits (see Kyle, 1984).

6 If the price were a function of individual orders, then anonymous traders could manipulate the price by submitting canceling orders. For example, a trader who wishes to purchase ten shares could submit a purchase order for 200 shares and a sell order for 190 shares. When the price is solely a function of the total order flow, such manipulations are not possible.

7 It is actually possible to think of the market maker as also a player in the game, whose payoff is minus the sum of the squared deviations of the prices from the true payoff.

8 More intuition for why λ_t is decreasing in n_t can be obtained from statistical inference. Recall that λ_t is the regression coefficient in the forecast of $\tilde{\delta}_{t+1}$, given the total order flow $\tilde{\omega}_t$. The order flow can be written as $a(\tilde{\delta}_{t+1}+\tilde{\varepsilon}_t)+\tilde{u}$, where $a(\tilde{\delta}_{t+1}+\tilde{\varepsilon}_t)$ represents the total trading position of the informed traders and $\tilde{u}$ is the position of the liquidity traders with $\text{var}(\tilde{u})=\Psi$. As the number of informed traders increases, a increases. For a given level of a, the market maker sets λ_t equal to $\lambda(a)=a/[a^2(1+\phi)+\Psi]$. This is an increasing function of a if and only if $a \leqslant [\Psi/(1+\phi)]^{1/2}$ which in this model occurs if and only if $n_t \leqslant 1$. We can think of the market maker's inference problem in two parts: first he uses $\tilde{\omega}_t$ to predict $a\tilde{\delta}_{t+1}$; then he scales this down by a factor of $1/a$ to obtain his prediction of $\tilde{\delta}_{t+1}$. The weight placed upon $\tilde{\omega}_t$ in predicting $a\tilde{\delta}_{t+1}$ is always increasing in a, but for a large enough value of a the scaling down by a factor of $1/a$ eventually dominates, lowering λ_t.

9 Interestingly, when $n_t=1$ the equilibrium is the same whether the informed trader takes λ_t as given or whether he takes into account the effect that his trading policy has on the market maker's determination of λ_t. In other words, in this model the Nash equilibrium in the game between the informed trader and the market maker is identical with the Stackelberg equilibrium in which the trader takes the market maker's response into account.

10 Our measure of volume is proportional to the actual expected volume if there is exactly one nondiscretionary liquidity trader; otherwise, the trading crossed between these traders will not be counted, and V_t^L will be lower than the true contribution of the liquidity traders. This presents no problem for our analysis, however, since the amount of this trading in any period is independent of the strategic behavior of the other traders.

11 Note that the amount of informed trading is independent of the precision of the signal that informed traders observe. This is due to the assumed risk neutrality of informed traders.

12 Note that we are assuming that the precision of the information, measured by the parameter $\phi=\text{var}(\tilde{\varepsilon}_t)$, together with the cost of becoming informed are constant over time. If the precision of the signal varied across periods, then there might also be a different cost to acquiring different signals. We would then need to specify a cost function for signals as a function of their precision.

13 In fact, the same equilibrium obtains if liquidity traders are assumed to respond to the entry of an informed trader, as will be clear below.

14 A comparative statics result analogous to part 3 is discussed by Kyle (1984).

15 Note that if indeed there is no trading by either the informed or the liquidity traders, then λ is undetermined if we interpret it as a regression coefficient in the regression of $\tilde{\delta}_{t+1}$ on $\tilde{\omega}_t^P$. However, with no liquidity trading the market maker must refuse to trade. This is equivalent to setting λ_t to infinity.

16 Note that in the model of section 4, where liquidity traders can allocate their trades, previous order flows must be included in the regression as well, since they (indirectly) provide relevant information in predicting $\tilde{\delta}_{t+1}$.

17 We have in fact searched over a number of possible candidates for (n_1, n_2, n_3) and have obtained the best fit with $(4, 1, 3)$.

18 It is straightforward to prove that the equilibrium among informed traders is always unique.

19 The case in which both are periods with high trading volume is completely analogous. Otherwise, the discussion can be modified in a straightforward manner.

References

Clark, P. K. (1973) "A Subordinated Stochastic Process Model with Finite Variance for Speculative Prices," *Econometrica*, 41, 135–55.

Foster, F. D. and Viswanathan, S. (1987) "Interday Variations in Volumes, Spreads and Variances: 1. Theory," *Working Paper 87-101*, The Fuqua School of Business, Duke University, October.

French, K. R. and Roll, R. (1986) "Stock Return Variances; the Arrival of Information and the Reaction of Traders," *Journal of Financial Economics*, 17, 5–26.

Glosten, L. R. and Milgrom, P. R. (1985) "Bid, Ask and Transaction Prices in a Specialist Market with Heterogeneously Informed Traders," *Journal of Financial Economics*, 14, 71–100.

Harris, L. (1986) "A Transaction Data Survey of Weekly and Intraday Patterns in Stock Returns," *Journal of Financial Economics*, 16, 99–117.

Jain, P. J. and Joh, G. (1986) "The Dependence Between Hourly Prices and Trading Volume," *Working Paper*, Wharton School, University of Pennsylvania.

Kyle, A. S. (1984) "Market Structure, Information, Futures Markets, and Price Formation." In *International Agricultural Trade: Advanced Readings in Price Formation, Market Structure, and Price Instability*, eds G. G. Storey, A. Schmitz, and A. H. Sarris (Boulder, CO, and London: Westview Press), pp. 45–64.

Kyle, A. S. (1985) "Continuous Auctions and Insider Trading," *Econometrica*, 53, 1315–35.

Marsh, T. A. and Rock, K. (1986) "The Transaction Process and Rational Stock Price Dynamics," *Working Paper*, University of California, Berkeley, CA.

Williams, J. (1987) "Financial Anomalies Under Rational Expectations: A Theory of the Annual Size and Related Effects," *Working Paper*, Graduate School of Business Administration, New York University.

Wood, R. A., McInish, T. H. and Ord, J. K. (1985) "An Investigation of Transaction Data for NYSE Stocks," *Journal of Finance*, 40, 723–41.

Chapter 20

B. Espen Eckbo

Background and Comments

Controlled experiments in corporate finance are rare. Financial economists must attempt to isolate the effects of variable X in real life, where there are always several other variables at work behind a screen of noise. When a clear fact emerges, there are usually several plausible competing explanations.

Turning to a fresh institutional setting often helps sort things out. The following paper by Espen Eckbo and Herwig Langohr provides a perfect example. The problem is to distinguish the effects on tender offers of (a) increased requirements for disclosure and (b) increases in the minimum tender offer period. The Williams Act changed (a) and (b) at the same time, and so it is difficult to separate their contributions to subsequent increases in offer premiums. However, in France, variable (a) *alone* was changed in 1970. Since offer premiums also increased in France after that change, the importance of disclosure requirements seems to be confirmed. Therefore our confidence in the importance of disclosure requirements in the United States is reinforced.

This illustrates one motive for the increasing pace of research on corporate finance outside the United States. The point of this research is not just to learn about other countries' systems; it also illuminates corporate behavior at home.

Author's Introduction

The paper reprinted here provides empirical estimates of the impact of (a) disclosure regulations and (b) the payment method on takeover premiums. The French institutional setting permits a first test of the proposition that increased requirements for information disclosure increase offer premiums when existing regulations already give potential rival bidders ample time to counterbid. The evidence strongly supports this proposition. The premium increase is shown to be driven by an increase in the total offer-induced revaluation of the target shares, with no change in the premium over the *post*-expiration target share price. The results also indicate that disclosure requirements deter public offers with below-average total gains, some of which turn to privately negotiated block trades which exempt the bidder from mandatory information disclosure.

With respect to the payment method, total offer premiums are shown to be significantly higher in all-cash than in all-stock offers, whether the offer is a minority buyout or transfers voting control. Further, a decomposition of the total offer premium shows that the impact of the payment method is again restricted to the total offer-induced revaluation of the target shares. This result fails to support traditional tax-based explanations for the impact of the payment method but is consistent with the proposition that successful bidders rationally anticipate a differential information effect of all-cash versus all-stock bids.

The possibility that information asymmetries determine the optimal payment method is explored further in Eckbo, Giammarino, and Heinkel (1990). Assuming that the bidder and target firms each have private information concerning the true values of their own securities, we identify a fully separating equilibrium where the true value of the bidder is revealed by the mix of cash and securities used as payment to the target. This theoretical result provides a possible justification for the existence of mixed offers. The model implies that the revealed bidder value is monotonically increasing and convex in the fraction of the total offer that consists of cash, a prediction which we examine using corporate acquisitions in Canada. In Canada mixed offers are relatively frequent and free of the tax-related options frequently characterizing mixed offers in the United States.

Some of the central effects of asymmetric information discussed in the above two papers also surface in the general context of corporate stock offerings. If the market cannot distinguish overvalued stocks from undervalued stocks *ex ante*, it anticipates adverse selection and possibly lowers the stock's secondary market price in response to the issue announcement. In Eckbo and Masulis (1989) we offer a "pecking order" hypothesis to explain how this adverse selection cost can influence the issuing firm's choice of equity flotation method. We then provide large-sample tests which help resolve the long-standing puzzle over US firms' reluctance to float new shares by means of subscription rights issued to current shareholders.

Finally, the time provided by the Batterymarch Fellowship was used to critically reexamine aspects of the "event study" methodology underlying much empirical research in corporate finance. In particular, Eckbo, Maksimovic, and Williams (1990) show that standard generalized least squares estimates of coefficients in cross-sectional regressions with announcement-induced abnormal stock returns as dependent variable are inconsistent. These estimates do not correctly reflect the distributional implication of the market's knowledge that managers initiate corporate events based on private information. We provide a consistent estimator and demonstrate using a sample of corporate takeover events that use of the proposed estimator substantially affects the empirical conclusions.

References

Eckbo, B. E., Giammarino, R. and Heinkel, R. (1990) "Asymmetric Information and the Medium of Exchange in Takeovers: Theory and Tests," *Review of Financial Studies*, 3: 4.

Eckbo, B. E., Maksimovic, V. and Williams, J. (1990) "Consistent Estimation of Cross-Sectional Models in Event Studies," *Review of Financial Studies*, 3: 3, 343–65.

Eckbo, B. E. and Masulis, R. W. (1989) "Adverse Selection and the Rights Issue," Unpublished Paper, University of British Columbia.

Bibliographical Listing

"Valuation Effects of Greenmail Prohibitions," *Journal of Financial and Quantitative Analysis*, forthcoming.

"Asymmetric Information and the Medium of Exchange in Takeovers: Theory and Tests" (with Ronald M. Giammarino and R. Heinkel), *Review of Financial Studies*, 3: 4, 1990.

"Competition and Wealth Effects of Horizontal Mergers." In *The Law and Economics of*

Competition Policy, eds F. Mathewson, M. Trebilcock and M. Walker (The Fraser Institute, 1990), ch. 9, pp. 297–332.

"Consistent Estimation of Cross-Sectional Models in Event Studies" (with Vojislav Maksimovic and Joseph Williams), *Review of Financial Studies*, 3: 3, 1990, 343–65.

"Adverse Selection and the Rights Issue" (with R. Masulis), Unpublished Paper, University of British Columbia, 1989.

"The Role of Stock Market Studies in Formulating Antitrust Policy Towards Horizontal Mergers: Comment," *Quarterly Journal of Business and Economics*, 28: 4, 1989, 22–38.

"F.I.R.A. and the Profitability of Foreign Acquisitions in Canada," Unpublished Paper, University of British Columbia, 1988.

"Gains to Acquiring Firms: Econometric Issues and US–Canadian Evidence," Unpublished Paper, University of British Columbia, 1988.

"The Market for Corporate Control: Policy Issues and Capital Market Evidence." In *Mergers, Corporate Concentration and Corporate Power in Canada*, eds R. S. Khemani, D. Shapiro and W. T. Stanbury (Halifax, Nova Scotia: The Institute for Research on Public Policy, 1988), ch. 7, pp. 143–225.

Information Disclosure, Method of Payment, and Takeover Premiums

Public and Private Tender Offers in France

B. ESPEN ECKBO and HERWIG LANGOHR

1 Introduction

The expected return from acquisition activity depends on whether the bidder's initial information advantage can be maintained throughout the bidding process. If the resources needed to generate takeover gains are available to potential rival bidders, the information in the initial bid will stimulate competition for the target shares, increasing the price necessary for success. This possibility underlies the concern that disclosure regulations deter acquisition activity, potentially undermining the efficiency of the corporate sector.[1] In the first part of this study, we provide new empirical evidence on the effect of disclosure rules on offer premiums and abnormal stock returns based on cash tender offers for control of publicly traded target firms in France.

Rational bidders, facing the risk that information in the initial offer will stimulate competing bids, may react by implementing offer strategies designed to protect their information advantage. Such strategies may involve attempting to acquire a foothold in the target before launching the takeover, negotiating with target management, presenting a two-tiered offer designed to overcome free-rider problems when the target is widely held (Grossman and Hart, 1980a; Comment and Jarrell, 1987) and, of

Reproduced from *Journal of Financial Economics*, 24: 2, October 1989, 363–403.

Professor Herwig Langohr is at INSEAD, France. We are grateful for the comments and suggestions made by Nathalie Dierkens, Pierre Hillion, Bruno Husson, Ronald Masulis, John McConnell, seminar participants at INSEAD, the University of Alberta, UCLA, the University of British Columbia, the University of Oregon, the University of Southern California, the American, European, and French Finance Association meetings, and, in particular, Michael Jensen and Richard Ruback (the editors) and the referee, Wayne Mikkelson. We thank the French stockbroker association (CAC), Slimane Echihab, and Martine Delcour for assistance in collecting the data. Financial support from INSEAD and the Ministry of Finance and Corporate Relations of the Province of British Columbia is also gratefully acknowledged.

particular interest in this paper, selecting a particular payment method (cash and/or securities in the bidder firm). There is theoretical support for the proposition that the means of payment can play a strategic role in deterring competition and signal the true value of the bidder firm under asymmetric information (Hansen, 1987; Fishman, 1989; Eckbo, Giammarino, and Heinkel, 1990).[2] Evidence is also growing that both the level and division of takeover gains are systematically related to the payment method (Wansley, Lane, and Yang, 1983; Huang and Walkling, 1987; Travlos, 1987; Asquith, Bruner, and Mullins, 1988; Eckbo, 1988; Franks, Harris, and Mayer, 1988; Eckbo, Giammarino, and Heinkel, 1990). In the second part of this paper, we provide new empirical tests of the impact of the payment method on offer premiums and abnormal stock returns in both tender offers for control and minority buyouts.

In their study of the impact of disclosure rules on takeover bids, Jarrell and Bradley (1980) find that the average premium over the pre-offer price in cash tender offers increased from 32 percent to nearly 53 percent after the passage of the US Williams Act in July 1968.[3] Schipper and Thompson (1983) report that a sample of frequent acquirers on average earned significantly negative abnormal returns over the months surrounding announcements related to the introduction of the Williams Act. This is consistent with market expectations that the Williams Act would be costly for bidder firms, which is also the conclusion of Jarrell and Bradley (1980). Asquith, Bruner, and Mullins (1983) and Bradley, Desai, and Kim (1988) report significantly lower average abnormal returns to bidder firms after 1968, which further supports the proposition that the Williams Act has increased competition among bidders.[4]

The studies above do not show that the disclosure provisions of the Williams Act are the only – or the most important – factor explaining this evidence. The Williams Act also increased the minimum tender offer period from zero to 10 days, in itself an economically important change. A substantial delay in the execution of the tender offer gives potential rival bidders valuable time to collect the information needed to construct competing offers. Thus the delay requirements permit production of information that may generate higher valued bids during the auction for the target shares.[5] An analogous argument is made by Jarrell (1985), who reports that delaying the execution of a tender offer by suing the bidder on average substantially increases the final offer price received by successful targets.

Disclosure regulations similar to those in the Williams Act were introduced in France in 1970. However, these regulations left unchanged a 4 week minimum tender offer period in effect since 1966. Thus our French institutional setting permits tests of the proposition that disclosure regulations increase offer premiums when existing regulations already give potential rival bidders ample time to counterbid. In our sample of successful cash tender offers for control, we document a statistically significant increase in the average offer premium over the pre-offer target share price after 1970, from 34 to 73 percent. We also present evidence on the two components of this premium: the offer-induced revaluation of the target shares and the premium over the post-expiration price, reflecting the value of the option to tender. Empirically, the increase in the premium over the pre-offer price is driven entirely by the offer-induced revaluation of the target shares; there is no evidence of a change in the value of the option to tender.

An increase in the cost of public tender offers (due to disclosure regulations) causes bidders to substitute toward privately negotiated block trades if the voting power in the target is such that a single block trade can transfer control. Apparently, there was an increase in the number of such private tender offers in France after 1970, prompting their regulation in 1973. Since then, privately negotiated controlling-block trades must be followed by a mandatory 15 day offer for the remaining (any or all) target shares at the block price. However, the bidder in a private tender offer is exempted from the disclosure regulations governing the public tender offer procedure. On this basis it is interesting to find that the average offer premium in control-oriented cash takeover bids in the post-1970 period is significantly higher in public than in private tender offers (73 versus 27 percent).

Bidder abnormal returns are on average indistinguishable from zero both before and after 1970. Since the average gains to targets are significantly higher after 1970, this suggests that total takeover gains are larger after the regulatory change. This outcome is consistent with the argument that disclosure regulations have deterred offers that, on average, produce lower total gains than offers that survive mandatory information disclosure.[6]

In examining the impact of the payment method, we argue that any compensation for the realization of a personal capital gains tax liability should be reflected in the value of the option to tender, while the information effect of the payment method will cause an offer-induced revaluation of the target shares. In a sample of public tender offers for voting control after 1970, we find that the offer-induced revaluation is significantly higher when the payment is all cash than when it is all stock in the bidder firm. The average premium over the post-expiration target share price, however, is indistinguishable across the two payment methods, a result that fails to support the hypothesis that all-cash offers compensate for a relative personal tax disadvantage. Bidder firm abnormal returns are on average indistinguishable from zero in both all-cash and all-stock offers. This result is similar to recent evidence on takeover bids in

Canada (Eckbo, 1988) and the United Kingdom (Franks, Harris, and Mayer, 1988), but it contrasts with the significantly negative average market reaction reported for all-stock mergers in the United States (Travlos, 1987; Asquith, Bruner, and Mullins, 1988).

Through a sample of minority buyouts, we also examine whether the superior performance by targets in all-cash offers is limited to transactions involving transfer of control. The bidders in our minority buyouts all control enough of the target voting shares (on average 80 percent) to put in place the preferred production/investment policy without the formal consent of minority shareholders. Interestingly, we find that the average offer-induced revaluation in minority buyouts shows the same systematic dependence on the payment method that we observe for control-oriented takeover bids.

The rest of the paper is organized as follows. In section 2 we summarize the institutional characteristics of public and private tender offers for publicly traded target firms in France. Sample characteristics and estimation procedures are detailed in section 3. In section 4 we present average abnormal returns based on the total samples of successful and unsuccessful public tender offers for control, private tender offers, and minority buyouts, thus providing a perspective on the overall valuation effects of French tender offers. The effect of disclosure regulations on tender offer premiums in cash offers for control is presented in section 5. The effect of the payment method on offer premiums is estimated in section 6. Section 7 concludes the paper.

2 Tender Offers in France: Institutional Characteristics

The French stock market is an auction market operating under the general rule that all trades must be executed through a broker at the final auction (floor) price.[7] Before 1966, the rule made no exception for public takeover bids, preventing tender offers at a premium over the market price, with the predictable result that no such bids took place.[8] To encourage public tender offers, the French Minister of Economics and Finance and the French Stock Brokers' Association (Compagnie des Agents de Change (CAC)) established in 1966 a procedure under which cash tender offers for control, conditional on prior authorization by the CAC, can be executed off the exchange floor with the CAC acting as an auctioneer.[9] The CAC determines control as a *de facto* situation, unless control is explicitly defined under French corporate law.[10]

The CAC can reject the bidder's application to use the tender offer procedure if it views the offer price and the number of target shares sought as unreasonable.[11] The offer starts when the CAC announces its terms.

During the offer period, which is required to be at least 4 weeks, the CAC monitors the auction. Shareholders can transmit sell orders to financial intermediaries until the offer expiration date. After this date, the CAC collects the sell orders and corresponding share certificates from brokers and counts the total number of shares tendered. After the final count is reached, the CAC publicly announces the offer outcome. In more than 90 percent of the tender offers in our sample, the announcement came 2 weeks after the expiration-day week. The time between the expiration date and the CAC's announcement is sometimes used to solicit additional target shares if the initial response is unsatisfactory.

The bidder is allowed to increase the offer price once by at least 5 percent during the first 20 days of the offer period (all tendered shares automatically participate in the price increase) but it is not allowed to extend the offer expiration date, which is announced by the CAC at the beginning of the offer period. Rival bids exceeding the initial offer price by at least 5 percent are permitted during the offer period, in which case all prior sell orders are cancelled and the initial bidder is allowed to respond.[12] Rules introduced in 1978 prohibit a bidder from making another public offer to acquire additional target shares during the 12 months immediately following expiration of the initial offer period.

In 1970 the public tender offer procedure was made available for control-oriented security exchange offers in which the bidder pays target shareholders in stocks and/or bonds, and for complete minority buyouts in which the bidder's prior holdings in the target are at least 50 percent. Further, to increase the costs of speculating on the outcome of the offer, regulations introduced in 1970 require that the CAC be informed daily of insider or principal shareholder trades in the bidder and target securities during the offer period. While the offer is outstanding, margin requirements for target share trades are raised to 100 percent, private trades in the target shares are prohibited, and target share forward and options transactions are suspended.[13]

The 1970 regulations also impose substantial disclosure requirements on both bidder and target firms. For the first time, the two firms must disclose "all important facts" for target shareholders to make "informed decisions," including the bidder's prior ownership in the target, the rationale behind (and financing of) the offer, shareholdings of members of the target's board of directors, and the target board's evaluation of the offer. Additional relatively minor disclosure requirements were subsequently introduced in 1973 and 1978. As of 1973, bidders are required to disclose a detailed justification for the offer price or exchange ratio as well as the ownership structure, research policy, business policy orientation, production/investment strategy, and forecast end of year sales and earnings for every firm represented by a security given to the target firm in an exchange offer. The target firm must disclose similar information about itself. As of 1978, the bidder firm must also disclose the identity of any shareholder owning more than 5 percent of its common stock and a detailed description of its subsidiaries' business activities. The target board must disclose its vote structure concerning the tender offer, and target board members who are also shareholders must disclose their intended reponse to the offer.

In 1973 a rule was implemented that effectively converts a successful private tender offer involving a controlling block of shares into a public tender offer for 100 percent of the target's shares. According to this new regulation, the size of the block, the block price, and the identity of the buyer and seller must be publicly disclosed on the same day that the block trade is executed. Further, during the 15 days following the block trade, the buyer must be prepared to accept all additional shares tendered to him at the block trade price. The parties involved in the controlling-block trade are otherwise exempt from the disclosure requirements governing public tender offers.

Between 1970 and 1978 the public tender offer procedure was gradually made available to a broader spectrum of acquisitions. For example, in 1972 a "simplified" procedure that has fewer disclosure requirements than the regular tender offer procedure was introduced to complete buyouts of relatively small minority shareholdings. Further, the CAC does not centralize the sell orders or declare the outcome of the offer. The minimum offer period is 20 trading days and no competing bids or changes in the initial bid are allowed while the offer is outstanding.[14] As of 1973, it is also possible to use the public tender offer procedure to become a minority holder in the target firm, provided that the minority holding is at least 15 percent. In 1975 the public tender offer procedure was made available to bidders who own a majority of the target's shares and who seek to reinforce the majority position by acquiring an additional 15 percent (but not all) of the shares.[15]

3 Data and Estimation Procedures

3.1 Sample characteristics

Our sample period starts with the first cash public tender offers for control of a French target firm in 1966 and ends in 1982. Information on control-oriented security exchange offers as well as minority buyouts became publicly available with the regulatory reform in 1970, and data on private tender offers became available just prior to their regulation in 1973. A total of 306 public and private tender offers for voting control and minority buyouts took place over the sample period 1966–82.[16] The population of

306 assumes that an offer that has successive price increases by the initial bidder, or that receives competing bids, is counted as one offer only. During the period 1966–82 tender offers were only rarely contested: in our database there are less than ten contests with multiple bidders, and none in which the target management openly resisted the takeover bid. Of the 306 takeover bids, 256 offers qualify for inclusion in our database. Seven offers are excluded because of missing information on one or more offer parameters, which include the offer price and the numbers of target shares held, sought, tendered, and purchased,[17] 27 cases are excluded as a result of our minimum restriction on the availability of stock prices necessary to estimate abnormal stock returns, and 16 offers are excluded because we lack information on the payment method in the transaction.

Table 20.1 lists the annual distribution of the sample of exchange-listed bidder and target firms, classified by the type of offer. The target firms (which are all publicly traded) are listed on the Paris Stock Exchange in 211 of the 256 cases; the remaining targets are listed on the Lyons Exchange, the Marseilles Exchange, or the Lille Exchange. Of the 256 bidders, 139, representing 100 firms, are listed at the time of the offer.[18]

Of the 119 public tender offers for voting control, 70 are all cash and 49 are securities exchange offers. Of the 44 minority buyouts, in which the bidder's prior holding in the target exceeds 66 percent, 29 are all cash.[19] The 93 private tender offers for voting control are all-cash offers. Thus, of the 256 offers in the database, 192 are all-cash offers and in the remaining 64 cases the bidders offer to exchange securities (stocks and/or bonds) in their own firms for the target shares.[20]

We define a "successful" offer as one in which the bidder (a) purchases at least the minimum of target shares sought or (b) if no minimum was specified, purchases at least 50 percent of the maximum number of target shares sought. Although condition (b) is somewhat arbitrary, it is not restrictive, as the percentage of the target shares actually purchased in unsuccessful offers is small in comparison with the percentage purchased in successful offers (on average 12 versus 60 percent in public offers for control). With this definition, 29 of the 256 offers in the database, all control-oriented public tender offers, are unsuccessful. Since our sample contains nearly the entire population, a reasonable estimate of the *ex post* success rate is therefore 76 percent (90 of 119) for control-oriented public tender offers over the period 1966–82. All the private tender offers are necessarily classified as successful, since only those transactions that actually took place appear in our data sources. Further, table 20.1 overstates the success rate for the minority buyouts, since our sample selection criteria eliminated seven buyouts that would have been classified as unsuccessful under the definition above.

Table 20.2 shows the average values of the total equity of the bidder and

Table 20.1 Annual distribution of public and private tender offers for control and of minority buyouts for the total sample of 256 publicly traded French target firms in the period 1966–1982

Year of offer	*212 offers for control*[a]					*44 minority buyouts,*[b] *all public, all successful*	
	119 public offers				*93 private offers, all successful*[c]		
	90 successful[c]		*29 unsuccessful*				
	Cash	*Securities*[d]	*Cash*	*Securities*[d]	*Cash*	*Cash*	*Securities*[d]
1966	1	0	1	0	0	0	0
1967	3	0	4	0	0	0	0
1968	5	0	4	0	0	0	0
1969	4	0	2	0	0	0	0
1970	1	7	2	0	0	3	0
1971	1	2	0	0	0	2	3
1972	6	2	1	2	3	4	0
1973	3	9	0	1	8	1	0
1974	4	4	0	0	7	2	2
1975	4	3	1	2	7	4	1
1976	4	4	0	0	9	1	2
1977	3	5	2	1	9	4	2
1978	2	2	0	0	9	1	3
1979	4	0	2	0	9	2	0
1980	0	2	4	0	12	1	1
1981	2	0	0	0	9	3	1
1982	0	3	0	0	11	1	0
1966–82	47	43	23	6	93	29	15

The sample is classified by the outcome of the transaction and by the method of payment (cash versus securities in the bidder firm).

[a]An offer to transfer control is one in which the bidder owns less than 67 percent (voting control) of the target shares before the offer and seeks to acquire voting control.

[b]In a minority buyout the bidder seeks 100 percent of the target and owns 67 percent or more of the target before the offer.

[c]A "successful" offer is one in which the bidder firm purchases at least the minimum number of shares specified as a condition for buying any shares at all. If no minimum is specified, an offer is "successful" if the bidder purchases at least 50 percent of the maximum number of shares sought. For the private tender offers, we count the block traded as the minimum number of target shares sought by the bidder firm. Thus all the private offers are by definition successful.

[d]In a securities offer the bidder pays for the target shares using one or more types of securities (possibly in combination with a cash payment). Of the 64 securities offers in the total sample, 49 involve exchanging bidder shares for the target shares, while in 15 cases the bidder offers to exchange straight or convertible bonds. In 11 of the 64 securities offers the payment is a mix of cash and securities. All the private tender offers are cash offers.

Table 20.2 Average market value of total equity 8 weeks before the tender offer announcement, the percentage of the target shares held by the bidder before the offer, the percentage tendered, and the percentage purchased for the total sample of 227 successful public and private tender offers for publicly traded French target firms, 1966–1982

	90 successful public offers for control[a]				*Private offers*	*44 minority buyouts*		
	All–cash offers 1/66–12/69 (N = 13)	*All–cash offers 1/70–12/82 (N = 34)*	*Common-stock offers*[b] *1/70–12/82 (N = 31)*	*Bond offers*[c] *1/72–12/82 (N = 12)*	*All-cash for control 1/72–12/82 (N = 93)*	*All-cash offers 1/70–12/82 (N = 29)*	*Common-stock offers 1/70–12/82 (N = 12)*	*Bond offers 1/70–12/82 (N = 3)*
A *Market value of total equity of publicly traded bidder and targets (million francs)*[d]								
Target firms	39.7	48.1	130.0	445.7	115.5	99.7	123.1	252.0
Listed bidder firms	490.7	1413.6	595.1	1869.2	1870.0	9413.3	1146.1	n.a.[e]
	(N = 7)	(N = 12)	(N = 26)	(N = 7)	(N = 45)	(N = 15)	(N = 9)	
Bidder/target	12.3	29.4	4.6	4.2	16.2	94.4	9.3	n.a.[e]
	(N = 7)	(N = 12)	(N = 26)	(N = 7)	(N = 45)	(N = 15)	(N = 9)	
B *Percentage of target shares held, tendered, and purchased*								
Percentage held	14.0	23.0	21.2	16.4	12.6	79.5	78.4	70.1
Percentage tendered	57.9	66.1	71.2	66.4	59.0	16.4	24.5	24.1
Percentage purchased	56.1	59.0	67.2	59.0	59.0	16.4	20.9	24.1
Purchased/tendered	0.97	0.89	0.94	0.89	1.00	1.00	0.85	1.00

[a]In the sample of 29 unsuccessful public offers for control (Jan 1966 to Dec 1982) the average equity values of the bidder and target firms are 930.1 million francs and 173.0 million francs, with a ratio of bidder-to-target value of 5.4, where 18 of the 29 bidders are publicly traded firms. Furthermore, for this category of offers, the average percentage of the target shares held before the offer is 10.5, the percentage tendered is 13.5, and the percentage purchased is 11.3 respectively. The average maximum percentage of the target shares sought by the bidder in these unsuccessful offers is 84.1.

[b]In five of the 31 stock offers, the total compensation also involves a small cash component.

[c]In four of the 12 bond offers, the total compensation also involves a small cash component.

[d]Number of publicly traded bidders in parentheses.

[e]None of the three bidders are publicly traded firms; thus the information is not available.

target firms, the percentage of the target shares held by the bidder before the offer, and the percentage tendered and purchased for eight subsamples of the total database. The ratio of the average bidder to target equity value is higher after January 1970 and generally higher in cash offers than in securities exchange offers. The average percentage of the target shares held by the bidder before the tender offer rises from 14 percent before January 1970 to 23 percent afterward. On average, the bidder ends up holding more than 70 percent of the target shares in all categories involving tender offers for control. The oversubscription in public offers is generally small, with an average of 80 percent or more of the tendered shares purchased. The typical offer attracts less than 100 percent of the target shares, even when the bidder is prepared to purchase any or all of the outstanding target shares, as, for example, in private tender offers during the mandatory 15 day offer period following the controlling-block trade.

3.2 *Estimation of offer premiums and abnormal stock returns*

Information on stock prices, dividends, and other distributions needed to compute offer premiums and security returns are not readily available in France and were collected from several sources.[21] For every offer in the sample, we recorded weekly (Friday to Friday) prices from week −53 relative to the week that the offer was made through week 52 relative to the week of expiration of the offer, that is, roughly 1 year of weekly data on either side of the total offer period. Adjustments were made in the returns for cash dividends as of the ex-dividend week and for splits and rights issues.[22]

Define P as the offer price and P_h as the market price of the target shares before any information about the tender offer is revealed to the market. We refer to $P - P_h$ as the "premium over the pre-offer price." This total premium can be written as the sum of two components:

$$P - P_h = (P - P_e) + (P_e - P_h) \tag{1}$$

where P_e is the post-expiration target share price. We refer to $P - P_e$ as the "premium over the post-expiration price," and $P_e - P_h$ as the "total offer-induced revaluation." In France, all oversubscribed offers must be executed *pro rata*, and so the before-tax value to tendering target shareholders of the premium over the post-expiration price is $\alpha(P - P_e)$, where $0 \leqslant \alpha \leqslant 1$ is the expected fraction of the tendered shares that the bidder will purchase. We refer to $\alpha(P - P_e)$ as the (*ex post*) "value of the option to tender."

A cash bid states the franc value of the offer price, while we use an estimate of the market value of securities that the bidder offers in exchange for the target shares.[23] Define week a as the week of the offer announcement and week e as the offer expiration week. Our event window runs from week $a-8$ through week $e+8$, which, given the minimum 4 week offer period in public tender offers, typically spans a period of 5 months.[24] The price P_{a-8} at the beginning of this event period is used as a proxy for P_{h}. The end price P_{e+8} is sufficiently removed from the offer expiration to qualify as a post-expiration price. The ratio of the number N_{p} of shares purchased to the number of shares tendered is used as a proxy for the value of α.[25]

The total offer-induced target revaluation is measured either as the relative price change $(P_{e+8} - P_{a-8})/P_{a-8}$ over the event window or as the market-adjusted abnormal stock return (including dividends) over the same period. Abnormal return estimates are based on return observations from week $a-52$ through week $e+52$ and the following market model:

$$r_{jt} = \alpha_j + \alpha_j' d_{jt} + \beta_j r_{\mathrm{m}t} + \beta_j' r_{\mathrm{m}t} d_{jt} + \sum_{n=1}^{6} \gamma_{jn} d_{nt} + \varepsilon_{jt}, \qquad t = a-52, \ldots, e+52, \tag{2}$$

where r_{jt} is the continuously compounded rate of return to firm j over week t, $r_{\mathrm{m}t}$ is the continuously compounded rate of return to the value-weighted market portfolio over week t, d_{jt} is a binary variable that takes a value of unity in the estimation period after the offer expiration week and zero otherwise, d_{nt} is a binary variable that takes a value of unity if t is in event period n (defined below) and zero otherwise, and ε_{jt} is a zero-mean distribution term assumed to be normally, identically, and independently distributed.

The coefficients α_j' and β_j' are estimated to control for a possible post-offer change in the firm's expected return if and only if the firm has at least ten return observations in the estimation period after the event period. While no adjustment is made for missing return observations in the estimation period outside the total event window $[a-8, e+8]$, missing price observations inside the event window are replaced assuming an abnormal return of zero. The substitution is based on parameter values of α_j and β_j estimated using observations in the pre-event period $[a-53, a-9]$ only. This return substitution allows estimation of the total abnormal return over the event period $[a-8, e+8]$. The CAC typically suspends trading in the bidder and target shares during the announcement week. Since we replace the resulting missing price observation with an estimate assuming zero abnormal return, most of the announcement effect shows up in week $a+1$, the first week of trading after the announcement.[26]

The event parameter γ_{jn} $(n = 1, \ldots, 6)$, multiplied by the number w_n of weeks in the event period, is the abnormal stock return to firm j over event period n. The six event subperiods are nonoverlapping and cover the total event window $[a-8, e+8]$. The first event subperiod is $[a-8, a-1]$, that is, γ_{j1} captures pre-offer leakage of information and, in general, any nonzero stock price performance before the offer. The second and third subperiods are week a and week $a+1$, capturing the announcement effect of the offer. The fourth and fifth subperiods cover the interim offer period $[a+2, e-1]$, and the week that the offer expires and the following week $[e, e+1]$. The sixth subperiod covers the 7 week period $[e+2, e+8]$ following expiration of the offer.[27] Finally, the abnormal return over the total event window $[a-8, e+8]$, computed as $\Sigma_{n=1}^{6} w_n\gamma_{jn}$, is our market-adjusted measure of the total offer-induced target revaluation.

In a sample of N firms, the equally weighted cross-sectional average abnormal return for the nth event period is computed as

$$\mathrm{AAR}_n = \frac{w_n}{N} \sum_{j}^{N} \gamma_{jn}. \tag{3}$$

AAR_n represents the average continuously compounded return from a strategy of investing an equal dollar amount in each of the N securities at the beginning of event period n with no further rebalancing over the event period (a buy and hold strategy). Under the null hypothesis of zero abnormal return, and presuming that the N events are independent, it follows that

$$z_n = \frac{1}{N^{1/2}} \sum_{j=1}^{N} \frac{\gamma_{jn}}{\sigma_{\gamma_{jn}}} \sim \mathrm{N}(0, 1), \tag{4}$$

where $\sigma_{\gamma_{jn}}$ is the standard deviation of γ_{jn}. When the true values of γ_{jn} and $\sigma_{\gamma_{jn}}$ are replaced with their ordinary least squares (OLS) estimates, this z statistic is approximately standard normal for large N.[28]

4 Abnormal Returns: Total Sample Results

Tables 20.3 and 20.4 report average abnormal stock returns in French takeover bids without specific reference to disclosure regulations or the payment method. The two tables partition the total database into successful and unsuccessful public tender offers for control, private tender offers for control, and minority buyouts. First, targets of successful and unsuccessful tender offers realize similar significant gains over the event window (13.5 versus 12.4 percent). Using US data, Bradley, Desai, and Kim (1983) show that initial offer-induced gains to targets in unsuccessful tender offers are reversed on average unless a subsequent bidder wins control within 2 years of the initial bid. We are unable to repeat this test, because none of the 29 unsuccessful targets in our sample received subsequent offers. Of course, if the low *ex post* frequency of repeat offers

Table 20.3 Percentage average abnormal return for 256 French target firms in the period 1966–1982

Event period[a]	*Successful public tender offers for control (N = 90)*	*Unsuccessful public tender offers for control (N = 29)*	*Successful private tender offers for control (N = 93)*	*Successful public tender offers, minority buyouts (N = 44)*
$n = 1$: pre-offer period	2.96	1.70	3:32	3.13
$[a-8, a-1]$	(1.26, 61.4)	(0.71, 62.1)	(2.00, 53.8)	(1.23, 54.5)
$n = 2$: offer announcement[b]	0.77	0.33	3.46	0.14
$[a, a]$	(2.11, 44.3)	(0.28, 41.4)	(8.83, 54.8)	(0.25, 50.0)
$n = 3$: offer announcement + 1[b]	16.48	15.68	9.47	22.26
$[a+1, a+1]$	(37.57, 72.7)	(18.10, 72.4)	(22.28, 60.2)	(34.18, 79.5)
$n = 4$: interim period	2.26	1.75	−1.21	1.33
$[a+2, e-1]$	(0.87, 47.7)	(−0.08, 55.2)	(−0.96, 33.3)	(1.05, 61.4)
$n = 5$: offer expiration	−2.55	−2.34	−2.65	−0.20
$[e, e+1]$	(−5.23, 36.4)	(−2.33, 37.9)	(−4.90, 22.6)	(−0.08, 43.2)
$n = 6$: post-expiration period	−6.37	−4.75	−3.87	−3.50
$[e+2, e+8]$	(−2.99, 40.9)	(−1.77, 41.4)	(−2.58, 46.2)	(−0.84, 36.4)
Total event period	13.54	12.36	8.53	23.16
$[a-8, e+8]$	(5.13, 65.9)	(2.64, 62.1)	(4.31, 54.8)	(6.47, 79.6)

Abnormal return for firm j over event period n is based on the OLS estimates of the coefficients γ_{jn} $(n = 1, \ldots, 6)$ in the following market model:

$$r_{jt} = \alpha_j + \alpha_j' d_t + \beta_j r_{mt} + \beta_j' r_{mt} d_t + \sum_{n=1}^{6} \gamma_{jn} d_{nt} + \varepsilon_{jt}, \qquad t = a - 52, \ldots, e + 52,$$

where r_{jt} and r_{mt} are the continuously compounded weekly rates of return to firm j and the value-weighted market index, d_t is a dummy variable that takes on a value of unity in the estimation period after the expiration of the offer and zero otherwise, and the six dummy variables d_{nt} take a value of unity in each of six nonoverlapping event periods defined in relation to the offer announcement (week a) and offer expiration (week e), and zero otherwise. The z value and the percentage of the sample with positive abnormal return are given in parentheses.

a, offer announcement week; e, offer expiration week.

[a]Missing returns in the total event period (week $a-8$ through week $e+8$) are replaced assuming zero abnormal performance based on estimates of α and β from the period week $a-52$ through week $a-9$ relative to the offer announcement. Since γ_{jn} represents the weekly abnormal return over event period n, the firm's total abnormal return is found by multiplying γ_{jn} by the number of weeks in period n. The number of weeks is identical across firms except in the interim period (event period $n = 4$). Ninety percent of the public offers for control have a 4 week offer period (which is the mandatory minimum), while the average offer period is 4.3 for this sample. The private tender offers have a minimum 15 day (2 week) offer period, and the average offer period in this sample is 2.2 weeks.

[b]The stock exchange commission typically suspends trading in the bidder and target shares in the week of the offer announcement. Since we replace the resulting missing price observation assuming an abnormal return of zero, the announcement effect almost uniformly shows up in week $a+1$, the first week of trading after the announcement. For all cases in our database, a trading price is available in week $a+1$.

Table 20.4 Percentage average abnormal return for 139 French bidder firms in the period 1966–1982

Event period[a]	*Successful public tender offers for control (N = 52)*	*Unsuccessful public tender offers for control (N = 18)*	*Successful private tender offers for control (N = 45)*	*Successful public tender offers, minority buyouts (N = 24)*
$n = 1$: pre-offer period	−0.73	2.92	−2.15	−0.89
$[a-8,\ a-1]$	(0.27, 56.6)	(1.26, 50.0)	(−0.93, 44.4)	(−0.30, 48.0)
$n = 2$: offer announcement[b]	0.16	0.87	0.82	−0.54
$[a, a]$	(0.04, 52.8)	(1.07, 62.5)	(1.52, 55.6)	(−0.52, 44.0)
$n = 3$: offer announcement + 1[b]	−0.29	1.08	0.14	−0.96
$[a+1, a+1]$	(0.18, 47.2)	(1.53, 37.5)	(0.40, 46.7)	(−1.13, 36.0)
$n = 4$: interim period	−1.23	−5.06	1.57	−2.40
$[a+2, e-1]$	(−1.25, 49.1)	(−2.05, 37.5)	(1.73, 57.8)	(−1.24, 52.0)
$n = 5$: offer expiration	−0.37	−0.75	0.94	1.66
$[e, e+1]$	(−0.87, 39.6)	(−1.11, 37.5)	(1.50, 55.6)	(1.54, 44.0)
$n = 6$: post-expiration period	−0.75	0.13	−0.42	−1.45
$[e+2, e+8]$	(−0.53, 43.4)	(0.22, 50.0)	(−0.60, 42.2)	(−1.15, 44.0)
Total event period	−3.21	−0.82	0.90	−4.58
$[a-8, e+8]$	(−0.79, 35.8)	(0.35, 50.0)	(0.19, 53.3)	(−1.32, 36.0)

See footnotes to table 20.3.

is equated with the market's expectations *ex ante*, it also follows that the gains to unsuccessful targets shown in table 20.3 are unrelated to anticipations of a change in control through a future takeover bid. If so, the gains could represent an information effect (causing the revaluation of previously undervalued resources) or gains from anticipated changes in target management following the unsuccessful takeover bid.

Second, in the vernacular of Bradley (1980), the evidence in table 20.3 does not support the "corporate raiding" argument that holds that the average successful bidder is expected to transfer wealth from *ex post* minority shareholders. In contrast, the evidence shows that target shareholders earn significantly positive abnormal returns from successful control-oriented offers – both public and private – and from minority buyouts (event window abnormal returns are 13.5 percent, 8.5 percent, and 23.1 percent respectively).

Third, the results contradict the "inside information" argument that the bidder typically sets the offer price below his private post-expiration target share value, as proponents of disclosure regulations often argue. The significant decline in the target share price with the expiration of the offer (event parameters γ_5 and γ_6) implies that the bidder on average incurs a loss on the shares purchased. This, of course, does not mean that acquiring firms do not profit from the tender offer. For example, in synergistic offers, the underlying synergy is presumed to have a value-increasing effect on the shares of both firms.

Fourth, table 20.4 fails to uncover statistically significant gains or losses to bidder firms in any of the four offer categories. The significantly negative value of γ_4 in the sample of 18 unsuccessful bidders is indirect evidence that takeovers are valuable to bidder firms, and explains the negative price adjustment as the market (presumably) starts to realize that the offer will fail. There is no direct confirmation of this hypothesis, however, as the abnormal returns to the 52 successful bidders in public tender offers for control are indistinguishable from zero.[29]

Fifth, targets in successful public and private tender offers experience a statistically significant average price decline in the event period $e+2$ through $e+8$ (event parameter γ_6 in table 20.3). Closer inspection reveals that this price drop coincides with the CAC's announcement of the offer outcome. In our estimation procedure, week e represents the offer expiration date announced by the CAC at the beginning of the offer period. However, week e is not necessarily the final offer week. After week e but before the CAC formally announces the offer outcome, a period that typically lasts 2 weeks,[30] the bidder frequently enlists the aid of the CAC, financial intermediaries, and brokers to attract additional target shares. The exact length of the period between the expiration date and the offer outcome announcement date is not known by the market until the CAC formally announces the outcome. As a result, the negative impact of the offer expiration is reflected in the average values of both γ_5 and γ_6. Since we use P_{e+8} as a proxy for the post-expiration equilibrium price P_e, the empirical results presented below fully reflect the impact of the expiration of the offer.

5 Offer Premiums and Disclosure Regulations

Disclosure regulations raise the direct transaction costs of making a bid and reduce the expected return from acting on private information that the target resources are undervalued. As a result, the regulations are expected to deter some otherwise marginally profitable bids.[31] In addition, the regulations can affect the division of the total takeover gains between the bidder and target shareholders in offers that survive mandatory information disclosure. Previously undisclosed information that the target resources are undervalued in their current or best alternative use creates expectations of higher valued offers, increasing the offer-induced target revaluation. Alternatively, the bidder and target firms may be locked in a bilateral monopoly, in which case greater knowledge of the source of the takeover gains gives the target additional bargaining power. To the extent that disclosure regulations produce this information, we expect to see an increase in the premium over the *post*-expiration target share price, reflecting additional rents from the supply of control.[32]

We first provide empirical estimates of the average total offer premium and its two components based on cash public tender offers for control before and after the 1970 disclosure regulations. We subsequently compare these estimates with the average offer premium in private offers after 1970. As in the public offers, the bidder in private offers pays with cash and acquires voting control of the target. As mentioned earlier, however, the bidder in a private offer is not required to disclose substantive information.

5.1 Public cash tender offers before versus after January 1970

Table 20.5 shows that the average (median) public tender offer premium over the pre-offer price increased from 33.8 (31.9) percent in 1966–9 to 73.3 (59.0) percent over the period 1970–82. In franc values, the average premium increased from 7.5 million to 15.2 million (median values of 2.1 and 8.8 million). The table also reveals that the bulk of the premium increase occurred in the offer-induced target revaluation rather than in the premium over the post-expiration price. The former increased from 17.0 to 46.7 percent (median values of 19.0 and 35.8 percent), and the latter from 15.2 to 23.7 percent (median values of 13.6 and 16.1 percent). The increase in the average value of the tender option from 14.7 to 21.1 percent

Table 20.5 Mean (median) offer premiums and abnormal returns in 140 successful all-cash public and private tender offers for control of publicly traded French target firms in the period before and after the January 1970 change in disclosure regulations

Definition of offer premium	*Public tender offers* Sample period 1/66–12/69 (N = 13)	*Public tender offers* Sample period 1/70–12/82 (N = 34)	*Private tender offers, sample period 1/72–12/82 (N = 93)*
A Premium over pre-offer price[a]			
$(P - P_{a-8})/P_{a-8}$ (%)	33.8	73.3	27.4
	(31.9)	(59.0)	(18.3)
$N_p(P - P_{a-8})$ (million francs)	7.5	15.2	1.6
	(2.1)	(8.8)	(2.9)
B Premium over post-expiration price[b]			
$(P - P_{e+8})/P_{e+8}$ (%)	15.2	23.7	14.6
	(13.6)	(16.1)	(5.6)
$\alpha(P - P_{e+8})/P_{e+8}$ (%)	14.7	21.2	14.6
	(13.3)	(13.1)	(5.6)
$N_p(P - P_{e+8})$ (million francs)	4.1	9.4	1.4
	(1.0)	(4.4)	(0.7)
C Total offer-induced target revaluation			
$(P_{e+8} - P_{a-8})/P_{a-8}$ (%)	17.0	46.7	18.7
	(19.0)	(35.8)	(6.5)
$N_p(P_{e+8} - P_{a-8})$ (million francs)	3.4	5.8	0.2
	(1.1)	(4.9)	(0.7)
D Percentage average abnormal stock return (*z* value, percentage positive)[c]			
Target firm			
Week $a + 1$	16.2	28.1	9.5
	(13.7, 100.0)	(41.8, 82.4)	(22.3, 60.2)
Weeks $a - 8$ through $e + 8$	15.3	28.5	8.5
	(2.3, 75.0)	(6.4, 79.4)	(4.3, 54.8)
Bidder firm[d]			
Week $a + 1$	1.0	0.6	0.1
	(1.2, 71.4)	(1.3, 66.7)	(0.4, 46.7)
Weeks $a - 8$ through $e + 8$	−0.2	−0.1	0.9
	(0.1, 42.9)	(0.1, 41.7)	(0.2, 53.3)

a, offer announcement week; *e*, offer expiration week.

[a] P is the offer price, P_{a-8} is the target price 8 weeks before the offer announcement (week a), and N_p is the number of target shares purchased by the bidder.

[b] $\alpha(P - P_{e+8})/P_{e+8}$, where $\alpha = F_p/F_t$, is the *ex post* value of the option to tender, F_p is the fraction of the target shares purchased, F_t is the fraction of the target shares tendered, and P_{e+8} is the target share price 8 weeks after the expiration of the offer (week e).

[c] Abnormal returns are computed using the market model described in table 20.3. The abnormal return in week $a + 1$ is represented by γ_3 in the market model regression, while the abnormal return over the total event period $[a - 8, e + 8]$ is given by the sum of the six event parameters weighted by the total number of weeks in each of the six subperiods of the total event window.

[d] These average abnormal returns are based on a total of seven publicly traded bidders in the sample of 13 public offers prior to 1970, 12 bidders in the sample of 34 public offers after 1969, and 45 bidders in the sample of 93 private offers after 1971.

(median value virtually unchanged at 13.3 and 13.3 percent) is somewhat less than the increase in the premium over the post-expiration price, reflecting in part the slight post-1970 increase in the rate of oversubscription.[33] In sum, we find that the January 1970 disclosure regulations were followed by a substantial increase in the average offer-induced target revaluation and only a moderate increase, if any, in the average premium over the post-expiration price. The statistical significance of these sample differences is confirmed by the cross-sectional regressions discussed below.

Table 20.6 reports the annual time series behavior of the mean total offer premium in the sample of 47 successful cash public tender offers. The average premium in the post-1969 period is relatively evenly distributed, with the single largest premium occurring in the one case that took place in 1970. As noted in the table, the maximum offer premium was 42 percent in 1967, 36 percent in 1968, and 53 percent in 1969. Thus the offer premiums associated with the two cases in 1970 and 1971 both exceed the maximum in the sample of 13 offers before 1970. Moreover, the average premium over the pre-offer price associated with the 11 offers in 1970–3 is 88.4 percent, which is significantly higher than the 33.8 percent average for the 13 cases in 1966–9 but indistinguishable from the average over the entire post-1969 period. Thus, although the average offer premiums in 1972 and 1974 are relatively moderate, the evidence supports the hypothesis that the January 1970 disclosure regulations had an immediate impact.

Table 20.7 reports the results of cross-sectional regressions of offer premiums on offer characteristics. The regression model is estimated across the total sample of 163 cash tender offers for control and includes the natural logarithm $\ln V_T$ of the target's total equity value, the fraction F_h of the target shares held by the bidder before the offer and the fraction F_p purchased, and dummy variables for the pre-1970 period ($D_{-70} = 1$), private tender offers ($D_{PRIV} = 1$), and unsuccessful offers ($D_{FAIL} = 1$). The size variable is included to capture the scale of the offer, and is expected to have a negative effect on the *percentage* offer premium. The bidder realizes an offer-induced gain on his prior holding in the target which, in the presence of competition, tends to be transferred to target shareholders. Thus F_h is predicted to have a positive effect on offer premiums in bids for control. If target shareholders have heterogeneous expectations about the post-offer target share price, or if they face different potential capital gains tax liabilities, the supply curve of tendered target shares will be upward sloping.[34] An upward-sloping supply curve is consistent with the fact that less than 100 percent of the target shares are tendered in the typical tender offer (table 20.2) despite the substantial average offer premium. Thus we expect F_p to have a positive effect on offer premiums.

Table 20.6 Annual average offer premium measured relative to the target price 8 weeks prior to the week of offer announcement in the total sample of 47 successful cash public tender offers for publicly traded French targets in the period 1966–1982[a]

Year of offer	*No. of offers*	*Premium over pre-offer price* $(P - P_{a-8})/P_{a-8}$ *(%)*
A Period without disclosure regulations[b]		
1966	1	19.0
1967	3	30.8
1968	5	28.7
1969	4	46.3
1966–9	13	33.8
		(31.9)
B Period with disclosure regulations		
1970	1	141.7
1971	1	62.5
1972	6	41.6
1973	3	107.6
1974	4	40.3
1975	4	61.4
1976	4	127.2
1977	3	98.6
1978	2	96.4
1979	4	60.4
1980	0	–
1981	2	34.8
1982	0	–
1970–82	34	73.3
		(59.0)

Median values in parentheses.

[a] P is the offer price and P_{a-8} is the target share price 8 weeks before the week of the offer announcement (week a).

[b] In 1967, 1968, and 1969 the maximum premiums were 42 percent, 36 percent, and 53 percent respectively.

The dependent variables of the three regressions in panel A of table 20.7 are the premium over the pre-offer price, the premium over the post-expiration price, and the total offer-induced target revaluation. The first regression shows that the premium over the pre-offer price (a) decreases with ln V_T, (b) is essentially unrelated to both F_h and F_p, (c) is significantly lower for pre-1970 offers and for private tender offers, and (d) is as high in unsuccessful as in successful offers. The significant impact of D_{-70} confirms the picture provided earlier by the sample average in tables

Table 20.7 Ordinary least squares estimates of the effect on offer premiums and abnormal stock returns of the size of the target's total equity, the fractions of the target shares held prior to the offer and purchased by the bidder, whether the offer is made before or after the January 1970 change in disclosure regulations, whether the offer is public or private, and whether the offer is successful or fails, for the total sample of 163 cash tender offers for control of publicly traded French target firms in the period 1966–1982[a]

Dependent variable	a_0	a_1	a_2	a_3	a_4	a_5	a_6	R^2	*F value*
A *Offer premium*									
1 Premium over pre-offer price,	2.31	−0.11	−0.11	0.24	−0.34	−0.40	0.02	0.20	6.24
$(P-P_{a-8})/P_{a-8}$	(4.09)	(−3.47)	(−0.48)	(1.12)	(−2.66)	(−4.13)	(0.11)		
2 Premium over post-expiration	−0.14	0.01	0.21	0.37	−0.04	−0.06	0.09	0.03	0.77
price, $(P-P_{e+8})/P_{e+8}$	(−0.26)	(0.21)	(0.93)	(1.81)	(−0.32)	(−0.71)	(0.52)		
3 Total offer-induced target	2.55	−0.11	−0.46	−0.26	−0.35	−0.28	−0.06	0.14	4.01
revaluation, $(P_{e+8}-P_{a-8})/P_{a-8}$	(4.28)	(−3.49)	(−1.88)	(−1.15)	(−2.56)	(−2.71)	(−0.34)		
B *Abnormal stock return*									
4 Listed bidder firms	0.01	0.00	−0.02	−0.01	0.01	−0.01	0.01	0.04	0.45
($N=76$), week $a+1$	(0.15)	(0.08)	(−0.55)	(−0.26)	(0.30)	(−0.34)	(0.39)		
5 Listed bidder firms ($N=76$),	−0.49	−0.02	−0.16	−0.22	−0.06	−0.00	−0.03	0.10	1.22
weeks $a-8$ through $e+8$	(−1.60)	(−1.34)	(−1.88)	(−0.94)	(−0.01)	(−0.36)	(−0.20)		
6 Target firms week $a+1$	0.97	−0.04	0.01	0.05	−0.06	−0.16	−0.02	0.14	4.03
	(3.44)	(−2.94)	(0.06)	(0.44)	(−0.96)	(−3.28)	(−0.19)		
7 Target firms, weeks	1.32	−0.07	0.08	0.07	−0.04	−0.14	−0.00	0.05	1.29
$a-8$ through $e+8$	(2.11)	(−2.04)	(0.33)	(0.28)	(−0.26)	(−1.29)	(−0.01)		

Model: $Y = a_0 + a_1 \ln V_T + a_2 F_h + a_3 F_p + a_4 D_{-70} + a_5 D_{PRIV} + a_6 D_{FAIL}$

The t values are in parentheses.

[a]The variables are defined as follows: P, offer price; P_{a-8}, target share price 8 weeks before the offer announcement week (week a); P_{e+8}, target share price 8 weeks after expiration of the offer (week e); ln V_T, logarithm of the value of the target firm's total equity in week $a-8$; F_h, fraction of the target shares held by the bidder prior to the offer; F_p fraction of the target shares purchased by the bidder; D_{-70}, a dummy variable that equals unity if the offer is made before the January 1970 change in disclosure regulations and zero otherwise; D_{PRIV}, a dummy variable that equals unity if the offer is a private tender offer and zero otherwise; D_{FAIL}, a dummy variable that equals unity if the offer failed (as defined in table 20.1) and zero otherwise.

20.5 and 20.6. The regression is significant with an R^2 of 0.20 and an F statistic of 6.24. Regressions 2 and 3 reveal that this significance is driven almost exclusively by the total offer-induced target revaluation.

The premium over the post-expiration price (regression 2) is essentially unrelated to all the explanatory variables (with the possible exception of F_p), and produces an R^2 of 0.03 and an F value of 0.77. When the total target revaluation is used as dependent variable (regression 3), however, the values of the estimated coefficients are again significant and almost identical with the parameter values emerging from the regression with the premium over the pre-offer price. This regression is also significant with an R^2 of 0.14 and an F value of 4.01. In sum, the regression results of panel A of table 20.7 confirm that the increase in the premium over the pre-offer price after the January 1970 change in disclosure regulations is statistically significant and driven by an increase in the total offer-induced revaluation.

Panel B of table 20.7 reports cross-sectional regressions of abnormal stock returns to bidder and target firms over week 1 and weeks $a-8$ through $e+8$. Regressions 4 and 5, which use the abnormal return to bidder firms as the dependent variable, are both insignificant (F statistics of 0.45 and 1.22). This confirms the total sample findings of table 20.4, as well as those of table 20.5, that the average abnormal return to bidder firms is uniformly indistinguishable from zero.

Regressions 6 and 7 use the abnormal return to the target firm as the dependent variable. Regression 6 is significant (R^2 of 0.14 and F value of 4.03) but does not capture any association between week 1 abnormal return and the time period of the offer, coefficient a_4. Regression 7 is insignificant (R^2 of 0.05 and F value of 1.29). In evaluating the discrepancy between the results in panels A and B, note that the abnormal return over week 1 (regression 6) is conceptually different from the offer-induced revaluation used in regression 3.[35] Moreover, while the abnormal return to the target firm over the total event period (regression 7) is conceptually equivalent to the offer-induced revaluation used in regression 3, the general lack of power of regression 7 suggests that its dependent variable is a relatively noisy estimate of the simple measure of the offer-induced revaluation used in regression 3, with the additional variability reflecting noise in the estimated market model parameters.

The evidence on the abnormal return to bidder firms fails to reject the proposition that, on average, competition grants most (if not all) of the takeover gains to targets both before and after the introduction of disclosure regulations.[36] The logical implication is that disclosure regulations that increase the cost of takeovers will deter some bids (a truncation effect). The evidence further shows that the sample mean of the distribution of offer-induced target revaluations is significantly higher after the introduction of disclosure rules. Jointly with the evidence on bidder firms, this is consistent with the proposition that, on average, tender offers deterred by disclosure rules produce lower total gains than tender offers that survive disclosure (that is, truncation of marginally profitable takeovers).[37]

5.2 *Public versus private cash tender offers after January 1970*

Referring back to table 20.5, panel D, we can see that bidders in private as well as public tender offers earn on average statistically insignificant abnormal returns over both week 1 and the total event period $a-8$ through $e+8$. Thus the abnormal performance of successful bidder firms does not provide any evidence that the 1970 change in disclosure regulations has materially affected the distribution of bidder gains in private versus public offers. There is some indication, however, that the 1970 regulation of public offers led to an increase in the frequency of the alternative private offer procedure. Although data on private tender offers before 1972 are not publicly available, we base this conjecture on official statements indicating that the subsequent 1973 regulation of private offers was intended to make substitution of the private offer procedure for the public offer procedure less attractive.[38]

Table 20.5 also shows a significant difference between the average gains to targets in public and private cash tender offers after 1970. The average premium over the pre-offer price in the sample of 93 private tender offers is 27.4 (median 18.3) percent, which contrasts with the 73.3 percent average for public offers. The lower total premium in private offers reflects primarily a lower offer-induced revaluation of the target shares, which averages 18.7 (median 6.5) percent. This offer-induced revaluation is indistinguishable from the 17.0 (median 19.0) percent average revaluation in public tender offers before 1970, but significantly less than the 46.7 (median 35.8) percent average in public offers after disclosure regulations took effect.

In contrast, the average premium over the post-expiration price is 14.6 (median 5.6) percent, which is indistinguishable from the corresponding premium in public tender offers before 1970 (average 15.2 percent, median 13.5 percent) and somewhat smaller than the average value of 23.7 (median 16.1) percent in public offers from 1970 onward. Interestingly, the latter indicates that, after 1970, the seller of a controlling block of shares typically extracted a *smaller* control premium in a private tender offer than what is typically paid in a public offer. A similar conclusion emerges from a comparison of the values of the tender option, $\alpha(P-P_e)/P_e$, which controls for the fact that only public offers can be oversubscribed. For private offers, the average (median) option value is 14.6 (5.6) percent, compared with 14.7 (13.3) percent in the sample of public offers before 1970 and 21.2 (13.1) percent in public offers from 1970 onward.

The sign and significance of the regression coefficient a_5 in table 20.7, which multiplies the dummy variable for private offers, give partial support to the above conclusions. In panel A, a_5 is negative and significant in regressions 1 (where the dependent variable is the premium over the pre-offer price) and 3 (total offer-induced revaluation) but insignificant in regression 2 (premium over post-expiration price). Target firm abnormal returns are also significantly lower in private than in public offers during week 1 (coefficient a_5 in regression 6) but not over the total event period (regression 7).

Since the evidence fails to reject the hypothesis that bidders earn zero abnormal returns in either private or public offers, the significantly smaller target returns in private offers are consistent with the proposition that total takeover gains are on average smaller in private than in public offers.[39] If public offers deterred by disclosure regulations tend to move to the private offer procedure, this evidence further supports the earlier conclusion that disclosure regulations have probably deterred offers with relatively small total gains.

It is also interesting that the evidence of lower target gains in the average private tender offer appears despite the substantially higher target ownership concentration in this offer category.[40] This finding runs somewhat counter to the argument that, in diffusely held targets, competition among shareholders for the control premium tends to induce individual shareholders to tender "too soon" in relation to a perfectly coordinated reponse (e.g. De Angelo and Rice, 1983). However, recall that private tender offers are offers for any or all of the target shares over a mandatory 15 day period after the controlling-block trade has been executed. In other words, the bidder in a private offer does not have the option to restrict the number of target shares purchased. This option is valuable when the bidder needs only a majority of the target votes to implement the intended post-offer change in the target. In these cases, the risk of excess supply of target shares at the controlling-block price reduces the equilibrium offer price in a private relative to a public offer.[41]

6 Offer Premiums and the Payment Method

There are several reasons for expecting that the level and division of gains in corporate takeovers depend on the method of payment. In France, target shareholders pay capital gains tax if the shares are tendered for cash, whereas payment in securities allows deferral of taxes.[42] Thus, in a cash offer, the bidder must offer extra compensation equal to the difference between the immediate tax liability and the present value of future (deferred) taxes. This tax hypothesis predicts that the before-tax value of the premium over the post-expiration target share price, which dictates the incentive to tender, is higher in cash offers than in securities exchange offers.[43] Furthermore, the choice of financing may have non-tax-related valuation effects. For example, Myers and Majluf (1984) show that the use of equity can convey unfavorable information, while Jensen (1986) argues that the use of cash can increase value by obviating potential agency problems associated with excessive retention of cash ("free cash flow"). Hansen (1987), Fishman (1989) and Eckbo, Giammarino, and Heinkel (1990) also demonstrate that the choice of payment method can convey information under conditions of asymmetric information. Although we do not attempt to distinguish empirically between these non-tax-based valuation arguments, they lead us to expect a higher offer-induced revaluation in cash than in stock offers for both the bidder and the target firm.

Below, we first compare offer premiums and abnormal returns in public all-cash and all-securities offers for control. We subsequently make the same comparison for minority buyouts. The sample period is restricted to 1970–82, the period for which securities exchange offers and minority buyouts are available for study (table 20.1).

6.1 Public tender offers for control

Columns 1 and 2 of table 20.8 list the average and median offer premiums and abnormal returns in the samples of 34 all-cash and 31 all-stock offers after 1970.[44] The table reveals a striking difference in the offer premiums in the two samples. The average (median) premium over the pre-offer price is 17.2 (19.0) percent when the payment is all stock, compared with 73.3 (59.0) percent for all-cash offers. The average franc value of the total offer premium multiplied by the number of target shares purchased is 15.2 million in all-cash offers versus 6.9 million in stock exchange offers.

Table 20.8 also shows that the average premium over the post-expiration price is almost identical across the two payment methods: 22.5 percent and 23.7 percent (medians 20.0 percent and 16.1 percent), respectively. Thus the difference in the offer premiums over the pre-offer price across all-cash and securities exchange offers is driven by a difference in the total offer-induced revaluation in the two offer categories. The average (median) total revaluation is −1.1 (0.4) percent in stock offers and −1.8 (0.3) percent in bond offers, compared with the 46.7 (35.8) percent for the all-cash offers.

While surprising, our finding of an approximately zero total offer-induced target revaluation in securities exchange offers appears to hold

Table 20.8 Mean (median) offer premiums and abnormal returns in 84 successful public tender offers for control and minority buyouts in France, classified by the payment method, in the period 1970–1982

	Offers for control			*Minority buyouts*	
Definition of offer premium	*Payment in cash only*[a] *(N = 34)*	*Payment in common stock (N = 31)*	*Payment in bonds (N = 12)*	*Payment in cash only (N = 29)*	*Payment in common stock (N = 12)*
A *Premium over pre-offer price*[b]					
$(P - P_{a-8})/P_{a-8}$ (%)	73.3	17.2	34.9	38.3	9.0
	(59.0)	(19.0)	(55.2)	(35.6)	(17.1)
$N_p(P - P_{a-8})$ (million francs)	15.2	6.9	38.2	6.0	5.7
	(8.8)	(5.4)	(15.4)	(0.8)	(4.0)
B *Premium over post-expiration price*[c]					
$(P - P_{e+8})/P_{e+8}$ (%)	23.7	22.5	38.5	9.2	3.2
	(16.1)	(20.0)	(33.7)	(6.1)	(14.5)
$\alpha(P - P_{e+8})/P_{e+8}$ (%)	21.2	21.2	34.3	9.2	2.7
	(13.1)	(17.0)	(30.9)	(6.1)	(12.0)
$N_p(P - P_{e+8})$ (million francs)	9.4	12.4	54.1	1.4	6.9
	(4.4)	(4.8)	(46.2)	(0.2)	(1.4)
C *Total offer-induced target revaluation*					
$(P_{e+8} - P_{a-8})/P_{a-8}$ (%)	46.7	−1.1	−1.8	27.8	7.4
	(35.8)	(0.4)	(0.3)	(22.0)	(7.5)
$N_p(P_{e+8} - P_{a-8})$ (million francs)	5.8	−5.5	−15.9	4.5	−1.2
	(4.9)	(0.1)	(0.1)	(0.7)	(1.3)

D Percentage average abnormal stock return (z value, percentage positive)[d]					
Target firm					
Week $a+1$	28.1	5.4	12.1	28.7	12.1
	(41.8, 82.4)	(6.6, 54.8)	(7.1, 60.0)	(36.7, 85.7)	(8.0, 66.7)
Weeks $a-8$	28.5	3.9	−0.0	33.2	5.6
through $e+8$	(6.4, 79.5)	(1.2, 54.8)	(−0.2, 60.0)	(7.4, 89.2)	(0.7, 66.7)
Bidder firm[e]					
Week $a+1$	0.6	−0.9	−1.2	−0.8	−1.1
	(1.3, 66.7)	(−0.9, 34.6)	(−1.2, 28.6)	(−0.5, 40.0)	(−1.1, 33.3)
Weeks $a+1$	−0.1	−3.6	−11.8	−5.6	−1.0
through $e+8$	(0.1, 41.7)	(−0.7, 34.6)	(−1.3, 14.3)	(−1.0, 40.0)	(−0.6, 33.3)

a, offer announcement week; e, offer expiration week.

[a]This column repeats the third column of table 20.5.

[b]P is the offer price, P_{a-8} is the target price 8 weeks prior to the offer announcement (week a), and N_p is the number of target shares purchased by the bidder.

[c]$\alpha(P - P_{e+8})/P_{e+8}$, where $\alpha = F_p/F_t$, is the *ex post* value of the option to tender, F_p is the fraction of the target shares purchased, F_t is the fraction of the target shares tendered, and P_{e+8} is the target share price 8 weeks after the expiration of the offer (week e).

[d]Abnormal returns are computed using the market model described in table 20.3. The abnormal return in week $a+1$ is represented by γ_3 in the market model regression, while the abnormal return over the total event period $[a-8, e+8]$ is given by the sum of six event parameters weighted by the total number of weeks in each of the six subperiods of the total event window.

[e]These average abnormal returns are based on a total of 12 publicly traded bidders in the sample of 34 all-cash offers for control, 26 bidders in the sample of 31 all-stock offers, seven bidders in the sample of 12 bond offers, 15 in the sample of cash minority buyouts, and nine in the sample of 12 stock minority buyouts.

with alternative definitions of the post-expiration price P_e. Wansley, Lane, and Yang (1983), in the context of takeovers in the United States, argue that a relatively small offer-induced target revaluation in a securities exchange offer can simply reflect a measurement problem. That is, while a cash offer can be executed over a relatively short time, the US Securities and Exchange Commission requires that securities offered in exchange for the target shares be registered before the transaction is completed. A lengthy pre-registration process can cause information about the forthcoming offer to leak to the market, which attenuates the abnormal returns measured in relation to the offer announcement. Although this may be a problem when comparing abnormal stock returns in all-cash and securities exchange offers in the United States, we do not observe a materially different registration period for all-cash than for securities offers in France. Also, French law explicitly requires the regulatory agencies to keep information about a forthcoming offer secret until the offer has been formally approved and announced. Thus this particular regulatory argument does not confound our comparison of cash and securities exchange offers in France.

Also, shareholders of bidder firms in France can refuse to authorize the issuance of stocks promised in a securities exchange offer *after* the offer has been made by management and target shareholders have accepted. That is, the securities exchange commission grants the bidder management the right to offer target shareholders common stock which is yet to be authorized in order to avoid leakage of information about a forthcoming takeover bid from the stock authorization process itself. In principle, we would expect bidder shareholders to exercise this *ex post* veto right in accepted offers when they believe that management is overpaying for the target. However, the relatively low offer premiums in stock offers are almost certainly not explained by the existence of this veto right: first, the average offer premium over the pre-offer price in the six unsuccessful (and potentially vetoed) exchange offers in our database is only 15 percent, that is, lower than the average offer premium of 22.5 percent in successful bids. Second, as seen from table 20.8, the abnormal stock returns to bidders in both cash and stock offers are indistinguishable from zero.[45] There is no evidence that bidders in all-stock offers perform better than bidders in all-cash offers.

To analyze these findings further, table 20.9 reports the results of cross-sectional regressions of the offer premiums and abnormal returns for the total sample of 139 public tender offers during 1970–82. The regression model includes the natural logarithm $\ln V_T$ of the target's total equity value and dummy variables for payment with common stock in the bidder firm or a combination of cash and stock ($D_{STOCK} = 1$), minority buyouts ($D_{MBO} = 1$), and unsuccessful offers ($D_{FAIL} = 1$). As regression coefficient

Table 20.9 Ordinary least squares estimates of the effect on offer premiums and abnormal stock returns of the size of the target's total equity, the payment method, and whether the offer is for control or a minority buyout for the total sample of 139 public tender offers for publicly traded French target firms in the period 1970–1982[a]

Dependent variable	a_0	a_1	a_2	a_3	a_4	R^2	*F value*
A *Offer premium*[b,c]							
1 Premium over pre-offer	1.30	−0.04	−0.39	−0.21	−0.17	0.23	9.84
price, $(P - P_{a-8})/P_{a-8}$	(2.73)	(−1.33)	(−5.08)	(−2.81)	(−1.66)		
2 Premium over post-expiration	−0.26	0.03	−0.00	−0.14	−0.14	0.08	2.74
price, $(P - P_{e+8})/P_{a-8}$	(−0.74)	(1.40)	(−0.03)	(−2.39)	(−1.81)		
3 Total offer-induced target	1.42	−0.06	−0.37	−0.10	0.05	0.24	10.36
revaluation $(P_{e+8} - P_{a-8})/P_{a-8}$	(3.04)	(−2.12)	(−4.86)	(−1.32)	(0.46)		
B *Abnormal stock return*							
4 Listed bidder firms ($N = 82$),	0.02	−0.00	−0.02	−0.01	0.00	0.03	0.61
week $a + 1$	(0.27)	(−0.17)	(−1.35)	(−0.78)	(0.09)		
5 Listed bidder firms ($N = 82$),	0.37	−0.02	−0.06	−0.02	0.02	0.05	1.09
weeks $a - 8$ through $e + 8$	(1.32)	(−1.30)	(−1.29)	(−0.38)	(0.25)		
6 Target firms,	0.55	−0.02	−0.18	0.05	−0.03	0.20	8.08
week $a + 1$	(2.17)	(−1.15)	(−4.30)	(1.32)	(−0.47)		
7 Target firms,	0.92	−0.04	−0.21	0.06	−0.13	0.14	5.41
weeks $a - 8$ through $e + 8$	(2.21)	(−1.57)	(−3.05)	(0.85)	(−1.46)		

Model: $Y = a_0 + a_1 \ln V_T + a_2 D_{STOCK} + a_3 D_{MBO} + a_4 D_{FAIL}$

t values are in parentheses.

[a] The variables are defined as follows: P, offer price; P_{a-8}, target share price 8 weeks before the offer announcement week (week a); P_{e+8}, target share price 8 weeks after expiration of the offer (week e); $\ln V_T$, logarithm of the value of the target firm's total equity in week $a - 8$; D_{STOCK}, a dummy variable that equals unity if the payment method is common stock in the bidder firm or a combination of cash and stock and zero otherwise; D_{MBO}, a dummy variable that equals unity if the offer is a minority buyout and zero otherwise; D_{FAIL}, a dummy variable that equals unity if the offer failed (as defined in table 20.1) and zero otherwise.

[b] When the regression is restricted to the sample of minority buyouts only, excluding D_{MBO} and D_{FAIL}, coefficient a_2 becomes −0.32 (t value of −2.44) when the dependent variable is the premium over pre-offer price (regression 1), −0.03 ($t = 0.33$) with the premium over post-expiration price as the dependent variable (regression 2) and −0.29 ($t = 2.72$) with the total offer-induced target revaluation as the dependent variable (regression 3). Thus the negative value of a_2 shown in this table is driven by the minority buyouts as well as by the tender offers for control.

[c] When the regression is restricted to successful cash offers only, excluding D_{STOCK} and D_{FAIL}, coefficient a_3 becomes −0.36 (t value of −3.12) in regression 1 (premium over pre-offer price), −0.14 ($t = -2.31$) in regression 2 (premium over post-expiration price), and −0.20 ($t = -1.70$) in regression 3 (total offer-induced target revaluation).

a_2 in panel A shows, the payment method is statistically significant, with a t value of -5.08 in regression 1 (with the premium over the pre-offer price as dependent variable) and -4.86 in regression 3 (with the total offer-induced revaluation as dependent variable). The parameter estimate is virtually identical in the two regressions and indistinguishable from zero in the regression with the premium over the post-expiration price as the dependent variable (regression 2). Overall, regressions 1 and 3 explain a significant portion of the total variation in the dependent variables, with R^2 values of 0.23 and 0.24 respectively and F statistics of 9.84 and 10.36 respectively. Since the premium over the post-expiration price is statistically indistinguishable for the two payment methods, we cannot conclude that the larger premium over the pre-offer price in all-cash offers is driven by compensation demanded by target shareholders for giving up the option to defer capital gains taxes. The sample of 12 bond offers in column 2 of table 20.8 also provides evidence against the tax hypothesis. Like stock offers, payment in bonds of the bidder firms allows target shareholders to continue to defer capital gain taxes on the sale. The average premium over the post-expiration price in bond offers is 38.5 (median 33.7) percent, that is, somewhat higher than in the comparison sample of all-cash offers.

Although the average abnormal return to bidder firms is indistinguishable from zero in both offer categories, the average franc value of the total offer premium, multiplied by the number of target shares purchased, is 15.2 million francs in all-cash offers versus 6.9 million in all-stock offers. The total gains in all-cash offers are thus larger than the total gains in all-stock offers. This finding is consistent with both the information-signaling and agency-cost hypotheses referred to above. The evidence does not provide strong support for these hypotheses, however, since we have failed to identify a significant signaling benefit to the average bidder firm, and since our tests do not incorporate information on the existence of free cash flow in either the bidder or the target firm.

6.2 *Minority buyouts*

As shown in columns 4 and 5 of table 20.8, the average (median) offer premium over the pre-offer price is 38.3 (35.6) percent for the sample of 29 all-cash minority buyouts and 9.0 (17.1) percent for the 12 stock exchange buyout offers. The average (median) premium over the post-expiration price for the two offer categories is 9.2 (6.1) percent and 3.2 (14.5) percent respectively, while the total offer-induced revaluation is 27.8 (22.0) percent and 7.4 (7.5) percent respectively. The premium over the pre-offer price and the total revaluation are both significantly higher in all-cash buyouts, whereas the premium over the post-expiration price is statistically indistinguishable across cash and stock exchange buyouts (see footnote b to table 20.9 for the respective *t* values).[46]

Thus the payment method effect observed for control-oriented tender offers carries over to minority buyouts. This finding suggests that the difference in payoff structures between cash and securities exchange offers is relevant in developing an optimal bidding strategy. As before, however, there is no direct support for this conjecture from the average performance of bidder firms. In minority buyouts, as well as in control-oriented tender offers, the abnormal performance of bidder firms is indistinguishable from zero regardless of the means of payment in the transaction.

Finally, for all-cash offers the total offer premium is significantly lower in minority buyouts than in control-oriented offers (38.3 versus 73.3 percent). This time, however, the premium over the post-expiration price appears to drive the difference. The minority buyout regression coefficient a_3 in panel A of table 20.9 is statistically significant, with a *t* value of −2.81 in regression 1 (with the premium over the pre-offer price as dependent variable) and −2.39 in regression 2 (with the premium over the post-expiration price as the dependent variable). It is insignificantly different from zero with a *t* value of −1.32 in regression 3 (where the total offer-induced revaluation is the dependent variable).[47]

7 Conclusions

In this paper we have presented empirical estimates of the effects of disclosure regulations and the payment method on offer premiums and abnormal stock returns in public and private tender offers in France over the period 1966–82. Disclosure regulations governing public tender offers were introduced in 1970 without changing the 4 week minimum tender offer period in effect since 1966. In the sample of successful cash tender offers in which the bidder acquires voting control of the target firm, we find a statistically significant increase in the average premium over the pre-offer target share price from 34 to 73 percent following the 1970 disclosure regulations. This increase is driven primarily by an increase in the total offer-induced revaluation of the target shares. There is no evidence that the regulations have changed the component of the offer premium that reflects the value of the option to tender (as measured by the premium over the post-expiration price). Our evidence also fails to reject the hypothesis that bidder firms earn zero offer-induced abnormal stock returns both before and after 1970. Overall, our results are consistent with the hypothesis that disclosure regulations have deterred tender offers that, on average, produce lower total gains than offers that survive mandatory information disclosure.

An increase in the cost of public offers (due to disclosure requirements) causes bidders to substitute toward privately negotiated controlling-block trades, provided that a single target shareholder can transfer control. As of 1973, privately negotiated controlling-block trades must be followed by a public offer to purchase any or all target shares at the block price over a 15 day period. In contrast, the bidder in a private tender offer is not required to disclose substantive information. We find that the average premium over the pre-offer price in private bids after 1970 is 27 percent, which is significantly lower than the 73 percent average in public offers. This finding lends further support to the proposition that the French disclosure requirements for public offers have deterred some public offers with below-average total gains, some of which have sought the alternative private offer procedure. Gains to bidder firms in private offers are statistically indistinguishable from zero.

We also document that the average premium over the pre-offer price is significantly higher in all-cash than all-stock-exchange offers (73 versus 17 percent in public tender offers for voting control). Again, the difference is driven by the offer-induced revaluation of the target shares. The average premium over the post-expiration price is virtually identical across offers with the two payment methods (24 versus 23 percent), which suggests that the payment method effect does not stem from a need to compensate target shareholders for a potential capital gains tax liability. Bidder firm abnormal returns are on average indistinguishable from zero in both all-cash and all-stock offers.

Finally, our evidence challenges the proposition that a larger revaluation of the target shares in cash offers necessarily reflects relatively large synergy gains in this particular category of bids. "Synergy gains" is typically used as a generic term for the value created by the improvement in the firm's production/investment strategy after the takeover. It is natural to assume that the bidder must acquire voting control of the target to implement a substantial change in the firm's operating policy. In this context, it is interesting that the average offer premium in the minority buyouts in our database exhibits the same systematic dependence on the payment method that we observe for control-oriented tender offers. In our sample of minority buyouts, the bidder's prior holding in the target is on average 80 percent of the voting shares, and no less than 67 percent, which in France constitutes absolute voting control. If we interpret the target revaluation in minority buyouts as an information (rather than a synergy) effect, this evidence supports the hypothesis that the bidder's choice of payment method depends partly on the information asymmetry between the bidder and the target before the tender offer, and that the payment method *per se* conveys information to the market.

Appendix

Summary of major regulatory changes governing public and private tender offers to purchase shares of publicly traded firms in France in the period 1966–1982[a]

Offer procedure	*Date of regulatory reform (m/d/y)*	*Summary of major restrictions*
1 Restrictions on the use of alternative tender offer procedures		
1.1 Regular tender offer (not available prior to 4/4/66)	4/4/66[b]	Bidder must (a) hold less than 20 percent of the target shares prior to the offer, (b) seek control over the target (as defined by CAC), and (c) pay in cash
	1/23/70[c]	Bidder is allowed to pay in securities
	3/15/73, 10/10/73[d]	Bidder's prior holding in target can be greater than 20 percent. However, the bidder must acquire a majority of the target shares or control
	5/2/75[e]	Bidder must seek control and a minimum of 15 percent of the target shares
	8/13/78, 11/13/78[f]	Bidder must seek control and *either* (a) at least 10 percent of the target shares and 5 million francs worth of target shares *or* (b) at least 20 million francs worth of target shares
1.2 Minority buyouts using regular tender offer procedure (not available prior to 1/23/70)	1/23/70[e]	Bidder must (a) hold at least 50 percent of the target shares prior to the offer and (b) seek 100 percent of the target shares
1.3 Minority buyouts using simplified tender offer procedure (not available prior to 2/22/72)	2/22/72[g]	Prior to the offer the bidder must (a) hold at least 90 percent of the target shares *or* (b) hold all except at most 15,000 of the target shares *or* (c) hold all except at most 2 million francs worth of target shares. The bidder must seek 100 percent of the target
	5/2/75[e]	Restrictions (b) and (c) above are changed from 15,000 shares to 2,000 shares and from 23 million francs to 5 million francs
	8/13/78, 10/3/78[f]	Restriction (a) above is changed from 90 percent to 67 percent and restrictions (b) and (c) are dropped entirely
1.4 Purchases of up to a minority interest using the regular	3/15/73, 10/10/73[d]	Bidder acquires (a) a minimum of 15 percent of the target shares and (b) at most a minority interest in the target

continued

Offer procedure	*Date of regulatory reform (m/d/y)*	*Summary of major restrictions*
tender offer procedure (not available prior to 3/15/73)	8/13/78, 10/3/78[f]	Restriction (a) above is changed from 15 percent to at least 10 percent and 5 million francs *or* at least 10 million francs worth of target shares. Use of securities as method of payment is ruled out
1.5 Privately negotiated controlling-block trades (no restrictions prior to 3/15/73)	3/15/73, 10/10/73[d]	Any private tender offer executed through a block trade is converted to a public tender offer for 100 percent of the target shares at the block trade price
2 Restrictions in effect while the tender offer is outstanding		
2.1 Regular tender offer procedure	4/4/66[g]	Minimum offer period is 1 month
	1/23/70[c]	Bidder has the option to increase the value of the initial bid once by a minimum of 5 percent during the first 20 days of the offer period. Competing bids are allowed up to the day before the expiration day of the initial offer, in which case the initial bidder is allowed to counterbid. Competing bids and counterbids must exceed the initial offer by at least 5 percent. Initial bidder cannot extend the initial expiration day. Initial bidder can withdraw from offer only if competing bid materializes. Target shareholders can withdraw already tendered shares only if competing bid materializes. During the offer period, target forward and options quotations are suspended and margin on target share forward trades is lifted to 100 percent
	3/15/73, 10/10/73[d]	Target share limit orders expire with offer. Dealer transactions are not permitted during offer period. Dealers must close existing positions before expiration of offer. Target share trade secrecy is repealed. All insider trades and trades involving 5 percent or more of the target shares are published
	5/2/75[e]	The target firm may not trade during the offer period to "significantly reinforce" its position in the takeover (i.e. significant share repurchases are excluded)

Offer procedure	*Date of regulatory reform (m/d/y)*	*Summary of major restrictions*
	8/13/78 10/3/78[d]	Competing bids are generally allowed only during the first 10 days of the initial offer period. After the expiration of the initial bid, the initial bidder must wait at least 1 year before launching another bid for the same target shares
2.2 Minority buyouts using the regular tender offer procedure	1/23/70[c]	Same rules as those governing the regular tender offer procedure in general
2.3 Minority buyouts using the simplified procedure	2/22/72[g]	No competing bids are allowed during the offer period. Bidder cannot increase his own bid. No restrictions on trades in the target shares during the offer period
2.4 Purchases of up to a minority interest using the regular tender offer procedure	3/15/73	Same rules as those governing the regular tender offer procedure in general
2.5 Privately negotiated controlling-block trades	3/15/73, 10/10/73[d]	None of the restrictions governing the regular tender offer procedure, except that the target share margin requirement is raised to 100 percent during a 15 day mandatory price support period that starts the day of the block trade. During the price support period, the buyer of the block must accept all additional target shares tendered at the block price
3 Disclosure rules[h]		
3.1 Regular tender offer procedure	1/23/70[c]	Bidders must disclose "all important facts" for shareholders' choice, including the exact motive behind and financing of the offer
		Targets must disclose "all important facts" for shareholders' choice, including the board's recommendation concerning the offer
	3/15/73, 10/10/73[d]	Bidders must disclose the issue status of securities offered in an exchange bid, and, for *each* security offered, the capital structure, investment policy over next 5 years, principal markets and market shares, subsidiaries and shareholdings, management

continued

Offer procedure	*Date of regulatory reform (m/d/y)*	*Summary of major restrictions*
		compensation schemes, business policy orientation, and sales and earnings forecasts of underlying business operation
		Targets must disclose the same information about capital, ownership structure, and operations as the bidder must disclose for each security offered in exchange offer
	8/13/78, 10/3/78[f]	Regardless of the method of payment, bidders must disclose principal activities and products, share ownership of more than 5 percent, a 5 year financial report, and sales and earnings forecast
		Targets: no additional requirements (beyond the 1973 rules)
3.2 Minority buyouts using regular tender offer procedure	1/23/70[c]	Same disclosure requirements as those governing the regular tender offer procedure in general
3.3 Minority buyouts using the simplified offer procedure	2/22/72[g]	Same disclosure requirements as those introduced for the regular tender offer procedure on 1/23/70
	3/15/73, 10/10/73[d]	Same disclosure requirements as those introduced for the regular tender offer procedure
	8/13/78, 10/13/78[f]	Simplified minority buyouts essentially exempted from the additional disclosure requirement imposed on the regular tender offer procedure
3.4 Purchases of up to a minority interest using the regular tender offer procedure	3/15/73, 10/10/73[d]	Same disclosures rules as those governing the regular tender offer procedures in general
	8/13/78, 10/3/78[f]	Essentially exempted from all the major disclosure rules governing the regular tender offer procedure in general
3.5 Privately negotiated controlling-block trades	3/15/73, 10/10/73[d]	No disclosure requirements

[a]Institutions involved in enforcing the regulations described in this appendix include the CAC and the COB. For all types of offers discussed here, the bidder must obtain prior authorization to go ahead with the offer from the CAC and the COB who verify that the offer complies with existing regulations. The CAC judges whether an offer constitutes an attempt to acquire "control." The CAC generally plays the role of auctioneer in the public tender offer, and publicly announces the identity of the bidder and target firms, the terms of the offer (including revised or competing bids), and (with the exception

of privately negotiated controlling-block trades and simplified minority buyouts) the outcome of the offer.

[b]Letters of April 4, July 6, and November 29, 1966, between the CAC and the French Minister of Economics and Finance.

[c]COB, General Ruling on public tender offers, *Journal Officiel de la République Française* (henceforth *Journal Officiel*), January 23, 1970; CAC. Addendum to CAC general regulation, *Journal Officiel*, January 23, 1970.

[d]CAC, Addendum to CAC general regulation, *Journal Officiel*, March 15, 1973; COB, Note on the interpretation and application of COB. General ruling on public tender offers, *COB Monthly Bulletin 46*, February 1973; COB, General ruling on controlling-block trades, *Journal Officiel*, March 17, 1973; CAC, CAC general regulation, *Journal Officiel*, August 24, 1973; COB, General instruction on information schedule, October 1973.

[e]COB, General ruling on public tender offers, *Journal Officiel*, May 1, 1975.

[f]COB, General ruling on public cash and exchange offers, *Journal Officiel*, August 13, 1978; COB, Instruction concerning the application of rule D5 of COB general ruling on public tender offers, October 3, 1978.

[g]CAC, Addendum to CAC general regulation, *Journal Officiel*, February 11, 1972.

[h]Disclosure regulations are enforced by assigning the bidder and target management certain fiduciary responsibilities *vis-à-vis* their shareholders. The rules impose an *ex post* penalty on attempts to release misleading information.

Notes

1 "[T]ake-overs, like bankruptcy, represent one of Nature's method of eliminating deadwood in the struggle for survival. A more open and more efficiently responsive corporate society can result" (Samuelson, 1970, p. 505).

2 Jensen (1986) argues that the payment method may in part be driven by agency cost considerations.

3 The disclosure provisions of the Williams Act require the bidder in cash tender offers for 10 percent or more of voting stock to disclose any plans to liquidate the target firm, merge it, or make any changes in its basic corporate structure. In 1970, these requirements were extended to securities exchange (stock for stock) offers and 5 percent acquisitions. Smiley (1975) estimates that the disclosure requirements have raised direct transaction costs of a tender offer by as much as 25 percent.

4 As argued by Nathan and O'Keefe (1989), it is also possible that the post-1968 increase in average offer premiums and decrease in average bidder gains are driven by (as yet unspecified) factors unrelated to the Williams Act. Examining the annual time series behavior of average offer premiums, they find no substantial increase until after 1972, that is, some time following the passage of the Williams Act.

5 The auction is open since the Williams Act also specifies that target shareholders who have tendered their shares to one bidder firm can withdraw them should a higher valued offer be made by another firm before the minimum offer period for the initial offer has elapsed. Further, any upward revision in an outstanding offer must be applied to those shareholders who have already tendered at the previous terms.

6 A similar inference is made by Jensen and Ruback (1983, p. 29) in their review of studies of the Williams Act.

7 The auction market operates as follows. From the opening of the exchange until 12 noon, brokers collect buy and sell orders. At noon, the specialists, who are responsible for clearing the markets for their respective securities, determine the price at which the maximum number of transactions can be executed. Any excess demand or supply is then cleared in an auction that lasts until the exchange closes. Each specialist auctions out one company's shares at a time, and so the number of simultaneous auctions equals

the number of specialists in the market. Brokers participate in the auctions exclusively as agents and are not allowed to intervene as principals. The auction system prevents the broker from executing an order at a price different from the floor price.

8 See Bradley (1980) and Grossman and Hart (1980a) for a discussion of the necessary conditions for a tender offer to succeed.

9 A chronological summary of the rules and regulations discussed in this section is provided in the appendix, which includes relevant references.

10 French corporate law determines the number of corporate voting rights needed to implement certain changes in a firm's organization, including replacement of members of the board of directors and merging with another firm. Two-thirds (plus one) of the voting rights constitutes absolute control, a rule that historically has *not* been altered by means of corporate charter supermajority provisions such as those seen in the United States. A simple majority (50 percent of the votes plus one) is sufficient to replace the board of directors, whereas a two-thirds majority is needed to vote a merger with another firm. See Fleuriet (1977), for example, for a survey of the French corporate law in effect during our sample period.

11 Historically, the CAC has occasionally refused to authorize a tender offer on the grounds that the offer price was too low.

12 As of 1978, rival bids are permitted only during the first 10 days of the 1 month offer period.

13 In France, short selling of shares takes place by means of forward contracts that expire or are marked to market at the end of each month. Thus the short seller does not physically deliver the shares until month end. A relatively small fraction of all French publicly listed companies trade in this forward market, and for the remaining companies short selling is impossible.

14 Under the 1972 rules, a bidder may use the simplified procedure if two of the following three conditions are met: (a) the bidder holds at least 90 percent of the target shares; (b) the number of target shares not held by the bidder is 15,000 or less; (c) the market value of the target shares not held by the bidder does not exceed 2 million francs. In 1975, the 15,000 share rule was changed to 20,000, the 2 million franc maximum was increased to 5 million, and dealer transactions in the target shares during the offer period were prohibited. In 1978, the 90 percent rule was relaxed to two-thirds of all target shares, and the required amount of information disclosure was further reduced.

15 The regulations summarized above concern the tender offer *process*. Before October 1977 no French institution had the authority to prevent an acquisition on the basis of the possible impact of the takeover on product market competition. As of that date, however, the bidder must also be prepared to submit proof that the acquisition does not "harm competition."

16 Source: CAC, *Année Boursière Exercise*, 1965–82, and Commission des Opérations en Bourse (COB), 1er–15ème Rapport au Président de la République Exercises, *Journal Officiel de la République Française*, 1968–82.

17 Data sources for the various offer parameters are as follows; CAC, *Année Boursière Exercises*, 1965–82, vols 5–20; CAC, *Décision et Avis de la Chambre Syndicale*, 1965–82; COB, 1er–15ème Rapport au Président de la République Exercises, *Journal Officiel de La République Française*, 1968–82; CAC, Service Statistique, 1984 (fiches individuelles d'entreprise); DAFSA, Les Microfiches sur les Actionnaires et les Participations 1976–82; DAFSA, *Les Liaisons Financières*, vols 1 and 2, 1966–77.

18 The source of the stock exchange listing is CAC, Cote Officielle, Cours Officiel et Authentique, 1966–83.

19 Note 10 motivates the 66 percent threshold used to define a minority buyout. In our

sample, the mean percentage of the target shares held by the bidder before the offer is 79 in the group of minority buyouts and 21 in the group of control-oriented public tender offers.

20 Of the 64 exchange offers, 43 are public offers for control. Of these, 31 are stock exchange offers (five mixed with cash) and 12 are bond offers (four mixed with cash). Of the 15 minority buyout exchange offers, 12 involve common stock and in three cases bonds are the means of payment.

21 First, we used the 1982 and 1984 versions of a data tape issued by the CAC that covers weekly stock returns to firms listed simultaneously on the Paris forward and spot markets between 1967 and 1982. This tape, which also contains a small sample of firms listed exclusively on the spot market, covers only a small number of the firms in our database. The tape does not maintain a record of delisted securities. Second, we obtained data from a tape maintained by the CAC since 1977 which covers all officially listed securities and preserves the historical record of delisted securities. Third, and most importantly, information was collected manually from various issues of CAC, Cote Officielle, Cours Officiels et Authentique, 1965–82, and CAC, *Année Boursière Exercises*, 1966–82.

22 Since the bulk of the stock return data had to be collected by hand and given our objective of analyzing a comprehensive set of takeover transactions, we chose to work with weekly rather than daily stock returns. Daily returns have an advantage when longer return intervals "hide" the market reaction to the event under study. Given the large and significant abnormal returns reported below, however, this is not likely to be an important consideration in this paper. This suspicion is confirmed by the results reported by Husson (1986), which are based on daily stock returns and approximately half the takeovers in our database.

23 Specifically, in a stock exchange offer, we use the stock price on the last trading day before expiration of the offer to construct the offer price. If the stock is not publicly traded, we use the value of the bid as stated in the data sources listed above. The value of bidder bonds offered as a means of payment is estimated using the following algorithm:

$$\hat{B} = (B + T_1 C)\exp(-rT_1) + T_2 C,$$

where B is the first observed market price of the bond after expiration of the offer, C is the bond's coupon, T_1 is the number of days from the offer expiration date through the date B is observed divided by 365, T_2 is the number of days of (unpaid) coupon accrued at the offer expiration day divided by 365, and r is the daily (annualized) average overnight interbank interest rate. In our database B is observed either within the offer expiration month or in the subsequent month. If B is observed within the offer expiration month, then r is the average interest rate for this month. If B is observed in the month following the expiration month, then r is the weighted average of the monthly averages in the two consecutive months.

24 For 90 percent of the public tender offers in the sample, the tender offer period equals the mandatory minimum of 4 weeks, while the mean offer period in this sample is 4.3. The average offer period in the sample of private tender offers is 2.2 weeks, that is, slightly above the 15 day mandatory minimum for this offer category. None of the targets in the data is delisted before week $e + 8$.

25 There is virtually no change in the empirical results if we use the number of shares sought, instead of N_p, in constructing the proxy for α, as these two quantities are virtually identical in most cases.

26 For all offers in the database, a trading price is available in week $a + 1$.

27 Since the intercept dummy d_{jt} overlaps with the abnormal return dummy d_{6t}, the estimated value of γ_6 could understate the true abnormal return in the post-expiration period. As it turns out, however, none of our conclusions is altered if one starts the intercept dummy after event week $e+8$, or if this dummy variable is eliminated.

28 Since the event period dummies in equation (2) are orthogonal, the z value for the sum of two event parameters that measure abnormal return over periods of different length, for example, γ_1 and γ_2, is computed as

$$z_{1+2} = \frac{1}{N^{1/2}} \sum_{j=1}^{N} \frac{w_1\gamma_{j1} + w_2\gamma_{j2}}{(\sigma^2_{\gamma_{j,1+2}})^{1/2}}$$

where $\sigma^2_{\gamma_{j,1+2}} = w_1^2\sigma^2_{\gamma_{j1}} + w_2^2\sigma^2_{\gamma_{j2}}$.

29 As shown in table 20.2, the bidder is typically more than ten times the size of the target. Since the power of stock returns to register a given dollar gain decreases with the size of the bidder, it is possible that the generally insignificant abnormal returns reflect a measurement problem due to relative size. Eckbo (1988) reports evidence consistent with the presence of a size-related measurement problem when measuring gains to bidder firms in a large sample of US and Canadian acquisitions.

30 In our sample, the outcomes of 64 percent of the public tender offers were announced in week $e+2$, 20 percent in week $e+3$, and 10 percent in week $e+4$. One outcome was announced in week $e+7$.

31 Disclosure regulations can also *increase* the information advantage for some bidder firms because antifraud provisions, backed by significant penalties on material misstatements and omissions, generally increase the credibility of information that the bidder discloses. A more credible signal can improve the bidder's bargaining position with the target as well as reduce the possibility of costly uninformed bidding by rival firms. See also Grossman and Hart (1980b).

32 See DeAngelo and Rice (1983) for discussion of the conditions under which tendering target shareholders may be able to extract a control premium from the bidder firm.

33 The percentage of the tendered target shares purchased by the bidder declined from 97 percent before 1970 to 89 percent in the sample period after January 1970 (table 20.2).

34 Rosenfeld (1982) and Bradley, Desai, and Kim (1988) analyze the supply curve of tendered target shares (the former study in the context of share repurchase offers).

35 The abnormal return over week 1 reflects both the offer-induced revaluation and the value of the tender option, attenuated by any prior leakage of information about the forthcoming offer. Panel D of table 20.5 shows an increase in the average abnormal returns to targets from approximately 16 to 28 percent after January 1970.

36 The z values in table 20.5 for event period $a+1$ are 1.2 for bidders before 1970 and 1.3 for bidders after 1969, both of which fail to reject the null hypothesis of zero average abnormal returns. Note, however, that 71.4 percent of the bidders before 1970 and 66.7 percent after 1969 have positive abnormal returns. Under the null, the expected fraction of firms with positive abnormal returns is 0.5 with variance $(0.5 \times 0.5)/N$. Reflecting the small sample sizes ($N=7$ before 1970 and $N=12$ after 1969), a two-sided t test based on the percentage positive also fails to reject the null hypothesis.

37 While not reported in table 20.5, this proposition is supported when looking at the franc value of the sum of the average abnormal return to bidder and target firms as well.

38 The 2 week mandatory price support period imposed on private tender offers in 1973 was intended to (translated) "favor the increased use of the *public* tender offer

procedure," COB, 1974, Sixième Rapport au Président de la République Année 1973, p. 150 (emphasis added).

39 A similar conclusion follows from an analysis of the franc value of the sum of the average abnormal returns to bidder and target firms.

40 Although we do not have direct evidence on ownership structure, recall that all targets of private tender offers are controlled by a single blockholder.

41 Formally, for a given post-expiration price P_e, the bidder seeking only a controlling block of shares is indifferent between a public tender offer price of P and a private tender offer price of $P_p = \alpha P + (1 - \alpha) P_e$, which implies that $P_p < P$ if the offer is expected to be oversubscribed ($\alpha < 1$). The condition $P_p < P$ is also acceptable to the controlling-block seller provided that collusion with minority shareholders is ruled out.

42 If the tendering shareholder is a corporation and if the corporation purchased the target shares within 2 years prior to the offer, the realized capital gain is treated as general business revenue and taxed at the 50 percent corporate income tax rate. If the shares have been held for more than 2 years, the realized capital gain is considered long term and taxed according to a flat rate of 15 percent. If the tendering shareholder is an individual, any capital gains realized before December 31, 1978 are fully tax exempt. After this date (and throughout the rest of our sample period) the taxation of realized capital gains depends on the total value of the securities sold. If the total value is less than 150,000 francs, any capital gain is free. If the value exceeds this limit, the tax rate is a flat 15 percent. There is an exception to this rule if the individual realizes gain from what is considered "speculative selling" (a term referring in particular to short selling). In this case, if the individual's portfolio turnover ratio (that is, the ratio of the value of the shares sold to the total value of the portfolio) exceeds 2.6, the individual must choose between a flat tax rate of 30 percent and the individual's marginal tax rate on ordinary income.

43 During our sample period, cash and securities exchange offers were given identical accounting treatment for the purpose of corporate taxes. Thus accounting-related tax benefits on the corporate level, such as, for example, those discussed by Carleton et al. (1983) and Gilson, Scholes, and Wolfson (1988) in the context of takeover bids in the United States, are not a determinant of the payment method in our French sample.

44 Column 1 reproduces, for convenience, the information in the third column of table 20.5. In five of the 31 all-stock offers, the means of payment is a mixture of cash and common stock. The cash component in each of these five offers represents less than 50 percent of the total compensation given to target shareholders. Because of the small sample, we do not present separate results for mixed offers. See Eckbo, Giammarino, and Heinkel (forthcoming) for a theoretical and empirical analysis of mixed cash–stock offers.

45 The z values in table 20.8 for event period $a+1$ are 1.3 for the 12 listed bidders in the sample of 34 all-cash offers and -0.9 for the 26 listed bidders in the sample of 31 all-stock offers, both of which fail to reject the null hypothesis of zero average abnormal returns. Moreover, 66.7 percent of the bidders offering cash and 34.6 percent of the bidders offering stock have positive abnormal returns. The hypothesis that either one of these two percentages equals the expected value of 50 cannot be rejected at the 10 percent level of significance. However, there is some indication that the two percentages are different from each other; the t value of the difference (66.7 – 34.6) is 1.84, which is significant at the 10 percent level.

46 Our estimate of the offer-induced revaluation in minority buyouts is comparable with the evidence reported by Dodd and Ruback (1977) for their sample of 19 "clean-up" offers (which they define as offers where the bidder owns at least 50 percent of the

target prior to the offer). Targets in their "clean-up" offers on average earn 17.4 percent abnormal return over the offer announcement month, compared with an average of 20.8 percent for targets in 136 tender offers for control.

47 As stated in note c of table 20.9, identical conclusions emerge when the cross-sectional regression is restricted to successful cash offers only, excluding the dummy variables D_{STOCK} and D_{FAIL}.

References

Asquith, P., Bruner, R. and Mullins, D. (1983) "The Gains to Bidding Firms from Merger," *Journal of Financial Economics*, 11, 121–40.

Asquith, P., Bruner, R. and Mullins, D. (1988) "Merger Returns and the Form of Financing," Unpublished Paper, Harvard University.

Bradley, M. (1980) "Interfirm Tender Offers and the Market for Corporate Control," *Journal of Business*, 53, 345–76.

Bradley, M., Desai, A. and Kim, E. H. (1983) "The Rationale Behind Interfirm Tender Offers: Information or Synergy?" *Journal of Financial Economics*, 11, 183–206.

Bradley, M., Desai, A. and Kim, E. H. (1988) "Synergistic Gains from Corporate Acquisitions and Their Division Between the Stockholders of Target and Acquiring Firms," *Journal of Financial Economics*, 21, 3–40.

Carleton, W. T., Guilkey, A. K., Harris, R. S. and Stewart, J. F. (1983) "An Empirical Analysis of the Role of the Medium of Exchange in Mergers," *Journal of Finance*, 38, 813–26.

Comment, R. and Jarrell, G. (1987) "Two-tier and Negotiated Tender Offers: The Imprisonment of the Free-Riding Shareholder," *Journal of Financial Economics*, 19, 283–310.

DeAngelo, H. and Rice, E. M. (1983) "Antitakeover Charter Amendments and Stockholder Wealth," *Journal of Financial Economics*, 11, 329–60.

Dodd, P. and Ruback, R. (1977) "Tender Offers and Stockholder Returns: An Empirical Analysis," *Journal of Financial Economics*, 5, 351–74.

Eckbo, B. E. (1988) "Gains to Bidder Firms: Methodological Issues and U.S.–Canadian Evidence," Unpublished Paper, University of British Columbia.

Eckbo, B. E., Giammarino, R. and Heinkel, R. (1990) "Asymmetric Information and the Medium of Exchange in Takeovers: Theory and Tests," *Review of Financial Studies*, 3: 4.

Fishman, M. (1989) "Preemptive Bidding and the Role of the Medium of Exchange in Acquisitions," *Journal of Finance*, 44, 41–57.

Fleuriet, M. (1977) *Pouvoir et finance d'enterprise droit et practiques* (Paris: Dalloz).

Franks, J. R., Harris, R. S. and Mayer, C. (1988) "Means of Payment in Takeovers: Results for the U.K. and the U.S." In *Corporate Takeovers: Causes and Consequences*, ed. A. Auerbach (Chicago, IL: University of Chicago Press for the National Bureau of Economic Research).

Gilson, R. J., Scholes, M. S. and Wolfson, M. A. (1988) "Taxation and the Dynamics of Corporate Control: The Uncertain Case for Tax-Motivated Acquisitions." In *Knights, Raiders and Targets: The Impact of the Hostile Takeover*, eds J. C. Coffee, Jr, L. Lowenstein, and S. Rose-Ackerman (New York: Oxford University Press).

Grossman, S. and Hart, O. (1980a) "Takeover Bids, the Free Rider Problem, and the Theory of the Firm," *Bell Journal of Economics*, 11, 42–64.

Grossman, S. and Hart, O. (1980b) "Disclosure Law and Takeover Bids," *Journal of Finance*, 35, 323–34.

Hansen, R. G. (1987) "A Theory for the Choice of Exchange Medium in the Market for Corporate Control," *Journal of Business*, 60, 75–95.
Huang, Y.-S. and Walkling, R. A. (1987) "Target Abnormal Returns Associated with Acquisition Announcements: Payment, Acquisition Form, and Managerial Resistance," *Journal of Financial Economics*, 19, 329–49.
Husson, B. (1986) "The Gains from Take-Over Operations: The French Case," Unpublished Paper, C.E.S.A. de Jouy en Josas, Paris.
Jarrell, G. A. (1985) "The Wealth Effects of Litigation by Targets: Do Interests Diverge in a Merge?" *Journal of Law and Economics*, 28, 151–77.
Jarrell, G. A. and Bradley, M. (1980) "The Economic Effects of Federal and State Regulations of Cash Tender Offers," *Journal of Law and Economics*, 23, 371–407.
Jensen, M. C. (1986) "Agency Costs of Free Cash Flow, Corporate Finance and Takeovers," *American Economic Review*, 76, 323–9.
Jensen, M. C. and Ruback, R. (1983) "The Market for Corporate Control: The Scientific Evidence," *Journal of Financial Economics*, 11, 5–50.
Myers, S. C. and Majluf, N. S. (1984) "Corporate Financing and Investment Decisions when Firms Have Information that Investors Do Not Have," *Journal of Financial Economics*, 13, 187–221.
Nathan, K. S. and O.Keefe, T. B. (1989) "The Rise in Takeover Premiums: An Exploratory Study," *Journal of Financial Economics*, 23, 101–19.
Rosenfeld, A. (1982) *Repurchase Offers, Information-Adjusted Premiums and Shareholder Response*, MERC Monograph, Series MP-8201 (Rochester, NY: University of Rochester).
Samuelson, P. (1970) *Economics*, 8th edn (New York: McGraw-Hill).
Schipper, K. and Thompson, R. (1983) "Evidence on the Capitalized Value of Merger Activity for Acquiring Firms," *Journal of Financial Economics*, 11, 85–119.
Smiley, R. (1975) "The Effect of the Williams Amendment and Other Factors on Transactions Costs in Tender Offers," *Industrial Organization Review*, 3, 138–45.
Travlos, N. G. (1987) "Corporate Takeover Bids, Method of Payment, and Bidding Firms' Stock Returns," *Journal of Finance*, 42, 943–63.
Wansley, J., Lane, W. and Yang, H. (1983) "Abnormal Returns to Acquiring Firms by Type of Acquisition and Method of Payment," *Financial Management*, 12, 16–22.

Chapter 21

Chi-fu Huang

Background and Comments

Chi-fu Huang is best known for his theoretical analyses of the properties of capital market equilibrium. These include analysis of individuals' lifetime consumption and investment strategies under uncertainty (see his paper with John Cox, chapter 4 in this book).

In the following paper he takes up a quite different topic – auctions of US Treasury bills. This is a topic that should have been studied to death. However, until Bikhchandani and Huang's paper, no one had thought through the properties of an auction in which winning bidders (Treasury securities dealers in this case) immediately resell to less well-informed investors. Before the investors buy, they can learn from observing the bids. This affects what they are willing to pay, which in turn feeds back into the dealers' optimal bidding strategy.

The authors' treatment is entirely theoretical. A simple numerical example illustrating the likely size of this feedback effect would have been helpful. However, even very small percentage changes are worth our attention when many hundreds of billions of dollars of Treasury bills are issued every year. Moreover, purely theoretical treatments can help sellers predict which types of auctions are likely to work in particular circumstances, or to understand the pros and cons of auctions versus other selling mechanisms.

There are many other possible applications. For example, some types of public utility securities have traditionally been sold by competitive bidding rather than negotiated underwriting. However, utility managers seem to avoid competitive bidding when allowed to do so. Why? Is there some fault in the design of that bidding process, in which a single winning syndicate takes all of the issue?

Several nonregulated companies have experimented with auctions for debt issues. The issues have been successfully floated, but the procedure has never caught on. Why not? Why are we unable to design an auction to reduce the extremely high underwriting and underpricing costs of initial public offerings of common stock (Ritter, 1987)?

We need more theoretical papers like the one that follows to get to the bottom of questions like these.

Reference

Ritter, J. (1987) "The Costs of Going Public," *Journal of Financial Economics*, 19, December, 269–81.

Author's Introduction

One of the major advances in economic theory in the 1980s has been a deeper understanding of one of the oldest forms of economic institutions: the auctions. See Wilson (1988) for a recent survey. To date, auctions account for a large volume of economic and financial activities. The US Department of the Interior uses a sealed bid auction to sell mineral rights on federally owned properties. Every week, the US Department of the Treasury uses a sealed-bid auction to sell Treasury bills worth billions of dollars. Many other financial activities, although not explicitly conducted as auctions, can nevertheless be thought of as auctions; see, for example, an analysis of sales of seasoned new issues in Parsons and Raviv (1985).

One common feature shared by such financial activities is that there exist active resale or secondary markets for the objects for sale. This is true, for example, for Treasury bills and for seasoned new issues. This resale aspect, however, may make existing auction theories inapplicable. The case in point is the Treasury bill auctions.

In Treasury bill auctions, there are about 40 primary dealers of government securities who regularly participate in the weekly auction. They submit *competitive* sealed bids that are price–quantity pairs. Others, usually individual investors, can submit *noncompetitive* sealed bids that specify quantity only. The noncompetitive bids, small in quantity, always win. The primary dealers compete for the remaining bills in a discriminatory auction. That is, the demands of the bidders, starting with the highest price bidder down, are met until all the bills are allocated. The winning competitive bidders pay the unit price they submitted. All the noncompetitive bidders pay the quantity-weighted average price of all the winning competitive bids. After the auction, the Department of the Treasury announces some summary statistics about the bids submitted. These include total tender amount received, total tender amount accepted, highest winning bid, lowest winning bid, quantity-weighted average of winning bids, and the split between competitive and noncompetitive bids.

The Treasury bills are then delivered to the winning bidders and can be resold in an active secondary market. Since primary dealers are large financial institutions, they tend to have private information about the demand for Treasury bills and the future term structure of interest rates. Thus the summary statistics about the bids announced by the Department of the Treasury may convey information that is not yet publicly known to the secondary market participants. Thus, when submitting their bids in the auction, the primary dealers would take into account the impact of their bids on the resale price. This "signaling" aspect is what is missing in the existing literature and is the primary focus of this paper.

Apart from the existence of resale markets, Treasury bill auctions differ from existing models of auctions in another respect. Before the weekly auction, there is an active forward market for the bills to be auctioned. Treasury bills are auctioned off every Monday. Starting on the Tuesday before the auction date, forward contracts on Treasury bills are traded among the 40 odd primary dealers who will participate in the auctions. The bid and ask prices of the forward contracts are common knowledge among the bidders. Several questions arise here.

First, how does the existence of forward markets affect bidders' behavior in the auction? Second, suppose that there exists an equilibrium with nontrivial transactions in the forward markets. How well does the forward price aggregate bidders' diverse private information? Third, would the information revealed through the forward price weaken the winners' curse and lead to higher expected revenue for the auctioneer? Finally, can there be manipulation of forward prices in that a bidder receiving a good signal submits a low demand in the forward market to conceal his information and thus wins at a lower bid than otherwise in the subsequent auction? I hope to investigate some of these questions in my future research.

References

Parsons, J. and Raviv, A. (1985) "Underpricing of Seasoned Issues," *Journal of Financial Economics*, 14, 377–97.

Wilson, R. (1988) "Strategic Analysis of Auctions," *Working Paper*, Graduate School of Business, Stanford University.

Bibliographical Listing

"A Variational Problem Arising in Financial Economics" (with John C. Cox), *Journal of Mathematical Economics*, forthcoming.

"Continuous Time Stopping Games with Monotone Reward Structures" (with L. Li), *Mathematics of Operations Research*, 15: 3, August 1990, 496–507.

"On Intertemporal Preferences with a Continuous Time Dimension II: The Case of Uncertainty" (with A. Hindy), *Working Paper 2105-89*, Sloan School of Management, Massachusetts Institute of Technology, 1989.

"Optimal Consumption and Portfolio Policies When Asset Prices Follow a Diffusion Process" (with John C. Cox), *Journal of Economic Theory*, 49: 1, October 1989, 33–83.

"A Continuous Time Portfolio Turnpike Theorem" (with John C. Cox), *Working Paper 3117-88*, Sloan School of Management, Massachusetts Institute of Technology, September 1988.

Foundations for Financial Economics (with R. H. Litzenberger) (Amsterdam: Elsevier, 1988).

"Nonnegative Wealth, Absence of Arbitrage, and Feasible Consumption Plans" (with Philip H. Dybvig), *Review of Financial Studies*, 1: 4, 1988, 377–401.

Auctions with Resale Markets: An Exploratory Model of Treasury Bill Markets

SUSHIL BIKHCHANDANI and CHI-FU HUANG

1 Introduction

In this paper we develop an exploratory model for Treasury bill auctions. In these auctions, there are two types of bidders. There are about 40 *competitive bidders*, mainly primary dealers and large financial institutions, who submit sealed bids that are price–quantity pairs. The *noncompetitive bidders*, primarily individual investors, submit sealed bids that specify quantity only (less than a prespecified maximum). The noncompetitive bids, usually small in quantity,[1] always win. The competitive bidders compete for the remaining bills in a discriminatory auction. That is, the demands of the bidders, starting with the highest price bidder down, are met until all the bills are allocated. The winning competitive bidders pay the unit price that they submitted. All the noncompetitive bidders pay the quantity-weighted average price of all the winning competitive bids. After the auction, the Department of the Treasury announces some summary statistics about the bids submitted. These include the total tender amount received, the total tender amount accepted, the highest winning bid, the lowest winning bid, the proportion of winning bids accepted at the lowest price, the quantity-weighted average of winning bids, and the split between competitive and noncompetitive bids. The Treasury bills are then delivered to the winning bidders and can be resold at an active secondary market.

Reproduced from *Review of Financial Studies*, 2: 3, 1989, 311–39.

Sushil Bikhchandani is Assistant Professor at the John E. Anderson School of Management, University of California at Los Angeles. We thank John Cox and Margaret Meyer for helpful conversations. We are grateful to Chiang Sung for answering many of our questions on the organization of Treasury bill auctions. We would also like to acknowledge helpful comments from Michael Brennan and seminar participants at City College of New York, Duke University, Princeton University, Stanford University, the University of California at Los Angeles, and the Summer Meeting of the Econometric Society in 1989.

Competitive bidders are large institutions, who tend to have information about the term structure of interest rates that is better than the information possessed by investors in the secondary markets. The buyers on the resale market have access to public information, including information revealed by the Department of the Treasury about the bids submitted in the auction. To the extent that bids submitted reveal the private information of the competitive bidders, the resale price in the secondary market will be responsive to the bids. This creates an incentive for the primary dealers to signal their private information to the secondary market participants. This information linkage between the actions taken by the competitive bidders in the auction and the resale price is absent in existing models of common value auctions (e.g. Milgrom and Weber, 1982a) and is the primary focus of this paper.[2]

The revenue-maximizing mechanism for selling Treasury bills was a subject of debate in the early 1960s. Friedman (1960) proposed that the Department of the Treasury should switch from a discriminatory auction to a uniform price auction for the sale of Treasury bills. Apart from the fact that uniform price auctions would induce bidders to reveal their true demand curves, Friedman asserted that discriminatory auctions encouraged collusion and discouraged smaller bidders from participating. Both Goldstein (1960) and Brimmer (1962) disputed Friedman's contention. Smith (1966), on the basis of a mathematical model, concluded that uniform price auctions yield greater revenues. Unlike Smith's model, our model is game theoretic in that each bidder's beliefs about the others' bids are confirmed in an equilibrium, and we model the information linkage between the primary auction and the secondary market. Like Smith, our analysis provides support for Friedman's proposal that the Treasury bill auction should be uniform price.

The results of this paper may also be helpful in analyzing other types of auctions with resale markets such as art auctions, in which bidders have correlated values. If a painting by Van Gogh is auctioned at a price much higher than expected, then one might expect this and other paintings by Van Gogh to be sold at higher prices in the future. In addition, many other financial transactions, although not explicitly conducted as auctions, can nevertheless be thought of as implicitly carried out through auctions; see, for example, the analyses of the sales of seasoned new issues in Parsons and Raviv (1985) and of the market for corporate control in Tiemann (1986). One feature often shared by these financial transactions is that there exist active resale or secondary markets for the objects for sale. Our analysis here may be helpful in understanding such markets.

The rest of this paper is organized as follows. In section 2 we develop a model of competitive bidding with a resale market. The competitive bidders are risk neutral and have private information about the true value of the objects. After the auction the auctioneer publicly announces some information (the prices paid by the winning bidders, for example) about the auction, and the winning bidders then sell the objects in the secondary market. Although the primary motivation of this model is the Treasury bill market, there are many institutional details that are absent. For instance, we require that competitive bidders demand at most one unit of the object, instead of being allowed to choose quantity, and we do not model the effect of any forward contracts and close substitutes (such as last week's Treasury bills) owned by competitive bidders on their bidding strategies. In this paper we focus on one aspect of the Treasury bill market – the informational linkage of the resale market and the primary auction.

In section 3 we analyze discriminatory auctions in which the winning bids and the highest losing bids are revealed at the end of the auction. The equilibrium bids we obtain are higher than those derived in Milgrom and Weber (1982a) because primary bidders have an incentive to signal.

A key insight gained from the theory of common valuation auctions without resale markets is that, the greater the amount of information revealed in an auction, the greater is the expected revenue for the auctioneer since this weakens the *winners' curse*. Thus, loosely speaking, if the auctioneer has private information, he can increase his expected revenue by announcing his private information before the auction. However, when there is a resale market which creates an incentive for the bidders to signal, the auctioneer may reduce the bidders' incentive to signal and thus decrease his expected revenue if he announces his private information. Sufficient conditions for the public announcement of the auctioneer's private information to increase his expected revenue are provided.

In sections 4 and 5, we consider a uniform price auction in which the rule for determining the winning bidders is identical with that in the discriminatory auction but the winning bidders pay a uniform price equal to the highest losing bid. The existence of an equilibrium depends in part on the kind of information about the auction publicly revealed by the auctioneer. If, as we assumed for discriminatory auctions, the winning bids are announced, then we show by example that there may exist an incentive for the bidders to submit arbitrarily large bids in order to deceive the secondary market buyers. Bidders in a discriminatory auction do not have such an incentive since, upon winning, they must pay what they bid. However, a symmetric Nash equilibrium always exists in the uniform price auction, provided that only the price paid by the winning bidders is announced (and thus bidders have no incentive to signal).

Next, we turn to the question of the auctioneer's revenues. The key insight from the theory of auctions without resale markets mentioned above is also useful here. Without resale markets, uniform price auctions yield higher revenues than discriminatory auctions, since in the former the price is linked to the information of the highest losing bidder. When there are resale markets in which the buyers draw inferences about the true value from the bids and the winning bids *are* announced, there is an additional factor which works in the same direction, namely that in a uniform price auction it is cheaper to bid high in order to signal a high realization of private information, since conditional upon winning a bidder does not pay what he bids. Therefore, in our model as well, uniform price auctions result in greater expected revenues for the auctioneer when an equilibrium exists.

We also provide plausible sufficient conditions for the auctioneer's revenues under a uniform price auction, in which only the price paid by winning bidders is announced, to be greater than under a discriminatory auction, in which all the winning bids are announced. Section 6 contains concluding remarks. All proofs are in an appendix.

2 The Model

Consider a common value auction in which n risk-neutral bidders (the dealers who submit competitive bids in Treasury bill auctions) bid for k identical indivisible objects, with $n > k$. The true value of the objects is the same for all the bidders and is unknown to them at the time they submit their bids. Each bidder privately observes a signal about the true value, based on which he submits a bid. We assume that there are no noncompetitive bids. In section 6 we indicate how noncompetitive bids can be incorporated in our model. Throughout we assume that each bidder demands (or is allowed) at most one unit of the object.

The primary dealer's interest in the objects being auctioned is solely for the purpose of resale in the secondary market. We assume that the primary dealers' personal (consumption) valuations of the object are always sufficiently lower than the valuations of the resale market buyers that they would prefer to resell the objects rather then consume them. For instance, the primary bidders may have capital constraints so that unless they sell this week's Treasury bills they may not be able to participate in next week's auction. Since, as we shall establish, primary bidders make positive expected profits in the auction, they might prefer to sell the Treasury bills at their expected value conditional on all publicly known information.

If instead we assume that the primary bidders' personal value of the object is at the same level as that of the resale buyers, then if all the private information of the winning primary bidders is not revealed after the primary auction, the primary bidders will never sell the object if the expected value of the object conditional on all public information and their privately known information is greater than the resale price, and will always sell when their expected value is strictly less than the resale price. Therefore the resale market buyers will make strictly negative expected profits and the resale market will break down. Hence we preclude this possibility. For similar reasons we assume that primary bidders can participate in the resale market only as sellers, and not as buyers.

After the auction the auctioneer publicly announces some information about the auction. For simplicity we assume that the winning bids and the highest losing bid submitted in the auction are publicly announced. In the case of the uniform price auction, there may not exist an equilibrium if the winning bids are revealed at the end of the auction. Therefore we also analyze uniform price auctions when the winning bids are not announced and only the price paid by the winning bidders is announced.

We allow the possibility that some additional information about the value of the objects for sale may become publicly available after the bids are submitted but before the opening of the secondary market. The k winners in the primary auction then sell the objects to risk-neutral buyers on the secondary markets. The buyers on the secondary markets do not have access to any private information about the true value. They infer what they can from the information released by the auctioneer about the primary auction, and any other publicly available information. Thus, regardless of the secondary market mechanism – an auction or a posted price market – the resale price will be the expected value of the object conditional on all publicly available information.

The n risk-neutral bidders will be indexed by $i = 1, 2, \ldots, n$. The true value of each object being auctioned is a random variable $\tilde{V}$. Each bidder i has a common prior on $\tilde{V}$ and observes a private signal $\tilde{X}_i$ about the true value. Let $\tilde{P}$ denote any other information that becomes public after the auction is over but before the resale market meets. We shall assume, except when otherwise stated, that given $\tilde{P}$ the bidders' signals are not uninformative about the true value, that is, $E[\tilde{V}|\tilde{P}] \not\equiv E[\tilde{V}|\tilde{X}_1, \tilde{X}_2, \ldots, \tilde{X}_n, \tilde{P}]$. If this condition is violated, for example when $\tilde{P} \equiv \tilde{V}$, our model reduces to the usual common value auction without a resale market.

Let $f(v, p, \mathbf{x})$ denote the joint density function of $\tilde{V}$, $\tilde{P}$, and the vector of signals $\tilde{\mathbf{X}} \equiv (\tilde{X}_1, \tilde{X}_2, \ldots, \tilde{X}_n)$. It is assumed that f is symmetric in the last n arguments. Let $[\underline{v}, \bar{v}] \times [\underline{p}, \bar{p}] \times [\underline{x}, \bar{x}]^n$ be the support of f, where $[\underline{x}, \bar{x}]^n$ denotes the n-fold product of $[\underline{x}, \bar{x}]$. Note that we do not rule out the possibility that the support of the random variables is unbounded from either above or below. Further, it is assumed that all the random variables in this model are *affiliated.* That is, for all $\mathbf{x}, \mathbf{x}' \in [\underline{x}, \bar{x}]^n$, $v, v' \in [\underline{v}, \bar{v}]$, and $p, p' \in [\underline{p}, \bar{p}]$,

$$f[(v, p, \mathbf{x}) \vee (v', p', \mathbf{x}')] f[(v, p, \mathbf{x}) \wedge (v', p', \mathbf{x}')] \geqslant f(v, p, \mathbf{x}) f(v', p', \mathbf{x}'),$$

where $\vee$ denotes the componentwise maximum and $\wedge$ denotes the componentwise minimum. Affiliation is said to be strict if the above inequality is strict. Affiliation implies that if H is an increasing[3] function then $E[H(\tilde{V}, \tilde{P}, \tilde{X}_1, \tilde{X}_2, \ldots, \tilde{X}_n) | c_i \leqslant \tilde{X}_i \leqslant d_i, i = 1, \ldots, n]$ is an increasing function of c_i, d_i. The reader is referred to Milgrom and Weber (1982a) for other implications of affiliation. We further assume for simplicity that if H is continuously differentiable then

$$E[H(\tilde{V}, \tilde{P}, \tilde{X}_1, \tilde{X}_2, \ldots, \tilde{X}_n) | c_i \leqslant \tilde{X}_i \leqslant d_i, i \leqslant n]$$

is continuously differentiable in c_i and d_i, for all $c_i, d_i \in [\underline{x}, \bar{x}]$, with the convention that the derivative at $\underline{x}$ is the right-hand derivative and that at $\bar{x}$ is the left-hand derivative. Moreover, we shall assume that $(\tilde{V}, \tilde{P}, \tilde{X}_1, \ldots, \tilde{X}_n)$ are strictly affiliated so that if H is strictly increasing in any of $(\tilde{V}, \tilde{P}, \tilde{X}_1, \ldots, \tilde{X}_n)$, say in $\tilde{X}_1$, then $E[H(\tilde{V}, \tilde{P}, \tilde{X}_1, \tilde{X}_2, \ldots, \tilde{X}_n) | c_i \leqslant \tilde{X}_i \leqslant d_i, i \neq 1]$ is strictly increasing in c_i and d_i for all $c_i, d_i \in [\underline{x}, \bar{x})$.

3 Discriminatory Auction

In a discriminatory auction the bidders submit sealed bids and the k highest bidders win the auction. A winning bidder pays the price that he or she bids. In this section we show that when the bidders' private signals are *information complements*,[4] in a sense to be defined later, there exists a symmetric Nash equilibrium with strictly increasing strategies in the bidding game among the primary dealers. Unlike the auctions examined by Milgrom and Weber (1982a), the affiliation property alone is not sufficient for the existence of a Nash equilibrium. Intuitively, when the motive of the primary bidders is to resell in a secondary market in which the buyers know some or all of their bids (or a summary statistic based on their bids), there exists an incentive for the primary bidders to bid more than they otherwise would and thus signal their private information. This is because, by affiliation, the resale value is responsive to the bids submitted to the extent that the bids reveal the private information received by the primary bidders. If each bidder's incentive to signal increases with his information realization, then there exists an equilibrium in strictly increasing strategies. It is the information complementarity of the bidders' signals with respect to the true value that ensures that the bidders' incentive to signal increases with their information realizations and enables them to sort themselves in a separating equilibrium. We also show that if secondary markets participant's beliefs are *monotone*, in a sense to be defined, then there exists a unique symmetric equilibrium.

In a model where bidders participate in an auction for final consumption of the objects, Milgrom and Weber (1982a) show that the auctioneer's expected revenue can be increased if he precommits to truthfully reporting his private information about the objects for sale before the auction, provided that his private information is affiliated with the bidders' private information. This follows since, by publicly announcing his information, the auctioneer introduces an additional source of affiliation among the primary bidders' private information and thus weakens the winners' curse. Hence the bidders compete more aggressively and the expected selling price is increased. However, in our model with a resale market this result is not necessarily true. A portion of the bid submitted by a bidder is attributed to his incentive to signal to the resale market participants. If the auctioneer's private information is a "substitute" for the bidders' information, announcing that information will reduce the responsiveness of the resale price to the bidders' information. This in turn reduces the incentive for the bidders to signal and may cause the expected selling price to fall. However, when the auctioneer's private information is a "complement" to that of the bidders, it is always beneficial for the auctioneer to announce his private information.

3.1 Existence of a symmetric Nash equilibrium

By the hypothesis that $f(v, p, \mathbf{x})$ is symmetric in its last n arguments, this is a symmetric game. Thus it is natural to investigate the existence of a symmetric Nash equilibrium. We examine the game from bidder 1's point of view. The analysis from the viewpoints of the other bidders is symmetric.[5] Note that, at the time when bidder 1 submits his bid, he only observes his private information $\tilde{X}_1$. Thus a strategy for bidder 1 is a function of $\tilde{X}_1$. Bidder i's strategy is denoted $b_i : [\underline{x}, \bar{x}] \to \mathbb{R}$. We begin our analysis by deriving the first-order necessary conditions for an n-tuple $(\hat{b}, \ldots, \hat{b})$ to be a Nash equilibrium in strictly increasing and differentiable strategies, when buyers in the secondary market believe that $(\hat{b}, \ldots, \hat{b})$ are the strategies followed in the bidding.

Since buyers in the secondary market do not have access to private information about the true value, the resale price is the expectation of $\tilde{V}$ conditional on all public information. As mentioned earlier, to simplify the analysis we assume that the auctioneer announces the prices paid by winning bidders (that is, the winning bids) and the highest losing bid.[6] Suppose that bidders $i = 2, \ldots, n$ adopt the strategy $\hat{b}$, and that bidder 1 receives information $\tilde{X}_1 = x$ and submits a bid equal to b. Then, if bidder 1 wins with a bid b, the resale price will be

$$\begin{aligned} r^{\mathrm{d}}[\hat{b}^{-1}(b), \tilde{Y}_1, \ldots, \tilde{Y}_k, \tilde{P}] &\equiv E[\tilde{V} \mid \tilde{X}_1 = \hat{b}^{-1}(b), \hat{b}^{-1}[\hat{b}(\tilde{Y}_1)], \ldots, \hat{b}^{-1}[\hat{b}(\tilde{Y}_k)], \tilde{P}] \\ &= E[\tilde{V} \mid \tilde{X}_1 = \hat{b}^{-1}(b), \tilde{Y}_1, \ldots, \tilde{Y}_k, \tilde{P}], \end{aligned} \tag{1}$$

where $\hat{b}^{-1}$ denotes the inverse[7] of $\hat{b}$ and $\tilde{Y}_j$ is the jth-order statistic of $(\tilde{X}_2, \ldots, \tilde{X}_n)$. Note that if $\tilde{P} \equiv \tilde{V}$, $r^{\mathrm{d}}[\hat{b}^{-1}(b), \tilde{Y}_1, \ldots, \tilde{Y}_k, \tilde{P}] \equiv \tilde{V}$, and our model reduces to an ordinary common value auction without a resale market. Define

$$v^{\mathrm{d}}(x', x, y) \equiv E[r^{\mathrm{d}}(x', \tilde{Y}_1, \ldots, \tilde{Y}_k, \tilde{P}) | \tilde{X}_1 = x, \tilde{Y}_k = y]. \tag{2}$$

By our hypothesis about strict affiliation, both r^{d} and v^{d} are strictly increasing in each of their arguments (provided that, given $\tilde{P}$, the bidders' signals are not uninformative about $\tilde{V}$). The expected profit for bidder 1 when $\tilde{X}_1 = x$ and he submits a bid equal to b is

$$\begin{aligned}
&\Pi^{\mathrm{d}}(b|x) \\
&\quad \equiv E[\{r^{\mathrm{d}}[\hat{b}^{-1}(b), \tilde{Y}_1, \ldots, \tilde{Y}_k, \tilde{P}] - b\}1_{\{b \geqslant \hat{b}(\tilde{Y}_k)\}} | X_1 = x] \\
&\quad = E[E[\{r^{\mathrm{d}}[\hat{b}^{-1}(b), \tilde{Y}_1, \ldots, \tilde{Y}_k, \tilde{P}] - b\}1_{\{b \geqslant \hat{b}(\tilde{Y}_k)\}} | \tilde{X}_1, \tilde{Y}_k] | \tilde{X}_1 = x] \\
&\quad = E[\{v^{\mathrm{d}}[\hat{b}^{-1}(b), \tilde{X}_1, \tilde{Y}_k] - b\}1_{\{b \geqslant \hat{b}(\tilde{Y}_k)\}} | \tilde{X}_1 = x] \\
&\quad = \int_{\underline{x}}^{\hat{b}^{-1}(b)} \{v^{\mathrm{d}}[\hat{b}^{-1}(b), x, y] - b\} f_k(y|x)\, dy,
\end{aligned}$$

where the second equality follows from the law of iterative expectations and $f_k(y|x)$ denotes the conditional density function of $\tilde{Y}_k$ given $\tilde{X}_1$. Taking the first derivative of $\Pi^{\mathrm{d}}(b|x)$ with respect to b gives

$$\begin{aligned}
\frac{\partial \Pi^{\mathrm{d}}(b|x)}{\partial b} &= \{v^{\mathrm{d}}[\hat{b}^{-1}(b), x, \hat{b}^{-1}(b)] - b\} f_k[\hat{b}^{-1}(b)|x]\{\hat{b}'[\hat{b}^{-1}(b)]\}^{-1} \\
&\quad - F_k[\hat{b}^{-1}(b)|x] \\
&\quad + \{\hat{b}'[\hat{b}^{-1}(b)]\}^{-1} \int_{\underline{x}}^{\hat{b}^{-1}(b)} v_1^{\mathrm{d}}[\hat{b}^{-1}(b), x, y] f_k(y|x)\, dy,
\end{aligned} \tag{3}$$

where $\hat{b}'(x)$ is the derivative of $\hat{b}(x)$, $F_k(y|x)$ is the conditional distribution function of $\tilde{Y}_k$ given $\tilde{X}_1$, and v_1^{d} is the partial derivative of v^{d} with respect to its first argument. For $(\hat{b}, \ldots, \hat{b})$ to be a Nash equilibrium, it is necessary that $\hat{b}$ be a best response for bidder 1 when bidders $i = 2, \ldots, n$ adopt strategy $\hat{b}$ and the resale market participants believe that all bidders adopt $\hat{b}$. That is, relation (3) must be zero when $b = \hat{b}(x)$:

$$\begin{aligned}
0 &= \left.\frac{\partial \Pi^{\mathrm{d}}(b|x)}{\partial b}\right|_{b = \hat{b}(x)} \\
&= [v^{\mathrm{d}}(x, x, x) - \hat{b}(x)] f_k(x|x)[\hat{b}'(x)]^{-1} - F_k(x|x) \\
&\quad + [\hat{b}'(x)]^{-1} \int_{\underline{x}}^{x} v_1^{\mathrm{d}}(x, x, y) f_k(y|x)\, dy.
\end{aligned} \tag{4}$$

Rearranging (4) gives an ordinary differential equation

$$\hat{b}'(x) = [v^{\mathrm{d}}(x, x, x) - b(x)] \frac{f_k(x \mid x)}{F_k(x \mid x)} + \int_{\underline{x}}^{x} v_1^{\mathrm{d}}(x, x, y) \frac{f_k(y \mid x)}{F_k(x \mid x)} \,\mathrm{d}y. \qquad (5)$$

Note that, by the definition of v^{d} and the law of iterative expectations,

$$v^{\mathrm{d}}(x, x, y) = E[\tilde{V} \mid \tilde{X}_1 = x, \tilde{Y}_k = y]. \qquad (6)$$

In addition to (5), there are two other necessary conditions that $\hat{b}$ must satisfy: (a) $v^{\mathrm{d}}(x, x, x) \geqslant \hat{b}(x)$, $\forall x \in [\underline{x}, \bar{x}]$; (b) $\hat{b}(\underline{x}) = v^{\mathrm{d}}(\underline{x}, \underline{x}, \underline{x})$. Condition (a) follows since expected profit for bidder 1 has to be positive in equilibrium. Condition (b) follows from (a) and the fact that, if $\hat{b}(\underline{x}) < v^{\mathrm{d}}(\underline{x}, \underline{x}, \underline{x})$, then by slightly increasing the bid to $b(\underline{x}) + \varepsilon$ when $\tilde{X}_1 = \underline{x}$, expected profit can be raised from zero to some strictly positive amount.

The solution to (5) with the boundary condition $\hat{b}(\underline{x}) = v^{\mathrm{d}}(\underline{x}, \underline{x}, \underline{x})$ is

$$\hat{b}(x) = v^{\mathrm{d}}(x, x, x) - \int_{\underline{x}}^{x} L(u \mid x) \,\mathrm{d}t(u) + \int_{\underline{x}}^{x} \frac{h(u)}{f_k(u \mid u)} \,\mathrm{d}L(u \mid x), \qquad (7)$$

where

$$L(u \mid x) = \exp\left[-\int_{u}^{x} \frac{f_k(s \mid s)}{F_k(s \mid s)} \,\mathrm{d}s \right]$$

$$t(u) = v^{\mathrm{d}}(u, u, u) \qquad (8)$$

$$h(u) = \int_{\underline{x}}^{u} v_1^{\mathrm{d}}(u, u, y) f_k(y \mid u) \,\mathrm{d}y.$$

Note that $L(u \mid x)$ and $t(u)$ are increasing functions of u and thus are measures on $[\underline{x}, \bar{x}]$. We shall show in what follows that $\hat{b}(x)$ of (7) also satisfies condition (a), maximizes expected profit under the hypothesis that $(\tilde{X}_1, \ldots, \tilde{X}_n, \tilde{P})$ are *information complements* with respect to $\tilde{V}$, and is strictly increasing.

Definition 1 Random variables $(\tilde{Z}_1, \ldots, \tilde{Z}_m)$ are said to be information complements with respect to another random variable $\tilde{T}$ if

$$\frac{\partial^2 \phi(z_1, \ldots, z_m)}{\partial z_i \partial z_j} \geqslant 0, \qquad \forall i \neq j, \forall z_1, \ldots, z_m$$

where

$$\phi(z_1, \ldots, z_m) \equiv E[\tilde{T} \mid \tilde{Z}_1 = z_1, \ldots, \tilde{Z}_m = z_m].$$

Thus the random variables $(\tilde{X}_1, \ldots, \tilde{X}_n, \tilde{P})$ are information complements with respect to $\tilde{V}$ if the marginal contribution to the conditional expectation of $\tilde{V}$ of a higher realization of $\tilde{X}_i$ is larger the higher the realization of any other $\tilde{X}_j$ or $\tilde{P}$. This information complementarity condition is satisfied by a large class of distributions. For example, if $\phi(z_1, \ldots, z_m)$ is linear in the z_i, then $(\tilde{Z}_1, \ldots, \tilde{Z}_m)$ are information complements. Thus if $(\tilde{T}, \tilde{Z}_1, \ldots, \tilde{Z}_m)$ are multivariate normally distributed, then $(\tilde{Z}_1, \ldots, \tilde{Z}_m)$ are information complements with respect to $\tilde{T}$. We give three examples of strictly affiliated random variables that also satisfy the information complementarity condition.

Example 1 Let $(\tilde{T}, \tilde{Z}_1, \ldots, \tilde{Z}_m)$ be multivariate normally distributed with density function $g(t, z_1, \ldots, z_m)$. Let Σ be the variance–covariance matrix of these random variables, and assume that Σ^{-1} exists and has strictly negative off-diagonal elements. It is easily verified that $\partial^2 \ln g / \partial t \partial z_i > 0$ and $\partial^2 \ln g / \partial z_i \partial z_j > 0$ for $i \neq j$. Theorem 1 of Milgrom and Weber (1982a) then implies that $(\tilde{T}, \tilde{Z}_1, \ldots, \tilde{Z}_m)$ are strictly affiliated. Since $E[\tilde{T} | \tilde{Z}_1, \ldots, \tilde{Z}_m]$ is linear in the $\tilde{Z}_i$, $(\tilde{Z}_1, \ldots, \tilde{Z}_m)$ are information complements with respect to $\tilde{T}$.

In addition to the multivariate normally distributed random variables, there is a large class of distributions with linear conditional expectations. The following is an example.

Example 2 Let $\tilde{Z}_i, i = 1, \ldots, m$ be independent conditional on $\tilde{T}$ and distributed according to a gamma distribution given $\tilde{T} = t$:

$$g_i(z_i | t) = \begin{cases} \dfrac{(1/t)^\alpha}{\Gamma(\alpha)} z_i^{\alpha - 1} \exp\left(-\dfrac{z_i}{t}\right) & \text{if } z_i > 0 \\ 0 & \text{otherwise} \end{cases}$$

where $\alpha > 0$, $t > 0$, and Γ is the gamma function. Let $1/\tilde{T}$ also be distributed according to a gamma distribution with a density

$$h\left(\frac{1}{t}\right) = \begin{cases} \dfrac{\sigma^\gamma}{\Gamma(\gamma)} \left(\dfrac{1}{t}\right)^{\gamma - 1} \exp\left(-\dfrac{\sigma}{t}\right) & \text{if } t > 0 \\ 0 & \text{otherwise} \end{cases}$$

where $\gamma > 0$ and $\sigma > 0$. Using theorem 1 of Milgrom and Weber (1982), we verify that $(\tilde{T}, \tilde{Z}_1, \ldots, \tilde{Z}_m)$ are strictly affiliated. Direct computation yields

$$E[\tilde{T} | \tilde{Z}_1, \ldots, \tilde{Z}_m] = \frac{\sum_{i=1}^m \tilde{Z}_i + \sigma}{m\alpha + \gamma - 1}.$$

Thus $(\tilde{Z}_1, \ldots, \tilde{Z}_m)$ are information complements with respect to $\tilde{T}$.

Note that the prior distribution of $\tilde{T}$ in example 2 is an element of the family of "conjugate distributions" of gamma distributions (DeGroot, 1970, ch. 9). Other distributions with linear conditional expectations can be constructed similarly. Interested readers should consult Ericson (1969) and DeGroot (1970).

The following example gives random variables that are strict information complements.

Example 3 Let $\tilde{Z}_i$, $i = 1, 2, \ldots, m$, be independent conditional on $\tilde{T}$ with density

$$g_i(z_i \mid t) = \begin{cases} \dfrac{z_i^{at}}{at+1} & \text{if } z_i, t \in (0,1) \\ 0 & \text{otherwise.} \end{cases}$$

The density of $\tilde{T}$ is

$$h(t) = \begin{cases} \dfrac{(n+1)a}{(a+1)^{n+1} - 1} (at+1)^n & \text{if } t \in (0,1) \\ 0 & \text{otherwise.} \end{cases}$$

It is easily verified that $\partial^2 \ln g_i(z_i \mid t)/\partial z_i \partial t > 0$, $\forall z, t \in (0,1)$. Theorem 1 of Milgrom and Weber (1982) implies that g_i satisfies the strict affiliation inequality. The same theorem also shows that

$$g(t, z_1, z_2, \ldots, z_m) = \begin{cases} h(t) \prod_{i=1}^{m} g_i(z_i \mid t) & \text{if } z_1, z_2, \ldots, z_m, t \in (0,1) \\ 0 & \text{otherwise} \end{cases}$$

is strictly affiliated. Direct computation yields

$$\begin{aligned} \phi(z_1, z_2, \ldots, z_m) &\equiv E[\tilde{T} \mid \tilde{Z}_1 = z_1, \tilde{Z}_2 = z_2, \ldots, \tilde{Z}_m = z_m] \\ &= \frac{(\prod_{i=1}^{m} z_i)^a}{(\prod_{i=1}^{m} z_i)^a - 1} - \frac{1}{a \ln(\prod_{i=1}^{m} z_i)} \end{aligned}$$

for $z_1, z_2, \ldots, z_m \in (0,1)$. Finally, we can also verify that $\partial^2 \phi(z_1, z_2, \ldots, z_m)/\partial z_i \partial z_j > 0$ for all $i \neq j$ if $a \in (0,1)$.

The following lemma is a direct consequence of the definition of information complementarity. All proofs are in the appendix.

Lemma 1 Suppose that $(\tilde{X}_1, \ldots, \tilde{X}_n, \tilde{P})$ are information complements with respect to $\tilde{V}$. Then $v_1^{\mathrm{d}}(x, x', y)$ is strictly increasing in x' and y, where v_1^{d} denotes the partial derivative of v^{d} with respect to its first argument.

The following proposition shows that if $(\tilde{X}_1, \ldots, \tilde{X}_n, \tilde{P})$ are information complements with respect to $\tilde{V}$, then $\hat{b}$ of (7) satisfies condition (a), that is, $v^{\mathrm{d}}(x, x, x) \geqslant \hat{b}(x)$, $\forall x \in [\underline{x}, \bar{x}]$.

Proposition 1 Suppose that $(\tilde{X}_1, \ldots, X_n, \tilde{P})$ are information complements with respect to $\tilde{V}$. Then $v^{\mathrm{d}}(x, x, x) \geqslant \hat{b}(x)$, $\forall x \in [\underline{x}, \bar{x}]$, and the inequality is strict for $x > \underline{x}$, where $\hat{b}$ is defined in (7).

A corollary of proposition 1 is that $\hat{b}$ is strictly increasing. Thus our assumption that resale market buyers can invert the primary bids to obtain the bidders' signal realizations is justified.

Corollary 1 The strategy $\hat{b}$ defined in (7) is strictly increasing.

Before proceeding, we first record two lemmas that are direct consequences of the definition of affiliation.

Lemma 2 (Milgrom and Weber, 1982a) $F_k(y \mid x)/f_k(y \mid x)$ is decreasing in x.

Lemma 3 Let $x' \geqslant x \geqslant y$. Then $F_k(y \mid x')/F_k(x \mid x') \leqslant F_k(y \mid x)/F_k(x \mid x)$. That is, the distribution function $F_k(\cdot \mid x')/F_k(x' \mid x')$ dominates the distribution function $F_k(\cdot \mid x)/F_k(x \mid x)$ in the sense of first-order stochastic dominance.

The main result of this section is as follows.

Theorem 1 The n-tuple $(\hat{b}, \ldots, \hat{b})$, with $\hat{b}$ as defined in (7), is a Nash equilibrium of the discriminatory auction provided that $(\tilde{X}_1, \ldots, \tilde{X}_n, \tilde{P})$ are information complements with respect to $\tilde{V}$.

When bidders in the discriminatory auction participate only for the purpose of consumption, Milgrom and Weber (1982a) have indentified a symmetric Nash equilibrium with a bidding strategy

$$b^{\mathrm{d}}(x) = v^{\mathrm{d}}(x, x, x) - \int_{\underline{x}}^{x} L(u \mid x) \, \mathrm{d}t(u) \tag{9}$$

where $L(u \mid x)$ and $t(u)$ are as defined in (8). The bidding strategy for the purpose of resale identified in theorem 1 is strictly higher than b^{d} for every $x \in (\underline{x}, \bar{x}]$ by an amount equal to

$$\int_{\underline{x}}^{x} \frac{h(u)}{f_k(u \mid u)} \, \mathrm{d}L(u \mid x),$$

the magnitude of which depends on the responsiveness v_1^d of the resale value to the submitted bid.[8] It is this informational link between the resale value and the bids submitted by bidders in the discriminatory auction that gives the bidders an incentive to signal. Of course, since $\hat{b}$ is strictly increasing, the resale buyers can invert the bids announced by the auctioneer to obtain the private information of the bidders and, as in Ortega-Reichart (1968) and Milgrom and Roberts (1982), in equilibrium no one is deceived.

It is worth emphasizing that the primary bidders benefit if the resale market buyers are better informed about the true value. If, for instance, $\tilde{P} \equiv \tilde{V}$ or if $\tilde{P}$ "contains" all the relevant information in $\tilde{X}_1, \tilde{X}_2, \ldots, \tilde{X}_n$, then there would be no signaling incentive for the bidders and the expected price(s) in the auction would be lower. We might expect the "informativeness" of $\tilde{P}$ to increase with the length of the time period between the end of the primary auction and the start of the resale market.

Next we establish that the symmetric equilibrium identified above is the unique symmetric equilibrium if secondary market buyers' beliefs satisfy a monotonicity condition. The beliefs of the secondary market buyers about the bidders' private information are said to be *monotone* if they are nondecreasing in the bids submitted. For instance, if the secondary market buyers believe that bidder 1's private information lies in the interval $[x_1^l(b), x_1^u(b)]$ when bidder 1 bids b, then the monotonicity condition on beliefs would imply that $x_1^l(\cdot)$ and $x_1^u(\cdot)$ are nondecreasing functions.[9] Since bidders with higher realizations of their private information would expect higher resale prices, it is natural to expect them to bid more. Therefore monotonicity of beliefs seems to be a natural restriction to impose. Of course when bids are in the range of the equilibrium bidding strategies, beliefs are obtained by inverting the bidding strategies.

Since a symmetric equilibrium is a natural focal point in a game with symmetric players and as shown below $(\hat{b}, \ldots, \hat{b})$ is the only symmetric equilibrium in nondecreasing strategies when the resale buyers' beliefs are monotone, we shall use this equilibrium when comparing expected revenues between a discriminatory auction and a uniform price auction.

Theorem 2 If the secondary market buyers have monotone beliefs, then $(\hat{b}, \hat{b}, \ldots, \hat{b})$, where $\hat{b}$ is as defined in (7), is the unique symmetric equilibrium in nondecreasing strategies.

3.2 *Public announcement of the auctioneer's information*

Suppose that the auctioneer has private information about $\tilde{V}$, represented by a random variable $\tilde{X}_0$. We shall consider the impact of announcing $\tilde{X}_0$ before the auction on the expected selling price. Let $\bar{b}(\cdot\,; x_0)$ be a symmetrical equilibrium bidding strategy conditional on $\tilde{X}_0 = x_0$. It is assumed that $\bar{b}(\cdot\,; x_0)$ is increasing and differentiable in x. If bidder 1 bids b and wins then the resale price in this case will be

$$p^{\mathrm{d}}[\bar{b}^{-1}(b; x_0), \tilde{Y}_1, \ldots, \tilde{Y}_k, \tilde{P}; x_0] \equiv E[\tilde{V} | \tilde{X}_1 = \bar{b}^{-1}(b; x_0), \tilde{Y}_1, \ldots, \tilde{Y}_k, \tilde{P}, \tilde{X}_0 = x_0],$$

where $\bar{b}[\bar{b}^{-1}(b; x_0); x_0] = b$. Putting

$$w^{\mathrm{d}}(x', x, y; x_0) \equiv E[p^{\mathrm{d}}(x', \tilde{Y}_1, \ldots, \tilde{Y}_k, \tilde{P}; x_0) \,|\, \tilde{X}_1 = x, \tilde{Y}_k = y, \tilde{X}_0 = x_0],$$

it is straightforward to show that $\bar{b}(x; x_0)$ must satisfy

$$\bar{b}'(x; x_0) = [w^{\mathrm{d}}(x, x, x; x_0) - \bar{b}(x; x_0)] \frac{f_k(x \,|\, x; x_0)}{F_k(x \,|\, x; x_0)} + \int_{\underline{x}}^{x} w_1^{\mathrm{d}}(x, x, y; x_0) f_k(y \,|\, x; x_0)\, \mathrm{d}y, \tag{10}$$

where $f_k(y \,|\, x; x_0)$ denotes the conditional density of $\tilde{Y}_k$ given $\tilde{X}_1 = x$ and $\tilde{X}_0 = x_0$. In addition, the boundary condition $\bar{b}(\underline{x}; x_0) = w^{\mathrm{d}}(\underline{x}, \underline{x}, \underline{x}; x_0)$ must be satisfied. The solution to (10) with this boundary condition is

$$\bar{b}(x; x_0) = w^{\mathrm{d}}(x, x, x; x_0) - \int_{\underline{x}}^{x} L(u \,|\, x; x_0)\, \mathrm{d}t(u; x_0) + \int_{\underline{x}}^{x} \frac{h(u; x_0)}{f_k(u \,|\, u; x_0)}\, \mathrm{d}L(u \,|\, x; x_0), \tag{11}$$

where

$$L(u \,|\, x; x_0) = \exp\left\{ - \int_{u}^{x} \frac{f_k(s \,|\, s; x_0)}{F_k(s \,|\, s; x_0)}\, \mathrm{d}s \right\}$$

$$t(u; x_0) = w^{\mathrm{d}}(u, u, u; x_0)$$

$$h(u; x_0) = \int_{\underline{x}}^{u} w_1^{\mathrm{d}}(u, u, y; x_0) f_k(y \,|\, u; x_0)\, \mathrm{d}y.$$

Next, we define conditional information complements.

Definition 2 Random variables $(\tilde{Z}_1, \ldots, \tilde{Z}_m)$ are said to be information complements conditional on random variable $\tilde{Y}$ with respect to random variable $\tilde{T}$ if

$$\frac{\partial^2 \phi(z_1, \ldots, z_m, y)}{\partial z_i \partial z_j} \geqslant 0, \qquad \forall i \neq j,\ \forall z_1, \ldots, z_m,\ \forall y$$

where

$$\phi(z_1, \ldots, z_m, y) \equiv E[\tilde{T} | \tilde{Z}_1 = z_1, \ldots, \tilde{Z}_m = z_m, \tilde{Y} = y].$$

If $(\tilde{X}_1, \tilde{X}_2, \ldots, \tilde{X}_n, \tilde{P})$ are information complements conditional on $\tilde{X}_0$ with respect to $\tilde{V}$, then a proof identical with that of theorem 1 shows that $\bar{b}$ defined in (11) is a symmetric equilibrium strategy. This is stated without proof in the following proposition.

Proposition 2 The n-tuple $(\bar{b}(\cdot\,; x_0), \ldots, \bar{b}(\cdot\,; x_0))$, with $\bar{b}(\cdot\,; x_0)$ as defined in (11), is a Nash equilibrium of the discriminatory auction when the auctioneer announces $\tilde{X}_0 = x_0$, provided that $(\tilde{X}_1, \ldots, \tilde{X}_n, \tilde{P})$ are information complements conditional on $\tilde{X}_0$ with respect to $\tilde{V}$ and the resale market participants believe that all the bidders follow strategy $\bar{b}(\cdot\,; x_0)$.

Note that the existence of an equilibrium does not depend on whether $(\tilde{X}_0, \tilde{X}_1, \ldots, \tilde{X}_n, \tilde{P})$ are information complements with respect to $\tilde{V}$. There exists a Nash equilibrium as long as $(\tilde{X}_1, \tilde{X}_2, \ldots, \tilde{X}_n, \tilde{P})$ are information complements conditional on $\tilde{X}_0$ with respect to $\tilde{V}$. Our main result in this subsection will be that the expected selling price under the policy of always reporting $\tilde{X}_0$ cannot be lower than that under any other reporting policy provided that $(\tilde{X}_0, \tilde{X}_1, \ldots, \tilde{X}_n, \tilde{P})$ are information complements with respect to $\tilde{V}$.[10] We first show, in the next proposition, that $\bar{b}(x; x_0)$ is an increasing function of x_0.

Proposition 3 Suppose that $(\tilde{V}, \tilde{X}_0, \tilde{X}_1, \ldots, \tilde{X}_n, \tilde{P})$ are affiliated and that $(\tilde{X}_0, \tilde{X}_1, \ldots, \tilde{X}_n, \tilde{P})$ are information complements with respect to $\tilde{V}$. Then $\bar{b}(x; x_0)$ is an increasing function of x_0.

The main result of this section is as follows.

Theorem 3 Suppose that $(\tilde{V}, \tilde{X}_0, \tilde{X}_1, \ldots, \tilde{X}_n, \tilde{P})$ are affiliated and that $(\tilde{X}_0, \tilde{X}_1, \ldots, \tilde{X}_n, \tilde{P})$ are information complements with respect to $\tilde{V}$. A policy of publicly revealing the seller's information cannot lower, and may raise, the expected revenue for the seller in a discriminatory auction.

Given proposition 3, the proof of theorem 3 mimics that of Milgrom and Weber (1982a, theorem 16) and is omitted. The interested reader is referred to Bikhchandani and Huang (1988) for details.

Theorem 3 depends critically on the fact that under its hypothesis $\bar{b}(x; x_0)$ is increasing in x_0. When $(\tilde{X}_0, \tilde{X}_1, \ldots, \tilde{X}_n, \tilde{P})$ are not information complements, $\bar{b}(x; x_0)$ may not be an increasing function of x_0, and revealing $\tilde{X}_0$ may reduce the bidders' incentive to signal. This in turn may lower the expected revenue for the seller even though $(\tilde{X}_0, \tilde{X}_1, \ldots, \tilde{X}_n, \tilde{P})$ are affiliated.

4 Uniform Price Auction

In a uniform price auction the bidders submit sealed bids and the k highest bidders win the auction. The price that they pay is equal to the $(k+1)$th highest bid. Initially we obtain a candidate for a symmetric Nash equilibrium under the assumption that after the auction the auctioneer reveals the winning bids and the highest losing bid, that is, the price paid by the winning bidders. If any of the lower bids are also revealed, our results remain unchanged.

We first obtain strategies that satisfy first-order necessary conditions for a symmetric Nash equilibrium. Next we show that when there exists a symmetric equilibrium in the uniform price auction, the auctioneer's expected revenues at this equilibrium are greater than at the symmetric equilibrium of the discriminatory auction. The intuition behind this result is as follows. From the theory of auctions without resale markets we know that, compared with a discriminatory auction, a greater amount of information is revealed during a uniform price auction. This weakens the winners' curse in the uniform price auction and results in greater revenues for the auctioneer. In addition when the primary auction and the resale markets are informationally linked, as in our model, it is cheaper to submit higher bids in the uniform price auction in order to signal to the resale market buyers. This in turn further increases the expected revenues from uniform price auctions.

However, the second of these two factors – the fact that in a uniform price auction the price paid by a bidder conditional upon winning does not increase as his bid is increased – can result in nonexistence of equilibrium in a uniform price auction. If the resale price is very responsive to the bids submitted there may exist an incentive for the bidders to submit arbitrarily large bids and upset any purported equilibrium. In the last part of this section we show by example that this is indeed possible, and more generally we show that when $k = 1$ and $\tilde{P}$ is a constant there does not exist any Nash equilibrium in strictly increasing pure strategies.

4.1 Necessary conditions for a symmetric equilibrium

As in the discriminatory auction, each primary bidder's strategy is a function from $[\underline{x}, \bar{x}]$ to the real line. Suppose that $(b_0, b_0, \ldots, b_0)$ is a Nash equilibrium in strictly increasing and differentiable strategies, when buyers in the secondary market believe that all bidders use b_0. If all other bidders use strategy b_0, bidder 1 receives information $\tilde{X}_1 = x$ and submits a bid equal to b; then if bidder 1 wins the resale price is

$$\begin{aligned} r^{\mathrm{u}}[b_0^{-1}(b), \tilde{Y}_1, \ldots, \tilde{Y}_k, \tilde{P}] &\equiv E[\tilde{V}|\tilde{X}_1 = b_0^{-1}(b), b_0^{-1}[b_0(\tilde{Y}_1)], \ldots, b_0^{-1}[b_0(\tilde{Y}_k)], \tilde{P}] \\ &= E[\tilde{V}|\tilde{X}_1 = b_0^{-1}(b), \tilde{Y}_1, \ldots, \tilde{Y}_k, \tilde{P}]. \end{aligned} \tag{12}$$

Note that $r^{\mathrm{u}}(\cdot) = u^{\mathrm{d}}(\cdot)$ and is strictly increasing in all its arguments. If bidder 1 wins the auction, the expected resale price conditional on $\tilde{X}_1$ and $\tilde{Y}_k$ is

$$v^{\mathrm{u}}[b_0^{-1}(b), x, y] \equiv E[r^{\mathrm{u}}[b_0^{-1}(b), \tilde{Y}_1, \ldots, \tilde{Y}_k, \tilde{P}] \,|\, \tilde{X}_1 = x, \tilde{Y}_k = y]. \tag{13}$$

By strict affiliation, v^{u} is strictly increasing in its arguments. From the definition of v^{d} it follows that

$$v^{\mathrm{u}}(x', x, y) = v^{\mathrm{d}}(x', x, y) \qquad \forall x', x, y. \tag{14}$$

We show below that b_0 must be given by the following equation:

$$b_0(x) = v^{\mathrm{u}}(x, x, x) + \frac{h(x)}{f_k(x\,|\,x)}, \tag{15}$$

where $h(x)$ is as defined in (8).

If $X_1 = x$ and bidder 1 bids b, his expected profit is

$$\begin{aligned} &\Pi^{\mathrm{u}}(b\,|\,x) \\ &\equiv E[\{r^{\mathrm{u}}[b_0^{-1}(b), \tilde{Y}_1, \ldots, \tilde{Y}_k, \tilde{P}] - b_0(\tilde{Y}_k)\}1_{\{b \geqslant b_0(\tilde{Y}_k)\}}|\tilde{X}_1 = x] \\ &= E[E[\{r^{\mathrm{u}}[b_0^{-1}(b), \tilde{Y}_1, \ldots, \tilde{Y}_k, \tilde{P}] \\ &\quad - b_0(\tilde{Y}_k)\}1_{\{b \geqslant b_0(\tilde{Y}_k)\}}|\tilde{X}_1, \tilde{Y}_k] \,|\, \tilde{X}_1 = x] \\ &= E[\{v^{\mathrm{u}}[b_0^{-1}(b), \tilde{X}_1, \tilde{Y}_k] - b_0(\tilde{Y}_k)\}1_{\{b \geqslant b_0(\tilde{Y}_k)\}}|\tilde{X}_1 = x] \\ &= \int_{\underline{x}}^{b_0^{-1}(b)} \{v^{\mathrm{u}}[b_0^{-1}(b), x, y] - b_0(y)\}f_k(y|x)\,\mathrm{d}y. \end{aligned} \tag{16}$$

Taking the first derivative of $\Pi^{\mathrm{u}}(b|x)$ with respect to b gives

$$\begin{aligned} \frac{\partial \Pi^{\mathrm{u}}(b|x)}{\partial b} &= \{v^{\mathrm{u}}[b_0^{-1}(b), x, b_0^{-1}(b)] - b\}f_k[b_0^{-1}(b)|x]\{b_0'[b_0^{-1}(b)]\}^{-1} \\ &\quad + \{b_0'[b_0^{-1}(b)]\}^{-1} \int_{\underline{x}}^{b_0^{-1}(b)} v_1^{\mathrm{u}}[b_0^{-1}(b), x, y]\,f_k(y|x)\,\mathrm{d}y \end{aligned} \tag{17}$$

where $b_0'(x)$ is the derivative of $b_0(x)$ and v_1^{u} is the partial derivative of v^{u} with respect to its first argument. For $(b_0, \ldots, b_0)$ to be a Nash equilibrium, it is necessary that relation (17) be zero when $b = b_0(x)$. That is,

$$\begin{aligned} 0 &= b_0'(x) \left.\frac{\partial \Pi^{\mathrm{u}}(b|x)}{\partial b}\right|_{b = b_0(x)} \\ &= [v^{\mathrm{u}}(x, x, x) - b_0(x)]\,f_k(x|x) + \int_{\underline{x}}^{x} v_1^{\mathrm{u}}(x, x, y) f_k(y|x)\,\mathrm{d}y \end{aligned} \tag{18}$$

where we use the assumption that b_0 is strictly increasing. Rearranging terms implies that $b_0(x)$ is as defined in (15).

In a uniform price auction without resale markets Milgrom and Weber (1982a) show that the symmetric Nash equilibrium bidding strategy is $b^{\mathrm{u}}(x) = v^{\mathrm{u}}(x, x, x)$. As in discriminatory auctions, the bidding strategy b_0 is strictly higher than b^{u}, for every $x \in (\underline{x}, \bar{x}]$, by an amount which depends on the responsiveness v_1^{u} of the resale value to the submitted bid.

4.2 Revenue comparison with the discriminatory auction

Next we show that, when there exists a symmetric equilibrium in the uniform price auction, it generates strictly greater expected revenues than the symmetric equilibrium of the discriminatory auction.[11]

Theorem 4 When $(b_0, \ldots, b_0)$ is a symmetric Nash equilibrium in the uniform price auction, the expected revenue generated at this equilibrium is strictly greater than the expected revenue at the symmetric equilibrium of the discriminatory auction.

4.3 Possibility of nonexistence of equilibrium

In this subsection we illustrate the possibility that strong signaling incentives on the part of the bidders may lead to nonexistence of a pure strategy Nash equilibrium when winning bids are announced in a uniform price auction. First we present an example in which $\max\{\tilde{X}_1, \tilde{X}_2, \ldots, \tilde{X}_n, \tilde{P}\}$ is a sufficient statistic of $(\tilde{X}_1, \tilde{X}_2, \ldots, \tilde{X}_n, \tilde{P})$ for the posterior density of $\tilde{V}$. Although in this example the random variables are only weakly affiliated, it illustrates the difficulties that arise when the resale price is very responsive to the winning bids.

Example 4 Suppose that all the bids are announced after a uniform price auction. The prior marginal density of $\tilde{V}$ is uniform with support $[0, 1]$. The random variables $(\tilde{X}_1, \tilde{X}_2, \ldots, \tilde{X}_n, \tilde{P})$ are identically distributed and are independent conditional on $\tilde{V}$, and their conditional density is uniform on $[0, \tilde{V}]$. Let $\tilde{Z} = \max\{\tilde{X}_1, \tilde{X}_2, \ldots, \tilde{X}_n, \tilde{P}\}$. It is readily confirmed that $E[\tilde{V}|\tilde{X}_1, \tilde{X}_2, \ldots, \tilde{X}_n, \tilde{P}] = E[\tilde{V}|\tilde{Z}]$. Clearly, the resale price will be equal to $E[\tilde{V}|\tilde{Z}]$, and

$$\begin{aligned} E[\tilde{V}|\tilde{Z}] &\geqslant \tilde{Z} \\ E[\tilde{V}|\tilde{Z} = 1] &= 1. \end{aligned} \tag{19}$$

Let $(b_1, b_2, \ldots, b_n)$ be a candidate Nash equilibrium, with b_i strictly increasing. We limit our attention to weakly undominated strategies and thus $0 \leqslant b_i(\tilde{X}_i) \leqslant 1$. Let $\Pi^{\mathrm{u}}(b|x)$ be bidder 1's expected payoff when he bids b and $\tilde{X}_1 = x$. Then it is easily verified that if $x < \bar{x}$

$$\Pi^{\mathrm{u}}[b_1(x)|x] \leqslant \Pi^{\mathrm{u}}[b_1(\bar{x})|x], \tag{20}$$

since if bidder 1 bids $b_1(\bar{x})$ he will always win whenever he would have with a bid of $b_1(x)$, and pay the same price. In addition he will also win whenever the kth highest bid of the others' bid is in $(b_1(x), b_1(\bar{x}))$. Moreover, since b_1 is strictly increasing, (19) implies that the resale price if he bids $b_1(\bar{x})$ is equal to unity which is at least as large as the resale price if he wins with a bid of $b_1(x)$. The inequality in (20) is strict as long as there is a nonzero probability that the kth highest bid is in the interval $(b_1(x), b_1(\bar{x}))$.

Thus the only candidate Nash equilibrium appears to be a somewhat degenerate one in which at least one of the bidders, say bidder 1, always bids unity, and at least $n-k$ bidders bid sufficiently low that they never win, and the $n-k$ lowest bid is low enough that bidder 1 always maximizes his profits by bidding unity. However, if there is any strictly positive cost of participating in the auction (such as an entry fee or a bid preparation cost), then the $n-k$ bidders who never win at this equilibrium will not participate in the auction.

Next we show that if $k=1$ and $\tilde{P}$ is totally uninformative about $\tilde{V}$, then there does not exist a symmetric Nash equilibrium in strictly increasing strategies. Essentially when there is only one object and no other information becomes public after the auction, there exists a large incentive for the bidders to submit high bids, since the resale price is very responsive to the winning bid.

Proposition 4 Suppose that $k=1$ and that $\tilde{P}$ is independent of $\tilde{V}$. Then if the winning bid and the highest losing bid are announced there does not exist a Nash equilibrium in strictly increasing strategies.

However, there are other examples for which an equilibrium exists. For instance if $\tilde{V}$ is uniform on $[0,1]$ and $\tilde{X}_1$ is uniform on $[\tilde{V},1]$, then $v_1^{\mathrm{u}}(\cdot,\cdot,\cdot) \equiv 0$, and the equilibrium strategy is to bid $b_0(x) = v^{\mathrm{u}}(x,x,x)$. Whether there exist intuitive sufficient conditions under which an equilibrium exists remains an open question.

5 Uniform Price Auction Without Signaling

Since there exists a possibility of nonexistence of equilibrium in a uniform price auction with signaling, in this section we analyze uniform price auctions when the winning bids are not announced. Thus the bidders do not have an incentive to signal their private information, since if they win their bids are not revealed. Even without the signaling incentive, we are able to show that in at least two scenarios the expected revenue generated by this uniform price auction is higher than that generated by the discriminatory auction discussed in section 3. We believe that the first scenario is plausible for the case of the Treasury bill market.

5.1 Existence of a symmetric Nash equilibrium when the winning bids are not announced

We show below that there exists a symmetric Nash equilibrium in strictly increasing and differentiable strategies $(b^\star, b^\star, \ldots, b^\star)$ when buyers in the secondary market believe that all bidders use $b^\star$. Suppose that bidders $i = 2, \ldots, n$ adopt the strategy $b^\star$ and bidder 1 receives information $\tilde{X}_1 = x$ and submits a bid equal to b. If bidder 1 wins, the resale price is

$$\hat{r}^{\mathrm{u}}(\tilde{Y}_k, \tilde{P}) \equiv E[\tilde{V} | \tilde{Z}_{k+1} = \tilde{Y}_k, \tilde{P}] \\ = E[\tilde{V} | \tilde{X}_1 \geqslant \tilde{Y}_k, \tilde{Y}_k, \tilde{P}],$$

where $\tilde{Z}_j$ is the jth order statistic of $(\tilde{X}_1, \tilde{X}_2, \ldots, \tilde{X}_n)$. The equality follows from the fact that the signals are identically distributed. $\hat{r}^{\mathrm{u}}$ is strictly increasing in both its arguments. If bidder 1 wins the auction, the expected resale price conditional on $\tilde{Y}_k$ and $\tilde{X}_1$ is

$$\hat{v}^{\mathrm{u}}(x, y) \equiv E[\hat{r}^{\mathrm{u}}(\tilde{Y}_k, \tilde{P}) | \tilde{X}_1 = x, \tilde{Y}_k = y].$$

By strict affiliation, $\hat{v}^{\mathrm{u}}$ is strictly increasing in its arguments. Thus, if $X_1 = x$ and bidder 1 bids b, his expected profit is

$$\hat{\Pi}^{\mathrm{u}}(b|x) \equiv E[[\hat{r}^{\mathrm{u}}(\tilde{Y}_k, \tilde{P}) - b^\star(\tilde{Y}_k)] 1_{\{b \geqslant b^\star(\tilde{Y}_k)\}} | X_1 = x] \\ = E[E[[\hat{r}^{\mathrm{u}}(\tilde{Y}_k, \tilde{P}) - b^\star(\tilde{Y}_k)] 1_{\{b \geqslant b^\star(\tilde{Y}_k)\}} | \tilde{X}_1, \tilde{Y}_k] | \tilde{X}_1 = x] \\ = E[[\hat{v}^{\mathrm{u}}(\tilde{X}_1, \tilde{Y}_k) - b^\star(\tilde{Y}_k)] 1_{\{b \geqslant b^\star(\tilde{Y}_k)\}} | \tilde{X}_1 = x]. \quad (21)$$

Define

$$b^\star(x) \equiv \hat{v}^{\mathrm{u}}(x, x). \quad (22)$$

Note that $b^\star$ is strictly increasing. We show that $(b^\star, b^\star, \ldots, b^\star)$ is an equilibrium.

Theorem 5 The n-tuple $(b^\star, b^\star, \ldots, b^\star)$ is a Nash equilibrium in the uniform price auction provided that resale market buyers believe that all the bidders follow the strategy $b^\star$.

Milgrom and Weber (1982a) have shown that the price paid by winning bidders in a uniform price auction when bidders participate for the purposes of consumption is $E[\tilde{V} | \tilde{X}_1 = \tilde{Y}_k, \tilde{Y}_k]$. We show in the next lemma that the price paid by winning bidders in the uniform price auction in our model is greater than this. This is true even though the primary bidders do not have a signaling motive.

Lemma 4 With probability one, the price paid by winning bidders in a uniform price auction with a resale market is greater than that in a uniform price auction without resale markets (in which the bidders participate for consumption). That is

$$b^{\star}(\tilde{Y}_k) > E[\tilde{V} | \tilde{X}_1 = \tilde{Y}_k, \tilde{Y}_k]$$

with probability one.

The "true value" of the object for the primary bidders is the resale price. Thus, if no additional information becomes available after the auction, that is, if $\tilde{P}$ is constant, the winners' curse on the primary bidders is weakened. Since there is no signaling motive, we would expect the bids in the primary auction to increase when $\tilde{P}$ is constant (or when $\tilde{P}$ is independent of $(\tilde{V}, \tilde{X}_1, \tilde{X}_2, \ldots, \tilde{X}_n)$). This is proved in the next lemma.

Lemma 5 With probability one, the bids in the uniform price auction strictly increase when $\tilde{P}$ is constant, that is, when no additional information (other than about the bids submitted in the auction) becomes public after the auction.

5.2 *Revenue comparison with the discriminatory auction*

We obtain two sets of sufficient conditions under which the expected revenues generated at the symmetric equilibrium of the uniform price auction obtained in the previous subsection are greater than the expected revenues at the symmetric equilibrium of the discriminatory auction of section 3. The first set seems plausible for the case of Treasury bill auctions.

The following theorem states that if the public information $\tilde{P}$ is not very informative about the true value of the objects, the uniform price auction generates higher expected revenue than the discriminatory auction.

Theorem 6 There exists a scalar $M > 0$ such that if $\partial \hat{r}^{u}(y, p)/\partial p \leqslant M$ for all $y, p \in [\underline{x}, \bar{x}] \times [\underline{p}, \bar{p}]$, then the uniform price auction without signaling generates strictly higher expected revenue than the discriminatory auction with signaling at their respective symmetric equilibria.

In words, theorem 6 says that if the *ex post* public information $\tilde{P}$ has little impact on the resale price conditional on the information released from the uniform price auction, then the auctioneer's expected revenue is higher in the uniform price auction even when winning bids are not announced. This is true even though there is no signaling aspect in the uniform price auction. In the case of the Treasury bill auction, bids are submitted before 1:00 p.m. every Monday. The results of the auction are announced around 4:30 p.m. and the resale market comes into play. We would expect that any public information that normally arrives between 1:00 p.m. and 4:30 p.m. would not be very informative about $\tilde{V}$ conditional on the results of the earlier auction.

The following theorem gives an alternative scenario under which once again the uniform price auction generates higher revenues. Essentially it says that, if the signaling motive of the bidders is not strong, then the uniform price auction generates higher expected revenue.

Theorem 7 Suppose that $(\tilde{V}, \tilde{X}_1, \ldots, \tilde{X}_n)$ are strictly affiliated. There exists a scalar $M > 0$ such that if $\partial r^{\mathrm{d}}(x, y_1, \ldots, y_k, p)/\partial x \leqslant M$ for all $x, y_1, \ldots, y_k, p \in [\underline{x}, \bar{x}]^{k+1} \times [\underline{p}, \bar{p}]$, then the uniform price auction without signaling generates strictly higher expected revenue than the discriminatory auction with signaling at their respective symmetric equilibria.

A scenario where theorem 7 is applicable is when the public information $\tilde{P}$ is very informative about the true value $\tilde{V}$. Then the impact of $\tilde{X}_1$ on the resale price will be small when bidder 1 wins. However, this scenario does not seem to be plausible in the case of Treasury bill auctions.

6 Concluding Remarks

This paper is an exploratory study of competitive bidding when there exists a resale market which is informationally linked to the bidding. We have shown that there exists a symmetric Nash equilibrium in discriminatory auctions when winning bids and the highest losing bid are announced provided that the relevant variables are affiliated and are information complements. This is the only symmetric equilibrium when the resale market buyers have monotone beliefs. If his information is complementary to that of the bidders, the auctioneer will increase his expected revenue by precommitting to announce his private information before the auction. We know little about the general impact of the *ex post* information $\tilde{P}$ on the signaling motive of bidders. For the case of Treasury bill markets this is not important since we believe that very little additional information becomes publicly available in the short time period between the closing of the Treasury bill auction and the opening of the resale market. A related question which is of greater importance for Treasury bill auctions is whether there exist plausible scenarios in which the auctioneer can increase expected revenue by announcing his private information after the auction (and before the secondary markets convene) rather than before the auction. These warrant further investigation.

We established the possibility of nonexistence of an equilibrium in a uniform price auction when winning bids are announced. However, when there exists a symmetric equilibrium, it generates greater expected revenues than the symmetric equilibrium in a discriminatory auction. We also showed that there exists a symmetric Nash equilibrium in a uniform price auction when only the highest losing bid is announced, so that there is no signaling incentive for the bidders. Two scenarios are provided where the uniform price auction without signaling generates strictly higher expected revenue for the auctioneer than the discriminatory auction.

Some implications of our model deserve attention. First, it is easy to incorporate noncompetitive bids in our model, provided that the total amount j of noncompetitive bids is common knowledge before the auction. We can model the primary auction as one with n bidders and $k + j$ objects, j of which are awarded to noncompetitive bidders at the average price. The preceding analysis remains unchanged. The expected profits of the noncompetitive bidders are positive and equal to the *ex ante* expected profits of the competitive bidders. There is a prespecified minimum and maximum quantity for each noncompetitive bid, which may be the reason that resale market buyers do not buy Treasury bills through noncompetitive bids, and it may also explain why competitive bidders do not submit only noncompetitive bids while avoiding (presumably costly) information collection.[12] Second, the fact that *ex ante* expected profits of the bidders are strictly positive (except in uniform price auctions without signaling, when $\tilde{P}$ is uninformative about $\tilde{V}$) implies that, in expectation, the average price in the auction is strictly less than the resale price. This comparison has been empirically documented by Cammack (1986). Third, as pointed out in section 3.1, the primary bidders benefit if the resale market buyers are better informed about the true value, since it decreases the bidders' signaling incentive.

There are several possible extensions of our model. First, in the Treasury bill auction, the primary bidders submit price–quantity pairs and demand more than one unit of the Treasury bill. This feature is missing in our model. Second, one week before the conduct of the weekly Treasury bill auction, forward contracts of the Treasury bills to be auctioned are traded among the primary bidders. The relationship among the forward prices, bids submitted, and the resale price needs to be investigated. Third, there exists a wide variety of close substitutes of Treasury bills carried as inventories by primary bidders. These close substitutes may have a significant effect on the interplay between the forward markets and the weekly auction. We hope to investigate some of these issues in our future research.

Appendix

Proof of lemma 1

The joint density of $(\tilde{V}, \tilde{P}, \tilde{X}_1, \tilde{Y}_1, \ldots, \tilde{Y}_{n-1})$ is

$$(n-1)!f(v, p, x, y_1, \ldots, y_{n-1})1_{\{y_1 \geqslant y_2 \geqslant \cdots \geqslant y_{n-1}\}}.$$

As a consequence, the conditional density of $\tilde{V}$ given $(\tilde{P}, \tilde{X}_1, \tilde{Y}_1, \ldots, \tilde{Y}_{n-1})$ is

$$\frac{f(v, p, x, y_1, \ldots, y_{n-1})}{f(p, x, y_1, \ldots, y_{n-1})} 1_{\{y_1 \geqslant y_2 \geqslant \cdots \geqslant y_{n-1}\}}.$$

Thus $(\tilde{P}, \tilde{X}_1, \tilde{Y}_1, \ldots, \tilde{Y}_k)$ are information complements. Let r_1^{d} denote the derivative of r^{d}, which is defined in (1), with respect to its first argument. It is then easily verified that $r_1^{\mathrm{d}}(x, y_1, \ldots, y_k, p)$ is a strictly increasing function of p, y_j, $\forall j$. Next note that

$$v_1^{\mathrm{d}}(x, x', y) = E[r_1^{\mathrm{d}}(x, \tilde{Y}_1, \ldots, \tilde{Y}_k, \tilde{P}) | \tilde{X}_1 = x', \tilde{Y}_k = y].$$

Theorem 5 of Milgrom and Weber (1982a) then implies, by affiliation, that $v_1^{\mathrm{d}}(x, x', y)$ is a strictly increasing function of x' and y. ■

Proof of proposition 1

We first write

$$\begin{aligned} v^{\mathrm{d}}(x, x, x) - \hat{b}(x) &= \int_{\underline{x}}^{x} L(u|x)\, \mathrm{d}t(u) - \int_{\underline{x}}^{x} \frac{h(u)}{f_k(u|u)}\, \mathrm{d}L(u|x) \\ &= \int_{\underline{x}}^{x} L(u|x) \\ &\quad \times \left[v_1^{\mathrm{d}}(u, u, u) + v_2^{\mathrm{d}}(u, u, u) + v_3^{\mathrm{d}}(u, u, u) - \frac{h(u)}{F_k(u|u)} \right] \mathrm{d}u. \end{aligned} \tag{A1}$$

By the hypothesis that $(\tilde{X}_1, \ldots, \tilde{X}_n, \tilde{P})$ are information complements with respect to $\tilde{V}$ and lemma 1, $v_1^{\mathrm{d}}(u, u, u) \geqslant v_1^{\mathrm{d}}(u, u, y)$ for $y \leqslant u$. It follows that

$$\frac{h(u)}{F_k(u|u)} = \int_{\underline{x}}^{u} v_1^{\mathrm{d}}(u, u, y) \frac{f_k(y|u)}{F_k(u|u)}\, \mathrm{d}y \leqslant v_1^{\mathrm{d}}(u, u, u).$$

Substituting this relation into (A1) gives

$$v^{\mathrm{d}}(x, x, x) - \hat{b}(x) \geqslant \int_{\underline{x}}^{x} L(u|x)[v_2^{\mathrm{d}}(u, u, u) + v_3^{\mathrm{d}}(u, u, u)]\, du \geqslant 0.$$

Note that the above inequality is strict for $x \in (\underline{x}, \bar{x}]$ since $v_2^{\mathrm{d}} > 0$ and $v_3^{\mathrm{d}} > 0$ by strict affiliation. ■

Proof of corollary 1
We shall show that $\hat{b}'(x) > 0$, $\forall x > \underline{x}$. From proposition 1 we have $v^{\mathrm{d}}(x, x, x) - \hat{b}(x) > 0$, $\forall x > \underline{x}$. The proof is completed by inserting this in (5) and noting that $v_1^{\mathrm{d}} > 0$. ∎

Proof of lemma 3
By affiliation we have for $\beta \geqslant \alpha$, $x' \geqslant x$

$$f_k(\alpha|x')f_k(\beta|x) \leqslant f_k(\alpha|x)f_k(\beta|x').$$

Thus for $x \geqslant y$

$$\int_y^x \int_{\underline{x}}^y f_k(\alpha|x')f_k(\beta|x)\,\mathrm{d}\alpha\,\mathrm{d}\beta \leqslant \int_y^x \int_{\underline{x}}^y f_k(\alpha|x)f_k(\beta|x')\,\mathrm{d}\alpha\,\mathrm{d}\beta,$$

which is equivalent to

$$F_k(y|x')[F_k(x|x) - F_k(y|x)] \leqslant F_k(y|x)[F_k(x|x') - F_k(y|x')].$$

Rearranging terms gives

$$\frac{F_k(y|x')}{F_k(x|x')} \leqslant \frac{F_k(y|x)}{F_k(x|x)}.$$

∎

Proof of theorem 1
Let $x' \leqslant x$. Recall from (4) that

$$\begin{aligned}
0 &= \frac{\partial \Pi^{\mathrm{d}}[\hat{b}(x')|x']}{\partial b} \\
&= [\hat{b}'(x')]^{-1} F_k(x'|x') \\
&\quad \times \left\{ [v^{\mathrm{d}}(x', x', x') - \hat{b}(x')] \frac{f_k(x'|x')}{F_k(x'|x')} - \hat{b}'(x') + \int_{\underline{x}}^{x'} v_1^{\mathrm{d}}(x', x', y) \frac{f_k(y|x')}{F_k(x'|x')}\,\mathrm{d}y \right\} \\
&\leqslant [\hat{b}'(x')]^{-1} F_k(x'|x') \\
&\quad \times \left\{ [v^{\mathrm{d}}(x', x, x') - \hat{b}(x')] \frac{f_k(x'|x)}{F_k(x'|x)} - \hat{b}'(x') + \int_{\underline{x}}^{x'} v_1^{\mathrm{d}}(x', x, y) \frac{f_k(y|x')}{F_k(x'|x')}\,\mathrm{d}y \right\} \\
&\leqslant [\hat{b}'(x')]^{-1} F_k(x'|x') \\
&\quad \times \left\{ [v^{\mathrm{d}}(x', x, x') - \hat{b}(x')] \frac{f_k(x'|x)}{F_k(x'|x)} - \hat{b}'(x') + \int_{\underline{x}}^{x'} v_1^{\mathrm{d}}(x', x, y) \frac{f_k(y|x)}{F_k(x'|x)}\,\mathrm{d}y \right\} \\
&= \frac{F_k(x'|x')}{F_k(x'|x)} \frac{\partial \Pi^{\mathrm{d}}[\hat{b}(x')|x]}{\partial b}
\end{aligned}$$

where the first inequality follows from proposition 1, lemma 1, and lemma 2, and the second inequality follows from lemma 3. That is, when $\tilde{X}_1 = x$ and bidder 1 bids $b = \hat{b}(x') \leqslant \hat{b}(x)$, his expected profit can be raised by bidding higher. Similar arguments show that

$$\frac{\partial \Pi^{\mathrm{d}}[b(x')|x]}{\partial b} \leqslant 0$$

for $x' \geqslant x$. As a consequence, $\Pi^{\mathrm{d}}(b|x)$ is maximized at $b = \hat{b}(x)$. Finally, since $\Pi^{\mathrm{d}}[\hat{b}(\underline{x})|x] = 0$ for all x, we have $\Pi^{\mathrm{d}}[\hat{b}(x)|x] > 0$ for all $x > \underline{x}$, by strict affiliation. We have thus shown that $\hat{b}(x)$ is the best strategy for bidder 1 when he observes $\tilde{X}_1 = x$, when bidders $i = 2, 3, \ldots, n$ follow $\hat{b}$, and when the resale market participants believe that all the bidders follow $\hat{b}$. ■

Proof of theorem 2

Suppose that $(b_s, b_s, \ldots, b_s)$ is a symmetric equilibrium in nondecreasing strategies. Therefore b_s is differentiable almost everywhere. Thus, as in Milgrom and Weber (1982a, theorem 14), the proof is complete once we establish that b_s must be strictly increasing and continuous. Hence b_s must satisfy the differential equation (5) and the only solution to this is $\hat{b}$ of (7).

First, suppose that b_s is not strictly increasing. That is, there exist $x_a < x_b$ such that $b_s(x) = c$, $\forall x \in [x_a, x_b]$. The resale price if bidder 1 wins with a bid b is

$$r^{\mathrm{s}}(b, \tilde{B}_1, \ldots, \tilde{B}_k, \tilde{P}) = E[\tilde{V}|\tilde{b}_1 = b, \tilde{B}_1, \ldots, \tilde{B}_k, \tilde{P}],$$

where $\tilde{b}_1$ is the random variable which denotes bidder 1's bid and $\tilde{B}_l$ is the lth-order statistic of the others' equilibrium bids, $(b_s(\tilde{X}_2), \ldots, b_s(\tilde{X}_n))$. Since b_s is nondecreasing, B_l is affiliated with all the other random variables in the model. Analogous to v^{d} we define the conditional expected resale price if bidder 1 wins:

$$v^{\mathrm{s}}(b, x, \beta) \equiv E[r^{\mathrm{s}}(b, \tilde{B}_1, \ldots, \tilde{B}_k, \tilde{P})|\tilde{X}_1 = x, \tilde{B}_k = \beta].$$

The affiliation and monotone beliefs of the resale market buyers imply that r^{s} and v^{s} are nondecreasing in all arguments. The expected profit for bidder 1 when $\tilde{X}_1 = x \in [x_a, x_b]$ and he submits an equilibrium bid $b_s(x) = c$ is

$$\begin{aligned}\Pi^{\mathrm{s}}(c|x) = {} & E[[v^{\mathrm{s}}(c, \tilde{X}_1, \tilde{B}_k) - c]\, 1_{\{\tilde{B}_k < c\}}|\tilde{X}_1 = x] \\ & + \Pr\{\text{bidder 1 wins} \mid \tilde{B}_k = c, \tilde{b}_1 = c\} \\ & \times E[[v^{\mathrm{s}}(c, \tilde{X}_1, \tilde{B}_k) - c]\, 1_{\{\tilde{B}_k = c\}}|\tilde{X}_1 = x] \end{aligned} \tag{A2}$$

where the probability that bidder 1 is declared a winner given that there is a tie is the expectation of the number of objects left after those who bid more than c have been assigned objects divided by the number of bidders (including bidder 1) who bid c. Since $b_s(x) = c$, $\forall x \in [x_a, x_b]$, both this probability and the probability of the event $\{\tilde{B}_k = c\}$ are strictly positive (and strictly less than unity). We must have $v^{\mathrm{s}}(c, x_a, c) \geqslant c$ or else a bid $b_s(x_a) = c$ results in negative profits when $\tilde{X}_1 = x_a$. Therefore, by strict affiliation, for any $x_0 \in (x_a, x_b]$ there exists $\varepsilon_1 > 0$ (which depends on x_0) such that $v^{\mathrm{s}}(c, x_0, c) > c + \varepsilon_1$. Thus the second expression in (A2) is strictly positive for $x = x_0$. If instead of c bidder 1 bids slightly more when $\tilde{X}_1 = x_0$, there is a discontinuous jump in his probability of winning since, if $\tilde{B}_k = c$, bidder 1 will now win with probability one. Since beliefs are monotone, $v^{\mathrm{s}}(c', x_0, \cdot) \geqslant v^{\mathrm{s}}(c, x_0, \cdot)$, $\forall c' > c$. Therefore there exists $\varepsilon_2 > 0$ such that a bid of $b_s(x_0) + \varepsilon_2$ leads to greater expected profits than $b_s(x_0)$. This contradicts our assumption that b_s is an equilibrium strategy. Therefore b_s must be strictly increasing.

Next suppose that b_s has a discontinuity at x_d. Consider the case where $\lim_{x\uparrow x_d} b_s(x) < b_s(x_d)$. Since b_s is strictly increasing and can be inverted we shall write $v^s(x', x, y)$ instead of $v^s(b, x, \beta)$ where $b_s(x') = b$ and $b_s(y) = \beta$. Then the continuity of v^s implies that for small enough $\varepsilon > 0$

$$\begin{aligned}\Pi^s[b_s(x_d)|x_d] &= E[[v^s(x_d, x_d, \tilde{Y}_k) - b_s(x_d)]\,1_{\{\tilde{Y}_k \leqslant x_d\}}|\tilde{X}_1 = x_d] \\ &< E[[v^s(x_d - \varepsilon, x_d, \tilde{Y}_k) - b_s(x_d - \varepsilon)]\,1_{\{\tilde{Y}_k \leqslant x_d - \varepsilon\}}|\tilde{X}_1 = x_d] \\ &= \Pi[b_s(x_d - \varepsilon)|x_d],\end{aligned}$$

which contradicts our assumption that $b_s(x_d)$ is an equilibrium bid.

The possibility that $\lim_{x\downarrow x_d} b_s(x) > b_s(x_d)$ can be ruled out similarly. ■

We record a technical lemma before proving proposition 3.

Lemma A1 (Milgrom and Weber, 1982a) Let $\rho(z)$ and $\sigma(z)$ be differentiable functions for which (a) $\rho(\underline{x}) \geqslant \sigma(\underline{x})$ and (b) $\rho(z) < \sigma(z)$ implies $\rho'(z) \geqslant \sigma'(z)$. Then $\rho(z) \geqslant \sigma(z)$ for all $z \geqslant \underline{x}$.

Proof of proposition 3

Let $x_0 \geqslant x_0'$. By affiliation we know that

$$\bar{b}(\underline{x}; x_0) = w^d(\underline{x}, \underline{x}, \underline{x}; x_0) \geqslant \bar{b}(\underline{x}, x_0') = w^d(\underline{x}, \underline{x}, \underline{x}; x_0').$$

If we can show that $\bar{b}(x; x_0) < \bar{b}(x; x_0')$ implies $\bar{b}'(x; x_0) \geqslant \bar{b}'(x; x_0')$, then the proposition follows from lemma A1. Suppose that $\bar{b}(x, x_0) < \bar{b}(x; x_0')$. As generalizations of lemmas 1, 2, and 3, we have that $w_1^d(x, x', y; x_0)$ is increasing in both y and x_0, $F_k(y|x; x_0)/f_k(y|x; x_0)$ is decreasing in x_0 and that $F_k(\cdot|x; x_0)/F_k(\cdot|x; x_0)$ dominates $F_k(\cdot|x; x_0')/F_k(\cdot|x; x_0')$ in the sense of first-degree stochastic dominance. Then

$$\begin{aligned}\bar{b}'(x; x_0) &= [w^d(x, x, x; x_0) - \bar{b}(x; x_0)]\,\frac{f_k(x|x; x_0)}{F_k(x|x; x_0)} \\ &\quad + \int_{\underline{x}}^{x} w_1^d(x, x, y; x_0)\,\frac{f_k(y|x; x_0)}{F_k(x|x; x_0)}\,\mathrm{d}y \\ &\geqslant [w^d(x, x, x; x_0') - \bar{b}(x; x_0')]\,\frac{f_k(x|x; x_0')}{F_k(x|x; x_0')} \\ &\quad + \int_{\underline{x}}^{x} w_1^d(x, x, y; x_0')\,\frac{f_k(y|x; x_0')}{F_k(x|x; x_0)}\,\mathrm{d}y \\ &= \bar{b}'(x; x_0'),\end{aligned}$$

which was to be shown. ■

Proof of theorem 3

Given proposition 3, the proof of theorem 3 mimics that of Milgrom and Weber (1982a, theorem 16).

Define

$$W(x,z) \equiv E[\bar{b}(x;\tilde{X}_0)\,|\,\tilde{Y}_k \leqslant x, \tilde{X}_1 = z],$$

which is the expected price paid by bidder 1 when the auctioneer publicly reveals $\tilde{X}_0$, conditional on bidder 1 winning when $\tilde{X}_1 = z$ and bidder 1 bids as if $\tilde{X}_1 = x$. By proposition 3 and the hypothesis that $\tilde{X}_0$ and $\tilde{X}_1$ are affiliated, $W_2(x,z) \geqslant 0$. Note that, by symmetry, the expected revenue for the seller under the policy of publicly reporting $\tilde{X}_0$ is k times

$$\begin{aligned}
&E[\bar{b}(\tilde{X}_1;\tilde{X}_0)|\{\tilde{Y}_k \leqslant \tilde{X}_1\}]\\
&\quad = E[E[\bar{b}(\tilde{X}_1;\tilde{X}_0)|\tilde{Y}_k \leqslant \tilde{X}_1, \tilde{X}_1]\,|\{\tilde{Y}_k \leqslant \tilde{X}_1\}]\\
&\quad = E[W(\tilde{X}_1,\tilde{X}_1)|\{\tilde{Y}_k \leqslant \tilde{X}_1\}],
\end{aligned}$$

where the first equality follows from the law of iterative expectations and the second from the definition of W. If $\tilde{X}_0$ is not reported, the expected revenue for the seller is k times

$$E[\bar{b}(\tilde{X}_1)|\{\tilde{Y}_k \leqslant \tilde{X}_1\}].$$

If we can show that $W(x,x) \geqslant \bar{b}(x)$, then we are done. We shall utilize Milgrom and Weber (1982, lemma 2). Note first that, by the law of iterative expectations,

$$\begin{aligned}
W(\underline{x};\underline{x}) &= E[\bar{b}(\underline{x};\tilde{X}_0)|\tilde{Y}_k \leqslant \underline{x}, \tilde{X}_1 = \underline{x}]\\
&= E[w(\underline{x},\underline{x},\underline{x};\tilde{X}_0)|\tilde{Y}_k = \underline{x}, \tilde{X}_1 = \underline{x}]\\
&= E[E[\tilde{V}|\tilde{X}_0, \tilde{X}_1 = \underline{x}, \tilde{Y}_k = \underline{x}]\,|\,\tilde{Y}_k \leqslant \underline{x}, \tilde{X}_1 = \underline{x}]\\
&= v(\underline{x},\underline{x},\underline{x}) = \bar{b}(\underline{x}).
\end{aligned}$$

Now we claim that $W(x,x) < \bar{b}(x)$ implies $\mathrm{d}W(x,x)/\mathrm{d}x \geqslant \bar{b}'(x)$. Note first that if bidder 1, prior to learning $\tilde{X}_0$ but after observing $\tilde{X}_1 = x$, were to commit himself to some bidding strategy $\bar{b}(z;\cdot)$, his optimal choice would be $z = x$, since $\bar{b}(x;x_0)$ is optimal when $\tilde{X}_0 = x_0$. Thus $\hat{W}(z,x)$ at $z = x$ will have to satisfy the first-order condition

$$W_1(x,x) = [v(x,x,x) - W(x,x)]\,\frac{f_k(x|x)}{F_k(x|x)} + \int_{\underline{x}}^{x} v_1(x,x,y)\,\frac{f_k(y|x)}{F_k(x|x)}\,\mathrm{d}y. \tag{A3}$$

Then

$$\begin{aligned}
\bar{b}'(x) &= [v(x,x,x) - \bar{b}(x)]\,\frac{f_k(x|x)}{F_k(x|x)} + \int_{\underline{x}}^{x} v_1(x,x,y)\,\frac{f_k(y|x)}{F_k(x|x)}\,\mathrm{d}y\\
&\leqslant [v(x,x,x) - W(x,x)]\,\frac{f_k(x|x)}{F_k(x|x)} + \int_{\underline{x}}^{x} v_1(x,x,y)\,\frac{f_k(y|x)}{F_k(x|x)}\,\mathrm{d}y\\
&\leqslant W_1(x,x) + W_2(x,x) = \frac{\mathrm{d}W(x,x)}{\mathrm{d}x}
\end{aligned}$$

where the first equality follows from (6), the first inequality follows from the hypothesis that $W(x, x) < \hat{b}(x)$, and the second inequality follows from (A3) and the fact that $W_2(x, x) \geqslant 0$. The assertion then follows from Milgrom and Weber (1982, lemma 2). ■

Proof of theorem 4

Let $P^{\mathrm{u}}(x)$ denote the expected price paid by bidder 1 in a uniform price auction, conditional upon winning, when bidders use strategy b_0 and $\tilde{X}_1 = x$. That is

$$P^{\mathrm{u}}(x) \equiv \int_{\underline{x}}^{x} b_0(y) \frac{f_k(y|x)}{F_k(x|x)} \, \mathrm{d}y$$

$$= \int_{\underline{x}}^{x} \left[v^{\mathrm{u}}(y, y, y) + \frac{h(y)}{f_k(y|y)} \right] \frac{f_k(y|x)}{F_k(x|x)} \, \mathrm{d}y. \tag{A4}$$

If $P^{\mathrm{d}}(x)$ denotes the corresponding expected price when bidders use strategy $\hat{b}$ in a discriminatory auction then

$$P^{\mathrm{d}}(x) \equiv \hat{b}(x) \tag{A5}$$

$$= \int_{\underline{x}}^{x} \left[v^{\mathrm{d}}(y, y, y) + \frac{h(y)}{f_k(y|y)} \right] \mathrm{d}L(y|x)$$

$$= \int_{\underline{x}}^{x} b_0(y) \, \mathrm{d}L(y|x) \tag{A6}$$

where the first equality follows from using integration by parts on (7) and the second from (14). Note that $L(u|x)$ and $F_k(y|x)/F_k(x|x)$ are probability distributions on $[\underline{x}, x]$. Then, since $b_0(y)$ is increasing, the proof is complete if we can show that $F_k(y|x)/F_k(x|x)$ stochastically dominates $L(u|x)$ in the sense of first order, that is,

$$\frac{F_k(y|x)}{F_k(x|x)} \leqslant L(u|x), \qquad \forall y.$$

Since

$$\ln[F_k(y|x)] = \int_{\underline{x}}^{y} \frac{f_k(s|x)}{F_k(s|x)} \, \mathrm{d}s$$

we have

$$F_k(y|x) = \exp\left[\int_{\underline{x}}^{y} \frac{f_k(s|x)}{F_k(s|x)} \, \mathrm{d}s \right].$$

Therefore

$$\frac{F_k(y|x)}{F_k(x|x)} = \exp\left[- \int_{y}^{x} \frac{f_k(s|x)}{F_k(s|x)} \, \mathrm{d}s \right]$$

$$\leqslant \exp\left[- \int_{y}^{x} \frac{f_k(s|s)}{F_k(s|s)} \, \mathrm{d}s \right]$$

$$= L(y|x)$$

where the inequality follows from lemma 2. ■

Proof of proposition 4

Let $(b_1, b_2, \ldots, b_n)$ be a candidate for Nash equilibrium where $b_i: [\underline{x}, \bar{x}] \mapsto \mathbb{R}$ are strictly increasing. We shall show that if bidder j uses strategy b_j, $j = 2, 3, \ldots, n$, and the resale market buyers believe that each bidder i uses strategy b_i, $i = 1, 2, \ldots, n$, then bidder 1 has an incentive to deviate from $b_1(\tilde{X}_1)$. In fact we shall show that when $\tilde{X}_1 = x$ bidder 1's profits are *minimized* at a bid of $b_1(x)$.

The price that bidder 1 faces is

$$\tilde{B}_1 \equiv \max\{b_2(\tilde{X}_2), b_3(\tilde{X}_3), \ldots, b_n(\tilde{X}_n)\}.$$

Since the b_i are strictly increasing, $\tilde{X}_1$ and $\tilde{B}_1$ are strictly affiliated and $\tilde{B}_1$ is atomless. We assume, for simplicity, that $\tilde{B}_1$ has a density function. The expected resale price if bidder 1 wins with a bid equal to b is[13]

$$r^{\mathrm{u}}[b_1^{-1}(b), \tilde{B}_1] \equiv E[\tilde{V} \mid \tilde{X}_1 = b_1^{-1}(b), \tilde{B}_1]$$

The expected profit for bidder 1 if $\tilde{X}_1 = x$ and he bids $b_1(x')$ is

$$\begin{aligned} \Pi^{\mathrm{u}}(x' \mid x) &\equiv E[[r^{\mathrm{u}}(x', \tilde{B}_1) - B_1] 1_{\{b_1(x') \geqslant \tilde{B}_1\}} \mid \tilde{X}_1 = x] \\ &= \int_{\underline{b}}^{b_1(x')} [r^{\mathrm{u}}(x', \beta) - \beta] g(\beta \mid x) \, \mathrm{d}\beta, \end{aligned}$$

where $\underline{b} \equiv \min\{b_2(\underline{x}), b_3(\underline{x}), \ldots, b_n(\underline{x})\}$, and $g(\cdot \mid x)$ is the conditional density of $\tilde{B}_1$ given $\tilde{X}_1 = x$. The first-order necessary condition for b_1 to be an equilibrium strategy is

$$\begin{aligned} \left.\frac{\partial \Pi^{\mathrm{u}}(x' \mid x)}{\partial x'}\right|_{x' = x} &= \{r^{\mathrm{u}}[x, b_1(x)] - b_1(x)\} g[b_1(x) \mid x] \\ &\quad + \int_{\underline{b}}^{b_1(x)} r_1^{\mathrm{u}}(x, \beta) g(\beta \mid x) \, \mathrm{d}\beta = 0, \end{aligned}$$

where $r_1^{\mathrm{u}}(x, \beta)$ denotes the derivative of r^{u} with respect to its first argument.

Let $x' > x$. Then by strict affiliation

$$\begin{aligned} 0 &= \{r^{\mathrm{u}}[x', b_1(x')] - b_1(x')\} g[b_1(x') \mid x'] + \int_{\underline{b}}^{b_1(x')} r_1^{\mathrm{u}}(x', \beta) g(\beta \mid x') \, \mathrm{d}\beta \\ &< g[b_1(x') \mid x'] \\ &\quad \times \left(\{r^{\mathrm{u}}[x', b_1(x')] - b_1(x')\} + \int_{\underline{b}}^{b_1(x')} r_1^{\mathrm{u}}(x', \beta) \frac{g(\beta \mid x)}{g[b_1(x') \mid x]} \, \mathrm{d}\beta \right) \\ &= \frac{g[b_1(x') \mid x']}{g[b_1(x') \mid x]} \frac{\partial \Pi(x' \mid x)}{\partial x'}. \end{aligned}$$

Similarly, we can show that, for $x' < x$,

$$\frac{\partial \Pi(x' \mid x)}{\partial x'} < 0.$$

Thus for any $x \in [\underline{x}, \bar{x}]$, $\Pi^{\mathrm{u}}(x' \mid x)$ achieves a global minimum at $x' = x$! ■

Proof of theorem 5
Given that bidders $2, 3, \ldots, n$ use $b^\star$, we can rewrite (21) as

$$\hat{\Pi}^{u}(b|x) = \int_{\underline{x}}^{b^{\star-1}(b)} [\hat{v}^{u}(x, y) - \hat{v}^{u}(y, y)]\, f_k(y|x)\, \mathrm{d}y, \tag{A7}$$

where $f_k(y|x)$ is the conditional density of $\tilde{Y}_k$ given $\tilde{X}_1$. Since, by strict affiliation, $\hat{v}^{u}$ is strictly increasing in both arguments, the integrand in (A7) is positive if and only if $x > y$. Thus bidder 1's profits are maximized when he wins if and only if $\{\tilde{X}_1 \geqslant \tilde{Y}_k\}$. Therefore bidder 1's profits are maximized[14] if he uses the strategy $b^\star$. ■

Proof of lemma 4
From the definition of $b^\star$ we have, if $\tilde{Y}_k \neq \bar{x}$,

$$\begin{aligned} b^\star(\tilde{Y}_k) &\equiv E[E[\tilde{V}|\tilde{X}_1 \geqslant \tilde{Y}_k, \tilde{Y}_k, \tilde{P}]\,|\,\tilde{X}_1 = \tilde{Y}_k, \tilde{Y}_k] \\ &> E[E[\tilde{V}|\tilde{X}_1 = \tilde{Y}_k, \tilde{Y}_k, \tilde{P}]\,|\,\tilde{X}_1 = \tilde{Y}_k, \tilde{Y}_k] \\ &= E[\tilde{V}|\tilde{X}_1 = \tilde{Y}_k, \tilde{Y}_k], \end{aligned}$$

where the inequality follows from strict affiliation, and the equality from the law of iterative expectations. Note that the strict inequality above is an equality when $\tilde{Y}_k = \bar{x}$, which is a zero probability event. ■

Proof of lemma 5
Let $b^\star$ be the equilibrium bidding strategy when $\tilde{P}$ is a strictly affiliated random variable, and let $b_c^\star$ be the equilibrium bidding strategy when $\tilde{P}$ is constant. Then since

$$E[E[\tilde{V}|\tilde{X}_1 \geqslant \tilde{Y}_k, \tilde{Y}_k]\,|\,\tilde{X}_1, \tilde{Y}_k] = E[\tilde{V}|\tilde{X}_1 \geqslant \tilde{Y}_k, \tilde{Y}_k],$$

we have

$$\begin{aligned} b_c^\star(x) &\equiv E[E[\tilde{V}|\tilde{X}_1 \geqslant \tilde{Y}_k, \tilde{Y}_k]\,|\,\tilde{X}_1 = x, \tilde{Y}_k = x] \\ &= E[\tilde{V}|\tilde{X}_1 \geqslant x, \tilde{Y}_k = x] \\ &= E[\tilde{V}|\tilde{Z}_{k+1} = x], \end{aligned} \tag{A8}$$

where the last equality follows since the signals are identically distributed. Next, when $x \neq \bar{x}$,

$$\begin{aligned} b^\star(x) &\equiv E[E[\tilde{V}|\tilde{X}_1 \geqslant \tilde{Y}_k, \tilde{Y}_k, \tilde{P}]\,|\,\tilde{X}_1 = x, \tilde{Y}_k = x] \\ &= E[E[\tilde{V}|\tilde{Z}_{k+1}, \tilde{P}]\,|\tilde{Z}_k = x, \tilde{Z}_{k+1} = x] \\ &< E[E[\tilde{V}|\tilde{Z}_{k+1}, \tilde{P}]\,|\tilde{Z}_k \geqslant x, \tilde{Z}_{k+1} = x] \\ &= E[E[\tilde{V}|\tilde{Z}_{k+1}, \tilde{P}]\,|\tilde{Z}_{k+1} = x] \\ &= E[\tilde{V}|\tilde{Z}_{k+1} = x] \\ &= b_c^\star(x), \end{aligned}$$

where the first equality follows since the signals are identically distributed, the inequality follows from strict affiliation, the second equality follows from the definition of Z_k, and the last equality follows from (A8). When $x = \bar{x}$, which is a zero probability event, the above strict inequality becomes an equality. Thus the assertion of the lemma is proved. ■

Proof of theorem 6

By symmetry, the expected revenue for the auctioneer is equal to n times the unconditional expected payment of bidder 1. Let $\hat{R}^{\mathrm{u}}$ and R^{d} denote the expected revenue of the auctioneer under uniform price auction and under discriminatory auction respectively. Then

$$\begin{aligned}\hat{R}^{\mathrm{u}} &= n \times E[b^{\star}(\tilde{Y}_k)1_{\{\tilde{X}_1 \geqslant \tilde{Y}_k\}}]\\ &= k \times E[b^{\star}(\tilde{Y}_k)|\tilde{X}_1 \geqslant \tilde{Y}_k]\\ R^{\mathrm{d}} &= n \times E[\hat{b}(\tilde{X}_1)1_{\{\tilde{X}_1 \geqslant \tilde{Y}_k\}}]\\ &= k \times E[\hat{b}(\tilde{X}_1)|\tilde{X}_1 \geqslant \tilde{Y}_k].\end{aligned}$$

Note that the total unconditional expected profits for bidders in equilibrium for the uniform price auction and for the discriminatory auction are respectively

$$\begin{aligned}&n \times E[[\hat{r}^{\mathrm{u}}(\tilde{Y}_k, \tilde{P}) - b^{\star}(\tilde{Y}_k)]\, 1_{\{\tilde{X}_1 \geqslant \tilde{Y}_k\}}]\\ &\quad = k \times E[\tilde{V}|\tilde{X}_1 \geqslant \tilde{Y}_k] - \hat{R}^{\mathrm{u}}\end{aligned}$$

and

$$\begin{aligned}&n \times E[[r^{\mathrm{d}}(\tilde{X}_1, \tilde{Y}_1, \ldots, \tilde{Y}_k, \tilde{P}) - b^{\star}(\tilde{X}_1)]\, 1_{\{\tilde{X}_1 \geqslant \tilde{Y}_k\}}]\\ &\quad = k \times E[\tilde{V}|\tilde{X}_1 \geqslant \tilde{Y}_k] - R^{\mathrm{d}}.\end{aligned}$$

Thus, before bidders receive their private information, the two auctions are constant-sum games between the auctioneer and the bidders, with total payoff equal to $k \times E[\tilde{V}|\tilde{X}_1 \geqslant \tilde{Y}_k]$. If we put

$$\hat{r}^{\mathrm{u}}(\tilde{Y}_k) \equiv E[\tilde{V}|\tilde{X}_1 \geqslant \tilde{Y}_k, \tilde{Y}_k],$$

it is easily seen that

$$E[\hat{r}^{\mathrm{u}}(\tilde{Y}_k, \tilde{P}) - \hat{r}^{\mathrm{u}}(\tilde{Y}_k)|\tilde{X}_1 \geqslant \tilde{Y}_k, \tilde{Y}_k] = 0,$$

and hence

$$E[\hat{r}^{\mathrm{u}}(\tilde{Y}_k, \tilde{P}) - \hat{r}^{\mathrm{u}}(\tilde{Y}_k)|\tilde{X}_1 \geqslant \tilde{Y}_k] = 0.$$

Thus

$$R^{\mathrm{o}} \equiv k \times E[\hat{r}^{\mathrm{u}}(\tilde{Y}_k)|\tilde{X}_1 \geqslant \tilde{Y}_k] > R^{\mathrm{d}} = k \times E[\hat{b}(\tilde{X}_1)|\tilde{X}_1 \geqslant \tilde{Y}_k],$$

since the (unconditional) expected profit of a bidder in a discriminatory auction is always strictly positive by strict affiliation.

For ease of exposition, we assume that the support of $\tilde{P}$ is finite. Then

$$M \equiv \frac{R^{\mathrm{o}} - R^{\mathrm{d}}}{k(\bar{p} - \underline{p})}$$

is strictly positive. We shall show that if $\partial\hat{r}^{\mathrm{u}}(y, p)/\partial p \leqslant M$ for all $y, p \in [\underline{x}, \bar{x}] \times [\underline{p}, \bar{p}]$, then $\hat{R}^{\mathrm{u}} \geqslant R^{\mathrm{d}}$. First note that by affiliation $\partial\hat{r}^{\mathrm{u}}(y, p)/\partial p \geqslant 0$. Thus

$$\begin{aligned}\hat{r}^{\mathrm{u}}(\tilde{Y}_k, \tilde{P}) &\geqslant \hat{r}^{\mathrm{u}}(\tilde{Y}_k, \bar{p}) - M(\bar{p} - \tilde{P})\\ &> \hat{r}^{\mathrm{u}}(\tilde{Y}_k) - M(\bar{p} - \underline{p}),\end{aligned}$$

where the strict inequality follows from the assumption of strict affiliation. Hence

$$\hat{r}^{\mathrm{u}}(\tilde{Y}_k) - \hat{r}^{\mathrm{u}}(\tilde{Y}_k, \tilde{P}) < \frac{R^{\mathrm{o}} - R^{\mathrm{d}}}{k},$$

and thus

$$\begin{aligned} -b^{\star}(\tilde{Y}_k) &= -E[\hat{r}^{\mathrm{u}}(\tilde{Y}_k, \tilde{P}) | \tilde{X}_1 = \tilde{Y}_k, \tilde{Y}_k] \\ &< \frac{R^{\mathrm{o}} - R^{\mathrm{d}}}{k - \hat{r}^{\mathrm{u}}(\tilde{Y}_k)}. \end{aligned}$$

Taking expectations of the above expression conditional on $\{\tilde{X}_1 \geqslant \tilde{Y}_k\}$ gives

$$\hat{R}^{\mathrm{u}} = k \times E[b^{\star}(\tilde{Y}_k) | \tilde{X}_1 \geqslant \tilde{Y}_k] > R^{\mathrm{d}},$$

which was to be shown. ■

Proof of theorem 7

From Milgrom and Weber (1982a, theorem 15) and the hypothesis that $(\tilde{V}, \tilde{X}_1, \tilde{X}_2, \ldots, \tilde{X}_n)$ are strictly affiliated, it follows that

$$\begin{aligned} D \equiv\ & k \times E[E[\tilde{V} | \tilde{X}_1 = \tilde{Y}_k, \tilde{Y}_k] | \tilde{X}_1 \geqslant \tilde{Y}_k] \\ & - k \times E[E[\tilde{V} | \tilde{X}_1, \tilde{Y}_k = \tilde{X}_1] - \mathcal{J}(\tilde{X}_1) | \tilde{X}_1 \geqslant \tilde{Y}_k] > 0, \end{aligned}$$

where

$$\mathcal{J}(x) \equiv \int_{\underline{x}}^{x} L(u|x)\, \mathrm{d}t(u)$$

and where $t(u)$ and $L(u|x)$ are as defined in (8).[15]

Let $M \equiv D / (kE[\tilde{X}_1 | \tilde{X}_1 \geqslant \tilde{Y}_k])$. We now show that, with M as defined, the theorem is true. First we recall from lemma 4 that, with probability one,

$$b^{\star}(\tilde{Y}_k) > E[\tilde{V} | \tilde{X}_1 = \tilde{Y}_k, \tilde{Y}_k].$$

Therefore

$$E[b^{\star}(\tilde{Y}_k) | \tilde{X}_1 \geqslant \tilde{Y}_k] > E[E[\tilde{V} | \tilde{X}_1 = \tilde{Y}_k, \tilde{Y}_k] | \tilde{X}_1 \geqslant \tilde{Y}_k]$$

and

$$k \times E[b^{\star}(\tilde{Y}_k) | \tilde{X}_1 \geqslant \tilde{Y}_k] - k \times E[E[\tilde{V} | \tilde{X}_1, \tilde{Y}_k = \tilde{X}_1] - \mathcal{J}(\tilde{X}_1) | \tilde{X}_1 \geqslant \tilde{Y}_k] > D. \tag{A9}$$

Next note that

$$E[\tilde{V} | \tilde{X}_1, \tilde{Y}_k = \tilde{X}_1] - \mathcal{J}(\tilde{X}_1) = \hat{b}(\tilde{X}_1) - K(\tilde{X}_1),$$

where $\hat{b}$ is defined in (7) and

$$K(x) \equiv \int_{\underline{x}}^{x} \frac{h(u)}{f_k(u|u)}\, \mathrm{d}L(u|x),$$

and where $h(u)$ and $L(u|x)$ are as defined in (8). Next the hypothesis that $\partial r^{\mathrm{d}}(x, y_1, \ldots, y_k, p) / \partial x \leqslant M$ for all $x, y_1, \ldots, y_k, p$ implies that

$$k \times K(x) \leqslant M \times k \times x.$$

Hence

$$k \times E[K(\tilde{X}_1)|\tilde{X}_1 \geqslant \tilde{Y}_k] \leqslant D. \tag{A10}$$

Substituting (A10) into (A9) gives

$$k \times E[b^{\star}(\tilde{Y}_k)|\tilde{X}_1 \geqslant \tilde{Y}_k] > k \times E[\hat{b}(\tilde{X}_1)|\tilde{X}_1 \geqslant \tilde{Y}_k],$$

which was to be shown. ■

Notes

1 In the first half of 1989, with an inverted yield curve, the noncompetitive bids increased significantly. For example, in the auction on June 26 noncompetitive bids accounted for about 4 percent of the total amount tendered and about one-sixth of the total amount accepted.

2 For an analysis of bidding with a resale market when the valuations of the bidders are common knowledge, see Milgrom (1987).

3 Throughout this paper, we shall use weak relations. For example, increasing means nondecreasing, positive means nonnegative, etc. If a relation is strict, we shall say, for example, strictly increasing.

4 The reader will see that our notion of information complementarity is different from that in Milgrom and Weber (1982b).

5 To simplify the analysis we arbitrarily assume throughout that in case of a tie the winner is not chosen randomly. Rather, bidder 1 is declared the winner. This assumption is inconsequential. The equilibrium strategy will remain unchanged if we assume that, in the case of a tie, the winner(s) is (are) chosen from the tied bidders at random.

6 If some of the other losing bids, or some function of them, are also announced all the results remain unchanged.

7 If $b < \hat{b}(\underline{x})$ then $\hat{b}^{-1}(b) = \underline{x}$ and if $b > \hat{b}(\bar{x})$ then $\hat{b}^{-1}(b) = \bar{x}$. Thus we only need to consider values of b that lie in the range of $\hat{b}$.

8 If $\tilde{P} \equiv \tilde{V}$ there is no signaling motive and the equilibrium strategy is as specified in (9), since $r^{d}(\cdot) \equiv \tilde{V}$ and thus $v_1^{d}(\cdot) \equiv 0$ and $h(\cdot) \equiv 0$. Also, when $\tilde{P}$ is "very informative" about $\tilde{V}$ the signaling motive is weak. For example, if we let $\tilde{P}_n \equiv \tilde{V} + \varepsilon_n$ where ε_n is, say, uniformly distributed on $[-1/n, 1/n]$, then as n increases the resale price becomes less responsive to the players' bids and in the limit the incentive to signal disappears.

9 In the symmetric equilibrium of theorem 1, the resale buyers beliefs are monotone (since $\hat{b}$ is increasing) with $x_1^{l}(b) = x_1^{u}(b) = \hat{b}^{-1}(b)$. For $b > \hat{b}(\bar{x})$, $x_1^{l}(b) = x_1^{u}(b) = \bar{x}$, and for $b < \hat{b}(\underline{x})$, $x_1^{l}(b) = x_1^{u}(b) = \underline{x}$.

10 Note that this assumption is stronger than the conditional information complementarity required for the existence of Nash equilibrium.

11 An argument similar to that in theorem 2 establishes that b_0 is the only candidate for a symmetric equilibrium when the resale market buyers have monotone beliefs. This remark also applies to the symmetric equilibrium we shall obtain in section 5.

12 By renormalizing the units, we can assume that each competitive bidder demands exactly $m > 1$ or zero units. This allows us to keep the prespecified maximum demand of noncompetitive bidders at a level less than that of competitive bidders.

13 We assume here that the identity of the winning bidder is also disclosed. In our earlier analysis, since we restricted attention to symmetric equilibria, such an assumption was not necessary.

14 If $\tilde{P}$ is independent of $\tilde{X}_i$, or if there is no post-auction public information, then $\hat{v}^{u}$ is constant in its first argument and no bid gives bidder i an expected profit greater than zero. However, $(b^{\star}, \dots, b^{\star})$ remains an equilibrium.

15 Note that to prove this we also need a technical lemma that is slightly different from lemma 6. Let $\rho(z)$ and $\sigma(z)$ be differentiable functions for which (a) $\rho(\underline{x}) \geqslant \sigma(\underline{x})$ and (b) $\rho(z) \leqslant \sigma(z)$ implies $\rho'(z) > \sigma'(z)$. Then $\rho(z) > \sigma(z)$ for all $z > \underline{x}$. The reader should convince herself/himself that this is indeed true.

References

Bikhchandani, S. and Huang, C. (1988) "Auctions with Resale Markets: A Model of Treasury Bill Markets," *Working Paper*, University of California at Los Angeles.

Brimmer, A. (1962) "Price Determination in the United States Treasury Bill Market," *Review of Economics and Statistics*, 44, 178–83.

Cammack, E. (1986) "Evidence on Bidding Strategies and the Information Contained in Treasury Bill Auctions," *Working Paper*, University of Chicago.

DeGroot, M. (1970) *Optimal Statistical Decisions* (New York: McGraw-Hill).

Ericson, W. (1969) "A Note on the Posterior Mean of a Population Mean," *Journal of The Royal Statistical Society*, 31, 332–4.

Friedman, M. (1960) *A Program for Monetary Stability* (New York: Fordham University Press), pp. 63–5.

Goldstein, H. (1960) "The Friedman Proposal for Auctioning Treasury Bills," *Journal of Political Economy*, 70, 386–92.

Milgrom, P. (1987) "Auction Theory." In *Advances in Economic Theory, Proceedings of the 5th World Congress of the Econometric Society*, ed. T. Bewley (Cambridge: Cambridge University Press).

Milgrom, P. and Roberts, J. (1982) "Limit Pricing and Entry Under Incomplete Information: An Equilibrium Analysis," *Econometrica*, 50, 443–59.

Milgrom, P. and Weber, R. (1982a) "A Theory of Auctions and Competitive Bidding," *Econometrica*, 50, 1089–122.

Milgrom, P. and Weber, R. (1982b) "The Value of Information in a Sealed-Bid Auction," *Journal of Mathematical Economics*, 10, 105–14.

Ortega-Reichart, A. (1968) "Models of Competitive Bidding under Uncertainty," Ph.D. Dissertation, Stanford University.

Parsons, J. and Raviv, A. (1985) "Underpricing of Seasoned Issues," *Journal of Financial Economics*, 14, 377–97.

Smith, V. (1966) "Bidding Theory and the Treasury Bill Auction: Does Price Discrimination Increase Bill Prices?" *Review of Economics and Statistics*, 48, 141–6.

Tiemann, J. (1985) "Applications of Auction Games in Mergers and Acquisitions: The White Knight Takeover Defense," Mimeo, Graduate School of Business Administration, Harvard University.

Index

Index compiled by Elan David Garonzik